The Beauty of Baudelaire

The Beauty of Baudelaire

The Poet as Alternative Lawgiver

ROGER PEARSON

OXFORD
UNIVERSITY PRESS

Great Clarendon Street, Oxford, OX2 6DP,
United Kingdom

Oxford University Press is a department of the University of Oxford.
It furthers the University's objective of excellence in research, scholarship,
and education by publishing worldwide. Oxford is a registered trade mark of
Oxford University Press in the UK and in certain other countries

© Roger Pearson 2021

The moral rights of the author have been asserted

First Edition published in 2021

Impression: 1

All rights reserved. No part of this publication may be reproduced, stored in
a retrieval system, or transmitted, in any form or by any means, without the
prior permission in writing of Oxford University Press, or as expressly permitted
by law, by licence or under terms agreed with the appropriate reprographics
rights organization. Enquiries concerning reproduction outside the scope of the
above should be sent to the Rights Department, Oxford University Press, at the
address above

You must not circulate this work in any other form
and you must impose this same condition on any acquirer

Published in the United States of America by Oxford University Press
198 Madison Avenue, New York, NY 10016, United States of America

British Library Cataloguing in Publication Data

Data available

Library of Congress Control Number: 2021931967

ISBN 978-0-19-284331-9

DOI: 10.1093/oso/9780192843319.001.0001

Printed and bound in Great Britain by
Clays Ltd, Elcograf S.p.A.

Links to third party websites are provided by Oxford in good faith and
for information only. Oxford disclaims any responsibility for the materials
contained in any third party website referenced in this work.

for

Tommy, Frasier, Mitchell, Sophie
(the future)
and Vivienne
(always)

Approchons, et tournons autour de sa beauté.
                    ('Le Masque', l. 16)
l'idée de beauté, qui est le but le plus grand et le plus noble du poème.
                    ('Notes nouvelles sur Edgar Poe', ii. 329)

*****

Alfred de Vigny a écrit un livre [*Stello*] pour démontrer que la place du poète n'est ni dans une république, ni dans une monarchie absolue, ni dans une monarchie constititutionnelle; et personne ne lui a répondu.
                    ('Edgar Allan Poe, sa vie et ses ouvrages', ii. 250)
Or le poète n'est d'aucun parti. Autrement, il serait un simple mortel.
                    (Draft preface to *Les Fleurs du Mal*, i. 182)
La Poésie est ce qu'il y a de plus réel, c'est ce qui n'est complètement vrai que dans *un autre monde*.
                    ('Puisque réalisme il y a', ii. 59)

*****

La loi de l'écrivain, ce qui le fait tel, ce qui, je ne crains pas de le dire, le rend égal et peut-être supérieur à l'homme d'État, est une décision quelconque sur les choses humaines, un dévouement absolu à des principes.
                    (Balzac, 'Avant-propos' to *La Comédie humaine*)
Un poète doit être plus utile qu'aucun citoyen de sa tribu. Son œuvre est le code des diplomates, des législateurs, des instructeurs de la jeunesse.
                    (Lautréamont, *Poésies*)

Preface

> L'homme y passe à travers des forêts de symboles
> Qui l'observent avec des regards familiers.
> ('Correspondances', ll. 3–4)
>
> pour être juste, c'est-à-dire pour avoir sa *raison d'être*, la critique doit être partiale, passionnée, politique, c'est-à-dire faite à un point de vue exclusif, mais au point de vue qui ouvre le plus d'horizons.
> (*Salon de 1846*, ii. 418)

'Puissent les vrais chercheurs nous donner [. . .] cette joie singulière de célébrer l'avènement du *neuf!*' (ii. 407). As we mark the bicentenary of Baudelaire's birth in 1821, the urgent plea of this final sentence from the *Salon de 1845* assumes fresh resonance. Is there really anything more, anything *new*, to be said about the life's work of perhaps France's greatest lyric poet? I believe so.

This account of Baudelaire's writings started out as a chapter in my still-envisaged volume on *Alternative Legislators: The Poet as Lawgiver in Nineteenth-Century France* but soon outgrew its intended context. I now present it as a comprehensive stand-alone study: of Baudelaire's critical writings, of his verse poetry in *Les Fleurs du Mal*, and of his prose poetry in *Le Spleen de Paris*. As the subtitle indicates, my principal emphasis derives from an ambition to situate Baudelaire's work within an ongoing tradition of poetic 'lawgiving' in France that did not end with those Romantic magi, Lamartine, Hugo, and Vigny, but continues, in my view, to this day. I trust nevertheless that this emphasis has not led to a tendentious or narrowly focused study but rather to a new and potentially reinvigorating perspective on a body of writing that is itself familiar, perhaps only too familiar, to anyone with an interest in poetry.

In my earlier book, *Unacknowledged Legislators: The Poet as Lawgiver in Post-Revolutionary France*[1] I focused on the work of Chateaubriand, Staël, Lamartine, Hugo, and Vigny. Mindful of Paul Bénichou's magisterial investigations of French Romanticism and of the ways in which he employs the model of a lay priest to shape his account of various nineteenth-century French poets and prose writers, I emphasized instead the role of the poet as lawgiver. Unlike 'legislator' the term 'lawgiver' contains a fruitful ambiguity that seems to me to shed valuable light on the nature of poetic expression. The word 'legislator' etymologically denotes

---

[1] Oxford: Oxford University Press, 2016.

someone who bears or carries the law, who brings it to others, and so is analogous with 'lawgiver' in implying that the laws already exist and have simply to be conveyed, brought as a gift like Tables or Tablets from the top of a mountain. Yet perhaps the more common understanding is of a 'lawgiver' who 'gives, i.e. makes or promulgates, a law or code of laws; a legislator' (*Oxford English Dictionary*). In the present book, as previously in *Unacknowledged Legislators*, I see the term 'lawgiver' as highlighting a fundamental tension in poetic writing between passive transmission and active creation. Does the poet resemble Moses, receiving the Laws from God and handing them down to humankind? Or does the poet more closely resemble Orpheus, actively employing the power of poetry—of harmony— to bring order where there was originally chaos? Or perhaps both at once? As Wordsworth writes in Book Second of *The Prelude*, 'the first Poetic spirit of our human life' '[c]reates, creator and receiver both, | Working but in alliance with the works | Which it beholds' (ll. 273–5). For Baudelaire this coexistence of passivity and creativity is absolutely central and informs his recurrent theoretical statements about poets and artists as what I shall call 'double agents': on the one hand, human beings who are necessarily subject to the laws of human nature, and, on the other, human beings who observe and analyse this state of subjection and, through willed effort, create imagined and alternative legislations.

While French poets and prose writers of the Romantic period have more usually been associated with the Mosaic model, and are indeed so associated by Bénichou, I tried to show how they themselves were conscious of this tension between receipt and invention and how they were each in their own various ways no less Orphic than Mosaic in their understanding of the nature of poetic creation. I presented my five chosen authors as 'unacknowledged legislators of the World', as Shelley puts it at the end of his *Defence of Poetry* (1821), because each of them did indeed write and live their lives as poets and prose writers who expected to be able to influence the course of public life through their writing and instead found themselves variously outlawed, exiled, self-exiled, and/or increasingly sidelined by the official legislators of their time, from the earliest days of the Revolution and then under the many and various political regimes that came and went in France throughout the nineteenth century. Long before Verlaine wrote his celebrated articles on 'les poètes maudits'—but also very long after such other famous exiles as Ovid, Dante, Tasso, and Camoëns—these five authors knew the cost of resistance.

In this book I approach Baudelaire as an 'alternative lawgiver'. By this I mean, first, that he differs from his predecessors (and this is indeed familiar ground for all who know his work) by not seeking—or believing desirable or even feasible— an overtly public or political function for his poetry, whether in verse or prose. Not so, of course, for his writings on painting or music. His first two *Salons* (of 1845 and 1846) are energetic manifestos for change, and in writing (favourably) about Wagner he was participating in a very public and political battle. But, second—and as these qualifications suggest—I mean that for all that he did not see himself as offering religious, moral, or political guidance to his readers, he did have very clear and firmly held views on the nature and function of art and, above all perhaps, on the nature of the relationship between art and morality. These led him to offer in his writings an 'alternative' way of thinking about how we human beings might envisage our own human condition, which he sees as a condition of melancholy, and how we do, may, or could respond to its difficulties. And so, third, I mean that Baudelaire—with wholly conscious intent—offers an alternative moral vision to the Roman Catholic doctrine of sin that was so deeply embedded in the society and culture of his day and which had dominated Western lives for many centuries past.

Central to this alternative moral vision is Baudelaire's account of 'le Mal', which, as we shall see, he presents in terms not of Christian 'evil' but of a secular 'ill-being', a condition of melancholy that he considers to be 'irremediably' synonymous with the business of living. But central also to this alternative moral vision is the value Baudelaire ascribes to human creativity: our active capacity to conjure from the 'destruction' wrought by time and depression new ways of seeing and feeling, new patterns of understanding, new harmonies—in short, what he calls 'le Beau' or 'la Beauté'. Beauty for Baudelaire is not something intrinsic in the world, not a glimpse of the 'Sublime' or the 'Divine', but an effect of perception that he came to call 'conjecture': a quickening of interest, a sense of new possibilities, of new shapes and of new 'ideas' (in its etymological sense of 'forms') as they come tantalizingly and intriguingly into view.

For this reason the 'laws' of Baudelaire's beauty are both found and made: rooted in the world of human experience but drafted by a poet in the innovative legislations of a sonnet or a prose poem. And for the reader also the 'beauty of Baudelaire' is both found and made: it is there in the words he uses, but—and I believe that for him this was what was most important—it is there also in what we make of those words. Since a beautiful painting is, as he writes in the *Salon de 1846*, simply nature reflected in the eyes of an artist, then, he says, the best form of art criticism will be an account of how that painting is reflected in the mind of an intelligent and sensitive viewer—so that the best such account might well take the form of an elegy or a sonnet. Well, this book is no sonnet. But I hope nevertheless that it may itself be read not as the work of someone trying to lay down the law about how to read Baudelaire but as an invitation to reread and rethink *Les Fleurs du Mal* and *Le Spleen de Paris*—and, just possibly, with the feeling that even now these works have somehow only just been written.

The Queen's College, Oxford
9 April 2021

Acknowledgements

I would like to express particular thanks to the two anonymous readers engaged by Oxford University Press to review my submitted manuscript. The scholarly expertise and close attention that they brought to their assessments provided me with invaluable alternative perspectives on my work, and their detailed comments and suggestions have saved me from many errors and helped me substantially to complete a less imperfect book. I would also like to thank the staff of the Taylorian and Bodleian libraries in Oxford for doing so much and in such difficult recent circumstances to provide and maintain access to the resources on which academic research depends.

Contents

A Note on References and Abbreviations   xvii

Introduction: An Unacknowledged Legislator?   1

PART I RESISTANCE

1. The Poet of Resistance   21
2. The Poet-Artist as Double Agent   47
3. The Poet-Artist as Performer   68

PART II MELANCHOLY

4. Melancholy and Baudelaire   91
5. Melancholy and Satan   108
6. Lesbos and Limbo: Towards *Les Fleurs du Mal*   127
7. The Beauty of Ill-Being: From Sappho to Satan   159
8. *Les Fleurs du Mal* (1857/1861): New Beginnings   182
9. *Les Fleurs du Mal* (1857/1861): New Endings   207
10. Melancholy and the Poetic Act: Decomposition and Composition   228

PART III IMAGINATION

11. Imagination and Resistance: The Case of Poe   243
12. The Government of the Imagination: The *Salon de 1859*   265
13. Imagination and Conjecture: Gautier and Hugo   286
14. Imagination and Suggestion: Wagner, Guys, Delacroix   307

PART IV POETRY IN VERSE

15. The Poetry of Passion: Sex, Beauty, and Verse   335
16. The Performance of Melancholy: The Duel and the Waltz   362

17. Versification and the Poetic Idea	384
18. Poetry in the City: Melancholy and Time in 'Tableaux parisiens'	406
19. The Poet and the City: The Seer as Sightseer in 'Tableaux parisiens'	434

PART V PROSE POETRY

20. The Inauguration of the Prose Poem	457
21. Prose Poetry and the Press: The Poetics of Resistance	485
22. The Question of Intent: Mystification and Perplexity	505
23. The Voice of the Stranger: Reality and Imagination	533
24. The Poet in the World: Empathy and Performance	553
25. The Beauty of the Prose Poem	572
Conclusion: Beauty and the Poet as Alternative Lawgiver	594
Bibliography	619
Index	639
General Index	645

A Note on References and Abbreviations

Unless otherwise stated, all references to Baudelaire's work will be to *Œuvres complètes*, ed. Claude Pichois (2 vols, Paris: Gallimard [Bibliothèque de la Pléiade], 1975-6). These will be given in the main text and in the form (ii. 000), denoting volume and page number.

In the case of the posthumously published notes traditionally known as the *Journaux intimes*, Pichois's editorial work has since been complemented in *Fusées, Mon cœur mis à nu, et autres fragments posthumes*, ed. André Guyaux (Paris: Gallimard [Folio classique], 2016). References to both editions will be given in the footnotes.

For the correspondence, all references will be to *Correspondance*, ed. Claude Pichois and Jean Ziegler (2 vols, Paris: Galllimard [Bibliothèque de la Pléiade], 1973) and given in the main text in the form (*Corr.*, ii. 000).

In quotations all use of italics or of the upper case for emphasis derives from the quoted text unless otherwise stated. The symbol [-] indicates a paragraph break.

In the case of Baudelaire's verse I have provided the line number(s) for all quotations. In the case of the prose poems in *Le Spleen de Paris* I give page references only in the case of the longer poems and otherwise refer simply to poem titles.

One purpose of this book is to offer close readings of Baudelaire's poems, prose poems, and critical writings, all of which—and in particular the poems of *Les Fleurs du Mal*—have over more than a century and a half been read and discussed many, many times. My own readings are, to the best of my ability, informed by the critical and editorial work of others, duly recorded in the Bibliography. Rather than provide detailed lists in the footnotes, I have made specific reference to this work only where I owe a particular debt, where I have found a fortuitous overlap, where I explicitly engage in debate with another critic, or where I think my own discussion might usefully be complemented by another interpretation or contrasted with it. In the event I have found it helpful to include more extensive and detailed reference to the critical literature on the prose poems than on Baudelaire's other writings, and this largely because the critical debates surrounding *Le Spleen de Paris* are in general of more recent date and as yet less consensual than those prompted by his other works.

Introduction

An Unacknowledged Legislator?

S'il y a quelque gloire à n'être pas compris, ou à ne l'être que très peu, je peux dire, sans vanterie, que, par ce petit livre, je l'ai acquise et méritée d'un seul coup.

(draft preface for *Les Fleurs du mal*, i. 184)

POLITIQUE. Je n'ai pas de convictions, comme l'entendent les gens de mon siècle, parce que je n'ai pas d'ambition. [-] Il n'y a pas en moi de base pour une conviction. [...] Cependant, j'ai quelques convictions, dans un sens plus élevé, et qui ne peut pas être compris par les gens de mon temps.

(*Mon cœur mis à nu*)[1]

Baudelaire on Trial

Ceci est du nouveau: poursuivre un livre de vers! Jusqu'à présent la magistrature laissait la poésie fort tranquille.

(Flaubert, in a letter to Baudelaire, 14 August 1857)[2]

Que l'artiste agisse sur le public, et que le public réagisse sur l'artiste, c'est une loi incontestable et irrésistible.

(*Salon de 1859*, ii. 619)

Literature and the law did not always see eye to eye in Second Empire France. Famously, following the serialized publication of *Madame Bovary* at the end of 1856, its author was prosecuted for an 'outrage à la morale publique et religieuse et aux bonnes mœurs' but acquitted on 7 February 1857. Following the publication of *Les Fleurs du Mal* on 25 June 1857 Baudelaire was indicted on the same charge and on 20 August exonerated of irreligion but found guilty of obscenity. Six poems were banned on the grounds that they 'conduisent nécessairement à l'excitation

---

[1] *Fusées, Mon cœur mis à nu, et autres fragments posthumes*, ed. André Guyaux (Paris: Gallimard [Folio classique], 2016), 85; i. 680.

[2] *Correspondance*, ed. Jean Bruneau and Yvan Leclerc (5 vols, Paris: Gallimard [Bibliothèque de la Pléiade], 1973–2007), ii. 758.

des sens par un réalisme grossier et offensant pour la pudeur' (i. 1182).[3] Flaubert had written to Baudelaire on 13 July to thank him for sending a copy of *Les Fleurs du Mal*, and again on 14 August to express concern about the trial, and on 23 August—but too late—to recommend a possible line of defence: namely, that Baudelaire's lawyer might quote in court some smutty verse by the enormously popular poet and songwriter Pierre-Jean de Béranger, who had recently died on 16 July and been accorded the honour of a state funeral. If a national treasure can write like that, how can they condemn the author of *Les Fleurs du Mal*? 'Tenez-moi au courant de votre affaire,' Flaubert urges his fellow-writer: 'Je m'y intéresse comme si elle me regardait personnellement.'[4]

On 18 October, in *L'Artiste*, Baudelaire published his long-intended review of *Madame Bovary*, perhaps delayed by preparing for his own trial,[5] and then found himself summoned to appear before the public prosecutor to be asked just exactly what he meant by it (see *Corr.*, i. 436).[6] What he meant by it was 'Bravo!': to Flaubert, of course, for 'son excellent livre' (ii. 76) but also to the French judicial system! For in acquitting the author of *Madame Bovary* they had honoured Beauty:

> Ce souci remarquable de la Beauté, en des hommes dont les facultés ne sont mises en requisition que pour le Juste et le Vrai, est un symptôme des plus touchants [...] En somme, on peut dire que cet arrêt, par sa haute tendance poétique, fut définitif; que gain de cause a été donné à la Muse, et que tous les écrivains, tous ceux du moins dignes de ce nom, ont été acquittés dans la personne de M. Gustave Flaubert. (ii. 77)

Throughout his review Baudelaire revels in the ironies of the situation, not least that his review should have appeared so late—indeed almost exactly one year after the first instalment of *Madame Bovary* had appeared in the *Revue de Paris* (on 1 October 1856). For instead of heralding a new talent in the customary manner of

---

[3] On the trial of *Madame Bovary*, see Dominick LaCapra, *Madame Bovary on Trial* (Ithaca, NY: Cornell University Press, 1982). On the trial of *Les Fleurs du Mal*, see i. 1176–224, and also Michele Hannoosh, 'Reading the Trial of the *Fleurs du mal*', *Modern Language Review*, 106 (2011), 374–87. (I discuss this article in detail in Chapter 22.) On both trials see Yvan Leclerc, *Crimes écrits: La Littérature en procès au XIXe siècle* (Paris: Plon, 1991); Elisabeth Ladenson, *Dirt for Art's Sake: Books on Trial from 'Madame Bovary' to 'Lolita'* (Ithaca, |NY: Cornell University Press, 2007), chs 1 and 2; Gisèle Sapiro, *La Responsabilité de l'écrivain: Littérature, droit et morale en France (XIXe–XXIe siècle)* (Paris: Éditions du Seuil, 2011), 196–239; and William Olmsted, *The Censorship Effect: Baudelaire, Flaubert, and the Formation of French Modernism* (New York: Oxford University Press, 2016).

[4] *Correspondance*, ed. Bruneau and Leclerc, ii. 759.

[5] Rosemary Lloyd has suggested that Baudelaire initially intended to publish the review *before* his own trial as a pre-emptive form of defence. See her *Baudelaire's Literary Criticism* (Cambridge: Cambridge University Press, 1981), 83.

[6] Under a law passed in 1852 it was forbidden to discuss censorship cases in the press. See Scott Carpenter, *Acts of Fiction: Resistance and Resolution from Sade to Baudelaire* (University Park, Pa: Pennsylvania State University Press, 1996), 127.

an enthusiastic reviewer—'l'écrivain prophète, celui qui annonce le succès, qui le commande, pour ainsi dire, avec l'autorité de l'audace et du dévouement'—he finds himself in the somewhat otiose position of an 'écrivain retardaire' (ii. 76). The excellent M. Gustave Flaubert now has no need of his support since so many 'artistes' (Baudelaire's choice of term is eloquent), including 'quelques-uns des plus fins et des plus accrédités', have already garlanded the novel with praise. But such a johnny-come-lately position has its own advantages. Not only is he able to make some new observations of his own and to add support to existing plaudits,[7] his role is that of a presiding magistrate summing up at the end of a trial:

> Plus libre, parce qu'il est seul comme un traînard, il a l'air de celui qui résume les débats, et, contraint d'éviter les véhémences de l'accusation et de la défense, il a ordre de se frayer une voie nouvelle, sans autre excitation que celle de l'amour du Beau et de la Justice.   (ii. 76)

Brandishing the language of the courts ('commande', 'autorité', 'accrédités') this poet—who himself has *not* been acquitted—thus assumes the role of judge; and his first act—'[p]uisque j'ai prononcé ce mot splendide et terrible, la Justice'—is to judge the judiciary itself and, with wild effusion, to 'remercier la magistrature française de l'éclatant exemple d'impartialité et de bon goût qu'elle a donné dans cette circonstance' (ii. 76-7).

Henceforward in this review there are three magistratures at work: the official one, here lauded with heavy irony; that of literary critics, including Baudelaire; and that of Flaubert and his novel. The first is sarcastically commended for saving *Madame Bovary* from the flames of book-burning zealots who have overstepped the mark in their devotion to public morality, and by the same token praised for exhibiting that very quality of impartiality so effectively demonstrated by the novel itself:

> Sollicitée par un zèle aveugle et trop véhément pour la morale, par un esprit qui se trompait de terrain,—placée en face d'un roman, œuvre d'un écrivain inconnu la veille,—un roman, et quel roman! le plus impartial, le plus loyal,—un champ, banal comme tous les champs, flagellé, trempé, comme la nature elle-même, par tous les vents et tous les orages,—la magistrature, dis-je, s'est montrée loyale et impartiale comme le livre qui était poussé devant elle en holocauste.   (ii. 77)

---

[7] Ladenson points out that in fact '[t]he one reader whose assessment diverges radically from the rest during this period is Charles Baudelaire' and this because he steps outside the terms of a judicial debate that was predicated by both prosecution and defence on a shared belief that literature should be spiritually uplifting and thereby have a beneficial effect on the morals of its readers. See *Dirt for Art's Sake*, 34.

But let there be no doubt: *Madame Bovary* owes its success not to the notoriety of the trial or the 'wisdom' of the judges but to its own merits and to the sound judgement of other writers: 'les approbations de tous les lettrés lui appartenaient depuis longtemps' (ii. 77). As to Baudelaire, the presiding judge and critic, he now substitutes himself for the official magistrature by assessing the novel in the light of what *he* believes to have been Flaubert's aims. In the trial itself the case had turned on the novelist's intentions: had he sought to denigrate marriage and present what the prosecuting counsel Ernest Pinard called 'l'adultère dans toute sa poésie'?[8] Neither. Instead Baudelaire offers his own alternative judicial assessment, presenting Flaubert as 'un esprit bien nourri, enthousiaste du beau' who, in despair at the contemporary vogue for 'le Réalisme', set himself the challenge of producing a work of literary art by treating the most clichéd subject matter in 'un style nerveux, pittoresque, subtil, exact' (ii. 80). This Flaubert was motivated by an ambition for aesthetic innovation and not for the promotion of a feel-good morality.

Continuing with his playful deployment of multiple magistratures Baudelaire ridicules those critics who have, precisely, complained of the novel's failure to pronounce judgement, to come up with some closing statement that might usefully direct readers as they strive to reach a verdict on the life and suicide of Emma Bovary:

> Plusieurs critiques avaient dit: cette œuvre, vraiment belle par la minutie et la vivacité des descriptions, ne contient pas un seul personnage qui représente la morale, qui parle la conscience de l'auteur. Où est-il, le personnage proverbial et légendaire, chargé d'expliquer la fable et de diriger l'intelligence du lecteur? En d'autres termes, où est le réquisitoire?   (ii. 81)[9]

The position of Baudelaire as the representative of an alternative judiciary is clear:

> Absurdité! Éternelle et incorrigible confusion des fonctions et des genres!—Une véritable œuvre d'art n'a pas besoin de réquisitoire. La logique de l'œuvre suffit à toutes les postulations de la morale, et c'est au lecteur à tirer les conclusions de la conclusion.   (ii. 81–2)[10]

In short, readers must judge for themselves.

---

[8] On Pinard's closing statement for the prosecution, see Ladenson, *Dirt for Art's Sake*, 37–8.

[9] Flaubert himself plays on this readerly expectation at the end of the novel when he has Charles Bovary remark to Rodolphe Boulanger that '[c]'est la faute de la fatalité', thereby quoting back at Rodolphe the cynical words with which, in the letter breaking off their relationship, Emma's lover had previously sought to excuse his behaviour. See my 'Flaubert's Style and the Idea of Literary Justice', *Dix-Neuf*, 17: 2 (July 2013), 156–82 (174).

[10] Cf. Baudelaire's subsequent comment in a letter to Algernon Charles Swinburne of 10 Oct. 1863 in which he chides the English poet for having (in his review of *Les Fleurs du Mal* in the *Spectator* in Sept. 1862) rather overdone his defence of the work against the charge of immorality: 'Je ne suis pas si *moraliste* que vous feignez obligeamment de le croire. Je crois simplement (comme vous, sans doute) que tout poème, tout objet d'art *bien fait* suggère naturellement et forcément une *morale*. C'est l'affaire

According to Baudelaire's own celebrated judgement on *Madame Bovary*, Flaubert chose 'la femme adultère' to be his central character as part of this self-imposed challenge to tackle clichéd subject matter. In the event, while seeking imaginatively to inhabit her innermost feelings and motives, the writer found himself unable to prevent his heroine from becoming a man:

> Il en est résulté une merveille; c'est que, malgré tout son zèle de comédien, il n'a pas su ne pas infuser un sang viril dans les veines de sa créature, et que madame Bovary, pour ce qu'il y a en elle de plus énergique et de plus ambitieux, et aussi de plus rêveur, madame Bovary est restée un homme. Comme la Pallas armée, sortie du cerveau de Zeus, ce bizarre androgyne a gardé toutes les séductions d'une âme virile dans un charmant corps féminin. (ii. 81)

By implication Flaubert has turned her into himself: 'Madame Bovary, c'est moi'.[11] Whereupon Baudelaire proceeds to do exactly the same. First, he itemizes Emma's allegedly 'masculine' traits: (i) a predominance of imagination ('faculté suprême et tyrannique') over unthinking sentiment; (ii) energy, decisiveness, a 'mystical' combination of reason and passion; and (iii) an 'immoderate' desire to seduce and dominate others by whatever means ('jusqu'au charlatanisme du costume, des parfums et de la pommade')—like a dandy. And yet, he says, she gives herself to men who are not worthy of her, 'exactement comme les poètes se livrent à des drôlesses' (ii. 82). Emma, it seems, is a poet—a parallel then made explicit as Baudelaire proceeds to describe (iv) the 'tempérament équivoque de madame Bovary' (ii. 83). For the nuns at her convent school Emma as a young girl already possessed 'une aptitude étonnante à la vie, à profiter de la vie, à en conjecturer les jouissances;—voilà l'homme d'action!'; and this vivid imagination, this power of *conjecture*, is what leads to the fusion in her mind of urgent sexual longing with intense religious fervour:

> Cependant la jeune fille s'enivrait délicieusement de la couleur des vitraux, des teintes orientales que les longues fenêtres ouvragées jetaient sur son paroissien de pensionnaire; elle se gorgeait de la musique solennelle des vêpres, et, par un paradoxe dont tout l'honneur appartient aux nerfs, elle substituait dans son âme au Dieu véritable le Dieu de sa fantaisie, le Dieu de l'avenir et du hasard, un Dieu de vignette, avec éperons et moustaches;—voilà le poète hystérique. (ii. 83)[12]

---

du lecteur. J'ai même une haine très décidée contre toute *intention* morale exclusive dans un poème' (*Corr.*, ii. 325).
[11] Baudelaire's review has been thought by some to be the source of Flaubert's famous but apocryphal comment. See Lloyd, *Baudelaire's Literary Criticism*, 92 and n. 29.
[12] Lloyd points out that this description of stained-glass windows is absent from *Madame Bovary* and owes more to Baudelaire's own childhood memories (*Baudelaire's Literary Criticism*, 96).

From this it would appear that for Baudelaire the poetic imagination derives from a 'nervous' temperament ('tout l'honneur appartient aux nerfs') and is symptomatic of a potentially pathological state that can be identified with 'hysteria'. Accordingly he concludes by appearing to praise Flaubert's novel now not only for its impartiality but for its originality in foregrounding a physical and mental condition that continues to baffle medical opinion:

> L'hystérie! Pourquoi ce mystère physiologique ne ferait-il pas le fond et le tuf d'une œuvre littéraire, ce mystère que l'Académie de médecine n'a pas encore résolu, et qui, s'exprimant dans les femmes par la sensation d'une boule ascendante et asphyxiante (je ne parle que du symptôme principal), se traduit chez les hommes nerveux par toutes les impuissances et aussi par l'aptitude à tous les excès. (ii. 83)

There is good reason to suppose that Baudelaire is here writing also about his own temperament, and perhaps even, by implication, about 'le fond et le tuf' of *Les Fleurs du Mal*. As Claude Pichois notes (and as will be seen below in Parts I and III where I discuss Baudelaire's articles on Delacroix, Poe, Gautier, Wagner, and Constantin Guys), Baudelaire the critic writes most revealingly about himself when ostensibly writing about other writers and artists.[13] Similarly, for a more recent critic, Patrick Née, this reference to the mystery of 'hysteria' as potentially able to constitute the substance of a literary work deserves particular note as a possible key to the relationship between Baudelaire's own temperament and his aesthetic theory and practice.[14] In the first of his two articles Née takes a number of symptoms of 'hysteria' as it was then understood and diagnosed—*angustia* (breathlessness, constriction of the chest, the widely attested sensation alluded to by Baudelaire of 'une boule ascendante et asphyxiante'), 'hysterical tears' (mentioned in Baudelaire's article on Marceline Desbordes-Valmore (ii. 149)), and a 'defence mechanism' blocking empathy—and finds them explicitly or implicitly manifest in a number of poems. Noting Baudelaire's statement dated 23 January

---

[13] See ii. 1071: 'Là où Baudelaire réussit le mieux, donc avec un rare bonheur, c'est dans la critique d'identification. [. . .] il ne frôle pas les écrivains dont il parle: il se fait eux-mêmes, au risque—risque de toute critique d'identification—de se perdre en eux ou de les obliger de trop ressembler à lui.' Cf. also ii. 1070: 'Sa propre esthétique, c'est au contact de l'œuvre de Delacroix que Baudelaire l'a élaborée et au contact de l'œuvre de Wagner qu'il l'a précisée, imaginant son œuvre propre au travers des œuvres de ceci.'

[14] See Patrick Née, 'Du "poète hystérique" chez Baudelaire', *L'Année Baudelaire*, 16 (2012), 111–30, and 'Baudelaire et l'hystérie en son temps (1800–1860)', *Revue d'histoire littéraire de la France*, 116 (2016), 841–56. In 'Du poète "hystérique"' Née states: 'Baudelaire, à partir des années 1850, n'a cessé d'organiser sa théorie et sa pratique poétiques en relation avec les conceptions nosographiques de la médecine de la première moitié de son siècle' (113). For the medical background he refers his reader specifically to Juan Rigoli, *Lire le délire: Aliénisme, rhétorique et littérature en France au XIXe siècle* (Paris: Fayard, 2001), and Nicole Edelman, *Les Métamorphoses de l'hystérique: Du début du XIXe siècle à la Grande Guerre* (Paris: Éditions La Découverte, 2003).

1862 that '[j]'ai cultivé mon hystérie avec jouissance et terreur',[15] he wonders how anyone can 'cultivate' 'une pathologie subie et redoutée' and speculates not only that Baudelaire may have aimed for a 'transmutation de l'*hystérie* en *poétique de l'hystérie*' but also that this is what he means in 'L'Irrémédiable' by 'la conscience dans le Mal'. Née concludes:

> tout se passe comme si, *hystérique*, Baudelaire voulait bien l'être par le truchement de son *je* lyrique, au titre d'une acuité accrue de l'imagination et d'une surexcitation de la créativité, mais non pas au titre d'un diagnostic touchant sa personne, qui l'enfermerait pathologiquement dans la cage aux névrosés.[16]

In his second article Née returns to Baudelaire's suggestion that 'l'hystérie' might provide the substance of a literary work—'[c]itation capitale à bien des égards'—and sees it now as part of a defence of the poetic imagination. Situating Baudelaire's view of 'hysteria' as 'poetic' (whether it be his own putative condition or that of Emma Bovary) within the context of nineteenth-century psychiatry and adducing numerous antagonistic comments made by Baudelaire in respect of the opinions held by contemporary specialists such as Baillarger, Lélut, Brierre de Boismont, and Moreau de Tours on the subject of the pathological status of 'hysterical' hallucination, Née sees Baudelaire as conducting '[u]n vrai combat [...] contre une annexion pure et simple de cette paradoxalement précieuse "hystérie" par une trop conquérante extension de la "folie"'.[17]

In other words, innovative poets are not madmen, and they need to defend themselves against this age-old slur that dates back at least as far as Socrates' view of the eponymous rhapsode in Plato's *Ion*: 'A poet, you see, is a light thing, and winged and holy, and cannot compose before he gets inspiration and loses control of his senses and his reason has deserted him.'[18] Baudelaire for his part was deeply opposed to this idea of 'inspiration' as the source of poetic beauty, principally because of his own conviction, shared with Delacroix and Gautier, that artistic success is the product of concerted effort and carefully acquired technique, but

---

[15] *Fusées*, ed. Guyaux, 125, and i. 668.
[16] 'Du "poète hystérique"', 121, 130. See also n. 3 to p. 125, where Guyaux notes that when (in 1866) doctors diagnosed Baudelaire's failing health as evidence of 'hystérie', he shared his scepticism with Sainte-Beuve: 'Un autre [médecin] me dit pour toute consolation que je suis *hystérique*. Admirez-vous comme moi l'élastique de ces grands mots bien choisis pour voiler notre ignorance de toutes choses?' (letter of 15 Jan. 1866, *Corr.*, ii. 583). Three weeks later, in a letter to his friend and the future editor of his posthumous *Œuvres complètes*, Charles Asselineau, it appears that this diagnosis was understood to include the threat of aphasia, from which Baudelaire was to suffer one further month later after a major stroke left him partly paralysed and deprived of the power of speech: 'Le mal persiste. Et le médecin a prononcé le grand mot: hystérie. En bon français: je jette ma langue aux chiens' [a slang expression for speechlessness] (letter of 5 Feb. 1866, *Corr.*, ii. 587).
[17] 'Baudelaire et l'hystérie en son temps', 843.
[18] *Ion*, 534b. See Plato, *Early Socratic Dialogues*, ed. Trevor J. Saunders (rev. edn, London: Penguin Books, 2005), 55. See also my *Unacknowledged Legislators: The Poet as Lawgiver in Post-Revolutionary France: Chateaubriand-Staël-Lamartine-Hugo-Vigny* (Oxford: Oxford University Press, 2016), 21.

also because the cliché of the vatic poet offers ammunition to all the magistrates and doctors who would like to marginalize poets as either criminal or crazy. The guardians of civil and medical laws have their own ways of describing and understanding and regulating the world of human experience, of how it is and how it should be—in short, what is good for us; and they do not like poets suggesting alternatives.

I will return to this question of the relationship between mental health and poetry in Chapter 4. For the moment it is clear that Baudelaire's review of *Madame Bovary* constitutes not only a celebration of Flaubert but a defence of the poetic imagination—and the self-defence of a poet who had been found guilty of obscenity. For Baudelaire—here writing, therefore, as both judge and defence counsel—the court had used the wrong criteria, an inappropriate legislation. The Poet obeys other laws: not only the laws of art ('l'amour du Beau') but the laws of life itself as alternatively perceived and understood by the creative imagination. In bringing a charge against *Madame Bovary* for offending public decency, the prosecutor had been seeking not only to condemn adultery but also, Baudelaire implies, to outlaw the 'alternative' (allegedly 'hysterical') thinking of a woman with the spirit and imagination to want more from life than the platitudes of marriage. And that same prosecutor, following the same legislation and informed by the same mindset, had successfully secured the condemnation of poems that depict the alternative sexuality of Sappho and her companions on the island of Lesbos.[19] But Baudelaire wants an alternative sort of reader, one who can think outside the witness box of Second Empire France and understand the meanings of *Les Fleurs du Mal* from within—the reader whom he addresses in a sonnet first published in 1861 and which for a time was most probably intended to serve as the epigraph to the second edition, the 'Épigraphe pour un livre condamné'. This reader will understand that the 'poète hystérique' is actually an alternative lawgiver:

> Lecteur paisible et bucolique,
> Sobre et naïf homme de bien,
> Jette ce livre saturnien,
> Orgiaque et mélancolique.
>
> Si tu n'as fait ta rhétorique
> Chez Satan, le rusé doyen,
> Jette! tu n'y comprendrais rien,
> Ou tu me croirais hystérique.

---

[19] Née discusses the gendering of 'hysteria' in the latter part of 'Baudelaire et l'hystérie en son temps', 848–56. See also Ladenson, *Dirt for Art's Sake*, 74, on this connection between some of the banned poems ('Lesbos', 'Femmes damnées (Delphine et Hippoltye)') and Baudelaire's account of Emma Bovary's sexuality.

> Mais si, sans se laisser charmer,
> Ton œil sait plonger dans les gouffres,
> Lis-moi, pour apprendre à m'aimer;
>
> Âme curieuse qui souffres
> Et vas cherchant ton paradis,
> Plains-moi!... Sinon, je te maudis!

But Baudelaire did not in the end include this epigraph, with its ironic twist on the rhetorical device of the *captatio benevolentiae*, no more than he ever published any of his draft prefaces to the collection. Constantly he was tempted to explain himself, yet resolutely he remained true to his conviction that the work must speak for itself, just as readers also must decide for themselves: 'La logique de l'œuvre suffit à toutes les postulations de la morale, et c'est au lecteur à tirer les conclusions de la conclusion.'

Baudelaire as Lawgiver?

> Si j'avais voté, je n'aurais pu voter que pour moi.
> (letter to Narcisse Ancelle, 5 March 1852 (*Corr.*, i. 188))
>
> Quant à moi qui sens quelquefois en moi le ridicule d'un prophète [...]
> (*Fusées*, f. 22)[20]

So if it's up to the reader, how can the poet be a lawgiver? It may seem perverse to affiliate Baudelaire, the reputed fountainhead of 'modern' French poetry, to the age-old tradition of the poet as lawgiver. Unlike his most influential and immediate predecessors in the history of French poetic theory and practice— Chateaubriand, Staël, Lamartine, Hugo, and Vigny—he shows little apparent sign of wishing to offer moral, political, or religious guidance to his readers. He is no Moses, nor does he ever take Moses as a model—except once, in 'L'Héautontimorouménos', where the poet states his intention to provoke tears by striking his victim as though he were the Prophet smiting the rock and bringing forth water (Exodus 17: 5–6 and Numbers 20: 7–13).[21] Moreover he was privately scathing of Hugo's grandiose adoption of the prophet's role: 'Hugo-Sacerdoce a

---

[20] *Fusées*, ed. Guyaux, 75; i. 667. The posthumously published text of *Fusées* is thought to have been compiled between 1855 and 1862 (see i. 1468).

[21] On the important differences between these two biblical accounts and the consequences for a reading of 'L'Héautontimorouménos', see Kate Etheridge, '"Grâces sataniques": Laughter, Redemption, and Poetic Self-Awareness in *Les Fleurs du Mal*', in Charlie Louth and Patrick McGuinness (eds), *Gravity and Grace: Essays for Roger Pearson* (Cambridge: Legenda (Modern Humanities Research Association), 2019), 70–84 (81).

toujours le front penché;—trop penché pour rien voir, excepté son nombril'; and he wryly scorns the influence of the Hugolian example: 'Qu'est-ce qui n'est pas un sacerdoce aujourd'hui? La jeunesse elle-même est un sacerdoce,—à ce que dit la jeunesse.'[22] More publicly, in 'Le Vin des chiffonniers',[23] the lofty figure of the poet-lawgiver has become a drunken down-and-out, a ragpicker '[b]utant, et se cognant aux murs comme un poète' (l. 6)—a kind of 'tatterdemalion Jean-Jacques', in Richard Burton's apt phrase.[24] Blithe in his garrulous ardour to the threat of police informers—whom he regally regards as 'ses sujets' (l. 7)—this rubbish-tip revolutionary pours out his heart to all who would listen to his 'glorieux projets' (l. 8):

> Il prête des serments, dicte les lois sublimes,
> Terrasse les méchants, relève les victimes,
> Et sous le firmament comme un dais suspendu
> S'enivre des splendeurs de sa propre vertu.
>
> (ll. 9–12)

Our 'modern' Baudelaire, by contrast, rejects the didactic and the overtly ideological. Whether in verse or prose this Baudelaire is the poet of 'suggestion', of brevity and obliquity, of subtle implication rather than magisterial pronouncement, let alone drunken declamation. He is also the disabused political idealist who dedicates *Les Fleurs du Mal* to his friend Théophile Gautier, the champion of Art for Art's Sake; and he is the reader, art-lover, concert-goer, and critic who admired not only Gautier but Poe, Delacroix, and Wagner for their innovative techniques and single-minded dedication to their chosen art forms. Surely the great innovation of Baudelaire was, precisely, to reject the Romantic figure of the poet as *vates*, of the poet not only as someone with a superior ability to wield the everyday instrument of human language but also as a unique and privileged individual who is privy to superior insights and truths that enable him—authorize him—to lay down the law and lead his people towards the promised land of a brighter, better future?

In *Unacknowledged Legislators* I examined the textual reality behind this mythical figure and identified, from the work of five central literary figures of

---

[22] *Fusées*, ed. Guyaux, 72; i. 665.

[23] Dating back at least to 1851, this poem was first published in 1854 in the wonderfully entitled periodical *Jean Raisin, revue joyeuse et vinicole*. See i. 1047–9, and Luc Badesco, 'Baudelaire et la Revue Jean Raisin: La Première Publication du "Vin des chiffonniers"', *Revue des sciences humaines*, 85 (Jan.–Mar. 1957), 57–88. For discussion of the poem see in particular Richard D. E. Burton, *Baudelaire and the Second Republic: Writing and Revolution* (Oxford: Clarendon Press, 1991), ch. 6, and Ross Chambers, 'Recycling the Ragpicker: "Le Vin des chiffonniers"', in William J. Thompson (ed.), *Understanding 'Les Fleurs du Mal': Critical Readings* (Nashville: Vanderbilt University Press, 1997), 176–91. On the social and historical context see Antoine Compagnon, *Les Chiffonniers* (Paris: Gallimard, 2017).

[24] Burton, *Baudelaire and the Second Republic*, 246.

the Romantic period in France, four principal strands in the role of the poet as lawgiver: the poet as politician; the poet as champion of justice; the poet as moral and religious commentator; and the poet as 'officiant of uncertainty'.[25]

Under the first heading of 'the poet as politician' Baudelaire clearly marks a radical departure in that as a writer he sought no political role in the life of the nation, neither as a participant in parliamentary governance (Chateaubriand, Lamartine, Hugo) nor as a polemical activist deeply engaged in public affairs (Staël) nor even as an occasional lobbyist (Vigny). But does that mean that he had no interest in politics? For a long time it was orthodox to believe that the idealistic young man who had fought with the Parisian workers on the barricades of June 1848 had been disillusioned by the failure of that resistance and by the betrayal, on the part of the newly installed government of the Second Republic, of the very ideals that had sparked the earlier revolution, in February, and put an end once and for all to monarchical rule in France. Following Louis-Napoléon's *coup d'état* on 2 December 1851 (timed to coincide with the anniversary of the battle of Austerlitz, his uncle's most decisive victory) Baudelaire refused to participate in the sham elections of 29 February 1852 and explained why in a letter to his legal guardian, Narcisse Ancelle:

> Vous ne m'avez pas vu au vote; c'est un parti pris chez moi. LE 2 DÉCEMBRE m'a *physiquement dépolitiqué. Il n'y a plus d'idées générales.* Que *tout Paris* soit *orléaniste*, c'est un fait, mais cela ne me regarde pas. Si j'avais voté, je ne n'aurais pu voter que pour moi. Peut-être l'avenir appartient-il aux hommes *déclassés*?
> (*Corr.*, i. 188)

As far as he is concerned, all political debate is now over: those who once supported the Orleanist monarchy of Louis-Philippe have successfully turned the clock back, leaving him in a minority of one. And yet seven years later, in a letter to his friend the photographer Nadar on 16 May 1859, Baudelaire reveals what a number of commentators have since shown to be true: 'Je me suis vingt fois persuadé que je ne m'intéressais plus à la politique, et à chaque question grave, je suis repris de curiosité et de passion' (*Corr.*, i. 578).

Owing in particular to the work of Walter Benjamin, Dolf Oehler, David Kelley, Pierre Pachet, Richard Burton, Steve Murphy, and Pierre Laforgue,[26] we now have access to a much more nuanced and well-informed picture of the many different ways in which Baudelaire's writings are inflected—whether in sympathy or in opposition—both by the political and economic issues of his day[27] and, more

---

[25] See *Unacknowledged Legislators*, 573–86.   [26] See Bibliography for full details.
[27] On the socio-economic issues, see also Margueritte S. Murphy, *Material Figures: Political Economy, Commercial Culture, and the Aesthetic Sensibility of Charles Baudelaire* (Amsterdam and New York: Rodopi, 2012).

generally, by the political thinking of others (for example, Rousseau, De Maistre, and Proudhon). As Oehler puts it (and as translated by Rosemary Lloyd): 'It is part of Baudelaire's modernity that he reacted with extreme sensitivity to the political and social movements of his time and it is part of his sensitivity that he, like Flaubert, distanced himself from those clichés with which his contemporaries expressed their aspirations, viewpoints, political programmes, historical philosophy and so forth.' Moreover, Oehler adds: 'The despair, the spleen, that is expressed in so many of his poems is not simply metaphysical, but also has a completely concrete political and social basis.'[28] What emerges most clearly from these critical accounts, perhaps, is Baudelaire's recurrent propensity to think outside the narrow parameters of conventional political definitions and ephemeral contemporary struggles. While he may have shared in the enthusiasms of the Left in the run-up to the 1848 Revolution, as he then shared also in the widespread sense of disillusion that followed,[29] Baudelaire more often viewed political action and political aspirations against the broader backdrop of an immutable human nature—and from the perspective of his own increasingly bitter scepticism about the possibility of moral or social progress. In this, as Pierre Laforgue observes, he had much in common (and not only his dress sense) with the contemporary figure of the dandy: 'un personnage en rupture avec ses semblables et n'existant que dans une sorte de solitude radicale par rapport à ses contemporains'.[30]

For this reason Baudelaire is not so much a champion of justice (my second characteristic of the unacknowledged legislator)—even though *Le Spleen de Paris* demonstrates considerable empathy with the dispossessed of contemporary society—as he is a witness to the possibility of alternative forms of justice, including what Flaubert calls a 'literary justice'.[31] He may have been prepared to acknowledge publicly (though not in private correspondence with his mother (see *Corr.*, ii. 254)) that Hugo's *Les Misérables* served a useful reforming purpose in drawing attention to the injustice of poverty undergone by a large proportion of the French population, but he was not ready to subordinate his own art to a purpose of this kind, no matter how just the particular cause.

Unlike his influential predecessors Baudelaire had no public agenda. For Chateaubriand, literature—and poetry in particular—had a key role to play in

---

[28] Dolf Oehler, 'Baudelaire's Politics', in Rosemary Lloyd (ed.), *The Cambridge Companion to Baudelaire* (Cambridge: Cambridge University Press, 2005), 14–30 (15, 24).

[29] This widespread experience of disillusion lies at the heart of Flaubert's *L'Éducation sentimentale* (1869) and has been eloquently analysed in its literary manifestations by Ross Chambers in his *Mélancolie et opposition: Les Débuts du modernisme en France* (Paris: Corti, 1987).

[30] See his *Politiques de Baudelaire: Huit études* (Paris: Eurédit, 2014), 206. In his introduction to this collection of essays (pp. 9–20) Laforgue still feels obliged to argue how essential it is to 'save' Baudelaire from critics who continue to 'dehistoricize' him and to discuss even his celebrated 'modernité' in complete isolation from the particulars of his nineteenth-century context. Laforgue himself sees Baudelaire's politics as fundamentally and lastingly 'socialiste', arguing that his 'pulsions maistriennes elles-mêmes, que nous ne nions pas, sont intégrées dans son socialisme' (20).

[31] See my 'Flaubert's Style and the Idea of Literary Justice', 166.

the restoration of the Christian faith to its rightful and beneficent place at the centre of national life, just as for Staël literature—and poetry in particular (first in *Corinne* and then in *De l'Allemagne*)—had a key role to play in 'completing' the Revolution by promoting republican ideals of freedom, altruism, and community amongst her readers (what she calls 'enthousiasme'). As Lamartine and Hugo shifted their political stance, at different speeds and in different guises, from Right to Left, they continued to place literary endeavour at the service of their ideological convictions and political ambitions in ways that are quite alien to Baudelaire's aesthetic theory and practice. Of the five writers in question only Vigny, with whom Baudelaire developed a brief but strong personal rapport in 1861, can be seen—both in *Stello* and in his own career as a writer—to anticipate Baudelaire's adoption of a consciously separatist and 'resistant' role for the poet within society. In Vigny's case, of course, the famous prescriptions of his Docteur Noir—'séparer la vie poétique de la vie politique', 'Seul et libre, accomplir sa mission'—precisely bespeak a quasi-religious 'mission': the poet's pastoral role as the accumulator and preserver of human wisdom. For its author *Les Destinées* constitutes the newest Testament, the recorded witness of 'l'Esprit pur' for a secular, post-Christian age. But is not *Les Fleurs du Mal* somewhat similar? The Devil's Testament, perhaps? For Baudelaire's famous collection, conceived and in part already written during the same decade as the majority of Vigny's *Destinées* (the 1840s), and completed and published one year after Hugo's own greatest achievement as a poet-lawgiver, *Les Contemplations* (1856), can be seen to spring from a similar ambition to offer a post-Christian alternative to the Bible. Indeed, might not Vigny and Hugo each have said of their own works, as Baudelaire claimed of *Les Fleurs du Mal*, that it was 'destiné à représenter L'AGITATION DE L'ESPRIT DANS LE MAL' (i. 195)?

The case for Baudelaire as a poet-lawgiver soon gathers momentum when we consider him not as a political legislator or as a champion of justice but as a 'moral and religious commentator' and as an 'officiant of uncertainty'. With the latter phrase I wanted to encapsulate a crucial trend in French Romanticism whereby the traditional belief that a poet has access to some higher ('divine') truth underwent a significant change as the source of poetic authority shifted from God to man. As I wrote: 'with this shift poets begin to see it as their purpose to point not towards an absolute truth that can now, thanks to them, be known, but rather to some realm of the unknown that makes our present fund of human knowledge a petty and risible thing. No longer priests, they have become the officiants of uncertainty.'[32]

In arguing the case for Baudelaire as an 'alternative lawgiver' I therefore begin (in Part I) by discussing Baudelaire's strategies of 'resistance' as he seeks to carve

---

[32] *Unacknowledged Legislators*, 582.

out an authentic and independent role for the poet (and, more broadly, the artist) in the bourgeois society of post-1830 France. I investigate how he rejects all claims for the moral 'usefulness' of poetry but rejects also the doctrine of 'l'art pour l'art', and how he insists instead on the moral seriousness of art: a moral seriousness that derives its legitimacy simultaneously—ambiguously and problematically—from the poet's attention to the 'laws' of nature, on the one hand, and, on the other, from the poet's own willed creations of aesthetic order in the face of nature. For Baudelaire—and here I pay particular attention to his essay on caricature, *De l'essence du rire*, and to his prose poem 'Une mort héroïque'—the poet is a performer and 'double agent', enacting the melancholy of the human condition as though in ignorance of the futility of his performance in a pointless world but in the process knowingly creating patterns of 'beauty' that, for the reader or spectator, reinvest that pointless world with interest and a multiplicity of meaning.

I then go on (in Part II) to examine the question of melancholy and the ways in which *Les Fleurs du Mal* provides a secular (but theologically inflected) moral commentary on our human condition.[33] I argue for the need to see 'le Mal' not in terms of 'evil' but as an amoral and unreligious term denoting the 'ill-being' of our melancholic condition, itself predicated on the 'tragedy of desire'—and of which Satan, having known Heaven and 'resisted' God, who cast him into Hell, is the symbolic representative. In presenting this argument I treat *Les Fleurs du Mal* not as a definitive entity but as a work in progress, something necessarily 'abandoned' (in Valéry's well-known formulation) rather than 'finished', and I follow it like a river from its source in a collection provisionally entitled *Les Lesbiennes* (1845–7) and then *Les Limbes* (1851), through its 'pre-edition' in 1855 and the first and second editions of 1857 and 1861, to the posthumous and 'unfinished' third edition of 1868. While it is customary to privilege the 1861 edition as the nearest

---

[33] Baudelaire's religious opinions have understandably generated considerable debate. In his own day the very sensitivity of the question may explain why neither his work nor his correspondence provides any definitive evidence of what he may or may not have 'believed' (in the religious sense), particularly in relation to the Christian faith, and since then some critics have taken advantage of this lack of firm statement to approach Baudelaire from their own particular religious viewpoint. My own view of a secular Baudelaire is based on a reading of all his published work and correspondence, but I have found the following of particular use: George Blin, *Baudelaire* (Paris: Gallimard, 1939), 209–17, where Blin makes a robust case that Baudelaire was not a Roman Catholic: 'rien ne saurait justifier l'effort de toute une littérature catholique pour annexer Baudelaire. Non, il n'a pas connu "le frisson de la croix"' (209–10); 'Il est clair que Baudelaire n'a pas pratiqué. Je doute même qu'il ait beaucoup prié' (213); 'c'est toujours par défi, par polémique, contre quelqu'un que Baudelaire se révèle "fervent catholique"' (215); and Alain Vaillant, *Baudelaire, poète comique* (Rennes: Presses universitaires de Rennes, 2007), 88–99, where in a section entitled 'La mystique antireligieuse' Vaillant makes a similarly robust case that Baudelaire was a non-believer. On Baudelaire's specific attitudes to sin, see Bertrand Marchal, 'La Nature et le péché', *Études baudelairiennes*, 12 (1987), 7–22, and also Jean Dubray, *Pascal et Baudelaire* (Paris: Classiques Garnier, 2011), 133–59. For some useful surveys of the critical reception of Baudelaire's religious views, see Antoine Compagnon, *Baudelaire devant l'innombrable* (Paris: Presses de l'Université de Paris-Sorbonne, 2003), 21–8; Jean-Pierre Jossua, 'Quelques interprétations de la religion de Baudelaire', *Recherches de science religieuse*, 94 (2006), 169–91; and Guyaux (ed.), *Baudelaire: Un demi-siècle de lectures des 'Fleurs du mal' (1855–1905)* (Paris: PUPS [Presses de l'Université Paris-Sorbonne], 2007), 130–6.

to a definitive version we have, this being the last to be published during Baudelaire's lifetime, I believe nevertheless that by adopting a more holistic and 'organic' approach to the various manifestations of what we call *Les Fleurs du Mal*, we are granted a clearer and more nuanced picture both of its constituent elements and of its celebrated 'secret architecture'.

In particular I shall show how the significant structural changes that Baudelaire made to the collection between 1857 and 1861, through the addition and reordering of poems, serve an equally significant shift in the poetic argument, such that where in the 1857 edition the poet proposes a resigned acceptance of melancholy and death, in the 1861 edition he advocates a resistance to melancholy and death through the power of the creative imagination and (in the newly added 'Hymne à la Beauté') the power of a new form of beauty. Indeed, in the *Salon de 1859*, written and published during this crucial period in Baudelaire's career as a writer, he describes a process of pictorial composition that closely resembles the process of poetic transformation that he himself was then undertaking:

> Un bon tableau, fidèle et égal au rêve qui l'a enfanté, doit être produit comme un monde. De même que la création, telle que nous la voyons, est le résultat de plusieurs créations dont les précédentes sont toujours complétées par la suivante; ainsi un tableau conduit harmoniquement consiste en une série de tableaux superposés, chaque nouvelle couche donnant au rêve plus de réalité et le faisant monter d'un degré vers la perfection. (ii. 626)

In tracing the evolution of *Les Fleurs du Mal* and its coming-into-being I do not wish to imply some easy access to a body of coherent and unambiguous authorial intentions, still less a certain knowledge (notoriously elusive in Baudelaire's case) of when particular poems were first drafted and/or later revised.[34] I intend rather to approach the poems on their own terms and according to a rough chronology of their publication *as well as* in respect of their situation within successive structurings of the evolving work. In this way it becomes possible to identify and trace particular thematic preoccupations and insistent patterns of imagery that may become occluded by undue attention to the ordering of a particular edition. The view of *Les Fleurs du Mal* that emerges from such an approach is ultimately less 'architectural' than 'kaleidoscopic' (the analogy Baudelaire used to describe *Le Spleen de Paris*), and perhaps therefore more in keeping with the relativism that is fundamental to Baudelaire's world-view—and to his conception of beauty.[35]

---

[34] For a detailed overview see the appendix 'Dates of Texts' in David Evans, *Rhythm, Illusion and the Poetic Idea: Baudelaire, Rimbaud, Mallarmé* (Amsterdam: Rodopi, 2004), 339–42.

[35] Steve Murphy makes a similar point in his introduction to the multi-authored *Lectures des 'Fleurs du Mal'*: 'ne pas croire qu'il est possible de fixer et figer le texte littéraire en lui imposant un sens objectif et définitif' (Murphy (ed.), *Lectures de Baudelaire: 'Les Fleurs du Mal'* (Rennes: Presses universitaires de

In Part III, I turn temporarily away from *Les Fleurs du Mal* in order to discuss Baudelaire's critical writings of the period 1855-63—on Poe, Gautier, Hugo, Wagner, and Constantin Guys—and to show how he comes to adopt this new faith in the imagination as a form of 'government', ruling us with *new* ways of perceiving the world of human experience, and also as an instrument of 're-creation' with which what is destroyed by time and mortality can be reassembled as a fresh form of life, the life of art and beauty. In particular I foreground his now recurrent use of the term 'conjecture' with which he seeks to describe the ways in which beauty, far from being some self-sufficient attribute (as described in 'La Beauté'), is principally an enriching and provocative effect of surmise: or, as he describes it in 'Hymne à la Beauté', 'un Infini que j'aime et n'ai jamais connu'. In this way—through the creation of beauty for others—the poet-lawgiver as 'moral and religious commentator' is also an 'officiant of uncertainty'.

In Part IV I return to *Les Fleurs du Mal* and discuss it now less from the point of view of melancholy than from this new perspective of a 're-creative' beauty, here deployed specifically in lyric verse. I examine the so-called 'love poems' within the context of the revised framework of the 1861 edition, seeing them less as poems about 'love' than as poems exemplifying the poetic creation of beauty, before then focusing—in Chapter 17—on the various prosodic techniques with which Baudelaire seeks to construct what he calls the 'idée poétique'. (Those who would prefer to have an overview of the poet's handling of versification before embarking on my account of *Les Fleurs du Mal* could read this chapter between Chapters 5 and 6.) After this I pass to the 'poetry of the city' in 'Tableaux parisiens', showing how the poet finds new ways of articulating the relationship between melancholy and beauty within a symbolic urban context and how the traditional figure of the poet as vatic seer is transformed into the poet as sightseer, observing the mysteries of the City in phantasmagorical and quasi-visionary dreamworks of verse.

From this I pass in turn, in Part V, to the prose poems of *Le Spleen de Paris*, itself unfinished and comprising only fifty of the hundred poems once envisaged by its ambitious but increasingly ailing author. After initial discussions of Baudelaire's inauguration of this new form of literary writing in 'Le Crépuscule du soir' and 'La Solitude', first published in 1855, and of the relationship between the prose poem and the world of journalism in which it was born and lived, I present a poet-lawgiver who now casts off the mantle of the 'moral and religious

Rennes, 2002), 10). In so doing he was explicitly taking his cue from Ross Chambers who, a decade earlier, had advocated the same principle for Baudelaire's work as a whole: 'it is the Baudelairean corpus in its totality, as well as individual texts, that we need to learn to consider less a coherent body of work and more an assemblage energized by desire. The corpus is not woven together like a text, but traversed, torn and tattered by many different "lines of flight"' ('Perpetual Abjuration: Baudelaire and the Pain of Modernity' (review article of Burton, *Baudelaire in 1859*, and Maclean, *Narrative as Performance*), *French Forum*, 15: 2 (May 1990), 169-88 (186)).

commentator', sending up this role in a riotous flurry of maxims and apothegms and turning the 'officiant of uncertainty' into a festive clown, at once a master of mystification and the instrument of a delicious and suspenseful perplexity. Here there now emerges the 'voice of the stranger', lending insistent new forms of expression to the experience of melancholy, performing a whole series of new roles as the most elusive of poet-narrators, and producing an extraordinary new form of literary beauty: that is, a form of discourse that militantly resists the conceptual frameworks of orthodox moral, religious, political, philosophical, and aesthetic thinking and simply goes it alone, a law unto itself in a minority voice of one.

* * * * *

Throughout this book I envisage a Baudelaire for whom beauty, being an effect, can constitute an instrument of emancipation: a mode of reception in which the reader is invited to participate in the writer's own response to the world and to take that response forward in their own terms and within the context of their own historical, political, and cultural situation. For this writer who was so opposed to facile proclamations of faith in Progress and Democracy and Morality, poetry nevertheless represented a genuinely powerful means of enlisting the moral and imaginative engagement of human beings in the mystery of our lives. For him poetry is a fundamentally democratic medium: less the statement of a truth than a request for empathy ('Plains-moi!...Sinon, je te maudis!'), not only a gift of beauty but an invitation to create it, not something to be taken as read but as something to be read and reread as though for the first time, and with ever-changing effects: a legislation to be voted on, passed, revised, or repealed, and to be voted on again. It is no accident that *lex* and *legere*—law and reading—derive from the same etymological root.

Nor is it an accident that there have been quite so many different responses to Baudelaire's work over the many years since it was first published. As Jean-Claude Mathieu wrote in 1972: 'Chaque individu, chaque époque, chaque classe a produit "un" Baudelaire, celui qu'il lui était possible de comprendre et utile d'admettre.'[36] For André Guyaux, writing in 2003, there have been essentially three successive Baudelaires: 'le poète du Mal', 'le poète de la mort', and 'le poète observateur du monde'.[37] In the same year, under the heading of 'Légendes des *Fleurs du Mal*', Antoine Compagnon identifies a whole *dramatis personae* but in no particular order, conceding that to some extent they overlap: 'le réaliste', 'le satanique', 'le décadent', 'le symboliste', 'le classique', 'le catholique', 'le moderne', 'le réactionnaire', 'le "superpoète"', 'l'essentiel', 'le postmoderne'. All these 'images'

---

[36] '*Les Fleurs du Mal' de Baudelaire* (Paris: Hachette, 1972), 108.
[37] 'Avant-propos', in André Guyaux and Bertrand Marchal (eds), '*Les Fleurs du Mal*': *Actes du colloque de la Sorbonne des 10 et 11 janvier 2003* (Paris: Presses de l'Université Paris-Sorbonne, 2003), 7–8.

of Baudelaire are available to today's readers, Compagnon maintains, though he himself identifies three principal ones: 'le décadent', 'le classique', and 'le moderne'. But above all he cautions, rightly, against the critical tendency to present each new Baudelaire as the real Baudelaire. Rather, we should return to the text, to 'un Baudelaire *littéral*': 'C'est le Baudelaire dont on ne sait que faire, celui d'un vers toujours déconcertant en dépit de toutes les épithètes.'[38] And Michel Brix, writing in 2007, sounds a similarly valuable note of warning to any critic proposing to write about Baudelaire for the first time: 'Seul le critique fraîchement débarqué en baudelairisme peut rêver qu'il va découvrir l'œuf de Colomb, mettre tout le monde d'accord et produire la lecture *exacte* et *définitive* des *Fleurs du Mal*.'[39]

In other words, we should listen to Baudelaire's own insistent and repeated statements that in responding to the beauty of a work of art we have to reach our own verdicts on the basis of 'la logique de l'œuvre', of its own internal legislations. As he notes in the *Salon de 1846* (about painting but it could also be about a poem): 'Chercher la poésie de parti pris dans la conception d'un tableau est le plus sûr moyen de ne pas la trouver. Elle doit venir à l'insu de l'artiste. Elle est le résultat de la peinture elle-même; car elle gît dans l'âme du spectateur, et le génie consiste à l'y réveiller' (ii. 474). Or as he had written in a review earlier that year: 'C'est que la poésie d'un tableau doit être faite par le spectateur.—Comme la philosophie d'un poème par le lecteur' (ii. 9).

---

[38] Compagnon, *Baudelaire devant l'innombrable*, 9–39 (38 for the quotation). For Baudelaire's critical reception, see W. T. Bandy (ed.), *Baudelaire Judged by his Contemporaries (1845–1867)* (New York: Columbia University, 1933), later translated (where necessary), revised, and republished as W. T. Bandy and Claude Pichois (eds), *Baudelaire devant ses contemporains* (Monaco: Éditions du Rocher, 1957); A. E. Carter, *Baudelaire et la critique française 1868–1917* (Columbia: University of South Carolina Press, 1963); and Guyaux (ed.), *Baudelaire: Un demi-siècle de lectures des 'Fleurs du mal'*, in which Guyaux's 'Préface' (pp. 11–139) provides a detailed historical survey.

[39] Michel Brix, 'Claude Pichois et l'interprétation de Baudelaire', *L'Année Baudelaire*, 9/10 (2007), 71–7 (72).

PART I
RESISTANCE

La première affaire d'un artiste est de substituer l'homme à la nature et de protester contre elle. Cette protestation ne se fait pas de parti pris, froidement, comme un code ou une rhétorique; elle est emportée et naïve, comme le vice, comme la passion, comme l'appétit.
(*Salon de 1846*, ii. 473)

1
The Poet of Resistance

> Monsieur, vous sentez-vous assez fort pour aimer un merdeux qui ne pense pas comme vous?
>
> (*Corr.* ii. 501)

The Poet as Contrarian

> Le vrai poète,—une vérité habillée d'une manière bizarre, un paradoxe apparent, qui ne veut pas être coudoyé par la foule, et qui court à l'extrême orient quand le feu d'artifice se tire au couchant.
>
> ('Notes nouvelles sur Edgar Poe', ii. 322)

'Vous savez', Baudelaire wrote to Sainte-Beuve from Brussels in March 1865, 'que je peux devenir dévot par contradiction (*surtout ici*)' (*Corr.* ii. 491). This comment to an old friend who knew him well epitomizes a central feature of Baudelaire's work: resistance through contrariness. The pursuit of the new, the ambition to 'extraire la *beauté* du Mal' (i. 181), the experiment of writing poetry in prose, all attest to Baudelaire's deep-seated aversion to the orthodox, the status quo, and the universally acknowledged. *Pauvre Belgique!* is itself an extraordinary onslaught on everything he hates: 'Esprit d'obéissance et de CONFORMITÉ' (ii. 857). 'On pense en commun', he laments: 'C'est-à-dire qu'on ne pense pas' (ii. 859). And Belgians don't just think alike: 'Ils et elles ne pissent qu'en bande.' 'Donc', he concludes, 'tout dissident est de mauvaise foi' (ii. 858). But Belgian bad faith is Baudelaire's contrarian integrity. Dissidence, contradiction: etymologically, to think and feel separately, to speak against...like 'allegory' (etymologically, 'other speak'), or the art of perceiving and describing human experience in fresh ways that point to other meanings and possibilities, to an elsewhere and an otherwise. This is the poet as alternative lawgiver, as otherly wise, proposing truths that have been obscured by conformism, piety, pretension, laziness, or mere quotidian familiarity, and proclaiming to fellow human beings how we might feel and think *differently*.[1]

---

[1] Cf. Mallarmé's formulation in *La Musique et les Lettres*: '*Autre chose*...ce semble que l'épars frémissement d'une page ne veuille sinon surseoir ou palpite d'impatience, à la possibilité d'autre chose' (Mallarmé, *Œuvres complètes*, ed. Bertrand Marchal (2 vols, Paris: Gallimard [Bibliothèque de la Pléiade], 1998–2003), ii. 67).

Baudelaire's most enthusiastic expression of this spirit of poetic resistance came in 1851, in his preface to the work of his friend Pierre Dupont (1821–70), the songwriter and working-class hero who had been sentenced to seven years' exile from France for his socialist lyrics. Not yet wholly drained of the political idealism that had inspired him during the events of the 1848 Revolution, Baudelaire celebrates the power of the poet or songwriter to offer an alternative, to take the reader to a 'utopia' or 'non-place' that constitutes a negation of the multiple iniquities of the here and now:

> C'est une grande destinée que celle de la poésie! Joyeuse ou lamentable, elle porte toujours en soi le divin caractère utopique. Elle contredit sans cesse le fait, à peine de ne plus être. Dans le cachot, elle se fait révolte; à la fenêtre de l'hôpital, elle est ardente espérance de guérison; dans la mansarde déchirée et malpropre, elle se pare comme une fée du luxe et de l'élégance; non seulement elle constate, mais elle répare. Partout elle se fait négation de l'iniquité. (ii. 35)

Here poetic resistance carries a specifically political charge: this is poetry as revolutionary protest song, and even if Baudelaire subsequently loses faith in all prospect of social improvement through political action, his sense that poetry remains a powerful 'counter-power' within the body politic remains firm. In this, and particularly in his conception of poetry as a form of reparation ('elle répare'), he anticipates Seamus Heaney's conception of poetry as a form of 'redress'.[2]

But a more familiar note of Baudelairean resistance, at once jaundiced and ironic, had been struck five years earlier, in the short text entitled 'Conseils aux jeunes littérateurs' that he published in 1846 and in which (having just turned 25) he casts himself preposterously in the role of a maternal Mme de Warens teaching his fellow young Rousseaus how to dress properly. Implicitly mocking the very idea that aspiring writers should follow precepts, he issues deadpan advice that simultaneously debunks Romantic notions of the poet-genius and sends up bourgeois good sense with withering antiphrasis. Literary success is not a question of luck but persistence; 'inspiration' is not born of orgiastic excess ('cet odieux préjugé' (ii. 18)) but of a healthy diet and daily application; financial gain makes the effort all worthwhile; do not get into debt, though it is fine to pretend that one is; etc. As to the writing of poetry, this is to be especially commended as a reliable, long-term investment. Even the bourgeoisie bows to its superior status, particularly as poetry fulfils our most pressing need: 'Quoi d'étonnant, d'ailleurs, puisque tout homme bien portant peut se passer de manger pendant deux jours,—de

---

[2] See Heaney, *The Redress of Poetry* (London: Faber and Faber, 1995), especially pp. 1–16. I discuss this in my Conclusion.

poésie, jamais? [-] L'art qui satisfait le besoin le plus impérieux sera toujours honoré' (ii. 19). If only...[3]

This implausible prospect of a well-fed middle class espousing the spiritual values of poetic endeavour reappears in 1851 in Baudelaire's article on 'Les Drames et les romans honnêtes'. Scathingly dismissive of the 'grande fureur d'honnêteté [qui] s'est emparée du théâtre et aussi du roman' (ii. 38), Baudelaire sees this as a bourgeois reaction against the perceived excesses and 'immorality' of poets and artists (as depicted, for example, in Dumas *père*'s *Kean ou Désordre et génie* (1836)). He focuses on the ridiculous plot of Émile Augier's verse comedy *Gabrielle* (1849), in which a wife, temporarily contemplating elopement with an admirer who has spoken to her of love whereas her (otherwise perfect) husband speaks to her only of business, is finally brought to her senses by the said husband's eloquence and realizes that he is the 'real' man in her life: 'Ô père de famille, ô poète, je t'aime!' (ii. 1097). And this real man is a lawyer:

> Un notaire! La voyez-vous, cette *honnête* bourgeoise, roucoulant amoureusement sur l'épaule de son homme et lui faisant des yeux alanguis comme dans les romans qu'elle a lus! Voyez-vous tous les notaires de la salle acclamant l'auteur qui traite avec eux de pair à compagnon, et qui les venge de tous ces gredins qui ont des dettes et qui croient que le métier de poète consiste à exprimer les mouvements lyriques de l'âme dans un rythme réglé par la tradition! Telle est la clef de beaucoup de succès. (ii. 39)[4]

For Baudelaire this equation of poetry with good, sensible bourgeois behaviour (Augier was a principal figure in the so-called École du bon sens) represents an act of revenge on the part of the professional classes who had been deeply outraged by the doctrine of 'l'Art pour l'Art' expounded by Gautier in his preface to *Mademoiselle de Maupin* (1835) and who therefore sought to capitalize on the more excessive behaviour of some members of the Jeune-France and others in order to ridicule poets as disorderly wasters. For Gautier, as for Vigny, the lawyer is the anti-poet;[5] and in Baudelaire's case an anti-poet profoundly implicated in a regime of political and financial governance that privileges money, marriage, and rules, and relies for its stability on a deeply hypocritical ethos of keeping up

---

[3] For further comment on this text see Bernard Howells, 'The Portrait of the Artist in 1846', in his *Baudelaire: Individualism, Dandyism and the Philosophy of History* (Oxford: Legenda, 1996), 3–27.

[4] Cf. Hippolyte Taine's sarcastic comment on this play: 'Avis aux avoués, notaires, banquiers, employés, magistrats, tous gens d'affaires comme le mari; ils sont tenus d'être poètes deux fois par mois pour garder leurs femmes' (quoted by Pichois, ii. 1097). When Baudelaire reused this section of the article in his 1859 article on Gautier, the 'notaire' became an 'avocat': see Pichois's comment, ii. 1133 (n. 2 to p. 114).

[5] On Vigny's depiction of Robespierre as the lawyer and anti-poet in *Stello* (1832) and similarly of the députés in *De Mademoiselle Sedaine et de la propriété littéraire* (1841), see *Unacknowledged Legislators*, 526–9, 541–8.

appearances. Hence, also in 1851, the provocative challenge issued to these guardians of public law and order. Will they condemn the wine-induced inebriation that is akin to the intoxication of artistic creativity?

> Et cependant dites, en votre âme et conscience, juges, législateurs, hommes du monde, vous tous que le bonheur rend doux, à qui la fortune rend la vertu et la santé faciles, dites, qui de vous aura le courage impitoyable de condamner l'homme qui boit du génie? ('Du vin et du hachisch', i. 379)

But where Vigny seeks to play the bourgeoisie at its own game by arguing that art is a product with economic value and that its producers therefore deserve the same rights (and respect) as other producers,[6] Baudelaire adopts a more contrarian line of resistance, rejecting Guizot's famous mantra of self-enrichment but also refusing to espouse a clichéd bohemian disdain for money per se. For him, in 1851, the July Monarchy's obsession with financial gain (in particular as the only route to the [male] right to vote) has been profoundly at odds with the richness to be had from a shared communality of spiritual purpose:

> la fameuse parole: 'enrichissez-vous', légitime et vraie en tant qu'elle implique la moralité, la niait par ce seul fait que elle ne l'affirmait pas. La richesse peut être une garantie de savoir et de moralité, à la condition qu'elle soit bien acquise; mais quand la richesse est montrée comme le seul but final de tous les efforts de l'individu, l'enthousiasme, la charité, la philosophie, et tout ce qui fait le patrimoine commun dans un système éclectique et propriétariste, disparaît. (ii. 27–8)

In a society based on property and the pursuit of wealth, and governed by lawyers, the poet is the guardian of our spiritual heritage, which—following Staël—Baudelaire here equates with 'enthousiasme' and aligns, as she does, with altruism and independent intellectual enquiry. And for this very reason the poet is ostracized within his own community. '[L]a France n'est pas poète', Baudelaire writes in his article on Gautier in 1859: 'elle éprouve même, pour tout dire, une horreur congéniale de la poésie' (ii. 124). The poet represents difference and resistance, the rejection of the 'tyrannie contradictoire' of a terrible conformism: 'Ici, chacun veut ressembler à tout le monde, mais à condition que tout le monde lui ressemble. [...] De là, la ruine et l'oppression de tout caractère original' (ii. 125). All innovation is suspect: 'Aussi ce n'est pas seulement dans l'ordre littéraire que les vrais poètes apparaissent comme des êtres fabuleux et étrangers; mais on peut dire que dans tous les genres d'invention le grand homme ici est un monstre' (ii. 125). The once noble and public calling of poetry has become an underground activity: 'Aimons donc nos

---

[6] See *Unacknowledged Legislators*, 544–5.

poètes secrètement et en cachette' (ii. 125).[7] Indeed to be a poet may even mean being not quite French: 'Par sa raillerie, sa gausserie, sa ferme décision de n'être jamais dupe, [Gautier] est un peu Français; mais s'il était tout à fait Français, il ne serait pas poète' (ii. 127). Still less, of course, if he were Belgian.

In contradiction and resistance lies the new nobility. From the start Baudelaire's critical writings reflect a determination that the artist shall be different. The *Salon de 1845*, for example, begins by emphasizing the merit of originality ('M. Delacroix est décidément le plus original des temps anciens et des temps modernes' (ii. 353)) and ends, as I have mentioned, with an aspiration to the new: 'Puissent les vrais chercheurs nous donner l'année prochaine cette joie singulière de célébrer l'avènement du *neuf!*' (ii. 407). Writing about Dupont in 1851 he regards the poet's resistance as marching in step with a political resistance to injustice, but ten years later, in his article on Wagner, Baudelaire no longer trusts such an easy equation between poetic and political rebellion.[8] Thus he applauds the composer of *Tannhaüser* for his perception that artistic originality depends on a fundamental attitude of non-compliance and also for his willing embrace of the persistent and painful sense of dissatisfaction consequent on such an attitude ('cette facilité à souffrir, commune à tous les artistes et d'autant plus grande que leur instinct du juste et du beau est plus prononcé' (ii. 787)). But he can no longer accept the premise of Wagner's 'opinions révolutionnaires': 'Possédé du désir suprême de voir l'idéal dans l'art dominer définitivement la routine, il a pu (c'est une illusion essentiellement humaine) espérer que des révolutions dans l'ordre politique favoriseraient la cause de la révolution dans l'art' (ii. 787). Not for Baudelaire, therefore, Hugo's notorious definition of Romanticism as 'le libéralisme en littérature' (in the preface to *Hernani* (1830)). Indeed here in the essay on Wagner Baudelaire points rather to an earlier mismatch between political and artistic movements, with Restoration sympathizers like the young Hugo and Lamartine favouring artistic freedoms and the liberals sticking to the rules of Classicism. Art and politics do not go hand in hand, no more than his own admiration for Wagner's music implies any acceptance of his ideological programme.

As demonstrated by his comments on wealth, Baudelaire's resistance is altogether more subtle and more insidious. In his address 'Aux bourgeois' at the beginning of the *Salon de 1846*, he returns to the double-edged polemic of the 'Conseils aux jeunes littérateurs' and now presents some of his barbs as serious statements. Rather than simply rejecting bourgeois rule, he accepts it—albeit in

---

[7] Cf. similar comments made by Flaubert to Louise Colet in Dec. 1852: 'Il faut *déguiser la poésie* en France; on la déteste', and again in July 1853: 'Or, dans ce charmant pays de France, le public n'admet la poésie que déguisée' (*Correspondance*, ed. Bruneau and Leclerc, ii. 209, 385–6).

[8] Patrick McGuinness has demonstrated this non-alignment of poetic and political resistance later in the century in his *Poetry and Radical Politics in Fin de Siècle France: From Anarchism to Action Française* (Oxford: Oxford University Press, 2015).

terms that imply its absence of moral authority: 'Vous possédez le gouvernement de la cité, et cela est juste, car vous êtes la force' (ii. 415). The bourgeois are in power, and with that power, he contends, goes a responsibility towards the claims of art: 'Mais il faut que vous soyez aptes à sentir la beauté; car comme aucun d'entre vous ne peut aujourd'hui se passer de puissance, nul n'a le droit de se passer de poésie' (ii. 415).

His earlier comment in the 'Conseils' about the inability of human beings to live without poetry is now reinforced and proffered in all seriousness: 'Vous pouvez vivre trois jours sans pain;—sans poésie, jamais; et ceux d'entre vous qui disent le contraire se trompent: ils ne se connaissent pas' (ii. 415). Those (on the Left) who believe the bourgeois incapable of aesthetic sensibility are self-righteous hypocrites, 'des pharisiens'. Rather the professional middle classes must be taught to 'sentir et [...] jouir', and that is the function of art: 'L'art est un bien infiniment précieux, un breuvage rafraîchissant et réchauffant, qui rétablit l'estomac et l'esprit dans l'équilibre naturel de l'idéal' (ii. 415–16). Like a nice cup of hot cocoa it is just what the weary lawmaker or businessman needs at the end of a long day:

> Vous en concevez l'utilité, ô bourgeois,—législateurs, ou commerçants,—quand la septième ou la huitième heure sonnée incline votre tête fatiguée vers les braises du foyer et les oreillards du fauteuil. [-] Un désir plus brûlant, une rêverie plus active, vous délasserait alors de l'action quotidienne. (ii. 416)

The tone here is that of a soothing nanny or dutiful wife and the setting reassuringly and fittingly domestic, but beneath the irony Baudelaire means it: and his message is essentially a secular version of that proposed by Chateaubriand in his *Génie du christianisme*. Human beings have fundamental spiritual needs that can be met by art.

In taking this line Baudelaire is here engaging in one of the 'transgressions créatrices', to use Pierre Bourdieu's phrase, by which he seeks to redraw the cultural map of his time.[9] Rather than rely on the easy polarities of political Left and Right, of artists and bourgeoisie, and rather than fall in with his fellow bohemians and vilify and condemn the bourgeois as philistine, Baudelaire states what could be viewed as in fact the most desirable outcome: a cultivated ruling class sympathetic to his own advocacy of imagination and creativity as important social values. In this respect 'Aux bourgeois' anticipates his candidacy for election to the Académie française (in 1861–2) where this has been seen as a mocking challenge intended to unmask the reality that the Academy's own laws of taste and literary decorum prevent it from recognizing true literary merit. Bourdieu

---

[9] See the section entitled 'Baudelaire nomothète' in Pierre Bourdieu, *Les Règles de l'art: Genèse et structure du champ littéraire* ([1992] rev. edn, Paris: Éditions du Seuil, 1998), 106–18 (108).

describes Baudelaire's candidacy as simultaneously 'sérieuse et parodique',[10] terms which might also serve for 'Aux bourgeois'. With pseudo-deference Baudelaire defends the bourgeois against those detractors who consider them unfit to enjoy and appreciate art just because they do not—or have no time to—understand the technical aspects of its production. Rather they have every right to devote their leisure time to art, and indeed have shown themselves—whether as 'roi, législateur ou négociant'—to be the friends of art in creating private collections or in founding museums and galleries. Indeed, in their own way, they have constituted an avant-garde!

> Vous vous êtes associés, vous avez formé des compagnies et fait des emprunts pour réaliser l'idée de l'avenir avec toutes ses formes diverses, formes politique, industrielle et artistique. Vous n'avez jamais en aucune noble entreprise laissé l'initiative à la minorité protestante et souffrante, qui est d'ailleurs l'ennemie naturelle de l'art. [-] Car se laisser devancer en art et en politique, c'est se suicider, et une majorité ne peut pas se suicider. (ii. 416)

As resistance fighter and alternative lawgiver Baudelaire is here adopting a powerful tactic, shaming his opponents into becoming his accomplice in the pursuit of artistic innovation—just as in the opening poem of *Les Fleurs du Mal* the poet challenges his reader to abandon pretence and recognize the truth that is about to be unfolded: 'Hypocrite lecteur,—mon semblable,—mon frère'. If the ruling class is to maintain the allegiance of the electoral majority and consolidate its hold on power, it will have to welcome the new—that is, the wished-for 'naïveté' and 'originalité' of art in its depiction of the 'héroïsme de la vie moderne', which, first mooted in the *Salon de 1845*, constitute the agenda of the *Salon de 1846*.[11]

The Poet as Artist and Outlaw

> Et aujourd'hui, qu'est-il, l'artiste ce frère antique du poète?
> (*Salon de 1859*, ii. 611)

Much of Baudelaire's thinking about the nature of art, and particularly about its source and function, is focused on painting and is conducted within his articles on the Salons, on other exhibitions, and on particular artists (Delacroix, Guys). But it is legitimate to read his various statements and arguments with reference also to

---

[10] Bourdieu, *Les Règles de l'art*, 108.
[11] For further discussion of Baudelaire's views on art and the bourgeoisie see Gretchen van Slyke, 'Les Épiciers au musée: Baudelaire et l'artiste bourgeois', *Romantisme*, 55 (1987), 55–66.

poetry since the central issues he addresses pertain to both painting and poetry (as well as sculpture and music) and because he clearly sees all the arts as intimately related forms of Art. The term 'poésie' itself transcends the purely literary and denotes that which appeals to the imagination, whether in nature itself or through the medium of an individual art form. In the *Salon de 1859*, for example, during his discussion of portraiture, Baudelaire states the core tenet of his own aesthetic theory in just these terms and as though it will already be very familiar to his readers: 'Parce que je réclame sans cesse l'application de l'imagination, l'introduction de la poésie dans toutes les fonctions de l'art [...]' (ii. 657).

Like Gautier, known for his so-called 'transpositions d'art', Baudelaire saw art forms as interchangeable. Thus, in the *Salon de 1846*, he refers to some of Hugo's poems as 'tableaux' that are coldly symmetrical, while by contrast he praises Delacroix's canvases as 'poèmes' (ii. 431). In *Exposition universelle. 1855. Beaux-Arts* Baudelaire condemns Hugo again for his lack of warmth and suggestiveness: 'M. Victor Hugo est un grand poète sculptural qui a l'œil fermé à la spiritualité' (ii. 593), thus tarring him with the same brush as sculpture itself (which he describes in the *Salon de 1846* as '[b]rutale et positive comme la nature' (ii. 487)). In 'L'Œuvre et la vie d'Eugène Delacroix' (1863) by contrast, the eponymous artist is quite simply 'le type du peintre-poète' (ii. 751), and Baudelaire comments with approval on a new-found solidarity between the arts: 'C'est, du reste, un des diagnostics de l'état spirituel de notre siècle que les arts aspirent, sinon à se suppléer l'un l'autre, du moins à se prêter réciproquement des forces nouvelles' (ii. 744).[12]

For Baudelaire the poet is an artist, and if the lawyer is the anti-poet, so too are the experts who lay down the law about art: 'ces "modernes professeurs-jurés" d'esthétique', as Baudelaire (adapting Heine) calls them in *Exposition universelle*. Already in the *Salon de 1845* he had praised one painting, albeit strategically,[13] for having been produced 'avec une grande naïveté—sans aucune prétention d'école ni aucun pédantisme d'atelier' (ii. 397), just as, more enthusiastically, he had commended Corot for 'la naïveté et l'originalité' (ii. 389) of his art. 'Naïveté' is a recurrent word of approval in Baudelaire's art criticism of this period, borrowed from Delacroix himself,[14] and by it he means a kind of innocence and individuality of vision deriving from the artist's 'tempérament', informed and enabled by skilful technique but independent of all prescriptive rule and normative fashion. Hence in the *Salon de 1846* the unfavourable comparison of Hugo the verse poet with Delacroix the superior 'poet' in paint. The former is 'un ouvrier beaucoup

---

[12] Cf. his comments in 'Théodore de Banville' (1861): 'La poésie moderne tient à la fois de la peinture, de la musique, de la statuaire, de l'art arabesque, de la philosophie railleuse, de l'esprit analytique, et, si heureusement, si habilement agencée qu'elle soit, elle se présente avec les signes visibles d'une subtilité empruntée à divers arts' (ii. 167).

[13] See ii. 1283, n. 1 to p. 397.

[14] See Margaret Gilman, *Baudelaire the Critic* ([1943] New York: Octagon Books, 1971), 35–40.

plus adroit qu'inventif, un travailleur bien plus correct que créateur', while the latter is 'quelquefois maladroit, mais essentiellement créateur' (ii. 431). Hugo's skills smack of the Academy—indeed 'M. Hugo était naturellement académicien avant que de naître' (ii. 431)—while Delacroix's art displays the 'insolence' of genius: 'Ses œuvres, au contraire, sont des poèmes, et de grands poèmes naïvement conçus' (ii. 431). Baudelaire defines in a footnote what he means: 'Il faut entendre par la naïveté du génie la science du métier combinée avec le "gnôti séauton" [know thyself], mais la science modeste laissant le beau rôle au tempérament' (ii. 431).[15] For Baudelaire Delacroix thus represents an ideal combination of art and life: 'Delacroix est, comme tous les grands maîtres, un mélange admirable de science,—c'est-à-dire un peintre complet,—et de naïveté, c'est-à-dire un homme complet' (ii. 435).

Just as Baudelaire seeks to move beyond the facile binaries of wealth versus moral worth and bourgeois philistinism versus bohemian culture, so here, too, he employs the concept of 'naïveté' to escape the binary of rule-observance and creative originality—and thus by implication to erase the supposed demarcation line between Classicism and Romanticism. For him the key distinction lies between the professor and the practitioner: what matters is not the aesthetic theories of the former but the technical know-how of the latter, 'la science du métier'. In this respect, and despite his being 'quelquefois maladroit', Delacroix is Baudelaire's ideal artist:

> Delacroix part donc de ce principe, qu'un tableau doit avant tout reproduire la pensée intime de l'artiste, qui domine le modèle, comme le créateur la création; et de ce principe il en sort un second qui semble le contredire à première vue,—à savoir, qu'il faut être très soigneux des moyens matériels d'exécution.   (ii. 433)

A seeming contradiction is thus reconciled since the careful acquisition of technique is the means to a more effective, rapidly spontaneous capture of artistic vision: 'il est important que la main rencontre, quand elle se met à la besogne, le moins d'obstacles possible, et accomplisse avec une rapidité servile les ordres divins du cerveau: autrement l'idéal s'envole' (ii. 433). Later, in *Le Peintre de la vie moderne* (1863), it will be the fast pace of modern life in the city that requires a commensurate speed of execution on the part of Constantin Guys (ii. 686). Indeed if the artist's vision is not to escape capture, artistry itself needs to become a kind of second nature:

> C'est la peur de n'aller pas assez vite, de laisser échapper le fantôme avant que la synthèse ne soit extraite et saisie; c'est cette terrible peur qui possède tous les grands artistes et qui leur fait désirer si ardemment de s'approprier tous les moyens d'expression, pour que jamais les ordres de l'esprit ne soient altérés par

---

[15] Cf. his subsequent reference in the *Salon de 1846* to 'la naïveté, qui est la domination du tempérament dans la manière' (ii. 491).

les hésitations de la main; pour que finalement l'exécution, l'exécution idéale, devienne aussi inconsciente, aussi *coulante* que l'est la digestion pour le cerveau de l'homme bien portant qui a dîné. (ii. 699)

Baudelaire returns to this theme on a number of occasions, and not only when discussing Delacroix.[16] Most notably, the perception of a need to found originality of vision upon solidity of technique is seen as a defining characteristic of Poe: 'C'est un fait très remarquable qu'un homme d'une imagination aussi vagabonde et aussi ambitieuse soit en même temps si amoureux des règles, et capables de studieuses analyses et de patientes recherches' ('Edgar Allan Poe, sa vie et ses ouvrages' (1852), ii. 273). In the *Salon de 1859*, where imagination becomes the central focus, Baudelaire stresses also how important it is not to let the technical mastery show: 'mieux on possède son métier, moins il faut s'en prévaloir et le montrer, pour laisser l'imagination briller dans tout son éclat' (ii. 612). And by the time of his review of Cladel's *Les Martyrs ridicules* (1861) Baudelaire's rejection of the traditional idea of poetic inspiration is categoric: 'l'inspiration, en un mot, n'est que la récompense de l'exercice quotidien.' Like an apprentice acrobat the would-be genius 'doit [. . .] risquer de se rompre mille fois les os en secret avant de danser devant le public' (ii. 183).

Implicit in this preference for the rule of thumb over the prescriptions of aesthetic theory is a strong conviction that the production of art necessarily precedes the business of criticism. 'La poésie a existé, s'est affirmée la première,' Baudelaire writes in his Wagner essay, 'et elle a engendré l'étude des règles. Telle est l'histoire incontestée du travail humain' (ii. 793). The critic or aesthetic theorist is always one step behind the innovations of the visual artist or poet, which is why poets make for the best critics (ii. 793) and why the production of art according to pre-existing theories or rules is intrinsically doomed, and indeed risible: for example, as he argues in the *Salon de 1846*, the application of moral criteria in the production and assessment of historical landscape painting or the institutional adherence to the rules of neo-classical tragedy at the Comédie-Française, 'le théâtre le plus désert de l'univers' (ii. 480).

Original art—'naive' art—is by definition dismissive of convention and initially resistant to critique, as Baudelaire asserts in *Exposition universelle*, where he takes the literal internationalism of the exhibition as a metaphor for the disorientating effect of diversity on hidebound minds. How can we adapt to the foreignness of the new when our usual frameworks of reference are founded on the local familiarities of the old? His answer is that we must reject these frameworks ('[a]ucun voile scolaire, aucun paradoxe universitaire, aucune utopie pédagogique' (ii. 576)), submit to what we might now call cultural jet-lag or

---

[16] See, for example, his account of Gautier's linguistic abilities in 'Théophile Gautier' (1859), ii. 118. For further similar comments on Delacroix, see 'L'Œuvre et la vie d'Eugène Delacroix' (1863), ii. 746-7.

future-shock ('les étonnements du débarquement sont grands, [...] l'accoutumance est plus ou moins longue, plus ou moins laborieuse'), and robustly embrace 'un monde nouveau d'idées' (ii. 576). To journey into the unknown is to be born again: 'tout ce monde d'harmonies nouvelles entrera lentement en lui [i.e. the putative 'cosmopolitan' traveller towards the new], le pénétrera patiemment [...] toute cette vitalité inconnue sera ajoutée à sa vitalité propre'. Cultural 'travel' not only broadens the mind: it vivifies and indeed enhances our capacity to express what it means to be alive: 'quelques milliers d'idées et de sensations enrichiront son dictionnaire de mortel' (ii. 577).

Perhaps sensitive to the irony that he himself—since publication of the *Salon de 1846*—risks being seen as the kind of 'insensé doctrinaire du Beau' whom he here ridicules (ii. 577), Baudelaire wryly narrates his own conversion from the would-be aesthetic pedagogue into the champion of 'naïveté'. Like many he tried to 'm'enfermer dans un système pour y prêcher à mon aise', and tried even, within this system, to be flexible and non-doctrinaire: 'toujours mon système était beau, vaste, spacieux, commode, propre et lisse surtout' (ii. 577). But he has found that life and art have constantly given the lie to his pronouncements, which he has repeatedly been obliged to abjure: 'toujours un produit spontané, inattendu, de la vitalité universelle venait donner un démenti à ma science enfantine et vieillotte, fille déplorable de l'utopie' (ii. 577). Try as he might to adjust the criteria informing his system of judgement, beauty has constantly eluded the grasp of his definitions, 'le beau multiforme et versicolore, qui se meut dans les spirales infinies de la vie' (ii. 578). And so he has given up the struggle: 'je me suis contenté de sentir; je suis revenu chercher un asile dans l'impeccable naïveté' (ii. 578). Good art springs from life itself, so that beauty and aesthetic 'legislation' are necessarily opposites: 'il y a dans les productions multiples de l'art quelque chose de toujours nouveau qui échappera éternellement à la règle et aux analyses de l'école!' (ii. 578). The shock of the new—'[l']étonnement'—'est une des grandes jouissances causées par l'art et la littérature'. Hence, now, the famous assertion: '*Le beau est toujours bizarre*' (ii. 578).[17]

---

[17] This sentence, italicized as though it were a quotation, paraphrases the statement made by the English philosopher and statesman Francis Bacon (1561-1626) that 'there is no excellent beauty, that hath not some strangeness in the proportion' (in 'Of Beauty', *Essays*, no. 43), which in turn is slightly misquoted by Edgar Allan Poe in his narrative *Ligeia* (1838; trans. into French, 1855 [see ii. 1369, n. 2 to p. 578]): '"There is no exquisite beauty", says Bacon [...,] speaking truly of all the forms and *genera* of beauty, "without some strangeness in the proportions [*sic*]"'. (See *Collected Works of Edgar Allan Poe*, ed. Thomas Ollive Mabbott (3 vols, Cambridge, Mass. and London: The Belknap Press of Harvard University Press, 1969-78), ii. 311-12.) Poe substitutes 'exquisite' for 'excellent' again when he quotes Bacon in his article 'Anastatic Printing' (*Broadway Journal*, 12 April 1845), where he adds this gloss: 'The philosopher has reference, here, to beauty in its common acceptation; but the remark is equally applicable to all the forms of beauty—that is to say, to every thing which arouses profound interest in the heart or intellect of man. In every such thing, strangeness—in other words *novelty*—will be found a principal element; and so universal is this law that it has no exception even in the case of this principal element itself. Nothing, unless it be novel—*not even novelty itself*—will be the source of very intense excitement among men.' Cf. the *Salon de 1859*: 'le Beau est *toujours* étonnant' (ii. 616).

By this, as he here explicitly states, Baudelaire does not mean anything 'wilfully' or 'coldly' bizarre, but rather that the bizarre—'un peu de bizarrerie, de bizarrerie *naïve*, non voulue, *inconsciente*' (my emphases)—is the essential ingredient in art: 'son immatriculation, sa caractéristique' (ii. 578). Thus the strange, the unsettling, the unthought, the unlegislated-for—in a word, beauty[18]—become the very source of art's legitimacy, its badge of registration; and by the same token the would-be aesthetic legislator loses his own putative authority: 'Le *professeur-juré*, espèce de tyran-mandarin, me fait toujours l'effet d'un impie qui se substitue à Dieu' (ii. 578). With this remark Baudelaire gives a new twist to the Romantic concept of the poet as divine lawgiver. To lay down the law for art is to be an 'atheist', is to deny the inherent, infinite, and *surprising* diversity of human existence from which art itself derives:

> Or, comment cette bizarrerie, nécessaire, incompressible, variée à l'infini, dépendante des milieux, des climats, des mœurs, de la race, de la religion et du tempérament de l'artiste, pourra-t-elle jamais être gouvernée, amendée, redressée, par les règles utopiques conçues dans un petit temple scientifique quelconque de la planète, sans danger de mort pour l'art lui-même? (ii. 578–9)

'[U]n petit temple scientifique' (such, perhaps, as the École des Beaux-Arts): aesthetic theory is a false religion when placed beside the true faith of 'la naïveté'; and it spells death for art, whereas art itself means life and creativity. As Baudelaire later puts it in *Fusées*, f. 1: 'Ce qui est créé par l'esprit est plus vivant que la matière.'[19] Thus art is a law unto itself, and so the artist or poet must be an outlaw, an agent of the surprisingly, disturbingly, endlessly new.

But herein lies a problem. If we grant the autonomy of art, what then of the artist's own autonomy? Is the artist an active or passive participant in the production of art? And, whether active or passive, what exactly is the artist doing if art exceeds all explicit descriptive and prescriptive lawmaking? Simply and unconsciously following the existing inherent but unstated laws of art, its 'naïveté'? Or in fact, whether knowingly or unknowingly, modifying those laws and perhaps even introducing new ones? And finally, and most importantly, are these 'laws' of art perhaps indistinguishable from the laws of nature itself? Is it perhaps the true function of the poet and artist to articulate the patterns that structure the universe, the fundamental laws of harmony that govern every aspect of the world and of our existence within it: what Mallarmé later called 'un compte exact de purs motifs rythmiques de l'être'?[20]

---

[18] Cf. the terms of Poe's own definition of beauty in the previous note: 'all the forms of beauty—that is to say, [...] every thing which arouses profound interest in the heart or intellect of man'.

[19] *Fusées*, ed. Guyaux, 51; i. 649.

[20] See Mallarmé, *Œuvres complètes*, ii. 294, and my *Mallarmé and Circumstance: The Translation of Silence* (Oxford: Oxford University Press, 2004), 132.

In *Le Peintre de la vie moderne* (1863) Baudelaire highlights the paradoxical nature of this situation when presenting the dandy—for whom living is a work of art—as an outlaw of passionate and independent spirit who nevertheless heeds a higher set of laws: 'Le dandysme, qui est une institution en dehors des lois, a des lois rigoureuses auxquelles sont strictement soumis tous ses sujets, quelles que soient d'ailleurs la fougue et l'indépendance de leur caractère' (ii. 709). Indeed, as the contrarian who serves the noble cause of art, the dandy—and with him the poet-artist—constitutes the true hero of modern life:

> Que ces hommes se fassent nommer raffinés, incroyables, beaux, lions ou dandys, tous sont issus d'une même origine; tous participent du même caractère d'opposition et de révolte; tous sont des représentants de ce qu'il y a de meilleur dans l'orgueil humain, de ce besoin, trop rare chez ceux d'aujourd'hui, de combattre et de détruire la trivialité. (ii. 711)

This profound tension within Baudelaire's conception of the artist and, more particularly, of the poet is already evident in *Exposition universelle* where he argues on the one hand that the artist must ignore the rules, obey the promptings of 'tempérament', and seek 'la naïveté': 'L'artiste ne relève de lui-même' (ii. 581), and on the other that art itself is governed by a mysterious 'law' that defies understanding and to which all artists are subject: 'Je ne connais pas de problème plus confondant pour le pédantisme et le philosophisme, que de savoir en vertu de quelle loi les artistes les plus opposés par leur méthode évoquent les mêmes idées et agitent en nous des sentiments analogues' (ii. 580). In this way the work of art is seen to spring both from the artist's own individual self and yet also to tap in to ideas and feelings that transcend the individual and speak to the 'laws' of our shared humanity—and in particular to what Baudelaire, in the *Salon de 1859*, calls 'cette grande loi d'harmonie générale' (ii. 626).

The *Salon de 1859* constitutes a powerful reassertion of the rights of the imagination in the face of an increasingly dominant Realist aesthetic. In the section entitled 'Le Gouvernement de l'imagination' Baudelaire draws particularly on his conversations with Delacroix to outline the 'préceptes' (ii. 626) by which the imaginative artist takes the raw material of nature, its vocabulary ('La nature n'est qu'un dictionnaire', the painter has told him (ii. 624)), and selects—much as a poet 'composes' in language—those elements that are most appropriate to the expression of his particular 'conception', thereby conferring on these chosen elements 'une physionomie toute nouvelle' (ii. 625). Painters here are said to be 'obeying' their imagination (imagination is governing *them*) and yet at the same time to be consciously employing their carefully acquired skills and techniques in the service of 'l'idée génératrice' (ii. 625): 'Comme un rêve est placé dans une atmosphère qui lui est propre, de même une conception, devenue composition, a besoin de se mouvoir dans un milieu coloré qui lui soit particulier' (ii. 625).

Imagination itself now governs the composition of the painting according to the laws of colour combination. For example, yellow, orange, and red are commonly known (Baudelaire asserts) to evoke notions of joy and riches, of glory and love, but there are 'des milliers d'atmosphères jaunes ou rouges, et toutes les autres couleurs seront affectées logiquement et dans une quantité proportionnelle par l'atmosphère dominante' (ii. 625). And so the 'government' of the imagination is a very precise affair: 'L'art du coloriste tient évidemment par de certains côtés aux mathématiques et à la musique' (ii. 625). Accordingly these 'préceptes', these rules of painterly thumb, must be fully understood and heeded by the artist, just as the poet must be mindful of the rules of rhetoric and versification:

> Car il est évident que les rhétoriques et les prosodies ne sont pas des tyrannies inventées arbitrairement, mais une collection de règles réclamées par l'organisation même de l'être spirituel. Et jamais les prosodies et les rhétoriques n'ont empêché l'originalité de se produire distinctement. Le contraire, à savoir qu'elles ont aidé l'éclosion de l'originalité, serait infiniment plus vrai. (ii. 626-7)

These rules are not those of any 'petit temple scientifique', therefore, but of the imagination itself, of our 'spiritual being'. And yet they are not immutable: 'Tous ces préceptes sont évidemment modifiés plus ou moins par le tempérament varié des artistes' (ii. 626).

Here, then, Baudelaire argues not only that poets and artists must reject the rules imposed by the Academy or by current taste or prevailing prejudice about the true purpose of art (as he himself does, for example, in the unpublished draft article 'Puisque réalisme il y a'), and not only that, like the dandy, they must reject these rules the better to heed the 'higher' laws of art, but also that they can bend the 'natural' laws of art according to the dictates of their own temperament. In his discussion of Wagner, by contrast, Baudelaire returns to his emphasis on the existence of a 'higher' set of laws to which the 'naive' artist is absolutely subject. Poetry, he says, is 'incomplete' if written merely from instinct. Rather—and this is why 'tous les grands poètes deviennent naturellement, fatalement critiques' (ii. 793)—poets need to analyse their poetic work in order to 'découvrir les lois obscures en vertu desquelles ils ont produit' (ii. 793). Here, too, he returns to the question (raised earlier in *Exposition universelle*) of how and why artists of very differing techniques and methods are nevertheless able to prompt human beings to very similar intellectual or emotional reactions through their art, and he uses the performance of the overture to *Lohengrin* as a kind of test case, comparing the accounts given of it by Wagner and Liszt with his own in an attempt to prove that 'la véritable musique suggère des idées analogues dans des cerveaux différents' (ii. 784). In sum, the composer, painter, or poet must play a double role: 'naïvement' giving expression to their own 'temperamental' conceptions of reality while yet being conscious of—and by implication knowingly heeding—the fundamental laws that 'naturally' govern their creative acts. In the words of 'L'Irrémédiable', then, the artist is engaged in a kind of '[t]ête-à-tête sombre et limpide', or what one might call 'la conscience dans l'Art'.

The Poet as Moralist

> La poésie [...] n'a pas d'autre but qu'elle-même.
> ('Notes nouvelles sur Edgar Poe', ii. 333)[21]

To say, as Baudelaire does in *Exposition universelle*, that 'l'artiste ne relève de lui-même' is to say that the truly original artist or poet owes little to predecessors: 'Dans l'ordre poétique et artistique, tout révélateur a rarement un précurseur' (ii. 581). His comment, therefore, does not signal any adherence to art merely for its own sake. In his 1851 preface to Dupont's works Baudelaire rejects that option categorically as a dead-end and a false 'elsewhere': 'La puérile utopie de l'école de l' "art pour l'art", en excluant la morale, et souvent même la passion, était nécessairement stérile' (ii. 26). Art is not merely about formal experiment or the pursuit of some impersonal formal perfection. Such an attitude is 'en flagrante contradiction avec le génie de l'humanité' (ii. 26): art *is* a moral enterprise and profoundly rooted in the human condition.[22] Similarly in 'L'École païenne' (1852), where he discusses the recent trend to promote the poetry of ancient Greece and its alleged ideal of an impersonal beauty, he warns that '[l]e goût immodéré de la forme pousse à des désordres monstrueux et inconnus' (ii. 48). Here, too, he sees undue focus on poetic form as a dead-end: 'Le temps n'est pas loin où l'on comprendra que toute littérature qui se refuse à marcher fraternellement entre la science et la philosophie est une littérature homicide et suicide' (ii. 49). Poetry is a moral discourse, engaged like the natural sciences and philosophy in coming to a clearer understanding of our human condition and the world we inhabit. It is about *us*, and so, in *Exposition universelle*, and in characteristically contrarian manner, he rejects the rejection of Romantic confessionalism, arguing that there is nothing wrong with the expression of a poetic subjectivity as long as the *je* in question speaks for humanity at large: 'Le poète, placé sur un des points de la

---

[21] This statement recurs, with 'poésie' and 'elle-même' capitalized, in the section of the 'Notes nouvelles sur Edgar Poe' that Baudelaire includes as an inserted quotation in his subsequent article on Théophile Gautier published in *L'Artiste* (13 Mar. 1859). See ii. 113.

[22] Later, in his 1859 article on Gautier, the Baudelaire who had opposed 'l'Art pour l'Art' insists that '[l]a part du Beau dans *Mademoiselle de Maupin* était excessive' but nevertheless maintains that its author 'avait le droit de la faire telle' (ii. 112). For Baudelaire the laudable purpose of that novel—at a time (1835) when many were calling for literary art to serve a pedagogic and/or political purpose—was to depict 'non pas la fureur de l'amour, mais la *beauté* de l'amour et la *beauté* des objets dignes d'amour, en un mot l'enthousiasme (bien différent de la passion) créé par la beauté' (ii. 112). He thus exonerates Gautier from the charge of mere formalism by presenting his fictional account of the pursuit of beauty as the depiction of a commendable human aspiration.

circonférence de l'humanité, renvoie sur la même ligne en vibrations plus mélodieuses la pensée humaine qui lui fut transmise; tout poète véritable doit être une incarnation' (ii. 27).

Fifty years after first publication of the *Génie du christianisme* Baudelaire here echoes the Chateaubriand who had seen the poet-lawgiver not only as a latter-day Moses but also as a new Jesus. For Chateaubriand, Christ stands in direct line of descent from Amphion, Orpheus, and Solon, all of them *nomothètes* articulating '[u]ne belle musique appelée Loi' in the service of moral and political governance.[23] But where, as Chateaubriand believes, Christ and his Church seek to guide humanity towards a love of harmony that is called moral virtue,[24] Baudelaire's poet as 'incarnation' is a more purely Orphic nomothete as he seeks to articulate and order the potentially chaotic 'vibrations' of human experience for the benefit of humanity at large. In this respect his conception of the poet's function is more closely aligned with Shelley's (and through Shelley, with Staël's).[25] For Shelley, in the *Defence of Poetry*, 'man is an instrument [like an Aeolian lyre] over which a series of external and internal impressions are driven [...] But there is a principle within the human being, and perhaps within all sentient beings, which acts otherwise than in the lyre, and produces not melody alone, but harmony by an internal adjustment of the sounds or motions thus excited to the impressions which excite them.' For Shelley this principle is imagination, the ability to take the tunes played upon us and to synthesize or harmonize them: 'It is as if the lyre could accommodate its chords to the motions of that which strikes them, in a determined proportion of sound; even as the musician can accommodate his voice to the sound of the lyre.'[26] Thus both Shelley and Baudelaire see the poet as

---

[23] Chateaubriand, *Génie du christianisme*, ed. Pierre Reboul (2 vols, Paris: Garnier-Flammarion, 1966), i. 83. By equating lyric and law Chateaubriand is implicitly recalling the ancient Greek term *nomos*. See my *Unacknowledged Legisators*, 20–1: 'The perception of a common ground between poetry and law has a long history. From the earliest days of ancient Greek poetry this perception was expressed in the term *nomos*, meaning at once "local custom" and "melodic pattern". Common to both meanings was the sense of due and proper order. From its original meaning of "local custom" *nomos* acquired the further meanings of "norm" and "law. [...]. In its meaning of "melodic pattern" *nomos* was superseded by *harmonia*, indicating a generalized rather than localized system of patterning in music and poetry which were themselves then regarded as virtually identical. The double meaning of *nomos* (law and musico-poetic pattern) plays an important part in those sections of Plato's dialogues that debate the role of the poet in society, notably in the *Republic* and the *Laws*. In these discussions the work of the public legislator and the work of the poet are seen as analogous in that each is seeking to establish and promulgate rules and patterns that are in accordance with some fundamental *nomos* governing the universe as a whole. But if the lawgiver and the poet are analogous, they are also rivalrous; and for Plato/Socrates the *nomoi* of the philosopher-king must prevail over the harmonies of the poet in the interests of the greater good. The common ground is also a battleground. [-] At issue on this battleground is one central question: who speaks with authority? Should we heed the poet-musician or the philosopher-legislator (whom Plato, following Thucydides, calls a *nomothêtes*)?' For further discussion see the first section of Chapter 2 below, and *Unacknowledged Legislators*, 20–3.

[24] For full discussion see *Unacknowledged Legislators*, 109–11.

[25] See *Unacknowledged Legislators*, 296.

[26] See *A Defence of Poetry*, in Donald H. Reiman and Neil Fraistat (eds), *Shelley's Poetry and Prose* (2nd edn, New York and London: Norton, 2002), 511.

bringing human beings into harmony with our own lived experience, as attuning humanity to the *nomoi* of the world or universe at large.

For the nomothete the substance and shape of a melody or harmony are necessarily one and the same. For this reason Baudelaire, like Flaubert, insists repeatedly on the unity of what are conventionally called 'form' and 'content'. Poetic patterns are not mere decoration but constitute thought (and feeling) itself. In the prefatory essay on Dupont, it is true, Baudelaire states a firm preference for heartfelt opinion over virtuosic and over-sophisticated technical skill ('ce "voluptuosisme" armé de mille instruments et de mille ruses' (ii. 27)), praising Auguste Barbier in particular for his passionate political engagement and forgiving him his unfinished sentences and inadequate rhymes (just as he had earlier in the *Salon de 1846* forgiven Delacroix for being 'quelquefois maladroit', and this on the grounds that he is 'essentiellement créateur'). But there is clearly an element of special pleading in the Dupont preface on behalf of a writer and person whom Baudelaire admires but whose prosodic technique is flawed, and, as we have seen, he is usually more inclined to regard polished technique as a necessary means to the effective expression of artistic vision. Indeed in his article on Barbier ten years later he takes the satirist to task for privileging ideas over expression and asserts firmly: 'l'idée et la forme sont deux êtres en un' (ii. 143).

Thus, just as Baudelaire rejects 'l'Art pour l'Art' and with it any undue emphasis on the formal, especially when manifest in the virtuosic deployment of traditional technique (for example, by the Hugo of *Les Orientales*), so too he opposes any insistence on 'content', especially when this content is moralistic, politically tendentious, or variously philosophical. To say that art is a moral enterprise is not to say that art should preach, and Baudelaire frequently inveighs against the belief that art in general or poetry in particular should play an overtly ideological or didactic role. In his critique of Barbier he describes the privileging of ideas over form as leading quite simply to 'l'anéantissement de la poésie' (ii. 143). In his 1859 article on Gautier he wearily rejects Cousin's 'fameuse doctrine de l'indissolubilité du Beau, du Vrai et du Bien' (ii. 111),[27] just as in his earlier 'Notes nouvelles sur Edgar Poe' (1857) he had denounced all those who believe that 'le but de la poésie

---

[27] Victor Cousin's influential lectures on aesthetics, first given during the early years of the Restoration, had been available in various published versions from the late 1820s onwards and first appeared in definitive form in *Du vrai, du beau et du bien* in 1853. For him the primary source of art was God, so that each of the three elements in this trinity of 'le vrai, le beau, and le bien' is grounded in the divine. Since they share a common source, each therefore reflects the other, but none, being subsidiary to the divine, has priority over the other. On Baudelaire's dismissive comment, see Paulo Tortonese, 'Baudelaire et la philosophaillerie moderne', in André Guyaux and Sophie Marchal (ed.), *La Vie romantique: Hommage à Loïc Chotard* (Paris: Presses de l'Université Paris-Sorbonne, 2003), 483–522, where Tortonese shows that Cousin never argued for the 'indissolubilité' of this trinity and that, as the preceding sentence in the article indicates ('Je ne sais quelle lourde nuée, venue de Genève, de Boston, ou de l'enfer, a intercepté les beaux rayons du soleil de l'esthétique'), Baudelaire may here be thinking more specifically of the work of the Swiss illustrator Rodolphe Töppfer (1799–1846) and/or of the Bostonian writer Ralph Waldo Emerson (1803–82).

est un enseignement quelconque, qu'elle doit tantôt fortifier la conscience, tantôt perfectionner les mœurs, tantôt *démontrer* quoi que ce soit d'utile' (ii. 333). Here again Hugo (this time of *Châtiments* and *Les Contemplations*) is the villain, paradoxically winning admiration from 'notre race antipoétique' by 'introduisant de force et brutalement dans sa poésie ce qu'Edgar Poe considérait comme l'hérésie moderne capitale,—*l'enseignement*' (ii. 337).

Earlier still, in 'Edgar Allan Poe, sa vie et ses ouvrages' (1852)—and before Hugo had published those two collections—Baudelaire had described this 'heresy' simply as 'l'idée d'utilité directe' (ii. 263). Here he quotes Poe himself as saying that while it is not the primary purpose of poetry to be 'useful' (because in the first instance 'elle s'adresse au sens du beau et non à un autre' (ii. 263)), poetry may yet incidentally be so. Just as an industrial building may well, Poe contends, fulfil its primary purpose of efficient functionality and yet also be aesthetically pleasing, so too poetry may be both beautiful and, as it were, incidentally useful: 'Que la poésie soit subséquemment et conséquemment utile, cela est hors de doute, mais ce n'est pas son but; cela vient *par-dessus le marché*' (ii. 263). But here Baudelaire does not interpret Poe further nor say in what he himself believes this incidental or supplementary utility of poetry might consist.

On the particular subject of moral utility he is similarly adamant but unspecific. One year earlier, in 'Les Drames et les roman honnêtes', he had railed against the reduction of art to the level of propaganda, whether on behalf of 'l'école bourgeoise' or 'l'école socialiste': 'Moralisons! moralisons! s'écrient toutes les deux avec une fièvre de missionnaires' (ii. 41). Is art useful, he asks: 'Oui. Pourquoi? Parce qu'il est l'art.' His particular argument here is simply that what is beautiful cannot be immoral: 'Je défie qu'on me trouve un seul ouvrage d'imagination qui réunisse toutes les conditions du beau et qui soit un ouvrage pernicieux' (ii. 41). In his 1861 article on Hugo, however, he appears to moderate his condemnation of the latter's 'heretical' didacticism: 'Il ne s'agit pas ici de cette morale prêcheuse qui, par son air de pédanterie, par son ton didactique, peut gâter les plus beaux morceaux de poésie' (ii. 137). Instead he commends Hugo for his compassionate depiction of human suffering ('la voix profonde de la charité' (ii. 136)), which he identifies with an acceptable kind of second-order moralizing:

> une morale inspirée qui se glisse, invisible, dans la matière poétique, comme les fluides impondérables dans toute la machine du monde. La morale n'entre pas dans cet art à titre de but; elle s'y mêle et s'y confond comme dans la vie elle-même. Le poète est moraliste sans le vouloir, par abondance et plénitude de nature. (ii. 137)

Like some musical accompaniment (ii. 136), Hugo's tonality of 'bonté' is here described in terms that recall Baudelaire's aesthetic ideal of 'naïveté': that is to say, something involuntary and implicit, a sort of second nature ('comme dans la vie elle-même', 'abondance et plénitude de nature'), a gentle, underlying tune of moral harmony, a reassuring *nomos*. What Baudelaire continues to reject, therefore, is the Hugolian 'bonté' but not the presence of a 'moral tone', and in *Les Fleurs du Mal* his own second-order moralizing will turn, as we shall see, on the particular conception of 'le Mal' that he there seeks to express and illustrate.

This contrast between overt and second-order moral commentary recurs one year later when Baudelaire comes to review *Les Misérables*. He begins by reproducing the long passage from his 1861 article that describes Hugo as being 'moraliste sans le vouloir' but notes that in this case he must amend its penultimate sentence: 'car dans *Les Misérables* la morale entre directement *à titre de but*' (ii. 218). Quoting Hugo's prefatory statement that such books as his shall have their use for as long as the man-made injustice of mass poverty and lack of education endures, Baudelaire evinces sympathy for this 'livre de charité' (ii. 224) and agrees that the problem of widespread poverty needs to be brought forcibly to the attention of 'une société trop amoureuse d'elle-même et trop peu soucieuse de l'immortelle loi de fraternité' (ii. 224).

Moreover he defends Hugo against the charge that his social conscience has been rather too recently acquired, citing some of his early plays as evidence to the contrary, and arguing also that it would be 'parfaitement monstrueux' for a mature writer *not* to be moved and disturbed by 'cette tache noire que fait la pauvreté sur le soleil de la richesse' (ii. 219). Whereas a young poet may be more disposed, 'dans son exubérante jeunesse', to celebrate the joys of life and to glory in his art, it is natural that '[l]'âge mûr [...] se tourne avec inquiétude et curiosité vers les problèmes et les mystères', with the result that the one crucial difference between the younger and older poet is this: 'c'est de savoir si l'œuvre d'art doit n'avoir d'autre but que *l'art*, si l'art ne doit exprimer d'adoration que pour *lui-même*, ou si un but, plus noble ou moins noble, inférieur ou supérieur, peut lui être imposé' (ii. 219).

Baudelaire here seemingly reinforces the traditional distinction between 'l'Art pour l'Art' and a form of art that bespeaks some (other) particular purpose, and indeed concedes that 'nous pensons exactement comme l'auteur, que *des livres de cette nature ne sont jamais inutiles*' (ii. 224). Where he differs, however, and as his final paragraph makes clear, is in his rejection of the notion of moral progress as the purpose and/or result of art: 'Hélas! du Péché Originel, même après tant de progrès depuis si longtemps promis, il restera toujours bien assez de traces pour en constater l'immémoriale réalité!' (ii. 224).

This view that poetry should not seek to improve people but can and must instead be in some way 'involuntarily' moral is one which Baudelaire had aired also in the notes he prepared for his lawyer during the trial of *Les Fleurs du Mal*:

> Il y a plusieurs morales. Il y a la morale positive et pratique à laquelle tout le monde doit obéir. [-] Mais il y a la morale des arts. Celle-ci est tout autre, et depuis le commencement du monde, les Arts l'ont bien prouvé. (i. 194)

This in turn recalls Baudelaire's statement back in 1846 (in his review of Senneville's *Prométhée délivrée*) that poetry must have its own 'involontary philosophy': 'La poésie est essentiellement philosophique; mais comme elle est avant tout *fatale*, elle doit être involontairement philosophique' (ii. 9), which he follows up with a comment that could come straight from Flaubert's correspondence: 'Or, la grande poésie est essentiellement *bête*, elle *croit*, et c'est ce qui fait sa gloire et sa force' (ii. 11). Art simply *is* and *does*, and such moral or intellectual 'content' as it may display derives directly from its nature as art, from art as a second nature. For, as he states in the *Salon de 1846*: 'La nature n'a d'autre morale que le fait, parce qu'elle est la morale elle-même' (ii. 480). The best art, like nature, has a morality of its own, which it is up to the individual reader or spectator to derive unaided from it. For this reason it is fundamentally inappropriate, indeed illegitimate, to subject a work such as *Madame Bovary* to an actual trial since (as we saw in the Introduction) the laws under which it should be judged are inherent in the work itself. Every successful work of art, like nature itself, contains its own individual and unique legislation.[28]

In his unpublished essay entitled 'L'Art philosophique', Baudelaire similarly condemns the kind of pictorial or plastic art that seeks to replace the book 'pour enseigner l'histoire, la morale et la philosophie', and he advocates instead a form of pure art ('suivant la conception moderne') which he defines famously thus: 'C'est créer une magie suggestive contenant à la fois l'objet et le sujet, le monde extérieur à l'artiste et l'artiste lui-même' (ii. 598). Here again we see Baudelaire the contrarian escaping the intellectual straitjacket of a conventional binary, in this case of 'l'Art pour l'Art' versus didactic art. For him, whether it be painting or poetry, art is neither useless nor useful in any everyday sense: rather it is both 'pure' and possessed of serious moral purpose. And his account of its 'suggestive magic' in 'L'Art philosophique' also recalls his concept of 'naïveté', this time by advocating a form of representation of the world that both mirrors the world and yet springs from the artist's own temperament, from the artist as 'incarnation' of the human.

And so the poet-artist as lawgiver and moralist comes once more into view as a double agent. Passively he gains access, from the perspective of his own inner being, to ideas and feelings that are putatively shared by all of us; and actively, now not only conscious of the laws of art that govern his creativity but conscious also of 'la morale' and 'la philosophie' that 'involuntarily' govern his 'conceptions' of the

---

[28] For this reason, and again in an interesting parallel with Flaubert, Baudelaire condemns the lack of authorial impersonality in Léon Cladel's *Les Martyrs ridicules*: 'Le discours est très éloquent et très enlevant; malheureusement la note personnelle de l'auteur, sa simplicité révoltée, n'est pas assez voilée. Le poète, sous son masque, se laisse encore voir. Le suprême de l'art eût consisté à rester glacial et fermé, et à laisser au lecteur tout le mérite de l'indignation. L'effet d'horrreur en eût été augmenté. Que la morale officielle trouve ici son profit, c'est incontestable; mais l'art y perd, et avec l'art vrai, la vraie morale: la suffisante, ne perd jamais rien' (ii. 186).

world, he gives concerted expression to his own particular way of seeing that derives from the laws of his own temperament. Thus, for example, a man who lives his own life (and by implication the same life as others lead) as a dialectic of 'vaporisation' and 'centralisation'[29]—of self-abandonment and willed effort, of empathy and self-consciousness, of acquiescence in desire and doomed attempts to resist it—will knowingly and artfully display the world of universal human experience as a reflection of his own unique and individual struggle, of his own ineluctable fate.

The Poet as Nomothete

> un être si bien doué pour comprendre l'harmonie, une sorte de prêtre du Beau.
> ('Le Poème du hachisch', in *Les Paradis artificiels*, i. 432)
> une loi suprême et omnicompréhensive
> ('Victor Hugo', ii. 138)

Whatever the terms of his assertions, Baudelaire's principal argument is that art must be true to itself as art, which means also being true to nature in some manner more fundamental than the mere mimetic reproduction of nature's surface. Art must draw its inspiration from the fundamental rhythms of the physical world itself, and this is what Baudelaire praises in Hugo (in 1861 and with implicit reference to *Les Contemplations*) when he describes him as being, 'dès le principe, l'homme le mieux doué, le plus visiblement élu pour exprimer par la poésie ce que j'appellerai le *mystère de la vie*' (ii. 131). Nature presents itself to our attention as a puzzling composite of various aspects, each vying simultaneously for our intellectual and emotional engagement: 'forme, attitude et mouvement, lumière et couleur, son et harmonie' (ii. 132), and the poet's task is to 'orchestrate' our resultant 'impressions'. Thus:

> La musique des vers de Victor Hugo s'adapte aux profondes harmonies de la nature; sculpteur, il découpe dans ses strophes la forme inoubliable des choses; peintre, il les illumine de leur couleur propre. Et, comme si elles venaient directement de la nature, les trois impressions pénètrent simultanément le cerveau du lecteur. De cette triple impression résulte la *morale des choses*. (ii. 132)

These deep harmonies, this 'morale des choses', constitute the *nomoi* that the poet as nomothete must perceive and articulate, the sounds, shapes, and colours of the sensual world. Not long before this, in one of his projected prefaces to *Les Fleurs du Mal*, Baudelaire had intended to discuss 'comment la poésie touche à la

---

[29] *Fusées*, ed. Guyaux, 79; i. 676.

musique par une prosodie dont les racines plongent plus avant dans l'âme humaine que ne l'indique aucune théorie classique' (i. 183), and to examine also the ways in which poetry is not only musical but also geometric, espousing the shapes and patterns of physical reality in its own prosodic structures and rhythms:

> la phrase poétique peut imiter (et par là elle touche à l'art musical et à la science mathématique) la ligne horizontale, la ligne droite ascendante, la ligne droite descendante; [...] elle peut monter à pic vers le ciel, sans essoufflement, ou descendre perpendiculairement vers l'enfer avec la vélocité de toute pesanteur; [...] elle peut suivre la spirale, décrire la parabole, ou le zigzag figurant une série d'angles superposés [...]. (i. 183)

Even by the mere juxtaposition of adjective and noun the poet can 'exprimer toute sensation de suavité ou d'amertume, de béatitude ou d'horreur' in ways that recall the skill of a painter, or a masterchef, or a cosmeticist (i. 183). Thus poetry is not so much 'about' nature or the material world of the senses as *part* of it, an instrument capable of prompting sense impressions of its own.

Baudelaire never completed such a preface, but in some respects this article on Hugo may be read as its replacement and as a preface to the 1861 edition of *Les Fleurs du Mal*. As we shall see, Baudelaire there presents a very different *nomos* at work in the universe of human experience, not the ascending trajectory of harmony, love, and redemption from matter that is set out in *Les Contemplations* but a descending spiral of desire and dissatisfaction leading to death. But his account of Hugo here reveals much about how Baudelaire envisages the underlying nature and function of the poet's role as nomothete:

> Le vers de Victor Hugo sait traduire pour l'âme humaine non seulement les plaisirs les plus directs qu'elle tire de la nature visible, mais encore les sensations les plus fugitives, les plus compliquées, les plus morales (je dis exprès sensations morales) qui nous sont transmises par l'être visible, par la nature inanimée, ou dite inanimée; non seulement, la figure d'un être extérieur à l'homme, végétal ou minéral, mais aussi sa physionomie, son regard, sa tristesse, sa douceur, sa joie éclatante, sa haine répulsive, son enchantement ou son horreur; enfin, en d'autres termes, tout ce qu'il y a d'humain dans n'importe quoi, et aussi tout ce qu'il y a de divin, de sacré ou de diabolique. [-] Ceux qui ne sont pas poètes ne comprennent pas ces choses. (ii. 132)

This final comment underlines the importance of the insight into the poet's function here being expressed by Baudelaire. 'La morale des choses', 'sensations morales': once again transcending a familiar binary opposition, here of body and spirit, he is suggesting that the purpose of poetry is to convey what, later in the

Hugo article, he calls the moral 'atmosphere' (ii. 136) of our lived reality and which in Hugo's poetry derives from 'l'esprit de justice et de charité' (ii. 136). Here, at this earlier point in the article, he is saying that Hugo is able not only to translate the visible world into words but also to interpret the sensations and impressions we receive from the physical world within a framework that 'translates' them into human terms, and indeed situates them within a dialectic of the divine/sacred and the diabolical—or, as *Les Fleurs du Mal* suggests, of 'spleen et idéal'.

Baudelaire now alludes to Fourier's theory of universal analogy, to Swedenborg's neo-Platonist philosophy of 'correspondances', and to Lavater's phrenology, but he does so not by way of necessarily subscribing to their ideas (as has so often been thought) but rather to suggest (i) that in his role as moral interpreter of the physical world the poet is engaged in a task that is shared with the philosopher and the scientist (as in 'L'École païenne' he had earlier said it should be); (ii) that this poetic task derives from a didactic tradition that is no less time-honoured than theirs (cf. his reference to 'tous les excellents poètes dans lesquels l'humanité lisante fait son éducation aussi bien que dans la contemplation de la nature' (ii. 133)); and (iii) that in pursuing this task the poet aspires to standards of precision and rigour every bit as high as those demanded of the mathematician or natural scientist. Hence the much-quoted question and answer that follow:

> Or qu'est-ce qu'un poète (je prends le mot dans son acception la plus large), si ce n'est un traducteur, un déchiffreur? Chez les excellents poètes, il n'y a pas de métaphore, de comparaison ou d'épithète qui ne soit d'une adaptation mathématiquement exacte dans la circonstance actuelle, parce que ces comparaisons, ces métaphores et ces épithètes sont puisées dans l'inépuisable fonds de l'"universelle analogie', et qu'elles ne peuvent êtres puisées ailleurs. (ii. 133)

But what marks the poet out from all other (moral, philosophical, scientific) interpreters of nature is a superior command of language, and here Hugo provides the perfect model. Like the prophet Ezekiel whom God provides with a book to eat so that he may thereafter speak His words to the house of Israel (Ezekiel 2: 9–10, 3: 1–3), Hugo ('le plus visiblement élu') has seemingly swallowed a dictionary of the French language, with the result that 'le lexique français, en sortant de sa bouche, est devenu un monde, un univers coloré, mélodieux et mouvant' (ii. 133). With this 'prophetic' gift the poet speaks not God's words so much as the language of nature itself, the *nomos*: 'De cette faculté d'absorption de la vie extérieure, unique par son ampleur, et de cette autre faculté puissante de méditation est résulté, chez Victor Hugo, un caractère poétique très particulier, interrogatif, mystérieux et, comme la nature, immense et minutieux, calme et agité' (ii. 134). In particular Hugo is able to convey the 'mystery' itself without seeking to resolve or dispel it in the manner of some Enlightenment champion of reason:

> Voltaire ne voyait de mystère en rien, ou qu'en bien peu de choses. Mais Victor Hugo ne tranche pas le nœud gordien des choses avec la pétulance militaire de Voltaire; ses sens subtils lui révèlent des abîmes; il voit le mystère partout. Et de fait où n'est-il pas? (ii. 134)[30]

There is, then, a mysterious and complex order inherent in nature that it is the poet's function to uncover and express in all its mysteriousness and all its complexity: what Baudelaire later in his article describes as 'une loi suprême et omnicompréhensive' (ii. 138). When he asserts 'cette vérité que tout est hiéroglyphique' (ii. 133), he means not that the world can be read (or presented) by the poet as a system of easily decipherable signs (for example, of one-to-one correspondences between the physical and the moral) but rather that the poet needs to observe nature (and in particular human nature) with an innocence of vision—a 'naïveté'—that allows access to fundamental *nomoi* which may be obscured by pre-programmed (moral, moralistic, philosophical, religious) interpretations: 'nous savons que les symboles ne sont obscurs que d'une manière relative, c'est-à-dire selon la pureté, la bonne volonté ou la clairvoyance native des âmes' (ii. 133). As an 'incarnation' of nature, positioned on its circumference, the poet must see and hear (like Hugo the 'voyant' and 'écho sonore') the structures and rhythms that govern the universe. These shall be the source and benchmark of his truthfulness, of his quasi-mathematical rigour, not the systems of professors or philosophers, nor yet, for that matter, of religious doctrine. The laws that the poet follows shall be the laws of nature itself, which must not be infringed.

But if nature is, as Baudelaire wrote in the *Salon de 1846*, '[b]rutale et positive', if the 'morale' inherent in nature is one of cruelty and destruction—in short, 'le Mal', then how shall the artist proceed in his representation of these laws? There is a key passage in the 'Notes nouvelles sur Edgar Poe' where Baudelaire is paraphrasing Poe's essay *The Poetic Principle* and takes Poe's argument in a new direction. The relevant passage in Poe reads:

> Just as the Intellect concerns itself with Truth, so Taste informs us of the Beautiful while the Moral Sense is regardful of Duty. Of this latter, while Conscience teaches the obligation, and Reason the expediency, Taste contents herself with displaying the charms:—waging war upon Vice solely on the ground of her deformity—her disproportion—her animosity to the fitting, to the appropriate, to the harmonious—in a word, to Beauty;[31]

---

[30] Cf. *Mon cœur mis à nu* where Baudelaire describes Voltaire as '*l'anti-poète*, le roi des badauds, le prince des superficiels, l'anti-artiste' (*Fusées*, ed. Guyaux, 95; i. 687).

[31] Edgar Allan Poe, 'The Poetic Principle', in *Poems and Essays* (London and New York: Dent [Everyman's Library], 1975), 97.

while Baudelaire paraphrases the second half of this passage as follows:

> Aussi, ce qui exaspère surtout l'homme de goût dans le spectacle du vice, c'est sa difformité, sa disproportion. Le vice porte atteinte au juste et au vrai, révolte l'intellect et la conscience; mais, comme outrage à l'harmonie, comme dissonance, il blessera plus particulièrement certains esprits poétiques; et je ne crois pas qu'il soit scandalisant de considérer toute infraction à la morale, au beau moral, comme une espèce de faute contre le rythme et la prosodie universels. (ii. 334)

This last assertion (from 'et je ne crois pas [...]') is Baudelaire's own and points very precisely to the crux of the challenge he sets himself in *Les Fleurs du Mal* to 'extraire la *beauté* du Mal' (i. 181). The problem is ultimately an aesthetic one: how to reconcile the dissonance of our existential ills with the harmony of art?

For Baudelaire, nature at its most fundamental level stages a dialectic of life and death, of creativity and destruction. The artist as nomothete must paint the destruction and yet by the very act of creation *resist* and *protest*, substituting human endeavour for the passive processes of nature: 'la première affaire d'un artiste est de substituer l'homme à la nature et de protester contre elle. Cette protestation ne se fait pas de parti pris, froidement, comme un code ou une rhétorique; elle est emportée et naïve, comme le vice, comme la passion, comme l'appétit' (*Salon de 1846*, ii. 473). This resistance through creativity is thus itself a kind of second nature: not something undertaken out of obedience to externally imposed laws or a set of rules (whether of rhetoric or prosody) but as a visceral, instinctive response that is no less powerful and innate ('naïve') than 'vice' itself: art as passion, as appetite, as life. The dissonance of 'le Mal'—the dissonance that *is* 'le Mal'—must be met with the harmony of a different *nomos*, of those rhythms and patterns that Baudelaire sees displayed, for example, in Delacroix's handling of colour and which he locates in nature itself. For why is it, he asks in *Mon cœur mis à nu*, that people take such endless pleasure in gazing at the sea?

> Parce que la mer offre à la fois l'idée de l'immensité et du mouvement. Six ou sept lieues représentent pour l'homme le rayon de l'infini. Voilà un infini diminutif. Qu'importe s'il suffit à suggérer l'idée de l'infini total? Douze ou quatorze lieues (sur le diamètre), douze ou quatorze de liquide en mouvement suffisent pour donner la plus haute idée de beauté qui soit offerte à l'homme sur son habitacle transitoire.[32]

Rather than our quotidian spectacle of decay and time-dictated endings, the sea here offers the observer an *un*ending prospect of suggestiveness, as also do the man-made ships that sail upon it:

---

[32] *Fusées*, ed. Guyaux, 106; i. 696.

> Je crois que le charme infini et mystérieux qui gît dans la contemplation d'un navire, et surtout d'un navire en mouvement, tient, dans le premier cas, à la régularité et à la symétrie qui sont un des besoins primordiaux de l'esprit humain, au même degré que la complication et l'harmonie,—et, dans le second cas, à la multiplication successive et à la génération de toutes les courbes et figures imaginaires opérées dans l'espace par les éléments réels de l'objet. [-] L'idée poétique qui se dégage de cette opération du mouvement dans les lignes est l'hypothèse d'un être vaste, immense, compliqué, mais eurythmique, d'un animal plein de génie, souffrant et soupirant tous les soupirs et toutes les ambitions humaines.[33]

As Baudelaire notes just before this, in *Fusées*, f. 17, the 'beauty' of this sight derives from the banal being suddenly invested with a deeper significance: 'Dans certains états de l'âme presque surnaturels, la profondeur de la vie se révèle tout entière dans le spectacle, si ordinaire qu'il soit, qu'on a sous les yeux. Il en devient le symbole.'[34] In the case of the ship, not only does the sight of it answer to a fundamental human need by entrancing the viewer with a quasi-musical display of satisfyingly complex harmonic relations at both a literal and a figurative level, it also prompts the 'poetic idea' of 'eurythmic' suffering—of 'le Mal' perceived not as dissonance but as a form of animal genius and organic rhythm. The ship appears as the symbol of human desire ('toutes les ambitions humaines') with all its attendant pain and suffering, but also of human desire played out according to fundamental and orderly patterns that transform dissonance into harmony. Rather like the 'idée poétique' and 'hypothèse' of *Les Fleurs du Mal* itself perhaps ... the testimony of a poetic persona living out the 'sighs' and 'ambitions' of human destiny, irremediably and passively subject to the myriad manipulations of the Devil-Puppeteer ('C'est le Diable qui tient les fils qui nous remuent!' ('Au lecteur', l. 13)) and yet, as poetic voice, the active embodiment of 'eurhythmic' being. Like the poet-moralist, therefore, the poet as nomothete emerges also as a double agent: part of nature, yet substituting himself for nature; undergoing natural process and yet protesting against it; powerless yet resistant.

---

[33] *Fusées*, ed. Guyaux, 70; i. 663–4. Cf. *Les Paradis artificiels*, where Baudelaire describes in very similar terms the state of reverie induced by hashish in the mind of a poet: 'L'idée de beauté doit naturellement s'emparer d'une place vaste dans un tempérament spirituel tel que je l'ai supposé. L'harmonie, le balancement des lignes, l'eurythmie dans les mouvements, apparaissent au rêveur comme des nécessités, comme des *devoirs*, non seulement pour tous les êtres de la création, mais pour lui-même, le rêveur, qui se trouve, à cette période de la crise, doué d'une merveilleuse aptitude pour comprendre le rythme immortel et universel' (i. 432).
[34] *Fusées*, ed. Guyaux, 64; i. 659.

2
The Poet-Artist as Double Agent

> L'artiste n'est artiste qu'à la condition d'être double et de n'ignorer aucun phénomène de sa double nature.
>
> (*De l'essence du rire*, ii. 543)

Baudelaire in Context

> Des poètes illustres s'étaient partagé depuis longtemps les provinces les plus fleuries du domaine poétique.
>
> (draft preface to *Les Fleurs du Mal*, i. 181)

Before focusing further on this conception of the poet as having a double nature it is important to recall both the context in which Baudelaire was writing and also the terms of the age-old debate about the role of the poet to which he was contributing in his critical writings and, as we shall see presently, by his own poetic practice.

From earliest times a defining function of the poet has been to communicate to fellow human beings some special insight into the laws that govern our shared universe. As mentioned in Chapter 1, the ancient Greek term *nomos* meant both civil law and musical harmony. In this double meaning it was central to Plato's discussions of the poet's role in society, and the importance of the relationship *between* the two meanings of the word may be inferred, for example, from Socrates' contention in the *Republic* that 'one can never change the ways of training people in music without affecting the greatest political laws' (*Republic*, 424c).[1] Similarly, in the *Laws*, the Athenian proposes that 'no one shall sing a note, or perform any dance-movement, other than those in the canon of public songs, sacred music, and the general body of chorus performances of the young—any more than he would violate any other "nome" [*nomos*] or law' (*Laws*, 800a).[2] Hence Socrates' pronouncement in the *Republic* that 'hymns to the gods and eulogies of good people are the only poetry we can admit into our city' (607a).[3] It is precisely because of their central political importance within the life of the

---

[1] Plato, *Republic*, trans. C. D. C. Reeve (Indianapolis and Cambridge, Mass.: Hackett, 2004), 108.
[2] Plato, *Laws*, ed. Trevor J. Saunders (rev. edn, London: Penguin Books, 2004), 241.
[3] *Republic*, trans. Reeve, 311.

Republic that Socrates/Plato wishes to banish all poets who do not heed this requirement. For Plato the only permissible *nomothêtes* is the philosopher-legislator who will act as Guardian within the ideal Republic. But poets have other ideas: they want to sing from their own hymn sheet, to offer their own take on the *nomoi* that govern our world and our behaviour within it.

This idea of the poet as nomothete or lawgiver was central to the discussion of the poet's function during the post-revolutionary period in France, and in particular to the underlying belief shared by Chateaubriand, Staël, Lamartine, Hugo, and Vigny that the poet's art was profoundly implicated in the moral, political, and religious life of the nation. Chateaubriand's *Génie du christianisme* springs directly from the conviction that a poet (for him a writer in prose as well as verse) may articulate a Christian vision of the universe—of the moral harmony in God's Creation—in such a way as to convince his reader of its truth through an appeal to feeling rather than reason and so contribute to the restoration of monarchical and Christian rule in a country torn apart by the Terror and the fanatical pursuit of republican ideals. For him the events of 1789 derived from a deep-seated sense of dissatisfaction and longing that is endemic within the human condition, which he calls 'mélancolie'. If this longing—that can be finally assuaged only in the Christian afterlife—is not to cause further social disruption, then it must be mitigated in the here and now by the poet, who can, in alliance with the Christian Church, offer the spiritual solace that comes from contemplation of the incomprehensible wonders of nature and of a harmony and moral perfection beyond the terrestrial. For Chateaubriand, as for the early Lamartine, the poet is the spokesman for a Christian God, offering glimpses of heaven as we flounder in our slough of doubt and despond.

But for Staël, as for the later Lamartine—the former a Protestant deist with little time for the hereafter, and the latter a self-professed 'Christian rationalist' or, more accurately, a deist who wonders if God is just a word for the mystery of the unknown—the poet is the voice of humanity here on earth, one who gives persuasive and uplifting expression to our shared concerns and aspirations and who can help to 'complete' the Revolution by inspiring and fostering a sense of altruism and community. What is endemic for Staël, as it was for Rousseau, is pity, an instinctive desire to reach out to others in the name of reason and in the name of all that is best in human beings: what she calls 'enthousiasme'. Her 'God within us' is not so much divine as what we might call our 'better nature'. Instead of Chateaubriand's negative melancholy and the Christian perspective that sees the human condition as inferior to the life that awaits us after death, the author of *Corinne* proposes a positive melancholy, not a *mal du siècle* but a state of 'rêveuse indolence'—comparable with Baudelaire's 'féconde paresse' ('La Chevelure')—prompted by a perceived discrepancy between the limitless bounty of our sensual experience and the limited spiritual and expressive powers with which we seek to encompass it. For Staël the poet speaks not of some transcendent and invisible realm but rather in eloquent celebration of a tangible and visible present existence, of a temporal plenitude to be enjoyed by our mortal selves, what she calls the 'apotheosis' of man. As she puts it in *De l'Allemagne*, the poetry of enthusiasm is like a cloud of incense that is to be understood not as having been bestowed by God from above but instead as rising up from below, from us, as the expression of human aspiration and human insight. Human beings are part of nature, and nature speaks through the poet.

So too, eventually, for Hugo. At first (in his preface to the first edition of *Odes et poésies diverses*) he sees the function of poetry as threefold: as the conduit for a royalist and Christian world-view, as the expression of his own soul, and as a form of visionary insight beneath the surface of reality: 'La poésie, c'est tout ce qu'il y a d'intime dans tout.'[4] For a long time he remained conflicted between the public and private functions of poetry until, in the figure of Olympio, he reconciled them within a broader conception of the poet as visionary and prophet: the poet of *Les Contemplations* who recounts both his own personal history and the history of human suffering as parallel narratives of moral progress towards an eventual universal redemption. In his poetic creation Hugo's poet apes God's own act of Creation, itself dependent on language ('Fiat lux'), such that in the end it matters little whether the language of creation is God's or the poet's. The Word is the word is the world.

Just as Staël's 'enthusiasm' places God firmly within *us*, so Vigny responds with disdain to what he perceives as God's silence and focuses exclusively on a purely human knowledge. In *Les Destinées* he wants—as Staël also had wanted, following her encounter with the secular lyric of Goethe and Schiller—to take poetry not back to the world of ancient Greece (as Leconte de Lisle seeks in part to do in his *Poèmes antiques* (1852)) but forward to a third, post-Christian stage of moral freedom and human independence from the gods. Vigny's muse is Éva, the mortal embodiment of pity and the female companion to his own 'Esprit pur', his secular version of the Holy Spirit; and for him *Les Destinées* represents (as mentioned above in the Introduction) a third Testament, the New Testament of Man and the endpoint in a trinitarian progression towards a new kind of poetry, which he calls 'enthousiasme cristallisée'. The poet is not a mouthpiece for divine truth but the encapsulator and transmitter of purely human wisdom and compassion for the benefit of posterity.

Each of these writers was, in their own individual ways, a nomothete, expounding what they considered to be fundamental moral, political, philosophical, and religious truths about the human condition. At the heart of their endeavours lay an ambition to explain and improve the lives of human beings, whether through

---

[4] Victor Hugo, *Œuvres complètes*, ed. Jacques Seebacher, Guy Rosa, et al. (15 vols, Paris: Robert Laffont, 1985–90), *Poésie*, i. 54.

writing or political engagement or both. Since the Christian Church had been performing this task for some 1,800 years,[5] it is no surprise that they saw a particular need to define the poet's function in relation to the Christian faith itself, responding to it whether by adherence (Chateaubriand), variation (Lamartine and Hugo with their own particular gospels of love), or substitution (the secular 'enthusiasm' of Staël and Vigny). In this respect Baudelaire was no different. Born in 1821 he began writing poems in the 1830s, and many of those that he subsequently published in 1857 in the first edition of Les Fleurs du Mal were drafted and/or completed during the 1840s: that is, during a period when the agenda of Chateaubriand's Génie du christianisme and the best-selling works of the young Royalists Lamartine, Hugo, and Vigny were still fresh in the public mind and constituted the acme of post-revolutionary poetic endeavour. But Baudelaire was different in what he wanted to say: the poet as contrarian chose to write against this prevailing trend, and even (so he claims, perhaps disingenuously) for the simple sake of doing so. As he records in a projected preface to the second (or, possibly, third) edition of Les Fleurs du Mal:

> Des poètes illustres s'étaient partagé depuis longtemps les provinces les plus fleuries du domaine poétique. Il m'a paru plaisant, et d'autant plus agréable que la tâche était plus difficile, d'extraire la beauté du Mal. Ce livre, essentiellement inutile et absolument innocent, n'a pas été fait dans un autre but que de me divertir et d'exercer mon goût passionné de l'obstacle. (i. 181)

This insistence on the 'uselessness' of his work pays implicit homage to Gautier's preface to Mademoiselle de Maupin, just as the reference to difficulty overcome recalls Gautier's more recent statements in 'L'Art' in Émaux et camées.[6] The idea of creating a work of art as the response to a challenge is itself perhaps not disingenuous, however, given that this is exactly how Baudelaire imagines Flaubert as having undertaken Madame Bovary: 'une gageure, une vraie gageure, un pari, comme tous les œuvres d'art' (ii. 81). As to the 'poètes illustres' who have monopolized 'les provinces les plus fleuries du domaine poétique', here Baudelaire

---

[5] Cf. Staël's preface to Delphine (1802) where she reminds readers of what she had tried to achieve in De la littérature (1800): 'comme le christianisme date de dix-huit –siècles, et nos chefs-d'œuvre en littérature seulement de deux, je pensais que les progrès de l'esprit humain en général, devaient être comptés pour quelque chose, dans l'examen des différences entre la littérature des anciens et celle des modernes' (Delphine, ed. Béatrice Didier (2 vols, Paris: Flammarion, 2000), i. 55).

[6] In the preface to Mademoiselle de Maupin Gautier's rejection of a 'useful' moral and social function for art is summarized in his famous assertion that 'Il n'y a de vraiment beau que ce qui ne peut servir à rien; tout ce qui est utile est laid, car c'est l'expression de quelque besoin.' See Théophile Gautier, Romans, contes et nouvelles, ed. Pierre Laubriet (2 vols, Paris: Gallimard [Bibliothèque de la Pléiade], 2002), i. 230. The opening stanza of 'L'Art' (first published in 1857 and incorporated as the final poem in the 1858 edition of Émaux et camées) reads: 'Oui, l'œuvre sort plus belle | D'une forme au travail | Rebelle, | Vers, marbre, onyx, émail.' See Gautier, Œuvres poétiques complètes, ed. Michel Brix (Paris: Bartillat, 2004), 570.

is recalling Sainte-Beuve's suggestion at the time of the trial of *Les Fleurs du Mal* that he defend his choice of subject matter on the ground that everything else had been written about! 'Tout était pris dans le domaine de la poésie', his friend had written:

> Lamartine avait pris les *cieux*, Victor Hugo avait pris la *terre* et plus que la *terre*. Laprade avait pris les *forêts*. Musset avait pris la *passion et l'orgie* éblouissante. D'autres avaient pris le *foyer*, la *vie rurale*, etc. [-] Théophile Gautier avait pris l'Espagne et ses hautes couleurs. Que restait-il? [-] Ce que Baudelaire a pris. [-] Il y a été comme forcé. (i. 790)[7]

For all the humour of Sainte-Beuve's suggestions we have here a glimpse of how writers and artists then as now have to situate themselves within a context of competing visions, and for Baudelaire that context was the context of the poet as lawgiver—in which he would inaugurate a new 'province fleurie'.

Just as the term *nomos* has from earliest times denoted an intimate relationship between poetry and the law, so too, and also from earliest times,[8] the term *nomos* has begged a powerful question: is the 'lawfulness' or harmony proposed by a nomothete, whether in legislative or poetico-musical form, truly inherent in the universe or in fact mere human invention? This question echoes insistently through discussions of poetry during the first half of the nineteenth century, and writers negotiate the ambiguity of the poetic function differently.[9] Chateaubriand claims poetic authority explicitly from God and yet does not present the poet as a mere passive recipient of divine truth. His poet is an active moral and political leader, but one nevertheless who proceeds not in the manner of Orpheus, as though imposing order on chaos, but rather of a Moses guiding his errant readerly flock *back* to the perception of a divine and pre-existent harmony in the world. (Chateaubriand seeks similarly in his memoirs to mask the discrepancy between a supposedly 'revealed' religious truth and his own humanly created narrative of divine providence.)

For Staël, receptive to Kant's critique of Lockean epistemology and his view that our human perception of reality is shaped by innate conceptual structures, the poet is at once actor and observer, part of nature and celebrant of nature. For her the poet's special task is to record those epiphanic moments in which a human being experiences some profound sense of harmony with and in the world: 'Il se

---

[7] Sainte-Beuve, 'Petits moyens de défense tels que je les conçois [18 ou 19 août 1857]', in Guyaux (ed.), *Baudelaire: Un demi-siècle de lectures des 'Fleurs du mal'*, 213–14 (213). Sainte-Beuve here expands on similar comments he had made to Baudelaire in a letter of 20 July 1857: see Guyaux (ed.), *Baudelaire: Un demi-siècle de lectures des 'Fleurs du mal'*, 175–7 (175).
[8] See *Unacknowledged Legislators*, 20 n. 15.
[9] See *Unacknowledged Legislators*, 25–30, 579–82.

sent au milieu des merveilles du monde comme un être à la fois créateur et créé, qui doit mourir et ne peut cesser d'être.'[10] If, as Kant had argued, a sense of the divine—the sense of a spiritual otherness—is imprinted in our modes of perception and is stimulated by what we call beauty, then we are at once the recipient and the source of mysterious spiritual intimations—and ultimately their only source, even though we may call that other dimension 'God'. Such moments constitute the 'apotheosis' of man: etymologically, the 'completion' of man as God.

As to the verse poets themselves, Lamartine gradually abandons the poetic persona of God's spokesman on earth, evident particularly in the *Méditations poétiques*, and begins increasingly to see poetry as the means to a secular expression of the mystery of human experience. Like Staël he comes to view the poet as a force of nature, like a nightingale, part of the physical world and yet endowed with a voice with which to express the harmonies of the world and to 'half-create' them: 'celui qui achève la création en la contemplant, en l'animant et en l'exprimant'.[11] Hugo, similarly, talks of poetry as part 'meditation' and part 'inspiration', that is, part active invention and part passive reception. For him the poet as lawgiver is the genius who is sent on a mission and yet also chooses to go: 'Le volontaire nécessaire'; just as he is, similarly, the participant in table-turning who listens to voices from the beyond only to discover that they simply tell him what he has already thought. Likewise Vigny talks of inspiration and the poet's 'mission' but quickly locates the source of this inspiration and this mission solely within our secular terrestrial reality. The poet's work springs exclusively from the human brain: 'La hauteur, la profondeur et l'étendue de son œuvre et de sa renommée future sont égales aux trois dimensions de son cerveau.—Il est par lui-même, il est lui-même, et son œuvre est lui.' And for Vigny the age of 'l'Esprit pur' has dawned at last because we have finally realized that heaven itself is simply the product of this human brain: 'La race humaine se refroidit en ce qui touche le surnaturel. Elle a fini par comprendre que sa *Pensée* est la *créatrice* des mondes invisibles.'[12]

For all that each of these five writers is therefore conscious of a profound tension at the heart of the poetic function—prophecy or invention, receptiveness or effort, inspiration or perspiration—none sees this as inherently problematic or disabling. Whether God or human nature is the source of truth and therefore of poetic authority, the resultant discourse is seen as grounded outside the writer's own individual act of writing. But with Baudelaire—and with Flaubert—the

---

[10] Staël, *De l'Allemagne*, ed. Simone Balayé (2 vols, Paris: Garnier Flammarion, 1968), i. 207. See *Unacknowledged Legislators*, 269.

[11] Lamartine, *Cours familier de littérature* (28 vols, Paris: Chez l'auteur, 1856–70), IVe Entretien, i. 267. The term 'half-create' is from Wordsworth's 'Lines written a few miles above Tintern Abbey' (1798), where he describes himself as a 'lover' 'of all the mighty world | Of eye and ear, both what they half-create | And what perceive'. Cf. my reference in the Preface to his account in *The Prelude* of the 'poetic Spirit' as 'creator' and 'receiver'.

[12] For the textual references to Hugo and Vigny and for further discussion see *Unacknowledged Legislators*, 580–1.

situation changes radically. Both acknowledge that there is a world 'out there', a world of 'nature' and human experience, which it is the writer's function somehow to express, but they are both acutely conscious of the problematic relationship between nature and art and in a way that their predecessors were not. For Chateaubriand—the celebrated stylist known as the 'enchanteur'—language could offer a faithful representation of a harmonious world, just as for Staël the poet's eloquence allowed for the expression of what the ordinary mortal could only feel but not articulate. Lamartine may initially have worried (in the *Méditations poétiques*) that human language was inadequate to the task of celebrating the divine, but his own poetic fluency, both in the *Méditations* and in his *Harmonies poétiques et religieuses*, gave the lie to such doubts. Hugo felt few such doubts, eventually becoming confident enough, in *Les Contemplations*, to be the Creator of his own Creation. And Vigny's favourite analogies for poetry—the diamond, the pearl, the elixir, the navigational chart—all point to the valuable expressive and transformative power of poetic language, worked on by the poet as though by nature itself so that the compressed and brilliant truth of reality may come quasi-organically into everlasting view.

But for Baudelaire the double nature of the poet-artist—unconscious participant in life, conscious creator of artefact—is a source of perpetual anxiety. For him it is not enough to say that art represents nature and derives its authority from the fidelity of its representation. Because what, after all, *is* nature? In the *Salon de 1859* he ridicules the 'doctrinaires' of Realism for their blithe confidence:

> Cependant il eût été plus philosophique de demander aux doctrinaires en question, d'abord s'ils sont bien certains de l'existence de la nature extérieure, ou, si cette question eût paru trop bien faite pour réjouir leur causticité, s'ils sont bien sûrs de connaître *toute la nature*, tout ce qui est contenu dans la nature. Un oui eût été la plus fanfaronne et la plus extravagante des réponses.   (ii. 620)

And wherein lies fidelity? Certainly not in the simple reproductions and simulations of literary or painterly 'Realism' or (in Baudelaire's view) of photography. Where then? In the expression of something beneath or beyond or above nature? Art as 'surnaturalisme'? But who is to say if these visions are not just the products of art? Yet who, also, is to say that such visions are not more 'true' than nature itself? Nature is mindless and cruel and base, while human creativity can transform it through the power of the individual imagination. Man, though part of nature, is superior to nature, and so too, in a similar manner, is art. In the works of Chateaubriand, Staël, Lamartine, Hugo, and Vigny we can see the source of a poet's authority gradually cease to be God and become located with increasing conviction in the mind, spirit, and imagination of the human being. But now with Baudelaire we see that source of authority shift again, from man in nature to man as conscious creator and transformer *of* nature, to man as artist. This is the artist who must *protest* against nature and 'substitute man for nature'. The true 'hero of modern life' is a resistance hero.

The Poet-Artist as Double Act

> Tous les grands poètes deviennent naturellement, fatalement, critiques.
> ('Richard Wagner et *Tannhaüser* à Paris', ii. 793)

One way to see Baudelaire's view of the poet-artist, therefore, is as a riposte to the kind of antagonism expressed in Plato's *Ion*. As mentioned briefly in the Introduction, Socrates/Plato seeks to undermine the authority of the poet as a potential rival to the philosopher-lawgiver by contending that Ion, as an inspired rhapsode subject to the *furor divinus*, is necessarily out of his mind and so cannot judge rationally whereof he speaks. Baudelaire, by contrast, may be viewed as trying to combat this dismissal of the poet as mere plaything of the muses by emphasizing the element of willed and conscious effort in the production of art, even to the extent of denying the idea of 'inspiration' altogether: 'l'inspiration, en un mot, n'est que la récompense de l'exercice quotidien' (ii. 183).[13] Indeed he wonders, in characteristically contrarian style, if the real issue with inspiration is not how it comes but how it ceases: 'L'inspiration vient toujours quand l'homme le *veut*, mais elle ne s'en va pas toujours quand il le veut.'[14] His most emphatic statement on this matter comes at the very end of 'Du vin et du hachisch' (1851) where he quotes Auguste Barbereau (1799–1879), a musician and conductor who had six years earlier published a book on the theory and practice of musical composition. Barbureau, it seems, was no drinker:

> J'étais auprès de lui dans une société dont quelques personnes avaient pris du bienheureux poison, et il me dit avec un accent de mépris indicible: 'Je ne comprends pas pourquoi l'homme rationnel et spirituel se sert de moyens artificiels pour arriver à la béatitude poétique, puisque l'enthousiasme et la volonté suffisent pour l'élever à une existence supra-naturelle. Les grands poètes, les philosophes, les prophètes sont des êtres qui par le pur et libre exercice de la volonté parviennent à un état où ils sont à la fois cause et effet, sujet et objet, magnétiseur et somnambule.'

---

[13] By way of exception, however, Baudelaire, in 'Quelques caricaturistes étrangers' (1857/8), finds the paintings of Brueghel the Elder impossible to account for other than as a form of hallucination: 'Quel artiste pourrait composer des œuvres aussi monstrueusement paradoxales, s'il n'y était poussé dès le principe par quelque force inconnue? En art, c'est une chose qui n'est pas assez remarquée, la part laissée à la volonté de l'homme est bien moins grande qu'on ne le croit' (ii. 573); and he defies anyone to explain the 'capharnaüm diabolique et drolatique' of his paintings other than as the product of 'une espèce de grâce spéciale et satanique' (ii. 573).

[14] *Fusées*, ed. Guyaux, 64; i. 658.

And Baudelaire concludes: 'Je pense exactement comme lui' (i. 398). Here again is the duality of the poetic state as others had described it, whether it be Wordsworth ('half-create') or Staël ('un être à la fois créateur et créé') or Hugo ('le volontaire nécessaire'), but now seen for the first time as a state to be induced at will by the poet-artist. The most familiar expression of this ambition comes in *Le Peintre de la vie moderne* where Baudelaire defines genius as 'l'enfance retrouvée à volonté', a formulation which reprises the argument of 'Le Génie enfant' in *Les Paradis artificiels*:[15] that is, the poet-artist is defined by a capacity to recover consciously the joy of a child's unconscious pristine wonder at the world.

In essence Baudelaire's position is this: the poet-artist is a part of nature and his role is to depict, knowingly, how it looks and feels to be unknowingly part of nature, part of life. Art is therefore a kind of feigned innocence (he does after all describe *Les Fleurs du Mal* as 'absolument innocent' (i. 181)!)—or 'naïveté'. In the *Salon de 1846*, as we have seen, this 'naïveté' constitutes an early version of the later 'enfance retrouvée à volonté'. On the one hand, in his account of Delacroix's originality, he quotes Heine's use of the term 'surnaturaliste' in order to describe how Delacroix is able to describe nature as it were from the inside, from inside his own soul: 'En fait d'art, je suis surnaturaliste. Je crois que l'artiste ne peut trouver dans la nature tous ses types, mais que les plus remarquables lui sont révélés dans son âme, comme la symbolique innée d'idées innées, et au même instant' (ii. 432). On the other hand, he stresses how the poet-artist is indeed not some vapid dreamer but a conscious craftsman who seeks to reproduce the *nomos* of his own existence within nature: 'Ainsi l'idéal n'est pas cette chose vague, ce rêve ennuyeux et impalpable qui nage au plafond des académies; un idéal, c'est l'individu redressé par l'individu, reconstruit et rendu par le pinceau ou le ciseau à l'éclatante vérité de son harmonie native' (ii. 456).

Not *the* ideal, therefore, but *an* ideal: that is to say, an individual vision consciously created by the individual artist but on the basis of that unique and involuntary relationship with the world that Baudelaire calls 'tempérament'. Thus 'Chaque individu est une harmonie. [...] Chaque individu a donc son idéal' (ii. 456). Hence his sarcastic condemnation of those who impose a set of extrinsic moral constraints on art—be it on historical landscape painting or on neo-classical tragedy. Whereas Baudelaire himself believes that 'La nature n'a d'autre morale que le fait, parce qu'elle est la morale elle-même', for these misguided theorists and aesthetic legislators 'il s'agit de la reconstruire et de l'ordonner d'après des règles plus saines et plus pures, règles qui ne se trouvent pas dans le pur enthousiasme de

---

[15] See 'Un mangeur d'opium' in *Les Paradis artificiels*: 'le génie n'est que l'enfance nettement formulée, douée maintenant, pour s'exprimer, d'organes virils et puissants' (i. 498). Later Baudelaire describes how De Quincey as a student at Oxford recalled his childhood 'mais avec la richesse poétique qu'y ajoutait maintenant un esprit cultivé, déjà subtil, et habitué à tirer ses plus grandes jouissances de la solitude et du souvenir' (i. 505). Cf. also *Exposition universelle*: 'La peinture est une évocation, une opération magique (si nous pouvions consulter l'âme des enfants!)' (ii. 580).

l'idéal, mais dans des codes bizarres que les adeptes ne montrent à personne' (ii. 480). This is the wrong sort of lawgiving.

'Naïveté', 'harmonie native', and now 'le pur enthousiasme de l'idéal'. For Baudelaire the term 'idéal' implies no moral perfection but denotes rather what pertains to the non-material realm of the imagination: in *De l'essence du rire*, for example, he glosses the phrase 'une certaine faculté créatrice' as 'une idéalité artistique' (ii. 535). At issue here, therefore, is a creativity free of all extraneous requirements and born of an 'enthusiasm' that no longer betokens (as the word's etymology suggests) 'God within us' but rather, as already for Staël, of 'the human within us'. It is within the realm of this 'pure enthusiasm', then, that the poet-artist must look for guidance in the act of 'reconstructing' or 'ordering' nature in art; and this guide is the 'harmonie native' that unites the poet-artist's own temperament with the world itself, a *nomos* governing self and other. Thus in the celebrated debate between 'dessinistes' and 'coloristes' that is articulated within the *Salon de 1846* and conducted in support of Delacroix over Ingres, the colourists epitomize Baudelaire's attempted solution to the problem of representing nature consciously but 'naïvely': 'les coloristes, les grands coloristes, dessinent par tempérament, presqu'à leur insu' (ii. 458). But in that 'presqu[e]' lies the entire problem of the double nature of the artist.

This duality remains problematic even when it becomes the key to Baudelaire's theory of comedy, itself the basis for his definition of 'modern' art. In *De l'essence du rire* Baudelaire argues that there was no laughter in paradise, only unthinking joy: 'La joie est *une*. Le rire est l'expression d'un sentiment double, ou contradictoire; et c'est pour cela qu'il y a convulsion' (ii. 534). Laughter derives from self-consciousness, from some (entirely putative and random) 'fall' ('l'accident d'une chute ancienne, d'une dégradation physique et morale' (ii. 528)), and springs also from a fundamental human conceitedness ('un certain orgueil inconscient' (ii. 531)). We laugh (as Hobbes had previously contended) out of a sense of superiority over something or someone else: 'Idée satanique s'il en fut jamais!' (ii. 530)—'satanic' because we have been tempted into believing in that superiority and thus into the sin of pride. As Baudelaire puts it in a further variation on the story of the Garden of Eden: 'le comique est un des plus clairs signes sataniques de l'homme et un des nombreux pépins contenus dans la pomme symbolique' (ii. 530). Laughter is born of the contradiction in man's double nature, of a Pascalian disparity between 'grandeur' and 'misère': 'misère infinie relativement à l'Être absolu dont il possède la conception, grandeur infinie relativement aux animaux' (ii. 532). And Baudelaire appears to take some delight in associating this 'Satanic' laughter with Christianity itself and its doctrine of the 'fallen' state of man: 'c'est en nous, chrétiens, qu'est le comique' (ii. 534). Indeed thanks to the New Covenant we now have more to laugh about: 'C'est pourquoi je ne trouve pas étonnant que nous, enfants d'une loi meilleure que les lois religieuses antiques, nous, disciples favorisés de Jésus, nous possédions plus d'éléments comiques que la païenne antiquité' (ii. 533). Once again, the contrarian steps outside a traditional binary: rather than Christ and the Devil being opposites, Christianity has given us Satan.

But there is also a duality within comedy itself, one that Baudelaire explicitly maps onto the opposition between moralistic literature and 'l'Art pour l'Art'[16] and which also anticipates his distinction between the 'positiviste' and the 'imaginatif' in the *Salon de 1859*. One type of comedy is 'le comique ordinaire', which he dubs 'le comique significatif' and associates with Molière and Voltaire. The other is the comedy of the grotesque, which he calls 'le comique absolu' and associates with Rabelais.[17] The former is mere imitative representation and addresses human reason, while the latter, 'se rapprochant beaucoup plus de la nature, se présente sous une espèce *une*, et qui veut être saisie par intuition' (ii. 536). The former (which, in English, we might consider to be 'wit') makes us smile or laugh on the basis of some intellectual realization that may not necessarily be immediate, while the grotesque makes us laugh suddenly and spontaneously (for example, the comedy of farce and slapstick). One could perhaps see in this insistence on the unitary nature of the grotesque a kind of nostalgia for the prelapsarian joy of paradise, but Baudelaire is quick to correct such an impression: 'Le comique ne peut être absolu que relativement à l'humanité déchue' (ii. 536). Nevertheless this 'comique absolu' is clearly related to 'naïveté', 'harmonie native', and 'le pur enthousiasme de l'idéal'. It, too, is the artistic expression of something natural, an art of (feigned) unselfconsciousness: 'Il faut ajouter qu'un des signes très particuliers du comique absolu est de s'ignorer lui-même' (ii. 542); and it, too, constitutes a higher form of art: 'L'essence très relevée du comique absolu en fait l'apanage des artistes supérieurs qui ont en eux la réceptibilité suffisante de toute idée absolue' (ii. 536). Thus the superior artist resembles the dandy who dresses and behaves beautifully while wearing an expression that declares such beauty of dress and behaviour to be the most natural thing in the world.

Here, at the end of *De l'essence du rire*, Baudelaire confronts once more the problematic double nature of the artist, in this case the professional comic actor or 'comédien' who knowingly turns himself into the object that will provoke the 'comique absolu'. Just as beauty is not inherent in what is perceived but an effect within the perceiver, so too laughter is an effect: 'C'est du choc perpétuel de ces deux infinis [i.e. 'grandeur' and 'misère'] que se dégage le rire. Le comique, la puissance du rire est dans le rieur et nullement dans l'objet du rire' (ii. 532).[18] Accordingly the role of the comic performer is to simulate ignorance of this

---

[16] 'Il y a entre ces deux rires, abstraction faite de la question d'utilité, la même différence qu'entre l'école littéraire intéressée et l'école de l'art pour l'art' (ii. 535).
[17] For a probing analysis of the inconsistencies in Baudelaire's use of this distinction in *De l'essence du rire*, see J. A. Hiddleston, 'Baudelaire et le rire', *Études baudelairiennes*, 12 (1987), 85–98.
[18] An observation repeated at the end of the essay: 'c'est spécialement dans le rieur, dans le spectateur, que gît le comique' (ii. 543).

disparity in order to provoke the 'absolute' laughter that the unwittingly 'grotesque' would also provoke. In this he epitomizes 'tous les phénomènes artistiques qui dénotent dans l'être humain l'existence d'une dualité permanente, la puissance d'être à la fois soi et un autre' (ii. 543). The performer of the 'comique absolu' will be funny only if members of the audience believe that he is unaware of his absurdity (and thus can delight in their own superiority), a phenomenon that Baudelaire summarizes as 'cette loi d'ignorance' (ii. 543) before ending his essay by defining the artist as subject to the *opposite* law: 'de même que, par une loi inverse, l'artiste n'est artiste qu'à la condition d'être double et de n'ignorer aucun phénomène de sa double nature' (ii. 543). The 'absolute' comic actor is aware of pretending but must further pretend not to be thus aware; while conversely the artist may often believe that art is not a pretence but must always remember that it is. The artist may like to think that art is spontaneous intuition, that art is natural; but art is art, a conscious, positive act of creation. And yet to be conscious of the conscious nature of human creativity is in itself a necessary, 'natural' part of our very nature, of our double nature, so that such knowledge, far from being disabling, can and must be willingly accepted and put to use.

It is in this way, therefore, that the artist most eloquently 'incarnates' the human condition and gives expression to the fundamental law of division—between instinct and reflection, between base desire and spiritual aspiration—that defines our 'double nature'. The poet-artist is necessarily double—a performer and a critic—and a central issue in Baudelaire's aesthetic theory is this: how can the authentic artist be a conscious creator without forgoing the direct link with experience itself, with that immediate sense of unconscious immersion in reality that Baudelaire calls 'naïveté'? Genius may be defined as childhood recovered at will, but adults know—must not forget, perhaps cannot forget—that they nevertheless remain adults. Such also, in Les Fleurs du Mal, is 'la conscience dans le Mal'. As moral beings we are subject to the 'deux postulations simultanées' that Baudelaire describes in Mon cœur mis à nu: 'l'une vers Dieu, l'autre vers Satan. L'invocation à Dieu, ou spiritualité, est un désir de monter en grade; celle de Satan, ou animalité, est une joie de descendre.'[19] We may perceive this disparity in terms of failure and loss, of a perpetual human inadequacy that gives rise to melancholy; or we can accept it—'Soulagement et gloire uniques' ('L'Irrémédiable', l. 39)—as constitutive of our double nature, as the very definition of the human, and meet it humanly, face on, not looking for solutions in the hereafter or in transcendence, but in the here and now, in the immanent reality of human experience, and above all in the reality of human creativity and the power of the human imagination to transcend the world of the given in favour of another world, of 'un Infini que j'aime et n'ai jamais connu' ('Hymne à la Beauté', l. 24). In this way Les Fleurs du

---

[19] *Fusées*, ed. Guyaux, 88; i. 682–3.

Mal may be seen as exemplifying a form of positive resistance to 'le Mal' through the medium of art. Rather than present 'le Mal' as a flaw to be overcome or to be repented of, Baudelaire's collection embraces it—catalogues it, portrays it, enjoys it, laments it—within the framework of an artistry that precisely, in ways to be examined later in this study, give the lie to it. What is 'irremediable' in life may be partially or wholly resisted through art, that other form of life.

Baudelaire as Comic Artist?

Le comique est un élément damnable et d'origine diabolique.
(*De l'essence du rire*, ii. 528)

Baudelaire's theory of the comic has led several critics to consider whether his own poetry in verse and prose may therefore itself be considered 'comic'. At first sight this may appear a strange term to apply to a writer more usually associated with melancholy and bitter despair. But, as the essay *De l'essence du rire* suggests, the source of both comedy and melancholy is the same: the awareness of our 'fallen' state, our human consciousness of a disparity between what could be and what is, of a world in which 'l'action n'est pas la sœur du rêve' ('Le Reniement de saint Pierre', l. 30). Thus those critics who see Baudelaire as 'comic' are essentially identifying the fundamental dualism at the heart of his work that is manifest in his familiar binaries of 'spiritualité' and 'animalité, 'surnaturalisme' and 'ironie', or 'vaporisation' and 'centralisation'. John W. MacInnes, for example, writes that '[w]hat I have named the comical element in Baudelaire's verse resides in the irresolvable tension between poetic aspiration and suspicion', the 'suspicion' in question being the 'profound suspicion that the writing subject can never coincide with its transcription of a "moment of being"; that is, that it can never achieve the language of immediate and full sense to which it aspires.' MacInnes argues that Baudelaire's poet is 'comic', therefore, because he writes as though such plenitude were possible and yet also in the knowledge that it is not, with the result that his poems 'resist being located under the simple sign of either irony or sincerity [...] and suggest that it is only by submitting to the desire for a fantasmatic control over language that the poet comes to know the extent to which the self is fragmented in its quest for a specular stabilization of the world in meaning'.[20] Like comic artists pretending that they don't know they're funny, so the 'comic' poet writes as though he had one single, unified identity even though he discovers with each speech act that he hasn't.

---

[20] *The Comical as Textual Practice in 'Les Fleurs du Mal'* (Gainesville, Fla: University of Florida Press, 1988), 126.

Critical consideration of Baudelaire as a 'comic' poet has centred mostly on the art of caricature. Thus, for example, Ainslie Armstrong McLees in her book *Baudelaire's 'Argot plastique': Poetic Caricature and Modernism*[21] seeks to demonstrate how the caricaturist's traditional combination of visual incongruity, moral commentary, and social critique may be found also in Baudelaire's poetry, where it prepares for the modernism of T. S. Eliot and others through a provocative subversion of poetic tradition and the introduction of 'urban poetry'. Similarly, in her own book on Baudelaire and caricature,[22] Michele Hannoosh has shown through a series of acutely attentive readings how Baudelaire's theory of laughter as set out in *De l'essence du rire* not only informs his two essays on caricature—'Quelques caricaturistes français' and 'Quelques caricaturistes étrangers'—but also provides the basis for his theory of the modern, adumbrated in the *Salon de 1846* and fully articulated in *Le Peintre de la vie moderne*.[23] Her arguments are compelling, and I would like to dwell on them here, together with those presented by Alain Vaillant in his book *Baudelaire, poète comique*,[24] as a way of relating this conception of the poet as comic artist to my own hypothesis of the poet as alternative lawgiver.[25]

Hannoosh argues that for Baudelaire the comic art of caricature (whose purpose is to present 'in a work of beauty the image of moral and physical ugliness' (p. 104)) offers a model for modern art and indeed for all art:

> the peculiar oxymoronic nature of *comic art*, which [Baudelaire] treats as a contradiction in terms, represents in boldly exaggerated form, like a good caricature, the dualism of art itself, the contradiction inherent in all artistic

---

[21] Athens, Ga, and London: University of Georgia Press, 1989.

[22] Michele Hannoosh, *Baudelaire and Caricature: From the Comic to an Art of Modernity* (University Park, Pa: Pennsylvania State University Press, 1992). Page references will be given in the main text.

[23] Cf. also her earlier discussion of Baudelaire's short article 'Peintres et aquafortistes' (1862), in Michele Hannoosh, 'Etching and Modern Art: Baudelaire's *Peintres et aquafortistes*', *French Studies*, 43 (1989), 47–60. There she examines the 'close relation between [Baudelaire's] conception of etching and his aesthetic thought overall' (p. 47) under four headings: (i) 'the essentially personal nature of etching, which ensures that the artist's individual temperament is conveyed through this work'; (ii) 'the technical training and expertise that it demands'; (iii) 'its aristocratic quality, making it appeal to artists and literati rather than to a larger public'; (iv) 'its capacity to express especially well an urban beauty and to produce an art of the city' (pp. 47–8). She concludes that '*Le Spleen de Paris* realizes fully the late aesthetic that Baudelaire formulates in the essay on etching—an urban poetry translating the artist's visions of modern life in a free but controlled form, a highly personal and thus aristocratic art, difficult and unsettling in its contrasts, its range of tones, and its irony. *Peintres et aquafortistes* poses a radical challenge to the modern artist, offering this relatively minor form as a model by which to define the possibilities of a new form altogether, and of a distinctly modern pictorial and literary art' (pp. 57–8).

[24] (Rennes: Presses universitaires de Rennes, 2007). Page references will be given in the main text.

[25] In *Baudelaire's Prose Poems: The Practice and Politics of Irony* (Oxford: Oxford University Press, 1999) Sonya Stephens also discusses Baudelaire's theory of the comic in relation to the art of caricature and with particular reference to his prose poems. I allude to some aspects of her account in Part V.

creation, as in mankind—at once diabolical and divine, real and ideal, ugly and beautiful, temporal and enduring, inferior and superior. (p. 3)

For Hannoosh, Baudelaire's distinction between the 'comique significatif' and the 'comique absolu' as a criterion for the classification and evaluation of caricature thus maps directly onto his distinction (introduced in the *Salon de 1846* and developed in *Le Peintre de la vie moderne*) between the transitory and the eternal[26] and prepares for the combination of the two that informs his celebrated definition: 'La modernité, c'est le transitoire, le fugitif, le contingent, la moitié de l'art, dont l'autre moitié est l'éternel et l'immuable' (ii. 695). Key to Hannoosh's pioneering argument is the fact that for Baudelaire duality and unity are not opposites:

> Baudelaire specifies that duality is a contradiction of unity and not its opposite: as with colo[u]r and line, rational analysis has separated the two, but the distinction does not exist in reality. As this passage[27] suggests, unity in fact consists in duality, variety, and difference; the contradiction lies, like all contradiction, in the human perception of the two. The world is in this sense a 'vast system of contradiction' [i. 546], a 'unified' network of contradictory, interrelated elements.
> (p. 260)

For her, therefore, Baudelaire's essays on laughter and caricature invalidate any account of his aesthetic as being 'essentially nostalgic, based on a longing for a primordial wholeness (linguistic, psychological, or metaphysical)' (p. 3).[28] Rather this aesthetic is based on 'the vast theological metaphor' of the Fall, and his essays 'bring out [...] the essential humanity or [...] the "fallenness" of art—an idea with evident Romantic origins, but involving a radical realignment of values':

---

[26] For example, she quotes (on p. 13) Baudelaire's discussion of Goya in 'Quelques caricaturistes étrangers' where he makes a distinction between 'historical' and 'artistic' caricaturists: 'C'est là ce qui marque le véritable artiste, toujours durable et vivace même dans ces œuvres fugitives, pour ainsi dire suspendues aux événements, qu'on appelle *caricatures*; c'est là, dis-je, ce qui distingue les caricaturistes historiques d'avec les caricaturistes artistiques, le comique fugitif d'avec le comique éternel' (ii. 568).

[27] In section vii ('De l'idéal et du modèle') of the *Salon de 1846*, ii. 455-6: 'Quoique le principe universel soit un, la nature ne donne rien d'absolu, ni même de complet; je ne vois que des individus. Tout animal, dans une espèce semblable, diffère en quelque chose de son voisin, et parmi les milliers de fruits que peut donner un même arbre, il est impossible d'en trouver deux identiques, car ils seraient le même; et la dualité, qui est la contradiction de l'unité, en est aussi la conséquence.' Here Baudelaire adds a footnote: 'Je dis la contradiction, et non pas le contraire; car la contradiction est une invention humaine.'

[28] As an example of the critical thinking she has in mind, cf. Max Milner's comment: 'La métaphore baudelairienne nous apporte la nostalgie d'une unité irrémédiablement perdue plutôt que le pressentiment d'une unité à reconquérir'. See his 'Baudelaire et le surnaturalisme', in *Le Surnaturalisme français: Actes du colloque organisé à l'Université Vanderbilt les 31 mars et le 1er avril 1978* (Neuchâtel: Éditions de la Baconnière, 1979), 31-49 (48). Cf. also Georges Poulet: 'La philosophie de la lumière chez Baudelaire obéit aux mêmes lois que son esthétique. Elle exprime finalement la condition de l'homme, rêvant le parfait dans l'imparfait', in *La Poésie éclatée: Baudelaire/Rimbaud* (Paris: Presses universitaires de France, 1980), 65.

Here it becomes the necessary (and fertile) condition of art, and art understood not as a *pis-aller* effort to regain an original perfection, but as the positing of that very perfection. The absolute exists only from the fallen, imperfect perspective of mankind; the image of oneness is born of the dualism of the comic; absolute beauty, like the category of *comique absolu*, is relative, a product of the historical and contingent. (p. 3)

When Baudelaire states in *De l'essence du rire* that 'les phénomènes engendrés par la chute deviendront les moyens du rachat' (ii. 528), he means (Hannoosh argues) that art achieves 'wholeness' precisely by articulating the divided and fragmentary nature of human experience. This allows Hannoosh to contest Walter Benjamin's account of Baudelaire's 'allegorical genius'[29] as consisting only in 'embodying and exposing the division and fragmentation of the modern subject, representing and revealing the terrifying and exhilarating otherness of modern experience' and to argue instead that for Baudelaire comic art (and, by extension, 'modern' art) proposes also 'the means of transcending the very alienation which the dualism of the comic and the "brokenness" of allegory express' (pp. 4–5), 'a modern solution to the alienation of modern life itself'. 'The dualism of the comic artist', she writes, 'becomes the source of a peculiarly modern unity, the artist's capacity for *dédoublement*, that is, to be simultaneously self and other' (p. 5). While she agrees with Paul De Man (in 'The Rhetoric of Temporality') that Baudelairean *dédoublement* 'does not effect a synthesis of the self or unify the self', she argues nevertheless for a Baudelairean irony that is positive and redemptive ('les moyens du rachat'):

> The 'wholeness' of the self is created by the division in the ironic self, which transcends dualism by entering fully into it, maintaining it in the extreme, demonstrating the limitations of the self and redefining it in its relations to others, and creating the conditions by which others do the same. (p. 5)

For her the 'tension' noted by MacInnes between 'aspiration' and 'suspicion' is thereby resolved. Further, she sees this doubling of the comic artist as being 'enacted for the benefit of the audience' (p. 5) and comparable with 'the self-generating and self-reflexive experience of the *flâneur* in a "communion" with the crowd' (her reference here is to the prose poem 'Les Foules'). Finally, although Hannoosh is predominantly concerned throughout her book with Baudelaire's

---

[29] See Walter Benjamin, 'Baudelaire or the Streets of Paris', in *Paris—The Capital of the Nineteenth Century*, trans. Quintin Hoare, collected in Benjamin, *Charles Baudelaire: A Lyric Poet in the Era of High Capitalism*, trans. Harry Zohn (London and New York: Verso, 1973), 170–2: 'Baudelaire's genius, which drew its nourishment from melancholy, was an allegorical one. With Baudelaire, Paris for the first time became the subject of lyrical poetry. This poetry is no local folklore; the allegorist's gaze which falls upon the city is rather the gaze of the alienated man' (p. 170).

aesthetic theory and the importance of his contribution to the subsequent history of art and art criticism, she ends her discussion by pointing to *Le Spleen de Paris* as a demonstration of Baudelaire's theory of the comic, itself expressed in the dedicatory letter to Arsène Houssaye that introduced some of the poems when they were published in *La Presse* in 1862:

> The aesthetic of the fragmentary that the 'Dédicace' advances may thus be understood according to the comic model of unity in dualism and the relativity of the absolute. The *Petits Poèmes en prose* do not abolish unity but propose a new conception of it, a unity dependent on fragmentation, an ideal literally born of the fragmented but interconnecting ('croisement', 'rapports') and kaleidoscopic experiences, the *correspondances* of the modern city. Baudelaire's figure of the truncated serpent puts forward a new *ars poetica* [...]. (p. 315)

This move beyond Benjamin is well founded, I believe, except in its emphasis on the notion of 'redemption'. Hannoosh sees Baudelaire as 'revers[ing] the "orthodox" story of degradation, making the product of the Fall the very means of redemption and thus affirming the salutary value of comic art'. In this way, she argues, Baudelaire 'converts a standard Christian argument *against* comedy—the pleasure taken in a reminder of the Fall—into an apologia for it, according to an equally central Christian doctrine: sin itself, in the Augustinian tradition, is a calling back to the path of righteousness' (p. 20). Wittily, she sees Baudelaire the theorist as himself a comic performer: 'in exploiting the theological model *à outrance* [...] he employs an essentially comic technique, making one of the oldest of myths state a radically new principle: the status of comic art, and notably caricature, as a "high' art, one especially well suited to the paradoxes and contradictions of the modern temperament' (p. 11).

But wherein lies 'redemption'? Surely not in a Baudelairean art that would 'call us back to the path of righteousness?' When Hannoosh subsequently discusses *Le Peintre de la vie moderne*, she uses the term again, describing 'the city depicted by Guys' as being 'the locus of the comic' and 'thus encompass[ing] the means not only of corruption but of redemption too, the awareness and exploitation of dualism, the *flâneur*'s interaction with the innumerable forms and beings that meet the eye' (p. 252). Here 'redemption' lies more persuasively in 'awareness', and she goes on to show, accurately, how Baudelaire sees the value of Guys's Parisian sketches as deriving from the 'considérations morales' (ii. 708) to which they give rise. In this way, like Benjamin but from a different angle, she seeks to 'redeem' Baudelaire himself from his reputation as a reactionary in thrall to Joseph de Maistre:

> the essays on caricature [...] demonstrate how the most radical aesthetic of the time could base itself on the most apparently conservative, indeed reactionary, of

metaphysical and moral theories, which in the poet's own words repudiated the positivism of eighteenth-century enlightened philosophy and the social progressive doctrines of his own era in favo[u]r of the pervasive myth of original sin.

(p. 255)

In essence, then, Hannoosh is arguing that the poet as 'comic artist' makes a virtue of necessity, acknowledging and incorporating the 'fallenness' of the human condition within an unhypocritical form of art that does not seek to conceal it or hanker after some putative prelapsarian perfection. And she sees moral value in that lack of hypocrisy, and also suggestiveness, arguing that these 'considérations morales' 'have an immediacy and richness of meaning that defy the attempts of verbal description—temporal, restrictive, and exclusive—to reproduce them' (p. 253). More than that, she envisages 'a morality deriving from the art itself, the moral considerations that it inspires in the viewer' (p. 254) and that 'the essays on caricature integrate the moral and the aesthetic, positing the moral value of all true aesthetic experience, the impression of unity of the dualistic *comique absolu*' (p. 255). But since her focus is on Baudelaire's aesthetic theory of caricature, she legitimately stops short of speculating further on exactly what sort of 'morality' or 'moral considerations' might be so inspired, or about how such art, this 'modern' art, may itself offer *within Baudelaire's own work* an alternative vision of the world, not just food for moral reflection upon what *is* but also a journey down those 'profondes avenues' of the kind opened up by Delacroix's paintings for 'l'imagination la plus voyageuse' (ii. 431): in other words, that particular form of 'rêverie' that Baudelaire himself mentions in his dedicatory letter as being the source of *Le Spleen de Paris*.

This idea of the poet as a comic artist has also been taken up by Alain Vaillant in his book *Baudelaire, poète comique*, where, unlike Hannoosh, he does indeed seek to demonstrate how Baudelaire's poetry may itself be seen as 'comic', and in the process he makes some remarkably bold claims about Baudelaire's place within the history of French (and even world) literature. Presenting Baudelaire as 'le premier artiste à avoir fait du rire le médium privilégié de la communication lyrique' (p. 293), Vaillant follows Hannoosh (to whom he refers but with whom he does not explicitly debate) in seeing *De l'essence du rire* as central to Baudelaire's aesthetic: 'cette esthétique moderne du comique dont Baudelaire s'est fait à la fois le théoricien et le premier créateur' (p. 137). He views this aesthetic as being wholly coherent and also unchanging (p. 22). Indeed Vaillant argues similarly that all of Baudelaire's verse poems (in *Les Fleurs du Mal*) say more or less the same thing: 'La doctrine, l'univers personnel et le système de représentations de Baudelaire sont extraordinairement stables et cohérents. En puisant dans un stock limité de motifs, d'images, et de convictions, tous les poèmes disent, avec quelques variations artistiques, *à peu près* la même chose' (p. 271). This is so, he contends, because 'le rire fonde [...] l'esthétique secrète de chaque poème' as well intervening also 'à la jointure des poèmes' (i.e. 'between' the poems as they are arranged and juxtaposed in the two collections of 1857 and 1861). Indeed 'le rire est *entre* les poèmes avant que d'y venir s'y loger' (p. 271). These unnuanced assertions permit Vaillant to conclude that 'Baudelaire reste, seul de son espèce et par excellence, le *poète comique* de la littérature française' (p. 313).

In reaching this conclusion Vaillant argues that Baudelaire's own 'comique absolu' in *Les Fleurs du Mal*[30] is born of an 'impasse métaphysique': namely, that body and spirit remain eternally divided and cannot be harmonized. Interpreting the Baudelairean motif of prostitution as the 'prostitution' of the spirit accepting to be part body in order to act within and upon the world, he sees this metaphysical impasse as manifest in four areas of Baudelairean preoccupation: the affect of sexual passion; an anti-religious mysticism; his political philosophy; and his aesthetics. Focusing especially on this last area, Vaillant equates 'vaporisation' and 'centralisation' with 'surnaturalisme' and 'ironie' and finds in this double binary the motor force of Baudelaire's own 'comique absolu' and of the melancholy expressed and indeed 'embodied' in *Les Fleurs du Mal*: 'En un mot, *Les Fleurs du Mal* ont *matérialisé* la mélancolie', and this because 'la seule manière conséquente de dépasser l'aporie métaphysique est, par le rire, de suggérer l'image d'une matière qui soit comme habitée, animée par le regret de ce qui lui manque, irrévocablement' (p. 150). Like Hannoosh, therefore, Vaillant sees salvation and redemption in the simple acceptance—by the poet as comic artist—of our 'fallenness', of the 'prostitution' of the spirit in the material: 'Point de salut, donc, hors de la matière, plus exactement d'une matière sublimée par la capacité surnaturaliste de l'artiste ou du poète, sans que, pour autant, cette sublimité esthétique enlève rien à son immanence essentielle' (p. 166). But, as this statement suggests, Vaillant is more inclined than Hannoosh to see beyond simple acceptance or awareness as the means of redemption and to allow also for a poetic 'sublimation' of our material reality.

Perhaps Vaillant's boldest claim, however, is that Baudelaire thereby substituted the poet as comic artist for the Romantic figure of the poet as priest and prophet:

> Baudelaire est donc ce singulier romantique pour qui le rire (contenu et latent, plutôt que sonore et éclatant) joue le rôle qui est celui de la voix lyrique chez les autres poètes. Le poète romantique façon Lamartine ou Hugo se voulait prêtre, prophète ou messie. Il y a aussi, au sens chrétien du terme, une vraie Passion du rire chez Baudelaire: à la fois sujet rieur et objet de dérision, Baudelaire s'offre comme victime sacrificielle au public, pour lui faire partager ses extases d'imagination à travers la surface ironique de ses images versifiées. Plutôt que le poète

---

[30] Vaillant is curiously dismissive of Baudelaire's prose poetry in *Le Spleen de Paris*, which he does not discuss as evidence of a comic artistry. See in particular pp. 252–3.

moderne ou post-moderne qui utilisera l'art baudelairien de la brièveté pour renouveler la pratique romantique de la confidence intime, le poète des *Fleurs du Mal* préfigure l'humoriste qui, face à son public, communie avec lui par le rire qu'il déclenche et dont il est la première cible. Or l'humour professionnel est une création du XIXe siècle finissant, née dans les parages du *Chat noir* et des cabarets monmartrois, à l'initiative de poètes passés directement du baudelairisme spleenétique au satanisme tout aussi baudelairien du rire. (pp. 292-3)

As precursor of the professional cabaret comedian the poet as comic artist is thus seen here to fulfil a public role as sacrificial victim,[31] offering himself up for ridicule as a manifestation of the 'comique absolu'—'sorte de Buster Keaton poétique' (p. 146)—both laughing at himself[32] and causing others to laugh at him. But in so doing, Vaillant argues, Baudelaire's poet distances himself from his reader and thereby breaks absolutely with the Romantic lyric tradition that sees poetry as a form of intimate confession predicated on an unproblematic and transparent communication between a poet and reader who are partners in a universal community of human suffering and human understanding: 'cette sorte de poésie où le "je" dit à la fois la présence authentique d'un homme singulier (l'auteur) et sa vocation à l'absolue universalité et assure ainsi une communication idéale, intime et pourtant publique, entre soi et le monde' (p. 292). Baudelaire's poet, he alleges, can no longer play the role of such a mediator and now stands for 'une incommunicabilité tranquillement assumée mais poétiquement transfigurée' (p. 292). As the butt of laughter ('contenu et latent') and as sacrificial victim this poet is thus seen by Vaillant as a Christ-like figure ('Il y a, au sens chrétien du terme, une vraie Passion du rire chez Baudelaire'), mocked and even vilified by his fellow human beings but now stripped of any mediatory role (between God and man), save only in the revelation of his own 'extases d'imagination' insofar as these may be glimpsed beneath the ironic surface of his verse.

But what about 'Au lecteur' at the beginning of *Les Fleurs du Mal* and its famous final line: 'Hypocrite lecteur,—mon semblable,—mon frère?'? May it not be that Baudelaire's poet retains his role as mediator—as lawgiver—by continuing to 'embody' the human condition: the human condition no longer as perceived through the lens of the Christian story of crucifixion and redemption but as now viewed instead through the very different lens of a secular imagination? As we saw earlier in *Exposition universelle*, Baudelaire himself rejects the rejection of Romantic confessionalism, arguing that there is nothing wrong with the expression of a poetic subjectivity as long as the *je* in question speaks for humanity at large: 'tout poète véritable doit être une incarnation'. It follows, then, that

---

[31] Hannoosh proposes the same analogy. See *Baudelaire and Caricature*, 71.
[32] Vaillant does not mention that this would break the 'loi d'ignorance' that, in Baudelaire's analysis, underpins the 'comique absolu'.

Baudelaire's poet may indeed be seen as a 'comic' artist but only insofar as he is a performer of 'fallenness', of melancholy, and a performer who, like the comedian of *De l'essence du rire*, must remember that he is a double agent.

The comic artist knows that the 'comique absolu' arises only when the object of laughter is ignorant of its own ridiculousness, a ridiculousness that derives from its dual or fallen nature. And so, in order to be funny, the comic artist simulates this ignorance in a deadpan performance of the grotesque and absurdly comic. But artists, by an inverse law, can only properly be artists if they remain constantly aware of their own double nature *as artists*: that is, as both a real human being and a performer pretending to be a real human being. If we were to extend the implications of this 'inverse' law further, then we could say that whereas comic artists have to pretend that they are not performing and therefore that they are seemingly not aware of the 'fallenness' of the human condition, then the artist himself has to pretend that there is no division between being human and being a performer whereas all the while he knows that there is: that he is part 'individu', expressing his own unique 'tempérament' in the service of a 'pur enthousiasme de l'idéal', *and* that he is also part craftsman and conscious creator of art.

3
The Poet-Artist as Performer

> Fidèle à son douloureux programme, l'auteur des *Fleurs du Mal* a dû, en parfait comédien, façonner son esprit à tous les sophismes comme à toutes les corruptions.
> (Baudelaire's footnote to 'Révolte' in *Les Fleurs du Mal* (1857), i. 1076)

The Baudelairean poet-artist is thus a double agent, and the dualism he embodies is not only our divided human nature (the 'deux postulations') but also his own dualism *qua* artist as both mortal human and artistic performer. The objective of the Baudelairean poet-artist is not laughter, however, but 'beauty': that is to say, a perceptual response in the spectator or reader that may be variously characterized as a quickening of interest, surprise, excitement, heightened and sustained attention, perhaps also wonderment and surmise. Beauty as shock and awe. Beauty is the opposite of ennui and consists in a temporary state of 'ivresse', that is, the ephemeral experience of a sensual, emotional, intellectual, and/or spiritual intensity of being.

How, then, is the poet-artist to provoke this experience of beauty in the reader? How is he to 'perform'? If, in order to achieve the 'comique absolu', the comic artist of the grotesque makes his audience laugh by appearing not to know that he is or looks grotesque, then the poet-artist must similarly, in order to create the experience of beauty, appear not to know that his performance *is* one of beauty. If the objective is to 'extract' beauty from 'le Mal', then the poet-artist must present 'le Mal' as though only 'le Mal' existed. And yet as artist he must remain aware of the fundamental tension within his own double nature. As a human being he represents mortality and death, and yet as an artist he represents creativity and life. Thus his double nature itself embodies a tension between, on the one hand, the loss and destruction wrought by time and death, and, on the other, the recoveries and recreations able to be effected through memory and imagination. He is both melancholic and not melancholic, a 'contradiction'.

In this book I shall therefore now be arguing that, for Baudelaire, poetry is constituted by a 'performance' of melancholy in which the creativity and positivity implicit in the act of artistic performance 'contradict' (that is, speak against by speaking other) but do not deny or minimize the destructiveness and decay at the heart of human experience. And in that paradoxical display of creativity and positivity, as these become manifest to the reader, lies the particular beauty of Baudelaire. Baudelairean allegory is not brokenness and fragmentation but the fullness and multiplicity of an alternative *logos*, of alternative imaginative visions: 'tout, même l'horreur, tourne aux enchantements' ('Les Petites Vieilles', l. 2).[1] Baron Haussman may be changing the face of Paris, leaving the poet and swan of 'Le Cygne' seemingly exiled and bereft, but the human imagination can also effect its own transformations. In 'Le Cygne' the changing city may reinforce a sense of transience that simultaneously confirms the poet's *un*changing melancholy at the sight of change itself: 'Paris change! mais rien dans ma mélancolie | N'a bougé!' ('Le Cygne', ll. 29–30). And yet within that state of melancholy the poet's memory continues to do its creative work, if only by constructing new memorials to pain: 'palais neufs, échafaudages, blocs, | Vieux faubourgs, tout pour moi devient allégorie, | Et mes chers souvenirs sont plus lourds que des rocs' (ll. 30–2). In this way the poetic imagination may be seen less as redeeming 'le Mal' and more as 'resisting' it, 'protesting' against 'nature' (in the sense of 'the way things are') and replacing the passive acceptance of our human lot with an active affirmation of our human superiority and our capacity to 'substitute' our own allegories for '[l]e spectacle ennuyeux de l'immortel péché' ('Le Voyage', l. 88).

If the double agency of Baudelaire's comic artist is to be seen as a model for that of the poet-artist, then the sense of superiority over nature that fuels the laughter prompted by the 'comique absolu' stems now from the power of the imagination to distance us from our 'fallen' human reality and to resist the melancholy caused by our awareness of that reality. Similarly, where the comic artist must perform as though unaware of his own absurdity, so the poet-artist must appear not to realize that the melancholy and despair he is performing are belied by the very creativity of the poetic act. The poet—and in the case of *Les Fleurs du Mal* and *Le Spleen de Paris* this therefore means the living, flesh-and-blood Baudelaire himself—may, for all we know or do not know, be obeying the 'inverse' law whereby he remains always conscious of being both 'fallen' human being and artistic performer. But in the 'performance' of the poet we readers see only the performance—a performance not now of the grotesque (as it is for the 'absolute' comic artist) but of melancholy. And in the case of Baudelaire's poet-artist this means a verbal performance in which a deadpan faith in creativity silently gives the lie to our deadly awareness of the pointlessness of all human enterprise. In this way the beauty of Baudelaire prefigures Samuel Beckett's famous definition of literary art as 'the expression that there is nothing to express, nothing with which to express, nothing from which to express, no power to express, no desire to express, together with the obligation to express'.[2] And for Baudelaire—with his recurrent references

---

[1] Baudelaire's conception and use of allegory has been historically contextualized and very thoroughly examined by Patrick Labarthe in *Baudelaire et la tradition de l'allégorie* (Geneva: Droz, 1999; rev. edn, 2015). For Labarthe, '[l]'allégorie comme trope procède toujours [...] d'une expérience du réel marqué par le négatif' ([1999] 614).

[2] Samuel Beckett, *Proust/Samuel Beckett: Three Dialogues/Samuel Beckett & Georges Duthuit* (London: John Calder, 1965), 103.

to effort and hard work and the need for accomplished craftsmanship—that 'obligation to express' appears to have been strongly felt.

Two accounts of artistic performance in Baudelaire's work serve especially to illustrate this perception of the poet-artist as performer and double agent—and of the poet-artist as alternative lawgiver. In the first of these the protagonist is at once Orpheus and Christ, in the second a resistance hero. Both of these performers are outcasts of a kind, the one an impoverished wanderer, the other an indicted conspirator. Each is only too aware of the fragility of life and the possibility of death, but each transcends this grim awareness through an artistic performance that is transitory but also eternal in its capacity to allow both performer and audience momentarily to forget the very passage of time and the inevitability of death—because they have forgotten, thanks to the artist's skill, that indeed this performance is *only* art. But in that temporary oblivion lies a merciful alternative to 'la conscience dans le Mal'.

Beauty as 'Ivresse'

> Et cependant dites, en votre âme et conscience, juges, législateurs, hommes du monde, vous tous que le bonheur rend doux, à qui la fortune rend la vertu et la santé faciles, dites, qui de vous aura le courage impitoyable de condamner l'homme qui boit du génie?
> ('Du vin et du hachisch', i. 379)

In 'Du vin et du hachisch' Baudelaire tells a story about the celebrated Italian violinist Niccolò Paganini (1782–1840) and how he was accustomed, in the days before he became famous, to travel about in the company of a Spanish guitarist giving impromptu concerts in the many places and countries they visited, like wandering minstrels: 'Ce qu'il y a eu de jouissances et de poésie dans cette vie de troubadour, nul ne le saura jamais' (i. 385). The guitarist—'qui était fort buveur' (i. 384)—epitomizes Baudelaire's ideal of the poet-artist as one who 'protests' against nature:

> Mon Espagnol avait un talent tel, qu'il pouvait dire comme Orphée: 'Je suis le maître de la nature.' [-] Partout où il passait, raclant ses cordes, et les faisant harmonieusement bondir sous le pouce, il était sûr d'être suivi par une foule. Avec un pareil secret on ne meurt jamais de faim. On le suivait comme Jésus-Christ. Le moyen de refuser à dîner et l'hospitalité à l'homme, au génie, au sorcier, qui a fait chanter à votre âme ses plus beaux airs, les plus secrets, les plus inconnus, les plus mystérieux! (i. 384)

Paganini and the guitarist part company, but the guitarist continues to wander, alone. Chancing one day on a fellow Spaniard working beside a graveyard as a sculptor of marble tombs, he falls in with his compatriot and fellow-drinker—and possessor of a violin that he is barely able to play. Having invited his compatriot to accompany him at his advertised concert, the deeply intoxicated guitarist listens as the reluctant and equally intoxicated violinist plays an excruciating tune ('Bacchus en délire taillant de la pierre avec une scie' (i. 386)), whereupon he, the guitarist, takes the tune and improvises upon it in a performance of sublime confidence and power:

> Tout à coup, une mélodie énergique et suave, capricieuse et une à la fois, enveloppe, étouffe, éteint, dissimule le tapage criard. [...] La guitare s'exprime avec une sonorité énorme; elle jase, elle chante, elle déclame avec une verve effrayante, et une sûreté, une pureté inouïes de diction. (i. 386)

Human agency is replaced by the agency of art itself as melody and instrument each in turn becomes the subject of these sentences.[3] Thanks to the wine, this artist performs as though he were indeed Orpheus, 'le maître de la nature': transcending the raucous dissonance of the man who merely decorates death with marble tombs and instead giving harmonious expression to life in the deepest and most complex 'tunes of the soul'. His music has the appearance of being not art but life itself, and is duly received with 'un enthousiasme immense'. Yet this music is never to be repeated, just as the guitarist himself then vanishes into oblivion, never to be heard of again. The death of the artist, of this master of nature, seems to betoken the death of nature itself:

> Et maintenant où est-il? Quel soleil a contemplé ses derniers rêves? Quel sol a reçu sa dépouille cosmopolite? Quel fossé a abrité son agonie? Où sont les parfums enivrants des fleurs disparues? Où sont les les couleurs féeriques des anciens soleils couchants? (i. 386)

For it is thanks to the Orphic musician that the beauty of flowers and sunsets lives on as though perpetuated in intoxicating perfume and fairy-tale picture-books... or in poetry like *Les Fleurs du Mal*. Dissonance and death are met with resistance and the protest of eurhythmic art. And if it is true, as Baudelaire writes in relation to Théodore de Banville, that '[t]out poète lyrique, en vertu de sa nature, opère fatalement un retour vers l'Éden perdu' (ii. 165), it follows also that it is in the very knowledge of his double nature—as freely creative artist as well as doomed created being—that Baudelaire's lyric poet may find solace for Eden's loss. There may be

---

[3] Baudelaire returns to this idea in 'Le "Confiteor" de l'artiste': 'toutes ces choses pensent par moi, ou je pense par elles [...] elles pensent [...] mais musicalement et pittoresquement, sans arguties, sans syllogismes, sans déductions' (i. 278). For further discussion see the final section of Chapter 25 below, 'Life's Harmonies, or the Beauty of Rhythm'.

joy in paradise, but in real life beauty can spring from melancholy. For beauty is what brings the dead back to life.

Or keeps the soon-to-be-dead alive, for a time...

Beauty as Resistance

> Fancioulle fut, ce soir-là, une parfaite idéalisation, qu'il était impossible de ne pas supposer vivante, possible, réelle.
> ('Une mort héroïque', i. 321)

In 'Une mort héroïque', the much-discussed prose poem from *Le Spleen de Paris*, the eponymous hero is Fancioulle, 'un admirable bouffon'. Party to a plot against the ruling Prince whose favourite artist he is, the clown, together with his co-conspirators, is found out and condemned to death. When Fancioulle is billed to perform one of his greatest roles, and it is thought that his co-conspirators will also attend, the rumour circulates that the Prince is minded to pardon the criminals. But the narrator for his part thinks it 'infiniment plus probable' that the Prince wants to assess the theatrical talents of a person performing while under sentence of death and has decided to conduct a *physiological* experiment to determine to what degree a performing artist's professional skills may be affected by such exceptional circumstances. In the event Fancioulle, apparently untroubled by these circumstances, delivers a superlative performance such that neither he nor the audience give further thought to his or anyone else's impending death. But the Prince, though enthused by the performance, begins to look pale, as though filled with jealousy or resentment at Fancioulle's power over his audience. A young page boy, in whose ear the Prince whispers, smiles mischievously and leaves. Soon afterwards a *coup de sifflet* is heard—a sharp, prolonged signal of disapproval—and a child runs away down a corridor, audibly suppressing his giggles. Fancioulle, interrupted, falls dead. Did the whistle—'rapide comme un glaive'—achieve what the executioner would in any case later have effected? Did the Prince indeed intend this very outcome? Maybe, maybe not. Did he subsequently miss Fancioulle? The narrator considers it 'doux et légitime' to believe so. What is certain is that the co-conspirators were 'effacés de la vie' that very night, and that no subsequent mime artist who performed at court was able to rival Fancioulle in skill or princely favour.

This richly suggestive text has prompted more commentary than any other prose poem in *Le Spleen de Paris*, such that one critic has wondered if that ultimately is not its very point, its resistance to closure.[4] Within the present

---

[4] See Maria Scott, *Baudelaire's 'Le Spleen de Paris': Shifting Perspectives* (Aldershot: Ashgate, 2005), 148: 'What is most disconcerting about "Une mort héroïque", namely the impossibility of deciphering

discussion I would like nevertheless to suggest ways in which we may read 'Une mort héroïque' as an allegory of the poet-artist as performer and double agent, and also of the poet-artist as alternative lawgiver. For here in operation is that very 'loi d'ignorance' that Baudelaire posits in *De l'essence du rire* as being essential to the 'comique absolu'. In the view of Michele Hannoosh in *Baudelaire and Caricature* Fancioulle heeds this law to the extent of breaking the inverse law of remembering his double nature as both person and artist: 'Fancioulle becomes his role, and the step is fatal. He falls victim to the illusion of his own art, the illusion of unity'.[5] Therefore he cannot be regarded as representative of the Baudelairean ideal of the artist, even though the narrator himself suggests that he can:

> Fancioulle me prouvait, d'une manière péremptoire, irréfutable, que l'ivresse de l'Art est plus apte que toute autre à voiler les terreurs du gouffre; que le génie peut jouer la comédie au bord de la tombe avec une joie qui l'empêche de voir la tombe, perdu, comme il est, dans un paradis excluant toute idée de tombe et de destruction. (i. 321)

For Hannoosh this is pure sentimentalism. Fancioulle's (alleged) failure to fulfil the conditions of comic art 'is hidden under a heavy, almost oppressive, layer of sentimentality that, like the art itself, deceives and bewitches the reader':

> To take the statement as positive is to put ourselves in the position of the audience within the poem, mistaking the Prince's sadistic manipulation for a charitable act of clemency. It is to fall victim to the sentimentalism of Fancioulle himself. The clichés, rather, signal the irony: Fancioulle's comedy destroys the

---

its allegory in any definitive way, may provide the very key to its allegory. However, the paradoxical nature of this assertion itself invites a renewed recognition of the text's (heroic?) resistance to closure.' The most influential commentaries on 'Une mort héroïque' include: Jean Starobinski, 'Sur quelques répondants allégoriques du poète', *Revue d'histoire littéraire de la France*, 67 (1967), 402–12, and *Portrait de l'artiste en saltimbanque* (Geneva and Paris: Éditions d'Art Albert Skira and Flammarion, 1970), 83–6; Ross Chambers, '"L'Art sublime du comédien" ou le regardant et le regardé: Autour d'un mythe baudelairien', *Saggi et richerche di letteratura francese*, 10 (1971), 189–260 (248–51); Vivien L. Rubin, 'Two Prose Poems by Baudelaire: "Le Vieux Saltimbanque" and "Une mort héroïque"', *Nineteenth-Century French Studies*, 14: 1–2 (1985–6), 51–60; J. A. Hiddleston, *Baudelaire and 'Le Spleen de Paris'* (Oxford: Clarendon Press, 1987), 15–19; Peter Schofer, '"Une mort héroïque": Baudelaire's Social Theater of Cruelty', in Claude Kurt Abraham et al. (eds), *Theater and Society in French Literature* (Columbia: University of South Carolina [French Literature Series, 15], 1988), 50–7; Nathaniel Wing, 'Poets, Mimes and Counterfeit Coins: On Power and Discourse in Baudelaire's Prose Poetry', *Paragraph*, 13 (1990), 1–18; Hannoosh, *Baudelaire and Caricature* (1992), 53–8; Steve Murphy, 'La Scène parisienne: lecture d'"Une mort héroïque" de Baudelaire', in Keith Cameron and James Kearns (eds) *Le Champ littéraire, 1860–1900* (Amsterdam: Rodopi, 1996), 49–61, republished in a revised version in *Logiques du dernier Baudelaire: Lectures du 'Spleen de Paris'* (Paris: Honoré Champion, 2003), 113–60; Stephens, *Baudelaire's Prose Poems*, 150–9; Debarati Sanyal, 'Conspiratorial Poetics: Baudelaire's "Une Mort héroïque"', *Nineteenth-Century French Studies*, 27: 3–4 (1999), 305–22; and Patrick Labarthe, *Patrick Labarthe présente 'Petits Poèmes en prose' de Baudelaire* (Paris: Gallimard [Foliothèque], 2000), 73–8.

[5] Hannoosh, *Baudelaire and Caricature*, 56.

dualism of comic art and fails to accomplish its purpose, that is, reminding mankind of its inferiority relative to an omnipotent absolute, death. Comic art by definition is meant to present an image of mortality (and thus redemption), and this is *precisely* what Fancioulle's art does not do. Instead, it inspires an intoxicating and dangerous oblivion that hides the abyss, a joy that keeps him from seeing his mortality, a paradise that excludes these very ideas but in which he is, significantly, *perdu*. Baudelaire uses a word heavy with theological connotations of damnation to suggest, under cover of praise, the flaw in Fancioulle's art. The problem lies not in the conventional Romantic division between the sublimity of art and the intrusive, disillusioning forces of reality, but in Fancioulle's failure to maintain that very dualism that is the *sine qua non* condition of comic art and [...] of art in general.[6]

Hannoosh's reading has been influential,[7] and so I would like to spend some time contesting it in order then to present an alternative reading—a reading that will inform the rest of the discussion in this book—and one which builds on Jean Starobinski's earlier interpretation of this particular passage about 'l'ivresse de l'art':

L'art, on le voit, n'est pas une efficace opération de salut, mais une pantomime sublime au bord de la tombe, voilant, pour un instant seulement, *les terreurs du gouffre*. [...] Baudelaire, qui a fait de l'art son idéal, doute du pouvoir rédempteur de la beauté. Sur la crête où il surplombe l'abîme, l'artiste, en sa plus émouvante réussite, est une apparition infiniment fragile. Il ne *tient* pas sous le coup de sifflet. Le bouffon, autoportrait de Baudelaire lui-même, figure, sous une forme à peine parodique, le vertige mortel auquel l'artiste est exposé, non seulement parce qu'il a osé attenter à la personne du maître (du Père), mais parce qu'il subit le manque d'*être* qui s'attache à la nature illusoire de l'art.[8]

---

[6] Hannoosh, *Baudelaire and Caricature*, 54–5.
[7] Stephens, for example, takes it as the basis for her own account of 'Une mort héroïque' as an example of 'literary caricature' in which she views the Prince and the narrator as succeeding in maintaining a 'superior, ironic artistic stance' and Fancioulle as failing to 'sustain the necessary *dédoublement*' (see *Baudelaire's Prose Poems*, 156). Scott, by contrast, remains non-committal, referring her readers simply to Hannoosh's 'very interesting reading' (see *Baudelaire's 'Le Spleen de Paris'*, 142 n. 74).
[8] *Portrait de l'artiste*, 86. In an earlier version of his reading Starobinski had rejected this Freudian reading of the Prince as a father figure: 'La donnée initiale est la révolte contre le pouvoir, le refus violent que l'artiste oppose à son maître. (N'allons pas imposer ici une interprétation psychologique trop grossière et parler de révolte contre le Père. N'allons pas non plus, dans un facile recours aux références biographiques, affirmer que Baudelaire fait allusion à ses sentiments révolutionnaires de 1848.)' ('Sur quelques répondants allégoriques du poète', 407). Chambers largely accepts Starobinski's reading(s) but stresses the element of ultimate failure, seeing the *coup de sifflet* as marking the end of the Romantic notion that art can triumph over death: 'En montrant ainsi l'artiste le plus sublime [i.e. Fancioulle] soumis, comme un simple "amuseur"[,] à la mort, Baudelaire marquait clairement le passage du Romantisme, avec sa croyance démesurée en la divinité du génie, à la modernité post-romantique, toujours marquée par les velléités, devenues nostalgies, de l'époque antérieure, mais

First, Hannoosh's charge of 'sentimentalism'[9] would seem to be based on the narrator's comment that prefaces his account of what Fancioulle has 'proved' to him about the nature and function of art: 'Ma plume tremble, et des larmes d'une émotion toujours présente me montent aux yeux pendant que je cherche à vous décrire cette inoubliable soirée' (i. 321). But should we necessarily consider the narrator's allegedly sentimental language as invalidating his statement about the power of art and, in this instance, of the 'comique absolu'? And especially when in *De l'essence du rire* Baudelaire himself writes in similar terms of the disparity between the power of a comic performance and the inability of the writer to convey it: 'Avec une plume tout cela est pâle et glacé. Comment la plume pourrait-elle rivaliser avec la pantomime?' (ii. 540)?[10] There Baudelaire is describing pantomime as the epitome of the 'comique absolu': 'La pantomime est l'épuration de la comédie; c'en est la quintessence; c'est l'élément comique pur, dégagé et concentré' (ii. 540). And Fancioulle himself is the master of this art: 'Le sieur Fancioulle excellait surtout dans les rôles muets ou peu chargés de paroles' (i. 321). As to 'the sentimentalism of Fancioulle himself' there is simply no evidence for it in the text, and no evidence in particular that he himself shares the allegedly 'sentimental' conviction of 'les esprits superficiels' (i. 320) among the populace that the Prince may be intending to pardon him if he performs well.

Second, Hannoosh had not previously argued, let alone demonstrated, that for Baudelaire the purpose of comic art lies in 'reminding mankind of its inferiority relative to an omnipotent absolute, death' or that 'comic art by definition is meant

---

constamment rongée par l'ironie, la lucidité, le doute qui font de tout art une dérision, une pauvre chose en présence des vérités incontrovertibles de la condition humaine. De la mort de Fancioulle à celle du comédien dans *La Peste*, il n'y a qu'un petit pas à franchir' ('"L'Art sublime du comédien"', 251). Starobinski, for his part, later published a further reading of the text in which he, too, lays more emphasis on the effects of the *coup de sifflet*. See 'Le Prince et son bouffon', in Jean Starobinski, *L'Encre de la mélancolie* (Paris: Éditions du Seuil, 2012), 499–513 (513), where the section entitled 'Bandello et Baudelaire' (506-13) constitutes a slightly revised version of 'Bandello et Baudelaire (*Le Prince et son bouffon*), first published in *Le Mythe d'Étiemble: Hommages, études et recherches: inédits* (Paris: Didier Érudition, 1979), 251–59: 'C'est donc l'art, à travers Fancioulle, qui est mis à mort, qui est *exécuté*, par le coup de sifflet. [...] Il est évident que Fancioulle et le Prince trahissent l'un et l'autre les exigences du Beau, et que l'Art ne peut que périr de cette double trahison' (513).

[9] Echoing Leo Bersani's claim that this passage 'brings us perilously close to the clichéd sentimentality of "Bénédiction" and "Élévation"'. See his *Baudelaire and Freud* (Berkeley, Los Angeles, and London: University of California Press, 1977), 133.

[10] This parallel is noted by Stephens (*Baudelaire's Prose Poems*, 156-7). A further parallel may be seen between Baudelaire's own comment that 'avec une plume tout cela est pâle et glacé' and the narrator's description of the Prince in 'Une mort héroïque as his expression slowly changes during the performance: 'je contemplais le visage du Prince, sur lequel une pâleur nouvelle s'ajoutait sans cesse à sa pâleur habituelle, comme la neige s'ajoute à la neige' (i. 322). Within the prose poem this added pallor makes of the Prince a mirror-image of the clown with his traditional white make-up. (On the possible role in the composition of 'Une mort héroïque' of the famous contemporary mime-artist Jean-Gaspard Deburau (1796–1846) see Murphy, *Logiques du dernier Baudelaire*, 121–8.) Starobinski notes also a parallel with 'Le Vieux Saltimbanque' where the narrator comments after observing the deep gaze with which the mountebank observes his surroundings: 'Je sentis ma gorge serrée par la main terrible de l'hystérie, et il me sembla que mes regards étaient offusqués par ces larmes rebelles qui ne veulent pas tomber' (i. 296). See Starobinski, 'Sur quelques répondants allégoriques du poète', 412.

to present an image of mortality (and thus redemption)'. This insistence appears to be imported here to lend weight to her critique of Fancioulle's performance as inauthentically comic, even though she has already shown how '[t]he Clown Fancioulle bears a strong resemblance to the English Pierrot' (53) and has described how for Baudelaire 'the boisterous English Clown [...] represents in every respect the excess, jubilance, violence, and absurdity of the "comique absolu"' (48). Certainly for Baudelaire, as Hannoosh convincingly argues, comic art derives from an acknowledgement of human limitations, including our mortality, but nowhere does he maintain that the 'comique absolu' depends on a constant awareness of the ubiquity and inevitability of death. We are comic because of the discrepancy we encounter between reality and our dreams and pretensions, albeit death places an ultimate limitation on all our terrestrial ambitions. But in any case Fancioulle's art *does* present an image of mortality, as the Prince himself recognizes 'pendant qu'il applaudissait ostensiblement les talents de son vieil ami, l'étrange bouffon, qui bouffonnait si bien la mort' (i. 322).

This unorthodox use of 'bouffonner' as a transitive verb makes the meaning of this statement ambiguous, suggesting perhaps both that Fancioulle mocks death by performing comedy in the face of the threat of death (his own execution) and also that Fancioulle offers a comic performance *of* death in the ambiguity of his 'convulsions' (to be discussed below).[11] What is certain is that Fancioulle is performing while under sentence of death, a fact known to his audience—including especially his co-conspirators who are under similar sentence. Indeed it is these circumstances that the Prince may have engineered expressly in order to see how a comic artist performs in such a situation—which in another sense, of course, is the situation in which all of us, artists and non-artists, have to perform the very act of living, knowing that we must die but not knowing when. Death will always have the last laugh.

Third, the 'loi d'ignorance' posited by Baudelaire in *De l'essence du rire* relates to the comic performer who, in order to achieve the 'comique absolu', must, while being aware that he is funny, pretend not to be. As Hannoosh accepts, Fancioulle observes this law in that the audience is induced into seeing only the performance and not a man who knows he is performing, still less a man who is sentenced to death and pretending not to know that. In fact Fancioulle represents the artist (clown, actor, poet) as the consummate double agent: the 'comédien' who can convince the spectator that he, the actor, does not know he is acting. The narrator of 'Une mort héroïque' insists on how great such a performance might be and how Fancioulle in fact has achieved this:

---

[11] Cf. Mallarmé's 'Mimique' in which Pierrot has tickled his wife to death and proceeds after her funeral to re-enact her convulsive death with the convulsions of his own, real death. See my *Mallarmé and Circumstance*, 64–6.

Quand on dit d'un comédien: 'Voilà un bon comédien', on se sert d'une formule qui implique que sous le personnage se laisse encore deviner le comédien, c'est-à-dire l'art, l'effort, la volonté. Or, si un comédien arrivait à être, relativement au personnage qu'il est chargé d'exprimer, ce que les meilleures statues de l'antiquité, miraculeusement animées, vivantes, marchantes, voyantes, seraient relativement à l'idée générale et confuse de beauté, ce serait là, sans doute, un cas singulier et tout à fait imprévu. Fancioulle fut, ce soir-là, une parfaite idéalisation, qu'il était impossible de ne pas supposer vivante, possible, réelle. (i. 321)

Fourth, Hannoosh argues that Fancioulle has forgotten himself in his role and thus infringed the 'inverse' law whereby the comic artist must remember his dual role as both real person and performing artist. In this case, she argues, Fancioulle has not only forgotten himself in his role but also thereby inspired in his audience 'an intoxicating and dangerous oblivion that hides the abyss, a joy that keeps him from seeing his mortality, a paradise that excludes these very ideas'. But, like almost every other commentator, she omits to consider what his comic role actually consists in. In the text we are told, first, that 'Fancioulle devait jouer l'un de ses principaux et de ses meilleurs rôles' (i. 320) and subsequently that he excelled especially in 'les rôles muets ou peu chargés de paroles, qui sont souvent les principaux dans ces drames féeriques dont l'objet est de représenter symboliquement le mystère de la vie' (i. 321). The text then continues: 'Il entra en scène légèrement et avec une aisance parfaite, ce qui contribua à fortifier, dans le noble public, l'idée de douceur et de pardon' (i. 321). Fancioulle's role, therefore, is the symbolic representation of the 'mystery of life',[12] and so perfect is his performance from the start that the audience is fooled into thinking that he believes in the possibility of his being pardoned. But there is no evidence that he himself believes this nor, as Hannoosh contends, that he has forgotten that he may soon die: no evidence, therefore, that he has ceased to be aware of his double nature as both living person and performing artist.

There follows the narrator's account of what constitutes a perfect performance: namely, one in which the performance stands in relation to the 'personnage qu'il est chargé d'exprimer' in exactly the same degree as the greatest statues of antiquity would stand to the 'idée générale et confuse de la beauté' were they miraculously brought to life and enabled to walk and see ('miraculeusement animées, vivantes, marchantes, voyantes')—which in itself would represent 'un cas singulier et tout à fait imprévu'. Cutting through the narrator's cumbersome analogy one may infer that Fancioulle is to be thought of as bringing a lifeless

---

[12] As Starobinski notes ('Quelques répondants allégoriques du poète', 408.) Cf. also Schofer, 'Baudelaire's Social Theater of Cruelty', 52. The expression of 'le mystère de la vie' is precisely what Baudelaire had praised Hugo for two years earlier in his article of 1861 (as noted by Hiddleston, *Baudelaire and 'Le Spleen de Paris'*, 16).

object of potential and ill-defined beauty to life; or, as the narrator himself puts it more directly: 'Fancioulle fut, ce soir-là, une parfaite idéalisation, qu'il était impossible de ne pas supposer vivante, possible, réelle.' But who, then, *is* the 'personnage' whom he has been charged with 'expressing' as part of his symbolic representation of the 'mystery of life'? Perhaps none other than the artist as double agent, both living person and accomplished performer, at once subject to the constraints of the real and yet able to reshape them through art.

Certainly the narrator implies as much in his description of Fancioulle's performance and his own response to it. For he can see what others cannot:

> Ce bouffon allait, venait, riait, pleurait, se convulsait, avec une indestructible auréole autour de la tête, auréole invisible pour tous, mais visible pour moi, et où se mêlaient, dans un étrange amalgame, les rayons de l'Art et la gloire du Martyre. Fancioulle introduisait, par je ne sais quelle grâce spéciale, le divin et le surnaturel, jusque dans les plus extravagantes bouffonneries. (i. 321)

Thus Fancioulle obeys both the 'loi d'ignorance' by appearing to be unaware of the pretence of his performance *and* the 'loi inverse' that demands of the artist that he remain always conscious of his double nature—because it is this very dualism that he here performs. On the one hand, he enacts the 'mystery of life' by his movements on stage, by his laughter and his tears, and by his buffooning 'convulsions' that could betoken either (or both) delight and anguish, laughter and sobbing, perhaps even orgasm and the throes of death. (When he does die, '[il] ouvrit ensuite la bouche comme pour respirer convulsivement' (i. 322)). On the other hand, he brings an added imaginative dimension to this 'performance' of life, suggesting that life is more than simply an emotional drama oscillating between laughter and tears, comedy and tragedy: he brings 'le divin et le surnaturel'.

For the narrator this combination represents 'un étrange amalgame', as though the aureola or golden crown traditionally associated with Christ, the Virgin Mary, and martyred saints were here composed of both the radiance of art and the quasi-religious halo or 'glory' that symbolizes the self-sacrifice of the artist who suffers for his art. All that the narrator—and Baudelaire—claims at this point in the text is that the 'intoxication' of art (which we might define as the power of the imagination to transform the real) is better suited (than, say, the intoxications of sexual passion or drugs or alcohol) to *veil* the terrors of the gulf (the grim physical and psychological realities of our human existence, including melancholy and the indisputable fact of our inevitable mortality), and that Fancioulle has demonstrated (in the experimental 'laboratory' circumstances set up by his Prince) that the artist-genius can indeed create art even in the closest possible proximity to death—and do so with a joyful faith in the value of creativity that blocks out, if only for a moment, all idea of mortality and destruction. The result of that faith and of that creativity is 'beauty', which is indeed an 'idée générale et confuse' for it is available to the 'general' public but touches each of us in our own particular way. Beauty here consists in the effect of Fancioulle's performance on his courtly audience, including the all-powerful and cynical Prince:

> Tout ce public, si blasé et si frivole qu'il pût être, subit bientôt la toute-puissante domination de l'artiste. Personne ne rêva plus de mort, de deuil, ni de supplices. Chacun s'abandonna, sans inquiétude, aux voluptés multiples que donne la vue d'un chef-d'œuvre d'art vivant. Les explosions de la joie et de l'admiration ébranlèrent à plusieurs reprises les voûtes de l'édifice avec l'énergie d'un tonnerre continu. Le Prince, lui-même, enivré, mêla ses applaudississsements à ceux de sa cour. (i. 322)

So the artist rules through the alternative dominion of art and the power of beauty, and this particular artist has himself conspired against the official ruler of a princely dominion. The name 'Fancioulle' translates the Italian 'fanciullo', meaning 'young boy', but the word 'fanciullo' (like 'infant') in turn derives from the Latin 'infans = not speaking'. These meanings suggest, therefore, a certain childlike innocence—the 'naiveté' of the *Salon de 1846*—while also implying that Fancioulle's principle means of artistic expression is non-verbal performance rather than verbal description or analysis: Fancioulle is a silent symbolic performer of the mystery of life. But he is also a political dissident whose dissidence, we are told at the beginning of the prose poem, springs from melancholy. The narrator, himself a verbal performer, presents this fact with ironic naivety, noting with seeming dismay that 'pour les personnes vouées par état au comique, les choses sérieuses ont de fatales attractions' and almost apologizing for having to suggest that performing artists, even clowns, can have political opinions:

> bien qu'il puisse paraître bizarre que les idées de patrie et de liberté s'emparent despotiquement du cerveau d'un histrion, un jour Fancioulle entra dans une conspiration formée par quelques gentilshommes mécontents. (i. 319)

To think that a mere 'bouffon' should resist the tyranny of the state and submit instead to the 'despotism' of ideas! No wonder Fancioulle was only '*presque* un des amis du Prince' (i. 319; my emphasis). As these opening remarks suggest, the narrator is himself play-acting here, adopting the patronizing and dismissive tone of a reactionary conformist the better to ridicule this very conformism. And who are these gentleman-malcontents with whom Fancioulle has conspired? The narrator proceeds with mock relief to tell us:

> Il existe partout des hommes de bien pour dénoncer au pouvoir ces individus d'humeur atrabilaire qui veulent déposer les princes et opérer, sans la consulter, le déménagement d'une société. (i. 319)

Here himself imitating an 'homme de bien' in denouncing Fancioulle to *us*, this narrator sounds like a parody of Chateaubriand, dismissing the instigators of the 1789 Revolution as mere melancholics who have turned society upside down—and without a word of consultation!—more or less because they felt a bit irritable and down in the dumps. 'D'humeur atrabilaire': the narrator seems to be adopting the now long-outdated theory of the humours ('atrabilaire', from the Latin 'ater=black' and 'bilis=bile', is a synonym for 'mélancolique') in order to dismiss political dissidence as a form of mental disorder when in fact, as the example of Fancioulle unequivocally illustrates, moral resistance is an essential and healthy part of the authentic artist's public function.

By contrast the Prince himself is the wrong sort of artist. In one sense he is unremarkable, almost Mr Everyman: 'Le Prince n'était ni meilleur ni pire qu'un autre' (i. 319), but 'une excessive sensibilité' (i. 319) has rendered him—'en beaucoup de cas'—more cruel and despotic than others. He is himself a double agent, both connoisseur and practitioner: '[a]moureux passionné des beaux-arts, excellent connaisseur d'ailleurs', 'véritable artiste lui-même' (i. 320), and like Fancioulle he is also melancholic ('il ne connaissait d'ennemi dangereux que l'Ennui' (i. 320)). But he cares not a jot for ethics or his fellow human beings: the narrator describes him as '[a]ssez indifférent relativement aux hommes et à la morale'. Rather he is a Sadean figure ('il était vraiment insatiable de voluptés'), resistant to tyranny (as Fancioulle is) but in his case to the tyranny of boredom, craving new pleasures and experiences, and 'monstrous' in his choice of means:

> les efforts bizarres qu'il faisait pour fuir ou pour vaincre ce tyran du monde lui auraient certainement attiré, de la part d'un historien sévère, l'épithète de 'monstre', s'il avait été permis, dans ses domaines, d'écrire quoi que ce fût qui ne tendît pas uniquement au plaisir ou à l'étonnement, qui est une des formes délicates du plaisir. (i. 320)

This reference to a perverse censorship effected in the fastidious cause of pleasure and surprise, along with the mention of torture in the account of what the audience is enabled to forget as they watch Fancioulle's performance, suggests that this particular princely tyrant is himself worth resisting through the agency of art, which, by its cunning obliquities of preterition and irony and allegory and a miming that speaks louder than words, can elude the despotism of being told what and what not to say or what and what not will give pleasure. Sadean, this exquisite Prince thus also assumes a somewhat Satanic air as the pleasure-seeking despot who 'tient les fils qui nous remuent', delighting in pulling the strings within his very own puppet-theatre but, like some manic theatre-director with big ideas, deeply frustrated by its paltry dimensions. Again the narrator's parodically reactionary voice may be heard, here in the notion that a young Nero might be well intentioned or that Providence may lack foresight:

Le grand malheur de ce Prince fut qu'il n'eut jamais un théâtre assez vaste pour son génie. Il y a de jeunes Nérons qui étouffent dans des limites trop étroites, et dont les siècles à venir ignoreront toujours le nom et la bonne volonté. L'imprévoyante Providence avait donné à celui-ci des facultés plus grandes que ses États. (i. 320)

If Fancioulle is the artist of life, then the Prince is the artist of death, eventually 'disappearing' the remaining conspirators, 'effacing' them from life and rubbing them out of the picture. But as the artist of death (for whom the young page-boy— 'l'enfant'—therefore represents his new, wordless, whistling agent, a *compliant* Fancioulle) the Prince is condemned to everlasting melancholy, since, as the final words of the prose poem relate, he was never again to favour another mime-artist as greatly as he had favoured his 'almost-friend' Fancioulle. Nevermore... As the counterpart of 'le roi d'un pays pluvieux' of the third 'Spleen' poem in *Les Fleurs du Mal* ('Du bouffon favori la grotesque ballade | Ne distrait plus le front de ce cruel malade' (ll. 7–8)) he is the man who has everything and nothing: the theatre of his dominion is too small, and he has destroyed his favourite plaything. He may wield the power of life and death, and yet he is left jealous and resentful by being outperformed by Fancioulle, this 'chef-d'œuvre vivant' (322), who also wields the power of life and death in his celebration of 'le mystère de la vie' and his ability to veil, temporarily, the horrors and mortality of our human condition. Both the Prince and Fancioulle are melancholics, but while the Prince of Death orders theatrical spectacles for his *own* pleasure and contentment, the true artist is he who, like Baudelaire himself, performs for the benefit of others. The one rules despotically out of self-interest and brings destruction; the other employs 'la toute-puissante domination de l'artiste' and causes joy and admiration. One employs the violence of suppression and execution and erasure; the other provokes the violence of a thunderous enthusiasm and the indelible memory of an 'inoubliable soirée'.[13]

But what of the third artist in 'Une mort héroïque', the narrator himself? Is he perhaps also a model of the poet-artist as double agent? As already noted, he seems at the beginning of the prose poem to serve as an ironic spokesman for reactionary opinion (How can a clown be interested in patriotism or liberty? Political unrest is just irresponsible grumpiness, etc.). At the same time he appears almost over-insistent on his own judiciousness: '*Presque* un des amis', 'Je croirais volontiers que le Prince fut *presque* fâché' (i. 319; my emphases), 'De telles suppositions non exactement justifiées, mais non absolument injustifiables, traversèrent mon esprit' (i. 322), 'Il est permis d'en douter', 'Il est doux et

---

[13] This opposition of erasure and inscription is noted by Scott, *Baudelaire's 'Le Spleen de Paris'*, 147.

légitime de le croire' (i. 323).[14] Moreover he is fond of asserting his own clearsightedness: 'pour ceux qui, comme moi, avaient pu pénétrer plus avant dans les profondeurs de cette âme curieuse et malade' (i. 320), 'auréole invisible pour tous, mais visible pour moi' (i. 321), 'pour un œil clairvoyant' (i. 322). How could we not trust such a man, especially as he is so ready *not* to give answers where none exist: 'C'est un point qui n'a jamais pu être éclairci' (i. 320).[15] Except that we may perceive some pomposity here, and also vanity, not to mention the knowing superiority that comes with a well-delivered, if archly italicized pun: '[le Prince] voulait profiter de l'occasion pour faire une expérience physiologique d'un intérêt *capital*' (i. 320). There is a certain stiff formality about this narrator, a kind of antiquarian fustiness to suggest that he himself may be the 'historien sévère' who would call the Prince a 'monstre' (i. 320). And there is, too, a suspect quaintness and old-world charm about the manner of his narration. The anonymous Prince of an anonymous principality, the Fool with a symbolic name (cf. Shakespeare's Feste), the stately unfolding of time: 'Enfin, le grand jour arrivé', 'Depuis lors'... We are in the world of the fairy-story, but a melancholic fairy-story in which everyone lived (if they lived) *un*happily ever after.

In other words, the narrator is a highly overt performer of his narrative art. But, if he is a double agent, what then is he pretending not to know? Quite simply, the important message that this prose poem, *pace* Scott, very clearly but very implicitly imparts. As Debarati Sanyal has suggested, the narrator is himself a 'coconspirator', and his 'self-erasing speculations' may be seen as suggestive of 'the complex negotiations of an oppositional voice striving to be heard in a censored domain' (315).[16] The narrator is conspiring with Fancioulle to resist both the tyranny of the Prince and the tyranny of boredom, that is, both censorship and melancholy. 'Hard power' in the person of the Prince believes that it owns the artist and seeks further to annex the dominion of art through a pretence of friendship and approbation even while pursuing its own egotistical pleasures. But the 'soft power' of art resists this appropriation by putting on its own show and by resisting melancholy through the beauty it effects on the audience at large.[17]

---

[14] Schofer notes nevertheless the contrast between this cautiousness and the narrator's 'categorical' assertions about Fancioulle's performance ('Fancioulle me prouvait, d'une manière péremptoire, irréfutable [...]'). See 'Baudelaire's Social Theater of Cruelty', 53.

[15] For Scott the narrator in this text thus epitomizes the 'resistance to closure' that may provide 'the very key to its allegory'. See above, n. 2.

[16] Sanyal, 'Conspiratorial Poetics', 315. Cf. also Murphy, *Logiques du dernier Baudelaire*, 159: 'Baudelaire [...] se permet un récit allégorique qui, construit en trompe-l'œil, n'en fournit pas moins un acte d'opposition culturelle. [-] L'implicite, dans 'Une mort héroïque', doit être débusqué par le lecteur; la vérité donnée explicitement se révèle fallacieuse.'

[17] Cf. Stephens, *Baudelaire's Prose Poems*, 151: 'what we have in "Une mort héroïque" is, in fact, a power play, not only political, in fact not essentially political at all. The real conflict between the Prince and Fancioulle (and the narrator) is one of artistic power.'

Fancioulle himself dies for his resistance, though by the very nature of his death—which resembles a clowning performance—he is able to resist the 'désapprobation inattendue' signalled by the whistle-blow right up until the very last moment of his final, convulsive breath:

> Fancioulle, secoué, réveillé dans son rêve, ferma d'abord les yeux, puis les rouvrir presque aussitôt, démesurément agrandis, ouvrit ensuite la bouche comme pour respirer convulsivement, chancela un peu en avant, un peu en arrière, et puis tomba roide mort sur les planches. (i. 322)

Is this a real death or the performance of a death? Shaken and woken from the 'dream' of his performance (and the private world of his imagination) Fancioulle paradoxically closes his eyes, but then opens them again—wider than ever, as though more 'clairvoyant' than ever within the renewed dream of his art—and duly completes his performance of 'le mystère de la vie' in the only way such a mystery can ever end: with death. As the narrator has told us, this Prince permits only what will afford him 'le plaisir et l'étonnement'. But while here the pleasure and satisfaction are all his, the surprise is all with Fancioulle and with his audience: the fatal shock of a rude awakening, like the punch in the back that rouses the cloud-gazing poet from his rêverie in 'La Soupe et les nuages' or the sensation of a blow to the stomach from a pickaxe undergone by the blithe narrator of 'La Chambre double' when the spectre of Time comes knocking on his door like a bailiff calling in a debt. The 'ivresse' of joyous aesthetic pleasure ('[l]es explosions de la joie et de l'admiration' (i. 322)) cannot last forever, no more than the 'parfaite idéalisation' of the mimed performance that brings it into being.

But the narrator—and the written word—can and do last. Unlike Fancioulle and the 'gentilshommes mécontents' with whom he conspired, the narrator, this other co-conspirator, is alive to tell his tale: overtly in the verbal language that Fancioulle eschews, but also silently, like a mime, in the implications that lie beneath the whiteness of the page and that we can read between the lines. For this is the story of a heroic death:[18] the story of a poet-artist who believed in the soft power of art, who believed that melancholy could be resisted by the imagination, and who brought temporary relief from such melancholy by creating an effect of beauty: 'Chacun s'abandonna, sans inquiétude, aux voluptés multipliées que donne la vue d'un chef-d'œuvre vivant' (i. 322). Unlike the Prince—'insatiable

---

[18] *Pace* Hiddleston, who refers to the prose poem's 'gratingly ironic title' (*Baudelaire and 'Le Spleen de Paris'*, 18). Hiddleston sees Fancioulle as 'a charlatan', as 'still only a fool, his art a mere "drame féerique"', and, like Hannoosh after him, considers the alleged "veiling of the abyss" to be 'illusory' (18). Cf. also Richard Stamelman, 'The Shroud of Allegory: Death, Mourning, and Melancholy in Baudelaire's Work', *Texas Studies in Literature and Language*, 25: 3 (Fall, 1983), 390–409 (393): 'In the prose poem "Une Mort héroïque", [Baudelaire] shows the fatal consequences of an artistic performance that suppresses the consciousness of death in order to lose itself in the perfection of a symbolic, ideal art.'

de voluptés' (i. 320)—Fancioulle's audience is granted the multiple satisfactions consequent on 'l'ivresse de l'Art', and so too, in a different way, are we as readers of this prose poem with all its rich and suggestive multiplicities of meaning.

* * * * *

If the narrator of 'Une mort héroïque' is a kind of mime-artist, then so too is the poet of *Les Fleurs du Mal* a kind of performer. As the moment approached for the publication of the second edition of *Les Fleurs du Mal* Baudelaire was minded to write a preface to the work in which he would explain himself, and particularly in the light of the notorious court proceedings that had followed publication of the first edition in 1857. In the end, having drafted three such prefaces (i. 181–4), he appears to have despaired of a fair hearing from those who were determined to condemn him:

> je me suis arrêté devant l'épouvantable inutilité d'expliquer quoi que ce soit à qui que ce soit. Ceux qui savent me devinent, et pour ceux qui ne peuvent ou ne veulent pas comprendre, j'amoncellerais sans fruit les explications. (i. 182)

He would simply give his performance, therefore, seemingly ignorant of what he was doing.

In these draft prefaces two key motifs recur: resistance and performance. Repeatedly Baudelaire laments the 'vulgarité' and 'bêtise' of his age and mocks the despotism of its doxa: belief in Progress and the natural goodness of man, insistence that art must be morally improving, faith in God. It would have been so easy to play the game: 'Le Diable. Le péché originel. Homme bon. Si vous vouliez, vous seriez le favori du Tyran' (i. 182): so easy, in other words, to have been a non-resistant Fancioulle. And indeed, to his shame, he has sometimes weakened, he has worn the make-up of the *bien-pensant*:

> Car moi-même, malgré les plus louables efforts, je n'ai su résister au désir de plaire à mes contemporains, comme l'attestent en quelques endroits, apposées comme un fard, certaines basses flatteries adressées à la démocratie, et même quelques ordures destinées à me faire pardonner la tristesse de mon sujet. (i. 184)[19]

---

[19] He may here be thinking, for example, of the note he appended at the last moment to the 'Révolte' section of *Les Fleurs du Mal*, with particular respect to 'Le Reniement de saint Pierre' (first published in 1852 and very nearly incurring a public prosecution (see i. 1075)). He almost immediately regretted his action and thought the note 'détestable' (see i. 1076). The note reads: 'Parmi les morceaux suivants, le plus caractérisé a déjà paru dans un des principaux recueils littéraires de Paris, où il n'a été considéré, du moins par les gens d'esprit, que pour ce qu'il est véritablement: le pastiche des raisonnements de l'ignorance et de la fureur. Fidèle à son douloureux programme, l'auteur des *Fleurs du mal* a dû, en parfait comédien, façonner son esprit à tous les sophismes comme à toutes les corruptions. Cette déclaration candide n'empêchera pas sans doute les critiques honnêtes de le ranger parmi les théologiens de la populace et de l'accuser d'avoir regretté pour notre Sauveur Jésus-Christ, pour la Victime éternelle et volontaire, le rôle d'un conquérant, d'un Attila égalitaire et dévastateur. Plus d'un adressera sans doute au ciel les actions de grâces habituelles du Pharisien: "Merci, mon Dieu, qui n'avez pas permis que je fusse semblable à ce poète infâme!"' (i. 1075–6).

But for the most part he can take pride in his contrarian stance. For example, he has tried to question a facile and uncritical acceptance of Christian doctrine about divine love and the existence of the Devil: 'Il est plus difficile d'aimer Dieu que de croire en lui. Au contraire, il est plus difficile pour les gens de ce siècle de croire au Diable que de l'aimer. Tout le monde le sert et personne n'y croit. Sublime subtilité du Diable' (i. 182–3). But, much more importantly, he has tried to write effective and original poetry, and that has upset people too: 'Je sais que l'amant passionné du beau style s'expose à la haine des multitudes' (i. 181). And in the third of these draft prefaces he sets out a programme whereby through a series of carefully defined actions 'l'artiste peut s'élever à une originalité proportionnelle' (i. 183): observance of prosodic rules that are seen as springing from the fundamental music of the soul; observance of French prosodic rules in particular, which have a 'mysterious' and 'unacknowledged' power; observance of the essential need for rhyme and the importance of rhythmic shape; acknowledgement of the power of syntax, even the simple collocation of adjective and noun, to convey the nuance of human experience, etc. (i. 183). There is an *art* of poetry, a 'méthode' (i. 184), and he could teach anyone in twenty lessons how to write a verse tragedy or an epic poem.

This is the poet as supreme artist, not a subjective melancholic bent on misery and lament, but a craftsman possessed of 'cette insensibilité divine!' (i. 183–4) and writing about the human condition from an impersonal and quasi-Olympian perspective. Always ready for a challenge, Baudelaire even proposes one day to demonstrate the excellence of his 'méthode' by employing it in 'la célébration des jouissances de la dévotion et des ivresses de la gloire militaires, bien que je ne les aie jamais connues' (184)! Readers, he says, have been determined to consider the author of *Les Fleurs du Mal* to be every bit as wicked as the terrible things his poems describe: 'On m'a attribué tous les crimes que je racontais' (i. 182). But they have failed absolutely to see that poetry is a performing art, a craft or skill with which the poet 'enacts' the human condition—in Baudelaire's case, in all its ugliness and horror. He never set out either to shock or *not* to shock the (allegedly) innocent ('Ce n'est pas pour mes femmes, mes filles ou mes sœurs que ce livre a été écrit; non plus que pour les femmes, les filles ou les sœurs de mon voisin.' (i. 181)), and he is indifferent as to whether his poetry may be thought of as having a good influence or a bad influence on its readers. It is simply art.

In the projected preface to the third edition (i. 184–6) Baudelaire returns to some of these themes: the lack of understanding among commentators and his perverse pride in being 'unacknowledged'; the pointlessness of trying to explain himself; and ultimately his distaste at the thought of taking his readers 'behind the scenes': 'Mène-t-on la foule dans les ateliers de l'habilleuse et du décorateur, dans la loge de la comédienne?' (i. 185) Why on earth would he, an artist, want to show everyone how it's all done? Why reveal all the sordid tricks of his trade?

> Montre-t-on au public affolé aujourd'hui, indifférent demain, le mécanisme des trucs? Lui explique-t-on les retouches et les variantes improvisées aux répétitions, et jusqu'à quelle dose l'instinct et la sincérité sont mêlés aux rubriques [in the sense of 'ruses', 'tricks'] et au charlatanisme indispensable dans l'amalgame de l'œuvre? Lui révèle-t-on toutes les loques, les fards, les poulies, les chaînes, les repentirs, les épreuves barbouillées, bref toutes les horreurs qui composent le sanctuaire de l'art? (i. 185)

The sanctuary of art is the make-up room, where the performing artist puts on the slap. Just like Fancioulle. Indeed in these prefaces Baudelaire clearly relishes the idea that as a poet he is a play-actor, a double agent composed of 'sincerity' and 'charlatanry'. He himself may have experienced 'toute sensation de suavité ou d'amertume, de béatitude ou d'horreur' (i. 183), but with rhyme and metre, syntax and stanza he can simulate them too. He has enjoyed conspiring against conventional good taste and listening to all the dumb things that have been said about him. Indeed, contrarian that he is, he has thrived on it: 'j'ai un des ces heureux caractères qui tirent une jouissance de la haine et qui se glorifient dans le mépris. Mon goût diaboliquement passionné de la bêtise me fait trouver des plaisirs particuliers dans les travestissements de la calomnie' (i. 185). A travesty after all is just another role. And anyway how 'real' in the end is the 'real' Baudelaire? What if this *enfant terrible* were actually as pure as the driven snow?! It's a nice thought:

> Chaste comme le papier, sobre comme l'eau, porté à la dévotion, comme une communiante, inoffensif comme une victime, il ne me déplairait pas de passer pour un débauché, un ivrogne, un impie et un assassin.

Walter Benjamin quotes this passage in his *Arcades Project* and prefaces it with just three words: 'Baudelaire as mime'.[20]

In the end Baudelaire did not publish a preface to *Les Fleurs du Mal*. In any case, as he told his publisher Michel Lévy in August or September 1862, the whole idea of explaining his poetic 'méthode' clever trick by clever trick was really just a joke: 'cette sérieuse bouffonerie'. Much better to use Gautier's recent article about him instead! (*Corr.* ii. 257; i. 1168). And much better also to let the poems of *Les Fleurs du Mal* speak for themselves—as a poetic performance where what matters is not whether the poet is writing an autobiography (like Hugo's *Les Contemplations*) but what the poetry itself says and what effects it may have on its potential readers.

---

[20] Walter Benjamin, *The Arcades Project*, trans. Howard Eiland and Kevin McLaughlin (Cambridge, Mass., and London: Belknap Press of Harvard University Press, 1999), 330.

In what follows I aim to describe this 'performance'. For, within the 100 poems (plus the prefatory 'Au lecteur') of the 1857 edition or the 127 poems that make up the 1861 edition of *Les Fleurs du Mal*, Baudelaire the double agent may be seen to simulate human self-abandonment to desire and destruction while yet knowingly exercising his own conscious creativity in the simulation of that abandonment. Like the dandy who defies the rules of quotidian convention the better to heed the higher laws of self-conscious art, so the poet of *Les Fleurs du Mal* rejects the orthodoxy that poetry cannot come from the ugly or the depraved and heeds the higher rule of art, of creativity as 'une idéalité artistique' (ii. 535) that allows him to produce a 'eurythmic' harmony through the poetic deployment of rhyme, rhythm, and image. In this way the art of *Les Fleurs du Mal* is analogous with the 'comique absolu' inspired by the grotesque insofar as 'dans ce cas-là le rire est l'expression de la supériorité, non plus de l'homme sur l'homme, mais de l'homme sur la nature' (ii. 535). And perhaps it is this harmony—this *nomos*— that provides the answer to Baudelaire's question about how different artists with different techniques nevertheless end up inspiring a communality of response amongst those who attend to their art. For through art we are all brought to some fundamental sense of order and meaningfulness in the universe, a sense of 'justesse' to set against the apparent dissonance of our divided, alienated, dystopian selves, a truthfulness that combines 'le vrai, le bien, et le beau' in a new form of poetic justice.

PART II
MELANCHOLY

Le mot mélancolie, consacré dans le langage vulgaire, pour exprimer l'état habituel de tristesse de quelques individus, doit être laissé aux moralistes et aux poètes, qui, dans leurs expressions, ne sont pas obligés à autant de sévérité que les médecins.

(Étienne Esquirol, 'Mélancolie')[1]

Dans la culture d'Occident, et durant des siècles, la mélancolie a été inséparable de l'idée que les poètes se faisaient de leur propre condition.

(Jean Starobinski, *La Mélancolie au miroir*, 12)

---

[1] *Dictionnaire des sciences médicales par une société de médecins et de chirurgiens* (60 vols, Paris: Pankoucke, 1818–22), xxxii (1819), 147–83 (148).

4
Melancholy and Baudelaire

> ce misérable dictionnaire de mélancolie et de crime
> (draft dedication of *Les Fleurs du Mal*, i. 187)
>
> ce livre saturnien, | Orgiaque et mélancolique
> ('Épigraphe pour un livre condamné', ll. 3–4)

Melancholy

> l'éternelle Mélancolie
>
> (*Salon de 1859*, ii. 669)

Melancholy has a long and complex history.[1] Today the words 'melancholy' and 'mélancolie' have lost much of their original force, now suggesting no more than a calm, quiet state of unhappy reflection, a vague or regretful longing, a wistfulness, a sadness without apparent cause. But historically 'melancholy', like 'mélancolie', is a vernacular version of the ancient Greek *melankholia*, from *melas*,

---

[1] The classic history of melancholy remains Raymond Klibansky, Erwin Panofsky, and Fritz Saxl, *Saturn and Melancholy: Studies in the History of Natural Philosophy, Religion, and Art* (London: Nelson, 1964). For succinct accounts see Kenneth Davison, 'Historical Aspects of Mood Disorders', *Psychiatry*, 5: 4 (2006), 115–18, and A. J. Lewis, 'Melancholia: A Historical Review', *Journal of Mental Science*, 80 (1934), 1–42. On melancholy in antiquity see also Jacques Jouanna, 'Aux racines de la mélancolie: La Médecine grecque est-elle mélancolique?', in Jean Clair and Robert Kopp (eds), *De la Mélancolie* (Paris: Gallimard, 2007), 11–51. On melancholy in the nineteenth century, see G. E. Berrios, 'Melancholia and Depression during the 19th Century: A Conceptual History', *British Journal of Psychiatry*, 153: 3 (1988), 298–304. For the context of nineteenth-century French psychiatry see Jan Goldstein, *Console and Classify: The French Psychiatric Profession in the Nineteenth Century* (Cambridge: Cambridge University Press, 1987). On the interrelationship of medical and literary accounts of mental disorders in nineteenth-century France, see Tony James, *Dream, Creativity, and Madness in Nineteenth-Century France* (Oxford: Oxford University Press, 1995), and Juan Rigoli, *Lire le délire: Aliénisme, rhétorique et littérature en France au XIXe siècle* (Paris: Fayard, 2001). On the medical treatment of melancholy see Jean Starobinski, *Histoire du traitement de la mélancolie des origines à 1900* (Basel: Geigy, 1960). Starobinski (1920–2019), a qualified doctor, former specialist in mental health treatment, and historian of medicine, as well as being a distinguished literary scholar and historian of art, is one of the few critics to focus on the presentation of melancholy in literature, and particularly in relation to Baudelaire, notably in *La Mélancolie au miroir: Trois Lectures de Baudelaire* (Paris: Julliard, 1989). *L'Encre de la mélancolie* (Paris: Éditions du Seuil, 2012) provides a comprehensive collection of his writings on melancholy over more than fifty years, beginning with his *Histoire du traitement de la mélancolie* (a thesis submitted to the Faculty of Medicine at the University of Lausanne in 1959/60) and containing some twenty-five articles, including five on Baudelaire under the title 'Rêve et immortalité mélancolique' (pp. 419–540).

melan = black + *khole* = bile, and the Latin *melancholia*: namely, a medical condition corresponding in some part[2] to what we might now call 'depression' or 'clinical depression'. This condition is characterized, in varying degrees of intensity, by multiple and conflicting feelings: of irrational fear or anxiety, of guilt and remorse, of hopelessness, self-loathing, despondency, apathy, boredom, and loss of the will to live—all of which are to be found depicted, usually from the perspective of a first-person poetic persona, in *Les Fleurs du Mal*.

Accounts of depression are to be found in ancient Egyptian and Indian texts,[3] as well as in the Old Testament.[4] While since earliest times the condition has often been attributed to external cosmic forces (most notably the influence of the planet Saturn) or to supernatural causes (evil spirits, angry gods), Pythagoras (*c*.570–*c*.495 BC) and Empedocles (*c*.494–*c*.434 BC) are acknowledged as the first to propound the so-called humoral theory, associating the four 'humours' of the body—blood, phlegm, yellow bile, and black bile—with the four seasons, with four qualities (dry, wet, hot, cold), and with four temperaments (sanguine, phlegmatic, choleric, melancholic), while holding in general that good mental health requires these four humours to be in a state of equilibrium. Hippocrates (*c*.460–*c*.370 BC), in turn, was the first to identify what he called 'melancholia' as a mental disorder caused by an excessive accumulation of black bile in the body.

Flash forward to the beginning of the nineteenth century, and despite the intervening centuries of advancing sophistication in the understanding of mental disorders, the humoral theory was still so deeply embedded in attitudes to melancholy that the pioneering French psychiatrist Étienne Esquirol (1772–1840) felt obliged in 1819 to warn readers of the *Dictionnaire des sciences médicales* of its inadequacy while yet also conceding its partial validity: 'Il est certain que le mot mélancolie, même dans l'acception des anciens, offre souvent à l'esprit une idée fausse, car la mélancolie ne dépend pas toujours de la bile.'[5] The humoral account of melancholy was finally superseded in the course of the nineteenth century as medical opinion sought to distinguish more rigorously, in both theory and nomenclature, between 'normal' and pathological states of 'melancholy'.[6] By the end of the century, and notably in the work of the eminent

---

[2] For a detailed account of why 'melancholia' and depression cannot be directly equated, see Jennifer Radden, 'Is This Dame Melancholy? Equating Today's Depression and Past Melancholia', *Philosophy, Psychiatry, and Psychology*, 10: 1 (March 2003), 37–52.

[3] See Jennifer Radden (ed.), *The Nature of Melancholy: From Aristotle to Kristeva* (Oxford: Oxford University Press, 2000), p. x.

[4] See Davison, 'Historical Aspects of Mood Disorders', 115.

[5] Étienne Esquirol, 'Mélancolie', in *Dictionnaire des sciences médicales par une société de médicins et de chirurgiens* (60 vols, Paris: Panckoucke, 1818–22), xxxii (1819): 147–83 (148). See also, Goldstein, *Console and Classify*, 156–7.

[6] See Radden, 'Introduction: From Melancholic States to Clinical Depression', in Radden (ed.), *The Nature of Melancholy*, 3–51, in which she sketches 'a nineteenth-century shift whereby the hitherto encompassing category of melancholy divides, leaving a sharper distinction between the despondent moods and temperamental differences of normal experience, on the one hand, and, on the other, the

German psychiatrist Emil Kraepelin (1856-1926) that provided the foundation of modern psychiatry, the terms 'depression' and 'depressive states' had come to replace 'melancholy', while 'melancholia' survived only to designate a sub-type of psychotic depression occurring in the elderly.[7] The word 'mélancolie' itself, as Esquirol had wished (see epigraph to Part II above), was abandoned to the mouths and pens of 'moralists and poets.'[8]

This was only fair, for it was in fact poets—and in particular French poets (notably Alain Chartier)—of the late medieval period who first gave currency to the term 'melancholy' as the description of a temporary state of sadness or depression that is independent of any pathological or physiological circumstances.[9] Being characterized by gloomy introspection, such 'melancholy' came by extension to be associated particularly with a state of heightened self-awareness, as may be seen in Milton's poem 'Il Penseroso' (1645/6). Here the poet calls on his imagined goddess 'Melancholy' to be his muse and to reward his 'thoughtful' devotion to her by granting him a vision of the divine—or, as he also puts it: 'Till old experience do attain | To something like prophetic strain' (ll. 173-4).[10] In this aspiration Milton's poet is drawing on the Renaissance ideal of the solitary contemplative thinker, 'a type of man foreign to the Middle Ages, the "homo literatus" or "Musarum sacerdos", who in public and private life was

---

clinical disorder of melancholia, which has come to be associated with the clinical depression of our own time' (4-5).

[7] See Berrios, 'Melancholia and Depression', 300. Curiously the *Dictionnaire historique de la langue française*, ed. Alain Rey (3 vols, Paris: Dictionnaires Le Robert, 1998) states under 'Dépression' that the first use of this word in a psychological sense occurs in 1867, 'chez Baudelaire', but gives no source reference. More usually the first use of the term in French is associated with the noted psychiatrist and expert on epilepsy (itself consistently identified with 'melancholia' since ancient times) Louis Delasiauve (1804-93) in a scientific paper of 1856.

[8] The humoral theory nevertheless proved difficult to eradicate. Writing in 1934 A. J. Lewis, an assistant medical officer at the Maudsley Hospital in London, notes: 'there has been in recent times fresh interest in the doctrine of temperaments, most active and justified where depression and mania are in question; there has even been a revival in France of the long-rejected theory that black bile is the source of melancholy' ('Melancholia: A Historical Review', 1-2).

[9] See Klibansky, Panofsky, and Saxl, *Saturn and Melancholy*, 217: 'The term "melancholy", ever more widely used in popular late medieval writings, was, specially in France, eagerly adopted by writers of belles-lettres in order to lend colour to mental tendencies and conditions. In doing this they gradually altered and transferred the originally pathological meaning of this notion in such a way that it became descriptive of a more or less temporary "mood"' (217-18).

[10] See Klibansky, Panofsky, and Saxl, *Saturn and Melancholy*, 231: 'What emerges here is the specifically "poetic" melancholy mood of the modern; a double-edged feeling constantly providing its own nourishment, in which the soul enjoys its own loneliness, but by this very pleasure becomes again more conscious of its solitude, the "joy in grief", the "mournful joy", or "the sad luxury of woe", to use the words of Milton's successors. This modern melancholy mood is essentially an enhanced self-awareness, since the ego is the pivot round which the sphere of joy and grief revolves'. Only with Milton and his successors, it is argued, does it become possible to 'actually revel in the sweet self-sufficiency of the melancholy mood': melancholy is transfigured by the imagination into 'an ideal condition, inherently pleasurable, however painful—a condition which by the continually renewed tension between depression and exaltation, unhappiness and "apartness", horror of death and increased awareness of life, could impart a new vitality to drama, poetry and art' (pp. 232, 233).

responsible only to his own mind.'[11] Here, in modern guise, is the age-old figure of the poet as *vates*, a 'priest of the Muses'[12] and poet-lawgiver who now through melancholic contemplation gains access to a special truth for which he can provide the literary expression: the poet as 'modern genius'.[13] Such had Dante been, described by Boccaccio as 'malinconico e pensoso' (melancholy and thoughtful),[14] and such would Baudelaire—for whom Dante was an important model—also be.

Prefacing her anthology of excerpted writings on melancholy from Aristotle to Kristeva, Jennifer Radden notes how '[f]or most of western European history, melancholy was a central cultural idea, focusing, explaining, and organizing the way people saw the world and one another and framing social, medical, and epistemological norms', but how '[t]oday, in contrast, it is an insignificant category, of little interest to medicine or psychology, and without explanatory or organizing vitality.'[15] For her, Freud's essay on 'Mourning and Melancholia' (1917) marks the 'watershed' moment, constituting at once the end and 'completion' of a centuries-old tradition while ushering in a 'new type of theorizing'. Consequently, she warns that with melancholy having now 'lost its definitive and vital role', we may tend to minimize the importance of this erstwhile 'central cultural idea' and 'at some cost'.[16] And this is certainly true if we want to understand the 'vital' role of melancholy in Baudelaire's 'alternative legislation' and quite what he himself, within the context of nineteenth-century French and European culture, understood melancholy to be, both in itself and in its relation to aesthetic beauty.

Yves Bonnefoy offers a similar perspective in his preface to Starobinski's *La Mélancolie au miroir*, where he makes a very large claim for the importance of melancholy as a topic for critical study and describes the condition as a 'désordre de l'âme':

---

[11] Klibansky, Panofsky, and Saxl, *Saturn and Melancholy*, 245.

[12] The description of poets as 'musarum sacerdotes' derives originally from Horace.

[13] See Klibansky, Panofsky, and Saxl, *Saturn and Melancholy*, 247: 'The birth of this new [Renaissance] humanist awareness took place, therefore, in an atmosphere of intellectual contradiction. As he took up his position, the self-sufficient "homo literatus" saw himself torn between the extremes of self-affirmation, sometimes rising to hubris, and self-doubt, sometimes sinking to despair; and the experience of this dualism roused him to discover the new intellectual pattern, which was a reflection of this tragic and heroic disunity—the intellectual pattern of "modern genius".'

[14] See Klibansky, Panofsky, and Saxl, *Saturn and Melancholy*, 254. The authors note also how '[i]n the twenty-first canto of the *Paradiso*, it is the sphere of Saturn in which the "anime speculatrici", led by Peter Damian and St Benedict, appear to the poet; and from it the shining ladder of contemplation rises to the vision of the Deity' (255). In their view, however, Milton's debt was not to Dante (*c*.1265–1321) but to the early Renaissance humanist scholar (and Catholic priest) Marsilio Ficino (1433–99), 'who really gave shape to the idea of the melancholy man of genius and revealed it to the rest of Europe—in particular to the great Englishmen of the sixteenth and seventeenth centuries—in the magic chiaroscuro of Christian Neoplatonic mysticism' (255).

[15] Radden (ed.), *The Nature of Melancholy*, p. vii.

[16] Radden (ed.), *The Nature of Melancholy*, pp. vii, viii.

rien n'est certes plus justifié que cette sorte d'étude, car la mélancolie est peut-être ce qu'ont de plus spécifique les cultures de l'Occident. Née de l'affaiblissement du sacré, de la distance qui croît entre la conscience et le divin, et réfractée et reflétée par les situations et les œuvres les plus diverses, elle est l'écharde dans la chair de cette modernité qui depuis les Grecs ne cesse de naître mais sans jamais en finir de se dégager de ses nostalgies, de ses regrets, de ses rêves. D'elle procède ce long cortège de cris, de gémissements, de rires, de chants bizarres, d'oriflammes mobiles dans la fumée qui passe par tous nos siècles, fécondant l'art, semant la déraison—celle-ci déguisée parfois en raison extrême chez l'utopiste ou l'idéologue.[17]

For Bonnefoy melancholy is thus neither simply a personal mood nor a form of mental illness but a deep-seated (Western) cultural condition, a nostalgia for the sacred and a self-conscious sense of lack that has beset human beings ever since the days of ancient Greece, and a yearning moreover that is dangerously manifest in the extremism of utopian visions and ideological purities. As I have discussed elsewhere,[18] Chateaubriand saw in this condition the cause of the French Revolution, and today's observers might wish similarly to identify it, albeit under some other name (such as 'populism'), as a cause of current political longings—for lost sovereignty, past greatness, fundamentalist orthodoxy. Melancholy is not just personal but political, and in this respect Baudelaire's 'melancholy' is no different. For this alternative lawgiver, as we shall see, moral progress depends on how we deal with melancholy, and—as Bonnefoy himself suggests ('fécondant l'art')—it is in art rather than politics that this 'melancholy' may be able to have *beneficial* effects: as it might be, in the form of 'les fleurs du Mal'.

From Radden's anthology there emerges a rich historical landscape of melancholy that, for all the variety of its geographical, cultural, and linguistic contexts, nevertheless exhibits a remarkably stable and enduring topography, an 'iterative effect' that Radden considers 'deeply and perhaps unexpectedly conservative'. Instead of 'older theories, meanings, and associations' being 'superseded and eventually replaced by newer conceptions', conflicting accounts of the condition persist in parallel down the ages:

> Melancholy is seen to result from earthly things—bile and dryness; astronomical movements (especially those of the planet Saturn); and supernatural influences, the work of the Devil. Particularly since the modern period, it is also regarded as the result of social and psychological occurrences—too much creativity, idleness, or grief [...] different and contrary meanings of melancholy and melancholia

---

[17] Yves Bonnefoy, 'Préface', in Starobinski, *La Mélancolie au miroir*, 7–8.
[18] See *Unacknowledged Legislators*, 100–7.

seem to accumulate and coexist, creating ambiguity and resonance as the centuries go by. Melancholy is both a normal disposition and a sign of mental disturbance; it is both a feeling and a way of behaving. It is a nebulous mood but also a set of self-accusing beliefs.[19]

It begins to look as if 'melancholy' may simply be our word for the difficulties of living, for what Baudelaire refers to in his poem 'Semper eadem' as 'le mal de vivre'.

As Radden notes, there exists also a whole iconographic tradition relating to melancholy, in which Albrecht Dürer's engraving entitled 'Melencolia I' (1514) and Delacroix's 'Le Tasse en prison' (1839) occupy pride of place.[20] The former provides the original and principal object of study for the authors of *Saturn and Melancholy*.[21] For them the figure of melancholy depicted in 'Melencolia I' derives not only from Ficino's conception of the melancholic contemplative as a modern 'musarum sacerdos' but also from the depiction of melancholy in medieval iconography as equivalent to the Christian sin of 'accidie' (or 'acedia'), that is, the deadly sin of sloth manifesting as a neglect of the Christian duty to work and pray.[22] But they argue that in 'Melencolia I', rather than Christian sinfulness,

---

[19] Radden (ed.), *The Nature of Melancholy*, p. ix. Radden's analysis has found subsequent confirmation in the work of the Danish film director and screenwriter Lars von Trier whose so-called 'Depression Trilogy' consists of *Antichrist* (2009), *Melancholia* (2011), and *Nymphomaniac* (2013).

[20] See Radden (ed.), *The Nature of Melancholy*, pp. x–xi, 30–2. Delacroix's painting is known variously in English as 'Tasso in the Madhouse' or 'Tasso in the House of the Insane'. Radden notes how in the nineteenth century this 'long and distinguished pictorial tradition' (p. x) began to incorporate 'another kind of portrait of melancholia [...] that illustrating medical textbooks. Engravings, drawings, paintings, and finally photographs now sought to convey the melancholic patient in sharply realistic terms' (p. xi). Her book contains numerous illustrations to exemplify this tradition, itself an important context for Baudelaire's poem 'Le Squelette laboureur'.

[21] They contend that Dürer's engraving owes a crucial debt to the figure of the melancholic contemplative elaborated by Ficino and argue that if 'Dürer was the first to raise the allegorical figure of Melancholy to the plane of a symbol, this change appears now as the means—or perhaps the result—of a change in significance: the notion of a "Melencolia" in whose nature the intellectual distinction of a liberal art [in this case, geometry, or the art of measurement in its broadest applications, itself traditionally associated with Saturn] was combined with a human soul's capacity for suffering could only take the form of a winged genius' (Klibansky, Panofsky, and Saxl, *Saturn and Melancholy*, 318; and for the link between geometry and Saturn, see p. 333). For them the 'greatness of Dürer's achievement' lay in the fact that 'he conceived the melancholy of intellectual men as an indivisible destiny in which the differences of melancholy temperament, disease, and mood fade to nothing, and brooding sorrow no less than creative enthusiasm are but the extremes of one and the same disposition. The depression of *Melencolia I*, revealing both the obscure doom and the obscure source of creative genius, lies beyond any contrast between health and disease' (349).

[22] See Klibansky, Panofsky, and Saxl, *Saturn and Melancholy*, 300–2. In medieval Christian theology melancholy had been held to derive directly from the Fall of Man in the Garden of Eden. For some thinkers, notably Hildegard of Bingen, the humoral theory of melancholy combined with the Book of Genesis to produce a view of melancholy as a sickness of both body and mortal soul. For her, melancholy 'was born in the first fruit of Adam's seed out of the breath of the serpent when Adam followed its advice by devouring the apple' and melancholy then 'curdled in his blood'. (Quoted in Klibansky, Panofsky, and Saxl, *Saturn and Melancholy*, 79.) See also Davison, 'Historical Aspects of Mood Disorders', 115: 'the Christian Church was developing the concept of accidie [or acedia], one of the seven deadly sins, which shared many of the features of Melancholia, but with an emphasis on sloth

Dürer is depicting 'the melancholy of an imaginative being, as distinct from that of the rational or the speculative, the melancholy of the artist and of the artistic thinker, as distinct from that which is political and scientific, or metaphysical and religious'.[23] As to Delacroix, it was from him that Baudelaire drew particular inspiration for his treatment of melancholy in poetry, and it was about that particular painting that he wrote one of his first—and also (in a revised version) final—poems, 'Sur *Le Tasse en prison* d'Eugène Delacroix'.

Baudelaire's Melancholy

J'ai cultivé mon hystérie avec jouissance et terreur.

('Hygiène', i. 668)

In what follows I shall argue that *Les Fleurs du Mal* presents the radically original account of a 'melancholy' or state of 'depression' that is neither a mere mood nor yet a treatable medical condition with its own particular aetiology. For Baudelaire 'melancholy' is not an aberrant mental state, a 'disorder', but the irremediable, default experience of all humanity. I shall propose that 'le Mal' is his term for this condition, seen at once as akin to a sickness (or, as I shall suggest, a state of 'ill-being')[24] and as a form—newly defined—of 'evil'. In his customary fashion he seeks to resist and transcend traditional binaries: for example, the very opposition of health and illness, or of science and poetry (as foregrounded by Esquirol), just as he also seeks to escape the straitjacket of traditional Christian doctrine and terminology and in particular the binary of good and evil. For him, as we shall see, 'melancholy' or 'le Mal' is not some 'fallen' or 'sinful' state that may be cured/redeemed by penance and the pursuit of virtue, but is rather the inescapable truth of which our painful awareness may nevertheless be palliated by the creativity of art itself and indeed the 'work' of artistic creation. In particular, he resisted the Christian concept of acedia, of which (as we shall also see) 'Au lecteur' offers at once a parodic description and a secular redefinition.

---

and apathy, and regarded as induced by demons. It was conceived as a sinful affliction that required correction by confession or, possibly, manual labour. Women sufferers were at risk of being burned as witches. Some authorities, however, ventured to recommend seeking help from a physician rather than a priest.' On the relationship between ancient Greek 'melancholy' and Christian 'acedia' see Hélène Prigent, 'Mélancolie antique: Une philosophie de l'image?', in Clair and Kopp (eds), *De la mélancolie*, 75–93. For a particularly incisive account of 'acedia' in its relation to melancholy in the works of Dante and Petrarch (as well as of Proust and Roland Barthes), see Jennifer Rushworth, *Discourses of Mourning in Dante, Petrarch, and Proust* (Oxford: Oxford University Press, 2016), 18–53, 72–82.

[23] Klibansky, Panofsky, and Saxl, *Saturn and Melancholy*, 360.

[24] Cf. John E. Jackson's reference to 'mal-être' in *Baudelaire* (Paris: Le Livre de poche, 2001), 95.

As Jean Starobinski observes, Baudelaire seldom uses the word 'mélancolie' itself in his poetry, fearing perhaps that it would connote something rather more hackneyed and stereotypically 'Romantic' than he had in mind.[25] Instead—and perhaps also for syllabic and other prosodic reasons—he preferred the terms 'ennui' and 'spleen'. Certainly some of Baudelaire's own comments reflect this view that all talk of melancholy is tiresome posturing or sentimental claptrap: for example, when in 1852 he dismisses Musset and others as members of *'l'École mélancolico-farceuse'* (ii. 51) or when in the *Salon de 1859* he thanks the painter Chifflart for having avoided 'toutes les fadaises de la mélancolie apprise' (ii. 649). And yet not only is the experience of melancholy clearly at the heart of *Les Fleurs du Mal*, so too does it inform the prose poems, known under the title *Le Spleen de Paris*. 'La mélancolie *apprise*': what Baudelaire offers, precisely, is an alternative to received and reductive notions about this staple of early nineteenth-century art and literature. His account of melancholy is different: it is 'neuf'.

For Baudelaire the experience of melancholy is intrinsic to our everyday lives, and perhaps even the defining feature of our human condition, and so it is at once central to his art as a poet and to his role as an alternative lawgiver. No doubt one might speculate about the biographical reality that may have informed this poetic project. Yves Bonnefoy, for one, has surmised that Baudelaire's early contraction of syphilis may account for the insistent presence of death in his poetry,[26] and one could suppose also that, for a man who may often have contemplated suicide[27] and seems to have attempted it at least once (on 30 June 1845, aged 24), the experience of melancholy was intrinsic to his own life.[28] Indeed one might even wonder whether his disdain for 'les fadaises de la mélancolie apprise' may not derive from a bitter awareness of the discrepancy between the vapid affectation of young men palely loitering in fashionable simulation of the *mal du siècle* and the 'gouffre' of an all-encompassing mental suffering.

---

[25] *La Mélancolie au miroir*, 15–16, where Starobinski notes nevertheless that Baudelaire makes uninhibited use of the word and its cognates in both his correspondence and his critical writings.

[26] See Bonnefoy's celebrated preface to *Les Fleurs du Mal*, in Baudelaire, *Œuvres complètes*, ed. Lloyd James Austin (2 vols, Paris: Club du meilleur livre, 1955), reproduced in Bonnefoy, *L'Improbable, suivi d'Un rêve fait à Mantoue et autres essais* (rev. edn, Paris: Mercure de France, 1980), 29–38, and *Sous le signe de Baudelaire* (Paris: Gallimard, 2011), 11–18.

[27] Cf. his comment in a letter to his mother of 20 Apr. 1860: 'Je t'en supplie, ménage-moi donc les reproches. Songe donc que depuis tant, tant d'années, je vis sans cesse au bord du suicide' (*Corr.*, ii. 25). Cf. also similar comments, again to his mother, in the following year: *Corr.*, ii. 140, 151.

[28] Cf., for example, this earlier account in a letter to his mother of 30 Dec. 1857: 'Certainment, j'ai beaucoup à me plaindre de moi-même, et je suis tout étonné et alarmé de cet état. Ai-je besoin d'un déplacement, je n'en sais rien. Est-ce le physique malade qui diminue l'esprit et la volonté, ou est-ce la lâcheté spirituelle qui fatigue le corps, je n'en sais rien. Mais ce que je sens, c'est un immense découragement, une sensation d'isolement insupportable, une peur perpétuelle d'un malheur vague, une défiance complète de mes forces, une absence totale de désirs, une impossibilité de trouver un amusement quelconque. [...] Je me demande sans cesse: à quoi bon ceci? À quoi bon cela? C'est là le véritable esprit de spleen.—Sans doute, en me rappelant que j'ai déjà subi des états analogues et que je me suis relevé, je serais porté à ne pas trop m'alarmer; mais aussi je ne me rappelle pas être tombé jamais si bas et m'être traîné si longtemps dans l'ennui' (*Corr.*, i. 437–8).

Certainly this awareness lies at the heart of his early prose narrative *La Fanfarlo* (1847), in which the young protagonist Samuel Cramer is presented as one who meretriciously adopts the role of the melancholic only to end up afflicted by the terrible reality of this condition. Thus at the outset he is but a dandy of melancholy, performing and perfecting this noble role for himself alone: 'comédien par tempérament,—il jouait pour lui-même et à huis clos d'incomparables tragédies, ou, pour mieux dire, tragi-comédies'; 'Une larme lui germait-elle dans le coin de l'œil à quelque souvenir, il allait à sa glace se regarder pleurer' (i. 554). Then he goes public, seeking to seduce the genuinely (but temporarily) melancholic Mme de Cosmelly with the miseries of his dark poems (under their caricatural title *Les Orfraies*) and an extravagantly gloomy account of the human condition: our journey under a setting sun across a barren wasteland of dead passions and sterile reason, and with naught to imbibe but 'le poison de l'ennui' (562).

Having reduced his victim to satisfactorily copious and uncontrollable floods of tears, Cramer—'l'un des derniers romantiques que possèdent la France' (571)—surveys his work: 'le brutal et hypocrite comédien était fier de ces belles larmes; il les considérait comme son œuvre et sa propriété littéraire' (i. 562). The artist in Cramer is drawn to the combination of beauty and melancholy that is Mme de Cosmelly: 'cette belle mélancolique' (559), who comes to sit sadly in the Jardin du Luxembourg, 'la tête inclinée par une mélancolie gracieuse et presque étudiée, vers les fleurs de la plate-bande' (i. 558). (Perhaps his 'charmante victime' is also something of an actress?)[29] But this latter-day Dante mucks up, sending the real actress La Fanfarlo (mistress of Mme de Cosmelly's husband) a sonnet intended for his own putative beloved ('où il louait en style mystique sa beauté de Béatrix' (i. 569))[30] and subsequently curing Mme de Cosmelly of her blues by taking La Fanfarlo away from M. de Cosmelly and unintentionally restoring marital harmony. Dissonant co-habitation, by contrast, is to be his own fate: 'Samuel connut toutes les tortures de la jalousie, et l'abaissement et la tristesse où nous jette la conscience d'un mal incurable et constitutionnel,—bref, toutes les horreurs du mariage vicieux qu'on nomme le concubinage' (i. 580). Now he knows the truth of the condition whereof he so glibly spoke: 'aussi, dans le ciel où il régnait, son amour commençait d'être triste et malade de la mélancolie du bleu, comme un royal solitaire' (i. 578). Like the 'roi d'un pays pluvieux' of 'Spleen [iii]' he 'has' La Fanfarlo but possesses nothing—only 'une sorte de lorette ministérielle' (i. 580) getting plumper by the day as she prepares to give birth to another man's twins.

The contrast between real suffering and a confected Romantic melancholy is thus central to *La Fanfarlo*, and in a text that bears multiple traces of Baudelaire's

---

[29] For discussion of the complex interplay between 'sign and substance' in *La Fanfarlo*, see Nathaniel Wing, 'The Poetics of Irony in Baudelaire's *La Fanfarlo*', *Neophilologus*, 49: 2 (April 1975), 165–89.

[30] On Baudelaire's possible debt to Balzac's *Béatrix* for the outline of his plot, see i. 1413–14.

own lived experience it can be difficult to determine where its author himself precisely stands. Indeed Baudelaire may most resemble his protagonist in this very elusiveness, for as the narrator says of Cramer: 'avec ce diable d'homme, le grand problème est toujours de savoir où le comédien commence' (i. 572). For Claude Pichois *La Fanfarlo* is the work of a putatively pre-melancholic Baudelaire (despite that suicidal moment of two years earlier),[31] but there can be little doubt that Baudelaire had his own 'black dog'.[32] 'Au moral comme au physique', he writes in the posthumously published notes known under the title *Hygiène*, 'j'ai toujours eu la sensation du gouffre, non seulement du gouffre du sommeil, mais du gouffre de l'action, du rêve, du souvenir, du désir, du regret, du remords, du beau, du nombre, etc.'[33] A sense of emptiness and meaninglessness, of 'the Absurd' perhaps (in Camus's sense), has invaded even his most treasured domains ('le rêve', 'le beau'), but he has tried to engage with his depression and make it his own: 'J'ai cultivé mon hystérie avec jouissance et terreur.'[34] Here is the key impulse from which Baudelaire's poetry springs: the determination to counter passivity with activity, to challenge boredom and depression with the interest of art.

In this celebrated passage he records also how he appears to have experienced some first sign of the physical and/or mental incapacity that would later afflict him after his major stroke in early 1866: 'Maintenant j'ai toujours le vertige, et aujourd'hui 23 janvier 1862, j'ai subi un singulier avertissement, j'ai senti passer sur moi *le vent de l'aile de l'imbécillité*' (i. 668). As several commentators have pointed out, these comments are mirrored, in some cases almost *verbatim*, in 'Le Gouffre', a sonnet that appeared some five weeks later on 1 March in *L'Artiste* (and was subsequently included in the 'Nouvelles *Fleurs du Mal*' published in *Le Parnasse contemporain* in March 1866):

> Pascal avait son gouffre, avec lui se mouvant.
> —Hélas! tout est abîme,—action, désir, rêve,
> Parole! et sur mon poil qui tout droit se relève
> Mainte fois de la Peur je sens passer le vent.

---

[31] '*La Fanfarlo* respire le bonheur. Elle appartient à cette époque de sa vie littéraire où Baudelaire n'avait pas encore découvert le guignon' (i. 1415). The autobiographical elements in the text are discussed by Pichois in his 1957 edition of the text (Monaco: Éditions du Rocher).

[32] A term coined by Samuel Johnson. See Davison, 'Historical Aspects of Mood Disorders', 116.

[33] *Fusées*, ed. Guyaux, 125; i. 668.

[34] On Baudelaire's use of the term 'hystérie' see *Fusées*, ed. Guyaux, 417 n. 3. See also Pierre Laforgue, 'Baudelaire, Flaubert, ou hystérie et réalisme', in Laforgue, *Ut pictura poesis: Baudelaire, la peinture et le romantisme* (Lyon: Presses universitaires de Lyon, 2000), 73–82. In essence the term may be read here as shorthand for 'mental disorder', but a more precise, nosological understanding of the term is proposed by Née in 'Du "poète hystérique" chez Baudelaire' and 'Baudelaire et l'hystérie en son temps (1800–1860)'. For further discussion of what was understood by the term 'hystérie' within the context of French nineteenth-century psychiatry, see Goldstein, *Console and Classify*, *passim*, but especially 322–35.

> En haut, en bas, partout, la profondeur, la grève,
> Le silence, l'espace affreux et captivant...
> Sur le fond de mes nuits Dieu de son doigt savant
> Dessine un cauchemar multiforme et sans trêve.
>
> J'ai peur du sommeil comme on a peur d'un grand trou,
> Tout plein de vague horreur, menant on ne sait où;
> Je ne vois qu'infini par toutes les fenêtres,
>
> Et mon esprit, toujours du vertige hanté,
> Jalouse du néant l'insensibilité.
> —Ah! ne jamais sortir des Nombres et des Êtres!

Here is the irrational fear characteristic of depression, and to which Baudelaire refers frequently in his letters of this period (see i. 1115 n. 6), an experience also of nightmarish horror and boundless void from which the poet (and in this case, it would unambiguously seem, Baudelaire himself) would like to escape through becoming 'insensible'. The poem thus recalls 'Obsession', first published in May 1860, where the poet similarly seeks oblivion ('Car je cherche le vide, et le noir, et le nu!' (l. 11)) but also in vain. As Claude Pichois notes, the last line of 'Le Gouffre' is open to several interpretations: (i) 'May I never leave the realm of Numbers and Beings!'; (ii) 'What torment it is never to leave the realm of Numbers and Beings!'; (iii) 'If only it had been possible never to leave the realm of Numbers and Beings', this third reading being his (and my own) preferred interpretation.[35] For Baudelaire and/or the poetic persona of 'Le Gouffre' the problem is nothingness and the inescapable awareness of a yawning abyss:[36] if he cannot forgo consciousness, even in sleep, then he would rather that the world about him were ordered and structured ('des Nombres') and filled with life and living beings ('des Êtres'). Rather like Dürer's despondent figure, perhaps, gazing fiercely into the distance while vainly grasping her instrument of measurement...[37]

The personal reality underlying 'Le Gouffre' may also perhaps be inferred from the revisions that Baudelaire carried out between 1862 and 1866 to his early sonnet 'Sur *Le Tasse en prison* d'Eugène Delacroix'. Begun in 1842 and then dated 'Février 1844' (see i. 1150–1) the earlier version exists only in a manuscript copy, but Baudelaire returned to it after his brush with 'le vent de l'aile de l'imbécillité' and altered it significantly for publication, initially in the *Revue*

---

[35] See i. 1115–16. Also Née, 'Du "poète hystérique"', 120.
[36] Such, it appears, as Pascal himself *literally* experienced, about which Baudelaire would have learnt from Sainte-Beuve: see ii. 1115 n. 5.
[37] Baudelaire refers to Dürer on four occasions in his published work (i. 441; ii. 375, 582, 600) but only in passing, and never directly to the engraving itself. In the *Salon de 1845* he praises Louis Janmot's painting *Fleur des champs* (1845) for its depiction of '[c]ette simple figure, sérieuse et mélancolique, et dont le dessin et la couleur un peu crue rappellent les anciens maîtres allemands, ce gracieux Albert [*sic*] Dürer' (ii. 375).

nouvelle (1864) and then in *Les Épaves* (1866). The poem presents an ekphrasis of Delacroix's portrayal of Tasso incarcerated in what used to be called a 'lunatic asylum'. The central topos here is of poetic genius as a form of melancholia,[38] and Baudelaire's revisions are instructive. In the earlier version (see i. 1151) he presents Delacroix's Tasso as being distracted from his writing ('Déchirant sous ses pieds un manuscrit usé' (l. 2)) by the prospect of losing his reason: 'Le poète au cachot [. . .] | Mesure d'un regard que la démence enflamme, | L'escalier du vertige où s'abîme son âme' (ll. 1, 3–4). This fear has been brought on by the other inmates of the asylum and their own melancholic symptoms (confusion, unfounded fears, horrific visions): 'Les rires enivrants dont s'emplit la Prison, | Vers l'étrange et l'absurde invitent sa raison— | Le doute l'environne, et la peur ridicule, | Et la longue épouvante autour de lui circule—' (ll. 5–8). This Tasso is himself the classic melancholic, sadly preoccupied with his own inner world ('Ce triste prisonnier, bilieux et malsain, | Qui se penche à la voix des songes' (ll. 9–10)), but one who resists melancholy through vigilant reason and effort despite the present (and perhaps only temporary) frustration of his dreams: 'Ce rude travailleur, qui toujours lutte et veille, | Est l'emblème d'une âme, et des rêves futurs, | Que le Possible enferme entre ses quatre murs!' (ll. 12–14).

In the later version, Tasso's melancholy seems more terrible and the asylum a metaphor for the prison of his own condition—and here explicitly for the poet-persona of this poem's *own* condition. From the beginning Tasso is described as 'maladif' (l. 1); his foot is now 'convulsif' as it rolls his manuscript around on the floor, and his gaze flares with 'terreur' at the vertiginous prospect of madness. But instead of being a 'rude travailleur, qui toujours lutte et veille', he is now the genius and dreamer who finds himself trapped by a horrible reality ('Ce génie enfermé dans un taudis malsain' (l. 9), 'Ce rêveur que l'horreur de son logis réveille' (l. 12)). As such he has become the 'emblem' not merely of a dreamer hemmed in by the four walls of the possible but of a poet suffocated by the four walls of the real, and

---

[38] On this association of genius with melancholia, see not only Klibansky, Panofsky, and Saxl, *Saturn and Melancholy*, *passim*, but also Radden (ed.), *The Nature of Melancholy*, 12–17. Radden writes: 'The famous question from Aristotle's *Problems* (i.e. 'Why is it that all men who have become outstanding in philosophy, statesmanship, poetry or the arts are melancholic, or are infected by the diseases arising from black bile?') [. . .] is echoed throughout the centuries until the eighteenth, although with subtle shifts. From enabling agent, for example, melancholy becomes the noxious side effect of creativity and intellectual prowess—"spleen". By the nineteenth century, emphasis on the compensations of melancholy returns again; we see it forcefully conveyed in Delacroix's portrayal of the elevated suffering of the poet Tasso' (p. 12). In *Problems* it is claimed that melancholy (seen as a potentially benign admixture of black bile in the blood) is the source of poetic inspiration and vatic wisdom: 'those in whom (*the black bile*) is considerable and cold become sluggish and stupid, whereas those in whom it is very considerable and hot become mad, clever, erotic, and easily moved to spiritedness and desire, and some become more talkative. But many too, owing to this heat being near the location of the intelligence, are affected by diseases of madness or inspiration, whence come Sibyls and Bakides and all the inspired persons, when (*the condition*) comes not through disease but through natural mixture. Maracus the Syracusan was even a better poet when he was insane.' See Aristotle, *Problems*, ed. and trans. Robert Mayhew and David C. Mirhady (2 vols, Cambridge, Mass.: Harvard University Press, 2014), ii. 287 [Book xxx, ch. 1].

of a very real condition: 'Voilà bien ton emblème, Âme aux songes obscurs, | Que le Réel étouffe entre ses quatre murs!' (ll. 13-14).

In Delacroix's painting Tasso is depicted seated and semi-slumped, his head supported by his left hand and lower arm as he rests his left elbow on the headrest of his chaise longue (a pose that recalls the traditional iconography of melancholy before and since 'Melencolia I'). In this way he could be thought to be listening to voices, the voices of his dreams, which the first version of the poem describes as 'la voix des songes, dont l'essaim | Tourbillonne, ameuté derrière son oreille' (ll. 10-11). But in the second version the equivalent lines—'Ces grimaces, ces cris, ces spectres dont l'essaim | Tourbillonne, ameuté derrière son oreille' (ll. 10-11)—might seem more applicable to the figures grouped on the left-hand side of the painting, inmates of the asylum peering at him through the barred entrance to his cell—one of whom stretches an arm between the bars, at once pointing to and just touching a page of manuscript that has remained on the chair. But these figures appear neither to grimace nor to scream nor to be particularly ghostlike. A more plausible reading is that Baudelaire has made the nature of Tasso's dreams more horrific, and thus Tasso himself so oppressed by his tortured imaginings that he can no longer write. In this respect the author of *Jerusalemma liberata* has become also an emblem for the writer of this poem, who addresses himself in the second person ('ton emblème') and finds in Tasso's experience a mirror-image of his own subjection to forces and visions beyond his control and beyond his understanding ('aux songes obscurs'). In other words, had the younger, ambitious Baudelaire who had lamented in 'Le Reniement de saint Pierre' that 'l'action n'est pas la sœur du rêve' now become the older, ailing Baudelaire who has looked the 'terreurs du gouffre' fully in the face?

Starobinski and Baudelaire

> L'intuition poétique de Baudelaire, sur bien des aspects, anticipe sur ce que les cliniciens apprendront à reconnaître.
> (Jean Starobinski, 'Les Proportions de l'immortalité')

Such biographical speculations must necessarily remain just that: speculative. For the reader of Baudelaire's work what matters is the poetry itself—his 'performance' of melancholy—and how we may most coherently understand the many words, themes, images, and poetic patterns that structure and inform it: in fact, those very 'Nombres' and 'Êtres' that are the work of the creative imagination itself. Of all commentators Jean Starobinski has devoted the most sustained attention to Baudelaire's representations of melancholy.[39] In *La Mélancolie au*

---

[39] See above n. 2. But see also Stamelman, 'The Shroud of Allegory'; Robert Kopp, 'Le Spleen baudelairien: De la mélancolie à la dépression', in Clair and Kopp (eds), *De la Mélancolie*, 171-89; and

miroir he offers a bifocal perspective on Baudelairean melancholy: in its relation to pictorial art, and as an essentially *reflexive* condition repeatedly associated with the image of the mirror. Starobinski finds ample evidence in Baudelaire's poetic and critical works of the writer's constant awareness and detailed knowledge of the philosophical and iconographic tradition within which he is engaging with the condition of melancholy.[40] In the preamble to his brilliant reading of 'Le Cygne' ('ce grand poème de la mélancolie') Starobinski dwells in particular on the iconographic figure of the 'tête penchée' (such as Delacroix's Tasso) and on depictions of the melancholic subject as being variously in thrall to ecstatic vision or sunk in solitary torpor and despair: 'Exaltation et abattement: cette double virtualité appartient à un même tempérament, comme si l'un de ces états extrêmes était accompagné par la possibilité—péril ou chance—de l'état inverse.'[41] But he shows also how a number of traditional and even hackneyed melancholic motifs and themes—tombs, ruins, statues, bereavement, loss, exile, self-mirroring in water, etc—inform Baudelaire's account of statuary in the *Salon de 1859* and are newly mobilized and reinvigorated in 'Le Cygne' (completed in the same year) to evoke a condition that is simply too fundamental to our human condition to be left unspoken for fear of uttering a cliché.[42]

This insight is characteristic of Starobinski's approach to Baudelairean melancholy. He is interested in—and admiring of—how Baudelaire as a creative writer finds new ways to articulate an age-old condition. Often his focus is on the poet's artistry, as when he points in *Les Fleurs du Mal* to a recurrence of pairing whereby poems (for example, 'L'Héautontimorouménos' and 'L'Irrémédiable', 'Alchimie de la douleur' and 'Horreur sympathique') mirror each other, or when he notes how individual poems achieve their own internal reflexivity by being split in two ('L'Irrémédiable', 'Le Cygne').[43] He identifies a thematic mirroring of irony and melancholy ('ce poison noir') in 'L'Héautontimorouménos',[44] describing how the dissonance of melancholy (man out of tune with the world) is manifest in the inner dissonance of irony ('la discorde intrapsychique où l'Ironie personnifiée prend figure d'ennemi intime') and how the initial expression of externally directed dissatisfaction and aggression (sadism) mirrors itself subsequently within the poem in the torturing of self (masochism).[45] At the same time he is careful to link artistic procedures such as mirroring to broader thematic issues within the

the many valuable contributions of Ross Chambers. Cf. also Julia Kristeva's assertion in *Soleil noir: dépression et mélancolie* (Paris: Gallimard, 1987): 'il n'est d'imagination qui ne soit, ouvertement ou secrètement, mélancolique' (15).
[40] See *La Mélancolie au miroir*, 50, 65.   [41] See *La Mélancolie au miroir*, 56, 47.
[42] 'A partir de ces éléments anciens, qui tiennent presque du lieu commun, Baudelaire fera, dans "Le Cygne", un tableau d'une surprenante nouveauté. Il ressaisira [...] le sens d'une attitude trop souvent imitée pour n'être devenue objet de moquerie, mais liée à des valeurs affectives trop fondamentales pour n'avoir pas été, d'âge en âge, reformulées dans leur vérité par les artistes et les poètes.' (*La Mélancolie au miroir*, 52.)
[43] *La Mélancolie au miroir*, 27–8, 43, 58.   [44] *La Mélancolie au miroir*, 29–38.
[45] *La Mélancolie au miroir*, 33.

melancholic tradition. Thus in discussing 'L'Irrémédiable' he relates the various images of falling and imprisonment back to the poetry and painting, respectively, of Dante and Caspar David Friedrich, while foregrounding how the poem articulates the 'irremediable' schism at the core of melancholy, an insuperable division of the self between 'cœur' and 'miroir': '"Un cœur", en devenant "son miroir", se scinde pour se faire *autre* en face de lui-même.'[46]

In a number of other publications Starobinski's 'bifocal' approach has been evident also as he combines analysis of the poet's literary art with suggestive discussion of Baudelaire's intuitive anticipation of more recent psychiatric and psychoanalytic approaches to melancholy. Thus he addresses Baudelaire's accounts of dream, at once an essential ingredient in Romantic theories of creativity and then later a central focus of Freudian psychoanalysis. In associating dream experience with poetic creativity (for example, in 'Rêve parisien' and 'La Chambre double') the poet is seemingly perpetuating a Romantic commonplace, and yet here too, as in 'Le Cygne', he brings a new perspective, in this case by focusing on the *interruption* of dream, on the terrible return to reality and the inescapable, endlessly repeated waking prospect of death. Indeed sleep is itself seen as a form of death, and dream one manifestation of the 'gouffre': for even in sleep we cannot escape terrifying visions, just as for the living the worst nightmare of all might be the impossibility of dying. Or worse still, perhaps the 'after-death' is a place of endless labour (as in 'Le Squelette laboureur') so that even work and effort, traditionally (and religiously) advocated antidotes to melancholy during life, become part of a terrible, endless repetition, of an eternal melancholy.[47]

In similar vein Starobinski discusses the motif of a 'living death' in terms of a 'psychosis' of melancholy, reading the second 'Spleen' poem ('J'ai plus de souvenirs que si j'avais mille ans...') in the light of modern clinical accounts of depression and showing how 'l'intuition poétique de Baudelaire, sur bien des aspects, anticipe sur ce que les cliniciens apprendront à reconnaître'.[48] In his

---

[46] *La Mélancolie au miroir*, 39–45 (44).
[47] Jean Starobinski, 'Baudelaire metteur en scène', in *L'Encre de la mélancolie*, 421–35, formerly published as 'Rêve et immortalité chez Baudelaire', *Corps écrit*, 7 (1983), 45–56. (Starobinski acknowledges a parallel here with the discussions in Jackson, *La Mort Baudelaire*).
[48] 'Les Proportions de l'immortalité', in *L'Encre de la mélancolie*, 437–54 (444), formerly published under that title in *Furor*, 9 (May 1983), 5–19. This possibility underlies the subsequent overview provided by Pierre Dufour, '*Les Fleurs du Mal*: Dictionnaire de mélancolie', *Littérature*, 72 (1988), 30–54, in which Dufour finds that '[l]a conformité de la fantasmatique baudelairenne au tableau clinique de la mélancolie est en effet si grande dans tout le recueil qu'elle susciterait presque le soupçon': namely, 'Baudelaire mimerait-il, comme le pense Starobinski, les attitudes de la mélancolie "grâce à ce qu'il appelait son hystérie"?' (34). (This quotation is from Starobinski, 'Les Rimes du vide': see below, n. 55.) For Dufour *Les Fleurs du Mal* presents not an 'incurable' melancholy but a melancholy 'qui se maîtrise elle-même sur la scène de l'écriture' and thus (in Freudian terms) a kind of 'semi-sublimation' (36). He contends further that 'pratiquement tous les poèmes des [*Fleurs du Mal*] comportent un ou plusieurs éléments relevant de l'image culturelle de la mélancolie, tandis que quelques poèmes seulement ("L'Héautontimorouménos", "Le Cygne", "La Géante", "La servante au grand cœur...") illustrent directement la théorie freudienne de "Deuil et mélancolie" (36)', and, in

analysis of 'Horreur sympathique' he demonstrates how Baudelaire paradoxically depicts the melancholy of an 'âme vide' by deploying a 'plenitude' of rich rhymes on 'vide' ('avide', 'livide', 'Ovide', etc.) so that 'la richesse d'élocution contredit l'indigence impliquée (au niveau référentiel) par le mot "vide".'[49] Here (in an article published in a journal of psychoanalysis) Starobinski goes so far as to emphasize the potentially therapeutic function of a poetic response to melancholy (itself perceived as mental disorder). Thus, in relation to 'Horreur sympathique' he writes:

> Si Baudelaire reste fidèle à l'organisation rimée, ce n'est pas seulement par docilité esthétique, mais bien davantage parce que les contraintes traditionnelles de la versification lui permettent de surmonter des pulsions destructrices et déstructurantes, d'en différer la menace par le seul fait de lui donner forme. Dans la forme rigoureuse du sonnet, dire la destruction bâtit un objet indestructible: dire le vide se développe en un discours sans lacune.[50]

Later, in Parts III and IV, I shall take up this idea but in order to suggest that Baudelaire envisages poetic creativity as an effective response to melancholy seen not as an illness (still less a temporary mood) but as a universal human condition of 'ill-being'. At the same time I shall argue that it is the very fragmentation or 'disintegration' of human experience (wrought by repetition and the passage of time) that paradoxically enables the 'reintegration' of that experience through the power of the imagination and by conscious and concerted literary effort.

Finally, in another article published in the same journal of psychoanalysis, Starobinski examines the (frequent) presence of statues in pictorial depictions of melancholy and claims that 'Baudelaire est sans doute le poète qui a le plus obstinément interrogé le regard des statues.'[51] He notes in particular how in Baudelaire's discussion of statuary in the *Salon de 1859* many of the statues appear to watch over the observer as though issuing silent commands—indeed as though, like the super-ego, commanding silence: 'Lecteurs psychanalystes', he writes teasingly, 'vous serez peut-être tentés de lire dans ce commandement celui du refoulement et de la perlaboration.'[52] For Starobinski the silent gaze of the statue— and of the sphinx—speaks to Baudelaire subliminally of melancholy: 'L'expérience

---

similar vein: 'Aimée et redoutée, la mort est, en tout cas, le maître-mot du "dictionnaire de mélancolie", comme elle est pour Freud le "maître suprême"' (42).

[49] 'Les Rimes du vide', in *L'Encre de la mélancolie*, 455-69 (456), formerly published as 'Les Rimes du vide: Une lecture de Baudelaire', *Nouvelle revue de psychanalyse*, 11 (1975), 133-43.

[50] 'Les Rimes du vide', 458. Cf. 'Les Proportions de l'immortalité', 443-4, where Starobinski envisages a similarly compensatory, but not explicitly therapeutic, function for poetry: 'Mais le poème ["Spleen [II]"] qui dit cet effacement de la vie saura vivre d'une *autre vie*. Ce qu'il déclare mort, il l'élève à la vie sonore d'un texte.'

[51] 'Le Regard des statues', in *L'Encre de la mélancolie*, 471-98 (485), formerly published in *Nouvelle revue de psychanalyse*, 50 (1994), 45-64.

[52] 'Le Regard des statues', 486.

mélancolique est au premier chef un condensé d'agression et de souffrance: elle est en même temps [...] une sensation de déperdition vitale, de pétrification.' And Starobinski reads 'A une passante' (in which the passing woman is 'Agile et noble, avec sa jambe de statue' (l. 5)) as a supremely eloquent account of the birth of melancholy: 'Cet attachement à un passé désormais impossédable, cette inaptitude à s'en détacher, cette volonté d'inverser l'impossibilité en un fantôme de possibilité, c'est sans doute l'une des plus magnifiques expressions qui aient jamais été données de la conversion de l'état amoureux en état mélancolique.'[53]

Starobinski thus offers many subtly modulated readings of Baudelaire's poetic evocations of melancholy, itself understood sometimes as illness,[54] sometimes as a mood of longing and regret. But he stops short of discussing how melancholy sits within the particular frameworks of *Les Fleurs du Mal* and *Le Spleen de Paris*, or within the broader context of Baudelaire's philosophical, religious, and moral thought. Nor, other than to say that the 'plenitude' of poetic form may fill the 'vide' at the heart of melancholy, does he analyse the relationship between melancholy and art. Never, to my knowledge, does he consider *why*, for Baudelaire, melancholy is an essential attribute of beauty. Even when discussing the role of the artist in 'Une mort héroïque', for example, Starobinski treats the melancholic nature of the Prince—as well as the conspiratorial association of Fancioulle himself with 'ces individus d'humeur atrabilaire' (i. 319)—as incidental within a putative allegory of the death of art.

In Chapter 5, therefore, I shall focus in turn on a number of these broader questions: the relationship between melancholy and beauty; how Baudelaire's conception of melancholy differs from that of his immediate (Romantic) predecessors; how he sees melancholy in relation to what he calls 'le Malheur' and 'le Mal'; and, finally, how as an alternative lawgiver he proposes a form of response to melancholy that might enable us to achieve some measure of moral progress through art.

---

[53] 'Le Regard des statues', 497, 496.
[54] Starobinski is reluctant nevertheless to identify Baudelaire himself with such illness, and concludes 'Les Rimes du vide' with a statement of his position (at least in 1975): 'Je ne tiens nullement à faire de Baudelaire, poète du spleen, un mélancolique. Je préférerais dire qu'il mime admirablement—avec le secours de ce qu'il appelait son 'hystérie'—les attitudes de la mélancolie et ses mécanismes profonds' (469).

5
Melancholy and Satan

ô Satan, patron de ma détresse

('Épilogue [I]', l. 5)

Melancholy and Beauty

Ces sublimes défauts qui font le grand poète. La mélancolie, toujours inséparable du sentiment du beau, et une personnalité ardente, diabolique.

(ii. 238)[1]

For Baudelaire melancholy is a necessary element in our experience of beauty and constitutes a defining feature of modern art. Already in the *Salon de 1846* he identifies melancholy as the key attribute of Delacroix's paintings, describing it as 'cette mélancolie singulière et opiniâtre qui s'exhale de toutes ses œuvres, et qui s'exprime et par le choix de sujets, et par l'expression des figures, et par le geste, et par le style de la couleur' (ii. 440). Indeed it is this all-pervasive melancholy that has made Delacroix 'le vrai peintre du XIXe siècle' (ii. 440). In his essay on Banville, fifteen years later, Baudelaire considers this poet to be 'un parfait "classique"' (ii. 169) precisely because melancholy is absent from his work: 'Comme l'art antique, il n'exprime que ce qui est beau, joyeux, noble, grand, rythmique' (ii. 168). Dissonance and discordance, irony, nostalgia, regret... all the ingredients that Baudelaire here identifies as characteristic of the 'atmosphère satanique ou romantique' of contemporary art are missing. In his 1859 essay on Gautier, Baudelaire had traced this modern melancholy back to Chateaubriand ('Chateaubriand a chanté la gloire douloureuse de la mélancolie et de l'ennui' (ii. 117)), but here he names Beethoven as the artist who first began to 'remuer les mondes de mélancolie et de désespoir incurable amassés comme des nuages dans

---

[1] This comment on Byron occurs in unpublished notes for a riposte to the critic Jules Janin, who in 'Henri Heine et la jeunesse des poètes' (*L'Indépendance belge*, 12 and 13 Feb. 1865) had condemned Heine and other 'foreign' poets for their ironic and melancholic verse and championed the cheerfulness of French poets such as Béranger. 'Pourquoi donc toujours la joie?', Baudelaire writes: 'Pourquoi la tristesse n'aurait-elle pas sa beauté? Et l'horreur aussi? Et tout? Et n'importe quoi?' (ii. 237). And he cites 'Byron, Tennyson, Poe et Cie' as '[é]toiles de première grandeur' in the '[c]iel mélancolique de la poésie moderne' (ii. 237).

le ciel intérieur de l'homme' (ii. 168). And his proposed genealogy of nineteenth-century melancholy continues with Maturin in the novel, Byron in poetry, and Poe in both poetry and what Baudelaire calls 'le roman analytique' and we might term the 'novel of ideas'. This is the literature of Lucifer, 'le Lucifer latent qui est installé dans tout cœur humain' (ii. 168), a form of 'art moderne' that is defined by its 'tendance essentiellement démoniaque' (ii. 168). But Banville has set his face against this 'atmosphère satanique ou romantique' by ignoring the double nature of the artist (and of man) and deciding simply—'comme un original de la nature la plus courageuse'—to 'chanter la bonté des dieux' (ii. 168-9). His poetry thus constitutes 'un retour très volontaire vers l'état paradisiaque' (ii. 168) but *without* the accompanying ironic awareness that this paradise has been lost.

Not so for Baudelaire, as he makes clear in *Fusées*, f. 16, his most extended (but unpublished) reflection on the nature of beauty.[2] This piece begins with a famous and central definition: 'J'ai trouvé la définition du Beau,—de mon Beau. C'est quelque chose d'ardent et de triste, quelque chose d'un peu vague, laissant carrière à la conjecture.' As befits the idea that beauty is an effect, Baudelaire is thus careful to define beauty in its effect on *him* ('de mon Beau'), and in a move that is crucial to a coherent reading of *Les Fleurs du Mal* Baudelaire begins at once to explain his definition by focusing on male sexual desire in its response to female 'beauty': 'un visage de femme. Une tête séduisante et belle'. The sight of this 'tête de femme' (not of itself beautiful, we recall, but in this case appearing so to the aroused male) inspires a confusing mixture of feelings, thoughts, and imaginings:

> c'est une tête qui fait rêver à la fois,—mais d'une manière confuse,—de volupté et de tristesse; qui comporte une idée de mélancolie, de lassitude, même de satiété,—soit une idée contraire, c'est-à-dire une ardeur, un désir de vivre, associé avec une amertume refluante, comme venant de privation ou de désespérance. Le mystère, le regret, sont aussi des caractères du Beau.

Once again, what appears to be a binary opposition—ardour/sadness—turns out to be a false distinction. At first the male gaze perceives the possibility of sexual pleasure ('volupté') but also and simultaneously ('à la fois') post-coital 'tristesse', a form of 'mélancolie' here associated with exhaustion and satiety. By supposed contrast the 'tête de femme' may also inspire ardour and a desire to live, as though sexual desire constituted a form of affirmation and renewal, except that this ardour may simply be prompted by frustration and desperation: sex as a palliative to lack of sex. The melancholy that is for Baudelaire necessarily a part of modern

---

[2] Guyaux *Fusées*, ed. Guyaux, 61–3; i. 657–8. Guyaux suggests, on the basis of the manuscript, that Baudelaire may have been preparing this text for publication (ed. Guyaux, 10).

perceptions of beauty thus springs from what we might call the 'tragedy of desire':[3] we want because we lack, and in anticipating the satisfaction of desire we already perceive the return of that lack, in an endless loop that becomes a downward spiral into ennui and the living death that is the lack of all desire. In this case, for the man observing the woman, her own appearance of melancholy represents a kind of vainglorious challenge, as though he might be the answer to an ex-maiden's prayers: 'cette idée de volupté, qui dans un visage de femme est une provocation d'autant plus attirante que le visage est généralement plus mélancolique'.

Even when, for the heterosexual male gaze, the face or head in question is that of another man, here too for Baudelaire any perception of beauty will derive from a similar combination:

> cette tête contiendra aussi quelque chose d'ardent et de triste,—des besoins spirituels, des ambitions ténébreusement refoulées,—l'idée d'une puissance grondante, et sans emploi,—quelquefois l'idée d'une insensibilité vengeresse (car le type idéal du Dandy n'est pas à négliger dans ce sujet),—quelquefois aussi,—et c'est l'un des caractères de beauté les plus intéressants—le mystère, et enfin (pour que j'aie le courage d'avouer jusqu'à quel point je me sens moderne en esthétique), *le Malheur*.

Once again desire, and in particular frustrated or doomed (non-sexual) desire, is central to the combination: 'besoins spirituels', 'ambitions [...] refoulées', 'puissance grondante, et sans emploi'. The beauty of the dandy, it is suggested, may

---

[3] In using the phrase 'tragedy of desire' I have in mind a quite different 'tragedy' from that envisaged by D. J. Mossop in his *Baudelaire's Tragic Hero: A Study of the Architecture of 'Les Fleurs du Mal'* (Oxford: Clarendon Press, 1961). There, on the basis of some highly moralistic and religiously orthodox assumptions that, in my view, are wholly absent from Baudelaire's thinking, Mossop argues that 'the poet-hero' of *Les Fleurs du Mal* 'becomes a man whose instinctive tastes in pleasurable excitement (the Ideal) become more and more degraded insofar as they make excitement and pleasure itself conditional upon an ever-increasing admixture of pain. In the language of psychology, he develops [a] marked sado-masochistic complex [...] This vice is of the greatest importance in the architecture since it constitutes the poet-hero's tragic "flaw". It is the perversion of his aspiration towards the Ideal, which is, or should be, his noblest attitude' (19). Similarly, the 'poet-hero' 'finds that the conflict between the values of appetence and those of religious morality is contained in another conflict between the latter and aesthetic values. It is in this clash of values that God and Satan join battle for the soul of the poet-hero, and from it Baudelaire develops the tragic action' (27). For Mossop, 'the poet-hero's search for his ideal of relative beauty [...] is the same as his ideal of vice' (212), and 'the entire tragedy presented by *Les Fleurs du Mal* turns upon this very fact, for the same experiences which serve the poet-hero so well in the noble activity of writing poetry, nevertheless spell his moral and spiritual ruin' (217). As will become evident in Chapter 6, my conception of the 'tragedy of desire' differs also from that of Jacques Dupont, who in 'Baudelaire et Colette: Du côté de Lesbos', *L'Année Baudelaire*, 5 (1999), 155–67, writes of the 'femmes damnées' that 'leur démesure, leur dérèglement essentiel fait d'elles des figures tragiques, dont le destin catastrophique sanctionne l'*hybris*, témoigne de la faute principielle et originaire, de l'*hamartia* sans laquelle l'univers tragique ne saurait exister' (157–8). Where he argues that Baudelaire 'ne s'intéressait, en dernière instance, aux "Lesbiennes" que comme avatar singulier d'une révolte contre la nature, comme des créatures touchées du stigmate d'une énergie du désir' (166), I shall contend that for Baudelaire lesbian sexuality is both 'natural' and, like heterosexual desire, therefore a form of hell.

spring from the perception in the viewer that a cold and impassive exterior that shuns human contact and proclaims a total independence of self bespeaks a bruised sensibility and a spirit of vengeance manifesting as the determination to reject all future attainment of the fulfilling sentimental life that has been denied him in the past.[4] The melancholy of these subjects—woman, man, dandy—thus derives (in the observer as well as in the observed subjects themselves) from an awareness of lack, loss, failure, and impossibility.

An important element in the effect of beauty occasioned by these perceptions of another person's melancholy is the unknownness ('le mystère') to the observer of the *particular* causes of this 'tristesse', and so it is precisely in this way that the misfortune of another (*'le Malheur'*) can become a stimulus to speculation on the part of the viewer: a source of curiosity and interest, a source of imaginings, a source of poetry. And indeed of painting also, since in *Exposition universelle* Baudelaire takes this conception of 'le Malheur' as a potent source of aesthetic beauty and places it at the heart of his account of Delacroix's depiction of women. Whether historical or religious subjects like Cleopatra, Mary Magdalen, or the Virgin Mary, or else literary figures such as Shakespeare's Ophelia and Desdemona or Goethe's Gretchen, Delacroix has transformed these seemingly public and well-known women into 'des femmes d'intimité' (ii. 594), women of mystery and misfortune: 'On dirait qu'elles portent dans les yeux un secret douloureux, impossible à enfouir dans les profondeurs de la dissimulation. Leur pâleur est comme une révélation des batailles intérieures' (ii. 594). And it is this misfortune, presented as an illness, that becomes the source of their fascination for the viewer: 'ces femmes *malades* du cœur ou de l'esprit ont dans les yeux le plombé de la fièvre ou la nitescence anormale et bizarre de leur *mal*, dans le regard, l'intensité du surnaturalisme' (ii. 594; my emphases).

Melancholy and misfortune thus lend them an unnaturally intense brightness of eye (also a symptom of fever) that implies some visionary power and thereby also, therefore, the putative existence of some other domain beyond the quotidian and the visible. (For example, just *what* is causing the Mona Lisa to smile like that?) For Baudelaire this makes Delacroix the exemplary painter of 'la femme moderne', and especially of 'la femme moderne dans sa manifestation héroïque, dans le sens infernal ou divin' (ii. 594). The modern woman is the heroine of her 'inner battles', conflicted as she is (no more and no less than her male counterpart) by the 'deux postulations simultanées' of spiritualité and animality, and such women are rendered 'heroic' (as Baudelaire puts it here in sexist, stereotypical terms that are characteristic of his day) 'par le charme de leur crime ou l'odeur de la sainteté'. The mystery of their 'painful secrets' leads the viewer to look beyond the surface of their visual appearance and plumb the depths or explore the

---

[4] In the next section of *Fusées* (f. 17) Baudelaire characterizes this, in English, as 'Self-purification and anti-humanity' (*Fusées*, ed. Guyaux, 65; i. 659).

heights—at any rate, to imagine the mysterious beyond ('surnaturalisme')—of their inscrutable inner lives. In this respect Delacroix's women may be compared with Baudelaire's own 'femmes damnées' on the island of Lesbos as they gaze thoughtfully and mysteriously into the distance: 'Comme un bétail pensif sur le sable couchées, | Elles tournent leurs yeux vers l'horizon des mers' ('Femmes damnées', ll. 1–2).

In *Fusées*, f. 16 Baudelaire may ironize the 'modernity' of this view of beauty ('pour que j'aie le courage d'avouer jusqu'à quel point je me sens moderne en esthétique'), just as he self-deprecatingly concedes that others may see him as 'obsessed' by it (i. 658), but it is nonetheless fundamental to an understanding of *Les Fleurs du Mal* and in particular of the place of Satan in Baudelaire's thinking about melancholy and beauty. He ends *Fusées*, f. 16 by promoting melancholy over joy as the true 'companion' of beauty, rather as in *De l'essence du rire* he sees laughter rather than joy as the more appropriate (and perhaps only possible) response to our melancholic condition: 'Je ne prétends pas que la Joie ne puisse pas s'associer avec la Beauté, mais je dis que la Joie est un des ornements les plus vulgaires,—tandis que la Mélancolie en est pour ainsi dire l'illustre compagne, à ce point que je ne conçois guère [...] un type de Beauté où il n'y ait du *Malheur*.' And thus, 'obsessed' as he is with this interconnectedness of beauty and misfortune, Baudelaire is led to conclude that 'le plus parfait type de Beauté virile est *Satan*,—à la manière de Milton'. Satan, and in particular Milton's Satan in *Paradise Lost*, is the angel who resisted, who knew the joy of heaven but wanted more, wanted to *know* more. This is the Satan who revolted against God and was banished from heaven, Satan as Lucifer, the angel of light who was cast into outer darkness, and a Satan whose 'beauté virile' thus derives from 'des besoins spirituels', 'des ambitions [...] refoulées', 'l'idée d'une puissance grondante, et sans emploi'. In short, this is the Satan who for Baudelaire epitomizes modern melancholy, or what had come to be known, since Chateaubriand, as the *mal du siècle*.

Melancholy in Context

> cette coupable mélancolie qui s'engendre au milieu des passions, lorsque ces passions, sans objet, se consument d'elles-mêmes dans un cœur solitaire.
>
> (Chateaubriand, *Génie du christianisme*, i. 310)[5]

For Chateaubriand and Mme de Staël, as for Baudelaire also, melancholy is the status quo, the very condition of modern man. For these earlier writers, as for

---

[5] *Génie du christianisme*, ed. Pierre Reboul (2 vols, Paris: Garnier-Flammarion, 1966).

Vigny and Banville, paradise was ancient Greece: a present existence in which the poet sang joyously and spontaneously of nature, of man's place within nature and of the gods we invented to personify and domesticate the forces that shape our lives. With Christianity came a fall: the new belief in a life after death, a belief that in its turn serves to make the life *before* death seem inadequate—a source of melancholy. For Chateaubriand and Mme de Staël melancholy is thus (like Baudelaire's laughter) the invention of Christianity, and the human condition, from being a state of joyful, pagan celebration, has become a search for solace and solution: for Chateaubriand, as a Roman Catholic, to be found not only in religion itself but especially in the sense of divine mystery imparted by Christian art; for Mme de Staël, a Protestant, to be found in 'enthousiasme'—her faith in human altruism and the possibility of moral and social progress—and in the secular celebration of human life exemplified by the lyric verse of Goethe and Schiller. For Vigny, the best response to melancholy lay in combining a former pre-Christian 'simplicity' with the new post-Christian, self-conscious 'seriousness' of 'l'Esprit pur', the unflinching intellectual acceptance of human suffering and mortality without false hope of an afterlife. In the work of both Staël and Vigny there is thus an explicit ambition to escape Chateaubriand's exclusive antithesis of pagan versus Christian and to move towards a third, post-Christian stage in human development—and in the case of Staël in particular (who has so often and so unhelpfully been seen as 'pre-Romantic') towards a new form of 'post-Romantic' poetry.

In Staël's analysis 'Classical' poetry equates to a pagan, materialist, outward-looking apprehension of the physical world, 'Romantic' poetry to a Christian, spiritualist, inward-looking response: 'les modernes ont puisé, dans le repentir chrétien, l'habitude de se replier continuellement sur eux-mêmes'.[6] 'Classical' poetry knows nothing of 'cette réflexion inquiète'[7] that characterizes 'Romantic' poetry and which the ancients would have regarded as a form of madness. Staël wants to take literature, and poetry in particular, not only beyond slavish adherence to the literary models of ancient Greece and Rome but also beyond the influence of Christianity and its introspective feelings of guilt and melancholy—and towards a literature informed by human positivity and a secular sense of the divine. In her view (in both *De la littérature* and *De l'Allemagne*) this Christian inspiration in art is comparatively recent and to be seen as temporary, due now to be superseded within the onward march of progress, and not, as for Chateaubriand and other counter-Enlightenment thinkers, something temporarily lost during the Revolution and waiting to be reinstalled in perpetuity. At the same time, in *De l'Allemagne*, Staël presents the poetry of Goethe as representing the third stage in a putative historical progression from poetry to philosophy and

---

[6] *De l'Allemagne*, ed. Balayé, i. 212.   [7] *De l'Allemagne*, ed. Balayé, i. 212.

then forwards to poetry once more, but a new kind of poetry in which naivety is a superior form of knowledge and strength:

> on retrouve dans ses poésies beaucoup de traces du caractère des habitants du Midi; il est plus en train de l'existence que les septentrionaux; il sent la nature avec plus de vigueur et de sérénité; son esprit n'en a pas moins de profondeur, mais son talent a plus de vie; on y trouve un certain genre de naïveté qui réveille à la fois le souvenir de la simplicité antique et de celle du Moyen Âge: ce n'est pas la naïveté de l'innocence, c'est celle de la force.[8]

This account of Goethe's 'strong' naivety in turn recalls Staël's treatment of melancholy some ten years earlier in *Corinne* where, by way of countering the model of Chateaubriand's 'negative' melancholy (the *mal du siècle* experienced by René and Chateaubriand himself, and also by Corinne's British lover, Lord Nelvil), she conceives of a 'positive' melancholy to which her eponymous heroine gives expression. Within the symbolic geography of that novel, Corinne—half-English, half-Italian—argues for a southern rather than a northern melancholy:

> Ce n'est pas que le midi n'ait aussi sa mélancolie; dans quels lieux la destinée de l'homme ne produit-elle pas cette impression! mais il n'y a dans cette mélancolie ni mécontentement, ni anxiété, ni regret. Ailleurs, c'est la vie qui, telle qu'elle est, ne suffit pas aux facultés de l'âme; ici, ce sont les facultés de l'âme qui ne suffisent pas à la vie, et la surabondance des sensations inspire une rêveuse indolence dont on se rend à peine compte en l'éprouvant.[9]

For Chateaubriand it had been (in his *Essai sur les révolutions* (1797)) this melancholic sense of lack (of anxiety, discontent, regret) that had brought about the French Revolution and needed to be assuaged by a reinstated Christianity if the fanatical violence of the Terror was not to be repeated. For Staël, from her progressive perspective, it was important to posit an alternative logic. Accordingly she envisages a putative prelapsarian joy in human life ('la surabondance des sensations') not as lost but as ever-present—if we can but find the spiritual and intellectual means (Goethe's 'strong' naivety) to attune ourselves to the plenitude of our sensual life, of our physical existence in nature. Chateaubriand's 'vague des passions' becomes her 'rêveuse indolence', but one that can be raised to a level of conscious and fulfilling 'enthousiasme' by poetry itself.

As Staël's use of the Schillerian concept of naivety indicates, Baudelaire's approach to the relationship between melancholy and poetry is deeply imbued with the terms of the Chateaubriand–Staël debate, and he takes elements from

---

[8] *De l'Allemagne*, ed. Balayé, i. 234.
[9] *Corinne*, ed. Simone Balayé (Paris: Gallimard [Folio classique], 1985), 287–8.

both writers as he comes to his own original conception of melancholic beauty. But his particular approach is founded on what might be termed a 'supra-Christian' view. Once again refusing familiar binaries (pagan/Christian, good/evil, ephemeral/eternal) he takes the Christian terminology of Original Sin as shorthand for man's 'irremediable' subjection to what I have called the 'tragedy of desire' (and which I discuss further below in relation to *Les Fleurs du Mal*). Unlike Chateaubriand and Staël Baudelaire does not look to some historical cause for our melancholy (such as the advent of Christianity): it is a simple fact of human life and springs repeatedly from the fundamental nature of human desire. For him Satan is not only 'le plus parfait type de Beauté virile' but also the very model of the divided human being: one who knows both heaven and hell, the angel who had everything and yet rebelled because he would not accept the heavenly status quo, the contrarian who wanted an alternative. Indeed his name derives from the Hebrew for 'adversary' or 'one who resists'. As the Satan of the Old and New Testaments he is both pre-Christian and Christian, but as 'Satan' or 'le Diable' or 'le Démon' in *Les Fleurs du Mal* he is eternal and contemporary: what today we might call the 'elephant in the room'—seemingly absent, denied even, but insidiously present. Or as Baudelaire puts it in a projected preface to *Les Fleurs du Mal* (and as quoted earlier): 'Il est plus difficile d'aimer Dieu que de croire en lui. Au contraire, il est plus difficile pour les gens de ce siècle de croire au Diable que de l'aimer. Tout le monde le sert et personne n'y croit. Sublime subtilité du Diable' (i. 182–3).[10]

'Le Satan de Bénichou'

> le Satan de Baudelaire est avant tout le Satan méchant.
>
> (Paul Bénichou)

Baudelaire is absent from Paul Bénichou's classic investigation of French Romanticism, which ended in 1995 with his account of Mallarmé as its 'dernier héros spirituel'.[11] But in a lecture given at the Sorbonne in 1996 on 'Le Satan de Baudelaire'[12] Bénichou situates the poet squarely within the Romantic tradition, and for the reason that he was indeed a poet-lawgiver: 'étant lui-même romantique, [Baudelaire] croyait que la poésie devait rendre compte de la condition

---

[10] Cf. a similar comment in Baudelaire's notes on *Les Liaisons dangereuses* (ii. 68). For a possible source, see Max Milner, *Le Diable dans la littérature française de Cazotte à Baudelaire (1772–1861)* (2 vols, Paris: Corti, 1960), ii. 440–1.

[11] Paul Bénichou, *Selon Mallarmé* (Paris: Gallimard, 1995), 46.

[12] This lecture was published posthumously in André Guyaux and Bertrand Marchal (eds), *'Les Fleurs du mal': Actes du colloque de la Sorbonne, des 10 et 11 janvier 2003* (Paris: Presses de l'Université de Paris-Sorbonne, 2003), 9–23.

humaine, à sa manière, comme la religion et la philosophie'.[13] Earlier, in *L'École du désenchantement: Sainte-Beuve, Nodier, Musset, Nerval, Gautier* (1992), Bénichou had presented the authors named in his title (itself derived from Balzac) as representative of a generation who felt alienated by the materialist values of the Bourgeois Monarchy and now despaired of their own power to change the society they lived in. At the end of that book he had also briefly identified a subsequent generation of writers, a 'second Romanticism'—including Baudelaire, Flaubert, Banville, and Leconte de Lisle—in whom 'disenchantment' was replaced by simple 'pessimism' and a bitter, hopeless sense of the writer's isolation and irrelevance within society. In 'Le Satan de Baudelaire' Bénichou resumes his narrative (intending perhaps finally to complete the book on Baudelaire that he had always meant to write)[14] and grounds this 'pessimism' in the widespread disillusionment that followed the 1848 Revolution: 'La France, vers 1850, avait désabusé les poètes de la mission idéale qu'ils s'étaient attribuée. Les poètes répondaient à l'humanité qui les rejetait en la maudissant et au Dieu qui les désespérait en désespérant de lui. Le retour du vieux démon chez Baudelaire annonce sa volonté misanthropique et pessimiste.'[15]

While explicitly stating that he is not here undertaking to define Baudelaire's religious beliefs other than in respect of Satan, Bénichou nevertheless presents a Baudelaire whose poetry and thinking are predicated on a traditional Christian view of evil: 'le Satan de Baudelaire est avant tout le Satan méchant';[16] so that in presenting this evil Baudelaire has found a way to emulate the great poet-lawgivers of Romanticism: 'Baudelaire est le seul qui ait conquis la postérité, au même titre que ses aînés, pour avoir osé s'emparer du mal dans un esprit de vérité en même temps que de poésie. Il a agrandi le romantisme d'une large région de la nature humaine et de la société, et il a prolongé magnifiquement Hugo dans cette direction.'[17] In Bénichou's view Baudelaire did sincerely wish *Les Fleurs du Mal* to be seen as the work of a Catholic writer (rather than for such an interpretation simply to provide him with a convenient defence against prosecution), and he maintains that the poet emerges from all his published writings as 'une sorte de catholique qu'on appellerait aujourd'hui intégriste et ennemi des institutions de son siècle'.[18] Nevertheless Bénichou does concede the disparate and sometimes contradictory nature of Baudelaire's statements concerning religion, noting especially a number of blasphemous passages (in 'Les Aveugles', 'Les Petites Vieilles', 'Don Juan aux enfers', 'Le Rebelle', 'Les Litanies de Satan') in which God is denounced as a tyrant and Satan glorified, most notably in the 'Prière' at the end of 'Les Litanies de Satan' which, Bénichou argues, presents 'un programme de

---

[13] 'Le Satan de Baudelaire', 12.   [14] I am indebted to José-Luis Diaz for this information.
[15] See *Unacknowledged Legislators*, 37–8, and 'Le Satan de Baudelaire', 12.
[16] 'Le Satan de Baudelaire', 11.   [17] 'Le Satan de Baudelaire', 12.
[18] 'Le Satan de Baudelaire', 18.

philosophie humanitaire: la science, au lieu d'être un péché, devient la chose essentielle, le pilier de la doctrine'.[19]

Bénichou concludes therefore that '[l]e Diable de Baudelaire est double': one half is 'le Mal sans le remède de Dieu', the other is 'le Bien quand Dieu a été rejeté'.[20] But for Bénichou these two 'faces' of Satan are contradictory and therefore symptomatic not only of the great 'disarray' of 'disenchanted' Romanticism but also of a conflicted Baudelaire: 'Baudelaire est, sous le Prince des Ténèbres, catholique sans espoir et ne peut retrouver l'espoir qu'avec un Dieu défait et un Satan disculpé, qui ne mérite d'ailleurs plus son nom. Ceci nous donne une figure transparente de l'Humanité sortie de tutelle.'[21] Here Bénichou contemplates the vista of a secular intellectual emancipation of the kind that he had hitherto placed firmly at the heart of his account of French Romanticism, and particularly of his discussion of the work of Quinet and Michelet in *Le Temps des prophètes*, whose humanitarian ideals, like those of the later Lamartine and the later Hugo, he champions. But—and here is perhaps why Bénichou never did write his book on Baudelaire—the poet of *Les Fleurs du Mal* is supposedly not to be counted among these secular prophets: 'Le temps pouvait s'ouvrir d'une Humanité non voilée, bâtissant, si elle pouvait, sa justification sur ses propres efforts. Ce projet, soutenable ou non, n'était certainement pas dans l'esprit de Baudelaire.'[22] 'Le Satan de Baudelaire' ends with the reflection that what the (first generation of French) Romantics tried to do was to maintain the 'validity' of the traditional distinction between Good and Evil by replacing the 'supernatural scenario' of God and the Devil with a purely symbolic 'mythology'. But, sadly: 'ce que Baudelaire nous montre, aussitôt après eux, c'est l'échec de leur entreprise. Ce qui doit remplacer la mythologie défunte du Bien et du Mal est, aujourd'hui encore, à peine en vue.'[23]

For Bénichou, Baudelaire's two-faced Satan thus represents a failure to reconcile the existence of evil in a godless world with the good that can come from non-religious intellectual enquiry—as it were, from having eaten of the Tree of Knowledge ('la science, au lieu d'être un péché, devient la chose essentielle'). It is certainly true that, at least following Louis-Napoléon's coup d'état of 2 December 1851, Baudelaire was too much of a sceptic about moral and political progress for him to have espoused the kind of humanitarian programme for literature that Bénichou himself so passionately believed in and increasingly despaired of. But I shall seek to show that Baudelaire's scepticism is not the same as pessimism or despair, and that the poet of *Les Fleurs du Mal* and *Le Spleen de Paris* did espouse and enact a *positive* function for literature: not the humanitarian doctrine of Bénichou's intellectual heroes but a strictly literary

---

[19] 'Le Satan de Baudelaire', 22–3.   [20] 'Le Satan de Baudelaire', 23.
[21] 'Le Satan de Baudelaire', 23.   [22] 'Le Satan de Baudelaire', 23.
[23] 'Le Satan de Baudelaire', 23.

programme—an alternative lawgiving—in which poetry is proffered as a locus of reconciliation between our melancholy recognition of 'le Mal' and the intellectual and aesthetic opportunities that arise from this very possibility of self-knowledge. For Baudelaire, I shall argue, poetry is indeed of benefit to humanity: not to society at large but to the individual, not for the greater good but for the private good—a private good that may combine with other private goods to constitute a new community, if not of hope, then of honesty: 'Hypocrite lecteur,—mon semblable,—mon frère.' In my view Baudelaire's Satan is not the Satan of Catholic homilies but a combination of the Satan of Genesis and the Satan of Milton: Lucifer, the angel of light who *resisted* God.[24]

Melancholy, 'le Malheur', and 'le Mal'

Je n'aurais pas fini de sitôt, si je voulais énumérer tous les beaux et bons côtés de ce qu'on appelle vice et laideur morale[.]
(*Choix de maximes consolantes sur l'amour*, i. 550)

l'ardeur du désir [...] cette humeur, hystérique selon les médecins, satanique selon ceux qui pensent un peu mieux que les médecins, qui nous pousse sans résistance vers une foule d'actions dangereuses ou inconvenantes.
('Le Mauvais Vitrier', i. 286)

Satan is, of course, associated with 'evil' and is indeed a paradoxical figure within French Romanticism.[25] But in addressing the 'melancholy beauty' of *Les Fleurs du Mal* it is necessary to be clear about Baudelaire's use of certain terms, such as 'spleen', 'malheur', and 'mal'. 'Spleen' itself is relatively straightforward and may be read as a synonym for melancholy. By privileging this term, deriving from the humoral theory in which the spleen is the source of bile, Baudelaire specifically foregrounds the physical and innate character of melancholy, showing the human propensity to depression as being not the product of Christianity—still less what Christianity can 'cure'—but an experience inherent in human life itself, something in our blood. The terms 'malheur' and 'mal' are more problematic, however, not

---

[24] Bénichou acknowledges this particular Satan at the very beginning of his lecture, describing him as 'legendary' because he is not to be found in either the Old or the New Testaments. While acknowledging that Baudelaire was well aware of his 'legendary' or non-biblical status, Bénichou subsequently omits this figure of Satan as rebellious angel from his discussion.

[25] Cf. Damian Catani's comment on the role of Satan in what he terms 'early "Satanic" Romanticism': 'Satan was thus a paradoxical figure: both the traditional, biblical incarnation of evil, and the perfect contemporary agent of the good who had the requisite power and charisma to embody and articulate modern man's deep-seated spiritual and psychological frustrations'. See Catani, *Evil: A History in Modern French Literature and Thought* (London: Bloomsbury, 2013), 36. The classic study remains Milner, *Le Diable dans la littérature*: on Baudelaire see ii. 423–83.

least because in the case of 'malheur' as well as 'mal' Baudelaire sometimes capitalizes them and sometimes not.[26] So far we have seen Baudelaire refer to 'le Malheur' in terms of misfortune, pain, and suffering—from whatever cause, but including especially that of thwarted desire or ambition. And, as we have also seen, he goes so far as to say (in *Fusées*, f. 16) that he cannot envisage beauty without some element of this suffering. Yet pain and suffering are forms not only of 'le Malheur' but also of 'le Mal', in the sense that they are ills, negative and unwelcome aspects of the human condition—but without the strong moral sense of 'evil' that also attaches to the word 'mal', especially when capitalized as though to assert its traditional metaphysical and theological meanings.[27] For Baudelaire human suffering is 'evil' in the sense that Leibniz referred to 'necessary' evils, an aspect of existence that is intrinsic within life itself and not an effect of divine or human will.

It is important to retain this sense of 'le Mal' as 'ill-ness' when reading *Les Fleurs du Mal* because the poems in the collection so often depict what is legally and/or theologically defined as evil (for example, as 'crime' or 'sin') that we may be led (as so many of Baudelaire's readers have been) to see this 'mal' as 'wickedness', something 'immoral' apparently gloried in and perhaps even approved of by the poet (both as persona and as Baudelaire himself). But as his use of the term 'spleen' suggests—not to mention the frequent references to digestion in his art criticism[28] or the manuscript notes entitled 'Hygiène. Conduite. Méthode. Morale'[29]—Baudelaire had a deep sense of human existence as a physical as well as a moral or mental activity. Indeed it would be a critical truism to point out the extraordinary prominence of sensual experience in *Les Fleurs du Mal*. If happiness can be said to derive from a state of well-being, so for him suffering—physical and mental pain or anguish—may be defined as a state of 'ill-being'. In fact *The Flowers of Ill-Being* might well be a better English translation of his famous title than the usual *The Flowers of Evil*. And this question of the meaning of 'le Mal' takes us to the heart of Baudelaire's role as an alternative lawgiver. In the notes he prepared for the legal defence of his work in 1857 he claims that it was 'destiné à représenter L'AGITATION DE L'ESPRIT DANS LE MAL' (i. 195). A book must be judged as a whole, he argues, and possible instances of blasphemy or obscenity must be set against contrasting evidence of piety ('des élancements vers le Ciel')

---

[26] On this question see *Fusées*, ed. Guyaux, 44–5.
[27] See i. 797, where Pichois notes that in his correspondence Baudelaire almost always ('environ neuf fois sur dix') spells 'Mal' with a capital, even when using a lower-case f for 'fleurs', so that '*Mal* indique bien la dimension métaphysique du recueil.' Cf. also Compagnon, *Baudelaire devant l'innombrable*, 13: 'Baudelaire met toujours un *M* majuscule au *Mal*, dans le titre *Les Fleurs du Mal*, pour insister sur la valeur théologique du terme, c'est-à-dire sur le péché originel.'
[28] See, for example, the comment in *Le Peintre de la vie moderne* on the need for the artist to acquire technical skills 'pour que finalement l'exécution, l'exécution idéale, devienne aussi inconsciente, aussi "coulante" que l'est la digestion pour le cerveau de l'homme bien portant qui a dîné' (ii. 699).
[29] *Fusées*, ed. Guyaux, 123–7; i. 668–75.

and chaste propriety ('des fleurs platoniques'). Clearly he hopes to persuade his *bien-pensant* Catholic judges that what he has represented in these poems is a commendable human struggle against our inherent propensity to sin, but another reading might be that he has sought to depict the pain and suffering of the 'ill-being' that derives from the fundamental impetus of desire—which is not in itself to be condemned, still less repented of, but rather accepted as an integral and 'irremediable' part of being human. Desire is the life-force, and it hurts.

This is why the poet can begin the second of the two draft 'Épilogues' to the 1861 edition of *Les Fleurs du Mal* by describing himself as 'Tranquille comme un sage et doux comme un maudit' (i. 191), just as he begins the first by stating how 'Le cœur content, je suis monté sur la montagne'. Despite the faint, ironic echo of Moses' ascent of Mount Sinai to receive the laws of God, the mountain in question here is an unidentified hilltop vantage point from which to observe the city of Paris: 'la ville en son ampleur, | Hôpital, lupanar, purgatoire, enfer, bagne, | Où toute énormité fleurit comme une fleur' ('Épilogue, I', ll. 2–4)—the Paris that now, in this 1861 edition and thanks to the newly added 'Tableaux parisiens', has become the representative city of 'le Mal'.

The scenario of this poem recalls Vigny's poem 'Paris' (1831), in which the poet takes an anonymous traveller to the top of a tower to show him the quasi-apocalytic spectacle of 'Paris by night'. Playing God to the traveller's Moses yet focusing exclusively on the 'ici-bas', the poet presents a vision of feverish mental activity as human minds burn the midnight oil: this city is a forge of intellectual effort in which innovative thinkers (implicitly but unambiguously Lamennais, Constant, and the Saint-Simonians) are shaping a molten future into 'un monde tout nouveau' (l. 160). Faced with this awesome spectacle, the traveller is overcome with fear that such millenarian programmes may carry within them the seeds of future destruction, but the more sanguine poet retains his faith in intellectual enquiry while noting that only two things in life are certain: 'LA SOUFFRANCE ET LA MORT' (l. 238).[30]

Baudelaire's poet-observer in 'Épilogue [I]', by contrast, begins by addressing his thoughts to Satan, 'patron de ma détresse' (l. 5), and seeks intoxication and rejuvenation in the spectacle before him, like an ageing lecher in the arms of an old mistress: in this case, of the 'énorme catin' that is Paris, with its 'charme infernal' (l. 9). The terza rima of 'Épilogue [I]' recalls *The Divine Comedy* and suggests that the poet here is to Satan as Dante was to Virgil, being shown the inferno that is Paris, a prison-house of desire with its brothels and its hospitals, its 24/7 bacchanal of sex and syphilis, and all the innumerable pleasures 'Que ne comprennent pas les vulgaires profanes' (l. 15). Satan is the poet's patron, and desire is both

---

[30] For further discussion of 'Paris', see *Unacknowledged Legislators*, 517–21.

sacred (because it is a necessary part of being human) and also—'Hypocrite lecteur'—delectable. The poet acknowledges that he is in a state of 'détresse'—the ill-being of human existence—but rather than lament what he sees ('je n'allais pas là pour répandre un vain pleur' (l. 6)), he embraces the causes of this 'détresse'—of this 'tristesse'—with provocative ardour. And in the final two stanzas he addresses his city-mistress directly: 'Je t'aime, ô capitale infâme!' (l. 13).

In the incomplete draft that is 'Épilogue [II]' the poet make a similarly direct address to the city of desire ('Tes débauches sans soif et tes amours sans âme' (l. 4)) as well as a similar declaration of love ('Je t'aime, ô ma très belle, ô ma charmante...' (l. 2)), but this time he attributes the quest for intoxication to the city itself: 'Ton goût de l'infini, | Qui partout, dans le mal lui-même, se proclame...' (ll. 5–6). Desire and the quest for the infinite are two sides of the same, human coin, just as heaven and hell have been the two domiciles of Satan—and just as in 'Femmes damnées' ['Comme un bétail pensif...'] the sexually tormented inhabitants of Lesbos are described as '[c]hercheuses d'infini' (l. 23). Here in 'Épilogue [II]', following a long list of the many places, people, and activities that constitute the 'charme infernal' of this teeming, agitated, infernal city, the poet closes by addressing all these places, people and activities in the following well-known lines:

> Ô vous! soyez témoins que j'ai fait mon devoir
> Comme un parfait chimiste et comme une âme sainte.
> Car j'ai de chaque chose extrait la quintessence,
> Tu m'as donné ta boue et j'en ai fait de l'or.
>
> (i. 192)

Not only has the poet carried out an alchemical process of transformation, producing both an 'elixir' (agent of rejuvenation)[31] and precious gold (emblem of beauteous matter and lasting value), but he has fulfilled a saintly duty, the duty of the lawgiver described in the poem 'Lesbos' (the second poem in the 'Fleurs du mal' section of the 1857 edition and one of the six poems banned by the court): 'Car Lesbos entre tous m'a choisi sur la terre | Pour chanter le secret de ses vierges en fleurs' (ll. 41–2). Paris—'où toute énormité fleurit comme une fleur'—may have replaced Lesbos as the site of 'le Mal', but the alternative poet-lawgiver's holy task is constant: to bear witness, to display the realities of our 'irremediable' moral degradation, and to extract a melancholy beauty from that in which the 'profane' see mere ugliness and immorality.

In the end Baudelaire did not include an 'Épilogue' in the 1861 edition of *Les Fleurs du Mal*, but these drafts demonstrate how the new vision contained within

---

[31] On Vigny's view of poetry as an elixir, see *Unacknowledged Legislators*, 547–8.

its satanic verses (as well as a vision of 'le spleen de Paris' that will later require prose) continues to reflect—and indeed has grown out of—the 'secret' of Lesbos. This 'secret' will be discussed presently, but for the moment we might note also for future reference that the 'fleurs' in question in both 'Épilogue [I]' ('où toute énormité fleurit comme une fleur') and 'Lesbos' ('ses vierges en fleurs') are manifestations of—are forms of beautiful organic growth arising out of—'le Mal' and not in the first instance the poems themselves.

Melancholy and Progress

> La poésie et le progrès sont deux ambitieux qui se haïssent d'une haine instinctive, et, quand ils se rencontrent dans le même chemin, il faut que l'un des deux serve l'autre.
> (*Salon de 1859*, ii. 618)

In placing Satan and the question of 'le Mal' or 'le Malheur' at the heart of his poetic project Baudelaire is thus being a contrarian poet-lawgiver but a poet-lawgiver nonetheless. If his account of melancholy owes something to the negative *mal du siècle* of Chateaubriand he nevertheless rejects the Christian religion as a framework of belief and solace. But by the same token, and as a reader of De Maistre, he also firmly rejects Staël's Rousseauist belief in the innate goodness of man and with it any facile faith in the inevitability of moral and social progress. Human beings in their natural state are predisposed by animal need and base instinct to suffer and to 'sin': that is, to commit acts that will bring 'le Malheur' either on themselves or on others, or on both. This is what Baudelaire calls Original Sin, and, as he proclaims at the end of his review of Hugo's *Les Misérables*, he considers it ultimately ineradicable (ii. 224).

But, as this comment leaves open, perhaps some small measure of progress *may* be possible, something implied also by these comments in *Mon cœur mis à nu*: 'Il ne peut y avoir de progrès (vrai, c'est-à-dire moral) que dans l'individu et par l'individu lui-même'; 'Théorie de la vraie civilisation. [-] Elle n'est pas dans le gaz, ni dans la vapeur, ni dans les tables tournantes, elle est dans la diminution des traces du péché originel'; 'Pour que la loi du progrès existât, il faudrait que chacun voulût la créer; c'est-à-dire que quand tous les individus s'appliqueront à progresser, alors, et seulement alors, l'humanité sera en progrès.'[32] What Baudelaire objects to—and as may also be inferred from the strong emphasis on moral and mental effort to be seen both in his personal writings and in his comments on the artist's acquisition of technical skill—is the moral and mental laziness of those who count

---

[32] *Fusées*, ed. Guyaux, 87, 107, and 121; i. 681, 697, and 707.

on the inevitability of progress without doing anything at all themselves to secure it: 'La croyance au progrès est une doctrine de paresseux, une doctrine de *Belges*. C'est l'individu qui compte sur ses voisins pour faire sa besogne.'[33]

Such moral progress as may be possible will perhaps come from *individual* efforts to resist what (in writing about Poe) he calls the 'fatal law' of our moral degradation: 'cette loi fatale qui nous enchaîne, nous domine, et se venge de la violation de son insupportable despotisme par la dégradation et l'amoindrissement de notre être moral' (ii. 287-8). And one key element in that resistance is precisely self-awareness, 'la conscience dans le Mal', so that self-consciousness— the very source of melancholy—can become the means, if not necessarily to a remedy, then at least to a form of bitter dignity. Just as Vigny resolves to accept the human condition without complaining, least of all to God, so too Baudelaire resolves to look the full awfulness of our condition in the face, without fear, without hypocrisy, without lament ('je n'allais pas là pour répandre un vain pleur'). As the 'Prière' at the end of 'Les Litanies de Satan' illustrates, his own vision of a future return to paradise depends precisely on a willing embrace of knowledge, a journey which therefore requires to be undertaken in the company of Satan: 'Fais que mon âme un jour, sous l'Arbre de Science, | Près de toi se repose, à l'heure où sur ton front | Comme un Temple nouveau ses rameaux s'épandront!' (ll. 49-51). It may or may not be the case that '[t]out poète lyrique, en vertu de sa nature, opère fatalement un retour vers l'Éden perdu', but Baudelaire undertakes to make that fateful journey strictly 'en connaissance de cause'.

This is the lesson of 'L'Irrémédiable', the penultimate poem in the 'Spleen et idéal' section of the 1861 edition of *Les Fleurs du Mal*. Here the poet presents throughout its first eight stanzas what the eighth stanza itself describes as 'Emblèmes nets, tableau parfait | D'une fortune irrémédiable, | Qui donne à penser que le Diable | fait toujours bien tout ce qu'il fait!' The Devil, paradoxically, is good at his job. But we, no less paradoxically, can find relief in observing him at work:

> Tête-à-tête sombre et limpide
> Qu'un cœur devenu son miroir!
> Puits de Vérité, clair et noir,
> Où tremble une étoile livide,
>
> Un phare ironique, infernal,
> Flambeau des grâces sataniques,
> Soulagement et gloire uniques,
> —La conscience dans le Mal!
>
> (ll. 33-40)

---

[33] *Fusées*, ed. Guyaux, 87; i. 681. See also similar comments in *Exposition universelle*, ii. 580, and in 'Notes nouvelles sur Edgar Poe', ii. 324-5.

The self-consciousness at the root of the *mal du siècle*—what Chateaubriand had seen as an incapacitating *excess* of knowledge—becomes the new light and the new lighthouse: not the light of Christ but the empowering light of human self-knowledge; and not the lighthouse of guidance and warning to others so much perhaps as a wry 'note to self'.

Earlier in *Les Fleurs du Mal*, in 'Les Phares', Baudelaire compares a selection of artists—Rubens, Da Vinci, Rembrandt, Michelangelo, Puget, Watteau, Goya, and Delacroix—to a series of beacons transmitting a single message across the vast spaces of the centuries from human witness to human witness:

> Car c'est vraiment, Seigneur, le meilleur témoignage
> Que nous puissions donner de notre dignité
> Que cet ardent sanglot qui roule d'âge en âge
> Et vient mourir au bord de votre éternité!
> ('Les Phares', ll. 41–4)

These artists, too, have extracted beauty from 'le m/Mal' and in so doing provided solace:

> Ces malédictions, ces blasphèmes, ces plaintes,
> Ces extases, ces cris, ces pleurs, ces *Te Deum*,
> Sont un écho redit par mille labyrinthes;
> C'est pour les cœurs mortels un divin opium!
> ('Les Phares', ll. 33–6);

and not only solace but also a warning, a command even, and an appeal for help as though each were indeed one of us, hunters after truth and salvation but lost in the darkness of a forest:

> C'est un cri répété par mille sentinelles,
> Un ordre renvoyé par mille porte-voix;
> C'est un phare allumé sur mille citadelles,
> Un appel de chasseurs perdus dans les grands bois!
> ('Les Phares', ll. 37–40)

But from a Baudelairean perspective (and contrary to usual readings of this poem) these 'phares' have a suspect air, being artists praised from the point of view of the traditional poet-lawgiver who looks to art as a form of witness and moral guidance. As the references to 'Seigneur', '*Te Deum*', and 'divin' demonstrate, we are here being reminded of how we have conventionally looked on our human response to 'le Malheur' within a Christian context, and we are being invited also perhaps to recall Hugo's 'Les Mages' (published one year earlier) or the already published poems that would later make up Vigny's posthumously published collection *Les Destinées*. For Hugo the role of the poet-artist is to light the way of progress down the ages and into the future; for Vigny the poet offers solace to contemporary and future readers by depicting the dignity of a quasi-Stoic acceptance in the face of ineluctable human suffering. But this is not how Baudelaire sees the poet-artist. At the end of 'L'Irrémédiable' we are offered instead a 'phare ironique, infernal': an intimate lighthouse of self, and a torch—'Flambeau des grâces sataniques, | Soulagement et gloires uniques'—that has taken its flame from the fires of infernal and tormenting self-knowledge to light our way with the possibility of an alternative, satanic salvation. This lighthouse is 'ironique' because its light issues from a knowing self-reflexion, a mirrored illumination that may nevertheless still fulfil the traditional function of a lighthouse in helping us to steer away from the reefs of complacent hypocrisy or suicidal despair—an alternative form of guidance, therefore, 'une étoile livide' by which we may chart our course during 'le voyage' of human existence: the star that is the knowledge of our irremediable condition, of '[l]e spectacle ennuyeux de l'immortel péché' ('Le Voyage', l. 88).

For Baudelaire, therefore, the only plausible form of moral progress will derive from this self-knowledge (cf. 'Il ne peut y avoir de progrès (vrai, c'est-à-dire moral) que dans l'individu et par l'individu lui-même'), and in 'Au lecteur'— first published in 1855 and with which all editions of *Les Fleurs du Mal* begin—the poet could scarcely be more overt about his role as an alternative lawgiver. Baudelaire's reader, it seems, needs to be taught how to read the poems that will follow and in particular how to approach this new and alternative account of our moral being, this 'loi fatale' of our 'degradation'—etymologically a 'stepping down'—towards moral collapse and eventually death: 'Chaque jour vers l'Enfer nous descendons d'un pas' ('Au lecteur', l. 15). This reader may be familiar with the other accounts of 'le m/Mal' and 'le Malheur' that have been offered not only by the Church but also by many poets since the Revolution. In Chateaubriand, Staël, Lamartine, Hugo, Desbordes-Valmore, Vigny, to name but the most canonical, the themes of human suffering, religious doubt, social deprivation, turpitude, bereavement, are everywhere present. 'Les misérables'? Their name, it seems, is legion. But for many, and perhaps all, of these poets (in the broad sense of the word) there remains room for change: Chateaubriand's restoration of Christianity, Staël's 'completion' of the Revolution, the quasi-Christian gospel of love embraced and preached by Lamartine and Hugo, Desbordes-Valmore's appeals for compassion and understanding, Vigny's accumulated wisdom.

But for Baudelaire there is little or no room for change. For him the integrity— the non-hypocrisy—of poetry lies in the open-eyed, no-holds-barred portrayal of our desire-bound lives, of our wretched pursuit of lasting fulfilment against the tides of tedium and time and across the shifting sands of our own fecklessness; and one important aspect of the poet's integrity lies in offering that portrayal not as the picture of others (as, say, in Hugo's 'Les Malheureux' in *Les Contemplations* or indeed in *Les Misérables*) but as the picture of himself. For all that Hugo declares to his reader in the preface to *Les Contemplations* (which postdates 'Au lecteur') that what appears to be mere autobiographical fact is actually universal truth ('Ah! insensé, qui crois que je ne suis pas toi'), Baudelaire had already gone one step further: 'Hypocrite lecteur,—mon semblable,—mon frère.' In this invitation to complicity he stands less with Hugo than with Staël and Desbordes-Valmore, for whom the very act of writing constitutes a form of progress by creating and sustaining a community of fellow-marginals—mostly but not exclusively women themselves—through a 'private' sharing of experience and opinion.[34] In place of the official, the patriarchal, and the orthodox an alternative world-view is offered up as palliative and stimulus to resistance. In Baudelaire's case the argument runs that we are all 'sinners', and that we must all acknowledge that what we fear most is not sin but boredom, not death so much as the dead hand of routine and the death of desire ... the thought that there is nothing new under the sun. And this in turn will open up the new avenue of 'progress' implicitly proposed by *Les Fleurs du Mal*: the use of the imagination as a means to the revitalization of human experience. In life we are in death, but in art we are in life.

I shall now be looking, therefore, at Baudelaire's depiction of the 'tragedy of desire' and his use of a poetic persona as double agent: the melancholic and the artist, a human being who is helplessly prey to depression and a poet who in some sense has its measure, its poetic measure: 'Sois sage, ô ma Douleur, et tiens-toi plus tranquille' ('Recueillement', l. 1). For Baudelaire, poetry is 'le Mal' recollected in tranquillity.

---

[34] On this aspect of Staël's writing, see *Unacknowledged Legislators*, 220–1. For Desbordes-Valmore, see the preface to her *Bouquets et prières* (1843).

6
Lesbos and Limbo
Towards *Les Fleurs du Mal*

Vivre est un mal. C'est un secret de tous connu

('Semper eadem', l. 4)

There were, as is well known, three separate editions of *Les Fleurs du Mal*: the first, in 1857, containing 101 poems,[1] from which Baudelaire was obliged after the notorious trial to remove six;[2] the second, in 1861, comprising 127 poems and including a new section entitled 'Tableaux parisiens'; and a third, posthumous edition published in 1868 and including, at the editorial behest of Baudelaire's close friend and literary executor Charles Asselineau, an additional fourteen poems.[3] It is customary when discussing *Les Fleurs du Mal* to focus more or less exclusively on the 1861 edition on the grounds that this is in some sense definitive, being the last to be published within Baudelaire's lifetime. But the banned poems—and particularly the three that came from the section 'Fleurs du Mal' that bears almost the same title as the whole collection[4]—are important to an understanding of the poetic coherence informing the 1857 collection and, perhaps

---

[1] 'Au lecteur' is unnumbered, serving therefore as an introduction to a collection of 100 poems which, by their number, perhaps recall the 100 cantos that make up Dante's *Divine Comedy* and also anticipate the 100 prose poems that Baudelaire intended to publish as one collection.

[2] 'Lesbos', 'Femmes damnées. Delphine et Hippolyte', 'Le Léthé', 'À celle qui est trop gaie', 'Les Bijoux', and 'Les Métamorphoses du vampire'. All six poems were later republished in Brussels in 1866 as part of *Les Épaves*, the distribution of which publication in France was the subject of a court case in Lille two years later, resulting in Baudelaire's publisher Auguste Poulet-Malassis being fined 500 francs and given a one-year prison sentence. See i. 812–13. The French ban on these poems was lifted only in 1949, thanks to a new law specifically drafted in 1946 to address these poems: see Leclerc, *Crimes écrits*, 275–81.

[3] Baudelaire published a selection of fifteen poems under the title NOUVELLES *FLEURS DU MAL* in the fifth issue of *Le Parnasse contemporain* (31 Mar. 1866), comprising some poems already published in *Les Épaves* and others published separately in reviews. A sixteenth, 'Le Couvercle', appeared separately in the 18th issue (30 June 1866), and all sixteen were published together, as NOUVELLES *FLEURS DU MAL* in the collected first volume of *Le Parnasse contemporain* (Oct. 1866). For the March issue Baudelaire had insisted that '*Nouvelles Fleurs du mal* doit être écrit de telle façon que FLEURS DU MAL soit un titre distinct du mot NOUVELLES' (see i. 813), and in both the March issue and the collected volume the poems are preceded by the title 'NOUVELLES *FLEURS DU MAL*'. Clearly Baudelaire wanted these poems to be considered not as a new collection, separate from and thus a sequel to *Les Fleurs du Mal*, but rather as individual poems to be read in addition to and belonging with *Les Fleurs du Mal*. Cf. the earlier model of Lamartine's *Nouvelles méditations poétiques* (1823).

[4] 'Lesbos', 'Femmes damnées. Delphine et Hippolyte', and 'Les Métamorphoses du vampire'. The remaining three—'Le Léthé', 'À celle qui est trop gaie', and 'Les Bijoux'—were part of 'Spleen et idéal' (numbers 30, 39, and 20 respectively in the 1857 edition).

even more importantly, the thinking that lay behind Baudelaire's poetic project, dating back as it does to the 1840s. This thinking may also be inferred from the two titles that he initially considered for his work: *Les Lesbiennes* and *Les Limbes*.

For, as is also well known, *Les Fleurs du Mal* developed out of a collection of poems that was first advertised, from October 1845 until January 1847, under the title *Les Lesbiennes*, and notably on the cover of the *Salon de 1846*: 'Pour paraître prochainement *Les Lesbiennes*, poésies par Baudelaire Dufaÿs'. A new title, *Les Limbes*, was first advertised from November 1848, in *L'Écho des marchands de vins*, for a collection of poems due to be published on 24 February 1849 (the first anniversary of Louis-Philippe's abdication and the end of the July Monarchy) and 'destiné à représenter les agitations et les *mélancolies* de la jeunesse moderne' (i. 793; my emphasis). This launch date for *Les Limbes* was not observed, and eventually, in 1851, Baudelaire published a selection of eleven poems under this title in *Le Messager de l'Assemblée*.[5] But *Les Limbes* was in turn abandoned as a title[6] when on 1 June 1855, in the *Revue des Deux Mondes*, there appeared a new selection of eighteen poems (including three from *Les Limbes*)[7] under the new title—suggested to Baudelaire by the writer and critic Hippoltye Babou—of *Les Fleurs du Mal*.[8]

Women, Flowers, Wine

Quelquefois dans un beau jardin | Où je traînais mon atonie
('A celle qui est trop gaie', ll. 17–18)

The title *Les Lesbiennes* was doubtless intended to grab the attention of potential readers, exploiting the ambiguity of the term 'lesbiennes'—female inhabitants of Lesbos, female homosexuals—with the effect of being at once learned and scandalous. The traditional term for a gay woman had been 'une tribade', and the poem 'Femmes damnées' ['Comme un bétail pensif sur le sable couchées...'] originally began 'Les Tribades en rond sur le sable couchées...'.[9] But the term 'les

---

[5] 'Pluviôse irrité contre la ville entière...', 'Le Mauvais moine', 'L'Idéal', 'Le Mort joyeux', 'Les Chats', 'La Mort des artistes', 'La Mort des amants', 'Le Tonneau de la Haine', 'De profundis clamavi', 'La Cloche fêlée', and 'Les Hiboux'.

[6] Michael J. Tilby has shown that the most probable reason was the publication in Poitiers in 1852 of *Les Limbes, poésies intimes de Georges Durand recueillies et publiées par son ami T. Véron* (of which Théodore Véron was himself the author). See his '*Les Fleurs du Mal* in Limbo: The Non-appearance of *Les Limbes* Revisited', *French Bulletin*, 36 [no. 135] (Summer 2015), 20–4. See also Marie-Christine Natta, *Baudelaire* (Paris: Perrin, 2017), 387–8.

[7] 'Au lecteur', 'Réversibilité', 'Le Tonneau de la Haine', 'Confession', 'L'Aube spirituelle', 'La Destruction', 'Un voyage à Cythère', 'L'Irréparable', 'L'Invitation au voyage', 'Mœsta et errabunda', 'La Cloche fêlée', 'L'Ennemi', 'La Vie antérieure', 'De profundis clamavi', 'Remords posthume', 'Le Guignon', 'Le Vampire', and 'L'Amour et le crâne'.

[8] See i. 797.

[9] See Claude Pichois and Jean Ziegler, *Charles Baudelaire* (rev. edn, Paris: Fayard, 2005), 273 and n. 2.

Lesbiennes' was just then becoming current as an alternative 'code' word,[10] for example in the title of a long poem entitled *Les Lesbiennes de Paris* published anonymously in 1845, naming a number of prominent women as gay, stanza by stanza, to which further stanzas were added in succeeding years, 'outing' other women.[11]

Lesbianism itself, as many commentators have noted, was not a new literary topic, and it had figured just recently in the work of three prominent writers: Musset's *Gamiani, ou deux nuits d'excès* (1833),[12] Balzac's *La Fille aux yeux d'or* (1833–5), and Gautier's *Mademoiselle de Maupin* (1835). But in the unfinished draft of an early poem ('Tous imberbes alors, sur les vieux bancs de chênes…' (i. 206–7)) that he sent to Sainte-Beuve at some point during the period 1843–5 Baudelaire alludes to the female homosexuality described in Diderot's *La Religieuse* (first published in France in 1796) and links it explicitly with melancholy. The poem begins by evoking adolescent misery in unsurprising and perhaps parodic terms ('Nous traînions tristement nos ennuis, accroupis | Et voûtés sous le ciel carré des solitudes' (ll. 4–5); 'Qui de nous, en ces temps d'adolescences pâles, | N'a connu la torpeur des fatigues claustrales' (ll. 13–14)) before swiftly changing gear and evoking steamy sexual longings (and perhaps activity) as it focuses in turn on the particular anguish of summer's stultifying heat and the misty monotony of autumn:

> Saison de rêverie, où la Muse s'accroche
> Pendant un jour entier au battant d'une cloche;
> Où la Mélancolie, à midi, quand tout dort,
> Le menton dans la main,[13] au fond du corridor,—
> L'œil plus noir et plus bleu que la Religieuse

---

[10] Cf. Gustave Planche slightly later in a letter of 27 Jan. 1853 referring to 'une passion de la même nature que celle de Sapho pour les jeunes Lesbiennes' in order to describe the nature of the actress Marie Dorval's interest in Victor Hugo's mistress, Juliette Drouet. (See i. 794, n. 1.) As this suggests, 'les Lesbiennes' was at the time in some ways a *less* explicit term than 'tribade'. For further contextual discussion see Graham Robb, *La Poésie de Baudelaire et la poésie française 1838–1852* (n.p.: Aubier, 1993), 169–86. On Claude Pichois's rejection of this sexual meaning of 'lesbienne' in the Pléiade edition (i. 793–4), see Antoine Compagnon's defence of Pichois in his 'Notes sur notes', in *Baudelaire toujours: Hommage à Claude Pichois*, *L'Année baudelairienne*, 9–10 (2005–6), 105–12 (105–8). But for the most recent and authoritative account, see André Guyaux, 'Des "habitantes de l'île de Lesbos"?', *L'Année Baudelaire*, 22 (2018), 107–14. Guyaux provides ample evidence of the recent and contemporary use of 'lesbienne' in a sexual sense and argues that Baudelaire consciously exploited the dual meaning of the word (female inhabitant of Lesbos, female homosexual) as a way of protecting himself against charges of indecency.

[11] See *Les Fleurs du Mal*, ed. Antoine Adam (Paris: Garnier frères, 1961), 411–12.

[12] *Gamiani* was published anonymously but is traditionally attributed to Musset (as being an account of his lover George Sand).

[13] Starobinski notes the emblematic character of this pose in the iconography of melancholy (*La Mélancolie au miroir*, 19) and refers his reader to Klibansky et al., *Saturn and Melancholy*. For Starobinski's own commentary on this poem and some accompanying illustrations, see *La Mélancolie au miroir*, 17–22.

> Dont chacun sait l'histoire obscène et douloureuse,
> —Traîne un pied alourdi de précoces ennuis,
> Et son front moite encor des langueurs de ses nuits.
>
> (ll. 25–32)

And so it continues, in lines that, when slightly revised, would become the fourth stanza of 'Lesbos':

> —Et puis venaient les soirs malsains, les nuits fiévreuses,
> Qui rendent de leur corps les filles amoureuses,
> Et les font aux miroirs—stérile volupté—
> Contempler les fruits mûrs de leur nubilité—[.]
>
> (ll. 33–6)

Beset by what Baudelaire suggestively evokes as 'ce conflit de molles circonstances' (l. 41), the melancholic adolescent in his boarding-school identifies with the abused nun in her convent, an identification that prefigures the poet's subsequent self-alignment with the female inhabitants of Lesbos. Already at the age of 15, and 'vers le gouffre entraîné' (l. 48), he had read *René*, and then he discovered Sainte-Beuve's *Volupté* (1834)—'Livre voluptueux, si jamais il en fut' (l. 56).[14] In detailing the effects of this book on his earlier melancholic self, the poet—who in this case is transparently Baudelaire himself—presents an account of melancholy that combines sexual frustration, mystical longing, and religious doubt: 'Tout abîme mystique est à deux pas du Doute' (l. 46). Melancholy is both magic potion and deadly poison ('Le breuvage infiltré, lentement, goutte à goutte' (l. 47)), a malady bestowed by destiny (l. 67) that he must henceforth make his own, like Samuel Cramer practising before his mirror:

> Et devant le miroir j'ai perfectionné
> L'art cruel qu'un Démon en naissant m'a donné,
> —De la Douleur pour faire une volupté vraie,—
> D'ensanglanter son mal et de gratter sa plaie.
>
> (ll. 68–71)

In focusing on Lesbos Baudelaire is thus less concerned with gay sex than with melancholy, and at the same time also with what Sappho and the inhabitants of Lesbos represent: namely, poetry, and a moral code (which the first-person voice in 'Lesbos' calls a 'religion') that pre-dates Christianity and so offers a contrarian

---

[14] In Sainte-Beuve's semi-autobiographical novel the first-person narrator, Amaury—now a priest on his way to America—relates the story of his former life in terms of a struggle between sensuality and spirituality during which powerful sexual desire is transformed into spiritual ardour. In his melancholy introspection Amaury resembles other representatives of the *mal du siècle* such as René, Obermann, Adolphe, and Musset's 'enfant du siècle'.

alternative to Christian ethics. Of particular importance in this regard is the 'Fleurs du Mal' section within the 1857 edition of Les Fleurs du Mal (and still, though to a lesser extent, within the 1861 edition). For the poems in this section help to show what—from the very beginning of the project that became Les Fleurs du Mal—Baudelaire understands by the term 'le Mal': that is, the 'Mal' of which these poems are to constitute the floral (i.e. poetic) representation and/or product.

That the 'flowers' in question were at first principally the poems themselves is suggested by 'L'Âme du vin', a poem dating back to 1843/4 and, having at one time been intended for Les Limbes,[15] eventually first published in 1850. After the first, introductory line this poem comprising six quatrains of alexandrines consists exclusively of the song sung by the 'soul' of wine from within the bottles, or 'bodies', that contain it. By way of expressing gratitude to the labourers who produced it through their sweat and toil on a hellish, sun-baked hillside, the 'âme du vin' describes its delight at descending to its 'death' within the 'sweet tomb' that is the warming chest of an exhausted vineyard-worker rather than continuing to 'live' within the glass prison of its bottle (l. 3) and the cold cellars in which these bottles are stored (l. 12). Adopting a language of revolutionary solidarity that echoes the verse of Pierre Dupont ('Homme, vers toi je pousse, ô cher désherité, | [...] | Un chant plein de lumière et de fraternité!' (ll. 2, 4)), the voice of wine offers its own self-sacrifice—in an irreverent echo of Christ sacrificing his life that others may live[16]—as a means to the secular redemption of the worker who is 'usé par ses travaux' (l. 10). In a parody of the Mass itself— 'Entends-tu retentir les refrains des dimanches | Et l'espoir qui gazouille en mon sein palpitant?' (ll. 13–14)—wine will be 'glorified' (l. 16) by the worker-worshipper sitting contentedly at his own domestic altar/table and observing how wine stimulates renewed sexual desire in his wife and restores colour and strength to his frail-looking son. For the pious, wine represents the blood of Christ, but here for this secular 'holy family' it simply brings health, renewal, and life—and, for the worker-poet himself—flowers:

> En toi je tomberai, végétale ambroisie,
> Grain précieux jeté par l'éternel Semeur,
> Pour que de notre amour naisse la poésie
> Qui jaillira vers Dieu comme une rare fleur!
>
> (ll. 21–4)

As though it were the food of the gods, or, as in the parable of the sower, the seed that fell on fertile soil, wine shall inspire the poet to dedicate his own creations to the principle of creativity itself. Wine is life: not something to be stored up and

---

[15] See i. 1045.
[16] Cf. 'Le Vin des chiffonniers' which ends by describing wine as the 'fils sacré du Soleil!'

coldly preserved for the future, but rather something to be shared and 'sacrificed' to nourish others. The point of wine—as of beauty, as of poetry—lies in its effect. Wine goes off, just as flowers wither, and yet they can be preserved in bottle and scent-bottle alike. But these bottles must be opened—just as poems are not exquisite exhibits to be laid down in books but words to be read in solidarity by fellow human beings as the potential means to a renewal of vitality.

'L'Âme du vin' was placed at the beginning of the section entitled 'Le Vin' in both the 1857 and 1861 editions of Les Fleurs du Mal, and its floral image is echoed in the last line of 'La Mort des artistes', which in the 1857 edition was placed last in 'La Mort' and thus in Les Fleurs du Mal as a whole. This time the voice of the poem is that of the frustrated artist, a sculptor, who laments the difficulty of artistic production as he tries repeatedly to give adequate expression to his artistic vision ('Pour piquer dans le but, de mystique nature' (l. 3)). Speaking for himself alone in the first stanza but then for other sculptors in the second, he predicts that they will 'wear out' their souls and have to destroy many a failed attempt '[a]vant de contempler la grande Créature | Dont l'infernal désir nous remplit de sanglots!' (ll. 7–8). Some will never succeed, and only one hope remains for these particular 'sculpteurs damnés et marqués d'un affront' (l. 10): 'C'est que la Mort, planant comme un soleil nouveau, | Fera s'épanouir les fleurs de leur cerveau!' (ll. 13–14). Placed at the end of the 1857 edition these lines clearly relate to the title of the collection and imply a rhetoric of modesty as the poet seemingly acknowledges his own failure—as though his own anthology (etymologically, a gathering or collection of flowers) has been doomed by the very 'Mal' of which it speaks.

But it is equally the case, as in the draft 'Épilogues' for the 1861 edition, that Baudelaire's flowers are a metaphor for certain manifestations of 'le Mal' within life itself, as if poetry were to be seen as the wine organically produced from the fruiting flowers of a living vine—or indeed, as in 'Le Flacon' and elsewhere, a perfume that captures and perpetuates floral scents. For the Baudelaire of the 1840s this was already the case, since the women of Lesbos—from whom the whole collection could indeed be said to grow—are themselves compared to flowers. And so these particular 'fleurs du Mal' offer an important point of access into the alternative lawgiving of Les Fleurs du Mal as a whole and its depiction of the melancholy of desire. So, too, does the 'fleur du Mal' that is the banned poem 'A celle qui est trop gaie'. Where, as we shall see, the poet regards the women of Lesbos as his sisters because he shares their melancholy, so here the poet turns a creature of joy into 'ma sœur' (the last two words of the poem) by imbuing her with his own 'Mal'. This beautiful woman is the embodiment of health, laughter, sunshine, and fresh air, and her brightly coloured 'toilettes' put poets in mind of 'un ballet de fleurs' (l. 12)—which is enough to make this particular poet hate her as much as he loves her (l. 16). The contrast between her floral gaiety and his own depression (he is a 'passant chagrin' (l. 5)) proves too much to bear. Just as sometimes, while wandering in a beautiful garden full of the fresh greenery of spring, his melancholic heart has been 'humiliated' by this 'insolence' of Nature and he has vented his anger by lashing out at a flower, so now he would revenge himself on this woman's joy by 'infusing' her one night with his own venomous disease through the sexual act.[17] By his love-making he will bruise and wound her startled flesh (ll. 30–2), crushing and poisoning beauty ('en faisant mal à la fleur' perhaps) in a manner that constitutes the precise opposite of his poetic ambition to create a 'fleur du Mal'.

From Lesbos to Limbo: 'Fleurs du Mal', or the Melancholy of Desire

> Lesbos au blanc rivage, où l'on dit qu'autrefois
> Les premiers chants humains mesurèrent les voix[.]
> Une vague y jeta comme un divin trophée
> La tête harmonieuse et la lyre d'Orphée.
> (Vigny, 'Hélena', in Poèmes [1822], ll. 435–8)

Baudelaire's quest for the new, for a poetic elsewhere, begins in Lesbos, the final resting place of the head and lyre of a dismembered Orpheus and the mythical birthplace of poetry—and at the same time the home of Sappho, the great poet of ancient Greece whom Plato called the tenth muse and whose name had long been associated with female homosexuality. Thus Baudelaire begins where the Orphic father of poetry left off and by taking the mother of poetry as his new model.

The poet-lawgivers who preceded Baudelaire in France both before and after the Revolution of 1789 had all looked to ancient Greece in search of some kind of founding authority for their work and public role. Whether it was the mythological figures of Orpheus and Amphion, or the reforming political leaders Solon and Lycurgus, poets and thinkers were keen to foreground these models as avatars of their own ambitions for the role of the writer. Rousseau, Condillac, and Marmontel, among others, had explicitly recalled and celebrated these earlier examples of poetry's centrality within the body politic, and their post-

---

[17] In the manuscript version of this poem, sent (unsigned) by Baudelaire to Mme Sabatier in Dec. 1852, the last line contained the word 'sang' instead of 'venin'. When the poem was subsequently included along with other banned poems and hitherto unpublished poems in *Les Épaves* Baudelaire added the following note, referring to the 1857 trial of *Les Fleurs du Mal*: 'Les juges ont cru découvrir un sens à la fois sanguinaire et obscène dans les deux dernières stances. La gravité du Recueil excluait de pareilles "plaisanteries". Mais "venin" signifiant spleen ou mélancolie, était une idée trop simple pour des criminalistes. [-] Que leur interprétation syphilitique leur reste sur la conscience' (i. 157). Adam takes Baudelaire's denial of obscenity at face value (ed. cit., 434 n. 1), but Pichois notes with amusement that this particular interpretation is Baudelaire's alone (i. 1133 n. 3). Just as *Les Épaves* was an attempt to circumvent French censorship, so Baudelaire's note constitutes an oblique debowdlerization of his own work.

revolutionary heirs had followed their example, if not their appointed models. For those intent on a counter-Enlightenment programme of 'restoration'—in particular Chateaubriand, soon followed by the young Royalists Lamartine and Hugo—the prophets of the Old Testament were more appropriate forebears, and none more so than Moses to whom God had delivered the Tables or Tablets of the Law on Mount Sinai. For Staël these various role-models, whether pagan or Judaeo-Christian, were all inappropriately male. As to Sappho, she wrote a play about her—but about the Sappho of whom myth tells that she killed herself for the unrequited love of a boatman (Phaon), and so a play about another exceptional woman (like Delphine and Corinne) brought to unhappiness and death by love for a man unequal to her gifts. Instead Staël took the model of the Latin poet Corinna, rival of Pindar, as the matrix for her modern poet-lawgiver Corinne.[18]

In turning to Lesbos for his initial poetic focus Baudelaire is making a key strategic move within the literary context of the 1840s. Some counter-Enlightenment polemicists, such as Bonald and Ballanche, had made much of the fact that in earliest times the poet's influence was achieved and maintained entirely through the oral medium, and so for them ancient Greece represented a kind of pre-Gutenberg paradise in which it was still possible to police public discourse effectively in the interests of sound governance. For those of the early post-revolutionary period who believed and argued that language was a divine (and hence necessarily truth-bearing) gift, ancient Greece was thus a model of patriarchal power in which the word of God had been delivered to human beings who knew best how to govern in God's name. In turning to Lesbos the Baudelaire of the 1840s was therefore not only turning his back on the whole Christian tradition within which Chateaubriand and his young Romantic followers were seeking to renew French society and French poetry, he was also choosing a different ancient Greece: not the ancient Greece of Plato and the philosopher-king, but the ancient Greece of Sappho—not a concept but a real human being, not a man but a woman, and a woman whose intimate lyrics bespeak the mindset of an alternative lawgiver.

Relatively little is known for certain about Sappho, even though in recent decades the Oxyrynchus Papyri have offered up further fragments of her work. Born on the island of Lesbos sometime between 630 and 615 BC, she died there c.570 BC. She may have spent part of her life living in political exile in Sicily before returning to Lesbos in 581 BC. Very little of her work has survived, but it is clear from multiple sources, including Plato, that her poetry was held in very high esteem. In respect of her sexuality some external evidence as well as the content of some of her surviving poetry has been taken to suggest that she was gay, and it is this association that has led to the uses of the term 'sapphism' and 'lesbianism' to denote female homosexuality.

---

[18] See *Unacknowledged Legislators*, 227 and n. 7.

What matters here is what Baudelaire knew or thought about Sappho and the island of Lesbos. Clearly he will have known of its time-honoured mythical status as the birthplace of poetry (and the epigraph above from Vigny's 'Héléna' of 1822 suggests a common cultural knowledge). At the same time there can be no doubt that he has our modern sense of 'lesbianism' in mind throughout many of the poems that made up 'Fleurs du Mal' in the 1857 edition. Thus the poet of 'Fleurs du Mal', and by implication, in the 1857 edition, of *Les Fleurs du Mal* as a whole, presents himself in 'Lesbos' not as Moses or Solon or Lycurgus but as the initiate of Lesbian mystery. In taking Sappho as his muse he is rejecting the role of the poet-lawgiver as public spokesman and political leader and adopting instead the guise of a young priest admitted to the black mystery of sexual desire and privy to the 'secret' that informs its apparently contradictory nature: 'Des rires effrénés mêlés aux sombres pleurs' ('Lesbos', l. 44). He will be the poet of human suffering at its most intimate and conflicted, the poet who goes back to the Orphic origins of poetry as he prepares to offer a radically new and contrarian account of human experience, the poet who wants to place the realities of sexual desire at the heart of our moral experience and, in so doing, to redefine and supersede the Christian concept of sin ('péché' is the first noun to be repeated in 'Au lecteur' and thus in *Les Fleurs du Mal*). By choosing ancient Greece as his site he also implies—in a new twist on counter-Enlightenment thinking—that the pre-Christian era offers proximity to a 'divine' truth that the 'fall' of Christianity has since obscured from view.

This truth is presented in 'Lesbos',[19] and in the accompanying poems about lesbian experience: 'Femmes damnées. Delphine et Hippolyte' and 'Femmes damnées' ['Comme un bétail pensif...']. In 'Lesbos' Baudelaire depicts the island as the site of 'voluptés grecques' and the home of a female community given over to sexual activity that brings both pleasure and pain: the pleasure of momentary satisfaction and the pain of renewed desire. This sexual activity—explicitly homosexual (ll. 11–15) and involving both cunnilingus (ll. 6–10) and masturbation (ll. 16–20)—is presented as entirely natural, a celebration of love such that 'Vénus à bon droit peut jalouser Sapho' (l. 14). Venus may thus be 'within her rights', but so too are the lesbians acting legitimately within theirs, albeit the sexual activity of these women is presented as being subject to a code quite different from that to which the modern world may be accustomed. Love in Lesbos is a trade-off between pleasure and suffering, and not something to which notions of good and evil, virtue and vice, can or should be applied. Here, quite unambiguously, is the poet as alternative lawgiver, offering us access to this other 'religion' that has no need of the concept of righteousness in matters of sexual activity, still less of a moral dichotomy between heaven and hell as eventual sites of reward and

---

[19] First published in *Les Poètes de l'amour*, ed. Julien Lemer (Paris: Garnier frères, 1850).

punishment for behaviour here on earth. For this 'religion' its heaven and its hell are the pleasure and anguish of sexual desire:

> Que nous veulent les lois du juste et de l'injuste?
> Vierges au cœur sublime, honneur de l'archipel,
> Votre religion comme une autre est auguste,
> Et l'amour se rira de l'Enfer et du Ciel!
> Que nous veulent les lois du juste et de l'injuste?
>
> Car Lesbos entre tous m'a choisi sur la terre
> Pour chanter le secret de ses vierges en fleurs,
> Et je fus dès l'enfance admis au noir mystère
> Des rires effrénés mêlés aux sombres pleurs;
> Car Lesbos entre tous m'a choisi sur la terre.
>
> (ll. 36–45)

The poet as alternative lawgiver is thus an initiate into the 'religion' and 'dark mystery' of Lesbos: that is, an initiate into the experience of a sacred pre-lapsarian sexuality that knows not guilt and yet is privy, in its virginal innocence, to the black torment of desire and to the mysterious confusion of laughter and tears, of pleasure and pain, attendant upon it. An initiate since childhood (and so a male version of the more familiar figure of the young girl being trained for her role as temple priestess in ancient Greece) the poet is the chosen one (like Moses) and calls on the women (addressed simply as 'Lesbos') to ignore traditional patriarchal disapproval of their 'religion' ('Laisse du vieux Platon se froncer l'œil austère' (l. 21))—this 'religion' that is their female sexual freedom and independence—and to realize instead that in their pleasure lies also their punishment and thus their metaphorical 'pardon' (ll. 22, 26). For in seeking pleasure ('l'excès des baisers' (l. 22)) and then still more pleasure ('des raffinements toujours inépuisés' (l. 24)) they undergo the infinite martyrdom of desire: 'Tu tires ton pardon de l'éternel martyre, | Infligé sans relâche aux cœurs ambitieux | Qu'attire loin de nous le radieux sourire | Entrevu vaguement au bord des autres cieux!' (ll. 21–4). And so the scales of justice look quite different in Lesbos, measuring as they do not good and evil but happiness and suffering:

> Qui des Dieux osera, Lesbos, être ton juge
> Et condamner ton front pâli dans les travaux,
> Si ses balances d'or n'ont pesé le déluge
> De larmes qu'à la mer ont versé tes ruisseaux?
> Qui des Dieux osera, Lesbos, être ton juge?
>
> (ll. 31–5)

Explicitly setting himself up against the lawgiving of Plato and his philosopher-king, the poet is also ready, in the name of this Lesbian 'mystery', to forgive

Sappho herself for abandoning the women of Lesbos in her subjection to heterosexual desire. This is the Sappho of myth and legend (and of Staël's play) who was cursed by a jealous Venus and made to fall in love—an unreciprocated but consummated 'love'—with the boatman Phaon (to whom Venus had given a magic ointment that made him appear irresistibly attractive), and the Sappho who threw herself off a cliff in order to put an end to the torment of her insatiable sexual desire. Now (ll. 46-55) the poet presents himself as the ever-vigilant lookout, scanning the seas for the return of her body to a forgiving Lesbos[20] and reflecting on the nature of this 'man-woman' and her own extraordinary combination of beauty and 'Malheur':

> De la mâle Sappho, l'amante et le poëte,
> Plus belle que Vénus par ses mornes pâleurs!
> —L'œil d'azur est vaincu par l'œil noir que tachette
> Le cercle ténébreux tracé par les douleurs
> De la mâle Sappho, l'amante et le poëte.
>
> (ll. 56-60)

Here Sappho epitomizes Baudelairean melancholy: she is more beautiful than Venus *because* of her suffering, while from the repeated collocation of 'l'amante et le poëte' we may infer that her poetry speaks not of public matters but of the terrible reality of private desire—the sexual desire that is common to both sexes and transcends gender difference, just as the male poet (as poetic persona and not as Baudelaire himself) who has been chosen to speak for the women of Lesbos is implicitly her mirror image, a 'femelle poëte', and perhaps even the ghost of Orpheus himself and a fellow homosexual.[21] And Sappho epitomizes Baudelairean melancholy also as a sacrificial victim, as a proto-Satanic figure—the original 'femme damnée'—whose fall ushers in an eternity of lament over an immutable human condition:

---

[20] According to myth, lovers seeking respite from their passion might leap into the sea from a cliff on the island of present-day Lefkadia, being 'cured' if they survived the leap, and 'cured' in a different way (like Sappho) if they did not. In 'Lesbos' the poet keeps watch on this cliff ('au sommet de Leucate' (ll. 46, 50)) to observe if the sea will return Sappho's body to 'Lesbos, qui pardonne' (l. 53). Since the island of Lesbos lies just off the coast of Turkey in the north Aegean Sea, and Lefkadia lies off the western coast of Greece in the Ionian Sea, the requirement of geographical accuracy has clearly been overruled by poetic licence.

[21] In Ovid, *Metamorphoses*, Book X, it is said that Orpheus was killed by the women of Thrace for reasons of thwarted desire and revenge because after the death of Eurydice he had forsworn heterosexual relationships in favour of relations with boys.

On the 'substitution' of a male poet for the absent Sappho as emblematic of a Lesbos that is a 'lieu dépoétisé, qui aujourd'hui n'est plus qu'un espace de mélancolie', see Pierre Laforgue, 'Lesbos, ou érotique et poétique chez Baudelaire', in Laforgue, *Œdipe à Lesbos: Baudelaire, la femme, la poésie* (Paris: Eurédit, 2002), 177-88 (187).

> —De Sappho qui mourut le jour de son blasphème,
> Quand, insultant le rite et le culte inventé,
> Elle fit son beau corps la pâture suprême
> D'un brutal dont l'orgueil punit l'impiété
> De celle qui mourut le jour de son blasphème.
>
> (ll. 66–70)

Sappho has been 'impious', 'insulting' the religion of lesbian sexual independence while also blaspheming (through self-subjugation to a man) against the sacred equality enjoyed by its adherents. She herself may perhaps be forgiven (by 'Lesbos, qui pardonne') since her blasphemy was the work of a jealous Venus, goddess of heterosexual passion, but the damage has been done. The inhabitants of Lesbos now know that sexual desire can be fatal, that it can drive someone to seek mercy in death (Sappho, we are told, throws herself off the cliff '[p]our savoir si la mer est indulgente et bonne' (l. 55)); and so the innocence of these 'Vierges au cœur sublime' has been lost, in a pre-Christian version of the Fall, through knowledge of the 'deathly' potential of sexual desire:

> Et c'est depuis ce temps que Lesbos se lamente,
> Et, malgré les honneurs que lui rend l'univers,
> S'enivre chaque nuit du cri de la tourmente
> Que poussent vers les cieux ses rivages déserts!
> Et c'est depuis ce temps que Lesbos se lamente!
>
> (ll. 71–5)

The poem thus ends on a note of tragic inevitability and irremediable recurrence ('chaque nuit'), a sense that within the wasteland of human experience the passing of time is not linear but cyclical—like the structure of the stanzas in 'Lesbos'—and brings only an endlessly repeated sequence of desire and death. This is the lamentable truth of Lesbos, 'le secret de ses vierges en fleurs': of its virgins who are not deflowered but who instead flower in a full expression of their female sexuality and yet cannot escape the 'loi fatale' of a downward spiral towards that ultimate leap into the sea of death. For them, as for the poet, life is one long process of bereavement, of grieving for the loss of Sappho as leader and celebrant of their island paradise: 'l'amante'/'lamente'... the homophone bears eloquent witness to the condition of these 'fleurs du Mal'.

In the second of the poems from the 1857 'Fleurs du Mal' section that were banned from subsequent publication, 'Femmes damnées. Delphine et Hippolyte', the poet's own childhood initiation into the 'noir mystère' of Lesbos is replaced by the sexual initiation of Hippolyte by Delphine and her consequent experience of desire as nightmare and abyss. The setting of this poem is simply a bed, but the names of the two female lovers[22] imply that we are here being offered the scenario of one particular relationship between two inhabitants of Lesbos. Once again Baudelaire presents sexual experience within an alternative moral framework: these women are 'damned' not because a Christian doctrine forbids homosexuality or states that it is sinful to engage in sexual activity that is not for the conjugal purpose of human reproduction but because once they (and by extension any of us) have tasted pleasure, they (and we) want more of it: satisfaction brings its own torment, its own hell. This is the central moral paradox of Baudelaire's Lesbos, and, more generally, of Baudelaire's world: an existence without desire is a sterile world of ennui, and yet desire—which is life—carries within it the seeds of destruction, condemning us—as one desire dies or is satisfied—to another and another, in an endless cycle of lament. Here in this poem Delphine has just initiated Hippolyte into sexual pleasure. For Hippolyte this represents a loss of innocence (ll. 1-8), while Delphine is depicted as a predatory animal savouring its triumph over 'sa pâle victime' (l. 21) and yet demanding gratitude for the gentleness of her procedures. She seeks to convince Hippolyte that her loss of innocence with another woman—which here *is* presented as a deflowering ('L'holocauste sacré de tes premières roses' (l. 27))—must be preferable to the alternative of subjection to the violent phallic sexuality of a male lover:

> Mes baisers sont légers comme ces éphémères
> Qui caressent le soir les grands lacs transparents,
> Et ceux de ton amant creuseront leurs ornières
> Comme des chariots ou des socs déchirants[.]
>
> (ll. 29-32)

Hippolyte for her part professes neither ingratitude nor repentance (l. 42) but rather 'malheur': 'je souffre et je suis inquiète' (l. 43), 'mon trouble et mon effroi' (l. 50). Indeed, herself a 'fleur du Mal', it is this very 'malheur' that now enhances her beauty (as was the case also with Sappho):

> De ses yeux amortis les paresseuses larmes,
> L'air brisé, la stupeur, la morne volupté,
> Ses bras vaincus, jetés comme de vaines armes,
> Tout servait, tout parait sa fragile beauté.
>
> (ll. 9-12)

---

[22] 'Hippolyte' might translate either Hippoltyus or Hippolyta, thus creating a potentially androgenous figure to mirror the 'man-woman' that is Sappho or the male poet of 'Lesbos' who is the chosen initiate of L/lesbians.

Her first experience of sexual pleasure has opened up a vista of nightmare ('de lourdes épouvantes | Et de noirs bataillons de fantômes épars' (ll. 45-6)) and a tormented sense of the destructiveness of desire, which she is nevertheless ('les paresseuses larmes') unable to resist:

> Toi que j'aime à jamais, ma sœur d'élection,
> Quand même tu serais une embûche dressée
> Et le commencement de ma perdition!
>
> (ll. 54-6)

Like the poetic 'je' of 'Lesbos' Delphine at once rejects any equation between this 'perdition' and the perdition of traditional Christian doctrine. 'Qui donc devant l'amour ose parler d'enfer?' (l. 60), she asks:

> Maudit soit à jamais le rêveur inutile
> Qui voulut le premier, dans sa stupidité,
> S'éprenant d'un problème insoluble et stérile,
> Aux choses de l'amour mêler l'honnêteté!
>
> (ll. 61-4)

Sexual passion, she is arguing, has nothing to do with notions of vice or virtue. It is a simple, 'insoluble' fact of life in the face of which philosophical or theological constructs are sterile, such as the very concept of 'hell' as a place of punishment for wickedness. But for Baudelaire it does very much have to do with a different kind of hell, the one experienced by Hippolyte herself: 'Je sens s'élargir dans mon être | Un abîme béant; cet abîme est mon cœur!' (ll. 75-6). Burning with volcanic, all-consuming desire this heart has become a 'monstre gémissant' (l. 78), insatiable and itself incapable of quenching the thirst for vengeance of the gods ('la soif de l'Euménide' (l. 79)); and for Hippolyte the only way out is total surrender to her newly kindled passionate desire for Delphine, a surrender that is tantamount to an embrace of death: 'Je veux m'anéantir dans ta gorge profonde | Et trouver sur ton sein la fraîcheur des tombeaux!' (ll. 83-4) As for Sappho, so here the only resort is to cast herself into the yawning abyss of her sexual longing.

Now the poet intervenes, and in a voice that differs markedly from the poetic voice of 'Lesbos'.[23] This poet is angry and sarcastic, despising the vain attempts of these women to deny and/or escape the 'hell' of desire, but also repeating the argument of 'Lesbos' that any punishment for these sexual acts derives not from

---

[23] Walter Benjamin sees this difference as a contradiction pointing to an 'inextricable confusion' in Baudelaire's attitude to lesbianism (in *Charles Baudelaire: A Lyric Poet in the Era of High Capitalism*, 93), while Dupont refers to an 'exploration contrastée' ('Baudelaire et Colette', 158). Auguste Poulet-Malassis, Baudelaire's publisher, claimed that these final five stanzas of the poem were added at the last moment in an (unsuccessful) attempt to forestall prosecution (see i. 1127).

some divine or man-made ethical system but from the 'loi fatale' of desire itself: 'Ombres folles, courez au but de vos désirs; | Jamais vous ne pourrez assouvir votre rage, | Et votre châtiment naîtra de vos plaisirs' (ll. 90–2). The metaphorical pardon of 'Lesbos' has here become a more literal 'châtiment', and the poet takes up Hippolyte's own reference to an insatiable thirst and compares sexual desire to rabies, an illness that makes its victim crave the very thing that will exacerbate the illness: 'L'âpre stérilité de votre jouissance | Altère votre soif [...]' (ll. 97–8). There is no more telling image than this in *Les Fleurs du Mal* for the 'ill-being' that Baudelaire places at the centre of the human condition.[24] Desire engages us in a vicious circle, here a downward spiral of degradation and 'crime': 'Descendez, descendez, lamentables victimes, | Descendez le chemin de l'enfer éternel' (ll. 85–6). And yet the poet ends with a sudden reversal of perspective on the rabies of desire by mocking these 'femmes damnées' for their doomed attempt to run away from themselves:

> Loin des peuples vivants, errantes, condamnées,
> À travers les déserts courez comme les loups;
> Faites votre destin, âmes désordonnées,
> Et fuyez l'infini que vous portez en vous!
>
> (ll. 101–4)

In other words, we are all rabid and we must drink the water of desire (in our thirst for the infinite) since it is in our nature to do so—and even though it will make us thirstier still. The 'âpre stérilité' of these women's 'jouissance' derives not just from the fact that gay sex is non-reproductive but more especially from the inescapable truth that a desire satisfied is a kind of death, leading to further destruction— within the eternal cycle of melancholy.[25]

These particular themes are taken up again in two poems: the third (unbanned) 'Lesbian' poem, also entitled 'Femmes damnées' ['Comme un bétail pensif sur le sable couchées...'], and 'La Destruction', the poem with which the 'Fleurs du Mal' section opens in both the 1857 and the 1861 editions of *Les Fleurs du Mal*.[26] In this 'Femmes damnées' the poet begins by depicting the inhabitants of Lesbos (though the place itself is not named in the poem) as wholly surrendering to their physical

---

[24] Cf. Baudelaire's description in the *Salon de 1846* of the effect of prolonged exposure to licentious images: 'Vous est-il arrivé, comme à moi, de tomber dans de grandes mélancolies, après avoir passé de longues heures à feuilleter des estampes libertines? Vous êtes-vous demandé la raison du charme qu'on trouve parfois à fouiller ces annales de la luxure, enfouies dans les bibliothèques ou perdues dans les cartons des marchands, et parfois aussi de la mauvaise humeur qu'elles vous donnent? Plaisir et douleur mêlés, amertume dont la lèvre a toujours soif!' (ii. 443).

[25] The association between melancholy and rabies dates from antiquity, when it was thought that the spleen dominated in the organism of a dog. See Rufus of Ephesus, *On Melancholy*, ed. Peter E. Pormann (Tübingen: Mohr Siebeck, 2008), 41, 91. On the dog featured in Dürer's *Melencolia I* see Walter Benjamin, *The Origin of German Tragic Drama*, trans. John Osborne (London: NLB, 1977), 152.

[26] I discuss this poem at the beginning of Chapter 7.

being while yet gazing into the distance as though reflecting on the spiritual implications of their situation:

> Comme un bétail pensif sur le sable couchées,
> Elles tournent leurs yeux vers l'horizon des mers,
> Et leurs pieds se cherchant et leur mains rapprochées
> Ont de douces langueurs et des frissons amers.
>
> (ll. 1–4)

This opening stanza is followed by a sequence of stanzas in which four different modes of sexual desire are evoked: as a timid, innocent first experience (ll. 5–8); as susceptible of being controlled and resisted, within the landscape of St Antony's own experience of the temptations of the flesh (ll. 9–12); as a terrible fever ('leurs fièvres hurlantes') causing a remorse that can only be alleviated by alcohol ('Ô Bacchus, endormeur des remords anciens!') (ll. 13–16) in the same way as the rabid desperately thirst for water; and finally as a sado-masochistic experience of cruelty and delight combining the 'écume du plaisir' (suggestive also of the foaming mouth of the rabid) and the 'larmes des tourments'. Here, as with the 'douces langueurs' and 'frissons amers' of the first stanza, we are shown the co-presence of pleasure and pain that had constituted the 'noir mystère' of which the poet of 'Lesbos' is the chosen initiate.

The poem ends by echoing the 'infini que vous portez en vous' of the banned 'Femmes damnées' while also implicitly introducing the theme of limbo:

> Ô vierges, ô démons, ô monstres, ô martyres,
> De la réalité grands esprits contempteurs,
> Chercheuses d'infini, dévotes et satyres,
> Tantôt pleines de cri, tantôt pleines de pleurs,
>
> Vous que dans votre enfer mon âme a poursuivies,
> Pauvres sœurs, je vous aime autant que je vous plains,
> Pour vos mornes douleurs, vos soifs inassouvies,
> Et les urnes d'amour dont vos grands cœurs sont pleins!
>
> (ll. 21–8)

In medieval Christian theology 'Hell' was divided into four separate areas: the hell of the damned; purgatory, where souls are purged before entering Heaven; the limbo of the Fathers, that is, of the Old Testament patriarchs who could not enter Heaven until 'freed' by the crucifixion and death of Christ;[27] and the limbo of the Infants, where unbaptized babies and very young children go after death.

---

[27] As is evident in Dante's description of limbo in the *Divina Commedia*, this region has also been thought to be inhabited by the great writers and thinkers of pre-Christian antiquity.

Common to these last two is the idea of a hell for the innocent, for those who die without being members of Christ's Church but who in God's eyes are blameless. Baudelaire's 'femmes damnées' are depicted as such persons, innocent and yet subject to the hellish torture of desire, conflicted beings who accede to—indeed crave—the promptings of the flesh, and yet suffer the agonies of regret and remorse on account of their very subjection to these promptings for which they bear no moral responsibility.

In these final two stanzas of the unbanned 'Femmes damnées' the poet resumes the role of 'brother' and initiate that he had claimed in 'Lesbos'. Like Christ entering the limbo of the Fathers to free chosen pagans and patriarchs from their temporary hell, but even more like Orpheus entering the Underworld in a vain attempt to rescue Eurydice, the poet's soul conducts a journey into the 'enfer' that these women are experiencing: not the Christian 'Hell' that comes after death, but the secular hell of conflicted human desire that imprisons the living. This conflictedness is epitomized in the chiastic structure of l. 21: 'Ô vierges, ô démons, ô monstres, ô martyres'. These women are virgins in the sense that they have not slept with men but also in the sense that they are innocent and blameless—like martyrs, destroyed for their devotion to an outlawed religion. In this case, as asserted in 'Lesbos', this is the 'religion' of innocent (homo)sexuality, but it is also the 'devotion' that desire demands of us all.

To the eyes of the *bien-pensants* (like the frowning and austere Plato) such 'devotion' is demonic and monstrous, but these women—'chercheuses d'infini' and 'De la réalité grands esprits contempteurs'—understand things better. If they are demonic, it is because of the irresistible nature of human passion, and if they are monstrous, it is not because of their homosexuality but because of the very hybridity of desire—its pleasure and its pain, its purity and its destructiveness. The poet for his part loves and pities these women in equal measure, as 'sisters' and soul-mates, partners perhaps in his own tormented thirst for the infinite. Like them he is contemptuous of everyday banal reality, and he identifies fully with these 'chercheuses d'infini' and with the predicament encapsulated in the bitter paradox of the poem's last line: 'les urnes d'amour dont vos grands cœurs sont pleins!' The poet celebrates the women's willingness to embrace their 'rabid' condition and to seek the 'infinite' within a pursuit of pleasure that they know will also bring them pain. They have a great capacity for passion, and yet that passion carries death within it, like a funeral urn, the death that is implicit in every desire. And perhaps also there is the sense here of the death of the idea of 'love' as capable of being anything other than sex—and, even then, sex not as innocent pleasure but sex as violence, cruelty, and ultimately (as we shall see in 'Un voyage à Cythère') a form of narcissism and solipsism.

But 'satyres'? How can these women be likened to the priapic companions of Dionysus, half-human, half-goat, and unflagging pursuers of the very Maenads who in one version of the myth are said to have dismembered Orpheus? Within the context of l. 23, however, following 'chercheuses' and 'dévotes', the masculine noun 'satyres' assumes a feminine air, designating these 'femmes damnées' who are themselves Bacchic devotees of wine, women, and (Sapphic) song, and who also are half-human, half-animal in that they are divided between their physical longings and that pursuit of the infinite that has them gazing pensively towards 'l'horizon des mers'.

In fact the 'gender-bending' of the word 'satyres' is part of a broader strategy in both 'Fleurs du Mal' and *Les Fleurs du Mal* whereby the male poet not only empathizes with the female inhabitants of Lesbos but begins to substitute himself for them. This is most clearly the case in 'Le Léthé', another of the banned poems and which figured as poem 30 in 'Spleen et idéal' in the 1857 edition. This poem can be read as following on from Hippolyte's final speech in the banned 'Femmes damnées' (ll. 75–84), and especially from her final wish: 'Je veux m'anéantir dans ta gorge profonde, | Et trouver sur ton sein la fraîcheur des tombeaux!' Like the women of the unbanned 'Femmes damnées' the poet as first-person male subject here describes himself as 'Martyr docile, innocent condamné' (l. 19). His sexual longing is blameless, and he is a willing, 'teachable' martyr to its cause, even though he knows that it condemns him to the innocent hell of insatiable desire. Within this impossible limbo he seeks escape from the torment of desire in an oblivious sleep resembling death (ll. 9–10), a suicidal extinction to be preceded (as in Hippolyte's case) by sexual climax: 'L'oubli puissant habite sur ta bouche, | Et le Léthé coule dans tes baisers' (ll. 15–16). Delphine's 'gorge profonde' now becomes 'l'abîme' of the poet's mistress's bed (l. 14). For both Hippolyte and the poet of 'Le Léthé' orgasm brings ecstasy and 'death', so that sexual desire is seen here as a fate both feared and welcomed, and the source of a pleasure all the more exquisite for the pain it brings:

> À mon destin, désormais mon délice,
> J'obéirai comme un prédestiné;
> Martyr docile, innocent condamné,
> Dont la ferveur attise le supplice [...].
>
> (ll. 17–20)

Repeatedly the poet aspires to disappear *into* his mistress: to sink his trembling fingers into 'l'épaisseur de ta crinière lourde' (l. 4); to bury his 'tête endolorie' in her skirts (ll. 5–6); to 'engloutir' his sobs in her bed (ll. 13–14). As though thus repeatedly reliving the act of penetration in his state of post-coital anguish, this poet-lover wants also to recapture the moment of his own 'fleur du Mal' as both a smell and a memory ('respirer, comme une fleur flétrie, | Le doux relent de mon amour défunt' (ll. 7–8)) that will serve as the narcotic substance that can send him to sleep. The poem closes on the shocking image[28] of the poet—now baby-like and

---

[28] The poem was banned on account of this stanza. See i. 1130.

by implication ready, therefore, to begin again—sucking the means of oblivion ('Le népenthès[29] et la bonne ciguë' (l. 22)) from the breast of his mistress 'Qui n'a jamais emprisonné de cœur' (l. 24). Whereas at the beginning of the poem he had sought her embrace ('Viens sur mon cœur, âme cruelle et sourde') and revelled in her casual cruelty ('Tigre adoré, monstre aux airs indolents'), now he returns this cruelty (in his sarcastic reference to the 'bouts charmants de cette gorge aiguë') and proclaims her powerlessness ('Qui n'a jamais emprisonné de cœur') by escaping into his own imaginary death—or simply into the oblivion of one more sexual act. The rancour (l. 21) he feels on account of her heartless control over him—that is, on account of the adored tiger-like grip of desire itself and its insidiously monstrous effects, as well as the pain caused both by the anguish of longing and the 'tristesse' of satisfaction ('mes sanglots apaisés' (l. 13))—is now 'drowned' and forgotten in the river of Lethe that is the 'petite mort' of orgasm: 'le Léthé coule dans tes baisers' (l. 16). And the sleep-death for which the poet-lover longs turns out to be the impossible dreamworld that is the sexual possession of an inanimate beauty unaccompanied by melancholy:

> Je veux dormir! dormir plutôt que vivre!
> Dans un sommeil aussi doux que la mort,
> J'étalerai mes baisers sans remord
> Sur ton beau corps poli comme le cuivre.
>
> (ll. 9–12)

The reality of desire, however—both here and in the 'Lesbian' poems with which 'Le Léthé' thematically belongs—is the lingering scent of 'une fleur flétrie, | Le doux relent de mon amour défunt'.

This relationship between desire and death informs all the 'Fleurs du Mal' poems. The idea of martyrdom that figures in the depiction of the women of Lesbos and of the male poet of 'Le Léthé' is also evoked in 'Une martyre. Dessin d'un maître inconnu', the poem placed between 'La Destruction' and the Lesbos poems in all editions. As the 'transposition d'art' of an imaginary drawing or painting (cf. the reference to 'la toile' (l. 11)) it presents the lurid scene of a sexual martyrdom, depicting the decapitated body of a young woman lying on a bed while her severed head reposes on the bedside table 'comme une renoncule' (l. 17). In its reliance on a certain type of Gothic horror, complete with murder, ghosts, and sumptuous airless chamber, it evokes recent or contemporary takes on the violent realities of sexual desire (comparable, for example, with the scenarios of Balzac's *La Fille aux yeux d'or* (see i. 1059)) and so serves as a kind of chronological bridge, following the timeless allegory of 'La Destruction', by anticipating

---

[29] Nepenthes (from the ancient Greek meaning 'no grief') was a plant extract that was held to dispel melancholy through forgetfulness. See Starobinski, *Histoire du traitement*, 20–1.

within the immediacy and present tense of ekphrasis the Sapphic martyrdoms of Lesbos to be depicted in the poems that follow. Similarly, it serves to introduce the presentation of women as 'fleurs du Mal', already mooted in 'La Destruction', not only through the comparison of a severed head to a ranunculus but also through the setting itself: a bedroom as warm and stuffy as a greenhouse (l. 5), in which 'des bouquets mourants dans leurs cercueils de verre | Exhalent leur soupir final' (ll. 7–8). Moreover the 'loi fatale' of desire is here already manifest as the observing poet wonders if the dead woman, despite her youth, had not perhaps already reached the end of that downward spiral of lust in a final paroxysm of self-abandonment:

> Elle est bien jeune encor!—Son âme exaspérée
> Et ses sens par l'ennui mordus
> S'étaient-ils entr'ouverts à la meute altérée
>   Des désirs errants et perdus?
>
> (ll. 41–4)

In her frustration and her boredom—that choosy monster of 'Au lecteur' ('ce monstre délicat' (l. 39))—has she finally yielded like exhausted, bitten prey to a rabid pack of errant and directionless desires? And has some vindictive lover, whose hunger she herself has failed to satisfy, instead sought to assuage '[l]'immensité de son désir' (l. 48) in one final, posthumous penetration of her 'chair inerte et complaisante' (l. 47)? Who can tell? But what is certain is that the tragedy of desire exceeds the conventional understanding of those who may mock, pry, or legislate:

> —Loin du monde railleur, loin de la foule impure,
> Loin des magistrats curieux,
>   Dors en paix, dors en paix, étrange créature,
>   Dans ton tombeau mystérieux;
>
> (ll. 53–6)

and certain also that both the woman and her lover are in some sense initiates of this mystery of destructive desire and thus united unto and into death:

> Ton époux court le monde, et ta forme immortelle
>   Veille près de lui quand il dort;
> Autant que toi sans doute il te sera fidèle,
>   Et constant jusques à la mort.
>
> (ll. 57–60)

The poet here is the alternative lawgiver, adopting a voice of understanding and tolerance and even solidarity with this couple that has lived the full logic of desire, and singing a consoling requiem for this truncated martyr to sex and ennui... albeit with the ironic implication that the male lover's future fidelity will take the form of a terrible haunting memory of necrophilia.

As 'Les Deux Bonnes Sœurs' suggests, coming after the Lesbos poems (or, in 1861, the single Lesbos poem), lust and death are ultimately synonymous, as synonymous as sisters or a same-sex couple. The allegorical figures of 'La Débauche et la Mort' are 'deux aimables filles' (l. 1)—girls or prostitutes?—and comparable with two lesbian lovers, seemingly full of libido and life ('Prodigues de baisers et riches de santé' (l. 2)), but also tattered and threadbare, and without issue: 'Dont le flanc toujours vierge et drapé de guenilles | Sous l'éternel labeur n'a jamais enfanté' (ll. 3-4). And, as in the Lesbos poems, the male poet presents himself as a privileged and sympathetic witness to this reality, from which now even remorse is absent (l. 8). With irony and perhaps some mischievous glee the poet as alternative lawgiver describes himself as might an outraged bourgeois depict the man who would soon be charged with offending public decency: for he is the 'Poëte sinistre, ennemi des familles, | Favori de l'enfer, courtisan mal renté' (ll. 5-6). But his alternative law is still the same: the conflicted and oxymoronic nature of sexual experience, here seen as comprising 'De terribles plaisirs et d'affreuses douceurs' (l. 11).

Throughout the sonnet any supposed difference—between debauch and death, between the living and the already destroyed—is instead submerged in an insistent coupling at both the lexical and prosodic levels. Not only are debauch and death 'deux aimables filles' but the 'Tombeaux et lupanars' are both 'charmilles' (l. 7), just as 'la bière et l'alcôve' are 'comme deux bonnes sœurs' (10)—a phrase bearing the key analogy foregrounded in the poem's title and positioned so as to qualify also the coupling of 'De terribles plaisirs et d'affreuses douceurs' that follows. And are these eponymous *sisters* merely siblings, or are they perhaps also—as suggested by the 'blasphèmes fécondes' (l. 9) that issue from bier and bed alike—nuns (like the eponymous protagonist of Diderot's *La Religieuse* mentioned in 'Tous imberbes alors, sur les vieux bancs de chênes...'), childless virgins and initiates of that 'religion' of sexuality previously mentioned in the Lesbos poems? That debauch and death are indeed synonymous is then confirmed in the closing tercet when, leaving allegory and the metaphor of lesbianism behind, the male poet speaks out from the present of his own anguished experience and calls upon debauch to bury him and for death to graft the dark cypress of the graveyard onto the diseased myrtle of love, a plant sacred to Aphrodite/Venus and symbolic of love's supposedly enduring flowering. In the hell of sexual desire all distinction— between life and death, the pagan and the Christian, the sacred and the defiled—is reduced to nought. And, at the prosodic level—the crossed rhymes of the quatrains, the twin couplets of the tercets (cdd cee)—as also at the thematic level, all semblance of duality and difference turns out to be cyclical and a form of repetition, leading to ennui and death. 'Nous offrent tour à tour' (l. 10): whether it be sex or death itself, the apparent newness of the experience is—for the poet as it was for the women of Lesbos—simply the same old mixture of satisfaction and distress. The pleasures are 'terribles' and the sweet moments of gentleness and peace equally 'affreuses': both are 'fleurs du Mal'.

As the sequence of twelve poems that constitutes the 'Fleurs du Mal' section in the 1857 edition gradually unfolds, all explicit mention of lesbianism ceases, and the poet's own experience of sexual desire becomes the main focus. In 'La Fontaine de sang' his life-blood serves as a drinking fountain to quench the implicitly rabid and vampiric lust of 'ces cruelles filles!' (l. 14), who are reminiscent of the 'deux aimables filles' of debauch and death in 'Les Deux Bonnes Sœurs'.[30] His knowledge that debauch and death are one fills him with terror (l. 10), but when he seeks the oblivion of sleep through drinking, he finds that the wine simply renders his perceptions even more acute—like trying to sleep on a bed of nails: a bed of nails that ironically serves to draw fresh blood to be drunk by 'ces cruelles filles'. In 'Allégorie', by contrast, 'une femme belle et de riche encolure' (l. 1) knows no such terror: 'Elle rit à la Mort et nargue la Débauche, | ces monstres' (ll. 5–6) and seems to personify lust: 'cette vierge inféconde | Et pourtant nécessaire à la marche du monde' (ll. 13–14). Like the inhabitants of Lesbos for whom the conventional distinction of good and evil is irrelevant in matters of sexuality, 'Elle ignore l'Enfer comme le Purgatoire' (l. 17). Death itself holds no fears for her, inspiring neither hatred nor remorse (l. 20), merely something to be approached as a new beginning ('Ainsi qu'un nouveau-né' (l. 20))—just one more resurrection of eternal desire.[31]

Ultimately, therefore, the poet is alone. In 'La Béatrice' he is not the privileged companion being guided through Dante's paradise by an ideal of womanhood but the inhabitant of a scorched earth ('des terrains cendreux, calcinés, sans verdure' (l. 1)), mocked by demons and laughed at by '[l]a reine de mon cœur au regard nonpareil' (l. 28) as his anti-Beatrice consorts freely with these demons upon whom she occasionally bestows 'quelque sale caresse' (l. 30). In 'Un voyage à Cythère' the island of love proves similarly bleak: 'une pauvre terre' (l. 8), 'cette île triste et noire' (l. 5), 'Un désert rocailleux troublé par des cris aigres' (l. 19)—and all the bleaker for the insistent contrast within the poem between the island's mythical reputation as a floral paradise of amorous rapture and its true status as the 'Eldorado banal de tous les vieux garçons' (l. 7). Rather than housing the temple of Aphrodite with its sacred cult and alluring semi-clad priestess, herself 'amoureuse de fleurs' (l. 22), this sorry place offers instead the horrific spectacle of

---

[30] On this connection see i. 1064 n. 4.

[31] While it may appear, in these two poems, that the focus on lesbianism has vanished, nevertheless it may be that here the poet has begun to demonstrate the fraternal, or indeed sisterly, relationship with the inhabitants of Lesbos that he affirmed in 'Lesbos'. For Pierre Laforgue, in a reading that he fears may seem 'scandaleuse', 'La Fontaine de sang' collapses gender difference by the implicit equation of a syphilitic's penile blood loss and a woman's menstrual flow, with the pun of 'sanglant' | 'sans gland' reinforcing the parallel. See his 'Flots de sang et rythmiques sanglots ou Éros et physiologie dans "La Fontaine de sang"', in Laforgue, *Œdipe à Lesbos*, 203–15 (208; 214 n. 5).

LESBOS AND LIMBO 149

a gibbet complete with the dangling, decomposing corpse of a man and a flock of 'féroces oiseaux' (l. 29) intent on pecking the skeleton bare before marauding animals below can take their turn to feed on its meat. Why has the man been hanged? 'En expiation de tes infâmes cultes', the poet tells him, '[e]t des péchés qui t'ont interdit le tombeau' (ll. 43–4). The love celebrated at the altar of Aphrodite may or may not have once been an idyllic rose garden filled with cooing doves and amorous sighs (ll. 15–17), but now 'Cythère n'était plus qu'un terrain des plus maigres' (l. 18): sexual passion has become the occasion of guilt and infamy, 'sinfulness' and the forfeit of a decent burial. And for the poet this hanged man is *his* allegory:

> Pour moi tout était noir et sanglant désormais,
> Hélas! et j'avais, comme en un suaire épais,
> Le cœur enseveli dans cette allégorie.
>
> (ll. 54–6)

Thus the poet's own 'embarquement pour Cythère' has brought him not to some Watteauesque '[i]le des doux secrets et des fêtes du cœur' (l. 9) but instead face to face with his own image as a degraded and putrescent victim of desire, akin to the monstrous, martyred women of Lesbos and like them condemned to know the terrible reality of their moral selves. Each man, each woman, it seems, *is* an island. For such is the Baudelairean journey of love:

> Dans ton île, ô Vénus! je n'ai trouvé debout
> Qu'un gibet symbolique où pendait mon image...
> —Ah! Seigneur! donnez-moi la force et le courage
> De contempler mon cœur et mon corps sans dégoût!
>
> (ll. 57–60)

To travel outwards towards the object of desire, to the elsewhere of an apparently separate being, turns out to be a doomed return to self: difference has once again vanished away. Love for another becomes hatred of self. In other words, this is a journey towards 'la conscience dans le Mal'—a task requiring all the more strength and courage for the fact that, as the following poem 'L'Amour et le crâne' makes clear, such self-awareness threatens to annihilate the poet completely.

The 'Fleurs du Mal' section ends with this remarkable tailpiece[32] depicting Cupid seated upon the skull of humanity and blowing bubbles from its rapidly

---

[32] According to the subtitle the poem describes a 'Vieux cul-de-lampe', that is, a 'tailpiece' or engraved design or drawing which a printer might include in the space remaining at the end of a page (for example, at the end of a chapter). Here the ekphrasis of 'L'Amour et le crâne' serves a similar function in rounding off the 'Fleurs du Mal' section (in both the 1857 and 1861 editions). In reality it

diminishing contents. From Cupid's mouth come fragile and evanescent globes that burst as quickly as 'un songe d'or' (l. 12), while from the mouth of the poet come the printed words that record the skull's alarm:

> —Ce jeu féroce et ridicule,
> Quand doit-il finir?
> Car ce que ta bouche cruelle
>   Éparpille en l'air,
> Monstre assassin, c'est ma cervelle,
>   Mon sang et ma chair!
>
>   (ll. 15–20)

Once again, love means death but now less because debauch signals the death of desire through repetition than because the lover's own knowledge of its deathliness saps his will to live, sucks the life-blood from him like birds pecking at a corpse or like 'ces cruelles filles' quenching their thirst with the blood from the bed of nails on which he lies, as though he were racked with anguished self-awareness. Or like the vampire-woman of the banned poem 'Les Métamorphoses du vampire' (which in the 1857 edition comes between 'La Béatrice' and 'Un voyage à Cythère') who sucks not only the poet's blood (l. 24) but also the very marrow from his bones (l. 17). For the poet sexual congress brings death, and in this case brings death to his vampiric partner also, for, as he discovers on waking, she has been reduced to a bloodless, fleshless pile of skeletal disjecta membra (l. 25). Woman, man, straight, gay, living, dead... it all ultimately comes to the same.

Les Limbes (1851): The Melancholy of Non-difference

> les limbes insondés de la tristesse
>
>   (*Salon de 1846*, ii. 440)

Baudelaire thus presents the sexual act—the culmination of desire—not as creation but as destruction, not a sharing of potentially generative pleasure but a sapping of the life-force or a murderous exchange of fluids. Supposedly a celebration and affirmation of life, for the future as also within the present itself, sex constitutes instead a living death, and therefore perhaps a kind of limbo. In 'Allégorie', as we have seen, the personification of lust 'ignore l'Enfer comme le Purgatoire', and in the Lesbos poems the women are innocent martyrs to the hellish torture of desire. If limbo (from the Latin 'limbus', meaning edge or

---

appears that the poem was based on an engraving (see i. 1074–5). For the engraving itself see ed. Adam, ed. cit., p. liv.

boundary) is a liminal state, so too is human life itself—a condition of melancholy in which disappointment follows upon aspiration and fulfilment in a ceaseless and unbreakable cycle. Mallarmé's sonnet of homage to Verlaine entitled 'Tombeau' ends by describing death as 'un peu profond ruisseau calomnié', suggesting that the poet's physical demise is, as it were, a mere blip on the cardiac monitor recording the health of his reputation and the posthumous glory of his work. Baudelaire's account of death might be thought the mirror image of this. For him, similarly, death does not mark a radical caesura in time but rather an indeterminate transition between two very similar states—but, in his case, of 'ill-being'. Hence the significant number of poems in Les Fleurs du Mal that either present human life as a form of living death or else describe a putative afterlife that simply perpetuates the experience of our mortal condition.

Several of these poems constitute the great majority of the group of eleven sonnets that Baudelaire published under the title of Les Limbes in 1851.[33] Indeed the only exception is 'Le Tonneau de la Haine', which instead articulates the theme of rabies that occurs in the Lesbos poems and presents hatred as a thirst for vengeance every bit as unquenchable as sexual desire. On the one hand, hatred is a leaking barrel, akin to the perforated vessels with which the Danaids were condemned to endlessly futile water-carrying, a barrel that cannot be filled even with the blood and tears of the dead, and even if 'Le Démon' (l. 5) were somehow to resuscitate 'ses victimes' (l. 7) and squeeze them dry all over again. On the other hand, hatred is also the drunk who drinks from that barrel and with every drink feels his thirst return in yet more compelling form, like the Hydra, the serpentine monster of the lake of Lerna at the entrance to the Underworld that grew two heads for every one that was cut off.[34] Like the barrel itself this drunk can never be (ful)filled, and hatred is thus a kind of vicious circle: the more one hates, the more one hates, world without end. A kind of hell, a kind of limbo.

But the remaining ten poems in Les Limbes focus on the uncertain relationship between life and death, constantly blurring the distinction between them. Some depict life as a living death, like 'De profundis clamavi',[35] in which the lover pleads for mercy from within the depths of the abyss into which his heart has fallen: a 'gouffre obscur' (l. 2), 'un univers morne' (l. 3), 'un pays plus nu que la terre polaire' (l. 7). Like the scorched earth of 'La Béatrice' or the barren rock of 'Un voyage à Cythère' this is a landscape of melancholy, of depression and ill-being, an 'anti-earth' in which the sun is cold (ll. 5, 10) and the darkness is 'immense' (l. 11). Indeed the reference to Proserpina and her six-monthly alternation of abode

---

[33] For valuable contextual discussion, see Robb, La Poésie de Baudelaire et la poésie française 1838–1852, 187–209.
[34] Starobinski notes that Sophocles uses the term 'melancholos' (i.e. black bile) to describe the blood of the hydra of Lerna. See Histoire du traitement, 23.
[35] Originally entitled 'La Béatrix' in Les Limbes, and subsequently 'Le Spleen' when republished in the Revue des Deux Mondes (1855).

between this world and the Underworld (ll. 5–6) suggests that the landscape of the poem is that of the Underworld itself, the limbo of the lover's despair: a pre-Creation world ('semblable au vieux Chaos' (l. 11)) without fauna or flora or water (l. 8), a grim domain ever-present to the lover's waking consciousness as the skein of time slowly unwinds (l. 14). If only, like an animal, he could seek oblivion 'dans un sommeil stupide' (l. 13).

Compare with this the lover of 'L'Idéal', whose heart is 'profond comme un abîme' (l. 9) and for whom only Lady Macbeth ('âme puissante au crime' (l. 10)) or Michelangelo's sculpture of Night can offer any remotely convincing artistic representation of his lover's ideal. And compare also the eponymous protagonist of 'Le Mort joyeux', who seeks oblivion not in sleep but in death itself—as though it were his natural habitat ('comme un requin dans l'onde' (l. 4)). For this melancholic figure life already so closely resembles death that he simply wants to dig his own grave among the snails and lay himself down as fodder for the worms. What joy that would be! He hates the accoutrements of death that mark it out as something distinctive and separate from life (tombs, testaments, tears); he would rather his corpse were simply pecked to pieces by the birds (ll. 7–8), like that of the hanged man in 'Un voyage à Cythère'. And perhaps the worms will kindly tell him if in death as in life he must suffer further: 'Et dites-moi s'il est encor quelque torture | Pour ce vieux corps sans âme et mort parmi les morts!' (ll. 13–14).[36] 'Corps' and 'mort(s)' here rhyme as insistently as life and death themselves resemble each other. Or as insistently as 'morts' and 'efforts' at the end of 'La Cloche fêlée',[37] in which the poet compares his own voice to the death rattle of a wounded soldier trapped under a pile of corpses and unable to move, animate yet motionless, dying even as he undertakes 'd'immenses efforts' (l. 14). Like a defective church bell incapable of filling the cold night air with its peals, the poet's soul is likewise cracked and his poetic voice enfeebled (ll. 9–11): he, too, is alive but dying, dying of the effort of living and soon to be dead, doomed to silence just as with the poem's end his own poetic strain will cease.

The poet of 'La Cloche fêlée' in turn resembles the first-person persona of 'Le Mauvais Moine', inhabiting death and yet unable to give it artistic life. Where once the monks of old decorated their cloisters with paintings of the Christian story, and in particular of the Resurrection ('Plus d'un illustre moine [...], | Prenant

---

[36] Baudelaire develops this possibility further in 'Le Squelette laboureur' (first published in 1860 before becoming the ninth of the 'Tableaux parisiens' in the 1861 edition of Les Fleurs du Mal). Here a chance sighting among the Parisian bouquinistes of some old anatomical drawings (in 'cadaverous' books that are themselves like ancient mummies) leads him to gaze at 'écorchés' (cutaways) and skeletal outlines of the body at work and to wonder if these symbolize the prospect of an afterlife ('Dans quelque pays inconnu' (l. 29)) in which we shall all be condemned to eternal hard labour and an absence of rest: 'Voulez-vous (d'un destin trop dur | Épouvantable et clair emblème!) | Montrer que dans la fosse même | Le sommeil promis n'est pas sûr [...]?' (ll. 21–4). Cf. Jackson, La Mort Baudelaire, 109: 'l'au-delà est pensé sur le mode du Même'.

[37] Entitled 'Le Spleen' in Les Limbes and simply 'La Cloche' in 'Les Fleurs du Mal' (1855).

pour atelier le champ des funérailles, | Glorifiait la Mort avec simplicité' (ll. 5–8)), death is instead his own soul's everlasting and seemingly inescapable habitat: 'Mon âme est un tombeau que, mauvais cénobite, | Depuis l'éternité je parcours et j'habite' (ll. 9–10). Where the poet's voice was weak and his soul cracked, the monk is simply lazy—unwilling or unable to make the merest effort towards the artistic representation of the 'spectacle vivant de ma triste misère' (l. 13).[38] But how could he? For how might the living spectacle of a living death actually look? (As the poet of 'L'Irréparable' asks insistently: 'Peut-on illuminer un ciel bourbeux et noir?' (ll. 21, 25).) Like the poet incapacitated by melancholy the 'mauvais moine' is trapped in a limbo, an intermediate space of ill-being between life and death, action and inaction, expression and silence.

The remaining poems in Les Limbes dwell similarly on this blurring of the distinction between life and death. In 'Pluviôse irrité...', the first of the four poems that Baudelaire subsequently entitled 'Spleen' in the 1857 edition of Les Fleurs du Mal, what is literally inanimate or dead is metaphorically alive, while the supposedly animate is either dead or nearly so. Rain is personified as a petty, spiteful god, copiously spilling mortality over the 'inhabitants' of the nearby cemetery: the clock has a cold, the smoking log sings falsetto, playing cards engage in sinister chat about a love that is dead. At the beginning of the sestet the poem turns on an ambiguity between the animate and inanimate: 'Le bourdon se lamente' (l. 9). A bumble-bee bemoaning its fate (perhaps of imprisonment by a baffling pane of glass), or the tenor-bell of a nearby church lugubriously tolling, doubtless in sympathy with 'la cloche fêlée'? Or is this simply a literalization of the idiomatic expression 'avoir le bourdon', the human feeling of being depressed, of almost not caring whether one lives or dies? The only unambiguously living creature in the poem is a cat, who is nevertheless 'maigre et galeux' (l. 6), ill nourished and diseased and implicitly half-dead. But not as dead as the 'vieux poëte', whose ghost wanders in the gutter like the cat itself, which meanwhile, like a person, cannot get comfortable in its bed. A half-living feline, a dead old poet with a 'living' ghost and a 'triste voix' that can still be heard...the borderline between the animate and inanimate has all but disappeared.

So it has also in 'Les Chats' and 'Les Hiboux' in which the cats and the owls are living creatures and yet evince the quietude and immobility of the dead. In both poems the impassiveness of these creatures bespeaks a wisdom that privileges meditation over action, as with noble dignity and patience—'Jusqu'à l'heure mélancolique' ('Les Hiboux', l. 6)—they await the inevitable darkness and the endless sleep of 'un rêve sans fin' ('Les Chats', l. 11). The sphinx-like cats and the owls who resemble 'des dieux étrangers' (l. 3) both appear to be in

---

[38] The monk is a victim of acedia, the so-called 'maladie des moines' that Baudelaire later read about in the psychiatrist Brierre de Boismont's book *Du suicide et de la folie suicide* (1856). See *Fusées*, ed. Guyaux, 61; i. 656. See also Starobinski, *Histoire du traitement*, 51–6.

silent communication with a realm that transcends human enterprise, and their eyes—starry and mystical in the case of the cats, red and darting in the case of the owls—imply a level of knowledge and insight beyond the capacity of us paltry humans with our passing fancies and restless desires. The world of cats and owls, it seems, is a limbo also, located somewhere between the sub-human and the suprahuman, a parallel universe greatly superior to our own melancholy condition of restless desire: 'L'homme ivre d'une ombre qui passe | Porte toujours le châtiment | D'avoir voulu changer de place' ('Les Hiboux', ll. 12–14).

In the remaining two poems from *Les Limbes*, 'La Mort des artistes' and 'La Mort des amants', the overlap between life and death is a source of irony, mocking any illusory faith in death's redemptive powers. In the former case, as already discussed, death is the locus for the realization of an impossible dream of artistic achievement, a prospect so overtly improbable that it suggests the very impossibility of artistic perfection *tout court*. In the latter poem, a sonnet comprised of lilting decasyllables, we are presented with the no less improbable scenario of an earthly idyll of love being 'reanimated' (l. 13) after death by a faithful, joyful angel. The two lovers are as torches, reflected in each other's mind, a picture of perfect harmony that can be unproblematically recreated after the peaceful transition of death during 'Un soir fait de rose et de bleu mystique' (l. 9). But the first-person plural voice of this poem seems to represent the perspective of love's own illusion: the silent first-person voice of the poet himself may not necessarily be complicit in such a vision. More overtly, in 'La Mort des artistes' the first-person voice of the octave, both singular and plural, knows only the difficulty of artistic production. In the sestet this voice distances itself, in the third person, from those artists—in particular, sculptors—who hope that death may paradoxically allow 'les fleurs de leur cerveau' (l. 14) to bloom at last.[39]

In the 1857 edition of *Les Fleurs du Mal* these two poems make up two-thirds of the final section, entitled 'La Mort', where they are joined by 'La Mort des pauvres'. Where 'La Mort des amants' articulates the traditional topos of lovers being reunited in death, 'La Mort des pauvres' may appear to offer a no less traditional view of death as a release from life's suffering:

> C'est la Mort qui console, hélas! et qui fait vivre;
> C'est le but de la vie, et c'est le seul espoir
> Qui, comme un élixir, nous monte et nous enivre,
> Et nous donne le cœur de marcher jusqu'au soir.
>
> (ll. 1–4)

---

[39] This holds true for the 1851 version (see i. 1091–2) in which the octave differs significantly from that which figures in the versions of 1857 and 1861.

Without the later addition to 'La Mort' in 1861 of three further poems—'La Fin de la journée', 'Le Rêve d'un curieux', and 'Le Voyage'—these three sonnets could conceivably be read as presenting three positive expectations: the continuing bliss of the lovers, the 'reward in heaven' meted out to the deserving poor, and, in 'La Mort des artistes', an implicit prospect that posterity will see perfection where the perfectionist sculptor himself sees only present failure. Read in this light, 'La Mort des artistes' would thus represent (as suggested above) a rhetoric of modesty whereby (in 1857) the poet of *Les Fleurs du Mal* signs off with a declaration of his own inadequacy and the fond hope that perhaps—whether on publication or later, following his own death—these poems will one day be thought better than he dares to believe. But the elements of irony, improbability, and hyperbole in these three poems are already (in 1857) too strong for such readings to be convincing, and especially in the terrible paradox expressed in those opening lines of 'La Mort des pauvres' that death is the purpose of life. In reality the life of the poor is also limbo, a place of suffering for the innocent. '[P]auvres et nus' (l. 11), constantly struggling to survive, they long for 'l'auberge fameuse' of the afterlife '[o]ù l'on pourra manger, et dormir, et s'asseoir' (ll. 7–8). But the implausibility of their desperate faith in posthumous comfort is suggested by the fantastical nature of the angel's 'doigts magnétiques' that will conjure up for the destitute not only rest but also 'le don des rêves extatiques' (ll. 9–10), and suggested further by the extravagant terms in which death is described in the second tercet: 'la gloire des dieux', 'le grenier mystique', 'la bourse du pauvre et sa patrie antique', 'le portique ouvert sur les Cieux inconnus!' We may perhaps conclude that this vision of a compensatory death, being presented as in 'La Mort des amants' in the first-person plural, represents the perspective of deprivation's own illusion and not the poet's own belief.

An ironic reading of these three poems is reinforced within the context of 'La Mort' in the 1861 edition where they are followed by 'La Fin de la journée', 'Le Rêve d'un curieux', and 'Le Voyage'. In the first of these the poet presents the figure of 'Le Poëte' as comparable with 'les pauvres' in welcoming death (in the metaphorical guise of night) as a source of rest after the tumult of life ('La Vie, impudente et criarde' (l. 3)) and also as a release from hunger and shame. His heart now already filled with 'songes funèbres' (l. 11), this Poet simply wants— rather like the protagonist of 'Le Mort joyeux'—to lie down and wrap himself in the draperies of darkness: 'Ô rafraîchissantes ténèbres!' (l. 14). In this case, therefore, death does not offer illusory new possibilities—of eternal love, of compensation, of artistic perfection—but simply a 'refreshing' oblivion, an escape from life. In itself, as we then learn from 'Le Rêve d'un curieux', death is a nonevent. The poet, apparently continuing the narrative of 'La Fin de la journée' and now wrapped in darkness, recounts his dream of dying, re-enacting also the familiar cycle of desire. As though, like the poet in Keats's 'Ode to a Nightingale' who is 'half in love with easeful Death', the eponymous 'curieux' of

Baudelaire's poem anticipates this new experience with all the liminal ambivalence of the women of Lesbos: 'C'était dans mon âme amoureuse, | Désir mêlé d'horreur, un mal particulier' (ll. 3-4); 'Angoisse et vif espoir' (l. 5); 'Plus allait se vidant le fatal sablier, | Plus ma torture était âpre et délicieuse' (ll. 6-7). But as in life, so in death... Having awaited this new experience like a child impatiently willing the curtain to rise on some exciting spectacle, the dreaming poet finds the 'vérité froide' (l. 11) of death itself altogether unsurprising, curtain-rise as total let-down: 'Eh quoi! n'est-ce donc que cela? | La toile était levée et j'attendais encore' (ll. 13-14).[40]

As we shall see in more detail later, this message pre-empts and undermines the putative excitement at the end of 'Le Voyage' where death will be presented as a further (doomed) attempt to experience novelty. As on the island of Lesbos, so here also on the threshold of death does the scenario of ill-being—of the 'mal particulier'—remain the same: desire followed by satisfaction followed by disappointment. But now, once death has been experienced, there is by implication not only nothing new under the sun but also nothing new within the darkness: there is nothing left that we have not already wanted and found wanting. In the bitter light of these three final poems in the 1857 and 1861 editions of *Les Fleurs du Mal*, the visions of death offered in the earlier three poems emerge as all the more illusory, clichéd, and trite—and therefore unambiguously ironic.

In these ways the figure of limbo serves the portrayal of melancholy as the experience of a liminal space between life and death, and no doubt for this reason Baudelaire thought for some time of including his two 'crepuscular' poems in *Les Limbes*.[41] In the event 'Le Crépuscule du soir' was published separately in 1852 before being placed directly before 'Le Crépuscule du matin' in the 'Spleen et idéal' section of the 1857 edition of *Les Fleurs du Mal*. In the 1861 edition, where they are included within 'Tableaux parisiens', they are set apart (as nos 95 and 103), serving ostensibly to articulate a division between Paris by day and Paris by night but more evidently signalling the limbo status of a city that never sleeps—of a twenty-four-hour city in which day and night are as indistinguishable, therefore, as life and death.

That Paris never sleeps reprises the theme of a living death in that the coming night is presented (in 'Le Crépuscule du soir') as offering no rest or respite for those who suffer torment ('Les esprits que dévore une douleur sauvage' (l. 8)), for those who seek answers ('Le savant obstiné dont le front s'alourdit' (l. 9)), or for those who are just plain exhausted ('l'ouvrier courbé qui regagne son lit' (l. 10)). Worse than that perhaps, the night exacerbates the tragedy of daytime desire: 'l'homme impatient se change en bête fauve' (l. 4)). Appetites, whether

---

[40] Cf. 'L'Irréparable': 'Mais mon cœur, que jamais ne visite l'extase, | Est un théâtre où l'on attend | Toujours, toujours en vain, l'Être aux ailes de gaze!' (ll. 48-50).
[41] See i. 795.

digestive ('On entend ça et là les cuisines siffler' (l. 21)) or sexual ('La Prostitution s'allume dans les rues' (l. 15)) or digestive-cum-monetary ('Les tables d'hôte, dont le jeu fait les délices' (l. 23)) continue to be whetted and seemingly sated in the ceaseless poltergeist tumult of a malign economy: 'Cependant des démons malsains dans l'atmosphère | S'éveillent lourdement, comme des gens d'affaire, | Et cognent en volant les volets et l'auvent' (ll. 11–13). Desire is devils' business, a fraudulent transaction whereby he who thinks he receives is all the while being impoverished—as though by death itself: '[La Prostitution] remue au sein de la cité de fange | Comme un ver qui dérobe à l'Homme ce qu'il mange' (ll. 19–20). Bought sex as thieving worm... Like the serpent-devil of the Garden of Eden, whom God condemned for making the first human beings eat of the Tree of Knowledge ('upon thy belly shalt thou go, and dust shalt thou eat all the days of thy life' (Genesis 3:14)), seductive dusk—'le soir charmant' (l. 1), 'Ô soir, aimable soir' (l. 5)—tiptoes in like a criminal's accomplice (ll. 1–2), offering pleasure for sale while devouring our living corpse and robbing us of life. For darkness is the domain of theft ('Et les voleurs, qui n'ont ni trêve ni merci, | Vont bientôt commencer leur travail, eux aussi' (ll. 25–6)), and night-time the pitiless agent of death ('C'est l'heure où les douleurs des malades s'aigrissent! | La sombre Nuit les prend à la gorge' (ll. 31–2)), denying all us inmates of the hospital which is life that longed-for end-of-day solace of domestic repose and a well-fed companionship: 'Plus d'un | Ne viendra plus chercher la soupe parfumée, | Au coin du feu, le soir, auprès d'une âme aimée' (ll. 34–6).

Just as in 'La Mort des pauvres' the illusory 'auberge fameuse' and 'grenier mystique' that are the afterlife appear unlikely to bring food and rest to the destitute, so dusk will bring no respite or comfort to the ailing patients of this symbolic hospital. And so 'Le Crépuscule du soir' ends on a bleak note: 'Encore la plupart n'ont-ils jamais connu | La douceur du foyer et n'ont jamais vécu!' Here is the ultimate paradox of ill-being: those who die shall not even have lived. As the beguiling pleasures of the night start into life, with theatres opening and orchestras tuning up (l. 22), so the poet bids himself be calm: 'Recueille-toi, mon âme, en ce grave moment, | Et ferme ton oreille à ce rugissement' (ll. 29–30). It is the poet's role, it seems, to bear witness to the truth: that the coming of the night—of death—betokens not release or delight but simply yet more misery in this house of want we call life. All he can do, as later in 'Recueillement', is to gather himself in and be still.

Similarly, in 'Le Crépuscule du matin', dawn means not hope and renewal but simply the return of the same-old, and it ends (and the 'Tableaux parisiens' section with it in the 1861 edition) by echoing 'Le Squelette laboureur': 'Et le sombre Paris, en se frottant les yeux, | Empoignait ses outils, vieillard laborieux'. Life is routine and eternal hard labour. Seemingly the early morning is a time for new beginnings, but in reality it represents the return of conflict, be it the awaking barracks (l. 1), or the soul's 'combats' with the body (ll. 7–8), or the 'torture' of sexual desire (announced by the adolescent's wet dream (ll. 3–4)). It is the moment not of reinvigorated perception but of fading dreams ('L'air est plein du frisson des choses qui s'enfuient' (l. 10)) and of a paradoxical combination of relief ('Comme un visage en pleurs que les brises essuient' (l. 9)) and loss ('Et l'homme est las d'écrire et la femme d'aimer' (l. 11)). Literature and love are of the night, illuminated by the lamp (ll. 5–6), while daylight—seen here to triumph over the lamp rather than (as is traditional) over the night—brings a crude illumination to bear on a harsh reality. Women who loved are now women as worn-out sex-workers (ll. 13–14) or cold, starving destitutes (ll. 15–16), some undergoing an agonizing parturient labour of their own (l. 18) in a grim anticipation of the final agony that awaits us all: 'Et les agonisants dans le fond des hospices | Poussaient leur dernier râle en hoquets inégaux' (ll. 22–3).

Whether it be 'Le Crépuscule du soir' or 'Le Crépuscule du matin', the cries of pain and anguish are the same. Be it night or day, life is work, exhaustion, death. While the prostitutes lie gaping, open-mouthed, in 'leur sommeil stupide' (l. 14), their clients, too, are spent. As the manual labourer grabs his tools before setting out on another's day toil, so 'Les débauchés rentraient, brisés par leurs travaux' (l. 24). We are all shiftworkers hot-bedding and hot-desking in this twilight world of ill-being. Limbo may be the abode of poets in Dante's *Inferno*, but in *Les Fleurs du Mal* it is the hospice of us all, including the poet himself: 'Et l'homme est las d'écrire'. Baudelaire's alternative poet-lawgiver—for all that the inhabitants of Lesbos may have singled him out—is no different from the rest of humanity. And Satan now, not Sappho or Orpheus, shall be his role model. Where Orpheus journeyed to the Underworld in search of his lost Eurydice but failed to bring her back because he doubted and looked back, now the poet inhabits a limbo and will pray to Satan to release him. Captive like Eurydice herself within the 'gouffre' of melancholy, he hopes for a return to life.

7
The Beauty of Ill-Being
From Sappho to Satan

De la mâle Sapho, l'amante et le poète
                                  ('Lesbos', ll. 56, 60)
Gloire et louange à toi, Satan
                                  ('Les Litanies de Satan', l. 46)

In examining Baudelaire's aesthetics under the heading of 'Resistance' it became clear that a recurrent feature of his thinking lay in the collapsing and superseding of binary oppositions in a manner that anticipates Derridean deconstruction. The figure of limbo may now be seen as a particularly powerful means of restructuring conventional apprehensions of human experience. Life and afterlife, pleasure and pain, day and night, self and other... all these seeming opposites become the undifferentiated aspects of a single phenomenon, a limbo existence that Baudelaire calls 'le Mal': human life as 'ill-being', 'le mal de vivre'. For the Baudelaire of the 1840s and early 1850s Lesbos and Sappho had provided similarly powerful tropes for a poet who was seeking the 'new' and adopting the role of alternative lawgiver against a backdrop of Christian, and specifically Catholic, orthodoxy. Lesbos, limbo, Sappho: each provides an alternative. Sexual desire, branded by Christians the sin of lust when pursued outside the legitimizations of heterosexuality and marital procreation, is presented as an innocent martyrdom, a living hell; the Christian faith in an afterlife of Hell, purgatory, and/or Heaven is replaced by a conflicted awareness of the living death that is human existence in the here and now; and the poet-lawgiver as Old Testament prophet and political leader now takes on the role of Sapphic initiate, privy to the 'religion' of private passion, to its tormenting pleasures and the deathly spiral of desire. In place of heterosexuality we have a homosexuality that stands in for all sexuality, for same-sex relations remain same-species relations; in place of the putative sequence of life and afterlife we have an existence that is simultaneously life and non-life; and in place of poetry as the Mosaic or Hugolian vista of a promised land we have poetry as 'la conscience dans le Mal', songs of martyred innocence and melancholic beauty that express the 'loi fatale' of our moral degradation and the tragedy of desire. For, as 'Un voyage à Cythère' makes clear, our journey to the island of

The Beauty of Baudelaire: The Poet as Alternative Lawgiver. Roger Pearson, Oxford University Press. © Roger Pearson 2021.
DOI: 10.1093/oso/9780192843319.003.0008

love brings each of us not towards the release of an absorption in the Other but merely to the mirror-image of our own damned self. According to the laws of 'le Mal' same-species love is also necessarily self-hatred.

'Les Fleurs du Mal' (1855): Towards the Beauty of Melancholy

> Chose curieuse et vraiment digne d'attention que l'introduction de cet élément insaisissable du beau jusque dans les œuvres destinées à représenter à l'homme sa propre laideur morale et physique!
> (*De l'essence du rire* (1855), ii. 526)

As we have seen, the women of Lesbos represent an experience of sexual desire to which the poet is not only an initiated and sympathetic witness but also himself tormentedly subject. Baudelaire's portrayal of these women—these 'fleurs du Mal'—transcends the particular circumstances of geography, epoch, and gender, and takes on a more explicitly universal and timeless significance by coming after 'La Destruction', the poem that opens the 'Fleurs du Mal' section of *Les Fleurs du Mal* in both the 1857 and 1861 editions. Nowhere is Baudelaire's perception of the intimate connections between sexuality, melancholy, and poetry more evident than in this allegorical sonnet.[1]

'La Destruction' was originally entitled 'La Volupté' when it was first published in 1855 in the *Revue des Deux Mondes*. There it figures among the eighteen poems that Baudelaire published under the new title of 'Les Fleurs du Mal',[2] and in many ways it constitutes a kind of programme for the later, completed edition of *Les Fleurs du Mal* while also foreshadowing the argument of *Les Paradis artificiels* (1860).

La Destruction

Sans cesse à mes côtés s'agite le Démon;
Il nage autour de moi comme un air impalpable;
Je l'avale et le sens qui brûle mon poumon
Et l'emplit d'un désir éternel et coupable.

Parfois il prend, sachant mon grand amour de l'Art,
La forme de la plus séduisante des femmes,

---

[1] I use the term 'sonnet' to include poems that in French are called 'quatorzains' and which, by containing more than five rhyme pairs, do not strictly conform to the requirements of the Petrarchan sonnet. For discussion of Baudelaire's use of the sonnet form, see Chapter 17.

[2] For a list of these poems see Chapter 6, n. 6. This unitalicized title, between quotation marks, is used here to distinguish this 1855 selection of poems from the 1857 and 1861 editions of *Les Fleurs du Mal*.

> Et, sous de précieux prétextes de cafard,
> Accoutume ma lèvre à des philtres infâmes.
>
> Il me conduit ainsi, loin du regard de Dieu,
> Haletant et brisé de fatigue, au milieu
> Des plaines de l'Ennui, profondes et désertes,
>
> Et jette dans mes yeux pleins de confusion
> Des vêtements souillés, des blessures ouvertes,
> Et l'appareil sanglant de la Destruction!

This demon is a precursor of the Satan who will take centre stage both in 'Au lecteur', itself included in the 1855 'Les Fleurs du Mal', and in the 'Révolte' section of *Les Fleurs du Mal*. In 'La Destruction' the demon serves as a representative of 'le Mal', an 'evil' spirit to be implicitly contrasted with a daemon—that friendly guiding spirit (also known as a familiar or genius) who is sometimes invoked by the poets and philosophers of ancient Greece. Baudelaire's 'Démon' is the demon of desire, associate of the 'démons malsains' of 'Le Crépuscule du soir' but here also clearly comparable with the Satan who unsuccessfully tempted Christ during his forty days of fasting in the wilderness. But 'La Destruction' offers a different slant on this biblical story, for here it is not abstinence but submission to the devil's temptation that causes the poet to end up, exhausted, upon the vast, deserted plains of boredom that bear the hallmarks of a crime scene. Far from the reach of divine watchfulness the poet's own gaze is filled with the 'confusion' of this terrible place to which his particular demon has guided him: soiled clothing that speaks of violence and perhaps of sexual activity, open wounds that betoken loss of blood and life,[3] and the bloody instrument of Destruction that may suggest a guillotine while also offering a parallel with the gallows from which the amorous traveller of 'Un voyage à Cythère' (also included in the 1855 'Les Fleurs du Mal') finds his corpse dangling and already half-devoured by ferocious birds. The landscape of boredom is a place of emptiness surrounded by limitless horizons of nothingness, yet it contains also the ruins of murderous—breath-taking— desire. To live is to breathe, and for the poet the demon of desire—impalpable but ever-present—inhabits the very air he breathes: 'un désir éternel et coupable'. As the poet is led further and further into this landscape of destruction, he gasps and pants for air—like an increasingly frenzied lover perhaps—eager for satisfaction and yet thereby also for the death of his desire and the onset of ennui. Like the wine-drinker and hash-smoker and consumer of laudanum in *Les Paradis*

---

[3] In the former case some editors have seen an allusion to masturbation (see i. 1058 n. 7), though this is dismissed by Adam (ed. cit., 408 n. 1). In the latter case a possible reading of 'blessure' as a metaphor for female genitalia is suggested by comparison with the final two stanzas of 'A celle qui est trop gaie' where this connection is overt (see i. 1058 n. 8). The possible meanings of the last two lines of the poem are discussed in detail in Jonathan Culler, 'Baudelaire's Destruction', *MLN* 127: 4 (Sept. 2012), 699–711.

artificiels, he has drunk 'infamous' love potions and inhaled the devil's air, but his looked-for paradise has proved illusory, a wasteland that serves only to make the ill-being of life seem all the more destructive and sterile.

But how has the poet been thus tempted? Through his 'grand amour de l'Art'. Like some shape-shifting djinn from the *Arabian Nights*, the demon of desire has assumed the form of the most alluring of women, tricking the poet into believing that in seeking sex he is actually pursuing beauty and thus his own true calling. In this respect the poet of 'La Destruction' foreshadows (within the ordering of the 1857 'Fleurs du Mal' section of *Les Fleurs du Mal*) the Sappho of 'Lesbos', 'l'amante et le poète', a victim of the magic potion that has made Phaon seem handsome and caused her simultaneously to betray the female inhabitants of Lesbos and her own calling as a poet. As for Baudelaire's poet, he has listened only too willingly to his own demon's 'spécieux prétextes de cafard': a hypocrite's pretexts, but also the pretext of depression itself.[4] As 'Au lecteur' (with which the 1855 'Les Fleurs du Mal' begins) suggests, 'l'Ennui' is our ugliest 'vice' (ll. 32–3), at once insidious like this shape-shifting demon of desire ('il ne pousse ni grands gestes ni grands cris' (l. 34)) and wholly destructive ('Il ferait volontiers de la terre un débris | Et dans un bâillement avalerait le monde' (ll. 35–6)).

The poet of 'La Destruction' is fooled into believing not only that sex is beauty but also that its pursuit may end his depression, and yet—as the poet of 'Au lecteur' makes plain to no less of a hypocrite (the reader)—that way lies only further melancholy and an artificial paradise of paradoxical destruction: 'C'est l'Ennui!—l'œil chargé d'un pleur involontaire, | Il rêve d'échafauds en fumant son houka' (ll. 37–8). Desire is destructive: natural, 'irremediable', so difficult to resist... but destructive. And here it is 'coupable', not within the framework of a Catholic doctrine of sin (though this may also be so) but because it causes the poet to 'sin' against his 'grand amour de l'Art', against the canon of creativity (as the opposite of destruction). Yet, as will be true of the whole of *Les Fleurs du Mal* and as will be discussed more fully later, the poet's ultimate fidelity to his 'grand amour de l'Art' is manifest in the artistry—indeed in the very existence—of the poem itself. Poetry is the 'counter-law', the alternative, willed ascent in response to the 'loi fatale' of our moral 'dégradation', our relentless 'stepping down' towards boredom and death.

The demon of desire in 'La Destruction' is a close cousin of both 'le Diable' and 'Satan Trismégiste' in 'Au lecteur'. The former—'le Diable qui tient les fils qui nous remuent!' (l. 13)—is the puppeteer who makes us dance to his tune; the latter is the obverse of Hermes Trismegistus, the god of magic and alchemy[5] and also the

---

[4] Both Adam (ed. cit., 409 n. 4) and Pichois (i. 1058 n. 4) insist that 'cafard' is to be taken only in the sense of 'hypocrite', but the double meaning including 'avoir le cafard = to be depressed' seems wholly viable in this context.

[5] 'Satan Trismégiste' is thus the forerunner of the 'Hermès inconnu' of 'Alchimie de la douleur' (l. 5), first published in 1860.

god of writing. In this way 'Satan Trismégiste' represents both the 'destroyer' and yet also the alchemical principle of transformation that Baudelaire's own poetic writing applies in reverse through its creative acts. In 'Au lecteur' the poet introduces his reader in the following terms to the 'genius' who presides over our world of ill-being:

> Sur l'oreiller du mal c'est Satan Trismégiste
> Qui berce longuement notre esprit enchanté,
> Et le riche métal de notre volonté
> Est tout vaporisé par ce savant chimiste.
>
> (ll. 9–12)

Rather than granting us the secret of how to turn base metal into gold, this alternative alchemist—the demon of desire—transforms our will into vapour, the vapour of the devilish air we breathe in 'La Destruction', and imposes the 'loi fatale' of our stepping down into destruction and boredom, our Hell on earth: 'Chaque jour vers l'Enfer nous descendons d'un pas' (l. 15). As the poem suggests, we may talk of remorse and repentance (ll. 3, 5) and even confess our sins (ll. 5–6), but we lack the courage to deny ourselves ('nos repentirs sont lâches'). Meanwhile a whole 'peuple de Démons' makes orgiastic merry in our brains (l. 22), like Cupid blowing bubbles in 'L'Amour et le crâne', and the vaporous air we breathe becomes the condensed liquid of Death, gradually filling our lungs and drowning us (ll. 23–4). If we lack the courage to resist desire, it is also only cowardice that holds us common mortals back from greater evil: 'le viol, le poison, le poignard, l'incendie' (l. 25). Rape, murder, arson,... we ourselves may not commit these acts, such is the banality of our own quotidian evil ('Le canevas banal de nos piteux destins' (l. 27)), but we thrill to the excitement and the horror of it all, for such is our imperative and overriding need not to be bored. In 'Au lecteur' the recurrent lists of accumulating nouns (ll. 1, 25, 29–30) and adjectives (ll. 31, 33) underscore the sense of an ironic multiplicity, of a world rich in apparent difference and interest but that yet may be swallowed up in a single yawn of *in*difference. Ennui— 'ce monstre délicat' (l. 39)—is a fussy eater, and there may be nothing within the whole wide world that can satisfy the monstrous, all-devouring appetite of its desire.

In the 1855 'Les Fleurs du Mal' 'Au lecteur' serves the prefatory function that it will later fulfil in the completed editions. The poet addresses his reader directly, establishing an early complicity by setting out the parameters of our melancholic existence and implying, through this final insistence that boredom is our greatest vice,[6] that in reading the poems to follow the reader may paradoxically avoid this

---

[6] Bénichou comments: 'On se demande pourquoi l'Ennui est le principal des péchés. C'est qu'il s'agit d'un vieux péché catholique qu'on appelle l'*acedia* et qui est le péché d'incuriosité absolue, qui conduit

very sin of acedia by taking an interest in 'La sottise, l'erreur, le péché, la lésine' (l. 1). In other words, and anticipating the argument of 'L'Irrémédiable', Satan himself offers us the 'Soulagement et gloire uniques' of 'la conscience dans le Mal'. Furthermore it is suggested by the new overall title of 'Les Fleurs du Mal' (now replacing both *Les Lesbiennes* and *Les Limbes*) that this 'conscience dans le Mal' may in some way be associated with—and perhaps even productive of—beauty.

Already evident in the presentation of the women of Lesbos as 'fleurs', this association of melancholy and beauty now takes on a new importance in the 1855 grouping of poems. In 'L'Ennemi', for example, time—the eponymous enemy— has taken away the poet's storm-tossed youth and left him with an autumn garden that contains 'bien peu de fruits vermeils' (l. 4) and now lies mortally cratered by torrential rain ('des trous grands comme des tombeaux' (l. 8)). But, thanks to a post-diluvian cultivation of the new ('il faut employer la pelle et les râteaux | Pour rassembler à neuf les terres inondées' (ll. 6–7)), from this landscape of melancholy and destruction future flowers perhaps may grow: 'Et qui sait si les fleurs nouvelles que je rêve | Trouveront dans ce sol lavé comme une grève | Le mystique aliment qui ferait leur vigueur?' (ll. 9–11). In 'Le Guignon' such flowers more explicitly figure the poet's own art, his labour of Sisyphus (ll. 1–4). As he treads his solitary way down the beaten track of time that leads to death, so perhaps he may uncover some hidden, off-piste beauty:

> —Maint joyau dort enseveli
> Dans les ténèbres et l'oubli,
> Bien loin des pioches et des sondes;
>
> Mainte fleur épanche à regret
> Son parfum doux comme un secret
> Dans les solitudes profondes.
>
> (ll. 9–14)[7]

And as the poet of 'La Vie antérieure' confirms, this is the new and secret beauty of melancholy, born of '[l]e secret douloureux qui me faisait languir' (l. 14).[8]

The most striking feature of the 1855 'Les Fleurs du Mal' is the introduction of what we might call 'anti-melancholy', that is, the exploration of states of being or activity that may serve variously to offer a permanent alternative to melancholy or

---

à mépriser le souci de Dieu et qui menace surtout les moines vivants dans la solitude' (Bénichou, 'Le Satan de Baudelaire', 13). Cf. 'Spleen (J'ai plus de souvenirs que si j'avais mille ans...'), l. 17: 'L'ennui, fruit de la morne incuriosité'.

[7] These tercets rework to new thematic purpose a well-known quatrain from Thomas Gray's 'Elegy Written in a Country Churchyard': 'Full many a gem of purest ray serene | The dark unfathomed caves of ocean bear: | Full many a flower is born to blush unseen, | And waste its sweetness on the desert air' (ll. 53–6). See i. 859–60.

[8] 'L'Ennemi', 'Le Guignon', and 'La Vie antérieure' were subsequently grouped together in 'Spleen et idéal' in both editions of *Les Fleurs du Mal*.

else a temporary escape from it, an escape nevertheless whose ultimately illusory nature only further exacerbates the condition. The second poem in the grouping, following 'Au lecteur', is 'Réversibilité', in which Baudelaire plays implicitly on a supposed Catholic doctrine (most probably derived by him from De Maistre) according to which the suffering of the innocent may serve to expiate the sinfulness of the wicked.[9] Here, in a poem that Baudelaire had earlier sent to Apollonie Sabatier, the poet addresses an unnamed woman as the muse of 'anti-melancholy': 'Ange plein de bonheur, et de joie et de lumières!' (ll. 21, 25). She is also the angel of 'gaieté' (ll. 1, 5), 'bonté' (ll. 6, 10), 'santé' (ll. 11, 15), and 'beauté' (ll. 16, 20). But from her angelic vantage-point can she ever have witnessed or known all the various manifestations of 'le Mal' that are here set out in a reprise of the listing technique of 'Au lecteur': anguish, hatred, sickness, ageing? The questioning is rhetorical, readable as a series of reproaches for the beloved's indifference to her lover's suffering (see i. 915) but also as a way of contrasting the implausibility of her goodness with an exhaustive account of 'le Mal'.

The poem ends, however, with a display of the poet's own virtue. Just as an elderly King David was presented with a young virgin who might warm his dying blood 'but the king knew her not' (1 Kings: 1, 1–4; cf. 'Réversibilité', ll. 22–3), the poet asks only that his beloved pray for him—a request that in itself suggests that her goodness may already have gone some small way towards redeeming him. But the illusory nature of her perfection—and of such redemption—is suggested by 'Confession' (placed after it in *Les Fleurs du Mal* but separated from it by 'Le Tonneau de la Haine' in the 1855 grouping) in which she, albeit apparently in one single, faltering moment of doubt, 'confesses' that 'rien ici-bas n'est certain' (l. 26); that 'l'égoïsme humain' (l. 28) is endemic in our condition, no matter how it disguises itself; and that female attempts to conceal the ageing process ('c'est un dur métier que d'être belle femme [...] c'est le travail banal | De la danseuse folle et froide qui se pâme | Dans un sourire machinal' (ll. 29–32)) are doomed: 'tout craque, amour et beauté' (l. 34). Her amorous endeavours, she believes, will soon be consigned to eternal oblivion (ll. 35–6)—except that the poet, ironically, now finds himself often recalling 'cette confidence horrible chuchotée | Au confessional du cœur' (ll. 39–40) and here records it, as it were for all time, in the poem itself. From a moment of despair springs an enduring memory perpetuated in art.

In 'L'Aube spirituelle', nonetheless, the poet returns to the redemptive theme of 'Réversibilité' and the renewed possibility of an 'anti-melancholy'. As those who have spent the night in debauch observe the bright new dawn now 'entering into society' with 'l'Idéal rongeur' (l. 2), there occurs 'l'opération d'un mystère vengeur'

---

[9] See i. 915–16. In particular De Maistre employed the idea in order to incorporate the slaughter of innocent people during the Terror within a providentialist narrative that values this slaughter as partially expiating the sins committed by the Revolution in abolishing the divine right of kings and executing Louis XVI. See *Unacknowledged Legislators*, 307.

(l. 3) whereby '[d]ans la brute assoupie un ange se réveille' (l. 4). Here the dark, demonic vengeance of 'Le Tonneau de la Haine' has become the sunrise of an angelic atonement, just as the image of being eaten away by remorse as though by worms (with which image later in 'Les Fleurs du Mal' 'L'Irréparable' begins and 'Remords posthume' hauntingly ends)[10] is here instead the gnawing insistence of the 'Idéal rongeur'. Similarly, the poet's 'gouffre' of despair (for example, in 'De profondis clamavi') becomes here the 'reverse' 'gouffre' (l. 7) of a hitherto inaccessible spiritual heaven that opens up before the man of melancholy ('l'homme terrassé qui rêve encore et souffre' (l. 6)) and draws him ineluctably in. Now the poet's insistent memory of his beloved ('chère Déesse, Être lucide et pur' (l. 8)) is no longer that of her 'horrible' confession but rather a 'souvenir plus clair, plus rose, plus charmant' (l. 10). As in 'Le Crépuscule du matin', sunlight 'blacks out' the artificial light of human beings (in this case 'la flamme des bougies' (l. 12)), a sunlight that here equates to the 'Âme resplendissante' (l. 14) of the woman he loves, her shining spirit with its eternal capacity to triumph over the brutish and the debauched. Sunrise no longer symbolizes, as it does in 'Le Crépuscule du matin', the repetitiveness of a banal quotidian cyclicity, but rather the endless possibility of spiritual renewal.

If 'L'Aube spirituelle' proclaims the existence of an alternative and redemptive moral universe of 'anti-melancholy', so also in similar fashion do various poems in the 1855 'Les Fleurs du Mal' that call up the vista of an alternative landscape, somewhere in the past or elsewhere in the present, in which beauty peaceably co-habits with 'le Mal'. In 'La Vie antérieure' the poet is beset by '[l]e secret douloureux qui me faisait languir', but his surroundings are those of an exotic paradise, a harmonious maritime world of sunsets and waves and unclothed slaves gently fanning his brow with cooling palm-leaves: 'C'est là que j'ai vécu dans les voluptés calmes' (l. 9). But this is all in the past, while his secret pain no doubt lives on.

The most idyllic example of a present elsewhere comes in 'L'Invitation au voyage' where, as the refrain reminds us, a peaceful sensual fulfilment again is key: 'Là, tout n'est qu'ordre et beauté,|Luxe, calme et volupté.' Here, too, there is harmony and a sense of belonging, even of homecoming to a native hearth: 'Tout y parlerait | À l'âme en secret | Sa douce langue natale' (ll. 24–6). But this elsewhere remains just that, an elsewhere: 'Mon enfant, ma sœur, | Songe à la douceur | D'aller là-bas vivre ensemble! (ll. 1–3)'—and an elsewhere that appears to offer in the future simply a 'beautiful' mirror image of a painful and conflicted present reality: 'Les soleils mouillés | De ces ciels brouillés | Pour mon esprit ont les charmes | Si mystérieux | De tes traîtres yeux, | Brillant à travers leurs larmes' (ll. 7–12). Sunshine and showers scarcely speak of a calm voluptuousness.

---

[10] Cf. also the first stanza of 'Au lecteur': 'Et nous alimentons nos aimables remords, | Comme les mendiants nourrissent leur vermine' (ll. 3–4).

Moreover, along the canals of this ideal (Dutch)[11] destination, even the tethered boats—'Dont l'humeur est vagabonde' (l. 31)—seem to evoke the 'treacherous' fickleness of the beloved herself, temporarily moored but ready to wander. Simultaneously these boats may suggest that the poet himself desires to travel only and above all—as the boats themselves do—in order to satisfy the every whim of a demanding mistress: 'C'est pour assouvir | Ton moindre désir | Qu'ils viennent du bout du monde' (ll. 32–4). For all that the lovers' hotel room might contain '[l]es plus rares fleurs' (l. 18), 'le Mal' of amorous tensions and an inescapable 'égoïsme humain' will thus remain only too plainly visible in its 'miroirs profonds' (l. 22).[12]

In the 1855 'Les Fleurs du Mal' 'L'Invitation au voyage' is followed by 'Moesta et errabunda' (in French, 'triste et vagabonde'), which takes up this combination of imagined idyll and melancholic reality. In this case the poet addresses himself to 'Agathe', asking her if in her heart she ever imagines herself away from the black ocean of 'l'immonde cité' (l. 2) and surrounded instead by a sunlit ocean that is 'Bleu, clair, profond, ainsi que la virginité' (l. 4). Such is the poet's empathy that Agathe's imagined yearning becomes the poet's own urgent desire to flee: 'Emporte-moi, wagon! enlève-moi, frégate!' (l. 11). Theirs is a vale of tears ('ici la boue est faite de nos pleurs!' (l. 12)), and the longing for an elsewhere seems all the more desperate because of it: 'Comme vous êtes loin, paradis parfumé' (ll. 16, 20). As the reference to 'virginité' already suggests, this particular paradise is characterized by innocence ('Tout n'est qu'amour et joie' (l. 17)), for this is 'le vert paradis des amours enfantines' (ll. 21, 25), the paradise lost of childhood ('[l]'innocent paradis, plein de plaisir furtifs' (ll. 26, 30)), and a paradise already 'plus loin que l'Inde et que la Chine' (l. 27).

But is this paradise lost? In his reading of 'Moesta et errabunda' Jean Starobinski notes that each of the first four stanzas begins with a question or implied wish that goes unanswered and contends that the repetition of these opening lines as the final line of each stanza (the poem consists of six quintils) reinforces a sense of loss and impossibility: 'Dans "Moesta et errabunda", il n'y a pas de *revenir* vers Agathe [...] Il n'y pas de départ non plus. [...] Aucune réponse n'est reçue, c'est l'interrogation ou l'imploration qui se répète.'[13] But one

---

[11] This is made explicit only in the prose poem 'L'Invitation au voyage'.

[12] In 'Ciel brouillé', first published in 1857 in *Les Fleurs du Mal* (where as no. 46 it immediately precedes 'L'Invitation au voyage'), the changeable nature of the poet's mistress ('Ô femme dangereuse' (l. 13)) is conveyed by a similar use of landscape, complemented by a four-stanza structure corresponding to the four seasons of the year.

[13] See his published lecture 'Le Poème de l'invitation' in Jean Starobinski, *Le Poème de l'invitation, précédé d'un entretien avec Frédéric Wandelère et suivi d'un propos d'Yves Bonnefoy* (Geneva: La Dogana, 2001), 51–88 (81). Starobinski also discusses the possible intertextual presence in this poem of some lines by André Chénier, and, by extension, of the Horatian model of the 'poem of invitation'. This in turn raises the further possibility that the poet's evocation of a childhood past is here mirrored by the evocation of a poetic past, even of an innocent literary (pre-revolutionary) period when it was possible to evoke the joys of nature without irony.

might argue that when in the final two stanzas the poet asks of the lost paradise: 'Peut-on le rappeler avec des cris plaintifs, | Et l'animer encor d'une voix argentine, | L'innocent paradis plein de plaisirs furtifs?' (ll. 28–30), the answer is 'yes'. For the poet has just done precisely this in his poem: with his own 'cris plaintifs' ('enlève-moi, frégate') and a silver-tongued listing of myriad delights: 'Les courses, les chansons, les baisers, les bouquets, | Les violons vibrant derrière les collines, | Avec les brocs de vin, le soir, dans les bosquets' (ll. 22–4)—a floral, sylvan idyll of wine and song and accommodating shrubbery. Here for the first time in Baudelaire's published work is the idea that the beauty of a child's vision of the world, later to be foregrounded at the beginning of 'Le Voyage', can be recovered through art, the idea as he later puts it that 'le génie n'est que l'enfance retrouvée à volonté'.[14] In this way we see emerging in the 1855 'Les Fleurs du Mal' the possibility of a synergy between melancholy and beauty, for in depicting that for which we melancholically long it is necessary to paint a picture of paradise, even if through the very act of painting that paradise our loss may come to seem all the more acute and unbearable.

As 'Moesta et errabunda' also demonstrates, in an alternative synergy of 'réversibilité', we cannot turn back the clock but we can remember. In this respect the poem constitutes a counterpart to 'Remords posthume' and 'L'Irréparable', for in Baudelaire's gradually developing poetic and moral vision remorse now stands as the melancholic obverse of memory, the memory that can bring us a world of the 'idéal' (interpreted as the creativity of the imagination) with which to alleviate our spleen. In 'Remords posthume' the poet returns to his device of illustrating the reality of the living by imagining the existence of the dead, in this case by telling his mistress ('courtisane imparfaite' (l. 12))—with the bitter sarcasm of an unloved lover, and as though he were her future tomb speaking—that there will be no point in her regretting in death her inability to love while she was alive. 'Remords posthume' is itself that future tomb: 'Le tombeau, confident de mon rêve infini | (Car le tombeau toujours comprendra le poète)' (ll. 9–10). The poet's own sonnet will constitute 'un monument construit en marbre noir' (l. 2) and serve to immobilize these faithless, vagabond feet that are wont to 'courir leur course aventureuse' (l. 8)), just as it will ensure that 'ma belle ténébreuse' (l. 1) shall forever be remembered as a lady of the night. The poetic tomb shall comprehend (understand and contain) not only the poet but his heartless mistress too so that the melancholic lover may gain revenge through the beauty of an imaginary and eternal remorse.

In 'L'Irréparable'[15] remorse is the worm that eats away at us while we are alive just as real worms will devour us when we die. This is memory as destruction, an old enemy (l. 7)) as terrible as time itself, and weighing us down ('pareil au

---

[14] On Baudelaire's treatment of childhood, see Rosemary Lloyd, *The Land of Lost Content: Children and Childhood in Nineteenth-Century French Literature* (Oxford: Oxford University Press, 1992), 101–8.
[15] In its 1855 version this poem was entitled 'A la Belle aux cheveux d'or', an allusion to a *féerie* in which the poem's original (unnamed) addressee, the actress Marie Daubrun, had starred some years previously (see i. 931–2).

mourant qu'écrasent les blessés' (l. 13) just like the wounded soldier who is smothered beneath 'un grand tas de morts' in 'La Cloche fêlée' or here the 'soldat brisé' (l. 18) who fears his corpse may soon be devoured by wolf or crow (in the manner of the dangling, half-pecked remains in 'Un voyage à Cythère'). To feel remorse is to be haunted by the 'irreparable', the constant deadly thought that some deed cannot be undone, a terrible blackness in which the light of hope in some inn of future comfort has been snuffed out: 'Le Diable a tout éteint aux carreaux de l'Auberge!' (l. 30). To feel remorse is to despair of redemption, of an afterlife beyond a present of bleak suffering. Instead the poet—'cet esprit comblé d'angoisse' (l. 12)—is damned to live forever with 'l'irrémissible' (l. 32). Though he may fondly recall a play in which a beautiful fairy (the part once played by Marie Daubrun) was able to '[t]errasser l'énorme Satan' (l. 47), now in the theatre of his own heart—'que jamais ne visite l'extase' (l. 48)—he waits in vain (like the poet of 'Le Rêve d'un curieux') for his own equivalent of 'l'Être aux ailes de gaze!' (l. 50). But the angel of 'Réversibilité' is absent from this scenario, on a stage ultimately dominated by Satan. If, at the beginning of the poem, remorse resembles a worm, it also recalls the snake in the Garden of Eden: 'le vieux, le long Remords, | Qui vit, s'agite et se tortille' (ll. 1–2). In stanzas 3 and 7 the poet addresses his laments neither to an angel nor to a fairy but to a 'belle sorcière', and yet it seems that 'le Mal' is not so easily to be magicked away.

The 1855 'Les Fleurs du Mal' thus combines earlier themes with new ones that will be central to the later, completed collections. Indeed the grouping includes three poems published previously in *Les Limbes*, thus reprising former themes in a new context: for example, the comparison of desire to rabies ('Le Tonneau de la Haine') and the characterization of life as a living death ('La Cloche fêlée', 'De profundis clamavi'). At the same time it includes three poems ('La Destruction', 'Un voyage à Cythère', 'L'Amour et le crâne') that will become part of the 'Fleurs du Mal' section of *Les Fleurs du Mal* where they complement the Lesbos poems by depicting sexual desire as a pathway to death. These characterizations of the tragedy of desire are now complemented by the trope of a blood-sucking, life-taking vampirism,[16] an image here applied not only to a lover ('Le Vampire') but also to time itself ('L'Ennemi')—so that the idea of time robbing us of the past and leading us fatally towards death becomes an important new aspect of Baudelaire's presentation of melancholy. As 'Le Guignon' records, the passage of time is

---

[16] In the manuscript of poems that Baudelaire sent to Théophile Gautier sometime between Sept. 1851 and the beginning of Jan. 1852 for possible publication in the *Revue de Paris*, and known as the 'Douze poèmes' (see i. 806–7), two poems—'Les Métamorphoses du vampire' and 'La Fontaine de sang'—are the first to articulate this image, both being later included in the 'Fleurs du Mal' section of *Les Fleurs du Mal*. 'Les Métamorphoses du vampire' was one of the six poems banned from subsequent publication. The other ten poems in the manuscript were: 'Le Crépuscule du matin', 'Le Crépuscule du soir', 'La Mendiante rousse' (*sic*), 'La Rançon' (not later included in *Les Fleurs du Mal*), 'Le Vin des chiffonniers', 'Le Reniement de saint Pierre' (first published separately in the *Revue de Paris* in Oct. 1852), 'Bohémiens en voyage', 'La Mort des pauvres', 'Le Guignon', and 'Un voyage à Cythère'.

particularly inimical to the artist, and the poet readily adopts the ancient Hippocratic aphorism 'ars longa, via brevis' ('L'Art est long et le Temps est court' (l. 4)). Moreover the 'Spleen et idéal' section of *Les Fleurs du Mal* will subsequently end (in 1861) with 'L'Horloge' in which the theme of vampiric time recurs (l. 12) and the clock calls on the listener to resist the destructive alchemy of Satan Trismegistus with the mineral extraction of a willed life: 'Les minutes, mortel folâtre, sont des gangues | Qu'il ne faut pas lâcher sans en extraire l'or!' (ll. 15–16). Within this time-limited context, therefore, the demon's temptation of the poet in 'La Destruction', luring him away from creative artistry into the arms of women, seems all the more destructive.

In these ways the 1855 'Les Fleurs du Mal' takes us close to the major themes and images of *Les Fleurs du Mal*, and of its major new section, 'Spleen et idéal'. Instead of lesbianism we now have the poet's own tormented erotic experience. The use of limbo as an image for the interchangeability of life and death and, more broadly, of the indifferentiation or universal sameness of life itself is now complemented by the idea of 'reversibility', with which the poet explores what might be called the potential 'dynamic' of duality (rather than the illusory nature of the differences implied by binary oppositions). Might it be that the creativity of art can in some way compensate for the destructiveness of 'le Mal'? Might there be a beauty to be wrought from melancholy just as at the heart of all beauty there is always melancholy? At the same time the grouping of poems within 'Les Fleurs du Mal' begins to adumbrate that within *Les Fleurs du Mal*, in particular the so-called 'love cycles'. 'De profundis clamavi' ('Le Spleen'), 'Le Vampire', and 'Remords posthume' are thought to have been inspired by Jeanne Duval; 'Réversibilité', 'Confession', and 'L'Aube spirituelle' were originally sent to Apollonie Sabatier; and 'L'Invitation au voyage' and 'L'Irréparable' ('A la Belle aux cheveux d'or') spring from Baudelaire's relationship with Marie Daubrun. 'Moesta et errabunda', addressed to 'Agathe', in turn foreshadows that group of poems in 'Spleen et idéal' in which the poetic persona (and no doubt Baudelaire himself)—still irremediably subject to the shape-shifting temptations of 'La Destruction'—draws inspiration from individual women, several of whom are named.[17]

Most notably of all, Baudelaire's account of the melancholy of desire, whether on the island of Lesbos or in the poet's own heart, has become an investigation of the relationship between sexuality and artistic creativity, between 'la forme de la plus séduisante des femmes' and 'mon grand amour de l'Art'. In 'La Destruction' this duality is presented firmly as an 'either/or', with the apparent implication that the poet should choose art over love, creativity over destruction. Yet perhaps, as so

---

[17] In the 1861 edition, poems 59–64. See i. 938 where Pichois questions the traditional description of this grouping as 'le cycle des héroïnes secondaires' on the grounds that '[e]n fait, ces héroïnes ont eu, à un moment, à un instant peut-être, la même importance que Jeanne, Mme Sabatier ou Marie Daubrun. Mais chacune n'a inspiré à Baudelaire qu'un poème'.

often in Baudelaire's work, an apparent 'either/or' is a 'both' that transcends the choice: namely, an art born of destruction—and in a process that will be proclaimed at the end of 'Une charogne': 'j'ai gardé la forme et l'essence divine | De mes amours décomposés'. The very 'dégradation' wrought by desire—that is to say, a disintegration and a decomposition as well as a 'stepping down'—may actually in turn facilitate an imaginative alchemy of recomposition and reintegration through aesthetic creativity.

'Douze poèmes' (1851-2/1857): Enter Satan

Ô Satan, prends pitié de ma longue misère!
('Les Litanies de Satan')

This relationship between ephemeral desire and lasting art, recalling (from the *Salon de 1846*) and anticipating (in *Le Peintre de la vie moderne*) Baudelaire's definition of 'modern' art in terms of an interdependence of the transitory and the eternal, will soon provide the key articulation of the structure of 'Spleen et idéal' and, more broadly, the central dialectic of 'le Mal' and 'les fleurs'. But in the so-called 'Douze poèmes' of 1851-2 it is already manifest in individual poems: for example, in 'La Mendiante rousse' (later 'À une mendiante rousse') where the poet demonstrates with quasi-exhibitionist virtuosity how to see beyond poverty to beauty, and also—with rather less virtuosity—in 'La Rançon'. Here, somewhat improbably, Baudelaire's poet prepares for the Day of Judgement, considering what 'ransom' a man may be asked to pay for his deliverance from life. What shall be the fruit of his time on earth?

For these earthly labours he has but two fields to till: 'L'un est l'Art, et l'autre l'Amour' (l. 9), and he must stand ready at the end of the day to show God 'des granges | Pleines de moissons' and 'des fleurs | Dont les formes et les couleurs | Gagnent le suffrage des Anges' (ll. 14–16). But Baudelaire himself does not believe in any such Day of Judgement. There is no need to 'rendre le juge propice, | Lorsque de la stricte justice | Paraîtra le terrible jour' (ll. 10–12), for there are no eternal laws by which we shall all be judged, still less perhaps a God to judge us. For the 'loi fatale' of moral degradation is descriptive not prescriptive in its legislation—just like the 'lois éternelles de la destruction'.[18] In 'Bohémiens en voyage' and 'Le Reniement de saint Pierre', both among the 'Douze poèmes', the

---

[18] See Baudelaire's comment on Pierre Dupont: 'Il y a dans son esprit une certaine force qui implique toujours la bonté; et sa nature, peu propre à se résigner aux lois éternelles de la destruction, ne veut accepter que les idées consolantes où elle peut trouver des éléments qui lui soient analogues' (ii. 172). And cf. Sade: 'La destruction étant une des premières lois de la nature, rien de ce qui détruit ne saurait être un crime.' (Quoted from *La Philosophie dans le boudoir* in Marcel Ruff, *L'Esprit du mal et l'esthétique baudelairienne* (Paris: Armand Colin, 1955), 57–8.)

poet rejects the existence of God. Inspired by an engraving by Jacques Callot (1592-1635), 'Bohémiens en voyage' describes these 'bohemians'—gypsies or travellers representing not only the 'alternative' artists of 'la Bohème' but also mankind at large—as having yesterday set off on a purely terrestrial journey towards death. Taking with them their own 'harvest' of children, carried on their backs or latched to female breasts, these men walk without illusion: 'Promenant sur le ciel des yeux appesantis | Par le morne regret des chimères absentes' (ll. 7-8). No God watches over them, only a wayside cricket who sings louder at their approach and mother Nature (in the shape of the pagan earth goddess Cybele (l. 11)) who '[f]ait couler le rocher et fleurir le désert' (l. 12): songs and flowers to sustain these travellers as they head towards their final destination, 'L'empire familier des ténèbres futures' (l. 14). Baudelaire's 'bohemians' may constitute a 'tribu prophétique' (l. 1), but as they journey forward in imitation of Moses and the Israelites, it is not Moses but nature herself—'qui les aime' (l. 11)—who smites the rock to bring forth water that will quench their thirst and in order also to irrigate the sterile earth that flowers therein may grow. For their only Promised Land is familiar death. Gypsies may be celebrated as 'prophetic' fortune-tellers, but poets are the true clairvoyants.

Such is this particular poet-lawgiver's prophecy, as it is also in 'Le Reniement de saint Pierre'. In this more stridently atheistic poem, which will become the first of three poems in the 'Révolte' section of *Les Fleurs du Mal*,[19] the poet infers from the suffering of the innocent on earth ('[l]es sanglots des martyrs et des suppliciés' (l. 5)) not the 'reversibility' of a vicarious atonement but rather the existence of a God for whom such sobbing—and cursing and blaspheming (ll. 1, 4)—is sweet music to His ears, 'une symphonie enivrante' (l. 6) lulling Him to sleep like some tyrant who has gorged on meat and wine (l. 3). Where is the God of mercy and forgiveness? Even Jesus doubted Him in the Garden of Olives (ll. 9-12)... And the poet now addresses a melancholic and only too human Christ ('ton crâne où vivait l'immense Humanité' (l. 16)), tortured on the Cross and remembering his own lost paradise of hope, the 'éternelle promesse' of which he was the messenger as he rode into Jerusalem along a flower-strewn path on Palm Sunday (ll. 21-4) and as he cast out the money-lenders from the temple '[o]ù tu fus maître enfin' (ll. 25-7). Perhaps, suggests the poet with his own impiety, Christ felt some remorse for having duped mankind with his 'dream': 'Le remords n'a-t-il pas | Pénétré ton flanc plus avant que la lance?' (ll. 27-8). Was he not, in fact, crucified by *doubt*? Ending on a note of sarcastic and petulant defiance, and employing the least lyrical and most irreverent of tones, the poet identifies with St Peter in denying Christ himself: 'Saint Pierre a renié Jésus... il a bien fait!' (l. 32). Since this is a world in which even the most noble of desires can never be satisfied, the

---

[19] When originally published in the *Revue de Paris* in Oct. 1852 this poem was officially condemned for being irreligious but in the event not legally prosecuted. See i. 1077.

poet will himself be glad to leave it: 'Certes, je sortirai, quant à moi, satisfait | D'un monde où l'action n'est pas la sœur du rêve' (ll. 29–30)—relieved to escape rather than happy to live on, say, in the fond hope of some compensatory afterlife in which desire and fulfilment are always sisters. And so this poet, like Satan, is a rebel, a 'révolté', ready to live by the sword of blasphemy and die by it (l. 31)! God may or may not exist, but in rejecting the divinity of Christ the poet rejects God anyway.

This absence of God from the universe, perceived in 'Bohémiens en voyage' as a source of melancholy ('le morne regret des chimères absentes'), will later be implied also in 'Les Aveugles' (published in 1860 and then included in 'Tableaux parisiens' in 1861) where the poet describes these unsighted people gazing upwards at the sky even as they walk blindly forward in their darkness and—'plus qu'eux hébété' (l. 13)—rhetorically asks: 'Que cherchent-ils au Ciel, tous ces aveugles?' (l. 14). For now the poet's stance is more aggressively contrarian, the blasphemy of a poet who has thrown in his lot with St Peter (ironically—and etymologically—the 'rock' upon which Christ built his Church) and with Satan, the rebellious angel of 'le Mal'. Subsequently he will identify with that other rebel, Cain (in 'Abel et Caïn', first published in Les Fleurs du Mal (1857) as the second poem in 'Révolte'):[20] Cain, the first son of Adam and Eve, whose sacrifice of the fruit of *his* labours (cf. 'La Rançon') was rejected by God; who slew his younger brother Abel, whose sacrifice God had accepted; and who thus became the first human being to become an instrument of death. The poet of 'Abel et Caïn' ends by exhorting Cain's descendants to join him in rejecting God: 'Race de Caïn, au ciel monte, | Et sur la terre jette Dieu!' (ll. 31–2). But the blasphemy of 'Révolte' will be complete only with the third poem, 'Les Litanies de Satan',[21] in which the poet adopts the incantatory style of religious liturgy and combines a parody of the Miserere (Psalm 51 begins: 'Have mercy upon me, O God') with the repetitive character of a litany, listing Satan's attributes in couplets that are punctuated by an insistent refrain: 'Ô Satan, prends pitié de ma longue misère.' By this refrain Satan is addressed as a kind of patron saint of melancholy (cf. 'ô Satan, patron de ma détresse' in 'Épilogue (I)'), but here because, as the couplets demonstrate, he is also a model of resistance ('qui, vaincu, toujours te redresses plus fort' (l. 5)) and a rallying point for all who suffer, that is, for Baudelaire's own 'misérables' who have been banished like Adam and Eve from a paradise on earth as Satan himself was cast out from Heaven. What better patriarch or Early Father of the Church could there be to follow than this 'Père adoptif de ceux qu'en sa noire colère | Du paradis terrestre a chassés Dieu le Père' (ll. 43–4)?

---

[20] The political implications of 'Abel et Caïn' suggest that this poem may date back to the period 1848–52 (see Adam, ed. cit., 422), while 'Les Litanies de Satan' may be contemporary with it (see i. 1083). Both poems thus belong with the group of poems so far considered from 'Les Fleurs du Mal' (1855) and the so-called 'Douze poèmes', including 'Le Reniement de saint Pierre'.

[21] Max Milner notes of this poem in particular that it owes much to a contemporary fashion for blasphemous verse. See Le Diable dans la littérature française, ii. 431–2.

This is Satan as Lucifer ('le plus savant et le plus beau des Anges' (l. 1)), the Prince of Darkness exiled from Heaven (l. 4), wronged and yet unbowed (l. 5), possessed of all knowledge ('Toi qui sais tout' (l. 7)) since he has experienced Hell ('grand roi des choses souterraines' (l. 7)) as well as Heaven and is therefore able to understand and relieve human suffering ('Guérisseur familier des angoisses humaines' (l. 8)). He above all can inspire those who know only ill-being or rejection to reach for Paradise through sexual passion (ll. 10–11), just as he can offer wretched human beings hope through the prospect of death (ll. 13–14) and set an example to the condemned in how to retain the moral high ground (ll. 16–17). As 'king of the subterranean' he knows (as does the poet of *Les Fleurs du Mal*) the whereabouts of precious stones and metals (ll. 19–20, ll. 22–3), that is, of hidden value and undiscovered beauty; as Prince of Darkness he can protect the somnambulist (ll. 25–6), us blind human beings who walk in darkness; as magician he can ensure the charmed life of a drunk (ll. 28–9).[22] To the weak he has given the means to make gunpowder with which to mount their own defence (ll. 31–2); on the rich he has brought opprobrium (ll. 34–5), while he has inspired young women to love the ragged heroes of the revolutionary cause and nurse their wounds (ll. 37–8). This is Satan as resistance leader, and a Satan who helps us all: providing the stick on which the wandering exile leans or the lamp by whose light the inventor creates the new, and acting as father confessor to all who resist ('conspirateurs') as he does to all who are caught ('pendus') (ll. 41–2). *Pace* Bénichou, this is not 'le Satan méchant' but 'le Satan rebelle'.

Glory be to Satan...Instead of God the Father this is Satan the Father: 'Confesseur' (l. 41), 'Père adoptif' (l. 43), an alternative god to whom the poet appeals insistently for compassion like the resistance fighter he, the poet, also is, seeking a solution to his melancholic plight. Satan...who for this poet of melancholy can be the only plausible addressee of his all-important closing 'Prière'—with its parody of St John's vision of God's throne in the Book of Revelation:[23]

> Gloire et louange à toi, Satan, dans les hauteurs
> Du Ciel, où tu régnas, et dans les profondeurs
> De l'Enfer, où, vaincu, tu rêves en silence!
> Fais que mon âme un jour, sous l'Arbre de Science,
> Près de toi se repose, à l'heure où sur ton front
> Comme un Temple nouveau ses rameaux s'épandront!
>
> (ll. 46–51)

---

[22] Cf. i. 1085 n. 4: 'Baudelaire inverse le dicton qui veut qu'il y ait un dieu pour les ivrognes.'

[23] 'And every creature which is in heaven, and on the earth, and under the earth, and such as are in the sea, and all that are in them, heard I saying, Blessing, and honour, and glory, and power, be unto him that sitteth upon the throne[.]' Revelation 5: 13.

Only Satan truly knows how it feels to lose Paradise, and only through Satan can the poet ever hope to return there. The tree of melancholy knowledge—'la conscience dans le Mal'—shall be the new temple of a secular redemption ('Flambeau des grâces sataniques'), and its boughs—recalling Palm Sunday ('le dimanche des Rameaux')—shall spread over the flower-strewn path of a new entry into Jerusalem for the poet as alternative lawgiver. Hence the frontispiece that Baudelaire at one stage sought to include in the second edition of *Les Fleurs du Mal*, which would have depicted '[u]n *squelette arborescent, l'arbre de la science du bien et du mal*, à l'ombre duquel fleurissent les sept péchés capitaux sous la forme de plantes allégoriques' (*Corr.* ii. 87). The words here are those of Baudelaire's publisher, Auguste Poulet-Malassis, but the intention was his own: that the engraver Félix Bracquemond depict the Tree of Knowledge as a skeletal emblem of human mortality casting its shade over the flora of ill-being. In the event a similar engraving, by Félicien Rops, figured as the frontispiece to *Les Épaves*, together with an 'explication' (again by Poulet-Malassis): 'Sous le Pommier fatal, dont le tronc-squelette rappelle la déchéance de la race humaine, s'épanouissent les Sept Péchés Capitaux, figurés par des plantes aux formes et aux attitudes symboliques. Le Serpent, enroulé au bassin du squelette, rampe vers ces *Fleurs du mal*.'[24] The engraving shows us flowers but the italics point to the poems: melancholy is beautiful in both life and art.

Les Fleurs du Mal (1857): 'La Satanica Commedia'?

> Il y a du Dante, en effet, dans l'auteur des *Fleurs du mal*, mais c'est du Dante d'une époque déchue, c'est du Dante athée et moderne, du Dante venu après Voltaire[.].
>
> (Jules Barbey D'Aurevilly, '*Les Fleurs du mal* par M. Charles Baudelaire')[25]

> There is no other book of poems in which the poet as such presents himself with so little vanity and so much force. This fact provides a basis for the frequent comparison with Dante.
>
> (Walter Benjamin, *The Arcades Project*)[26]

Before the publication of *Les Fleurs du Mal* in 1857 Baudelaire had published—or, as in the case of the 'Douze poèmes', had prepared for publication—36 of the 101

---

[24] The description continues by explaining other details. See i. 812–3 for the full text and the circumstances surrounding the publication of *Les Épaves*.
[25] See André Guyaux (ed.), *Baudelaire: Un demi-siècle de lectures des 'Fleurs du Mal'*, 196. Requested by Baudelaire himself following publication of the first edition of *Les Fleurs du Mal* on 25 June 1857, Barbey's review article is dated '24 juillet 1857'.
[26] Trans. Eiland and McLaughlin, 324 [J53, 4].

poems that would make up the completed edition.[27] As is well known, this first edition of Les Fleurs du Mal comprised 'Au lecteur' and then five sections of widely divergent length: 'Spleen et idéal' (77 poems), 'Fleurs du mal' (12), 'Révolte' (3), 'Le Vin' (5), and 'La Mort' (3). The fact that the first edition includes exactly 100 poems (plus the prefatory poem 'Au lecteur') suggests that Baudelaire might have had Dante's Divine Comedy (with its 100 cantos) as a model. Similarly, his wish for a frontispiece depicting the seven deadly sins recalls the second part of Dante's Comedy in which Mount Purgatory consists of seven layers that each in turn correspond, from the bottom up, to the seven sins of pride, envy, anger, sloth, avarice, gluttony, and lust. Where Balzac had recently constructed a Comédie humaine (1842), perhaps Baudelaire had in mind a Comédie satanique?[28] Baudelaire knew the Divine Comedy particularly from the prose translation of Pior Angeli Fiorentino, first published in 1840 and which he describes in a note to the first edition of the Salon de 1846 as 'la seule bonne pour les poètes et les littérateurs qui ne savent pas l'italien'.[29] In the Salon de 1846 Baudelaire notes Delacroix's 'goût irrésistible pour Dante, que Shakespeare seul balance peut-être dans son esprit' (ii. 437) and begins his account of Delacroix's art with Le Dante et Virgile aux enfers (now more commonly known as La Barque de Dante) first exhibited in 1822, emphasizing the furore stirred by 'ce beau tableau, vrai signal d'une révolution' (ii. 428). He devotes several pages to the painting, and ends by quoting, in Fiorentino's translation, the fourth canto of Inferno in which Dante, guided by Virgil, visits limbo and observes the shades of Homer, Horace, Ovid, and Lucan.

Clearly his own focus on limbo in Les Limbes suggests a desire to provide a sequel or at least an alternative to Dante's Inferno, Purgatory, and Paradise, and perhaps even to break down the distinction between these three posthumous spaces—since, as we have seen, he seeks in these particular poems to undermine the very difference between life and death. In Les Limbes the poem later entitled 'De profundis clamavi' in the completed editions bears the title of 'La Béatrix', suggesting an ironic contrast between this poet imploring 'Toi, l'unique que j'aime' (l. 32) from the depths of the 'gouffre obscur où mon cœur est tombé' (l. 2) and Dante's poet for whom Beatrice replaces the pagan Virgil at the end of Purgatorio and becomes his guide to the beatific vision of Paradiso. Baudelaire's

---

[27] On 20 April 1857 the following poems appeared in the Revue française: 'La Beauté', 'Avec ses vêtements ondoyants et nacrés...', 'Je te donne ces vers...', 'Tout entière', 'Le Flambeau vivant', 'Harmonie du soir', 'Le Flacon', and 'Le Poison'. On 10 May 1857 L'Artiste published 'Franciscae meae laudes', 'L'Héautontimorouménos', and 'L'Irrémédiable'.

[28] The figurine by Ernest Christophe that is the subject of Baudelaire's poem 'Le Masque' was originally entitled 'La Comédie humaine' when exhibited at the 1859 Salon but was later renamed 'Le Masque' by Christophe by way of tribute to Baudelaire's poem. See i. 874-6.

[29] See ii. 1300 nn. a and 1 to p. 438. He would doubtless also have been familiar with the partial, verse translation of the Comedy by Antony Deschamps (brother of Émile Deschamps), published in 1829.

poet is sunk in melancholy rather than the orthodox Christian sinfulness from which the poet's soul in the *Divine Comedy* is led, through inferno and purgatory, towards a vision of God on his throne (comparable therefore with that parodied in the 'Prière' at the end of 'Les Litanies de Satan'). Indeed in the 1855 'Les Fleurs du Mal' 'La Béatrix' is re-entitled 'Le Spleen', while the poem later entitled 'Le Vampire' is here given the title of 'La Béatrice'. Now the contrast between Baudelaire's poet and Dante's is all the more stark, with the purity of Beatrice being superseded by a blood-sucking mistress who is compared to a 'un troupeau hideux | De démons'.[30] These particular allusions to the *Divine Comedy* are elided in *Les Fleurs du Mal*, in particular with the new title of 'De profundis clamavi' turning the poet-lover of that poem into a latter-day St John the Baptist crying in the wilderness of his own pain—albeit a wilderness that more closely resembles the Underworld of Greek mythology.

The intertextual presence of Dante's *Divine Comedy* in *Les Fleurs du Mal* is further suggested by the compendious quality of Baudelaire's collection, which he himself referred to in his original draft dedication of the work to Théophile Gautier as 'ce misérable dictionnaire de mélancolie et de crime' (i. 187). In Dante's work the seven deadly sins of *Purgatorio* are matched by the seven virtues of *Paradiso*: that is, the four so-called cardinal virtues of prudence, fortitude, justice, and temperance, together with the three theological virtues of faith, hope, and charity. What we find in *Les Fleurs du Mal* is the conspicuous absence of such virtues and the omnipresence of the seven deadly sins of Rops's frontispiece. Thus the four cardinal virtues are expressed throughout the collection almost exclusively as negatives: incaution and abandon; cowardice and fecklessness; unfairness and cruelty; excess and lack of self-control. The three theological virtues, similarly, are roundly rejected, most notably in 'Révolte'. Instead of faith there is unbelief: for example, the absence of God in 'Bohémiens en voyage', the rejection of Christ, and by implication God also, in 'Le Reniement de saint Pierre', and the incitement of 'Abel et Caïn' to dethrone God in his Heaven. Instead of faith in God there is faith in Satan, the adoptive father of 'Les Litanies de Satan' who alone understands our human predicament. Instead of hope we have melancholy—the melancholy of despair, depression, spleen—and the absence of any belief in a heavenly afterlife. Rather than paradise, forever lost, death offers only an illusory spectacle of hope ('Le Rêve d'un curieux', 'La Mort des artistes') and is in reality no more than a banal gateway onto corporeal decomposition ('Le Mort joyeux') and a blessed oblivion—for the destitute ('La Mort des pauvres') and for the poet ('La Fin de la journée'). Indeed death *is* our only hope, a lovely dead end: 'C'est le but de la vie, et c'est le seul espoir' ('La Mort des pauvres', l. 2). And instead of charity, or love, there is hatred, the unfillable barrel of 'Le Tonneau de la Haine'.

---

[30] Amended to 'forte comme un troupeau | De démons' in 1857.

Rather than love as the pure and tender devotion of one to another, as affection or selfless altruism, there is love as sexual antagonism, the desire to possess and the failure to possess, love as cruelty, as a sado-masochistic confusion over whether the greater pleasure is to be had from the receipt or the administration of pain. As 'Un voyage à Cythère' suggests, the journey of love towards another person ends in self-disgust. In Bénédiction', the opening poem of 'Spleen et idéal', a grateful mother's love for her new-born child—allusively compared with the joy of the Virgin Mary following the Annunciation ('Puisque tu m'as choisie entre toutes les femmes' (l. 9; cf. Luke 1: 42)—is replaced by the outraged disgust and loathing of the poet's own mother, now delivered of her 'monstre rabougri' (l. 12). Where a Christian would receive God's love and bestow it in turn on her offspring, this vehement mouthpiece for a Satanic gospel substitutes hatred for love: 'Je ferai rejaillir ta haine qui m'accable | Sur l'instrument maudit de tes méchancetés' (ll. 13–14).

Preceding 'Bénédiction', the prefatory 'Au lecteur' introduces the 'dictionary of melancholy' that is *Les Fleurs du Mal* by using the device of listing discussed earlier, suggesting not only a dictionary or catalogue or litany (as in 'Les Litanies de Satan'), but also a catechism. A religious catechism has most usually taken the form of a series of questions and answers by which religious teaching is orally impressed on the memory and so indoctrinated, but it may also take the form of a compendium. Thus the *Catechism of the Catholic Church*, promulgated by Pope John Paul II in 1992,[31] presents itself instead as a summary, in book form, of the beliefs of the Catholic faithful and as a work of reference. In this respect it constitutes a form of lawgiving and itself defines the process of 'catechesis' as 'an *education in the faith* of children, young people and adults which includes especially the teaching of Christian doctrine imparted, generally speaking in an organic and systematic way, with a view to initiating the hearers into the fullness of Christian life' (*Catechism*, [section] 5).

The article concerning 'Sin' defines sin as 'an offence against reason, truth, and right conscience; it is failure in genuine love for God and neighbour caused by a perverse attachment to certain goods'; and the article goes on to quote St Augustine's definition of sin as 'an utterance, a deed, or a desire contrary to the eternal law' (*Catechism*, 1849). Sinfulness is unlawfulness. Though it does refer to and define the cardinal and theological virtues (*Catechism*, 1805–9, 1812–29), the 1992 *Catechism of the Catholic Church* makes no mention of the 'seven deadly sins', but states rather that 'there are a great many kinds of sins' and quotes the New Testament on 'the works of the flesh': 'Now the works of the flesh are plain: fornication, impurity, licentiousness, idolatry, sorcery, enmity, strife, jealousy,

---

[31] For the version published in English, see *Catechism of the Catholic Church* (Vatican City: Libreria Editrice Vaticana, 1993). References are henceforth included in the main text by section number.

anger, selfishness, dissension, factions, envy, drunkenness, carousing, and the like [...] those who do such things shall not inherit the Kingdom of God' (*Catechism*, 1852). On the other hand, it does distinguish carefully between venial, mortal, and eternal sin.[32]

At the beginning of *Les Fleurs du Mal* the poem 'Au lecteur' serves as an alternative catechism, the summary of a new legislation: 'La sottise, l'erreur, le péché, la lésine, | Occupent nos esprits et travaillent nos corps' (ll. 1–2)—a descriptive rather than prescriptive legislation with which to understand the human condition as the poet himself sees it. For him, as for the Catholic believer, sinfulness is constituted by a failure of will: 'le riche métal de notre volonté' (l. 11) has been vaporized by Satan Trismegistus, and the road to Hell is paved with good intentions: 'Et nous alimentons nos aimables remords, | Comme les mendiants nourrissent leur vermine' (ll. 3–4), 'Nos péchés sont têtus, nos repentirs sont lâches' (l. 5). Call it remorse, call it repentance, we may 'confess' our sins but only the better to sin again: 'Nous nous faisons payer grassement nos aveux, | Et nous rentrons gaiement dans le chemin bourbeux, | Croyant par de vils pleurs laver toutes nos taches' (ll. 6–8). Just as we are content to feed our remorse by sinning further, so we exact from avowal the rich reward of a clean conscience with which to start once more down the slippery path. We do not repent in authentic Christian fashion but instead lament our melancholic lot with crocodile's tears as though these might wash away our failure to resist the call of desire—and as though, 'Hypocrite lecteur', we did not want to heed that call again. These 'vils pleurs' are reminiscent of Lesbos and the 'noir mystère | Des rires effrénés mêlés aux sombres pleurs' into which the poet has been initiated since he was a child, but here the word 'vils' suggests a degree of self-loathing at his own hypocrisy, at *our* hypocrisy. And the greatest vice ('un plus laid, plus méchant, plus immonde!' (l. 33)) in our monstrous menagerie of vices is 'l'Ennui', acedia or a total failure not only of will but also of desire.

But the most important parallel with Dante's work in *Les Fleurs du Mal* (1857), and which will be reinforced in the 1861 edition, is the structure of the journey, a key element in Baudelaire's arrangement of the poems in the collection. For, as has often been noted, this progresses from birth (in 'Bénédiction') to death (in the final section 'La Mort') and so implicitly recounts the story of our human life as a melancholic journey here on earth—of this human life that is also a living death. In the 1857 edition this narrative comprises several more or less discrete stages: the illusions and disillusions of sexual passion ('Spleen et idéal'); the exclusive pursuit of (non-reproductive) sexual pleasure ('Fleurs du mal'); the rejection of

---

[32] See *Catechism*, 1854–64. In section 1860 it is stated that 'Sin committed through malice, by deliberate choice of evil, is the gravest [mortal sin]', and in section 1864 that 'eternal' sin is committed when 'one deliberately refuses to accept [God's] mercy by repenting, rejects the forgiveness of his sins and the salvation offered by the Holy Spirit.'

God ('Révolte'); and the quest for oblivion, first in alcohol ('Le Vin') and then finally in death ('La Mort'). This movement from birth to death also structures 'Spleen et idéal' (1857) itself, which leads from the birth and sunrise of 'Bénédiction' and 'Le Soleil' and the effortless *survol* of 'Élévation' to a final group of seven poems that evoke descent, rejection, and the night-time of death—together with some ironic forms of terrestrial repose.

Thus, following 'Le Tonneau de la Haine' with its depiction of the rabies of vengeance, the poet of 'Le Revenant' imagines returning as a ghost not to watch over his bed-companion but to frighten her. In 'Le Mort joyeux', as we have seen, the poet wants to dig his own grave and lie down happily to rest among the worms, whereas in 'Sépulture' he imagines being buried by some random 'bon chrétien' and lying there listening to the enduring 'Mal' above: wolves howling and starving witches shrieking, dirty old men labouring towards orgasm, dark villains plotting. In 'Tristesses de la lune' the moon shines lazily like a beautiful woman distractedly masturbating herself to sleep, while the poet piously catches her occasional, furtive tear and places it in his heart far from the eyes of the sun.[33] In this and the final two poems of 'Spleen et idéal' (1857) the emphasis is on the coming of repose through art and imagination: here the watchful repose of a poet ('Un poète pieux, ennemi du sommeil' ('Tristesses de la lune', l. 11)) finding beauty where he can; in 'La Musique' the repose of a poet without illusions who responds to music like a ship to the sea, and as human beings to life—first rocked by the fair winds and stormy convulsions of passion, then becalmed on the flat mirror of hopelessness; and finally, in 'La Pipe', the repose of a smoker whose mental suffering is eased by 'un puissant dictame' (l. 12)—in English, dittany—an aromatic flowering plant known for its medicinal properties:

> J'enlace et je berce son âme
> Dans le réseau mobile et bleu
> Qui monte de ma bouche en feu,
>
> Et je roule un puissant dictame
> Qui charme son cœur et guérit
> De ses fatigues son esprit.
>
> (ll. 9–14)

Recalling the houka-smoking figure of 'l'Ennui' at the end of 'Au lecteur', this poem thus rounds off 'Spleen et idéal' (1857) with the implication that for the poet-artist the 'paradis artificiel' of a drug-induced dream may offer the best remedy for someone who is 'comblé de douleur' (l. 5)—just as for the reader the

---

[33] This detail suggests an ironic intertextual allusion to Vigny's 'Éloa' in which an angel is formed from the tear shed by Christ upon the death of Lazarus.

best remedy for boredom may perhaps lie in the trip of imagination that comes from rolling a poetic spliff from a 'fleur du Mal'.

As these poems suggest, the 'story' of the 1857 edition of *Les Fleurs du Mal*, and of the 'Spleen et idéal' section in particular, is also and more particularly the story of the poet-artist and his response to the Satanic *curriculum vitae* of 'le Mal'. Where are the flowers of beauty to be found amidst this universal melancholy? In a parody of the Annunciation 'Bénédiction' proclaims the birth of the poet-artist—and presents the bitter (and comic) laments of his mother who is far from convinced that like Mary she is 'blessed among women' for giving birth to a poet; while in the final poem in the collection, 'La Mort des artistes', the only posthumous prospect for artists is the 'espoir, étrange et sombre' (l. 12) that perhaps 'la Mort, planant comme un soleil nouveau, | Fera s'épanouir les fleurs de leur cerveau!' (ll. 13–14). This in turn echoes 'Le Soleil', placed after 'Bénédiction' in 1857, in which the poet's task is associated with sunrise and recalls the sun itself, which—'ainsi qu'un poëte'—'ennoblit le sort des choses les plus viles' (l. 18).

This journey from birth to death, for mankind and for the poet-artist, is thus an important element in the shape and meaning of *Les Fleurs du Mal* (1857). But the framework extends further than these few poems. From the seven poems with which 'Spleen et idéal' (1857) ends—from 'Le Tonneau de la Haine' to 'La Pipe'—there emerges more extensive evidence of a crucial device: the balancing of counterparts between the beginning and end of the section so that no one poem or group of poems may be said to have the last word. In one way this marks an advance on the collapsing of difference characteristic of *Les Limbes* and perhaps constitutes an adaptation of the principle of 'réversibilité' operative in the 1855 'Les Fleurs du Mal' where, for example, 'L'Invitation au voyage' has its spleen counterpart in 'Un voyage à Cythère'. Be that as it may, this dialectical relationship between the beginning and end of 'Spleen et idéal', as well as of the whole collection, will be further strengthened in the 1861 edition, and with poems—as Baudelaire's famous remarks to Vigny about the work's 'architecture' indicate—that were specifically written for the purpose. And it is the poetic argument advanced within this extended framework that constitutes Baudelaire's alternative lawgiving in *Les Fleurs du Mal*. Where the teleology of Dante's *Divine Comedy* is founded on a faith in God and the truth of our eventual redemption from sin through Christ, Baudelaire's Satanic Comedy has no such teleology. Our human condition is 'irremediable', and so there can be no happy ending either for us or for *Les Fleurs du Mal*—only, as 'Le Voyage' will make clear in 1861, an endless melancholic quest for the new.

In Chapters 8 and 9 I shall examine in detail the ways in which the structural changes made to *Les Fleurs du Mal* between 1857 and 1861 articulate a revised poetic argument about the nature and function of beauty within a newly conceived relationship between melancholy and poetry.

8
Les Fleurs du Mal (1857/1861)
New Beginnings

> Et ces maudites *Fleurs du mal* qu'il faut recommencer! [...] et cela pour obéir à la volonté de trois magistrats niais[.]
> (Letter to Mme Aupick, 19 Feb. 1858)

The 'Architecture' of *Les Fleurs du Mal*

> le cadre singulier que j'avais choisi.
> (Letter to Alfred de Vigny, c.16 Dec. 1861)
>
> il y a ici *une architecture secrète*, un plan calculé par le poète, méditatif et volontaire. [...] Elles sont moins des poésies qu'une œuvre poétique *de la plus forte unité*.
> (Jules Barbey D'Aurevilly, 'Les *Fleurs du Mal* par M. Charles Baudelaire' [1857])[1]

So far I have approached *Les Fleurs du Mal* chronologically, stealing up on it from a distance through the various stages of its prehistory and tentatively inferring a continuity of evolution from the title of *Les Lesbiennes* through the title and constituent poems of *Les Limbes* to the 1855 'Les Fleurs du Mal', and including also the twelve poems that Baudelaire submitted to Théophile Gautier in late 1851/early 1852 for publication in the *Revue de Paris*. Turning now to the two editions of *Les Fleurs du Mal* published within Baudelaire's lifetime, it is important to be clear about the overall structure of the work as this has a major bearing on Baudelaire's evolving conception of his role as a poet, and specifically of his role as an alternative poet-lawgiver. For what, quite, did Baudelaire mean when he wrote to Vigny in December 1861, after publication of the second edition of *Les Fleurs du Mal*, with these frequently quoted words: 'Le seul éloge que je sollicite pour ce livre est qu'on reconnaisse qu'il n'est pas un pur album et qu'il a un commencement et une fin. Tous les poèmes nouveaux ont été faits pour être adaptés au cadre singulier que j'avais choisi'?[2]

---

[1] Guyaux (ed.), *Baudelaire: Un demi-siècle de lectures*, 197.
[2] Letter to Alfred de Vigny, c.16 Dec. 1861, *Corr.* ii. 196.

From this statement it is clear that the 1857 edition had already been carefully structured, and with a 'cadre singulier'. It is also clear from Baudelaire's letter to his mother in February 1858 that he had seen that edition as definitive:

> Et ces maudites *Fleurs du mal* qu'il faut recommencer! Il faut du repos pour cela. Redevenir poète, artificiellement, par volonté, rentrer dans une ornière qu'on croyait définitivement creusée, traiter de nouveau un sujet qu'on croyait épuisé, et cela pour obéir à la volonté de trois magistrats niais, dont un *Nacquart*![3]

For by now Baudelaire had begun to write prose poems, two of which ('Le Crépuscule du soir', 'La Solitude') had been published in 1855, and so he had already begun to move away from verse even as his short collection 'Les Fleurs du Mal' was being published almost simultaneously in the *Revue des Deux Mondes*. In 1857, two months after publication of *Les Fleurs du Mal*, he republished those two prose poems, together with four others, in *Le Présent* under the title *Poèmes nocturnes*. And so, ironically, we may have the magistrates to thank for the augmented, second edition of *Les Fleurs du Mal* and for Baudelaire's renewed creativity in verse of the kind evident in 'La Chevelure' and some of the poems of 'Tableaux parisiens' (notably 'Le Cygne', 'Les Sept Vieillards', and 'Les Petites Vieilles').

It is evident from his comments to Vigny that Baudelaire aimed to produce more than a random anthology, but so, too, had some of his immediate predecessors, including Vigny himself. His *Poèmes antiques et modernes* (1826) offers a brief, emblematic history of poetry in three stages, from ancient Greece through the Christian Middle Ages to a secular present, a narrative he then later stages as the history of humanity in *Les Destinées* (published posthumously in 1864).[4] The majority of verse collections hitherto published in France since the Revolution had each been loosely linked by a particular theme or tone, such as Lamartine's *Méditations poétiques* (1820) and *Harmonies poétiques et religieuses* (1830), Hugo's *Les Orientales* (1829) and *Les Feuilles d'automne* (1830), and Musset's *Contes d'Espagne et d'Italie* (1829). Sometimes the title would foreground a unity of poetic form, as with Desbordes-Valmore's *Élégies et romances* (1819) or Hugo's *Odes et ballades* (1826; 1828). In the latter, however, there is already evidence of an attempt to order the poems in such a way—here in separate 'books' with effects of contrast and symmetry—in order to complement the individual poems with an overarching poetic argument. Indeed Hugo appears to have wanted also to link his succeeding collections of verse with poems of anticipation or recall, as well as by explicit statement in his prefaces.[5] Eventually, in *Les Contemplations* (1856), he achieved the most elaborate and detailed poetic architecture—certainly during the nineteenth

---

[3] *Corr.* i. 451. On the identity of Nacquart, see n. 4 to *Corr.*, i. 422.
[4] See *Unacknowledged Legislators*, 509–22, 552–60.
[5] See *Unacknowledged Legislators*, 407–10, 421–2, 424–5.

century and, arguably, in the history of French poetry—before following that up with the mosaic of 'petites épopées' in the three 'series' of *La Légende des siècles*. In *Les Contemplations* he simulates the bipartite structure of the Bible, with each 'testament' ('Autrefois' and 'Aujourd'hui') consisting of three 'books', in order to present a quasi-autobiographical account of the poet's journey from childhood innocence ('Aurore') through young love ('L'Âme en fleur') to adult struggle ('Les Luttes et les rêves'), a journey savagely interrupted by the death of the poet's daughter and his temporary loss of religious faith ('Pauca meae'), before the journey is resumed through renewed contact with his fellow human beings ('En marche') and ends with his faith restored and a vision of ultimate redemption ('Au bord de l'infini').

Published one year later, the first edition of *Les Fleurs du Mal* reads almost like a response to *Les Contemplations*: instead of a journey from innocence through death towards redemption, we are given a journey from birth to death as a downward spiral. Where Hugo's collection traces a progression from one kind of poetry (the lyric as idyll and romance) to another (the lyric as revelation, in the manner of the last book of the New Testament), Baudelaire also—as we are about to see—uses his collection, already in 1857 but even more so in 1861, to substitute one kind of poetry—and one kind of poet—for another. Indeed it may be that it was the interference of the judiciary that prompted him to adopt a more overt role as alternative lawgiver in the 1861 edition. For why *did* Baudelaire revise and supplement the 1857 edition of *Les Fleurs du Mal*? Now fully engaged with the new medium of the prose poem he could simply have left out the banned poems and then republished. Yet in his letter to his mother of February 1858, nearly six months after the trial, Baudelaire seems to assume that substantial alterations are necessary as a consequence of the banning of those particular six poems. As we have seen, those poems sprang from the very source of *Les Fleurs du Mal*, namely *Les Lesbiennes*, and thus from the poet's initial ambition to present human beings as the 'innocent martyrs' of sexual desire. This emphasis is gradually overtaken by the theme of limbo, and then by a preoccupation with the relationship between melancholy and beauty that takes centre ground in the 1855 'Les Fleurs du Mal' and in *Les Fleurs du Mal* (1857) itself. But if we now examine the changes to the collection that Baudelaire made between 1857 and 1861 we shall see that he has become even more adamant about the function of poetry as a mode of resistance and that he overtly substitutes for the traditional figure of the poet as *vates* laying down the law for others a new role for the poet as one who invites readers to feel, think, and imagine for themselves.

Before undertaking this analysis, however, it is important to stress the shifting and approximate nature of the overall structure of *Les Fleurs du Mal*, whether in its first or second editions.[6] I am not persuaded, for example, that Baudelaire

---

[6] The role of Charles Asselineau, Baudelaire's literary executor, in the ordering of the third edition makes all inference of Baudelairean intention from its structure highly problematic.

aimed for any rigid numerical patterning in his arrangement of the poems.[7] But already in the cases of *Les Limbes* and the 1855 'Les Fleurs du Mal' it is evident that a certain thematic unity may account for the choice and grouping of the poems, just as sometimes the ordering of the poems appears to suggest an unfolding sequence or argument. Although much doubt exists as to the dates of composition and/or revision of many of the poems, some are known to have been written at a particular time and even as a group (such as those sent anonymously to Apollonie Sabatier), while others simply belong together through a communality of theme and image. As we can see also from the existence of the 'Douze poèmes', Baudelaire appears during the early to mid-1850s to have accumulated a portfolio of poems—newly written, long written but newly revised, drafted but as yet incomplete—from which he drew for publication in small selections or that he held ready, or nearly ready, for a later, more substantial collection that would eventually be published as *Les Fleurs du Mal*. As I shall suggest in Chapter 17, many of the poems in this collection relate to each other through a technique of concatenation whereby particular words or images create links and echoes between adjacent poems, thereby complementing their self-sufficiency with the suggestion of a quasi-musical progression of theme and variation. Nevertheless, as I now propose to show, there is every reason to agree with Barbey d'Aurevilly's insistence on the 'secret architecture' of *Les Fleurs du Mal* and on its status as 'une œuvre poétique *de la plus forte unité*'.

A New Poetry

> Nous avons [...] des beautés de langueur.
> ('J'aime le souvenir de ces époques nues...', ll. 29, 32)

As 'Au lecteur' makes clear, the poet of *Les Fleurs du Mal*—of this 'Satanica Commedia'—differs radically from the poet of Dante's *Divine Comedy* in that, rather than being guided (by Virgil and Beatrice), he himself is now the guide, Satan's cicerone ever at our elbow as we read our way towards 'La Mort'. Furthermore, in presenting this catechism of an alternative legislation the poet-guide of 'Au lecteur' is enacting a new role for the poet: the initiate into the dark mystery of Lesbos can no longer be a poet-lawgiver on the model of Lamartine and Hugo. Within the context of the 1855 'Les Fleurs du Mal' (which contains 'Au lecteur') this substitution of one kind of poet-lawgiver for another is not fully manifest, but very soon it will serve to structure both 'Spleen et idéal' and *Les Fleurs du Mal* as a whole, first in the 1857 edition and then, even more markedly,

---

[7] Cf., for example, James R. Lawler, *Poetry and Moral Dialectic: Baudelaire's 'Secret Architecture'* (Madison-Teaneck: Fairleigh Dickinson University Press, 1997).

in the edition of 1861. Setting aside the removal of the six banned poems, the major differences between the first and second editions of Les Fleurs du Mal consist in (i) a recasting of the end of 'Spleen et idéal', (ii) the reordering of the sections, (iii) the inclusion of 'Tableaux parisiens', and (iv) the addition of three poems to 'La Mort'. I shall examine these areas of difference in turn and with a view to establishing a particular narrative for the evolution of Les Fleurs du Mal in terms of a gradually more explicit and insistent presentation of the poet as alternative lawgiver. Where the poems relating to Lesbos depicted the anguish of desire—'le Mal'—within a non-Christian moral framework and the poems of Les Limbes subsequently presented this 'mal de vivre' as a collapse of the difference between life and death, the poems of the 1855 'Les Fleurs du Mal' began, as we have seen, to articulate a new relationship between 'le Mal' and art. Now, in 'Spleen et idéal' this relationship becomes fundamental, as does the poet's overt adoption of his new role.

In the first edition of Les Fleurs du Mal the section entitled 'Spleen et idéal' enacts the 'story' of 'La Destruction', which told of the poet being distracted from his 'grand amour de l'art' by the seductive beauty of women and the lure of sexual passion. But 'Spleen et idéal' develops this scenario by implying that the destructive may become the constructive. Broadly speaking, the section moves from a questioning of the poet's role and the nature of beauty through a portrayal of the spiral—or tragedy—of desire and towards a new aesthetic of melancholy. We have already seen how the first poem, 'Bénédiction', provides a comic opening to the section as the poet's mother laments her melancholic lot and resolves to consider the birth of her monstrous son as an expiation of her sins, anticipating the son's own acceptance of suffering as a blessing. Against this backdrop it is therefore difficult to read the poet's own extravagant self-importance as anything other than an ironic deflation of his traditional role as a poet-lawgiver and as the prophet who goes unrecognized in his own country, the unacknowledged legislator.[8] Like Christ, it seems, he has been sent into this world 'par un décret des puissances suprêmes' (l. 1) and to fulfil their 'desseins éternels' (l. 18). Though rejected by his mother, this 'Enfant déshérité' (l. 22) is no Nervalian 'Desdichado' beset by the 'soleil noir de la mélancolie' but a cheerful chap who 's'enivre du soleil' (l. 22) 'sous la tutelle invisible d'un Ange' (l. 21) and finds ambrosia and nectar wherever he goes. Like some jolly Orpheus he plays with the wind and chats with the clouds (l. 25), and like a merry Christ '[il] 's'enivre en chantant du chemin de la croix' (l. 26).

[8] Cf. i. 833 for Pichois's summary: 'les commentateurs sont d'accord pour y reconnaître avant tout les éléments bien attestés d'un thème romantique: le génie, le poète sont maudits par la société; cette malédiction est le signe de la vocation, donc de bénédiction. Sentiment de la différence et de la solitude; de l'incompréhension et de la persécution. On se rappelera, entre autres, Stello et Moïse de Vigny.' This seems to me to miss the point that Baudelaire begins Les Fleurs du Mal precisely by lampooning what had become clichés.

No true Calvary for him, then, only the glorious paradise of a sunny day. Suffering and sadness cannot touch him, and even his guiding spirit weeps to see him skipping along, 'gai comme un oiseau des bois' (l. 28). Like the Démon in 'La Destruction', his wife (!) or female companion would like to lure him away from the true path, tarting herself up like an idol to usurp the object of his usual 'hommages divins' (l. 44) and ready to tear his heart out and feed it to her pet (ll. 49–52). But this aggravatingly smug and self-satisfied poet is not to be deflected from his blithe and noble path, and nor can he in his high-minded piety be brought to see the reality of human suffering and the righteous anger of mankind at the injustice of our condition:

> Vers le Ciel, où son œil voit un trône splendide,
> Le Poète serein lève ses bras pieux,
> Et les vastes éclairs de son esprit lucide
> Lui dérobent l'aspect des peuple furieux[.]
>
> (ll. 53–6)

By a perverse logic that implicitly mocks the principle of 'réversibilité' as well as more traditional Christian teaching relating to humility and repentance, this poet blesses God for granting us suffering as a 'divin rémède à nos impuretés' (l. 58), for in mortification lies the road to (a rather suspect) spiritual ecstasy: 'la meilleure et la plus pure essence | Qui prépare les forts aux saintes voluptés!' (ll. 59–60). Bring it on, the poet seems to say, secure in the knowledge of his own illustrious place in the scheme of things—a scheme of things that strongly recalls the royalism of early Romantic poet-lawgivers:

> Je sais que vous gardez une place au Poète
> Dans les rangs bienheureux des saintes Légions,
> Et que vous l'invitez à l'éternelle fête
> Des Trônes, des Vertus, des Dominations.
>
> (ll. 61–4)

In exceptional suffering lies the 'noblesse unique' (l. 65) that justifies the poet's own 'couronne mystique' (l. 67). So exceptional indeed is our good poet that not even all the jewels of ancient Palmyra, or the pearls in the sea, or even precious metals as yet unknown, could suffice to create 'ce beau diadème éblouissant et clair' (l. 72): 'Car il ne sera fait que de pure lumière, | Puisée au foyer saint des rayons primitifs' (ll. 73–4).

As readers we may now begin to sympathize with the poet's mother and understand why God himself 'la prend en pitié' (l. 4). For this poet inhabits a fool's paradise, blissfully ignorant of the negative alchemy of pain (to be described later in 'Alchimie de la douleur') and aspiring to the possession of an absurd halo (that he will later lose in the prosaic mud of 'Perte d'auréole' in *Le Spleen de Paris*). The 'Bénédiction' of the title is a false blessing, whether it be that of the mother's 'election' as the producer of this sanctimonious poet, or that of the poet himself arrogantly and outrageously, indeed blasphemously, blessing God—'Soyez béni, mon Dieu' (l. 57), he says, as though he alone were worthy of him and fit to bless the Almighty—and generally spouting moral nonsense. For to bless God for giving us suffering is rather like saying, as we read in 'La Mort des pauvres', that the only hope in life is death.

In the 1857 arrangement of 'Spleen et idéal' 'Bénédiction' is followed by 'Le Soleil', which also ironizes a traditional view of the poet and a form of poetry that similarly minimizes the spectacle of human suffering, and once again with a suspect sunshine. No longer the saintly lawgiver of 'Bénédiction', this poet is the bringer of solace and beauty in a harsh and hostile world. In the first section of the poem (ll. 1–8), as the unrelenting heat of a 'soleil cruel' (l. 3) beats down on field and city alike, the poet unostentatiously goes about his business, a 'promeneur solitaire' who trusts to serendipity, sniffing out rhymes as though they were floral scents (l. 6), stumbling across words as though they were uneven paving-stones (l. 7) and bumping into lines of verse 'depuis longtemps rêvés' (l. 8). In the second section (ll. 9–16) the deictic ambiguity of the opening phrase—'[c]e père nourricier' (l. 9)—initiates a merging of sun and poet so that what may be the sun's beneficent effects (restoring colour to anaemic cheeks (l. 9), or youthful gaiety to the halt and the lame (l. 13)) appear also to be the work of poetry. Instead of the vengeful mother of 'Bénédiction' we have this nursing father[9] who 'éveille dans les champs les vers comme les roses' (l. 10): real roses and poetic flowers, real worms aerating the soil and a poet's lines of verse. Other actions of the sun-poet are similarly both literal and metaphorical: 'Il fait s'évaporer les soucis vers le ciel, | Et remplit les cerveaux et les ruches de miel' (ll. 11–12), where 'soucis' are potentially dew-drained marigolds as well as cares,[10] and human brains are filled like honeycombed hives with the sweet harvest of Plato's 'honeyed Muse'.[11] Likewise the sun may command the crops to grow and ripen (l. 15): 'Dans le cœur immortel qui toujours veut fleurir!' (l. 16).

The hyperbole and overt contrivance of these twin-purpose images begin to appear parodic, with this sunny, life-enhancing poet of nature coming to seem less and less 'natural' and increasingly the begetter of monstrous artifice and a source of comedy.[12] The insistent collocation of named or implied flowers (ll. 6, 10, 11,

---

[9] For a reading of 'Bénédiction' and 'Le Soleil' in terms of Freud's Oedipus complex, see Pierre Laforgue, *Œdipe à Lesbos*, 71–83.
[10] The double meanings of 'vers' and 'soucis' are noted by Ross Chambers, 'Baudelaire et l'espace poétique: A propos du "Soleil"', in Yves Bonnefoy et al., *Le Lieu et la formule: Hommage à Marc Eigeldinger* (Neuchâtel: Éditions de La Baconnière, 1978), 111–20 (114–15).
[11] See *Unacknowledged Legislators*, 20.
[12] For Ross Chambers this 'little series of puns is instructive' in that '[t]hey exemplify the kind of simultaneity of double reference (country-city, nature-culture) that is otherwise the sun's prerogative

12, 16) with the word 'vers' (ll. 8, 10, 11) foregrounds a stereotypical association of poetry with beauty that this collection entitled *Les Fleurs du Mal* will go on to redefine, not least by its rejection of the conventions of Romantic nature poetry. In the third section of the poem (ll. 17-20), which focuses now on city rather than field, the sun and the poet are demerged by a comic reversal which has the 'natural' sun proceeding 'ainsi qu'un poète' (l. 17) and passing unimpeded, in commendably egalitarian fashion, through palace and hospital alike—there, with modest majesty (l. 19), to bestow a nobility upon '[l]es choses les plus viles' (l. 18). This section lends itself to two contradictory but not necessarily self-cancelling readings. On the one hand, there is the suggestion that the beauty of poetry may be superficial: everything looks better in the sunshine, even hospitals, but the reality of 'le Mal' has not gone away. To 'ennoble' it sounds like the poet of 'Bénédiction' glorifying suffering but lacking all true understanding of it. Similarly, sunshine may, like poetry, be a great leveller, to be enjoyed by all human beings irrespective of their social rank, but once again this may be to deny the terrible reality of social division.

On the other hand, it is true that one of the principal innovations of *Les Fleurs du Mal* is precisely to let the ugly and the vile and the 'unpoetic' take their place in the sun. Indeed it will be through the artifice of art that the reality of our irremediable melancholy is eloquently and unflinchingly conveyed. The tripartite structure of 'Le Soleil' might be said, therefore, to narrate a welcome substitution of the poet for the sun and thus of art for nature: a cruel sun oppresses a wandering poet; a 'nourishing' sun and a beneficent poet work in tandem; the sun follows the poet's lead, and nature imitates art. Perhaps the poem suggests that poetry can indeed produce beauty in an ugly world, not by passively expressing the pre-existent beauty of nature but by being art—the creative art of melancholy that rhymes 'chloroses' with 'roses' (ll. 9-10)[13] and 'béquilles' with 'filles' (ll. 13-14).[14]

[...]. But they are also facile ("vers"), so contrived ("soucis"), or so banal ("miel") that what they emphasize in the end is the ungainliness of the poet's own *démarche*, corresponding in this way to his lurching progress along the street. Thus they reinforce the general sense of noise and mediocrity that this section [of the poem] conveys.' See *An Atmospherics of the City: Baudelaire and the Poetics of Noise* (New York: Fordham University Press, 2015), 47-8. From this reading Chambers extrapolates the principal thesis advanced in his book: 'These mediating lines tell us that noise is the inescapable accompaniment to city life that the poet of the modern must face in his effort to make beauty from the mundane. The question for Baudelaire, in future poems, will be, then, no longer how to produce harmonious verses that deny the presence and power of noise and seek to cancel it out, but rather how to incorporate this defining noisiness of urban life into an aesthetics that might somehow be capable of doing justice to noise's pervasive and inescapable, if mostly ignored, presence. How to envisage a noisy form of beauty, or the beauty of noise? How to produce a certain supernaturalism out of a world no longer benignly governed so much as it is subject to forces of disorder, entropy, and chaos; and this by virtue of its involvement in time, extension, the problematics of mediation, as well [...] as the destructive force that is history?' (49)

[13] The same rhyme is employed in 'L'Idéal', ll. 5, 7.

[14] This reading of 'Le Soleil' is supported by the poem's subsequent position in the 1861 edition as the second poem in 'Tableaux parisiens'. Here it follows 'Paysage', which introduces these 'Tableaux parisiens' by explicitly proclaiming the replacement of nature poetry (epitomized by Virgil's eclogues) with the emphatic artifice (and architecture) of a new, urban poetry. For further discussion see

In the 1857 'Spleen et idéal' 'Le Soleil' is followed by 'Élévation' and 'Correspondances', both of which have so often been taken at face value as expressions of a 'noble' view of the poet's role: that is, of the poet as an exceptional individual gifted with superior insight into spiritual reality. But just as 'Bénédiction' and 'Le Soleil' cast doubt respectively on the roles of divine lawgiver and nature poet, so too here the poet as *vates* comes under critical scrutiny. Like the 'Poète serein' of 'Bénédiction' and the poet with his quasi-regal right of entry at the end of 'Le Soleil, the poet of 'Élévation' gaily knows no obstacle: 'Mon esprit, tu te meus avec agilité, | [...] | Tu sillonnes gaiement l'immensité profonde | Avec une indicible et mâle volupté' (ll. 5, 7–8). Yet the poet who addresses his soaring spirit in this way does so because he sees such 'elevation' as a form of escapism: 'Envole-toi bien loin de ces miasmes morbides; | Va te purifier dans l'air supérieur (ll. 9–10). Half of the poet—the half that is conscious of his own insertion in material reality—is all too conscious of a darker and more proximate reality:

> Derrière les ennuis et les vastes chagrins
> Qui chargent de leurs poids l'existence brumeuse,
> Heureux celui qui peut d'une aile vigoureuse
> S'élancer vers les champs lumineux et sereins[.]
>
> (ll. 13–16)

The poet's spirit may soar in flight, but this is also a flight *from* another form of truth, the truth of human suffering. And there is a note of wistfulness here, as though the poet of 'Élévation' envies the effortless ease of his own, quasi-Keatsian 'blithe spirit':

> Celui dont les pensers, comme des alouettes,
> Vers les cieux le matin prennent un libre essor,
> —Qui plane sur la vie, et comprend sans effort
> Le langage des fleurs et des choses muettes!
>
> (ll. 17–20)

But he himself perhaps is unable to leave humanity so readily behind. Once again we have the suggestion, as in 'Le Soleil', that nature poetry is oblivious to the reality of human misery. It may sing charmingly of flora and the mute realm of the non-human, but what matters are the 'ennuis' and 'vastes chagrins' of those who can speak: what we really need are the flowers of human melancholy.

A similar contrast is presented in 'J'aime le souvenir de ces époques nues...', the poem which follows 'Correspondances' in both the 1857 and 1861 editions.

Chapter 18. For an alternative reading of 'Le Soleil' as turning on the distinction between poetry as 'found' and poetry as 'made', see Chambers, 'Baudelaire et l'espace poétique', 118–19.

Here the effortless ease of the ideal 'blithe spirit' is associated with ancient times, while 'Le Poète [d']aujourd'hui' (l. 15) 'sent un froid ténébreux envelopper son âme' (l. 18). The two epochs are divided by the Fall. The prelapsarian world is associated with sunshine, artlessness, nakedness, health, abundance, unsullied female beauty, and an absence of mendacity and anxiety. But the world of 'Aujourd'hui' is characterized by darkness, horror, clothed concealment, monstrosity, ridicule, bodily deformation, and a female condition of pallor, debauch, and 'toutes les hideurs de la fécondité!' (l. 28). 'Le Poète [d']aujourd'hui' pays homage to the 'youth' of the world (l. 36) in terms that recall the innocent spiritual vision at the end of 'Élévation' and thereby cast doubt on its present relevance:

> Et qui va répandant sur tout, insouciante
> Comme l'azur du ciel, les oiseaux et les fleurs,
> Ses parfums, ses chansons et ses douces chaleurs!
>
> (ll. 38–40)

The 'agilité' of the poet's spirit in 'Élévation' is now seen to be akin to the untroubled 'agilité' of Adam and Eve before the Fall (l. 3), whereas today's poet speaks for 'les races maladives' (l. 34). Not for him, therefore, a paradise of sweet-smelling flowers and pastoral song. Where once it was the sun (as Phoebus) that gilded the stone of statues (l. 2), now it is the artist who must cast his own crepuscular light upon the cankerous faces of his fellow human beings and illuminate the melancholy of our fallen condition with a new kind of beauty:

> Nous avons, il est vrai, nations corrompues,
> Aux peuples anciens des beautés inconnues:
> Des visages rongés par les chancres du cœur,
> Et comme qui dirait des beautés de langueur[.]
>
> (ll. 29–32)

'Correspondances'

> ce qu'une religion mystique appelle la *correspondance*
>
> (*Corr.*, i. 336)

What, then, of 'Correspondances', perhaps the best known and certainly one of the most frequently cited poems from *Les Fleurs du Mal*?

> La Nature est un temple où de vivants piliers
> Laissent parfois sortir de confuses paroles;
> L'homme y passe à travers des forêts de symboles
> Qui l'observent avec des regards familiers.

> Comme de longs échos qui de loin se confondent
> Dans une ténébreuse et profonde unité,
> Vaste comme la nuit et comme la clarté,
> Les parfums, les couleurs et les sons se répondent.
>
> Il est des parfums frais comme des chairs d'enfants,
> Doux comme les hautbois, verts comme les prairies,
> —Et d'autres, corrompus, riches et triomphants,
>
> Ayant l'expansion des choses infinies,
> Comme l'ambre, le musc, le benjoin et l'encens,
> Qui chantent les transports de l'esprit et des sens.

Critical opinion has sometimes accorded this poem a quasi-official status as the unambiguous statement of a neo-Platonist metaphysical and aesthetic programme underlying *Les Fleurs du Mal* as a whole. At its heart is ostensibly the idea that the material world corresponds to—symbolizes, is a simulacrum of—some hidden spiritual and perhaps divine reality. According to this reading Baudelaire is simply an accepting heir to the thought of eighteenth-century Illuminists such as Swedenborg and of German idealism as transmitted by Staël (in *De l'Allemagne*), and therefore a poet firmly in the Romantic tradition of Lamartine and Hugo.[15] Following in the path first sketched out by Jean Pommier in *La Mystique de Baudelaire*,[16] Lloyd Austin argued in *L'Univers poétique de Baudelaire: Symbolisme et symbolique* that Baudelaire's 'symbolism' substitutes for a traditional religious 'symbolique' (in which the material world corresponds to some higher, metaphysical or transcendental reality) a form of 'symbolisme' in which a complex network of sense impressions serves to express and 'correspond to' the complexity of human emotional and intellectual experience. 'Pour Baudelaire', Austin writes, 'le symbole est désormais un rapport essentiellement subjectif établi par l'imagination dans son activité librement créatrice.'[17] More recently, Jonathan Culler has shown how, far from simply espousing the poetics of Lamartine and Hugo—for whom divine Creation is a text to be deciphered and reproduced by the poet—Baudelaire is in fact subverting and departing from this poetics.[18]

---

[15] In their authoritative biography of Baudelaire, first published in 1987, Claude Pichois and Jean Ziegler comment that 'écrire le sonnet "Correspondances", où est évoquée la "ténébreuse et profonde unité" du monde, c'est adhérer à une pensée romantique et socialiste qui veut réintégrer l'homme dans le cosmos'. See Pichois and Ziegler, *Baudelaire* (1996 edn), 239. This assessment is quoted verbatim by Marie-Christine Natta in 2017 (*Baudelaire*, 237) as the expression of a continuing consensus.

[16] (Paris: Belles Lettres, 1932; repr. Geneva: Slatkine, 1967).

[17] (Paris: Mercure de France, 1956), 172. Austin claims that Baudelaire did initially believe in the possibility of a 'symbolique' of the traditional kind but that 'c'est sur la ruine de ses espoirs religieux que s'est édifié [*sic*] sa nouvelle construction poétique' (54).

[18] 'Intertextuality and Interpretation: Baudelaire's "Correspondances"', in Christopher Prendergast (ed.), *Nineteenth-Century French Poetry: Introductions to Close Reading* (Cambridge: Cambridge University Press, 1990), 118–37.

Culler notes of line 5, for example, that 'Baudelaire's echo seems to disrupt the one-to-one correspondence between natural sign and spiritual meaning that the other [writers] promote.'[19] Culler's focus is on the methodology and problematics of intertextual reading, and he adduces several further intertextual 'echoes' in Baudelaire's poem, notably the fourth canto of *Inferno* and its forest of limbo. But his questioning of the Romantic intertext is of especial relevance to the positioning of 'Correspondances' as the fourth poem in 'Spleen et idéal'.

For, like the poems that accompany it, this sonnet contributes to the gradual substitution of one view of the poet for another. Already, for example, it is evident that the two tercets anticipate 'J'aime le souvenir de ces époques nues...' in distinguishing between the innocent and the corrupt, an antithesis previously figured in 'Élévation' as a distinction between pure air on high and 'miasmes morbides' (l. 9) down below. The 'parfums frais comme des chairs d'enfants' of 'Correspondances' are of a piece with the morning delights (l. 18) of 'Élévation' and the 'natives grandeurs' (l. 16) of 'J'aime le souvenir...', while 'l'existence brumeuse' (l. 14) of the former and 'ce noir tableau plein d'épouvantement' (l. 19) of the latter belong with 'd'autres [parfums], corrompus, riches et triomphants' in 'Correspondances'. In both 'Élévation' and 'J'aime le souvenir...' the pure and the innocent are situated at a distance from the poet—respectively, high up or in the past—while the voice of the 'Poète [d']aujourd'hui' is situated, in an implied expression of solidarity, within the fallen and 'corrupt' condition of a suffering humanity here and now. This is to say that the acknowledgement of 'spleen' as the default human condition—that is, 'la conscience dans le Mal'—requires the construction of a new form of aesthetic 'idéal', one that is here presented in the last four lines of 'Correspondances' and which will later, in 1861, be affirmed more explicitly in 'Hymne à la Beauté'.

In the first quatrain of 'Correspondances' the poet adopts the calm voice of a seemingly irrefutable lawgiving authority as he states an apparently unproblematic truth: Nature, capitalized as though itself to be revered, is a temple, a place of worship, in which living pillars '[l]aissent parfois sortir de confuses paroles' as though God's truth, the truth of Nature, were not immediately comprehensible by mere mortals but can be heard in tantalizing snatches by the superior audition of a poet.[20] So perhaps, and particularly because of the famous precedent of Chateaubriand's comparison of a North American forest to a cathedral both in *René* and (even more lyrically) at the end of his *Génie du christianisme*, Nature is like a wood through the trees of which we catch glimpses of the sky and the divine

---

[19] 'Intertextuality and Interpretation', 121.
[20] See i. 845 n. 3 for an account of this interpretation. As an example of such poetry, cf. Hugo's poem 'Que la musique date du seizième siècle': 'Écoute la nature aux vagues entretiens. | Entends sous chaque objet sourdre la parabole. | Sous l'être universel vois le éternel symbole' (*Les Rayons et les ombres*, no. 35, ll. 114–16). On Hugo's presentation of the poet as a listener and 'écho sonore', see *Unacknowledged Legislators*, 424–5.

light of God. Perhaps the pillars—trees or architectural supports—represent symbols: as a pillar connects floor to ceiling and links the 'ici-bas' with 'là-haut', so Nature is full of symbols that bind the material and spiritual together in sacred unity. By its etymology, after all, a 'symbol' throws or brings two things together; and in the Christian Church 'symbol' is also the term used for the Apostle's Creed that unites Christians as members of the one community, a body of beliefs and a form of legislation.

Continuing with his grand allegory the poet describes how 'l'homme', within this temple that is Nature or the world about him, passes through (as the Christian envisages passing through life towards a better place) surrounded by these symbols 'Qui l'observent avec des regards familiers'. But already, and as Culler notes, we can see how Baudelaire is skewing and subverting the clichéd notion of a comfortable world of signs inhabited by human beings readily able to see the presence of God. 'Regards familiers' connotes not only a suspect comfort zone but also a potential disdain on the part of the symbols themselves. They seem to know *us* well, but can we necessarily understand *them* as we pass through life? These forests of symbols begin to represent a possible source of confusion, even a loss of human direction as 'l'[h]omme' wanders round in circles having seen these same old trees many times before. Perhaps the world is a perplexing, unknowable place, a place of imperfect language, an inarticulate and uncommunicative environment quite unlike that imagined at the end of 'Élévation' in which a certain type of poet 'comprend sans effort | Le langage des fleurs et des choses muettes!'

This possibility of an inarticulate world is foregrounded once more in the second quatrain as the poet turns from 'vertical' correspondences to the notion of 'horizontal' correspondences and subverts the idea of a vast universe in which God's design is everywhere apparent and God himself presides over the duality of darkness and light. God's world is supposedly a place of difference within unity. Smell, colour, and sound (that is to say, the differentiations that we experience through our senses) are said to 'se répondre', to speak to and answer each other. But they do so, we are told, only in the manner of long and distant echoes that 'se confondent': that is, of echoes that become confused and merge into one another in a dark and deep unity, a vast unity like 'la nuit' and 'la clarté'.[21] In other words, supposed difference becomes 'indifference' (as it became so frequently in *Les*

[21] Cf. Paul de Man, 'Anthropomorphism and Trope in the Lyric', in his *The Rhetoric of Romanticism* (New York: Columbia University Press, 1984), 239–62: 'For the vastness of the night is one of confusion in which distinctions disappear, Hegel's night in which A=A because no such thing as A can be discerned, and in which infinity is homogeneity. Whereas the vastness of light is like the capacity of the mind to make endless analytical distinctions, or the power of the calculus to integrate by ways of infinitesimal differentiation. The juxtaposition of these incompatible meanings is condensed in the semantic ambiguity of "se confondent", which can designate the bad infinity of confusion as well as the fusion of opposites into synthetic judgements. That "echoes", which are originally the disjunction of a single sensory unit or word by the alien obstacle of a reflection, themselves re-fuse into a single sound [...] again acts out the dialectic of identity and difference, of sensory diffuseness and intellectual precision' (244–5).

Limbes), the undifferentiated blankness of darkness or brightness that may well be the equivalent not of God's eloquent majesty but of a godless silence and a melancholy world.

This juxtaposition of a naive religious idealism and a more sceptical secularism[22] is repeated in the tercets by the contrast set up between two types of 'parfum'; and once again the simplicity of syntax and calm voice of authority belie a deeper irony. On the one hand, we have the simple fresh smell of a child, except that the insistence on flesh (rather than, say, skin), together with the disconcerting use of the plural, makes the image disturbingly literal and thereby subverts conventional, saccharine images of the 'cher enfant'. 'Doux comme les hautbois' introduces the celebrated theme of synaesthesia, so often considered a vital aspect of the programmatic character of this poem despite the fact that synaesthetic effects appear only rarely in *Les Fleurs du Mal*.[23] It is true that 'doux' and 'vert' are terms that are regularly applied to scent and that when we smell things we do not usually think of oboes or the greenness of meadows (the smell of grass possibly, but not the colour green). But there is perhaps something too idyllic, too pat, about these images of fresh scent. At the same time 'hautbois'—a woodwind instrument indeed in that the very word homophonically connotes 'haut(s) bois'—may more immediately recall the clichéd Chateaubriandesque image of Nature as a religious building with tall trees; while 'verts comme les prairies' seems at once too banal a simile and almost a jingle, a mere poetic convenience (given the internal rhyme of 'verts' and 'prairies'). May there even be a sly and mocking reference to innocent pastoral verse ('vers comme les prairies')?

On the other hand, juxtaposed with these 'parfums frais'—and introduced after a suspenseful dash at the beginning of l. 11 that seems to promise a final flourish, a glimpse perhaps in the last four lines of this sonnet of the kind of 'correspondances' the poet actually *does* believe in—we have 'd'autres [parfums]' that are 'corrompus, riches et triomphants, | Ayant l'expansion des choses infinies'. Unlike the long and distant echoes that collapse in on one another as though in an undifferentiated darkness or brightness, these 'parfums' expand outwards. Such smells may be 'corrompus': that is, redolent of the decomposition or process of organic decay that leads inevitably from fresh childhood to rotting death, and redolent also therefore of the smell of time passing, of the smell of melancholy. At the same time these smells are 'riches': that is, much deeper and richer than the simplicity and imaginative poverty of the images of children and oboes and meadows and all the other possibilities of twee Romantic pastoral. And they are

---

[22] *Pace* Graham Robb, who argues that 'la prétendue rupture entre les deux quatrains [...] n'existe que si l'on prend le titre au sens swedenborgien'. See *La Poésie de Baudelaire et la poésie française*, 148–51 (149).

[23] As already noted by Austin: see *L'Univers poétique*, 55, 190, 235, 287. Also Culler, 'Intertextuality and Interpretation', 130–1, where Culler refers his own reader to Sandro Genovali, *Baudelaire, o della dissonanza* (Florence: La Nuova Italia, 1971), 137–47.

'triomphants': that is, triumphant over time and oblivion in their overpowering strength and capacity to endure rather than fade upon the breeze into the nothingness of indifferentiation. In 'La Destruction' an 'air impalpable' burns our lungs with the torment of panting desire, but here we learn that the pungent smell of rotting that is borne upon the Satanic air we breathe (cf. the 'miasmes morbides' of Élévation) offers other, endless possibilities: 'l'expansion des choses infinies'.

But from what do these other smells derive, these smells described in the final line—and with a grammatical ambiguity that has the description apply to both the smell and its source—'[q]ui chantent les transports de l'esprit et des sens'? They come from amber, musk, benzoin, and incense. Three of these are tree resins, while the fourth is derived from the deer that roam the forests: all four of these sources produce perfume.[24] Thus the poet who has rejected the traditional role of the poet-lawgiver, deciphering Nature as the text of God's Creation, chooses to give us by way of an alternative not the 'ombre' of worn-out Romanticism but 'ambre'; not Chateaubriand's forest but the resins and perfumes it supplies; not trees as living pillars that '[l]aissent parfois sortir de confuses paroles' but real trees whose gummy secretions can transport the mind and senses; not incense as it is used in Christian churches but a joss-stick poetics that celebrates the senses as well as the spirit, and indeed transports the spirit by means of the senses. Here the senses are no longer a source of sin but the means to a convincing 'élévation' of the spirit. As for musk, this has a long medical history as an antidote to melancholy.[25]

'Transport' is etymologically synonymous with 'metaphor', and the poem can also be seen to replace dead metaphor ('La Nature est un temple')[26] with live metaphor ('d'autres [parfums...q]ui chantent'), just as it follows unsurprising simile ('Comme de longs échos') with disturbing comparisons ('comme des chairs d'enfant'). Instead of the exhausted tropes of a Hugolian or Lamartinian Romanticism the poet presents us with arresting and suggestive images that offer new 'correspondances' within the complex variety of our sensual experience: in short, 'correspondances' that restore life and vigour to difference and militate

---

[24] The *Oxford English Dictionary* provides the following definitions. Amber: 'A hard, translucent fossilized resin, typically yellow, orange, or brown in colour, used for jewellery and ornaments since ancient times and also in perfumery and traditional medicine.' Musk: 'A reddish brown substance with a strong, persistent odour secreted by a gland of the male musk deer [...] and highly prized in perfumery.' Benzoin: 'A dry and brittle resinous substance, with a fragrant odour and slightly aromatic taste, obtained from the *Styrax benzoin*, a tree of Sumatra, Java, etc. It is used in the preparation of benzoic acid, in medicine, and extensively in perfumery.' Incense: 'An aromatic gum or other vegetable product, or a mixture of fragrant gums and spices, used for producing a sweet smell when burned.' Cf. the verse poem 'L'Invitation au voyage': 'Les plus rares fleurs | Mêlant leurs odeurs | Aux vagues senteurs de l'ambre' (ll. 18–20).

[25] See Starobinski, *Histoire du traitement*, 139. Cf. Baudelaire's early evocation of melancholy in 'Tous imberbes alors sur les vieux bancs de chêne...': '—Quand la sombre Vénus, du haut des balcons noirs, | Verse des flots de musc de ses frais encensoirs' (ll. 39–40) (i. 207).

[26] On the clichéd character of this metaphor, see i. 845 n. 1.

against the *in*differentiation that characterizes the limbo of melancholy. These are analogies not to be accepted as holy writ but as food for thought. 'Ambre', 'musc', 'le benjoin', 'l'encens': put those in your readerly pipe and smoke them, the poet of 'Correspondances' seems to say, conscious that 'parfum' derives etymologically from Latin 'per fumus' = to smoke, and then you, too, reader, can imitate the allegorical figure of Ennui dreamily smoking its houka in 'Au lecteur' or the poet of 'La Pipe' (the final poem in the 1857 'Spleen et idéal') with his 'puissant dictame | Qui charme son cœur et guérit | De ses fatigues son esprit' (ll. 12–14). Smoke it or smell it, but above all inhale! Let the spirit take flight on the rich corruptions of melancholy and the triumphant perfumes of 'la conscience dans le Mal'. Poetry consists not in according unproblematic metaphysical meaning to nature but in attending to its secretions and emanations. For these shall be the means of transport as we embark upon our journeys of the imagination.[27]

'Correspondances' itself orchestrates sense impressions knowingly. It begins with sound (ll. 1–2), continues with sight (ll. 3–4), and returns to sound (ll. 5–6) before combining sight and sound with smell (l. 8). Then, after focusing on smell (ll. 9–13), while mixing in sound ('hautbois') and sight ('verts comme les prairies'), it ends with an emphasis on song—the song of poetry that offers 'l'expansion des choses infinies'. Instead of the 'confuses paroles' of competing metaphysical and religious explanations, poetry offers us a different sort of indeterminacy: the richness of difference and a proliferation of connections within the infinitely disparate. Trees are not just the anonymous constituent wherewithal of a forest: each tree has a name, and each produces a substance that also has a name. And these names, including that of the deer's own secretion, have an expansive resonance that springs from the word itself: be it the monosyllabic incontrovertibility of 'musc' or the ambiguity of 'ambre' ('expanded' not only semantically by its double meaning of amber and ambergris[28] but also aurally by its sounded terminal 'e'), or the exotic unfamiliarity of 'benjoin'. Even the more familiar 'encens' takes on a suggestive air, rhyming the conventionally religious with the faintly illicit implications of 'sens', which are reinforced by the homophonic presence of 'sang' that serves as a framing echo of the 'chairs d'enfants' at the beginning of the sestet. Indeed these aural and semantic uncertainties (chairs/chers, verts/vers, ambre [jaune]/ambre [gris], sens/sang) exemplify a creative rather than sterile form of linguistic 'confusion'. If 'les sons se répondent', they

---

[27] For further discussion of Baudelaire's use of the term 'correspondance' in relation to his theories of the imagination, see Part III.
[28] 'Ambergris': 'a wax-like substance having a brownish grey colour and a sweet earthy scent, formed as a natural secretion in the bile duct of sperm whales, which is occasionally found floating in the sea or washed up on coasts around the Atlantic, Indian, and western Pacific oceans, and has long been used in perfumery' (*Oxford English Dictionary*). A perfume made from bile, therefore, like a poetry born of melancholy!

do so less as echoes merging into one another ('Dans une ténébreuse et profonde unité') than as rhymes productive of new and provocative juxtapositions. As though to emphasize the importance of rhyme, and of this final rhyme in particular, the sonnet ends 'irregularly' with a couplet. The rhyme scheme of the Petrarchan form, unlike that of the Shakespearean, traditionally avoids a closing couplet, but here this couplet serves to assert that 'correspondance' is a poetic and not a philosophical issue. Where 'paroles' and 'symboles' may have rhymed unproblematically in the first quatrain, reinforcing the old idea of nature as a readable divine language of signs, now these linguistic signs take on a new and more complex life of their own, lingering like perfume in the air of a melancholic mental world: 'corrompus, riches et triomphants'. For the poet of 'Correspondances' poetry is the art of such language, offering not an unmediated facsimile of natural beauty (as mocked in 'Le Soleil' and 'Élévation') but a distillation of its perfumes contained within the 'flacon' of verse—as well as the creation of a jewelled beauty from the extracted resin of 'le Mal', like amber taken from the trees of Chateaubriand's extinct Romantic forests. And the temple that is nature will be replaced by the 'Temple nouveau' imagined in the 'Prière' at the end of 'Les Litanies de Satan', the temple created by the branches of the Tree of Knowledge.

A New Beauty

J'eusse aimé [...] Parcourir à loisir ses magnifiques formes [...]
('La Géante', ll. 5, 9)

Approchons, et tournons autour de sa beauté.
('Le Masque', l. 16)

Thus the opening poems in 'Spleen et idéal' (1857) dismantle the received models of the poet as divine lawgiver and as celebrant of nature, and now in 'Correspondances' dismantle both of these together. Instead we begin to glimpse the poet of melancholy who seeks a new kind of beauty and a new kind of poetry. This is the 'Poète [d']aujourd'hui' of 'J'aime le souvenir...' who recognizes the achievements of an innocent past but must now acknowledge 'ces inventions de nos muses tardives', or what he calls 'des beautés de langueur'. Against the backdrop of these opening five poems, those that follow in the 1857 edition reflect further movement from the past to the present and from the old to the new: the suspect luminaries of 'Les Phares' give way to the modern melancholics of 'La Muse malade', 'La Muse vénale', and 'Le Mauvais Moine'. For the poet of 'La Muse malade' his muse of ill-being has been overtaken by 'le Mal' and left speechless by the horrors of her nightmare visions; and—in a reversal of 'J'aime le souvenir...'—he longs for her to recover the 'healthy' powers of Christian and pagan inspiration. Indeed, in a reversal also of 'Correspondances', he longs for a sweeter smell:

> Je voudrais qu'exhalant l'odeur de la santé
> Ton sein de pensers forts fût toujours fréquenté,
> Et que ton sang chrétien coulât à flots rythmiques
>
> Comme les sons nombreux des syllabes antiques,
> Où règnent tour à tour le père des chansons,
> Phœbus, et le grand Pan, le seigneur des moissons.
>
> (ll. 9–14)—

for a sweeter smell, then, and also for a sweeter sound, the poetry of sunshine and pastoral that he has earlier rejected in 'Le Soleil' and 'Élévation'. His muse may be 'malade', but that is now how things must be for this temporarily recidivist poet of the new.

And this indeed he recognizes in 'La Muse vénale', where a poetry of Christian inspiration is presented as inauthentic, a hypocritical performance undertaken in order to pay the bills. But for his indigent muse (who lives in a palace that is perhaps therefore the modern equivalent of Mount Parnassus, a dwelling-place of unfunded splendour) the choice is either that or some equally hypocritical poetry of laughter and merriment that denies the reality of our melancholy condition. The former, at least, will please the *bien-pensants* and the well-to-do and therefore earn her more ('Récolteras-tu l'or des voûtes azurées?' (l.8)), while the latter will merely content the vulgar, penniless poor:

> Il te faut, pour gagner ton pain de chaque soir,
> Comme un enfant de chœur, jouer de l'encensoir,
> Chanter des *Te Deum* auxquels tu ne crois guère,
>
> Ou, saltimbanque à jeun, étaler tes appas
> Et ton rire trempé de pleurs qu'on ne voit pas,
> Pour faire épanouir la rate du vulgaire.
>
> (ll. 9–14)

Either way she will prostitute her art. She can be like the innocent choirboy pretending to praise God while he plays with the censer (as opposed to making good use of the incense as in 'Correspondances'), or she can be like some starving, fairground performer—even a shameless stripper ('étaler tes appas')—who cheers up the masses and palliates their spleen ('la rate') with a 'fleur du Bien' rather than the 'fleur du Mal' that would be an honest expression of the 'pleurs qu'on ne voit pas'.

If, then, the new poet of melancholy must forsake Christian inspiration and the poetry of nature and joy, what is left? Little or nothing, it would seem from a reading of 'Le Mauvais Moine', only the 'spectacle vivant de ma triste misère' (l. 13). But, like some lazy monk who should really be painting his monastery walls with inspiring murals, he finds it hard to get excited by the prospect. And yet even then, for the poet of 'Le Guignon', from within the depths of melancholy new aesthetic possibilities beckon ('Maint joyau', 'Mainte fleur'), and perhaps in the memories of a (literally and metaphorically) exotic past ('La Vie antérieure'). But at the same time ('Bohémiens en voyage') the past may be a place of lack ('le morne regret des chimères absentes' (l. 8)), just as in the future there is only death. As to the eternal present of the human condition (in 'L'Homme et la mer'), life is a bitter gulf of flux and struggle, like the sea upon which we human beings like to gaze as though peering into the mirror of our souls—and a sea that is reluctant to yield up the secrets of its 'richesses intimes' (l. 11). The emphasis here, however, is not on the illuminating power of this comparison (in accordance with the first quatrain of 'Correspondances') nor on the presence of potential hidden riches (as it is in 'Le Guignon') but on the blatant and everlasting spectacle of the destructiveness of both man and nature—'sans pitié ni remord' (l. 14)—and on the murky depths of the human soul.

This emphasis on 'le Mal' remains in the two poems that follow. In 'Don Juan aux enfers' we move from a murderous sea to the 'onde souterraine' (l. 1) of the Underworld and the river Styx across which, in scenes reminiscent of Dante and Delacroix,[29] Charon conveys an untroubled and unrepentant Don Juan to Hell. In 'Châtiment de l'orgueil' this priapic pride is followed by the Satanic hubris (l. 10) of a theologian to whom it occurs—and in an implicit parallel with the alternative poet-lawgiver of Les Fleurs du Mal—that just as he has, by his brilliant exegesis and preaching of the Christian gospel, brought his indifferent flock to a vision of Heaven, so and with similar success he could just as easily reverse the process (and the Christian story with it), and reduce 'Jésus, petit Jésus!' (l. 11) to the status of 'un fœtus dérisoire!' (l. 14). But after hubris comes nemesis, and this theologian who has revelled in the manipulative powers of his intellect and eloquence promptly loses his reason and is consigned—in an implicit parallel with Lucifer cast out of Heaven—to a mental prison of darkness and silence. Now an outcast—'Sale, inutile et laid comme une chose usée' (l. 25)—he himself has become the butt of ridicule.

Within the sequence of 'Spleen et idéal' in both the 1857 and 1861 editions of Les Fleurs du Mal these two poems ('Don Juan aux enfers' and 'Châtiment de l'orgueil') may be read as ironic introductions to the work of this alternative poet-lawgiver, who is about to devote a large number of poems to the subject of sexual passion as the expression of a Satanic reality. Is he himself guilty of hubris (he seems to ask, in mock ignorance of the answer) in thus resisting the accepted Cousinian view of art as the expression of a divine reality[30] and in seeking to

---

[29] See i. 867–8. [30] See Chapter 1, n. 27.

substitute the beauty of his own 'fleurs du Mal'? In the four poems that immediately follow he now turns his attention to the nature of beauty itself. In 'La Beauté', where Beauty speaks for herself, the poet presents a type of beauty that is exactly of the kind that he himself will not speak for:[31] a type of monumental beauty that keeps its stony distance from mere mortals, at once regal and inscrutable, a blankness and a stillness that eschew emotion, beauty as idealization ('Car j'ai [...] | De purs miroirs qui font toutes choses plus belles' (ll. 12-13)), and a beauty ultimately that suggests a certain vacuity reminiscent of the second quatrain of 'Correspondances' ('Vaste comme la nuit et comme la clarté'): 'Mes yeux, mes larges yeux aux clartés éternelles!' (l. 14). But the poet rejects this kind of beauty that is based on rules ('Les poètes [...] | Consumeront leurs jours en d'austères études' (ll. 9,11)) and on rules that have to be submissively learnt by 'ces dociles amants' (l. 12). If this poet is to be 'docile' (that is, teachable), then he will be taught by life itself. How can such a beauty ('Et jamais je ne pleure et jamais je ne ris' (l. 8)) accommodate the torment and conflicted emotions of Lesbos or the 'Mal' of which the poet himself is the prime representative? This beauty—akin to the kind of beauty Baudelaire excoriates in 'L'École païenne'—is bogus and superficial: 'mes grandes attitudes, | Que j'ai l'air d'emprunter aux plus fiers monuments' (ll. 9-10). This is a beauty of arrogance and facile pseudo-rhyme ('Je suis belle, ô mortels!' (l. 1)), of inflexible fancy ('comme un rêve de pierre' (l. 1)) and heartless cruelty ('mon sein, où chacun s'est meurtri tour à tour' (l. 2)), a hubristic beauty even, to set beside the figures of Don Juan and the crazy theologian.

This personification of beauty as a woman continues in 'L'Idéal' and 'La Géante'. In the former the suffering poet requires stronger aesthetic meat: not 'ces beautés de vignettes' (l. 1), 'Ces pieds à brodequins, ces doigts à castagnettes' (l. 3), still less the limp and bloodless ladies of Paul Gavarni's illustrations: 'Car je ne puis trouver parmi ces pâles roses | Une fleur qui ressemble à mon rouge idéal' (ll. 7-8). For this poet melancholy is not be prettified. His 'fleur du Mal' must have the beauty of red-blooded passion or a monstrous darkness, of Lady Macbeth or Michelangelo's sculptured depiction of Night in the form of a woman writhing 'paisiblement' as Titans sink their teeth into her breasts.

The beauty of melancholy must be violent, larger—but not finer—than life, not a haughty, distant, impersonal beauty but a beauty that gathers us in with a warm, protective embrace. Instead of the regal beauty of 'La Beauté', proud to be 'un sphinx incompris' and to inspire 'un amour | Éternel et muet ainsi que la matière' (ll. 3-4), the poet looks now instead to the beauty of 'La Géante', a young giantess with whom he would like to have lived '[c]omme aux pieds d'une reine un chat voluptueux' (l. 4). At the feet of *this* queen he will readily place himself, voluptuously, ready to be stroked. As in 'L'Idéal' this is beauty as enlargement and

---

[31] For a reading of 'La Beauté' along similar lines, see Jennifer Yee, '"La Beauté": Art and Dialogism in the Poetry of Baudelaire', *Neophilologus*, 102: 1 (2018), 1-14.

distortion, a beauty of the body as well as of the soul ('J'eusse aimé voir son corps fleurir avec son âme' (l. 5)), an experimental and shape-shifting beauty ('Et grandir librement dans ses terribles jeux' (l. 6)), a beauty whose mysteriousness is not 'incompris' but demands excitingly to be known ('Deviner si son cœur couve une sombre flamme | Aux humides brouillards qui nagent dans ses yeux' (ll. 7–8)). And deep in this beauty lies darkness and the fire of passion, beneath the tears: the beauty of melancholy. Unlike the bruising breast of 'La Beauté', this young giantess offers a bosom of comfort and protection, allowing the poet to 'Dormir nonchalamment à l'ombre de ses seins, | Comme un hameau paisible au pied d'une montagne' (ll. 13–14). Here, in a new form of pastoral, he can shelter from the burning 'soleils malsains' (l. 11) of his existential summer.

But is 'La Géante' a poem about beauty or the record of a sexual fantasy? Or indeed both? At this point in the 1857 'Spleen et idéal', from 'La Beauté onwards, the emphasis gradually shifts from the personification of beauty as a woman to the depiction of sexual relations with women who are perceived as beautiful. For Baudelaire, as *Fusées*, f. 16 makes clear, sexual and aesthetic attraction are closely interrelated. Moreover, as 'La Destruction' will later describe at the beginning of the 'Fleurs du Mal' section, this interrelationship can be seen in terms of the poet's submission to temptation by a 'Démon' who exploits his love of art in order to lead him into the barren landscape of sexual desire. Something of this transition between art and sex is already evident in 'La Beauté' in which Beauty is characterized by the frigidity of a monument, and more evident still in 'L'Idéal' where the poet's artistic ideal is exemplified by two women who combine literature (Lady Macbeth) and sculpture (Michelangelo's depiction of Night as a female nude). In 'La Géante' the woman in question is allegedly a product of nature, but in an imaginary past: 'Du temps que la Nature en sa verve puissante | Concevait chaque jour des enfants monstrueux' (ll. 1–2); and yet here Nature's power to conceive is itself born of the poet's own imagination.

In the 1857 edition 'La Géante' is followed by 'Les Bijoux', one of the six poems banned from subsequent publication (in this case because of the allegedly 'lascivious' nature of stanzas 5, 6, and 7).[32] The arresting opening hemistich suggests that the transition from art to sex is complete: 'La très-chère était nue' (note also the homophonic presence of 'la chair était nue'), but at once we see that the poet's attraction is as much aesthetic as sexual. Here is a living nude presenting herself to the poet's gaze like a 'femme d'Alger' in a Delacroix painting:

> et, connaissant mon cœur,
> Elle n'avait gardé que ses bijoux sonores,
> Dont le riche attirail lui donnait l'air vainqueur
> Qu'ont dans leurs jours heureux les esclaves des Mores.
>
> (ll. 1–4)

[32] See i. 1133–4.

This is sex as art: the woman may be the poet's slave (cf. also l. 9: 'Elle était couchée et se laissait aimer') and resemble a tamed tiger (l. 13) but she makes *him* the slave to her body ('vainqueur'; and cf. l. 10: 'Et du haut du divan elle souriait d'aise')) by enhancing the beauty of her nakedness with the artifice of jewels. Since, as in Diderot's novel *Les Bijoux indiscrets*, these 'jewels' are also a well-known French euphemism for genitals, the fusion of the sexual and the aesthetic is here total and allows for the subsequent account of the poet's 'extase' (l. 7) to be read simultaneously as an account of the sexual act or the description of a rather risqué tableau vivant: 'elle essayait des poses, | Et la candeur unie à la lubricité | Donnait un charme neuf à ses métamorphoses' (ll. 14–16); 'Je croyais voir unis par un nouveau dessin | Les hanches de l'Antiope au buste d'un imberbe' (ll. 25–6).[33] Indeed the poet's own poem seems to ape her shifting poses with its smooth succession of varied similes: 'Polis comme de l'huile, onduleux comme un cygne' (l. 18), and with a daring choice of Bacchic metaphor to match the arousing spectacle before him:

> Et son ventre et ses seins, ces grappes de ma vigne,
> S'avançaient, plus câlins que les Anges du mal,
> Pour troubler le repos où mon âme était mise[.]
>
> (ll. 20–2)

The final stanza clinches this fusion of the sexual and the artistic with its own sly, post-coital performance of the fading fires of passion:

> —Et la lampe s'étant résignée à mourir,
> Comme le foyer seul illuminait la chambre,
> Chaque fois qu'il poussait un flamboyant soupir,
> Il inondait de sang cette peau couleur d'ambre!

Neither sexual participant is present: not the poet who had earlier expressed his 'furious' love for 'Les choses où le son se mêle à la lumière' (l. 8), nor the 'ange du Mal' (cf. l. 21) with whom he has sated his 'fury'. No jewellery sparkles, for the lamp has died: no jewellery dances with a 'bruit vif et moqueur' (l. 5), for its wearer is still. Only the dying embers in the grate are left to perform their own *son et lumière*, emitting a human sigh and casting a blood-red gleam across an amber skin. Are we to understand that now that the 'ange du Mal' has done her work the fires of Hell beckon? Has real blood been spilled by an *untamed* tiger? This final stanza is not a dénouement but an artwork: a 'tableau mourant' full of suggestive signs oozing like resinous amber to be fashioned into the jewellery of the poem

---

[33] Here the word 'buste' itself fuses the aesthetic and the real by meaning at once a sculptor's bust (the head and upper body of a person) and the torso of a living person, and in particular female breasts.

itself. Like this naked woman wearing make-up ('Sur ce teint fauve et brun le fard était superbe!' (l. 28)) it offers us both an unvarnished spectacle of sexual desire and the artifice of an imaginary 'fleur du Mal'.

It is therefore possible that Baudelaire saw this group of poems that present a fusion of art and sex as effecting a transition between the opening considerations of the poet's role and the so-called cycles of 'love poems' that begin with 'Parfum exotique'.[34] This is suggested further by a comparison with the 1861 edition in which 'Les Bijoux', having been banned, was replaced by 'Le Masque', followed by 'Hymne à la Beauté'. The latter will be discussed in Chapter 9, but 'Le Masque' itself may be seen to fulfil a similar function to 'Les Bijoux' in presenting a combination of sexual attraction and aesthetic performance: in this case the ekphrasis of a 'Statue allégorique dans le goût de la Renaissance' by the sculptor Ernest Christophe.[35] Where in 'Les Bijoux' a living woman is seen as a work of art, here the statue of a woman is viewed as though she were real: 'Cette femme, morceau vraiment miraculeux' (l. 4). Just as in 'La Géante' the poet's gaze lingers on his imaginary giantess and 'ses magnifiques formes' that are both sexually exciting and aesthetically pleasing, so here the poet observes how '[d]ans l'ondulation de ce corps musculeux | L'Élégance et la Force abondent, sœurs divines' (ll. 2–3). Like the bed-companion of 'Les Bijoux', at once slave and regal presence, so the woman of this statue 'Est faite pour trôner sur des lits somptueux | Et charmer les loisirs d'un pontife ou d'un prince' (ll. 6–7). Where the bed-slave derives an 'air vainqueur' from her jewelled magnificence and higher position on the bed, the woman of the statue is an 'être doué de tant de majesté' (l. 14), and every feature of her face—her smile, her gaze—proclaims 'avec un air vainqueur: | "La Volupté m'appelle et l'Amour me couronne!"' (ll. 12–13).

Thus, as also in 'La Beauté' as well as in 'Les Bijoux', beauty is once more associated with authority and sexual power. In 'La Beauté' that power is limited since the type of beauty in question (cold, lifeless, forbidding) appears ultimately vacuous and sterile, while in 'Les Bijoux' the power is transitory, lasting only as long as it takes to sate the fury of passion. Here beauty is presented as two-faced, wearing a mask behind which ('Approchons, et tournons autour de sa beauté' (l. 16)) the sculptor has cleverly concealed her other, true face: 'La véritable tête, et la sincère face | Renversée à l'abri de la face qui ment' (ll. 23–4). And this face is

---

[34] Both Adam (ed. cit., 303) and Pichois (i. 1134) wonder if 'Les Bijoux' in fact marks the start of the cycle of poems inspired by Jeanne Duval, but one could suggest the same about 'La Géante', which precedes it and also derives from a similar inspiration. The evidence of the 1861 edition suggests that Baudelaire did envisage these poems as being principally about the nature of beauty since in 1861 the newly added 'Hymne à la Beauté' is there placed immediately after them, summarizing and concluding the poet's reflections on different types of beauty before 'Parfum exotique' initiates the so-called 'love cycles'.

[35] On this statue see Stéphane Guégan, 'À propos d'Ernest Christophe: D'une allégorie l'autre', in Guyaux and Marchal (eds), *'Les Fleurs du Mal': Actes du colloque de la Sorbonne des 10 et 11 janvier 2003*, 95–106.

weeping, bitterly and with the very tears that the protagonist of 'La Muse vénale' also chose to conceal. But how can she weep like this when she is so beautiful and wields such power, the poet asks himself, before—idiot that he is—suddenly understanding why. She weeps on account of her *mal de vivre*:

> —Elle pleure, insensé, parce qu'elle a vécu!
> Et parce qu'elle vit! Mais ce qu'elle déplore
> Surtout, ce qui la fait frémir jusqu'aux genoux,
> C'est que demain, hélas! il faudra vivre encore!
> Demain, après-demain et toujours!—comme nous!
>
> (ll. 32-6)

The poet feigns disapproval and shock as he moves round the statue, evoking the newly perceived discrepancy with his own sudden shift in tone from quaintly hyperbolic apostrophe to anatomical precision and a rhyme that replaces vapid Romantic cliché with the language of a medical manual:

> Ô blasphème de l'art! ô surprise fatale!
> La femme au corps divin, promettant le bonheur,
> Par le haut se termine en monstre bicéphale!
>
> (ll. 17-19)

Beauty, it seems, has two heads: one, like that in 'La Beauté', a 'beauté parfaite | Qui mettrait à ses pieds le genre humain vaincu' (ll. 29-30), and the other, shedding a magnificent stream of tears that runs straight to the poet's own 'cœur soucieux' (ll. 25-6):

> Ton mensonge m'enivre, et mon âme s'abreuve
> Aux flots que la Douleur fait jaillir de tes yeux!
>
> (ll. 27-8)

Only now do we see that the beauty of the mask was a false beauty, a 'visage mignard' (l. 1) that recalls the rococo 'beautés de vignettes' of 'L'Idéal', and wearing an ecstatic expression of 'Fatuité' accompanied by an overtly theatrical 'long regard sournois, langoureux et moqueur' (l. 10). The beauty of the real face beneath the mask, by contrast, displays the beauty of melancholy, and the poet is moved and intoxicated by the contrast between false beauty and the reality of human suffering, and also by the poignant, artful attempt of the woman-statue ('[t]on mensonge' (l. 27)) to conceal the terrible truth of the human condition beneath a charming air of 'gentillesse' (l. 15). Both faces lie, but the lie of the real face tells a deeper truth. By revealing the depth of suffering behind an appearance of smug rapture the sculptor has seemingly defiled the divinity of art ('Ô blasphème de l'art!'), but in fact he has created a work of beauty that in its truthfulness and its acknowledgement of 'le Mal' speaks to all of us ('comme nous'). As we learn in the prose poem 'Une mort héroïque', beauty, or 'l'ivresse de l'art', can only ever hope to 'veil' the terrors of the abyss, and this is the allegory that both Christophe and the poet of 'Le Masque' have produced. In 'Les Bijoux' the 'ivresse' of sexual pleasure served a similar function but could not last. Here in 'Le Masque' the 'ivresse' prompted in the poet by the statue is perpetuated in the poem itself, his own lasting tribute not only to the dedicatee, Ernest Christophe, but to the necessary relationship between beauty and melancholy.

9
Les Fleurs du Mal (1857/1861)
New Endings

[. . .] et une fin.

(*Corr.*, ii. 196)

New Frames for Old

Comme un beau cadre ajoute à la peinture | [. . .] |
Je ne sais quoi d'étrange et d'enchanté[.]

"('Le Cadre', ll. 1–3)

As we have seen, the overall framework of *Les Fleurs du Mal* traces a journey from birth to death, a pattern that also serves in 1857 to structure 'Spleen et idéal' itself, where we move from the birth and sunrise of 'Bénédiction' and 'Le Soleil' and the effortless *survol* of 'Élévation' to a final group of seven poems that evoke a downward trajectory towards night-time and death.[1] As we also have now seen in more detail, the first twenty poems of the 1857 'Spleen et idéal' trace an evolution from tradition to innovation in the poet's thinking about his own role and the nature of beauty. In the 1861 edition 'Le Soleil' is replaced with 'L'Albatros', which reinforces the existing framework by complementing 'Bénédiction' and 'Élévation' more explicitly than 'Le Soleil'. The mother's rejection of the poet in 'Bénédiction' is followed by society's rejection in 'L'Albatros', thus foregrounding another stereotypical Romantic view of the poet as the unacknowledged genius. Similarly, the mother's bitter lament at the birth of 'cette dérision' ('Bénédiction', l. 6) leads on to the crewmen's merciless ridiculing of the ungainly albatross ('qu'il est comique et laid!' (l. 10)). On the other hand, the final stanza of 'L'Albatros' ('Le Poète est semblable au prince des nuées' (l. 13)) now serves as a transition towards the stereotype of 'Élévation', the poet of superior and universal understanding.[2]

---

[1] See Chapter 7.
[2] For discussion of 'L'Albatros' as evidence of Baudelaire's evolving aesthetic and his rejection of Romantic stereotypes, see Margaret Gilman, '"L'Albatros" again', *Romantic Review*, 41: 2 (Apr. 1950), 96–107, and Susan Blood, 'Mimesis and the Grotesque in "L'Albatros"', in William J. Thompson (ed.), *Understanding 'Les Fleurs du Mal': Critical Readings* (Nashville and London: Vanderbilt University

Replacing 'Les Bijoux', 'Le Masque' is followed by 'Hymne à la Beauté', which also reinforces the existing framework by presenting the poet's manifesto of beauty in preparation for what will follow. Although by this title likening his poem to a hymn, as if he were affiliating himself to a Lamartinian tradition of quasi-religious verse, the poet here steps radically outside this tradition by presenting beauty not as an objective quality or phenomenon (epitomizing the inherent divinity of Creation) but as a subjective effect. Hence the simple but arresting analogy with which the poem opens and which prepares for the later section 'Le Vin':

> Viens-tu du ciel profond ou sors-tu de l'abîme,
> Ô Beauté? ton regard, infernal et divin,
> Verse confusément le bienfait et le crime,
> Et l'on peut pour cela te comparer au vin.

(ll. 1-4)

Coming after poems that concertedly align sexual attraction and aesthetic pleasure ('La Beauté', 'L'Idéal', 'La Géante', 'Le Masque'), the beauty in question here is also both the beauty of woman and the beauty of art. As the source of an effect, the beauty of woman resembles wine by its capacity to inspire both good and evil ('le bienfait et le crime'), both cowardice and courage (l. 8), but the source—woman— is as enigmatic as the combination of beauty and melancholy in art. Her eye reflects sunset as well as sunrise (l. 5), and she exudes the scents of a stormy evening (l. 6): the messages are mixed. As to her provenance and moral character these are irrelevant, for Beauty simply *is* authority (as in 'La Beauté' and 'Les Bijoux'). Destiny follows her skirts like a faithful dog (l. 10); she holds sway, randomly, irresponsibly, untouchably, proudly (ll. 11-16): she attracts, destructively (ll. 17-22). But the whole point of Beauty, both as woman and as art, is to offer moments in which the world seems temporarily less ugly and when time hangs less heavily on our mortal condition. Beauty is not the embodiment of perfection like Dante's Beatrice, guiding the poet towards a permanent Paradise, but a source of intoxication, like wine, offering temporary respite from 'les terreurs du gouffre':

> Que tu viennes du ciel ou de l'enfer, qu'importe,
> Ô Beauté! monstre énorme, effrayant, ingénu!
> Si ton œil, ton souris, ton pied, m'ouvrent la porte
> D'un infini que j'aime et n'ai jamais connu?

Press, 1997), 1-15. Blood notes (p. 5) that Flaubert intended to include the poem in the *Sottisier* of *Bouvard et Pécuchet*.

De Satan ou de Dieu, qu'importe? Ange ou Sirène,
Qu'importe, si tu rends,—fée aux yeux de velours,
Rythme, parfum, lueur, ô mon unique reine!—
L'univers moins hideux et les instants moins lourds?

(ll. 21–8)

Here is the credo of the poet as alternative lawgiver, as initiate of the 'black mystery' of Lesbos. Like Sappho and her sister 'martyres' this beauty is at once 'monstrous' and ingenuous, and 'les lois du juste et de l'injuste' are irrelevant. Christian dualities of heaven and hell, good and evil, God and Satan are immaterial; like the women of Lesbos the poet is here himself a 'chercheur d'infini', and this particular type of beauty comprises the sound, smell, and light with which to transform the world of drab quotidian experience. Casting fairy magic from eyes of velvet, this queenly Beauty is the imagination itself: 'Mystérieuse faculté que cette reine des facultés!' (*Salon de 1859*)—the imagination of the poet, but more especially of the reader.

In reframing the 1857 'Spleen et idéal' for the second edition Baudelaire left the ordering of poems 1–51 (from 'Bénédiction' to 'Causerie') largely unaltered. 'Le Masque' and 'Hymne à la Beauté' are substituted for the banned 'Les Bijoux', while 'Le Léthé' and 'A celle qui est trop gaie', also banned, are removed. 'La Chevelure', 'Duellum', 'Le Possédé', and the four poems that constitute 'Un fantôme' are added. Of these, 'La Chevelure' complements 'Parfum exotique' in that both relate back to the tercets of 'Correspondances' and illustrate how smell may provoke an exotic journey of memory and imagination. The others fill out the end of the first cycle of 'love poems' (22–39) by evoking the lovers' hatred ('Duellum'), the demonic character of the poet's mistress ('Le Possédé'), and the poet's reflections on her absence ('Un fantôme'). But after 'Causerie' the alterations are more far-reaching: fifteen new poems are added, the final seven poems are brought forward and included largely in reverse order, and a new final grouping of seven poems provides a radically new ending for 'Spleen et idéal' and thereby modifies the significance of its framework substantially.

Where in 1857 the final seven poems served to make the structure of 'Spleen et idéal' mirror the overall structure of *Les Fleurs du Mal* as a movement from birth to death, from upward aspiration towards downbeat acceptance and ironic repose, the 1861 ending of 'Spleen et idéal marks a change of gear whereby a full-blooded embrace of melancholy becomes itself a new starting-point (as then exemplified by the poems of 'Tableaux parisiens' in which a city serves as the symbolic *locus* of 'le Mal').[3] And this progression is in turn mirrored by the new ending to *Les Fleurs du*

---

[3] See Chapters 18 and 19. For a reading of these seven poems as expressing 'a more thorough thinking through of the logic and consequences of the impossibility of redemption', see Joseph Acquisto, *The Fall Out of Redemption: Writing and Thinking Beyond Salvation in Baudelaire, Cioran, Fondane, Agamben, and Nancy* (New York and London: Bloomsbury, 2015), 37–47 (37).

Mal as a whole, where the three poems added to 'La Mort'—'La Fin de la journée', 'Le Rêve d'un curieux', and 'Le Voyage'—substantially alter the overall poetic argument of the collection by also embracing melancholy and death as a new beginning.

As has sometimes been argued, the final seven poems in the 1861 'Spleen et idéal' may be seen as intended counterparts of poems that figure at the beginning of the section: namely, 'Obsession' ('Correspondances'); 'Le Goût du néant' ('Élévation'); 'Alchimie de la douleur' ('Bénédiction'); and 'Horreur sympathique' ('Correspondances', 'Don Juan aux enfers'). These are followed by 'L'Héautontimorouménos' (the only one of the seven coming from the 1857 edition, where it followed 'Causerie' as no. 52), 'L'Irrémédiable', and 'L'Horloge'. But it would be wrong to see the first four of these final seven poems simply as negative versions of earlier, positive statements of the poet's art since these, as we have seen, are themselves already ironic treatments of Romantic stereotypes. So, too, in fact are these later counterparts but from the opposite direction, exaggerating and undermining a certain type of nihilistic Romantic melancholy that the poet here rejects as strongly as he had previously ironized and rejected the alternative of 'idealism': that is, the poet as blessed by suffering, or the nature poet with a privileged insight into the divine script of Creation. Once again Baudelaire resists simplistic duality.

'Obsession'

Mais les ténèbres sont elles-mêmes des toiles

(l. 12)

The ambivalence of these last seven poems at the end of 'Spleen et idéal' (1861) may be observed initially in the case of 'Obsession', which is usually read as the apparent 'spleen' counterpart of an 'idéal' 'Correspondances':[4]

Grands bois, vous m'effrayez comme des cathédrales;
Vous hurlez comme l'orgue; et dans nos cœurs maudits,

---

[4] But see De Man, 'Anthropomorphism and Trope in the Lyric', where De Man comments that 'the two sonnets complement each other like the two halves of a *symbolon*' (253-4) and argues that 'the relationship between "Correspondances" and "Obsession" touches upon the uncertain status of the lyric as a term for poetic discourse in general. The lyric's claim of being song is made explicitly in "Correspondances" ("qui *chantent* les transports...''), whereas "Obsession" howls, laughs, and speaks but does not pretend to sing' (254). For a clarifying commentary on De Man's essay, see Barbara Johnson, 'Anthropomorphism in Lyric and Law', *Yale Journal of Law and the Humanities*, 10: 2 (1998), 549-74, where she describes it as 'both [h]yperbolic and elliptical' and as 'one of the most difficult, even outrageous, of his essays' (551). See also Kevin Newmark's analysis of De Man's essay in his *Beyond Symbolism: Textual History and the Future of Reading* (Ithaca, NY and London: Cornell University Press, 1991), 201-30.

> Chambres d'éternel deuil où vibrent de vieux râles,
> Répondent les échos de vos *De profundis*.
>
> Je te hais, Océan! tes bonds et tes tumultes,
> Mon esprit les retrouve en lui; ce rire amer
> De l'homme vaincu, plein de sanglots et d'insultes,
> Je l'entends dans le rire énorme de la mer.
>
> Comme tu me plairais, ô nuit! sans ces étoiles
> Dont la lumière parle un langage connu!
> Car je cherche le vide, et le noir, et le nu!
>
> Mais les ténèbres sont elles-mêmes des toiles
> Où vivent, jaillissant de mon œil par milliers,
> Des êtres disparus aux regards familiers.

'Obsession' mirrors the two-stage argument of 'Correspondances'. In the latter the poet rejects a neo-Platonist model of 'correspondance' between our material world and a transcendent spiritual reality in favour of a more elusive form of suggestive interconnection between the sensual and the imaginary. Here in 'Obsession' the poet appears to accept the possibility of a correspondence between nature and man that approximates to the Romantic idea of the pathetic fallacy but wants to blank it, only to find another kind of correspondence taking its place. He describes how, far from being a willing participant (as in the final tercet of 'Correspondances') in the transports of mind and senses brought on by rich scents and aromas, he feels 'obsessed' (from the Latin *obsidere* = to besiege) by a natural world that seems to speak to him only of suffering and the vanity of human enterprise. Unlike those poets who take comfort in the perception that nature's 'emotions' are in harmony with their own, this poet finds himself surrounded by sights and sounds that are only too familiar as reminders of our inadequacy and our mortality. So insistently is he 'besieged' that even at night he is unable to blot out this world, and instead he involuntarily projects onto the black canvas of nocturnal darkness thousands upon thousands of unfamiliar images: phantoms of the past perhaps ('[d]es êtres disparus'), or simply the strange, bizarre, and unfamiliar images of dream and nightmare. But we recall that for Baudelaire 'le beau est toujours bizarre'. Are we then to understand perhaps that while nature speaks to the poet only (and in very familiar terms) of his melancholic condition, his own 'eye' or vision can be the source—*is* the source—of myriad alternative representations of 'le Mal'? The oneiric spectacles of 'Tableaux parisiens' ('Les Sept Vieillards', 'Les Petites Vieilles', 'Le Jeu', 'Rêve parisien') will subsequently confirm that it can.

As in 'Correspondances' the first stanza takes up the stock Romantic comparison of a forest to a place of religious worship: no longer here a temple but a cathedral, in continuing implicit allusion to Chateaubriand's celebrated analogy.

The opening monosyllables of 'Grands bois' may suggest the thunderous chords of a cathedral organ (l. 2) as the wind howls in the branches, and these natural sounds are echoed in the human heart: 'nos cœurs maudits', which, because of the proximity of 'cathédrales', may be heard also as 'chœurs maudits'. Our human hearts, the poet alleges, are chambers of eternal grief, echoing the *De profundis* sung by the cathedral choirs of nature: that is, the Latin version of Psalm 130, one of the so-called Penitential Psalms, in which the psalmist expresses his faith and hope in God.[5] But the echo is imperfect, for the reference to *eternal* grief implies an absence of faith in redemption, just as the only music to be heard now is the alliterative vibration of a death rattle. 'Cathédrales' has dwindled to the mere echo of 'râles', while '*De profundis*' itself is a defective rhyme for 'maudits'.[6] Thus instead of the 'confuses paroles' of 'Correspondances' we have here an imperfect communication between nature and the human heart that belies any Christian idea of harmony between God and man.

The assertive tone of the first stanza is taken up in the second, which begins with three staccato monosyllables (recalling 'Grands bois vous [...]') and where the plurals of the first stanza are replaced by the bare singularities of 'je' and 'te'. The poet has become the solitary representative of a defeated humanity in a storm-tossed world, and the gale that implicitly causes the great woods to howl now explicitly makes the ocean roar with a sound resembling the bitter laughter of human beings[7] as they hurl insults at the deity from amidst their sobs. The depths of 'De Profundis' are here mirrored in the watery deeps, just as the echoing 'eau' of 'les échos de vos *De Profundis*' is taken up in 'Océan' and the subsequent 'sanglots'. For here also is the 'eau' of 'ô' ('ô nuit'), the language of exclamatory misery (the poem contains four exclamation marks) and complementing the pained exhalation of a death rattle. This poet's world echoes with endless agony and bitter postlapsarian laughter, just as the turbulence and despair of human experience is reflected in the parallel syntactic structures of the quatrains. Each begins and ends with a simple paratactic statement, after which a shorter paratactic statement in the second line is then followed by the syntactic disruption of inversion (ll. 2–4, ll. 6–8) and the metrical disruption of

---

[5] In Latin the psalm begins: 'De profundis clamavi ad Te, Domine' (Out of the depths have I cried unto thee, O Lord). Verse 7 reads, in the King James Version: 'Let Israel hope in the Lord: for with the Lord there is mercy, and with him is plenteous redemption.'

[6] By ending in a sounded [s] where 'maudits' does not. Cf. the first rhyme of 'La Cloche fêlée' where the inadequacy of the poet's 'bell' is displayed in the opening rhyme of 'hiver' and 's'élever', which is only technically permissible on account of 's'élever' being followed by a vowel at the beginning of the following line. In *Baudelaire and the Poetics of Craft* (Cambridge: Cambridge University Press, 1988) Graham Chesters suggests apropos this and other examples of a so-called *rime normande* (or rhyme for the eye) that 'Baudelaire compensates for their phonetic frailty by endowing them with a thematic function' (see 95–6). But one could perhaps more plausibly argue that the 'phonetic frailty' is employed precisely to illustrate the theme of the poet's sense of failure and inadequacy.

[7] Possibly an allusion to an image in the work of Aeschylus. See i. 980, and 981 n. 5.

enjambement (ll. 6–7) before resolution is provided in the last line by the deferred arrival of a main verb. This disruption and deferral are particularly marked in the second quatrain where the phrase 'tes bonds et tes tumultes' appears first to be the supplementary object of 'hais', only then to figure (in apposition to 'les') as the object of 'mon esprit [...] retrouve' so that the idea of retrieval is enacted in the syntax itself. And so, like intermittent gusts of wind or the bounding waves of the sea, the verse mirrors both the rhythms of nature and the fluctuating emotions of humankind, from fear to the sad acceptance of an alliterative mortality, or from hatred to the bitter deflation reflected in a bathetic enjambement: 'ce rire amer | De l'homme vaincu'.

In the first tercet the focus switches from the world of sound to the world of sight, and from the actuality of the present to an alternative, hypothetical realm of nothingness. The sound of bitter laughter lingers in the echoing syllables of 'plairais' (themselves reminiscent of 'verts comme les prairies' in 'Correspondances') as the poet longs for a night without stars and without the starlight that speaks in a 'langage connu'. This metaphorical image of hearing what he sees provides a transition from the sounds of the octave to the sights of the sestet (while briefly recalling the idea of synaesthesia mooted in 'Correspondances') and also foregrounds the dual nature of language, and therefore poetry, as something both seen and heard: a text in which what we read with our eyes is accompanied by a play of sound (homophony, rhyme, alliteration, patterns of contrast and repetition) that may complement or skew the silent meaning of the words. In this case the poet wants to shut his eyes and block his ears to the message of the stars. But what might this 'known language'—another element in a 'besieging' world of signs—be telling him? Of God in his Heaven and the wonderful beauty of Creation? Of Christ who was sent to lighten our darkness? Of a Pascalian 'disproportion de l'homme' and the petty insignificance of human beings in a vast cosmos where God is invisible? At any rate, this language is known and familiar, like the 'forêts de symboles' of 'Correspondances' that observe mankind 'avec des regards familiers'. And it is a language that the poet rejects—perhaps because it simply exacerbates his bitter sense of being 'vanquished', of being (as we are about to learn five poems later) 'irremediably' subject to 'le Mal'. 'Car je cherche le vide, et le noir, et le nu!': the monosyllabic character of this insistence (as of its addressee, 'ô nuit!') bears witness at once to the poet's determination and to his despair, doomed as he irredeemably is never to escape all these echoes and signs and symbols of the wretchedness of our melancholic condition.

But... and here the deferral of the *volta* from the beginning of the sestet to the beginning of the final tercet adds poignancy to the poet's expression of impotence (an 'If only...' to be followed now, finally, by a 'But in fact...'): this glimpse of nothingness is momentary, and the obsession returns. The darkness turns out to be a series of blank canvases on which are cast, in an ironic version of Christian resurrection, the living images of vanished beings who refuse to die.[8] Instead of death there is life: instead of 'où vibrent de vieux râles' we have 'Où vivent, jaillissant de mon œil par milliers'. And so the poem comes full circle: just as in the first quatrain the cursèd hearts emitted echoes of the '*De profundis*' to be heard in woods and cathedrals, so from the poet's eye spring forth thousands of unknown, departed, forgotten, unfamiliar beings, the assembled host of the dead bearing implicit witness to the paradoxical 'eternity' (cf. 'éternel deuil') of transience and human mortality. And now, with its final flourish of 'regards familiers' that directly recalls 'Correspondances', the poem adds a crucial twist to its depiction of a poet's doomed attempts at escape from 'la conscience dans le Mal'. In each preceding stanza we have had an image or expression of return and reminder, and thus of repetition and retrieval: respectively, the echoes, 'mon esprit les retrouve en lui', 'un langage connu', and 'aux regards familiers'. But on this occasion, in the last line, we have the suggestion that if the poet can project onto the black canvas of despair images and insights that have been rescued from the oblivion of habituated perception, then perhaps he can, by the power of his imagination, create 'un langage *in*connu'—the language, as 'Hymne à la Beauté' has it, of an 'Infini que j'aime et n'ai jamais connu'.

For Baudelaire, beauty must always be 'bizarre' and 'étonnant' if it is (as in 'Correspondances') to 'transport' the mind and senses of poet and reader alike. Perhaps, then, there may arise from the 'echo chamber' of the poet's 'cœur maudit' a new music and a new, secular version of the inauthentic Christian psalm that sings of faith in a redemption and an afterlife that can never come. Not a 'penitential' psalm, therefore, but a poem that expresses 'la Conscience dans le Mal' and finds value in these secular resurrections of what is dead and gone. Through the work of memory and imagination, the creativity of art can paint pictures on the walls of a prison-world under mortal siege. The term 'jaillissant' suggests that this creativity is involuntary, with beauty springing unbidden and even unwanted from the poet's eye. But an ambiguity remains. Perhaps, as is suggested in 'Un mangeur d'opium' ('d'apercevoir, ou plutôt de créer'),[9] this involuntary creativity of the opium-eater and the child is also in some sense willed, or at least can be so willed by the poet for whom genius is 'l'enfance retrouvée à volonté'. Indeed the four 'Spleen' poems that precede 'Obsession' in

---

[8] Adam (ed. cit., 365, n. 4) and Pichois (i. 981, n. 1) note the parallel with 'Les Ténèbres' (in the newly added quartet of sonnets entitled 'Un fantôme'): 'Dans les caveaux d'insondable tristesse [...] | Je suis comme un peintre qu'un Dieu moqueur | Condamne à peindre, hélas! sur les ténèbres' (ll. 1, 5–6), which in turn, it should be added, recalls 'Le Mauvais Moine' and the poet-monk who is too idle to paint the walls of his monastery. Both editors note a further parallel with 'Un mangeur d'opium' in *Les Paradis artificiels* where Baudelaire/De Quincey describes how the opium-eater shares with the child 'la singulière faculté d'apercevoir, ou plutôt de créer, sur la toile féconde des ténèbres tout un monde de visions bizarres' (i. 480).

[9] See n. 8.

the 1861 edition—with their rich transformations of ennui into the least familiar of scenes and images—would confirm that it can.

Embracing 'le Mal'

> Puits de Vérité, clair et noir
>
> ('L'Irrémédiable', l. 35)

As the first of the seven poems that round off the 1861 'Spleen et idéal', 'Obsession' therefore constitutes an important new element in Baudelaire's 'cadre singulier', a manifesto that takes up where 'Hymne à la Beauté' left off. The three poems that follow similarly echo earlier poems and express the active acceptance of 'la conscience dans le Mal'. In 'Le Goût du néant' the poet occupies the superior vantage-point he once envied in 'Élévation', but in so doing he no longer seeks to turn away from 'les ennuis et les vastes chagrins' of our terrestrial existence. Rather: 'Je contemple d'en haut le globe en sa rondeur | Et je n'y cherche plus l'abri d'une cahute' (ll. 13–14). No longer seeking shelter or escape from 'le Mal', he has renounced the struggle and now lacks the spur of 'L'Espoir' (ll. 1–2); spring, love, pleasure... nothing smells or (as the title also suggests) tastes of anything (ll. 7–10). All interest has gone, as it has also from the rhymes of the poem (where the same two rhymes are repeated throughout), and time holds the poet's ageing, stiffened body in its icy grip like snow (ll. 11–12). Recalling the 'homme vaincu' of 'Obsession' he is an 'Esprit vaincu, fourbu!' (l. 6), exhausted and ready for the avalanche of death to bear him away. But his parting rhetorical question hangs in the air: 'Avalanche, veux-tu m'emporter dans ta chute?' Release may not quite be yet at hand.

In 'Alchimie de la douleur' the poet moves on from this spirit of defeatedness in the face of 'le Mal', this willing acceptance of death. He must live, and so his poetry is the poetry of pain, the addressee of this poem. While other poets may look to Nature with ardour (like Lamartine or Hugo perhaps) and celebrate it as 'Vie et splendeur!' (l. 4), he sees Nature—as he has already in 'Obsession'—as the place of mortality, a 'Sépulture'.[10] Unlike the absurd poet of 'Bénédiction' for whom suffering is a God-given blessing, here is the poet of 'le Mal'—'[l]e plus triste des alchimistes' (l. 8)—for whom pain turns gold into base metal and paradise into hell (ll. 9–10). Whether other poets have their head in the clouds (a stereotype later taken up also in the prose poem 'La Soupe et les nuages'), he sees a cloud as a burial shroud containing the corpse of someone dear and now departed

---

[10] The poem 'Sépulture', placed fourth from last in the 1857 'Spleen et idéal', now serves in the 1861 edition to usher in the final sequence of sixteen poems that focus on death and despair and culminate in positive acceptance of 'le Mal' and the affirmation of life.

(ll. 11–12): 'Et sur les célestes rivages | Je bâtis de grands sarcophages' (ll. 13–14). His poems are like tombs constructed on the edge of heaven, imaginary resting-places within an inescapable terrestrial realm for all the victims of time and mortality: not castles in the air, but homes for the dead constructed from the vapours of imagination. Even within 'le Mal', then, he is still a builder who commemorates those who have lived: within melancholy he remains an active creator. From a taste *of* 'le Néant' he has developed a taste *for* 'le Néant'.

In 'Horreur sympathique' this acceptance of 'le Mal' is expressed more strongly still. Addressing himself initially as though he were the Don Juan of 'Don Juan aux enfers' now approaching Hell after a lifetime of debauch (ll. 1–4), he examines his own 'âme vide' against the symbolic backdrop of a storm-wracked sky.[11] The poet feels exiled as Ovid was from his 'paradis latin' (l. 8), but unlike Ovid he will voice no lament. He therefore rejects the stereotypical role of the misunderstood genius and unacknowledged legislator. Yes, he is 'insatiablement avide | De l'obscur et de l'incertain' (ll. 5–6) (cf. 'un Infini que j'aime et n'ai jamais connu'), and in his explorations beyond the lucidity of the familiar he may be guilty of the hubris or 'orgueil' (l. 10) of a Don Juan or a contrarian theologian (in 'Châtiment de l'orgueil'). And yes, this poet of clouds first revealed in 'Alchimie de la douleur' here recognizes that the banks of black cumulonimbus in the skies above may represent the funeral procession of his dreams, or the jagged shorelines (l. 9) of impossible destinations. But, like Don Juan, he has no regrets: 'Et vos lueurs sont le reflet | De l'enfer où mon cœur se plaît' (ll. 13–14). In 'Obsession' the poet rejected the pathetic fallacy of a Nature that has feelings and instead found himself projecting his own memories and imaginings onto the darkness before him. Here, faced with the void of his own soul and the memory of a 'tormented' destiny (l. 2), and firmly embracing a new poetic mode that he terms 'horreur sympathique', the poet imposes his own form of Satanic correspondence on the natural world, his own 'sympathy for the Devil'.[12] His hubris 'mirrors itself' (l. 10) in the stormy sky, while the gleams of lightning are ostensibly not lightning at all but reflections of the hellfire of 'le Mal' in which his heart is now content to have its being. The vision before him has its source neither in God nor in nature but in his own moral self. Thus, in the sestet where he may appear to be addressing the sky, the poet is in effect in dialogue with himself: his sentient self and his conscious self joined, like two separate persons, in a sympathetic fellowship of horror.

---

[11] Adam (ed. cit., 367) and Pichois (i. 983) both posit a reminiscence of Delacroix's recent painting of 'Ovide chez les Scythes', but the sky described in the poem more closely evokes that in 'La Barque de Dante', itself referenced in 'Don Juan aux enfers'.

[12] In an interview published by *Rolling Stone* (14 Dec. 1995) Mick Jagger stated that the song 'Sympathy for the Devil' (1968) was written by him and 'taken from an old idea of Baudelaire's, I think, but I could be wrong. Sometimes when I look at my Baudelaire books, I can't see it in there. But it was an idea I got from French writing. And I just took a couple of lines and expanded on it. I wrote it as sort of like a Bob Dylan song.' He mentions Jean-Luc Godard's film of the same title, also made in 1968, which includes footage of the Rolling Stones recording the song.

In 'Horreur sympathique', therefore, the external world is devoid of inherent meaning or symbolic purport. Such meaning as there may be derives solely from the poet: the horror is all his. In this respect the poem exemplifies the 'deux qualités littéraires fondamentales' identified by Baudelaire in *Fusées*: 'surnaturalisme et ironie'.[13] The poet goes beyond nature—the material world, the given, the familiar, his *own* nature—and indeed lays interpretation upon it, but he does so in terms of the dissonance, or 'irony', at the heart of human experience. In 'Le Reniement de saint Pierre' this world is described as one in which 'l'action n'est pas la sœur du rêve' (l. 30). Here similarly in 'Horreur sympathique' the dissonance lies between the poet's 'rêves' and the realities of a 'destin tourmenté', between being '[i]nsatiablement avide' (l. 5) and knowing the 'vide' of a libertine heart. Here once more is the tragedy of desire, and here also, as the next poem 'L'Héautontimorouménos' now suggests, is the 'loi d'ignorance' set out in *De l'essence du rire*. 'Irony'/'ironie' derives from the ancient Greek *eirōn* = dissembler, and 'eironeia' = simulated ignorance' and designates a discrepancy: between truth and falsehood, reality and appearance, or, as in *De l'essence du rire* and elsewhere in Baudelaire, between the 'naïveté' of our experience of 'le Mal' and a creativity that can only proceed if it pretends—like the buffoon who in order to be entertainingly ridiculous has to pretend that he does not know that he is ridiculous—that it will not be undone by that very 'Mal'.

This is the poet-artist as double agent, and we see him at his most anguished and yet also his most committed in 'L'Héautontimorouménos'. Unlike in *De l'essence du rire* it is through tears and not laughter that this poet-performer will know if he has succeeded in his 'irony': that is, if his reader can be convinced by this portrayal of a human being suffering the hell of 'le Mal', even if that same reader is aware that the poet, as an artist, himself knows this suffering to be simulated. By being dedicated (in 1861)[14] to a particular reader ('J.G.F.', whom some have taken to be Jeanne Duval)[15] this poem foregrounds its function of eliciting response (as the comic performer does) from an audience or readership, and in this respect it recalls the direct address of 'Au lecteur'. In the first three stanzas the poet presents himself as Moses, that most hallowed model of the poet as legislator, but here the Moses who smote the rock and brought forth water for the thirsting Israelites in their exile.[16] Baudelaire's Moses states his intention to smite the rock of his reader's eye and bring forth 'les eaux de la souffrance' (l. 6). Without feeling any emotion himself, neither anger nor hatred, this conscious artist will, like a butcher (l. 2), land his blow with skill. And the resultant tears will

---

[13] See *Fusées*, ed. Guyaux, 63; i. 658.
[14] In the 1857 edition the poem, undedicated, is placed earlier, as no. 52, after 'Causerie', which is commonly thought to end the cycle of poems concerning Marie Daubrun.
[15] See in particular i. 986–7, and Yves Bonnefoy, 'Que signifie J.G.F.?', *L'Année Baudelaire*, 9–10 (2005–6), 65–70, reprinted in *Sous le signe de Baudelaire*, 331–9.
[16] See 'Introduction', n. 21.

irrigate the Sahara (l. 5) of his arid existence by renewing his faith in the efficacy of his art and the value of his creative desire:

> Mon désir gonflé d'espérance
> Sur tes pleurs salés nagera
>
> Comme un vaisseau qui prend le large,
> Et dans mon cœur qu'ils soûleront
> Tes chers sanglots retentiront
> Comme un tambour qui bat la charge!
>
> (ll. 7–12)

The following stanzas are most often read, rightly, as an account of 'la conscience dans le Mal': of a poet who is at once wound and knife (l. 21) because he both suffers the inevitable ill-being of human existence but also exacerbates that suffering by being aware of its inescapable causes and its irremediable persistence. As the title indicates, this is the poet not only as double agent but as self-executioner, someone for whom the writing of poetry is a form of self-harm. The poet epitomizes dissonance: he is 'un faux accord | Dans la divine symphonie' (ll. 13–14) and the site of a most paradoxical 'Ironie' (l. 15). For this self-knowledge of dissonance is a poison that is also his life-blood (l. 18), a creature that shakes him and voraciously bites him (ll. 15–16), like some mordant Satanic serpent perhaps, but which is also the poet himself as the blood-sucking vampire of his own heart (l. 25), drawing sustenance from self-destruction. But if the poet is his own executioner, then the addressee of the first three stanzas is perhaps the poet himself, condemned to an eternal conversation with himself (as in 'Horreur sympathique'), the eternal victim of his own self-consciousness and irony. But as a human being engaged in the depiction of 'le Mal', he is also 'executing' the reader (and not just 'J.G.F.') of whom he is a mirror image: 'Hypocrite lecteur,—mon semblable,—mon frère'. He may claim to resemble a mirror in which a shrew gazes at her own reflection (ll. 19–20), but he is also providing a mirror within which all of mankind may conduct their own self-scrutiny, their own 'conscience dans le Mal'.

The poet ends by presenting himself as an outcast ('Un de ces grands abandonnés') and a vampire who can only laugh, not smile.[17] Within the terms of *De l'essence du rire* this may be read positively: the poet cannot distance himself intellectually (and by implication inauthentically) from the reality of our divided nature but rather must experience it to the full both in life and in art in a Rabelaisian celebration of the grotesque. Not for him the 'comique significatif', therefore, only the 'comique absolu'. And this is the lesson of 'L'Irrémédiable': 'la

---

[17] Adam (371 n. 7) suggests that Baudelaire derived this idea from his reading of Maturin's *Melmoth*.

conscience *dans* le Mal!', and not 'la conscience *du* Mal' (my emphases). In this poem the poet tells in the third person of an angel falling from an azure heaven into the muddy, leaden waters of the river Styx, the river of ancient Greek mythology that divides the living from the dead (and which in this respect, therefore, is itself a kind of limbo). This 'fall' is thus in the first instance a fall into mortality, while being at the same time reminiscent of the fall of Lucifer (the original 'grand abandonné') from light into darkness. This Lucifer, we may infer, is also the poet himself: 'Un Ange, imprudent voyageur | Qu'a tenté l'amour du difforme' (ll. 5-6).

At the end of *Les Fleurs du Mal* the newly added poem 'Le Voyage' will summarize a journey that begins in a paradise of childhood delight, but here the poet has fallen from the Platonic realm of the Idea:

> Une Idée, une Forme, un Être
> Parti de l'azur et tombé
> Dans un Styx bourbeux et plombé
> Où nul œil du Ciel ne pénètre[.]
>
> (ll. 1-4)

Within Platonic philosophy the 'Idea' is a form, the 'being' of which material existence presents a simulacrum and is therefore already at one remove from its source. Unlike those artists who espouse a traditional neo-Platonic conception of aesthetic perfection as deriving from some combination of 'le Vrai, le Bien et le Beau', this poet has been tempted by the new, which must necessarily be imperfect and 'difforme': not a 'rêve' but a 'cauchemar' (l. 7), not coherent shape but a crazy turbulence ('un gigantesque remous | Qui va chantant comme les fous' (ll. 10-11)), a place impenetrable by the shape-finding sightedness of Heaven. Where in 'La Destruction' the poet is tempted away from his art by the lure and allure of erotic beauty, here he is tempted by what appears to be the very opposite of beauty: darkness, chaos, monstrosity, the hell of our mortal contingency. Like the women of Lesbos he is condemned by the law of moral degradation to 'step down' into the damp, dark hole of the 'gouffre':

> Un damné descendant sans lampe,
> Au bord d'un gouffre dont l'odeur
> Trahit l'humide profondeur
> D'éternels escaliers sans rampe[.]
>
> (ll. 17-20)

And there he is trapped, like a ship in ice (ll. 25-6), in an inescapable gaol (l. 28): the prison-house of mortality and 'le Mal': 'une fortune irrémédiable' (l. 30). This Underworld is no blazing inferno but a cold, wet dungeon.

And yet this poet who has left perfection behind has discovered perfection in the new, in his own perfect rendering of the Devil's own perfection:

> Emblèmes nets, tableau parfait
> D'une fortune irrémédiable,
> Qui donne à penser que le Diable
> Fait toujours bien tout ce qu'il fait!
>
> (ll. 29–32)

Like the apostate apostle of 'Le Reniement de saint Pierre' this poet, too, has done well to renounce the accepted and the traditional—in this case the Platonic Idea—and indeed in doing so he has followed the advice he once gave to the women of Lesbos (in the 1857 edition): 'Laisse du vieux Platon se froncer l'œil austère' ('Lesbos', l. 21). The eye (and Idea) of Plato is 'austere' (from the ancient Greek 'auein' = to dry), a baleful, dessicating eye,[18] but now the new eye of the poet—and of the tear-filled eye of the reader in 'L'Héautontimorouménos'[19]—is able to transform the 'humide profondeur' of this damp, dark hole into a water-filled well of truth lit by Satan's torch, a new 'idéal' illuminated by spleen:

> Tête-à-tête sombre et limpide
> Qu'un cœur devenu son miroir!
> Puits de Vérité, clair et noir,
> Où tremble une étoile livide,
>
> Un phare ironique, infernal,
> Flambeau des grâces sataniques,
> Soulagement et gloire uniques,
> —La conscience dans le Mal!
>
> (ll. 33–40)

The poet, already Lucifer, is now here also Orpheus, an Orpheus who has journeyed into the Underworld of 'le Mal' and returned not with Eurydice—the beloved other sought by human passion—but, like the poet who travels to the island of Cythera, the truth about his own human reality. In 'Un voyage à Cythère', as we saw, the poet is also a 'self-executioner', a man who finds his own condemned corpse hanging from a gibbet. But it was he who created that 'emblème net', that 'tableau parfait | D'une fortune irrémédiable'. He is the perfect double agent.

---

[18] The quality of dryness has habitually been associated with melancholy. See Chapter 4.
[19] 'Pour abreuver mon Saharah' (l. 5). Cf. the other (but there implicit) reference to Moses smiting the rock in 'Bohémiens en voyage', ll. 11–12.

Here in 'L'Irrémédiable'—following on from 'Obsession' and the four intervening poems—the poet explicitly proclaims his new aesthetic of beauty in melancholy, and the poem is positioned as though it were a conclusion drawn from all the preceding poems in 'Spleen et idéal' (as 'emblèmes nets' and 'tableaux parfaits' of 'le Mal'). It contributes therefore to the frame that is completed with 'L'Horloge', as though the poet had found his true calling ('Soulagement et gloire uniques') and now is filled with a new resolve. Knowledge is not disabling but empowering. We know that Time will always win ('c'est la loi' (l. 18)), but we do *have* time. Yes, time is sucking our blood dry (l. 12) and each instant of time devours a piece of our allotted portion of 'délice' (ll. 7–8), but over and against the law of Time there is an alternative law, the law of alchemy, the law of creation: 'Les minutes, mortel folâtre, sont des gangues | Qu'il ne faut pas lâcher sans en extraire l'or!' (ll. 15–16). The poet of *Les Fleurs du Mal* who has set out to extract beauty from 'le Mal' is the poet who ends 'Spleen et idéal' not on a note of pessimism (as Pichois suggests, i. 990) but on a note of affirmation and determination, indeed of courage. 'Meurs, vieux lâche! il est trop tard!' (l. 24); death will come, one day, randomly ('le divin Hasard' (l. 21)), and it will be too late for virtue (our still virgin bride! (l. 22)) and for repentance too, that last refuge of the desperate ('oh! la dernière auberge!'). Too late because that is all there is: no further life—no afterlife—can follow that accidental moment. But it will be too late only if we have been cowards and lacked the courage to look 'le Mal' in the face and to live with it, within it—and *still* find value. 'Les minutes [...] sont des gangues': most of life is gangue ('the unwanted or valueless material of a mineral deposit, surrounding or mixed with the ore' (*OED*)), but we can do something with the nuggets. We can live those moments to the full, and we can make poems with them. And so, ironically, 'Spleen et idéal' ends with a call to virtue, to the theological virtue of fortitude.

This message of faith in the transformative power of art is what Baudelaire intended to stress with the final couplet of his second draft 'Épilogue' to this 1861 edition of *Les Fleurs du Mal* (ii. 191–2). Having praised Paris for its 'goût de l'infini, | Qui partout, dans le mal lui-même, se proclame' (ll. 6–7), he calls on its inhabitants to bear witness that he, too, has found the infinite within 'le Mal' and gold within the dirt:

> Ô vous! soyez témoins que j'ai fait mon devoir
> Comme un parfait chimiste et comme une âme sainte.
> Car j'ai de chaque chose extrait la quintessence,
> Tu m'as donné ta boue et j'en ai fait de l'or.
>
> (ll. 31–4)

As an epilogue, this poem would, like the alternative draft 'Épilogue [I]'— addressed to Satan (l. 6) and written in contemplation of a Paris '[o]ù toute énormité fleurit comme une fleur' (l. 5)—have figured directly after 'La Mort', and thus after 'Le Voyage' in particular, as a way of recalling the end of 'Spleen et idéal' and of reaffirming the 'alchemical' power of the poetic imagination. But instead Baudelaire chose to let the collection end with 'Le Voyage'. In many ways this poem restates the lesson of 'L'Horloge' while also providing an overview of the journey from birth to death that is sketched both in 'Spleen et idéal' and in *Les Fleurs du Mal* as a whole. In particular it comes after the other two poems added to 'La Mort' in 1861: 'La Fin de la journée' and 'Le Rêve d'un curieux'. In these the poet looks on death respectively as a blessed release or as his one last chance of experiencing something new and exciting. Following the disappointment of 'Le Rêve d'un curieux' ('La toile était levée et j'attendais encore'), 'Le Voyage' offers a commentary on this perennial human quest for the new and on how we undertake it even though we know it will fail.

'Le Voyage': The Tree of Desire

Désir, vieil arbre à qui le plaisir sert d'engrais

('Le Voyage', l. 70)

Divided into eight sections, 'Le Voyage' begins in the paradise that is the intoxication of children for whom everything is new and whose imaginative hunger is easily sated. They make no distinction between the world of reality and the world of dreams: the young child has but to gaze at a map or a print illustration and 'L'univers est égal à son vaste appétit' (l. 2). This, by implication, is the paradise we 'fallen' adults have lost as we embark on the journey of grown-up life, already implicated in the downward spiral of desire with its endless round of urge and disappointment:

> Un matin nous partons, le cerveau plein de flamme,
> Le cœur gros de rancune et de désirs amers,
> Et nous allons, suivant le rythme de la lame,
> Berçant notre infini sur le fini des mers[.]
>
> (ll. 5–8)

Even as we set out on our quest for the new, our hearts are festering with the rancour and resentment bred by earlier disillusion and with present desires that are already embittered by that knowledge of coming failure, of a finitude that will deny our thirst for the infinite and for the 'universal' satisfaction of the child. Some set out in order to escape—a place, a past, or, like Odysseus and his sailors fleeing Circe, the tyranny of some sexual subjection (ll. 9–16). But others set out with no particular purpose in view, unthinkingly, because it is in their nature to do so:

Mais les vrais voyageurs sont ceux-là seuls qui partent
Pour partir; cœurs légers, semblables aux ballons,
De leur fatalité jamais ils ne s'écartent,
Et, sans savoir pourquoi, disent toujours: Allons!'

(ll. 17-20)

These are the poet's own fellow-travellers, cloud-builders (recalling the poet of 'Alchimie de la douleur' and 'Horreur sympathique') who set out in hope and as yet innocently oblivious (like a naive young conscript) to the destruction that awaits:

Ceux-là dont les désirs ont la forme des nues,
Et qui rêvent, ainsi qu'un conscrit le canon,
De vastes voluptés, changeantes, inconnues,
Et dont l'esprit humain n'a jamais su le nom!

(ll. 21-4).

In the second section the poet describes how, whether we travel to escape or simply in order to travel, we are all subject to the same experience: moving on but turning in circles, searching, desiring, restlessly seeking rest, and driven by inexhaustible hope—not for paradise in the afterlife, as a Christian might hope, but simply for fulfilment in the present (ll. 25-32). But our soul is a like a three-masted ship hastening under full sail towards some ideal destination only to founder on the rock of illusion:

Chaque îlot signalé par les hommes de vigie
Est un Eldorado promis par le Destin;
L'Imagination qui dresse son orgie
Ne trouve qu'un récif aux clartés du matin.

(ll. 37-40).

Each of us is like a drunken sailor, 'inventeur d'Amériques' (l. 43), but espying only a mirage that merely serves to render the 'gouffre' of human existence all the more dire (ll. 41-4).[20] Imagining these metaphorical sailors now as real travellers, the poet calls on them in the third section to share the rich jewels of their experience 'pour égayer l'ennui de nos prisons' (l. 54). Where in 'Obsession' the poet's own eye had projected a myriad visions onto the black canvas of

---

[20] Or like an old tramp trudging through the mud, finding a Capuan paradise in the lowliest hovel (ll. 45-8). In French 'les délices de Capoue' denotes the lure of a delightful resting-place that will drain the traveller of the will for further effort. The reference is to Hannibal's campaign in Italy during which his decision to overwinter in Capua in Campania led to his defeat by the Romans.

the darkness, here the poet wants the sailors themselves to project their own memories 'sur nos esprits, tendus comme une toile' (l. 55). Speaking for us all, the poet wants to set sail—'sans vapeur et sans voile' (l. 53)—before the wind of an imagination stirred by these travellers' tales. But the sailors' reply (section IV) is not encouraging: they have seen all sorts, but they have also been bored, just as they are bored when they return home. The bathetic, caesura-deferring matter-of-factness of their response speaks volumes about the reality that awaits excited *Wanderlust*: 'Nous nous sommes souvent ennuyés, comme ici' (l. 60). Their own excitement has been mixed with anxiety ('une ardeur inquiète' (l. 63)) and the growing knowledge that reality will always fall short of their dreams:

> Les plus riches cités, les plus grands paysages,
> Jamais ne contenaient l'attrait mystérieux
> De ceux que le hasard fait avec les nuages.
> Et toujours le désir nous rendait soucieux!
>
> (ll. 65–8)

In fact they have learnt the lesson of Lesbos, and the sailors break off from replying to the poet to address desire itself and to demonstrate that they have learnt this lesson—namely, that they now know, having desired and travelled, that a desire satisfied simply fuels further desire and thus further anxiety, in an endless demonstration of the law of diminishing returns:

> —La jouissance ajoute au désir de la force.
> Désir, vieil arbre à qui le plaisir sert d'engrais,
> Cependant que grossit et durcit ton écorce,
> Tes branches veulent voir le soleil de plus près!
>
> (ll. 69–72)

But can this process go on for ever? 'Grandiras-tu toujours, grand arbre plus vivace | Que le cyprès?' (ll. 73–4). Human desire is like a perennial plant ('vivace'), but its perennial 'vivacity' begins to resemble that other, paradoxical 'vivacity' of the cypress tree, symbol of mourning in classical antiquity and symbol of death's eternity in the graveyard. As each desire dies, so does it enact the mortality in which all human journeys end. Indeed, this tree begins also to resemble a new Tree of Knowledge—not of Good and Evil, but of the nature of desire and the 'irremediable' condition to which mankind is subject.

'Pourtant' (l. 74)...And yet...Now addressing the poet once more, and all those for whom he speaks ('Frères qui trouvez beau tout ce qui vient de loin!' (l. 76)), the sailors report that they have brought back sketches from their travels 'pour votre album vorace' (l. 75), images of a fabled Indies that they have actually seen, of elephant idols and jewelled thrones and fairy palaces that would ruin even the most desirous of Western bankers (l. 80), and women with painted nails and teeth. Not to mention 'des jongleurs savants que le serpent caresse' (ll. 77–83)— those brothers-in-art of our own minstrel poet with his knowing accessions to Satan's caress.

But for our poet such news is not enough: 'Et puis, et puis encore?' (l. 83). Section V consists solely of this question, in itself the epitome of our insatiable desire for more. 'O cerveaux enfantins!' comes the sailors' mocking retort, as they bring us back from the Indies to the central lesson they have learnt and that we ourselves should learn:

> Pour ne pas oublier la chose capitale,
> Nous avons vu partout, et sans l'avoir cherché,
> Du haut jusques en bas de l'échelle fatale,
> Le spectacle ennuyeux de l'immortel péché[.]
>
> (ll. 85–8)

The world is boring and uninteresting because of this inescapable, 'irremediable' spectacle of 'immortal sin': not the Christian sin of which we can repent and in Heaven be redeemed and free, but our inherent human capacity to self-destruct through our inability to resist desire. Man and woman both are each and everywhere a slave to desire: woman ('esclave vile, orgueilleuse et stupide') is enslaved by the pursuit of her own beauty ('Sans rire s'adorant et s'aimant'), while man, for all his illusions of power ('tyran goulu, paillard, dur et cupide'), is enslaved by the slave that is woman ('[e]sclave de l'esclave') (ll. 89–92). In this brief but all-encompassing précis of the human condition, five of the seven deadly sins are on view: pride, gluttony, lust, wrath (in the cruelty of 'dur'), and greed. Only envy and sloth are missing, the latter appearing at once in the following stanza: 'Le poison du pouvoir énervant le despote' (l. 95). And the sailors continue with what they will describe at the end as being 'du globe entier l'éternel bulletin' (l. 108): the exultant executioner and the sobbing martyr, bloodfests and abject peoples who love the whip; (ll. 93–6); religions like Christianity all busily scaling the heavenly heights while the saints get their kicks out of horsehair shirts and a bed of nails (ll. 97–100); and humanity at large, full of big talk and believing it can do anything ('L'Humanité bavarde, ivre de son génie' (l. 101)),[21] then discovering that it cannot and furiously blaming God with all the crazy arrogance of its former hubris: 'O mon semblable, ô mon maître, je te maudis!' (l. 104). The least deluded members of the human race, the sailors conclude, are those who—perhaps like the poet

---

[21] Commentators have read this as a rejection of contemporary beliefs in 'Progress', and linked it to the (ironic) dedication of the poem to Maxime Du Camp, whose collection of poems *Chants modernes* (1855) had celebrated the growth of democracy and scientific discoveries as evidence of progress.

himself—flee the madding crowd ('le grand troupeau parqué par le Destin') and take refuge in 'l'opium immense!' (ll. 105–8).

In Section VII the poet now reflects on the sailors' 'bulletin': 'Amer savoir, celui qu'on tire du voyage!' (l. 109). Whether one travels or refuses to travel, there is no escaping the monotony and repetition of life: 'Une oasis d'horreur dans un désert d'ennui!' (l. 112), a monotony and repetition born of Time, 'l'ennemi vigilant et funeste' (l. 115). And yet we will never learn. Even when Time eventually leads us to the shores of 'la mer des Ténèbres' (l. 125), we will doubtless embark on that last journey '[a]vec le cœur joyeux d'un jeune passager' (l. 125), and our heads filled with all sorts of notions about lotus-eating and days that never end, about loyal friends and faithful wives welcoming us, like Pylades and Electra, with the outstretched arms of love (ll. 127–36). We cannot know for sure, but the implicit lesson must be that once again we will be sadly disappointed. Nevertheless, travel we must: and in the two stanzas that make up the eighth and final section of the poem, the poet calls on Captain Death to weigh anchor and bear us away into that glorious unknown:

> Ô Mort, vieux capitaine, il est temps! levons l'ancre!
> Ce pays nous ennuie, ô Mort! Appareillons!
> Si le ciel et la mer sont noirs comme de l'encre,
> Nos cœurs que tu connais sont remplis de rayons!
>
> Verse-nous ton poison pour qu'il nous réconforte!
> Nous voulons, tant ce feu nous brûle le cerveau,
> Plonger au fond du gouffre, Enfer ou Ciel, qu'importe?
> Au fond de l'Inconnu pour trouver du *nouveau!*
>
> (ll. 137–44)

But this is sheer bravado, bordering on the bitterest sarcasm—and far from the peace and joy with which true Christian penitents might leave 'le Mal' behind and go to meet their maker. The old loop of desire has begun again: we are simply bored and we want some excitement, so let's give death a go. Darkness is everywhere, but our young and joyful hearts are full of the rays of hope. Give us the poison that will bring release from the endless round that is life. Our minds are filled with feverish desire for the new,[22] and who cares *where* we go? Just somewhere different... our tired brains need a change of scene!

---

[22] As noted by Mario Richter and stressed by Steve Murphy, 'Le Voyage' ends (and with it *Les Fleurs du Mal*) by rhyming 'cerveau' and 'nouveau', just as in the 1857 edition the collection ended with 'La Mort des artistes' and the same rhyme in reverse order: 'nouveau', 'cerveau'. See Mario Richter, 'Réflexivité et représentation du poète dans *Les Fleurs du Mal*', in Steve Murphy (ed.), *Lectures de Baudelaire: 'Les Fleurs du Mal'* (Paris: Presses universitaires de Rennes, 2002), 71–88 (88 n. 21), and Murphy, 'Au lecteur. (Bribes de problématiques en guise d'introduction)', in Murphy (ed.), *Lectures des 'Fleurs du Mal'*, 9–32 (15–16).

As if! As if we'll find the new! For has not 'Le Rêve d'un curieux' already told us that death will be the greatest of non-events: 'La toile était levée et j'attendais encore.' Thus ends *Les Fleurs du Mal*: with death and with a bitterly ironic awareness of the perennial nature of human desire, at once doomed but indomitable, indomitable but deeply foolish. Life is over, and still we want the new... But one crucial positive emerges nevertheless from these two stanzas, and does so thanks to the new framework put in place by Baudelaire for the 1861 edition. 'Plonger au fond du gouffre, Enfer ou Ciel, qu'importe? | Au fond de l'Inconnu pour trouver du *nouveau!*': these words directly recall the last two quatrains of 'Hymne à la Beauté', also newly added, and so suggest that it is through art, and art alone, that we can find the new and set sail for the 'Inconnu': 'Que tu viennes du ciel ou de l'enfer, qu'importe, | Ô Beauté!'; 'De Satan ou de Dieu, qu'importe?'; 'un Infini que j'aime et n'ai jamais connu'. But whereas at the end of 'Le Voyage' the poet accepts the reality of '[l]e monde, monotone et petit' (l. 110) and gives himself up to Time and mortality, the poet of 'Hymne à la Beauté' has found in Beauty the means to render 'L'univers moins hideux et les instants moins lourds'. The law of Art trumps the law of Time, the law of Nature.

But how? Not just because, banally, the products of art outlive us mortals; certainly not because the artist can idealize the world, omitting the ugly and photoshopping the passably tolerable; but by resisting the passivity of entropy and decay with the human activity of creation. It is *because* Time destroys that Art can create and recreate—and recreate not merely what was but create new things from old. And so the italicized and exclamatory last word of *Les Fleurs du Mal*, brandished like a protest banner, asks us to look back at what we have read and to realize that we have indeed been made to look at 'le Mal' in a new light, by the light of the Imagination. Old binaries have been superseded: 'du ciel ou de l'enfer, qu'importe?', 'De Satan ou de Dieu, qu'importe?' The poet's role is no longer to provide an account of the world in terms of Christianity and its laws. What matters now is the poet's own account of a voyage beyond the known, beyond those 'regards familiers' of 'Correspondances' and those old stereotypes of the poet as divine lawgiver and reader of nature. And from that voyage he returns to you, his reader—his 'semblable'—with a careful record of what he has seen in a realm beyond the quotidian:

> Pourtant nous avons, avec soin,
> Cueilli quelques croquis pour votre album vorace,
> Frères qui trouvez beau tout ce qui vient de loin!

In this the poet-traveller resembles no one more than Constantin Guys, the sketch-artist of Paris celebrated in *Le Peintre de la vie moderne*, but before that the illustrator employed by the *Illustrated London News* to send back sketches of the Crimean War—and to reveal the reality that belies that naive conscript's fondest dreams.

10
Melancholy and the Poetic Act
Decomposition and Composition

> Et qui ne s'est nourri des choses du tombeau?
> ('Danse macabre', l. 42)
>
> Toute forme créée, même par l'homme, est immortelle. Car la forme est indépendante de la matière, et ce ne sont pas les molécules qui constituent la forme.
> (*Mon cœur mis à nu*)[1]
>
> [L'imagination] décompose toute la création, et [...] elle crée un monde nouveau, elle produit la sensation du neuf.
> (*Salon de 1859*, ii. 621)

In his article entitled 'L'Encre de la mélancolie'[2] Jean Starobinski examines the ways in which various poets have sought a palliative to melancholy in the writing of poetry. Arguing from a poem in Du Bellay's *Les Regrets* (1558) he contends that whereas melancholy is destructive rather than creative, it nevertheless establishes a lack that is of itself expressive. In Du Bellay's words: 'Je ne chante [...], je pleure mes ennuis, | Ou, pour dire mieux, en pleurant je les chante, | Si bien qu'en pleurant souvent je les enchante'. For Starobinski, melancholy creates a kind of non-space ('le défaut d'espace ou l'espace sans "orient"') from which the musical language of poetry opens up 'orientations', perspectives onto spaces of possibility:

> la parole mélodieuse devient à la fois la compensation symbolique et la traduction sensible, abolissant le sens des mots dans l'apparent non-sens de la 'phrase' musicale, organisant un espace propre qui, pour la conscience prisonnière, est la promesse d'une ouverture, et, pour la conscience errante, conquête rythmée d'un horizon demeuré jusqu'alors amorphe et irrespirable.[3]

---

[1] *Fusées*, ed. Guyaux, 118, and i. 705.
[2] Jean Starobinski, 'L'Encre de la mélancolie', *Nouvelle Revue française*, 21 (March 1963), 410–23; reprinted as '"Un éclat sans fin pour mon amour"', in *L'Encre de la mélancolie*, 611–23.
[3] '"Un éclat sans fin"', 619.

In the case of a poem by Charles d'Orléans (1394–1465),[4] he notes by way of contrast how such 'symbolic compensation' may take the form not of song but of ink. In this poem the black bile of melancholy is poetically figured as the darkness of an empty well from which the poet, in his thirst for comfort, seeks in vain to draw the clean water of hope. This black bile is then figured also as the ink with which he writes, only for 'Fortune' to come and tear up his page and cast the shreds of paper down into the selfsame empty well of melancholy. To write, it briefly seems, is to transform 'l'impossibilité de vivre en possibilité de dire', but even the act of writing is subject to the wanton destructiveness of melancholy. Nevertheless, as Starobinski notes: 'L'on remarquera sans doute que Charles d'Orléans réussit exquisement ce poème qui décrit l'échec de l'écriture.' Playfully he wonders if perhaps the poet used a different sort of ink or if in fact the ink of melancholy, by its very blackness, acquires the power to reflect the light and so becomes like the silvering of a mirror, enabling it to project an image... of light itself, the light of Lucifer! And he quotes Shakespeare—both in the original (from Sonnet 65): 'That in black ink my love may still shine bright', and in Yves Bonnefoy's translation: 'L'encre, noire, un éclat sans fin pour mon amour'—to suggest, explicitly, that Shakespeare is evoking the miraculous possibility of saving the memory of a love from the ravages of time through the act of writing, and, implicitly, that the beauty of Charles d'Orléans's poem belies the melancholic failure of which it speaks.[5]

Can poetry offer a palliative to melancholy? And if so, how? By the simple acts of awareness and acceptance, 'la conscience dans le Mal'? By serving as a written record in defiance of time? By presenting a beauty of shape and form where to the melancholic mind all seems shapeless and confused? For Baudelaire, no doubt all of these. But for him it is above all the creative act that constitutes the most effective riposte to 'l'appareil sanglant de la Destruction', and the creative act not just—even though these are essential—as effort or hard work.[6] For Baudelaire what counts above all is the transformative power of the creative act, the freedom of the imagination—the reader's as well as the poet's—to *compose* or *recompose* new worlds from the debris of our melancholic plight. Hence his comment in *Mon*

---

[4] 'Ou puis parfont de ma merencolie | L'eaue d'Espoir que ne cesse tirer, | Soif de Confort la me fait désirer, | Quoy que souvent je la treuve tarie. [-] Necte la voy ung temps esclercie, | Et puis après troubler et empirer, | Ou puis parfont de ma merencolie | L'eaue d'Espoir que ne cesse tirer. [-] D'elle trempe mon ancre d'estudie, | Quant j'en escrips, mais pour mon cuer irer, | Fortune vient mon pappier dessirer, | Et tout gecte par sa grant felonie | Ou puis parfont de ma merencolie.'
[5] '"Un éclat sans fin"', 622–3.
[6] *Pace* John E. Jackson: 'la poésie des *Fleurs du Mal* semble toujours garder, malgré tout, la ressource d'un élan irrépressible par lequel, s'emparant d'un vis-à-vis, Baudelaire se lie à lui, pour le meilleur comme pour le pire et consacre dans cette proximité difficile le triomphe d'une vraie sacralité du travail poétique.' See *Baudelaire et la sacralité de la poésie* (Geneva: Droz, 2018), 131. Cf. p. 9: 'c'est la réussite de l'œuvre qui assure la rédemption du poète', and p. 65: 'le sujet [of "Le Mauvais Moine"] s'exhorte [...] à faire de son état spleenétique le point de départ du *travail poétique* qui seul lui permettra d'accéder à son "salut" de créateur.'

cœur mis à nu: 'Toute forme créée, même par l'homme, est immortelle. Car la forme est indépendante de la matière, et ce ne sont pas les molécules qui constituent la forme.'[7] Often in accounts of *Les Fleurs du Mal* critics have seen 'spleen' and 'idéal' as opposites, with the experience of 'spleen' being viewed as a failure to capture the 'idéal' (defined as that which we most ardently desire or aspire to). But in Baudelaire's lexicon the term 'idéal' refers to the creativity of the human mind and its capacity to reconfigure the real, to make new 'forms', to fashion a new poetic 'Idée'.

In this connection it is important to recall Baudelaire's stated aim as being, within *Les Fleurs du Mal*, to 'extraire la *beauté* du Mal'. Beauty lies *within* 'le Mal' and is not something separate or overlaid upon it. Hence also his assertion that melancholy is 'toujours inséparable du sentiment du beau' (ii. 238). And this, too, is why, for example, 'Obsession' is not a 'spleen' version of the 'idéal' 'Correspondances' but the reverse mirror-image of a complex symbiosis. For Baudelaire 'spleen' and 'idéal' each constitutes a frame of mind: respectively, an effect of melancholy and negativity, a state of ill-being ('le Mal'), and an effect of heightened perception and positivity, a state of beauty ('les fleurs'). Melancholy is an awareness of time and loss within life, while beauty is an awareness of the possibility of renewal within the context of our mortality. Art is not the opposite of life but of death. For Baudelaire the effect of beauty successfully counterbalances the effect of melancholy by virtue of the alternative lawgiving of a liberating imagination, a lawgiving that proposes new shapes and patterns into which to fit the contingencies of 'le Mal' and that, in addition, invites readers—as we shall see in Part III—to adopt and enlarge on a poetics of 'conjecture' and to seek shapes and patterns of their own.

The first simile in *Les Fleurs du Mal* is instructive in this regard: 'Et nous alimentons nos aimables remords, | Comme les mendiants nourrissent leur vermine' ('Au lecteur', ll. 3–4). As reflexive human beings we allow remorse and regret to feed on us by dwelling on them repeatedly in our minds, as though savouring 'le Mal' and, with apparent perverseness, taking pleasure in our fallen state even as it eats away at us: 'La sottise, l'erreur, le péché, la lésine, | Occupent nos esprits et travaillent nos corps' (ll. 1–2). Like flea-ridden beggars we are destitute hosts to the vermin of a parasitic melancholy. In our minds 'un peuple de Démons' conducts an orgy ('ribote'), like stomach worms writhing in our gut ('fourmillant, comme un million d'helminthes' (ll. 21–2)). And yet, paradoxically, in reflecting upon loss and death and what might have been and what we might or should have done, we keep the past alive and perhaps imagine, fondly, a better, different, alternative future (cf. 'nos aimables remords')—rather as the corpse in 'Une charogne' provides food for maggots and the continuance of life.

---

[7] This comment was written no earlier than 1859. See i. 1491.

In that poem we are shown how—on a fine summer's morning—melancholy gives rise to creative art in the same manner as death brings life.[8] First, the animal corpse, lying thoroughly dead on an inorganic deathbed of dry minerality ('un lit semé de cailloux' (l. 4)), emits its insubstantial organic deathliness ('suant les poisons', '[s]on ventre plein d'exhalaisons'); then, like meat being cooked by the sun, it renders matter unto matter and reassumes its molecular multiplicity and fluidity: 'Le soleil rayonnait sur cette pourriture, | Comme afin de la cuire à point, | Et de rendre au centuple à la grande Nature | Tout ce qu'ensemble elle avait joint' (ll. 9–12). What was dead and coldly composite now blossoms like a flower in the sunshine of new possibilities: 'Et le ciel regardait la carcasse superbe | Comme une fleur s'épanouir' (ll. 13–14). What is rotting feeds the hungry: flies buzz eagerly above black battalions of maggots oozing from the '*vivants* haillons' of flesh (ll. 17–20; my emphasis), and a dog waits, anxiously, angrily, to resume its meal of carrion (ll. 33–6). What was once frozen in *rigor mortis* ('les jambes en l'air, comme une femme lubrique' (l. 5)) has become warm and liquid, rising and falling, squirting and bubbling (ll. 21–2): no longer just an 'objet' (l. 1) but a living and breathing organism: 'On eût dit que le corps, enflé d'un souffle vague, | Vivait en se multipliant' (ll. 23–4).

As the second half of the poem begins, what once was silent emits 'une étrange musique' (l. 25), like the sound of wind or running water (l. 26) or like the sound of a winnower's basket as it separate chaff from the grain (ll. 27–8)—as though there has already been a harvest and one day soon there will be another. A metamorphosis is under way as nature shifts its shapes: 'Les formes s'effaçaient et n'étaient plus qu'un rêve, | Une ébauche lente à venir, | Sur la toile oubliée, et que l'artiste achève | Seulement par le souvenir' (ll. 29–32). Time, too, is on the turn: the erstwhile identifying features of the corpse are as the remnants of some forgotten dream, or like the outline of a painting once begun and since neglected, but still full of possibility and ready to be taken up once more if the artist can but supplement the absent subject with the memory of how it once had looked. With this painterly analogy—and following the transformation of mere noise into 'strange music'—the parallel between the processes of the natural cycle and the procedures of artistic creativity becomes overt, and culminates in the closing stanza: 'Alors, ô ma beauté! dites à la vermine | Qui vous mangera de baisers, | Que j'ai gardé la forme et l'essence divine | De mes amours décomposés!' (ll. 45–8). The poet's 'beloved', his companion and mistress, his flesh-and-blood

---

[8] Cf. Jean-Pierre Richard, 'Profondeur de Baudelaire', in *Poésie et profondeur* (Paris: Éditions du Seuil, 1955), 91–162 (134): 'Rien de plus fécond qu'un beau cadavre, telle est la leçon, mal comprise, de "La Charogne" (*sic*).' (Noted by Jackson, *La Mort Baudelaire*, 66–7). See also Yves Charnet, '"L'Orage rajeunit les fleurs": Lettre à Claude Pichois', in Guyaux and Marchal (eds), *'Les Fleurs du Mal': Actes du colloque de la Sorbonne des 10 et 11 janvier 2003*, 41–52, where Charnet writes (in relation to 'Une charogne' and a number of other poems) of '[l]énergie ruineuse', '[l]a vitalité mortifère', '[l]a vitalité résurrectionniste' (49), 'cette ruineuse vitalité', and 'cette poétique de la destruction créatrice' (50), and depicts Baudelaire as '[c]hoisissant de faire de la création avec de la destruction' (52).

beauty, will die soon enough, and her body will rot beneath the grass and 'les floraisons grasses' that draw their nutrients from it—just as the poet's imagination will draw sustenance from the memory of this and other women he has known and his verse will feed off them like worms. The 'decomposition' wrought by loss, decay, and death will be countered by the 'composition' that is a poem: the destruction of 'les vers' becomes the construction of 'le vers'.[9]

'Vermine' derives etymologically from Latin 'vermina= les vers',[10] and the wordplay on 'ver(s)' has long been a favourite of poets. In *Les Fleurs du Mal* there is frequent mention of worms and vermin as perverse emblems of vitality within 'le Mal' of our mortal condition. We find the enslaved lover, bound to his bloodsucking mistress '[c]omme aux vermines la charogne' ('Le Vampire', l. 11), or, in a reversal of roles, the predatory lover pursuing his 'belle' '[c]omme après un cadavre un chœur de vermisseaux' ('Je t'adore à l'égal...', l. 8). In the city of 'Le Crépuscule du soir' Prostitution scavenges in the dirt '[c]omme un vers qui dérobe à l'Homme ce qu'il mange' (l. 20): desire is a deadly consumption. In 'Spleen, ii' ('J'ai plus de souvenirs que si j'avais mille ans...') we find the recurrent motif of our living bodies being eaten away by melancholy and remorse as though we were already dead: 'Je suis un cimetière abhorré de la lune, | Où comme des remords se traînent de longs vers | Qui s'acharnent toujours sur mes morts les plus chers' (ll. 8-10). Where once perhaps the poet's remorse fed on him like worms or like the fleas on a beggar, now he is a cemetery in which real worms feed, like remorse, on the bodies of those that are dearest to him. Moreover, within the context of an insistent repetition of 'morts'—ll. 6-7 describe the poet's brain as 'une pyramide, un immense caveau, | Qui contient plus de morts que la fosse commune'—the word 'remords' makes remorse itself seem like a series of repeated deaths,[11] as though this melancholic man who feels older than a thousand years had also died a thousand deaths. In 'Le Mort joyeux', by contrast, the poet bids the worms have *no* remorse as, joyously, he imagines laying himself unceremoniously down to eternal rest beneath the grass: 'À travers ma ruine allez donc sans remords' (l. 12): 'Ô vers! noirs compagnons sans oreille et sans yeux, | Voyez venir à vous un mort libre et joyeux; | Philosophes viveurs, fils de la pourriture' (ll. 9-11). Like the maggots of 'Une charogne' these worms are the living 'philosophical' symbols of a

---

[9] Cf. Victor Brombert, '"Le Cygne" de Baudelaire: douleur, souvenir, travail', in *Études baudelairiennes*, 3 (1973), 254-61: 'C'est que, dans la conscience baudelairienne, création et désintégration sont inévitablement accouplées. L'effort artistique est nécessairement recréation (sinon anti-création): il dépend du principe de désintégration, et ne peut opérer que dans la mesure où les formes s'effacent' (261).

[10] See *Dictionnaire historique de la langue française*: 'Vermine s'est dit de toutes sortes de petites bêtes nuisibles (serpents, souris, etc.), acception encore relevée au début du XVIIe siècle.—Il désigne surtout (1172-4) l'ensemble des insectes parasites de l'homme et des animaux (puces, poux, etc.) [...] Par figure, *vermine* a le sens de "personne méprisable (fin XIVe s.) et s'emploie comme terme collectif (1576) pour l'ensemble des individus considérés comme nuisibles à la société.—L'emploi métaphorique en argot pour "avocat" (1837) est sorti d'usage, mais des emplois insultants sont encore possibles.'

[11] See Jackson, *La Mort Baudelaire*, 112-13.

life emerging from death, the filial issue of rot and decomposition—like the lines of verse themselves, inky black companions without eyes or ears: the print on the page, born of melancholy and set to accompany the poet into eternity.

This idea of life arising organically out of death in a form of secular resurrection appears early in Baudelaire's work and is present in a number of poems already discussed. It is central in 'L'Âme du vin', dating from 1843/4: wine is the product of harvest and hard work, and from the prison of its bottle the liquid would prefer to be released so that, in being consumed and 'dying' within the chest of the exhausted vineyard-worker, it will itself paradoxically live and bring life: restoring health to the poet-worker's son, stimulating sexual desire in his wife (perhaps leading to the creation of a new life), and inspiring the poet-worker himself so that from *their* union—the poet's love for wine—a new poem may be 'born' and spring up 'comme une rare fleur!' This image in turn recurs in 'La Mort des artistes', which closes the 1857 Les Fleurs du Mal and itself ends with the last, desperate hope of the artists doomed never to complete their imagined masterpiece for as long as they live: 'C'est que la Mort, planant comme un soleil nouveau, | Fera s'épanouir les fleurs de leur cerveau!' (ll. 13–14). This may simply imply a hope for posthumous recognition, but it may also suggest that only by accepting our mortal condition can the artist succeed and come to see the imagined artwork finally blossom under the 'soleil noir' of melancholy.[12] Only by accepting 'le Mal' can the artist's endeavour flower and achieve a form of temporary immortality: like the fruit that becomes wine to be drunk, or like the flower itself that becomes a scent on the breeze ('Parfum exotique') or is distilled into a perfume to be released from a bottle of its own ('Le Flacon'). The grape and the flower, picked and pressed, offer, like a moment of reality seized by the imagination and distilled into words, the means to a temporary immortality, a 'quintessence'.[13]

'Vermine' is thus part of a broader thematic preoccupation with decomposition as that which enables life, of the disjunct and fragmented as evidence of a necessary dismantling before the 'work' of art can begin. Reality itself has to decompose—whether literally through death, or metaphorically through the passage of time and the effect of forgetting, or indeed of that process of 'degradation' that Baudelaire identifies as a law of our moral life. In Le Peintre de la vie moderne we learn that Constantin Guys does not sketch from life but rather from memory, so that the precise detail of what he observes may fall away to reveal the essential shapes and patterns that underlie what he has seen. A similar process occurs in dream, as Baudelaire notes in a letter of March 1860: 'le rêve, qui sépare et décompose, crée la *nouveauté*' (Corr., ii. 15). Only through the 'death' of the real, of our habitual perceptions, of the 'regards familiers', can the new be revealed by the artist in a form of alternative lawgiving. For the melancholic the world is a

---

[12] See Jackson, La Mort Baudelaire, 24–5.
[13] Cf. 'Épilogue [II]', l. 33: 'Car j'ai de chaque chose extrait la quintessence' (i. 192).

place of contingency and clutter[14] while for the artist it is a place of 'harmony' and 'eurhythmic' necessity, a place of beauty. If we define lawgiving as the act of assembling the contingent within a pattern (as a scientist seeks to identify a law of nature) or of promoting (and sometimes prescribing) a given pattern as an instrument of intellectual or moral or indeed aesthetic guidance (or necessity), then we can see Baudelaire as an 'alternative' lawgiver in that precisely he seeks to disassemble the familiar in order to propose a different set of patterns wherein we may situate the mess—or 'le Mal'—of our human condition. For Delacroix nature is just a dictionary (ii. 624–5), an atomized reality from which the artist assembles his composition as though he were translating the language of dream (ii. 625). So, too, for this poet of melancholy.

In the case of Baudelaire's poetry nowhere is this process of decomposition and composition more evident than in the four poems themselves entitled 'Spleen'. The earliest of these, 'Pluviôse, irrité contre la ville entière...', was first published in 1851, while the remaining three appeared first in the 1857 *Les Fleurs du Mal*. More than any others in the collection each of these poems conveys the poet's feelings of melancholy in the form of a dream or nightmare vision,[15] a 'reassembly' of reality not as narrative or realistic description but as a collection of images— of 'tableaux'—which figure the world as an illustration of the melancholic's disparate perspective: mortality, graves, tombs, dungeons, skeletons, blackness, darkness, lack of sunlight, lack of moonlight, coldness, pallor, ghostliness, opacity (fog, mist, smoke), fire without heat, desert without heat, sunset, hunger, disease, restlessness, irritation, lament, dirt, malodorousness, elderliness, oppressiveness, heaviness, clutter, emptiness, vast space, unmapped space, worms, withered flowers, datedness, stone, colourlessness, oblivion, heedlessness, worthless

---

[14] Starobinski notes that the iconography of melancholy traditionally depicts the melancholic as surrounded by 'objets épars' and comments that '[l]a pire des mélancolies, c'est alors de ne pouvoir passer outre, de rester captif du bric-à-brac'. In 'Le Cygne', he argues, the poet assembles a 'tableau parisien' out of such clutter: 'le tableau aura recomposé ce qui s'offrait et continue de s'offrir sous l'aspect de la décomposition' (*La Mélancolie au miroir*, 65, 66).

[15] Robert Kopp has suggested that in the fourth 'Spleen' poem Baudelaire derived his imagery from Alexandre Brière [or Brierre] de Boismont's clinical records of cases of pathological melancholy ('voire la dépression') in his study on suicide, *Du suicide et de la folie suicide* (Paris: Germer Baillière, 1856). See Kopp, 'Le Spleen baudelairien', 185. In *Du suicide* Brière de Boismont takes a resolutely reactionary, counter-Enlightenment approach to his topic, blaming recent high suicide rates on human pride and egotism and a growing rejection of God and Christianity. For him melancholy/depression results from a new cult of the self and represents the major problem of the age: 'Enfin, les temps modernes, en propageant le doute, en exaltant l'orgueil, en faisant de l'amour de soi, du scepticisme et de l'indifférence, une sorte de code à l'usage du grand nombre, ont donné une nouvelle impulsion au suicide' (p. 45). He estimates that there have been some 40,000 suicides in France between 1830 and 1846, and some 110,000 since the beginning of the century, arguing that if one were to take into account all the deaths that looked like accidents but weren't, the true figure is nearer three times as high (p. 44). Baudelaire refers to this work in *Fusées* (ed. Guyaux, 61; ii. 656), raising the possibility that in the fourth 'Spleen' poem and perhaps in other poems also the poet as double agent and performer was actively simulating the imagination of the mentally ill and giving expression to what later came to be known as the Unconscious.

power, empty prestige, rain, impotence, sadness, incuriosity, boredom, cruelty, exhaustion, corruption, rot, bloodlessness, dementia, timidity, disorientation, silence, spiders, homelessness, defeat, tears, subjection...an inventory of 'le Mal' and a dictionary of depression, but all composed into poems and stanzas and couplets and even into the fixed form of a sonnet, and harmonized with metre and rhythm and rhyme and caesuras and alliterations and assonance.

Insofar as these images or ideas are ever linked, the connection is usually ironic or bathetic. The first image of all—'Pluviôse, irrité'—sets the tone: not the wrath of the gods but the irritation of this pseudo-deity, Pluviosus, reminiscent of one month of the Revolutionary Calendar but here a petulant tyrant, tipping coldness and darkness over cemetery and suburb alike. 'À grands flots' suggests water, but his urn, funereal by implication, contains—like Du Bellay's well of melancholy—only emptiness and mortality. (Cf. also 'Spleen', iv. 4: 'Il nous verse un jour noir plus triste que les nuits'.) A similar effect of bathos is repeated in the first line of 'Je suis comme le roi d'un pays pluvieux...': I, the melancholic, am master of all I survey, but it is not a pretty picture. The world of the 'Spleen' poems is a world out of joint, of disconnect and misconnect: the dead 'inhabit' the graveyard (i. 3), and a ghost feels the cold (i. 8); the Sahara is misty (ii. 21), and the sky is a lid (iv. 1). Vitality appears only in the form of a skewed personification that animates the inanimate—a log singing, a clock with a cold, playing cards that chat (i); days that limp (ii)—or in the grotesque caricatures of allegory: Pluviôse and his pouring, Hope as a bat bumping its head on the rafters (iv. 8).

The melancholy world of the 'Spleen' poems is not only a world out of joint but also a place of absence, loss, failure, and impossibility. In 'Spleen i' humanity is present only as remnant: the graveyard corpses, the wandering soul of an old poet, the belongings of an elderly, dropsical woman. In 'Spleen ii' the past is also gone but now leaves an immense burden of memory—like a chest of drawers filled to overflowing with written records of that past, or an old boudoir bearing witness to a prettiness long gone and a present boredom of such oppressive weight that 'living matter' (ii. 19) has been reduced to a block of solid, stationary, forgotten granite. In 'Spleen iii' failure and impossibility are the keynotes: the impotence of the poet and the inability of others to quicken his interest. In 'Spleen iv', the oppressive weight of boredom is felt particularly as a prison: the prison of a physical reality that constrains and immobilizes, and a prison of the mind and soul in which the only movement is the funeral procession of melancholic thought. And the world of the 'Spleen' poems, out of joint, is also out of tune, a world without the very music of poetry that here paradoxically gives expression to it. A poet's soul keens with the sad voice of a shivering wraith (i. 8), while a damp log sings falsetto to accompany a wheezing clock (iv. 9–10); poems and songs are not heard but bundled away in a drawer (ii. 3); living matter is now but the rock of an old sphinx grumpily 'singing' in the dying rays of the sun (ii. 22–4); the grotesque ballad of a clown falls flat (iii. 7); church bells jump about in fury, howling towards heaven (iv. 13–14); funeral cortèges are silent, 'sans tambours ni musique' (iv. 17).

But as all these examples suggest, the world of the 'Spleen' poems—in anticipation of Surrealist collage—is a world rich in imagery and replete with an allusiveness that takes us here, there, and everywhere: a clock, a fireplace, a chest of drawers, a sitting-room, a boudoir, a house, a church, a city, a country, a desert, the far horizon; the 1789 Revolution, eighteenth-century pastels, a royal court, classical Rome, ancient Egypt. As for the child at the beginning of 'Le Voyage', so too for the poet's imagination: 'L'univers est égal à son vaste appétit.' Walter Benjamin wrote in *The Origin of German Tragic Drama* that 'the only pleasure the melancolic permits himself, and it is a powerful one, is allegory'.[16] But for Benjamin allegory—by which he means simile, metaphor, and the transformations of the poetic imagination—represents an exile from the 'real' world, the 'alienation' of the human being within a capitalist economy of commodity and fetish, an emblem of permanent destruction: 'Baudelaire's allegory bears traces of the violence that was necessary to demolish the harmonious façade of the world that surrounded him': 'That which the allegorical imagination has fixed upon is sundered from the customary contexts of life: it is at once shattered and preserved. Allegory holds fast to the ruins. Baudelaire's destructive impulse is nowhere concerned with the abolition of what falls to it.'[17] But I would argue that for Baudelaire the function of the poetic act is to 'compose' or 'recompose' that which has been 'decomposed' by time and the law of moral degradation: to offer new laws, under the 'government of the imagination', whereby his readers may perceive and interpret the world of human experience afresh.

Can we see this '(re)composition' as a form of secular redemption? Joseph Acquisto has recently argued not. Critics have frequently acknowledged the ways in which Baudelaire's language and thought is imbued with the arguments and terminology of Catholic doctrine but without sharing the faith on which it is based.[18] But Acquisto goes further by insisting on Baudelaire's rejection of the very notion of redemption, whether Christian or secular, and even through art: '[t]he narrative of esthetic redemption has to be refused just as systematically as its political or religious equivalents in order to draw all of the consequences of the move beyond redemption'.[19] Clearly there is absolutely no evidence that

---

[16] Benjamin, *The Origin of German Tragic Drama*, trans. Osborne, 185.

[17] Benjamin, *The Arcades Project*, 329 (J55a, 3; J56, 1). To the second of these noted comments Benjamin adds a reference to J55, 6: 'On the Christian determination of allegory: it has no place in the cycle "Révolte".'

[18] See, for example, Jackson, *La Mort Baudelaire*, 61: 'Non seulement l'auteur des *Fleurs du Mal* est nourri de toutes les formes de la liturgie et du credo catholiques—comme en témoignent tant de poèmes, à commencer par le premier du recueil—mais il a aussi très largement intériorisé la substance théologique de cette tradition dont il reste héritier. L'*ambiguïté* théologique du poème baudelairien naît justement de cet emploi d'un lexique religieux dans un texte qui n'en réassume pas nécessairement les présupposés.'

[19] *The Fall Out of Redemption*, 6.

Baudelaire ever believed in the orthodox Christian prospect of an eternal salvation of our souls, as promised by Christ and to be achieved by the repentance of our sins. If by 'redemption' one means some secure and lasting existential state of deliverance from 'le mal de vivre', then equally clearly Baudelaire offers no such thing—and certainly not through art. But if by 'redemption' one means, as its etymology indicates, a 'buying back'—as a sinner 'buys back' his soul through repentance—then perhaps Baudelaire's poetic act of composition from the decomposed may be seen as the 'buying back' of life from death,[20] and this through the agency of the imagination.

Poetry for Baudelaire, in both verse and prose, is not a means of 'holding fast to the ruins', as Benjamin argues, even if the ruins are everywhere visible, but rather a form of salvation through salvage and reassembly: as it were, 'quelques croquis pour votre vorace album', the sketches brought back by the sailors in 'Le Voyage' from the endlessly disappointing journeys of life. This is not to say, with Vigny, that poetry resembles the newly drawn map of uncharted waters, a treasure of accumulated wisdom to be carefully sealed in a bottle and cast adrift upon the random currents of time and found one day by some lucky mariner-reader. Rather, for Baudelaire, the flotsam and jetsam of human experience are there to be collected and refashioned by the imagination into objects of 'beauty' such that they become the stimuli of future imaginative conjecture and of further salvage and reassembly.

For this reason we might legitimately see Baudelaire's beauty as a form of 'la rédemption par le travail' (i. 441) that he foregrounds at the end of 'Le Poème du hachisch' in Les Paradis artificiels (1860), itself his only finished work. I will examine this text in greater detail in the Conclusion, but for the moment we can note how the *work* of art—in the sense that artists work, shape, fashion their material—is presented as an alternative to the disappointments and inadequacies of drug-use as a means of satisfying 'le goût de l'infini' (the title of the first section of 'Le Poème du hachisch') by which we are all driven and which, for Baudelaire, is synonymous with the search for beauty. Thus he ends 'Le Poème du hachisch' (in which drug-use produces, therefore, the wrong sort of 'poème') by recalling his inaugural description (in its opening paragraphs) of the kind of epiphanic, 'paradisiacal' moment in which '[l] homme gratifié de cette béatitude, malheureusement rare et passagère, se sent à la fois plus artiste et plus juste' (i. 401) and by recapping briefly on the frantic quest for 'toutes les substances, même dangereuses' (i. 441) by means of which human beings hope to relive such moments. But, Baudelaire contends, 'l'homme n'est pas si abandonné, si privé de moyens

---

[20] Cf. Mallarmé's choice of vocabulary in his letter to Maurice Barrès of 10 Sept. 1885: 'Tout est vain en dehors de ce *rachat* par l'Art, et l'on reste un filou. L'Art implique cela et un théâtre éternel, où passeront des générations' (my emphasis). See Stéphane Mallarmé, *Correspondance 1854–1898*, ed. Bertrand Marchal (Paris: Gallimard, 2019), 567.

honnêtes pour gagner le ciel, qu'il soit obligé d'invoquer la pharmacie et la sorcellerie'. He then proceeds to paint the allegorical scene of a man ('dirai-je un brahmane, un poète, ou un philosophe chrétien?') who has made it to the top of 'l'Olympe ardu de la spiritualité', a summit that recalls both Raphaël's fresco (in the Stanza della Signatura in the Vatican) of Apollo playing his modern lyre on the summit of Mount Parnassus and also Mantegna's oil painting (in the Louvre) of Mars and Venus also on Mount Parnassus, where the Muses dance as Apollo plays his classical lyre and a drunken Vulcan fulminates with jealousy:

> autour de lui, les Muses de Raphaël ou de Mantegna, pour le consoler de ses longs jeûnes et de ses prières assidues, combinent les danses les plus nobles, le regardent avec leurs plus doux yeux et leurs sourires les plus éclatants; le divin Apollon, ce maître en tout savoir [...] caresse de son archet les cordes les plus vibrantes.

At the bottom of the mountain in Baudelaire's own imaginary painting, as though in Hell ('dans les ronces et dans la boue'), are the tortured victims of drug addiction: 'la troupe des humains, la bande des ilotes, simule les grimaces de la jouissance et pousse des hurlements que lui arrache la morsure du poison'. Meanwhile, from his Olympian and Parnassian vantage-point, the man—now explicitly 'le poète attristé'—looks down and reflects on the meaning of the scene before him:

> Ces infortunés qui n'ont ni jeûné, ni prié, et qui ont refusé la rédemption par le travail, demandent à la noire magie les moyens de s'élever, d'un seul coup, à l'existence surnaturelle. La magie les dupe et elle allume pour eux un faux bonheur et une fausse lumière; tandis que nous, poètes et philosophes, nous avons régénéré notre âme par le travail successif et la contemplation; par l'exercice assidu de la volonté et la noblesse permanente de l'intention, nous avons créé à notre usage un jardin de vraie beauté. Confiants dans la parole qui dit que la foi transporte les montagnes, nous avons accompli le seul miracle dont Dieu nous ait octroyé la licence!

Here is Baudelaire's secular version of redemption from the 'sin' of pursuing beauty other than through the medium of art. 'Surnaturalisme' is not to be achieved by magic means but by hard work, here ironically likened to the abstinence and self-mortification of a Christian penitent. As though answering the magistrates who themselves saw in *Les Fleurs du Mal* only 'les grimaces de la jouissance', the poet insists on the artist's strength of will and nobility of purpose in creating 'un jardin de vraie beauté'—a paradise on earth 'à notre usage'—in which beauty is bestowed by the flowers of ill-being. If faith can move mountains, then here the faith in question is a faith in art and the mountain is Parnassus, home to the nine muses. Art is the miracle, the miracle of human creativity, for which God himself has granted the licence of authority that mere magistrates have recently taken it upon themselves to withdraw from this alternative lawgiver.

As we will now see, the Baudelaire who transformed the first edition of *Les Fleurs du Mal* into the second edition between 1857 and 1861—and radically altered its 'architecture'—was a Baudelaire stung by legal condemnation into a new and far-reaching conception of the imagination as a political instrument capable of the most powerful and subversive effects. Already I have discussed how Baudelaire's account of melancholy offers a radical alternative to the Christian doctrine of evil. Now, in Part III, I will examine how he came to envisage imagination itself as an alternative way of thinking and as a riposte to censorship and the laws laid down by the state. In Part IV I will complete my account of *Les Fleurs du Mal* before turning in Part V to the alternative lawgiving of *Le Spleen de Paris*. But for the moment we can reflect on the uplifting figure of Baudelaire as a good monk. Where the eponymous voice of 'Le Mauvais Moine' reflects sadly in the final tercet:

> Ô moine fainéant! quand saurai-je donc faire
> Du spectacle vivant de ma triste misère
> Le travail de mes mains et l'amour de mes yeux?

the author of 'Le Poème du hachisch' can consider himself not sinfully lazy but redeemed by work, not degenerate but regenerate ('nous avons regénéré notre âme'), not someone 'qui fait néant' but a poet who, with the noblest of intentions, has created something from nothing, found poetry in melancholy, and extracted beauty from 'le Mal': 'nous avons créé à notre usage un jardin de vraie beauté'.

PART III
IMAGINATION

Il y a bien longtemps que je dis que le poète est *souverainement* intelligent, qu'il est *l'intelligence* par excellence,—et que *l'imagination* est la plus *scientifique* des facultés, parce que seule elle comprend *l'analogie universelle*, ou ce qu'une religion mystique appelle la *correspondance*.
    (Letter to Alphonse Toussenel, 21 January 1856 (*Corr.*, i. 336))

la plus honorable et la plus utile des facultés morales
(Salon de 1859, ii. 622)

cette faculté *cardinale*
(Salon de 1859, ii. 623)

11
Imagination and Resistance
The Case of Poe

Il fut donc une admirable protestation[.]
('Notes nouvelles sur Edgar Poe', ii. 321)

In Part II I examined Baudelaire's conception of the human experience of melancholy and the gradual evolution in his literary treatment of this experience in the poems that eventually became *Les Fleurs du Mal*. Where at first, in the poems about Lesbos and lesbianism, he set out to depict the melancholy that derives from the downward spiral of desire and its ever-diminishing returns, his focus then shifted, in *Les Limbes*, to a portrayal of melancholy as an anguished perception of indifferentiation in which life is perceived as a living death. Subsequently, in the 1855 'Les Fleurs du Mal', he began to introduce the possibility of an 'anti-melancholy', of a form of beauty that can be 'extracted' from the irreparable sense of ill-being, or 'le Mal', which he held to be synonymous with our human condition. This beauty is envisaged not as an immutable quality inherent within the phenomenal world but as a psychological and moral response—in both the poet and the reader—such that the fundamental pointlessness and hopelessness of the human condition is offset by a renewed awareness of connection between its disparate attributes and the possibility afforded by art, and by poetry in particular, to find and/or create new patterns—that tension between the found and the made remains crucial—through the agency of the imagination. In *Les Fleurs du Mal* (1857) the acceptance of our condition of ill-being is figured as a willing embrace of Satan and reflected in the structure of both 'Spleen et idéal' and the collection as a whole in terms of a more or less passive acceptance of our sad and sorry state: a life of vain desire and inevitable loss leading always unto death. Such solace as there may be lies only in the smoker's pipe (at the end of 'Spleen et idéal') or in those fond, illusory prospects, entertained by lovers or the poor or artists, for some kind of payback after death: respectively, erotic reunion; some food and rest at last; ultimate and deserved acclaim.

But in *Les Fleurs du Mal* (1861) a more active and willed resistance comes into view. The poet as alternative lawgiver, already introduced in the opening poems of 'Spleen et idéal' (1857) as one who writes a new kind of poetry expressive of this acceptance of 'le Mal', now exhibits a more overtly militant opposition to the destructiveness of desire and the dire erosions of time. New emphasis is placed on the power of poetry to reassemble the *disjecta membra* of our scattered failures and sundry disappointments, to gather up the flotsam and jetsam of our ill-being and make of it by human will alone—by art—something new and interesting and *alive*: the poetry of words that feast on mortal lack like maggots on a corpse. By means of the imagination contingency and clutter are transformed, for both poet and reader, into the beauty of a poem, into a shapeliness that provides further food for thought—and a reason to care.

Before discussing (in Part IV) the further changes Baudelaire made between 1857 and 1861 to the structure, content, and poetic argument of *Les Fleurs du Mal* (which will then be followed by an account of the poet as lawgiver in the prose poems of *Le Spleen de Paris*, the first of which were published in 1855) it will be helpful to examine the major critical writings he published during the surrounding period (1855-63): his essays on Poe ([1852], 1856, 1857), the *Salon de 1859*, his articles on Gautier (1859, 1861), Hugo (1861), and Wagner (1861), and finally his analysis of the work of Constantin Guys in *Le Peintre de la vie moderne* (1863). Together these writings bear witness to a range of significant developments in Baudelaire's conception of the functions of art and beauty, and in particular to a crucial new emphasis on the role of the creative imagination.[1]

* * *

For Baudelaire 'Imagination' means resistance: in part, as we shall now see, an expression of political resistance, and, in greater part, an instrument of resistance within our irremediable condition of melancholy. And 'Imagination' means 'poetry', whether in verse or prose, whether in painting, music, or sculpture. As he writes in the *Salon de 1859*: 'je réclame sans cesse l'application de l'imagination, l'introduction de la poésie dans toutes les fonctions de l'art' (ii. 657). For as he writes also, in his essay on Gautier three months earlier: 'L'Imagination seule contient la poésie' (ii. 115). So important is this human faculty that often, as he does here, Baudelaire gives it a capital letter. Like 'le Mal'. And we shall now see in his developing response to the work of Edgar Allan Poe (1809-49) how Baudelaire saw the 'Imagination' as key to the public role of the poet as alternative lawgiver. For, in his account, the life and works of Poe exemplify the power of the Imagination in two ways: in its capacity to resist and subvert normative thinking, and in its power to confront the destructive effects of melancholy by constructing new worlds.

Baudelaire first encountered Poe's work in translation, in 1847, and at once sought out the originals. He began to translate some of Poe's prose himself (Mallarmé would later translate the poems)[2] and published his own version of

---

[1] On the particular importance of the year 1859 see Richard D. E. Burton, *Baudelaire in 1859: A Study in the Sources of Poetic Creativity* (Cambridge: Cambridge University Press, 1988). Margaret Gilman notes that before the *Salon de 1859* Baudelaire had made little use of the term 'imagination': see her *Baudelaire the Critic*, 119-22.

[2] See Mallarmé, *Œuvres complètes*, ed. Marchal, ii. 723-820.

Magnetic Revelation in 1848. In his short presentation of that text he focuses particularly on its 'philosophical' content, associating Poe with some big names from the world of narrative fiction (Diderot, Sterne, Laclos, Hoffmann, Goethe, Balzac) while applying to them collectively the aesthetic theories of 'tempérament' and of beauty as 'étonnement' that he had elaborated in his two *Salons* of 1845 and 1846. Thus Poe is said to have 'étonné, surtout étonné, plutôt qu'ému ou enthousiasmé' (ii. 247), and his narrative technique, like that of all these novelists and *nouvellistes*, is described as 'la conséquence même de [son] tempérament': 'Tous ces gens, avec une volonté et une bonne foi infatigable, décalquent la nature, la pure nature.—Laquelle?—La leur' (ii. 247). Clearly Baudelaire's aim here is to confer prestige on his new discovery by this association with celebrated writers, but at the same time he describes the whole group in terms that equally clearly spring from his own particular enthusiasm for Poe and for the specific reason (at this early stage) that prompted it: Poe's interest in the phenomenon of animal magnetism and, more broadly, his overriding ambition to posit original and 'astonishing' laws of nature.

Mindful of Diderot's materialist speculations, of Goethe's scientific enquiries and his novel about 'elective affinities', of Hoffmann's interest in mental disorder and the 'fantastic', and, above all, of Balzac's wide-ranging preoccupation with the paranormal and his ambition to establish one overarching and unifying theory of body–mind relations, Baudelaire identifies Poe with this array of 'philosophical' writers as a collective of would-be lawgivers seeking the new and the strange:

> ils visent généralement à l'étonnant. Dans les œuvres de plusieurs d'entre eux, on voit la préoccupation d'un perpétuel surnaturalisme. Cela tient [...] à cet esprit primitif de 'chercherie', qu'on me pardonne le barbarisme, à cet esprit inquisitorial, esprit de juge d'instruction, qui a peut-être ses racines dans les plus lointaines impressions de l'enfance. (ii. 248)

Like examining magistrates and filled with childlike curiosity, these writers investigate the domain of the spiritual or non-material ('surnaturalisme') in search of new laws, just as others—'naturalistes enragés'—subject the human soul to minute examination 'comme les médecins le corps' (ii. 248). In short, today's writers are comparable with scientists probing the mysteries of nature: 'Unité de l'animal, unité de fluide, unité de la matière première, toutes ces théories récentes sont quelquefois tombées par un accident singulier dans la tête des poètes, en même temps que dans les têtes savantes' (ii. 248).

As Baudelaire continued to translate Poe's prose works over a period of more than fifteen years, so his interpretative understanding of Poe evolved in concert with his own independent thinking about the role of the poet and the nature of poetry. This understanding is set out in three key texts: 'Edgar Allan Poe, sa vie et ses ouvrages', 'Edgar Poe, sa vie et ses œuvres', and 'Notes nouvelles sur Edgar Poe', and together they constitute not only an assessment of Poe but also a kind of self-portrait. For in Poe Baudelaire had found a kindred spirit. As he explained to Théophile Thoré in a letter of 20 June 1864: 'Savez-vous pourquoi j'ai si patiemment traduit Poe? Parce qu'il me ressemblait' (*Corr.* ii. 386).[3] Indeed he seems to signal this self-portraiture obliquely at the end of the first part of 'Edgar Allan Poe, sa vie et ses ouvrages' when he pokes fun at the American poet Henry Wadsworth Longfellow for finding prolixity in Poe's writing: 'Il est plaisant, avec son "abondance", le prolixe auteur d'*Évangeline*. Prend-il donc Edgar Poe pour un miroir?' (ii. 267). Not only did Baudelaire share Poe's conviction that literary creation depends not on inspiration but on a conscious and controlled process of composition directed towards the production of an effect upon the reader, but also, and perhaps even more importantly, he identified strongly with Poe's own situation: of abandonment, isolation, and alienation, of financial difficulty and alcohol dependency, of angry nonconformism and bruising reception (this even before the trial of *Les Fleurs du Mal*). And in the three panels of this self-portrait we shall see a move from predicament to remedy, from the situation of the persecuted lawgiver to the affirmation of the power of the Imagination. But the subject of the portrait nevertheless remains constant: the poet as resistance hero. As Baudelaire writes of Poe but could have said of himself: 'Il fut donc une admirable protestation' (ii. 321).

'Edgar Allan Poe, sa vie et ses ouvrages' (1852)

Il semble que Poe veuille arracher la parole aux prophètes, et s'attribuer le monopole de l'explication rationnelle.

(ii. 283)

'Edgar Allan Poe, sa vie et ses ouvrages' was first published in two parts as an article in the *Revue de Paris* in March and April 1852.[4] Baudelaire then drew on it for material when composing both the introduction (entitled 'Edgar Poe, sa vie et

---

[3] But cf. his unpublished draft 'Avis du traducteur', also from the early to mid-1860s, where he describes Poe more tentatively as 'un homme qui me ressemblait un peu, par quelques points, c'est-à-dire une partie de moi-même' (ii. 348).

[4] In writing this article Baudelaire drew information and sometimes wording from two sources in particular, both published in the *Southern Literary Messenger* (based in Richmond, Virginia): an obituary of Poe by John Reuben Thompson and, more importantly, a long review by John M. Daniel of a recently published edition of Poe's collected works. For the texts of these sources and discussion of Baudelaire's use of them see W. T. Bandy's authoritative edition of the article (*Edgar Allan Poe: sa vie et ses ouvrages* (Toronto and New York: University of Toronto Press, 1973)) and Claude Pichois's editorial comments and notes in ii. 1205–16. In my discussion I have taken care to distinguish Baudelaire's own particular arguments, comments, wordings, and emphases from those to be found in his sources, including the works of Poe himself. On the reception of Poe in France see James Lawler, *Edgar Poe et les poètes français* (Paris: Julliard, 1989), and the brief account by Lois Davis Vines, 'Poe in France', in Lois Davis Vines (ed.), *Poe Abroad: Influence, Reputation, Affinities* (Iowa City: University of Iowa Press, 1999), 9–17.

ses œuvres') to his first volume of translations of Poe's stories, entitled *Histoires extraordinaires* (1856), and then the 'Notes nouvelles sur Edgar Poe' that served as the introduction to the second volume, *Nouvelles Histoires extraordinaires* (1857), and in which he undertakes specifically to analyse Poe's 'opinions philosophiques et littéraires' (ii. 318). In both 'Edgar Allan Poe' and 'Edgar Poe' Baudelaire begins his account by comparing his subject to a jailbird and perpetual outlaw who had recently appeared before a French court bearing the words 'pas de chance' tattooed on his forehead—'comme un livre son titre' (ii. 249, 296)[5]—and duly been found guilty in confirmation of this latter-day mark of Cain. For there are writers like that: 'Il y a dans l'histoire littéraire des destinées analogues, de vraies damnations,—des hommes qui portent le mot 'guignon' écrit en caractères mystérieux dans les plis sinueux de leur front' (ii. 296; cf. ii. 249). And Poe is one of them. More particularly, Baudelaire affiliates him to the poet-outcast of Vigny's *Stello* (1832) whose status as doomed outsider remains unchanged whatever the vagaries of society's political arrangements:

> Un écrivain célèbre de notre temps a écrit un livre pour démontrer que le poète ne pouvait trouver une bonne place ni dans une société démocratique ni dans une aristocratique, pas plus dans une monarchie absolue ou tempérée.
> (ii. 297; cf. ii. 250, where Vigny is explicitly named.)

For Baudelaire, Poe's experience of the democratic society of the United States confirms Vigny's thesis since it offers the example of 'une tyrannie bien plus cruelle et plus inexorable que celle d'un monarque, qui est celle de l'opinion' (ii. 252; cf. ii. 299). In 1852 Baudelaire writes: 'la Démocratie a bien ses inconvénients, [...] malgré son masque bienveillant de liberté, elle ne permet peut-être pas toujours l'expansion des individualités, [...] il est souvent bien difficile de penser et d'écrire dans un pays où il y a vingt, trente millions de souverains' (ii. 251–2), while in 1856 his revised wording emphasizes not so much the restriction placed on the development and expression of an individual viewpoint as the loss of subtlety and complexity consequent on that restriction: 'Impitoyable dictature que celle de l'opinion dans les sociétés démocratiques; n'implorez d'elle ni charité, ni indulgence, ni élasticité quelconque dans l'application de ses lois aux cas multiples et complexes de la vie morale' (ii. 297–8). Faced with the rigid doxa of normative opinion the writer's own new legislation risks being robbed of its originality and precision. Here, therefore, is a new name to add to the long list of persecuted geniuses:

---

[5] Where the wording of both texts is the same I give two page references. Where the meaning is essentially the same but the wording different I quote from the later text (on the traditional editorial grounds of preference for a revised version) but include a reference to the earlier one. Where a difference of wording creates significant disparities of emphasis or implication I quote from both texts.

j'ajoute un saint nouveau au martyrologue: j'ai à écrire l'histoire d'un de ces illustres malheureux, trop riche de poésie et de passion, qui est venu, après tant d'autres, faire en ce bas monde le rude apprentissage du génie chez les âmes inférieures. Lamentable tragédie que la vie d'Edgar Poe! (ii. 297; cf. ii. 250)

Is it not, Baudelaire wonders, as though society actually *needed* these writers as its sacrificial victims, ready to be slaughtered upon the altar of its own, contrary values— 'Le temps et l'argent, tout est là' (ii. 252); 'Le temps et l'argent ont là-bas une valeur si grande!' (ii. 299)—the better to 'consacrate' (i.e. defend or promote) those values:

> Existe-t-il donc une Providence diabolique qui prépare le malheur depuis le berceau,—qui jette avec *préméditation* des natures spirituelles et angéliques dans des milieux hostiles, comme des martyrs dans les cirques? Y a-t-il donc des âmes *sacrées*, vouées à l'autel, condamnés à marcher à la mort et à la gloire à travers leurs propres ruines?
>
> (ii. 296–7; cf. ii. 250, where the sentence ends 'à travers un sacrifice permanent d'elles-mêmes')

In both 'Edgar Allan Poe' and 'Edgar Poe' Baudelaire makes much of Poe's status as rebel ('Jamais homme ne s'affranchit plus complètement des règles de la société' (ii. 270)) and loner ('Poe était là-bas un cerveau singulièrement solitaire' (ii. 299)). Orphaned at the age of 2, raised, educated, and financially supported by John and Frances Allan, continually at odds with them over issues of behaviour and money, eventually (following John's remarriage after the death of Frances) estranged, disowned, and disinherited, Edgar Poe struggled constantly with poverty and alcoholism and died a relatively early death at the age of 40. For Baudelaire this alcoholism and this neglect of his own health were a manifestation not only of Poe's rejection of society and indeed of life ('Poe fuyait tout dans le noir de l'ivresse, comme dans le noir de la tombe' (ii. 271); cf. ii. 314: 'Poe fuyait tout dans le noir de l'ivresse comme dans une tombe préparatoire') but also of society's own rejection of *him*, the manifestation in fact of a more general condition of alienation experienced by writers as a whole. Whereas the libertine poets of the seventeenth century (Saint-Amant, Chapelle, Colletet) could carouse 'joyeusement' with men and women of the nobility in their shared, knowledgeable, and unproblematic delight in literature, by the time of Rétif de la Bretonne in the following century such carousing had an illicit, subversive air: 'L'école de Rétif boit, mais c'est déjà une école de parias, un monde souterrain' (ii. 272). Now, in the nineteenth century, the writer is shunned entirely: 'Aujourd'hui, l'ivrognerie littéraire a pris un caractère sombre et sinistre. Il n'y a plus de classe spécialement lettrée qui se fasse honneur de frayer avec les hommes de lettres' (ii. 272). Today's poets are left to their own devices, isolated even from one another by their own very absorption in the work of being a poet, or else simply, and more banally, by 'les haines d'école'. Post-prandial carousing has become a sad and solitary affair: 'Le dîner absorbé et l'animal satisfait, le poète entre dans la vaste solitude de sa pensée' and drinks in order to be reunited with his only true friends: 'il ne peut plus résister à l'espérance de retrouver dans la boisson les visions calmes ou effrayantes qui sont déjà ses vieilles connaissances' (ii. 272). And this is the reason also, Baudelaire concludes, that poets all smoke so much! Rather than the stimulus of human conversation and a community of literature, drink and tobacco now provide the poet's only paths into a newly solipsistic world of the imagination. As we read in 'Au lecteur': 'Il rêve d'échafauds en fumant son houka' (l. 38).

In 'Edgar Poe' Baudelaire drops this historical perspective from his account of Poe's alcoholism and instead further develops the idea that drinking allowed Poe to reconnect with the earlier products of his imagination, 'ses vieilles connaissances'. Indeed, he argues, this drinking could be seen as a kind of mnemonic aid and writerly technique:

> l'ivrognerie de Poe était un moyen mnémonique, une méthode de travail, méthode énergique et mortelle, mais appropriée à sa nature passionnée. Le poète avait appris à boire, comme un littérateur soigneux s'exerce à faire des cahiers de notes. Il ne pouvait résister au désir de retrouver les visions merveilleuses ou effrayantes, les conceptions subtiles qu'il avait rencontrées dans une tempête précédente; c'étaient de vieilles connaissances qui l'attiraient impérativement, et, pour renouer avec elles, il prenait le chemin le plus dangereux, mais le plus direct. Une partie de ce qui fait aujourd'hui notre jouissance est ce qui l'a tué. (ii. 315)

Now, therefore, for the Baudelaire of 1856, the writer dies not only as a sacrificial victim, uniting society in the defence of its threatened values, but also for us as readers, destroying himself even as he constructs works of art that will live on and answer to our readerly quest for 'jouissance'.

If Poe's alcoholism and early death bespeak the alienation of the writer in modern society ('la même transformation des mœurs, qui a fait du monde lettré une classe à part' (ii. 272)), so then too does the profound and even rebarbative melancholy that marks the work of this persecuted man, himself made famous by 'The Raven' with its cruelly insistent refrain 'Nevermore' (highlighted in the first epigraph to 'Edgar Poe, sa vie et ses œuvres' (ii. 296)): 'Les échos désespérés de la mélancolie, qui traversent les ouvrages de Poe, ont un accent pénétrant, il est vrai, mais il faut dire aussi que c'est une mélancolie bien solitaire et peu sympathique au commun des hommes' (ii. 269).[6] But for all that

---

[6] Cf. 'Edgar Poe': 'Sa personne était singulière, séduisante et, comme ses ouvrages, marquée d'un indéfinissable cachet de mélancolie' (ii. 309); and on his love poetry: 'La divine passion y paraît magnifique, étoilée, et toujours voilée d'une irrémédiable mélancolie' (ii. 312).

Poe is a doomed and melancholic genius, persecuted by American society just as Byron had been also by 'la haine britannique' (ii. 259), nevertheless as an artist he is no wild spirit. Yes, his life may have been 'déréglée et diabolique' (ii. 272), but this was a writer with a powerful imagination who knew the value of discipline and order in art. As Baudelaire writes in 1852: 'C'est un fait très remarquable qu'un homme d'une imagination aussi vagabonde et aussi ambitieuse soit en même temps si amoureux des règles, et capable de studieuses analyses et de patientes recherches' (ii. 273).

For Baudelaire, therefore, Poe is the very model of the poet as outlaw, of the writer as an alternative lawgiver pushing back against the materialist, mercantile, and utilitarian nature of 'barbaric' and 'uncivilized' American society by championing literary creativity and the power of the imagination:

> les États-Unis ne furent pour Poe qu'une vaste prison qu'il parcourait avec l'agitation fiévreuse d'un être fait pour respirer dans un monde plus amoral,—qu'une grande barbarie éclairée au gaz—et que sa vie intérieure, spirituelle, de poète ou même d'ivrogne, n'était qu'un effort perpétuel pour échapper à l'influence de cette atmosphère antipathique.' (ii. 297)[7]

But not for him the ease and licence of mere fantasy and drunken visions. Rather, he exemplifies the constructive imagination of an active, conscious artist seeking an effect, his celebrated 'totality of effect' and 'unity of impression': and thus he is an artist who resembles Baudelaire himself and one who, also like Baudelaire, rejects all those who would reduce the social utility of poetry to mere didacticism or propaganda. Employing his familiar tactic of foregrounding a truth by seemingly denying it, Baudelaire makes the parallel with his own case unambiguously clear in his account of Poe's public talks on 'The Poetic Principle':

> Il y a, depuis longtemps déjà, aux États-Unis, un mouvement utilitaire qui veut entraîner la poésie comme le reste. Il y a là des poètes humanitaires, des poètes du suffrage universel, des poètes abolutionnistes des lois sur les céréales, et des poètes qui veulent faire bâtir des 'workhouses'.[8] Je jure que je ne fais aucune allusion à des gens de ce pays-ci. Ce n'est pas ma faute si les mêmes disputes et les mêmes théories agitent différentes nations. Dans ses lectures, Poe leur déclara la guerre. (ii. 262)

---

[7] In the equivalent sentence in 'Edgar Allan Poe' he describes the United States as 'une vaste cage, un grand établissement de comptabilité' (ii. 251).

[8] This sentence borrows and translates a sentence from John Daniel's review in the *Southern Literary Messenger*.

Baudelaire ends 'Edgar Allan Poe, sa vie et ses ouvrages' by comparing Poe with Christ, applying to him the words of the Christian catechism: 'Il a beaucoup souffert pour nous' and writing an epitaph to place upon his tomb (Baudelaire's own 'Tombeau d'Edgar Poe' therefore, pre-dating Mallarmé's) in which he celebrates Poe's Christ-like status as a lawgiver:

> Vous tous qui avez ardemment cherché à découvrir les lois de votre être, qui avez aspiré à l'infini, et dont les sentiments refoulés ont dû chercher un affreux soulagement dans le vin et la débauche, priez pour lui. Maintenant, son être corporel purifié nage au milieu des êtres dont il entrevoyait l'existence, priez pour lui qui et qui sait, il intercédera pour vous. (ii. 288)

Poe has travelled the road of melancholy and explored the dark and mysterious recesses of human behaviour, not least the phenomenon of 'perverseness' of which Poe writes in *The Black Cat* (and here in Baudelaire's translation): 'N'avons-nous pas une inclination perpétuelle, en dépit de notre jugement, à violer ce qui est *la loi*, seulement parce que nous savons que c'est la loi? Cet esprit de perversité [...] de faire mal pour le seul amour du mal' (ii. 278). In his account of Poe's stories (ii. 275–82) Baudelaire foregrounds how frequently they turn on the discovery of new laws: here in *The Black Cat* the law of law-breaking and wanton cruelty, but elsewhere of encryption (*The Gold-Bug*) and gravity (*A Descent into the Maelström*), or the laws that govern 'la génération des idées' (*The Murders in the Rue Morgue*) or the workings of 'les mondes ultérieurs' (*Magnetic Revelation*) or mental illness (*Berenice*). He refers to this as Poe's 'conjecturisme' or 'probabilisme' (ii. 275) and likens him explicitly to a modern-day, 'rational' prophet-lawgiver: 'Il semble que Poe veuille arracher la parole aux prophètes, et s'attribuer le monopole de l'explication rationnelle' (ii. 283).

Here also, and pursuing the theme of lawgiving, Baudelaire dwells briefly on *Eureka* ('sans doute le livre chéri et longtemps rêvé d'Edgar Poe' (ii. 286)) and describes how this work 'prétend développer le procédé, et démontrer la loi suivant laquelle l'univers a revêtu sa forme actuelle visible, et trouvé sa présente organisation, et aussi comment cette même loi, qui fut l'origine de la création, sera le moyen de sa destruction et de l'absorption définitive du monde' (ii. 287). But he declines to comment further on this work, ostensibly for fear of misrepresenting Poe's ideas and thereby perhaps accidentally providing Poe's critics with further grounds for vilification, especially as the poet has already been accused of being a pantheist (instead of being a good God-fearing Christian). But, in so declining, Baudelaire thereby—and once again characteristically—raises the very question of Poe's religious beliefs, highlighting their (welcome) lack of orthodoxy and exonerating Poe from possible blame on the excellent grounds of an inconsistency (in other words, an innovative complexity) in his ideas: 'je puis affirmer que, comme bien d'autres grands hommes épris de logique, il se contredit quelquefois fortement, ce qui fait son éloge' (ii. 287).[9] As if this were not enough, Baudelaire stimulates his reader's interest further by issuing a solemn call for intellectual sobriety and judiciousness: 'Il faut le lire avec précaution et faire la vérification de ses étranges idées par la juxtaposition des systèmes analogues et contraires' (ii. 287). So, all is relative, even Christianity.

In the brief final section of 'Edgar Allan Poe', in which he likens Poe to Christ, Baudelaire alludes also to 'les illuminés', those philosophers and thinkers of the eighteenth and nineteenth centuries, whether in Europe or America,[10] who sought to find answers—'illumination'—to the mysteries of the universe *outside* the parameters of the traditional Christian Revelation, and he describes them as 'les plus grands des hommes' (ii. 288). By clear implication Poe, too, is an 'illuminé'— and perhaps Baudelaire also. For here at the end of his long article he himself turns lawgiver. He takes as the text of his secular sermon the axiom that 'Tout mystique a un vice caché' (ii. 287), a comment made to him first by a puritanical friend and then later by a bookseller of works on the occult who possesses inside knowledge of the only too human and physical failings (drunkenness, gluttony, sexual promiscuity) of his supposedly 'mystical' customers. Baudelaire then interprets this by stating his own version of original sin: 'Mon Dieu! [...] quelle est donc cette loi fatale qui nous enchaîne, nous domine, et se venge de la violation de son insupportable despotisme par la dégradation et l'amoindrissement de notre être moral?' (ii. 287–8). Why is it, he laments, that all intellectual and moral ambition, the honourable striving to transcend everyday 'niaiserie' and 'insouciance', should seemingly be punished by a 'fall' into the human weakness of base desire as though according to some underlying law of compensation or equivalence: 'L'homme sera-t-il éternellement si limité qu'une de ses facultés ne puisse s'agrandir qu'au détriment des autres?' (ii. 288).

Such striving is here presented in unequivocally political terms as a rising up against the tyranny of our seemingly immutable and fallen 'nature', as the violation of an unjust law and a breaking of chains, in short as a kind of criminal insurrection. But if indeed 'vouloir à tout prix connaître la vérité est un grand crime, ou au moins peut conduire à de grandes fautes'—as, seemingly, was the case with Poe and his alcoholism—then the appropriate response should be one not of condemnation and proscription but of compassion. And here, by a nice twist and perhaps ironically aping those same American puritans who condemn Poe, Baudelaire evokes the central Christian law of love in order to turn Poe into

---

[9] Cf. the later comment in 'Edgar Poe': 'Parmi l'énumération nombreuse des *droits de l'homme* que la sagesse du XIXe siècle recommence si souvent et si complaisamment, deux assez importants ont été oubliés, qui sont le droit de se contredire et le droit de *s'en aller*' (ii. 306). Cf. also Baudelaire's contribution to the album of Philoxène Boyer: 'Parmi les droits dont on a parlé dans ces derniers temps, il y en a un qu'on a oublié, à la démonstration duquel *tout le monde* est intéressé,—le droit de se contredire' (i. 709).

[10] See ii. 1216 n. 1 to p. 288.

Christ himself, and to turn his own admiration for Poe into a proclamation of quasi-Christian devotion to this poet who was crucified by his compatriots: 'Edgar Poe, ivrogne, pauvre, persécuté, paria, me plaît plus que calme et "vertueux", un Gœthe ou un W. Scott' (ii. 288).

'Notes nouvelles sur Edgar Poe' (1857)

L'Imagination est la reine des facultés[.]

(ii. 328)

In the 'Notes nouvelles sur Edgar Poe', by contrast, a text written some five years later, Baudelaire ends his account of Poe rather differently—by focusing not on Poe's persecution but on his resistance, the resistance of his imagination. Implicitly echoing Bonald's notorious comment that 'la littérature est l'expression de la société',[11] Baudelaire comments: 'Un semblable milieu engendre nécessairement des erreurs littéraires correspondantes. C'est contre ces erreurs que Poe a réagi aussi souvent qu'il a pu et de toute sa force' (ii. 328). So sacrosanct is the notion of usefulness in the United States ('l'idée [...] la plus hostile du monde à l'idée de beauté') that the typical critic there 'cherchera dans un livre de poésie les moyens de perfectionner la conscience' (ii. 328), whereas for Poe as critic and writer what matters in any given work is 'la perfection du plan' and 'la correction de l'exécution' (ii. 328). But these matter not in themselves but because they are the necessary attributes of a constructive Imagination, which Baudelaire now describes in terms that anticipate the central argument of the *Salon de 1859*:

> Pour [Poe], l'Imagination est la reine des facultés; mais par ce mot il entend quelque chose de plus grand que ce qui est entendu par le commun des lecteurs. L'Imagination n'est pas la fantaisie; elle n'est pas non plus la sensibilité, bien qu'il soit difficile de concevoir un homme imaginatif qui ne serait pas sensible. L'Imagination est une faculté quasi divine qui perçoit tout d'abord, en dehors des méthodes philosophiques, les rapports intimes et secrets des choses, les correspondances et les analogies. (ii. 328-9)

The Imagination is first and foremost a means of perception, of noting and bringing to attention—*without* reference to any particular philosophical framework (Fourier's, for example, or Swedenborg's)—a whole network of hitherto unremarked connections within the world. Not only is the imaginative writer

---

[11] See *Unacknowledged Legislators*, 309.

like a scientist, therefore; scientists themselves need to have the imagination of a poet: 'Les honneurs et les fonctions qu[e Poe] confère à cette faculté lui donnent une valeur telle (du moins quand on a bien compris la pensée de l'auteur), qu'un savant sans imagination n'apparaît plus que comme un faux savant, ou tout au moins comme un savant incomplet' (ii. 329).

Enacting Poe's own spirit of resistance Baudelaire begins the 'Notes nouvelles sur Edgar Poe' by defending his subject against the charge of decadence laid against him by traditionalist American critics. Neatly he points out that such a charge implies a quasi-biological historical process ('une échelle de littératures, une vagissante, une puérile, une adolescente, etc.' (ii. 320)) and that it is therefore illogical to blame writers for subjection to the inevitable: 'Ce terme (namely, 'Littérature de décadence') [...] suppose quelque chose de fatal et de providentiel, comme un décret inéluctable; et il est tout à fait injuste de nous reprocher d'accomplir la loi mystérieuse' (ii. 320). For all the *ex cathedra* solemnity of their 'parole académique', all that these 'professeurs jurés' (ii. 330) seem to be saying, therefore, is that it is 'shameful' to obey this law 'avec plaisir', and that (Baudelaire now includes himself amongst those so attacked) 'nous sommes coupables de nous réjouir dans notre destinée' (ii. 320). This traditionalist charge of decadence is here presented as a form of unjust lawgiving, at once a false oracle (cf. 'l'irréfutable oracle' (ii. 319)) and an illegitimate quasi-ecclesiastical excommunication ('j'entends ronfler l'anathème' (ii. 319)). As would-be guardians of a Delphic truth, these hidebound critics are but '[d]es sphinx sans énigme' standing watch before 'les portes saintes de l'Esthétique classique' (ii. 319). In short, and despite this motley array of Egyptian, Greek, and Christian models, *they* are the true barbarians, proclaiming loyalty to the habitual and the unsurprising. For them beauty comes in the form of a 'matrone rustique, répugnante de santé et de vertu, sans allure et sans regard, bref, *ne devant rien qu'à la simple nature*' (ii. 319), while Baudelaire for his part prefers a quite different sort of 'santé' and 'vertu' and a quite different sort of beauty:

> une de ces beautés qui dominent et oppriment le souvenir, unissant à son charme profond et originel toute l'éloquence de la toilette, maîtresse de sa démarche, consciente et reine d'elle-même,—une voix parlant comme un instrument bien accordé, et des regards chargés de pensée en n'en laissant couler que ce qu'ils veulent. (ii. 319)

In the remaining pages of the 'Notes nouvelles sur Edgar Poe' Baudelaire proceeds to deconstruct the illusory binaries upon which the authority of these false lawgivers is supposedly founded. Where Poe's critics condemn him in the name of civilization and a utilitarian literary agenda of moral progress, Baudelaire defends him in the name of a superior primitivism and a deeper moral insight. To admire a beauty owing only to 'la simple nature' is, paradoxically, to admire the monstrous ('La nature ne fait que des monstres' (ii. 325)), whereas 'toute la question est de s'entendre sur le mot "sauvages"' (ii. 325). Presumably mindful of Montaigne's essay 'Des cannibales' and making explicit reference to Rousseau's *Discours sur l'inégalité*, Baudelaire here promotes the 'savage' over the 'civilized'. He begins by appearing to concede to the racial prejudice of his antagonists, professing to be under no illusion about the sorry state of the Native American: 'Nul philosophe n'osera proposer pour modèles ces malheureuses hordes pourries, victimes des éléments, pâtures des bêtes, aussi incapables de fabriquer des armes que de concevoir l'idée d'un pouvoir spirituel et suprême' (ii. 325). But the irony is clear: ignorance of the Christian God and an inability to invent gunpowder do not a savage make.[12] But what does? The power of the imagination, or what Baudelaire here calls 'une faculté inventive' ((ii. 326). Unlike Rousseau, Baudelaire does not argue that civilization has corrupted the natural goodness of man but rather that it has diminished our resourcefulness and limited our knowledge:

> Mais si l'on veut comparer l'homme moderne, l'homme civilisé, avec l'homme sauvage, ou plutôt une nation dite civilisée avec une nation dite sauvage, c'est-à-dire privée de toutes les ingénieuses inventions qui dispensent l'individu d'héroïsme, qui ne voit que tout l'honneur est pour le sauvage? Par sa nature, par nécessité même, il est encyclopédique, tandis que l'homme civilisé se trouve confiné dans les régions infiniment petites de la spécialité. (ii. 325)

As to the notion of progress, this is predicated on the existence of a prior state of ignorance and turpitude from which humankind seeks to advance, whereas in fact, Baudelaire argues, belief in progress is itself the surest sign of decadence. '[C]ette grande hérésie de la décrépitude' (ii. 324), he calls it, before explaining further:

> L'homme civilisé invente la philosophie du progrès pour se consoler de son abdication et de sa déchéance; cependant que l'homme sauvage, époux redouté et respecté, guerrier contraint à la bravoure personnelle, poète aux heures mélancoliques où le soleil déclinant invite à chanter le passé et les ancêtres, rase de plus près la lisière de l'idéal. (ii. 325-6)

The 'civilized' posit a better future in order to mask and even excuse the reality of their own imperfect state, whereas 'savages' accept the state of melancholy consequent on an awareness of death and the passage of time—and, in so accepting, become poets reaching out creatively to the world of the imagination.

---

[12] For Montaigne the Christian God and the teaching of Christian missionaries are simply a respectable cover for plundering South American gold, and the physical victory of the colonizers, attributable to their technological superiority, is trumped by the moral superiority of the colonized.

There can be no doubt as to which of these two categories Baudelaire himself—this poet of 'spleen et idéal'—identifies with. For what does the savage lack since he is both lawgiver and artist?

> Il a le prêtre, il a le sorcier et le médecin. Que dis-je? Il a le dandy, suprême incarnation de l'idée du beau transportée dans la vie matérielle, celui qui dicte la forme et règle les manières. Ses vêtements, ses parures, ses armes, son calumet témoignent d'une faculté inventive qui nous a depuis longtemps désertés. Comparerons-nous nos yeux paresseux et nos oreilles assourdies à ces yeux qui percent la brume, à ces oreilles 'qui entendraient l'herbe qui pousse'? (ii. 326)

From the medicine man, or the witch doctor, or the shaman, the 'savage' can seek a form of guidance in the conduct of his life that knows no sharp and artificial divide between the sensual and the spiritual. At the same time the 'savage' himself is possessed of superior sensory powers that afford an intimate knowledge of the world about him, and possessed also of this 'faculté inventive' that enables him to transform its everyday attributes—clothes, accessories, weapons, smoker's pipe— into objects of beauty. Like Poe—and like Baudelaire—he has an imagination, therefore, that allows him to perceive 'les rapports intimes et secrets des choses'. And Baudelaire's deconstruction of the illusory binary of 'savage' and 'civilized' culminates in this supreme, apparent paradox that the 'savage' can be a dandy. Unlike the 'sphinx pédagogiques' (ii. 319) who crave only the beauty of 'la simple nature', Baudelaire's 'savage' seeks to exercise the power vested in the human imagination that enables it to penetrate the secrets of the world and to transform the natural. Thus does the 'savage' produce the kind of beauty Baudelaire had earlier chosen as his objective, a beauty that includes 'toute l'éloquence de la toilette' and that is 'maîtresse de sa démarche, consciente et reine d'elle-même'. The tables have been turned: the WASPs are in thrall to nature, while the Native Americans are creative masters and mistresses[13] of their own phenomenal world.

Just as the traditionalists are thus less civilized than the 'savages', so too they are infantile and immature in their rigid adherence to an obsolete classical aesthetic: 'Mais ce à quoi les professeurs jurés n'ont pas pensé, c'est que, dans le mouvement de la vie, telle complication, telle combinaison peut se présenter, tout à fait inattendue pour leur sagesse d'écoliers' (ii. 320). New and deeper moral insight, like that of Poe ('Aucun homme, je le répète, n'a raconté avec plus de magie les *exceptions* de la vie humaine et de la nature' (ii. 317), requires a new and more complex aesthetic. And so we have the further paradox of a supposedly 'young'

---

[13] In his brief, ensuing comparison of 'la sauvagesse' and 'la dame américaine' Baudelaire questions whether the former, despite her apparent, obedient subjugation as property of the male (like an animal 'sachant qu'il n'est que la moitié d'une destinée'), is to be judged inferior to the latter, whom Poe depicts as required by fashion to carry a purse the size of a giant cucumber: 'Il faut [writes Poe] que cette bourse soit assez vaste pour qu'elle y puisse enfermer tout son argent,—plus que toute son âme!' (ii. 326).

country whose arbiters of taste espouse an old aesthetic and thus begin where others have ended: 'Et alors leur langue insuffisante se trouve en défaut, comme dans le cas,—phénomène qui se multipliera peut-être avec des variantes—où une nation commence par la décadence, et débute par où les autres finissent' (ii. 320). Indeed these colonizers who think they can impose old rules on 'new' (but in fact even older) nations may well find themselves facing similar problems elsewhere: 'Que parmi les immenses colonies du siècle présent des littératures nouvelles se fassent, il s'y produira très certainement des accidents spirituels d'une nature déroutante pour l'esprit de l'école' (ii. 320). Playing on the word 'école' Baudelaire thus disdains 'schools' of writing or thought as precisely that: schoolground mentalities that depend on old legislations in order to cope with the new.

Intellectual and artistic maturity, on the other hand, lie elsewhere. If Poe exemplifies a 'littérature de décadence', then he is at one with the 'savage', this poet of sunset and melancholy. And in that sunset, at once literal and metaphorical, lie both an advance on the blazing obviousness of noon ('Ce soleil qui, il y a quelques heures, écrasait toutes choses de sa lumière droite et blanche' (ii. 320))— itself suggestive perhaps of the traditionalists' simplistic approach to the question of morality in art—and also the foretaste of a new artistic dawn. In celebration of this moment Baudelaire himself lays out his own poetic talents in richly textured prose as he narrates the birth of analogy and allegory:

> Dans les jeux de ce soleil agonisant, certains esprits poétiques trouveront des délices nouvelles: ils y découvriront des colonnades éblouissantes, des cascades de métal fondu, des paradis de feu, une splendeur triste, la volupté du regret, toutes les magies du rêve, tous les souvenirs de l'opium. Et le coucher du soleil leur apparaîtra en effet comme la merveilleuse allégorie d'une âme chargée de vie, qui descend derrière l'horizon avec une magnifique provision de pensées et de rêves.
> (ii. 320)

The traditionalists' beauty that 'ne d[oi]t rien qu'à la simple nature' is here contrasted with the beauty of a sunset replete with hidden meanings, the very emblem of Poe's imagination 'qui perçoit [...] les rapports intimes et secrets des choses, les correspondances et les analogies'. '[A]ccidents spirituels', 'dans le mouvement de la vie, telle complication, telle combinaison': what interests Poe—and Baudelaire—is precisely this 'magnifique provision de pensées et de rêves' that arises out of a quotidian, sharp-sighted imaginative investigation of the world around us.

Poe's 'savage' imagination thus separates him radically from the poetry of his American contemporaries, all of them intent, it seems, on the preservation of a worn-out aesthetic and the conduct of a moral mission. Again we have the paradox of a 'young' country that in fact shows every sign of decrepitude: 'Jeune et vieille à la fois, l'Amérique bavarde et radote avec une volubilité étonnante

(ii. 320), and again we have a country that looks very much like France: 'Croyez qu'elle [l'Amérique] possède des pédants qui valent bien les nôtres pour rappeler sans cesse l'artiste à la beauté antique, pour questionner un poète ou un romancier sur la moralité de son but et la qualité de ses intentions' (ii. 320). Within this context Poe stands out as the true resistance hero: 'Poe m'apparaît comme un Ilote qui veut faire rougir son maître' (ii. 321), a Helot ready to challenge the Spartan rule of puritan opinion by putting it to shame, by voicing his scorn for those sacred cows that are 'la démocratie, le progrès et la "civilisation"' and by endeavouring to rouse his passive, unthinking, uncritical compatriots from their state of 'crédulité' and 'badauderie' to an active awareness and embrace of 'la souveraineté humaine' (ii. 321)—a sovereignty vested in the imagination, 'reine des facultés'.[14]

'Car il ne fut jamais dupe!' (ii. 321). Thus, rousingly, begins the second of the four sections of the 'Nouvelles notes sur Edgar Poe', in which Baudelaire presents a particularly 'resistant' aspect of Poe's thinking: his belief in what Baudelaire calls 'la méchanceté naturelle de l'Homme' (ii. 322), but what Poe himself calls 'the spirit of perverseness' both in the short story *The Black Cat* (as mentioned briefly above) and in his essay-cum-narrative entitled *The Imp of the Perverse*.[15] Poe has in mind the experience of standing on 'the brink of a precipice' and wondering if we may perversely decide to throw ourselves off, and from this he extrapolates 'an innate and primitive principle of human action, a paradoxical something, which we may call "perverseness", for want of a more characteristic term'. For Poe, anticipating Gide's account of the 'acte gratuit' in *Les Caves du Vatican*, this 'propensity' is a '*mobile* without motive':

Through its promptings we act without comprehensible object; or, if this shall be understood as a contradiction in terms, we may so far modify the proposition as to say, that through its promptings we act, for the reason that we should *not*. In theory, no reason can be more unreasonable; but, in fact, there is none more strong. With certain minds, under certain conditions, it becomes absolutely irresistible. I am not more certain that I breathe, than that the assurance of the wrong or error of any action is often the one unconquerable *force* which impels us, and alone impels us to its prosecution. Nor will this overwhelming tendency

---

[14] Cf. Baudelaire's comment to Toussenel, included above as an epigraph to Part III: 'le poète est *souverainement* intelligent'.
[15] Baudelaire's translation of *The Imp of the Perverse* is placed first in the *Nouvelles Histoires extraordinaires*, which he is here introducing. In this story the protagonist commits a murder and, though he remains unsuspected, begins to consider the possibility that he might 'perversely' confess to the crime, eventually yielding, as though prompted by an 'invisible fiend', to an irresistible desire to confess—and to confess not from any sense of guilt but from an unaccountable and irrational urge to self-destruct. His translation of *The Black Cat* is placed second in the collection, a story in which, as Baudelaire describes in 'Edgar Allan Poe' (ii. 277–9), the 'esprit de PERVERSITÉ' is illustrated by the narrator's irrational cruelty towards his beloved cat, his killing of his wife as she tries to protect the cat, and the final, 'perverse' assistance the narrator provides to the police in revealing the whereabouts of her corpse and his own culpability.

to do wrong for the wrong's sake, admit of analysis, or resolution into ulterior elements. It is a radical, a primitive impulse—elementary.[16]

What interests Poe, therefore, is the existence of an instinct that is the direct opposite of the survival instinct, and in *The Black Cat* he specifically sees this 'propensity' in terms of Christian sin. In finally destroying his beloved cat (whose eye he has already previously gouged out) the narrator is potentially destroying his immortal soul:

> Of this spirit [of perverseness] philosophy takes no account. Yet I am not more sure than my soul lives, than I am that perverseness is one of the primitive impulses of the human heart—one of the indivisible primary faculties, or sentiments, which give direction to the character of Man. Who has not, a hundred times, found himself committing a vile or a silly action, for no other reason than because he knows he should *not*? Have we not a perpetual inclination, in the teeth of our best judgement, to violate that which is *Law*, merely because we understand it to be such? This spirit of perverseness, I say, came to my final overthrow. It was this unfathomable longing of the soul to *vex itself*—to offer violence to its own nature—to do wrong for the wrong's sake only—that urged me to continue and finally to consummate the injury I had inflicted upon the unoffending brute. One morning, in cool blood, I slipped a noose about its neck and hung it to the limb of a tree;—hung it with the tears streaming from my eyes, and with the bitterest remorse in my heart;—hung it *because* I knew that it had loved me, and *because* I felt it had given me no reason of offence;—hung it *because* I knew that in so doing I was committing a sin—a deadly sin that would so jeopardise my immortal soul as to place it—if such a thing were possible—even beyond the reach of the infinite mercy of the Most Merciful and Most Terrible God.[17]

But in referring to the narrator's immortal soul in *The Black Cat* Poe seeks not to make a point about Catholic doctrine but rather to demonstrate how the 'spirit of perverseness' may irrationally but irresistibly overtake a person even when this may endanger what he or she holds most dear: in this case, not only the narrator's cat and presumably his wife but also his immortal soul, and with it the prospect of eternal life. Even the instinct for posthumous 'survival' is powerless against the 'imp of the perverse'. Baudelaire, however, in paraphrasing Poe's 'spirit

---

[16] *The Imp of the Perverse*, in *Collected Works of Edgar Allan Poe*, ed. Mabbott, iii. 1220–1.
[17] *The Black Cat*, in *Collected Works of Edgar Allan Poe*, ed. Mabbott, iii. 852. Baudelaire's translation of this passage as included in 'Edgar Allan Poe, sa vie et ses ouvrages' (ii. 278) differs markedly but not significantly from his (more accurate) version of *Le Chat noir* included in *Nouvelles Histoires extraordinaires* (see Edgar Allan Poe, *Œuvres en prose*, traduction par Ch. Baudelaire, ed. Y.-G. Le Dantec (Paris: Gallimard [Bibliothèque de la Pléiade], 1951), 280–1).

of perverseness' as 'la méchanceté naturelle de l'Homme' (ii. 322), begins to transform Poe into himself. In the first instance he makes this move in order to prepare for his account of Poe as a 'non-dupe': the Poe who rejects the notion of moral progress, who accordingly rejects the idea of poetry as an instrument of moral edification to facilitate that progress, and who instead sees the aesthetic status and effects of poetry as paramount. But his paraphrase also allows him to smuggle in his own view of 'le Mal'—'la méchanceté' instead of 'la perversité'— and to attribute to Poe a certain slippage of terminology and argument that is entirely his own.[18]

Already Baudelaire's account of Poe's 'spirit of perverseness' may remind us of his own earlier portrayals of the spiral of desire, especially in the Lesbos poems: the powerlessness to resist desire, indeed the *desire* not to resist desire, the agonizing knowledge that in acceding to desire we shall, like a victim of rabies drinking water, only hasten the moment of our eventual destruction...and the very *pleasure* of self-destruction. Poe, for his part, is concerned exclusively with the perplexing irrationality or illogicality of this 'perverse' will to self-destruction ('the unfathomable longing of the soul to *vex itself*, 'to do wrong for the wrong's sake'), but in his paraphrase of Poe Baudelaire emphasizes more especially the allure of the dangerous and the forbidden, indeed of 'evil':

> Il y a dans l'homme, dit-il, une force mystérieuse dont la philosophie moderne ne veut pas tenir compte; et cependant, sans cette force innommée, sans ce penchant primordial, une foule d'actions humaines resteront inexpliquées, inexplicables. Ces actions n'ont d'attrait que *parce que* elles sont mauvaises, dangereuses; elles possèdent l'attirance du gouffre. Cette force primitive, irrésistible, est la Perversité naturelle, qui fait que l'homme est sans cesse et à la fois homicide et suicide, assassin et bourreau[.]   (ii. 322-3)

---

[18] Baudelaire's transformation of Poe's 'perverseness' into 'perversity' is accepted without comment by Gautier in his preface to the 1868 edition of the *Œuvres complètes*, where he describes Baudelaire's conception of 'perversité' both as being more or less the equivalent of original sin and also as something closely akin to Poe's account of 'perverseness': 'il ne pensait pas que l'homme fût né bon, et il admettait la perversité originelle comme un élément qu'on retrouve toujours au fond des âmes les plus pures, perversité, mauvaise conseillère qui pousse l'homme à faire ce qui lui est funeste, précisément parce que cela lui est funeste et pour le plaisir de contrarier la loi, sans autre attrait que la désobéissance, en dehors de toute sensualité, de tout profit et de tout charme. Cette perversité, il la constatait et la flagellait chez les autres comme chez lui-même, ainsi qu'un esclave pris en faute, mais en s'abstenant de tout sermon, car il la regardait comme damnablement irrémédiable. [...] Il haïssait le mal comme une déviation à la mathématique et à la norme' (see Guyaux (ed.), *Baudelaire: Un demi-siècle de lectures des 'Fleurs du mal'*, 478–9). The slippage from 'perverseness' to 'perversity' has been noted by Catherine Toal as a 'misinterpretation', which she situates within a rich discussion of Baudelaire's rewriting of Poe in some of his prose poems, itself situated within a wide-ranging and sophisticated account of literary treatments of violence (both personal and racial) in American and French literature and thought of the nineteenth and twentieth centuries. See her *The Entrapments of Form* (New York: Fordham University Press, 2016), 18–42.

Far from sticking closely to Poe's wording in *The Imp of the Perverse* he is here more or less quoting himself, from the poem 'L'Héautontimorouménos' ('The Self-Executioner') completed in 1855 and included as poem 52 in the first edition of *Les Fleurs du Mal*: 'Je suis la plaie et le couteau! | Je suis le soufflet et la joue! | Je suis les membres de la roue, | Et la victime et le bourreau!' (ll. 21–4). Physical and moral self-harm are central to Baudelaire's conception of 'le Mal', the work of the secular devil that is desire, and he now attributes to Poe's analysis of 'perverseness' a 'Satanic' dimension that is entirely of his own making, albeit inflected by the thought of Joseph de Maistre[19] (who is explicitly named at the end of the subsequent paragraph):

> car, ajoute-t-il [i.e. Poe], avec une subtilité remarquablement satanique, l'impossibilité de trouver un motif raisonnable suffisant pour certaines actions mauvaises et périlleuses, pourrait nous conduire à les considérer comme les suggestions du Diable, si l'expérience et l'histoire ne nous enseignaient pas que Dieu en tire souvent l'établissement de l'ordre et le châtiment des coquins[.]
> (ii. 323)

Where Poe uses the terms 'imp', 'fiend', and 'arch-fiend' to describe the 'spirit' of perverseness, Baudelaire in his translation of *The Imp of the Perverse* uses the single term 'démon', but here in the 'Notes nouvelles' he introduces a much more Catholic 'Diable'. Poe's 'perverseness' has become perversity—'la Perversité naturelle', 'la perversité primordiale de l'homme' (ii. 323)—and the approximate equivalent of original sin. Thus transformed, Poe's concept can now serve as a pretext for Baudelaire's scathing attack on all belief in innate human goodness and, with it, the new politics of 'socialisme' (ii. 324). How gratifying and indeed unexpected it is, Baudelaire proclaims, to observe this evidence of an 'antique sagesse' (ii. 323) issuing forth from so young a country:

> Il est agréable que quelques explosions de vieille vérité sautent ainsi au visage de tous ces complimenteurs de l'humanité, de tous ces dorloteurs et endormeurs qui répètent sur toutes les variations possibles de ton: "Je suis né bon, et vous aussi, et nous tous, nous sommes nés bons!" oubliant, non! feignant d'oublier, ces égalitaires à contresens, que nous sommes tous nés marquis pour le mal! (ii. 323)

Far from being born equal and equally good, we are all born subject to an *ancien régime* that is governed by the law of primordial perversity, the law of the marquis de Sade.[20] How absurd, therefore, to have faith in progress, and how wrong to believe that the function of poetry is moral improvement. How can we believe in

---

[19] See ii. 1237 (n. 3 to p. 323).   [20] Cf. ii. 1238 (n. 4 to p. 323).

the human capacity to improve its moral lot if we are our own worst enemies? When we are subject to this law of moral degradation dictating that for every upward aspiration there is a corresponding moment of descent into base desire and the 'gouffre' of self-destruction?

But what then *is* the proper function of poetry in the public sphere? Can poetry still be legitimately invested with ethical as well as aesthetic worth? Perhaps through the power of the imagination to understand the world by making new connections? Perhaps through a conception of beauty that sees it not as a quality of perfection inherent in the world (or indeed absent from it) but as a mode of perception in which hidden perspectives are revealed, offering alternative dimensions of understanding: beyond the quotidian, beyond the simple fact of mortality, beyond the known.

In the final section of the 'Notes nouvelles sur Edgar Poe' Baudelaire deconstructs one further illusory binary: of the useful and the beautiful. Beginning with a direct quotation from Poe's *Marginalia*, he introduces the idea that beauty is in fact a form of justice. For (writes Poe) if the Imagination is a means of perceiving hidden relations, then poets—members of the *genus irritabile vatum* (irritable race of poets) as Horace called them—are irritable not because of their temperament ('compris dans le sens vulgaire' (ii. 331)) but by virtue of the 'clairvoyance' that characterizes their more acute perceptions: 'Les poètes voient l'injustice, *jamais* là où elle n'existe pas, mais fort souvent là où des yeux non poétiques n'en voient pas du tout' (ii. 330-1). Thus, in Poe's words also, '[c]ette clairvoyance n'est pas autre chose qu'un corollaire de la vive perception du vrai, de la justice, de la proportion, en un mot du Beau' (ii. 331). If poets and artists are 'irritable', Poe argues, it is because their capacity to see beauty carries with it an 'exquisite' sense of beauty's opposite: 'Un artiste n'est un artiste que grâce à son sens exquis du Beau,—sens qui lui procure des jouissances enivrantes, mais qui en même temps implique, enferme un sens également exquis de toute difformité et de toute disproportion' (ii. 330). For Baudelaire this argument about the equivalence of beauty and justice constitutes 'une excellente et irréfutable apologie' (ii. 331) for all poets[21] and serves as a backdrop to this final section in which he proceeds (ii. 332-5) to offer extensive quotation and close paraphrase of key passages from Poe's essay *The Poetic Principle*, expounding an aesthetic that was also his own.[22] The moral value

---

[21] As discussed above in Chapter 1 under 'The Poet as Nomothete', Baudelaire adopts the idea as his own by supplementing his paraphrase of Poe with the following comment: 'et je ne crois pas qu'il soit scandalisant de considérer toute infraction à la morale, au beau moral, comme une espèce de faute contre le rythme et la prosodie universels' (ii. 334).

[22] Baudelaire is explicit about his source, but because he uses quotation marks only once and at the beginning of his summary (when citing Poe's statement about the long poem (ii. 332)) it can appear that the remainder of the summary contains Baudelaire's own words and sometimes even his own original thinking. Baudelaire's 'borrowing' from Poe verges on plagiarism when, in his 1859 article on Gautier he cites a very long passage from this section of 'Edgar Poe, sa vie et ses œuvres' as though indeed he were quoting himself, and not Poe: 'Il est permis quelque fois, je présume, de se citer soi-même, surtout pour éviter de se paraphraser. Je répéterai donc [...]' (ii. 112). A charitable

of poetry lies not in overt didacticism but in the crafted articulation of an original sensual and imaginative vision:

> Non seulement [Poe] a dépensé des efforts considérables pour soumettre à sa volonté le démon fugitif des minutes heureuses, pour rappeler à son gré ces sensations exquises, ces appétitions spirituelles, ces états de santé poétique, si rares et si précieux qu'on pourrait vraiment les considérer comme des grâces extérieures à l'homme et comme des visitations; mais aussi il a soumis l'inspiration à la méthode, à l'analyse la plus sévère. [...] Il affirmait que celui qui ne sait pas saisir l'intangible n'est pas poète[.]   (ii. 331)

Such a vision may seem more like a visitation from without, like some divine bestowal of grace, but actually this apparent 'inspiration' comes from within and depends on artistic technique for its expression and thus for its very existence. In the 'justice' of the vision lies the need for a similar 'justice' of expression: poetic health, or 'hygiene', requires the *mot juste*. And for Poe himself, as Baudelaire had remarked previously in 'Edgar Poe', the absence of such 'justice' must have constituted a living hell:

> Si vous ajoutez à cette vision impeccable du vrai, véritable infirmité dans de certaines circonstances, une délicatesse exquise de sens qu'une note fausse torturait, une finesse de goût que tout, excepté l'exacte proportion, révoltait, un amour insatiable du Beau, qui avait pris la puissance d'une passion morbide, vous ne vous étonnerez pas que pour un pareil homme la vie soit devenue un enfer, et qu'il ait fini mal; vous admirerez qu'il ait pu *durer* aussi longtemps.   (ii. 300)

Thus for Poe as also for Baudelaire the imagination is a form of resistance—'une admirable protestation'—against the false norms and false binaries by which the moral and artistic life of the nation are governed. Whereas in 'Edgar Allan Poe, sa vie et ses ouvrages' Baudelaire had presented his American kindred spirit as the persecuted genius, a quasi-Christian lawgiver crucified by conservatism and worthy of our compassion, in the 'Notes nouvelles sur Poe' he gives us a champion of the Imagination who finds justice in art and the perfection of his craft. Formal beauty is no mere surface charm but an indispensable means to the expression of a complex and revelatory moral and intellectual vision. For Baudelaire this poetry of the Imagination fulfils above all an exploratory and quasi-scientific role, uncovering the new rather than merely inculcating the old. Accordingly he ends the 'Notes

---

interpretation here would be to suggest that Baudelaire is so aware of thinking 'as one' with Poe that the question of authorship is irrelevant. I return to these particular translation-cum-paraphrases of *The Poetic Principle* below at the beginning of Chapter 13.

nouvelles' with a parting shot at both Victor Hugo and the prevailing moral and artistic climate of an 'anti-poetic' nation:

> toute âme éprise de poésie pure me comprendra quand je dirai que, parmi notre race antipoétique, Victor Hugo serait moins admiré s'il était parfait, et qu'il n'a pu se faire pardonner tout son génie lyrique qu'en introduisant de force et brutalement dans sa poésie ce qu'Edgar Poe considérait comme l'hérésie moderne capitale,—*l'enseignement.* (ii. 337)

For the contemporary critic, in America as in France, preoccupation with poetic and artistic form is suspect because it implies an unacceptable indifference to the inculcation of (orthodox) moral and religious lessons. But for Poe and Baudelaire it is the very purpose of art to resist such didacticism and to pursue less orthodox truths in the name of a higher justice. Soon, on 20 August 1857, Baudelaire would himself be arraigned before a court of law, like Poe before the court of American opinion, and there found guilty of infringing the orthodoxies of mid-nineteenth-century France. 'Pas de chance'...

12
The Government of the Imagination
The *Salon de 1859*

> Comme l'imagination a créé le monde, elle le gouverne[.]
> (*Salon de 1859*, ii. 623)
> cette imagination vive et ample, sensible, audacieuse, sans laquelle, il faut bien le dire, toutes les meilleures facultés ne sont que des serviteurs sans maîtres, des agents sans gouvernement.
> (*Peintres et aquafortistes* [1862], ii. 738)

Imagination and Creation

> l'âme qui jette une lumière magique et surnaturelle sur l'obscurité naturelle des choses[.]
> (*Salon de 1859*, ii. 645)

The concept of 'Imagination' provides the principal focus of the *Salon de 1859*: 'Je m'étais imposé de chercher l'Imagination à travers le Salon' (ii. 681). Hitherto in his writings, with the notable exception of the 'Notes nouvelles sur Poe', Baudelaire had made relatively little use of this familiar term, and yet here he insists that this concept has 'governed' his own writing of the *Salon de 1859* throughout its composition: 'l'idée principale qui a gouverné mon travail depuis le commencement, à savoir que les talents les plus ingénieux et les plus patients ne sauraient suppléer le goût du grand et la sainte fureur de l'imagination' (ii. 680). Skill and application are necessary attributes of the successful artist but in themselves they are insufficient without some breadth of scope and ambition and without what Baudelaire here calls the 'sainte fureur' of the imagination. By using this phrase he is overtly aligning himself with the traditional view of the poet as *vates*, a figure most famously depicted in Plato's *Ion*. There the vatic poet is ridiculed and rejected by Socrates as an inadequate alternative to the philosopher-king of the ideal Republic. But for Baudelaire great artists have need of the *furor divinus* if they—and we—are to see things differently. And society needs them.

Baudelaire always resisted any account of poetic 'inspiration' that undersold the critical acumen and conscious effort which he considered necessary to the creative

The Beauty of Baudelaire: The Poet as Alternative Lawgiver. Roger Pearson, Oxford University Press. © Roger Pearson 2021.
DOI: 10.1093/oso/9780192843319.003.0013

act. But equally he always saw technical expertise as secondary to the artist's main purpose: namely, to give expression to an originality of vision. In the *Salon de 1846*, as we saw in Part I, he calls this originality of vision 'naïveté': an 'innocence' and individuality of perspective deriving from the artist's own 'tempérament'. In the case of Delacroix he writes of a painting having to reproduce 'la pensée intime de l'artiste, qui domine le modèle, comme le créateur la création' (ii. 433). Unlike the poetic persona in *Les Contemplations* who presents himself as passively taking dictation, whether from nature itself or from 'la Bouche d'ombre', Baudelaire's artist actively gives voice to his own inner self, imposing his own vision on the real world that he is depicting. He is, as it were, his own source of inspiration, a lawgiver unto himself. When Baudelaire writes in the *Salon de 1846*, again with reference to Delacroix, of the painter's skilled hand executing 'avec une rapidité servile les ordres divins du cerveau: autrement l'idéal s'envole' (ii. 433), such language may suggest the age-old notion of divine inspiration, but now it is the artist's own brain that gives the orders. As to the 'idéal', this is not some Platonic Idea or Form, but a fleeting glimpse of some new pattern or connection within the phenomenal world that must be quickly seized and recorded, something uniquely perceived and constructed—imagined and created—by the artist's own eye and hand. Later, in *Le Peintre de la vie moderne*, Baudelaire will talk of the sketch-artist's fear 'de n'aller pas assez vite, de laisser échapper le fantôme avant que la synthèse n'en soit extraite et assise' and of his desire to have technical command of every expressive device 'pour que jamais les ordres de l'esprit ne soient altérés par les hésitations de la main' (ii. 699).

Here in the *Salon de 1859* the source of these 'ordres divins du cerveau' and these 'ordres de l'esprit' is identified as 'Imagination', a form of authority which is now seen in specifically public and implicitly political terms. In Part I we saw the ambiguity at the heart of Baudelaire's account of the creative act, whereby the work of art springs both from the artist's own individual 'tempérament' but also from the 'laws' of art, which in turn appear to derive from the 'laws' or *nomoi* that govern our shared human experience—and in particular what Baudelaire now calls 'cette grande loi d'harmonie générale' (ii. 626). In the aesthetic manifesto that is the *Salon de 1859*, and unlike in the earlier *Salons*, it is striking how Baudelaire presents 'Imagination' as the answer to a public problem and as offering an alternative form of government. In the first section of the *Salon* he diagnoses what is wrong with the 'modern' artist—namely, a *lack* of imagination: 'Discrédit de l'imagination, mépris du grand, amour (non, ce mot est trop beau), pratique exclusive du métier, telles sont, je crois, quant à l'artiste, les raisons principales de son abaissement' (ii. 612). The artist has been 'abased' by the positivism of the age and is in danger of forfeiting not only self-respect and prestige but the satisfaction of artistic expression itself:

> De jour en jour l'art diminue le respect de lui-même, se prosterne devant la réalité, et le peintre devient de plus en plus enclin à peindre, non pas ce qu'il rêve,

mais ce qu'il voit. Cependant *c'est un bonheur de rêver*, et c'était une gloire d'exprimer ce qu'on rêvait[.]   (ii. 619)

And in the second section Baudelaire blames the general public for the same failing, satirizng them ventriloquially as devotees of naturalistic representation ('Je crois à la nature et je ne crois qu'à la nature (il y a de bonnes raisons pour cela). Je crois que l'art est et ne peut être que la reproduction exacte de la nature' (ii. 617)) while mocking some for the limitations of their devotion: 'une secte timide et dissidente veut que les objets de nature répugnante soient écartés, ainsi qu'un pot de chambre ou un squelette' (ii. 617). Not for them *Les Fleurs du Mal*, then. A nice photograph would be so much better.

But, as we learn in the third section, the true dissident is Baudelaire himself, in his sect of one, a contrarian monarchist subject of 'la reine des facultés' and resistant to the tyrannical decrees of a Second Empire literal-mindedness that is also ventriloquially mocked: '"Nous n'avons pas d'imagination, et nous décrétons que personne n'en aura"' (ii. 620). Its blinkered adepts claim to seek only 'le Vrai' (ii. 616), but what would we say of a scientist who pursued the truth *without* imagination? 'Qu'il a appris tout ce qui, ayant été enseigné, pouvait être appris, mais qu'il ne trouvera pas les lois non encore devinées' (ii. 621). Many new laws of nature will thus remain undiscovered even as the decree of literal-mindedness is itself obeyed. For in fact: 'L'imagination est la reine du vrai, et le *possible* est une des provinces du vrai. Elle est positivement apparenté avec l'infini' (ii. 621). The language here is shot through with the terminology of governance ('lois', 'reine', 'province'), and Baudelaire now builds towards his most radical assertion. Only through imagination do we make sense of the world, and only through imagination, therefore, can we properly establish the laws whereby to live out these understandings. Or, as Baudelaire puts it: imagination has created the world and so has every right to govern it. The divine right of kings has been replaced by the secular right of 'cette reine des facultés' (ii. 620), and this queen has all the power of an army general: 'Mystérieuse faculté que cette reine des facultés! Elle touche à toutes les autres; elle les excite, elle les envoie au combat' (ii. 620). In modern parlance she multi-tasks: 'Elle est l'analyse, elle est la synthèse' (ii. 620).[1]

In fact this queen is a new God, recreating Creation just as Baudelaire now rewrites not only the Book of Genesis but also the opening verse of the Gospel according to St John. In the beginning was the Imagination, and the Imagination was with mankind, and the Imagination *was* mankind. For in the beginning the Imagination enabled us to make sense of our senses:

---

[1] Baudelaire thus combines the binary opposition set out in Shelley's *Defence of Poetry*, substituting his own binary of 'positivism/realism' v. imagination for Shelley's opposition of analytical reason and synthetic imagination. See *Unacknowledged Legislators*, 11.

> C'est l'imagination qui a enseigné à l'homme le sens moral de la couleur, du contour, du son et du parfum. Elle a créé, au commencement du monde, l'analogie et la métaphore. Elle décompose toute la création, et, avec les matériaux amassés et disposés suivant des règles dont on ne peut trouver l'origine que dans le plus profond de l'âme, elle crée un monde nouveau, elle produit la sensation du neuf. (ii. 621)

Without the human imagination the phenomenal world would be a collection of sundry, disparate, and meaningless objects, a piece of cosmic clutter, but instead the individual imagination creates the world afresh according to a new and different legislation that springs not from God but from the depths of the human soul. Thus the imagination may be said to add 'soul' to a soulless world, which (Baudelaire argues) is just what photography cannot do: 'Mais s'il lui [i.e. à la photographie] est permis d'empiéter sur le domaine de l'impalpable et de l'imaginaire, sur tout ce qui ne vaut que parce que l'homme y ajoute de son âme, alors malheur à nous' (ii. 619). And because this queen has created a new world, it is right that she should govern it: 'Comme elle a créé le monde (on peut bien dire cela, je crois même dans un sens religieux), il est juste qu'elle le gouverne' (ii. 621). Whereas in Christian terms the human soul bears witness to the presence of God and the divine hand of the Creator, in Baudelaire's terms the soul is the source of a creation that bears witness to the hand of the artist.

In the *Salon de 1859* Baudelaire thus makes his most explicit and far-reaching assertions to date regarding the poet's new, secular role as alternative lawgiver, and at the end of this section on 'La Reine des facultés' he adds sly emphasis to his passing reference to 'un sens religieux': 'Nous allons entrer plus intimement dans l'examen des fonctions de cette faculté *cardinale* (sa richesse ne rappelle-t-elle pas des idées de pourpre?)' (ii. 623). Instead of the Vatican's cardinals laying down the law of God we shall have the Imagination to govern our world, and instead of cardinal sins (and virtues) we shall look instead to this *cardinal* faculty for our instruction. For Imagination is not only the new Creator but also a moral guide: 'la plus honorable et la plus utile des facultés morales' (ii. 622). Indeed it is the source of a new ethics of empathy:

> Enfin elle joue un rôle puissant même dans la morale; car, permettez-moi d'aller jusque-là, qu'est-ce que la vertu sans imagination? Autant dire la vertu sans la pitié, la vertu sans le ciel; quelque chose de dur, de cruel, de stérilisant, qui, dans certains pays, est devenue la bigoterie, et dans certains autres le protestantisme.
> (ii. 621)

Instead of virtue without sky (or heaven), imagination offers a bigger picture—some blue-sky thinking—for the assessment of human behaviour and one that by implied antitheses conduces to softness, kindness, and fertile creativity.

Imagination thus may be the vehicle for a form of progressiveness ('le *possible* est une des provinces du vrai') that has nothing to do with the 'Progrès' beloved of Hugo and other utopian thinkers: rather, this is progressiveness as an openness to other things and other ways of thinking. For the imagination delights in alternatives. Non-Protestant countries, of course, include Catholic ones, and so the 'bigotry' in question here may belong to those three 'magistrats niais' who, out of a simple lack of imagination, caused Baudelaire to revise *Les Fleurs du Mal*. For a lack of imagination bespeaks a lack of critical acumen, in fact a lack of *judgement*: 'l'imagination, grâce à sa nature suppléante, contient l'esprit critique' (ii. 623). In 'La Reine des facultés' the Imagination is thus presented as a source of creative thinking that can potentially bring intellectual and moral progress and found a new governance based on compassion, understanding, and tolerance.

Imagination and Religion

> Je ne suis pas du tout honteux, mais au contraire très heureux de m'être rencontré avec cette excellente Mme Crowe[.]
>
> (ii. 624)

In the fourth section of the *Salon de 1859*, entitled 'Le Gouvernement de l'imagination', Baudelaire obliquely foregrounds his new agenda by feigning an anxiety that allows him to repeat it (and not just in the section-title therefore) and by appealing to the unlikeliest and most startling of authorities, the English novelist and spiritualist devotee Catherine Crowe, best-selling author of *The Night Side of Nature, or Ghosts and Ghost Seers* (1848):[2]

> Hier soir [Baudelaire tells his commissioning editor],[3] après vous avoir envoyé les dernières pages de ma lettre, où j'avais écrit, mais non sans une certaine timidité: 'Comme l'imagination a créé le monde, elle le gouverne', je feuilletais *La Face nocturne de la Nature* et je tombai sur ces lignes, que je cite uniquement parce qu'elles sont la paraphrase justificative de la ligne qui m'inquiétait.   (ii. 623–4)

By emphasizing his 'timidity' and implying some need to justify his 'worrying' statement, Baudelaire highlights the radical nature of this very proposition (namely, that the imagination has the right to govern the world since it created the world), a proposition whose far-reaching consequences might otherwise perhaps have passed unnoticed by the casual reader, and this despite the

---

[2] On Baudelaire's acquaintance with this work and the question of its influence, if any, on his thought, see ii. 1393–4.
[3] The *Salon de 1859* is subtitled 'Lettres à M. le directeur de la *Revue française*'.

thought-provoking parenthesis 'on peut bien dire cela, je crois, même dans un sens religieux'. Moreover, while repeating his assertion, Baudelaire quietly changes the wording, thereby making it more radical still. In 'La Reine des facultés' he had contended that the imagination, through its capacity to perceive order (analogy, metaphor), had in a sense 'decomposed' the original Creation ('toute la création') and created 'un monde nouveau', and so had the right to govern this new world. But now in repeating the comment he elides the idea of an original, 'preimaginary' Creation and moreover states a fact rather than a potentially legitimate state of affairs: 'Comme l'imagination a créé le monde, elle le gouverne.'[4] One reading of this would be that since imagination alone structures and makes sense of our world, then the imagination itself—the poetic imagination, and not the politicians and sundry other legislators who lay down the law—should govern it. And least of all the Church.

The teasing parenthetical allusion to 'un sens religieux' and the overtly punning description of imagination as 'cette faculté *cardinale*' prepare for the pivotal role of Catherine Crowe. For the true, radical, and unambiguously atheist thrust of Baudelaire's proposition now emerges paradoxically the more clearly for being concealed in the multiple ironies of the 'justification' supposedly provided by 'Mme Crowe'. Baudelaire translates her words as follows:

> Par imagination, je ne veux pas simplement exprimer l'idée commune impliquée dans ce mot dont on fait un si grand abus, laquelle est simplement *fantaisie*, mais bien l'imagination *créatrice*, qui est une fonction beaucoup plus élevée, et qui, en tant que l'homme est fait à la ressemblance de Dieu, garde un rapport éloigné avec cette puissance sublime par laquelle le Créateur conçoit, crée et entretient son univers   (ii. 624);[5]

and he then comments:

---

[4] *Pace* Marcel Raymond who refers to 'l'imagination, que Baudelaire se risque à présenter, dans les deux chapitres-clés du *Salon de 1859*, comme une forme dérivée, dégradée, du pouvoir créateur de Dieu'. See his 'Baudelaire et la sculpture', in *Journées Baudelaire. Actes du colloque [Namur-Bruxelles, 10–13 octobre 1967]* (Brussels: Académie royale de langue et de littérature françaises, 1968), 66–74 (68). *Pace* also Max Milner: 'le surnaturalisme ne saurait être réduit à une reconstruction du monde sans relation avec un ordre transcendant. Cette relation n'est pas la participation analogique à une plénitude entrevue [...] mais le creusement, au sein du langage et grâce à ses pouvoirs métaphoriques, d'une ouverture infinie, qui mime, qui dessine en creux [...] l'agilité originelle et le pouvoir unifiant de l'esprit créateur.' See his 'Baudelaire et le surnaturalisme', 31–49 (47–8).

[5] The original English, quoted by Baudelaire, reads: 'By imagination, I do not simply mean to convey the common notion implied by that much abused word, which is only *fancy*, but the *constructive* imagination which is a much higher function, and which, in as much as man is made in the likeness of God, bears a distant relation to that sublime power by which the Creator projects, creates, and upholds his universe' (ii. 624).

Je ne suis pas du tout honteux, mais au contraire très heureux de m'être rencontré avec cette excellente Mme Crowe, de qui j'ai toujours admiré et envié la faculté de croire, aussi développée en elle que chez d'autres la défiance.

Nowhere here does the enviably God-fearing Catherine Crowe in fact state that imagination governs—or may legimately govern—the world. She merely notes 'a distant relation' between the 'constructive' imagination of the artist and the 'sublime power' of the Creator, a parallel foregrounded by German idealists at the turn of the 18th/19th centuries and to be found subsequently as a commonplace of French Romanticism—and especially, as it so happens, in Hugo's *Les Contemplations*. For Mrs Crowe, on the contrary, it is the Creator who (in her own, English words) 'projects, creates, and upholds his universe'. In fact, therefore—and as Baudelaire's antiphrasis wryly implies—she represents the very opposite of his own view. By saying that he might have been ashamed but isn't of the apparent meeting of minds with this particular writer, he implicitly draws attention to the possible reasons for this shame: this writer is a woman who believes in ghosts, in God! (Perhaps these beliefs are synonymous? Is the Christian Resurrection in fact just a ghost story?) If he has 'admired' her capacity to believe, it is not because he has approved of it but rather because he has (in that other sense of the verb) wondered at it; if he has envied it, then that is because he himself does not believe (in either ghosts or God) and must live the torment of his incredulous melancholy without hope of divine 'upholding' or salvation.[6] The alleged 'meeting' or match between his own statements in 'La Reine des facultés' and the views of Mrs Crowe in fact belies a deeper and fundamental mismatch, and one that the poet is 'très heureux' to acknowledge in order the better to highlight—and with pride—the true nature of his own, secular agenda.

Having thus paid apparent but deeply ironic homage to this obscure spokesperson for a form of Christian orthodoxy, Baudelaire now turns to another source of wisdom in the shape of Delacroix, whom he nevertheless here omits to name explicitly—artfully implying that to cite a known religious sceptic such as Delacroix might here be impolitic, but thus foregrounding that scepticism by his own very discretion. Accordingly Baudelaire simply expounds the aesthetic theory of some anonymous 'homme vraiment savant et profond' (ii. 624) in order to set out his own theory of the imagination, which is predicated on a godless universe without intrinsic meaning. According to the unnamed Delacroix 'La nature n'est qu'un dictionnaire' (ii. 624),[7] a comment Baudelaire explicates first from the point of view of writing. Writers use a dictionary to ascertain the meaning(s) and origins

---

[6] Cf. Baudelaire's letter to his mother of 6 May 1861: 'Je désire de tout mon cœur (avec quelle sincérité, personne ne peut le savoir que moi!) croire qu'un être extérieur et invisible s'intéresse à ma destinée; mais comment faire pour le croire?' (*Corr.*, ii. 151).

[7] Cf. *Salon de 1846*: 'Pour E. Delacroix, la nature est un vaste dictionnaire dont il roule et consulte les feuillets avec un œil sûr et profond' (ii. 433).

of a given word, extracting from it the various components with which they may best express a meaning or tell a story. But the dictionary is not itself 'une composition dans le sens poétique du mot' (ii. 624).

Similarly for the painter the disparate constituents of the phenomenal world are as a vocabulary. Some artists—landscape artists, for example—will choose (as is alleged of literary realists) to depict simply what they see, as though copying words from the dictionary, suppressing their own personality in the name of faithfulness to reality but thereby committing 'un très grand vice, le vice de la banalité' (ii. 625). Great painters, by contrast, draw on the vocabulary contained within the dictionary of nature to 'translate' 'le langage du rêve' (ii. 625), starting from an 'idée génératrice' (ii. 625) and then composing their work (like a poem) according to 'cette grande loi d'harmonie générale' (ii. 626).[8] Indeed they allow themselves to be *governed* by the imagination. For the 'idée génératrice' to manifest itself most fully, this kind of painter allows one colour or tonality to dictate or call up another according to a precise logic of compatibility ('la loi sympathique qui les a associés' (ii. 626)) that is inherent in colour ('L'art du coloriste tient évidemment par de certains côtés aux mathématiques et à la musique' (ii. 625)). By following the laws inherent in art itself, artists each find the best means of expression for the unique 'lawgiving' of their own individual vision of the world, of their own 'creation'.

What seems here to be a straightforward analogy between writing and painting nevertheless masks a persistent and radical 'sens religieux' as Baudelaire continues to focus on this question of creation. Whereas Chateaubriand or Lamartine or Hugo believed in one original Creation that it is the poet's task to explore and celebrate through the art of poetry, Baudelaire is quite adamant that creations issue from the imagination of the beholder. His Genesis—'l'idée génératrice'— takes place in the artist's mind, as a 'dream' or vision that must be brought into being, 'created': 'Un bon tableau, fidèle au rêve qui l'a enfanté, doit être produit comme un monde' (ii. 626). Accordingly there is no one single Creation but multiple creations, a process of layering, indeed almost a process of evolution:

> De même que la création, telle que nous la voyons, est le résultat de plusieurs créations dont les précédentes sont toujours complétées par la suivante; ainsi un tableau conduit harmoniquement consiste en une série de tableaux superposés, chaque nouvelle couche donnant au rêve plus de réalité et le faisant monter d'un degré vers la perfection.' (ii. 626)

---

[8] Baudelaire repeats this analogy in his later section on landscape painters: 'La plupart [...] prennent le dictionnaire de l'art pour l'art lui-même; ils copient un mot du dictionnaire, croyant copier un poème. Or un poème ne se copie jamais: il veut être composé' (ii. 660-1).

Rather than some original divine perfection which the artist is unable to reproduce (as lamented, for example, in Lamartine's poem 'Dieu'), Baudelaire posits a perfection as the *endpoint* of a process of insistent work and harmonic superimposition: not a lost paradise, therefore, but an eventual palimpsest bearing witness to the unique and original vision of the artist and the various successive stages of the 'translation' by which the artist's dream becomes a figured reality.[9] How this process actually plays out will depend on 'le tempérament varié des artistes' (ii. 626), and there are various rules of thumb (as discussed earlier in Part I above) that will aid 'l'éclosion de l'originalité' (ii. 627). But the 'formule principale' is this:

> Tout l'univers visible n'est qu'un magasin d'images et de signes auxquels l'imagination donnera une place et une valeur relative; c'est une espèce de pâture que l'imagination doit digérer et transformer. Toutes les facultés de l'âme humaine doivent être subordonnées à l'imagination, qui les met en réquisition toutes à la fois. (ii. 627)

Artistic creation is thus a digestive process, during which the queen of faculties will enlist the others—our faculties of sight, hearing, taste, smell, and touch, of memory and reason—in the service of her governance. Imagination is the ultimate authority, a general sending troops into battle and now a commanding officer with the power to requisition—the power to govern.

Baudelaire ends the section on 'Le Gouvernement de l'imagination' by identifying two principal categories of artist: the 'réaliste' or 'positiviste', and the 'imaginatif'. The first simply says: 'Je veux représenter les choses telles qu'elles sont, ou bien qu'elles seraient, en supposant que je n'existe pas.' In other words: 'L'univers sans l'homme.' The second, by contrast, asserts: 'Je veux illuminer les choses avec mon esprit et en projeter le reflet sur les autres esprits' (ii. 627). This simple and traditional opposition[10] sets up an important dynamic that informs the remainder of the *Salon de 1859*, in which the Imagination's power to govern becomes the central theme. On the one hand, we have those artists who accept to represent things as they are—as it were, the status quo—and, on the other, we have those artists who can change the way we experience the world, and in particular the way in which we experience melancholy. In the next-but-one section, on portrait painting, the former category is associated with 'l'Âme de la Bourgeoisie'—'cette vilaine Âme, qui n'est pas une hallucination'—and the voice

---

[9] Cf. Baudelaire's eulogy of Delacroix in the following section: 'On pourrait dire que, doué d'une plus riche imagination, il exprime surtout l'intime du cerveau, l'aspect étonnant des choses, tant son ouvrage garde fidèlement la marque et l'humeur de sa conception. C'est l'infini dans le fini. C'est le rêve!' (ii. 636).
[10] See M. H. Abrams, *The Mirror and the Lamp: Romantic Theory and the Critical Tradition* (London, Oxford, and New York: Oxford University Press, 1971 [first published 1953]), *passim*.

of literal-mindedness that thinks a portrait is just a quasi-photographic likeness requiring neither effort nor skill. 'En vérité', the bourgeois sighs:

> les poètes sont de singuliers fous de prétendre que l'imagination soit nécessaire dans toutes les fonctions de l'art. Qu'est-il besoin d'imagination, par exemple, pour faire un portrait? Pour peindre mon âme, mon âme si visible, si claire, si notoire? Je pose, et en réalité c'est moi, le modèle, qui consens à faire le gros de la besogne. Je suis le véritable fournisseur de l'artiste. Je suis, à moi tout seul, toute la matière. (ii. 654)

With nice irony Baudelaire plays on the word 'matière' (subject matter) to make of this ugly bourgeois soul the voice of brute matter itself, and wryly notes: 'plus la matière est, en apparence, positive et solide, et plus la besogne de l'imagination est subtile et laborieuse' (ii. 655). The portrait-artist's subject requires to be imagined and created—'governed'—just as much as the brute matter of a landscape. And yes, Baudelaire asserts in the following section, 'l'imagination fait le paysage' (ii. 665); and indeed 'la plupart de nos paysagistes sont des menteurs, justement parce qu'ils ont négligé de mentir' (ii. 668). It is possible to conceive of a landscape without a human presence, but a landscape ('un assemblage de matière végétale ou minérale') needs 'un contemplateur pour en extraire la comparaison, la métaphore et l'allégorie' (ii. 660).

The use of the term 'contemplateur' here (rather than, say, 'observateur') suggests a possible further allusion to *Les Contemplations*, and here indeed Baudelaire appears to concede the Hugolian (and Christian) view that order exists in the universe independently of the observer. But he quickly turns aside any idea of divine providence by insisting that it is only the fortunate possibility of intelligent human perception that permits such order to exist: 'Il est certain que tout cet ordre et toute cette harmonie n'en gardent pas moins la qualité inspiratrice qui y est providentiellement déposée; mais, dans ce cas, faute d'une intelligence qu'elle pût inspirer, cette qualité serait comme si elle n'était pas' (ii. 660). Once again we have the idea that the imagination 'creates' the world: the landscape, in reality as in painting, comes into being 'par moi, par ma grâce propre, par l'idée ou le sentiment que j'y attache' (ii. 660). Not by the grace of God, therefore, but by the grace of the artist, by the artist's ability to 'translate' (ii. 660) an idea or feeling through the articulation of brute matter. Nature in itself is of no consequence: 'un site naturel n'a de valeur que le sentiment actuel que l'artiste y sait mettre' (ii. 660): 'il faut que tout cela devienne tableau par le moyen de l'impression poétique rappelée à volonté' (ii. 665).[11]

---

[11] The resemblance of this statement to the better-known definitions of genius as childhood (vision) recalled at will suggests that Baudelaire considers 'l'impression poétique' to be synonymous with a childlike innocence, or 'naïveté', of perception. The artist's imagination has to 'unlearn' its habitual perceptions in order to shed new and transformative light.

Imagination and Freedom

> Ainsi l'art est le seul domaine spirituel où l'homme puisse dire: "Je croirai si je veux, et si je ne veux pas, je ne croirai pas". (ii. 629)

Just as Baudelaire uses the transition from the third to the fourth sections (or letters) of the *Salon de 1859* to foreground the religious consequences of his aesthetic by a simulated timidity and a mock deference towards 'l'excellente Mme Crowe', so as he moves from 'Le Gouvernement de l'imagination' to the long section entitled 'Religion, histoire, fantaisie' he foregrounds his atheism while mock-disclaiming it:

> Disons donc simplement que la religion étant la plus haute *fiction* de l'esprit humain (je parle exprès comme parlerait un athée professeur de beaux-arts, et rien n'en doit être conclu contre ma foi) elle se réclame de ceux qui se vouent à l'expression de ses actes et de ses sentiments l'imagination la plus vigoureuse et les efforts les plus tendus. (ii. 628–9)

Already the title of the section quietly implies by its collocation with 'fantaisie' a scepticism about the objective truth of religion and history, a scepticism here further highlighted by the emphasis on 'fiction' and the implication of 'la plus haute *fiction*' that the human mind has produced many others. This scepticism is then developed in an account of religious painting that begins, characteristically, with a discussion of writing (here the poetic and dramatic art of Corneille's *Polyeucte*). Having ridiculed those who believe the function of art to be the accurate representation of 'things as they are', Baudelaire now implicitly draws a parallel with the literal-mindedness of those who consider that religious art can be successfully produced only by those who have religious faith: 'Erreur qui pourrait être philosophiquement démontrée, si les faits ne nous prouvaient pas suffisamment le contraire, et si l'histoire de la peinture ne nous offrait pas des artistes impies et athées produisant d'excellentes œuvres religieuses' (ii. 628). For, Baudelaire implies, 'religion' is no less of a fiction than the supposedly objective character of the phenomenal world assumed by the realist or positivist artist. The artist does not simply copy or record, but imagines—and performs his imaginings.

The dramatic role of Polyeucte, Baudelaire contends, initially required of the dramatist—and continues to require of the actor playing the part of this Christian martyr—'une ascension spirituelle et un enthousiasme beaucoup plus vif que tel personnage vulgaire épris d'une vulgaire créature de la terre, ou même qu'un héros purement politique' (ii. 629). And Baudelaire recalls the 'double agency' theory of *De l'essence du rire* in order to argue that an apparent sincerity of religious faith (like the faith of the lover, or the faith of the 'purely political hero') may—and certainly can—derive less from genuine conviction than from the need to convince:

> La seule concession qu'on puisse raisonnablement faire aux partisans de la théorie qui considère la foi comme l'unique source d'inspiration religieuse, est que le poète, le comédien et l'artiste, au moment où ils exécutent l'ouvrage en question, croient à la réalité de ce qu'ils représentent, échauffés qu'ils sont par la nécessité. (ii. 629)

In other words, the work of art (or the lover's declaration or the politician's oratory) is a performance born of the imagination and independent of any religious (or emotional, or political) belief on the part of the artist: 'Plus d'un écrivain religieux, naturellement enclin, comme les écrivains démocrates, à suspendre le beau à la croyance, n'a pas manqué d'attribuer à l'absence de foi cette difficulté d'exprimer les choses de la foi' (ii. 628). Art is a matter not of urgent and ostensibly objective truth (as the religious or politically engagé writer believes or implies) but a matter of imagination and expression and thus a domain of mental and spiritual freedom: 'Ainsi l'art est le seul domaine spirituel où l'homme puisse dire: "Je croirai si je veux, et si je ne veux pas, je ne croirai pas". La cruelle et humiliante maxime: "Spiritus flat ubi vult", perd ses droits en matière d'art' (ii. 629). The reference here is to the words addressed in John 3: 8 by Jesus to Nicodemus, 'a ruler of the Jews' and 'a master of Israel', who has come as the representative of a secular political and intellectually learned authority to investigate Christ's ability to perform miracles and indeed to acknowledge the divine source of this ability: 'for no man can do these miracles that thou doest, except God be with him' (3: 2) In his reply Christ asserts God's mysterious and unknowable power over mankind, the power of 'the Spirit': 'The wind bloweth where it listeth, and thou hearest the sound thereof, but canst not tell whence it cometh, and wither it goeth: so is everyone that is born of the Spirit.' But for Baudelaire this insistence on human ignorance and dependency is 'cruel' and 'humiliating': the imagination, not God, governs the world.[12]

But this freedom of the Imagination to believe what it will is not untrammelled, as Baudelaire makes clear in his remarks about 'fantaisie'. He introduces the term strategically, seemingly to cover a whole range of paintings at the Salon that do not fall under the conventional headings of 'religion', 'histoire', 'portrait', and 'paysage' but more importantly to highlight the true nature of the Imagination. He rejects the term 'peinture de genre' ('genre painting', or the depiction of

---

[12] For Hugo's take on John 3: 8, see 'Promontorium somniii', 651–2, and *Unacknowledged Legislators*, 496.

scenes from everyday life) as implying 'un certain prosaïsme' (ii. 644) and also the term 'peinture romanesque' as excluding the fantastic, and so plumps for 'fantaisie' while observing that this category demands the greatest caution and discrimination on the part of the viewer or critic: 'car la fantaisie est d'autant plus dangereuse qu'elle est plus facile et plus ouverte' (ii. 644). But this call for a disciplined severity of judgement acquires a suspect character in the light of the very analogies imaginatively employed to represent such 'fantaisie':

> dangereuse comme la poésie en prose, comme le roman, elle ressemble à l'amour qu'inspire une prostituée et qui tombe bien vite dans la puérilité ou dans la bassesse; dangereuse comme toute liberté absolue. (ii. 644)

Is the writer who had published his own first (two) prose poems in 1855 and four more in 1857 quietly mocking conservative disapproval of his aesthetic licence (and perhaps by implication—'comme le roman'—also of the alleged impropriety of Flaubert's *Madame Bovary*) by comparing his generic 'promiscuity' with the immaturity and base actions of a man of loose morals? Perhaps so, since he continues now with 'Mais' (rather than 'Car') as he embarks on a genuine critique of 'absolute licence':

> Mais la fantaisie est vaste comme l'univers multiplié par tous les êtres pensants qui l'habitent. Elle est la première chose venue interprétée par le premier venu; et, si celui-là n'a pas l'âme qui jette une lumière magique et surnaturelle sur l'obscurité naturelle des choses, elle est une inutilité horrible, elle est la première venue souillée par le premier venu. Ici donc, plus d'analogie, sinon de hasard; mais au contraire trouble et contraste, un champ bariolé par l'absence d'une culture régulière. (ii. 644–5)

Yes, Baudelaire is saying, the free play of the imagination is risky, but not because it can lead to genre-bending or allegedly naughty novels: rather, because it can produce the more terrible promiscuity of random associations, like some scruffy, motley field that could do with some regular ploughing and cultivation. Good art requires the presence of a 'soul' that is able to cast 'une lumière magique et surnaturelle sur l'obscurité naturelle des choses'. Artists can believe or not believe entirely as they please—in God, in democracy, in love, in prostitutes—but they must above all have the power to lighten the darkness of our obscure and contingent universe by creating analogies—pattern, order, meaningfulness— that transcend the messy, pointless juxtapositions of nature (by being 'surnaturelle') and effect a process of transformation that is at once wonderful and not immediately explicable (by being 'magique'). Where the 'réaliste' or 'positiviste' meekly accepts the status quo, the 'imaginatif' possesses the militant power to change our perceptions. In that sense the artist both creates and governs the world we live in.

Imagination and Sculpture

> Le fantôme de pierre [...] vous commande, au nom du passé, de penser aux choses qui ne sont pas de la terre.
>
> (ii. 670)

Not only do artists both create and govern the world we live in but, even better, they can take us 'Any where out of the world', as the title of the ante-penultimate prose poem in *Le Spleen de Paris* imperfectly has it[13]—an aesthetic possibility which, perhaps surprisingly, Baudelaire here associates with sculpture. In the *Salon de 1846* he had condemned this art form as 'ennuyeuse': partly on the grounds that the material substance of a sculpture is '[b]rutale et positive comme la nature' (ii. 487), and partly, he argues also, because the artist cannot control the ways in which the sculpture is seen. The sculptor tries (allegedly) to create from 'un point de vue unique' (ii. 487), but the observer's ability to move round a sculpture potentially allows the work to be viewed from 'cent points de vue différents, excepté le bon' (ii. 487). Chance effects of lighting may even permit the discovery of a beauty in the work that the artist had not intended. A painting, by contrast, imposes the artist's unique vision on the viewer: 'La peinture n'a qu'un point de vue; elle est exclusive et despotique: aussi l'expression du peintre est-elle bien plus forte' (ii. 487). But in the *Salon de 1859* this idea of a 'despotic' perspective being imposed by the artist is the very opposite of what Baudelaire now values: namely, the power of the work of art to inspire the imagination of the spectator (or listener or reader). In 1846 Baudelaire cared most about the originality of the artist's vision and the importance of getting the spectator to see it and share in it. But now, with a much more developed sense that beauty is an effect, he cares most about the nature of that effect—and the power of the imagination, as a form of libertarian, non-despotic government—to provoke wonder and speculative reflection.

For that reason it should not be seen as surprising that Baudelaire ends the *Salon de 1859* by dwelling on the capacity of sculpture to convey us in our imagination beyond the here and now. Relying on the very materiality of the earth as its medium, sculpture could be said to pose the greatest challenge to the

---

[13] The title is a quotation from Thomas Hood's poem 'The Bridge of Sighs' (1844) in which a homeless prostitute throws herself off Waterloo Bridge, a poem Baudelaire himself translated. See i. 1348. Also i. 269–71 and i. 1292. Cf. ii. 1399 on the reference to Hood in the *Salon de 1859* (ii. 638).

artist who wishes to transcend mere mimesis and, as Baudelaire puts it in 'La Mort des artistes', 'piquer dans le but, de mystique nature'.[14] Hence the reference in the *Salons* of both 1846 and 1859 (ii. 487, 671) to the facile delight taken by the unsophisticated in a piece of finely shaped wood or stone as opposed to the perplexity with which they respond to the less tangible representations of painting: 'Il y a là un mystère singulier qui ne se touche pas avec les doigts' (ii. 487). In 'La Mort des artistes'—with which the 1857 *Les Fleurs du Mal* ends but the 1861 edition will not—sculpture serves as a metaphor for the construction of an imaginary ideal, for our terrestrial dreams, that can never be realized on earth. The only hope left to us is that our 'brain-flowers' (l. 14) may bloom beyond death in the sunlight of the hereafter: that is to say, that the melancholy of the human condition is indeed 'irremediable' within the here and now. For this reason the change in Baudelaire's approach to sculpture in the *Salon de 1859* betokens a radically new faith in the remedial role of the Imagination in its encounter with 'le Mal'.

'Sculpture', the penultimate section of the *Salon de 1859* but followed only by a relatively brief 'Envoi', opens by painting word-pictures of a virtual sculpture park, a kind of 'musée imaginaire'. Where the Salon of 1859 was actually held in the Palais des Beaux-Arts on the avenue Montaigne in Paris, Baudelaire now takes his reader on an allegorical guided tour (ii. 669–70). Moreover, and as in the discussions of religious painting and, previously, of nature as the artist's dictionary, he begins (as indeed he will end) by foregrounding the medium of writing:

> Au fond d'une bibliothèque antique, dans le demi-jour propice qui caresse et suggère les longues pensées, Harpocrate, debout et solennel, un doigt posé sur sa bouche, vous commande le silence, et, comme un pédagogue pythagoricien, vous dit: Chut! avec un geste plein d'autorité. Apollon et les Muses, fantômes impérieux, dont les formes divines éclatent dans la pénombre, surveillent vos pensées, assistant à vos travaux, et vous encouragent au sublime.

Here, in a symbolic penumbral interior setting, removed from the outside world and surrounded by books, the studious reader (and writer)—the poet himself no doubt, but he does say 'vous' and so it could be 'nous'—is encouraged by the mythical authorities of ancient Greece to contemplate the sublime. Here in sculpted form are Harpocrates, the god of silence and of the 'Quiet, please' to be found in every library; of Apollo, the god of music and poetry and leader of the Muses; and, more obliquely present (in the figure with whom Harpocrates is compared), a teacher versed in the thought of Pythagoras—concerning the music of the spheres, perhaps, or that belief so central to Hugo's *Les Contemplations*, the possibility of metempsychosis or the transmigration of souls. Here are the poet's lares: imperious, authoritative, pedagogical figures, lawgivers all, standing watch

---

[14] In the 1857 version of 'La Mort des artistes' this line reads 'dans le but, mystique quadrature'.

over a poet's journey towards the 'sublime', towards something higher, something beyond the material, something else.

Outside, in a similarly penumbral and no less symbolic setting ('Au détour d'un bosquet, abritée sous de lourds ombrages'), stands a sculptured representation of the human condition: 'l'éternelle Mélancolie mire son visage auguste dans les eaux d'un bassin, immobiles comme elle'. The potential third-person observer of this sculpture is neither the poet nor 'vous' but could once again be each of us: 'Et le rêveur qui passe, attristé et charmé, contemplant cette grande figure aux membres robustes, mais alanguis par une peine secrète, dit: Voilà, ma sœur!' From this shady grove of many a Romantic sigh we then pass into an urban churchyard and the realm of death, presided over by 'la figure prodigeuse du Deuil'. At this point our imaginary guide, himself a lawgiver—and indeed a kind of ghost-writer—firmly directs our steps away from notions of Catholic sinfulness and the hurly-burly of our quotidian lives, and has us stop to reflect on mortality and the prospect of eternity:

> Avant de vous jeter dans le confessionnal, au fond de cette petite chapelle ébranlée par le trot des omnibus, vous êtes arrêté par un fantôme décharné et magnifique, qui soulève discrètement l'énorme couvercle de son sépulcre pour vous supplier, créature passagère, de penser à l'éternité!

Having deferred entry into the confessional and perhaps never entered it, we move from the church to visit the churchyard cemetery and are then bidden by the 'prodigieuse' sculpture of Mourning (as we shall see, itself a teacher) to reflect, in traditional terms, on the vanity of terrestrial ambitions and, in much less traditional and in fact writerly terms, to consider what lies beyond or 'out of' our mortal existence, a *je ne sais quoi*:

> Et au coin de cette allée fleurie qui mène à la sépulture de ceux qui vous sont chers, la figure prodigieuse du Deuil, prostrée, échevelée, noyée dans le ruisseau des ses larmes, écrasant de sa lourde désolation les restes poudreux d'un homme illustre, vous *enseigne* que richesse, gloire, patrie même, sont de pures frivolités, devant ce je ne sais quoi que personne n'a nommé ni défini, que l'homme n'exprime que par des adverbes mystérieux, tels que: peut-être, jamais, toujours! et qui contient, quelques-uns l'espèrent, la béatitude infinie, tant désirée, ou l'angoisse sans trêve dont la raison moderne repousse l'image avec le geste convulsif de l'agonie. (my emphasis)

Here Baudelaire implicitly recalls his earlier reference to religion as 'la plus haute *fiction* de l'esprit humain' and relativizes the Christian belief in eternal blessedness or eternal damnation (itself now rejected with horror, he contends, by a more rationalist tendency in contemporary thinking) as mere versions of a fundamental uncertainty about what lies beyond our temporal existence: a perhaps, a never, and an always. a *je ne sais quoi* that we cannot name or define but to which we can allude through art, whether through the silence of expressive sculpture or with the verbal language of poetry. As though to underline how art, not religion, can best speak to our sense of ontological mystery, Baudelaire's imaginary tour-guide now bids us be 'charmed' (and 'charm' derives etymologically from 'carmen' = song) by the music of fountains, to be nursed by them and further 'charmed' by the goddess of love and the goddess of eternal youth back into the domain of life and of the love from which new life is born:

> L'esprit charmé par la musique des eaux jaillissantes, plus douce que la voix des nourrices, vous tombez dans un boudoir de verdure, où Vénus et Hébé, déesses badines qui présidèrent quelquefois à votre vie, étalent sous des alcôves de feuillages les rondeurs de leurs membres charmants qui ont puisé dans la fournaise le rose éclat de la vie.

And finally, says our guide, wherever we look in life for the presence of sculpture we shall find it inviting us to look beyond life, not into the non-life of marmoreal death but into the other life of a real past and an imagined elsewhere. As we walk the streets of an ancient city—'une de celles qui contiennent les archives les plus importantes de la vie universelle'—our eyes will be drawn upwards and starwards ('sursum, ad sidera') into reflection upon human striving down the ages, and we will listen to innumerable stories being silently told:

> sur les places publiques, aux angles des carrefours, des personnages immobiles, plus grands que ceux qui passent à leurs pieds, vous racontent dans un langage muet les pompeuses légendes de la gloire, de la guerre, de la science et du martyre. Les uns montrent le ciel, où ils ont sans cesse aspiré; les autres désignent le sol où ils se sont élancés.

Now the ghost invites us, from out of the past, to reflect not on the future (and the eternity of death) but on the present, a present that has another dimension:

> Fussiez-vous le plus insouciant des hommes, le plus malheureux ou le plus vil, mendiant ou banquier, le fantôme de pierre s'empare de vous pendant quelques minutes, et vous commande, au nom du passé, de penser aux choses qui ne sont pas de la terre.

'Tel est le rôle divin de la sculpture', Baudelaire concludes, and he might have added: 'et de la poésie'. 'Qui ne peut douter', he continues, 'qu'une puissante imagination ne soit nécessaire pour remplir un si magnifique programme?' But from the realm of Baudelaire's prose allegory and his own flight of imagination we are now brought back to a sad reality, and the whole tenor of the remaining pages on sculpture, as throughout the *Salon de 1859*, is that contemporary artists are incapable of fulfilling this 'magnifique programme'. Not only do modern sculptors unduly privilege marble over bronze and clay as their chosen medium (ii. 670), but the majority simply lack the necessary imagination to lend brute matter the expressive power to be found in the sculptures of old ('des œuvres dont l'esprit s'étonne' (ii. 670)). *That* sculpture had the power of lyric poetry:

> Quelle force prodigieuse l'Égypte, la Grèce, Michel-Ange, Coustou et quelques autres ont mises dans ces fantômes immobiles! Quel regard dans ces yeux sans prunelle! De même que la poésie lyrique ennoblit tout, même la passion, la sculpture, la vraie, solennise tout, même le mouvement; elle donne à tout ce qui est humain quelque chose d'éternel et qui participe de la dureté et de la matière employée. (ii. 671)

We begin to see here the seeds of Baudelaire's famous definition of aesthetic modernity in *Le Peintre de la vie moderne* (1863): 'La modernité, le transitoire, le fugitif, le contingent, la moitié de l'art, dont l'autre moitié est l'éternel et l'immuable' (ii. 695). The purpose of art, whether in sculpture or poetry, is to approach the ephemera of everyday life ('le trot des omnibus')[15] with 'le goût du grand', to spot connections and similarities and patterns that point to a broader, timeless context, the bigger picture: what here in the *Salon de 1859* (ii. 621) as in 'Hymne à la Beauté' (l. 24) Baudelaire calls 'l'infini'. But for now, in the realm of sculpture, the requisite 'imagination profonde [...] fait trop souvent défaut' (ii. 672). Yes, there are exceptions—Franceschi's *Andromède*, Clésinger's *Taureau romain*, Just Becquet's *Saint Sébastien*—but in general there is a marked failure to meet those 'deux conditions essentielles' established by Poe: 'l'unité d'impression et la totalité d'effet' (ii. 674). Indeed the best of modern sculpture is missing from the exhibition: for example, two works by Ernest Christophe—*La Comédie humaine* and *Le Squelette*—which Baudelaire had seen in the artist's studio and about which he has written poems from which he here quotes: respectively, 'Le Masque' and 'Danse macabre', both first published in 1859 and subsequently included in the 1861 *Les Fleurs du Mal*.

Thus in the *Salon de 1859* Baudelaire ends his discussion of contemporary art with an ironic performative act: to see the best sculptures of the day we must imagine them, and in order to imagine them we have need of words, his own words, and in particular his own poetic words. The writerly work undertaken in the library at the beginning of this section is complete and now itself points to a

---

[15] Cf. 'Les Petites Vieilles', ll. 9–10: 'Ils rampent, flagellés par les bises iniques, | Frémissant au fracas roulant des omnibus'.

bigger picture. In 'La Mort des artistes' the art of sculpture constitutes a metaphor for melancholy and 'le Mal' in that it represents doomed desire:[16]

> Nous userons notre âme en de subtils complots,
> Et nous démolirons mainte lourde armature,
> Avant de contempler la grande Créature
> Dont l'infernal désir nous remplit de sanglots!
>
> (ll. 5–8)

The 'armature' being the wooden or metal support around which the sculpture is constructed, the pursuit of a desired object, whether in life or in art, is thus seen to involve (because we despair of success) the repeated destruction of the means by which we hope to achieve it. 'Creation', then, is a process of repeated acts of demolition and repeated new beginnings, and, for some, failure is inevitable:

> Il en est qui jamais n'ont connu leur Idole,
> Et ces sculpteurs damnés et marqués d'un affront,
> Qui vont se martelant la poitrine et le front,
>
> N'ont qu'un espoir, étrange et sombre Capitole!
> C'est que la Mort, planant comme un soleil nouveau,
> Fera s'épanouir les fleurs de leur cerveau!
>
> (ll. 9–14)

Only in the life hereafter will the pursued ideal be found and the sobs of melancholy finally cease. But here at the end of the *Salon de 1859*, and once again in relation to sculpture, Baudelaire suggests the possibility of overcoming melancholy through beauty, through the imagination. If melancholy derives from a sense of lack and impossibility, the experience of beauty—as an *effect*—derives from a sense of connection and meaningfulness, from the sense that the disparate elements of a contingent here and now can and do belong within some larger pattern. Where melancholy sees only transience and destruction, beauty is the experience of construction and permanence—a construction carried out by the imagination and a permanence provided by the medium of art. In 'Sculpture' Baudelaire's allegorical promenade takes us away from melancholy and death and the black emptiness of the after-death, and *back* towards life, whether it be the 'furnace' of sexual passion and 'le rose éclat de la vie' that brings colour to the 'membres charmants' of Venus and Hebe in their 'boudoir de verdure' (ii. 670), or the '*vitaï lampada*' (the torches of life) that illuminate the public sphere and its

---

[16] First published in 1851 and then significantly revised in the version that was placed at the end of the 1857 *Les Fleurs du Mal*, this poem takes sculpture as a paradigm of failed ambition in both versions.

emblematic instruments of human exploit: 'un outil, une épée, un livre, une torche' (ii. 670). And each 'fantôme de pierre', like a poem, calls on us to 'penser aux choses qui ne sont pas de la terre': to think not of what comes after but of what else there is or might be within the bigger picture of a *different* world. As Baudelaire puts it in 'Puisque réalisme il y a': 'La Poésie est ce qu'il y a de plus réel, c'est ce qui n'est complètement vrai que *dans un autre monde*' (ii. 59). 'L'autre monde' may be the term often used for the life hereafter within a Christian context, but here we have '*un* autre monde': another world, another sort of world, an alternative world, opened up to our blinkered and habituated perception by the imagination of an artist.

In this respect Baudelaire's inclusion of his own poems at the end of 'Sculpture' is instructive in another way. In relation to 'Danse macabre' (based on Christophe's sculpture 'Le Squelette') he writes specifically of his intention 'non pas d'*illustrer*, mais d'expliquer le plaisir subtil contenu dans cette figurine, à peu près comme un lecteur soigneux barbouille de crayon les marges de son livre' (ii. 679). Like Baudelaire the poet and like his ideal artist, Baudelaire the critic is not simply describing, 'illustrating', the statue, but metaphorically scribbling in its margins: he is not simply reproducing the world as it is ('puisque réalisme il y a') but annotating it (like a studious reader in that statue-filled library) and seeking to convey some of the 'plaisir subtil' it offers. The sculpture, or figurine, in question here is of a female skeleton all dressed up for a party. As Marcel Raymond has noted, the human skeleton is our own 'armature' and was for Baudelaire an object of increasing fascination. Indeed just before discussing Christophe's sculptures, Baudelaire also mentions Hébert's miniature sculpture of a young girl being kissed by a skeleton and refers to the latter as 'comme le plan du poème humain' (ii. 678).

For Raymond, Baudelaire's sculptures—his 'fantômes de pierre'—are all embodiments of what Baudelaire himself in describing Hébert's work calls 'l'idée vaste et flottante du néant': 'son fantôme est *plein de vide*' (ii. 678). Thus Raymond concludes: 'Dans son idée nouvelle de la sculpture, Baudelaire a rencontré de quoi satisfaire à la fois sa hantise de la condition mortelle de l'homme, son désir des choses qui ne sont pas de la terre, son besoin de réclamer sans cesse "l'application de l'imagination, l'introduction de la poésie dans toutes les fonctions de l'art"'.[17] But one might argue instead that for Baudelaire sculpture represents not so much the capacity of art to represent the 'néant' as the power of the imagination to incorporate death—and therefore melancholy—within life. As the skeleton supports our flesh and acts 'comme un plan du poème humain', so the fact of our mortality is the framework around which we must build our lives: not a cause for melancholy and despair, but a fact of life. As in the allegorical promenade and as in 'Danse macabre' poetry can take us from death back to life, from decay and

---

[17] See Raymond, 'Baudelaire et la sculpture', 74.

destruction and nothingness to a myriad imagined constructions and reconstructions of our terrestrial circumstances. After all, for the non-believer it is a skeleton not a soul that remains after death, and the skeleton not as a *memento mori* but as a *memento vitae*, a memory of the 'poème humain'. So, too, is a poem in verse or prose. Just as Baudelaire's city sculptures are not figures of emptiness but emblems of eloquence that tell of human endeavour and constitute essential parts of 'les archives les plus importantes de la vie universelle', so too for him poetry records the work of the poet's imagination and perpetuates its fleshed-out visions upon the skeletal armature of prosody. Poe had spoken of beauty as 'an ecstatic prescience of the glories beyond the grave'[18] and thus as a kind of foreknowledge: in Baudelaire's eyes beauty derives from a glimpsed knowledge of alternative glories before and besides the grave. For this reason imagination has the power to govern melancholy, and this, as we shall now see, because it can furnish the directionless desert of ennui with new, flower-filled avenues of conjecture.

[18] See below, Chapter 13 n. 2.

13
Imagination and Conjecture
Gautier and Hugo

> Je m'attache à ce mot 'conjecture', qui sert à définir, passablement, le caractère extra-scientifique de toute poésie.
>
> ('Victor Hugo', ii. 139)
>
> les conjectures éternelles de la curieuse humanité.
>
> ('Victor Hugo', ii. 139)

Melancholy and Imagination: Beyond Poe

> J'ai trouvé la définition du Beau—de mon Beau. C'est quelque chose d'ardent et de triste, quelque chose d'un peu vague, laissant carrière à la conjecture.
>
> (*Fusées*, f. 16)

Melancholy is marked by an experience of lack: of not having, of no longer having, of rather not having, of not worth having. Being characterized by an oppressive sense of familiarity and sameness, of habit and routine, it manifests in one especial symptom: 'l'ennui, fruit de la morne incuriosité' ('J'ai plus de souvenirs...', l. 17). Art, on the other hand—painting, sculpture, poetry, music—can rekindle curiosity through the work of the creative imagination and in so doing make the world seem (for artist and art-lover alike) a new and interesting place, no longer a hell of ill-being but a place in which it is good to be alive.

The terms 'conjecture' and 'suggestion' are central to Baudelaire's writing about imagination, particularly in the period between publication of the first and second editions of *Les Fleurs du Mal*, but also in the years after 1861 in which he continued to write a small number of poems, perhaps to be included in a third edition of *Les Fleurs du Mal*, and continued also, more particularly, to extend his portfolio of prose poems. Already in his 1852 article on Poe, as we saw earlier, he uses the terms 'conjecturisme' and 'probabilisme' (ii. 275) to describe the American writer's repeated attempts in his prose tales to establish new laws of nature. This is Poe the quasi-scientist, seeking out the 'exceptional' in human experience and using the 'exception' not to prove (in the sense of 'test') an old rule but to propose a new one: a modern-day lawgiver, in short, who wants to 'arracher la parole aux prophètes, et s'attribuer le monopole de l'explication rationnelle' (ii. 283). For Poe the imagination is 'la reine des facultés' because it has the power to perceive 'les rapports intimes et secrets des choses, les correspondances et les analogies' (ii. 329) and thus to enable a new understanding of human physical and psychological experience. In the third and fourth sections of the *Salon de 1859*, where he, too, describes the imagination as 'la reine des facultés', Baudelaire sees this human faculty in broader and less quasi-scientific terms as a form of creative and innovative thinking that can even, potentially, bring both intellectual and moral progress and found new procedures of public governance and private self-governance based on compassion, understanding, and tolerance. But what matters to Baudelaire is not so much the outcome as the process: the requirement, always, to think in *other* terms, to offer a conjecture, to search for the new. Hence in the section on 'Sculpture' the emphasis is on thinking *beyond* the physical and the terrestrial, the need to 'penser aux choses qui ne sont pas de la terre'.

Thus the value of sculpture as an art form lies now in its paradigmatic and indeed paradoxical power to make us imagine what lies beyond the material world—and, more specifically, what lies outside or beyond our habitual perceptions. In this respect Baudelaire appears to take his cue from the definition of beauty put forward by Poe in *The Poetic Principle*. For Poe (here cited from Baudelaire's paraphrase-cum-translation) 'le principe de la poésie est, strictement et simplement, l'aspiration humaine vers une beauté supérieure, et la manifestation de ce principe est dans un enthousiasme, une excitation de l'âme' (ii. 334);[1] and he describes this 'higher beauty' thus:

> C'est cet admirable, cet immortel instinct du Beau qui nous fait considérer la terre et ses spectacles comme un aperçu, comme une correspondance du Ciel. La soif insatiable de ce qui est au delà, et que révèle la vie, est la preuve la plus vivante de notre immortalité. (ii. 334)[2]

---

[1] 'It has been my purpose to suggest that, while this Principle itself is, strictly and simply, the Human Aspiration for Supernal Beauty, the manifestation of the Principle is always found in *an elevating excitement of the Soul*' (Edgar Allan Poe, *Selected Writings*, ed. David Galloway (Harmondsworth: Penguin Books, 1967), 511).

[2] Baudelaire here compresses Poe's argument substantially while bringing forward Poe's reference to beauty as a glimpsed foretaste of heaven (see the following note): 'An immortal instinct, deep within the spirit of man, is thus, plainly, a sense of the Beautiful. This it is which adminsters to his delight in the manifold forms, and sounds, and odours, and sentiments, amid which he exists. And just as the lily is repeated in the lake, or the eyes of Amaryllis in the mirror, so is the mere oral or written repetition of these forms, and sounds, and colours, and sentiments, a duplicate source of delight. But this mere repetition is not poetry. He who shall simply sing, with however glowing enthusiasm, or with however vivid a truth of description, of the sights, and sounds, and odours, and colours, and sentiments, which greet *him* in common with all mankind—he, I say, has yet failed to prove his divine title. There is still a something in the distance which he has been unable to attain. We have still a thirst unquenchable, to allay which he has not shown us the crystal springs. This thirst belongs to the immortality of Man. It is at once a consequence and an indication of his perennial existence. It is the desire of the moth for the

Here Poe is presenting a traditional Romantic view of the function of art as offering glimpses of the sublime, itself understood in Christian terms as an experience of the state of celestial perfection to be experienced in the life hereafter. For him, as also for Chateaubriand before him, the aesthetic experience of the sublime palliates a condition of melancholy understood as the anguished perception of lack:

> C'est à la fois par la poésie et *à travers* la poésie, par et *à travers* la musique que l'âme entrevoit les splendeurs situées derrière le tombeau; et quand un poème exquis amène les larmes au bord des yeux, ces larmes ne sont pas la preuve d'un excès de jouissance, elles sont bien plutôt le témoignage d'une mélancolie irritée, d'une postulation des nerfs, d'une nature exilée dans l'imparfait et qui voudrait s'emparer immédiatement, sur cette terre même, d'un paradis révélé.   (ii. 334)[3]

As I argued at the end of Chapter 12, however, Baudelaire goes beyond Poe in seeing beauty not as 'an ecstatic prescience of the glories beyond the grave' but rather as a glimpse of the alternative glories to be found in the here and now.

In seeking to account for the effect of beauty, Poe's distinction between 'excess of pleasure' and 'a certain, petulant, impatient sorrow' echoes (most probably unbeknownst to Poe) the crucial distinction made by Staël in *Corinne*[4] between two melancholies—the positive melancholy of the South and the negative melancholy of the North:

> Ce n'est pas que le midi n'ait aussi sa mélancolie; dans quels lieux la destinée de l'homme ne produit-elle pas cette impression! mais il y a dans cette mélancolie ni mécontentement, ni anxiété, ni regret. Ailleurs, c'est la vie qui, telle qu'elle est, ne suffit pas aux facultés de l'âme; ici, ce sont les facultés de l'âme qui ne suffisent pas à la vie, et la surabondance des sensations inspire une rêveuse indolence dont on se rend à peine compte en l'éprouvant.[5]

---

star. It is no mere appreciation of the Beauty before us—but a wild effort to reach the Beauty above. Inspired by an ecstatic prescience of the glories beyond the grave, we struggle, by multiform combinations among the things and thoughts of Time, to attain a portion of that Loveliness whose very elements, perhaps, appertain to eternity alone' (*Selected Writings*, ed. Galloway, 97–8).

[3] 'And thus when by Poetry—or when by Music, the most entrancing of the Poetic moods—we find ourselves melted into tears—we weep then—not [...] through excess of pleasure, but through a certain, petulant, impatient sorrow at our inability to grasp *now*, wholly, here on earth, at once and for ever, those divine and rapturous joys, of which *through* the poem, or *through* the music, we attain to but brief and indeterminate glimpses' (*Selected Writings*, ed. Galloway, 505).

[4] See my discussion in Chapter 5 ('Melancholy in Context').

[5] *Corinne*, ed. Balayé, 288. Cf. also *Delphine*: 'Il faut distinguer l'imagination qui peut être considérée comme l'une des plus belles facultés de l'esprit, et l'imagination dont tous les êtres souffrants et bornés sont susceptibles. L'une est un talent, l'autre une maladie; l'une devance quelquefois la raison, l'autre s'oppose toujours à ses progrès' (*Delphine*, ed. Didier, i. 56). See *Unacknowledged Legislators*, 257.

For Staël this distinction is all-important because it allows her to propose a new and secular function for poetry. For Chateaubriand and his fellow conservatives in the cause of the Counter-Enlightenment, melancholy—or the *mal du siècle*—is indeed characterized by feelings of discontent, anxiety, and regret (as exemplified by the figure of Oswald in *Corinne*, and by René, Obermann, and many other early nineteenth-century malcontents) and derives from a fundamental sense of lack in human experience (life as a vale of tears to be followed one day by a posthumous paradise) that can be met only by Christian faith and by a poetry that draws its inspiration from that faith. But for Staël (and Corinne) melancholy derives from an excess of delight in the world of sensual experience and an accompanying awareness that we with our limited spiritual capacities cannot quite, alas, encompass this excess. Instead of an absence to be filled there is a plenitude to be grasped, a plenitude that leaves us with what Keats described as a 'wild surmise' (in 'On First Looking into Chapman's Homer') and what Staël here calls 'une rêveuse indolence'[6]—and what Baudelaire in 'La Chevelure' (written and first published in 1858–9) calls a 'féconde paresse'.

While Baudelaire's poetics of conjecture may have its roots in the 'conjecturisme' of Poe, the fact remains that Poe pursues his conjectures predominantly in the domain of narrative fiction. On the subject of his poetry, by contrast, Baudelaire has very much less to say, even when, as in 'Edgar Allan Poe, sa vie et ses ouvrages', he is not specifically introducing the prose tales. There he allocates a mere single paragraph to Poe as a verse poet before devoting the remainder of the article to Poe as 'nouvelliste et romancier' (ii. 275). And his own decision to translate the stories and not the poems doubtless reveals where his true interest lay. (Indeed he considered 'The Bells' untranslatable (ii. 274).) In that single paragraph (ii. 274–5) Baudelaire presents Poe the verse poet as 'un homme à part' who represents 'presque à lui seul le mouvement romantique de l'autre côté de l'Océan': not the Romanticism of 'MM. Alfred de Musset et Alphonse de Lamartine', however, so beloved of 'des âmes tendres et molles', but rather a 'poésie, profonde et plaintive, [qui] est néanmoins ouvragée, pure, correcte et brillante comme un bijou de cristal.' Somewhat like Baudelaire's own, in fact—but evidently not as good: 'Sa poésie, condensée et laborieuse, lui coûtait sans doute beaucoup de peine, et il avait trop souvent besoin d'argent pour se livrer à cette voluptueuse et infructueuse douleur' (ii. 275)![7] In the introductions to his two volumes of translations Baudelaire leaves all reference to the poems until the very end of the 'Notes nouvelles sur Edgar Poe' (ii. 334–6), and then principally to focus on Poe's 'scandalous' account of the genesis of 'The Raven' (in his essay 'The

---

[6] For further discussion, see *Unacknowledged Legislators*, 233–7.
[7] Baudelaire perhaps derives this assessment from John Daniel's review (see above, Chapter 11 n. 4): 'As a poet we must contemplate in this poet an unfinished column. He wanted money too often and too much to develop his wonderful imagination in verse.'

Philosophy of Composition') in which he demonstrates how his 'choix du ton le plus poétique de tous, le ton mélancolique' (ii. 335) derived not from a spontaneous and genuine feeling of grief at the loss of a loved one but was instead a choice, and part of an intricate and consciously wrought process of poetic construction. But now, because he wants to present Poe as the worthy enemy of moral didacticism in poetry, Baudelaire reaffirms the untranslatability of his verse on the grounds of its unique quality and effectiveness: 'Ce n'est pas l'effusion ardente de Byron, ce n'est pas la mélancolie molle, harmonieuse, distinguée de Tennyson [...] C'est quelque chose de profond et de miroitant comme le rêve, de mystérieux et de parfait comme le cristal' (ii. 336) To the poetry of Poe is thus attributed the quality that Baudelaire treasures above all: a combination of clarity and mysteriousness that has to the power to provoke conjecture—and which he calls beauty.[8]

But what of other poets? It is a marked feature of Baudelaire's critical writings that he chooses to present his own aesthetic theories and opinions in relation to other artists and writers. Not for him, it seems, the official policy statement: unlike Lamartine, say, in *Des destinées de la poésie*, or Hugo in the preface to *Cromwell* or in *William Shakespeare*, or Mallarmé in *La Musique et les lettres*. Instead, just as at the end of 'Sculpture' he offers extracts from his poem 'Danse macabre' as a form of marginal scribbling on the work of Ernest Christophe, so too his critical writings take the form of commentaries situated alongside and in parallel with the artistic theories and productions of others: the exhibitors at the Salons of 1845, 1846, and 1859, the 'caricaturistes' (both French and foreign), Delacroix and Poe, and even Catherine Crowe. But, as this last example particularly attests, the artists and authors he writes about serve as proxies or foils, masks even, and sometimes as all three together: that is to say, an artist or writer with similar preoccupations but ultimately divergent aims and achievements. This is true also in Baudelaire's articles on Gautier, Hugo, Wagner, and Constantin Guys, and in each case the conjectural function of the imagination is paramount.

Gautier

Gautier, c'est l'amour exclusif du Beau, avec toutes ses subdivisions, exprimé dans le langage le mieux approprié.
('Théophile Gautier' (1859), ii. 117)

In his 1859 article on Théophile Gautier, the poet to whom *Les Fleurs du Mal* is famously dedicated ('Au poète impeccable, au parfait magicien ès lettres

---

[8] For further discussion of Baudelaire's views on Poe's verse, see P. M. Wetherill, *Charles Baudelaire et la poésie d'Edgar Allan Poe* (Paris: Nizet, 1962).

françaises'), Baudelaire celebrates his long-standing friend (ii. 104) once again as an ideal: 'un grand poète' (ii. 105) and 'UN PARFAIT HOMME DE LETTRES' (ii. 128). Like Poe, Gautier is celebrated for resisting (in the prefaces to *Albertus* (1832) and *Mademoiselle de Maupin* (1835) and in the novel itself) the 'heretical' use of literature for moral instruction and for championing instead the cause of beauty, 'l'amour exclusif du Beau' (ii. 111, 117). Indeed, as a celebrated art critic, he is beauty's lawgiver: 'ses comptes rendus des *Salons*, si calmes, si pleins de candeur et de majesté, sont des oracles pour tous les exilés qui ne peuvent juger et sentir par leurs propres yeux' (ii. 105). Beauty is at once Gautier's 'Idée fixe' (ii. 111) and his means of edification: 'Il n'y a pas d'homme qui pousse plus loin que lui la pudeur majestueuse du vrai homme de lettres, et qui ait plus d'horreur d'étaler tout ce qui n'est pas fait, préparé et mûri pour le public, pour l'édification des âmes amoureuses du Beau' (ii. 104). Thus does Gautier redeploy the trinity of Victor Cousin's 'fameuse doctrine de l'indissolubilité du Beau, du Vrai et du Bien', mere risible 'invention de la philosoperaillerie moderne' (ii. 111).[9] Whereupon Baudelaire, in order himself also to argue against Cousin's doctrine, resorts to quoting at some length from his earlier 'Notes nouvelles sur Edgar Poe', purportedly quoting his own words ('pour éviter de se paraphraser' (ii. 112)) but in fact, wittingly or unwittingly, quoting a paraphrase-cum-translation of Poe's own words in *The Poetic Principle*.[10] Baudelaire, it seems, is Poe who is Gautier who is Baudelaire.

Following these lengthy 'self-quotations' Baudelaire affirms his belief that 'l'Imagination seule contient la poésie' (ii. 115) and now asserts that Gautier is 'l'écrivain par excellence' (ii. 116) if by 'écrivain' is meant someone who produces '[des] travaux qui ressortent de l'imagination' (ii. 116). But whereas for Poe the imagination is a faculty governing all others and with them the world, in the case of Gautier imagination is principally a matter of language, of style: 'l'outil qui sert si bien cette passion du Beau' (ii. 117). Like Poe, Gautier is able to perceive the world in new ways, to see multiple 'correspondances' and 'analogies'. But in his case, rather than constituting evidence of his own quasi-scientific 'conjecturisme', this ability serves to present in perfect definition a world that invites conjecture from others:

> Si l'on réfléchit qu'à cette merveilleuse faculté [his linguistic ability] Gautier unit une immense intelligence innée de la *correspondance* et du symbolisme universels, ce répertoire de toute métaphore, on comprendra qu'il puisse sans cesse, sans fatigue comme sans faute, définir l'attitude mystérieuse que les objets de la

---

[9] See Chapter 1 n. 27.   [10] See Chapter 11 n. 22.

création tiennent devant le regard de l'homme. Il y a dans le mot, dans le *verbe*, quelque chose de sacré qui nous défend d'en faire un jeu de hasard. Manier savamment une langue, c'est pratiquer une espèce de sorcellerie évocatoire.

(ii. 117–18)[11]

Through his remarkable command of the French language Gautier 'evokes'—that is, calls up like a sorcerer summoning spirits—the phenomenal world and lends expression to its mute and mysterious 'attitude'. Thereby what he 'evokes' speaks, itself in turn, 'unequivocally' and 'provokes' the reader to conjectures comprising thought and memory:

> C'est alors que la couleur parle, comme une voix profonde et vibrante; que les monuments se dressent et font saillie sur l'espace profond; que les animaux et les plantes, représentants du laid et du mal, articulent leur grimace non équivoque; que le parfum provoque la pensée et le souvenir correspondants[.]   (ii. 118)

This in turn anticipates Baudelaire's account of the imagination three months later in the *Salon de 1859*:

> C'est l'imagination qui a enseigné à l'homme le sens moral de la couleur, du contour, du son et du parfum. Elle a créé, au commencement du monde, l'analogie et la métaphore. Elle décompose toute la création, et, avec les matériaux amassés et disposés suivant des règles dont on ne peut trouver l'origine que dans le plus profond de l'âme, elle crée un monde nouveau, elle produit la sensation du neuf.   (ii. 621)

But what Baudelaire here emphasizes most is Gautier's ability to find the right words in his 'evocations' of the world: 'Il y a dans le style de Théophile Gautier une justesse qui ravit, qui étonne, et qui fait songer à ces miracles faits dans le jeu par une profonde science mathématique' (ii. 118). And he recalls how in his youth he first encountered Gautier's writing style and was physically shaken ('me faisait tressaillir', 'une sorte de convulsion nerveuse' (ii. 118)) by 'la sensation de la touche posée juste, du coup porté droit' that characterized 'ce beau style' (ii. 118).[12] Like a painter's brush-stroke or the sculptor's chisel-blow Gautier's *mot juste* strikes home and renders the phenomenal world as it exactly but mysteriously is. For Baudelaire Gautier's imagination is here less about creating

---

[11] Cf. Baudelaire's comment in 'Théophile Gautier' (1861): 'il a exprimé, sans fatigue, sans effort, toutes les attitudes, tous les regards, toutes les couleurs qu'adopte la nature, ainsi que le sens intime contenu dans tous les objets qui s'offrent à la contemplation de l'œil humain' (ii. 152).

[12] Cf. 'Théophile Gautier' (1861) where Baudelaire describes him as 'un des maîtres les plus sûrs et les plus rares en matière de langue et de style' and ranks him with La Bruyère, Buffon, and Chateaubriand (ii. 152).

new worlds than about seeing with perfect clarity the extraordinary world we already inhabit and perceiving it as other. Furthermore, as these analogies with gambling suggest ('un jeu de hasard', 'ces miracles faits dans le jeu par une profonde science mathématique'), language provides the means to present the apparent contingencies of the human condition as though these were governed by rules or laws to which only the poet is privy.

In this respect Gautier is representative of a poetry that is politically resistant, a poetry shunned by 'la France' that prefers prose and facts and a literal-minded truth: 'Où il ne faut voir que le beau, notre public ne cherche que le vrai [...] la France n'est pas poète, elle éprouve même, pour tout dire, une horreur congéniale de la poésie. Parmi les écrivains qui se servent du vers, ceux qu'elle préférera toujours sont les plus prosaïques' (ii. 124). Compared with Lamartine and Hugo, Gautier is 'un homme *inconnu*' (ii. 105) because his verse lacks the 'condiment' of overt political reference that French readers believe allows poetry to speak to their own 'passions actuelles' and which they welcome in such poems as Hugo's 'Ode à la Colonne' or 'Ode à l'Arc de Triomphe' and in Barbier's *Iambes* (ii. 106). Gautier's 'condiment', however, is of a different order ('du choix le plus exquis et du sel le plus ardent') and makes little impression on the popular palate (ii. 106). Indeed, Baudelaire now corrects himself, no matter *how* political the 'condiment', France simply cannot stomach the *beauty* of verse: 'le Beau amène l'indigestion, ou plutôt l'estomac français le refuse immédiatement' (ii. 125), and this because the French mind is so wedded to its own particular theories about the public good: 'le caractère utopique, communiste, alchimique, de tous ses cerveaux, ne lui permet qu'une passion exclusive, celle des formules sociales, Ici, chacun veut ressembler à tout le monde, mais à condition que tout le monde lui ressemble' (ii. 125). Social utility is all and private otherness quite without consequence, especially that 'useless' otherness of poetry and, more generally, of beauty: 'De là, la ruine et l'oppression de tout caractère original. Aussi ce n'est pas seulement dans l'ordre littéraire que les vrais poètes apparaissent comme des êtres fabuleux et étrangers; mais on peut dire que dans tous les genres d'invention le grand homme ici est un monstre' (ii. 125). But against the tyranny of conformism and like-mindedness art can set an example in its commitment to the merits of originality and to the benefits of conjecture, of thinking differently. 'Aimons donc nos poètes secrètement et en cachette' (ii. 125): poetry is a form of political resistance and offers an alternative justice.

The insistence on beauty as the power to do linguistic justice to a mysterious but precise truth (in a new and subversive combination of Cousin's 'le vrai' and 'le beau') informs Baudelaire's admiration for Gautier's short stories and his art criticism alike. For him Gautier's stories are his greatest achievement, and for two reasons: because they are a form of poetry ('ce que j'appellerai la *nouvelle poétique*' (ii. 119)) and because they present the world we know as a new and alternative world: 'L'imagination du lecteur se sent transportée dans le vrai; elle respire le vrai; elle s'enivre d'une second réalité créée par la sorcellerie de la Muse' (ii. 121). Whether this be the sorcery of language or of 'the Muse', such 'magic' on the part of the 'parfait magicien ès lettres françaises' represents the transformative effect of the imagination, what in the *Salon de 1859* Baudelaire also calls the 'magic' of the soul: 'l'âme qui jette une lumière surnaturelle et magique sur l'obscurité naturelle des choses' (ii. 645). And not only can Gautier weave this magic through his own artistry, he is also wonderfully able to describe the effect of such magic: 'Nul n'a mieux su que lui exprimer le bonheur que donne à l'imagination la vue d'un bel objet, fût-il le plus désolé et le plus terrible qu'on puisse supposer. C'est un des privilèges prodigieux de l'Art que l'horrible, artistement exprimé, devienne beauté, et que la *douleur* rythmée et cadencée remplisse l'esprit d'une joie calme' (ii. 122-3).[13]

With this famous statement comes the first explicit evidence that Baudelaire had now come (in 1859) to recognize the possibility of a remedial or therapeutic function for art, the possibility that beauty can effect a transformation of horror and pain—of 'le Mal'—into an experience of 'calm joy'. Beauty can offer an antidote to melancholy, a form of resistance within the irremediable human condition. And in the penultimate section of his article he gives an account of Gautier's poetry that begins to sound like a new agenda, not least because it appears to constitute part of an ongoing dialogue, part explicit, part implicit, with Hugo. For Baudelaire there are two sides to Gautier's poetry, melancholy and consolation: 'Théophile Gautier a continué *d'un côté* la grande école de la mélancolie, créée par Chateaubriand. Sa mélancolie est même d'un caractère plus positif, plus charnel, et confinant quelquefois à la tristesse antique' (ii. 125). By way of evidence Baudelaire refers his reader to poems in *La Comédie de la Mort* and *España* 'où se révèlent le vertige et l'horreur du néant' (ii. 125). Indeed, Baudelaire contends: 'Il arrive même à ce poète, accusé de sensualité, de tomber en plein, tant sa mélancolie devient intense, dans la terreur catholique' (ii. 126).[14] But Gautier is original, he argues, in sounding a new note of consolation: '*D'un autre côté*, il a introduit dans la poésie un élément nouveau, que j'appellerai la consolation par les arts, par tous les objets pittoresques qui réjouissent les yeux et amusent l'esprit. Dans ce sens, il a vraiment innové; il a fait dire au vers français plus qu'il n'avait dit jusqu'à présent' (ii. 126).

Baudelaire is here foregrounding that emphasis on the visual that is so characteristic of Gautier's writing, and very often on the visual as mediated through the eyes of a painter. If 'le vertige et l'horreur du néant'—'le Mal'—are sufficiently present in Gautier's work to enrol him in the 'grande école de la mélancolie', the

---

[13] Cf. 'Théophile Gautier' (1861): 'il n'a aimé que le Beau; il n'a cherché que le Beau; et quand un objet grotesque ou hideux s'est offert à ses yeux, il a su encore extraire une mystérieuse et symbolique beauté!' (ii. 152).

[14] Cf. 'Théophile Gautier' (1861): 'Que de fois il a exprimé et avec quelle magie de langage! ce qu'il y a de plus délicat dans la tendresse et dans la mélancolie!' (ii. 150).

fact remains that they frequently manifest themselves at one remove, as depicted in art. Baudelaire refers his own reader specifically to Gautier's poems on Zurbarán and Valdès Leal (ii. 126), and if we follow his lead we may note in the poem 'Deux tableaux de Valdès Léal' how 'la consolation par les arts' stands in a kind of inverse causal relationship to the suffering that prompts it. The poet addresses the painter thus: 'Pour te montrer si gai, si clair, si coloriste, | Il fallait, à coup sûr, que tu fusses bien triste' (ll. 41–2).[15] It is important to note here that the 'consolation' derives not from any philosophical, religious, or moral framework but from art itself. In the case of poetry Baudelaire sees it as deriving from the rhythms of poetic language, and, in Gautier's verse, from a kind of stateliness and majestic placidity that can wrest 'calm joy' from the terrible realities of the human condition:

> Sa poésie, à la fois majestueuse et précieuse, marche magnifiquement, comme les personnes de cour en grande toilette. C'est, du reste, le caractère de la vraie poésie d'avoir le flot régulier, comme les grands fleuves qui s'approchent de la mer, leur mort et leur infini, et d'éviter la précipitation et la saccade. La poésie lyrique s'élance, mais toujours d'un mouvement élastique et ondulé. Tout ce qui est brusque et cassé lui déplaît, et elle le renvoie au drame ou au roman de mœurs. Le poète, dont nous aimons si passionnément le talent, connaît à fond ces grandes questions, et il l'a parfaitement prouvé en introduisant systématiquement et continuellement la majesté de l'alexandrin dans le vers octosyllabique (*Émaux et Camées*). (ii. 126)

'Majestueux/-euse' is a recurrent epithet in this article, sometimes characterizing Gautier himself ('la pudeur majestuese du vrai homme de lettres' (ii. 104); 'je le trouvai [...] déjà majestueux, à l'aise et gracieux dans des vêtements flottants' (ii. 107)) and sometimes his writings ('ses comptes rendus des *Salons*, si calmes, si pleins de candeur et de majesté' (ii. 105)). As these examples show, such majesty is repeatedly associated with calmness, authority, and integrity,[16] with regularity but also with fluidity and adaptability, and with an ease of movement and lightness of touch that are at the opposite pole to the fixity and tyranny of the contemporary French mindset as Baudelaire perceives it. If imagination is the queen of faculties, so the beauty of Gautier has an amiable sovereign power. Indeed this 'majesty' closely resembles the 'idée poétique' and 'eurhythmic' beauty of the ship described

---

[15] Théophile Gautier, *Œuvres poétiques complètes*, ed. Michel Brix (Paris: Bartillat, 2004), 424.
[16] Just as Baudelaire claimed of Poe that 'il ne fut jamais dupe' (ii. 321), so here he asserts Gautier's own resistance to the fads and poor imitations of contemporary cultural and intellectual life: 'Évidemment, à une époque pleine de duperies, un auteur [i.e. Gautier] s'installait en pleine ironie et prouvait qu'il n'était pas dupe. Un vigoureux bon sens le sauvait des pastiches et des religions à la mode' (ii. 111). At the end of the article he refers to 'sa ferme décision de n'être jamais dupe' (ii. 127).

in *Fusées*, f. 22, and both appear to embody some fundamental *nomos*, a complex harmony within the universe.[17] Here the manifestation of this poetic harmony is not a ship but the water upon which it sails, a great river placidly nearing the sea and with it the prospect of its own assumption into the boundless reach of the ocean. Poetry is the river of life perhaps, ending in death but also ready to survive as language—or, as Auden put it in his poem for W. B. Yeats, as '[a] way of happening, a mouth'. The water flows into the sea but the river mouth remains. Earlier in the article Baudelaire had mocked drawing-room conversations about poetry and noted sarcastically how if the cliché of a 'flowing' style ('son *style est coulant*') is so repeatedly and randomly applied to writers, this is doubtless because clear water is itself 'le symbole le plus clair de beauté pour les gens qui ne font pas profession de méditer' (ii. 105). But for Baudelaire the transparency of Gautier's poetry, like that of Poe's, is a clarity full of mystery, at once an invitation to conjecture and what in *Les Paradis artificiels* Baudelaire calls 'une merveilleuse aptitude pour comprendre le rythme immortel et universel' (i. 432). The still waters of Gautier run deep.

Hugo

>   un esprit rêveur et interrogateur
>
>   ('Victor Hugo', ii. 130)

In this article on Gautier of 1859 Baudelaire thus ostensibly nails his colours to the mast of Art for Art's sake—'l'amour exclusif du Beau'—but in fact invites his reader to reconsider in what such beauty consists and to understand Gautier's own art as transcending mere formalism. Melancholy—the 'vertige et horreur du néant'—is everywhere present in his work but mitigated by an insistent focus on the visual beauty of the world and by the consoling power of the poet's verbal imagination. Like the Spanish painters he so admires, Gautier is able to depict 'le Mal' and yet also to delight the eye and the mind with his depictions: in short, to 'extraire la *beauté* du Mal'. In this he anticipates Baudelaire himself, not only in his ambitions for *Les Fleurs du Mal* but also as the poet for whom poems about works of art, whether real or imagined, constitute an important element in his poetic enterprise (for example, 'Le Masque', 'A une Madone', 'Une gravure fantastique', 'Danse macabre', 'Une martyre', 'L'Amour et le crâne', 'Vers pour le portrait de M. Honoré Daumier', 'Sur *Le Tasse en prison* d'Eugène Delacroix'). But above all, Baudelaire contends, there is a depth to Gautier's poetic writing, a mysteriousness within clarity, that invites the participation of the reader's own imagination in this

---

[17] See my discussion in Chapter 1 ('The Poet as Nomothete').

'alternative' world that is opened up by the poet's skilful deployment of lexis and rhythm.

By presenting Gautier in this way Baudelaire was—as he flatteringly (and disloyally) confided to Hugo—minimizing Gautier's limitations and pursuing his own thoughts about the nature and function of poetry: 'Relativement à l'écrivain qui fait le sujet de cet article, et dont le nom a servi de prétexte à mes considérations critiques, je puis vous avouer *confidentiellement* que je connais les lacunes de son étonnant esprit' (*Corr.*, i. 597). But he was also implicitly setting up in opposition to Hugo himself as the most prominent representative of a very different kind of poetry, that of the poet-lawgiver who articulates a moral and religious vision of Progress. It is true that Hugo is openly mentioned by name several times in the article, and in seemingly favourable terms. Along with Chateaubriand and Balzac he is a major figure in the French pantheon (ii. 107, 117); Hugo and Gautier are France's answers to Shakespeare and Goethe (ii. 125); together with Sainte-Beuve and Vigny he renewed, indeed resuscitated, French poetry (ii. 110); in short, he is a quasi-mythical figure: 'Victor Hugo, grand, terrible, immense comme une création mythique, cyclopéen, pour ainsi dire, représente les forces de la nature et leur lutte harmonieuse' (ii. 117). But there is a sense here that Hugo—in 1859 still very much alive on the island of Guernsey and also, not least by virtue of his recent refusal of amnesty, the living symbol of republican opposition to the illegitimate empire of Napoléon III—is nevertheless somehow a figure from the past, a monument to former glories, a myth rather than a present, living poet of modernity. Moreover the comparison of this celebrated visionary poet of *Les Contemplations* to a one-eyed Cyclops might be thought something of a backhanded compliment.

But there is one particularly approbatory comment. Having disparaged the contemporary French reading public for requiring the condiment of political allusions in its poetry, Baudelaire further scorns it for being unaware of 'les parties mystérieuses, ombreuses, les plus charmantes de Victor Hugo' (ii. 106). Here is another Hugo, the poet of conjecture whom Baudelaire praises in his article of 1861. For Baudelaire there are essentially two Hugos: on the one hand, the portentous public commentator on the moral, political, and religious life of the nation and indeed of humanity at large, and, on the other—and for Baudelaire much more interestingly—the poet of mystery, the poet-lawgiver as the 'officiant of uncertainty'.[18] In taking the extraordinary step of requesting Hugo to provide a

---

[18] On the ambivalence of Baudelaire's attitude towards Hugo see André Ferran, *L'Esthétique de Baudelaire* (Paris: Hachette, 1933 [republished by Nizet, 1968]), 501–25, and Léon Cellier, *Baudelaire et Hugo* (Paris: Corti, 1970). See also Lloyd, *Baudelaire's Literary Criticism*, 159–89; André Guyaux, 'Baudelaire et Victor Hugo', in Elio Mosele (ed.), *George Sand et son temps: Hommage à Annarosa Poli* (3 vols, Geneva: Slatkine, 1994), i. 143–56; Pierre Laforgue, 'Baudelaire, Hugo et la royauté du poète: Le Romantisme en 1860', *Revue d'histoire littéraire de la France*, 96 (1996), 966–82; and Jean-Marc Hovasse, 'Les Signes de Hugo au cygne de Baudelaire', in Claude Millet, Florence Naugrette, and Agnès Spiquel (eds), *Choses vues à travers Hugo: Hommage à Guy Rosa* (Valenciennes: Presses

prefatory letter to his article on Gautier, due to be republished as a stand-alone pamphlet, he was in a sense provoking Hugo into deciding between these two types of poetry. In this request Baudelaire presents himself as the defender of the cause of art and, with seeming deference but punning impertinence, quietly challenges his illustrious correspondent to join him and indeed to move on, to 'progress':

> Je sais vos ouvrages par cœur, et vos préfaces me montrent que j'ai dépassé la théorie généralement exposée par vous sur l'alliance de la morale et de la poésie. Mais en un temps où le monde s'éloigne de l'art avec une telle horreur, où les hommes se laissent abrutir par l'idée exclusive d'utilité, je crois qu'il n'y a pas grand mal à exagérer dans le sens contraire. (*Corr.*, i. 597)

'Dépassé': he has infringed but also overtaken Hugo's conception of poetry as an instrument of moral and social improvement, and once again his praise is reserved for yesterday's man: 'J'ai voulu surtout ramener la pensée du lecteur [of his article] vers cette merveilleuse époque littéraire dont vous fûtes le véritable roi et qui vit dans mon esprit comme un délicieux souvenir d'enfance' (*Corr.*, i. 597).

In his reply Hugo firmly stood his ground:

> Vous ne vous trompez pas en prévoyant quelque dissidence entre vous et moi. Je comprends toute votre philosophie (car, comme tout poète, vous contenez un philosophe); je fais plus que la comprendre, je l'admets; mais je garde la mienne. Je n'ai jamais dit: l'Art pour l'Art; j'ai toujours dit: l'Art pour le Progrès. Au fond, c'est la même chose, et votre esprit est trop pénétrant pour ne pas le sentir. En avant! c'est le mot du Progrès; c'est aussi le cri de l'Art. Tout le verbe de la Poésie est là. *Ite*.[19]

Art itself, Hugo concedes, cannot progress in the sense that the perfect artistry of Aeschylus and Phidias can never be surpassed.[20] But it can be equalled, and to achieve this the artist must necessarily move with the times: 'Il faut déplacer l'horizon de l'Art, monter plus haut, aller plus loin, marcher.' And humanity at

---

universitaires de Valenciennes, 2008), 367–76. Guyaux notes in particular (p. 146 and n. 8) the extreme terms in which Baudelaire habitually expressed this ambivalence, from the description of Hugo as 'un âne de génie' during a conversation with Sainte-Beuve in 1847 to a letter of February 1865 in which he observes to Narcisse Ancelle that 'on peut en même temps posséder un *génie spécial* et être un *sot*. Victor Hugo nous l'a bien prouvé' (*Corr.*, ii. 459–60).

[19] For the full text of Hugo's letter of 6 Oct. 1859, from which this quotation is taken, see ii. 1128–9.

[20] Hugo claims only to have been 'one of the first' to argue this, perhaps uneasily conscious that the very same argument had been put forward more than half a century earlier by Staël. (See *De la littérature considérée dans ses rapports avec les institutions sociales*, ed. Gérard Gengembre and Jean Goldzink (Paris: Flammarion, 1991), 157.) Like Hugo she contends that while art cannot surpass earlier perfection, it can and must 'progress' (in the sense of 'move forward' rather than 'improve') along with humanity itself and aim for new perfections. See also *Unacknowledged Legislators*, 184.

large will move with the artist: 'Le poète ne peut aller seul, il faut que l'homme aussi se déplace. Les pas de l'Humanité sont donc les pas même de l'Art.—Donc, gloire au Progrès' (ii. 1129). Insidiously using Baudelaire's own work in support of his argument, Hugo contends that the poems Baudelaire has just sent with his letter of request—'Les Sept Vieillards' and 'Les Petites Vieilles'—themselves demonstrate such 'progress': 'Vous marchez. Vous allez en avant. Vous dotez le ciel de l'art d'on ne sait quel rayon macabre. Vous créez un frisson nouveau' (ii. 1129). But for Baudelaire artistic originality is not the same as 'Progress': the former bespeaks beneficial conjecture and the exploration of mystery, while faith in the latter represents dogmatism and unwarranted certainty, a foreclosing on the discovery of what we do not know.

This fundamental disagreement informs the ambivalence of Baudelaire's article on Hugo of 1861. Just as he had done in the article on Gautier, he once again presents Hugo as both public lawgiver and poet of mystery, a Hugo, therefore, at once ancient and modern. Now, however, he makes much more of the latter figure, contending that the leader of the Romantic movement in literature has recently moved in a new direction—a direction already taken by Baudelaire. Thus, on the one hand, the view of Hugo as yesterday's man is here strongly reinforced by the opening sentence: 'Depuis bien des années déjà Victor Hugo n'est plus parmi nous' (ii. 129). It is as though the famous exile were in fact already dead and gone.[21] Accordingly Baudelaire then opens his discussion by recalling the Hugo of yesteryear: the Parisian celebrity, seemingly ubiquitous, popping up regularly at social gatherings or else walking alone in the street, deep in thought: 'la statue de la Méditation qui marche' (ii. 130). Then as now he was the modern prophet: 'un homme très doux, très puissant, toujours maître de lui-même, et appuyé sur une sagesse abrégée, faite de quelques axiomes irréfutables' (ii. 129–30).[22] But Baudelaire accords Hugo this status as lawgiver only within the domain of literature itself and quietly but firmly excludes a wider influence: 'il exerçait une vraie dictature dans les choses littéraires' (ii. 129); among 'les littérateurs' 'Victor Hugo représentait celui vers lequel chacun se tourne pour demander le mot d'ordre. Jamais royauté ne fut plus légitime, plus naturelle' (ii. 131); 'un de ces esprits rares et providentiels qui opèrent, dans l'ordre littéraire, le salut de tous, comme d'autres, dans l'ordre moral et d'autres dans l'ordre politique' (ii. 131). So, by implication, he lacks the moral and political authority so commonly associated with him by fellow republicans. Hugo is no public saviour. Furthermore, the

---

[21] The impression is reinforced by the opening sentence of the second section of the article: 'Dans les temps, déjà si lointains, dont je parlais, temps heureux où les littérateurs étaient, les uns pour les autres, une société que les survivants regrettent et dont ils ne trouveront plus l'analogue, Victor Hugo représentait celui vers qui chacun se tourne pour demander le mot d'ordre' (ii. 131).
[22] This last remark has been read variously as a jibe against Hugolian intellectual complacency and as a sincere expression of admiration for an uncomplicated wisdom comparable with that of Delacroix. See Cellier, *Baudelaire et Hugo*, 174–5.

repeated comparison of his literary authority to that of a king ('le véritable roi', 'royauté [...] légitime') provides a sly reminder of Hugo's former but now abandoned royalism.

But yesterday's man is also today's man in two important respects: his cultural influence and his poetry of conjecture. Under the first heading Baudelaire pays tribute to Hugo's key role in inspiring the contemporary restoration of medieval cathedrals prompted initially by *Notre-Dame de Paris* (ii. 131) and, more especially, to his no less crucial role in the re-establishment of poetry itself as a source of widespread public enjoyment and engagement:

> Le mouvement créé par Victor Hugo se continue encore sous nos yeux [...] si aujourd'hui des hommes mûrs, des jeunes gens, des femmes du monde ont le sentiment de la bonne poésie, de la poésie profondément rythmée et vivement colorée, si le goût public s'est haussé vers des jouissances qu'il avait oubliées, c'est à Victor Hugo qu'on le doit. (ii. 131)

Under the second heading, of conjecture, he notes in Hugo's poetry an underlying continuity of purpose: 'Quand aujourd'hui nous parcourons les poésies récentes de Victor Hugo, nous voyons que tel il était, tel il est resté: un promeneur pensif, un homme solitaire mais enthousiaste de la vie, un esprit rêveur et interrogateur' (ii. 130). Despite the fundamental changes in his personal situation and in his political allegiance, the Hugo of *Les Contemplations* and the first series of *La Légende des siècles* is still the poet of 'La Pente de la rêverie' (1830), 'déjà si vieille de date' (ii. 137). Picking up on the division of *Les Contemplations* into two parts, 'Autrefois' and 'Aujourd'hui', Baudelaire appears here to accept the reality of Hugo's self-image as a vatic 'promeneur solitaire', communing now with the elements where once he had pensively strolled along city boulevards, the original flâneur:

> Comme Démosthène, il converse avec les flots et le vent; autrefois, il rôdait solitaire dans les lieux bouillonnants de vie humaine; aujourd'hui, il marche dans des solitudes peuplées par sa pensée. Ainsi est-il peut-être encore plus grand et plus singulier. Les couleurs de ses rêveries se sont teintées en solennité, et sa voix s'est approfondie en rivalisant avec celle de l'Océan. (ii. 130)[23]

---

[23] Baudelaire's scepticism about this self-image is nevertheless evident from his letters. Cf. for example his subsequent comment to Narcisse Ancelle on 12 Feb. 1865 when it was rumoured that Hugo was intending to move house from Guernsey to Brussels (where Baudelaire himself was now living): 'Il paraît que lui et l'Océan se sont brouillés. Ou il n'a pas eu la force de supporter l'Océan, ou l'Océan lui-même s'est ennuyé de lui. [...] J'ai encore plus d'orgueil que Victor Hugo, et je sens, je sais que je ne serai jamais si bête que lui' (*Corr.*, ii. 460).

Accordingly, the second section of the article constitutes a sustained tribute to Hugo as the supreme articulator of mystery, the poet without whom 'combien de sentiments mystérieux et profonds, qui ont été exprimés, seraient restés muets' (ii. 131). Baudelaire again appears sincere when making his famous assessment that 'Hugo était, dès le principe, l'homme le mieux doué, le plus visiblement élu pour exprimer par la poésie ce que j'appellerai le *mystère de la vie*' (ii. 131). Hugo possesses the requisite linguistic and poetic gifts, and, given his contemporary public image as the prophet on his rocky island listening to God, he seems most 'visibly' to fit the part of God's elect. One might argue that Baudelaire here claims only that Hugo had the wherewithal to express the 'mystery of life' and not that he actually did so, but there now follows the long passage, discussed above in Chapter 1, where Baudelaire presents Hugo as a *nomothete* who gives expression to the mysterious laws of the universe: the poet who confronts the 'mystère' of '[l]a nature qui pose devant nous' (ii. 131-2) and whose poetry 's'adapte aux profondes harmonies de la nature' (ii. 132); the poet who is not at all a simplistic or didactic moralist but one who can subtly convey 'la *morale des choses*' (ii. 132). This Hugo does indeed seem like the ideal poet: 'Aucun artiste n'est plus universel que lui, plus apte à se mettre en contact avec les forces de la vie universelle' (ii. 132); he respects 'l'*obscurité indispensable*' of what in the universe is indeed 'obscur et confusément révélé' (ii. 132); he commands 'un si magnifique répertoire d'analogies humaines et divines' (ii. 133), and, like Gautier, he is a master of the French language: 'J'ignore dans quel monde Victor Hugo a mangé préalablement le dictionnaire de la langue qu'il était appelé à parler; mais je vois que le lexique français, en sortant de sa bouche, est devenu un monde, un univers coloré, mélodieux et mouvant' (ii. 133). This tribute to Hugo as the poet of mystery reaches a climax in the final paragraph of the section: he has 'un caractère poétique, très particulier, interrogatif, mystérieux'; 'il voit le mystère partout'; through his art of verbal repetition he is able to convey 'l'énigmatique physionomie du mystère' (ii. 134), etc.

In the third section Baudelaire's tribute focuses on the 'universality' of Hugo's imagination, comparable with that of such great painters as Rubens and Veronese, Velásquez and Delacroix, who each possess 'une imagination et une faculté créatrice qui parle vivement à l'esprit de tous les hommes' (ii. 134). There is nothing that Hugo's art cannot encompass: 'c'est un génie sans frontières' (ii. 135). He is able to depict 'tout ce qu'il y a de plus doux et tout ce qui existe de plus horrible' (ii. 135), and he manages by language alone to bring everything to life: 'En tout, il met la palpitation de la vie' (ii. 135). Indeed, were he to depict a ship, his verse would achieve that very combination of the organic and the mechanical that, in *Fusées* f. 22, Baudelaire himself puts forward as an ideal of 'eurhythmic' beauty and here once again presents as being mysterious: 'ce caractère de volonté et d'animalité qui se dégage si mystérieusement d'un appareil géométrique et mécanique de bois, de fer, de cordes et de toile; animal monstrueux créé par l'homme, auquel le vent et le flot ajoutent la beauté d'une démarche' (ii. 135). In addition, Baudelaire praises the universality of Hugo's moral imagination—'l'atmosphère morale qui plane et circule dans ses poèmes' (ii. 136)—and commends a remarkable even-handedness, 'un caractère très manifeste d'amour égal pour ce qui est très fort comme pour ce qui est très faible' (ii. 136). And he rounds off this particular section with the account of Hugo's 'second-order moralizing' discussed in Chapter 1 above, not poetry as reprehensible 'enseignement' but 'une morale qui se glisse, invisible, dans la matière poétique, comme les fluides impondérables dans toute la machine du monde.' Thus: 'La morale n'entre pas dans cet art à titre de but; elle s'y mêle et s'y confond comme dans la vie elle-même' (ii. 137).

On the basis of *Les Contemplations*—which curiously, unlike *La Légende des siècles* in the next and final section, is never named—Baudelaire here seems to be setting out what he himself believes to be the true function of poetry in its relation to the 'mystery of life': that is, not only that it should be nomothetic in its pursuit of harmony, universal in its subject matter, and suffused with a moral atmosphere of justice and sympathy, but also conjectural. He begins by noting, with implicit reference to *Les Contemplations*, how in his depiction of '[l']excessif, l'immense, [...] toute la monstruosité qui enveloppe l'homme' (ii. 137) Hugo has begun in recent years to be affected by 'l'influence métaphysique qui s'exhale de toutes ces choses, curiosité d'un Œdipe obsédé par d'innombrables Sphinx' (ii. 137). Here identifying a continuity with the type of conjectural imagination that had earlier produced 'La Pente de la rêverie' ('ce poème enivrant' (ii. 137)), Baudelaire observes: 'On dirait que dès lors l'interrogation s'est dressée avec plus de fréquence devant le poète rêveur, et qu'à ses yeux tous les côtés de la nature se sont incessamment hérissés de problèmes' (ii. 137). 'Problème' is indeed a key word in Hugo's later poetry,[24] and Baudelaire begins to enumerate these 'problèmes' as a series of questions and conjectures, gently pastiching Hugo's own flamboyant rhetorical style as he does so:

> Comment le père *un* a-t-il pu engendrer la dualité et s'est-il enfin métamorphosé en une population innombrable de nombres? Mystère! La totalité infinie des nombres doit-elle ou peut-elle se concentrer de nouveau dans l'unité originelle? Mystère!

Indeed the word 'mystère' is itself now subjected to that Hugolian art of repetition to which Baudelaire had earlier alluded:

---

[24] See *Unacknowledged Legislators*, 453, 456, 464–6, 470.

Quel que soit le sujet traité, le ciel le domine et le surplombe comme une coupole immuable, d'où plane le mystère avec la lumière, où le mystère scintille, où le mystère invite la rêverie curieuse, d'où le mystère repousse la pensée découragée.

(ii. 137)

Instead, therefore, of the Hugo who believes that poetry can instruct its readers and contribute to moral progress, and the Hugo who in fact does put forward a very definite moral and religious philosophy in *Les Contemplations* (with its putative narrative of universal progression towards redemption), Baudelaire chooses now to present him as the speculative thinker: no longer the man who has the answers ('une sagesse abrégée, faite de quelques axiomes irréfutables') but the man who seeks them. And so, following the eulogy of Hugo as a nomothete, Baudelaire proceeds to use the example of Hugo as a poet of mystery in order to champion his own agenda for poetry as an authoritative form of imaginative speculation. Faced with all these mysteries Hugo's cosmic conjectures constitute an alternative to Newtonian science, a valuable form of 'gap-filling': 'Ah! malgré Newton et malgré Laplace, la certitude astronomique n'est pas, aujourd'hui même, si grande que la rêverie ne puisse se loger dans les vastes lacunes non encore explorées par la science moderne' (ii. 137–8). And this gap-filling extends to metaphysics: 'Très *légitimement*, le poète laisse errer sa pensée dans *un dédale enivrant de conjectures*. Il n'est pas un problème agité ou attaqué, dans n'importe quel temps ou par quelle philosophie, qui ne soit venu réclamer fatalement sa place dans les œuvres du poète' (ii. 138; my emphases). The domain of 'science'— in its double sense of science and knowledge, of the natural sciences and of all that we humans 'know'—is thus limited, and it is *legitimate* for human beings to explore beyond it:

S'abandonner à toutes les rêveries suggérées par le spectacle infini de la vie sur la terre et dans les cieux, est le droit légitime du premier venu, conséquemment du poète, à qui il est accordé alors de traduire, dans un langage magnifique, autre que la prose et la musique, les conjectures éternelles de la curieuse humanité.

(ii. 139)

In Baudelaire's assessment the great virtue of Hugo's cosmic reverie is that it remains speculative and never assumes 'la forme didactique, qui est la plus grande ennemie de la véritable poésie' (ii. 139). For the known is the enemy of true poetry:

Raconter en vers les lois *connues*, selon lesquelles se meut un monde moral ou sidéral, c'est décrire ce qui est découvert et ce qui tombe tout entier sous le télescope ou le compas de la science, c'est se réduire aux devoirs de la science et empiéter sur ses fonctions, et c'est embarrasser son langage traditionnel de l'ornement superflu, et dangereux ici, de la rime[.]   (ii. 139)

For Baudelaire, poetic form thus has a specific role to play in expressing the unknown, an idea already present in his discussion of Gautier. In his view Hugo's poetry had previously lacked this quality of conjecture, and displayed an undue preoccupation with form for form's sake, or at least with the demonstration of its own virtuosity. As we saw in Chapter 1, he condemns Hugo in the *Salon de 1846* as 'un ouvrier beaucoup plus adroit qu'inventif, un travailleur plus bien plus correct que créateur' and regrets particularly that in his poems 'il n'y a rien à deviner; car il prend tant de plaisir à montrer son adresse, qu'il n'omet pas un brin d'herbe ni un reflet de réverbère' (ii. 431). But now, it seems, there is more substance to Hugo's recent poetry, and, again gently pastiching his subject, Baudelaire makes a point of listing a large number of 'conjectures' with a combination of sustained rhetorical questioning and thunder-roll accumulation:

> L'éclosion des êtres est-elle permanente dans l'immensité comme dans la petitesse? Ce que nous sommes tentés de prendre pour la multiplication infinie des êtres ne serait-elle qu'un mouvement de circulation ramenant ces mêmes êtres à la vie vers des époques et dans des conditions marquées par une loi suprême et omnicompréhensive? La matière et le mouvement ne seraient-ils que la respiration et l'aspiration d'un Dieu qui, tour à tour, profère des mondes à la vie et les rappelle dans son sein? Tout ce qui est multiple deviendra-t-il un, et de nouveaux univers, jaillissant de la pensée de Celui dont l'unique bonheur et l'unique fonction sont de produire sans cesse, viendront-t-ils un jour remplacer notre univers et tous ceux que nous voyons suspendus autour de nous? (ii. 138)

Here is a view of God's Creation far removed from that presented in the Book of Genesis, a prospect of vast cyclical processes, of a repeated coming-into-being and going-out-of-being, of the 'mystery of life' as a kind of cosmic breathing in which 'Celui dont l'unique bonheur et l'unique fonction sont de produire sans cesse' begins to resemble the imagination itself, breathing new life into our tired perceptions, disassembling and reassembling the material universe in an endless series of shifting patterns—the imagination of Hugo himself as he explicitly seeks to 're-create' Creation in *Les Contemplations* as though he were the Deity himself.[25]

And what is the moral significance of this cosmic merry-go-round with its vast reaches of interplanetary and interstellar space? That, too, is the proper object of poetic conjecture:

> Et la conjecture sur l'appropriation morale, sur la destination de tous ces mondes, nos voisins inconnus, ne prend-elle pas aussi naturellement sa place dans les

---

[25] See *Unacknowledged Legislators*, 462–4.

immenses domaines de la poésie? Germinations, éclosions, floraisons, éruptions successives, simultanées, lentes ou soudaines, progressives ou complètes, d'astres, d'étoiles, de soleils, de constellations, êtes-vous simplement les formes de la vie de Dieu, ou des habitations préparées par sa bonté ou sa justice à des âmes qu'il veut éduquer et rapprocher progressivement de lui-même? Mondes éternellement étudiés, à jamais inconnus peut-être, oh! dites, avez-vous des destinations de paradis, d'enfers, de purgatoires, de cachots, de villas, de palais, etc?... (ii. 138)

In *Les Contemplations* Hugo surmises that human souls live a succession of corporeal lives, returning again and again in more or less material forms within the cosmos until such time as they shall—through goodness and love—have wholly purged themselves of matter. In 'Saturne' (Book III, 3), where the speculative 'songeur' is depicted leaning his elbows on the 'bord croulant du problème sans fond' (l. 4), the poet imagines the universe as the inside of a tomb (ll. 77–80) and Saturn in particular—the planet of melancholy—as a prison for wicked souls:

> Ceux-là, Saturne, un globe horrible et solitaire,
> Les prendra pour le temps où Dieu voudra punir,
> Châtiés à la fois par le ciel et la terre,
> Par l'aspiration et par le souvenir!
>
> Saturne! sphère énorme! astre aux aspects funèbres!
> Bagne du ciel! prison dont le soupirail luit!'
> ('Saturne' (*Les Contemplations*, iii. 3), ll. 57–62).

Extraordinary and monstrous as such imaginings may be, they are for Baudelaire emblematic of the epistemological power of the imagination and of the supreme value of poetic conjecture in the discovery of new 'laws' beyond the normal compass and orbit of our understanding:

Que des systèmes et des groupes nouveaux, affectant des formes inattendues, adoptant des combinaisons imprévues, subissant des lois non enregistrées, imitant tous les caprices providentiels d'une géométrie trop vaste et trop compliquée pour le compas humain, puissent jaillir des limbes de l'avenir, qu'y aurait-il, dans cette pensée, de si *exorbitant*, de si monstrueux, et qui sortît des limites légitimes de la conjecture poétique? Je m'attache à ce mot 'conjecture', qui sert à définir, passablement, le caractère extra-scientifique de toute poésie. (ii. 138-9)

Again, as with the ship of *Fusées*, we have the argument that the contingent may be governed by 'providential' laws that only the poetic imagination can perceive within the vast geometry of the cosmos, a universal *nomos*, 'une loi suprême et omnicompréhensive' (ii. 138) that only poetry can divine.

This, then, in 1861, is Baudelaire's poet: 'une âme collective qui interroge, qui pleure, qui espère, et qui devine quelquefois' (ii. 139); and it is this new Hugo who has demonstrated the potentially limitless reach of poetry's authority: 'Dans ces derniers temps il nous a prouvé que, pour vraiment limité qu'il soit, le domaine de la poésie n'en est pas moins, par le droit du génie, presque illlimité' (ii. 141). Conventional wisdom—that 'sagesse abrégée, faite de quelques axiomes irréfutables'—has its own limits and its own limitations: the 'limites légitimes' of poetic conjecture, by contrast, can embrace the seemingly monstruous, 'l'excessif, l'immense' that are the 'domaine naturel de Victor Hugo' (ii. 137). For Baudelaire, therefore, poetry (and all art) is the means by which human beings venture forth, forsaking the known in search of the unknown, relinquishing the safely wise to embrace the seemingly crazy. This for him, as he states in the *Salon de 1859*, is the fundamental alternative, the choice to be made:

> [...] l'intelligence humaine portant partout avec elle l'idée de la sagesse et le goût de la folie. Voilà bien l'immortelle antithèse philosophique, la contradiction essentiellement humaine sur laquelle pivote depuis le commencement des âges toute philosophie et toute littérature. (ii. 676)

And whereas quite recently (in 1855) Baudelaire had complained that 'M. Victor Hugo est un grand poète sculptural qui a l'œil fermé à la spiritualité' (*Exposition universelle*, ii. 593), now since publication of *Les Contemplations* and the first series of *La Légende des siècles* the prophet-lawgiver of Guernsey has become the very model of 'un esprit rêveur et interrogateur'.

14
Imagination and Suggestion
Wagner, Guys, Delacroix

> C'est le propre des œuvres vraiment artistiques d'être une source inépuisable de suggestions.
>
> ('Richard Wagner et *Tannhäuser* à Paris', ii. 794)

The words 'symbole' and 'conjecture', derived etymologically from ancient Greek and Latin respectively, have a similar meaning: a 'throwing together'—the perception of an analogy or other form of 'correspondance' or relationship between two things. In his discussion of the imagination throughout the period 1857–63—and in the poem 'Correspondances'—Baudelaire envisages the role of the poetic imagination as being not to determine a fixed relationship but to propose possible relationships. Whereas traditional 'symbolism' forecloses on speculation by inviting a 'translation' of symbols according to a pre-existing code (for example, as laid down by religious doctrine or hermeneutic convention), conjecture constitutes an open-ended consideration of signs and images free from assumption and preconception, a provisional putting of one and one together. For Baudelaire the role of the poet is not to assert but to *suggest*, itself derived etymologically from the Latin meaning to 'carry under(neath)'. In praising Hugo as the poet of conjecture and focusing on his taste for metaphysical questioning, he notes how '[l]a contemplation *suggestive* du ciel occupe une place immense et dominante dans les derniers ouvrages du poète' (ii. 137; my emphasis). Instead of the word 'conjecture', the terms 'suggestive' and 'suggestion' now come to the fore in the articles on Richard Wagner and Constantin Guys (published respectively in 1861 and 1863) to describe the creative and emancipatory function of the imagination. Moreover, whereas in the case of Hugo all the conjecture came from the poet himself, in the case of Gautier the emphasis had been on the conjecture of the reader, and this emphasis on the role of art in provoking an aesthetic response that is itself 'conjectural' resumes a central place in the discussions of Wagner and Guys.

Wagner

> Il reste encore incontestable que plus la musique est éloquente, plus la suggestion est rapide et juste, et plus il y a de chances pour que les

hommes sensibles conçoivent des idées en rapport avec celles qui inspiraient l'artiste.

('Richard Wagner et *Tannhaüser* à Paris', ii. 782)

Baudelaire's enthusiasm for the music of Richard Wagner (1813–83) dates back at least to 1849, when he describes him as 'celui que l'avenir consacrera le plus illustre parmi les maîtres' (*Corr.*, i. 157). This was the year in which Wagner briefly visited Paris, having fled Dresden where he had been outlawed as a revolutionary, and the year in which also, in two published essays *Die Kunst und die Revolution* (Art and Revolution) and *Das Kunstwerk der Zukunft* (The Art Work of the Future), Wagner set out his ideas for a *Gesamtkunstwerk*, or 'total work of art'.[1] Later, in his 'Lettre sur la musique', he recalls his early frustration at the fact that the society of his time regarded opera almost entirely as a form of commercial entertainment and its performance as the mere pretext for a pleasurable social occasion. Instead, he tells us, he resolved to 'tourner cette institution vers un but diamétralement opposé, c'est-à-dire l'appliquer à arracher un peuple aux intérêts vulgaires qui l'occupent tout le jour pour l'élever au culte et à l'intelligence de ce que l'esprit humain peut concevoir de plus profond et de plus grand'.[2] In pursuit of this aim he had looked for some model that would illustrate the exalted role that he envisaged for musical drama within public life, and, in a passage quoted by Baudelaire (ii. 789–90), he describes how he found it in the poet-lawgiver of ancient Greece:

> Je le trouvais, ce modèle, dans le théâtre de l'ancienne Athènes; là, le théâtre n'ouvrait son enceinte qu'à de certaines solennités où s'accomplissait une fête religieuse qu'accompagnaient les jouissances de l'art. Les hommes les plus distingués de l'État prenaient à ces solennités une part directe comme poètes ou directeurs; ils paraissaient comme des prêtres aux yeux de la population assemblée de la cité et du pays, et cette population était remplie d'une si haute attente de la sublimité des œuvres qui allaient être représentées devant elle, que les poèmes les plus profonds, ceux d'un Eschyle et d'un Sophocle, pouvaient être proposés au peuple et assurés d'être parfaitement entendus.

---

[1] In his article on Wagner Baudelaire notes that both these essays were as yet unavailable in French translation and that he had investigated the ideas underlying the composer's work, and especially his use of the leitmotif, by reading an English translation (published in 1855–6) of *Oper und Drama* (Opera and Drama), itself first published in 1852. In fact he appears to have relied on Wagner's 'Lettre sur la musique', first published in December 1860 as an introduction to some French translations of his libretti (see Richard Wagner, *Quatre poèmes d'opéras traduits en prose française, précédés d'une Lettre sur la musique* (Paris: Librairie nouvelle [A. Bourdilliat et Cie], 1861). (See ii. 786 [and n. 3], 1457.) In his 'Lettre sur la musique' Wagner summarizes the ideas expressed in his earlier essays, and Baudelaire quotes extensively from it in his article.

[2] 'Lettre sur la musique', 17.

Here, then, is Wagner the revolutionary in both politics and music who wants to mobilize all art forms jointly in a 'total' or 'complete' work of art, and a work that can play a central role in society by causing us to lift our eyes from trivial everyday concerns and encouraging us to explore the furthest reaches of the human imagination ('ce que l'esprit humain peut concevoir de plus profond et de plus grand'). And this is what mattered to Baudelaire: not so much Wagner's aesthetic and musical theories, still less his politics, but the *effect* of his music, and in particular its effect on *him*.

When Baudelaire first read Poe, he had thought he was reading himself: 'La première fois que j'ai ouvert un livre de lui, j'ai vu, avec épouvante et ravissement, non seulement des sujets rêvés par moi, mais des PHRASES pensées par moi, et écrites par lui vingt ans auparavant' (*Corr.*, ii. 386). Similarly, if more surprisingly, when Baudelaire first heard the music of Wagner, he felt as though he were hearing himself: 'D'abord il m'a semblé que je connaissais cette musique, et plus tard en y réfléchissant, j'ai compris d'où venait ce mirage: il me semblait que cette musique était *la mienne*, et je la reconnaissais comme tout homme reconnaît les choses qu'il est destiné à aimer' (ii. 1452). The first person to find this surprising was perhaps Wagner himself, to whom these words were addressed by Baudelaire in a letter (of 17 February 1860) that its writer presents as 'un cri de reconnaissance': an expression not only of gratitude, therefore, but also of recognition. In this famous piece of fan mail (see *Corr.*, 672-4, ii. 1452-3) the poet thanks the composer for being the occasion of '*la plus grande jouissance musicale que j'aie jamais éprouvée*' and expresses indignant sympathy with an artist who has daily been the subject of 'des articles indignes, ridicules, où on fait tous les efforts pour diffamer votre génie': 'l'indignation m'a poussé à vous témoigner ma reconnaissance; je me suis dit: je veux être distingué de tous ces imbéciles'. Conscious of the potential absurdity of his letter ('Je suis d'un âge où on ne s'amuse plus guère à écrire aux hommes célèbres') Baudelaire thus justifies it as an act of solidarity with a fellow artist and outlaw and with another unacknowledged genius.

But above all he clearly wants to tell Wagner about the feelings he himself had experienced during the recent concert performances (conducted by the composer himself) of pieces taken from *Tannhäuser* and *Lohengrin*:[3]

> le caractère qui m'a principalement frappé, ç'a été la grandeur. Cela représente le grand, et cela pousse au grand. J'ai retrouvé partout dans vos ouvrages la

---

[3] On 25 Jan., 1 and 8 Feb, at the Théâtre-italien. (See ii. 1456.) On the day before he wrote to Wagner, he had already described these feelings enthusiastically to his publisher Auguste Poulet-Malassis: 'Ça a été, cette musique, une des grandes jouissances de ma vie; il y a bien quinze ans que je n'ai pas senti pareil enlèvement' (*Corr.*, i. 671).

solennité des grands bruits, des grands aspects de la Nature, et la solennité des grandes passions de l'homme. On se sent tout de suite enlevé et subjugué.

(*Corr.*, i. 673)

This echoes the closing paragraph of the section on sculpture in the *Salon de 1859*, where Baudelaire insists that great art cannot spring from technique alone but requires 'le goût du grand et la sainte fureur de l'imagination' (ii. 680). There he had described how a sculpture situated in a public space can arrest your attention and 'command' you to 'penser aux choses qui ne sont pas de la terre' (ii. 670). Here in his letter to Wagner he describes the effect of his music in similar terms: 'J'ai senti toute la majesté d'une vie plus large que la nôtre.' More specifically, he has acceded to a state of what could be called 'sensual knowledge':

> J'ai éprouvé souvent un sentiment d'une nature assez bizarre, c'est l'orgueil et la jouissance de comprendre, de me laisser pénétrer, envahir, volupté vraiment sensuelle, et qui ressemble à celle de monter dans l'air ou de rouler sur la mer.[4]

Such feelings, he says, are comparable with those he has known under the influence of drugs: 'ces profondes harmonies me paraissaient ressembler à ces excitants qui accélèrent le pouls de l'imagination', and he attempts to describe his 'high' in abstract terms ('Il y a partout quelque chose d'enlevé et d'enlevant, quelque chose aspirant à monter plus haut, quelque chose d'excessif et de superlatif') before painting the verbal picture of a dark red colour ('ce rouge représente la passion') gradually changing through shades of a brighter red and pink into the 'incandescent' red of a furnace, itself traversé at the last by a single streak of white that is symbolic of 'le cri suprême de l'âme montée à son paroxysme' (*Corr.*, i. 673–4). This climax, at once sexual, spiritual, chromatic, and musical, constitutes 'la plus grande jouissance' that Baudelaire mentions to both Poulet-Malassis and Wagner: a moment of ecstasy, of beauty ('un Infini que j'aime et n'ai jamais connu'), in which the listener (or spectator, or reader) is transported elsewhere into the fourth dimension of 'une vie plus large que la nôtre'. A glimpse of grandeur, of the bigger picture.

In his letter Baudelaire informs Wagner that he has been trying hard to put these feelings into words ('J'avais commencé à écrire quelques méditations'), but he has found it difficult: 'j'ai reconnu l'impossibilité de tout dire' (*Corr.*, i. 674). But then, thirteen months later, on 13 March 1861, came the first night of *Tannhäuser* at the Paris Opera, followed by public controversy and protest, and, after two further performances, Wagner's decision to withdraw the opera. Baudelaire's article, 'Richard Wagner et *Tannhäuser* à Paris'—long pondered

---

[4] On the parallels with Baudelaire's poem 'La Musique' (first published in 1857), see i. 964–5.

and finished in a hurry—was published on 1 April 1861 in the *Revue européenne*.[5] In this article Baudelaire focuses from the start on the *effect* of Wagner's music: first, in the account of the controversy and starkly differing reactions with which Wagner's music has been met in both Germany and France; and, second, in relation to the question of aesthetic response in general and of musical expressivity in particular. Just as in his article on Gautier Baudelaire had sought to exculpate 'l'amour exclusif du Beau' from the charge of mere formalism, so here he begins by addressing the objection that music is an imprecise medium for the expression of non-musical reality: 'J'ai souvent entendu dire que la musique ne pouvait pas se vanter de traduire quoi que ce soit avec certitude, comme fait la parole ou la peinture' (ii. 781). Following the definition of the poet as 'un traducteur, un déchiffreur' (ii. 133) in the article on Hugo, the idea that art 'translates' reality here recurs insistently. While conceding the objection in part, Baudelaire maintains nevertheless that '[la musique] traduit à sa manière, et par les moyens qui lui sont propres' (ii. 781). Moreover the relative lack of precision is itself to be welcomed since it leaves room for the imaginative response of the listener: 'Dans la musique, comme dans la peinture et la musique et même dans la parole écrite, qui est cependant le plus positif des arts, il y a toujours une lacune complétée par l'imagination de l'auditeur' (ii. 781-2).

In this way music is particularly well suited to illustrating the kind of 'conjectural' or 'suggestive' beauty that Baudelaire has in mind and which he sees as the function of the poet as alternative lawgiver to create for his reader. But at the same time he is at pains also to emphasize the degree to which the artist's own 'translations' of reality shape this response: beauty is not wholly in the eye of the beholder. By way of providing quasi-scientific evidential proof of his assertion Baudelaire here undertakes a kind of experiment, juxtaposing three verbal responses to the overture to *Lohengrin*—Wagner's, Liszt's,[6] and his own—in order to demonstrate 'que la véritable musique suggère des idées analogues dans des cerveaux différents' (ii. 784). From this experiment he now concludes that 'suggestion' is the very means by which the artist conveys his own perspective: 'plus la musique est éloquente, plus la suggestion est rapide et juste, et plus il y a de chances pour que les hommes sensibles conçoivent des idées en rapport avec celles qui inspiraient l'artiste' (ii. 782). If this is possible, then it is because sound is, in and of itself, expressive, as is colour. Both are non-verbal instruments of meaning that achieve this expressivity through analogy—through 'throwing together' seemingly disparate but inherently interconnected elements of phenomenal reality. Indeed sound and colour are themselves able to suggest each other and, together,

---

[5] Baudelaire appears to have written the article between the first and second performances of *Tannhäuser* (13 and 18 March) and before the final performance on 24 March. The article was later published in pamphlet form with a *post-scriptum* ('Encore quelques mots') on 4 May. See ii. 1460-1, and n. 1 to ii. 808.

[6] In his *Lohengrin et Tannhäuser de Richard Wagner* (Leipzig: Brockhaus, 1851).

to suggest ideas: and all this because 'les choses [se sont] toujours exprimées par une analogie réciproque, depuis le jour où Dieu a proféré le monde comme une complexe et indivisible totalité' (ii. 784).

Despite some possible irony in the idea of a God 'proffering' rather than creating, this account of the world as originating (somehow) in the divine may seem less radical than those proposed in the *Salon de 1859*, where the human imagination alone perceives order and so may be said to create and 'govern' the world. Even more disconcertingly, Baudelaire now quotes in support of his contention the first two stanzas of his own poem 'Correspondances with their apparent endorsement of Swedenborg's neo-Platonic philosophy of 'correspondance' between the material and the spiritual. But here in the article Baudelaire is concerned above all with the 'meaning' and effect of music, not with any divine truth or pattern that may be inferred from the comparative observation of material phenomena. Particular sounds or musical notes, he contends, have the power to suggest things non-verbally—as well as to inspire the kind of 'sensual knowledge' he describes in his letter to Wagner—and this is obviously of importance to a poet who believes that verse achieves its effects through sound (assonance, alliteration, rhyme, rhythm) as well as semantics. In the stanzas he quotes from his own poem, the key line is therefore the last: 'Les parfums, les couleurs et les sons se répondent' (ii. 784)—not least because this chimes with Wagner's own theory of the *Gesamtkunstwerk*, the subject of the second section of Baudelaire's article. Just as the phenomenal world is apprehended in its 'complexe et indivisible totalité' by our five senses, so Wagner has sought to achieve 'une totalité d'effet' (ii. 790)—itself comparable with Poe's 'unity of impression'—by mobilizing music, word, and stage: 'depuis une déclamation notée et soulignée par la musique avec tant de soin qu'il est impossible au chanteur de s'en écarter en aucune syllabe, véritable arabesque de sons dessinée par la passion, jusqu'aux soins les plus minutieux relatifs aux décors et à la mise en scène' (ii. 790).

But for all that Wagner's operas each have a libretto and may thus be said to include poetry in the 'total work of art', Baudelaire prefers to stress the value of music as a form of non-verbal expression: 'Je tiens seulement à faire observer, à la grande louange de Wagner, que, malgré l'importance très juste qu'il donne au poème dramatique, l'ouverture de *Tannhäuser*, comme celle de *Lohengrin*, est parfaitement intelligible, même à celui qui ne connaîtrait pas le livret' (ii. 797). Moreover it is not only the overtures that have this expressive power, so also do the purely orchestral sections within the drama, such as the so-called Grand March in the second act of *Tannhäuser*: 'l'on peut lui appliquer le même éloge qu'aux deux ouvertures dont j'ai parlé, à savoir d'exprimer de la manière la plus visible, la plus colorée, la plus représentative, ce qu'elle veut exprimer' (ii. 797). And where the literary power of the libretto is already great, music makes it greater still, adding something that renders the expressive combination of words and music unsurpassable.

Such is the case, for example, in Tannhäuser's account of his journey to Rome: 'où la beauté littéraire est si admirablement complétée et soutenue par la mélopée, que les deux éléments ne font plus qu'un inséparable tout [...]; tout est dit, exprimé, traduit, par la parole et la musique, d'une manière si positive, qu'il est presque impossible de concevoir une autre manière de le dire' (ii. 797). Here Baudelaire appears to accept Wagner's own stated belief that music can achieve a level of expressivity that is denied to words alone: 'Wagner n'avait jamais cessé de répéter que la musique (dramatique) devait *parler* le sentiment, s'adapter au sentiment avec la même exactitude que la parole, mais évidemment d'une autre manière, c'est-à-dire exprimer la partie indéfinie du sentiment que la parole, trop positive, ne peut pas rendre' (ii. 786). Moreover, among the extensive quotations from Wagner's own writings, Baudelaire records his contention that 'conséquemment, par l'union intime de ces deux arts, on exprimerait avec la clarté la plus satisfaisante ce que ne pouvait exprimer chacun d'eux isolément' (ii. 789).

But what, then, is the effect of this heightened expressivity, of this 'suggestiveness'? A sense of 'grandeur' certainly, of horizons opened and extended, of imaginative reaches uncovered and explored, but also (as this last quotation from Wagner indicates) a very particular combination of clarity and inexpressibility, or mystery: in other words, that very combination which Baudelaire had identified as central to the poetry of Poe, Gautier, and Hugo.[7] Again Baudelaire quotes Wagner himself:

> Le caractère de la scène et le ton de la légende contribuent ensemble à jeter l'esprit dans cet état de *rêve* qui le porte bientôt jusqu'à la pleine *clairvoyance*, et l'esprit découvre alors un nouvel enchaînement des phénomènes du monde, que ses yeux ne pouvaient apercevoir dans l'état de veille ordinaire... (ii. 792)

As Baudelaire had argued in the *Salon de 1859*, art, through the agency of the creative imagination, makes the world look different. It brings novelty where once there had been familiarity and boredom, and it offers an experience of 'clearsightedness', of perceptual powers refreshed and reinvigorated so that now, as though for the first time, they have the true measure of the world. In discussing the overture to *Lohengrin* Baudelaire presents his own response in very similar terms to those of Wagner, notably in respect of the analogy with dream experience:

> Je me souviens que, dès les premières mesures, je subis une de ces impressions heureuses que presque tous les hommes imaginatifs ont connues, par le rêve,

---

[7] Cf. on Poe: 'C'est quelque chose de profond et de miroitant comme le rêve, de mystérieux et de parfait comme le cristal' (ii. 336); Gautier, whose linguistic clarity enables him to 'définir l'attitude mystérieuse que les objets de la création tiennent devant le regard de l'homme' (ii. 117); and Hugo: 'Quel que soit le sujet traité, le ciel le domine et le surplombe comme une coupole immuable, d'où plane le mystère avec la lumière, où le mystère scintille, où le mystère invite la rêverie curieuse' (ii. 137).

dans le sommeil. Je me sentis délivré *des liens de la pesanteur,* et je retrouvai par le souvenir l'extraordinaire *volupté* qui circule dans *les lieux hauts*[.]   (ii. 784)

He, too, can *see* better, see further (*'un immense horizon'*), more clearly, and beyond words:

Bientôt j'éprouvai la sensation d'une *clarté* plus vive, *d'une intensité de lumière* croissant avec une telle rapidité, que les nuances fournies par le dictionnaire ne suffiraient pas à exprimer *ce surcroît toujours renaissant d'ardeur et de blancheur.* Alors je conçus pleinement l'idée d'une âme se mouvant dans un milieu lumineux, d'une extase *faite de volupté et de connaissance,* et planant au-dessus et bien loin du monde naturel.   (ii. 784–5)

While the specifics of this response—with phrases italicized in preparation for Baudelaire's demonstration of parallel descriptions from Wagner and Liszt— relate only to the *Lohengrin* overture, the description of ecstasy as a combination of pleasure and knowledge has a wider application as the definition of beauty's effect, of 'suggestiveness'. And such an effect is transformative: 'J'avais subi (du moins cela m'apparaissait ainsi) une opération spirituelle, une révélation' (ii. 785).[8]

Guys

Il est le peintre de la circonstance et de tout ce qu'elle suggère d'éternel.
(*Le Peintre de la vie moderne,* ii. 687)

On supposera tout ce que j'ai à dire de sa nature, si curieusement et si mystérieusement éclatante, est plus ou moins justement suggéré par les œuvres en question; pure hypothèse poétique, conjecture, travail d'imagination.
(*Le Peintre de la vie moderne,* ii. 688)

In the case of Constantin Guys the 'suggestiveness' of beauty derives less from a transport of the soul than a journey of the mind. In each of the essays on fellow writers and artists that have so far been examined in the previous chapter and in

---

[8] For further discussion of Baudelaire's response to Wagner, see Margaret Miner, *Resonant Gaps: Between Baudelaire and Wagner* (Athens, Ga, and London: University of Georgia Press, 1995). On the broader question of Baudelaire's (limited) interest in music, see Claude Pichois's 'Notice' to the section entitled 'Critique musicale' in the *Œuvres complètes,* ii. 1451–60. Also Joycelynne Lonke, *Baudelaire et la musique* (Paris: Nizet, 1975).

this, Baudelaire himself adopts a voice of resistance, challenging an antagonistic *parti pris* in the name of an alternative and positive aesthetic. Gautier's formalism contains melancholy and mystery; Hugo's vatic certainty has been replaced by cosmic conjecture; Wagner's controversial innovations make music more, not less, expressive. With Guys the putative objections are ephemerality and triviality, and the counter-objection is that his works are suggestive and stimulate conjecture: 'Ce qui fait la beauté particulière de ces images, c'est leur fécondité morale. Elles sont grosses de suggestions' (ii. 722). Throughout *Le Peintre de la vie moderne* Baudelaire repeatedly asserts the suggestiveness of Guys's art, how his sketches invite us to consider the life and ethos of a given subject—the soldier, the dandy, the courtesan, the actress—and to reflect that each of them, in their own way, represents a particular kind of beauty and indeed that each of them, even the soldier, is actively engaged in the pursuit of beauty. Like a poet.

Constantin Guys (1802–92) was a Dutch-born illustrator and sketch artist, noted particularly for the many drawings of scenes from the Crimean War that he dispatched from the field of battle as a correspondent of the *Illustrated London News* and subsequently for his depictions (predominantly in etching and watercolour) of contemporary city life. Where in the essays on Gautier and Hugo Baudelaire had focused particularly on how poetry represents a universal human condition, and in his discussion of Wagner on the German composer's use of timeless legend, now he turns instead to the art of a specific place and time, presenting Guys as the 'peintre de la vie moderne'. The focus is no longer on 'la beauté générale' but on 'la beauté de circonstance et le trait de mœurs' (ii. 683), on the beauty to be derived from observing the world as it is today. Thus Baudelaire's reflections on Guys continue where the *Salon de 1846* left off, that is, with 'l'héroïsme de la vie moderne' and the assertion that today's world has its own aesthetic potential: 'on peut affirmer que puisque tous les siècles et tous les peuples ont eu leur beauté, nous avons inévitablement la nôtre. Cela est dans l'ordre' (ii. 493).

In his essay on Guys Baudelaire attempts to define what he means by 'modern' and in what ways a 'modern' art can achieve the 'suggestiveness' that he has now come to see as the defining feature of all authentic art. His first step is to make a virtue of necessity and to assert the importance of the 'presentness' of contemporary subjects as an essential aspect of their effect on the viewer, of their beauty: 'Le plaisir que nous retirons de la représentation du présent tient non seulement à la beauté dont il peut être revêtu, mais aussi à sa qualité essentielle de présent' (ii. 684). On the one hand, there is an observable, formal beauty—of shape, colour, and pattern—and, on the other, the spectacle, stimulating to the viewer's imagination and reflexive processes, of that formal beauty being exhibited by some new material presence that is manifest only in the contemporary world.[9] Hence—and

---

[9] Marielle Macé offers a compelling account of how Baudelaire, like Guys, sees the role of the artist as being to 'take responsibility' for the formal patterns by which life (including human life in the city)

before he addresses Guys's work itself—Baudelaire's immediate turn to the subject of fashion: the paradigmatic manifestation of the pursuit of beauty in the present. In order to relativize what might be considered the self-evident nature of present beauty—and thus to provide in advance a productively relativizing perspective on Guys's own sketches—Baudelaire discusses instead a series of fashion plates from the Revolutionary period (1789–99) whose subjects already appear quaintly dated and even ridiculous. But he invites us to look more closely and to think about what, say, the attire of a well-dressed man of the time might have to tell us about the ethos of that period:

> L'idée que l'homme s'est fait du beau s'imprime dans tout son ajustement, chiffonne ou raidit son habit, arrondit ou aligne son geste, et même pénètre subtilement, à la longue, les traits de son visage. L'homme finit par ressembler à ce qu'il voudrait être. (ii. 684)

Similarly, the dresses worn by women of the period may seem curiously lifeless and indeed all much the same, varying only in degrees of chic (or 'poésie' (ii. 684)) and vulgarity. But where once these outfits were animated and individualized by the living flesh of the wearer, now they can be revivified by our own creative imagination: 'La matière rendait ondoyant ce qui nous semble trop rigide. L'imagination du spectateur peut encore aujourd'hui faire marcher et frémir cette *tunique* et ce *schall*' (ii. 684). Just as it is possible to imagine a future costume drama in which these quaint clothes of yesteryear will, as worn by living, breathing actors and actresses, come alive and appear not at all quaint or risible, so the imagination can stage its own theatrical performance and bring the past to life: 'Le passé, tout en gardant le piquant du fantôme, reprendra la lumière et le mouvement de la vie, et se fera présent' (ii. 684). And just as the imagination may vivify the past, so too it can add further life to the living present, the drama of conjecture and surmise.

---

manifests itself, what she calls (acknowledging a debt to Michel Foucault) 'l'esthétique de l'existence' and defines both as 'cette prise en charge du "formel de la vie"' and as 'une attention morale à la façon dont une vie se joue dans des figures, des images, des rythmes'. In essence she sees the poet as discharging this responsibility by effecting an intensification of the expressivity inherent in these 'forms' of life. Having examined Baudelaire's attention to facial appearance, dress, and adornment, as well as to shaping or framing as means of intensification ('Il ne faut pas opposer, ici, une dynamique de l'image à une statique du contour, au contraire, la limite potentialise') she summarizes: 'C'est sans doute cela endosser la responsabilité des formes, les prendre en charge. L'œil, l'habit, la cadence, le désir, le rythme des choses, le rapport à soi et à la foule... tout converge dans cette poésie vers l'exigence d'une même responsabilité, qui est *in fine* morale, à l'égard des formes. C'est là le principe de l'esthétique de l'existence, qui repose sur un exercice de l'imagination dont Baudelaire fait un véritable stoïcisme: une capacité à voir rayonner les formes et à les seconder dans leur rayonnement, en leur traçant des bords artificieux pour augmenter leur éclat.' See Marielle Macé, 'Baudelaire, une esthétique de l'existence', *L'Année Baudelaire*, 18/19 (2014–15), 49–67 (50, 49, 57, and 60 respectively). Macé's comment on framing is derived from Martin Rueff, 'Le Cadre infini—sur la poétique baudelairienne', *Littérature*, 177 (2015), 21–37.

Part of the presentness and suggestiveness of the image of a well-dressed revolutionary lies therefore in the wearer's own criteria of beauty and, more generally, in the ethos of his behaviour: in short, 'la morale et l'esthétique du temps' (ii. 684). What we wear demonstrates who we want to be, what we want to be, how we think we should be: in short, beauty is an expression of desire. Hence Baudelaire's approval, albeit more grudging here than in the *Salon de 1846*,[10] of Stendhal's celebrated dictum: 'le Beau n'est que la promesse du bonheur' (ii. 686). Accordingly, Baudelaire contends, if one were to examine every passing fashion there has ever been throughout the history of France and to consider each fashion period in relation to 'la pensée philosophique dont celle-ci était le plus occupée ou agitée' (ii. 685), one would most probably discover two things: 'l'immortel appétit du beau' (ii. 685), and the smoothness of historical change: 'quelle profonde harmonie régit tous les membres de l'histoire' (ii. 685). A continuous narrative would emerge of gradually evolving expectations of beauty accompanied by slowly shifting intellectual and moral attitudes such that no period, no fashion—however 'monstrueux' or 'fou' it might appear to us now—would seem shocking or unexpected.

At one level, Baudelaire is merely echoing the view that beauty, being culturally and historically determined, is relative. Staël had already made this (at the time bold) claim in *De la littérature* (1800), largely on geographical and climatological grounds, and it informs French aesthetics throughout the first half of the nineteenth century (for example, in Stendhal's *Racine et Shakespeare* and Hugo's preface to *Cromwell*). But in characteristic manner Baudelaire is also arguing that the very knowledge of this relativity (on the part of both artist and observer) is itself part of beauty itself, part of artistic expression. He here explicitly rejects 'la théorie du beau unique et absolu' (ii. 685). Modernity means reflexivity, and if the artist is a double agent, so too is the work of art itself: 'le beau est toujours, inévitablement, d'une composition double, bien que l'impression qu'il produit soit une' (ii. 685). 'Modern' art recognizes this fact and does not seek to conceal its status as a double act: that is, as a thing of would-be timeless beauty produced within a particular historical and cultural moment. 'Modern' art is therefore an art aware of its own historicity, so that the way in which the work of modern art articulates that awareness becomes part of its suggestiveness, its beauty.

Baudelaire here repeats the 'modern' definition of beauty that he had proposed in the *Salon de 1846*:

Toutes les beautés contiennent, comme tous les phénomènes possibles, quelque chose d'éternel et quelque chose de transitoire,—d'absolu et de particulier. La

---

[10] Having defined Romanticism in accordance with Stendhal's own definition in *Racine et Shakespeare* as 'l'expression la plus récente, la plus actuelle du beau', Baudelaire further employs Stendhal's own phraseology: 'Il y a autant de beautés qu'il y a de manières habituelles de chercher le bonheur' (ii. 420).

> beauté absolue et éternelle n'existe pas, ou plutôt elle n'est qu'une abstraction écrémée à la surface générale des beautés diverses. L'élément particulier de chaque beauté vient des passions, et comme nous avons nos passions particulières, nous avons notre beauté.   (ii. 493)

Back then he had reflected on the artistic representation of the modern trend for men to dress only in black (frock coat, top hat, etc.), evident already in Dumas père's contemporary drama *Antony* (1831) and soon to be a controversial feature of Courbet's famous painting *Un enterrement à Ornans* (1849–50).[11] The beauty of black is at once historical and timeless, political and poetic, suggestive both of the alleged classlessness of the newly instituted 'bourgeois' monarchy and of a society in mourning, indeed of a world of universal and eternal melancholy:

> Remarquez bien que l'habit noir et la redingote ont non seulement leur beauté politique, qui est l'expression de l'égalité universelle, mais encore leur beauté poétique, qui est l'expression de l'âme publique;—une immense défilade de croque-morts, croque-morts politiques, croque-morts amoureux, croque-morts bourgeois. Nous célébrons tous quelque enterrement.   (ii. 494)

Here in *Le Peintre de la vie moderne* Baudelaire restates his former definition of beauty as 'double':

> Le beau est fait d'un élément éternel, invariable, dont la quantité est excessivement difficile à déterminer, et d'un élément relatif, circonstanciel, qui sera, si l'on veut, tour à tour ou tout ensemble, l'époque, la mode, la morale, la passion.
> (ii. 685)

But now he stresses that the 'particular' is not only unavoidable in art but also essential to beauty's effect:

> Sans ce second élément, qui est comme l'enveloppe amusante, titillante, apéritive, du divin gâteau, le premier élément serait indigestible, inappréciable, non adapté et non appropriée à la nature humaine.   (ii. 685)

And why is it essential? As Baudelaire himself recognizes ('J'ai plus d'une fois déjà expliqué ces choses' (ii. 686)), his answer is by now familiar: 'La dualité de l'art est une conséquence de la dualité de l'homme' (ii. 685–6).

In this way Baudelaire prepares the ground for his discussion of Constantin Guys as an exemplary 'peintre de la vie moderne' by presenting the ephemeral and

---

[11] See ii. 1323–4 nn. 3, 4, and 5.

the time-bound as a necessary ingredient in all art. At the same time, in the second section of the article ('Le Croquis de mœurs'), he anticipates the potential charge that Guys is concerned only with trivia by asserting the technical difficulty of recording the fleeting moments of quotidian life and by thereby implicitly enhancing the prestige of his work: 'il y a dans la vie triviale, dans la métamorphose journalière des choses extérieures, un mouvement rapide qui commande à l'artiste une égale vélocité d'exécution' (ii. 686). As to the objective itself, of recording contemporary life, Baudelaire describes it as 'cette énorme tâche, si frivole en apparence' (ii. 686) and notes how, brilliantly served by the recently invented art of lithography, this objective has already produced some great works of art: 'Nous avons dans ce genre de véritables monuments' (ii. 686–7). Whether it be Gavarni or Daumier, or indeed Balzac in the novel, the artist of the 'croquis de mœurs' has one all-important function, to make the contingent seem part of a bigger picture: 'il est le peintre de la circonstance et de tout ce qu'elle suggère d'éternel' (ii. 687). 'Suggestiveness' is the art of the alternative lawgiver, of situating the seemingly random within some newly perceived network of connection and as subject to a set of hitherto unformulated laws.

As though exemplifying this art of 'suggestiveness' in his own essay, Baudelaire now takes the figure of Constantin Guys himself as the 'circonstance' and infers from his works a generalized ('eternal') theory of what might be called art-within-life. Guys, it seems, is the most self-effacing of artists ('Grand amoureux de la foule et de l'incognito' (ii. 688)), never signing his own works, angry that Thackeray should have written an article in which he explicitly names him, and imploring Baudelaire not to do the same. He is, as it were, hidden behind his various drawings and watercolours, which nevertheless speak for him: 'tous ses ouvrages sont signés de son âme éclatante' (ii. 688). Indeed he begins to look like an emblematic figure representing that combination of clarity and mysteriousness that Baudelaire finds in Gautier's writing and Wagner's music. Referring to Guys he defends himself against the charge of having invaded his privacy precisely on the grounds that his sketches prompt conjecture, and in this case conjecture as to the nature of the person who produced them:

> pour rassurer complètement ma conscience, on supposera que tout ce que j'ai à dire de sa nature, si curieusement et si mystérieusement éclatante, est plus ou moins justement suggéré par les œuvres en question; pure hypothèse poétique, conjecture, travail d'imagination. (ii. 688)

But Guys is not so much an individual as an 'homme du monde', that is to say not a biographically definable entity who produces art on the basis of that individuality but an artist who understands and gives expression to the world as a whole, a sort of lawgiver: 'c'est-à-dire homme du monde entier, homme qui comprend le monde et les raisons mystérieuses et légitimes de tous ses usages' (ii. 689). In fact

Guy himself rejects the term 'artiste', believing that 'artists' tends to live in isolated communities, cut off from real life: 'L'artiste vit très peu, ou même pas du tout, dans le monde moral ou politique' (ii. 689). But in his case 'curiosité' constitutes 'le point de départ de son génie' (ii. 689): 'Il s'intéresse au monde entier; il veut savoir, comprendre, apprécier tout ce qui se passe à la surface de notre sphéroïde' (ii. 689)—like the convalescent hero of Poe's story *The Man of the Crowd*.

Once again Baudelaire is to be found sidestepping an obvious binary—here once more that of 'pure' and didactic art—by depicting an artist who shuns art for art's sake but whose interest in the world of human affairs prompts no philosophical or moral agenda. This artist, this 'man of the world', is simply possessed of an insatiable curiosity and desire to know, even about the trivial, as though he were himself a convalescent newly returned to health and vigour, gratefully savouring and treasuring life's every little circumstance: 'Le convalescent jouit au plus haut degré, comme l'enfant, de la faculté de s'intéresser vivement aux choses, même les plus triviales en apparence' (ii. 690). Like a child the artist is possessed of 'cette curiosité profonde et joyeuse' (ii. 690) and sees everything 'en *nouveauté*' (ii. 690). For Guys, as for the convalescent or the child, the world is only apparently trivial: in fact it is full of suggestion, inspiring his most passionate interest as he loses himself and his very identity in the crowd and becomes instead its reflector, comparable to 'un kaléidoscope doué de conscience, qui, à chacun de ses mouvements, représente la vie multiple et la grâce mouvante de tous les éléments de la vie' (ii. 692).

Hence perhaps Guys's own desire for anonymity as an artist: 'C'est un *moi* insatiable du *non-moi*, qui, à chaque instant, le rend et l'exprime en images plus vivantes que la vie elle-même, toujours instable et fugitive' (ii. 692). What Guys has found with his artist's eye is life itself, and each day he sets out across Paris in search of that life: 'Et il part! et il regarde couler le fleuve de la vitalité, si majestueux et si brillant' (ii. 692). What does he find? Not trivia and ephemera but a taste of the eternal, a teeming city life that is all movement and harmony, offering the eurhythmic beauty of the ship of *Fusées*: 'Il admire l'éternelle beauté et l'étonnante harmonie de la vie dans les capitales, harmonie si providentiellement maintenue dans le tumulte de la liberté humaine' (ii. 692). His eagle-eye takes in everything, the slightest change in vestimentary fashion, the myriad visual details of a passing regiment, and very soon the work of art is ready to emerge: 'dans quelques minutes, le poème qui en résulte sera virtuellement composé' (ii. 693). A sketch is a poem of life, just as life itself is a poem or a song: 'M. G[uys] restera le dernier partout où peut resplendir la lumière, retentir la poésie, fourmiller la vie, vibrer la musique' (ii. 693). Whereupon he returns home to commit his visual memories to the page, 'translating' his impressions onto paper with a force and accuracy that communicate themselves in turn to the imagination of the subsequent viewer of his work: 'et l'imagination du spectateur, subissant à son tour cette mnémonique si despotique, voit avec netteté l'impression produite par les choses sur l'esprit de M. G.. Le spectateur est ici le traducteur d'une traduction toujours claire et enivrante' (ii. 698). Again, that combination of clarity and suggestiveness: thanks to Guys '[l]a fantasmagorie a été extraite de la nature' (ii. 694)), as he not only records life but brings life to life ('en images plus vivantes que la vie elle-même').

By allowing memory to winnow out the inessential, Guys is trying to capture in his sketches that which Baudelaire calls 'modernité' (ii. 694), by which he means very specifically that (trivial, ephemeral) element in the circumstantial that reflects 'l'immortel appétit du beau': 'Il s'agit, pour lui, de dégager de la mode ce qu'elle peut contenir de poétique dans l'historique, de tirer l'éternel du transitoire' (ii. 694). Today's fashions, our modishness, our contemporary formulae for appearing and behaving at our best—in short, what we might now call our lifestyles and our mindsets—all bespeak a human desire to shape the givens of quotidian circumstance, to take control of what Sartre calls our 'facticity' and transform it in an act of constructive imagination that is also what we call 'art'. To be a 'peintre de la vie moderne' means not just to record the present by focusing on the circumstantial in the manner of the 'pûr flâneur' (ii. 694)—or indeed of the Realist—but more especially to identify and illustrate the ways in which human beings transform and *transcend* the present, and this in order to perpetuate such contemporary transformations—these creations of beauty—for the benefit of future generations (rather as the elegant Revolutionaries have been so perpetuated in engravings):

> En un mot, pour que toute *modernité* soit digne de devenir antiquité, il faut que la beauté mystérieuse que la vie humaine y met involontairement en ait été extraite. C'est à cette tâche que s'applique particulièrement M. G[uys].   (ii. 695)

Here it is no longer 'la fantasmagorie' but 'la beauté mystérieuse' that has been extracted from life, but the two are clearly synonymous: from the spectacle of the supposedly real and the allegedly self-evident there has been derived a dream-like and mysterious suggestiveness that for the observer of Guys's sketches constitutes beauty. In Baudelaire's analysis Guys makes apparent and visible an 'involuntary' and unconscious 'will to beauty' that informs the tumult of city life in particular and of human existence in general. If beauty here be defined as the effect derived from observing the present as a manifestation of the human urge to transform the present, then the 'beauté mystérieuse' (and 'fantasmagorie') that Guys extracts from modern life—just as Baudelaire once aimed to extract 'la *beauté* du Mal'—is in fact the beauty of desire, and here the beauty of our desire for beauty: that is, the suggestiveness of the different forms taken by this human capacity to lend shape and significance to the triviality of an ephemeral, contingent—and godless—life.

For Guys, in Baudelaire's opinion, is above all a painter of desire, and to view his sketches is to be prompted to a series of moral reflections on the ways in which desire manifests itself within the 'pomp' of life ('pomp' comes from the Greek *pompē* = procession):

> Pour définir une fois de plus le genre des sujets préférés par l'artiste, nous dirons que c'est *la pompe de la vie*, telle qu'elle s'offre dans les capitales du monde civilisé, la pompe de la vie militaire, de la vie élégante, de la vie galante. Notre observateur est toujours exact à son poste, partout où coulent les désirs profonds et impétueux, les Orénoques du cœur humain, la guerre, l'amour, le jeu; partout où s'agitent les fêtes et les fictions qui représentent ces grands éléments de bonheur et d'infortune.   (ii. 707)

Life is a parade, and each profession—including, and perhaps most especially, the 'oldest profession'—has, like each era, its own type of beauty, and one which reflects its own particular ethos: 'chacune tire sa beauté extérieure des lois morales auxquelles elle est soumise. [. . .] Le militaire, pris en général, a sa beauté, comme le dandy et la femme galante ont la leur, d'un goût essentiellement différent' (ii. 707). To observe, as Guys does, the ways in which a soldier or a dandy or a prostitute each is—and/or seeks to be—beautiful is therefore to be prompted into conjecture about the 'lois morales' that inform both their beauty and their aspirations to be beautiful.

In the case of the soldier Baudelaire pursues his own illustrative conjectures, inferring a characteristic military 'look' from the unique circumstances of army life. First, the soldier is used to surprises and knows also that he may soon die: 'Le signe particulier de la beauté sera donc, ici, une insouciance martiale, un mélange singulier de placidité et d'audace; c'est une beauté qui dérive de la nécessité d'être prêt à mourir à chaque minute' (ii. 707–8). Second, the soldier is childlike in that (a) he lives in an enclosed and protected community as does a schoolboy or monk, (b) his life is organized for him by a higher authority, and (c) his duty done for the day, he is easily entertained and enjoys violent games: hence 'le visage du militaire idéal devra être marqué d'une grande simplicité'. Baudelaire then goes on to itemize individual sketches by Guy depicting military personnel of different ages, rank, and training, but his overall conclusion is plain: 'Je ne crois pas exagérer en affirmant que toutes ces considérations morales jaillissent naturellement des croquis et des aquarelles de M. G.' (ii. 708). The suggestiveness of art entails conjecture, therefore, not only about the nature of the artist (what sort of man is Constantin Guys?) but about human nature in general and about individual human situations. Even the sketch has a moral seriousness that automatically ('naturellement') engages the viewer's mind and judgement. Indeed it may cause him or her to think about the nature of art itself.

Baudelaire ends his account of the dandy (in section ix) by commenting on how he has seemingly digressed from his discussion of Guys and yet in fact has precisely been engaging in just this type of moral reflection on Guys's work, and indeed with every justification: 'Les considérations et les rêveries morales qui surgissent des dessins d'un artiste sont, dans beaucoup de cas, la meilleure traduction que le critique en puisse faire; les suggestions font partie d'une idée mère, et, en les montrant successivement, on peut la faire deviner' (ii. 712). Echoing his earlier insistence that he is not talking about Guys the man but about Guys's art, this apparent temporary elision of his subject serves to underline how the beauty of a work of art lies not with its producer but with its receiver's interpretation. In this case, as with the soldier, Baudelaire show how the dandy's beauty is determined by a set of moral laws: 'Le dandysme, qui est une institution en dehors des lois, a des lois rigoureuses auxquelles sont strictement soumis tous ses sujets, quelles que soient d'ailleurs la fougue et l'indépendance de leur caractère' (ii. 709). And what drives the desire to be a dandy?

> Qu'est-ce donc que cette passion qui, devenue doctrine, a fait des adeptes dominateurs, cette institution non écrite qui a formé une caste si hautaine? C'est avant tout le besoin ardent de se faire une originalité, contenu dans les limites extérieures des convenances.   (ii. 710)

Like a poet writing an effective sonnet perhaps, the dandy strives to achieve the exceptional while scrupulously observing every known rule or norm that is conventionally held to govern his behaviour. Where the soldier lived like a monk, the dandy's daily toilette also resembles a monastic discipline, and dandyism itself a religion (ii. 711). Where the soldier showed impassivity and audacity in the face of death, the dandy demonstrates a similar spirit of resistance in the face of contingency. For all dandies the one true enemy is triviality: 'tous participent du même caractère d'opposition et de révolte; tous sont des représentants de ce qu'il y a de meilleur dans l'orgueil humain, de ce besoin, trop rare chez ceux d'aujourd'hui, de combattre et de détruire la trivialité' (ii. 711). But like the soldier who knows he must die, the dandy, too, is aware of destructiveness and failure and ephemerality, and so he epitomizes the modern artist as a hero of melancholy: 'Le dandysme est un soleil couchant; comme l'astre qui décline, il est superbe, sans chaleur et plein de mélancolie' (ii. 712). Here the implicit charge of triviality laid against Guys's choice of subject is finally laid to rest: for triviality is the enemy that we should all—ideally ('ce qu'il y a de meilleur dans l'orgueil humain')—resist: like the dandy, like the artist.

Finally Baudelaire turns to the beauty of woman: of woman as the object and goad of male desire, of woman as work of art, and of woman—despite the many misogynistic comments to be found throughout Baudelaire's work—as moral ideal. Here (in sections x–xii) it becomes apparent once more, as in the description of beauty in *Fusées*, f. 16, how for Baudelaire beauty is fundamentally a manifestation of desire: both sexual desire and the quasi-procreative, artistic desire to bring life to life. For the heterosexual male body and for the heterosexual male artist, woman is the potential source of greatest satisfaction: 'la source des plus vives, et même, disons-le à la honte des voluptés philosophiques, des plus durables jouissances' (ii. 713), 'cet être [...] pour qui, mais surtout *par qui* les artistes et les poètes composent leurs plus délicats bijoux' (ii. 713). Woman is the compelling cynosure of male effort, a kind of goddess: 'cet être terrible et incommunicable comme Dieu', 'une divinité, un astre, qui préside à toutes les conceptions du cerveau mâle' (ii. 713). Indeed for the male she represents the most potent stimulus to conjecture: 'c'est l'objet de l'admiration et de la curiosité la plus vive que le tableau de la vie puisse offrir au contemplateur' (ii. 713).

In Baudelaire's analysis woman epitomizes a 'will to beauty' that is inherent in the triviality and banality of life itself. Once again we find that mixture of clarity and mystery that was said to be characteristic of Gautier and Wagner, only now the clarity is represented in the alleged mindless transparency of the female: 'l'être dont nous parlons n'est peut-être incompréhensible que parce qu'il n'a rien à communiquer' (ii. 713). But woman does not represent a purely physical ideal, the 'bel animal' (ii. 713) of De Maistre's own misogynistic conception, nor yet the aesthetic ideal of some flawless perfection ('le type de beauté pure, tel que peut le rêver le sculpteur dans ses plus sévères méditations' (ii. 713)), but rather an effect comparable with that of art: 'le mystérieux et complexe enchantement' (ii. 713). For she is the work of her own art, and, like the tumultuous city itself in which Guys's women have their being, her beauty—a 'promesse de bonheur'—is comparable with that of the ship of *Fusées*, a harmonious combination of stasis and movement, of nature and artifice:

> La femme est sans doute une lumière, un regard, une invitation au bonheur, une parole quelquefois; mais elle est surtout une harmonie générale, non seulement dans son allure et les mouvement de ses membres, mais aussi dans les mousselines, les gazes, les vastes et chatoyantes nuées d'étoffes dont elle s'enveloppe, et qui sont comme les attributs et le piédestal de sa divinité; dans le métal et le minéral qui serpentent autour de ses bras et de son cou, qui ajoutent leurs étincelles au feu de ses regards, ou qui jasent doucement à ses oreilles. (ii. 714)

Female beauty is a combination of nature and art, of 'la femme et la robe', together constituting 'une totalité indivisible': 'Tout ce qui orne la femme, tout ce qui sert à illustrer sa beauté, fait partie d'elle-même' (ii. 714).

Pursuing his practice of inferring moral laws from a particular type of beauty, Baudelaire draws from Guys's depictions of women the 'considération morale' that the body, the 'natural', is bad where there is no accompanying will to beauty: that is, no desire to transform the natural, no evidence of the 'immortel appétit du beau', no urge to transcend the contingency and triviality of the present. Nature without art is bad, and imagination—the constructive imagination that knows, calculates, and creates—is what makes life good. And it takes a prophet, a lawgiver, to make this vital point to humanity, over and over again:

> Passez en revue, analysez tout ce qui est naturel, toutes les actions et les désirs du pur homme naturel, vous ne trouverez rien que d'affreux. Tout ce qui est beau et noble est le résultat de la raison et du calcul. Le crime, dont l'animal humain a puisé le goût dans le ventre de sa mère, est originellement naturel. La vertu, au contraire, est *artificielle*, surnaturelle, puisqu'il a fallu, dans tous les temps et chez toutes les nations, des dieux et des prophètes pour l'enseigner à l'humanité animalisée, et que l'homme, *seul*, eût été impuissant à la découvrir. Le mal se fait sans effort, *naturellement*, par fatalité; le bien est toujours le produit d'un art. Tout ce que je dis de la nature comme mauvaise conseillère en matière de morale, et de la raison comme véritable rédemptrice et réformatrice, peut être transporté dans l'ordre du beau. Je suis ainsi conduit à regarder la parure comme un des signes de la noblesse primitive de l'âme humaine. (ii. 715–16)

By implication, Rousseau—that false prophet—is wrong: natural man is wicked, goodness is acquired. But alongside that natural wickedness (Baudelaire's version of original sin) there exists a 'primitive' appetite for beauty. Beauty *is* redemptive, and the will to beauty, to transform the natural through art, is morally akin to virtue, *is* virtue. Fashion is thus a manifestation of the human goodness we call creativity (and that Baudelaire calls the 'idéal'):

> La mode doit donc être considérée comme un symtôme du goût de l'idéal surnageant dans le cerveau humain au-desssus de tout ce que la vie naturelle y accumule de grossier, de terrestre et d'immonde, comme une déformation sublime de la nature, ou plutôt comme un essai permanent et successif de réformation de la nature. (ii. 716)

Re-formation, not de-formation, re-creation as a response to the destruction inherent in our natural and material existence, a bringing of life to life: thanks to the vitality and creativity inherent in art, beauty is the one form of desire that resists death and destructiveness. And, as though to provoke his reader further after this radical revision of Cousinian aesthetics—and this deconstruction of the binary of nature and civilization (artifice is natural!)—Baudelaire presents fashion, and by extension the quest for beauty, as the expression of a 'titillating' desire to satisfy our spiritual longing. Each new passing fashion represents 'un effort nouveau, plus ou moins heureux, vers le beau, une approximation quelconque d'un idéal dont le désir titille sans cesse l'esprit humain non satisfait' (ii. 716). The pursuit of beauty constitutes our most effective resistance to melancholy.

Woman, thus, like the dandy and the artist, is herself a resistance hero, a noble representative of the human will to beauty: 'La femme est bien dans son droit, et même elle accomplit une espèce de devoir en s'appliquant à paraître magique et surnaturelle' (ii. 716–17). Indeed she can serve as a role model for the artist: 'C'est dans ces considérations que l'artiste philosophe trouvera facilement la légitimation de toutes les pratiques employées dans tous les temps par les femmes pour consolider et diviniser, pour ainsi dire, leur fragile beauté' (ii. 717). Make-up is art, and mascara is a woman's prosody, artifice that frames and deepens and provokes conjecture: 'ce cadre noir rend le regard plus profond et plus singulier, donne à l'œil une apparence plus décidée de fenêtre ouverte sur l'infini' (ii. 717). The true purpose of cosmetic transformation is not to simulate nature (for example, to maintain or restore the appearance of youth) but to improve upon nature, so that the effect of cosmetic beauty—the effect that *is* beauty—is to make you think about the nature of beauty itself, about human agency and the human ability to create and to transform. Beauty in that sense inspires us to resist—to resist nature, and time, and decay. Beauty teaches us to be human, to be active, to use our creative imagination. If we don't look good, slap on the slap, or at least the moisturizer: if we're feeling melancholic, imagine the world anew.

Now, in section xii ('Les Femmes et les filles'), Baudelaire returns to Guys and describes how—'s'étant imposé la tâche de chercher et d'expliquer la beauté dans la *modernité*'—he presents modern women who are 'très parées et embellies par toutes les pompes artificielles' (ii. 718), no matter from what walk of life they may come, and demonstrates through them that the pursuit of beauty is inherent in life itself. In the theatre Guys shows us not only the actresses but the well-to-do women watching them, themselves living works of art: 'elles sont théâtrales et solennelles, comme le drame ou l'opéra qu'elles font semblant d'écouter' (ii. 718). Resplendent in the ambient light that gleams on lustrous skin and sparkles in their jewels, these ladies—'[l]es unes, graves et sérieuses, les autres, blondes et évaporées'—sit like living portraits 'dans la loge qui leur sert de cadre' (ii. 718). To live is to perform, as we see also in Guys's sketches of public gardens in which 'elegant' families perambulate with an air of cosy satisfaction while young girls, resembling 'de petites femmes', pretend to pay formal calls on their companions, 'répétant ainsi la comédie donnée à domicile par leurs parents' (ii. 719). Further down the social ladder teenage actresses in fleapit theatres thrill to dress up in the silliest of costumes, while in cafés, too, life is a comedy. The man sits, perfectly tailored and coiffed, beside his mistress, her foot ostentatiously perched on a stool 'pour ressembler à une grande dame' (ii. 719), her tiny mouth filled with an enormous cigar: not so much a 'grande dame' as a 'grande drôlesse à qui il ne manque presque rien (ce presque rien, c'est presque tout, c'est la distinction)' (ii. 719). But for all their mindless pretension this couple, too, are works of art, not so much self-regarding as objects to be regarded:

> Est-il bien sûr qu'ils regardent? à moins que, Narcisses de l'imbécillité, ils ne contemplent la foule comme un fleuve qui leur rend leur image. En réalité, ils existent bien plutôt pour le plaisir de l'observateur que pour leur plaisir propre.
> (ii. 719)

In this they contrast with the female dancer to be found in music-halls and pleasure-gardens,[12] the emblem of a shady and illicit beauty ('l'image variée de la beauté interlope' (ii. 719–20)) and herself representative of the artist as double agent, being ostensibly oblivious to her own act of performance but in fact acutely attentive to how her performance is seen and, more especially, by whom: 'elles vont, elles viennent, passent et repassent, ouvrant un œil étonné comme celui des animaux, ayant l'air de ne rien voir, mais examinant tout' (ii. 719). The dancer can play a variety of roles to suit all tastes ('une élégance provocante et barbare', 'la simplicité usitée dans un meilleur monde' (ii. 720)), for she, too, is a living work of art ('elle darde son regard sous son chapeau, comme un portrait dans son cadre' (ii. 720)); and in her knowing deployment of beauty in the service of desire she is also a 'fleur du Mal': 'Elle représente bien la sauvagerie dans la civilisation. Elle a sa beauté qui lui vient du Mal, toujours dénuée de spiritualité, mais quelquefois teintée d'une fatigue qui joue la mélancolie' (ii. 720). As we see here, the moral experience of this seeker after beauty is not even worthy of the term 'melancholy', since she is devoid of any sophisticated perception of a mismatch between aspiration and reality. In truth, she is simply exhausted and ultimately incapable of disguising the nullity of her existence. She is an outsider, a kind of unwitting alternative lawgiver by virtue of the sheer inadequacy of her performance: 'Type de bohème errant sur les confins d'une société régulière, la trivialité de sa vie, qui est une vie de ruse et de combat, se fait fatalement jour à travers son enveloppe d'apparat' (ii. 720).

Hence the parallels that Baudelaire proceeds to draw between the work of a dancer—now described as a courtesan—and that of an actress, and between that of an actress and that of a poet. In the case of the actress the parallel arises because 'elle aussi, elle est une créature d'apparat, un objet de plaisir public' (ii. 720). For the dancer-courtesan the purpose of her beauty is sexual seduction and material reward, whereas for the actress 'la conquête, la proie, est d'une nature plus noble, plus spirituelle': 'Il s'agit d'obtenir la faveur générale, non pas seulement par la pure beauté physique, mais aussi par des talents de l'ordre le plus rare' (ii. 720). In this respect the actress resembles the poet in possessing 'une sorte de beauté professionnelle' (ii. 720), and each employs this beauty to secure the engagement and adherence of an audience.

Here, as we approach the end of *Le Peintre de la vie moderne*, Baudelaire's account of Guys begins to come full circle. Triviality, it seems, is the default of human existence, 'fatally' revealing itself no matter how 'beauty' may endeavour to conceal it. Triviality is the truth, and Guys has revealed it. But, faced with this triviality, beauty is all we have, as Baudelaire makes clear in the last two stanzas of

---

[12] Baudelaire uses the general term 'galeries' to denote all these establishments, a word that also translates as 'arcades'.

'L'Amour du mensonge' (first published in 1860 before being included in the 'Tableaux parisiens' one year later):

> Je sais qu'il est des yeux, des plus mélancoliques,
> Qui ne recèlent point de secrets précieux;
> Beaux écrins sans joyaux, médaillons sans reliques,
> Plus vides, plus profonds que vous-mêmes, ô Cieux!
>
> Mais ne suffit-il pas que tu sois l'apparence,
> Pour réjouir un cœur qui fuit la vérité?
> Qu'importe ta bêtise ou ton indifférence?
> Masque ou décor, salut! J'adore ta beauté.
>
> (ll. 17–24)

Melancholy itself may be vacuous, mere exhaustion, and life (as Shakespeare has it in *Macbeth*) 'a tale | Told by an idiot, full of sound and fury | Signifying nothing'. Those living portraits that are the young ladies at the opera sit silently ('l'éventail aux dents'), staring into the void ('l'œil vague ou fixe'), as do the café customers, imbeciles gazing out upon imbecility, seeing their fellow human beings in the crowd merely as a river of endless repetition reflecting their own vacuity. But Guys has made that vacuity interesting, suggestive, a stimulus to conjecture. Amongst all his many sketches that both literally evoke and metaphorically constitute 'cette galerie immense de la vie de Londres et de la vie de Paris' so that his pictorial art is itself a kind of pleasure garden or music hall performance, he presents 'les différents types de la femme errante, de la femme révoltée à tous les étages': a gamut of female sex workers stretching from the apprentice prostitute ('la femme galante, dans sa première fleur') to the brothel slaves owning and earning nothing from their slavery (ii. 720–1). Like the soldier and the dandy, these women as depicted by Guys have the power to make you think: 'Ce qui les rend précieuses et les consacre, c'est les innombrables pensées qu'elles font naître, généralement sévères et noires. [...] Ce qui fait la beauté particulière de ces images, c'est leur fécondité morale. Elles sont grosses de suggestions, mais de suggestions cruelles, âpres' (ii. 722). And anyone looking for a pornographic thrill will be disappointed, finding here nothing to excite 'une imagination malade': instead, only 'l'art pur, c'est-à-dire la beauté particulière du mal, le beau dans l'horrible' (ii. 722)—that is, something to stimulate a *healthy* imagination.

Thus, like Delacroix, Gautier, Hugo, and Wagner, Constantin Guys appears as an avatar of Baudelaire himself. The sketch artist is the true 'painter' of life as we now in modern, godless times perceive it to be: contingent, meaningless, trivial, a theatre of ill-being. By extracting beauty from 'le Mal' and by making the trivial interesting Guys provides a role model at once for the poet of *Les Fleurs du Mal* and for the author of *Le Spleen de Paris*. Not only has he demonstrated the presence of art within life by depicting the soldier and the dandy, the society lady and the music-hall tart, as all engaged in a performance of beauty, but he has through his art captured the vitality of life itself, harvesting the grapes of everyday *present* experience and deriving from their bitter juice the poetic means to a heady intoxication:

> Il a cherché partout dans la beauté passagère, fugace, de la vie présente, le caractère de ce que le lecteur nous a permis d'appeler la *modernité*. Souvent bizarre, violent, excessif, mais toujours poétique, il a su concentrer dans ses dessins la saveur amère ou capiteuse du vin de la Vie. (ii. 724)

Art is what captures the life of life, endowing it further with the vitality of the reader's own questionings and wonderings and offering the prospect of a fundamental *nomos* underlying the contingency and ill-being of our individual lives—as do the carriages that Guys so skilfully and repeatedly depicts (as we learn in the last section of the article, entitled 'Les Voitures'). Each carriage is quite plainly and convincingly a carriage: 'Toute sa carrosserie est parfaitement orthodoxe; chaque partie est à sa place et rien n'est à reprendre' (ii. 724). But what Guys has caught and rendered is the particular impression made by a carriage in movement, which once again, like Guys's beautiful woman, is reminiscent of the ship described in *Fusées*:

> Dans quelque attitude qu'elle soit jetée, avec quelque allure qu'elle soit lancée, une voiture, comme un vaisseau, emprunte au mouvement une grâce mystérieuse et complexe très difficile à sténographier. Le plaisir que l'œil de l'artiste en reçoit est tiré, ce semble, de la série de figures géométriques que cet objet, déjà si compliqué, navire ou carrosse, engendre successivement et rapidement dans l'espace. (ii. 724)

Within the static medium of pictorial art Guys has captured the movement of life and the passage of time itself.

Delacroix

> Delacroix est le plus *suggestif* de tous les peintres.
> (*L'Œuvre et la vie d' Eugène Delacroix* [1863], ii. 745).

For Baudelaire, then, the role of the imagination in the production of beauty is a complex form of resistance. As we saw in the case of Poe, the imagination can serve to resist and subvert normative thinking and to confront the destructiveness and negativity of melancholy ('nevermore') with the possibility of new creations.

The poet-artist pushes back against the ethos of a materialist and utilitarian society by affirming the spiritual power of the creative imagination and by demonstrating that beauty is not mere surface but a mode of perception that opens up new perspectives and provides alternative dimensions of understanding beyond the known and accepted. The imagination resists the government of orthodoxy and seeks emancipation from the tyranny of public opinion. In the *Salon de 1859* the imagination is presented as being itself an alternative form of government and the solution to a very public problem: namely, the positivist literal-mindedness to be found in society at large and evident particularly in the contemporary enthusiasm for Realism in both literature and painting.

Such literal-mindedness is predicated on an unthinking faith in an orderliness inherent in reality, perhaps even in a divine order within Creation, such that to see the world 'as it is' is at once to know it and to apprehend a self-evident truth. But such a faith is mere bigotry and blind preconception. The world *is* only as our imagination structures it for us, making sense of our senses: and thus, what the imagination creates, it may also govern and change—that is, govern and change in a spirit of provisionality and freedom, displaying and granting the existence of other possible structures and 'worlds' in a manner conducive to broad-mindedness, tolerance, and compassion. Unlike the hidebound 'positiviste' the 'imaginatif' has the power to alter our perceptions and indeed, as the example of sculpture demonstrates, to convey us beyond the here and now and to bid us contemplate 'les choses qui ne sont pas de la terre'. Such is the 'magnifique programme' of the imagination.

As we have now seen in the cases of Gautier and Hugo, of Wagner and Guys, this 'programme' relies on the power of conjecture, or more precisely the power of suggestiveness that provokes conjecture. Gautier may be the poet of Art for Art's Sake but from his preoccupation with beauty—his 'amour exclusif du Beau'—there results a remarkable combination of clarity and mystery. By virtue of an imagination that readily perceives multiple interconnections (correspondences and analogies) and thanks also to his extraordinary command of the French language Gautier is able to present the spectacle of the phenomenal world (and of the phenomenal world as represented in pictorial art) so precisely that its individual components appear in a wholly new light, inviting fresh conjecture and surmise (what Baudelaire describes as 'l'attitude mystérieuse que les objets de la création tiennent devant le regard de l'homme'). Whether he is dealing with our own real 'created' world or the world of objects depicted by creative artists, the 'justesse' of Gautier's verbal expression opens up new perspectives of imaginative understanding. In Hugo also, the Hugo not of vatic assertion but of cosmic speculation ('les parties mystérieuses, ombreuses, les plus charmantes'), this invitation to conjecture is paramount: an imagination that steps outside the known and the 'scientific' in order to explore the mysteries of the 'extra-scientifique', of the not-yet-known, and to find the new.

In both writers, therefore, language serves to point to something beyond language—akin to Baudelaire's 'Infini que j'aime et n'ai jamais connu'—just as in the music of Wagner and the sketches of Guys the artistic medium transcends its own boundaries in an enhanced capacity for expression. In Wagner's case the apparent imprecision of non-verbal music allows for a suggestiveness that in turn is perceived as a heightened form of perception, a 'clairvoyance' akin to the clarity and incontrovertibility of dream, in itself another domain of 'justesse'. And in Guys's case the apparent ephemerality and triviality of the sketch, in its subject matter as well as in its mode of production, belies an imaginative power of suggestion that Baudelaire characterizes as 'fécondité morale'. Guys has no philosophy to propound and yet his sketches are so much more than mere pretty pictures. Whether it be the figure of the soldier or the dandy, the courtesan or the actress, Guys's visual imagination is such that he silently demonstrates the 'lois morales' that govern the relationship between desire and dress: between how a person chooses to live and how their manner of dress reflects that choice. In fact it is by virtue of Guys's own imagination that we come to see how imagination informs the lives of us all and feeds our 'immortel appétit du Beau'. Where Baudelaire had sought to extract beauty from 'le Mal', Guys has extracted 'la fantasmagorie' and 'la beauté mystérieuse' from nature: that is, he has been able to capture and set down on paper new visions of quotidian reality having the clarity and mystery of a dream... much as Baudelaire himself does in 'Les Sept Vieillards' in 'Tableaux parisiens' and in some of the prose poems in *Le Spleen de Paris*.

In these various ways imagination can resist the defeatism of melancholy and reverse the downward spiral of desire in a rising curve of curiosity and conjecture. Suggestion is all, and Baudelaire returns to the idea in his obituary article following the death of Delacroix in August 1863. Already in the *Salon de 1846*, as we saw in Part I, he had praised Delacroix for paintings that open up 'de profondes avenues à l'imagination la plus voyageuse' (ii. 431). Now, in 'L'Œuvre et la vie d'Eugène Delacroix', where Baudelaire otherwise relies heavily on his own earlier writings for the production of this tribute, a new emphasis on suggestiveness is central to his posthumous assessment of the painter's achievement (as his use of italic implies): 'Delacroix est le plus *suggestif* de tous les peintres' (ii. 745). Where formerly Baudelaire had championed Delacroix as the painter of melancholy, now—like Gautier, Hugo, Wagner, and Guys—he is the artist of mystery:

> quel est donc ce je ne sais quoi de mystérieux que Delacroix, pour la gloire de notre siècle, a mieux traduit qu'aucun autre? C'est l'invisible, c'est l'impalpable, c'est le rêve, c'est les nerfs, c'est l'*âme*; et il a fait cela [...] sans autres moyens que le contour et la couleur[.]   (ii. 744)

Eschewing the precision of the 'dessin' and by means of shape and colour alone, Delacroix has produced a compelling record of human experience and in particular of human aspiration, and indeed of our 'grandeur': 'L'œuvre de M. Delacroix m'apparaît quelquefois comme une espèce de mnémotechnie de la grandeur et de la passion native de l'homme universel' (ii. 745). And Baudelaire pays especial tribute to '[c]e mérite très particulier et tout nouveau de M. Delacroix, qui lui a permis d'exprimer, simplement avec le contour, le geste de l'homme, si violent qu'il soit, et avec la couleur ce qu'on pourrait appeler l'atmosphère du drame humain, ou l'état d'âme du créateur' (ii. 745). '[C]e je ne sais quoi de mystérieux', 'l'invisible', 'l'impalpable', 'l'atmosphère du drame humain', 'l'état d'âme du créateur': all are attempts to describe in words what lies at the end of those long avenues of imaginative adventure opened up by Delacroix's paintings.

No wonder, Baudelaire claims finally (ii. 745), that more writers than artists turned up at the great man's funeral, for they understood him better. They knew that great painting, like poetry, depicts not what apparently is but rather 'ce qu'il y a de plus réel, [...] ce qui n'est complètement vrai que *dans un autre monde*' (ii. 59), another dimension of understanding towards which poets and painters continually reach out but which they can never wholly grasp. In part, as Baudelaire had earlier observed in *Exposition universelle*, this popularity among poets derived from the fact that Delacroix had drawn so widely on literature for his subjects, but it was the result also of the greater depth and finesse of his art: '[sa peinture] sait révéler des idées d'un ordre plus élevé, plus fines, plus profondes' (ii. 596). In the same article Baudelaire also recounts the story of Balzac one day observing a painting of a wintry peasant scene and being heard to wonder out loud whether the harvest was good and whether the inhabitants of a lowly dwelling had the means to pay their rent. Such art has the ability to 'faire vibrer, conjecturer et s'inquiéter' (ii. 579), and for Baudelaire this ability is often all that matters: 'Il m'arrivera souvent d'apprécier un tableau uniquement par la somme d'idées ou de rêveries qu'il apportent dans mon esprit' (ii. 579). That is what beauty does, just like that of *Madame Bovary*: 'ce livre, essentiellement suggestif, pourrait souffler un volume d'observations' (ii. 84).

PART IV
POETRY IN VERSE

Voici le maître-livre de notre poésie: *Les Fleurs du mal*. Jamais la vérité de parole, forme supérieure du vrai, n'a mieux montré son visage.

(Yves Bonnefoy)[1]

---

[1] 'Préface' [to *Les Fleurs du Mal*], in Baudelaire, *Œuvres complètes*, ed. Austin, reproduced in Bonnefoy, *L'Improbable et autres essais*, 31–40 (31) and in *Sous le signe de Baudelaire*, 11–18 (11).

15
The Poetry of Passion
Sex, Beauty, and Verse

Que j'ai gardé la forme et l'essence divine
De mes amours décomposés!
('Une charogne', ll. 47–8)

Baudelaire's 'love poetry'[1] provides us with an alternative legislation. Instead of sexual passion being seen within the context of Christian canon law concerning marriage or judged against the Roman Catholic doctrine of sin, Baudelaire situates it within his own moral philosophy of melancholy (as set out in Part II above) and in relation to his own conception of beauty: of beauty as an impermanent effect rather than an immutable quality, and of beauty in its potential role as a force for moral good in resisting the law of 'dégradation morale' that governs all human experience. At the end of Part II we saw how he envisages art, and more especially poetry, as an instrument of 'recomposition', allowing us to wrest newness and creativity from the tedium and sterility of melancholy. In this process the role of the imagination is key, and, as we have seen in Part III, Baudelaire attributes a central and all-powerful role to the imagination as the supreme human faculty by means of which we create and govern the world we inhabit. Imagination enables us to make sense of our contingent existence and transform its tawdry, random details into the essential components of a complex and harmonious structure, an alternative legislation.

Here in Part IV I shall examine Baudelaire's poetry in verse now less as an account of melancholy than as evidence of *how* melancholy offers the poet and the reader the possibility of beauty. Turning first to the subject of sexual passion I shall discuss how the poet's relationships with women, whether they be real or imagined, are shown to matter not as material for an autobiographical or pseudo-autobiographical record of erotic experience but rather as sources of imaginative activity and poetic work. Time and again we shall see how the multiple emotions stirred by 'love'—excitement, adoration, desperation, hurt, hatred, vindictiveness, blissful self-abandonment to destruction—turn the poet into an artist, provoking him into new perceptions and performances of beauty.

---

[1] Throughout this chapter I shall use single quotation marks to indicate that Baudelaire's treatment of 'love' has very little in common with traditional sentimental accounts of sexual relations.

The Beauty of Baudelaire: The Poet As Alternative Lawgiver. Roger Pearson, Oxford University Press. © Roger Pearson 2021.
DOI: 10.1093/oso/9780192843319.003.0016

Poetic language and prosodic constructs are his exemplary means of resistance to the 'Mal' of everyday life, his means of growing flowers in the garden of ill-being.

The Nature of 'Love'

> Comme j'entends le mot amour dans le sens le plus complet, je suis obligé d'exprimer quelques maximes particulières sur des questions délicates.
> ('Choix de maximes consolantes sur l'amour', i. 547)

The subject of sexual passion appears to have been central to Baudelaire's poetic project from the outset, and, as the Lesbos poems (first advertised in October 1845) indicate, sexual passion as a manifestation of the ill-being, or 'le Mal', from which the author of *Les Fleurs du Mal* would in due course explicitly claim to be 'extracting' beauty. As he notes jauntily at the beginning of his comic article 'Choix de maximes consolantes sur l'amour', published in March 1846: 'Si je commence par l'amour, c'est que l'amour est pour tous,—ils ont beau le nier,—la grande chose de la vie!' (ii. 546). (The same comment could perhaps also be made about the position of the 'love poems' within the structure of *Les Fleurs du Mal*.) In this article, written in part as a pastiche of Stendhal's *De l'amour* (1822), Baudelaire apes the Idéologues in their application of scientific method to matters of the heart. Soon, he assures his reader, it will be possible through further study of sympathetic attraction and Lavater's work on physiognomy to identify for each man '[v]otre maîtresse, la femme de votre ciel'.[2] Indeed he, Baudelaire, plans to compile—'énorme tâche' (i. 547)—a complete catalogue of 'les signes physiognomiques des femmes qui conviennent éternellement à tel ou tel homme' (i. 547), and he will call it *Le Catéchisme de la femme aimée*: the work he then advertises together with *Les Lesbiennes* on the cover of the *Salon de 1846*—the collection that would eventually turn into that other 'catechism', *Les Fleurs du Mal*.

Clearly he was joking, as he jokes also in 'Choix de maximes consolantes sur l'amour' in proffering advice to heterosexual men on their choice of sexual partner ('la femme nécessaire' (i. 547)). The northerner—'soifier d'idéal' (i. 547)—being used to the twin hardships of navigating fog-bound seas and forever trying to find the *aurora borealis*, should seek out the frigid since he obviously enjoys a challenge. The man from the Midi, however, having no time for secrets or mystery and being essentially an 'homme frivole', should content himself with the easier path of 'les femmes ardentes' (i. 547). As to young men who want one day to be

---

[2] On the possibility that the object of Baudelaire's courtship at this moment was Félicité, wife of his half-brother Alphonse, see Andrea Schellino, 'Existe-t-il un "cycle de Félicité" dans l'œuvre en vers de Baudelaire?', *Revue d'histoire littéraire de la France*, 117 (2017), 697–706 (702).

great poets„ well, they should avoid trying to be too clever: 'gardez-vous du paradoxe en amour' (i. 548). Drunken schoolboys may sing the praises of women who are fat, but such insincerity should be left to the 'école pseudo-romantique' (i. 548). Skinny ones, on the other hand...: 'la femme maigre est un puits de voluptés ténébreuses!' (i. 548). And beware of the power of association: if you start loving a woman disfigured by smallpox just because you have come to associate her with the melancholy beauty of Paganini's violin music, your next girlfriend will have to have a pock-marked face too. And so it goes. Don't hope to teach them to spell. Don't worry if they're not very smart: that way they think less and get fewer wrinkles. All very sexist, provocative, irreverent, and seemingly immature. Except that the cynical young analyst of love and sworn enemy of cant is already sketching his contrarian aesthetic. 'Sachez tirer parti de la laideur elle-même' (i. 548); 'Pour certains esprits plus curieux et plus blasés, la jouissance de la laideur provient d'un sentiment encore plus mystérieux, qui est la soif de l'inconnu, et le goût de l'horrible' (i. 548-9).

From very early on, and as the reference to Paganini suggests, Baudelaire associated sexual attraction with the pursuit—and creation—of aesthetic beauty. Already in 1841, during his brief stopover on the island of Mauritius, the 20-year-old *enfant terrible* composed (at her husband's request) a sonnet in honour of the beautiful Mme Autard de Bragard. In this poem, the first to be published under Baudelaire's own name (in 1845, entitled 'À une Créole', later amended to 'A une dame créole'), the poet evokes the sunlit, scent-filled landscape of palm trees and 'paresse' that will later figure in 'Parfum exotique' and 'La Chevelure' and speculates in Ronsardian vein that if this lady were one day to find herself on the banks of the Seine or the Loire, she would there most certainly inspire 'mille sonnets dans le cœur des poètes' (l. 13). Here the association of female beauty with a compulsion to represent or 'possess' this beauty in art is of an entirely traditional kind, albeit open to potential interpretation in Freudian terms as a form of displaced sexual desire. But in *La Fanfarlo*, first published in January 1847, the association lies at the centre of the plot, most especially in the climactic scene where the hero of this short fictional narrative, the poet Samuel Cramer, being about to witness the eponymous actress undress before him, promptly bids her put on the theatrical costume of Columbine, the role in which he had first seen and fallen in love with her. And don't forget the rouge, he shouts, as her maid sets off during a storm at three in the morning to secure the wherewithal to satisfy a poet's fantasy. For Cramer sex comes second—and procreation a very distant third—to the desire for aesthetic beauty:

l'amour était chez lui moins une affaire des sens que du raisonnement. C'était surtout l'admiration et l'appétit du beau; il considérait la reproduction comme un vice de l'amour, la grossesse comme une maladie d'araignée. (i. 577)

In Cramer's eyes a beautiful body is principally a work of art: 'Il aimait un corps humain comme une harmonie matérielle, comme une belle architecture, plus le mouvement' (i. 577). And in the case of La Fanfarlo herself the beauty in question—that is, the effect on him of her physical and theatrical presence—brings both the delight of imaginative surmise and the pain of melancholy. At first the female gaze (like the 'pensive' gaze of the 'Femmes damnées' ['Comme un bétail pensif...'] in 'Fleurs du Mal') presents a window onto the infinite: 'quand. [..]il la regardait, il lui semblait voir l'infini derrière les yeux clairs de cette beauté, et que les siens à la longue planaient dans d'immenses horizons' (i. 577). But then the lover, gazing on this gaze, feels increasingly isolated and alone:

> Du reste, comme il arrive aux hommes exceptionnels, il était souvent seul dans son paradis, nul ne pouvant l'habiter avec lui; et si, de hasard, il l'y ravissait et l'y traînait presque de force, elle restait en arrière: aussi, dans le ciel où il régnait, son amour commençait d'être triste et malade de la mélancolie du bleu, comme un royal solitaire. (i. 577–8)

The other—in this case a beautiful woman—offers him access to the 'exotic', to other places and other horizons; but at the same time that experience of an elsewhere is somehow his alone, something that cannot be shared ('nul ne pouvant l'habiter avec lui').[3] Here then we see, early in Baudelaire's writing career, the portrayal of sexual passion as a quest for the aesthetic and as an experience that for the poet necessarily entails the co-presence of 'idéal' and 'spleen'.

As to *Les Fleurs du Mal*, the account of sexual relations to be found there has been seen variously as illegal, immoral, licentious, and depraved. But at the very least it exhibits a perfectly clear logic. For Baudelaire the sexual instinct is part of our 'automatic' nature, of our animality, and as such part of 'le Mal'—or what he also calls 'original sin'. Hence his statement in 'Éloge du maquillage' (in *Le Peintre de la vie moderne*) that 'Le Mal se fait sans effort, *naturellement*, par fatalité' (ii. 715). Moreover, as he observes more privately in his unpublished *Fusées*, there may be pleasure to be had in embracing that 'fatal' or 'automatic' animality to the full: 'Moi, je dis: la volupté unique et suprême de l'amour gît dans la certitude de faire le *mal*.—Et l'homme et la femme savent de naissance que dans le mal se trouve toute volupté.'[4] This is not to say that sex is necessarily wicked or that supreme physical pleasure comes from being wicked (though for De Sade and

---

[3] Claude Pichois controversially suggests that this perception of an impossibility derives here from misogyny. See i. 1427, n. 1 to p. 578: 'La femme tient plus de la matière que de l'esprit. Baudelaire est un peu mahométan à cet égard.' In an alternative reading one might wonder if for Baudelaire the woman's gaze is not itself (as it is for the 'Femmes damnées') implicitly filled with a similar melancholy. Each of us, man and woman alike, may gaze into the other's eyes in search of love and infinite possibilities, but each will find only a reflection of their own fears and anxieties. Samuel Cramer may be 'exceptional', but each of us is exceptional—and alone.

[4] *Fusées*, ed. Guyaux, 55; i. 652.

others it may), but only that if we are to enjoy sex to the full we need to deliver ourselves up—body and no soul—to a purely physical and unthinking activity. But the corollary of this statement in 'Éloge du maquillage' must also be noted: 'le bien est toujours le produit d'un art' (ii. 715). Art and artifice, whether of make-up or poetry, constitute a force for good, and this because consciousness, self-consciousness, and the effort of resistance make us more than mere animals. As was evident in the previous chapter, the author of *Le Peintre de la vie moderne* sees artifice as a form of virtue.

In Baudelaire's contrarian account of 'love', the emotional relationships between man and woman (and woman and woman) that accompany the 'volupté' of sex are necessarily fraught with the imperatives of desire. Possession is all, although, as 'Le Possédé' makes clear, the one who desires to possess is himself (in the case of this particular poem, but as would a putative 'Possédée' also be) possessed by the desire itself and so by its object: an '[e]sclave de l'esclave', as Baudelaire phrases it in 'Le Voyage' (l. 92). It is 'in the nature' of sexual passion that the desires of the flesh 'fatally' determine the oscillations of devotion and indifference, commitment and rejection, dominance and acquiescence, warmth and coldness, affection and hatred, fond memory and bitter vengeance, that we find recorded in *Les Fleurs du Mal*, and particularly in 'Spleen et idéal' and 'Fleurs du Mal'. Here in all *its* nakedness is the reality of 'love' as a manifestation of the ill-being of our human condition. In *Fusées*, f. 3,[5] where he compares 'love' (meaning copulation) to a form of torture or a surgical operation, Baudelaire insists that a sexual relationship necessarily implies an unequal power relationship: 'Quand même les deux amants seraient très épris et très pleins de désirs réciproques, l'un des deux sera toujours plus calme ou moins possédé que l'autre. Celui-là, ou celle-là, c'est l'opérateur, ou le bourreau; l'autre, c'est le sujet, la victime.' 'Love', therefore, is perforce a game of winners and losers: 'Épouvantable jeu où il faut que l'un des joueurs perde le gouvernement de soi-même!' As to the cries and convulsions of the sexual act itself, are these not proof enough that 'love' is actually a form of death? Just observe its effects on the human face:

> Et le visage humain qu'Ovide croyait façonné pour refléter les astres, le voilà qui ne parle plus qu'une expression de férocité folle, ou qui se détend dans une espèce de mort. Car, certes, je croirais faire un sacrilège en appliquant le mot: extase à cette sorte de décomposition.

For Baudelaire, therefore, 'love' is nature, love is sex: it is frenzy, disharmony, and ugliness. 'Love' is decomposition. But the imagination can confer beauty on 'love', on nature, on sex, by the creation of harmony through art, that is, by a process of

---

[5] *Fusées*, ed. Guyaux, 53–4; i. 651.

composition and recomposition. Many accounts of Baudelaire's 'love poems' focus on what these poems tell us about the poet's supposed emotions and the state of his amorous relationships with a variety of women, but in fact these are more or less irrelevant. For the poetic 'je'—let alone for Baudelaire himself—these experiences are in the past, decomposed: they are history. What matters is their resurrection in the present tense of the poem:[6] what matters is the demonstration of a quasi-alchemical transmutation of memory into the eurhythmy of verse.

The Beauty of 'Love'

le beau, qui est la cause de l'amour

(*La Fanfarlo*, i. 577)

For Baudelaire's heterosexual male poet, as for his female inhabitant of ancient Lesbos, to be attracted to a woman is to be attracted by a certain form of 'beauty', by one or more physical and/or moral qualities that provoke desire and perhaps also what is commonly called 'love' (esteem, affection, loyalty, devotion). For Baudelaire the close interconnection that exists between sexuality and art springs from this love of 'beauty', whether it be in Sappho herself—'l'amante et le poëte'— or in the poetic 'je' of 'La Destruction' whom the 'Démon' beguiles ('sachant mon grand amour de l'Art') by adopting '[l]a forme de la plus séduisante des femmes'. In *Fusées*, f. 16, as we saw earlier also, Baudelaire defines beauty as an effect ('laissant carrière à la conjecture') by focusing on male sexual desire in its response to female physical beauty and on how that desire is inhabited from the outset by melancholy ('quelque chose d'ardent et de triste')—the melancholic knowledge that a desire satisfied is but the prelude to further desire and further torment. In 'La Destruction' it looks as if the poet must decide between sex and art as though between destruction and creativity, but in 'Une charogne', as we also saw, it seems as though the very 'decomposition' wrought by desire may actually facilitate an imaginative alchemy of recomposition through art.

The subject of sexual passion plays a central and complex role in the poems of *Les Fleurs du Mal*. In my earlier discussion (in Chapters 8 and 9) of the

---

[6] On this status of the poem as an event rather than as the record of an event, see Jonathan Culler, *Theory of the Lyric* (Cambridge, Mass.: Harvard University Press, 2015), 226: 'The fundamental characteristic of lyric, I am arguing, is not the description and interpretation of a past event but the iterative and iterable performance of an event in the lyric present, in the special "now" of lyric articulation. The bold wager of poetic apostrophe is that the lyric can displace a time of narrative, of past events reported, and place us in the continuing present of apostrophic address, the "now" in which, for readers, a poetic event can repeatedly occur. Fiction is about what happened next; lyric is about what happens now.' Culler acknowledges a debt (see 376 n. 43) to a similar statement by Alice Fulton ('Fiction is about what happens next. Poetry is about what happens now') in her *Feeling as a Foreign Language: The Good Strangeness of Poetry* (St Paul, Minn.: Greywolf Press, 1999), 7.

architecture of the collection and of the ways in which Baudelaire modified its 'cadre singulier' between the editions of 1857 and 1861 I ended my account of the opening frame of 'Spleen et idéal' at the point where in the 1861 edition the newly added poem 'Hymne à la Beauté' rounds off the initial group of poems (1–21) dealing with the poet and his pursuit of beauty and comes after a particular subgrouping of poems ('La Beauté', 'L'Idéal', 'La Géante', and 'Le Masque') in which the aesthetic is explicitly aligned with the sexual. In this way the reader is led into the long sequence of 'love poems' and invited to consider erotic experience essentially as synonymous with aesthetic experience. Furthermore, 'Hymne à la Beauté' exemplifies Baudelaire's characteristic side-stepping of traditional dualisms, here of beauty as being either divine (a manifestation of God within the sublime) or satanic (a lure and source of moral danger). For Baudelaire beauty is not exclusively one thing or the other: it may derive from multiple sources and may assume multiple guises. This ambiguity of beauty is emphasized from the outset:

> Viens-tu du ciel profond ou sors-tu de l'abîme,
> Ô Beauté? ton regard, infernal et divin,
> Verse confusément le bienfait et le crime,
> Et l'on peut pour cela te comparer au vin.
>
> (ll. 1–4)

Beauty simply *is* intoxication, and, like intoxication, it abolishes conventional distinctions and effects paradoxical inversions:

> Tu contiens dans ton œil le couchant et l'aurore;
> Tu répands des parfums comme un soir orageux;
> Tes baisers sont un philtre et ta bouche une amphore
> Qui font le héros lâche et l'enfant courageux.
>
> (ll. 5–8)

As the poem proceeds, this idea of 'confusion' (cf. 'confusément') or of the fusing of opposites is reinforced by repetition ('Sors-tu du gouffre noir ou descends-tu des astres? (l. 9)) and by further paradox. Like intoxication—and the government of the imagination—the alternative legislation of beauty defies necessity and subjects what supposedly *must* be to what otherwise—variously, randomly, come what may and what the hell—*might* and *can* be:

> Le Destin charmé suit tes jupons comme un chien;
> Tu sèmes au hasard la joie et les désastres,
> Et tu gouvernes tout et ne répond de rien.
>
> (ll. 10–12)

Above all, beauty brings life through a reconfiguration of death, at which it laughs. Horror and murderous destruction are now jewelled charms (bringing us luck and warding off misfortune), fit to adorn the proud belly of beauty in its amorous and seductive dance:

> Tu marches sur des morts, Beauté, dont tu te moques;
> De tes bijoux l'Horreur n'est pas le moins charmant,
> Et le Meurtre, parmi tes plus chères breloques,
> Sur ton ventre orgueilleux danse amoureusement.
>
> (ll. 13–16)

All that transiently is within our human existence rejoices to end up in beauty's embrace: like a dazzled mayfly happily welcoming an end to its day-long life in the immolation of a candle's flame, or an exhausted lover about to renounce his unequal struggle:

> L'éphémère ébloui vole vers toi, chandelle,
> Crépite, flambe et dit: Bénissons ce flambeau!
> L'amoureux pantelant incliné sur sa belle
> A l'air d'un moribond caressant son tombeau.
>
> (ll. 17–20).

In the last two stanzas of 'Hymne à la Beauté' the poet returns to his opening questions about the ambivalence inherent in the nature of beauty, but now to reject these questions out of hand. What matters is not the source of beauty but its effect, the intoxication and not the provenance of the wine:

> Que tu viennes du ciel ou de l'enfer, qu'importe,
> Ô Beauté! monstre énorme, effrayant, ingénu!
> Si ton œil, ton souris, ton pied, m'ouvrent la porte
> D'un Infini que j'aime et n'ai jamais connu?
>
> De Satan ou de Dieu, qu'importe? Ange ou Sirène,
> Qu'importe, si tu rends,—fée aux yeux de velours,
> Rythme, parfum, lueur, ô mon unique reine!—
> L'univers moins hideux et les instants moins lourds?
>
> (ll. 21–8)

Here is the credo of the poet as alternative lawgiver, as initiate of the 'black mystery' of Lesbos. Like Sappho and her sister 'martyres', this beauty is at once 'monstrous' and ingenuous, and 'les lois du juste et de l'injuste' are irrelevant. Christian dualities of heaven and hell, good and evil, God and Satan are immaterial. Like the women of Lesbos the poet is here himself a 'chercheur d'infini', and his 'Beauty' is of the kind that mobilizes the full range of our sensual experience—the rhythms and the scents, the gleam and the soft caress—in order to revivify our sorry world of drab quotidian experience. Casting spells of fairy magic from eyes of velvet, this queenly Beauty is the imagination itself: 'Mystérieuse faculté que cette reine des facultés!' (*Salon de 1859*)—the imagination of the poet, and of the reader too.

By here identifying three sources of beauty—hell, heaven, and the imagination—these two stanzas might be thought to introduce the 'love poems' of 'Spleen et idéal' in a more specific way. Much has been written about these poems and in particular about the possible identity of the woman or women in question. Three 'cycles' have traditionally been acknowledged (on the basis of the 1861 edition): (i) poems 22–39 (from 'Parfum exotique' to 'Je te donne ces vers...'); (ii) poems 40–8 ('Semper eadem' to 'Le Flacon', with 'Semper eadem' being seen more as a poem of transition between the first two cycles);[7] and (iii) poems 49–57 ('Le Poison' to 'A une Madone'). Considered to have been 'inspired' respectively by Baudelaire's relationships with Jeanne Duval, Apollonie Sabatier, and Marie Daubrun, these three cycles have also been seen to represent three different types of 'love': physical passion, platonic devotion, and the ambivalences of a less polarized attachment—and to demonstrate, each in turn, a recurrent progression in the experience of 'love' from anticipation and delight to disillusion, bitterness, and eventual resignation. A fourth grouping has also been identified (poems 58–64) in which the focus shifts rapidly over a succession of different women, some of whom are named (Sisina, Francisca/Françoise, Agathe, Marguerite). Where the women of the first three cycles had each 'merited' more than one poem, these individuals have a more miscellaneous air, being women variously admired ('Sisina') or possibly invented for a joke ('Franciscae meae laudes') or perhaps a childhood friend (Agathe in 'Moesta et errabunda') or else simply imagined as a floral symbol (Marguerite in 'Sonnet d'automne').

More particularly, perhaps, these poems—together with those that immediately follow, relating respectively to the moon, cats, owls, and a pipe—might be thought to confirm what is perfectly evident throughout every one of these 'love poems': namely, that the personal lives of these women matter little, if at all, to the poet, except insofar as they, mere 'love objects', provoke in him the effect of beauty and—'amours décomposés' that they are—become nourishment for his 'vers'. Indeed one might speculate that Baudelaire, like Guys in the case of Parisian scenes, chose to dispense with the obtrusive detail of live observation so that the work of memory—both in his own mind and as simulated by each poem—might

---

[7] See i. 905.

allow the 'forme' and 'essence divine' of a universal erotic experience to emerge more clearly.

The 'beloved' in Baudelaire's 'love poems' is thus no Beatrice, leading him to a paradise of spiritual bliss: rather she is, at most, a stimulus to conjecture and a prompt for the poetic imagination. Often it is her very coldness and indifference, her own apparent melancholy and indeed her silence, that provoke the poet's creativity and bring the prospect of a new kind of beauty. In short, what matters in these 'love poems' is not the love but the poem: the different ways in which the contingent experiences of our ephemeral lives are transformed by the imagination—and, here in 'Spleen et idéal', ephemeral lives that are specifically taken up with obtaining and recovering the intoxication of sexual passion: that is, our instinctive urge to perpetuate life through potential or actual procreation. But for Baudelaire it is poetry and not sex that confers new life—the life of beauty. As we saw earlier (in Chapter 8), the opening poems in 'Spleen et idéal' dismantle the received model of the poet as divine lawgiver and celebrant of nature and begin to substitute a poet of melancholy who seeks a new kind of beauty and a new kind of poetry: the poet as alternative lawgiver exploring the Satanic reality of human desire and responding to the 'irremediable' ill-being of the human condition through the affirmation of poetic creativity and the work of the imagination. As 'Correspondances' makes clear, the poet discards his vatic role in favour of a poetry of sensual delight and intellectual conjecture ('les transports de l'esprit et des sens') in which the stimulus of smells ('d'autres, corrompus, riches et triomphants') metaphorically equates to the heady promptings of memory and—now in the case of these 'love poems'—to the 'rich corruption' of the poet's 'amours décomposés'.

In both the 1857 and 1861 editions of 'Spleen et idéal' 'Parfum exotique' sets the tone at once: 'Quand, les deux yeux fermés, en un soir chaud d'automne, | Je respire l'odeur de ton sein chaleureux' (ll. 1–2). For this poet the beloved is a warm breast on which to lay his head (like a child as much as in his role as a lover) so that he may shut his eyes and take a trip of the imagination across the waves of its scent to a delightful island paradise that anticipates the paintings of Gauguin: hot sun, interesting fauna, flavoursome fruit, an uncomplicated place where lithe and vigorous men co-habit with no-nonsense women 'dont l'œil par sa franchise étonne' (l. 8). Indeed the poet's female companion is no more than—indeed simply *is*—the scent of the title, and he himself, '[g]uidé par ton odeur vers de charmants climats' (l. 9), leaves her behind in his pursuit of the 'ex-otic', of what is 'out of this place', elsewhere, or (as the later prose poem has it) 'Any where out of the world'. His eyes closed to present reality, the poet 'sees' (ll. 3, 10) his island and then its port: he has arrived. And now he smells not the body of his companion but the scent of leafy tamarind trees, which causes his nostrils to swell (l. 13) as though to accommodate this greater fullness of sensual experience (cf. 'l'expansion des choses infinies') and finally mingles in his soul with the sound of sailors singing—that is, with the songs of his fellow-travellers and brothers-in-art. Once more we find a movement from sex to aesthetics, from female lover to the business of poetry; and as in 'La Géante' (l. 13) the female breast is transformed from being the literal object of an ephemeral excitement into being the metaphorical source of a more long-lasting creativity and sense of peace—into a source of nourishment and life.

'La Chevelure'

> cet être [...] pour qui, mais surtout *par qui* les artistes et les poètes composent leurs plus délicats bijoux.
> (*Le Peintre de la vie moderne*, ii. 713)

Nowhere is this movement from sex to art more intricately described than in 'La Chevelure', and I shall now examine it in detail as a paradigm of Baudelaire's poetic practice. The poem was newly added to the 1861 edition and placed after 'Parfum exotique' as though to reinforce it by further inviting the reader to view the subsequent 'love poems' not as erotic or amatory literature but as a series of imaginative conjectures whereby the melancholy of desire and ill-being ('le Mal') becomes the stuff of poetry ('les fleurs'). Here in 'La Chevelure, as in 'Parfum exotique', the female companion is once again herself of little consequence, merely the source of sensual impressions that provoke a journey of the imagination—just as the poem itself, being also of little (and ultimately unknowable) biographical consequence, will instigate the imaginative journey of the reader. And, as in 'Parfum exotique', it is once more the scent of his bed-partner (in 'l'alcôve obsure' (l. 3)) that facilitates the poet's departure ('Le mien [namely, mon esprit] [...] nage sur ton parfum' (l. 10). Far from being 'ivre d'amour', the poet's 'tête' is 'amoureuse d'ivresse' as he prepares to plunge head first, literally and metaphorically, into the black waves of her hair and be carried away on an ocean of sensuous and poetic delight. He is in love not with a woman but with the intoxication that is beauty.

As its title appears to indicate, 'La Chevelure' is a poem about hair: that banal human attribute requiring tedious attention and as such an eloquent emblem of ennui and the 'unpoetic'. But by virtue of multiple analogies this everyday physical object is transformed by the poetic imagination into a magical talisman, a 'toison' (l. 1) comparable with the Golden Fleece sought by those other maritime travellers, Jason and the Argonauts. Waves of black hair are as the waves of a black ocean (l. 22) or an ebony sea (l. 14), breaking on the shore of a neck (l. 1): its swell (l. 13) and rolling motion (l. 23) bear the poet mentally away to far-off lands on a trip of heightened perceptions. Or hair is a 'forêt aromatique' (l. 8), full of the scents of 'langorous' Asia and 'burning' Africa (l. 6). It holds the promise at once of the exotic and of warm shelter, some busy foreign port perhaps (l. 16), or a dark tent offering seclusion and intimacy (l. 26), or an oasis (l. 34) in which the poet can rest and drink long draughts from the gourd of stored-up memories (ll. 34–5).

At the same time this poem may be read as the narrative of a sexual act, opening with the urgent approach and arrival of orgasm ('Extase!' (l. 3)) and ebbing through fond hopes of a repeat ('Saura vous retrouver' (l. 24)) towards the 'tristesse' of post-climactic doubt: 'N'est-tu pas l'oasis où je rêve, et la gourde | Où je hume à longs traits le vin du souvenir?' (ll. 34–5). More broadly, the poem stages the tragic spiral of desire, the joy of desire satisfied which is then followed by an immediate anxiety about the chances of ever satisfying that desire again: 'Longtemps! toujours! ma main dans ta crinière lourde | Sèmera le rubis, la perle et le saphir, | Afin qu'à mon désir tu ne sois jamais sourde!' (ll. 31–3). In this respect the poet's experience as recorded in the poem is a perfect illustration of Baudelaire's definition of beauty in *Fusées*, f. 16: 'quelque chose d'ardent et de triste [...] laissant carrière à la conjecture'. For while it is an unconfident lover who wonders if he will have to lavish jewels upon his mistress if she is again to answer to his desire, it is a knowing poet who realizes that for a banal object to delight a desirous imagination a second time it will require the aid of artifice. The effect of beauty must be wrought—but *can* be regained. In that sense the title 'La Chevelure' refers to the poem itself, 'fortes tresses' (l. 13) of versified memory in alexandrines now already strewn with the transformative jewels of simile and metaphor.

At the levels of narrative and description the poem relates the drama of passion as a journey from excitement to uncertainty, from multiple exclamation marks— of ecstasy and then perhaps of desperation—towards one single, terminal question mark. The poet has known momentary bliss but will that moment ever come again? Will he even be able to remember it? Already within the first stanza the outline of such a journey is evident as we move from the hyperbole and grand- iloquence of the opening lines to the bathos and prosaic rhythm of the last: 'Je la veux agiter dans l'air comme un mouchoir!' (l. 5). A traveller may wave a handkerchief as a sign of farewell, but does a poet shake a head of hair (as though perhaps it were already the artifice of a wig!) in order to make the memories fall out (as a perfumed handkerchief might release its scent)? Here the exclamation mark may suggest not only excitement but a joke in poor taste.

On the one hand, then, there has been a moment of ecstatic perfection in which the poet has been accorded an experience of timeless fulfilment and sensual plenitude in the here and now ('Tout un monde [...] | Vit dans tes profondeurs' (ll. 7–8)), and yet that timelessness turns out to be an illusion in the last stanza where the words (and exclamation marks) 'Longtemps! toujours!' suggest the desperate pleas of a poet who sees the moment of 'ivresse' receding and doubts if it will ever come again. Similarly, the poet's sense of plenitude is characterized by an impression of departure and even escape from the here and now: the 'alcôve obscure' (l. 3) where he lies beside the owner of this hair is itself a port from which he can set sail on a wide, imaginary sea. And yet in reality he is going nowhere, and the last stanza of the poem leaves him staring at this 'crinière lourde': no longer a Golden Fleece with curls of hair ('Ô boucles!' (l. 2)) tumbling down to the nape of the neck like white horses on the crest of a wave ('moutonnant' (l. 1), but now a heavy mane, a mere heap of horse hair, like a mattress. Where the opening images suggested a rich, animalistic sensuality (cf. also 'encolure'), now the hair seems dull and burdensome, no longer stimulating to the imagination and therefore much in need of artificial adornment.

While this poem may evoke the sexual act, the identity of the poet's bed-partner is nevertheless as obscure as the 'alcôve' in which the lovers lie. Nothing in the poem in fact tells us that the addressee of the poem is a woman, or even a human being: the poet is talking to the hair itself. Furthermore, 'Ô mon amour!' (l. 10) is as much an address to his feeling (cf. 'ma tête amoureuse d'ivresse') as it is to the 'forêt aromatique' of hair, still less to a flesh-and-blood beloved. So, too is the addressee of 'ô féconde paresse' (l. 24) a personification of the hair's effect ('mon esprit subtil [...] | Saura *vous* retrouver' (ll. 23–4; my emphasis)), in other words of beauty itself. 'Ô toison' (l. 1), 'Ô boucles!' (l. 2), 'tes profondeurs, forêt aromatique!' (l. 8), 'tu contiens, mer d'ébène' (l. 14), 'Cheveux bleus [...] Vous me rendez [...]' (ll. 26–7): so much apostrophe, but so little presence of a real live human being. By the end of the poem, where the possessive adjective in 'ta crinière lourde' (l. 31) (and, to a lesser extent, in 'vos mèches tordues' (l. 28)) might logically suggest the person whose hair has been so richly celebrated, we have nevertheless been led to see the hair as in some way self-sufficient and belonging to itself, and so it is the hair, as much as if not more than its owner, that will need to be decorated with jewels if it is to satisfy the poet's future 'desire'—that is, his imagination's need of intoxicating beauty.

In this way the final stanza offers us, like the poem as a whole, both 'ironie' and 'surnaturalisme': on the one hand, the poet's ironic knowledge that the good things in life never last (and that women must be bribed if they are to look on him again with favour), and, on the other, the poet's resistance through memory to the dominion of time and his 'recomposition' of nature by the concerted artifice of poetry itself. Out of the banality of hair came a moment of ecstasy, an epiphany of the imagination, beauty... a beauty that began to fade even as that ecstasy was reached. But out of this very experience of melancholy within delight the poet can summon a new and restorative beauty of his own, the harmony evident in the justly fashioned prosodic structures and metrical rhythms of 'La Chevelure'.

The poem consists of seven five-line stanzas (quintils) of alexandrines rhyming abaab, a scheme that combines *rimes croisées* (abab) and *rimes embrassées* (baab). If *rimes croisées* may be thought to contribute to a sense of onward movement and perhaps aspiration, *rimes embrassées* may similarly be thought to contribute to a sense of reflection and stasis, a turning-back-in-on and a form of self-containment.[8] This combination might then itself be thought to reflect the dual dynamic of this particular moment of ecstasy, consisting as it simultaneously does in a timeless sense of bliss and an anguished sense of transience. Such harmony of theme and poetic form may be seen also in the concentric stanzaic structure of the poem in which the first, third, fifth, and seventh stanzas convey movement and a concern for the future ('Je la veux agiter dans l'air comme un mouchoir'; 'J'irai là-bas'; 'Je plongerai ma tête'; 'ma main [...] | Sèmera') while the second and sixth stanzas evoke stasis and contentment within the present ('Tout un monde [...] | Vit'; 'Vous me rendez l'azur', 'Je m'enivre ardemment'). The fourth stanza, in the middle of the poem, contains no main verb and in that way represents a time out of time, the still centre of the poet's imaginary journey, a moment of arrival between two departures. The poet has reached port, itself an ambiguous place of stasis between journeys, a place where vessels 'glide' across a silken, golden water (are they coming or going?), at once under way and yet somehow motionless, their sails embracing the 'glory' of a pure and cloudless sky and the shimmer of eternal heat.

This harmonic tension between movement and stasis, between past, present, and future, is evident also at the level of individual stanzas. In the opening lines a series of exclamations at once betokens a single, timeless state of rapture but also builds in a crescendo of mounting excitement (and anticipatory climaxes) towards the ultimate climax of 'Extase!': 'Ô toison, moutonnant jusque sur l'encolure! | Ô boucles! Ô parfum chargé de nonchaloir!' The expostulatory rhythm of the apostrophe 'Ô toison' is followed by an early caesura, itself a high point and moment of stasis, to be followed ('moutonnant jusque sur l'encolure') by a rippling cadence across the conventional hemistichal line-break as the curls of hair tumble, seemingly prematurely, down towards the neck. Then come another apostrophe and another early caesura ('Ô boucles!'), then another exclamation ('Ô parfum chargé de nonchaloir!'), all culminating in 'Extase!' But now follows the anticlimax as the remainder of l. 3 and all of l. 4 effect a rhythmically and syntactically awkward transition from present bliss to future intention with a word order that generates its own confusion. 'Pour peupler ce soir l'alcôve obscure | Des souvenirs [...]': 'a dark alcove *of* memories' or 'to people a dark alcove *with* memories'? Are the memories already there or not? And will they indeed ever return? Now the dramatic line-breaks of ll. 1–3 give way to two alexandrines in which the traditional central caesura is markedly weak (after 'peupler' and 'agiter' respectively), and a final line that is almost prosaic in its bald statement of fact: 'Je

---

[8] On the question of attributing to rhyme schemes the 'ability to mean', see Clive Scott, *French Verse-Art: A Study* (Cambridge: Cambridge University Press, 1980), 128–36. See also Roy Lewis, *On Reading French Verse: A Study of Poetic Form* (Oxford: Clarendon Press, 1982), 112, and Chesters, *Baudelaire and the Poetics of Craft*, 98.

la veux agiter dans l'air comme un mouchoir!' The bathos of the handkerchief speaks to an anticlimax of poetic diction itself.

In this way Baudelaire builds melancholy and deflation into his account of the 'ivresse'—the beauty—experienced by the poet during his sensual immersion within the hair. For now we may note that even the grandiloquence of the opening lines is suspect, or at least ambiguous. The hair may resemble a fleece, and thus the Golden Fleece, but the immediate juxtaposition of 'toison' with 'moutonnant' creates an ironic contrast between myth and the animality of its literal source (again, further emphasized by 'encolure'). Is there perhaps also an effect of bathos in the opening exclamation 'Ô toison'? Where odes may traditionally begin with a personal address—'Ô toi'—this poem focuses on a 'toison', not a 'toi', so that the sound of [zon]—bringing it with the ghost rhyme of 'poison'—suggests something altogether different: less personal and 'loving' and more like a fall into danger. Similarly, the scent of this hair is 'chargé de nonchaloir': connoting perhaps initially a certain 'nonchalance' or unconcern that might suggest a state of contented bedroom ease, a moment of happy relaxation simulating the 'là-bas' (l. 11) in which 'l'arbre et l'homme, pleins de sève, | Se pâment longuement' (ll. 11–12). But in reality the scent is laden with 'nonchaloir', 'non-heat'. Is it perhaps already suggestive of a cold indifference (that of a sleeping bed-partner, of a quasi-corpse?) that anticipates the potential deafness to desire subsequently evoked in the last stanza of the poem. And what of 'Ô boucles!'? Apparently the most ecstatic of utterances, this apostrophe is also potentially playful, if not downright comic. O curls? O rings? O locks? Can hair really bear the weight of such grandiloquence, or is there here a touch of mock heroic? And if the poem *is* the hair ('La Chevelure'), are we then to see the letter o—which is so insistently present in these opening lines ('Ô toison', 'moutonnant', 'encolure', 'Ô boucles', 'Ô [parfum]', 'nonchaloir', 'Pour', 'soir', 'alcôve obscure') as a visual evocation of its curly rings? Are we even to hear the repeated [o] sound in 'Ô' (ll. 1–3, 10, 24) as an evocation of 'eau' and therefore of this sea/ocean of black waves?

Such playfulness and potential comedy are thus part of a broad tonal spectrum in the poem that stretches from 'surnaturalisme' to 'ironie', but a spectrum carefully contained within a complex harmonic structure in which metre and rhythm have major roles to play. Thus, following the disruptive early caesuras and syntactic inversion of the first stanza, combined with the matter-of-factness of l. 5, the traditional equilibrium of the classical alexandrine is restored in l. 6, with its balanced but contrasting geographical entities: 'La langoureuse Asie et la brûlante Afrique'. Ushering in the sensual bliss of the poet's imaginative journey, long, 'lazy' vowels evoke a supposed and stereotypical oriental torpor while sharp, staccato consonants may suggest the harshness of a burning African sun, before both continents combine within a perspective of great distance and elusive horizons: 'Tout un monde lointain, absent, presque défunt' (l. 7), where the repeated nasal sounds perhaps serve to reinforce a tonality of torpid reverie and insubstantial meanings. This tonality is at once offset, however, by the dramatic opening of the next sentence—'Vit dans tes profondeurs' (l. 8)—where the homophonic presence of 'vie' gives the lie to the 'presque défunt' of the previous line.⁹ After stasis and near-death (or near-sleep?) comes life and a sudden reawakening, thus contributing further to the tension in the poem between activity and inactivity, movement and stasis, excitement and repose. A similar effect is achieved twice in the following stanza: 'J'irai là-bas où l'arbre et l'homme, pleins de sève, | Se pâment longuement [...]'; 'Où les vaisseaux, glissant dans l'or et dans la moire, | Ouvrent leurs vastes bras', and indeed, as before, the verb of supposed action turns out ironically to be descriptive of a state: 'Vit', 'Se pâment', 'Ouvrent'. Paradise is a place of richness and plenitude but also of repose, a place of 'féconde paresse' (l. 24) and thus situated at the antipode of sterile ennui or 'spleen', a place perhaps for slowly going round in circles, like curls of hair.

This harmonic and thematic complexity can be seen at its fullest in l. 25, where the 'féconde paresse' is described further as 'Infinis bercements du loisir embaumé!', a line in which the careful chiastic structure (of adjective, noun, noun, adjective) encompasses a whole series of 'conjectures': the multiplication and endlessness of 'Infinis' as opposed to the singularity and closure of 'loisir embaumé'; the new beginnings of 'bercements' (connoting infancy and restorative sleep) as opposed to the dead end of 'embaumé' (the permanent sleep of the embalmed deceased); the movement of 'bercements' as opposed to the stillness and ease of 'loisir'. The whole duality of life and death, of activity and passivity, is contained here, as perhaps also is the duality of passive reverie and creative artistry. 'Fertile idleness', 'embalmed leisure': what better definitions could there be of Baudelaire's conception of poetry as an affirmation of the power of the imagination in the face of destructiveness, as an assertion of life and effort in response to death and melancholy? 'Loisir' (like 'leisure') derives from the Latin *licere* = to be permitted by law: a form of licit non-work, therefore, or licensed idleness, and ready to be embalmed: that is, treated with a healing ointment (as melancholy is by art?) or else preserved from decay and fragrantly perpetuated in 'balm', the liquid resin extracted from trees and comparable with those other resins—'l'ambre', 'le benjoin', or 'l'encens'—that are celebrated at the end of 'Correspondances' as having 'l'expansion des choses infinies'. The 'forêt de symboles' of old has become a new-style 'forêt aromatique', a source of lingering, insubstantial suggestiveness, of 'Infinis bercements', of intoxicating beauty.

'La Chevelure' demonstrates how a simple physical object can through the metamorphoses of the poetic imagination, a rich command of language, and the

---

⁹ A scatalogical reading of the poem might take 'vit' to be a noun (as a slang word for penis) and see references to pubic hair, the vagina, the penis, and sperm in, respectively, 'toison' (also 'forêt aromatique', 'boucles', 'les bords duvetés de vos mèches tordus'); 'encolure' (also 'port')'; '[Je plongerai ma] tête'; and 'sève'.

work of prosody become the central nexus in a world of proliferating opposites as well as a pivot on which the fundamental dynamic of human desire can be seen to turn. Animality and spirituality; the domestic and the exotic; inside and outside; midday and evening; light and darkness; spaciousness and confinement; heat and cold; life and death: all these antitheses are orchestrated within the unifying harmony of the poem. 'Comme d'autres esprits voguent sur la musique, | Le mien, ô mon amour, nage sur ton parfum' (ll. 9-10): as the poet's imagination journeys on the waves of the hair's aromas, so we readers journey on the musical waves of 'La Chevelure' as though we were listening to variations played upon a theme. The hair of the sleeping companion, with its undulating curls, is a place of rest, of comfort and protection, somewhere to bury one's own head and hide away; and yet it is also a place of activity and a means of conveyance to some other place. It is at once a port and an oasis. It resembles a fleece, something that clothes and yet something also to be sought, like a mythical treasure. Its curls suggest waves that move and tumble forwards, but these 'boucles' are also the circles of an eternal return (cf. 'boucler la boucle')—like the poem itself with its concentric stanzaic structure and its ultimate return to the word 'souvenir' (l. 35) that was in the first stanza its initial point of departure. And it resembles also a crumpled handkerchief, a banal, mundane accoutrement symbolic of a traveller's farewell and yet also itself a container, filled with the scents and memories that can launch a thousand ships.

As an aromatic forest the hair takes the poet into the deep reaches of its smells and then leads him to that other place where tree and poet—'pleins de sève', full of sap and creativity and full of the resin that will heal and perpetuate—may together yield themselves up to the heat in swooning acceptance. And that other place turns out to be a port, offering shelter and sustenance and the promise of further journeys: as does a tent (l. 26), a nomad's tent perhaps, and as does an oasis, itself also a place in which to drink, as was the port: 'où mon âme peut boire | À grands flots le parfum, le son et la couleur' (ll. 16-17)). And in that oasis the poet may draw refreshment from a gourd (again connoting both containment and travel), here the gourd of memories—the memories that sustain the poet on his journey through life and provide him with such moments of 'ivresse' as this. To remember is at once to imbibe and to breathe in the past, as though it were both a wine and a perfume ('où je hume à longs traits le vin du souvenir'); and to experience 'ivresse' is to experience beauty (cf. 'Hymne à la Beauté', l. 4: 'Et l'on peut pour cela te comparer au vin'). Similarly, perhaps, to read 'La Chevelure' is to drink from the gourd of its multiple poetic conjectures and to immerse our imagination in its intoxicating 'invitation au voyage': 'Je plongerai ma tête amoureuse d'ivresse | Dans ce noir océan où l'autre est enfermé' (ll. 21-2). For the beauty contained in the black ocean of poetic text and its dark tresses of jewelled verse offers us in the 'Infinis bercements du loisir embaumé' an alternative and more authentic reality: 'ce qui n'est complètement vrai que *dans un autre monde*'. The licit 'non-work' of poetry, its alternative lawgiving, can provide balm for melancholy through 'recreation'—the re-creation—of moments of ecstasy.

The Beauty of Resistance

La poésie lyrique ennoblit tout, même la passion[.]
(Salon de 1859, ii. 671)

Within the 1861 edition of *Les Fleurs du Mal* 'La Chevelure' thus takes up the subject of 'Parfum exotique' (an imaginary journey to an exotic place prompted by the scent from by a human body) while also echoing the poetic arguments of both 'Correspondances' and 'Hymne à la Beauté' concerning the nature and source of beauty. The prose version of 'La Chevelure'—'Un hémisphère dans une chevelure'[10]—differs in semantic content only slightly from 'La Chevelure', but it is notable that the noise of the port, which in 'La Chevelure' is conveyed simply by the adjective 'retentissant' (l. 16), is there said to be 'fourmillant de chants mélancoliques' (i. 300). In 'La Chevelure' this element of melancholy—absent from 'le chant des mariniers' at the end of 'Parfum exotique'—is supplied by bathos and by the closing allusions to the transience and potential irrecoverability of the poet's ecstasy. In this way 'La Chevelure' effects a transition from the unambiguous 'ivresse' of 'Parfum exotique' towards the poems of the so-called 'love cycles', which by contrast principally depict the tormented sexual passion that constitutes a major element in Baudelaire's catechism of ill-being. For, as he makes hyperbolically clear in the *Salon de 1859*, he harbours no illusions:

> Pour moi, si j'étais invité à représenter l'Amour, il me semble que je le peindrais sous la forme d'un cheval enragé qui dévore son maître, ou bien d'un démon aux yeux cernés par la débauche et l'insomnie, traînant, comme un spectre ou un galérien, des chaînes bruyantes à ses chevilles, et secouant d'une main une fiole de poison, de l'autre le poignard saignant du crime. (ii. 639)

'Love' means being devoured by love's own transport, being consumed by too much sex and too many sleepless nights, by exhaustion, murderous rage, and criminal intent. 'Love' is paradoxical impotence, a helpless subjection to lust: love is hatred, and self-hatred, a longing to destroy—and perhaps the fear of not longing at all.

But if, then, 'love' is actually sexual passion and a form of destruction, then its depiction in the art of poetry is itself a form of resistance, a way of turning 'le Mal'

---

[10] On the dating of 'Parfum exotique', 'Un hémisphère dans une chevelure', and 'La Chevelure', and on the traditional supposition that they were written in that order, see ii. 1321–2.

THE POETRY OF PASSION 353

of 'non-love' or 'nonchaloir' into a source of beauty. As we saw earlier, the relationship between sexual passion and the pursuit of beauty is introduced by the poems that immediately precede 'Parfum exotique' in the 1857 edition: 'La Beauté', 'L'Idéal', 'La Géante', and 'Les Bijoux', with the latter being replaced by 'Le Masque' and 'Hymne à la Beauté' in 1861. Thereafter the sequence of 'love poems' as established in the 1857 edition (nos 21-55, from 'Parfum exotique' to 'Moesta et errabunda') remains largely but not wholly unaltered in the 1861 edition (nos 22-57, from 'Parfum exotique' to 'A une Madone'). The banned poems 'Le Léthé' and 'A celle qui est trop vraie' are removed; 'Duellum' and 'Le Possédé' are added towards the end of the first cycle, as though to reinforce respectively the themes of hatred and powerlessness; 'Semper eadem' is inserted between the first and second cycles, perhaps to indicate by its Latin title (meaning 'always the same', where 'the same' is both a feminine singular and a neuter plural) that a change of sexual partner means not newness but repetition, a dreadful cyclicity: 'plus ça change, plus c'est la même femme'. Beyond these differences the majority of other changes to the 'love poems' as between the two editions occur at the end of the third cycle where 'L'Héautontimorouménos' is taken out and moved to form part of the closing frame of 'Spleen et idéal' and four new poems are inserted: 'Chant d'automne', 'A une Madone', 'Chanson d'après-midi', and 'Sisina'.[11]

The one remaining alteration is the addition of 'Un fantôme', a quartet of sonnets, towards the end of the first cycle, where it is placed before 'Je te donne ces vers...' and the newly inserted 'Semper eadem'. 'Un fantôme' is of great importance to a reading of the 'love poems' in *Les Fleurs du Mal* in that it strongly reinforces the idea of a close relationship between sexual passion and the pursuit of beauty through creative art. In the first of its four sonnets ('Les Ténèbres') the poet is alone within the darkness of his melancholy (ll. 1-4), talking to himself and eating his own heart out (ll. 7-8) in a torment of introspection and self-pity, like a painter condemned by a mocking God to paint upon darkness itself (ll. 5-6). Within this darkness the ghost of 'Elle' appears to him ('noire et pourtant lumineuse' (l. 14)), the spectral visitation of a remembered sexual beauty ('Un spectre fait de grâce et de splendeur', 'sa rêveuse allure orientale' (ll. 10-11)). In the second sonnet ('Le Parfum'), addressed now to the reader, the poet reflects on the intoxicating power of the sense of smell to conjure up memories: '[d]ans le présent le passé restauré' (l. 6). Like incense in a church or the long-lasting perfume from a sachet of musk, the scent from a lover's body is like a 'fleur exquise' (l. 8), a sweet-smelling flower of memory ready to be picked. The former lover, implicitly the spectral 'Elle', becomes present to the poet through the memory of an aromatic body—the lover's hair is itself a living sachet of perfume

---

[11] These last two are traditionally considered to constitute the beginning of the fourth cycle ('maladroitement appelé le cycle des héroïnes secondaires' (i. 938)), to which 'Sonnet d'automne' was newly added also in 1861.

and an 'encensoir de l'alcôve' (l. 10), exuding '[u]ne senteur [...] sauvage et fauve' (l. 11)—and also of the clothes ('mousseline ou velours' (l. 12)) that contain the body, themselves giving off the scent not only of a corporeal 'jeunesse pure' but also of fur: a fur that in this context (cf. 'sauvage et fauve') connotes not so much glamorous fur coats as a primitive, animal sexuality.

In the third sonnet ('Le Cadre') this particular suggestion is reinforced by the attribution to 'elle' (ll. 9, 10) of 'la grâce enfantine du singe' (l. 14), the closing phrase of a sonnet in which the body of 'Elle' has been further clothed, adorned, and 'furnished' by poetic memory: 'Ainsi bijoux, meubles, métaux, dorure, | S'adaptaient juste à sa rare beauté' (ll. 5–6). A natural beauty, strongly associated with a sexual 'rêveuse allure', has been enhanced—but not compromised ('Rien n'offusquait sa parfaite clarté' (l. 7)—by the precision (but only just!) of artistic creativity. These jewels, this furniture, these metals, this gilt, all serve to frame her 'rare' beauty—'Comme un beau cadre ajoute à la peinture' (l. 1)—and in thus setting it apart ('En l'isolant de l'immense nature' (l. 4)) art confers on this natural beauty the all-important power to provoke conjecture ('Je ne sais quoi d'étrange et d'enchanté' (l. 3)): once again, 'le beau est toujours bizarre'. Moreover, not only is this natural beauty not compromised, it/she appears to revel in the enhancement of its/her own new power: 'Même on eût dit parfois qu'elle croyait | Que tout voulait l'aimer; elle noyait | Sa nudité voluptueusement | Dans les baisers du satin et du linge' (ll. 9–12). Nature itself has found an ardent lover within the arms of sartorial embellishment. And so, as the fourth sonnet ('Le Portrait') concludes, the picture is complete: the ghostly 'Elle' (an 'amour décomposé') has been restored to life—with her beauty enhanced—by the power of memory and art, as though in four framed miniatures displayed upon the wall of the page. 'Je suis comme un peintre'...

But the poet's melancholy is not so easily to be overcome, for if his sexual passion has turned to ashes, so too will this 'portrait'. The fire of passion is subject to fire's own destructiveness: 'La Maladie et la Mort font des cendres | De tout le feu qui pour nous flamboya' (ll. 1–2). Even as the poet remembers the 'pleasure' and 'glory' (l. 14) of his sexual partner—her body ('ces grands yeux si fervents et si tendres', 'cette bouche où mon cœur se noya' (ll. 3, 4)) and the sexual relationship itself ('ces baisers puissants comme un dictame', 'ces transports plus vifs que des rayons' (ll. 5, 6)—he realizes that his 'portrait', drawn from memory, is in comparison with reality but 'un dessin fort pâle, aux trois crayons' (l. 8), a paltry, primitive sketch that is itself subject to a sad decay: 'Qui, comme moi, meurt dans la solitude' (l. 9). For, like him, this pencil drawing—and perhaps also, we may infer, this manuscript poem—will gradually fade: 'Et que le Temps, injurieux vieillard, | Chaque jour frotte avec son aile rude...' (l. 11). And so, from within this melancholy state, the poet's resistance ultimately assumes the tone of a doomed bravado: 'Noir assassin de la Vie et de l'Art, | Tu ne tueras jamais dans ma mémoire | Celle qui fut mon plaisir et ma gloire!' (ll. 12–14).

Time, of course, will eventually do just that, but perhaps not before further spectral manifestations of his sexual past are restored to the poet within the present where they may undergo the resuscitations of his poetic art. Certainly in the following poem, 'Je te donne ces vers...', before which Baudelaire chose to insert 'Un fantôme' in 1861, a traditional faith in the capacity of art to perpetuate our memory of the dead is confidently held, albeit with irony. Here the poet's former lover is also a ghost ('comme une ombre à la trace éphémère' (l. 11)), but in this case an 'Être maudit' (l. 9) who is no longer remembered by '[l]es stupides mortels qui t'ont jugée amère' (l. 13). But the poet does remember her and here dedicates his verses to this woman so that his future reader may find her as tiresomely elusive and coldly aloof as he has. To this end she, too, must be transformed into a work or instrument of art. He wants the memory of her to be like one of those 'fables incertaines' (l. 5), a story with an ambiguous moral, nagging away at the reader like the insistent twang of a dulcimer's strings, and also for this memory to hang by a 'fraternal' and 'mystical' little chain (like a dulcimer's accompanying drumstick perhaps) from the stringed instrument of the poet's own 'haughty' rhymes (l. 8)—as though she were dangling from the gibbet of his vengeful art. At the same time he verbally immortalizes her serene disregard for others in the image of a bronze statue with eyes of jet. An 'Être maudit' she is a fallen angel, but through art she becomes once more a 'grand ange'—yet with cold black eyes that make of her also, perhaps, an everlasting angel of death.

The inclusion and placing of 'Un fantôme' in the 1861 edition of *Les Fleurs du Mal* complements a rich network of echoes and anticipations within the structure of 'Spleen et idéal'. In 'Parfum exotique' the power of scent to inspire the imagination is seen wholly within the present, and only the context of 'un soir chaud d'automne' (l. 1) may suggest a melancholy awareness of time's passing. In 'La Chevelure', by contrast, the emphasis on memory already implies that very transience of the present and brings with it an attendant melancholic sense of impermanence, even though the poet's bedfellow still lies there (we may presume) by his side. In 'Un fantôme', by contrast, scent is exclusively a means to the resurrection of a dead past, implying that the sexual relationship evoked in the course of this first cycle of poems has now reached its end, leaving only the final act of ironic dedication to be completed in 'Je te donne ces vers...'. At the same time the references in 'Le Parfum' to musk and incense recall the poetics of smell outlined at the end of 'Correspondances', just as their source in this case—'ses cheveux élastiques et lourds' (l. 19)—recalls 'La Chevelure'. Similarly, the poet condemned to paint on darkness recalls the poet of 'Le Mauvais Moine' who could not paint at all, while both anticipate the poet of 'Obsession' who espouses the darkness only to find its black canvas peopled with the involuntary projections of his own mind's eye.

Within the remainder of this first cycle, as it stands in the editions of both 1857 and 1861, the pursuit of aesthetic beauty within the experience of 'love' takes many different forms, some paradoxical, others markedly grotesque. Where in 'Parfum exotique' the poet becomes a singing mariner, and in 'La Chevelure' a jeweller-to-be, now in 'Je t'adore à l'égal de la voûte nocturne...' the poet proudly assumes the identity of a 'choir' of singing earthworms attacking a corpse! The bed-companion of the previous two poems—sleeping, silent, but at least warm and still there—is here replaced by a sad, cold, elusive emblem of impossibility and death: the 'ornement de mes nuits' (l. 4). Now the black hair figures not the waves of an ocean but the vast, empty reaches of the night sky (l. 1). No longer filled with memories it is simultaneously a container of melancholy and an expanse of sorry sludge ('Ô vase de tristesse' (l. 2)). Where previously the companion had inspired the poet to embark on a journey towards an imaginary paradise, now she shows him—'ironiquement'—just how far removed he is from the 'immensités bleues' he craves (l. 6) even as he stretches out his arms to grasp them. And yet still he 'loves' her: 'Je t'adore' (l. 1), 'Et t'aime' (l. 3), 'Et je chéris' (l. 9), and 'loves' her all the more for the new source of beauty she offers: 'd'autant plus, belle, que tu me fuis' (l. 3), 'Jusqu'à cette froideur par où tu m'es plus belle!' (l. 9). She may be a 'bête implacable et cruelle!' (l. 9), but in the death-like frigidity of her unresponsiveness she offers not only an invigorating challenge ('Je m'avance à l'attaque, et je grimpe aux assauts' (l. 7)) but the prospect of artistic 'recomposition' through the sacred art of 'un chœur de vermisseaux', of life salvaged from death.

In 'Tu mettrais l'univers entier dans ta ruelle...' the poet takes up the idea of 'Je t'adore à l'égal de la voûte nocturne...' that his companion's cruelty offers him a new source of beauty and now sarcastically wonders if she realizes that she is a mere tool of nature, helping to shape a new genius! The addressee of this poem epitomizes sexual passion as promiscuity (l. 1), impurity (l. 2), voracious hunger (ll. 3–4), meretricious attraction (ll. 5–6), usurpation, and abuse (ll. 7–8). Here is sex as ignorance of beauty's law: 'Tes yeux [...] | Usent insolemment d'un pouvoir emprunté, | Sans connaître jamais la loi de leur beauté' (ll. 5, 7–8) This is sex as mechanical process and instrumentality, unperceiving and sterile, productive only of moral pain and a travesty of the (supposedly) beneficial medical practice of blood-letting as it sucks the very life out of the world: 'Machine aveugle et sourde, en cruautés féconde! | Salutaire instrument, buveur du sang du monde' (ll. 9–10). But she who thinks she knows everything ('ce mal où tu te crois savante' (l. 13)) is so ignorant of beauty's law that she fails to see how 'le Mal' can give birth to genius. For all the blood she has sucked, she should turn pale with horror to see how she—'âme cruelle' (l. 2), 'reine des péchés' (l. 16), 'vil animal' (l. 17)—is but an instrument of nature's secret and paradoxical design whereby even sterile lust can become the subject of a poem and a source of beauty. Really, she should be ashamed of herself, to spawn such sublime greatness from the midst of her filth: 'Ô fangeuse grandeur! sublime ignominie!' (l. 18). And this final line, separated off from the rest of the poem, provides a triumphant parting flourish as the poet flaunts that very genius she has borne: the grandiloquent apostrophe, the symmetrical hemistichs with their chiasmus of noun and adjective, the intricate repetitions and contrasts of sound ([g] + [ã] + [œ]; [ã] + [g] + [œ]) in the first hemistich, the mirrored [im/mi] and insistent [i]s of the second, the overall contrast of vocalic darkness and light ([ã] and [i]).

In these three poems that follow 'La Chevelure', therefore, the poet turns his lover's coldness and cruelty to artistic account, claiming explicitly (and showing demonstrably in the poems he writes) how he finds a new source of creativity in her sterility. In this way, implicitly, he takes revenge on her indifference. In 'Sed non satiata' he turns the tables again by affirming how *she* satisfies *him* while she herself can get no satisfaction. The poet's sense of fulfilment and plenitude, described in the octave, derives from the imaginative stimulus provided by his companion, the kind of stimulus already exemplified in 'Correspondances', 'Parfum exotique', and 'La Chevelure': a sensual excitement comparable to the effect of wine or drugs and manifest in his delighted embrace of the unfamiliar and the exotic. His companion is a strange deity, smelling of musk (again) and the tobacco of Havana, who puts the poet in mind of the mysterious practices of Afro/West Indian obi (or obeah): a sorceress herself perhaps and the product of dark arts and black magic (l. 4). But despite the association of obi with poisoning, the poet prefers the elixir of her passionate mouth to wine and opium, and finds solace for his melancholy as he drinks from the well of her eyes within this oasis of passion: 'Quand vers toi mes désirs partent en caravane, | Tes yeux sont la citerne où boivent mes ennuis' (ll. 7–8). But he cannot satisfy her, this 'démon sans pitié!' (l. 10), whose eyes blaze with voracious and unsated appetite, and he expresses this inability in a series of ironic twists on classical mythology. He cannot encompass her demonic passion, and so he cannot be the river Styx that encircles Hades nine times.[12] As a 'Mégère libertine' (Megaera being one of the three Eumenides or Furies and a byword for spiteful jealousy) she is at once possessive of him and yet promiscuous in her own behaviour—and indeed, by subsequent implication, with other women. But 'dans l'enfer de ton lit' (l. 14) he cannot play the role of Proserpine[13] to her Hades, king of the Underworld. Thanks to these skewed mythological references the poet of the sestet appears as something of a desperate and inadequate recycler of worn-out classical tropes as compared with the vigorous amateur of the bizarre and the exotic who is manifest in the octave: the adept of a new poetic magic and drinker of new poetic poisons, himself a kind of 'Faust de la savane' (l. 3).[14]

---

[12] The use of the verb 'embrasser' (l. 11) has encouraged a sexual reading of this line as the poet's (ironic) confession of his inability to bring his lover nine times to orgasm. See i. 886 n. 11.
[13] The resultant rhyme on '-pine' has also encouraged a secondary sexual reading. See i. 887 n. 13.
[14] In his fine reading of this poem Graham Chesters sees the rich rhymes on '-avane' in the octave as 'producing and supporting this sense of the rare and the bizarre'. See his *Baudelaire and the Poetics of Craft*, 91–4 (92).

The poet's ability to transform indifference into beauty is now, in 'Avec ses vêtements ondoyants...' and 'Le Serpent qui danse', associated with the art of the jongleur, or wandering minstrel, and in particular with the jongleur who can juggle a snake on the end of a stick. For such is the poet's new role, taking this serpent who is his demonic companion and transforming the undulating movements of her body into the sinuous rhythms of his verse. In the first of these two poems the beauty seems to be all hers: 'Avec ses vêtements ondoyants et nacrés, | Même quand elle marche on croirait qu'elle danse' (ll. 1–2), and yet at once the poet takes implicit ownership of the beauty as being himself its cause. For it is he who has seen the analogy ('on croirait qu'elle danse'), and she dances to his tune: 'Comme ces longs serpents que les jongleurs sacrés | Au bout de leurs bâtons agitent en cadence' (ll. 3–4). Like an empty, arid desert or a featureless sea oblivious to the suffering of mankind (ll. 5–7) this snake uncurls itself: 'Elle se développe avec indifférence' (l. 8). The woman's walk may be a dance, but in all she does she exhibits '[l]a froide majesté de la femme stérile' (l. 14). Again, coldness, indifference, sterility, 'comme un astre inutile' (l. 13); and, again, 'bejewelled' by the poet's creative imagination as he likens her shiny eyes to 'minéraux charmants' (l. 9) and finds not life or flesh but the hard, gleaming surfaces of a similarly mineral beauty: 'tout n'est qu'or, acier, lumière et diamants' (l. 12). As later in 'Un fantôme' where the frame of a picture is said to add '[j]e ne sais quoi d'étrange et d'enchanté' to the portrait, so here the poet finds a source of conjecture in 'cette nature étrange et symbolique' (l. 10), identifying in her the qualities of 'l'ange inviolé' and '[le] sphinx antique' (l. 11). Non-human, mythical, untouched and untouchable, stonily inscrutable, of ambiguous gender, potentially protective, potentially treacherous and destructive, a figment in the sky and a monument in the desert sand... The woman herself may respond to the poet with indifference, but just as nature itself turns mere carbon into diamonds, so he transforms this indifference into the multi-faceted subject of a sonnet. The art is his, the ennui all hers.

The Body of the Poem: 'Le Serpent qui danse'

Même quand elle marche on croirait qu'elle danse
('Avec ses vêtements ondoyants...', l. 2)

As if to demonstrate that it is the poet's art which has rendered sterility creative and invested blank stasis with the complex movement of verse, the next poem, 'Le Serpent qui danse', enacts what the first stanza of 'Avec ses vêtements ondoyants...' merely asserts. The poet now *is* the jongleur. The key comparison is placed in the central stanza, like a kernel:

THE POETRY OF PASSION 359

À te voir marcher en cadence,
    Belle d'abandon,
On dirait un serpent qui danse
    Au bout d'un bâton.

(ll. 17–20)

Comprising nine quatrains of alternating eight- and five-syllable lines, arranged in crossed rhymes of which the first is feminine, the poem ostensibly celebrates a woman's body: some of its individual parts—skin, hair, eyes, head, mouth, teeth— and its rhythmic motion. This focus is established at once in the opening lines: 'Que j'aime voir, chère indolente' | De ton corps si beau [...]', where the homophony of 'chère/chair' reinforces the corporeal emphasis. The image at the heart of the poem—of a snake writhing or 'dancing' at the top of a stick, held by a street-performer—suggests the movement of a tall/long swaying body, its head also gently 'writhing' as it walks. This in turn may suggest the very structure of this long, thin poem with its alternating rhythm of parisyllabic and imparisyllabic lines that follow one another in sinuous curves down the page. Meanwhile the image of a snake, identified with a serpent in both the title and the central stanza, recalls the serpent in the Garden of Eden and further connotes the possibility of a poisonous bite, in turn foreshadowing the climactic kiss at the end of the poem (and recalling the poisonous elixir of 'Sed non satiata').

Beautiful and deadly, this body is a site of ambiguity and uncertainty: of 'âcres parfums' (l. 6) and 'flots bleus et bruns' (l. 8), of two eyes 'où rien ne se révèle | De doux ni d'amer' (ll. 13–14) and that resemble 'deux bijoux froids où se mêle | L'or avec le fer' (ll. 15–16), of saliva that is compared to 'un vin de Bohême, | Amer et vainqueur' (ll. 33–4). But, as later in 'Ciel brouillé', such ambiguity is a source of fascination and delight. Once again, as in 'Parfum exotique' and 'La Chevelure', this body—its hair—sends the poet's soul on an imaginative journey as though across the waves of the sea (ll. 9–12). But here it is especially the rhythmic movement of the body that holds the poet in thrall, with the nasal vowels of the central rhyme 'cadence'/'danse' potentially evoking a sense of languorous ease that is anticipated and echoed respectively in the rhymes 'indolente'/'vacillante' (ll. 1, 3) and 'enfant/éléphant' (ll. 22, 24) (which is reinforced by 'Se balance' (l. 23) and echoed soon afterwards by 'se penche' (l. 25)).

In its structure, again as in 'La Chevelure', the poem combines linearity and circularity, producing at once a sense of forward movement and an impression of coiling repetition. As the poem itself unfolds (or 'se développe', as the previous poem has it), we move from 'voir' in the first line of the first stanza through 'voir' in the first line of the fifth to 'boire' in the first line of the ninth, from shimmering skin (l. 4) to twinkling stars (ll. 35–6), from setting sail in the morning, bound for a distant sky (ll. 9–12), to drinking the dark waters of a sea in which the stars of the night sky are reflected (ll. 33–6). As this body walks forward, therefore, we have a sense of travel, progression, and change. This is counterbalanced by the concentric arrangement of the stanzas, which by contrast suggest repetition and return. Coiled around the central stanza the third and seventh stanzas each evoke a sea journey, the former likening the poet's soul to a departing ship, the latter comparing the walking body to a slender vessel pitching and rolling. Furthermore, the second and eighth stanzas focus on the sea itself as an image for hair and saliva respectively, in each case with an insistent emphasis on discordant corporeality: the hair smells odd, and the saliva rises to the top of the teeth like the excess icemelt from grinding glaciers... Finally, the first and last stanzas of the poem are interconnected by overlapping patterns of sound and sense: the repeated [oi] of 'Je crois boire' (l. 33) recalls the beginning of the poem ('Que j'aime voir'), as does the rhyme of 'Bohême'/'parsème' (ll. 33, 35): 'vainqueur' (l. 34) recalls 'vin' (l. 33) and anticipates 'cœur' (l. 36), the last word of the poem and referring the reader back to 'Que j'aime'.

These elements of bathos (the smelly hair, the foaming mouth) themselves contribute to a further tension in the poem, namely between harmonious rhythm and dissonant detail—as if this beautiful languorous body were also slightly grotesque. Skin shimmers, but like a man-made material, a 'flickering' fabric; the jewel-eyes are cold, at once precious but unloving; the body's paradoxical burden of leisurely ease ('le fardeau de ta paresse' (l. 21)) causes the childlike head to sway from side to side, floppily, with the flabby softness ('mollesse' (l. 23)) of a young elephant. This dancing cadence begins therefore to look more like a lumbering gait, the lamest of shimmies. Indeed this tension between harmony and dissonance is reflected also in the metre in the contrast between the even balance of the octosyllabics and the contrasting 'limp' of the five-syllable lines that follow anticlimactically on—as though this body that moves so languidly were also gangling and awkwardly tall.

Compare also the progression of the rhymes, where the sense of impulsion created by the abab of the *rimes croisées* (with one foot, as it were, following the other) is sometimes accompanied in the rhyme words themselves by a similar alternation of (syllabic) expansiveness and sudden abbreviation: 'indolente'/'vacillante' followed respectively by 'beau'/'peau', 'profonde'/'vagabonde' by 'parfums'/ 'bruns'. The effect of this alternation is further enhanced by the lengthening effect of the mute e in the feminine a rhymes as contrasted with the end-stopping of the masculine b rhymes that bring their lines to an abrupt halt. In this way the walk once again resembles a limp, as the insistent use of enjambement also suggests. If we take four examples: 'Tes yeux, où rien ne se révèle | De doux ni d'amer'; 'On dirait un serpent qui danse | Au bout d'un bâton'; 'Se balance avec la mollesse | D'un jeune éléphant'; 'Qui roule bord sur bord et plonge | Ses vergues dans l'eau', we can see that in each case the *rejet* conveys a sense of falling short: respectively, an emptiness of expression; dancing, but on the end of a stick; swaying gently and softly like an animal as heavy as an elephant (however young); no longer sailing on an even keel but disappearing (however temporarily) beneath the waves. The penultimate stanza ends with similar bathos: 'Quand l'eau de ta bouche remonte | Au bord de tes dents'. Only at the end of the poem does the enjambement and the meaning of the *rejet* bring a sense of apparent success and continuation: 'Un ciel liquide qui parsème | D'étoiles mon cœur!' Only now does the body stop walking, and only now can the poet kiss his 'Belle d'abandon', his heart filling with starry delight as though he were himself the most childish of 'jeunes enfants'. But the reality is different: in drinking this bitter and irresistible potion of intoxicating saliva he is actually exchanging bodily fluids with a metaphorical snake. And now the metrical alternation of languorous ease and sharp interruption may put us in mind of a snake's own double nature, the slow, sinuous, seductive slide of its coiling body and the sudden twist of its small, eye-studded head—and the dart of its tongue between venomous fangs. Once again, therefore, the deadliness of 'love' has been resisted by the vivacity of the poet's imagination, its poison by the antidote of this poetic dance and the art of this particular 'jongleur'.

16
The Performance of Melancholy
The Duel and the Waltz

Deux guerriers ont couru l'un sur l'autre[.]
('Duellum', l. 1)
Valse mélancolique et langoureux vertige!
('Harmonie du soir', ll. 4, 7)

In the 1861 edition of *Les Fleurs du Mal*, as we have seen, the frame of 'Spleen et idéal' mirrors the overall frame of the collection. In the former the traditional poet of both ancient and Romantic conception (divine lawgiver, celebrant of nature, vatic interpreter) is replaced by a poet who accepts the irremediable reality of 'le Mal' and determines to make the best of our imperfect human condition. More broadly, the frame of the collection as a whole takes us from the 'satanic' recognition of 'l'Ennui' in 'Au lecteur' to the affirmation in 'Le Voyage' that the boredom consequent on our everyday familiarity with the world is indeed universal but can be palliated with metaphorical 'sketches' brought back from poetic journeys to the outer limits of our quotidian experience.

Now we are in position to observe that this overall progression is mirrored in this first cycle of 'love poems' (22–39), where, after the 'rivages heureux' (l. 3) of 'Parfum exotique', we move from the melancholic awareness of transience and of a potential failure of memory (at the end of 'La Chevelure') to the possibility of recovering the past through art itself ('Un fantôme'). By metaphorical association the intervening poems might therefore be read as a series of redolent moments, of '[parfums] corrompus, riches et triomphants' that recall earlier experiences and prompt conjecture in the present in accordance with the new poetics proposed at the end of 'Correspondances'. Similarly they might be seen as a series of jewels, like those listed at the end of 'La Chevelure' ('le rubis, la perle et le saphir'), with each poem a carefully fashioned adornment serving to render vanished ecstasies once more susceptible of answering to the poet's imaginative needs. In each case the analogy is with an object of human craft: the sketch, the jewel, the manufactured scent. In 'Parfum exotique' the 'odeur' of the woman's body and the 'parfum' of the tamarind trees are natural, as is the 'forêt aromatique' of the hair in 'La Chevelure', but the perfumes celebrated at the end of 'Correspondances' are processed from nature by human beings: 'l'ambre [gris]', 'le musc', 'le benjoin', 'l'encens'. Natural aromas fade, like the ecstasy of passion, but perfumery extracts a lasting essence that lingers even when, as in 'Le Flacon', the perfume bottle is seemingly empty: ' Il est de forts parfums pour qui toute matière | Est poreuse. On dirait qu'ils pénètrent le verre' (ll. 1–2). Poetry preserves 'l'essence divine' of the poet's 'amours décomposés', for these too 'pénètrent le [vers]'. And thus also does poetry 'extract' beauty from 'le Mal' as though it were a perfume.

As in 'Fleurs du Mal', so here in 'Spleen et idéal' the identity of the 'fleurs' is ambiguous: the women or the poems? But in both cases there is no need to resolve the ambiguity, for in a sense the women 'are' the poems. 'La Chevelure' both describes the effect of real hair and may be thought of as consisting in metaphorical jewelled tresses of verse, while in 'Le Serpent qui danse' the dancing snake is both the woman's body and the writhing rhythm of the poem's alternating metre. In 'Remords posthume' (later in the first cycle and discussed above in Chapter 7) the sonnet is likened to a tomb containing the future corpse of the poet's 'belle ténébreuse' (l. 1). The metrical feet of the poem will prevent his promiscuous and unfaithful lover's own feet from pursuing their 'course aventureuse' (l. 8), just as the worm-like verse will gnaw away at her ('Et le ver rongera ta peau' (l. 14)) like the remorse she never knew in life. The poet speaks as the voice of the tomb-poem (ll. 12–13), but contained in the black marble of its text are the remains of one who never knew 'ce que pleurent les morts' (l. 13): the value of life itself perhaps, or the love for which grief is the price we pay. In life she is in death, and in this poem she will live this death forever.

Except that poems—like marble monuments—do not last forever. As the poet concedes in 'Le Portrait' (the fourth sonnet in 'Un fantôme'), artworks are as subject to time and decay as anything else. But, as we saw, he ends that poem (and therefore 'Un fantôme') by proudly defying time: 'Noir assassin de la Vie et de l'Art, | Tu ne tueras jamais dans ma mémoire | Celle qui fut mon plaisir et ma gloire!' In so saying the poet might be seen as obeying the 'loi d'ignorance' identified in *De l'essence du rire*. There, as I discussed in Chapter 2, the most effective comic performer is the one who in order to be funny pretends not to know that he is funny. Like this 'comédien' the poet of 'Spleen et idéal' resists melancholy through the pursuit of aesthetic beauty even though he knows that poetry is ultimately as subject as anything else to the irremediable 'Mal' of the human condition. Thanks to Baudelaire's ordering of these poems in both the 1857 and 1861 editions the double agency of the poet-performer of melancholy becomes manifest: that is, a poet reduced by the 'original sin' of sexual passion to a state of suffering and melancholic despair, but at the same time a poet whose poetic work—both by its very existence and by its virtuosic display of invention and control—gives the lie to such despair. In Chapter 15 I discussed how the law of moral 'dégradation' governing the experience of sexual passion as inherently destructive is resisted by the use of language and prosody, the alternative legislation of beauty. In this chapter I shall examine how in 'Spleen et idéal' the poet's 'performance of melancholy' demonstrates that resistance with steadily increasing virtuosity and technical originality as he insistently foregrounds the duality of 'love' and poetry as both an antagonism and a potential harmony, as both a duel and a waltz.[1]

Melancholy versus Beauty

> Je sais l'art d'évoquer les minutes heureuses.
> ('Le Balcon', ll. 21, 25)

By its etymology 'passion' means 'suffering'. In the poems that follow 'Hymne à la Beauté' up to and including 'Le Serpent qui danse' the poet appears to suffer little and remains relatively upbeat. His companion is the one who is cruel, taciturn, sterile, and cold: doomed to be 'non satiata', she is the personification of melancholy. He the poet, on the other hand, has his imagination and his art and stands ready to counter silence with language and to match sterility with aesthetic creativity. In 'Avec ses vêtements ondoyants...' she is an 'astre inutile', but in 'Le Serpent qui danse' the poet's heart is filled with the guiding stars of imaginative delight as the result of his willing embrace of her treacherous allure. And, as discussed in Chapter 10, this emergence of creativity from destruction is the central idea of 'Une charogne' (which follows 'Le Serpent qui danse'). Nevertheless, as these 'love poems' follow one upon the other, the emphasis on the poet's own suffering increases: and the intense, 'passionate' feeling associated with a sexual relationship comes to include the suffering of hatred and a rabid thirst for vengeance. As 'Le Serpent qui danse' suggests, sexual passion is a poison, and, as 'Une charogne' savagely announces to the poet's companion, the bodily participants in sex will soon rot: 'Et pourtant vous serez semblable à cette ordure, | À cette horrible infection, | Étoile de mes yeux, soleil de ma nature, | Vous, mon ange et ma passion!' (ll. 37–40). In life we are in death.

As we also saw earlier (in Chapter 6), this theme is central to the poems first published under the title of *Les Limbes* (1851) in which 'De profundis clamavi' first appeared (under the title 'La Béatrix'). Thanks to its new title (quoting the beginning of Psalm 130) the poet ceases to be Dante and becomes a psalmist in search of mercy and redemption, a psalmist nevertheless who is no longer addressing God but instead begging the female source of his melancholy for

---

[1] This chapter therefore completes my commentary on 'Spleen et idéal', while my account of *Les Fleurs du Mal* as a whole will be completed in Chapters 18 and 19 by discussion of the 'Tableaux parisiens' section added to *Les Fleurs du Mal* in 1861. The intervening chapter (Chapter 17) will provide a full technical account of Baudelaire's poetic craft and could be read before or during a reading of this present chapter, which argues for the increasing 'visibility' of prosodic performance in the second half of 'Spleen et idéal'.

pity. Entitled 'Le Spleen' in the 1855 'Les Fleurs du Mal', in which the theme of mitigating melancholy through beauty becomes central (as discussed in Chapter 7), this poem is there followed, as it is here, by 'Le Vampire'. In both poems the suffering poet seeks release: in 'De profundis clamavi' a release from the hellish night of a dark depression, and in 'Le Vampire' from the bondage of his sexual desire and a relationship in which the blood-sucking lover drains his body dry. (In the 1857 edition these two poems were followed by 'Le Léthé', telling of the poet's yearning for the release of oblivion.) But no release is forthcoming. In 'De profundis clamavi' the poet can but sing his lament, while in 'Le Vampire' so great is the poet's subjection that even if his vampire were to be destroyed, he the poet would still resuscitate it with his kisses. This in turn might be read as a melancholic riposte to the positive message of 'Une charogne': namely, that in transforming melancholy through art the poet will not stop the vampire from feeding his memories, as a corpse feeds the maggots ('Le Vampire', l. 11), and that indeed his own 'vers' will simply lend new life to the suffering itself.

Here in 'Le Vampire', as in 'Une charogne', the poet's companion provides the corpse, but in 'Une nuit que j'étais près d'une affreuse Juive...' the two lovers lie together like corpses both: 'Comme au long d'un cadavre un cadavre étendu' (l. 2) (thus recalling 'Hymne à la Beauté' in which 'L'amoureux pantelant incliné sur sa belle | A l'air d'un moribond caressant son tombeau' (ll. 19–20)). In this case sleeping with a prostitute is presented as a form of living death, and the poet lies thinking of the lover ('la triste beauté dont mon désir se prive'(l. 4)) with whom he would have slept had she—'ô reine des cruelles!' (l. 13)—but shed a single tear of warm compassion to indicate that she had a heart. Even as he remembers her, and in particular the 'casque parfumé' of her hair ('dont le souvenir pour l'amour me ravive' (l. 8)), the poet-corpse must continue to deny himself possession of her sad beauty. Where coldness and cruelty formerly had represented a challenge and indeed a new delight for the poet (cf. 'Je t'adore à l'égal...'), now they are what prevent his return to life through memory and the restorative function of art. Instead, in 'Remords posthume' (which follows), his poetry will construct a cold monument for the woman who denied life. As will be evident again later in 'Alchimie de la douleur' ('Je bâtis de grands sarcophages' (l. 14)), the poet has become a builder of tombs.

So 'dead' is the poet's lover indeed that in 'Le Chat' ('Viens, mon beau chat...') the poet now turns to a cat as a substitute source of sensual delight. 'Je vois ma femme en esprit' (l. 9), he tells his 'beau chat', but she has become simply a reference point, providing analogies with which to describe an animal. Now it is the cat who has mineral eyes ('Mêlés de métal et d'agate' (l. 4): cf. 'Avec ses vêtements ondoyants...', l. 9), the cat whose hair he strokes and whose body he caresses, who exudes 'Un air subtil, un dangereux parfum' (l. 13). The poet bids the cat sheathe its claws (l. 2) just as in 'De profundis clamavi' and 'Remords posthume' he had sought mercy and compassion from his lover. Woman has become a medium through which to describe the inhuman: 'Son regard, | Comme le tien, aimable bête' (ll. 9–10), no longer a participant in living passion but now a means of art. In 'Duellum' the woman of flesh and blood ('Ma chère!' (l. 6)) has similarly been transformed from living reality into inhuman symbolic creature, in this case a mythical 'amazone inhumaine' (l. 13), just as her gender and existential experience—and the suffering of the lovers' mutual hatred—are transmuted into a stylized account of two duelling male warriors engaged in the most violent of armed struggles at the bottom of a dusty, thorn-filled ravine where lynx and leopard prowl.

As we approach the end of this first cycle of 'love poems' (which may be seen to close with 'Je te donne ces vers...' and the transitional 'Semper eadem') we find—in 'Duellum', 'Le Balcon', 'Le Possédé', and 'Un fantôme'—a twofold anticipation of the framing conclusions of 'Spleen et idéal' and *Les Fleurs du Mal*: respectively, acceptance of melancholy and 'le Mal', and faith in the palliative function of art and beauty. In 'Duellum' and 'Le Possédé', both added (as already noted) in 1861 (and added perhaps for this very purpose), the poet anticipates the willing acknowledgement of 'le Mal' stated in 'L'Irrémédiable'. In the final tercet of 'Duellum' he 'translates' the story of the two warriors locked in mortal combat thus:

> —Ce gouffre, c'est l'enfer, de nos amis peuplé!
> Roulons-y sans remords, amazone inhumaine,
> Afin d'éterniser l'ardeur de notre haine!

This, as in 'De profundis clamavi', is the 'gouffre' of ill-being: there a place of cold and darkness, here a dangerous ravine and a burning hell in which the poet duels with his female Amazon warrior and looks to hatred as the means of perpetuating the heat of their passion. This is what the human condition looks like, he says, for everybody (cf. 'de nos amis peuplé'!), and so why not accept that their sexual grappling is a form of belligerent wrestling ('Nos héros, s'étreignant méchamment, ont roulé' (l. 10))? To have sex is to make hate, not love. Young lovers ('une jeunesse en proie à l'amour vagissant' (l. 4)) wage the war of the sexes with sword and dagger, but soon their weapons are broken: 'Les glaives sont brisés! comme notre jeunesse, | Ma chère!' (ll. 5–6). But they can still fight tooth and nail ('les dents, les ongles acérés' (l. 6)), for such is the 'fureur des cœurs mûrs par l'amour ulcérés!' (l. 8). Sexual passion is an ulcer on the heart, but so be it: make hate and have no remorse.

In 'Le Possédé', similarly, the poet accepts 'le Mal' of sexual passion in its full satanic duality of tedium and pain: 'Il n'est pas une fibre en tout mon corps tremblant | Qui ne crie: "Ô mon cher Belzébuth, je t'adore!"' (ll. 13–14). On the one hand, the object of his passion ('Ô Lune de ma vie!' (l. 2)) represents the 'gouffre de l'Ennui' (l. 4): whether she be enveloped in darkness, asleep perhaps, or else wrapped up in in her own narcotic world (l. 3), whether silent or sombre, the poet cherishes her: 'Je t'aime ainsi!' (l. 5). But should she wake, like the sun rising, and choose to strut the stage of our bedlam world ('aux lieux que la Folie encombre' (l. 7)), then that, too, is fine: 'C'est bien! Charmant poignard, jaillis de ton étui!' (l. 8). Here is passion as murderous bewitchment, the blazing look that sparks desire in the boorish gaze of men (ll. 9–10). Whether she be moon or sun, 'nuit noire' or 'rouge aurore' (l. 12), the poet is possessed and happy to be possessed: 'Tout de toi m'est plaisir, morbide ou pétulant; | Sois ce que tu voudras [...]' (ll. 11–12). She is the devil—the Devil—incarnate, Beelzebub, prince of fallen angels, another Lucifer. She is 'le Mal'. Where in 'Le Vampire' the poet had sought release, now he worships unconstrained.

Intercalated with 'Duellum' and 'Le Possédé' the two poems 'Le Balcon' and 'Un fantôme' affirm the alternative message: the poet's faith in the beneficial power of art and in his own capacity as an artist. Of these four poems only 'Le Balcon' was present in the 1857 edition, suggesting that Baudelaire may have wished to contextualize (in the manner here suggested) and thereby relativize and temper its unusually blithe tone. In the 1857 edition, coming between 'Le Chat' and 'Je te donne ces vers...', 'Le Balcon' can be read as a triumphant, even sarcastic, celebration of memory over the reality of present suffering. What does the poet care about this woman who has now become for him less important than a cat and whose memory he wishes to perpetuate only as that of a rather tiresome 'être maudit'? He has his memories, and she has been transformed into the personification of memory itself, a maternal, life-giving source, the very best of mistresses: 'Mère des souvenirs, maîtresses des maîtresses' (l. 1)! As the mother of all memories she gives suck to the poetic vision of an earthly paradise. Not only is she the summa of shared sexual pleasure but also—uniquely in *Les Fleurs du Mal*—the emblem of warm tenderness and serene domestic bliss: 'Tu te rappelleras la beauté des caresses, | La douceur du foyer et le charme des soirs' (ll. 3–4). During winter evenings by the fire or summer nights on the balcony (ll. 6–7), poet and woman were once united in bodily delight and deep affection: 'Que ton sein m'était doux! que ton cœur m'était bon!' (l. 8). Here is love, here also indeed is a kind of poetry: 'Nous avons dit souvent d'impérissables choses' (l. 9). The intimacy is total: 'Je croyais respirer le parfum de ton sang' (l. 14). While she lies sleeping, her feet nestled in the poet's protective, undemanding, 'fraternal' hands (l. 19), and even in the darkness that 'partitions' (l. 16) them from the world (as she, too, is sequestered behind her closed eyelids), the poet can imagine the pupils of her eyes and drink of the delicious danger of her breath: 'ô douceur! ô poison!' (l. 18). To remember is to return to her body, like a child returning to the womb, for in this body lie her many beauties:

> Je sais l'art d'évoquer les minutes heureuses,
> Et revis mon passé blotti dans tes genoux.

> Car à quoi bon chercher tes beautés langoureuses
> Ailleurs qu'en ton cher corps et qu'en ton cœur si doux?
> Je sais l'art d'évoquer les minutes heureuses!
>
> (ll. 21-5).

Moreover, if we read 'balcon' in its slang sense of 'breasts', then the title of the poem foregrounds the dual importance of woman for this poet (as in 'La Géante'): as sexual partner and as source of metaphorical nourishment. To recall her 'beautés' is to find sustenance for further visions of beauty. Only in the final stanza is there a note of doubt about the power of memory, but a note that is quickly silenced by the closing affirmation of that very memory:

> Ces serments, ces parfums, ces baisers infinis,
> Renaîtront-ils d'un gouffre interdit à nos sondes,
> Comme montent au ciel les soleils rajeunis
> Après s'être lavés au fond des mers profondes?
> Ô serments! ô parfums! ô baisers infinis!

Within the context of the 1857 edition 'Le Balcon' can be read as a joyous celebration of the poet's memory and its capacity to relive the past as an idyll, an idyll born of art ('Je sais l'art d'évoquer les minutes heureuses') and one to set against the 'spleen' of 'Le Chat' and 'Je te donne ces vers...'. Within the context of the 1861 edition, however, and within the particular, newly added proximities of 'Duellum', 'Le Possédé', and 'Un fantôme', this reading requires adjustment. First, our recollection of the ending of 'La Chevelure' (also newly added) at the beginning of this first cycle lends extra force to the note of doubt sounded in the final stanza of 'Le Balcon'. In 'La Chevelure' the many exclamation marks were followed by a final question mark of uncertainty, whereas here in the last stanza of 'Le Balcon' the brief expression of uncertainty is followed by an exclamatory affirmation in which even the 'serments'—expressions of undying devotion (recalling the happy 'devoirs' of l. 2 and 'Nous avons dit souvent d'impérissables choses' (l. 9))—appear immune to irony by virtue of their immediate association with 'parfums' and 'baisers infinis'. But now, given 'La Chevelure', we may sense a new wistfulness in the last line of 'Le Balcon' with its evocation of an idyllic but vanished and potentially irrecoverable past. Second, and following on from this, we may find the insistence in 'Le Balcon' on the poet's art of recovering the past to be of greater consequence. Memory itself—this mother of invention—may require the midwifery of the poet's craft if it is to come alive once more. Third, and for this reason, the considerable prosodic virtuosity of 'Le Balcon' comes in 1861 to carry even greater symbolic weight, and in particular the use of a five-line stanza, or quintil, in which the first line is repeated as the last (as in 'Lesbos').

This prosodic 'return' reinforces the sense of a happy past being successfully recovered while also creating within each stanza an impression of enclosure and completion that sits well with the atmosphere of 'partitioned' contentment evoked within the poem as a whole. If doubt about the fidelity of memory is banished, then we owe this in large part to the poem's sustained tonality of sung delight: warm apostrophe ('vers toi, reine des adorées' (l. 13)), fond exclamation ('Que ton sein m'était doux!' (l. 8)), untroubled parataxis ('Tu te rappelleras la beauté des caresses' (l. 3)), all combine to create a sense of personal immediacy and of a readiness to love and to believe in the possibility of everlasting happiness. In short, the very opposite of melancholy. 'Je sais l'art d'évoquer les minutes heureuses': like a sorcerer calling up spirits, the poet can summon happy minutes with his skilful words, words with which to share 'd'impérissables choses'. Where subsequently in 'Un fantôme' (in 'Un portrait') there is fear that the sketch may fade but faith that the poet's memory shall not so fade, here by contrast memory may not rise again like the sun from the sea but we can be sure that the poet's own linguistic 'sorcellerie évocatoire' will bring us beauty—if not the 'beautés langoureuses' of woman herself, then the experience in words of what once was and could once more still be. The 'duellum' of melancholy and beauty knows no end.

Poems for an Angel

Sa chair spirituelle a le parfum des Anges[.]
('Que diras-tu ce soir...', l. 7)

In the 'love' poems that follow 'Semper eadem', this duel continues. The group of poems traditionally considered to be the second of the three 'love cycles' is the only one explicitly identified by Baudelaire as 'belonging' to a particular individual, namely Apollonie Sabatier.[2] In the first of these, 'Tout entière', the poet asserts the supremacy of beauty over 'le Mal' in terms that recall many of the motifs of the first cycle and anticipate the poet's later temptation by the Devil in 'La Destruction' at the beginning of 'Fleurs du Mal'. Here, in a poem that begins with prosaic simplicity and ends in high rhetoric, the poet playfully imagines that the 'Démon' called on him that morning in his room and tried to catch him out by asking which part of his lover's body ('Parmi les objets noirs ou roses | Qui

---

[2] See his letter to her of 18 Aug. 1857 (*Corr.*, i. 421–3 (423)). The poems in question are: 'Toute entière', 'Que diras-tu ce soir...', 'Le Flambeau vivant', 'A celle qui est trop gaie', 'Réversibilité', 'Confession', 'L'Aube spirituelle', 'Harmonie du soir', and 'Le Flacon'. Of these, the first and the last two were never sent to Mme Sabatier, as the others were, leading Claude Pichois to doubt Baudelaire's attribution and to propose a distinction between a 'cycle de Mme Sabatier' consisting of the six poems actually sent, and a larger, nine-poem 'cycle de l'Amour spirituel' (including 'A celle qui est trop gaie' banned in 1857 and thus absent from the 1861 edition of *Les Fleurs du Mal*) (see i. 909). For discussion of Baudelaire's relationship with Mme Sabatier see i. 906–9.

composent son corps charmant' (l. 7–8)) he finds the 'sweetest'. A reader may pruriently wonder, perhaps, about the anatomical identity of these 'objets noirs ou roses', but the poet for his part is not to be tricked into stating a preference: 'Puisqu'en Elle tout est dictame' (l. 11). Our gallant lover will not be seduced into lauding one body part in implicit denigration of another, for his beloved is beauty itself, an intoxicating corporeal harmony that inspires sensual satisfaction and aesthetic delight:

> Et l'harmonie est trop exquise
> Qui gouverne tout son beau corps,
> Pour que l'impuissante analyse
> En note les nombreux accords.
>
> Ô métamorphose mystique
> De tous mes sens fondus en un!
> Son haleine fait la musique,
> Comme sa voix fait le parfum!
>
> (ll. 17–24)

Like a latter-day Faust perhaps, confronted by Mephistopheles, or Satan ('l'Abhorré' (l. 10)), the poet has no need to sell his soul (cf. 'Ô mon âme!' (l. 9)) for he is already in possession of paradise. For him his lover is a quasi-narcotic remedy ('dictame'), and—like the poet of 'Parfum exotique' at the beginning of the first cycle—he knows neither doubt nor melancholy.

And why should he? For, as we learn in 'Que diras-tu ce soir...', this poet who was once a 'pauvre âme solitaire' (l. 1) and a 'cœur [...] flétri' has been brought back to life ('refleuri' (l. 4)) by this perfect creature. Indeed so perfect is she that he, a poet, even wonders what he will say: 'Que diras-tu ce soir [...] | À la très-belle, à la très-bonne, à la très-chère, | Dont le regard divin t'a soudain refleuri?' (ll. 1, 3–4). Where in 'La Destruction' the poet already loves art and is seduced into destructive sexual passion by pursuing that love in the shape of women, here by contrast woman represents something superior to sexual allure ('Sa chair spirituelle a le parfum des Anges' (l. 7)), a sweet authority (l. 6) whose gaze clothes the poet in clarity and light (l. 8), a spiritual presence that dances like a torch (l. 11) and commands the poet's own devotion to beauty: 'Je suis belle, et j'ordonne | Que pour l'amour de moi vous n'aimiez que le Beau' (ll. 12–13). Where in the first cycle the poet turned to beauty as an antidote to melancholy and his lover's coldness, here—situating himself within a long tradition of love poetry in which the beloved, herself perfect, inspires the poet's glorious but necessarily doomed attempts to equal that perfection in his art—this poet can but take pride in singing her praises (l. 5). For she, it seems, is the embodiment of every possible aesthetic, moral, and religious ideal: 'Je suis l'Ange gardien, la Muse et la Madone' (l. 14).

This in turn is underlined in 'Le Flambeau vivant' where the torch of a 'ghostly' presence dancing in the air like some paradoxically reliable will-o'-the-wisp has now come alive in the form of the beloved's blazing and protective gaze. Once again she is the seeming embodiment of moral and aesthetic perfection: 'Me sauvant de tout piège et de tout péché grave, | Ils [ses yeux] conduisent mes pas dans la route du Beau' (ll. 5–6). She is the instrument whereby the poet's soul is 'reawakened', and she, like the dancer of 'Que diras-tu…', is the artist setting an example to the poet: 'Vous marchez en chantant le réveil de mon âme' (l. 13).

The following three poems—'Réversibilité', 'Confession', and 'L'Aube spirituelle'—have already been discussed (in Chapter 7) within the context of the 1855 'Les Fleurs du Mal' where they were first published. Here they serve to articulate a moment of incipient doubt about this angelic perfection. In the 1857 edition 'A celle qui est trop gaie' preceded this trio, giving expression to the poet's petulant exasperation—even hatred (l. 16)—at the sheer excess of the woman's cheerful goodness and to his cruel wish to damage and poison her beautiful body ('T'infuser mon venin, ma sœur!' (l. 36)). But in the 1861 edition, from which that poem was banned, 'Le Flambeau vivant' is followed directly by 'Réversibilité' in which the poet wonders if this perfect woman—this 'Ange'—can truly understand the nature of 'le Mal'. As the angel of gaieté, kindness, good health, and beauty, has she really any knowledge whatsoever of 'le Mal' in all its various manifestations: anguish, shame, remorse, grief, boredom, terror, hatred, vengeance, illness, the fear of ageing, the dread of finding in a lover's eye that look that betrays an unwillingness to commit ('la secrète horreur du dévouement' (l. 18))? According to the doctrine of 'reversibility', the suffering of the innocent serves to atone for the sins of the wicked, but she does not suffer! And so all he can do is to ask her— 'Ange plein de bonheur, de joie et de lumières!' (l. 21)—to pray for him. Yet 'Confession' shows immediately that she does indeed know the meaning of human suffering when, in a discordant voice that is at once 'plaintive', 'bizarre' (l. 19) and 'criarde' (l. 25), she acknowledges—as though it were some dreadful family secret, like some ugly, unwanted child locked away in a cellar—that she understands 'le Mal': 'Que rien ici-bas n'est certain, | Et que toujours, avec quelque soin qu'il se farde, | Se trahit l'égoïsme humain' (ll. 26–8). Indeed she knows, too, that her own perfection is the product of art! For it is hard work being a beautiful woman, she confides: 'Que c'est un dur métier que d'être belle femme, | Et que c'est le travail banal | De la danseuse folle et froide qui se pâme | Dans un sourire machinal' (ll. 29–32); and she wonders really why she should even bother with beauty when nothing lasts, when oblivion chucks everything into the basket of eternity (ll. 35–6)?

So this confession—'cette confidence horrible, chuchotée' (l. 39)—is an acknowledgement of fundamental melancholy accompanied by a temporary loss of faith in the value of artifice, in the effort of putting on make-up and forcing a smile. But paradoxically it seems that this confession precisely makes this angel human and so, for the poet, she becomes now a different kind of ideal, one who represents—like Baudelaire's perfect performance artist—the pursuit of beauty *in spite of* 'la conscience dans le Mal'. This woman is in her own way an artist (like the women described in *Le Peintre de l'art moderne*), but, unlike this woman in her own dreadful moment of doubt, the poet by his very poem demonstrates his own continuing faith in the power of beauty and art to resist melancholy, to exist *despite* melancholy. Sexual passion may abate, and natural beauty may fade ('tout craque, amour et beauté' (l. 34)), but the poet still remembers this poignant moment of secular 'confession' as the lovers walked together through a moonlit Paris. He remembers it and records it in verse, like a sorcerer calling up the magic of the moon: 'J'ai souvent évoqué cette lune enchantée | Ce silence et cette langueur' (l. 37-8)). Furthermore this act of affirmation is repeated in the two poems that follow: 'L'Aube spirituelle' and 'Harmonie du soir'. Time may consign everything to the trash-can of history, but the poet can affirm the power of beauty by articulating its symbolic passage for his own artistic ends, proclaiming in turn a spiritual dawn and a glorious evening lit by the glow of eternal memory. Following the 'horrible' revelation of 'Confession', the poet awakes anew to the former brilliance of his 'chère Déesse' ('L'Aube spirituelle', l. 8), as though dazzled by the sunlight after a night of debauch—and by a sunrise that gives the lie to his doubts at the end of 'Le Balcon'. The sun *will* rise again. New vistas of imaginative possibility open up for 'l'homme terrassé qui rêve encore et souffre' (l. 6), as his former companion becomes a memory ('Ton souvenir plus clair, plus rose, plus charmant' (l. 10)) and so becomes another ghost, another 'amour décomposé': 'Ainsi, toujours vainqueur, ton fantôme est pareil, | Âme resplendissante, à l'immortel soleil!' (ll. 13-14).

In 'L'Aube spirituelle' memory is thus presented as a form of secular resurrection in the afterlife of the mind and here also as an after-death in the eternal sunshine of art—or what Seamus Heaney in 'Mossbawn. 1. Sunlight' (in *North*) calls a 'sunlit absence'. The Christian parallel is made more evident in 'Harmonie du soir', itself a kind of vesper, in which this memory[3] is said to gleam like a monstrance (l. 14)—the ornamental receptacle in which the consecrated host representing Christ's body is exhibited in Roman Catholic churches. In this famously virtuosic poem evening is celebrated as the time when flowers give off their scent in a moment of delicious melancholy, of a beauty shot through with the painful awareness of transience and the coming of night:

> Voici venir les temps où vibrant sur sa tige
> Chaque fleur s'évapore ainsi qu'un encensoir;

---

[3] On the biographical question of whether the memory in question is actually of Mme Sabatier see i. 919.

> Les sons et les parfums tournent dans l'air du soir;
> Valse mélancolique et langoureux vertige!
>
> (ll. 1–4)

The waltz of sounds and scents and memories—itself reminiscent of 'Correspondances' and comparable with the stanzaic 'waltz' of the poem's own repeated lines—is said to be played by a violin with a vibrato that recalls 'un cœur qu'on afflige' (ll. 6, 9), but also '[u]n cœur tendre' (ll. 10, 13)—the heart of one who, unlike the poet of 'Obsession', hates 'le néant vaste et noir!' (ll. 10, 13). This musical melancholy seeks the plenitude of harmony, evoked by the insistent assonance and alliteration of the poem and epitomized in the celebrated line: 'Le soleil s'est noyé dans son sang qui se fige' (ll. 12, 15). The sun is dead, drowned in its own coagulated blood and immolated on the great altar-table of the sky (ll. 8, 11), but it lives on in the mind and art of this 'cœur tendre' who, as darkness finally falls, '[d]u passé lumineux recueille tout vestige!' (l. 14)—that is, a heart who gathers in every last, dying ray of 'her' memory. And this light betokens the eternal flame of poetic recollection, a vesperal 'recueillement' that anticipates the poem 'Recueillement' intended for inclusion in a third edition of *Les Fleurs du Mal*: 'Sois sage, ô ma Douleur, et tiens-toi plus tranquille. | Tu réclamais le Soir; il descend; le voici' (l. 1).

Verse Dance

> Un musicien [Weber] a écrit l'*Invitation à la valse*; quel est celui qui composera l'*Invitation au voyage*, qu'on puisse offrir à la femme aimée, à la sœur d'élection?
>
> ('L'Invitation au voyage', in *Le Spleen de Paris*, i. 302).

Increasingly the reader of *Les Fleurs du Mal* may come to see the succeeding poems of 'Spleen et idéal'—and subsequently of the collection as a whole—less as the account of a duel between melancholy and beauty and more as the performance of a 'valse mélancolique' in which various recurrent themes and images 'circulate' and the dancing partners of melancholy and beauty take turns to lead—a kind of round dance combining repetitious circularity with rhythmic harmony. Certainly at this point in 'Spleen et idéal' the impression of cyclicity now emerges strongly as we move from the second to the third grouping of 'love poems' and as particular themes are repeated: the willing acceptance of the lethal potion that is 'love' ('Le Poison', recalling the end of 'Le Serpent qui danse' and, less directly, 'Le Possédé'); the woman's coldness that offers the poet a new kind of pleasure and a potential new source of aesthetic beauty ('Ciel brouillé', recalling 'Je t'adore à l'égal...'); the substitution of cat for woman ('Le Chat ['Dans ma cervelle se promène...']', recalling the earlier 'Le Chat ['Viens, mon beau chat...']'); the celebration of the woman's dress in combination with the rhythmic movements of her body ('Le Beau navire', recalling 'Avec ses vêtements ondoyants...' and 'Le Serpent qui danse'); the journey of the imagination prompted by the poet's companion ('L'Invitation au voyage', recalling 'Parfum exotique' and 'La Chevelure'); the experience of remorse as a destructive form of memory ('L'Irréparable', recalling 'Remords posthume'); the willing sacrifice of self to the destructive effects of sexual passion ('Causerie', recalling 'Le Possédé and, less directly, 'Le Vampire'); the poet's appeal for mercy ('Chant d'automne', recalling 'De profundis clamavi' and, less directly, 'Une nuit que j'étais...'); and, finally, the vengeful creation of a work of art with which to memorialize a lover's cruelty ('A une Madone', recalling 'Remords posthume' and 'Je te donne ces vers...').

Central to this thematic recurrence is the dual nature of memory itself as both the potential source of a bliss relived and as the nagging reminder not only of deeds that cannot be undone but of the 'irreversible' nature of time itself: of 'remords' as repeated 'morts', as repeated 'morsures'. This duality is the focus of 'Le Flacon', which serves as the transition between the second and third cycles much as 'Semper eadem' so served between the first and second. In 'Semper eadem' the poet laments that 'Vivre est un mal' (l. 4) and begs his cheerful companion not to ask questions about his own melancholy but to let him continue to enjoy the illusion of sweet love ('Laissez, laissez mon cœur s'enivrer d'un mensonge' (l. 12)). Consequently the second cycle of 'love poems' may be read as an account of the poet's desperate acquiescence in the 'mensonge' of a new relationship. In the case of 'Le Flacon', by contrast, the poet is more sourly aware of the transience of 'love' ('un vieil amour ranci, charmant et sépulcral' (l. 20)) and that his own memory, like an empty and discarded perfume-bottle, contains the record not of fond illusion but of a bitter truth.

'Le Flacon' consists of seven quatrains of alexandrines arranged, unusually, in rhyming couplets. Like 'La Chevelure', which also comprises seven stanzas (of five lines), the poem contains a central turning-point. In 'La Chevelure' the poem pivots on its fourth stanza, which, in the absence of a main verb, evokes the timeless paradise of a port, whereas here in the middle stanza of 'Le Flacon' the poem pauses in the present tense to gaze, Janus-like, both backwards and forwards, at two different types of memory and at two different experiences of 'love':

> Voilà le souvenir enivrant qui voltige
> Dans l'air troublé; les yeux se ferment; le Vertige
> Saisit l'âme vaincue et la pousse à deux mains
> Vers un gouffre obsurci de miasmes humains[.]

In the first three quatrains of the poem the act of memory is figured, positively, as the chance discovery of an old perfume-flask, contained in a small casket of oriental provenance or else lying in a dusty old wardrobe in some empty house. Where the casket has a rusting lock, also suggesting age and disuse, the wardrobe is itself a kind of perfume-bottle, being full of 'l'âcre odeur des temps' (l. 6). Like Chinese boxes, and perhaps also like this poem, the perfume-flask of memory is a container within a container—and a source of resurrection: 'un vieux flacon qui se souvient, | D'où jaillit toute vive une âme qui revient' (ll. 7–8). What was dead and forgotten is full of life, of the 'vie' to be heard in 'vive' and seen in 'revient'. What was asleep now awakes as dormant thoughts take wing, like butterflies emerging from their chrysalis-tombs ('chyrsalides funèbres' (l. 9)) to flutter upwards in resplendent shades of blue and pink and gold (ll. 9–12). Here is 'le souvenir enivrant qui voltige', a 'Vertige' that itself recalls the 'Valse mélancolique et langoureux vertige' of 'Harmonie du soir' (the preceding poem).

But now the ambiguity of 'l'air troublé', followed by 'les yeux se ferment', provides the moment of transition from positivity to negativity. The air filled with scent—and the mind filled with memories—is like air disturbed by the beating wings of a beautiful butterfly, and eyes are closed in surrender to the vertiginous power of smell and the dizzying swirl of a once dormant past. But in a moment of brutal and dramatic enjambement 'le Vertige | Saisit l'âme vaincue': a willing surrender to soaring delight has become a sudden capture and involuntary descent into 'un gouffre obscurci de miasmes humains'.[4] The resurrection of golden memories formerly represented by the birth of a butterfly is now the resurrection of the smelly body of Lazarus: 'Lazare odorant déchirant son suaire' (l. 18).[5] More literally, the memory of love as multicoloured swoon has clouded, leaving the poet not with a newly emerged butterfly but the corpse and ghost of something that once charmed and yet now reeks of death: 'le cadavre spectral | D'un vieil amour ranci, charmant et sépulcral' (ll. 19–20). And this is the memory with which the poet will forever be left, the stale perfume of which he becomes the everlasting but discarded container: 'Quand on m'aura jeté, vieux flacon désolé, | Décrépit, poudreux, sale, abject, visqueux, fêlé' (ll. 23–4). This bottle will be forever cracked, like the church bell of the poet's soul in 'La Cloche fêlée'.

Where in 'Remords posthume' the poet had created a tomb-poem to memorialize his unloving mistress, now he is himself that tomb, preserving the memory of 'love' as that most paradoxical experience: an amiable plague, a longed-for destruction, a cherished poison manufactured by angels. In short, the memory of a potion that brings both life and death:

---

[4] Cf. 'Élévation' where the poet would like to escape 'ces miasmes morbides' (l. 9) and looks with sarcastic envy on 'celui qui peut d'une aile vigoureuse | S'élancer vers les champs lumineux et sereins' (ll. 15–16). Cf. also that poet's envy of 'Celui dont les pensers, comme des alouettes, | Vers les cieux le matin prennent un libre essor' (ll. 17–18) with the evocation in 'Le Flacon' of these butterfly-memories 'Qui dégagent leur aile et prennent leur essor' (l. 11).

[5] Cf. John: 11: 39: 'Jesus said, Take ye away the stone. Martha, the sister of him that was dead, saith unto him, Lord, by this time he [Lazarus] stinketh: for he hath been dead four days.'

> Je serai ton cercueil, aimable pestilence!
> Le témoin de ta force et de ta virulence,
> Cher poison préparé par les anges! liqueur
> Qui me ronge, ô la vie et la mort de mon cœur!
>
> (ll. 25–8)

And, like the 'flacon', he the poet-tomb is contained within the further box that is the poem itself. Just as we saw how the title of 'La Chevelure' signified both the hair and the hair-like poem, and how 'Le Serpent qui danse' signifies both the sinuous sway of a body on the move and the alternating rhythmic shifts of the poem itself, so here also 'Le Flacon' *is* the poem. The analogy is foregrounded at once in the opening couplet: 'Il est de forts parfums pour qui toute matière | Est poreuse. On dirait qu'ils pénètrent le verre.' The wordplay on 'verre/vers' has already been noted, but the analogy between flask and poem—and more precisely between the glass bottle found in a box or wardrobe and the lines of verse contained within the 'box' of the poem as a whole—is evident also from the enjambement in which the absence of syntactic containment within the syllabic constraints of the alexandrine simulates the porosity of the bottle itself.[6] Furthermore, and given this opening to the poem, we may choose to see 'le Vertige' with its arresting capital letter as a further punning allusion to 'le vers' and thus also to the line of verse as the stalk of a flower ('tige'): of a 'fleur du Mal' from which is extracted the beautiful perfume of poetry. Are we perhaps also to reflect that at this very moment the 'air' or song of the poem itself becomes 'troublé' by the passage from 'idéal' to 'spleen', and perhaps even that the two hands (l. 15) with which 'le Vertige' pushes the poet's soul down into the human miasma of melancholy are akin to the transgressive couplets of the poem's unorthodox rhyme scheme? Be that as it may, the poem itself will live on—even after the poet himself is 'perdu dans la mémoire | Des hommes' (ll. 21–2)—as both testimony and testament to the conflicted character of erotic experience and to the sad truth that even the fondest memories go stale.

The account of memory in 'Le Flacon' sets the tone for this third cycle of 'love poems' in which the passage of time is a recurrent preoccupation (and one that culminates in 'L'Horloge' at the end of 'Spleen et idéal'). In 'Le Poison', as the poet gazes into the green eyes of his lover and tastes her venomous saliva in a kiss ('ta salive qui mord' (l. 17)), he accepts the intoxication of love's 'poison' with no regrets, full in the knowledge that it will bring him oblivion and—'charriant le vertige' (l. 19)—bear his giddy soul away on the implicit river of time towards the shores of death. In the four quatrains of 'Ciel brouillé', where stanzas 2–4 allude in turn to successive seasons of the year, the poet celebrates the quasi-seasonal

---

[6] This metrical 'porosity' is evident also in the repeated 'enjambement sur la césure' throughout the poem (see ll. 5, 6, 7, 13, 17, 22, 27, 28).

mutability of his lover's moods ('Alternativement tendre, rêveur, cruel', ll. 2-3)) and wonders, as he now revels in her resplendent autumn, whether he will be able also to delight in winter's cold: 'Adorerai-je aussi ta neige et vos frimas, | Et saurai-je tirer de l'implacable hiver | Des plaisirs plus aigus que la glace et le fer?' (ll. 13-16). Just as the interrogative doubt at the end of 'La Chevelure' represents a move away from the unalloyed pleasure of 'Parfum exotique', so here this question mark initiates a by now familiar and cyclical movement from affirmation towards melancholy. Nevertheless this movement is for the moment seemingly deferred by the celebratory descriptions of 'Le Chat' ('Cette voix, qui perle et qui filtre | Dans mon fond le plus ténébreux, | Me remplit comme un vers nombreux | Et me réjouit comme un philtre' (ll. 9-12)) and of 'Le Beau Navire' ('Je veux te raconter, ô molle enchanteresse! | Les diverses beautés qui parent ta jeunesse' (ll. 1-2)), as it is also by the sweet prospects of 'L'Invitation au voyage'. But the signs of danger are already everywhere apparent: the saliva that poisons; the freezing winter ('Ô femme dangereuse, ô séduisant climats!' ('Ciel brouillé', l. 13)); the fixed stare of the cat ('Le Chat', l. 40); the young woman of 'Le Beau navire' with arms like boa constrictors (ll. 33-6) and legs that torment the poet with desire like two witches stirring 'un philtre noir dans un vase profond' (ll. 29-32); and, not least, the 'traîtres yeux' (l. 11) that threaten the happy travel plans of 'L'Invitation au voyage' (l. 11).

By the time we reach the 'sorcière' of 'L'Irréparable' and its 'Être aux ailes de gaze' who never appears the waltz of melancholy is fully under way, and the poet now reflects insistently on what will follow autumn in this unceasing dance to the music of time: in 'Causerie' ('Vous êtes un beau ciel d'automne, clair et rose! | Mais la tristesse en moi monte comme la mer' (ll. 1-2)) and then immediately again in 'Chant d'automne' ('Bientôt nous plongerons dans les froides ténèbres; | Adieu, vive clarté de nos étés trop courts!' (ll. 1-2). The sense of an ending becomes acute: in 'Causerie' the poet's breast is 'un lieu saccagé | Par la griffe et la dent féroce de la femme' (ll. 6-7), while in 'Chant d'automne' he listens to the sound of wood being chopped and gathered in for the fires of winter. Indeed there has been a revolution: in 'Causerie' he compares his heart to 'un palais flétrie par la cohue' (l. 9), recalling the attack on the Tuileries Palace of 1792, while in 'Chant d'automne' the sound of falling logs recalls the erection of a scaffold for the chopping of heads: 'L'échafaud qu'on bâtit n'a pas d'écho plus sourd' (l. 10). The *ancien régime* of love's illusion crumbles as the Bastille of his mind is stormed ('Mon esprit est pareil à la tour qui succombe | Sous les coups du bélier infatigable et lourd' (ll. 11-12)' and the iron of winter enters his soul: 'Tout l'hiver va rentrer dans mon être: colère, | Haine, frissons, horreur, labeur dur et forcé' (ll. 5-6). The sunset of 'Harmonie du soir' ('Le soleil s'est noyé dans son sang qui se fige') has become the sunset of his own heart: 'Et, comme le soleil dans son enfer polaire, | Mon cœur ne sera plus qu'un bloc rouge et glacé' (ll. 7-8). And the sound of wood-cutting takes on a new association: 'Il me semble [...] | Qu'on cloue en grande hâte un cercueil quelque part. | Pour qui?' (ll. 13–15). The end is nigh: 'La tombe attend; elle est avide!' (l. 25)—'à vide' but also 'un vide' soon to be filled. All he can do now is ask for love, for a moment's mercy as the shadows lengthen:

> Et pourtant aimez-moi, tendre cœur! soyez mère,
> Même pour un ingrat, même pour un méchant;
> Amante ou sœur, soyez la douceur éphémère
> D'un glorieux automne ou d'un soleil couchant.
>
> (ll. 21–4)

But if this suggests a final appeal to the maternal comfort of the Virgin Mary, that idea is firmly dispelled at once by the blasphemy and vindictive poetic performance of 'A une Madone. *Ex-voto dans le goût espagnol*'. Here, as in 'Je te donne ces vers...', the poet ends this particular sequence of 'love poems' by creating a lasting memorial of hate, of anti-love. He speaks of building an underground altar in the depths of his misery and there placing, in a niche of blue and gold, the imaginary statue of his Madonna-cum-mistress ('pour toi, Madone, ma maîtresse' (l. 1)). His allegorical construct represents a settling of scores. Jealous, he will sculpt a cloak, lined with suspicion and embroidered with his own tears, which will conceal her charms as thoroughly as if she were encased in a sentry-box of vigilance. With the dress beneath the cloak he will wrap the white skin and pink flesh of her naked body as though in the kiss of his desire, moulding the garment carefully to the contours of her mounds and cleft. And with the satin slippers of his respect he will 'imprison' her feet 'dans une molle étreinte' (l. 21)—in a gesture that recalls 'Remords posthume' (and contrasts with the fraternal nestling of 'Le Balcon')—and place them on a pedestal. Of what? A silver moon may prove too difficult to sculpt, but there is always that serpent from the Garden of Eden:

> Je mettrai le Serpent qui me mord les entrailles
> Sous tes talons, afin que tu foules et railles
> Reine victorieuse et féconde en rachats,
> Ce monstre tout gonflé de haine et de crachats.
>
> (ll. 25–8)

And then he will worship at the altar of this 'mortelle Madone' (l. 10), surrounded by the heady scents (once more recalling 'Correspondances') of 'Benjoin, Encens, Oliban, Myrrhe' (l. 34).[7] But in case anyone should think that this Madonna with

---

[7] 'Oliban' (frankincense) and myrrh: both are aromatic resins and components of the holy incense ritually burned in ancient sacred temples and subsequently in Roman Catholic churches.

her foot on the serpent has triumphed over evil, he will complete his work of art ('pour compléter ton rôle de Marie' (l. 37))[8] with one last, brutal, and symbolic act:

> Volupté noire! des sept Péchés capitaux,
> Bourreau plein de remords, je ferai sept Couteaux
> Bien affilés, et, comme un jongleur insensible,
> Prenant le plus profond de ton amour pour cible,
> Je les planterai tous dans ton Cœur pantelant,
> Dans ton Cœur sanglotant, dans ton Cœur ruisselant!
>
> (ll. 39-44)

The 'jongleur' who once juggled a serpent on his stick has now become the knife-thrower as street performer, revenging himself on the sacred heart of 'le Mal' by turning its own weapons of moral mass destruction (the seven deadly sins) back upon it, ruthlessly and repeatedly putting the knife in with the stabs of an insistent 'dans ton cœur'. For all its allure and all its delights, 'love', it seems, is still lust, a greedy, gluttonous desire filled with anger and envy and pride, and endlessly ending in boredom. Sexual passion is all the passions, instruments with which to destroy a heart that pants with desire or sobs with pain—or bleeds from seven wounds. Where the second cycle ended with 'Le Flacon' in which the poet himself became the sepulchral memorial of love's poison, now once more it is his lover (as in 'Je te donne ces vers...' at the end of the first cycle) who shall be a monument to passion, this time as a grotesque icon of 'le Mal' and a statue crowned by poetry: 'Avec mes Vers polis, treillis d'un pur métal | Savamment constellé de rimes de cristal, | Je ferai pour ta tête une énorme Couronne' (ll. 7-9).

The Sense of an Ending

> Meurs, vieux lâche! il est trop tard!
>
> ('L'Horloge', l. 24)

'Causerie' is the point at which the order of the poems making up 'Spleen et idéal' undergoes the greatest change between 1857 and 1861. As already discussed, Baudelaire undertook significant revisions in this area: removing seven poems for inclusion in 'Tableaux parisiens';[9] bringing the seven final poems[10] forward so

---

[8] From the standpoint of a biographical reading this may constitute an allusion to Marie Daubrun's Christian name. But within the faux-Christian allegory of the poem the blasphemous suggestion might be that the mother of Christ was neither virgin nor chaste and that as a mortal woman she was wholly implicated in the 'sinful' human condition of our secular 'Mal'.

[9] 'Brumes et pluies', 'A une mendiante rousse', 'Le Jeu', 'Le Crépuscule du soir', 'Le Crépuscule du matin', 'La servante au grand cœur...', and 'Je n'ai pas oublié...'.

[10] 'Le Tonneau de la haine', 'Le Revenant', 'Le Mort joyeux', 'Sépulture', 'Tristesses de la lune', 'La Musique', and 'La Pipe'.

that—in a different order, now incorporating 'Les Chats' and 'Les Hiboux', and with the addition of 'Sonnet d'automne' and 'Une gravure fantastique'—they form a group between 'Moesta et errabunda' and 'La Cloche fêlée'; and, lastly, creating a final group of newly added poems around the now relocated 'L'Irrémédiable'.[11] More particularly, where the third love cycle had previously ended with 'L'Héautontimorouménos' (which becomes the antepenultimate poem in the 1861 'Spleen et idéal'), 'Causerie' is now followed by 'Chant d'automne' (which, as we have seen, takes up and repeats its themes of revolutionary destruction and the onset of winter), 'A une Madone' (in which the poet is no longer a 'bourreau de lui-même' but exclusively the 'bourreau de la femme aimée' (i. 985) depicted in the first three stanzas of 'L'Héautontimorouménos'), 'Chanson d'après-midi', and 'Sisina'. The inclusion of the latter two poems serves to introduce the fourth cycle of 'love poems'—the so-called 'cycle des héroïnes secondaires' (i. 938)— where (in most but not all of the poems) 'love' continues to be thematically treated as a manifestation of 'le Mal'.

In 'Chanson d'après-midi' the afternoon of the title echoes the motifs of autumn and sunset present in the third cycle, while the poet's reference to the object of his 'terrible passion' (l. 6) whom he worships 'Avec la dévotion | Du prêtre pour son idole' (ll. 7–8) recalls the murderous 'ex-voto' of the preceding poem, 'A une Madone'. So also do the satin shoes (l. 33) beneath which the poet now happily submits his entire being ('ma grande joie, | Mon génie et mon destin' (ll. 35–6)). More broadly, however, this unnamed woman ('Nymphe ténébreuse et chaude' (l. 16)) is a kind of composite lover, embodying many of the features to be found in earlier poems: her role not as 'ange' (l. 2) but as 'sorcière' (l. 4), recalling 'Sed non satiata'; her hair that puts the poet in mind of desert, forest, and balm (ll. 9–10) as in 'La Chevelure'; her flesh that smells like incense and has the charm of evening ('Parfum exotique', 'Harmonie du soir'); her 'paresse' (l. 18) that echoes the 'féconde paresse' of 'La Chevelure' and recalls the 'chère indolente' of 'Le Serpent qui danse', as do also 'La morsure et le baiser' (l. 28) with which she seeks to quench her rabid thirst (ll. 25–6) (cf. also 'Le Poison'). This is the poet's lover as unfathomable mystery ('Ta tête a les attitudes | De l'énigme et du secret' (ll. 11–12)), an unpredictable and seemingly random force that can destroy him one moment and console him the next (ll. 29–32). For all that she compounds his melancholy, she is seemingly also its only cure: 'Explosion de chaleur | Dans ma noire Sibérie' (ll. 39–40.

'Chanson d'après-midi' thus serves as transition towards a short sequence of poems that focus in turn on a series of individual women. In 'Sisina' (in reality Élisa Neri, a friend of Mme Sabatier), the poet celebrates a fearless and fearsome 'adventuress' with a warm, compassionate heart. 'Franciscae meae laudes'

---

[11] 'Obsession', 'Le Goût du néant', 'Alchimie de la douleur', 'Horreur sympathique', 'L'Héautontimorouménos', 'L'Irrémédiable', and 'L'Horloge'.

('Louanges de ma Françoise') was originally subtitled—and was so again in the posthumous third edition of *Les Fleurs du Mal* (1868)—'Vers composés pour une modiste érudite et dévote'. The dedicatee is unknown and may simply have been invented as the imaginary (and unlikely) object of this blasphemous poem in which Baudelaire pastiches the *Dies irae* (Day of Wrath), the sequence of sung Latin verse traditionally forming part of the Requiem Mass. Here he celebrates the redemption that is 'love'. The woman in question is a 'femina delicata' ('femme délicieuse' (l. 5)) of magnetic attractiveness (l. 9), and from her he will seek the kisses of a beneficent oblivion (ll. 7–8). By her agency all sins are pardoned (l. 6). She is a goddess (l. 12), guiding the poet and smoothing his path (ll. 13–14, 20, 24), a source of virtue (l. 16) and a fountain of eternal youth (l. 17), a chastity belt for the poet (l. 29)...and the provider of both bread and wine (ll. 32–3) for a most dubious Eucharist. The poems that follow this—'A une dame créole' (for Mme Autard de Bragard), 'Moesta et errabunda' (addressing an unidentified 'Agathe'), 'Le Revenant' ('ma brune'), and 'Sonnet d'automne' ('Marguerite')—have a miscellaneous air, creating the impression of a fading preoccupation with women as a source of aesthetic beauty (let alone of passionate climax) and preparing for a further transition towards poems about objects and 'spleen' and then eventually the seven 'framing' poems discussed earlier and that begin with 'Obsession'.

The newly added 'Sonnet d'automne' reprises the salient autumnal theme of the third cycle of 'love poems' and adds a valedictory (and self-contradictory) note: 'Je hais la passion' (l. 8). By now the poet knows his own heart (with its 'secret infernal' (l. 5)) and the terrible consequences of passion ('Crime, horreur et folie!' l. 12)), and he is only too familiar with Cupid and his bow: 'Je connais les engins de son vieil arsenal' (l. 11). And so he simply cannot go through all that again. Instead, he bids Marguerite: 'Aimons-nous doucement' (l. 9). No longer seeking to be 'cured' by the 'Explosion de chaleur' of 'Chanson d'après-midi', he seeks a soulmate in this daisy of late summer and autumn, an altogether different kind of 'fleur du Mal': 'Ô pâle marguerite! | Comme moi n'es-tu pas un soleil automnal, | Ô ma si blanche, ô ma si froide Marguerite?' (ll. 12–14). With its yellow centre and its rays of white petals this is a pale sun-like presence he can live with—like the moon of the newly positioned 'Tristesses de la lune' that follows. Here, as we saw earlier, the moon is compared to a woman ('une beauté' (l. 2)), a woman who is characterized by a now familiar 'paresse' (l. 1) and reclines on a bed of white satin casually caressing her own breasts before going to sleep (ll. 3–4). During the 'petite mort' of the intervening orgasm—'Mourante, elle se livre aux longues pâmoisons' (l. 6)—her gaze is filled with 'Les visions blanches | Qui montent dans l'azur comme des floraisons' (ll. 7–8), themselves recalling not only her white satin cushions but also the marguerite of the previous poem. As from time to time the woman/moon sheds 'une larme furtive' (l. 10), this tear is gathered in by '[u]n poëte pieux' like a shard of opal to be safely stored away in his heart and far from the eyes of the sun (ll. 13–14). Here again is beauty as ecstatic vision shot through with melancholy: 'quelque chose d'ardent et de triste' ready to be preserved in the poet's emotional memory bank and treasured in the jewel-box of his art.

And so, as we move on through poems about animals and objects ('Les Chats', 'Les Hiboux', 'La Pipe') towards 'La Cloche fêlée' and the 'Spleen' poems, the same sense of thematic familiarity persists: the mysterious stare of a cat ('Les Chats', recalling 'Le Chat ('Dans ma cervelle se promène...') and its association with the Sphinx (recalling 'La Beauté' and 'Avec ses vêtements ondoyants...'); the smoker's pipe ('La Pipe', recalling 'Au lecteur' and 'Le Possédé'); the poet as a sailor tossed or gently rocked upon a sea of music ('La Musique', recalling 'La Chevelure'). Here we encounter the seven poems with which the 1857 'Spleen et idéal' section ended and there represented (as together they evoke descent, rejection, and the night-time of death) a kind of winding down towards ironic forms of terrestrial repose ('Le Mort joyeux', 'Sépulture') and narcotic oblivion ('La Pipe', ll. 12–14). These poems are now so positioned as to be followed by 'La Cloche fêlée', which (as in the 1857 edition) serves to introduce the four 'Spleen' poems. Having only the repeated title 'Spleen' these poems resemble musical variations on a theme: the subject is ever the same, but the poetic treatment in each case is new.

Where in the 1857 edition these four poems were followed by 'Brumes et pluies' and 'L'Irrémédiable', with the former echoing the rain of 'Pluviôse, irrité contre la ville entière...' and the latter asserting the inevitability of melancholy and 'le Mal', now in the 1861 edition they are followed by the newly included 'Obsession' whose final tercet can perhaps be read as a description of the four 'Spleen' poems: 'Mais les ténèbres sont elles-mêmes des toiles | Où vivent, jaillissant de mon œil par milliers, | Des êtres disparus aux regards familiers.' In his melancholy state the poet yearns for oblivion, but that very melancholy—through memory and reflection—has projected a whole new set of images onto the black canvas of depression: images of people and things that had become so familiar (and tedious and boring) that they had disappeared from view. But as the 'Spleen' poems have just demonstrated, the poetic imagination can turn that very 'disappearance' to account, recomposing the decomposed in fresh patterns of interest. The forgotten and invisible become, through poetry, once again visible and memorable. This, soon, will lead on to the 'Tableaux parisiens' and the poetic transformation of the quotidian into the phantasmagorical. For the moment, however, 'Obsession' ushers in the newly constructed seven-poem ending of 'Spleen et idéal' in which 'le Mal' is wholeheartedly embraced as the source of a new poetics: of poetry as a 'taste' for nothingness, as a productive 'alchemy' of pain, as a pleasurable experience of hell ('Horreur sympathique', l. 14), and of poetry also as the acceptance of double agency ('L'Héautontimorouménos') and the irremediable nature of 'le Mal'.

At the same time the preceding 'Spleen' poems epitomize one of the most salient effects of 'Spleen et idéal' (and subsequently of *Les Fleurs du Mal* in its entirety). As the impression of repetitiveness and cyclicity grows, so the evidence of poetic virtuosity and innovation accumulates. At this point in the collection we note a gradual blurring and fading of the focus on women and 'love' and how the poems now take up once more (from 'Obsession' to 'L'Horloge) the opening questions about the role of the poet and his pursuit of beauty (culminating in 'Hymne à la Beauté). The poems that in the 1857 version of 'Spleen et idéal' had conveyed the sense of a gradual descent towards a resigned (if also ironic) acceptance of mortality and the inescapable march of time are now followed by the 'Spleen' poems and then, as though building on what these four poems have shown to be possible, a renewal of the poet's search for beauty. Time now is the one great enemy ('Meurs, vieux lâche! il est trop tard!'), and the ticking clock a call to arms—a summons to resist with the courage of art.

Thus, both at the level of overt analogy and at the level of poetic practice itself, the poet as moral commentator is counterbalanced by the poet as craftsman, and this in such a way that, over the unfolding sequence of poems that make up 'Spleen et idéal' and then *Les Fleurs du Mal* as a whole, we may come to see poetic craft as an 'alternative legislation', as an alternative way of figuring the ultimately irremediable and unchanging nature of human desire and human experience. 'Plus ça change, plus c'est la même chose'—except that, with regard to poetic technique, each poem is very precisely *not* the same. The poet cannot change the world—as perhaps the 'unacknowledged legislators' of an earlier period might have hoped to do—but they can change the way we look at it. We have already seen how the poet presents himself as a producer of artworks and artefacts: of the sketch and the portrait, of jewels and perfume. In the 1857 edition there is some evidence also of ekphrasis, that is, of poems in which the poet describes and transposes into poetic form a real or imaginary work of visual art: for example, 'Une martyre. Dessin d'un maître inconnu' and 'L'Amour et le crâne. Vieux cul-de-lampe'.[12] This presentation of the poet as artist and craftsman is reinforced in the 1861 edition by additional poems of this kind: by 'Le Masque' and 'Danse macabre', both dedicated to the sculpteur Ernest Christophe, and by 'A une Madone. *Ex-voto dans le goût espagnol*' and 'Une gravure fantastique'. The latter poem in particular, being newly inserted among the poems with which the 1857 'Spleen et idéal' ended, not only reinforces but also aestheticizes their common themes of spectral presence and sepulchral abode ('Le Revenant', 'Sépulture', 'Le Mort joyeux'). Here we are given the description of a 'fantastical' engraving depicting a ghost-rider on a ghost-horse, wielding his sabre as he rides around '[l]e cimetière immense et froid, sans horizon, | Où gisent, aux lueurs d'un soleil blanc et terne, | Les peuples de l'histoire ancienne et moderne' (ll. 12–14). All human death is here, encapsulated in the living cemetery that is art.

---

[12] Cf also those poems that explicitly or implicitly allude to actual works of art such as 'Don Juan aux enfers' and 'L'Idéal'.

17
Versification and the Poetic Idea

Quand il s'agit d'un poète, la facture de ses vers est chose considérable et vaut qu'on l'étudie, car elle constitue une grande partie de sa valeur instrinsèque.
(Théophile Gautier, 'Charles Baudelaire' (1868))[1]

Nul, parmi les grands et les célèbres, nul plus que Baudelaire ne connaît les infinies complications de la versification proprement dite.
(Paul Verlaine (1865))[2]

Je sens vibrer en moi toutes les passions | D'un vaisseau qui souffre.
('La Musique', ll. 9–10)

L'idée poétique qui se dégage de cette opération du mouvement dans les lignes est l'hypothèse d'un être vaste, immense, compliqué, mais eurythmique, d'un animal plein de génie, souffrant et soupirant tous les soupirs et toutes les ambitions humaines.
(*Fusées*, f. 22)[3]

Baudelaire's handling of the rules of French versification was for long a subject of controversy. Even Théophile Gautier, the 'poète impeccable' to whom *Les Fleurs du Mal* is dedicated, found it difficult, writing some six months after his friend's death, to explain how a poet so committed to precision and craft could have produced quite so many 'irregular' sonnets (so-called *sonnets libertins*). On the one hand, the author of the carefully faceted jewel-poems that make up *Émaux et camées* (1st edn, 1852) praises Baudelaire for his careful attention to the rules of French metre: 'La question de métrique, dédaignée par tous ceux qui n'ont pas le sentiment de la forme, et ils sont nombreux aujourd'hui, a été à bon droit jugée comme très importante par Baudelaire.'[4] Moreover, he recalls how on one occasion Baudelaire had been delegated to present him with a book of poems by two contemporary poets and had himself tut-tutted at the prosodic laxity of their sonnets (though perhaps the grateful recipient did not notice the tongue in

---

[1] Théophile Gautier, 'Préface aux *Œuvres complètes*' [1868], in Guyaux (ed.), *Baudelaire: Un demi-siècle de lectures*, 495.
[2] 'Charles Baudelaire', in *L'Art*, 30 Nov./23 Dec. 1865. See Verlaine, *Œuvres en prose complètes*, ed. Jacques Borel (Paris: Gallimard [Bibliothèque de la Pléiade], 1972), 599–612 (611).
[3] *Fusées*, ed. Guyaux, 70; i. 663–4. [4] Guyaux (ed.), *Baudelaire: Un demi-siècle de lectures*, 494.

Baudelaire's cheek). On the other hand, Gautier expresses bafflement at why any poet would choose a particular fixed form like the sonnet and then disregard its rules, in particular the traditional requirement of a Petrarchan sonnet that the rhymes of the first quatrain be repeated in the second (the so-called 'règle de la quadruple rime'):

> Pourquoi, si l'on veut être libre et arranger les rimes à sa guise, aller choisir une forme rigoureuse qui n'admet aucun écart, aucun caprice? L'irrégulier dans le régulier, le manque de correspondance dans la symétrie, quoi de plus illogique et de plus contrariant?[5]

In the first edition of *Émaux et camées* Gautier had himself created his own fixed form—quatrains of octosyllabic lines rhyming abab (in French terminology, *rimes croisées* or *rimes alternées*) where the first rhyme is always feminine (i.e. ending with a mute e)—and then stuck to it. That collection of eighteen poems[6] ends with 'L'Art' in which, by way of an epilogue (and in quatrains of alternating six- and two-syllable lines also rhyming abab and with the first rhyme feminine), the poet asserts that the impression of poetic beauty is enhanced by a perception of difficulty overcome: 'Oui, l'œuvre sort plus belle | D'une forme au travail | Rebelle | Vers, marbre, onyx, émail' (ll. 1–4). Here the difficulty of maintaining a regular rhyme scheme within short lines (and thus with little syllabic room for manoeuvre) illustrates the argument. But for Gautier such artifice must never appear contrived: 'Point de contraintes fausses!' (l. 5). Rather it should contribute to a sense that the work of versification has lent solid and permanent form to the evanescent play of the imagination: 'Sculpte, lime, ciselle; | Que ton rêve flottant | Se scelle | Dans le bloc résistant' (ll. 53–6). The poem is to resemble a sculpture, chiselled from the marble of an unyielding verse form, or else a cameo or enamel miniature crafted with exquisite precision. This, therefore, is the Gautier who cannot tolerate the *sonnet libertin*, whether composed by Baudelaire or anyone else:

> Chaque infraction à la règle nous inquiète comme une note douteuse ou fausse. Le sonnet est une sorte de fugue poétique dont le thème doit passer et repasser jusqu'à sa résolution par les formes voulues. Il faut donc se soumettre absolument à ses lois, ou bien, si l'on trouve ces lois surannées, pédantesques et gênantes, ne pas écrire de sonnets du tout.[7]

Versification is a legislation, and its laws must be obeyed.

---

[5] Guyaux (ed.), *Baudelaire: Un demi-siècle de lectures*, 496.
[6] Gautier subsequently added to the collection over the next two decades, and the final edition (in May 1872) contained forty-seven poems.
[7] Guyaux (ed.), *Baudelaire: Un demi-siècle de lectures*, 496.

Théodore de Banville was similarly alive to the unorthodoxy of Baudelaire's sonnet practice but adopted a more tolerant view. In his *Petit traité de poésie française* (1872) he sought to tidy up the legislation of prosody for his fellow poets, reaffirming, for example, the essential requirement of rhyme within the French verse tradition and, in the case of the sonnet, somewhat arbitrarily asserting that only one particular rhyme scheme (abba abba ccd ede) could be regarded as 'regular', though without necessarily proscribing other possibilities.[8] Indeed he allows that 'le Sonnet irrégulier a produit des chefs-d'œuvre' and adduces by way of evidence 'le merveilleux livre intitulé *Les Fleurs du Mal*'.[9]

In 1906 the critic Albert Cassagne published his classic study of Baudelaire's prosodic practice and took a different line. Yes, Baudelaire's sonnet practice is wayward, especially in the frequent neglect of the 'règle de la quadruple rime', but Gautier has missed the point: 'Illogique ou non, "l'irrégulier dans le régulier, le manque de correspondance dans la symétrie" était justement ce qui plaisait à Baudelaire.'[10] For Cassagne such irregularity bespeaks Baudelaire's desire to be different ('son goût de l'indépendance') and perhaps even a fundamental inability to conform ('son inaptitude à se plier à une forme régulière'), not least because he was in fact (Cassagne alleges) a 'médiocre rimeur'.[11]

Baudelaire's desire to be different has been demonstrated with great thoroughness by Graham Robb in his own classic study of Baudelaire's poetry as seen in relation to the verse of his day.[12] As Robb argues, the use of the *sonnet libertin* was extremely rare in France during the 1840s so that Baudelaire's extensive use of it constituted an important innovation in poetic practice[13] and indeed a form of 'provocation'[14] more shocking even than his choice of subject matter, not least his treatment of sexual relations.[15] Yet, as Robb also shows, this 'provocation' is carefully orchestrated. For example, while Baudelaire frequently disregards 'la règle de la quadruple rime', he always maintains the same rhyme scheme in both quatrains, thereby framing 'irregularity' in 'regularity' as though to demonstrate

---

[8] Cf. Evans, *Rhythm, Illusion and the Poetic Idea*, 65: 'Banville's stipulation [...] is a pure fiction which stubbornly maintains, in his usual playful manner, a fallacious hierarchy of absolute values of poeticity.'

[9] Banville, *Petit traité de poésie française* (rev. edn, Paris: Librairie de l'Écho de la Sorbonne, 1875), 174. For a discussion and detailed illustration of the 'irregularity' in Baudelaire's sonnet practice as anticipating the advent of *vers libre*, see Rosemary Lloyd, 'Baudelaire Sonneteer: Flare to the Future', in Patricia A. Ward (ed., with the assistance of James S. Patty), *Baudelaire and the Poetics of Modernity* (Nashville: Vanderbilt University Press, 2001), 101–23.

[10] Albert Cassagne, *Versification et métrique de Ch[arles] Baudelaire* (Paris: Hachette, 1906; repr. Geneva: Slatkine, 1982), 91.

[11] Cassagne, *Versification et métrique*, 91–2.

[12] Robb, *La Poésie de Baudelaire et la poésie française 1838–1852* (n.p.: Aubier, 1993). For Robb, following Claude Pichois and others, the majority of the poems in *Les Fleurs du Mal* had already been written, at least in draft form, by 1845 (see *La Poésie de Baudelaire*, 16–21).

[13] 'On peut donc affirmer que la presque totalité des sonnets du XIXe siècle ayant plus de deux rimes dans les quatrains a été composée par des poètes qui ont pu lire d'abord les sonnets libertins de Baudelaire dans la première édition des *Fleurs du Mal* en 1857' (*La Poésie de Baudelaire*, 233).

[14] Robb, *La Poésie de Baudelaire*, 236–7.   [15] Robb, *La Poésie de Baudelaire*, 349.

that he can obey rules if he so chooses but is consciously departing from established convention in order to exploit new possibilities and achieve new effects.[16] Contesting Cassagne's disparagement of Baudelaire's ability to rhyme, Robb shows by contrast how subtly he handled the whole business of rhyming. During the 1840s the concerted inclusion of rich rhymes—that is, rhymes that combine the basic and essential element of assonance with at least two further (vocalic or consonantal) homophonic elements—was much in vogue and, like the *sonnet libertin*, constituted a highly controversial innovation.[17] Not only did Baudelaire himself engage openly in this pursuit (as, for example, in 'Parfum exotique' and 'Sed non satiata', which probably date originally from the early 1840s)[18] but he also, more subtly, played on the expectations that his knowledgeable contemporary readers would have brought to their reading of rhyme. Thus, as Robb illustrates, in 'Que diras-tu ce soir...', a *sonnet libertin*, the opening (feminine) rhyme of 'solitaire' and 'très-chère' is not repeated in the second quatrain, but the words with which it could have been ('autoritaire' and 'claire') are otherwise present in the masculine rhyme of 'autorité' and 'clarté' (ll. 6, 8).[19]

This (like the other examples given by Robb) highlights how today, after well over a century of *vers libre*, we need to understand the formal properties of Baudelaire's poems within the context of the intricate prosodic rules he chose variously to observe, bend, or disregard—and to consider how these choices may contribute to the meaning of the poems. In the case of 'Que diras-tu ce soir...', for example, the poet wonders (as we saw earlier) how he will sing the praises of this woman who herself speaks—and commands—with such clear 'autorité' and 'clarté: 'Je suis belle, et j'ordonne | Que pour l'amour de moi vous n'aimiez que le Beau; | Je suis l'Ange gardien, la Muse et la Madone' (ll. 12-14). But just as this woman, here recalled as a memory, is envisaged therefore as a ghost ('Son fantôme dans l'air danse comme un flambeau' (l. 11)), so the poet is present in the poem not only through what he says and does but also, ghost-like, through what he does *not* say or do. As the poem relates, he wonders what *he* will say and ends up— apparently and ironically—simply recording what *she* says, except that, as the 'ghost rhyme' within 'autorité' and 'clarté' (i.e. 'autoritaire/claire') suggests, he does not quite say what he is expected to say. As it were, he may not have anything

---

[16] *La Poésie de Baudelaire*, 237. Cf. André Gendre, *Évolution du sonnet français* (Paris: Presses universitaires de France, 1996): 'Dans l'habitude d'introduire à [strophe 2] un nouveau couple de rimes, je devine une recherche de souplesse et de plasticité: ne rien perdre de la structure très serrée du sonnet, mais l'ouvrir à des harmoniques plus nombreuses, à des richesses sonores inattendues' (182).

[17] 'La rime riche est en 1840 ce qu'était l'enjambement en 1830: de tous les débats portant sur les aspects techniques de la poésie, c'est le plus important, par le nombre de fois qu'il apparaît, comme par les déclarations passionnées qu'il soulève' (*La Poésie de Baudelaire*, 279). Robb's reference to enjambement recalls Hugo's use of this 'irregular' device in the opening lines of his verse play *Hernani* (1830), a provocative 'anti-Classical' move that lit a touch-paper to a long-standing dispute among writers, critics, and arbiters of taste and led to the so-called 'battle' of *Hernani* in which physical blows were exchanged in the theatre itself as Romanticism 'triumphed' over Classicism.

[18] See i. 878, 884.   [19] *La Poésie de Baudelaire*, 310.

new to say, but he has found a new way to say it. And here is what we might call, using Baudelaire's formulation, the 'idée poétique' of the poem: an overt obeissance, as of a gallant lover, tempered by a discreet resistance and a self-affirming lawlessness. Similarly, we might add to our earlier reading of 'Sed non satiata'— the poet takes revenge on the woman's indifference by affirming how *she* satisfies *him* (by providing a new source of creativity) while she herself can get no satisfaction—by suggesting that the especial 'visibility' of rich rhyme in this poem precisely exemplifies this enhanced poetic creativity. Similarly, too, in 'Parfum exotique' the rich rhymes 'correspond' to the plenitude of the poet's sensual and imaginative—and indeed *poetic*—delight. As Graham Chesters has noted, the very artifice of the rich rhymes serves to 'suggest and stress the idea of poetic form'.[20] Here the 'poetic idea' is as much poetry itself as it is the power of smell to conjure up paradise.

One further important aspect of Robb's account of Baudelaire's handling of versification concerns the relationship between poetry and song, a hierarchical distinction that has obtained in French verse at least since Boileau. As Robb demonstrates,[21] Baudelaire drew innovatively on various formal attributes of song in the composition of his own poems: for example, the use of refrains, the quintil (i.e. the five-line stanza, in which the first line may be repeated as the last, as in 'Lesbos' or 'Le Balcon'), mixed metre, and the imparisyllabic line. Thanks to an early surviving draft of 'Une gravure fantastique' Robb is able to trace the process of transformation (previously analysed also by Felix Leakey and Alison Fairlie)[22] whereby Baudelaire transformed his original pastiche of popular song into a fourteen-line poem of alexandrines in *rimes plates* (eventually included in the 1861 edition of *Les Fleurs du Mal*), which Robb describes as 'un exemple étonnant de cette assimilation toujours plus profonde de la chanson'.[23] Even in the present century the award of the Nobel Prize in Literature to Bob Dylan (in 2016) has had the capacity to generate warm debate about the distinction between 'song' and 'poetry', and indeed about what we mean by 'literature'.[24] In Baudelaire's time, as in our own, the issue was bound up with controversy about the nature of high and low culture, which in turn begged questions of class and politics. But, as Robb argues, Baudelaire set no store by any rigid distinction between song and poetry.[25] For him what mattered were the formal devices to be found in song (for example, in the lyric works of Pierre Dupont, Marceline Desbordes-Valmore, and

---

[20] Chesters, *Baudelaire and the Poetics of Craft*, 20, 91–4. Chesters' study contains much valuable discussion of Baudelaire's use of rhyme and other sound patterning.
[21] See the chapter 'Baudelaire chansonnier' in *La Poésie de Baudelaire*, 243–78.
[22] For bibliographical references and also for Claude Pichois's own account of this poem see i. 967–9.
[23] *La Poésie de Baudelaire*, 268.
[24] See Alexandre Gefen, *L'Idée de littérature: De l'art pour l'art aux écritures d'intervention* (Paris: Corti, 2021), 9–13.
[25] *La Poésie de Baudelaire*, 248.

Béranger, among many others) and that he could put to use within his own poetry: 'Baudelaire, presque seul à son époque, a emprunté à la chanson des procédés pour les adapter à une poésie qui ne paraît avoir avec elle que des rapports tenus.'[26]

Robb's account of Baudelaire's poetic practice demonstrates, therefore, that a hitherto perceived 'waywardness' was in fact an energetic pursuit of the skilfully new, and this is also the main thrust of the more recent and most thorough account of Baudelaire's use of verse forms: Dominique Billy's Les Formes poétiques selon Baudelaire.[27] Building scrupulously on Robb's study, Billy offers a detailed statistical survey and commentary, chapter by chapter, on Baudelaire's use of rimes suivies (rhyming couplets), the distich (in 'Les Litanies de Satan' and 'Abel et Caïn'), the quatrain (whether in rimes plates, rimes alternées/croisées, or rimes embrassées), the quintil, and song, before devoting approximately two-fifths of his book to an exhaustive formal analysis of Baudelaire's sonnet practice and then ending with an analysis of 'Harmonie du soir'. Rather than 'provocation' Billy prefers to see Baudelaire as predominantly concerned with variety: that is, with taking established forms—and particularly the sonnet—and creating multiple new variations on their defining characteristics. What we have, then, is 'le souci d'une recherche esthétique' rather than 'une quelconque négligence':[28] neither 'une certaine désinvolture à l'égard des règles' (as proposed by Cassagne), nor 'une attitude provocatrice entretenue avec une belle constance' (as proposed by Robb), but 'un goût nettement marqué pour la variété'.[29] What we have, too, is a marked tension between the exploration and cultivation of variety, on the one hand, and a rigorous submission to self-imposed formal constraints on the other.[30] For Billy what mattered most to Baudelaire was his endless curiosity, free of dogmatism or preconception, about the 'potentialités' of versification.[31]

If versification is a legislation, then, for Baudelaire it was a legislation that needed at once to be respected, qua legislation, but also to be resisted and modified and even reinvented.[32] Robb contends, for example, that the individual poetic

---

[26] La Poésie de Baudelaire, 243. Cf. Claude Pichois's comments on Baudelaire's aspiration in the early 1850s towards a closer collaboration between poetry and song: 'Entre 1851 et 1854 on le voit cherchant cette collaboration à un niveau où il est difficile qu'elle s'établisse: s'il est tenté par la forme de la chanson, dont "L'Invitation au voyage" est avec "Le Jet d'eau" un merveilleux exemple, c'est qu'il souhaite cette renaissance de la poésie vraiment lyrique, dont de grands exemples avaient été donnés par Marot et par Ronsard' (ii. 1454). For an account of how Baudelaire's poetry has itself subsequently been turned into song, see Helen Abbott, Baudelaire in Song: 1880–1930 (Oxford: Oxford University Press, 2017). See also her earlier studies Between Baudelaire and Mallarmé: Voice, Conversation and Music (Farnham: Ashgate, 2009), and Parisian Intersections: Baudelaire's Legacy to Composers (Oxford and New York: Peter Lang, 2012).
[27] Dominique Billy, Les Formes poétiques selon Baudelaire (Paris: Honoré Champion, 2015).
[28] Billy, Les Formes poétiques, 402. [29] Billy, Les Formes poétiques, 258–9, 338.
[30] Billy, Les Formes poétiques, 335. [31] Billy, Les Formes poétiques, 403.
[32] Pace Roberto Calasso's unwarrantable assertion that '[f]ormal innovations did not appeal to him. With him, perhaps for the last time, the Alexandrine was the universal medium' and his equally unwarrantable reference to 'Baudelaire's threadbare and perhaps even a little "parochial" forms' (La Folie Baudelaire, trans. Alastair McEwen (London: Allen Lane, 2012 [first published in Italian in 2008]), 237, 238.

forms of 'Le Beau Navire', 'La Musique', 'Le Poison', and 'Le Goût du néant' are each unique not only within *Les Fleurs du Mal* but also (to his knowledge) in French poetry as a whole. Yet Baudelaire does not 'trumpet' these innovations, foregrounding them for their own sake as novelties, but rather employs each of them 'surreptitiously' in the service of a poetic idea. As Robb puts it: 'ce n'est pas Baudelaire qui nous a appris qu'"Harmonie du soir" est un pantoum, que "L'Invitation au voyage" est une berceuse, ou que "La Beauté" est un sonnet libertin'.[33] And this (as we saw in Chapter 1) is how Baudelaire himself talks about versification, not as an arbitrary constraint but as an aid (as the law of the land itself should doubtless be):

> Car il est évident que les rhétoriques et les prosodies ne sont pas des tyrannies inventées arbitrairement, mais une collection de règles réclamées par l'organisation même de l'être spirituel. Et jamais les prosodies et les rhétoriques n'ont empêché l'originalité de se produire distinctement. Le contraire, à savoir qu'elles ont aidé l'éclosion de l'originalité, serait infiniment plus vrai.
> (*Salon de 1859*, ii. 626–7)

For him, the rules of versification answer to a deep-rooted spiritual need that arises out of the way in which we human beings are mentally 'hardwired' in our perception of the world. And he makes a similar point in one of his draft prefaces for *Les Fleurs du Mal*, both in specific relation to metre and rhyme ('le rythme et la rime répondent dans l'homme aux immortels besoins de monotonie, de symétrie et de surprise' (i. 182)) and in more general terms ('la poésie touche à la musique par une prosodie dont les racines plongent plus avant dans l'âme humaine que ne l'indique aucune théorie classique' (i. 183)). For this reason the rules must be mastered if poetic expression is to be attempted at all: 'tout poète qui ne sait pas au juste combien chaque mot comporte de rimes est incapable d'exprimer une idée quelconque' (i. 183). Just as he insists on the fact that Delacroix's expert and hard-won command of the techniques of painting was an essential prerequisite to his ability to give adequate expression in the moment to a fleeting artistic vision, so Baudelaire considers that, far from dictating poetic composition or imposing some dreadful conformity, the rules of versification are there to serve the creative imagination of the individual poet-artist who may bend them at will: 'Tous ces préceptes sont évidemment modifiés plus ou moins par le tempérament varié des artistes' (ii. 626).[34]

---

[33] Robb, *La Poésie de Baudelaire*, 215.
[34] In his account of Baudelaire's techniques of versification (*Rhythm, Illusion and the Poetic Idea*, 19–86) David Evans argues that 'far from [being] a one-sided rebellion against a versificatory straitjacket, Baudelaire's poetry comes more and more to demonstrate a simultaneous drive towards both harmony and rhythmic irregularity' (63), and he analyses six 'sites of verse tension, the critical points at which the clash between anticipated regularity and actual irregularity might create a *faux*

The 'idée poétique' thus depends for its very existence on the knowing and alternative use of an existing prosodic legislation. In fact the poetic idea is just that, a fusion of 'idea' and 'form': 'l'idée et la forme sont deux êtres en un' ('Auguste Barbier', ii. 143).[35] Hence Baudelaire's celebrated statement to the Lyonnais critic Armand Fraisse in his letter of 18 February 1860:

> Quel est donc l'imbécile [...] qui traite si légèrement le Sonnet et n'en voit pas la beauté pythagorique? Parce que la forme est contraignante, l'idée jaillit plus intense. Tout va bien au Sonnet, la bouffonnerie, la galanterie, la passion, la rêverie, la méditation philosophique. Il y a là la beauté du métal et du minéral bien travaillés. Avez-vous observé qu'un morceau de ciel, aperçu par un soupirail, ou entre deux cheminées, deux rochers, ou par une arcade, etc., donnait une idée plus profonde de l'infini que le grand panorama vu du haut d'une montagne?
> (*Corr.*, i. 676)[36]

This is the Baudelaire who had experienced a meeting of minds with Poe on reading of the latter's own preference for brevity over length in a poem as the surer means to create a 'unity of impression' and 'totality of effect', and this also is the Baudelaire of 'Hymne à la Beauté' who values beauty for opening 'la porte | D'un Infini que j'aime et n'ai jamais connu'. The tighter the verse form, the more intense the idea and the more powerfully this can suggest 'l'expansion des choses infinies'.

Accordingly, the versification of *Les Fleurs du Mal* is indeed remarkable both for its variety and for its skilful modulations of constraint. 'Le Mal' may be irremediable and everywhere the same, but almost every poem is in some way— formally as well as lexically—different from every other.[37] In respect of metrical choice it is true that the alexandrine dominates. Of the 127 poems in the 1861 edition of *Les Fleurs du Mal* (counting 'Un fantôme' as one poem) 95 employ exclusively this metre, while in a further 7 poems of mixed metre it constitutes one

---

accord: 1. Disruption of the caesural accent and pause. 2. Rhythmical hiatus caused by adjacent accents. 3. Tension in the syllable count and effects of assymetry at the rhyme position. 4. Cases of *rejet* and *contre-rejet* (i.e. rhythmically problematic *enjambement*). 5. Rhyming and stanzaic irregularities in the sonnet form. 6. Questions of rhyme strength: reinforced or problematic rhymes' (40).

[35] Cf. *Exposition universelle*, ii. 576: 'l'immortel, l'inévitable rapport entre la forme et la fonction'.

[36] As Claude Pichois points out, Baudelaire had made a similar point one year earlier in the *Salon de 1859* in relation to a painting of seagulls by Octave Penguilly-l'Haridon: 'l'azur intense du ciel et de l'eau, deux quartiers de roche qui font une porte ouverte sur l'infini (vous savez que l'infini paraît plus profond quand il est plus resserré)' (ii. 653).

[37] Billy calculates that Baudelaire's sonnets exhibit 35 different rhyme schemes, 45 different combinations of rhyme and metre, and 50 different combinations of rhyme, metre, and rhyme gender (*Les Formes poétiques*, 259). Within the 1861 *Les Fleurs du Mal* I find only six small groupings of poems that share the same rhyme scheme, metre, and order of rhyme gender: (i) 'Duellum', 'Le Flambeau vivant', 'Causerie'; (ii) 'L'Idéal', 'Tristesses de la lune'; (iii) 'L'Ennemi', 'Que diras-tu ce soir...'; (iv) 'Correspondances', 'A une passante'; (v) 'Le Mauvais Moine', 'A une dame créole', 'Spleen (i)', 'Sisina', and 'La Mort des pauvres'; (vi) 'Parfum exotique', 'Sed non satiata'.

of two metres variously combined. But the alexandrine itself has its own flexibility, especially following the Romantics' 'dislocation' of its traditional binary structure,[38] and its twelve syllables permit constantly shifting permutations of multiple groupings and rhythmic patterns. Of the poems that do not contain alexandrines 17 use exclusively octosyllabic lines, while 2 ('La Mort des amants', and the four-part 'Un fantôme') have decasyllables,[39] and 1 ('Chanson d'après-midi) is made up of heptasyllabic lines.[40] There are 8 different combinations of mixed metre: 12/8 (alternating) in quatrains of *rimes croisées* ('Une charogne', 'Confession', 'Une martyre'); 12/8 (alternating) in quintils rhyming ababa ('L'Irréparable'); 12/8 in quatrains of *rimes plates* (consisting of 3 alexandrines followed by an octosyllabic line) ('Le Beau navire'); 12/7 (alternating) in quintils rhyming abbab ('Le Poison'); 12/5 (alternating) in sonnet form ('La Musique'); 10/8 (alternating) in sonnet form ('Le Chat' [no. 34]); 8/5 (alternating) in quatrains of *rimes croisées* ('Le Serpent qui danse', 'L'Amour et le crâne'); 7/4 in quatrains of *rimes plates* (consisting of three heptasyllbic lines followed by a four-syllable line) ('À une mendiante rousse'); 5/7 in three twelve-line stanzas rhyming aabccbddeffe and consisting in a metrical variation of 5,5,7 four times within the stanzas, each of which is followed by a separate couplet in heptasyllabic metre ('L'Invitation au voyage').

As to verse form, the sonnet may appear to dominate, being used in sixty poems (counting 'Un fantôme' now as four poems, and including poems of fourteen lines that employ fewer or more than five rhymes: that is, the so-called *quatorzains*).[41] But here, too, variety is the hallmark. As noted earlier, the orthodox Petrarchan sonnet as later defined by Banville in his *Petit traité de poésie française* (1872) should rhyme abba abba ccd ede, but only four poems in *Les Fleurs du Mal* (1861) do so: 'Parfum exotique', 'Sed non satiata', 'Le Possédé', and 'Le Cadre' (within 'Un fantôme').[42] Five other sonnets have these orthodox *rimes embrassées redoublées*

---

[38] Cf. Hugo, 'J'ai disloqué ce grand niais d'alexandrin', in 'Quelques mots à un autre' (l. 84) (*Les Contemplations*, i. 26).

[39] In 'La Mort des amants' the use of a decasyllabic line with a regular central caesura relates it to a traditional dance-song, the 'tarantara'. See Billy, *Les Formes poétiques*, 249–50, and Alain Chévrier, *Le Décasyllabe à césure médiane: Histoire du tarantara* (Paris: Garnier, 2011), 214–16. Also Jean Prévost, *Baudelaire: Essai sur la création et l'inspiration poétiques* (Paris: Mercure de France, 1953), 327.

[40] As a metre commonly found in song, the heptasyllabic line is thus appropriate in this '*Chanson d'après-midi*' (my italics). Billy notes also that the octosyllabics of 'Le Vin de l'Assassin' make of that poem a modern version of a sixteenth-century drinking song. See *Les Formes poétiques*, 111.

[41] Of these 60 sonnets 23 use the orthodox 5 rhymes. 1 sonnet ('Sonnet d'automne') has only 2 rhymes; 1 ('Je te donne ces vers...') has only four rhymes; 7 have 6 rhymes; 28 have seven rhymes.

[42] The last three were added in 1861. In the 1857 edition, therefore, only 'Parfum exotique' conformed to this prescription. Within that context the observance of an orthodox traditional Petrarchan rhyme scheme, together with the highest incidence of rich rhyme in the tercets of any sonnet in *Les Fleurs du Mal* (see Billy, *Les Formes poétiques*, 284) suggest a poetic 'perfection' that matches the lack of melancholy in the poem: as it were, a demonstration of poetic form as yet 'unfallen' and untainted by 'le Mal'. In 'Le Cadre' the orthodoxy is partially offset by the disruption of alternating rhyme gender.

in the octave,[43] while eleven have *rimes croisées redoublées*.[44] Otherwise, in the quatrains of his sonnets, Baudelaire employs four rhymes arranged abab cdcd or abba cddc in, respectively, eleven[45] and sixteen[46] cases. Occasionally he varies the rhyme scheme of the quatrains further, distributing the a and b (and sometimes c) rhymes 'irregularly' across the octave: abba baab in 'La Muse vénale', 'La Vie antérieure', and 'Je te donne ces vers...' (where he also re-employs the a rhyme in the tercets (aac dcd)); abba acca in 'Une nuit que j'étais...'; abab cbcb in 'Le Tonneau de la haine' (where he also re-employs the c rhyme in the tercets (cdc dee)); aabb aabb ('Brumes et pluies' and 'La Fontaine de sang', which therefore combine the orthodox practice of *rimes redoublées* with the unorthodox use of couplets in the quatrains); aabb ccdd ('Le Revenant'); and aabb ccbb ('Le Vin des amants'). In the tercets of these sixty sonnets, similarly, variety is once again the hallmark. Six combinations of c, d, and e rhymes are used; four combinations of d, e, and f rhymes; and seven combinations of e, f, and g rhymes.[47]

This brief statistical overview[48] already gives rise to certain interpretative possibilities. That 'Je te donne ces vers...' is one of only two poems with less than five rhymes adds a further ironic layer to this poem in which the poet refers to his own 'rimes hautaines' (l. 8) and to his intention that the memory of his lover shall 'hang' from them with tiresome repetitiveness (ll. 5–6). No one else but the poet will listen or respond to this 'Être maudit' (ll. 9–11), and now we see that his response takes the form of an unusually repetitive and therefore insistent rhyme

---

[43] 'Bohémiens en voyage', 'Remords posthume', 'Sonnet d'automne', 'La Pipe', 'La Mort des artistes'.

[44] 'La Muse malade', 'Le Mauvais moine', 'Sisina', 'A une dame créole', 'Le Mort joyeux', 'Spleen [i]', 'Horreur sympathique', 'Les Deux Bonnes Sœurs','La Mort des amants', 'La Mort des pauvres', 'Le Rêve d'un curieux'.

[45] 'Correspondances', 'La Beauté', 'Le Guignon', 'De profundis clamavi', 'L'Aube spirituelle', 'Les Chats', 'Les Hiboux', 'Alchimie de la douleur', 'Les Aveugles', 'A une passante', 'Le Vin du solitaire'.

[46] 'L'Ennemi', 'L'Idéal', 'La Géante', 'Avec ses vêtements ondoyants...', 'Le Chat' [no. 34], 'Duellum', 'Semper eadem', 'Que diras-tu ce soir...', 'Le Flambeau vivant', 'Causerie', 'Tristesses de la lune', 'La Musique', 'Sépulture', 'La Cloche fêlée', 'Obsession', 'La Destruction'.

[47] Billy notes that in 56 of the 60 sonnets the tercets contain 3 rhymes, while in 4 they contain only 2. He notes further that in exactly half of these 56 sonnets the tercets begin with a couplet while in the other half they end with a couplet. In three sonnets—'La Muse malade', 'De profundis clamavi', and 'La Cloche fêlée'—the tercets consist solely of rhyming couplets. See *Les Formes poétiques*, 341, 343, and 353 respectively.

[48] For further analysis of Baudelaire's versification, see Benoît de Cornulier, 'Métrique des *Fleurs du Mal*', in Martine Bercot et al., *'Les Fleurs du Mal': L'Intériorité de la forme. Actes du colloque du 7 janvier 1989* (Paris: SEDES, 1989), 55–76; 'Pour l'analyse du sonnet dans *Les Fleurs du Mal*', in Murphy (ed.), *Lectures de Baudelaire: 'Les Fleurs du Mal'*, 197–236; and 'La Versification des *Fleurs du Mal*', in *L'Atelier de Baudelaire. 'Les Fleurs du Mal': édition diplomatique*, ed. Claude Pichois and Jacques Dupont (4 vols, Paris: Champion, 2005), iv. 3543–65. See also Rachel Killick, 'Baudelaire's Versification: Conservative or Radical?', in Rosemary Lloyd (ed.), *The Cambridge Companion to Baudelaire* (Cambridge: Cambridge University Press, 2005), 51–68, and her '"Sorcellerie évocatoire" and the Sonnet in *Les Fleurs du Mal*, *Dalhousie French Studies*, 2 (1980), 21–39; David Scott, *Sonnet Theory and Practice in Nineteenth-Century France: Sonnets on the Sonnet* (Hull: University of Hull, 1977), and his 'Baudelaire, le sonnet et la poétique symboliste', *L'Année Baudelaire*, 4 (1998), 45–59; and Gendre, *Évolution du sonnet français*.

scheme. On the one hand, the relative difficulty of employing only four rhymes over fourteen lines implies a display of skill, while the marked unorthodoxy of the rhyme scheme itself (abba baab aac dcd) suggests the poet's own 'haughty' disregard for convention. In turn we might compare this combination of 'monotonie' and skill with the rhymes in 'Spleen ii' where, as Jean Prévost notes, lines 11–18 contain eight consecutive rhyme words all ending with [e], thereby creating a sense of repetitiveness and sameness that contributes to the central poetic idea of the poem (i.e. melancholy) and with the reference at the end of this sequence of rhymes to those long days when 'L'ennui, fruit de la morne incuriosité, | Prends les proportions de l'immortalité' (l. 17).[49] But three of these four rhyme-pairs are rich rhymes, and in the case of 'Boucher'/'débouché' in fact a so-called 'rime très riche' (because it has more than three rhyming elements): sameness and cleverness are combined, just as melancholy is expressed with art.

The same is true in 'Horreur sympathique', as Jean Starobinski has shown,[50] where the richness of the rhymes on 'vide'—'livide'/'vide', 'avide'/'Ovide'—give the lie to an alleged emptiness or absence, and where (one might add) the combination of negativity (stormy black sky, torment, exile, mourning) and positivity ('Je ne geindrai pas comme Ovide', 'l'Enfer où mon cœur se plaît'), itself foregrounded in the poem's title, is here mirrored in the 'spleen et idéal' of the poem's own form: its 'illegitimate' status as a *sonnet libertin*, on the one hand, and, on the other, the inventiveness of its rhymes (made the more apparent by the relative brevity of the octosyllabic metre). Indeed the word 'libertin' at the end of the first quatrain invites a reflexive reading:

> De ce ciel bizarre et livide,
> Tourmenté comme ton destin,
> Quels pensers dans ton âme vide
> Descendent? réponds, libertin.
>
> —Insatiablement avide
> De l'obscur et de l'incertain,
> Je ne geindrai pas comme Ovide
> Chassé du paradis latin.

This modern poet will not look on the storm-tossed sky of formal unorthodoxy as the emblem of a vacuous mind or an empty spirit beset by misfortune, nor yet as evidence of sad exile from the sunlit serenity of a classical paradise (as his critics might), but rather, being in constant pursuit of the new, the infinite, and the 'inconnu', as a vehicle for the willing embrace—and even celebration—of melancholy:

---

[49] See Prévost, *Baudelaire*, 316, and Billy, *Les Formes poétiques*, 34.
[50] See 'Les Rimes du vide: Une lecture de Baudelaire', and Billy, 285–6.

Cieux déchirés comme des grèves,
En vous se mire mon orgueil;
Vos vastes nuages en deuil
Sont les corbillards de mes rêves,
Et vos lueurs sont le reflet
De l'Enfer où mon cœur se plaît.

The poetic sky—not to mention the heaven of orthodox religion—is rent asunder, as are the conventions of the sonnet itself by this dramatic and transgressive enjambement across the tercets. Funereal black, it seems, is the new cerulean blue. In a world subject to 'le Mal' the dreams of the imagination must perforce be conducted as funeral processions bidding final farewell to the old and the passé: and this poet is proud to acknowledge his irremediably fallen status—riven in two like the land from the sea—just as he is happy in his Hell of rhyme-lit libertinage. 'Horreur sympathique': with his own new take on the eighteenth-century doctrine of the sympathetic imagination this poet can identify with the human condition as it is truly, honestly, non-hypocritically lived in all its horror.

As these examples show, the poetic idea—the fusion of 'idée' and 'forme'—can manifest itself in many different ways in Les Fleurs du Mal. Given the etymological roots of 'idée' (something 'seen', a form)[51] and of 'poétique' (something 'made' or 'fashioned'), the 'idée poétique' means less an intellectual argument or observation presented in verbal and versified form—akin to the classical view of poetry as a form of 'gift-wrapped' thought—than a created formal pattern in words that may betoken new and multiple meanings for the reader. If we look again at 'Un fantôme', unique in Les Fleurs du Mal as a poem comprising a group of poems and almost unique as being written exclusively in decasyllables ('La Mort des amants' is the only other example),[52] we can add to our earlier understanding of it as a celebration of the capacity of art to bring back the dead. As Patrick Labarthe has shown,[53] 'Un fantôme' constitutes a celebration of the sonnet form itself, now resurrected from its Renaissance heyday when the decasyllable was its default metre and before the 'loi de l'alternance des rimes' had been established as the norm by Ronsard. Hence perhaps the 'surreptitious' disregard for this law in

---

[51] This derivation is emphasized by Leconte de Lisle in his review of the second edition of Les Fleurs du Mal: 'les idées, en étymologie exacte et en strict bon sens, ne peuvent être que des formes et [...] les formes sont l'unique manifestation de la pensée'. See Guyaux (ed.), Baudelaire: Un demi-siècle de lectures, 342.
[52] 'Le Chat' [no. 34]' combines decasyllables with octosyllables.
[53] See Patrick Labarthe, 'De l'usage des archaïsmes dans Les Fleurs du Mal', in Relais: Dix études réunies en hommage à Georges Blin (Paris: Corti, 2002), 119-47, and 'Le "Tombeau de Jeanne": Lecture d'"Un fantôme"', in Yoshikazu Nakaji (ed.), Baudelaire et les formes poétiques (La Licorne [Presses universitaires de Rennes], 83 (2008), 79-95 (83-4). Also Billy, Les Formes poétiques, 250-1.

'Le Cadre', where the tercets begin with a masculine rhyme where they 'should' have continued with a feminine rhyme.⁵⁴

As Dominique Billy suggests, accepting Labarthe's demonstration of a conscious 'archaïsme prosodique', 'Un fantôme' represents something of a 'petit compendium des variétés du sonnet baudelairien'.⁵⁵ In this way one might also argue that the poet of 'Un fantôme' is enacting his own renaissance. Not only he is poetically performing the revivification of the ghost who is his former lover and bringing her once more into existence through an act of memory and poetic creation (albeit in a form that is subject to decay, like the lines of a pencil drawing), but he is also breathing new (and varied) life into an old verse-form that has fallen into desuetude. As though restaging the 'querelle des Anciens et des Modernes' the poem offers both the Renaissance 'antiquity' of the sonnet in its metre and in its brief lapse from alternating rhyme gender, and also the 'modernity' of Baudelaire's own concerted variations on its norms, making of this four-part poem a 'cadre' that confers '[j]e ne sais quoi d'étrange et d'enchanté' ('Le Cadre', l. 3) upon its many-layered poetic idea.

This participation of unusual prosodic features in the poetic idea is especially evident in the second half of 'Spleen et idéal', as though as that section moves more insistently and seemingly inevitably towards an acceptance of 'le Mal' and spleen, so it simultaneously insists on the power of poetic creativity, of 'l'idéal', the capacity of poetic form and the poetic imagination to generate the new. As Billy has shown,⁵⁶ the poem containing exclusively quatrains arranged in *rimes croisées*—even excluding, therefore, the additional use of this type of quatrain in the sonnets—constitutes the most common stanzaic pattern in the 1861 *Les Fleurs du Mal*. Indeed it is employed both in the first two poems of 'Spleen et idéal' ('Bénédiction', 'L'Albatros') and in the last poem in the whole collection ('Le Voyage') as though it were the default prosodic structure upon which other poetic forms are to be seen as variations. If we note also that seventeen of the twenty-four poems concerned employ exclusively the alexandrine, while in addition three employ the alexandrine as one of two 'mixed' metres ('Une charogne', 'Confession', 'Une martyre'), then, and more particularly, the quatrain of alexandrines in *rimes croisées* appears to be the 'baseline' from which other poetic forms, including the sonnet, might be seen as diverging. Just as Baudelaire begins 'Spleen et idéal', and therefore the collection as a whole, by mocking the Romantic figure of the poet as prophetic lawgiver and celebrant of nature and then substituting a new kind of poet who articulates 'des beautés inconnues', 'des beautés de langueur'

---

⁵⁴ See Billy, *Les Formes poétiques*, 251, 294–6.
⁵⁵ Billy, *Les Formes poétiques*, 251–2: 'pour les quatrains, renouvellement des rimes (I et IV), disposition alternée (IV), commutation [i.e. abba baab] (II); pour les tercets, disposition banvillienne [i.e. ccd ede] dans III, mais chute en rime plate dans les trois autres' (251).
⁵⁶ Billy, *Les Formes poétiques*, 72.

('J'aime le souvenir...', ll. 30, 32), so too *Les Fleurs du Mal* begins with poetic forms that evoke a more traditional prosody, such as might be found in the poetry of Lamartine, Hugo, and Vigny before 1840: namely, the longer poem comprised of alexandrines in *rimes plates* (like 'J'aime le souvenir...' itself) or in quatrains whether in *rimes croisées* ('Bénédiction', 'L'Albatros',[57] 'Les Phares') or in *rimes embrassées* ('Au lecteur', 'Élévation'). In this context 'Correspondances' then heralds an alternative beginning not only in its articulation of a new poetics of suggestive interconnection but also in its poetic form: as the first of sixty sonnets, a new prosodic baseline for a new kind of poetry, a poetry that privileges brevity and conjecture above expatiation and vatic pronouncement.

By attending to the distribution of poetic forms within *Les Fleurs du Mal* in this way, we may note also, as Billy does,[58] that the less common quatrain in *rimes embrassées* is itself evident at key structural points: in the prefatory 'Au lecteur' and in the three poems with which 'Spleen et idéal' ends ('L'Héautontimorouménos', 'L'Irrémédiable', and 'L'Horloge'). While it would be misleading to attach undue importance to such distributive patterns—since, for example, the octosyllabic metre of 'L'Héautontimorouménos' and 'L'Irrémédiable' links them also with the two preceding sonnets 'Alchimie de la douleur' and 'Horreur sympathique'—readers of the 1861 *Les Fleurs du Mal* may nevertheless be aware in the course of a sequential reading of 'Spleen et idéal' (and, to a lesser extent, of the collection as a whole) of a progression from the prosodically orthodox towards a more innovative and complex handling of versification. If we divide the 127 poems of the 1861 edition of *Les Fleurs du Mal* arbitrarily into four groups of 32, 32, 32, and 31 poems, we see, for example, that the incidence of the sonnet (counting 'Un fantôme' as one poem) remains relatively even (15, 15, 16, 11), as does the particular incidence of the sonnet in alexandrines (14, 12, 11, 8). But in other respects the degree of divergence from the 'norms' of the alexandrine, the quatrain, and uniform metre (isometry) increases markedly in the second quartile. Here the incidence of mixed metre peaks (2, 6, 2, 2), as does the use of the quintil (1, 5, 0, 0) and of decasyllabic metre (0, 6, 0, 1). Only here in this second quartile do we find three-line stanzas ('Franciscae meae laudes') and heptasyllabic metre employed (in three poems), while, as already noted, 'Le Beau Navire' and 'L'Invitation au voyage' represent unique combinations of prosodic features. Here, too, the use of the quatrain other than in sonnets is relatively rare: the quatrain of alexandrines in *rimes croisées* is used only in three cases, each with a particular variation (the line repetitions of 'Harmonie du soir', the mixed metre of 'Confession', and the division of 'Chant d'automne' into four and three stanzas);

---

[57] Newly added to the 1861 edition, 'L'Albatros' thus replaced the alexandrines in *rimes plates* of 'Le Soleil' with a no less orthodox poetic form.
[58] Billy, *Les Formes poétiques*, 108.

and no poem in this quartile that is not a sonnet employs the quatrain of alexandrines in *rimes embrassées*.[59]

If, less arbitrarily, we consider the distribution of poetic forms within 'Spleen et idéal' itself and divide the 85 poems of that section into groups of 21, 21, 21, and 22, then we see that the use of the quatrain of alexandrines in *rimes croisées* is concentrated in the first quartile (5 poems), while in the second it figures only with mixed metre (2 poems, with lines of 8 and 5, and 12 and 8, syllables respectively) and in the third only with some further variation as just described ('Harmonie du soir', 'Confession', 'Chant d'automne'). In the fourth quartile the form occurs just once, in the fourth 'Spleen' poem. As to the quatrain of alexandrines in *rimes embrassées*, the incidence is symmetrical (2, 0, 0, 2), albeit in the last of these four poems with the variation of 'Le Goût du néant' where the a rhyme of each of the three stanzas recurs also in the single lines intercalated between each stanza. Taking the distribution of poetic forms in 'Spleen et idéal' as a whole, then, we can see that the greatest divergence from the posited baseline norms occurs in the third quartile (from 'Le Flambeau vivant' to 'Le Revenant' inclusive) in which the reduced incidence of conventionally rhymed quatrains and of sonnets in alexandrines is offset by a high number of less usual forms: the quatrain in *rimes plates* ('Le Flacon', 'Ciel brouillé', 'Le Beau Navire'), four of the six quintils contained in the whole collection, the three-line stanza of 'Franciscae meae laudes', the heptasyllabic line of 'Chanson d'après-midi', and the unique combinations of 'L'Invitation au voyage'.

Turning back from these purely formal features towards the more traditional thematic grouping of these poems, it is notable that the more unusual and/or complex verse forms in *Les Fleurs du Mal* occur in the third and fourth cycles of 'love poems'. Already we have seen how, at the end of the first cycle, the unique composition of 'Un fantôme' complements (by exhibiting the poet's own prosodic skill) its poetic argument that art can 'recreate' what is dead. Similarly, towards the end of the second cycle, 'Harmonie du soir' celebrates the poetic act of memory in a poem of overt virtuosity, a virtuosity that then becomes particularly striking in the third cycle. Following 'Le Flacon', with its unorthodox use of quatrains in *rimes plates* and its complex concentric structure that recalls that of 'La Chevelure', 'Le Poison' is the only poem in *Les Fleurs du Mal* to combine alexandrines with heptasyllabic lines, 'Ciel brouillé' the only one of two (with 'À une mendiante rousse') to comprise exclusively masculine rhymes. 'Le Chat', by having the same title as an earlier poem, anticipates the 'Spleen' poems in demonstrating that each poem is unique even if it shares a title or a subject with another. Then come 'Le Beau Navire' and 'L'Invitation au voyage', prosodically

---

[59] It should be noted that 'Le Vampire', as no. 31, comes at the end of the first quartile but anticipates the divergences of the second with its unique form of six quatrains in which stanzas 1, 2, 4, and 5 have *rimes croisées*, and stanzas 3 and 6 *rimes embrassées*.

the most complex poems in *Les Fleurs du Mal*. 'L'Irréparable' is unique within the collection in using alternating lines of 12 and 8 syllables within the stanzaic form of the quintil. Four poems later 'Chanson d'après-midi' is the only poem written exclusively in heptasyllabic metre. 'Franciscae meae laudes' is the only poem written in three-line stanzas... and in Latin!

Prosody informs the meaning of all poems in verse. In the case of these particular poems in 'Spleen et idéal' innovative or experimental forms assume significance by demonstrating novelty and creativity in the face of what may come to seem, given the very cyclicity of these 'love poems', an increasingly repetitive thematics of 'le Mal'. In 'Le Poison' the combination of alexandrines with heptasyllabic lines serves, in conjunction with the repeated use of enjambement, to reinforce the poem's central poetic idea of increase: of supplementation, expansion, and excess. As wine may transform a hovel into a palace (ll. 1-5) or as opium may so expand our perceptual horizons that it '[r]emplit l'âme au-delà de sa capacité' (l. 10), so the lover's 'poisonous' gaze stimulates the poet's imagination ('Mes songes viennent en foule' (l. 14)) and the 'deadly' saliva of a kiss plunges his soul—'sans remord'—into oblivion. In each of the four five-line stanzas three alexandrines (as the first, third, and fifth lines) are 'supplemented' by two intercalated heptasyllabic lines in such a way as to suggest, variously, a liberation from constriction or restriction (the hovel, remorse), a broadening even of the limitless ('L'opium agrandit ce qui n'a pas de bornes, | Allonge l'illimité' (ll. 6-7)), or—as though the alexandrine itself could not be stopped—an unceasing flow ('le poison qui découle | De tes yeux, de tes yeux verts' (ll. 11-12); 'charriant le vertige, | La [i.e. mon âme] roule défaillante aux rives de la mort!' (ll. 19-20)). Arguably two intercalated parisyllabic lines might have produced a similar effect, except that the imparasyllabic (in this case heptasyllabic) line here reinforces—through its perceived 'lack' of a final syllable—a sense of unfinished business, of ongoing surmise and the prospect of as yet unknown possibilities, of a potentially unquenchable thirst (l. 15)... even unto death.

'Le Poison' is followed by 'Ciel brouillé', which takes up the quatrains in *rimes plates* of 'Le Flacon' but now transgresses the requirement to alternate masculine and feminine rhyme. The sky of 'love' has turned cloudy and confused, while the rules of versification have been blurred and muddled. Following 'Le Chat' [no. 51], 'Le Beau navire' takes up the quatrains of *rimes plates* of 'Le Flacon' and 'Ciel brouillé' but now varies this form metrically with each quatrain consisting of alexandrines in lines 1, 2, and 4 and octosyllabic metre in line 3 (thus echoing the octosyllables of 'Le Chat'). At the same time stanza 1 is repeated as stanza 4, stanza 2 as stanza 7, and stanza 3 as stanza 10 (the final stanza). The uneven metre recalls the rhythm of a pitching gait evoked in 'Le Serpent qui danse' while also echoing the poem that preceded it ('Avec ses vêtements ondoyants...'): 'Quand tu vas balayant l'air de ta jupe large, | Tu fais l'effet d'un beau vaisseau qui prend le large' ('Le Beau Navire', ll. 5-6, 25-6). Here the repetition of the stanzas is mirrored in the repetitions of the couplets and the rich rhymes, including one *rime homonyme* ('large'/'large'), as it is mirrored also by the internal rhymes of 'fais'/ 'effet' and 'beau vaisseau'. The poet's first stated purpose in the poem is to 'raconter [...] | Les diverses beautés qui parent ta jeunesse', so that the repetition suggested by the *rimes plates* and the use of whole stanzas as refrains serves to counterbalance the diversity evoked by the poem's function as a celebratory list: 'ton cou', 'Ta tête' 'Ta gorge', 'Tes nobles jambes', 'Tes bras'. Anatomical diversity ('Les diverses beautés') bespeaks a single beauty ('ta beauté'). The poet's other stated purpose is to 'peindre ta beauté| | Où l'enfance s'allie à la maturité' (ll. 15-16), a combination reflected in the phrase 'majestuese enfant' with which the repeated third stanza and therefore the poem itself ends. The 'alliance' of the 'majestic' alexandrine with the 'lighter' and traditionally more lyrical octosyllabic line may convey something of this duality. Dressed in her voluminous skirt the young woman proceeds like a ship under full sail, at once stately and yet gently at ease: 'Chargé de toile, et va roulant | Suivant un rhythme doux, et paresseux, et lent' (ll. 27-8), where this second line itself combines a diversity of epithet with an insistently even and repeated rhythm. Once again recalling the woman of 'Le Serpent qui danse', here we have the 'molle enchanteresse' addressed in the opening line of the poem (and again in l. 13), at once a source of magical and unsettling perceptions for the poet ('Ta tête se pavane avec d'étranges grâces' (ll. 10, 38)) and yet in herself calm and softly untroubled: 'D'un air placide et triomphant | Tu passes ton chemin, majestueuse enfant' (ll. 11-12, 39-40).

This combination of strange enchantment and quiet certainty (again we find that favoured Baudelairean combination of mystery and clarity) is further reflected in the poem, where the steadiness of its gradual unfurling as a complex song may deflect attention from the bizarreness of the stream of consciousness prompted by the poet's spellbound gaze. This woman who walks like a ship under sail has a bosom that breasts the waves of her silk blouse ('qui pousse la moire' (l. 17)) but simultaneously resembles a cupboard with convex doors that look like gleaming breastplates (ll. 18-20)...breastplates designed to protect but that here provoke, armed as they are with points of pink (l. 21)...a cupboard full of goodies ('Armoire à doux secrets, pleine de bonnes choses' (l. 22))...goodies to delight a childlike poet, who nevertheless has in mind rather more 'mature' (cf. ll. 1, 16) forms of adult intoxication ('De vins, de parfums, de liqueurs | Qui feraient délirer les cerveaux et les cœurs!' (ll. 23-4)). Clearly this 'molle enchanteresse' has woven her magic, and the poet soon registers his distrust by proposing the analogies discussed earlier: those alluring legs kicking the panels of her skirt forward as she walks, tormenting and exacerbating 'les désirs obscurs' like two witches stirring a black love potion in a vase; those young arms that could fend off any precocious young Hercules as though it were child's play (l. 33), arms as strong as boa constrictors with which to press a lover, this poet-lover, to her heart in a most stubborn and potentially fatal embrace (ll. 34-6)...

'Love' is dangerous, 'love' is 'le Mal', but here that reality has been transmuted into a form of hallucination within a complex and harmonious poetic structure. Like a ship. Both in itself and as a poem that may be thought to epitomize the complex and harmonious poetic structure of Les Fleurs du Mal as a whole, 'Le Beau Navire' perfectly reflects Baudelaire's description in Fusées, f. 22 of what he there specifically calls 'l'idée poétique':

> Je crois que le charme infini et mystérieux qui gît dans la contemplation d'un navire, et surtout d'un navire en mouvement, tient, dans le premier cas, à la régularité et à la symétrie qui sont un des besoins primordiaux de l'esprit humain, au même degré que la complication et l'harmonie,—et, dans le second cas, à la multiplication successive et à la génération de toutes les courbes et figures imaginaires opérées dans l'espace par les éléments réels de l'objet.—L'idée poétique qui se dégage de cette opération du mouvement dans les lignes est l'hypothèse d'un être vaste, immense, compliqué, mais eurythmique, d'un animal plein de génie, souffrant et soupirant tous les soupirs et toutes les ambitions humaines.[60]

Here in 'Le Beau Navire' we find—'dans le premier cas'—the regularity and symmetry of prosodic structure in the repetitions of couplet and rhyme, of rhythm and refrain. Beauty is at once singular and diverse, embodied in the sameness and difference of sounds and metre, in the broad array of unenterprising rhyme ('beauté'/'maturité'), rich rhyme ('grâces'/'grasses', 'clairs'/'éclairs'), virtuosic rhyme ('hercules'/'émules'), and reinforced rhyme ('la moire'/'la belle armoire'). The repetition of stanzas—itself a 'complication de l'harmonie'—suggests at once the repetition and the onward movement of a walk, and also an arrival (as the third repeated stanza closes the poem). At the same time—'dans le second cas'— we have the work of the imagination, the 'multiplication' and 'generation' of *imaginary* 'curves' and 'shapes' 'operated' by the 'real elements of the objects': in this case, the woman's body parts. And the 'poetic idea' is that of a poet who both 'recounts' (l. 1) and 'paints' (l. 3) the 'enchanting' effect of that body on his own body, heart, mind, and imagination.

In Baudelaire's description the ship under sail is a vast, complex, harmonious combination of moving parts, suggestive of a living creature that exhibits its creativity ('plein de génie') by generating a virtual geometry of shapes and patterns, and suggestive also of a living creature that experiences the full gamut of human melancholy: 'souffrant et soupirant tous les soupirs et toutes les ambitions'. The ship is beauty ('eurythmique'): beauty as an effect, beauty as creativity, and beauty as the tragedy of desire—what in Fusées, f. 16 Baudelaire

---

[60] Fusées, ed. Guyaux, 70; i. 663–4.

describes as 'des besoins spirituels, des ambitions ténébreusement refoulées' when defining beauty as 'quelque chose d'ardent et de triste'. In 'Le Beau Navire', therefore, the ship is not only the woman but also the poem, and, as poem, the articulation of a living poet's passions—like the poet of 'La Musique' who sets sail on a sea of music: 'Je sens vibrer en moi toutes les passions | D'un vaisseau qui souffre' (ll. 9–10). The poet is the poem is the ship is the woman.

For this reason the poem that follows it, 'L'Invitation au voyage', may be read as the invitation extended by all poems to their readers to embark on a journey of the imagination, to board the text and trust to the craft of verse to bear them across an imaginary sea. Already we have seen that this poem is not without evidence of 'le Mal' (in the 'traîtres yeux' (l. 11), the tears (l. 12), and the selfish whims implied by 'C'est pour assouvir | Ton moindre désir' (ll. 32–3)), but the predominant tone is one of innocent surmise and imagined delight. This tone derives in part from the evocation of the non-sexual in the opening line ('Mon enfant, ma sœur'), which recalls the 'jeunesse' and 'enfance' mentioned at the beginning of 'Le Beau Navire'. Here in 'L'Invitation au voyage' 'love' is imagined as a sweet co-habitation, a life of ease and untroubled fidelity even unto death (ll. 4–5). Once again the prospect of metaphorical 'ciels brouillés' (l. 8) is a source of enchantment rather than apprehension, perhaps even a prophylactic against boredom. So, too, the imagined décor of their future shared abode, at once reassuringly settled (the gleaming, cherished antique furniture) and excitingly suggestive (the rarest flowers, the faint scent of ambergris). Here the ceilings are 'rich' and the mirrors 'deep' (ll. 21–2), and the oriental splendour of the decoration implies mystery and an exoticism that is but a displaced homeliness mirroring theirs: 'Tout y parlerait | À l'âme en secret | Sa douce langue natale' (ll. 24–6). And there will be ships, ships that like to sail ('Dont l'humeur est vagabonde' (l. 31)), ships ready to bring all manner of satisfaction from the four corners of the world—like a poem that imagines what it might be like to live somewhere else.

But what kind of somewhere else? The triple refrain is insistent: 'Là, tout n'est qu'ordre et beauté, | Luxe, calme et volupté'. This may or may not be Holland with its canals (ll. 29, 37) and indifferent weather (ll. 6–8), but more importantly it represents the dreamworld of poetic creation, that 'autre monde' where poetry is true. And the unique poetic form of 'L'Invitation au voyage' marks it out as special. One feature of that uniqueness is its combination of two imparisyllabic metres of different lengths (5/7)—in itself a kind of 'alternative', enjambed alexandrine—so that the implication of 'incompletion' is ubiquitous within the poem. At the same time the preponderance of the five-syllable line, together with the use of a refrain, conveys the tone of a simple song, even of a lullaby. Here again the poetic idea is poetry itself: order and beauty, luxury, calm, and voluptuousness. This particular poem has a uniquely structured 'order' that possesses the calm beauty of symmetry and regularity. Even as it evokes the idea of luxury in its description of a sumptuous décor and the personal use of a supply chain of global commerce, so too it luxuriates voluptuously in the poetic: foregrounding the lyrical in its song-like form, exhibiting the riches of rhyme in lines that require it every fifth or seventh syllable, savouring the imagined otherness offered by simile (the country resembles his companion) and metaphor (the sun clothes the fields, the canals, the whole city, in gold and hyacinth-blue).

If the description of the beauty of a ship in *Fusées* may be applied to individual poems,[61] how much more may it be applied to the complex system of moving parts that is *Les Fleurs du Mal*. The collection may comprise individual poems, but it also produces effects of beauty through its overall organization. Most obviously, it is divided into separate sections. More interestingly, as we have seen, it is structured as a journey from birth to death. Indeed it is itself one long 'invitation au voyage' and ends, precisely, with 'Le Voyage', which is by a considerable margin the longest poem in the collection.[62] At the same time, as we have also seen, 'Spleen et idéal' is framed by two groupings (1–21, 79–85) that present a particular poetic argument about the nature of poetry, the quest for beauty, and the acceptance of 'le Mal'. Poems 79–85 echo and/or provide reversed mirror versions of some of the first poems in the section, whether thematically or lexically. The four cycles of 'love poems', like the subsequent poems about death and spleen, constitute further subdivisions within 'Spleen et idéal'. In 'Tableaux parisiens', as we shall see presently in more detail, the poems are arranged to reflect the day (86–94) and night (96–102) of city life, with 'Le Crépuscule du soir' (95) and 'Le Crépuscule du matin' (103) figuring the moments of transition in the twenty-four-hour day of Paris.

Thus, in the arrangement of the poems as well as in the individual poems themselves, there is regularity and symmetry within complex harmony. In this respect the overall collection may be seen as answering to that fundamental human need that Baudelaire describes in his draft preface as being already met by metre and rhyme, our 'immortels besoins de monotonie, de symétrie et de surprise'. At the same time, as in some complex living organism (cf. 'un animal de génie') the separate moving parts of *Les Fleurs du Mal* are held together by an all-encompassing system of concatenation, whereby neighbouring or nearly neighbouring poems are connected, whether by an image or a single word, like links in a chain.[63] There are a very large number of such links, most obviously in the shorter

---

[61] *Pace* Billy, who fears it would be 'prétentieux' to extrapolate from it in this way. See *Les Formes poétiques*, 145.

[62] It contains 144 lines (the square of its twelve-syllable alexandrines). Apart from 'Les Petites Vieilles' (84 lines) and 'Bénédiction' (76 lines), no poem in the 1861 edition of *Les Fleurs du Mal* has more than 60 lines.

[63] Cf. Baudelaire's comment on 'well-made' poetry in his article on Wagner: 'En effet, sans poésie, la musique de Wagner serait encore une œuvre poétique, étant douée de toutes les qualités qui constituent une poésie bien faite: explicative par elle-même, tant toutes choses y sont bien unies, conjointes, réciproquement adaptées, et, s'il est permis de faire un barbarisme pour exprimer le superlatif d'une qualité, prudemment "concaténées"' (ii. 803). On 'l'art comique de la concaténation' in the first two editions of *Les Fleurs du Mal*, see Vaillant, *Baudelaire, poète comique*, 272–89. For Vaillant 'les

sections where Paris or wine or Lesbos or impiety or death variously provide a focal point of reference. But 'Spleen et idéal', too, is replete with such interconnections: the flight of the albatross that precedes the soaring overview of 'Élevation'; the 'langage des fleurs' of 'Élevation' that contrasts with the 'confuses paroles' of 'Correspondances'; the 'parfum' in the penultimate line of 'Hymne à la Beauté', recalling the 'parfums' in the tercets of 'Correspondances' and followed at once by the subject of 'Parfum exotique', itself evoked again in the second line of 'La Chevelure' and anticipating the 'parfum mélangé de musc et de havane' in the second line of 'Sed non satiata' and also 'Le Parfum', the second poem in 'Un fantôme'... A long list of similar examples could be given, extending throughout the collection. Readers of *Les Fleurs du Mal* will be more or less conscious of these and similar anticipations and echoes of word and image as they proceed from one poem to the next, but it is important to note explicitly how this concatenation contributes to a quasi-musical structure of theme, variation, and reprise and thus to the overall harmony of the collection. For this may perhaps be the more appropriate way to envisage the unity or 'secret architecture' of the 1861 edition, seeing it not as some numerologically determined entity of precisely positioned elements but as a looser, more fluid arrangement of working parts (assembled and adjusted over many years) in which an overarching poetic argument, rethought between 1857 and 1861, provides a strong hermeneutic direction—towards acceptance of 'le Mal', towards celebration of the 're-creative' power of art and of poetry in particular—while being subtended by the swirls and eddies of poems that stand in some closer, more particular relationship one with another. Sometimes that relationship can be traced to some original biographical circumstance, as in the case of the poems sent to Apollonie Sabatier and grouped in the second cycle of 'love poems'. But in other cases, such as that of 'La Chevelure' for example (a poem written after publication of the first edition and added in 1861), one might plausibly infer an intentional reinforcement on Baudelaire's part of the effect of concatenation, in this case linking 'Correspondances', 'Parfum exotique', and 'Sed non satiata', poems already included in the first edition.

Be that as it may, the poetic idea of *Les Fleurs du Mal* consists not only in its moral arguments about the nature of 'le Mal' and about how we do and could respond to its ubiquity within human experience, but also in its complex formal orchestration of argument and illustration through the handling of poetic forms: of metre, rhythm, rhyme, stanzaic pattern, and verse form. By the time we reach the end of the collection and read in 'Le Voyage' of '[l]e spectacle ennuyeux de

---

phénomènes de la concaténation sont strictement locaux' (283), whereas for Randolph Runyon they are omnipresent. See his meticulously detailed analysis of the device in Randolph Paul Runyon, *Intratextual Baudelaire: The Sequential Fabric of 'Les Fleurs du Mal' and 'Spleen de Paris'* (Columbus, Oh.: Ohio State University Press, 2010). See also Margery Evans, *Baudelaire and Intertextuality: Poetry at the Crossroads* (Cambridge: Cambridge University Press, 1993), 121–38, for her discussion of the Wagnerian leitmotif and 'dissonant harmony' in relation to *Le Spleen de Paris*.

l'immortel péché', we may or may not have been persuaded of the 'irreparable' or 'irremediable' nature of 'le Mal'. But at the same time we shall have read 127 new, different, artfully designed verbal constructs, each representing a unique deployment of the creative imagination and each with its own particular and individual poetic idea. 'Plonger au fond du gouffre, Enfer ou Ciel, qu'importe? | Au fond de l'Inconnu pour trouver du *nouveau!*', read the last two lines of *Les Fleurs du Mal*. For the poet it is only through new imaginings and new verbal formations that such novelty may be satisfactorily and lastingly found.

18
Poetry in the City
Melancholy and Time in 'Tableaux parisiens'

>   Dessins auxquels la gravité
>   Et le savoir d'un vieil artiste,
>   Bien que le sujet en soit triste,
>   Ont communiqué la Beauté.
>
>   ('Le Squelette laboureur', ll. 5–8)
>
>   La pendule aux accents funèbres
>   Sonnait brutalement midi.
>
>   ('Rêve parisien', ll. 57–8)

The section entitled 'Tableaux parisiens' was added to the second edition of *Les Fleurs du Mal*, in which the existing sections were themselves reordered. In the first edition 'Spleen et idéal' is followed by 'Fleurs du Mal', 'Révolte', 'Le Vin', and 'La Mort'. This ordering implies a potential narrative, hingeing on the placing of 'La Destruction' at the beginning of 'Fleurs du Mal'. In 'Spleen et idéal' (1857) the poet sets out in pursuit of aesthetic beauty only to discover—through his susceptibility to the beauty of women—the ephemeral and destructive nature of 'love'. Through his anguished awareness of the downward spiral of sexual desire the poet then accedes to a more generalized consciousness of melancholy before entering into a crepuscular state of resigned acceptance and readiness for death. In 'Fleurs du Mal' (1857) 'La Destruction' recalls this narrative progression as a journey towards the desolate 'plaines de l'Ennui' (l. 11) and as the story of a poet whom a 'Démon', 'sachant mon grand amour de l'Art', has temporarily lured from the true path of aesthetic beauty. 'Une martyre' (subtitled 'Dessin d'un maître inconnu') then offers, in the form of pictorial art, a gruesome picture of 'l'appareil sanglant de la Destruction': a tableau of sexual desire as lust, violence, and murderous decapitation. In the Lesbos poems that follow, the male poet, now himself initiated into the horrors of desire, is qualified to understand the suffering of others, and in particular these conflicted companions in the martyrdom of sexual longing. 'Fleurs du Mal' ends by returning to the doomed figure of the poet himself: in 'Un voyage à Cythère' (for Lesbos, read Cythera, read universal sexual desire) and 'L'Amour et le crâne', itself an ekphrastic poem (subtitled 'Vieux cul-de lampe') to mirror 'Une martyre' and depicting the destructive effects of Eros on the poet, himself a martyr. Following these accounts of the human condition as a limbo for the innocent victims of desire, the remaining sections could be seen as proposing three responses: an outraged, blasphemous rejection of the Christian God and the Christian faith in love ('Révolte'); a search for something, anything, to deaden the pain ('Le Vin'); and the prospect of death itself as the only remaining source of hope ('La Mort').

As we have seen, the enlargement and rearrangement of the final third of 'Spleen et idéal' in the 1861 edition, together with the addition of three poems to 'La Mort', introduces a new potential narrative and a new poetic argument in which the poet resists the negativity and destructiveness of 'le Mal' by affirming the positivity and constructiveness of art and the capacity of the imagination to create beauty from melancholy. 'L'Irrémédiable' (repositioned and given new prominence as the penultimate poem in 'Spleen et idéal') foregrounds the poet's acceptance of 'le Mal' not now as resigned acquiescence but as active embrace. In turn the final three poems in 'La Mort' discredit death as a source of hope, reaffirm the immutable fallen reality of the here and now, and depict, notwithstanding this despair, the allegorical journeys of ever-departing, ever-desirous sailors who return from their travels with offerings of beauty: 'quelques croquis pour votre album vorace'.

The addition of a new section entitled 'Tableaux parisiens' to the 1861 edition of *Les Fleurs du Mal* constitutes an important part of this recasting of the whole collection and indeed follows directly on from the revised final third of 'Spleen et idéal'. Where in the first edition the poet had turned from his own experiences as recorded in 'Spleen et idéal' to the suffering of the inhabitants of Lesbos, whom he views as his sisters, now the poet turns to the inhabitants of Paris amongst whom in particular he hails the women of 'Les Petites Vieilles' as 'Ruines! ma famille! ô cerveaux congénères' (l. 81). Once more the poet as solitary subject of 'le Mal' looks to the community of others, no longer to a symbolic Greek island of antiquity representing the torment of sexual desire and the mythical birthplace of Western poetry, but now to the modern city as a symbolic locus of 'le Mal' as it is exhibited by a multiple array of people (old men, old women, the poor, the blind, the sick, the dying, a woman in mourning, gamblers, sex workers, a faithful servant)—and to the modern city as the source of an alternative, transgressive form of poetic writing that made Baudelaire himself wonder if he had gone too far. Hence his comment (towards the end of May 1859) on sending 'Les Sept Vieillards' to Jean Morel, co-editor of the *Revue française*: 'c'est le premier numéro d'une nouvelle série que je veux tenter, et je crains bien d'avoir simplement réussi à dépasser les limites assignées à la Poésie' (*Corr.* i. 583).

Following 'Tableaux parisiens' the newly positioned section entitled 'Le Vin' now serves as a continuation of this gallery exhibition of suffering humanity ('Le Vin des chiffonniers', 'Le Vin de l'assassin', 'Le Vin du solitaire', 'Le Vin des amants').[1] Providing further evidence of the concatenation described in the last chapter, 'Le Vin des chiffonniers', with its depiction of Parisian ragpickers, links back to 'Tableaux parisiens', while the final poem in the section, 'Le Vin des amants', anticipates the account of same-sex desire in 'Fleurs du Mal'. The inhabitants of Lesbos, once so central to the project that became *Les Fleurs du Mal*, have now become relatively incidental examples of the martyrdom of sexual passion within this more comprehensive dictionary of melancholy. Being no longer followed by 'Le Vin', the section entitled 'Révolte' consequently takes on greater importance as part of the ending of the collection. The broad panorama of melancholy is more or less complete, and the poet's response is twofold: revolt against any possible belief in the existence of a beneficent and loving God, and deep sarcasm about the fond hopes that people—lovers, the poor, frustrated artists—entertain about death. Death is simply the only thing left that we have not experienced, and like everything else it will doubtless prove to be a disappointment.

'Paysage'

> Je veux, pour composer chastement mes éclogues,
> Coucher auprès du ciel, comme les astrologues[.]
>
> ('Paysage', ll. 1–2)

As in the first edition of *Les Fleurs du Mal*, so in the second edition the turn from self to other following the end of 'Spleen et idéal' is accompanied by an explicit turn towards poetry as a form of fine art: previously with the 'dessin' of 'Une martyre', here with the 'tableaux' that make up this new second section of the collection. Where the revised 'Spleen et idéal' ends with 'L'Horloge' and the mocking words of Time: 'Meurs, vieux lâche! il est trop tard!', this new section begins (in 'Paysage') with a firm statement of creative will: 'Je veux', and goes on to assert the power of the poet-artist to govern Time itself. For in deepest, coldest winter he can make his own weather:

> Car je serai plongé dans cette volupté
> D'évoquer le Printemps avec ma volonté,
> De tirer un soleil de mon cœur, et de faire
> De mes pensers brûlants une tiède atmosphère.
>
> (ll. 23–6)

---

[1] For discussion of the political implications of these poems and also in relation to *Du vin et du hachisch*, see Burton, *Baudelaire and the Second Republic*, 185–219.

Following the depictions of sexual passion in 'Spleen et idéal' the poet now proposes to live chastely alone in his garret, where he will ostensibly enjoy the 'volupté' of artistic rather than sexual activity. As Ross Chambers has rightly noted, this chastity is suspect,[2] and indeed there is nothing chaste about the evident sexual charge of 'À une mendiante rousse', or the poet's prurient interest in the earlier sex lives of the 'petites vieilles', his instant attraction to the female passer-by of 'À une passante', his sexual taste for the skeletal ('Danse macabre', l. 20), and his interest in the 'chère indolente' of 'L'Amour du mensonge', whose heart, 'meurtri comme une pêche, | Est mûr, comme son corps, pour le savant amour' (ll. 11-12). Nevertheless 'Tableaux parisiens' does mark a break with the poetry of passion that constitutes such a significant part of 'Spleen et idéal'. Now the sunshine that the poet proposes in 'Paysage' to derive from the realm of his own emotional being becomes the subject of the following poem, 'Le Soleil', where the power of the sun serves as a metaphor for poetic activity, and where, as previously discussed, the poem subverts the poet's traditional role as celebrant of the natural world and, in foregrounding a new poetry of the city, celebrates the substitution of art for nature.

In 'Paysage', just as in the opening poems of 'Spleen et idéal' (which in 1857 included 'Le Soleil' as the second poem, following 'Bénédiction'), the poet presents himself as replacing the ancient with the modern, as being both an heir to Theocritus and Virgil but also a new kind of urban soothsayer: 'Je veux, pour composer chastement mes églogues, | Coucher auprès du ciel, comme les astrologues' (ll. 1-2). Virgil's *Eclogues* (also known as his *Bucolics*) were modelled on the *Idylls* of Theocritus, short pastoral poems[3] depicting everyday scenes (including scenes of passion) within the context of nature. Virgil, by contrast, employs the term 'eclogue' for poems in which the pastoral songs of shepherds evoke not only country life and rural amours but also the tumult of revolutionary politics in the city (of Rome). Baudelaire's new poet of the city appears to favour Theocritus, drawing imaginative inspiration from 'tout ce que l'Idylle a de plus enfantin' (l. 20) and excluding not only politics ('L'Émeute, tempêtant vainement à ma vitre' (l. 21)) but also (ostensibly) sexual desire ('chastement', 'enfantin'). But whereas both Theocritus and Virgil celebrate nature, this poet is focused on the paradox of an urban 'paysage' and of an urban astrology.

At the beginning of 'Spleen et idéal', as we saw, the poet's traditional role as celebrant and interpreter of nature is undermined in both 'Élévation' and

---

[2] See his 'Trois paysages urbains: Les Poèmes liminaires des *Tableaux parisiens*', *Modern Philology*, 80: 4 (May 1983), 372-89 : 'Ce mot [volupté], pourtant, qui (avec "mes pensers brûlants") vient dénier ironiquement la chasteté à laquelle le poète prétendait au premier vers, révèle assez que ce poème sur la puissance du rêve n'est pas, comme son lexique pourrait le faire croire, le poème de la volonté, mais celui du désir, du vouloir dans le sens pulsionnel' (380).

[3] The word 'Idyll/Idylle' derives from the ancient Greek 'eidyllion', a diminutive of 'eidos' = image, and so etymologically means the opposite of the 'bigger picture'.

'Correspondances'. In 'Élévation' the ostensible gift of being able to soar above the world and command an effortless overview and understanding of 'Le langage des fleurs et des choses muettes' equates to a suspect blindness and refusal to contemplate the 'miasmes morbides' of 'le Mal', while in 'Correspondances' the possibility of inferring some divine message or higher spiritual truth from nature appears equally in doubt and is replaced by the prospect of a sensual transcendence ('l'expansion des choses infinies') in the here and now. In the opening lines of 'Paysage' the poet as stargazer becomes a rooftop flâneur. Rather than scan the heavens and read the star signs in order to prophesy the future, he will examine the human workplace ('Je verrai l'atelier qui chante et qui bavarde' (l. 6)) and read the city as a second nature.

The urban skyline is a new seascape ('Les tuyaux, les clochers, ces mâts de la cité' (l. 7)) and the lamp in the window a new star in the sky (l. 10). Nothing bucolic here, and yet every bit as much of an invitation to muse and dream: 'Et les grands ciels qui font rêver d'éternité' (l. 8). Glimpsed between bell-tower and fluepipe (with its ascending urban river of smoke (l. 11)), the sky is no longer a heaven of divine meaning and stellar script but a space into which the poet can project his endless reverie and surmise, anticipating Baudelaire's subsequent question to Armand Fraisse (quoted in the previous chapter): 'Avez-vous observé qu'un morceau de ciel aperçu par un soupirail, ou entre deux cheminées, deux rochers, ou par une arcade, etc., donnait une idée plus profonde de l'infini que le grand panorama vu du haut d'une montagne' (*Corr.*, i. 676). Indeed this 'dream space' (cf. 'Et, voisin des clochers, écouter en rêvant' (l. 3)) is also that godless void into which the 'hymnes solennels' of the Christian churches below rise up only to be borne away on the wind (l. 4). Sky, not heaven, and a city sky at that: an alternative domain for the lawgiving of the poetic imagination.[4] In 'Les Aveugles' the habitual upward and unseeing gaze of the blind—'au Ciel' (l. 14)—serves as a metaphor for the mental blindness of seeking transcendental answers in the heavens rather than submitting our quotidian experience to the investigations of imaginative surmise: 'on ne les voit jamais vers les pavés | Pencher rêveusement leur tête appesantie' (ll. 7–8). But it is precisely downwards that this poet will direct his own gaze ('du haut de ma mansarde'), and from the cobbled streets of Paris that this melancholic poet ('Vois! je me traîne aussi! [. . .] plus qu'eux hébété' ('Les Aveugles', l. 13) will derive the wherewithal to dream.

The city itself, of course, is testimony to the power of human construction, replacing field and tree with street and tower, and as such it now represents the 'natural' habitat of a poet who can build and transform through his use of a constructive imagination. Moonlight may retain its own traditional clichéd capacity to 'verser son pâle enchantement' (l. 12), but he for his part intends to 'bâtir

---

[4] Cf. Chambers, 'Trois paysages urbains', 379: 'En s'opposant au ciel, "je" propose le poète comme substitut de Dieu'.

dans la nuit mes féeriques palais' (l. 16): natural magic pales beside the sumptuous enchantments of art. The seasons, noticeable even here in the city, may come and go, but the poet can shut himself away (l. 15) and turn the cold monotony of winter (l. 14) into the warm air of spring (l. 26)—death into life, melancholy into a season of renewal, 'le Mal' into spring flowers. Outdoor viewing and rooftop dreaming become indoor imaginings and deskbound creations in which nature and gardens and birdsong and love and innocent simplicity will figure only by kind permission of artifice:

> Alors je rêverai des horizons bleuâtres,
> Des jardins, des jets d'eau pleurant dans les albâtres,
> Des baisers, des oiseaux chantant soir et matin,
> Et tout ce que l'Idylle a de plus enfantin.
>
> (ll. 17-20)

By the light of his own lamp and the fire of his own thoughts (l. 26) he will create his own warm 'atmosphere' here on earth and breathe the alternative oxygen of poetry within the landscape of his mind—just like the child at the beginning of 'Le Voyage': 'L'univers est égal à son vaste appétit. | Ah! que le monde est grand à la clarté des lampes!' (ll. 2-3).

The Capital of Melancholy

> Je t'aime, ô capitale infâme!
>
> ('Épilogue [I]', l. 13)
>
> Ton goût de l'infini,
> Qui partout, dans le mal lui-même, se proclame...
>
> ('Épilogue [II]', ll. 6-7)

'Paysage' thus serves as a statement of intent, and in this it partly recalls the prefatory function of 'Au lecteur'. Moreover the two poems that follow it appear to complement this statement: 'Le Soleil', as already mentioned, by ironizing the traditional figure of the nature poet, and 'À une mendiante rousse' by celebrating the beauty to be found in the city, even in a beggar. But the 'beautifying' role of art presented in these three poems is itself suspect. In 'Paysage' the beautification is escapist and sentimental.[5] The poet looks down from his rooftop garret[6] on the

---

[5] Christopher Prendergast, in his *Paris and the Nineteenth Century* (Cambridge, Mass. and Oxford: Blackwell, 1992), refers to 'an ease that verges on the saccharine' (61). See also Chambers, 'Trois paysages urbains', 381: '[l]e sentimentalisme conventionnel de certaines images'.

[6] Prendergast sees Baudelaire as reproducing a hackneyed stereotype already typical of the period but as 'appear[ing] to do so without even a trace of ironic self-consciousness' (*Paris and the Nineteenth*

song and conversation of the workplace rather than empathizing directly with the sufferings of labour, as he will in 'Le Squelette laboureur'. He shuts his window to block out the 'Émeute' of social unrest, just as Gautier had done in *Émaux et camées* where, in his own prefatory poem, the champion of 'l'Art pour l'Art' blithely discounts the raging storm of the 1848 Revolution: 'Sans prendre garde à l'ouragan | Qui fouettait mes vitres fermées, | Moi, j'ai fait *Émaux et camées*'.[7] And the Idyll that the poet of 'Paysage' imagines himself writing, closeted away and hunched over a desk in the snug cosiness of his garret, has a distinctly ersatz and schmaltzy air: fountains 'weeping' into alabaster basins, birds twittering, tremulous blue horizons... Like the poet of 'Élévation' gaily rising above the 'miasmes morbides' down below, this poet has turned his back on the city, on reality, on 'le Mal'. Not so the poet of 'Le Crépuscule du soir' and 'Le Crépuscule du matin', of 'Les Sept Vieillards, 'Les Petites Vieilles', and 'Le Cygne'; not so the poet of 'Rêve parisien', who demonstrates more disturbingly how to 'bâtir dans la nuit mes féeriques palais' (l. 16).

In 'Le Soleil' the sun-poet does, admittedly, walk among his people, but here, as in 'Bénédiction at the beginning of 'Spleen et idéal', we encounter once more that old con-trick, the alleged nobility of suffering: 'Quand, ainsi qu'un poète, [le soleil] descend dans les villes, | Il ennoblit le sort des choses les plus viles, | Et s'introduit en roi, sans bruit et sans valets, | Dans tous les hôpitaux et dans tous les palais' (ll. 17–20). How very kind of the poet to grace such subject matter with his presence, and what compassion he shows for the plight of these poor souls. But such a poet is not Baudelaire (though he might be Hugo). Similarly, in 'À une mendiante rousse', we find another wrong turn. In a virtuoso pastiche of Ronsardian erotic verse Baudelaire presents the cliché of seeing beauty in poverty and so demonstrates by counter-example how *not* to write the poetry of the city. For him the art of the urban eclogue is, as he believes all art should be, transformative rather than revelatory. When he comes, as he now does in 'Tableaux parisiens', to paint his own gallery of the dispossessed (the fragile elderly, the blind, the dead, the forgotten servant, a thirsting swan) he will not be uncovering their latent beauty—like the alluring, freckled nakedness of the red-haired beggar-girl visible through her ragged clothing—but *creating* it by his own transformative artistic vision. In 'À une mendiante rousse', however, such transformation appears inauthentic, being at once stylistically overblown and oblivious to the wretchedness of its subject. The poet is himself penniless (ll. 51–2) and 'chétif' (l. 5), at once ostensibly qualified to empathize with the beggar-girl's condition but thereby also

---

Century, 60). Philippe Hamon argues for an ironic reading of this stereotype and of 'Paysage' as a whole (see his *L'Ironie littéraire* (Paris: Hachette, 1996), 99–101), while Patrick Labarthe prefers to see 'ambivalence' rather than irony, and wonders, unconvincingly, if '"Paysage" procéderait plutôt d'une tentative de "pastoralisation" de la ville?' See his 'Locus amoenus, locus terribilis dans l'œuvre de Baudelaire', *Revue d'histoire littéraire de la France*, 99 (1999), 1021–45 (1034).

[7] See Gautier, *Œuvres complètes*, ed. Brix, 443.

disqualified, by both his poverty and his scrawny build, from securing the girl's attention while she begs for the money with which to buy 'des bijoux de vingt-neuf sous' (l. 50). But even as he bids her dispense with artifice, for she has no need of it ('Va donc, sans autre ornement, | Parfum, perles, | diamant, | Que ta maigre nudité, | Ô ma beauté!' (ll. 53–6)), he himself completes a poem of singular prosodic and syntactic ornamentation in her honour, clothing the girl's nakedness in the rich poetic fabric of a Renaissance conceit. But unlike the jewel-verse of 'La Chevelure', a necessary artifice with which to recapture an experience of 'ivresse', this poetic display appears gratuitous and unfeeling: an expression of powerlessness on the part of a poet who cannot help his companion in poverty and indeed, quite unlike the poet of 'Le Cygne' and 'Les Petites Vieilles', is incapable of identifying with her even though he, too, is poor and ill-nourished. All he can say, it seems, is 'oh! pardon!' (l. 51).

For here is this pale and sickly-looking girl, with her 'jeune corps maladif' (l. 6), wearing heavy clogs (l. 12) and holed stockings (l. 17) and a ragged dress that hardly covers her (cf. 'un haillon trop court' (l. 13), 'des nœuds mal attachés' (l. 21)). How can she hope to fend off all the men who are endlessly touching her up (l. 28) or looking up her skirt as she climbs the stairs (ll. 35–6) or fondly thinking of what they might like to do to her in that tiny hideaway she calls home (ll. 39–40)? And here she is, too, reduced to offering herself for money to some ageing down-and-out slumped on the steps of a restaurant, a fellow-beggar desperate for food (ll. 45–8). And why offer herself? Not for food but so that she can buy herself a trinket, and thus—like the women later depicted in *Le Peintre de la vie moderne*—participate in that pursuit of beauty which for Baudelaire is the hallmark of a 'civilized' humanity.[8] In 'À une mendiante rousse' we are obliquely privy to all this information, but the poet-persona veils the harsh reality with a Cinderella fantasy built on allusions to courtly romance and the concerted use of archaic language and euphemistic rhetoric. Those groping hands are merely 'doigts lutins'; those prying eyes belong to young poets who, like flunkeys dancing attendance, would like to dedicate the first fruits (l. 34)—of what? their poetry? their own virginity?—to this queenly beauty; and the sex they unceremoniously seek in her hovel is graced with the specious elegance of a *fête galante*: 'Maint page épris du hasard, | Maint seigneur et maint Ronsard | Épieraient pour le déduit | Ton frais réduit!' (ll. 37–40).[9]

The poet of 'À une mendiante rousse' thus clearly suffers from cognitive dissonance: the girl should have faith in her own natural beauty, but meanwhile he has to write the most artificial of poems. The true poet of the city, on the other

---

[8] See Chapter 14, and in particular the discussion of Baudelaire's account of apparently 'uncivilized' 'natives' as dandies.

[9] 'Réduit' is usually translated into English as 'cubbyhole'. In medieval and sixteenth-century French usage 'déduit' meant 'pleasure', and in one of its accepted uses 'sexual pleasure' in particular. See *Dictionnaire de l'Académie française* (9th edition) under 'Déduit'.

hand, must in Baudelaire's view resemble the Constantin Guys who looks beyond his own self and can capture the world of human nature 'en images plus vivantes que la vie elle-même, toujours instable et fugitive' (ii. 692), the Guys thanks to whom '[l]a fantasmagorie a été extraite de la nature' (ii. 694). As in the case of 'le Mal' from which beauty is extracted, or the gangue of time in 'L'Horloge' '[q]u'il ne faut pas lâcher sans en extraire l'or!' (l. 16), the city provides the raw material from which beauty may be derived through a quasi-alchemical and transformative process of isolation and refinement—a process which the poet of the 'Tableaux parisiens' repeatedly likens to dreaming. Not the vague, Romantic dreaming of 'Paysage', nor the preciosity of 'A une mendiante rousse', but a nightmarish series of hallucinatory visions exhibiting the deformities of caricature. The swan with its 'gestes fous' ('Le Cygne', l. 34); the first of the seven old men with 'la tournure et le pas maladroit | [-] | D'un quadripède infirme' ('Les Sept Vieillards', ll. 24–5); the once desirable old women who are now 'monstres disloqués' ('Les Petites Vieilles', l. 5) with 'membres discords' that defy the geometric norms of a coffin-builder's craft (ll. 29–32), doll-like women (l. 13) that totter down the street in an involuntary dance, less puppets on a string than little doorbells being rung by some pitiless demon (ll. 15–16); the blind, who are also not quite human, 'Pareils aux mannequins; vaguement ridicules; | Terribles, singuliers comme les somnambules' ('Les Aveugles', ll. 2–3); and the poet himself, 'crispé comme un extravagant' ('A une passante', l. 6): each one crazy or misshapen or visually odd, all of them strange and disturbing. In 'Danse macabre', an account of Ernest Christophe's statuette of a female skeleton in party dress, the poet discounts accusations that this representation of womanhood is 'mere' caricature:

> Aucuns t'appelleront une caricature,
> Qui ne comprennent pas, amants ivres de la chair,
> L'élégance sans nom de l'humaine armature.
> Tu réponds, grand squelette, à mon goût le plus cher!
> (ll. 17–20)

For skeleton, for caricature, read the fundamental, irreducible reality of our human condition—a fundamental truth here revealed by the artifice of the grotesque, of the 'comique absolu' identified in *De l'essence du rire* (whose full title continues *'et généralement du comique dans les arts plastiques*). As we know also from Baudelaire's essays on the art of caricature, a genre made famous in nineteenth-century France by Daumier, Gavarni, and others, caricature is an antirealism, a transformation of reality that reveals a deeper truth. Indeed in the opening sentences of *Quelques caricaturistes français* (1857) Baudelaire pays tribute to the work of Carle Vernet in terms that proclaim an aesthetic theory (while also bearing witness to his own long-standing admiration for Balzac): 'Son œuvre est un monde, une petite *Comédie humaine*; car les images triviales, les croquis de la foule et de la rue, les caricatures, sont souvent le miroir le plus fidèle de la vie' (ii. 544).

For Baudelaire as poet-caricaturist, the Paris of 'Tableaux parisiens' is not so much the capital of France—home city both of himself and of the majority of his readers[10]—as the capital of melancholy, a symbolic city in which, after the egocentric travails of 'Spleen et idéal', the exocentric poet turns outwards to explore the world of others. In so doing he continues to encounter 'le Mal' and he continues to pursue beauty: not by passively finding something already extant but hitherto unseen (like the poet of 'Le Soleil' stumbling across rhymes), some hidden Parisian 'mystery' à la Eugène Sue or indeed à la Balzac himself (the kind of mystery perhaps intimated by the description of the closed shutters in 'Le Soleil' as 'abri des secrètes luxures' (l. 2)), and also not by venturing like the sun into hovel and hospital and ennobling the wretched (as Hugo had done in Book 3 of *Les Contemplations* and would do so again in *Les Misérables*), but by enacting the aesthetic of 'Une charogne': taking the 'decompositions' to be found in an emblematic site of our human subjection to the realities of time and death, and, like a poetic Haussmann, reshaping this urban 'Mal' in poetic constructions of his own, building 'féeriques palais' of imagery and prosody that invite conjecture and surmise. In the letter he wrote to Hugo when sending him a handwritten version of 'Le Cygne' in December 1859, Baudelaire makes the point explicitly: 'Ce qui était important pour moi, c'était de dire vite tout ce qu'un accident, une image, peut contenir de suggestions' (*Corr.*, i. 623).[11] And as he writes in 'Les Sept

---

[10] On the literary and journalistic tradition of the 'tableau de Paris', dating back at least to Louis-Sébastien Mercier's *Tableau de Paris* (1782-3), see Karlheinz Stierle, 'Baudelaires "Tableaux parisiens" und die Tradition des "tableau de Paris"', *Poetica* 6 (1974), 285-322, republished in English translation as 'Baudelaire and the Tradition of the *Tableau de Paris*', *New Literary History*, 11: 2 (Winter 1980), 345-61. For Stierle, Baudelaire's originality within the tradition lies in the 'transformation of perception' by the lyrical subjectivity of the flâneur (360-1). See also Stierle, *Der Mythos von Paris: Zeichen und Bewusstsein der Stadt* (Munich and Vienna: Carl Henser Verlag, 1993), trans. into French by Marianne Rocher-Jacquin as *La Capitale des signes: Paris et son discours* (Paris: Éditions de la Maison des sciences de l'homme, 2001), 411-560. On the tradition of the 'tableau de Paris', see also Prendergast, *Paris and the Nineteenth Century*, 184-6. On the broader context (and intertexts) of specifically poetic treatments of Paris see Pierre Citron, *La Poésie de Paris dans la littérature française de Rousseau à Baudelaire* (2 vols, Paris: Les Éditions de minuit, 1961). Note in particular his commentary on the clichés of the genre: 'Partout [...] chez les romantiques qui ont chanté Paris, se trouvent la pluie, la brume, la boue, les pavés, le bruit, les cloches, la nuit, le gaz et les réverbères, le jeu, la prostitution, les mansardes, les faubourgs. Là encore, les sources présumées s'évanouissent en se multipliant: l'on n'est plus en présence que de lieux communs' (ii. 352); and his argument that in Baudelaire these images, 'retrouvant leur indépendance, expriment une réalité autre que celle des romantiques' (ii. 353). Citron demonstrates the importance of Hugo's ode 'A l'Arc de triomphe' (in *Les Voix intérieures*) as an intertext, and comments that the last stanza of 'Les Sept Vieillards', 'si baudelairienne qu'elle soit par l'esprit, est un véritable centon de Hugo' (ii. 354). Citron's study gives the lie to Walter Benjamin's unfounded claim that '[w]ith Baudelaire, Paris for the first time became the subject of lyrical poetry'. See his 'Baudelaire or the Streets of Paris', in *Charles Baudelaire: A Lyric Poet in the Era of High Capitalism*, 170.

[11] By aiming to 'dire vite' Baudelaire aligns himself with Delacroix and Guys for whom, as he makes clear in his accounts of these artists, technical skill permits a rapidity of execution that facilitates the capture of a fleeting perception.

Vieillards', using an image that recalls the resins at the end of 'Correspondances', '[l]es mystères partout coulent comme des sèves' (l. 3): that is, mystery not as a secret to be uncovered but mystery as a 'sève' to rhyme with 'rêve', an aura of wondrousness to be conferred on the quotidian by an act of mental flânerie. The poet as ragpicker has become the poet as urban architect, the 'Architecte de mes féeries' of 'Rêve parisien' (l. 37).

Baudelaire's city thus offers not the beauty of freckles glimpsed beneath rags but the beauty of melancholic conjecture. But is this city Paris? From the title of the section it would seem so. But Paris is mentioned only four times by name:[12] in 'Le Cygne' ('Le vieux Paris n'est plus' (l. 7), 'Paris change!' (l. 29)); as the setting for the poet's flânerie in 'Les Petites Vieilles' ('Traversant de Paris le fourmillant tableau', l. 26)); and at the very end of the section, in the closing couplets of 'Le Crépuscule du matin', where the shivering dawn steals slowly over the Seine and 'le sombre Paris, en se frottant les yeux, | Empoignait ses outils, vieillard laborieux'. The river itself is named also in 'Danse macabre' ('Des quais froids de la Seine' (l. 53)), while the 'quais' of Paris are implied by the 'quais poudreux' (l. 2) of 'Le Squelette laboureur' where the anatomical engravings in old medical manuals are presumably to be found among the bouquinistes. In 'Le Cygne', with its two explicit mentions of 'Paris', the additional references to 'le nouveau Carrousel' and the Louvre serve to situate the location of the escaped swan very precisely. But in 'À une mendiante rousse' (ll. 47-8), where the phrase 'quelque Véfour | de carrefour' (ll. 47-8) alludes to two famous Parisian restaurants, the Grand Véfour and the Petit Véfour, both situated in the arcades of the Palais Royal, the reference owes something to the requirement of playful rhyming that characterizes this virtuoso poem while it serves also to point up a disparity between wealth and poverty by using this prestigious name as a synonym for any old restaurant to be found on the corner of any old street, and not necessarily in Paris.

In other poems within 'Tableaux parisiens' the urban setting is also less precisely identified: for example, in 'Les Sept Vieillards', the houses looming in the mist seem like 'les deux quais d'une rivière accrue' (l. 7), but this 'faubourg' (l. 12) is again not necessarily Parisian, no more than the 'vieux faubourg' of 'Le Soleil' (l. 1) or the 'rue assourdissante' of 'A une passante' (l. 1) or the 'cité' of 'Les Aveugles' (l. 10) or even the 'cité' (l. 7) of 'Paysage', which poem, as it so happens, may well have been first written about Lyon.[13] Even in 'Les Petites Vieilles', with its explicit reference to Paris, the poem opens with a broad reference to 'les plis sinueux des vieilles capitales' (l. 1) as the site of the poet's taste for urban observation, recalling 'Le Soleil' where the sun-poet 'descend dans les villes'

---

[12] And only once elsewhere in Les Fleurs du Mal, in 'Confession', l. 8.
[13] See Richard D. E. Burton, 'Baudelaire and Lyon: A Reading of "Paysage"', Nottingham French Studies, 28: 1 (March 1989), 26–38.

(l. 17). Since the city depicted in 'Rêve parisien' is seen in a dream, like the setting of 'Le Jeu', then the meaning of 'parisien' in this title—and indeed in the title 'Tableaux parisiens'—is, as Ross Chambers has shown, problematic: a dream experienced *in* Paris or *because of* Paris, or simply *by* a Parisian?[14]

There is evidence in fact that Baudelaire sought to attenuate the specifically Parisian aspect of these poems. Despite its Lyonnais origins 'Paysage' was originally published under the title 'Paysage parisien' (in 1857, in *Le Présent*), just as 'Les Sept Vieillards' was initially called 'Fantômes parisiens' before this title was then applied to a grouping of 'Les Sept Vieillards' and 'Les Petites Vieilles', but both references to Paris were subsequently dropped.[15] Indeed this is the point. The creator of these urban eclogues is transforming his subject through the imagination, extracting its phantasmagoria and showing us not a particular city but the City: a place of encounter in which a single individual comes into contact with the rest of humanity and with a universal condition of ill-being. Moreover those poems that appear not to be set in a city at all come later in the section, between the two dream experiences recorded in 'Le Jeu' and 'Rêve parisien', as though they, too, were accounts not of daytime reality but of nocturnal recollections and imaginings. The women depicted in 'Danse macabre' and 'L'Amour du mensonge' belong with the 'courtisanes vieilles' in the oneiric gambling-den of 'Le Jeu', itself only putatively urban. 'Je n'ai pas oublié...' recalls a childhood home, 'voisine de la ville' (l. 1), and an arguably dream-like scene that itself thus 'neighbours' a waking, urban reality—as though memory itself were a kind of dream, just as dream is made of memories. 'La servante au grand cœur...', by implication set in the same house, turns on the idea of the 'sleep' of the dead and the imagined return of a servant to the poet's bedroom to watch over him ('l'enfant grandi' (l. 20)) while he sleeps just as once she had watched over him as a child. Newly situated after 'La servante du grand cœur...', 'Brumes et pluies' reads like a sequel, with the seasons now wrapping the sleeping urban poet ('l'enfant grandi') in the shrouds of melancholy so that he has changed places with the deceased maid:

> Ô fins d'automne, hivers, printemps trempés de boue,
> Endormeuses saisons! je vous aime et vous loue

---

[14] See Ross Chambers, 'Are Baudelaire's "Tableaux parisiens" about Paris?', in Anna Whiteside and Michael Issacharoff (eds), *On Referring in Literature* (Bloomington and Indianapolis: Indiana University Press, 1987), 95–110. Chambers argues that 'one may conclude that the best sense attributable to the title is "Tableaux d'un Parisien"', but only on the understanding that the lyric subject ('[t]he *ego* who is the subject of the poetic utterance is the truly universal factor in *all* of the poems of the "Tableaux parisiens"') is a Parisian 'in the sense that Paris is less the place he writes about than *the place out of which he speaks*, and hence the place *in which* the poems are supposed to be understood— the place, in short, which gives point to the poetic text as an utterance, and hence does so not as mimetic object but as illocutionary situation' (99).

[15] See *Corr.*, i., 1018, n. 1 to p. 582.

> D'envelopper ainsi mon cœur et mon cerveau
> D'un linceul vaporeux et d'un vague tombeau.
>
> (ll. 1-4)

This symbolic City, then, is the capital of 'le Mal', as is evident from the two draft 'Épilogues' with which Baudelaire once thought to close the second edition of *Les Fleurs du Mal*. Both the 'Crépuscule' poems, included as part of 'Spleen et idéal' in the first edition, offer panoramic overviews of the ill-being to be witnessed in this city: in 'Le Crépuscule du soir' quasi-bestial sexual appetite, prostitution, gambling, robbery, and terminal illness; in 'Le Crépuscule de matin' debauch, exhaustion, poverty, and once again terminal illness. Now in the second edition, complimenting these overviews, the poems of 'Tableaux parisiens' focus also and more particularly on subgroups of suffering humanity: old men, old women, the blind; and, narrowing the focus still further, they in addition provide individual case studies: the first old man, hostile and aggressive, his eyes filled with hatred and malign intent, or the old woman who likes to sit and listen to a military band, or the woman in mourning (for a lover? for a relative? for a friend?) whom the poet passes in the street, or the labourer depicted in an anatomical engraving. Here are the 'monstres innocents' referred to by the narrator of 'Mademoiselle Bistouri' in *Le Spleen de Paris*, seemingly caricatural departures[16] from some impossible paradigm of a 'normal' humanity, at once innocent and monstrous like the female inhabitants of Lesbos: innocent because they are not responsible for their miserable condition, monstrous because they have been physically, emotionally, and/or psychologically damaged by the business of living and the imperatives of desire.

In 'Mademoiselle Bistouri' the poet-narrator speaks in the voice of a Christian believer even as his literary creator implies disbelief in the existence of a benign Creator:

> Quelles bizarreries ne trouve-t-on pas dans une grande ville, quand on sait se promener et regarder? La vie fourmille de monstres innocents.—Seigneur, mon Dieu! vous, le Créateur, vous, le Maître; vous qui avez fait la Loi et la Liberté; vous, le souverain qui laissez faire, vous, le juge qui pardonnez; vous qui êtes plein de motifs et de causes, et qui avez peut-être mis dans mon esprit le goût de l'horreur pour convertir mon cœur, comme la guérison au bout d'une lame; Seigneur, ayez pitié, ayez pitié des fous et des folles! Ô Créateur! peut-il exister

---

[16] Cf. Citron, *La Poésie de Paris*: 'Les créatures du Paris de Baudelaire sont des hommes, mais aussi autre chose: des monstres, comme ceux que Baudelaire aime à trouver chez Daumier, comme les sept vieillards, comme "la monstrueuse petite folle aux yeux verts" de "La Soupe et les nuages", ou comme "Mademoiselle Bistouri"' (ii. 375).

des monstres aux yeux de Celui-là seul qui sait pourquoi ils existent, comme ils *se sont faits* et comment ils auraient pu *ne pas se faire*? (i. 355-6)

As Ross Chambers remarks, '[t]his is *flâneur* prose with a sting in its tail',[17] and the sting is delivered by the poet as alternative lawgiver. In tones of desperation the poet-narrator of 'Mademoiselle Bistouri' seeks causes, not only for the deranged behaviour of Mademoiselle Bistouri herself but for the extraordinary and individual plights of suffering humanity. His opening question echoes the cliché of a 'mysterious' Paris, so prevalent in accounts of France's capital city, but already the ironies are apparent. Mademoiselle Bistouri is not just a 'bizarrerie' but an acute case of mental illness. Moreover the poet-narrator is no expert investigator, deserving respect for his discovery: the woman has simply accosted him randomly as he strolled—'à l'extrémité du faubourg'—beneath the gaslight of night-time Paris. Indeed the poet has reached not only the limits of the city but of his own understanding, and the mystery in this case is fundamental, at once existential and religious. On behalf of these 'fous' and these 'folles' our poet begs mercy of his Christian God, Creator of the world and Master of the universe, who endowed humankind with free will, dictated his Law to Moses, and thereafter has forborne to intervene in human affairs, save only at the last to pardon those who repent their sins: this God who is the author of divine Providence, the *fons et origo* of all causation. But with his final, necessarily rhetorical question (for God never answers) the poet plainly has his doubts, and the 'Créateur' is replaced by a new metaphysical entity: 'Celui-là seul', who knows why we human beings are here at all and how we can become so damaged (for according to the Christian doctrine of free will it is we and not God who are responsible, hence the emphasis in 'ils *se sont faits*' and '*ne pas se faire*'); 'Celui-là seul' who therefore also knows how we might avoid the universal ill-being of our pitiable condition. But perhaps no such transcendental know-all actually exists? Perhaps we need to approach the question from another angle and recognize, live with, the impossibility of such knowledge? And follow other laws?

Since Walter Benjamin numerous commentators, including Chambers, have seen Baudelaire's urban dispossessed in political terms, applying to them the Marxist term of 'alienation' and considering them as innocent victims of—as having been made 'monstrous' by—the commodifying, dehumanizing effects of nineteenth-century capitalism. Chambers himself summarizes this perspective as follows:

> The alienation that most *flâneur* writing existed to exploit, to mitigate or to deny is what [Baudelaire] persistently draws attention to, and he does so with an eye to

[17] Ross Chambers, 'Baudelaire's Paris', in Lloyd (ed.), *The Cambridge Companion to Baudelaire*, 101-16 (105).

pointing up what is pathological in the social reality it bespeaks: the ill or evil (*le mal*) that modern life exemplifies, but also diverts us from grasping or coming to grips with. In other words, he takes up the thematics of *flâneur* writing, but with a view to giving it a critical edge.[18]

For Chambers here, as elsewhere for others, the principal focus of 'Tableaux parisiens'—and, as we shall see in Part V, the principal focus of *Le Spleen de Paris* also—is on 'modern life' and on a 'social reality' that is necessarily a sociopolitical reality. I would argue, however, that just as the 'Tableaux parisiens'—and indeed *Le Spleen de Paris*—is not really about Paris, it is not really about 'modern life'. Rather Baudelaire is fulfilling an ambition that he had outlined in the *Salon de 1846* and would later set out more fully in *Le Peintre de la vie moderne*: namely, to derive material from his observation of contemporary life in order to portray a timeless and universal human condition. It is debatable, for example, whether any of the ill-being depicted in the 'Tableaux parisiens' can be attributed specifically to an urban environment, let alone a nineteenth-century Parisian one. The people of this city grow old, fall sick, and die; the people of this city want sex and barter sex; the people of this city want food and rest and shelter and the means to acquire them, even risking what they already have—whether it be their body (in sex work) or their money (in gambling), or else by stealing what others possess. All of this has been happening since time immemorial, in cities, in villages, in the countryside. Yes, this city is noisy, and yes, it is crowded, but so too, no doubt, was Babylon.[19]

It may be that some commentators, in their admiration for Baudelaire's analytic intelligence and exceptional literary skills, have been eager to rescue him from his sometime reputation as a Catholic right-wing reactionary: the friend of Pierre Dupont who lost faith in revolutionary politics, the enemy of 'Progress', the preacher of 'original sin', the reader of De Maistre. But in drawing attention so insistently to the putative illustrations of urban alienation in his work they may have distracted that attention from a wider context. For the condition of Baudelaire's dispossessed—the condition of 'le Mal'—is more evidently metaphysical and existential than it is social or political. Certainly in 'Tableaux parisiens' many inhabitants of this symbolic city are seen, like the poet-narrator of 'Mademoiselle Bistouri', as facing a crisis of faith. Take the swan, for example. As one who has escaped from his cage in a menagerie, he could perhaps be viewed as the symbolic victim of the economics of show and performance, a creature of nature abused by the demands of an urban audience, a commodity. But he is

---

[18] Chambers, 'Baudelaire's Paris', 105.
[19] On the 'implied Babylonian analogy' of 'Épilogue (I)', see Prendergast, *Paris and the Nineteenth Century*, 52.

exiled (or alienated) not only from his 'beau lac natal' ('Le Cygne', l. 22) but also from the sky—and its own putative divine inhabitant:

> Je vois ce malheureux, mythe étrange et fatal,
> Vers le ciel quelquefois, comme l'homme d'Ovide,
> Vers le ciel ironique et cruellement bleu,
> Sur son cou convulsif tendant sa tête avide,
> Comme il s'adressait des reproches à Dieu!
>
> (ll. 24-5)

Physically distorted by his anguish—and thus comparable perhaps with the albatross of 'Spleen et idéal' ('qu'il est comique et laid' ('L'Albatros', l. 10))—this swan, believed in myth to sing only at its death, is constrained to silent protest. Desperate for water, and so for storm and rain, it observes the mercilessly blue sky as an ironic and sarcastic response to its essential need: the sky is empty, and God does not listen, for indeed (as the homophony of 'tendant sa tête [à vide]' suggests) God may not even exist. The swan's silent, convulsed reproaches fall on divine deaf ears, just as the blank gaze of the blind in 'Les Aveugles', who are similarly grotesque and risible ('vaguement ridicules'), falls only on darkness. These disabled human beings direct their gaze seemingly at random: 'Dardant on ne sait où leurs globes ténébreux' (l.4))—two dark eye-worlds with which to sleepwalk their way through the 'noir illimité' (l. 9) of a godless existence: 'Leurs yeux, d'où la divine étincelle est partie' (l. 5). Their sky, too, is empty, even if they want to call it Heaven—perhaps like all human beings who want to stick with the old laws. Moreover the swan and the blind are not alone in their anguished perception of a godless universe. Witness the old men of 'Les Sept Vieillards': 'ces spectres baroques | Marchaient du même pas vers un but inconnu' ('Les Sept Vieillards', ll. 30-2). Or the old women, descendants of the first woman on earth and, like her, living their lives under the control of a cruel God: 'Où serez-vous demain, Èves octogénaires, | Sur qui pèse la griffe effroyable de Dieu?' ('Les Petites Vieilles', ll. 83-4). A good question, for, as we learn in 'Danse macabre', the walk of life is a dance of death in which we merrily reel into the unknown: 'Le branle universel de la danse macabre | Vous entraîne en des lieux qui ne sont pas connus!' (ll. 51-2).

Certainly the poet himself—who had started out in 'Paysage' by comparing himself to an astrologer finding meaning in the stars—is left existentially reeling by what he encounters in this city of 'le Mal', mostly notably at the end of 'Les Sept Vieillards'. This same poet of 'Paysage' who had firmly resolved to shut his door to the world outside has evidently ventured down into the street, out of curiosity: 'Fourmillante cité, cité pleine de rêves', '[l]es mystères partout coulent comme des sèves' (ll. 1, 3). But the dream turns into a phantasmagorical nightmare, a crazy hybrid of the Sorcerer's Apprentice and Snow White and the Seven Dwarfs, leaving him '[e]xaspéré comme un ivrogne qui voit double' (l. 45). He returns home and locks his door once more: 'épouvanté, | Malade et morfondu, l'esprit fiévreux et trouble, | Blessé par le mystère et par l'absurdité!' (ll. 46–8). The beguiling mystery of Paris also has a sting in its tale, threatening the poet with mental illness of his own and confronting him with a vision of 'absurdité', of successive figures looming up out of the fog like one generation after another, each old man exactly the same as the last and so resembling a 'Dégoûtant Phénix, fils et père de lui-même' (l. 43) in a monstrous parody of renewal and resurrection. The poet is left floundering, all at sea, nearly mad:

> Vainement ma raison voulait prendre la barre;
> La tempête en jouant déroutait ses efforts,
> Et mon âme dansait, dansait, vieille gabarre
> Sans mâts, sur une mer monstrueuse et sans bords!
>
> (ll. 49–52)

In 'Les Petites Vieilles' the poet ventures forth once again, this time 'obéissant à mes humeurs fatales' (l. 3), a puppet on the string of his stalker's obsession ('Ah! que j'en ai suivi de ces petites vieilles!' (l. 49)), no more free to direct his own path than these old women themselves who are buffeted by the wind and (like the poet) dancing 'sans vouloir danser' (l. 15). In 'Les Sept Vieillards' the old men present the poet with the horrific vision of eternity as an endless succession of treachery (l. 20), and he appeals to the reader, as had once done in 'Au lecteur', for fraternal solidarity:

> Que celui-là qui rit de mon inquiétude,
> Et qui n'est pas saisi d'un frisson fraternel,
> Songe bien que malgré tant de décrépitude
> Ces sept monstres hideux avaient l'air éternel!
>
> (ll. 37–40)

But now in 'Les Petites Vieilles' it is he the poet who expresses solidarity with the women, as he subsequently will do also in 'Fleurs du Mal' with the women of the unbanned 'Femmes damnées': 'Pauvre sœurs, je vous aime autant que je vous plains' (l. 26). On this occasion he adopts a paternal rather than a fraternal role ('Tout comme si j'étais votre père' ('Les Petites Vieilles', l. 75)), but the message of human solidarity is clear: 'Ruines! ma famille! ô cerveaux congénères' (l. 81).

These two subgroups of old men and old women represent contrasting human responses to the ill-being of our shared condition: bitterness and bile in the case of the former ('Hostile à l'univers plutôt qu'indifférent' ('Les Sept Vieillards', l. 28)), and resigned acceptance in the case of the latter: 'Telles vous cheminez, stoïques et sans plaintes, | A travers le chaos des vivantes cités' (ll. 61–2)—an acceptance of the kind just recently embraced by the poet himself in the closing poems of 'Spleen et idéal' and especially in 'L'Irrémédiable'. Initially reluctant to leave his garret sanctuary the poet-narrator of these two poems has come out into humanity and now shares compassionately in its sufferings: here directly with the old women, but earlier—as though slowly adapting to his new role as a member of the human community—through his memory of a swan. Crossing the newly created Place du Carrousel, between the Louvre and the Tuileries palace, and recalling a swan he had once seen at this very spot, the poet makes of this bird an emblem of human ill-being, like a star-sign for 'le Mal', betokening loss and lack and endless desire: 'Je pense à mon grand cygne [cf. hom. 'signe'], avec ses gestes fous, | Comme les exilés, ridicule et sublime, | Et rongé d'un désir sans trêve!' (ll. 34–6). And this in turn makes him think of others who cannot go home: Andromache, captive widow of Hector during the Trojan War; an emaciated and consumptive African woman longing for the coconut palms of her native continent; undernourished orphans; mariners marooned on an island; prisoners of war... 'à bien d'autres encor!' Here are the inhabitants of our global village of melancholy and ill-being: in short, 'quiconque a perdu ce qui ne se retrouve' (l. 45). And, as we learn in 'Les Petites Vieilles', the poet is one of them: 'celui que l'austère Infortune allaita!' (l. 36). But he, at least, *can* go home, to his garret, there to commemorate and bear poetic witness to a common suffering: 'Ainsi dans la forêt où mon esprit s'exile | Un vieux Souvenir sonne à plein souffle du cor!' ('Le Cygne', 49–50). Not the North American forest of Chateaubriand, God's natural cathedral, nor the 'forêts de symboles' mentioned in the first stanza of 'Correspondances', but, as in the last stanza of that poem, a forest of oozing resin, a place where '[l]es mystères partout coulent comme des sèves'.

The city of 'le Mal', the city of others of whom the poet himself is one, is a city of damaged human beings, of human detritus, akin to the rubbish tip of 'Le Vin des chiffonniers': 'un tas de débris, | Vomissement confus de l'énorme Paris' (l. 15–16). This is particularly evident in 'Les Petites Vieilles' where the women are not only 'Ruines' but '[d]es êtres [...] décrépits' (l. 4), 'monstres disloqués' (l. 5), '[m]onstres brisés, bossus, | Ou tordus' (ll. 6–7), and '[d]ébris d'humanité pour l'éternité mûrs!' (l. 72). Indeed they are barely alive. Already defeminized by the insistent use of masculine nouns ('êtres', 'monstres' 'débris'),[20] they now exist only as ghosts, mere wrinkled shades ('ombres ratatinées' (l. 69)) and shadows of the gracious or glorious women they once were (ll. 65–6). The old men, too, are damaged. The first one, and thus presumably also his six lookalikes, is 'cassé, son échine | Faisant avec sa jambe un parfait angle droit' ('Les Sept Vieillards', ll. 21–2); and they, too, are ghosts, 'ces spectres baroques' (l. 31). The city of 'le Mal' is a place of disability ('Les Aveugles') and injury (cf. the 'porteurs de béquilles' of 'Le Soleil' (l. 13) or the 'animaux blessés' to whom the old women

---

[20] As noted by Rachel Killick, 'Espaces du moi, espaces de la ville: Forme et signification dans quatre poèmes de "Tableaux parisiens"', *Essays in French Literature*, 39 (2002), 153–70 (156).

are compared ('Les Petites Vieilles', l. 14)), a place of sickness (the consumptive African woman, the beggar-girl with her 'jeune corps maladif') and terminal illness (in both the 'Crépuscule' poems).

Life itself might perhaps be thought of as a form of terminal illness, and the poet who measures his own condition against that of the blind is under no illusion: 'Vois! je me traîne aussi! mais, plus qu'eux hébété.' This city of existential ill-being is a place of flux, of disintegration and dissolution, like the rotting corpse of 'Une charogne', but it is also, by that very fact, a place of potential recomposition and reintegration, of salvage—or poetic 'Haussmannisation'. The river Seine runs through the city, like the river of tears that flows from the eyes of the widowed, exiled Andromache ('Le Cygne', l. 4) or of the many women who have also lost husbands and sons to war ('Les Petites Vieilles', ll. 45–8). But then there is that other river, the river of time, seemingly unstoppable and yet, through memory, reversible: 'Andromaque, je pense à vous'. The swan itself, lamenting its 'beau lac natal', confronts a 'ruisseau sans eau' in the Place du Carrousel, but for the poet of 'Le Cygne' his recollection of the widow of Hector lamenting her loss by the banks of the Trojan river Simoeis serves as a metaphorical river that irrigates the plain of his own 'mémoire fertile'. The river of time is also the river of memory.

The Capital of Time

> Fourmillante cité, cité pleine de rêves,
> Où le spectre en plein jour raccroche le passant!
> ('Les Sept Vieillards', ll. 1–2)

The city of 'Tableaux parisiens' is thus a symbolic locus of human existence, less a topography than a site of human convergence, less a socio-political reality than a poetic Place du Carrousel. In many of these poems the act of living is represented as a form of bodily movement through space: walking, strolling, passing, stumbling, even digging, and occasionally dancing—as though the poet were watching the human race going through its paces.[21] But this symbolic locus is also a city of time, of movement in, through, back, and forward in time, a haunted, haunting place of passage.[22]

The idea that Paris was the 'capital of the nineteenth century' was—in Baudelaire's own day and before being consecrated in Walter Benjamin's writings

---

[21] The word 'carrousel' originally designated equestrian exercises, with the derived sense of 'merry-go-round' being attested in French only from 1870. See Alain Rey (ed.), *Le Robert. Dictionnaire historique de la langue française*, art. 'carrousel'.

[22] *Pace* Citron: 'C'est une ville qui semble n'avoir pas d'existence temporelle', 'La Cité n'existe qu'au présent, et elle symbolise même le présent dans la mesure où elle représente la *modernité*' (*La Poésie de Paris*, ii. 358).

of the 1930s, including his *Passagenwerk* or 'Arcades Project'—part of a broader view of France's largest city as being 'variously capital of the century, Europe, nations, the earth and the universe'.[23] But in 'Tableaux parisiens' Baudelaire's city is more appropriately viewed as the capital of Time itself: and as a 'modern' capital in Baudelaire's specific use of that term, that is, in that it figures time as both 'fugitive' and 'eternal', as the experience both of fleeting moments and of a complex layering of remembered epochs. This city is not only an emblematic realm of life's passing, of desired futures turning rapidly into lost histories ('Ruines!'), of the 'passante' becoming the passé(e), it is also an agglomeration of human agency and construction across and down the ages. Traversed by the river of time as it flows ceaselessly in one direction towards the eternal sea of its own death, this city is also a place where past, present, and future rub shoulders like people passing in the street, coming and going, this way and that, and offering up random, frozen moments of perception—what Proust's Narrator at the end of *A la recherche du temps perdu* will later call 'un peu de temps à l'état pur':[24] images and tableaux to intrigue the eye and prompt a rich conjecture, in the manner of a dream. Comparable with the Place du Carrousel itself, as depicted in 'Le Cygne', this city constitutes a 'lieu de mémoire', a palimpsest of multi-levelled living in which a seemingly blank and empty space can nevertheless be underlain or filled with the memory of the bustling habitations and activities of former days. Time passes, leaving the melancholic with a sense of transience; time passes but nothing changes, leaving the melancholic with a sense of repetitiousness and boredom. Either way, a lose-lose situation: 'Paris change! mais rien dans ma mélancolie | N'a bougé!' ('Le Cygne', l. 29-30). This is Time as the enemy: 'Ô douleur! ô douleur! Le Temps mange la vie' ('L'Ennemi', l. 12). But in this city of time ghosts also tap you on the shoulder in broad daylight ('Les Sept Vieillards', l. 2). The past comes out to meet you, and time can be regained through memory, imagination, and art. Not only does the poet of 'Tableaux parisiens' make his own weather, as 'Paysage' implies, he also sets his own clock.

Directly positioned after 'L'Horloge' in the 1861 edition of *Les Fleurs du Mal*, the 'Tableaux parisiens' (poems 86-103) are carefully arranged to evoke the passage of time. Combining eight poems from the 1857 'Spleen et idéal'[25] with ten 'new' poems (all of which had been published in the interim) the section begins with a kind of prologue ('Paysage'), then moves from day to night

---

[23] See Prendergast, *Paris and the Nineteenth Century*, 6. Prendergast recalls Vigny's poem 'Paris' in which the city is described not only as 'le pivot de la France' but as 'l'axe du monde', and quotes Edmond Texier as 'manag[ing] to get most of the relevant clichés into a single paragraph, when in his *Tableau de Paris* [1852] he described Paris as "l'œil de l'intelligence, le cerveau du monde, l'abrégé de l'univers, le commentaire de l'homme, l'humanité faite ville"' (6-7).

[24] Marcel Proust, *A la recherche du temps perdu*, ed. Jean-Yves Tadié (4 vols, Paris: Gallimard [Bibliothèque de la Pléiade], 1987-9), iv. 451.

[25] 'Le Soleil', 'A une mendiante rousse', 'Le Crépuscule du soir', 'Le Jeu', 'Je n'ai pas oublié...', 'La servante au grand cœur...', 'Brumes et pluies', 'Le Crépuscule du matin'.

approximately halfway through with 'Le Crépuscule du soir' (no. 95) and ends with daybreak in 'Le Crépuscule du matin'. The resulting impression is of a city without rest and in which, night after day, day after night, the ticking clock of 'L'Horloge'—'Trois mille six cents fois par heure, la Seconde | Chuchote: *Souviens-toi!*' (ll. 9–10)—allows no let-up in the round-the-clock reality of 'le Mal'. As several critics have noted,[26] poems 87–94 are more concerned with daytime scenes and events (for example, the sunshine of 'Le Soleil', or the morning encounters of 'Le Cygne' (l. 14) and 'Les Sept Vieillards' (l. 5)), while poems 96–102 all evoke the evening or else a moonless night of charmless sex ('Brumes et pluies', ll. 13–14) and the nocturnal realm of dream ('Le Jeu', 'Rêve parisien'). And this diurnal cyclicity is overlaid with the rhythm of the seasons, from the anticipated winter and imagined spring of 'Paysage', through the hot summer sunshine of 'Le Soleil' (ll. 3–4), to the coming winter of 'La servante au grand cœur...' ('Et quand Octobre souffle' (l. 5)) and the miserable seasons of cold and wet evoked with funereal delight in 'Brumes et pluies', where the poet's apostrophe ('Ô fins d'automne, hivers, printemps trempés de boue' (l. 1)) brings us back once more to spring.

This sense of temporal cyclicity is evident throughout the section. In 'Les Sept Vieillards' the nightmare vision of old men popping up one after another out of the fog suggests a view of time in which the usual, slow replacement of one generation by another is so accelerated as to reveal the essential sameness of humanity through the ages such that each generation appears to be both the father and son of itself (l. 43) and such that life is but one long 'cortège infernal' (l. 44). In 'Les Petites Vieilles' the life-cycle is similarly accelerated and distorted. As the old women age, so they become smaller as though they were already preparing to occupy a coffin the size of a child's (ll. 21–2)—or even a cradle:

> Et lorsque j'entrevois un fantôme débile
> Traversant de Paris le fourmillant tableau,
> Il me semble toujours que cet être fragile
> S'en va tout doucement vers un nouveau berceau[.]
>
> (ll. 25–8)

Indeed they still—already?!—have the eyes of a young girl ('Ils ont les yeux divins de la petite fille | Qui s'étonne et qui rit à tout ce qui reluit' (ll. 19–20)), and the poet worries about their safety as if he were their father (l. 75). As envisaged in 'Paysage' this poetic city of Time thus turns the autumn of one's years into spring. It is a place where military bands perform in public gardens 'dans ces soirs d'or où

---

[26] See, for example, Chambers, 'Baudelaire et l'espace poétique', 113–14, where Chambers equates the two sequences respectively with 'le sentiment de l'absence de Dieu (c'est le monde diurne)' and 'celui de la présence de Satan (c'est le monde nocturne)'.

l'on se sent revivre' and '[v]ersent quelque héroïsme au cœur des citadins' (ll. 55-6). In 'À une passante' a momentary glance and a fleeting glimpse together constitute a similar potential turning-point of rebirth and renewal: 'Un éclair... puis la nuit!—Fugitive beauté | Dont le regard m'a fait soudainement renaître' (ll. 9-10), the possible beginning of a whole new 'cycle' of 'love': 'Ô toi que j'eusse aimé, ô toi qui le savais!' (l. 14). A woman dressed in black and in mourning for a death becomes a flash of lightning to lighten the poet's own darkness, as though the passage from night to day and back to night ('puis la nuit!') were once again as accelerated as the temporal process depicted in 'Les Sept Vieillards' and 'Les Petites Vieilles'.

In the beginning is the end, in the end is the beginning. Or not. In 'Le Squelette laboureur' the anatomical drawings depicting flayed or skeletal labourers prompt the poet to wonder if death is neither end nor beginning ('Qu'envers nous le Néant est traître; | Que tout, même la Mort, nous ment' (ll. 25-6)) and if we are all condemned to an eternity of hard labour. 'Danse macabre' might appear to suggest, on the contrary, that we mortals can get ready to party, but Christophe's statuette may more especially imply that even in life we are already just bone and no skin, let alone that flesh we all think so important but which in reality so quickly loses its bloom. Such conjectures recall the poems of *Les Limbes*, subsequently distributed through 'Spleen et idéal' and 'La Mort', in which melancholy is figured as a sense of indifferentiation between life and death.[27]

But in several poems, notably 'Le Cygne' and 'Les Petites Vieilles', time is not an endless sameness but a two-way street—and a street in which the movement of traffic is called art, and sometimes poetry. 'Le Cygne' begins, famously, with a thought: 'Andromaque, je pense à vous!' This thought is a thought in the present in that the poet, here beginning to write his poem, is thinking of Andromache—as is (and will be) the reader on reading this first line. But this is also an act of thinking related in the historic present of a narrative about the poet's recent walk through the newly laid-out Place du Carrousel when he remembered how in a more distant past he had seen a swan from a menagerie searching for water in the dust and had been put in mind of Andromache, herself captured, exiled, and deprived. This 'double present'—of writing and remembering—is repeated in the third stanza: 'Je ne vois qu'en esprit tout ce camp de baraques' (l. 9), where the poet both remembers now as he writes and also how previously on his walk he had remembered the busy fairground that had once occupied this site. This latter memory is developed further in the conventional narrative tenses of the imperfect and the past historic (ll. 13-28), together with the present tense of reported speech (l. 23), before the poet returns to his 'double present' (of writing and of his recent walk): 'Paris change! mais rien dans ma mélancolie | N' a bougé!', 'tout pour moi

---

[27] Or day and night. Baudelaire at one stage thought of including 'Le Crépuscule du soir' and 'Le Crépuscule du matin' in *Les Limbes*. See above, Chapter 6.

devient allégorie', 'mes chers souvenirs sont plus lourds que des rocs'. In the following stanza (ll. 33–6) the present tense is apparently the historic present of his walk ('Aussi devant ce Louvre une image m'opprime: | Je pense à mon grand cygne'), and this tense is then employed throughout the remainder of the poem: 'Je pense à la négresse', 'Je pense aux matelots'. But this present tense is also the 'double present' of writing as well as of the remembered walk such that the distinction itself blurs into irrelevance: to write this poem is to take a walk in the past, and to take a walk down a cultural memory lane.

In the narrative past (of the historic present) the sight of the swan preceded the thought of Andromache: 'Je pense à mon grand cygne [...] et puis à vous, | Andromaque', but within the structure of the poem that sequence is reversed. Like the fleeting glimpse of a woman passing in the street, a sudden, random thought has sprung up from the poet's cultural memory, the thought of this other woman, Andromache, also in mourning for her loss. In the first instance the poet's memory—prompted perhaps by a present melancholy of his own ('rien dans ma mélancolie | N'a bougé')—is of a story relayed down the ages to the present (and the future) in the poetic works of Homer, Euripides, Virgil, Ovid, and Racine.[28] Within the structure of the poem this sudden thought of Andromache in mourning by a river, a thought born of reading (epic and dramatic) poetry, is what *then* 'fecundates' this particular lyric poet's own 'mémoire fertile', his own personal memory of a real event in his own past, the sighting of the escaped swan in the now demolished Quartier du Doyenné. In this way the poem invites a view of time as a continuum along which memory and poetry facilitate a two-way traffic, here manifest in the 'double present' of the poet's tense usage and also in the further 'double present' of a combined personal and cultural memory. This combination is evoked in the final stanza:

> Aussi dans la forêt où mon esprit s'exile
> Un vieux Souvenir sonne à plein souffle du cor!
> Je pense aux matelots oubliés dans une île,
> Aux captifs, aux vaincus!... à bien d'autres encor!
>
> (ll. 49–52)

Now associating himself with the swan, as he similarly associates himself elsewhere with the old women and the beggar-girl, the blind and the female passer-by, the melancholic poet—as the inhabitant of a city—must needs situate his own exile metaphorically in the forest. Here it is the hunting horn of memory—of the memory of other people, of the living, the dead, and the imagined—that allows him to find his own bearings in the forest and to collaborate in his mind not with

---

[28] On the related idea of the city as a (historical and cultural) palimpsest, see Patrick Labarthe, 'Baudelaire, Paris et "le palimpseste de la mémoire"', *L'Année Baudelaire*, 18/19 (2014–15), 245–61.

the hunters but with the hunted: sailors punished by being left marooned, prisoners taken in war, all those who have been defeated in a struggle. The final hemistich closes the poem by opening up the future prospect of endless memories and endless conjectures, as though such mental journeys were a permanent feature of life in the city of time: 'Andromaque, je pense à vous! [...et] à bien d'autres encor!' These others are among the subjects of the following poems, of which many figure in the title or first line an individual or category of human beings that is being brought to mind—and brought back to life—by words: like the forgotten nanny of 'La servante au grand cœur...' whom the poet imagines leaving her eternal bed and returning on a cold December night to watch over him with a fond, maternal eye.

In 'Le Cygne' time is thus presented as a place of passage along which memory allows the poet to move backwards and backwards at will. Similarly in 'Les Petites Vieilles' the poet begins in a timeless present of repeated action: 'Je guette [...] | Des êtres singuliers, décrépits et charmants' (ll. 2-3), once again combining in a 'double present' the act of writing about these women and his continuing habit of following them through the streets of Paris, just as he combines in a further 'double present' his own personal memories of their appearance with the cultural memories that informed his attempts to imagine them in the guise of their younger selves. 'Éponine ou Laïs!' (l. 6), he wonders, remembering respectively the heroism of a Roman revolutionary's wife and the profession of a courtesan in ancient Greece. He maintains this 'double present' throughout the first two sections, exhibiting his 'modern' perspective by further comparing these women of today with the women of Greece and Rome in former times (ll. 37-40): one, once enamoured of Frascati wine now long since drunk, was like a Vestal virgin, sacred servant of the temple that is a Parisian bar;[29] another was an actress, priestess to Thalia, Greek muse of comedy, but whose name no one now remembers save the prompt who is buried beneath the earth as once he was buried beneath the stage; and another, some birdbrain celeb as might once have graced the shade of the flowering Tivoli gardens but whose own bloom has also long since faded. In the third section the poet then situates his observations of these elderly women within a perspective of retrospect: 'Ah! que j'en ai suivi de ces petites vieilles!' (l. 49) and switches to the imperfect of repeated action to describe one woman's regular evening attendance at the performance of a military brass band. Perhaps the widow of a soldier, like Andromache, this melancholic figure is herself a kind of exile, sitting 'Pensive [...] à l'écart sur un banc' (l. 52). Like the poet of 'Le Cygne' attending to the 'plein souffle du cor' of his memories, so too she listens to 'un de ces concerts, riches de cuivre' (l. 53), absorbed in her loss but desperate to imbibe the live spirit of heroism (l. 56) imparted by the band ('Humait avidement

---

[29] See i. 1019, n. 3 to p. 90.

ce chant vif et guerrier' (l. 58)) and to recover the past—perhaps her husband's past of firm discipline and noble exploit—by adopting an overtly military bearing: 'droite encor, fière et sentant la règle' (l. 57), 'Son front de marbre avait l'air fait pour le laurier!' (l. 60).

Here the poet remembers one woman remembering. In the fourth and final section he then proceeds to remember on behalf of all of them:

> Je vois s'épanouir vos passions novices;
> Sombres ou lumineux, je vis vos jours perdus;
> Mon cœur multiplié jouit de tous vos vices!
> Mon âme resplendit de toutes vos vertus!
>
> (ll. 77–80)

Where once (in 1851) Baudelaire had examined the consumption of wine and the smoking of hashish as the 'moyens de la multiplication de l'individualité' (i. 377), here the time travel of memory and imagination serves a similar purpose: 'Toutes m'enivrent!' (l. 41). And he completes his multiple vicarious conjectures by encompassing all of time in his comparison of these elderly ladies to the first woman: 'Où serez-vous demain, Èves octogénaires [...]?' (l. 83). As in 'Le Cygne' the poem thus ends by opening out onto a future, but in this case onto a future that we know must since have ceased—as the poet himself already fears: 'Mais moi, moi qui de loin tendrement vous surveille, | L'œil inquiet, fixé sur vos pas incertains' (ll. 73–4). In both cases the final note is one of compassion.

In 'Les Petites Vieilles' time is thus ultimately telescoped, along with all women who have ever lived, into a vision of the eternal feminine, whereas in a reverse process in 'Les Sept Vieillards' the sight of one old man turns into a proliferating nightmare vision of the eternal masculine. In this case the poet's time travel produces not compassion but disgust ('Dégoûtant Phénix' (l. 43)), not an exhilarating intoxication of the imagination but a negative 'ivresse' of which the symptoms are double vision, fever, and incipient insanity:

> Exaspéré comme un ivrogne qui voit double,
> Je rentrai, je fermai ma porte épouvanté,
> Malade et morfondu, l'esprit fiévreux et trouble,
> Blessé par le mystère et par l'absurdité!
>
> (ll. 45–8)

Here the multiplication is outside the poet's own agency ('[c]e sinistre vieillard qui se multipliait' (l. 36)) and threatens to continue into the future, the future of his own death ('Aurais-je, sans mourir, contemplé le huitième [?]' (l. 41), and this because it represents a paradoxical multiplication of sameness, a world without difference and a world without end: 'Ces sept monstres hideux avaient l'air éternel!' (l. 40). Each 'new' man is the same old man, '[s]osie inexorable, ironique et fatal' (l. 42), and the only cultural memory that comes to the poet's mind as he contemplates these men is of the Wandering Jew (l. 25). A mythical immortal man and thus an emblem of the never-endingly identical, this creation of medieval legend was held to have mocked Christ on his way to the Cross and to have been condemned to walk the earth until the Second Coming (of Christ).[30] As such, his proliferating figure in 'Les Sept Vieillards' bodies forth the poet's own melancholy as it exists *before* he first sets eyes on him: 'Je suivais, roidissant mes nerfs comme un héros | Et discutant avec mon âme déjà lasse, | Le faubourg secoué par les lourds tombereaux' (ll. 10–12). The heavy tumbrils already suggest the guillotine and the seemingly endless executions that took place (not far from the Place du Carrousel) on what was then called the Place de la Révolution (formerly the Place Louis XV, subsequently the Place de la Concorde). Moreover the men themselves seem almost to have been produced by the 'brouillard sale et jaune' by which the poet-flâneur is surrounded: 'un vieillard dont les guenilles jaunes | Imitaient la couleur de ce ciel pluvieux | ... | M'apparut' (ll. 13–17), as though they were shape-shifting spirits—or ghosts come to tap the melancholy poet on the shoulder.

Here, then, the poet does not move easily backwards and forwards in time but remains locked in a nightmare present of endless repetition: not the active and knowing producer of a 'double present' but the passive victim of 'double vision',[31] like that of a drunk who can only see a single object as though it were two—in a mockery of universal analogy: 'Les maisons, dont la brume allongeait la hauteur, | Simulaient les deux quais d'une rivière accrue' (ll. 6–7); 'un vieillard dont les guenilles jaunes | Imitaient la couleur de ce ciel pluvieux' (ll. 13–14); 'décor semblable à l'âme de l'acteur,| [-] | Un brouillard sale et jaune inondait tout l'espace' (ll. 8–9). All things, including poetic agency, look the same within the fog of melancholy. Whereas in 'Les Petites Vieilles' the plurality of women and the 'multiplication' afforded by the poet's vicarious emotional involvement in their past lives makes him want to see them again, here the multiplication of these old men bids fair to frighten him to death. Whereas the title of 'Les Petites Vieilles'

---

[30] This legend had quite recently been brought to the attention of the reading public by Eugène Sue's novel *Le Juif errant* (1844–5).

[31] For a very different account of Baudelaire's 'double vision' in relation to time, and one which puts the emphasis heavily on blurredness and incoherence, see Françoise Melzer, *Seeing Double: Baudelaire's Modernity* (Chicago: University of Chicago Press, 2011). For Melzer 'the poems of Baudelaire [...] record a double vision: one of the world as it was, and one as it is' (5–6), and she sees Baudelaire as unable to reconcile the two: 'Baudelaire's texts record his inability to focus on the same point with both eyes' (17). For her this double vision produces an 'unwilled [...] collision that reveals [...] what has been called Baudelaire's modernity—one that he did not fully understand, and that was frequently unwelcome' (21). In Melzer's view Baudelaire's 'melancholia is a mourning for a past he will not relinquish, but also a fear of a future that he sees as toxic' (195). In essence she accepts Benjamin's findings about the fragmentation and sense of 'alienation' present in Baudelaire's 'vision' of modern life but takes these as evidence not of percipience but of confusion: 'What I have been calling his double vision is the result, not of some clarity of thought born of a coherent perspective on the chaos of early modernity, but rather of the overlaying of disparate realities that remain, opposingly, in the poet's gaze' (248).

lumps all the women together and yet each one is different, the title of 'Les Sept Vieillards' promises differentiated individuality and yet each man is the same.[32] Number two is indistinguishable from number one:

> Son pareil le suivait: barbe, œil, dos, bâton, loques,
> Nul trait distinguait, du même enfer venu,
> Ce jumeau centenaire, et ces spectres baroques
> Marchaient du même pas vers un but inconnu.
>
> (ll. 29–32)

And identical twins become identical septuplets. No need to linger—in fact, better not—to see number eight.

Whereupon the poet returns home, by implication to the safe garret of 'Paysage', there to shelter from the mental storm (l. 50) of a deep psychological and metaphorically meteorological depression and perhaps to write this poem: to take back control (cf. 'Vainement ma raison voulait prendre la barre' (l. 49)) by creating the eurhythmy of these thirteen stanzas of crossed rhymes. Where there was endless proliferation, now there is measure and number and constraint.[33] The 'vieille gabarre | Sans mâts, sur une mer monstrueuse et sans bords!' (ll. 51–2) that was the poet's soul, a flat-bottomed barge adapted to city rivers and without a keel to steady it in the heavy seas of mental disarray, has been transformed into the ship of *Fusées*, an ark in which to sail upon the diluvian fog of the city of Time: 'Un brouillard sale et jaune *inondait* tout l'espace' (l. 9; my emphasis). Instead of the double vision of despair there can be the double vision of simile and metaphor, of a poetic city in which repetition creates difference not sameness: 'On eût dit sa prunelle trempée | Dans le fiel' (ll. 17–18), 'sa barbe à long poils, roide comme une épée' (l. 19); 'son bâton, parachevant sa mine, | Lui donnait la tournure et le pas maladroit | [-] D'un quadrupède infirme ou d'un juif à trois pattes' (ll. 22–4); 'il allait s'empêtrant, | Comme s'il écrasait des morts sous ses savates' (ll. 26–7). And instead of the double vision of despair there can be the 'double present' of writing and memory, or what Baudelaire in *Le Peintre de la vie moderne* will later call 'une contention de mémoire résurrectionniste, évocatrice, une mémoire qui dit à chaque chose: "Lazare, lève-toi!"' (ii. 699). Sometimes that double vision, a 'contention' or tension between past and present, nature and art—such as the co-presence of natural beauty and literary artifice in 'À une mendiante rousse'— may knowingly skew the focus as an object lesson in how not to write an urban eclogue, but elsewhere, and particularly in those poems that evoke the art of caricature, 'Tableaux parisiens' illustrates the claim made at the beginning of

---

[32] For an analysis of the ramifications of this difference see Ronjaunee Chatterjee, 'Baudelaire and Feminine Singularity', *French Studies*, 70 (2015), 17–32.

[33] This recalls 'Obsession' where the strict prosodic requirements of the sonnet form offset the proliferation of images ('jaillissant de mon œil par milliers') by which the poet is 'besieged'.

'Les Petites Vieilles': 'tout, même l'horreur, tourne aux enchantements' ('Les Petites Vieilles', l. 2).

If the poet of 'Le Cygne' observes that 'tout pour moi devient allégorie', he means in that context that his melancholy is so all-encompassing that everything he sees—in this case: 'palais neufs, échafaudages, blocs, | Vieux faubourgs' (ll. 30–1)—is just another version of the same old story about transience and the unstoppable march of time. Even Paris, his home, this ancient city, is changing! Life is a permanent building site, a constant reminder of impermanence. In this case the 'double vision' of allegory—seeing something and seeing what it means— is comparable with the endless series of old men emerging like wraiths from the fog, a vision of eternal sameness. But through the willed exercise of the imagination—'Je veux, pour composer chastement mes églogues'—the poet as alternative lawgiver has the power to create allegories (that is, forms of 'other-speak') which point not to sameness but to difference and to an endless proliferation of the new: in other words, the capacity to 'bâtir dans la nuit mes féeriques palais'.[34] As 'Rêve parisien' suggests, not least by the rude awakening with which it ends ('La pendule aux accents funèbres | Sonnait brutalement midi'), poetry can be a form of 'dream space', a time out of time, like the urban skies into which the new poet-seer of 'Paysage' aspires to gaze. With allegory this poet can hope to express the world differently for the benefit of others, to create an intoxicating sense of fresh discovery. As Baudelaire writes in *Les Paradis artificiels*: 'l'allégorie, ce genre si *spirituel*, que les peintres maladroits nous ont accoutumés à mépriser, mais qui est vraiment l'une des formes primitives et les plus naturelles de la poésie, reprend sa domination légitime dans l'intelligence illuminée par l'ivresse' (i. 430). Like the engraver celebrated in 'Le Squelette laboureur', the poet as alternative lawgiver will not so much speak truth (or say sooth) to power, as the seers and soothsayers (and astrologers) of old were called upon to do, as communicate beauty to melancholy: and he will do so in 'Dessins'—or 'Tableaux parisiens'—'auxquels la gravité | Et le savoir d'un vieil artiste, | Bien que le sujet en soit triste, | Ont communiqué la Beauté'. In these 'Tableaux parisiens', where the emphasis is on the poet's interaction with humanity at large, it is perhaps particularly appropriate to find this new emphasis on a shared memory and a shared history, and in particular on the shared memory of art, literature, and mythology and the shared beauty of poetry from Homer and Virgil to Ronsard and Racine. The poet-artist as double agent, communicating beauty to melancholy as though he were unaware that beauty also changes, fades, and dies, is the poet also as double visionary: present builder of fresh new verbal palaces out of the linguistic rubble of the past, the modern master of an ancient medium.

---

[34] *Pace* Stamelman, 'The Shroud of Allegory', 392, where, taking his cue from Benjamin, Stamelman sees allegory as 'the literary mode that posits an unbridgeable distance between itself and a referent that it can never fully signify or recover'. Cf. Benjamin: 'The allegories stand for that which the commodity makes of the experiences people have in this century' (*Arcades Project*, 328 [J55, 13]).

19
The Poet and the City
The Seer as Sightseer in 'Tableaux parisiens'

Aussi devant ce Louvre une image m'opprime.
('Le Cygne', l. 33)

As figured in 'Tableaux parisiens' the poet's relationship with the world around him is thus ambivalent, a by now familiar conflicted experience of 'spleen' and 'idéal': that is, of 'la conscience dans le Mal' with its associated feelings of despair and powerlessness in tension with a countermanding will to exercise the creative imagination. Coming after 'Spleen et idéal' this section may imply the poet's desire to escape from his own melancholic self-absorption by plunging into the world of others, but, if so, his desire is doomed, for like the traveller of 'Un voyage à Cythère' he simply comes upon images that reflect back to him the reality of his own mortal condition: 'À quiconque a perdu ce qui ne se retrouve' ('Le Cygne', l. 45). This is the negative sense of 'tout pour moi devient allégorie'. As he looks at others he is still looking at himself, self-consciously engaging in a dialogue with self that is in effect a monologue: 'Et discutant avec mon âme déjà lasse' ('Les Sept Vieillards', l. 11); 'Contemple-les, mon âme' ('Les Aveugles', l. 1); 'Recueille-toi, mon âme' ('Le Crépuscule du soir', l. 29). When he walks the foggy streets of the city this particular poet-flâneur remains the subject of his own ironic gaze: 'roidissant mes nerfs comme un héros' ('Les Sept Vieillards', l. 10), as he wryly tells us, a very nervous hero of modern life. Perhaps, like the army widow, he needs to listen to a military band. If dialogue is the emblematic activity of a city, of a life in community,[1] then this poet seems paradoxically drawn to those who live alone and speak to no one, or to images of the dead who cannot speak, or to a swan that cannot sing. The city is a place of groups, as the plural titles suggest ('Les Sept Vieillards', 'Les Petites Vieilles', 'Les Aveugles'), but for this poet it is the locus of individual isolation, of the kind represented by the haunting image of the swan desperately searching for the water of life. If it is true that one is never lonelier than in a city, then 'Tableaux parisiens' appears to illustrate that truth.

Read sequentially, the poems show the poet at first locking himself away in pursuit of his own writing ('Paysage'), then walking the streets ('il descend dans les

---

[1] See Prendergast, *Paris and the Nineteenth Century*, 23.

villes' ('Le Soleil', l. 17)), observing a beggar-girl ('À une mendiante rousse'), recalling a past scene when crossing the Place du Carrousel ('Le Cygne'), fleeing home in terror after a nightmare vision of old men emerging from the fog ('Je rentrai, je fermai ma porte, épouvanté' ('Les Sept Vieillards', l. 46)), then venturing out again to observe old women ('L'œil inquiet, fixé sur vos pas incertains' (l. 74)), and then the blind, and a woman in mourning, and a bouquiniste's anatomical drawings. At day's end, as darkness falls, he takes in the urban scene ('Le Crépuscule du soir') before withdrawing into an inner world of dream ('Le Jeu'), of imagination ('Danse macabre', 'L'Amour du mensonge'), and of memory ('Je n'ai pas oublié...'), 'La servante au grand cœur...'). Following an oblique celebration of sleep and darkness in 'Brumes et pluies' ('Endormeuses saisons!', 'l'aspect permanent de vos pâles ténèbres', ll. 2, 12), the poet records a further city dream in 'Rêve parisien' ('Le sommeil est plein de miracles!' (l. 5)) from which he awakes to an awful reality ('J'ai vu l'horreur de mon taudis' (l. 54)) before ending with an overview of the urban scene at dawn in 'Le Crépuscule du matin'—from which poem, for the first time in 'Tableaux parisiens', his own first-person voice is absent, as though he himself had been swallowed up in the anonymity of the city.

This in turn prepares for the ventriloquism of 'Le Vin' in which the poet briefly continues his exploration of the lives of others—the ragpicker, the murderer, the solitary, the lover—and in his own voice (except in the case of the ragpicker, that parody of a lawgiver) he acts out the suffering of each, a suffering here countermanded not by creativity but by the bravado and hubris induced by alcohol: 'Je m'en moque comme de Dieu, | Du Diable ou de la Sainte Table!' ('Le Vin de l'assassin', ll. 51-2); 'l'orgueil, ce trésor de toute gueuserie, | Qui nous rend triomphants et semblables aux Dieux!' ('Le Vin du solitaire', ll. 13-14); 'Partons à cheval sur le vin | Pour un ciel féerique et divin!' ('Le Vin des amants', ll. 3-4). In each case the drunk performs his own act of 'révolte', thinking he is God or indeed superior to God, but the poet seemingly knows better—until 'Révolte' itself, that is, where in these three poems the poet joins his fellow sufferers in similarly blasphemous protest and in his own poetic demonstrations of bravado and hubris.[2]

The poet's ambivalent relationship with the city in 'Tableaux parisiens' figures not only as a mirroring but also as an oscillation: between engagement and withdrawal and between activity and passivity. So, too, had his relationships with women in 'Spleen et idéal': now the ardent supplicant, now the rejected victim; now the vengeful ex-lover, now the resigned aspirant to calm. Here in 'Tableaux parisiens', in the realms both of the physical world and of his own inner reality, the poet is at once subject and object. Out in the world he is overwhelmed by the old men, feeling himself to be the victim of a plot or some evil happenstance

---

[2] The drunk's mockery of 'la Sainte Table' in 'L'Âme de l'assassin' links that poem back to the parody of the Eucharist in 'L'Âme du vin' so that together the two poems anticipate the blasphemy of 'Révolte'.

('Les Sept Vieillards', ll. 33–4), but in the case of the old women, for all that he is 'obéissant à mes humeurs fatales' ('Les Petites Vieilles', l. 3), he daily seeks them out and actively derives 'des plaisirs clandestins' (l. 76) from his vicarious involvement in their imagined pasts (ll. 77–80). Within his inner world the dream described in 'Le Jeu' comes to him unbidden: 'Voilà le noir tableau qu'en un rêve nocturne | Je vis se dérouler' (ll. 13–14), but in 'Rêve parisien', by contrast, he himself appears to have consciously created the dream. Indeed *he* is the painter of the tableau:

> Le sommeil est plein de miracles!
> Par un caprice singulier,
> J'avais banni de ces spectacles
> Le végétal irrégulier,
>
> Et, peintre fier de mon génie,
> Je savourais dans mon tableau
> L'enivrante monotonie
> Du métal, du marbre et de l'eau.
>
> (ll. 5–12)

Just as in 'La Chevelure' where the poet's experience of 'ivresse', of a quasi-timeless state of heightened perception and sensual satisfaction, is described as 'féconde paresse' and thus identified as the paradox of a productive passivity and inactivity, so here also the 'enivrante monotonie' of the oneiric cityscape—unlike the terrifying repetitiveness of the old men—provides a vision of exciting sameness, of an intoxicating lack of tonal and/or chromatic differentiation, and thus evokes also perhaps the delight of a beautiful melancholy wrought from the 'monotonous' regularity of verse.

But how has this come about? For an ambiguity remains. 'J'avais banni' suggests the artist's willed exclusion of messily organic nature from his tableau, just as later he describes how as '[a]rchitecte de mes féeries, | Je faisais, à ma volonté, | Sous un tunnel de pierreries | Passer un océan dompté' (ll. 37–40). Painter and architect he may be, and yet 'miracles' and 'un singulier caprice' suggest some other cause. Whether God or 'inspiration' or random whim may have been that cause, the ambiguity surrounding the creative act—as discussed earlier in this book—is plainly evident. Does the dream dream the poet, or does the poet dream the dream? Is he the passive seer, granted visions from above, or is he the active sightseer who creates them for us here below? The juxtaposition of 'À une passante' and 'Le Squelette laboureur' presents this (unanswerable) question through a particularly stark contrast. In 'À une passante' beauty has presented itself unsolicited to the poet, in a flash, and is just as quickly gone: 'Fugitive beauté | [...] | Ne te verrai-je plus que dans l'éternité?' (ll. 9–11). In 'Le Squelette laboureur', on the other hand, the beauty of these 'planches d'anatomie' has been finely wrought (ll. 5-8):

> Dessins auxquels la gravité
> Et le savoir d'un vieil artiste,
> Bien que le sujet en soit triste
> Ont communiqué la Beauté[.]
>
> (ll. 5-8)

But the unanswerable question is not even a question. The poet of 'Tableaux parisiens', as of both *Les Fleurs du Mal* and *Le Spleen de Paris*, is both finder and maker of beauty, a double agent: a flâneur who pretends to record chance encounters and strange circumstance, and an artist who constructs his tableaux with all the skill and gravity of ... a 'graveur'.

Seeing

> Tout pour l'œil
>
> ('Rêve parisien', l. 51)

Within the context of the revised, second edition of *Les Fleurs du Mal*, following the poems of 'Spleen et idéal', 'Tableaux parisiens' presents the poet no longer as a solitary seeker after beauty but as an individual immersed in the lives of others and as a poet-artist (and double agent) imaginatively engaged in the melancholic space-time of the city. As is epitomized in 'À une passante' the poet sees others and now also sees others seeing him, a meeting of eyes that instantaneously establishes a mysterious but unmistakable bond. With each new chance encounter and each new sudden memory the poet confronts an image of his own mortal condition and is united—in melancholic awareness of the realities of loss, pain, and decay—not only with a thirsting swan but with his fellow human beings, both men and women, both the quick and the dead. But with each new sighting of eye and mind there comes also a new stimulus to his poetic creativity, a series of conjectures and dreams, a collection of tableaux.

Seeing is a major motif in the 'Tableaux parisiens'. In 'Paysage', as discussed earlier, the poet chooses his symbolic vantage-point on high, like an astrologer trying to get a closer look at the heavens. But as he switches his gaze from the celestial to the terrestrial, the recurrence of the verb 'voir' bears witness to the non-transcendental focus of the poet as alternative lawgiver: 'Je verrai l'atelier' (l. 6), 'Il est doux [...] de voir naître' (l. 9), 'Je verrai les printemps' (l. 13). In the first two of these statements the act of seeing is literal and physical, but already in the third it is part literal (the poet will see the evidence of the changing seasons) and part metaphorical (he will experience the passing of time). The repetition of 'voir' is accompanied by a repetition of 'rêver': 'écouter en rêvant | Leurs hymnes solennels' (ll. 3–4), 'les grands ciels qui font rêver d'éternité' (l. 8), '[a]lors je rêverai des horizons bleuâtres' (l. 17). Within the narrative sequence of the poem, external observation is thus supplemented and then replaced by inner perception. Moreover, as these three uses of 'rêver' record, passive dreaming prompted by external phenomena (hymns, skies) is replaced by active dreaming, by an inner sight that creates its own object: in other words, by the imagination—the creative capacity that images our mental world. In this way the poet as inhabitant of a building becomes himself the builder: 'Pour bâtir dans la nuit mes féeriques palais' (l. 16), and the passive seer of ancient times becomes the active sightseer of a new kind of poetry. No longer the transmitter of eternal verities, he has become the poetic medium of fleeting quotidian visions.

In 'Tableaux parisiens' eyes are everywhere, like a Surrealist motif, whether it be the beggar-girl's breasts peeping out from her tattered dress ('Tes deux beaux seins, radieux | Comme des yeux' ('À une mendiante rousse', ll. 23–4)) or the lamp at dawn that resembles 'un œil sanglant qui palpite et qui bouge' in 'Le Crépuscule du matin' (l. 5).[3] In 'Je n'ai pas oublié...' the setting sun gazes in through the window, 'grand œil ouvert dans le ciel curieux' (l. 7), appearing to '[c]ontempler nos dîners longs et silencieux' (l. 8). The sun is the spectator while human life presents a picture, a tableau of quiet domestic life—perhaps resembling the Last Supper—in a little white house 'voisine de la ville (l. 1).[4] In 'À une passante', conversely, the eye is the sky, and a threatening sky at that with its nascent eye of the storm ('son œil, ciel livide où germe l'ouragan' (l. 7)). Life within this symbolic city of humanity is not only a two-way street but also a two-way spectacle, a matter of seeing and being seen, and thus once again a form of double vision.[5] Each moment is a potential tableau during which the effect of beauty strikes like lightning to illuminate the darkness of melancholy ('Un éclair... puis la nuit!' (l. 9)): an electrical and electrifying charge that sparks new life in the poet: 'Fugitive beauté | Dont le regard m'a fait soudainement renaître' (ll. 9–10).

Individual human beings are defined by the expression in their eyes: the beggar-girl glancing longingly at cheap costume jewellery ('À une mendiante rousse', ll. 49–50); the African woman with her 'œil hagard', desperately hoping to spot a

---

[3] Cf. Prendergast, *Paris and the Nineteenth Century*, 33: 'In "[Le] Crépuscule du matin", we are a long way from the purifying and unifying light that comes with daybreak over Wordsworth's London in "Westminster Bridge". The natural light that appears over Baudelaire's Paris is from the start poisoned by its passage through the artificial light of the gas lamps, the light of Evil rendered in the dramatically violent image of the bleeding eye.'

[4] The following poem, 'La servante au grand cœur...', ends with a similar tableau, there of the servant seated in nocturnal vigilance.

[5] Cf. Macé, 'Baudelaire, une esthétique de l'existence', 52: 'D'ailleurs les yeux eux-mêmes, chez Baudelaire, voient moins qu'ils ne sont à voir, comme des tableaux profonds.'

coconut palm in downtown Paris ('Le Cygne', ll. 42–3); the loving servant who once cared for the poet as a child and whom he now imagines returning to watch over him 'de son œil maternel' (l. 20); even the female skeleton in 'Danse macabre', whose deep eye-sockets—'faits de vide et de ténèbres' (l. 13)—can still be read: 'Le gouffre de tes yeux, pleins d'horribles pensées' (l. 37). People, including therefore the dead, are epitomized by their look—what they look like, how they look at others—such as the first old man 'dont l'aspect aurait fait pleuvoir les aumônes, | Sans la méchanceté qui luisait dans ses yeux' (ll. 15–16). He, too, appears with the suddenness of lightning as he looms up abruptly out of the fog (an abruptness reinforced by the enjambement across the stanza break) and instantly presents the poet with the sharpest image of hatred, violence, and treachery:

> Tout à coup, un vieillard [...]
>
> M'apparut. On eût dit sa prunelle trempée
> Dans le fiel; son regard aiguisait les frimas,
> Et sa barbe à long poils, roide comme une épée,
> Se projetait, pareille à celle de Judas.
>
> (ll. 13, 17–20)

Here a surface appearance of deserving poverty is belied by a gaze of bitter gall, while in the eyes of the elderly women an expression of penetrating shrewdness and dark wisdom is offset by a look of purest innocence and delight:

> [Ces monstres disloqués] ont des yeux perçants comme une vrille,
> Luisants comme ces trous où l'eau dort dans la nuit;
> Ils ont les yeux divins de la petite fille
> Qui s'étonne et qui rit à tout ce qui reluit.
>
> (ll. 17–20)

No wonder the poet has double vision. Now he in turn invokes the reader's eyes: 'Avez-vous observé [...]?' (l. 21), before returning to his own ocular activities: the glimpse ('lorsque j'entrevois' (l. 25)) and the sizing-up (ll. 29–32), as he wonders how coffin-makers cope with all these different corporeal shapes. But he cannot take his eyes off the eyes, for they bring beauty to his condition of melancholy:

> —Ces yeux sont des puits faits d'un million de larmes,
> Des creusets qu'un métal refroidi pailleta ...
> Ces yeux mystérieux ont d'invincibles charmes
> Pour celui que l'austère Infortune allaita!
>
> (ll. 33–6)

When he follows one particular woman, watching her as she listens to the military band, he observes how '[s]on œil parfois s'ouvrait comme l'œil d'un vieil aigle' (l. 59); and, in a further example of double vision, he observes himself watching all of them: 'Mais moi, moi qui de loin tendrement vous surveille, | L'œil inquiet, fixé sur vos pas incertains' (ll. 73-4). They are uncertain and so is he, an unsteady step matched by an unsteady gaze. Life with others is all in the mind's eye. Everyone else fails to 'see' the women: that is, no one recognizes them, a drunk makes an insulting pass at them, a young boy mocks them (ll. 65-8). As to the poet, he sees what he wants to see: 'Je vois s'épanouir vos passions novices' (l. 77) and can live vicariously through them: 'Je vis vos jours perdus' (l. 78)—where the ambiguity of 'je vis' (I live, I saw) itself enacts a double vision of present fantasy and visual access to the past.

In 'Les Aveugles', as already partly discussed, the physical ability to see and the mental capacity to make sense of the human condition underpin a parallel between the blind men walking in the street and a melancholic poet beset by existential doubt ('je me traîne aussi! mais, plus qu'eux hébété' (l. 13)) in a city given over to raucous self-indulgence and the darkness of pleasure (l. 12).[6] At one level this poem offers a 'negative' version of the poet's paradigmatic experience of life in the city as that of seeing and being seen: here the persons under observation physically cannot see him, while he for his part cannot see/understand them and what it is they might be searching for in the sky. The phrase '[c]omme s'ils regardaient au loin' (l. 6) enhances the poignancy of their melancholic situation, ironically recalling the stereotype of the blind seer with superior insight into the ways of destiny[7] and anticipating the description of the inhabitants of Lesbos at the beginning of 'Femmes damnées': 'Comme un bétail pensif sur le sable couchées, | Elle tournent leurs yeux vers l'horizon des mers' (ll. 1-2). The blind would do better, the poet implies, to 'look' down rather than up, like the poet of 'Paysage', and, like him in this poem, to gaze conjecturally, their head heavy with thought (and melancholy?), at the realities to be found at street level (ll. 7-8). That way, like the poet of 'Le Soleil', they might even trip over a rhyme or two and bump into a poem (cf. 'Le Soleil', ll. 6-8). At another level this situation mirrors in reverse the poet's relationship with the city. As his soul 'contemplates' the blind (l. 1), he calls on the city to 'see' (l. 13) him, to *lift* its eyes from its own blind pursuit

---

[6] 'Atrocité' (l. 12) derives etymologically from Latin 'ater, atrum' = black. (Cf. 'atrabilaire'.) This point is made in Peter H. Nurse, '*Les Aveugles* de Baudelaire', *L'Information littéraire*, 8 (Nov.-Dec. 1966), 219-22 (221), reprinted as 'Baudelaire, *Les Aveugles*', in Peter H. Nurse (ed.), *The Art of Criticism: Essays in French Literary Analysis* (Edinburgh: Edinburgh University Press, 1969), 193-203, and taken up in Ross Chambers, 'Seeing and Saying in Baudelaire's "Les Aveugles"', in Robert L. Mitchell (ed.), *Pre-Text, Text, Context: Essays on Nineteenth-Century French Literature* (Columbus, Oh.: Ohio State University Press, 1980), 147-56 (149).

[7] Chambers notes that because the blind are plural in number, 'the centrality of the single blind figure of the archetype has dissolved into a type of collective anonymity' ('Seeing and Saying in Baudelaire's "Les Aveugles"', 148).

of self-gratification and to behold the spectacle, in him, of its own moral bankruptcy and its own metaphysical perplexity.

In 'Le Cygne' and 'L'Amour du mensonge' the mind's eye also plays a central role. 'Je ne vois qu'en esprit tout ce camp de baraques' (l. 9), says the poet of 'Le Cygne', recalling a fair in the erstwhile Quartier du Doyenné,[8] and the poem as a whole establishes a strong parallel between physical and mental sight. As already discussed, the poet recalls in the present how, in another tableau moment, he once and suddenly saw a swan: 'Là, je vis, un matin [...] | Un cygne' (ll. 14, 17). And, like some new-style daytime astrologer who has seen a sign, he still retains it in his mind's eye, and he understands: 'Je vois ce malheureux, mythe étrange et fatal' (l. 24). What he has seen has already become another of the city's ghosts, a strange new, quasi-mythical emblem of melancholy. 'Je vois' and 'je pense' are now synonyms: 'Aussi devant ce Louvre une image m'opprime: | Je pense à mon grand cygne' (ll. 33–4; cf. also ll. 41, 51)). What was once a sight, something seen in the city, has become a mental image, a picture not in the Louvre but in his own mind, a 'tableau parisien'. Where at the end of 'Les Sept Vieillards' the poet fears that he's been seeing things, that he's seeing double, that he's going mad, the poet-sightseer of the 'Tableaux parisiens' does see things, does see double, and finds and makes a poem-dream as a result.

In 'Le Jeu' dream is presented as a form of 'clairvoyance', not the crystal-ball-gazing of fairground seers but a heightened form of perception, and of self-knowledge:

> Voilà le noir tableau qu'en un rêve nocturne
> Je vis se dérouler sous mon œil clairvoyant.
> Moi-même, dans un coin de l'antre taciturne,
> Je me vis accoudé, froid, muet, enviant,
>
> Enviant de ces gens la passion tenace,
> De ces vieilles putains la funèbre gaieté,
> Et tous gaillardement trafiquant à ma face,
> L'un de son vieil honneur, l'autre de sa beauté!
>
> (ll. 13–20)

The scene is a gambling-house-cum-brothel full of ageing whores and (like Dante's limbo perhaps) of 'poëtes illustres', of more old women and more old men. The latter are like male versions of the female skeleton in 'Danse macabre' (the poem that follows 'Le Jeu'), not autonomous living beings but vile bodies in the grip of deadly desire:

---

[8] See Roberto Calasso's eloquent evocation of this historical setting in *La Folie Baudelaire*, 47–51.

Autour des verts tapis des visages sans lèvre,
Des lèvres sans couleur, des mâchoires sans dent,
Et des doigts convulsés d'une infernale fièvre,
Fouillant la poche vide ou le sein palpitant[.]

(ll. 5-8)

The 'courtisanes vieilles' (l. 1) also look dead (cf. 'Pâles' (l. 2) and, like Christophe's statuette, wear jewels ('un cliquetis de pierre et de métal' (l. 4)) such as a beggar-girl might covet and such as might befit the exclusively mineral, inorganic city of 'Rêve parisien'. Once again the eye says it all: 'le sourcil peint, l'œil câlin et fatal' (l. 2): artifice and seductive wiles to facilitate the destiny of desire. Even the chandeliers ('de pâles lustres' (l. 9)) look ghostly in this chamber of death, like huge eyes ('d'énormes quinquets projetant leurs lueurs | Sur des fronts ténébreux des poètes illustres | Qui viennent gaspiller leurs sanglantes sueurs' (ll. 10-11))[9] gazing down with all the menace of the bloodshot eye of the lamp depicted in 'Le Crépuscule du matin' (l. 5).

For the melancholic poet silently observing himself watching from a corner (and 'accoudé' in a posture similar to that of the garret-dweller looking down on the city in 'Paysage'), this scene presents a 'noir tableau' of deadly temptation:

Et mon cœur s'effraya d'envier maint pauvre homme
Courant avec ferveur à l'abîme béant,
Et qui, soûl de son sang, préférerait en somme
La douleur à la mort et l'enfer au néant!

(ll. 21-4)

Permitted by his dream, in anticipation of Freud, to observe his own inner promptings with 'clairvoyance', the poet is frightened by his discovery that he actually envies these people who, in pursuing the excitements of sex and gambling, take a further gamble by risking not only further suffering in this life but the punishment of their immortal soul in the next. That the poet is frightened by this discovery implies that he considers this gamble dangerous and not to be undertaken.[10] What we have here, therefore, is a nightmare vision of people seeking their own destruction ('Courant avec ferveur à l'abîme béant' (l. 22)), a caricatural tableau of 'la passion tenace' (l. 17), of desire in its most grotesque form. For a poet who is constantly torn between powerless passivity and creative agency it may

---

[9] 'Quinquet' was a slang term for the eye, a punning usage to be found very soon afterwards in Mallarmé's 'Le Pitre châtié'. See my *Unfolding Mallarmé* (Oxford: Clarendon Press, 1996), 43.

[10] *Pace* Damian Catani: 'Though the poem ends on a note of moral equivocation, it opens up the possibility of a new post-Romantic subjectivity which is able to recuperate from urban vice a dynamic approach to existence that escapes the moral passivity of "ennui".' See his *Evil: A History*, 52.

therefore represent an option that he knowingly rejects in favour of the 'clairvoyance' afforded by the alternative legislation of his poem-dream.

In the dream world of 'Rêve parisien' sight is similarly all-important: 'terrible nouveauté! | Tout pour l'œil, rien pour les oreilles!' (ll. 51–2). In the opening stanza the 'terrible paysage', at once found and made by the poet's dreaming, has never been seen before ('Tel que jamais mortel n'en vit' (l. 2)), and, unlike the sorry image of the swan that 'oppresses' the poet in 'Le Cygne', it continues to delight the poet after he awakes: 'Ce matin encore l'image, | Vague et lointaine, me ravit' (ll. 3–4). At the end of the poem, after his dream sight, the poet paradoxically *opens* his eyes only to discover (like the poet of the prose poem 'Une chambre double'), the horrible reality of his quotidian surroundings ('En rouvrant mes yeux pleins de flamme | J'ai vu l'horreur de mon taudis' (ll. 53–4)) and to feel once more '[l]a pointe des soucis maudits' (l. 56). Dream sight has held melancholy at bay, and also time itself, for in his dream there was '[u]n silence d'éternité' (l. 52) that prevented him from hearing the ticking of the clock. But now for this late-riser the time for dream is up: 'La pendule aux accents funèbres | Sonnait brutalement midi' (ll. 57–8): the witching hour of day has sounded, and his eyes are filled with darkness. Non-sight awaits, the blindness of day, as well as a waking weariness akin to a sad and dreamless sleep: 'Et le ciel versait des ténèbres | Sur le triste monde engourdi' (ll. 59–60).

In 'L'Amour du mensonge' the poet comes upon a further emblem of melancholy in the guise of another female passer-by. *He* actively looks ('Quand je te vois passer, ô ma chère indolente' (l. 1), 'Quand je contemple [...] | Ton front pâle' (ll. 5–6)), and *she* passively looks: at once bored ('promenant l'ennui de ton regard profond' (l. 4)) and beautiful ('Qu'elle est belle! et bizarrement fraîche!' (l. 9)). The poet gazes especially at her eyes, filled with ennui but to him fascinating: 'tes yeux attirants comme ceux d'un portrait' (l. 8). 'Le beau est toujours bizarre': this woman, 'bizarrement fraîche', is already, even without his own poetic input, a work of art. The poem ends with two quatrains summarizing the aesthetic principle that is central to both 'Tableaux parisiens' and the second edition of *Les Fleurs du Mal*, and perhaps also to *Le Spleen de Paris*:

> Je sais qu'il est des yeux, des plus mélancoliques,
> Qui ne recèlent point de secrets précieux;
> Beaux écrins sans joyaux, médaillons sans reliques,
> Plus vides, plus profonds que vous-mêmes, ô Cieux!
>
> Mais ne suffit-il pas que tu sois l'apparence,
> Pour réjouir un cœur qui fuit la vérité?
> Qu'importe ta bêtise ou ton indifférence?
> Masque ou décor, salut! J'adore ta beauté.
>
> (ll. 17–24)

In his account of Delacroix as the master of modern melancholy Baudelaire had drawn attention to the women in his paintings whose beauty derives from the secret and mysterious suffering that has left its mark on their appearance. But here he envisages a melancholy that is both vacuous and beautiful, like the 'enivrante monotonie' of 'Rêve parisien'. The comparison of this vacuity to that of godless heavens links it to the various expressions of existential anguish and religious scepticism evident elsewhere in the 'Tableaux parisiens' so that the (emotional, moral, intellectual) nullity and disengagement of this beautiful woman (cf. 'ta bêtise ou ton indifférence') may be interpreted as representing the 'mystère' and 'absurdité' that so terrify the poet at the end of 'Les Sept Vieillards'. The 'truth' that the poet here wishes to flee may be a metaphysical one: not 'le Mal' or ill-being of the human condition itself, which he continues to confront and depict, but the inherently contingent and meaningless nature of human existence in the first place. Beauty, on the other hand, is that capacity still to be interested, still to care, despite our knowledge of this truth. If we are not to mirror the bored, empty gaze of this woman, then we ourselves must see with art: 'Masque ou décor, salut! J'adore ta beauté'. Whether the nullity be masked or decorated—masked like the destitution of the beggar-girl, decorated like the female skeleton—transformed it must be. In that transformation lies our 'salut', not a religious redemption from sin but an aesthetic response that is both a new way of seeing and a new way of thinking, a poetics of resistance. To engage in conjecture, to wonder and surmise, to fantasize and imagine, that is what the 'appearance' must stimulate us to do. And whatever does that—however blank or banal or even ugly (this woman is no longer in the first flush of youth...)—is what Baudelaire calls 'beauty'.

Painting

> Je me suis toujours plu à chercher dans la nature extérieure et visible des exemples et des métaphores qui me servissent à caractériser les jouissances et les impressions d'un ordre spirituel.
> ('Marceline Desbordes-Valmore' [1861], ii. 148)

> un kaléidoscope doué de conscience, qui, à chacun de ses mouvements, représente la vie multiple et la grâce mouvante de tous les éléments de la vie.
> (*Le Peintre de la vie moderne*, ii. 692).

'L'Amour du mensonge' thus ends like the prose poem 'Les Fenêtres' (i. 339), first published in 1863 and later collected in *Le Spleen de Paris*: it is not the objective truth that matters, if indeed such a truth exists, but the stimulus to conjecture afforded by the sight that has been seen. In the prose poem the poet gazes out over the rooftops of the city (like the poet of 'Paysage') and in an adjacent building sees a woman: 'une femme mûre, ridée déjà, pauvre, toujours penchée sur quelque chose, et qui ne sort jamais'. Observing her face, her clothing, her gestures, he imagines her story—'ou plutôt sa légende', as though this were not only a legend but a caption to go with the picture—and sometimes recounts it to himself, 'en pleurant'. Perhaps this may even be the poet's own story, for he comments that '[s]i c'eût été un pauvre vieux [sic] homme, j'aurais refait la sienne tout aussi aisément'. Certainly the image of a woman 'penchée sur quelque chose et qui ne sort jamais' directly recalls the poet's own self-image as a writer in 'Paysage', doors firmly shut and eyes resolutely lowered towards his desk (l. 22). 'Peut-être me direz-vous: "Es-tu sûr que cette légende soit la vraie?"', he speculates, and answers his own imagined question with the well-known reply: 'Qu'importe ce que peut être la réalité placée hors de moi, si elle m'a aidé à vivre, à sentir que je suis et ce que je suis?'[11]

Baudelaire's 'Tableaux parisiens' are not holiday snaps but mental and moral landscapes, framed perceptions of reality like a poem or a picture or the view through a window: not so much the view out as the view in, and even then not so much what you can see as what you cannot, quite, see. As the poet of 'Les Fenêtres' begins by saying: 'Celui qui regarde du dehors à travers une fenêtre ouverte, ne voit jamais autant de choses que celui qui regarde une fenêtre fermée.' Here is Baudelaire the anti-Realist once more proclaiming the superiority of the imagination over mimetic observation, the need to see through a glass darkly by the light of a single candle:

Il n'est pas d'objet plus profond, plus mystérieux, plus fécond, plus ténébreux, plus éblouissant qu'une fenêtre éclairée d'une chandelle. Ce qu'on peut voir au soleil est toujours moins intéressant que ce qui se passe derrière une vitre. Dans ce trou noir ou lumineux vit la vie, rêve la vie, souffre la vie.

This is the '[f]ourmillante cité, cité pleine de rêves' of 'Les Sept Vieillards', the city of other people's dreams and aspirations: an extraordinary anthill (cf. 'Le Crépuscule du soir', l. 16) of human activity and of a myriad stories, like those imagined in 'Les Petites Vieilles': 'Toutes m'enivrent' (l. 41).

In his art criticism Baudelaire had long since envisaged the city in these terms as a source of stimulus to the imagination. In the *Salon de 1846* he understood this in terms of being able to see beyond the familiar, in fact of being able to *see*: 'La vie parisienne est féconde en sujets poétiques et merveilleux. Le merveilleux nous enveloppe et nous abreuve comme l'atmosphère; mais nous ne le voyons pas'

---

[11] For an eloquent reading of 'Les Fenêtres' as the account of a '(re)birth' through observation, see Jean-Luc Steinmetz, 'Ontoscopie (sur "Les Fenêtres")', in André Guyaux and Henri Scepi (eds), *Lire 'Le Spleen de Paris'* (Paris: Presses de l'Université Paris-Sorbonne, 2014), 159–66.

(ii. 496). More recently, in the *Salon de 1859*, he had noted a lack of cityscapes among the paintings on display and described in detail just what such an urban 'paysage' might look like:

> un genre que j'appellerais volontiers le paysage des grandes villes, c'est-à-dire la collection des grandeurs et des beautés qui résultent d'une puissante agglomération d'hommes et de monuments, le charme profond et compliqué d'une capitale âgée et vieillie dans les gloires et les tribulations de la vie. (ii. 666)

From this description one could infer that Baudelaire did specifically envisage at least some of the poems of 'Tableaux parisiens' as themselves carrying out this programme, not in offering poetic celebrations of well-known Parisian landmarks (as Hugo had done, for example, in his ode 'À l'Arc de Triomphe') but in depicting the moral landscape of the city as a reflection of 'les gloires et les tribulations de la vie'. In the *Salon de 1859* he cites with approval the recent etchings of Charles Meryon in terms that recall some of the visual ingredients of 'Paysage', first published two years earlier:

> J'ai rarement vu représentée avec plus de poésie la solennité naturelle d'une ville immense. Les majestés de la pierre accumulée, les clochers 'montrant du doigt le ciel',[12] les obélisques de l'industrie vomissant contre le firmament leurs coalitions de fumée [...] le ciel tumultueux, chargé de colère et de rancune, la profondeur des perspectives augmentée par la pensée de tous les drames qui y sont contenus[.] (ii. 666-7)

But for Baudelaire what matters is not the mimetic accuracy of Meryon's etchings but the way in which they capture 'la noire majesté de la plus inquiétante des capitales' (ii. 667) and their power to suggest the dramas of human existence. Landscape art must convey the moral atmosphere of a particular place or scene, and, as his comments on the nature of the artistic process in 'Le Gouvernement de l'imagination' earlier in the *Salon de 1859* make clear, the source of a painting (or any work of art, including a poem) lies in the artist not out in the world. This source is the 'idée génératrice', or 'idée poétique', which, once conceived in the artist's mind or 'temperament' in the form of a dream or vision, must be brought into being through a process of active creation: 'Un bon tableau, fidèle au rêve qui l'a enfanté, doit être produit comme un monde' (ii. 626). In the section entitled 'Le Paysage', on traditional landscape painting, Baudelaire comments that nature in itself is of no consequence: 'un site naturel n'a de valeur que le sentiment actuel que l'artiste y sait mettre' (ii. 660). Like the 'vieil artiste' in 'Le Squelette laboureur'

---

[12] A quotation from Wordsworth's *The Excursion*, derived by Baudelaire from Gautier: see ii. 1408 n. 6.

the poet has to 'communicate beauty' *to* the subject under observation, and this by recalling how the subject initially registered in his emotions (cf. 'la plus inquiétante des capitales') or his imagination, and then reproducing that essential effect (an effect of beauty, of the familiar appearing strange) through conscious artistic technique: 'il faut que tout cela devienne tableau par le moyen de l'impression poétique rappelée à volonté' (ii. 665).

This is precisely what Constantin Guys, celebrated four years later in *Le Peintre de la vie moderne*, is described as doing when he transforms the unnoticed strangeness of today's world into the durability of art:

> En un mot, pour que toute *modernité* soit digne de devenir antiquité, il faut que la beauté mystérieuse que la vie humaine y met involontairement en ait été extraite. C'est à cette tâche que s'applique particulièrement M. G[uys]. (ii. 695)

Like Delacroix before him[13] and like the poet of 'Une charogne',[14] Guys allows time to wipe from his memory the precise but incidental details of some Parisian figure or scene (a kind of information overload that would paradoxically blind him to its underlying formal and moral shape) and thus allows memory to retain and give back the innocence and unknowingness of 'first sight', which is also a childlike harmony of vision or 'ideal' sight',[15] so that he can better bring out the 'beauté mystérieuse' that human beings, involuntarily and unselfconsciously, have conferred by their own actions on the phenomenal world: that is, a dream-like and mysterious suggestiveness that for Baudelaire as the observer of Guys's sketches constitutes beauty. And this beauty consciously 'communicated' by the artist is, as Baudelaire insists repeatedly in his essay on Guys, synonymous with the human desire to understand other human beings and thereby our own place in the world: 'Je ne crois pas exagérer en affirmant que toutes ces considérations morales jaillissent naturellement des croquis et des aquarelles de M. G.' (ii. 708); 'Ce qui fait la beauté particulière de ces images, c'est leur fécondité morale' (ii. 722). And if this is so, then the proper response for the observer and critic of art is to articulate the considerations and reflections about the human condition to which these pictures of life give rise:

---

[13] 'Pour E. Delacroix, la nature est un vaste dictionnaire dont il roule et consulte les feuillets avec un œil sûr et profond; et cette peinture, qui procède surtout du souvenir, parle surtout au souvenir. L'effet produit sur l'âme du spectateur est analogue aux moyens de l'artiste'; 'J'ai déjà remarqué que le souvenir était le grand critérium de l'art; l'art est une mnémotechnie du beau: or, l'imitation exacte gâte le souvenir.' (*Salon de 1846*, ii. 433, 455.)

[14] 'Les formes s'effaçaient et n'étaient plus qu'un rêve, | Une ébauche lente à venir, | Sur la toile oubliée, et que l'artiste achève | Seulement par le souvenir.' ('Une charogne', ll. 29–32.)

[15] 'Tous les matériaux dont la mémoire s'est encombrée se classent, se rangent, s'harmonisent et subissent cette idéalisation forcée qui est le résultat d'une perception *enfantine*, c'est-à-dire d'une perception aiguë, magique à force d'ingénuité!' (*Le Peintre de la vie moderne*, ii. 694)

> Les considérations et les rêveries morales qui surgissent des dessins d'un artiste sont, dans beaucoup de cas, la meilleure traduction que le critique en puisse faire; les suggestions font partie d'une idée mère, et, en les montrant successivement, on peut la faire deviner. (ii. 712)

This statement made in 1863 echoes that with which Baudelaire proclaimed the originality of his own art criticism in the opening section of the *Salon de 1846* and asserted that the most effective response to a painting might take the form of a sonnet or an elegy (i. 418). There his point is that what makes a picture beautiful is the 'reflection' of reality through an artist's 'temperament', so that the best art criticism is likely to be that which emulates this process: that is, 'ce tableau réfléchie par un esprit intelligent et sensible' (i. 418). In 'Tableaux parisiens' the poet combines these two types of 'reflection' into one: creating word pictures that offer, through the lens or 'temperament' of melancholy, predominantly visual impressions of life in the real and metaphorical city of humanity while presenting these word pictures in poetic forms that echo their moral purport—or in what one might call a prosody of melancholy.

As discussed above in Chapter 17, a poem may be described as an 'idée poétique', a fusion of form and content in which 'idea' as notion and 'idea' as form operate together in a common purpose of expression. In 'Tableaux parisiens' this may be seen, for example, at the end of 'Brumes et pluies', where the unorthodox placing of a couplet at the end of a Petrarchan sonnet sits well with the bathetic tone of the poet's imagined remedy for depression: 'Si ce n'est, par un soir sans lune, deux à deux, | D'endormir la douleur sur un lit hasardeux' (ll. 13–14). In 'À une mendiante rousse' the first rhyme ('roux', 'trous') offers an immediate summary of the beggar-girl's salient features, the red hair and the ragged dress, while the ensuing dominance of rhyme in the remainder of the poem—thanks to a rapid incidence of rhyme that results from the shortness of the lines (7/4) and the (unconventional) use of couplets within quatrains—highlights poetic artifice itself in its contrast with the girl's natural beauty.

In 'Les Aveugles' the stuttering, interrupted rhythms (visually underlined by the repeated use of semicolons and exclamation marks) evoke both the tentative movements of the blind and the breathless anguish of the poet. In the second quatrain enjambement serves to dramatize the surprise that the blind should gaze upwards ('restent levés | Au ciel') and to call attention to a possible ironic homonym in the *rejet* ('Ô Ciel'), while in the following couplet the enjambement serves to reinforce a sense of downward movement through the emphatic positioning of the delayed infinitive: 'on ne les voit jamais vers les pavés | Pencher rêveusement leur tête appesantie'. In 'À une passante', similarly, broken rhythms (also foregrounded visually in *points de suspension* and a dash) convey the poet's excitement at his sudden vision of this '[f]ugitive beauté', while the staccato exclamations (and exclamation marks) at the beginning of the second tercet

('Ailleurs, bien loin d'ici! trop tard! *jamais* peut-être') capture the separate stages of the woman's gradual movement away from the poet and her eventual disappearance into the crowd.[16]

Many such examples could be adduced from 'Tableaux parisiens', but it is evident that in his evocations of city life Baudelaire makes particular use of prosodic features, and notably enjambement, that suggest dislocation and interruption. More broadly still it would seem that in the poems written after 1857 he effects an overt dismantling of traditional prosodic forms as a means of conveying the shifting shapes of broken lives and a changing city. It was while sending 'Les Sept Vieillards' to an editor that Baudelaire described this poem as the first in a new series in which he had 'simplement réussi à dépasser les limites assignées à la Poésie'. It cannot be known quite which poems, written and unwritten, belonged in this series, though presumably it included 'Les Petites Vieilles' and 'Le Cygne' and perhaps also 'Les Aveugles', 'À une passante', and 'Le Squelette laboureur' (on the grounds that these are grouped together between two poems—'À une mendiante rousse' and 'Le Crépuscule du soir'—that had already figured in the first edition of *Les Fleurs du Mal*). Nor can it be easily inferred quite which 'limits' of 'Poetry' Baudelaire believed himself to have transgressed and whether, within the fusion of the 'idée poétique', these limits related more to the subject matter or the form. But, as some critics have noted,[17] one particular feature of 'Les Sept

---

[16] For further discussion of 'formal experimentation' in 'A une passante', see Chambers, 'The Storm in the Eye of the Poem: Baudelaire's "A une passante"', in *Textual Analysis: Some Readers Reading*, ed. Mary Ann Caws (New York: Modern Language Association of America, 1986), 156–66 (164).

[17] See Graham Chesters, 'Baudelaire and the Limits of Poetry', *French Studies*, 32 (1978), 420–34, reprinted in revised form in *Baudelaire and the Poetics of Craft*, 145–61; Ross Chambers, 'Are Baudelaire's "Tableaux parisiens" about Paris?', 103–4 and 'Daylight Spectre: Baudelaire's "The Seven Old Men"', *Yale French Studies*, 125: 6 (2014), 45–65, material from which was subsequently incorporated into the same author's *An Atmospherics of the City: Baudelaire and the Poetic of Noise* (New York: Fordham University Press, 2015), ch. 4; and Daniel Finch-Race, 'Placelessness in Baudelaire's "Les Sept Vieillards" and "Les Petites Vieilles"', *Modern Language Review*, 110 (2015), 1011–26. From an ecocritical perspective Finch-Race pursues 'the hypothesis that the structure of poetry is influenced by environmental alterations, the shifting structure of a number of keystone pieces in the 1861 edition of *Les Fleurs du mal* can be equated to the demolition of the sinuous streets of old Paris in favour of capacious boulevards' (1013). In the case of 'Les Sept Vieillards' he identifies and analyses three key features: (i) 'the submersion of the caesura in the flow of a line due to the elision of an *e caduc*, creating a tighter juncture between the sixth and seventh syllables that diminishes medial accentuation'; (ii) 'enjambement within and between stanzas (along with concomitant *rejets* and *contre-rejets*)'; and (iii) 'the strategic use of rhyme that is not *riche* or *léonine*, indicating a weakening of the borders of verse'; and he seeks 'ultimately [to demonstrate] that the prosodic mechanisms at the heart of the "Tableaux parisiens" indicate a threshold for poetry that is analogous to the material transition represented by Haussmann's reconfiguration of Paris' (1015). Cf. also Killick, 'Baudelaire's Versification: Conservative or Radical', where she concludes her overview thus: 'Baudelaire is interested neither in the mechanical observance nor the unconsidered flouting of "rules". Rather, he harnesses the fundamental energies of versification as the driving force in the portrayal of what we might now define as a Modernist or even post-modern crisis of identity. Baudelaire's great achievement is not only to have encapsulated the crucial dilemma of attempted self-construction and persistent self-loss on the level of his images and themes but to have made the challenges and vicissitudes of versification an integral and organic part of his reflection on the human condition' (66).

Vieillards' is the way in which the grotesque, 'caricatural' misshapenness of the old men is reflected in the verse form. At one level this is straightforward: for example, the unorthodox use of enjambement across stanza breaks (rather than merely line breaks) on three occasions (ll. 8–9, 16–17, 24–5) to accompany the (disruptive and distorted) appearance of the first old man.[18] Further enjambement—across the caesura as well as the line and the stanza—reinforces this vision of 'la tournure et le pas maladroit | D'un quadrupède infirme', and there is even a direct correlation of subject and form here in the disrupted metre and metrical feet (cf. 'la tournure et le pas maladroit') and in the irregularity of the quatrains (cf. 'un quadrupède infirme').[19]

In this way Baudelaire creates prosodic tableaux of melancholy: tableaux in the sense of visual descriptions of people and places and objects, whether real and remembered ('Paysage', 'A une mendiante rousse', 'Danse macabre', 'Je n'ai pas oublié...', 'La servante au grand cœur...') or imagined and dreamt ('Le Jeu', 'Rêve parisien'); tableaux in the theatrical sense of frozen scenes in which a whole narrative situation and/or moral dilemma is encapsulated in one image ('Le Cygne', 'À une passante', 'Les Aveugles', 'Le Squelette laboureur'); tableaux featuring successive framed images, sugggestive of cartoon caricature and in unwitting anticipation of cinematography ('Les Sept Vieillards', 'Les Petites Vieilles'); and tableaux as prosodic displays in which disruption, dislocation, and breakage are not only visually apparent in the layout of the poem but also provide evidence of the poetic process whereby what is damaged or decayed or decomposed or destroyed is reconstructed on the page like the new buildings of Haussmann's Paris. But what these prosodic tableaux also depict is 'le chaos des vivantes cités' ('Les Petites Vieilles', l. 62), and in so doing they further threaten to transgress the 'limits' of poetry by substituting disorder for order. In this respect Baudelaire may be seen as confronting the same artistic dilemma as was to be faced by Flaubert in the writing of *L'Éducation sentimentale* (1869):[20] how to depict shapelessness (of lives, of time's passage, of history, of mental understanding) when the expressive power of art depends so crucially on the creation of pattern and design? In Baudelaire's terms, how to depict dissonance without endangering the harmony of verse? Or, more especially, how to create poetic harmony—beauty—without being unfaithful to the chaotic and the untidy and the unresolved?

His answer was the prose poem. In verse, order is the default, so that prosodic irregularity or disruption can be powerfully expressive of a disorderly subject. While particularly evident in some of the 'Tableaux parisiens' this may also be

---

[18] Cf. also 'Les Petites Vieilles', ll. 8–9, 16–17 ('Tout cassés | Qu'ils sont'), 40–1, 52–3.
[19] Ross Chambers has further suggested that 'Les Sept Vieillards' (comprising thirteen stanzas) has the form of 'a monstrous sonnet', being ' structured *as if* it were a sonnet; but a *strange* sonnet—one that is made of quatrains instead of single lines, and one singularly misshapen, flawed, noisy or deformed, having the structure 4+4/3+2.' See Daylight Specter', 55.
[20] See my 'Flaubert's Style and the Idea of Literary Justice', 156–82 (172–3).

seen elsewhere in *Les Fleurs du Mal*: for example, in the exclusive use of masculine rhymes in 'Ciel brouillé' where the 'scrambled' sky of a moody mistress also scrambles the rules of versification and where the bravado of a poet professedly ready to undergo the winter of her discontent is expressed in an exclusion of the feminine rhyme. But what if one were to change the default? Make prose the master medium in which to reflect on 'les gloires et les tribulations de la vie' but bring to it the principles of verse: of unity and division, of fixed form and quasi-fugal variation, of symmetry and contrast, of alternation, repetition, and cross-over, of observance and transgression? And in this way achieve new ways of seeing and being seen, of reading the world and being read as reading? Of being a new kind of lawgiver? By presenting an 'idée-mère'—a mental picture or insight like the image of a swan outside the Louvre—and then 'translating' it (in narrative or dialogue or discursive reflection) like a critic setting out 'successivement' the 'suggestions' and 'les considérations et les rêveries morales' to which it gives rise? Of being an alternative lawgiver, offering and provoking a series of conjectures that derive their authority and authenticity precisely from *not* laying down the law and from demonstrating how the provisionality of surmise, of our search for meaning, of our very desire for laws that explain and bring order—in other words, the excitement of conjecture that is beauty—most faithfully and truly answers to the random complexities and confusions of human life?[21]

At the end of 'Tableaux parisiens' the two final poems—'Rêve parisien' and 'Le Crépuscule du matin'—provide a telling contrast between pure artifice and a chaotic reality. In the former we are provided with a vision of the artist's self-confidence ('peintre fier de mon génie' (l. 9)) and in the latter of the artist's melancholic self-knowledge and sense of defeat ('L'air est plein du frisson des choses qui s'enfuient, | Et l'homme est las d'écrire' (ll. 10–11)). As the penultimate poem in 'Tableaux parisiens' 'Rêve parisien' portrays a kind of *nec plus ultra* of the essential qualities of a riverine city: water and hard surfaces. This cityscape of dream takes the form of a 'palais infini' (l. 14) in which the sole purpose of a limitless proliferation of no-expense-spared construction appears to be to contain and control the water (and the water of life?): 'Plein de bassins et de cascades | Tombant dans l'or mat ou bruni' (ll. 15–16), and even to immobilize it completely by magically (cf. l. 30) transforming it into glass and metal: 'Et des cataractes

---

[21] Ross Chambers sees a comparable shift taking place between *Les Fleurs du Mal* and *Le Spleen de Paris*, but in a move from harmony to what he calls 'noise', both as a literal reality in the urban setting and as the figure for a more generalized disorder: 'The question for Baudelaire, in future poems, will be, then, no longer how to produce harmonious verses that deny the presence and power of noise and seek to cancel it out, but rather how to incorporate this defining noisiness of urban life into an aesthetics that might somehow be capable of doing justice to noise's pervasive and inescapable, if mostly ignored, presence. How to envisage a noisy form of beauty, or the beauty of noise? How to produce a certain supernaturalism out of a world no longer benignly governed so much as it is subject to forces of disorder, entropy, and chaos; and this by virtue of its involvement in time, extension, the problematics of mediation, as well [. . .] as the destructive force that is history?' See *An Atmospherics of the City*, 48.

pesantes, | Comme des rideaux de cristal, | Se suspendaient, éblouissantes, | À des murailles de métal' (ll. 17–20). Water sleeps in pools, like mirrors (ll. 22–4), or spread out like sheets (l. 25) over a million leagues as far as the mind's eye can see ('Vers les confins de l'univers' (ll. 25–8)). Water is frozen like huge blocks of ice (l. 31), while rivers the size of the Ganges 'pour' silently into diamond chasms (ll. 33–6) and the tamed ocean passes through jewelled tunnels at the poet-architect's own behest (ll. 37–40). Solidified liquid is the only source of light: 'Le liquide enchâsssait sa gloire | Dans le rayon cristallisé' (ll. 43–4). There is no sun, there are no stars (ll. 45–6), yet blackness itself seems to gleam like a rainbow ('fourbi, clair, irisé' (l. 42).

In short, this is a city without people, without life. In the opening description—'ce terrible paysage, | Tel que jamais mortel n'en vit' (ll. 1–2)—the double sense of 'vit' (saw, lives off) both affirms the idea of the city as a picture, a sight to be seen, and asserts the impossibility of life in such a place. Without animal or vegetable ('J'avais banni [...] | Le végétal irrégulier' (ll. 7–8); 'Non d'arbres, mais de colonnades' (l. 21)) it is pure minerality: all metal and stone (ll. 12, 29), marble and gold (ll. 12, 16), and immobility. There is a multiplicity of pathways, both vertical and horizontal ('Babel d'escaliers et d'arcades' (l. 13)), but nobody, no thing, nothing moves. The one source of light is the poet's own dream, his 'feu personnel' (l. 48), illuminating 'ces mouvantes merveilles (l. 49) that appear to move and shift only as reflections cast by the flickering light of his imagination. Otherwise the nearest thing to a human being in this scene are the 'gigantesques naïades, | Comme des femmes' (ll. 23–4). Nature has been banned in all its messy, organic, animate forms: here is pure art, dream art, and it leaves the poet enchanted ('Ce matin encore l'image, | Vague et lointaine, me ravit' (ll. 3–4) even as he awakes—his eyes still filled with the flames (l. 53) from his 'feu personnel'—to the horrible reality of his hovel and feels '[l]a pointe des soucis maudits' once more enter his soul.

Should we read 'Rêve parisien' as a celebration of artifice or as a condemnation of art as lifeless and divorced from the human (as Baudelaire condemns 'l'Art pour l'Art' for being in 'L'École païenne')? Or perhaps as one pole in a duality of which the other is illustrated in the chaotic reality of 'Le Crépuscule du matin'? Not a city born of the creative imagination but one filled with the mess and noise of human existence. Whereas in 'Rêve parisien' there reigns ('terrible nouveauté!' (l. 50)) '[u]n silence d'éternité' (l. 52), here in 'Le Crépuscule du matin' life begins with noise: a reveille summoning life's warriors to action ('La diane chantait dans les cours des casernes' (l. 1)); a cock-crow that proclaims life's ill-being through images of tubercular and auditory rupture ('Comme un sanglot coupé par un sang écumeux | Le chant du coq au loin déchirait l'air brumeux' (ll. 19–20); and the dissonance and irregularity of the dying who fail to keep a steady rhythm as they breathe their last: 'Et les agonisants dans le fond des hospices | Poussaient leur dernier râle en hoquets inégaux' (ll. 22–3). Where previously there was the perfect art of dream from which it was painful to awake, now there is the sad reality of waking up in the morning only then to die. Here the whole of Paris is roused at cock-crow from its own dreams, from another reality (like that of poetry?), only to discover that they are awaking not to a plenitude but to an absence ('L'air est plein du frisson des choses qui s'enfuient', l. 10): the absence of men who write and women who love (as they both did in 'Spleen et idéal'), the absence of 'ces mouvantes merveilles' that hold a dreamer rapt. Poetry and creativity give way to the daytime world of poverty and mortality, and work: not the work of a dream painter but a sullen drudgery, the hard labour of living: 'Et le sombre Paris, en se frottant les yeux, | Empoignait ses outils, vieillard laborieux' (ll. 27–8). As we move from 'les bruns adolescents' (l. 4) at the beginning to this old man at the end, we are back in the world of time and the world of fog and illness and hospitals and exhaustion, back in a paradoxical place where the houses wake up (l. 12) and the prostitute ('la paupière livide') sleeps the sleep of death (ll. 13–14), where people rub their eyes as though in disbelief, as though obliged to banish the stardust from their vision. This is no rosy-fingered dawn, but 'l'aurore grelottante en robe rose et verte' (l. 25), moving along the Seine like a mendicant redhead in search of alms. Night and day, dream and reality, art and life: the poet-artist as painter and sightseer must honour them both.

PART V
PROSE POETRY

Sois toujours poète, même en prose. Grand style (rien de plus beau que le lieu commun).
('Notes précieuses')[1]
J'invoque la muse familière, la citadine, la vivante[.]
('Les Bons Chiens', i. 360)

---

[1] *Fusées*, ed. Guyaux, 131; i. 670.

20
The Inauguration of the Prose Poem

> un commencement de tentative nouvelle
> (letter to Alfred de Vigny, Dec. 1861 (*Corr.*, ii. 196))

On 1 June 1855, in the *Revue des Deux Mondes*, Baudelaire published the group of 18 verse poems that bore, for the first time, the title of 'Les Fleurs du Mal'. On 2 June 1855, he published his first two prose poems—'Le Crépuscule du soir' and 'La Solitude'.[1] We may tend to think of Baudelaire's prose poems as coming after his verse poems, and in this case they in fact did so—but only by a day! Indeed it has been suggested that the first two prose poems to be published by Baudelaire were not these but the prose versions of 'L'Âme du vin' and 'Le Vin des chiffonniers' that were included in 'Du vin et du hachisch' (1851).[2] This essay was published in the daily evening newspaper *Le Messager de l'Assemblée* in March 1851 and thus one month before the publication, in the same newspaper and on the writer's thirtieth birthday, of the eleven poems collected under the title *Les Limbes*. Before that only seven of his poems had appeared in print.[3]

It is, of course, true that Baudelaire's early career as a creative writer was focused principally on verse,[4] and many of the verse poems that were eventually collected in *Les Fleurs du Mal* were originally drafted and/or completed during the 1840s. The first prose poems, by contrast, would seem to have been conceived slightly later. But, as J. A. Hiddleston argues, 'the possibilities of some kind of overlap between the two genres are a preoccupation which dates from very early in his literary career'.[5] Already in *La Fanfarlo* (1847) we read of the young poet, Samuel Cramer, who tries at first and in vain to seduce Mme de Cosmelly by presenting her with a copy of

---

[1] In Charles Asselineau et al., *Fontainebleau: Paysages, légendes, souvenirs, fantaisies. Hommage à C. F. Denecourt* (Paris: Hachette, 1855), 78–80. The publication was officially registered in the *Bibliographie de la France* on 2 June 1855. (See i. 1024.)
[2] See Baudelaire, *Le Spleen de Paris. (Petits Poèmes en prose)*, ed. Jean-Luc Steinmetz (Paris: Le Livre de poche [Classiques], 2003), 9–10. See also Steinmetz, 'Une fable des origines', in Steve Murphy (ed.), *Lectures du 'Spleen de Paris'* (Rennes: Presses universitaires de Rennes, 2014), 97–104.
[3] 'A une dame créole' (May 1845), 'Don Juan aux enfers' (Sept. 1846), 'A une Malabaraise' (Dec. 1846), 'Les Chats' (Nov. 1847), 'L'Âme du vin' (June 1850), 'Châtiment de l'orgueil' (June 1850), and 'Lesbos' (July 1850).
[4] Steinmetz comments: 'Assurément le poète en lui l'emporte sur le prosateur; mais ses premières œuvres signalaient l'excellence de sa prose, et ce fait explique peut-être pourquoi, à partir d'un certain moment, une forme de poème en prose particulière lui devint si nécessaire' (Steinmetz (ed.), *Le Spleen de Paris*, 24).
[5] J. A. Hiddleston, *Baudelaire and 'Le Spleen de Paris'* (Oxford: Clarendon Press, 1987), 62.

his sonnets *Les Orfraies* but then has more success in convincing her of his sincerity when he begins to 'mettre en prose et à déclamer quelques mauvaises stances composées dans sa première manière' (i. 560). Not only does Cramer's prose recital echo earlier poems by Baudelaire himself but it also appears to anticipate later ones, such as 'Harmonie du soir' and 'Moesta et errabunda'.

After this inauguration of his prose poetry in 1855,[6] Baudelaire continued to add to his portfolio of prose poems at the same time as he was vigorously pursuing his objective of a verse collection. In August 1857, two months after publication of the first edition of *Les Fleurs du Mal*, he published (under the title *Poèmes nocturnes*) four new prose poems: 'L'Horloge', 'Un hémisphère dans une chevelure', 'L'Invitation au voyage', and 'Les Projets', together with 'Le Crépuscule du soir' and 'La Solitude', in *Le Présent*, a fortnightly review founded the previous month and focusing on contemporary literature and the fine arts. During the period between 1857 and 1861, when he was making major revisions and additions to *Les Fleurs du Mal*, Baudelaire continued to draft further prose poems with the result that in November 1861, in the *Revue fantaisiste*,[7] he published three new ones ('Les Foules', 'Les Veuves', 'Le Vieux Saltimbanque') and republished the existing six. By 1862 he was in a position to send twenty-six prose poems (including the nine already published, which in some cases had been substantially revised) for publication in the *feuilleton* section of *La Presse*. Thereafter new prose poems appeared at regular intervals: 9 in 1863; 9 in 1864; and 1 ('Les Bons Chiens') in 1865. In this same year, however, four others were rejected for publication, doubtless on the grounds of subject matter ('Le Galant Tireur', 'Assommons les pauvres!') or else perhaps a perceived triviality and/or absurdity ('La Soupe et les nuages', 'Perte d'auréole').[8] 'Mademoiselle Bistouri' was similarly refused in 1867. In 1866 no new prose poems were published, and in 1867 only one: 'Any where out of the world', which, adding irony to its title, was the last new prose poem to be published in Baudelaire's lifetime.[9]

We need therefore to envisage verse and prose as being for Baudelaire, from the beginning and indeed until the end,[10] two alternative modes of poetic

---

[6] Cf. Steinmetz's comment on the first publication of 'Le Crépuscule du soir' and 'La Solitude': 'Qu'ils aient revêtu à ses yeux un caractère inaugural, plusieurs indices engagent à le croire, entre autres leur publication jumelée à maintes reprises, les années suivantes (en 1857 et 1861), en tête de diverses séries de poèmes en prose, comme s'il souhaitait par là conserver le souvenir d'un commencement, d'un acte de naissance' (Steinmetz (ed.), *Le Spleen de Paris*, 10).

[7] Edited by Catulle Mendès, this twice-monthly periodical appeared first on 15 Feb. 1861 and ceased publication after the issue of 15 Nov. 1861.

[8] Writing to the publisher Julien Lemer on 13 Oct. 1865 Baudelaire acknowledges that perhaps twenty of his prose poems may be 'inintelligibles ou répulsifs pour le public d'un journal' (*Corr.*, ii. 534).

[9] For full details of the publication history of the prose poems, see Steinmetz (ed.), *Le Spleen de Paris*, 229-38.

[10] After the second edition of *Les Fleurs du Mal* was published in Feb. 1861 Baudelaire published a number of further poems: notably the fifteen poems that make up the 'Nouvelles *Fleurs du Mal*' published in *Le Parnasse contemporain* on 31 March 1866 ('Épigraphe pour un livre condamné',* 'L'Examen de minuit',* 'Madrigal triste',* À une Malabaraise', 'L'Avertisseur',* 'Hymne', 'La Voix', 'Le

expression—two different instruments for the creation of 'beauty'—and to see them as being always available to him, as they are to Samuel Cramer, in parallel one with the other. Moreover, within the prose poems taken as a collective whole and sometimes within individual prose poems themselves, there seems to be a clear division between, on the one hand, a focus on the relationship between beauty and melancholy (that is, on the principal subject matter of Les Fleurs du Mal), and, on the other, a focus on moral, political, and philosophical issues that aligns the poems more clearly with the preoccupations of contemporary journalism, with the prosaic world of newspapers and periodicals and reviews and ephemeral pamphlets in which Baudelaire had moved with much energy since his return from the Indian Ocean and to which as a critic of art and literature he himself so frequently contributed in print.

I shall return to the question of beauty and melancholy in the final three chapters of this book, and to the relationship between poetry and the press in the next. But for the moment it will be helpful to consider in closer detail Baudelaire's first two experiments with the form of the prose poem, 'Le Crépuscule du soir' and 'La Solitude', since these two poems respectively illustrate each of these two central strands of Le Spleen de Paris. At the same time we might usefully bear in mind how this new literary genre, inaugurated by Baudelaire,[11] anticipates Mallarmé's poème critique, a unique and innovative form of discourse that positions itself at once between and *beyond* the aesthetic and the polemical, the lyrical and the journalistic.[12] Here (for both poets) is a new kind of writing that

Rebelle',* 'Le Jet d'eau', 'Les Yeux de Berthe', 'La Rançon', 'Bien loin d'ici',* 'Recueillement',* 'Le Gouffre',* 'Les Plaintes d'un Icare'*). Of these Asselineau chose to include nine (here marked with an asterisk) in his posthumous, third edition of Les Fleurs du Mal (1868), along with 'La Prière d'un païen', 'Le Couvercle', and 'La Lune offensée'. Les Épaves, published in Belgium in 1866, contains not only the six poems from Les Fleurs du Mal that had been banned by the courts in 1857 but also a number of hitherto unpublished poems, some of which were written after 1861 (for example, 'Le Monstre' and 'Lola de Valence') and at least one of which ('Sur Le Tasse en prison') was, as we have seen, the heavily revised version of a much earlier text. After 1861, therefore, verse still continued to matter to Baudelaire, and the relative paucity of new poems, like the dwindling number of new prose poems, was no doubt a consequence of his increasingly poor health.

[11] On the prehistory of the 'poème en prose', see Nathalie Vincent-Munnia, Les Premiers Poèmes en prose: Généalogie d'un genre dans la première moitié du dix-neuvième siècle français (Paris: Champion, 1996). For her, as later for Steinmetz, Baudelaire did not invent the 'poème en prose' but was the first to use that term (attested already in the early eighteenth century) to designate and, in his writing practice, to exemplify and 'inaugurate' a distinct new form of literary expression: 'C'est [...] à partir de Baudelaire (et des années 1855-1869) que l'expression commence à perdre ce sens purement analogique et paradoxal pour devenir une formule plus uniformisée renvoyant à une entité poétique et générique et non plus seulement à une "manière" littéraire' (10); 'c'est Baudelaire qui inaugure ce sens moderne en le choisissant pour titre' (87). On the history and generic characteristics of the prose poem in France see Suzanne Bernard, Le Poème en prose de Baudelaire jusqu'à nos jours (Paris: Nizet, 1959); Tzvetan Todorov, 'La Poésie sans le vers', in Les Genres du discours (Paris: Éditions du Seuil, 1978), 116-31; Michel Sandras, Lire le poème en prose (Paris: Dunod, 1995); Yves Vadé, Le Poème en prose et ses territoires (Paris: Belin, 1996); and Michel Murat, 'Le Dernier Livre de la bibliothèque', in Murat, La Langue des dieux modernes (Paris: Classiques Garnier, 2012), 45-59.

[12] See Mallarmé, Œuvres complètes, ii. 277: 'une forme, peut-être, en sort, actuelle, permettant, à ce qui fut longtemps le poème en prose et notre recherche, d'aboutir, en tant, si l'on joint mieux les mots,

may be called 'poetic' not because it apes (though it may) certain features of traditional prosody (for example, in the quasi-stanzaic use of the paragraph) or because it sometimes emulates the high register of verse-language in its 'lyrical' deployment of repetition, hyperbole, apostrophe and other rhetorical devices, or even because it addresses topics stereotypically thought to be 'poetic' (solitude, sunset, transience, despair, death, dreaming, madness, fairies, imaginary journeys, painting, music, theatre, and poetry itself), but because this discourse is simply that of a *poet*: that is, of the alternative lawgiver who has forged a new language— what Richard Terdiman calls a 'counter-discourse'[13]—in order to give expression to an independent and 'resistant' perspective on all the other languages and perspectives by which poets and their readers are surrounded.

The credentials of this new kind of poet are eloquently described by Mallarmé in his Oxford and Cambridge lecture (1894) that was subsequently published as *La Musique et les Lettres* in 1895:

> Il importe que dans tout concours de la multitude quelque part vers l'intérêt, l'amusement, ou la commodité, de rares amateurs, respectueux du motif commun en tant que façon d'y montrer de l'indifférence, instituent par cet air à côté, une minorité; attendu, quelle divergence que creuse le conflit furieux des citoyens, tous, sous l'œil souverain, font une unanimité—d'accord, au moins, que ce à propos de quoi on s'entre-dévore, compte: or, posé le besoin d'exception, comme de sel! la vraie qui, indéfectiblement, fonctionne, gît dans ce séjour de quelques esprits, je ne sais, à leur éloge, comment les désigner, gratuits, étrangers, peut-être vains—ou littéraires.[14]

An ineloquent paraphrase of this passage might read as follows (and demonstrate the economical polysemy of Mallarmé):[15]

> In a society of human beings preoccupied with their own self-interest (in the form, amongst others, of interest rates, mortgages, investment returns) or with

---

que poème critique'. Mallarmé has in mind, and exemplifies in *Divagations*, a form of writing that combines the substance of a newspaper article with the compression and linguistic art more commonly associated with verse. For further discussion see my *Mallarmé and Circumstance*, 28–32.

[13] Richard Terdiman, *Discourse/Counter-Discourse: The Theory and Practice of Symbolic Resistance in Nineteenth-Century France* (Ithaca, NY: Cornell University Press, 1985).

[14] *Œuvres complètes*, ed. Marchal, ii. 72–3.

[15] But cf. also Barbara Johnson's careful translation of this passage: 'It is important that in any contest of multitudes for interest, amusement, or commodity, certain rare enthusiasts, respectful of the common motive insofar as they show indifference to it, institute, by following a different drummer, a minority: given that, however deep the furious conflict among citizens, under the sovereign eye, it adds up to unanimity—agreement, at least, that what they are devouring each other for matters. In any case, given the need for an exception, like salt! - a veritable one which, indefectibly, functions—there are in our time on earth a few minds, I'm not sure, to their credit, how to call them: gratuituous, foreign, maybe vain—or literary.' See Stéphane Mallarmé, *Divagations*, trans. Barbara Johnson (Cambridge, Mass., and London: The Belknap Press of Harvard University Press, 2007), 193,

amusement (perhaps leisure activities or simply a refusal to take a serious interest in the world) or with consumerism (the pursuit of the commodity, or simply the pursuit of convenience and the easy way out) it is important that a few individuals—just for the love of it, and manifesting a respectful and non-disparaging awareness of such everyday motives and patterns of behaviour precisely by showing no interest in them or affording them any overt attention—set themselves up, by this very appearance of being on the sidelines, as a kind of institutional minority; given that, whatever differences between citizens may be created by the furious conflict between them, they are all, when seen as part of one single sovereign body, of one mind—being in agreement, at least, that what they are tearing each other apart for actually matters: accordingly, given the desirability of the exceptional and the unorthodox, like a pinch of salt that adds savour to a dish, the one true exception that functions without fail derives from this earthly existence of a few minds who are (I don't quite know what elogious term to choose to describe them) gratuitous, alien, perhaps pointless—or literary.

The Baudelaire of *Le Spleen de Paris*, as of *Les Fleurs du Mal*, is just such a poet: an exception, unorthodox, undidactic (or 'gratuitous') but an awkward customer with his own individual moral and political takes on the human condition, not 'one of us' but an 'étranger' (like the subject of the first poem in *Le Spleen de Paris*), someone quite possibly of no use at all ('vain') and even vain in thinking he might be of use... Except that for both Baudelaire and Mallarmé such a poet clearly does matter, hugely, like literature itself. As we shall see, the poet of *Le Spleen de Paris* takes up his solitary position on the sidelines—or rather in the *feuilleton* at the bottom of a broadsheet page—and, in his minority of one, gives voice to his own perspective on a society that had torn itself apart in the 1848 Revolution and was still, in its aftermath, continuing to do so. Where the antagonists in this violent struggle are at least unanimous in a single belief—in this case, that who owns what and how much is the key to happiness and social cohesion (the so-called 'question sociale')—the poet proposes an alternative legislation which derives from the human right to be uncertain and to change one's mind, to wonder and speculate: the right—and freedom—to imagine and, in both senses of the verb, to own one's conjectures.

Against Nature, against the Light of Day: 'Le Crépuscule du soir' (1855)

mon âme est rebelle à cette singulière religion nouvelle[.]

(*Corr*. i. 248)

Baudelaire's first two published prose poems, 'Le Crépuscule du soir' and 'La Solitude', appeared in a book about the forest of Fontainebleau. Initiated and edited by his friend Fernand Desnoyers (1826–69), warden of the forest,[16] journalist, and poet, this volume was intended to honour Claude-François Denecourt (1788–1875) and to celebrate the work that Denecourt had carried out over some twenty years in mapping the forest of Fontainebleau, establishing and marking forest paths, and publishing guides for the benefit of fellow nature-lovers. Methodical and devoted in the service of this cause, Denecourt had been largely responsible for the growing popularity of the forest of Fontainebleau as a tourist attraction, notably for the well-to-do Parisians who came by train to find peace and fresh air, but also for painters and poets—and, as some of the contributions to the volume make clear, for lovers who sought sylvan camouflage and for the suicidal who needed a tree from which to hang themselves.

Where once Chateaubriand had travelled all the way to the forests of North America (as another contributor reminds his readers)[17] and there found the great natural cathedrals of God's Creation, Romantics and romantics now had only to make a relatively short journey from Paris to paradise: someone like George Sand, for example, whose contribution follows Baudelaire's.[18] In an extract taken from a letter she had written back in August 1837 Sand describes a happy day spent riding in the forest with her young son and how they delighted in everything that nature had to offer, the great oaks and the enormous rocks, the flowers and the butterflies, but above all the deep, deep silence. They took no map with them because, thanks to Denecourt, 'il est difficile de se perdre dans une forêt semée d'écriteaux'.[19] Here, then, was nature tamed and waymarked, nature as theme park, as a 'forêt de symboles' ready to observe the visitor 'avec des regards familiers'. As one anglophone contributor, Clara de Chatelain, writes in 'To the Hermit of the Forest': 'Twas God who reared this leafy world | On which we feast our ravished look:— | But Denecourt has each myth unfurled, | And taught us how to read its book.'[20] But, methodical as he was, Denecourt was not himself immune to the mystical. From time to time he would perform quasi-druidic ceremonies and dedicate an oak tree to a particular writer he admired, including Baudelaire.[21]

Such is the context in which Baudelaire's first two prose poems were published. Initially (at the turn of the year 1853–4) he had responded to Desnoyer's invitation

[16] See Marie-Christine Natta, *Baudelaire* (Paris: Perrin, 2017), 359.
[17] Théodore Pelloquet, 'La Forêt de Fontainebleau et M. de Chateaubriand', in *Fontainebleau*, 282–9.
[18] The contributors numbered 40 and also included Lamartine (in prose), Hugo ('A Albert Dürer', from *Les Voix intérieures*), Musset, Janin, Murger, Nerval, Gautier, and Banville.
[19] *Fontainebleau*, 81. Four years earlier, in August 1833 and before the installation of these signposts, she and Musset had got famously lost there. For this and further detailed information about Denecourt himself and about the volume compiled in his honour, see F. W. Leakey, 'A *Festschrift* of 1855: Baudelaire and the *Hommage À C. F. Denecourt*', in J. C. Ireson, I. D. Macfarlane, and Garnet Rees (eds), *Studies in French Literature Presented to H. W. Lawton* (Manchester: Manchester University Press, and New York: Barnes & Noble Inc., 1968), 175–202. On Sand and Musset see 177 and n. 8.
[20] Clara de Chatelain, 'To the Hermit of the Forest', in *Fontainebleau*, 63–5 (65).
[21] See *Corr.*, i. 837–8, and Natta, *Baudelaire*, 359.

to contribute by sending two previously published verse poems—'Le Crépuscule du soir' and 'Le Crépuscule du matin'—and by reminding him with sarcastic wit (the letter would be published with the poems) why he was not a nature poet:

> Mon cher Desnoyers, vous me demandez des vers pour votre petit volume, des vers sur la *Nature*, n'est-ce pas? sur les bois, les grands chênes, la verdure, les insectes,—sur le soleil sans doute? Mais, vous savez que je suis incapable de m'attendrir sur les végétaux et que mon âme est rebelle à cette singulière religion nouvelle, qui aura toujours, ce me semble, pour tout être *spirituel* je ne sais quoi de *shocking*. Je ne croirai jamais que 'l'âme des Dieux habite dans les plantes',[22] et quand même il y habiterait, je m'en soucierais médiocrement, et considérerais la mienne comme d'un bien plus haut prix que celle des légumes sanctifiés. J'ai même toujours pensé qu'il y avait dans la *Nature*, florissante et rajeunie, quelque chose d'impudent et d'affligeant. (*Corr.*, i. 248)

As several of the contributions to *Fontainebleau* demonstrate, the forest was especially associated with the opportunity to observe beautiful sunsets.[23] Charles Monselet's sixteen-line poem 'Soleil couchant', for example, begins (unconvincingly): 'La chaleur était forte. Aux feux de l'Occident | Le soleil retrempait son disque fécondant [...]'.[24] The choice of two poems about dusk and dawn was therefore seemingly appropriate, except that the willing poet undermines the virtue of his compliance by claiming that actually the forest twilight usually puts *him* in mind not of God but the city! Not for Baudelaire any Chateaubriandesque thoughts about the majesty of God's Creation and the wonders of nature but rather a keen attentiveness to the spectacles of our astonishing urban experience and the terrible reality of human suffering:

> Dans l'impossibilité de vous satisfaire complètement, suivant les termes stricts du programme, je vous envoie deux morceaux poétiques qui représentent à peu près la somme des rêveries dont je suis assailli aux heures crépusculaires. Dans le fond des bois, enfermé sous ces voûtes semblables à celles des sacristies et des cathédrales, je pense à nos étonnantes villes, et la prodigieuse musique qui roule sur les sommets me semble la traduction des lamentations humaines.[25]

---

[22] A quotation from the work of Victor de Laprade (1812–83), a pious, nature-loving poet in the tradition of Chateaubriand and Lamartine who succeeded to Musset's chair at the Académie française in 1858. See i. 1025.

[23] As it happens, it was these sunsets, observed from his house at Valvins on the opposite bank of the Seine, that Mallarmé would have particularly in mind in his accounts of the *drame solaire*, notably in his prose poem 'La Gloire'. See my *Mallarmé and Circumstance*, 38–9, 129–32.

[24] *Fontainebleau*, 69.

[25] Leakey makes the suggestion that Baudelaire did in fact have available some verse poems ('Le Soleil', 'Correspondances', 'Tristesses de la lune', 'J'aime le souvenir de ces époques nues...') that might have answered more obviously to Desnoyers's request for contributions about nature. See 'A *Festschrift* of 1855', 191.

As in 'Élévation', therefore, the poet as alternative lawgiver rejects the Romantic cult of nature and disowns the hackneyed persona, enlisted by Clara de Chatelain, of the poet who 'comprend sans effort | Le langage des fleurs et des choses muettes!' For Baudelaire what matters are the 'miasmes morbides', and his two 'Crépuscule' poems provided the nature-lovers of Fontainebleau with quite a list of twilight thoughts: on crime, human bestiality, prostitution, pain, poverty, exhaustion, and fatal illness.

Subsequently—and it is not known when or why[26]—Baudelaire sent Desnoyers two further poems, in prose, for inclusion in the volume. Perhaps he regretted the hasty and/or uncompromising character of his earlier response? And even a lack of courtesy towards Denecourt, the honorand? But still there is resistance and a reluctance to conform: Baudelaire was known as a verse poet, and verse poems were what were expected of him. The first of these prose poems, also called 'Le Crépuscule du soir'[27]—in itself a provocation in that its subject matter challenges the supposedly 'poetic' or 'lyrical' character of twilight—reads as follows (this first version being much shorter than the later, revised version):

> La tombée de la nuit a toujours été pour moi le signal d'une fête intérieure et comme la délivrance d'une angoisse. Dans les bois comme dans les rues d'une grande ville, l'assombrissement du jour et le pointillement des étoiles ou des lanternes éclairent mon esprit.
>
> Mais j'ai deux amis que le crépuscule rendait malades. L'un méconnaissait alors tous les rapports d'amitié et de politesse, et brutalisait sauvagement le premier venu. Je l'ai vu jeter un excellent poulet à la tête d'un maître d'hôtel. La venue du soir gâtait les meilleures choses.
>
> L'autre, à mesure que le jour baissait, devenait plus aigre, plus sombre, plus taquin. Indulgent pendant la journée, il était impitoyable le soir;—et ce n'était pas seulement sur autrui, mais sur lui-même que s'exerçait abondamment sa manie crépusculaire.
>
> Le premier est mort fou, incapable de reconnaître sa maîtresse et son fils; le second porte en lui l'inquiétude d'une insatisfaction perpétuelle. L'ombre qui fait la lumière dans mon esprit fait la nuit dans le leur.—Et, bien qu'il ne soit pas rare de voir la même cause engendrer deux effets contraires, cela m'intrigue et m'étonne toujours. (i. 1327–8)

---

[26] To my knowledge no critic or editor of these two prose poems comments on the matter. Leakey describes them simply as being 'sent at some later date, presumably' ('A *Festschrift* of 1855, 190). Baudelaire's statement in his letter to Desnoyers that 'la prodigieuse musique qui roule sur les sommets me semble la traduction des lamentations humaines' anticipates exactly the content of the second paragraph of the prose poem 'Le Crépuscule du soir' as revised for publication in 1862.

[27] It should be noted that in *Fontainebleau* (74–7) Baudelaire's two verse poems are presented under a common title, 'Les Deux Crépuscules', while each bears respectively the title of 'Le Soir' and 'Le Matin'.

THE INAUGURATION OF THE PROSE POEM 465

With its four short paragraphs of roughly equal length and stanzaic appearance this poem is simply and carefully structured: one paragraph on the poet's positive response to dusk, one paragraph each for the two differing negative responses of conveniently representative 'friends', and a final paragraph recording four different effects of dusk: madness, perpetual anxiety, mental illumination, and philosophical perplexity. The effect of simplicity is enhanced by the insistent use of parataxis so that the hypotaxis at the end of the third and fourth paragraphs suggests a growing and intrusive sense of complication, as though darkness were falling in the mind. The overall tone of the piece implies frankness and sincerity, but ironies and mysterious allusions abound. Is the second paragraph perhaps about Baudelaire himself, who by his initial reaction to Desnoyers's invitation had also transgressed the rules of friendship and politeness (toward Desnoyers as well as Denecourt)? The story of chicken-throwing, in itself comic and incongruous in this ostensibly solemn context, sounds like an in-joke. In the third paragraph we perhaps find Baudelaire again, the known depressive and author of melancholic poems, and the man subsequently described in the fourth paragraph as suffering from 'l'inquiétude d'une insatisfaction perpétuelle'. Or is this in fact a sarcastic depiction of those innumerable victims of the *mal du siècle*, wallowing in the endless and delicious misery of their melancholy? The first friend's failure to recognize his mistress rather than his wife—and which of them is the mother of the son?—adds a louche subtext to a potentially tragic story of mental illness, while the smug tone of the poet in his clever contrast of twilight ('l'ombre') bringing light to him and darkness to his two friends is undone by the obvious paradox of which he seems wholly unaware. If twilight brings illumination, why is he so 'intrigued' and 'alarmed' by the wholly unsurprising fact that the same cause can have two opposite effects?

These layerings of persona and the resultant ironic distance will be characteristic of many of the subsequent prose poems. That this poet is 'intrigued' recalls the positive role of conjecture in Baudelaire's poetics and anticipates its crucial role in *Le Spleen de Paris*. But here Baudelaire is principally and quietly questioning the easy Romantic assumption that the crepuscular reflections brought on by the spectacle of dusk are in themselves 'lyrical', a lovely form of melancholy that it is a positive delight to experience (provided one catches the train back to Paris in time). That the poet should be alarmed, on the other hand, by the philosophical problem of causation and the thought that a single cause may have two opposite effects exemplifies Baudelaire's ironic use throughout *Le Spleen de Paris* of first-person poetic personas whose opinions and attitudes can be variously unintelligent, bigoted, inconsistent, or just wilfully contentious—in short, often containing 'je ne sais quoi de *shocking*'. Baudelaire himself, of course, is just about the last person one would expect to be 'alarmed' by the contradictions of causation. Indeed contradiction—beauty in melancholy? poetry in prose?—is exactly the logical relationship upon which this contrarian resistance hero thrives. If twilight brings *him* illumination, then that is because he always sees things in at least two lights. As he does solitude also.

Against Advice: 'La Solitude' (1855)

> Ce Baudelaire est une pierre de touche: il déplaît invariablement à tous les imbéciles.
>
> (Hippolyte Castille)[28]

Along with sunsets the forest was famous for the opportunity it afforded people—and particularly the inhabitants of a noisy, dirty, densely populated city—to escape the madding crowd. Hence Sand's own delight: 'cette profonde solitude, ce solennel silence à quelques heures de Paris sont inappréciables'.[29] Baudelaire's second prose poem, 'La Solitude', is in fact presented in *Fontainbleau* as part of a diptych with 'Le Crépuscule du soir' by being framed as the response to a comment by the second 'friend' and by taking up once more the question of a dual causation. Again, this first version is much shorter than the later, revised text:

> Il me disait aussi,—le second,—que la solitude était mauvaise pour l'homme, et il me citait, je crois, des paroles des Pères de l'Église. Il est vrai que l'esprit de meurtre et de lubricité s'enflamme merveilleusement dans les solitudes; le démon fréquente les lieux arides.
>
> Mais cette séduisante solitude n'est dangereuse que pour ces âmes oisives et divagantes qui ne sont pas gouvernées par une importante pensée active. Elle ne fut pas mauvaise pour Robinson Crusoë; elle le rendit religieux, brave, industrieux; elle le purifia, elle lui enseigna jusqu'où peut aller la force de l'individu.
>
> N'est-ce pas La Bruyère qui a dit: 'Ce grand malheur de ne pouvoir être seul? ...'
> Il en serait donc de la solitude comme du crépuscule; elle est bonne et elle est mauvaise, criminelle et salutaire, incendiaire et calmante, selon qu'on en use, et selon qu'on a usé de la vie.
>
> Quant à la jouissance,—les plus belles agapes fraternelles, les plus magnifiques réunions d'hommes électrisés par un plaisir commun n'en donneront jamais de comparable à celle qu'éprouve le Solitaire, qui, d'un coup d'œil, a embrassé et compris toute la sublimité d'un paysage. Ce coup d'œil lui a conquis une propriété individuelle inaliénable. (i. 1329)

---

[28] See W. T. Bandy and Claude Pichois (eds), *Baudelaire devant ses contemporains* (Monaco: Éditions du Rocher, 1957), 7.
[29] *Fontainebleau*, 81.

As Baudelaire must have known, no doubt through Desnoyers but perhaps also from the author himself, Hippolyte Castille (1820–86)—a prolific novelist, journalist, and contemporary historian—had contributed to the volume a short prose piece entitled 'Sur la solitude'[30] in which he questions the assumption that the solitude offered by the forest of Fontainebleau is beneficial. Castille professes diffidence in approaching this topic on the grounds that Jean-Jacques Rousseau and his fellow Swiss, Johann Georg Zimmermann (1728–95), author of *Über die Einsamkeit* (*On Solitude* (1756)), had exhausted the topic. Nevertheless he believes that they have neglected to consider the disturbing mixture of feelings that may flow from being alone, whether at sea, on a mountain, or in a forest:

> cet étrange et complexe sentiment qui domine l'homme dans la solitude, toutes les fois que son imagination n'est pas absorbée par quelque sujet particulier. Il n'est personne, je crois, qui n'ait éprouvé, en pénétrant sous les sombres arcades d'une forêt, un mélange de charme et d'horreur. [...] La solitude, les bois, ne sont jamais complètement gais; les plus jolis rayons de soleil dans les feuilles n'empêchent pas que l'ombre verte tombe comme une mélancolie du dôme des grands arbres.[31]

Solitude is dangerous, an invitation to melancholy, and Castille berates poets, painters, and lovers for idealizing it. For why indeed *do* people hang themselves in the forest?

> Mais, ô rimeurs, ô peintres, ô amants! m'expliquerez-vous, au détour du chemin, ce sinistre pendu, dont l'ombre s'allonge en travers de la route, et qui, lui aussi, est venu choisir l'aimable solitude des bois et le vert rameau d'un chêne pour cette triste cérémonie?

Castille believes he has the answer:

> Il y a donc au fond des bois quelque volupté secrète, quelque joie funèbre et mystérieuse pour le malheureux lassé de frayer avec les humains! Ah! pour qu'on prenne le parti de se pendre à cette branche sous laquelle deux amants se sont assis, croyez-moi, il faut que la solitude ne soit pas tout grâce, tout bonté, tout béatitude; il y a des heures où elle apparaît plus amère que la mort.[32]

Baudelaire's prose poem 'La Solitude' may be read—at least in its first version and perhaps also (as we shall see) in its later, revised version—as a response to Castille, especially in view of its final sentence: 'Ce coup d'œil lui a conquis une propriété

---

[30] *Fontainbleau*, 84–9.   [31] *Fontainebleau*, 85.   [32] *Fontainebleau*, 86.

individuelle inaliénable.' In the months before the outbreak of revolution on 22 February 1848 Castille had founded and managed a journal entitled *Le Travail intellectuel: Journal des intérêts scientifiques, littéraires et artistiques*[33] whose sole *raison d'être* was to campaign in favour of intellectual property rights and, more generally, against state 'interference' in the commercial and intellectual 'marketplace' through protectionism and censorship. The question of property was then— and in 1855 continued to be—at the heart of political debate as nascent socialism and communism began to challenge the established order.[34] In 1847, a year of financial crisis in which both Lamartine and Marx published essays on the subject of a free market economy, Castille's campaign was conducted with the explicit support of the leading free-market theorists Frédéric Bastiat (1801–50), founder and editor of the periodical *Libre-Échange*, and his protégé Gustave Molinari (1819–1912), whose article 'De la production de la sécurité', published in 1849, is considered to constitute the first advocacy of so-called 'anarcho-capitalism'. To a modern eye their early versions of free market economics may suggest a politics of the right, and even the far right, but in 1847 the anti-statist 'liberalism' of Castille's *Le Travail intellectuel* secured the adherence of leading Republicans including Béranger and Michelet. 'La *propriété*, je le sais, les épouvante', states Castille in the second issue, and so he thanks them for publicly subscribing to his campaign in favour of the legal recognition of 'la propriété intellectuelle' as a 'contrepoids nécessaire, indispensable de la propriéte foncière'.[35]

---

[33] First published on 15 Aug. 1847 it appeared monthly on the same date up to and including 15 Feb. 1848.
[34] See Donald R. Kelley and Bonnie G. Smith, 'What was Property? Legal Dimensions of the Social Question in France (1789–1848)', *Proceedings of the American Philosophical Society*, 128: 3 (Sept. 1984), 200–30: 'no issue illustrated quite so clearly the divisions of post-Napoleonic Europe, and conservatives and liberals were quite as agitated on the question as radicals' (200). As Kelley and Smith argue, Napoleon's Code Civil of 1804 was 'the alpha and omega of practical discussions of basic institutions, especially of property, which was its dominant subject' (201). Following the so-called 'bourgeois' revolution of 1830 lawyers became the new aristocracy and indeed the new priesthood: 'a sort of secular clergy, for like their ancient Roman models the French jurists regarded themselves as "priests of the laws". Their scripture was the the Code, the class they served the "bourgeoisie conquérante", the doctrine they preached "the religion of property"' (202). On the other side of the political divide Pierre-Joseph Proudhon (1809–65) published his famous pamphlet *Qu'est-ce que la propriété?* in 1840 with its no less famous assertion that '[l]a propriété, c'est le vol'. In 1855 Henri Baudrillart, professor of political economy at the Collège de France, took Proudhon's asssertion as his starting-point before asserting the 'absolute' (or inalienable) character of property as laid down in the Code Civil and seeking to justify the moral basis of property as deriving from labour and meritorious effort (see Kelly and Smith, 'What was Property', 225).
[35] 'Réponse aux adhérents du *Travail intellectuel*', *Le Travail intellectuel*, no. 2 (15 Sept. 1847), 1–2 (1). A similar political situation obtained in Great Britain, as Clive Wilmer notes in his introduction to a selection of John Ruskin's writings, including *Unto this Last* (first published in 1862): 'in the nineteenth century political attitudes were not so neatly shared out between left and right as they are—or seem to be—today. Modern capitalist economics were then thought progressive, being associated with the expansion of personal liberty. A radical liberal, like John Stuart Mill, who championed democracy and the extension of personal rights and liberties, was also an advocate of doctrines which can be blamed for the degradations of the workhouse (Utilitarianism) and the extremes of Victorian poverty (laissez-faire). By contrast, Shaftesbury and Wilberforce, famous respectively for the Factory Acts and the abolition of slavery, were high Tories. State intervention in the economy and social welfare

In responding to Castille's 'Sur la solitude'[36] Baudelaire is in the first instance resisting the moralizing stance evident in his denunciation of the dangers of solitude. In this connection he will have been mindful of Castille's earlier and notorious condemnation of Balzac in an article published on 4 October 1846 in the Sunday weekly *La Semaine* (of which Castille was joint-editor). In this article Castille takes Balzac to task both for depressing his readers and for making vice seem attractive. Thus he begins by recording 'une profonde admiration pour l'artiste qui fouilla d'une main si ferme et si intelligente ces bas-reliefs du cœur humain, les passions' but then complains that this has left him, Castille, with 'une immense tristesse mêlée de mépris pour cette humanité dont un ciseau impitoyable vient de sculpter les difformités morales'. Indeed, he states, '[d]e ce mépris naît je ne sais quel dégoût de la vie qui vous domine durant plusieurs jours', such in fact that more than one reader, so Castille claims, has ended up retiring from the world and closing their curtains 'pour ne plus voir le soleil'. In a clear reference to the account of man's 'Fall' recorded in the Book of Genesis, Castille likens a novel by Balzac to 'un fruit magnifique et tentateur': 'quiconque y mord en garde longtemps l'amertume à la lèvre. Je défends sérieusement Balzac aux hypocondriaques.' To read the *Comédie humaine*, therefore, is to be led into unhealthy solitude and to fall into sin: 'On l'a dit depuis longtemps, M. de Balzac est le chantre du désespoir. À ceci nous n'ajouterons qu'un mot: le désespoir est immoral.' Moreover the blame for this state of affairs lies with art itself: 'chaque fois que M. de Balzac s'écarte du sens moral, on peut en accuser, neuf fois sur dix, son profond amour pour l'art'. Conscious of adopting a position that will upset 'les partisans de l'art pour l'art', Castille robustly proclaims his adherence to the neo-Platonist aesthetic philosophy propounded by Victor Cousin:

> tout œuvre d'art doit [...] tendre vers un but: *le Beau*. Mais le Beau ainsi que l'entendaient les Grecs, c'est-à-dire le Beau contenant l'âme du Bien. De là au sens moral, il n'y a pas loin. On pourrait victorieusement prouver que, dans toute œuvre parfaite, le beau, le sens moral et la logique sont toujours d'accord avec les règles de l'art, et concourent à sa perfection. Plus d'un sculpteur, plus d'un peintre, plus d'un poète ou d'un romancier catholiques romains, gagneraient à méditer la haute théorie du païen Platon.[37]

---

policies belonged to the right, for the right believed in the duty of government to govern—to secure social order and adminster justice impartially.' See John Ruskin, *'Unto this Last' and Other Writings*, ed. Clive Wilmer (rev. edn, London: Penguin Books, 1997), 23–4. I am grateful to Patrick McGuinness for bringing *Unto this Last* and this particular edition to my attention.

[36] As will be seen, the following discussion departs radically from Leakey's perception of a 'subtle affinity' between Baudelaire's views and Castille's 'thoughtful essay', let alone his assertion of 'an unexpected kinship of imagination' in relation to the image of the hanged man ('A *Festschrift* of 1855', 193, 194).

[37] Earlier in the article he has referred to Balzac as being 'catholique, apostolique et romain' (134). Castille's article ('Critique littéraire. Romanciers contemporains. I. M. H. de Balzac') is reproduced in Stéphane Vachon (ed.), *Balzac* (Paris: Presses de l'Université de Paris-Sorbonne [Collection Mémoire

Commenting on this at the time in the weekly journal *Le Tintamarre* Baudelaire described Castille's article—together with Balzac's reply on 11 October[38]—as 'un événement énorme' (ii. 1013), and its young author as 'éminemment cocasse' (ii. 1014). He paraphrases Balzac's defence against the charge of having made vice attractive: 'Si un jeune homme, en lisant *La Comédie humaine*, s'amourache des Lousteau et des Lucien de Rubempré, il est JUGÉ!!!'[39]—and gleefully adds: 'JUGÉ!!!! [-] Cependant le jeune Hippoltye est très innocent.'[40] Later returning to the subject of art and morality in his article 'Les Drames et les romans honnêtes', published in *Semaine théâtrale* on 27 November 1851, Baudelaire recalls this famous exchange of views, now describing Castille as '[u]n jeune écrivain qui a écrit de bonnes choses, mais qui fut emporté ce jour-là par le sophisme socialistique' (ii. 41).[41]

The irony here is rich. As Baudelaire well knew, Castille had by now, in the aftermath of the 1848 Revolution, deserted the cause of socialist reform and become an ardent upholder of 'the Law' in the person of Louis-Napoléon. This change of political clothing[42] is advertised by Castille himself in 'Sur la solitude' where he quotes at length from the 'Introduction' to his recently published *Histoire de la seconde République française*:

---

de la critique], 1999), 133–41. For these quotations see 133–5, 138. This last quotation is followed by a footnoted recommendation to read Plato's *Symposium*. As the opening paragraphs of the article make clear, this issue of *La Semaine* was intended as a relaunch, and so Castille was doubtless provoking controversy in order to draw attention to the journal.

[38] Reproduced in Balzac, *Écrits sur le roman*, ed. Stéphane Vachon (Paris: Librairie Générale Française [Le Livre de poche], 2000), 307–23.

[39] Balzac himself had written: 'Si, lisant *La Comédie humaine*, un jeune homme trouve peu blâmables les Lousteau, les Lucien de Rubempré, etc., ce jeune homme est jugé.' See *Écrits sur le roman*, ed. Vachon, 317.

[40] This perception of a disparity between Castille's pompous moralizing and his 'innocence' surfaced again obliquely in March 1856 when in a celebrated letter to his friend and fellow contributor to *Fontainebleau*, Charles Asselineau, Baudelaire describes at length a dream of his in which he leaves Castille outside in a carriage while he, Baudelaire, visits a brothel. See *Corr*. i. 338–41. On this dream see Michel Butor's celebrated commentary in his *Histoire extraordinaire: Essai sur un rêve de Baudelaire* (Paris: Gallimard, 1961).

[41] In both 1846 and 1851 Baudelaire makes plain his admiration for Balzac's reply (to the effect that art is moral not by being didactic or avoiding the depiction of immorality but by its presentation of moral complexity), and in the notes he wrote for his lawyer at the time of the trial of *Les Fleurs du Mal* he specifically advises him to read Balzac's letter and attend to its argument (i. 194). For further discussion of this public exchange between Castille and Balzac, see Arlette Michel, 'La Morale du roman: Balzac répond à Hippolyte Castille', *L'Année balzacienne*, 4 (2003), 225–47.

[42] Cf. Dolf Oehler, 'Messages disparus de Job: Hippolyte Castille', in *Le Spleen contre l'oubli. Juin 1848: Baudelaire, Flaubert, Heine, Herzen* (Paris: Payot et Rivages, 1996), 153–94: 'Castille [...] passe de l'écrivain engagé qui veut parler aux masses au polygraphe bonapartiste élitaire' (154). For Oehler, who notes Flaubert's view of him as a venal pen-pusher (153), Castille was essentially a trimmer and an opportunist: 'il n'y a de continuité ni dans son écriture ni dans ses opinions' (154). On his transition from socialist to supporter of Louis-Napoléon, Oehler comments further: 'par haine contre les bourgeois, des hommes comme Castille, avec plus ou moins de sincérité, ont léché les bottes de l'empereur qu'ils avaient copieusement raillé avant le coup d'État [...]. Castille et ses pareils appréciaient en lui celui qui avait renvoyé la bourgeoisie au fond de ses boutiques où elle se tiendrait plus tranquille que sur la place publique' (186).

Deux instincts puissants luttent éternellement au fond de l'âme humaine: l'instinct sauvage indompté, le moi irrationnel, c'est-à-dire la révolte; et l'instinct de l'association, du sacrifice, du devoir, c'est-à-dire la Loi. [-] Quand du haut d'un monument nos regards glissent au-dessus de la ville et découvrent les campagnes, quand nous entrons dans une forêt, quand, sur la plage, nos yeux se perdent parmi les profonds horizons des mers, un soupir s'échappe de notre poitrine; on dirait que nous nous souvenons d'une condition antérieure, dont les sensations n'ont plus en nous qu'un écho affaibli; nous voudrions prolonger cette vague réminiscence du premier homme, perpétuée dans toute l'humanité; notre tête se relève d'un mouvement brusque et léger, la brute se réveille. Tout à coup un son lointain, le son d'une cloche, nous fait tressaillir: c'est la religion; un roulement de tambour traverse les airs: c'est la patrie. Et si cela ne suffisait pas, la faim qui tord nos entrailles nous avertit que déjà la soupe fume sur la table, que les enfants impatients frappent les assiettes de leur cuiller, et que la ménagère inquiète est déjà deux fois venue regarder au seuil de la porte: c'est la famille. [-] Alors nous inclinons cette tête rebelle, nous nous acheminons à pas lents vers le grand bercail; puis nous hâtons la marche, et, en rentrant dans la commune, l'homme social, le citoyen a complètement repris conscience de ses devoirs.[43]

It would be difficult to imagine a more *bien pensant* statement of affiliation to the values of the Second Empire than this nor a mindset more calculated to provoke a greater resistance in Baudelaire. In Castille's 'Introduction' these comments come directly after he has posited a 'duel de la Liberté et de la Société' that is 'en quelque sorte antérieur à la formation des peuples' and which is fought 'dans le cœur même de l'homme'.[44] For him freedom and society are opposites, and in 'Sur la solitude' he quotes again from his history of the Second Republic: 'La lutte est entre la nature et la société, comme entre la liberté et le sacrifice'; and then, in case the readers of *Fontainebleau* should be in any doubt as to his own position, he adds: 'Or je n'hésite pas à mettre le sacrifice au-dessus de la liberté.'[45]

For Castille, therefore, the forest of Fontainbleau and the solitude that it offers to poets, painters, and lovers is a place of potential destruction akin to that brought about by the 1848 Revolution. It is a place of temptation, prompting atavistic memories of our savage state of freedom—'la liberté, cette déesse de la solitude, du malheur et de la révolte'[46]—before we were obliged by the social contract to hurry home before the soup gets cold. In short, it encourages the sigh-inducing perception of a lack, of something we once had and now inarticulately long for—in which view Castille precisely echoes the principal thesis of

---

[43] 'Sur la solitude', in *Fontainebleau*, 87–8, and *Histoire de la seconde République française* (4 vols, Paris: Victor Lecou, 1854–6), i. 11–12.
[44] *Histoire de la seconde République française*, i. 11.
[45] 'Sur la solitude', 88–9. Cf. *Histoire de la seconde République française*, i. 13.
[46] *Histoire de la seconde République française*, i. 13.

Chateaubriand's *Essai sur les révolutions* and his diagnosis of a human state of melancholy that causes revolutions and can best be assuaged (as Chateaubriand subsequently argues in his *Génie du christianisme*) by religious, and specifically Christian, faith. For Castille the forest means anarchy and unbridled individualism, an invitation to disrespect the Law. But for Baudelaire, resisting Castille's politics as much as his pious moralizing, there is an alternative legislation: that of the creative imagination.

In his sonnet 'La Destruction'—first published among 'Les Fleurs du Mal' the day before the prose poem 'La Solitude'—we find a similar 'démon [qui] fréquente les lieux arides', a Satanic seducer who lures the poet into the wilderness of solitude and boredom—'au milieu | Des plaines de l'Ennui, profondes et désertes' (ll. 10–11)—by exploiting his sexual attraction to women. Moreover the 'appareil sanglant de la Destruction' evoked at the end of that poem figures here in 'La Solitude' in the poet's acknowledgement that 'l'esprit de meurtre et de lubricité s'enflamme merveilleusement dans les solitudes'. But, as we saw in examining the other poems published for the first time in 1855 under the collective title of 'Les Fleurs du Mal', there is a new emphasis there on the creativity of the artist as an alternative to the destructiveness inherent in our human experience of time and desire. Accordingly, here in 'La Solitude', Baudelaire resists Castille's condemnation of poets and artists as being responsible for idealizing the experience of solitude and thereby, like Balzac, supposedly seducing readers and spectators into depression and sin. Faced with Castille's transformation of a socialist faith in community into a brutal suppression of individual freedom, Baudelaire here champions the rights of the solitary human being—as Castille himself had once done—over and against the claims of the collective. By the same token he defends the worth and integrity of poets and artists by turning the tables on Castille and using the language and imagery of free-market economics to make his point: the experience of sublimity afforded by a forest view is now an inalienable title deed. Here, truly, is something worth owning.

In this connection the reference to Robinson Crusoe is particularly instructive. By arguing that solitude is dangerous only for 'ces âmes oisives et *divagantes* qui ne sont pas gouvernées par une importante pensée active' (my emphasis), Baudelaire appears both to be acceding in part to Castille's argument and also to be echoing Castille's own concession towards the end of his essay that some people—runners, for example!—may draw peace and strength from the solitude of the forest:

> pour certains hommes, une course dans les bois est un calmant sans égal. Ceux-là sont des athlètes qui, dans le silence et l'isolement, savent puiser de fortes résolutions et rassembler leur vigueur défaillante. Mais pour quiconque ne sait

pas dompter le mauvais esprit de la solitude, les bois voudront toujours dire: assassinat, viol ou suicide.[47]

But in echoing Castille Baudelaire is once again turning the tables on him: silently mocking, through ostensible concession, the moralizing journalist's reliance on the age-old stereotype of poets and artists as solitary dreamers with their heads in the clouds and instead—in anticipation of Mallarmé's own *Divagations*—proposing that poets, too, may be capable of important and active thought, and indeed that 'oisiveté' and 'divagation' are precisely what permit thoughts of *real* importance. Perhaps the poet is like Robinson Crusoe: marooned on his island, isolated from society, and surviving a shipwreck (a revolution?) by constructing his own new habitat? The hero of Daniel Defoe's novel, first published in 1719 (and newly translated into French by Petrus Borel in 1836), had recently been adopted by Castille's friend and free-marketeer Frédéric Bastiat in his influential work of economic theory, *Harmonies économiques* (1850), as a means of illustrating his own models of labour and capital, of property, exchange, and value.[48] For Bastiat, Defoe's hero represents 'l'homme surmontant par son énergie, son activité, son intelligence, les difficultés de la solitude absolue',[49] a description echoed in Baudelaire's contention that '[la solitude] le rendit religieux, brave, industrieux; elle le purifia, elle lui enseigna jusqu'où peut aller la force de l'individu'.

In essence Bastiat is arguing for the social benefits of individual labour and for the legitimacy of private property based on that labour within a 'harmonious' community of individuals. Accordingly, what was then frequently termed 'philanthropie'—namely, the redistribution of wealth advocated by socialist and communist economic and political theory—was anathema to him: 'Prendre aux uns pour donner aux autres! Qu'il me soit permis de signaler ici le danger et l'absurdité de la pensée économique de cette aspiration, dite "sociale", qui fermentait au sein des masses et qui a éclaté avec tant de force à la révolution de Février.'[50] Similarly, Bastiat takes issue with Rousseau's account of the origins of society in the *Discours sur l'inégalité*, claiming that in his depiction of the happy state of 'natural man' Rousseau was obliged to make that happiness consist in 'la privation', whereas true happiness comes, as it does for Crusoe, in the gradual accumulation of 'capital'—in his case, the successive fashioning of more

---

[47] 'Sur la solitude', 88.
[48] In doing so Bastiat initiated a tradition in the field of economic theory that continues to this day. See Fritz Söllner, 'The Use (and Abuse) of Robinson Crusoe in Neoclassical Economics', *History of Political Economy*, 48: 1 (2016), 35–64. See also Michael White's article entry under 'Robinson Crusoe' in *The New Palgrave Dictionary of Economics* (London: Palgrave Macmillan, 2019: article first published in *The New Palgrave Dictionary of Economics*, 2nd edn, 2008).
[49] See Frédéric Bastiat, *Harmonies économiques* (Paris: Guillaumin & Cie, 1850), 118.
[50] *Harmonies économiques*, 156.

sophisticated tools and the progressive acquisition of more comfortable living conditions—and in the enjoyment ('jouissance') of these comforts, or 'property'.[51]

Castille ends his essay as he began it, by also thinking of Rousseau: 'Ajouterai-je que, pour un petit nombres d'âmes robustes et saines, les grands aspects de la nature sont un perpétuel *memento* qui ramène l'homme au profond, au social sentiment de l'égalité?'[52] Rousseau, as we know, believed that inequality began with the institution of property and the birth of 'l'homme social', now expelled from a state of nature in which all are equal, and his famous statement in the *Discours sur l'inégalité* is worth recalling in full since Baudelaire, too, surely has it in mind in 'La Solitude':

> Le premier qui ayant enclos un terrain, s'avisa de dire, 'ceci est à moi', et trouva des gens assez simples pour le croire, fut le vrai fondateur de la société civile. Que de crimes, de guerres, de meurtres, que de misères et d'horreurs n'eût point épargnés au Genre-humain celui qui arrachant les pieux ou comblant le fossé, eût crié à ses semblables. Gardez-vous d'écouter cet imposteur; Vous êtes perdus, si vous oubliez que les fruits sont à tous, et que la Terre n'est à personne[.][53]

Castille, as we have seen, staunchly believes in social obligation rather than individual freedom (believing these to be incompatible) and here ends his essay by revisiting his earlier account of our two (alleged) conflicting instincts: 'l'instinct sauvage indompté, le moi irrationnel, c'est-à-dire la révolte; et l'instinct de l'association, du sacrifice, du devoir, c'est-à-dire la Loi', and suggesting that solitude in nature can have a beneficial effect on the strong-minded by reminding us of our fundamental sameness—or equality—as human beings (presumably by removing us from the social/urban context in which our fundamental humanity is overlaid by hierarchical divisions of class, wealth, and power). Where Rousseau argued also that we have two basic instincts—but in his case these instincts being, the one, to secure our own survival, and the other, to feel compassion towards others—he rejected the Aristotelian contention that man is a social animal and granted only that family, rather than a more broadly social association, is natural (and therefore beneficial). For him society is born of reason not sentiment. By speaking of a 'sentiment social', Castille is silently redefining Rousseauism so that he can end his essay by enlisting the solitude of the forest of Fontainbleau in the cause of his new reactionary politics. In the preceding, penultimate paragraph of the essay he

---

[51] *Harmonies économiques*, 119–20, 255–7, 315–16. The second edition of *Harmonies économiques*, published posthumously in 1851, contains additional material, including further use of Crusoe as a model.

[52] 'Sur la solitude', 89.

[53] *Discours sur l'origine et les fondements de l'inégalité* (1754), in Rousseau, *Œuvres complètes*, ed. Bernard Gagnebin and Marcel Raymond (5 vols, Paris: Gallimard [Bibliothèque de la Pléiade], 1959–95), iii. 164.

suggests that forests can serve a useful and quasi-monastic purpose as a refuge for the weak-minded, for 'les grandes infortunes' and 'les âmes fatiguées'. There such people may go to enjoy the fresh air and the silence like consumptives partaking of remedial asses' milk. And, Castille adds: 'nous avons nos savants, nos poètes, nos peintres, nos musiciens, à qui ces bois sont nécessaires'.[54] Poets and artists, then, are sick, powerless to resist a savage, unbridled, irrational urge to revolt, while men like Castille are sound of mind and firm of social purpose, obedient to the call of religion, nation, and family. For them what counts is 'la soupe' rather than 'les nuages'.

Baudelaire, needless to say, sees things rather differently (as his own prose poem 'La Soupe et les nuages' will also later demonstrate), and the final paragraph of 'La Solitude' represents a direct rebuttal of Castille's position. The model of the industrious Robinson Crusoe who can create his own sustainable reality on the Island of Despair is now replaced by the figure of 'le Solitaire': the poet as a new kind of 'promeneur solitaire'[55] who lays claim not to land or property but to 'la sublimité d'un paysage'—as though, in a revision of Rousseau's narrative of appropriation, thereby founding a new society, a society of poets and artists and musicians and 'savants', and, for that matter, of lovers. And when it comes to 'la jouissance'—the term current in contemporary politico-economic accounts for the 'enjoyment' of the fruits of one's labours, of one's property[56]—then, says the poet of 'La Solitude', even the finest forms of social association ('les plus belles agapes fraternelles, les plus magnifiques réunions d'hommes électrisés par un plaisir') are as nothing compared with the individual's inalienable right to 'own' and 'enjoy' a perfect moment: the epiphany or 'moment privilégié' (as Joyce and Proust will later, respectively, call it) of a solitary walk in the forest, and a moment, as 'Correspondances' has it in its own consideration of forest walks, 'ayant l'expansion des choses infinies'. And this ownership is secured not under the 'Law' of Hippolyte Castille but by the alternative legislation of a poet.

In these ways the apparently straightforward and paratactic sentences of 'La Solitude' belie a more complex and partly hidden agenda, just as the very simplicity—and even banality—of the poet's moral conclusion ('Il en serait donc de la solitude comme du crépuscule; elle est bonne et elle est mauvaise, criminelle et salutaire, incendiaire et calmante, selon qu'on en use, et selon qu'on a usé de la vie') conceals a deeper lesson: the undesirability of being lectured at, and the need to resist all those who, like Castille, are constantly laying down the law for others. Indeed this was the main lesson of Frédéric Bastiat's impassioned pamphlet *La Loi* (1850) in which the free-marketeer inveighs against 'la fausse philanthropie' of

---

[54] 'Sur la solitude', 89.

[55] *Le Promeneur solitaire* was one of the titles Baudelaire briefly considered giving to his collection of prose poems. See *Corr.* ii. 207.

[56] On Baudelaire's recurrent use of the word in *Le Spleen de Paris*, see Murphy, *Logiques du dernier Baudelaire*, 370–4.

socialism (here redefining the redistribution of wealth as 'une spoliation légale') and resists what he regards as the excessive and unwarranted interference of ever-proliferating legislation in the life of the individual:

> Il faut le dire: il y a trop de grands hommes dans le monde; il y a trop de législateurs, organisateurs, instituteurs de sociétés, conducteurs de peuples, pères des nations, etc., etc. Trop de gens se placent au-dessus de l'humanité pour la régenter, trop de gens font métier de s'occuper d'elle.[57]

Castille, the new recruit to imperial law and order, has clearly not heeded his erstwhile colleague's warning.

Moreover, it seems, he has also been quoting the Church Fathers in support of his view that solitude is dangerous. So, not only does Castille seek to lay down the law himself, therefore, but he quotes another 'authority'—in this case the authority of the Early Church—in his own support. As the poet of 'La Solitude' now demonstrates, everyone can play that game, and so he himself quotes the seventeenth-century moralist and thinker Jean de La Bruyère (1645–96) who writes as follows in Les Caractères (1688):

> Tout notre mal vient de ne pouvoir être seuls: de là le jeu, le luxe, la dissipation, le vin, les femmes, l'ignorance, la médisance, l'envie, l'oubli de soi-même et de Dieu. [-] L'homme semble quelquefois ne se suffire pas à soi-même; les ténèbres, la solitude, le troublent, le jettent dans des craintes frivoles et dans de vaines terreurs; le moindre mal alors qui puisse lui arriver est de s'ennuyer. [-] L'ennui est entré dans le monde par la paresse; elle a beaucoup de part dans la recherche que font les hommes des plaisirs, du jeu, de la société. Celui qui aime le travail a assez de soi-même.[58]

So well known is this passage—and will have been to an educated French reader of 1855—that Baudelaire merely abbreviates the statement: 'N'est-ce pas La Bruyère qui a dit: "Ce grand malheur de ne pouvoir être seul?..."' A desire for succinctness may no doubt be the reason for this ellipsis, but La Bruyère's summary of the dangers of 'non-solitude' reads like a précis of 'Au lecteur', first published the day before 'La Solitude'. Perhaps Baudelaire wanted, in the persona of this particular prose poet in 'La Solitude', to avoid giving the impression that he himself has a law to lay down (as the poet-moralist of Les Fleurs du Mal nevertheless most clearly has), and this in order the more pointedly to reprove the opinionated Castille. For

---

[57] Frédéric Bastiat, La Loi (Paris: Guillaumin et Cie, 1850), 78.
[58] Jean de La Bruyère, Les Caractères, ou Les Mœurs de ce siècle, ed. Antoine Adam (Paris: Gallimard [Folio], 1975), 254–5.

every cause—solitude, say—can have two contrary, or apparently contrary, effects: such as, for example, 'le Mal' and an experience of the sublime.

In the absence of firm evidence that Baudelaire had read Castille's essay before composing and submitting 'La Solitude' to Desnoyers for publication, we cannot rely wholly on this possibility for a reading of the text. But even without such a supposition it is clear that the main thrust of 'La Solitude' in this first version of the prose poem lies in the poet's resistance against being lectured at, against people who state opinions and pronounce moral lessons as though these were self-evidently and unproblematically true. Like Flaubert who repeatedly asserted that 'la bêtise humaine consiste à vouloir conclure' and wrote in such a way as to avoid such conclusions and to achieve what he terms a kind of 'literary justice',[59] so Baudelaire uses the prose poem as a means of inviting more provisional and sophisticated consideration of a whole range of issues. Here in 'La Solitude' the simple matter of solitude and its various benefits and disbenefits for the individual human being gives on to much broader horizons. In the first paragraph the reference to the Church Fathers calls up the early history of the Christian Church during which one fundamental difference of theological opinion turned on whether it was better to seek God in solitude or in community. Some early followers of Christ, including some of the early Church Fathers, chose to live the life of a hermit in the desert (and are therefore sometimes referred to as the 'Desert Fathers'), and the desert, or 'wilderness', was itself known as a place of temptation, whether it be that in which Satan tempted Christ—as alluded to in Baudelaire's poem 'La Destruction'—or the eastern desert of Egypt where St Antony underwent his celebrated temptations of the flesh. Others, by contrast, chose to follow the so-called Rule of Saint Benedict and to live together in monastic communities.[60] This debate between the so-called eremetic and cenobitic traditions in the Church has a long history—as has the age-old question, at least since Plato, of the poet's rightful place in society. Does he belong in the Republic at all? Yes, but on the firm understanding that 'hymns to the gods and eulogies of good people are the only poetry we can admit into our city'?[61] Or is there a role for the poet as alternative *nomothetes*, a lone voice crying in the wilderness and representing a new Covenant?

As suggested by the references to Robinson Crusoe and the 'Solitaire' who lays claim to ownership of 'la sublimité d'un paysage', the question of the poet's rightful place is a political as well as a quasi-religious one. Should the poet extol the benefits of life in a strictly regimented social community—regimented whether by a recently instituted imperial rule or by the 'philanthropic' dictates of new

---

[59] See my 'Flaubert's Style and the Idea of Literary Justice'.
[60] In his article 'Sur la solitude' (*Fontainebleau*, 89) Castille likens the shelter afforded to weak-minded poets by the forest of Fontainebleau to that offered by the community of La Trappe to people in need of material and psychological assistance.
[61] Plato, *The Republic*, 607a. See my *Unacknowledged Legislators*, 20–3, for further discussion.

socialist or communist dispensations—or should the poet represent the private over and against the public, stand for the right to individual freedom of expression in the face of all manner of orthodox opinion and prejudice and lazy thinking? Should poets immerse themselves in the crowd, or should they lock themselves away like the poet of 'Paysage' or the prose poet of 'À une heure du matin': 'D'abord, un double tour à la serrure. Il me semble que ce tour de clef augmentera ma solitude et fortifiera les barricades qui me séparent actuellement du monde' (i. 287)? The barricades of 1848 have become the barricades of literary art, a brave defence against the imperialism of the orthodox.

Alone at Twilight: 'La Solitude' and 'Le Crépuscule du soir' (1862/4)

> La tombée de la nuit a toujours été pour moi le signal d'une fête intérieure et comme la délivrance d'une angoisse.
> ('Le Crépuscule du soir' [1855]).

We have come some distance from the simple question of whether the forest of Fontainebleau encourages suicide, and yet all these issues are raised by 'La Solitude', where the obvious truth of the poet's statement that solitude can be both beneficial and injurious throws into relief the even greater obviousness of the 'friend's' error and stupidity in pronouncing so unambiguously on the matter. Castille argued that poets idealize solitude and that *he* is the realist, but who can tell? As it might be, 'lequel est le vrai'?[62] In revising 'La Solitude' subsequently for publication in *La Presse*,[63] Baudelaire concertedly foregrounds this poetic resistance to the unambiguous assertion of a truth. Where previously the text had formed a diptych with 'Le Crépuscule du soir' by serving as a response to the second 'friend's' warning that solitude is dangerous, now the prose poem stands alone as the response to a 'gazetier philanthrope': that is, to a journalist of socialist persuasion, as well as a journalist who has 'generously' doled out unwanted moral advice to the poet. Castille may no doubt still have been in Baudelaire's mind as he created this figure, but the latter here stands more broadly for a whole body of 'progressive', 'humanitarian' public discourse.[64]

---

[62] The alternative title of 'Laquelle est la vraie?' is 'L'Idéal et le réel'. See *Le Spleen de Paris*, ed. Steinmetz, 236.
[63] 'La Solitude', together with 'Le Crépuscule du soir', were to have been published in their revised forms in the fourth group of prose poems submitted to Houssaye and subsequently rejected for publication. The revised version of 'Le Crépuscule du soir' was first published in *Le Figaro* on 7 Feb. 1864, while the revised version of 'La Solitude' first appeared published in the *Revue de Paris* on 25 Dec. 1864.
[64] This body of writing is the subject of Paul Bénichou, *Le Temps des prophètes: Doctrines de l'âge romantique* (Paris: Gallimard, 1977), the third of his magisterial account of French Romanticism. For a

THE INAUGURATION OF THE PROSE POEM 479

Now eight rather than four paragraphs in length, the revised version of 'La Solitude' devotes three of these additional paragraphs to this rejection of dogmatism:

> Il est certain qu'un bavard, dont le suprême plaisir consiste à parler du haut d'une chaire ou d'une tribune, risquerait fort de devenir fou furieux dans l'île de Robinson. Je n'exige pas de mon gazetier les courageuses vertus de Crusoé, mais je demande qu'il ne décrète pas d'accusation les amoureux de la solitude et du mystère.
>
> Il y a dans nos races jacassières des individus qui accepteraient avec moins de répugnance le supplice suprême, s'il leur était permis de faire du haut de l'échafaud une copieuse harangue, sans craindre que les tambours de Santerre ne leur coupassent intempestivement la parole.[65]
>
> Je ne les plains pas, parce que je devine que leurs effusions oratoires leur procurent des voluptés égales à celles que d'autres tirent du silence et du recueillement; mais je les méprise.

Loquacity, *ex cathedra* statement and decree, accusation and harangue: these are the multiple and ubiquitous symptoms of an 'anti-poetry' to be resisted by the cultivation of solitude, mystery, and silence—and scorn. 'Chacun sa volupté' (or 'jouissance'), the poet of 'La Solitude' proclaims, in apparent deference to egalitarianism, but now—in a revision and repositioning of the final paragraph of the first version of 'La Solitude'—there is a quite clear, satirical objection to the 'philanthropic' objectives of socialism to be seen in the poet's ridicule of the principle of sharing wealth:

> Je désire surtout que mon maudit gazetier me laisse m'amuser à ma guise: 'Vous n'éprouvez donc jamais,—me dit-il avec un ton de nez très apostolique,—le besoin de partager vos jouissances?' Voyez-vous le subtil envieux! Il sait que je dédaigne les siennes, et il vient s'insinuer dans les miennes, le hideux trouble-fête!

Here the poet's resistance to self-righteous and 'apostolic' opinion takes the form of a comically petulant individualism as he himself accuses the accursed journalist of the sin of envy and of seeking to gate-crash his party. For how, after all, *can* you share the fruits of solitude... unless perhaps in poetry? Once again the poet cites La Bruyère as an 'authority' on his side of the debate, but now adds in Pascal for

---

summary and discussion of Bénichou's arguments and conclusions, see my *Unacknowledged Legislators*, 32–44.

[65] The reference is to Antoine Joseph Santerre (1752–1809), a commanding officer in the National Guard during the Revolutionary period, who was thought by some to have ordered a drum roll in order to drown out Louis XVI's valedictory speech on the occasion of his execution in Jan. 1793.

good measure, the Pascal who contended that 'Presque tous nos malheurs nous viennent de n'avoir pas su rester dans notre chambre.' And this is also Pascal the religious thinker who espoused the teachings of Jansenism and of St Augustine, that most influential of the Early Fathers of the Church. Moreover, Pascal was a true (Christian) believer, unlike the 'maudit gazetier' who, 'comme tous les incrédules', quotes the Early Fathers simply to lend false authority to his 'oratorical effusions' as specious tub-thumper and worthless tinpot prophet. For such, the poet tells us and as Pascal reflected in his own 'cellule du recueillement', are 'ces affolés qui cherchent le bonheur dans le mouvement et dans une prostitution que je pourrais appeler *fraternitaire*, si je voulais parler la belle langue de mon siècle'. And here the revised version of 'La Solitude' ends, as did the first, with a veiled reference to Bastiat: in this case, the Bastiat who in *Capital et rente* (1849), a polemical pamphlet vigorously arguing against the political and economic theories of Proudhon, had employed the term *fraternitaire* as a pejorative characterization of socialism.[66]

---

[66] 'Eh bien! passons un peu par-dessus les modernes axiomes fraternitaires découverts par messieurs les socialistes', comments Jacques the woodworker in an imaginary dialogue with his fellow-woodworker Guillaume, who wants to borrow Jacques's plane for free on the grounds that 'l'on a proclamé la Fraternité?' The dialogue is intended by Bastiat to demonstrate the natural justice and socio-political legitimacy of being obliged to pay interest on a loan. See *Capital et rente* (Paris: Guillaumin & Cie, 1849), 32. I am indebted for this further allusion to Bastiat's work to Jean-Michel Gouvard, 'Sur les notions d'égalité, de fraternité et de citoyenneté dans *Le Spleen de Paris*', in Murphy (ed.), *Lectures du 'Spleen de Paris'*, 297–306 (304–6). On Bastiat's subsequent ironic critique of 'l'axiome fraternitaire "chacun pour tous"' in *Harmonies économiques*, see Alexandre de Vitry, 'Baudelaire et ses "frères|"', *Revue d'histoire littéraire de la France*, 119 (2019), 289–304 (295). As Andrea Schellino notes in his 'Baudelaire et la prostitution "*fraternitaire*". À propos de "La Solitude"' (*Méthode! Revue de littérature* [Université de Pau], 24 (Autumn 2014), 183–94 (see n. 48)), the word 'fraternitaire' was used by Proudhon himself: in *La Guerre et la paix: Recherches sur le principe et la constitution du droit des gens* (2 vols, Paris: E. Dentu, 1861), ii. 217, and in *Théorie de la propriété* (Paris: Librairie internationale, 1866), 49. Proudhon uses the term, not (as Schellino suggests) to critique his own earlier economic theories as sentimentally idealistic but to emphasize (perhaps by way of defending himself against the now deceased Bastiat's former attacks) the objective nature of these theories by contrast with what he remembers as the ineffectual good intentions much flaunted in the period 1848–51. In *La Guerre et la paix* he discusses how the problem of poverty could be addressed either by promoting economic growth or by redistribution: 'La première de ces solutions avait la faveur, non seulement de la bourgeoisie, mais des masses, non seulement des théories en vogue, mais de l'opinion.—Nous ne produisons pas assez, s'écriait-on de toutes parts; nous ne tirons pas du sol ce qu'il peut rendre; nous laissons dormir nos capitaux. Il ne s'agit pas de "rogner les habits, mais d'allonger les vestes...". Le mot fit fortune. Il y avait dans ce système quelque chose de *fraternitaire*, en apparence, en même temps que d'entreprenant, de conquérant, qui devait ravir conservateurs et démocrates et entraîner le gouvernement' (my emphasis). As to the second solution, 'on cria à la spoliation' (*La Guerre et la paix*, ii. 218)—the term used by Bastiat to denigrate the politics of redistribution. In *Théorie de la propriéte* Proudhon again uses the term 'fraternitaire' to imply something that merely appears to conform to the republican principles of 'liberté, égalité, fraternité': 'Mes études de réforme économique dans la même période [1848–51] ont surtout porté sur le *côté objectif* de la question. Nous étions débordés par la sensiblerie fraternitaire, communautaire; il semblait que la solution du problème du prolétariat fut simplement affaire de prédication et de propagande'. Baudelaire first uses the word 'fraternitaire' in the revised draft version of 'La Solitude' submitted to Houssaye in 1862 and so may conceivably have derived it not only from Bastiat's *Capital et rente* but from Proudhon's very recent use of it in *La Guerre et la paix*.

Like Bastiat the poet wants to resist this modish leftist rejection of the individual's right to go it alone. 'La solitude est mauvaise', the poet has been warned, because socialists and communists, not to mention bourgeois conformists and other adepts of 'Law and Order', want us all to toe the line, to fall into line, to accept the party line. But the poet is an 'étranger', with a beautiful language of his own: he has his own 'cellule du recueillement', not the quasi-monastic sylvan reaches of the forest of Fontainebleau but a post-Pascalian room of his own, a stanza—or carefully crafted prose poem—from which to share the fruits of solitary, nonconformist thinking with a like-minded reader, a person with imagination: 'l'âme oisive et divagante', perhaps, 'qui la peuple de ses passions et de ses chimères'. 'Chacun sa volupté', 'Chacun sa chimère'... In this way the poet of 'La Solitude'—like the Baudelaire of *Le Spleen de Paris*—supersedes the false binary of free-market economics and the socialist collective, of the individual and the group, by positioning himself as the Poet: working alone in silent reflection and yet then *publishing* this poem: a private person sharing the inalienable property of his thoughts by making them public and offering an alternative perspective on the world. And, as we shall see presently, where does he seek to publish these thoughts? In *La Presse*, whose very title seems to render it symbolic of *all* journalism and of all 'gazetiers philanthropes'.

In the case of 'La Solitude' we can see how the first version of the poem is much more deeply implicated in the social and political questions of the day than may at first appear, and how in the revised version the campaign of resistance to contemporary doxa—and more especially to the oppressive certainty with which public opinion-formers seek to impose those doxa—has itself become more militant and more outspoken. The art of poetry offers the one safe place of truth and refuge from the mad maelstrom of nineteenth-century social media. Accordingly, this sense of refuge and peace, stated categorically in the first sentence of the original version of 'Le Crépuscule du soir' ('La tombée de la nuit a toujours été pour moi le signal d'une fête intérieure et comme la délivrance d'une angoisse'), is here reaffirmed, in the revised version of this poem, in the more 'lyrical' and overtly 'poetic' language of ecstatic apostrophe: 'Ô nuit! ô rafraîchissantes ténèbres! vous êtes pour moi le signal d'une fête intérieure, vous êtes la délivrance d'une angoisse!' The two 'friends' of the first version remain, but now the first flings his chicken at the maître d'hôtel as though, like some crazy soothsayer of old, he had found in its entrails 'je ne sais quel insultant hiéroglyphe', while the perpetual dissatisfaction of the second has become firmly associated with an insatiable ambition for public honour ('tous les honneurs que peuvent conférer les républiques et les princes'). Each is subject to blinding self-obsession; the former so much so that eventually he can no longer recognize his closest relatives, the latter so much so that he becomes the object of his own fury. For the first friend, the end of day and the coming of night constitute an intolerable moment of reversion from a world of regulated sociability to a primitive domain of savagery: 'L'un méconnaissait alors tous les rapports d'amitié et de politesse, et maltraitait, comme un sauvage, le premier venu.' And so he goes out of his mind. For the second friend the transition from day to night marks a similarly problematic passage from the social to the unsociable: 'Indulgent et sociable encore pendant la journée, il était impitoyable le soir', and twilight brings anger ('rageusement') and confusion ('sa manie crépusculaire'). After dusk he is unable to live amicably with others or even with himself, so consumed is he by the wrong sort of imagination: 'la brûlante envie de distinctions imaginaires'. He is imprisoned by his own obsessive desire for public recognition, which can only be exacerbated by the close of the working day and its attendant opportunity to dwell feverishly, in the darkness, on what he lacks and has failed to achieve during the day just ended. Each man craves the esteem of others, neither can live with himself.

The solitary poet, on the other hand, welcomes this evening twilight as a moment of illumination, at once domestic and cosmic, and as a moment of glorious release: 'Dans la solitude des plaines, dans les labyrinthes pierreux d'une capitale, scintillement des étoiles, explosion des lanternes, vous êtes le feu d'artifice de la déesse Liberté!' It is lighting-up time, and the pyrotechnics of the poetic imagination can begin—as the ensuing two (and final) paragraphs of the poem proceed to demonstrate in their display of high linguistic register and elaborate analogical thinking. For the poet the pink remnants of fading sunlight and the ruddy flames of newly lit candelabra contrast with the gathering darkness in such as a way as to evoke a metaphorical twilight of emotional complexity, of 'tous les sentiments compliqués qui luttent dans le cœur de l'homme aux heures solennelles de la vie'. In addition, this sunset is like a dancer's dress made of dark, transparent gauze overlaid upon a skirt of dazzling aspect—in just the same manner as 'le noir présent transperce le délicieux passé', and in just the same way that 'les étoiles vacillantes d'or et d'argent, dont elle ["une de ces robes étranges de danseuses"] est semée, représentent ces feux de la fantaisie qui ne s'allument bien que sous le deuil profond de la Nuit'. If the coming of night is 'le signal d'une fête intérieure', here is the party of the poetic imagination in full swing: a word-dance against a backdrop of mourning. Only in the deepest darkness do the fireworks of fantasy burn truly bright.

This 'performance' of the poetic imagination with which the revised version of 'Le Crépuscule du soir' ends is itself part of a broader symbolic structure within the poem, and one that has been introduced since the first version of 1855. Now the poet takes up his own observation post within an imagined scene, smoking on a balcony—at once outside and yet adjacent to a room of his own, public yet private, conscious of the lives of others but alone with his thoughts—and poised between a mountain and a valley that invert the traditional hierarchy of heaven and hell:

Cependant du haut de la montagne arrive à mon balcon, à travers les nues transparentes du soir, un grand hurlement, composé d'une foule de cris discordants, que l'espace transforme en une lugubre harmonie, comme celle de la marée qui monte ou d'une tempête qui s'éveille.

From the mountain-top there comes to the poet not the example of Moses or the Tables of the Law but a great noise, a multitudinous discordance: 'je puis, quand le vent souffle de là-haut, bercer ma pensée étonnée à cette imitation des harmonies de l'enfer'. Up there in the blackness is a dark hospice for the dying, anticipating the 'deuil profond de la Nuit' with which the poem ends. Down below is peace and light: 'le repos de l'immense vallée, hérissée de maisons dont chaque fenêtre dit: "C'est ici la paix maintenant; c'est ici la joie de la famille!"' Hell on high, peace here on earth... From above comes the 'sinistre ululation' of 'les infortunés', shrieking like owls as though nightfall were 'un signal de sabbat', the inauguration of a devil's dance: down below, '[u]n grand apaisement se fait dans les pauvres esprits fatigués du labeur de la journée'. Meanwhile the poet smokes and contemplates the scene with equanimity, like these exhausted minds in whom 'leurs pensées prennent maintenant les couleurs tendres et indécises du crépuscule'. This tender indecision of twilight does not drive these exhausted workers to throw their chicken at a waiter, still less to lose their minds. Rather they enter, like the poet, into true possession of their mental faculties, freed from the false ambitions of daylight striving and able now to acknowledge the spectacle of duality and indeed of apparent contradiction before them. Twilight brings space: the space to feel and reflect, a paradoxical and contradictory space of transparent cloud ('à travers les nues transparentes du soir') across which the sound of discordant cries is for the poet somehow transformed into a lugubrious harmony, albeit a harmony filled with menace, as of a rising tide or a gathering storm.

The poem itself now reflects this transformation in its own progression: dwelling on the strange sufferings of the two friends in whom the coming darkness 'excites' such distress and prompts savagery and unreason, and then itself 'exploding' in the onset of this 'fête intérieure', this 'performance' of the poetic as a firework display within the mind and a deliverance from the anguish of melancholy and the prospect of death. Evening twilight marks the end of the harsh realities of the quotidian, and it inaugurates—'précurseur des voluptés profondes'—the prospect of coming glories (after 'les dernières gloires du couchant'), the spectacles born of poetry and dream. The menace of a gathering dusk is figured in the image of heavy drapes being drawn by an invisible hand across the sky from the East, marking the end of today's performance, but at once these drapes become mere gauze, a dark transparent veil (like 'les nues transparentes du soir') beneath which not a witches' sabbath but new and wondrous sights—born of memory ('sous le noir présent transperce le délicieux passé') and imagination ('ces feux de la fantaisie')—may burst forth like 'les splendeurs amorties d'une jupe éclatante', a poetic dance of light within the deep sadness of the night and the knowledge of our certain mortality.

In these ways the new literary form of the prose poem itself—this 'fête intérieure'—may be seen to enact a paradoxical harmony. For, like the poet's twilit balcony, it, too, is poised in between: between reality and imagination, between the quotidian and the fantastical, between oppression and liberation.[67] Situated in the mountainous shadow of death and suffering, in the shadow of 'le Mal', it occupies a vantage point from which to observe a contrasting vista of peace and joy within the intimate shelter of the valley below. At once a 'mi-lieu'[68] and a halfway-house between reason and unreason, between waking and dreaming, it is also a place of fruitful indecision, of veiled splendours and transparent clouds, of a gentle half-light: in short, a sweet spot ('Crépuscule, comme vous êtes doux et tendre!') between the tyranny of night as the conqueror of day ('l'agonie du jour sous l'oppression victorieuse de sa nuit') and the 'refreshment' of night ('O nuit! ô rafraîchissantes ténèbres!') as the liberator of the imagination. Here is the prose poem as the 'intrigued' and 'alarmed' reflection of a cause, such as life itself ('tous les sentiments compliqués qui luttent dans le cœur de l'homme'), that can have two contrary effects: melancholy and beauty. Here is the prose poem poised, like Pascal, between the 'infiniment grand' and the 'infiniment petit', between the vast imaginary reaches of the 'inconnu' and the paltry circumstance of the sadly terre-à-terre. And here is the prose poem manifesting that remarkable combination of clarity and mystery that Baudelaire found to be central to the work of Gautier and Wagner. For the poet in search of beauty, the prose poem is not only a room of his own but a 'chambre double' in which 'tout a la suffisante clarté et la délicieuse obscurité de l'harmonie' (i. 280).

---

[67] For a highly suggestive account of 'Le Crépuscule du soir' that sees this 'inbetweenness' in terms of the polarities of agency and passivity, emotion and affect, the human and the non-human (or non-anthropocentric), see Nikolaj Lübecker, 'Twenty-First Century Baudelaire? Affectivity and Ecology in "Le Crépuscule du soir"', *Modernism/modernity*, 27: 4 (Nov. 2020), 689–706.

[68] Cf. my account of Mallarmé's presentation of the prose poem as a 'mi-lieu' in *Mallarmé and Circumstance*, 104–9.

21
Prose Poetry and the Press
The Poetics of Resistance

> Comment avertir les gens, les nations?—avertissons à l'oreille les plus intelligents.
>
> ('Symptômes de ruines', i. 372)

Baudelaire's fifty completed prose poems were first brought together as a collection only after his death in 1867. Edited by Charles Asselineau and Théodore de Banville they appeared in 1869 as part of the fourth volume of his Œuvres complètes, published by Michel Lévy. Bearing the title *Petits Poèmes en prose*, they were presented in the order he himself had set out[1] and which corresponds in very large part to the order in which the poems had originally been published.[2] Forty-three of the fifty had first appeared in the press: some in reviews that were avowedly literary, such as the *Revue fantaisiste* and the *Nouvelle Revue de Paris*, but the majority in weekly or daily newspapers: for example, *Le Présent*, *La Presse*, *Le Figaro*, and, when Baudelaire later lived in Brussels (April 1864–July 1866), in *L'Indépendance belge*.

For a long time it was customary to approach Baudelaire's prose poems from the direction of poetry, not least because of his own reference (in the dedicatory letter to Arsène Houssaye) to Aloysius Bertrand's *Gaspard de la nuit: Fantaisies à la manière de Rembrandt et de Callot* (1842). In a series of short prose pieces themselves comprising brief, quasi-stanzaic paragraphs that combine dialogue and simple narrative, Bertrand evokes a late medieval world as though he were painting a collection of miniatures—or writing poems in prose. From this model Baudelaire claims to have derived the idea of employing a similar technique in the description of modern life—'ou plutôt d'*une* vie moderne et plus abstraite' (i. 275). But his prose poems have very little in common with Bertrand's—except for Satan. The eponymous Gaspard turns out to be the devil,[3] who is thus, through the

---

[1] See *Le Spleen de Paris*, ed. Steinmetz, 58, for a photograph of this manuscript list.
[2] In this and subsequent chapters, as in the previous one, I shall be discussing the prose poems largely in this traditional sequence, not in order to infer an intended narrative thread or thematic logic of the kind disavowed by Baudelaire in his dedicatory letter to Arsène Houssaye but rather in order to trace a chronological progression in his handling of this new literary form.
[3] See Aloysius Bertrand, *Gaspard de la nuit: Fantaisies à la manière de Rembrandt et de Callot*, ed. Henri Scepi (Paris: Gallimard [Folioplus Classiques], 2011), 27: '"Quoi! Gaspard de la Nuit serait?..."— "Eh! Oui...le diable!"'

etymology of 'Gaspard', the 'treasurer' of the night as well as being the fictional author of *Gaspard de la nuit* itself.[4] Compare the poet-narrator of 'Le Crépuscule du soir' who responds to the witches' sabbath of the mountain hospice by instead welcoming the coming of night as 'le signal d'une fête intérieure' and by celebrating the treasure of the stars as symbolic of 'ces feux de la fantaisie qui ne s'allument bien que sous le deuil profond de la Nuit'. As the condemned author of *Les Fleurs du Mal* Baudelaire now delights in presenting his prose poems, his own 'fantaisies', as yet another work of the Devil—indeed as the Devil himself, in the shape of the serpent to which, in the dedicatory letter to Houssaye, he famously compares the group of prose poems now to be published in *La Presse*. Moreover, they might even have been entitled *Les 666* and thus stamped with the devil's number, the so-called 'mark of the beast'.[5] And so if indeed *Le Spleen de Paris* is to be seen as a 'pendant' to *Les Fleurs du Mal*, as Baudelaire himself frequently (from December 1863 onwards) insisted it should be,[6] then perhaps this is because it represents another 'Satanica Commedia', but this time not in the shape of a hundred poems but a hundred cantos of prose[7]—and a prose that owes much to the world of the Parisian press.

Petits Poèmes en prose or *Le Spleen de Paris*?

J'aime les titres mystérieux ou les titres pétards.

(*Corr.*, i. 378)

---

[4] The opening chapter, signed 'Louis Bertrand', narrates how in a public park in Dijon this 'Louis Bertrand' meets an old man who lends him the manuscript of a book he has written about art, entitled *Gaspard de la nuit: Fantaisies à la manière de Rembrandt et de Callot*. When he tries to find the old man again in order to return it, he is told that this gentleman 'est en enfer, supposé qu'il ne soit pas ailleurs', which in turn prompts Louis to conclude: 'Si Gaspard de la Nuit est en enfer, qu'il y rôtisse, j'imprime son livre' (ed. Scepi, 27).

[5] See his draft letter to Houssaye: 'J'ai cherché des titres. Les 66. Quoique cependant cet ouvrage tenant de la vis et du kaléidoscope pût bien être poussé jusqu'au cabalistique 666 et même 6666...' (i. 365). Cf. Revelation 13: 18: 'Here is wisdom. Let him that hath understanding count the number of the beast: for it is the number of a man; and his number is Six hundred three-score and six.' Critical opinion now sees in these possible titles a debt to *Gaspard de la nuit*, which comprises six books and contains several texts themselves comprising six paragraphs. See Steve Murphy, 'De la prose poétique au poème en prose: Baudelaire, Bertrand et la confusion des genres', in Henri Scepi (ed.), *Le Genre et ses qualicatifs*, in *La Licorne*, 105 (2013), 81–109 (91). Murphy here (94–5) sees a further debt to *Gaspard de la nuit* in the spacing between paragraphs insisted on by Baudelaire for 'Le Crépuscule du soir' and 'La Solitude' when they were first published in *Fontainebleau*.

[6] See i. 1293 n. 2.

[7] In a letter to the publisher Pierre-Jules Hetzel on 8 Oct. 1863, where he overstates the number he has already written, Baudelaire reports that '[d]ans *Le Spleen de Paris*, il y aura cent morceaux—il en manque encore trente' (*Corr.*, ii. 324). On 4 May 1865, writing to Sainte-Beuve from Brussels, he expresses a similar ambition and a larger shortfall: 'Hélas! les *Poèmes en prose* [...] sont bien attardés. [...] Faire *cent* bagatelles laborieuses qui exigent une bonne humeur constante (bonne humeur nécessaire même pour traiter des sujets tristes), une excitation bizarre qui a besoin de spectacles, de foules, de musique, de réverbères même, voilà ce que j'ai voulu faire! Je n'en suis qu'à *soixante*, et je ne peux plus aller. J'ai besoin de ce fameux *bain de multitude* dont l'incorrection vous avez justement choqué' (*Corr.*, ii. 493).

When Baudelaire inaugurated the prose poem in 1855 with 'Le Crépuscule du soir' and 'La Solitude' there was no need for an overall title, but in 1857, when these two poems were republished in *Le Présent* along with four new poems ('L'Horloge', 'La Chevelure' [later 'Un hémisphère dans une chevelure'], 'L'Invitation au voyage', and 'Les Projets'), they bore the title *Poèmes nocturnes*. In his correspondence between 1857 and 1861 (and thus between the first two editions of *Les Fleurs du Mal*) Baudelaire refers repeatedly to his prose poems under this general title and describes them on one occasion as 'essais de poésie lyrique en prose', adding 'dans le genre de *Gaspard de la nuit*' (*Corr.* ii. 128).

As the term 'essais' suggests, he was very much aware of the experimental nature of these avowedly 'lyrical' texts and of their status as 'work in progress'. Here was the poet who thrived on challenge, who had 'extracted' beauty from 'le Mal' and now wanted to move on to the further challenge of producing *lyric* poetry in the medium of prose. But how can you have lyric (song) if you have no versification, no 'music'? By assertion perhaps, as in 'L'Horloge', where the poet likens his prose poem to a madrigal? By closely replicating the structure and imagery (and, initially, the title) of an existing verse poem, as in 'La Chevelure'? Or by combining, as in 'L'Invitation au voyage', a wide range of rhetorical and quasi-musical techniques (richness of vocabulary and intricacy of rhythm, high-register apostrophe, insistent patterns of alliteration and assonance) with an overt comparison of the poem to Weber's 'Invitation to the Waltz'? The epithet 'nocturnes', while redolent of a certain clichéd Romanticism (dating back to Young's *Night-Thoughts* (1742-5)), also recalls the famous solo piano pieces composed by Frédéric Chopin between 1827 and 1846 and so suggests, together with the prose poem 'Le Thyrse' (dedicated to Franz Liszt and first published in 1863), that Baudelaire may have envisaged an alternative lyricism or musicality in his prose poems. Versification is not indispensable in the creation of harmony or eurhythmy.

At the same time the title of *Poèmes nocturnes*—a 'titre mystérieux' rather than 'pétard'—may also have carried forward the idea presented in the prose poem 'Le Crépuscule du soir' (in both its first and final versions) that night-time itself inaugurates the 'fête intérieure' of the imagination, its dreamworks. Certainly in those four new poems published in 1857 the poetic and the nocturnal are foregrounded as the domain of the imagination and the key coordinates of its journeys: witness the poet-fantasist of 'Les Projets' who returns home at day's end and wonders: 'Pourquoi contraindre mon corps à changer de place, puisque mon âme voyage si lestement?'; the poet-lover of 'L'Horloge' who believes he has written a madrigal about finding eternity mirrored, at all hours of the day or night, in the eyes of his cat; the poet-lover of 'La Chevelure' ['Un hémisphère dans une chevelure'] whose seven paragraphs bear a close formal resemblance to seven stanzas as he immerses himself in 'la nuit de ta chevelure'; and that other traveller, the poet-dreamer of 'L'Invitation au voyage', who bids his 'cher ange' accompany him to the land of creativity, to the dreamworld of a new land of Cockaigne.

Subsequently, in 1861, Baudelaire can be seen (*Corr.* ii. 197, 207) trying out alternative titles—*La Lueur et la fumée, Le Promeneur solitaire, Le Rôdeur parisien*—with each one picking up (but perhaps too particularly?) on recognizable features of individual prose poems. *La Lueur et la fumée* chimes with the description of the dream-room of 'La Chambre double': 'Ici, tout a la suffisante clarté et la délicieuse obscurité de l'harmonie', implying perhaps (as suggested at the end of the last chapter) that we may read these prose poems as combining comprehensibility and difficulty in a new harmonic performance of certainty and doubt, of gleams of truths briefly alleged and soon gone up in smoke. *Le Promeneur solitaire* proclaims a perverse succession to Rousseau by an urban flâneur and solitary with a very different take on the idea of the natural goodness of human beings (as may be seen not only in 'La Solitude' but also in 'Le Gâteau' and 'Le Joujou du pauvre'), while *Le Rôdeur parisien* implies a similarly street-roaming role but with added emphasis on the specifically questing and local nature of the flânerie as though the poet were stalking the new along the city's boulevards. Now, as we shall see in more detail presently, the focus is on the relationship between the individual and the crowd. Of the three new prose poems published in the *Revue fantaisiste*, the second and third—'Les Veuves' and 'Le Vieux Saltimbanque'—dwell on the experiences (undergone by the widow and the ageing mountebank) of loss, marginalization from the community, and a reduction in status from participant to observer, while in the first—'Les Foules'—the artist proclaims a special capacity for empathy ('cette sainte prostitution de l'âme') that enables him to be at once self and other, alone yet of the crowd, a 'promeneur solitaire et pensif' who is also one of us... like a unique and original writer on the promiscuous page of a newspaper, and like a prose poem in the world of the press.

In 1862 Baudelaire sent twenty-six prose poems for publication in *La Presse* under the new title of *Petits Poèmes en prose*. Why this title? Perhaps because he was simply unable to come up with a thematic phrase (like *Les Fleurs du Mal*, itself in any case suggested by someone else) that would fit such a disparate array of texts? But there may have been another reason. In nineteenth-century usage the usual word for a short poem was a 'poésie' while the term 'poème' connoted longer texts in verse, usually of a narrative, dramatic, or philosophical kind. More particularly, the three young 'mages romantiques' who were held to have renewed lyric poetry in France—namely, Lamartine, Hugo, and Vigny—had each overtly associated themselves with one particular verse form as the vehicle for their originality: in Lamartine's case the elegy and in Hugo's the ode. Vigny had chosen the 'poème'. His first collection of verse poems was published in 1822 under the title *Poèmes*, which in subsequent editions became *Poèmes antiques et modernes*. In the preface to the 1837 edition Vigny claims that he was the first to compose this kind of verse in which 'une pensée philosophique est mise en scène sous une forme Épique ou Dramatique'.[8] Vigny had in fact devised a form of *short* verse poem (what he calls '[c]es perles si lentement formées')[9] that might narrate a story or stage a dramatic scene in order to present a moral and philosophical message. (Thus, in addition, *Les Destinées* is subtitled 'Poèmes philosophiques'.) In a diary entry of 1829 Vigny describes his intention more fully:

> Concevoir et méditer une pensée philosophique; trouver dans les actions humaines celle qui en est la plus évidente *preuve*; la réduire à une action simple qui se puisse graver en la mémoire et représenter en quelque sorte une statue et un monument grandiose à l'imagination des hommes, voilà où doit tendre cette poésie épique et dramatique à la fois.[10]

In December 1861 Baudelaire met Vigny in person. On 11 December, as the author of the recently published second edition of *Les Fleurs du Mal*, Baudelaire had declared his candidature for election to the Académie française (as though challenging it to confer honour where the magistrates judging the first edition had found criminal fault) and accordingly begun in the traditional way to call on its 'immortal' members in pursuit of their support. Following his afternoon visit, probably on 16 December, Baudelaire wrote to Vigny to thank him (*Corr.*, ii. 195–6) and (by way of electioneering) sent examples of his work: offprints of his recent articles on Gautier and Wagner, a copy of *Les Paradis artificiels*, and his last remaining deluxe vellum copy of the 1861 *Les Fleurs du Mal* (together with his famous assertion that it is not 'un pur album' but has been carefully structured). In addition, and as well as a copy of 'les poésies de Poe', he enclosed 'un vieux numéro de revue' containing some of his prose poems as evidence of 'un commencement de tentative nouvelle'. A few days later he wrote to Arsène Houssaye, long-time editor of *L'Artiste*, an illustrated weekly review, and now also literary editor of *La Presse*, a daily newspaper. Houssaye had suggested that he would publish the prose poems over several issues, alternating between the two publications, and an enthusiastic Baudelaire ('Votre idée [...] me sourit beaucoup') was updating him on his progress, and in particular on his search for an overall title: 'Je crois que j'ai enfin trouvé un titre qui rend bien mon idée: LA LUEUR ET LA FUMÉE [-] POÈME, EN PROSE [-] au minimum quarante poèmes, au maximum, cinquante. Dont douze sont faits', which he lists (*Corr.*, ii. 196–7). This use of the singular 'poème' is anomalous, particularly since the said 'poème' is to consist of a

---

[8] Vigny, *Œuvres complètes*, i. 5.
[9] Vigny, *Œuvres complètes*, ii. 1186. For discussion of Vigny's use of the crystal and the pearl as figures for a poetry of compressed wisdom, see *Unacknowledged Legislators*, 558–9.
[10] *Journal d'un poète*, in *Œuvres complètes*, ed. Fernand Baldensperger (2 vols, Paris: Gallimard [Bibliothèque de la Pléiade], 1948–50), ii. 891.

number of 'poèmes',[11] so it may be that Baudelaire here had in mind Vigny's own use of the term. Given that so many of the prose poems provide short narratives and/or evoke dramatic scenes, and given also that so many of them draw multiple (ironic) moral lessons, it is plausible to suppose that this meaning of 'poème' partly informs the new title *Petits Poèmes en prose*—and indeed may explain the addition of the otherwise redundant 'petits'.[12] For in their brevity lies also their modernity. Vigny, as the inventor of this type of miniature epic or drama, was an evident precursor of Hugo, the Hugo who from the late 1840s had envisaged a work entitled 'Petites épopées' and in 1859 had duly published the first volume of *La Légende des siècles* with the subtitle 'Histoire—Petites épopées'. As Baudelaire himself commented in his 1861 essay on Hugo (and mindful no doubt also of Poe's insistence on the literary power of brevity to create a 'totality of effect' and 'unity of impression'), this was 'le seul poème épique qui pût être créé par un homme de son temps pour des lecteurs de son temps'—and this because of its use of brevity:

> D'abord les poèmes qui constituent l'ouvrage sont généralement courts, et même la brièveté de quelques-uns n'est pas moins extraordinaire que leur énergie. Ceci est déjà une considération importante, qui témoigne d'une connaissance absolue de tout le possible de la poésie moderne. (ii. 140)[13]

As individual prose poems continued to be written, published, and republished after 1862, so Baudelaire's uncertainty about the title persisted both in print and in his correspondence. *Le Spleen de Paris* emerges with growing conviction from 1863 onwards, but *Petits Poèmes en prose* survives, on its own (in November 1864, in *L'Artiste*) or in contracted form as a subtitle in *Le Spleen de Paris. Poèmes en prose* (in February 1864, in *Le Figaro* and the *Revue de Paris*). In June 1866 *Petits Poèmes lycanthropes* figured as the collective title for 'La Fausse Monnaie' and 'Le Joueur généreux' (in the *Revue du XIXe siècle*) and may suggest, with a nod to Petrus Borel,[14] a poet who perhaps sees in the differing poetic personas of his

---

[11] The exact wording of this letter is subject to editorial doubt (see *Corr.*, ii. 752-3), but this formulation of the title and subtitle, including the singular use of 'poème', is textually certain.

[12] Pace Jean-Michel Gouvard, *Charles Baudelaire, 'Le Spleen de Paris'* (Paris: Ellipses, 2014), 25.

[13] It does not necessarily follow that Baudelaire himself wanted the prose poem to rival the epic, as suggested by Evans, *Baudelaire and Intertextuality*, 5-6. The 'intrigue de 6000 pages' to which Baudelaire refers in his draft notes for the dedicatory letter (i. 738) may more plausibly refer, exaggeratedly, to a novel, while in 'Les Bons Chiens' the shepherds of Virgil and Theocritus (authors of *Bucolics* and *Idylls* respectively, as we saw in the case of a similar reference in 'Paysage') are not 'the pastoral minstrels of traditional epic poets' (*Baudelaire and Intertextuality*, 5), even if Virgil did also write *The Aeneid*. For discussion of Baudelaire's approval of Hugo's 'short epics' in relation to Poe's views on the effects of brevity, see Dominique Combe, 'Le "poème épique condamné": Baudelaire, Hugo et Poe', in Guyaux and Marchal (eds), *'Les Fleurs du Mal': Actes du colloque de la Sorbonne des 10 et 11 janvier 2003*, 53-64.

[14] See Gouvard, *Charles Baudelaire, 'Le Spleen de Paris'*, 28-9.

prose poems a parallel with the mythological human ability to 'shape-shift'. And the idea of dreamwork itself persists in 'Onéirocritie', the title of one of three subsections (along with 'Choses parisiennes' and 'Symboles et moralités' (i. 366-7)) into which Baudelaire at one point thought of dividing the prose poems that remained to be written.[15] But eleven days later, in *L'Événement, Le Spleen de Paris* itself first appeared in print without the addition of *Poèmes en prose*, as a surtitle for 'La Corde', here being republished.

Nocturnal (and musical) melancholy, spleen, Paris, dreams, 'poèmes' with a moral, political, or philosophical lesson to impart: here are some (though by no means all) of the major ingredients to be found in these fifty prose poems, but in such various guises and combinations that it would indeed be difficult to invent a title that encapsulated them completely. Critics, for their part, have been no less divided in the matter. In her foundational study of the prose poem (1959) Suzanne Bernard preferred 'le titre (tellement suggestif!) de *Spleen de Paris*, que Baudelaire semble avoir préféré à partir de 1864',[16] and in this she was followed by Claude Pichois, as editor of the Pléiade edition (1975), for whom *Le Spleen de Paris* takes precedence as 'le seul titre attesté avec certitude durant les dernières années de la vie de Baudelaire' (i. 1299). Among subsequent commentators this preference has been shared by (among others) Hiddleston (1987), Murphy (2003), Maria Scott (2005), Krueger (2007), Gouvard (2014), and Kaplan (2015). *Petits Poèmes en prose*, on the other hand, has been preferred by Johnson (1979), Stephens (1999), Labarthe (2000), and Hannoosh (2011), and also, as editor, by Kopp (1969). Many editors (including Daniel-Rops, Lemaître, Ruff, Milner, Steinmetz, and later Kopp (2006) himself) have instead pursued an editorial compromise in the form of *Petits Poèmes en prose (Le Spleen de Paris)* or *Le Spleen de Paris: Petits Poèmes en prose*, perhaps in order, at their publishers' behest, to reassure potential purchasers that the two titles refer to one and the same book. Only Cervoni and Schellino (2017) have chosen to use *Le Spleen de Paris* on its own.[17]

So, which to choose? Like 'Tableaux parisiens', these fifty prose poems have very little to do specifically with Paris, except that they were written by a Parisian and published in the Parisian press. Alone among all the poet-narrators that of 'Le Vieux Saltimbanque' identifies himself as one who behaves 'en vrai Parisien'. The city itself is otherwise mentioned only twice by name as the actual setting of the poem: once, in 'Le Mauvais Vitrier', with its reference to 'la lourde et sale atmosphère parisienne', and once in 'Le Joueur généreux', where the poet mingles with a boulevard throng and bumps into the Devil, whom he follows down into a comic version of Hell described as 'une demeure souterraine, éblouissante, où

---

[15] Baudelaire appears to be using the term 'symbole' here in the same way as Vigny (who drafted a 'Livre des symboles et paraboles') in its theological sense of creed, compendium of doctrine, or religious rite (such as the Eucharist) and thus as similar to a parable. See *Unacknowledged Legislators*, 519-20.
[16] *Le Poème en prose de Baudelaire jusqu'à nos jours*, 103 n. 2.
[17] For full bibliographical details, see 'Bibliography'.

éclatait un luxe dont aucune des habitations supérieures de Paris ne pourrait fournir un exemple approchant'.[18] Many of the poems do clearly designate or obliquely evoke an urban setting: of streets and crowds and rooftop vistas, of residential buildings and public parks, of tobacconists and cafés and bars, of theatres and fairgrounds and shooting galleries, of urchins and stray dogs ('Un plaisant', 'Le Chien et le flacon', 'Le Mauvais Vitrier', 'À une heure du matin', 'Les Foules', 'Les Veuves', 'Le Vieux Saltimbanque', 'Le Joujou du pauvre', 'Les Projets', 'Les Yeux des pauvres', 'La Fausse Monnaie', 'Le Joueur généreux', 'La Corde', 'Les Vocations', 'Les Fenêtres', 'Portraits de maîtresses', 'Le Galant Tireur', 'Le Tir et le cimetière', 'Perte d'auréole', 'Mademoiselle Bistouri', 'Assommons les pauvres!'). But others are set by the sea ('La Belle Dorothée', 'Déjà!', 'Le Port') or in a mountainous region ('Le Gâteau', 'Le Crépuscule du soir'). One begins in China ('L'Horloge'), another is partly set in Belgium ('Les Bons Chiens'), and another tells of a nameless principality ('Une mort héroïque'). Several are situated simply in a no-man's-land of fable or allegory ('Le Désespoir de la vieille', 'La Chambre double', 'Chacun sa chimère', 'Le Fou et la Vénus', 'La Femme sauvage et la petite-maîtresse', 'Les Dons des fées', 'Les Tentations ou Eros, Plutus et la Gloire') or else in the non-place (or utopia!) of moral, philosophical, and aesthetic conjecture ('L'Étranger', 'Le "Confiteor" de l'artiste', 'La Solitude', 'Le Thyrse', 'Enivrez-vous', 'Le Désir de peindre', 'Les Bienfaits de la lune', 'Laquelle est la vraie?', 'Un cheval de race' [even if the woman does smell of the Midi], 'Le Miroir', 'La Soupe et les nuages', 'Any where out of the world'). And two are set in the expanding realms of imaginary space ('Un hémisphère dans une chevelure', 'L'Invitation au voyage').

But these categorizations are themselves open to debate since, for example, poems like 'Le Mauvais Vitrier' or 'Les Fenêtres' are clearly susceptible of allegorical readings in which the urban setting is quite incidental to the poem's possible meanings. In seeking to justify his preference for *Le Spleen de Paris* as the most appropriate title for the collection, Claude Pichois acknowledges some of these non-Parisian and non-urban features to be found in the poems but then interprets 'spleen' as a yearning to be *out of* Paris! Comparable with the *Sehnsucht* of the German Romantics, this yearning is specifically Parisian: 'Regret d'être à Paris, désir des ailleurs, mélancolie secrétée par la vie parisienne.' Pichois is thus able to conclude that '*Le Spleen de Paris* est un recueil de poèmes en prose marqué par un esprit parisien; dans les sentiments se reflète une âme parisienne et moderne, les sujets fussent-ils étrangers à Paris ou même exotiques' (i. 1300). But here the title is, to use Mallarmé's term, speaking too 'loudly'.[19] The city of *Le Spleen de Paris*,

---

[18] In 'La Belle Dorothée' the narrator wonders if Dorothée may be meeting a young French officer, of whom she will ask 'si les belles dames de Paris sont toutes plus belles qu'elle'.

[19] Cf. Mallarmé, 'Le Mystère dans les lettres', in *Œuvres complètes*, ed. Marchal, ii. 234: 'Appuyer, selon la page, au blanc, qui l'inaugure son ingénuité, à soi, oublieuse même du titre qui parlerait trop haut.'

while implicitly reflecting the Paris of Baudelaire's own experiences, is more profitably read, like the city of 'Tableaux parisiens', as a capital of melancholy: an emblematic site of human intercourse in which the ill-being of the poet and his fellow human beings now extends (that is, beyond the preoccupations of *Les Fleurs du Mal*) to include an acute sense of political, ethical, and even philosophical malaise. Confronted with numerous moral dilemmas and existential conundrums, within this symbolic human metropolis of widely differing situations and opinions and lifestyles and options, the poet is plunged into disorder and chaos, into a world of contingency and arbitrariness, into a 'human comedy' from which it may seem impossible to produce that harmony on which beauty depends for its existence: some creative ordering that can transform dissonance into eurythmy while remaining true to the reality of dissonance itself.

For my own part I shall refer to '*Le Spleen de Paris*', and on the grounds not only that over the past two decades this has now become the consensus choice, but also in part because this title has the character of an arbitrary signifier and so may be appropriate for a collection of texts that so insistently and radically cast doubt on the very act of asserting meaning—of laying down the law. In 'La Solitude', as we saw, the poet is a loner who resists the simplistic moralizing dictum of a journalist because he can see so many more aspects to the question at issue. Compare also the poet of 'Assommons les pauvres!' (written some ten years later and first published only posthumously), who spends a fortnight reading books that were all the rage 'il y a seize ou dix-sept ans'— that is, *circa* 1848—and dismisses 'toutes les élucubrations de tous ces entrepreneurs de bonheurs publics' as '[d]es formules de bonne femme'. The happiness of the greatest number has become a business, and politics a matter of churning out propaganda that simply serves to reinforce an endless confrontation of right and left: of 'ceux qui conseillent à tous les pauvres de se faire esclaves, et ceux qui leur persuadent qu'ils sont tous des rois détrônés'. But which is which? Socialism calls for obedience to the party line and persuades the poor that their sovereign rights have been stolen? Bourgeois liberalism and/or Second Empire imperialism demand obedience from the poor in the name of law and order and persuade them that they themselves, the rulers, have a divine right to rule like the monarchs of the *ancien régime*? By a linguistic sleight of hand, itself demonstrating the emptiness of all political terminology and ideology, the poet here makes his point against a prevailing public discourse and offers instead, in his own whimsical way, simply 'l'idée d'une idée, quelque chose d'infiniment vague'. As Richard Burton has shown, this poem (which ends with the question: 'Qu'en dis-tu, citoyen Proudhon?')[20] constitutes 'at one and the same time a celebration, parody, and subversion of [Proudhonian]

---

[20] This line was removed by Asselineau and Banville in the first complete edition of the prose poems for reasons of their own, and has been restored by recent editors (Steinmetz; Cervoni and Schellino).

discourse'.[21] For his own part Baudelaire admired Proudhon and had known him well.[22] What he is here demonstrating above all is the absurdity of placing unthinking faith in the kind of books 'où il est traité de l'art de rendre les peuples heureux, sages et riches, en vingt-quatre heures'. *Le Spleen de Paris* is no such book.

As a title, *Le Spleen de Paris* might therefore be seen as the formulation of a poetics of resistance to the false happiness and false wisdom peddled by the public discourse of the nation's capital and, more broadly and more 'eternally', by those who think they know best. The 'effusions oratoires' of the 'races jacassières' so despised by the poet of 'La Solitude' are here to be met with the jaundiced gaze of the sceptic and the *fumisterie* of a comic jester, just as their clichés and slogans—a 'prêt-à-parler' to match their 'prêt-à-penser'—are to be resisted by the language and art of a Poet. Just what Baudelaire thought he was up against is described by him in uncompromising—and indeed splenetic—terms within the private pages of *Mon cœur mis à nu*:

> Il est impossible de parcourir une gazette quelconque de n'importe quel jour ou quel mois ou quelle année, sans y trouver à chaque ligne les signes de la perversité humaine la plus épouvantable, en même temps que les *vanteries* les plus surprenantes de probité, de bonté, de charité, et les affirmations les plus effrontées relatives au progrès et à la civilisation.
>
> Tout journal, de la première ligne à la dernière, n'est qu'un tissu d'horreurs. Guerres, crimes, vols, impudicités, tortures, crimes des princes, crimes des nations, crimes des particuliers, une ivresse d'atrocité universelle.
>
> Et c'est de ce dégoûtant apéritif que l'homme civilisé accompagne son repas de chaque matin.—Tout, en ce monde, sue le crime[:] le journal, la muraille, et le visage de l'homme.
>
> Je ne comprends pas qu'une main pure puisse toucher un journal sans une convulsion de dégoût.[23]

Not just newspapers, then, but a whole world of crime and ideological deceit, of 'la perversité humaine la plus épouvantable', both as it is publicly displayed in all the bills and posters affixed to the walls of the city and as it may be read on the only too legible faces of its fallen people.

---

[21] Burton, *Baudelaire and the Second Republic*, 329.

[22] 'S'il était question d'art, oui, vous auriez raison de dire de Proudhon: Il est fou.—Mais en matière d'économie, il me paraît singulièrement respectable.' (Letter to Narcisse Ancelle, 8 Feb. 1865, *Corr.*, ii. 453.) Proudhon's death on 19 January 1865 may, in Burton's view, have prompted Baudelaire 'to confront head-on the complexity of his reactions to the man and his doctrine and, in so doing, to compose a text in which political and psychological ambivalences are fused with an intensity unique in his work' (*Baudelaire and the Second Republic*, 329).

[23] *Fusées*, ed. Guyaux, 118–19; i. 705–6.

Sacred Temple or Butterfly of War? The *Feuilleton* of *La Presse*

> Le Feuilleton est une puissance.
> (Frédéric Soulié, 'Le Feuilleton', *La Presse*, 1 July 1836)

Nowhere is the resistant character of Baudelaire's prose poems more directly and visibly evident than on the first page of the issue of *La Presse* published on 26 August 1862.[24] Founded in 1836 by Émile de Girardin, *La Presse* was the first 'penny press' daily newspaper in France, almost simultaneously challenged by *Le Siècle*.[25] By virtue of numerous advertisements and selling at half the price of his established rivals, Girardin soon achieved a large circulation, thereby revolutionizing the industry, upsetting vested interests, and defying pious assumptions about the role and importance of the press as he did so.[26] The French newspaper of the period consisted of a single broadsheet folded and thereby divided into four 'pages'. On the first three pages the layout was such that the upper three-quarters of the page contained material relating to political, economic, and social life: news bulletins and reports concerning domestic and international affairs, accounts of parliamentary business, excerpted transcripts of court cases, lists of stock market prices, notices of bankruptcies and deaths, theatre programmes, etc. The first column or columns in this upper part—or 'haut-de-page'—were occupied by the so-called 'premier-Paris', corresponding to our modern 'leader' or editorial. The bottom quarter of the page—the *feuilleton* (also known as the 'rez-de-chaussée')— was filled by reviews (of books, theatrical productions, etc.) or else by a short story or perhaps—and this was one of the major innovations of both *La Presse* and *Le Siècle*—an instalment of some serialized work of fiction. Alexandre Dumas's *La Comtesse de Salisbury* appeared in *La Presse* from mid-July to mid-September and proved so effective as a means of securing reader loyalty that the paper's second serialized novel, Balzac's *La Vieille Fille*, which appeared from late October to the end of November, was accorded space in the columns of the 'haut-de-page' under the traditional *feuilleton* heading of 'Variétés'.

---

[24] This may be accessed at <https://gallica.bnf.fr/ark:/12148/bpt6k479531x/f1.item>. A photograph of the front page for the following day, exhibiting a similar contrast, is provided in Philippa Lewis, *Intimacy and Distance: Conflicting Cultures in Nineteenth-Century France* (Cambridge: Legenda (MHRA), 2017), 85.

[25] Each newspaper began publication on 1 July 1836. The prospectus issue of *La Presse* appeared on 16 June, that of *Le Siècle* on 23 June. For a detailed account of Girardin's career by an extremely well-informed General Secretary of the Syndicat des journalistes, see Jean Morienval, *Les Créateurs de la grande presse en France: Émile de Girardin, H. de Villemessant, Moïse Millaud* (Paris: Éditions Spes, s.d. [1934]), 19–115.

[26] Cf. Odysse Barot, *Émile de Girardin, sa vie, ses idées, son œuvre, son influence* (Paris: Michel Lévy, 1866), where Barot (1830–1907), a journalist and novelist and an enthusiastic apologist for Girardin, comments: 'On en était encore à cette idée fausse qui fait du journal un trépied et du journaliste un grand-prêtre. "On venait proposer, dit un contemporain, de changer en un trafic vulgaire ce qui est une magistrature et presque un sacerdoce."—Étrange sacerdoce où le pontife est choisi par lui-même et sacré des ses propres main!' (37).

In *La Presse* of 26 August 1862 the *feuilleton* spreads over the first two pages (the 'ground floor' of the third page and most of the fourth page are filled with advertisements) and contains Baudelaire's dedicatory letter to Arsène Houssaye and nine of his prose poems: 'L'Étranger', 'Le Désespoir de la vieille', 'Le "Confiteor" de l'artiste', 'Un plaisant', 'La Chambre double', 'Chacun sa chimère', 'Le Fou et la Vénus', 'Le Chien et le flacon', and 'Le Mauvais Vitrier'. Above these the reader of the day would have found information, for example, about Garibaldi's campaign in Italy, the effect of the 1862 harvest on grain prices, and the delights of steeplechasing at Dieppe. *La Presse* specialized in bringing together excerpted statements, articles, and announcements from various official sources, including the government's own newspaper *Le Moniteur*, as well as from a broad spectrum of the wider domestic and international press (hence its own title).[27] On that particular day, for example, it quotes under 'Faits divers' an account in the British *Daily Telegraph* of a maritime disaster off the coast of Panama and a report by the British *Daily News* on the nature and extent of French possessions in Indochina.

The overall effect, as of daily newspapers today, is one of miscellany and polyphony: official government announcements, key political debates, and weighty editorial opinions on the affairs of the nation sit side by side, or column by column, with human interest stories and the latest bond market prices, not to mention advertisements (on 26 August) for vintage marsala, insect repellent, and a second-hand piano. Against this backdrop of random diversity Baudelaire's much-discussed dedicatory letter takes on a new meaning. This 'petit ouvrage dont on ne pourrait pas dire, sans injustice, qu'il n'a ni queue ni tête' begins to look like a mirror image, reflected upwards from the 'ground floor', of the contingent juxtapositions of public life in the world. For here, too, in the prose poems, we find political opinions and sweeping moral judgements lined up alongside seemingly banal anecdote, just as we can read of racehorses ('Un cheval de race') and shipping ('Le Port') and how the Chinese can tell the time of day from the eyes of a cat ('L'Horloge').

These particular parallels are, of course, themselves random, and none of these three prose poems in fact figures in this issue of *La Presse*, but the fact of reflection remains true. And, like all reflections, these prose poems at the bottom of the page offer a distorted, alternative representation of the world they mirror. Up above we have the mess and circumstance of everyday life, while down below we have a 'poetic' mess comprising all manner of parallel and contrast, of interconnection and incongruity, of pompous pronouncement and blatant contradiction. In the letter to Houssaye Baudelaire claims to have been inspired to his new art of the prose poem by the city itself: 'C'est surtout de la fréquentation des villes énormes,

---

[27] One of Girardin's first publications, *Le Voleur*, founded in 1828 as an illustrated literary magazine and published weekly, made a virtue of overtly 'stealing' the best articles and illustrations from other journals.

c'est du croisement de leurs innombrables rapports que naît cet idéal obsédant.' But one might wonder if it was not also his intimate knowledge of the contemporary press that gave rise to his 'tentative nouvelle'—and, eventually, to the title of *Le Spleen de Paris*.

The division of the broadsheet page into upper and lower 'floors' dates back to 28 January 1800 when it was first introduced by the *Journal des Débats*, a weekly newspaper founded in 1789 with the express purpose of reporting the debates in the newly formed Assemblée nationale. Initially its *feuilleton* was devoted principally to theatre reviews, but subsequently, in the hands of Étienne de Jouy, this section became known for offering an oblique take on public life through the inclusion of satirical sketches. When Girardin founded *La Presse* in 1836 he intended, by means of the contributions and commissioning work of his wife Delphine Gay (writing under the pseudonym of the vicomte de Launay) and with the participation of Théophile Gautier and many other writers affiliated to the Romantic cause, that its *feuilleton* would be a forum for the unorthodox and the subversive in the world of literature and the arts. Just as he proclaimed in its prospectus issue that *La Presse* would be addressed to readers of all political persuasions, so he was determined that his newspaper would cater similarly for all tastes and not just—indeed especially not—for those of the traditionally minded.

In its first issue, on 1 July 1836, the novelist and playwright Frédéric Soulié (1800–47) was entrusted with setting the tone, and he invites his readers to see the *feuilleton* not as a God or some all-powerful temple of taste complete with its sacred lawgivers but as a butterfly, spreading its pretty and insubstantial wings across the lower reaches of the newspaper. In making the former analogy he is targeting Jules Janin (1804–74), who had become theatre critic of the *Journal des Débats* in 1830 and whose *feuilleton* could make or break a new production. Had the *feuilleton* existed in ancient Rome, writes Soulié, it would have been worshipped like a god with its own temple, rites, and priests, and due sacrifice would have been made to its omnipotence:

> on eût immolé sur l'autel des romans, des tragédies, des poèmes, des acteurs et des danseuses; Jules Janin se serait promené dans Rome en robe de papier blanc, précédé de deux licteurs portant des faisceaux de plumes et, en sa qualité de grand-prêtre du Feuilleton, il eût possédé le droit d'arrêter la représentation d'un vaudeville, comme le grand-prêtre de Jupiter avait le droit de suspendre l'exécution des condamnés.

In place of such august lawgiving, seemingly invested with a power over life and death, Soulié proposes instead the harmless butterfly:

> s'il me fallait représenter le Feuilleton sous une forme palpable, tout ce que j'oserais me permettre de proposer à mes lecteurs, ce serait de se figurer le

Feuilleton sous l'aspect d'un vaste papillon. Au dos d'une plume qui simule le corps, attachez en guise d'ailes, les deux longues bandes de papier que vous lisez, et voilà notre papillon tout trouvé.

But this butterfly is in fact an agent of armed resistance, as we learn when Soulié ends his manifesto for the *feuilleton* with his own words of Jupiterian command: 'enseigne et vis en guerre'. While the *Journal des Débats* may have been responsible for introducing the new paginal layout, the fundamental nature of the *feuilleton* as a commentary on the literary and cultural life of the nation dates back, Soulié points out, at least to the days of the *Mercure français*, founded in 1611 and considered to be France's first literary gazette. Mindful of this much older tradition, carried forward in the *Mercure galant*, later the *Mercure de France* (which ceased publication only in 1825), Soulié contends that the modern *feuilleton* has lost sight of its role as an instrument of cultural commentary and innovative enquiry: 'ces choses [...] que le Feuilleton a abandonnés, d'autres qu'il n'a pas abordées'. Of the former he proposes a list that constitutes an alternative 'history' of the nation that the *feuilleton* alone can provide:

> Dans les premières, il faut ranger les études de mœurs, ces esquisses légères qui saisissent au vol la physionomie changeante d'un peuple, ces tableaux des habitudes, des modes, des exclusions, des préférences de chaque moment; cette peinture du salon, de la rue, de la boutique, du magasin, du bureau, du premier étage et de la mansarde, de la Chaussée d'Antin et du Marais, du faubourg Saint-Germain et du faubourg Saint-Marceau; cette observation des plaisirs et des intérêts qui préoccupent la vie intime, confidences que nous pourrions appeler les mémoires d'une nation, récits souvent plus intéressants que la solennelle histoire qui les domine.

As to topics so far untouched, he ends his manifesto with a call to arms:

> sois varié, il le faut; tu as tes entrées partout, dans le passé et dans le présent, en haut et en bas, à droite et à gauche; tu as le droit de mettre des habits de toutes formes et de toutes couleurs: depuis la veste bleu de ciel galonnée d'argent du coureur, jusqu'au frac noir brodé de vert de l'académicien; tu peux te montrer un sifflet ou un compas à la main; tu peux être grave et plaisant, tu as le droit de parler de Chateaubriand, et tu es forcé de parler du plus infime vaudevilliste; ton empire est immense; va donc, ouvre tes assises, prends tes pinceaux, embouche ta trompette, écoute aux portes, regarde aux fenêtres, entre partout, et après cela juge, peins, raconte; enseigne et vis en guerre.

In Girardin's newly founded *La Presse*, therefore, the spirit of innovation was alive on both 'floors' of the newspaper's page. As Marie-Ève Thérenty has noted in *La*

Littérature au quotidien, her wide-ranging account of relations between 'Literature' and the press in nineteenth-century France: 'Le feuilleton représente un monde à l'envers où les efforts de Girardin pour investir politiquement et idéologiquement le régime de la monarchie de Juillet sont en apparence minés.' On the one hand, his editorials—'le premier-Paris'—would customarily be proclaiming the benefits of 'le commerce, l'agriculture, l'industrie, les routes, les chemins de fer, les canaux, les banques, les assurances', while the *feuilleton* for its part 'ne cesse de demander plus de poésie, de fantaisie et de lettres, ne cesse de vitupérer contre "les marchands de filoselle et de pommes de terre"'.[28] In her view Girardin's plans for the *feuilleton* as the site of a counter-discourse therefore succeeded: 'Rapidement, la fine escouade enrôlée par Girardin fait de l'espace du feuilleton une case ironique, fantaisiste, littéraire qui parle au monde autrement que le haut-de-page et crée des effets polyphoniques tout à fait intéressants en jouant sur le contre-pied, l'antiphrase, les paradoxismes.'[29] Not only, therefore, did this visionary press baron help to found the tradition of the *roman-feuilleton*, but he also encouraged a form of 'alternative' journalism, 'une écriture du quotidien qui contrevient aux codes rhétoriques définis par la pratique fortement discursive du premier-Paris. [...] une articulation entre une écriture dit sérieuse et une écriture fantaisiste aux effets plus complexes.'[30]

Collusion or Resistance? The Prose Poem and the Press

Je désire surtout que mon maudit gazetier me laisse m'amuser à ma guise.

('La Solitude')

One may argue nevertheless that the *feuilleton* of *La Presse* does indeed only *apparently* undermine the rhetoric and preoccupations of the 'premier-Paris', since a thirst for change and reform drives them both, a desire—six years after the July Revolution and also six years after the opening night of Hugo's *Hernani*— to do things differently. Moreover the paginal division between political economy and the arts was in one sense merely typographic. As Thérenty and others have observed, the career journalist of more modern times did not then yet exist, and

---

[28] Marie-Ève Thérenty, *La Littérature au quotidien; Poétiques journalistiques au XIXe siècle* (Paris: Éditions du Seuil, 2007), 64. For the purposes of her analysis Thérenty distinguishes between 'la Littérature (le panthéon des auteurs canonisés et des chefs-d'œuvre reconnus par la postérité)' and 'la littérature (toutes les écritures, même mineures, et quelquefois journalistiques, qui relèvent d'une poétique)', 19, n. 15.
[29] Thérenty, *La Littérature au quotidien*, 28. For further information and discussion, see also Alain Vaillant and Marie-Ève Thérenty, *1836: l'an I de l'ère médiatique, étude littéraire et historique du journal 'La Presse' d'Émile de Girardin* (Paris: Nouveau Monde Éditions, 2001).
[30] Thérenty, *La Littérature au quotidien*, 28-9.

newspapers were written by people who (like Hippolyte Castille and Baudelaire himself) were variously and often simultaneously novelists, poets, historians, economists, and politicians (whether elected or merely aspirant).[31] As Thérenty argues, there was therefore in the press not only an overlap of personnel during the July Monarchy and the Second Empire but 'une profonde circularité entre les formes littéraires et les formes journalistiques, dues à la coïncidence essentielle entre les deux systèmes professionnels pendant quelques dizaines d'années'.[32]

For this reason she contends that the emergence of the prose poem as a new literary form derives entirely from the encounter between 'Literature' and journalism: 'Le genre du petit poème en prose est en effet indéfectiblement lié au journal. Il n'existe véritablement en tant que genre qu'à partir du moment où il se confronte avec cet univers médiatique.'[33] In particular she writes of the close connection between the short prose pieces contributed by poets such as Baudelaire (to whom she devotes nevertheless only two pages of analysis)—and later Théodore de Banville—and the 'chronique', a popular feature of many newspapers in which a regular column reported, usually from within an urban context, on some incident just recently observed or some anecdote or conversation just recently (over)heard. In the case of Banville, for example, the prose poems of his collection *La Lanterne magique* were pre-published in *Le Gil Blas* (in the second half of 1882) so as to alternate with a regular 'chronique' entitled 'Paris vécu'. Because these 'chroniques' usually took the form of generously spaced short paragraphs, especially if they were the account of a dialogue, the reader of the day, Thérenty contends, would have been led to minimize the 'charge poétique' of the prose poem and to see it as essentially just another 'chronique'.[34] In this way the prose poem served to blur the distinction between reality and fiction.

In relation to Baudelaire, and in particular to the prose poems he published in *La Presse* on 26 August 1862, Thérenty notes, for example, how closely 'Un plaisant' resembles 'l'anecdote typique mi-réelle, mi-fictive de la chronique de

---

[31] See Thérenty, *La Littérature au quotidien*, 13–19. Cf. Alain Vaillant's entry on Baudelaire in Dominique Kalifa, Philippe Régnier, Marie-Ève Thérenty, and Alain Vaillant, *La Civilisation du journal: Histoire culturelle et littéraire de la presse française aux XIXe siècle* (Paris: Nouveau Monde éditions, 2011), 1189–96: 'Baudelaire est le parfait exemple—banal du point de vue de son parcours, mais exceptionnel par son génie—de l'écrivain-journaliste du milieu du XIXe siècle: plus exactement de ces professionnels de la petite presse culturelle qui, entre poésie, critique littéraire ou artistique, fiction et chronique, sont les polygraphes de la *modernité*' (1189). See also Marie-Françoise Melmoux-Montaubin, *L'Écrivain-journaliste au XIXe siècle: Un mutant des lettres* (Saint-Étienne: Cahiers intempestifs, 2003). This kind of overlap or 'mutancy' may also be seen, for example, in the masthead of *Le Siècle*, which describes itself as a 'journal politique, littéraire et d'économie sociale'.

[32] Thérenty, *La Littérature au quotidien*, 18.

[33] Thérenty, *La Littérature au quotidien*, 262. Cf. also Jean-Pierre Bertrand, 'Une lecture médiatique du *Spleen de Paris*', in Marie-Ève Thérenty and Alain Vaillant (ed.), *Presse et plumes: Journalisme et littérature au XIXe siècle* (Paris: Nouveau Monde Éditions, 2004), 329–37: 'Selon un paradoxe bien baudelairien, le poème en prose s'offre donc comme un genre né de et pour la presse tout en étant un pied-de-nez à l'hypocrite lecteur du journal' (330).

[34] Thérenty, *La Littérature au quotidien*, 260.

nouvelle année', even to the extent that it ends with a moral as did many such 'chroniques'. Of 'Le Mauvais Vitrier' she writes that it, too, derives from 'la même esthétique hybride d'instantanés saisis sur le vif dans la rue et rendus grâce à une énonciation marquée d'observateur mâtiné de parleur.' So, too, 'Le Gâteau', published with the third group of prose poems in *La Presse* on 24 September: 'Les poèmes en prose fourmillent de choses vues, comme dans "Le Gâteau" et son micro-fait divers.'[35] Notwithstanding this overlap between the journalistic and the literary Thérenty argues for a clear difference between the 'chronique' and the prose poem on the basis of the moral lessons derived from the 'chose vue'. These literary versions of the 'chronique', she writes, 'tranchent incontestablement avec le reste de la production journalistique de l'époque. Leurs moralités les élèvent au rang de paradigme en proposant des règles de déchiffrement du réel,' which, she notes, are 'souvent inattendues et ambiguës chez Baudelaire'; and she quotes with approval the conclusion of another critic, Silvia Disegni, who sees in the prose poem the embodiment of Baudelaire's conception of 'modern art' as a combination of the transient and the eternal: 'Le poème en prose arrache la chronique à l'éphémère, à la péremption, à l'actualité, car la recherche formelle dérobe la nouvelle [i.e. the newly reported fact] au champ de l'information et du fugace pour lui donner une sorte d'éternité.'[36] For Thérenty herself Baudelaire's principal aim in writing prose poems was to give further and alternative expression to the duality of 'spleen et idéal': 'Le poème en prose balance entre l'idéal, les pays de Cocagne, les rêves de voilure et de mâture[,] et le spleen, celui-ci surgissant souvent à l'occasion de scènes banales du quotidien saisies dans la rue ou de petites scènes prosaïques et répétitives.' Accordingly she reads 'Perte d'auréole' as an allegory of Baudelaire's entry into the world of the press ('l'univers corrompu des journaux de boulevard') that bespeaks not 'une dégradation' but rather 'l'annonce d'une modification d'esthétique: la jonction entre un registre traditionnellement poétique et un autre relevant de l'univers journalistique'.[37] This relationship between the literary form of the prose poem and other more specifically journalistic forms like the 'chronique' or the 'chose vue' is for her, then, essentially one of 'collusion'.[38] Baudelaire's moral opinions may be 'souvent inattendues et ambiguës', she concludes (implicitly and unjustifiably conflating the author with

---

[35] Thérenty, *La Littérature au quotidien*, 260.
[36] Thérenty, *La Littérature au quotidien*, 261. Thérenty quotes from Silvia Disegni, 'Les poètes journalistes au temps de Baudelaire', in Silvia Disegni (ed.), *Poésie et journalisme au XIXe siècle en France et en Italie*, in *Recherches et travaux* [Grenoble], 65 (2005), 83–98 (90–1). See also Silvia Disegni, 'Poème en prose et formes brèves au milieu du XIXe siècle', in Marie-Ève Thérenty and Guillaume Pinson (eds), *Microrécits médiatiques: Les formes brèves du journal, entre médiations et fiction*, in *Études françaises*, 44: 3 (2008), 69–85. Cf. also Alain Vaillant's comment: 'la modernité n'est rien d'autre que l'esthétique issue de la culture médiatique', in his 'Métamorphoses littéraires. 2. La modernité littéraire', in Kalifa et al., *La Civilisation du journal*, 1523-31 (1523).
[37] Thérenty, *La Littérature au quotidien*, 260–1.
[38] Thérenty, *La Littérature au quotidien*, 13, 19.

his poet-narrators), but essentially these prose poems are new ways of expressing the duality of 'spleen et idéal' that he had already presented in verse.

Jean-Michel Gouvard has expanded on Thérenty's brief analysis of the parallels between Baudelaire's prose poems and contemporary journalistic forms by showing how some of the 'petits genres' identified by her are exemplified in *Le Spleen de Paris*: for example, the conversation (in 'Portraits de maîtresses' and 'Les Vocations'), the brief travelogue ('Le Gâteau', 'La Belle Dorothée', 'Déjà!'), the 'fait divers' ('La Corde'), and the 'écho mondain' ('Un plaisant', 'Le Miroir').[39] Moreover, as Gouvard also points out, a given prose poem may suggest more than one 'petit genre'. 'Un Plaisant', for example, recalls both the 'chronique de la nouvelle année' and the 'écho de Paris', while 'Perte d'auréole' combines elements of the 'chronique', the conversation, and the 'écho de Paris'. Gouvard sees in this mixing of journalistic techniques a refusal on Baudelaire's part simply to play the part of a journalist and instead the firm resolve of a literary artist to distance himself from the ephemeral quotidian world of the media ('restant en marge d'un monde dont elle refuse d'épouser le flux') and even to 'confront' this world in the form of a written embodiment of the poetic: 'il cherche à confronter, par les emprunts qu'il fait aux techniques journalistiques, la poésie avec l'un des vecteurs les plus puissants de la modernité naissante.'[40] But in the end, like Thérenty, Gouvard settles also for a form of collusion: 'Baudelaire emprunte à la presse et à ses procédés les figurations, (thématiques ou formelles), qui lui semblent adéquates pour exprimer la vision du monde qui est la sienne, lesquelles, par leur expression, contribuent en retour à forger l'image de ce monde, la manière même de le regarder.'[41]

Other critics, however, have suggested a less collusive or cooperative relationship between Baudelaire's prose poems and the world of journalism, mostly notably Graham Robb. Already in 1990 he was the first to call significant attention to the formal similarities between the prose poem and certain types of contemporary journalistic writing and to locate the origins of the prose poem and of Baudelaire's own use of it not in the versions of 'poetic prose' to be found in Chateaubriand's *Atala*, as Suzanne Bernard and Max Milner had done, or even in Aloysius Bertrand's *Gaspard de la nuit*, but in the daily press: 'Les abonnés du *Figaro* ou de *La Presse* auraient trouvé dans "Le Joujou du pauvre", dans "La Fausse Monnaie" ou dans "La Corde" des spécimens—provocants ou ambigus,

---

[39] See Jean-Michel Gouvard, '*Le Spleen de Paris* de Charles Baudelaire: Des "petits genres journalistiques" aux "petits poèmes en prose"', *Mémoires du livre/Studies in Book Culture*, 8: 2 (Spring 2017) <https://doi.org/10.7202/1039699ar>. The 'écho mondain' was a regular newspaper column, such as the popular 'Échos de Paris' section in *Le Figaro*, in which some newsworthy incident from life in 'high society' was reported for the amusement of readers.

[40] Gouvard, '*Le Spleen de Paris* de Charles Baudelaire: Des "petits genres journalistiques" aux "petits poèmes en prose"', 13.

[41] Gouvard, '*Le Spleen de Paris* de Charles Baudelaire: Des "petits genres journalistiques" aux "petits poèmes en prose"', 13.

mais bien reconnaissables—d'un genre assez répandu et qui s'insérait facilement dans les colonnes du journal: la "chose vue", l'anecdote transformée en moralité'.[42] Similarly, the prose poems that at one stage Baudelaire proposed to group under the headings 'Choses parisiennes' and 'Symboles et moralités' would have been read as 'des échantillons peut-être parodiques ou simplement excentriques de ce genre sentimental et moralisant'.[43] For Robb, furthermore, Baudelaire's prose poems bear the traces not only of some well-worn journalistic formulae of the day—the anecdote with a moral, the unusual scene or tableau illustrating a proverb or popular saying, the portrait of an anonymous passer-by, or, as in 'À une heure du matin', 'l'examen de conscience où l'écrivain raconte sa journée à des fins satiriques ou moralisantes'—but also of some surprisingly specific one-off topics treated in the recent or contemporary press (the comparison of a woman to a thoroughbred horse, the description of a mountebank). Even the images of the truncated snake and the kaleidoscope[44] were commonplace to describe collections of similar short prose pieces.[45]

Of particular interest to Robb are the tone and idiom of Baudelaire's prose poet, which he views as having been similarly borrowed: 'Son "flâneur" parisien adopte souvent le ton suffisant ou enjôleur des anecdotiers de la petite presse';[46] 'il nous semble que Baudelaire s'est assimilé, pour le transformer, non seulement le caractère pseudo-poétique de ces *tableaux*, mais aussi l'idiome complexe que lui et ses jeunes contemporains maniaient à l'époque où ils collectionnaient à leur tour des nouvelles à la main.'[47] For Robb this 'complex idiom'—evident, for example, in the work of Henry Murger, and notably in his *Scènes de la vie de bohème* (1851)-constituted a strategy whereby writers committed to the literary in its least journalistic forms could nevertheless write for a bourgeois readership in the press 'tout en affirmant, à travers la parodie, leur dignité de créateurs'. Key to this strategy was the employment of a range of conflicting linguistic registers, which Robb summarizes as follows: 'le calembour, un mélange d'actualité et

---

[42] See Graham Robb, 'Les Origines journalistiques de la prose poétique de Baudelaire', *Les Lettres romanes*, 14 (1990), 15-25 (17). Also Bernard, *Le Poème en prose*, 38, and Aloysius Bertrand, *Gaspard de la nuit*, ed. Max Milner (Paris: Gallimard, 1980), 9. Robb's article is not mentioned by Thérenty in *La Littérature du quotidien*.
[43] Robb, 'Les Origines journalistiques', 19.
[44] Baudelaire uses the former in his published dedicatory letter to Houssaye (i. 175) and the latter in a draft of this letter (i. 365).
[45] See Robb, 'Les Origines journalistiques', 17-19.   [46] Robb, 'Les Origines journalistiques', 18.
[47] Robb, 'Les Origines journalistiques', 19-20. Before the Revolution the 'nouvelle à la main' was a short manuscript newssheet, distributed like a conventionally printed newspaper and containing the latest news, gossip, or rumours. The term was current in the Second Empire press to describe 'les petites historiettes de boulevard racontées par la presse, souvent sous forme de dialogues'. See Thérenty, *La Littérature au quotidien*, 35 n. 31, and also 166, where she gives a more specific account of the term's usage: 'La nouvelle à la main raconte généralement une rencontre de journalistes sur le boulevard ou dans les cafés, une petite scène de sociabilité parsemée de noms propres et de personnalités, rythmée par un petit dialogue et close par un bon mot. Le journal fourmille donc de ses voix dérobées à l'oral, de ces conversations en apparence mimétiques mais refondées par la machine journalistique. Le journal devient la chambre d'échos du boulevard'.

d'allusions classiques, de lieux communs et de maximes déformées, d'argot et de préciosité, d'expressions familières et de mots savants [...] un langage qui fut sans doute difficilement compréhensible aux abonnés, mais qui n'en est pas moins fondé sur des locutions bourgeoises.'[48] Thus in Baudelaire's prose poems we find not Thérenty's 'collusion' with the press but a subversive strategy, what Robb calls 'une ironie tenant de la pantomime', a parodic adoption of bourgeois journalistic discourse that transforms it into a form of private, 'bohemian' slang: 'une sorte d'argot [...] une langue de *déclassés* qui a conservé sa vocation primitive: n'avoir de sens complet que pour des initiés se trouvant dans un monde hostile'.[49]

For Robb also, therefore, Baudelaire's art of the prose poem derives not from some putative pleasure found in the poetic prose of a Chateaubriand or an Aloysius Bertrand but from what he calls an 'antagonism' towards the pompous and self-righteous lawgiving of journalists like Hippolyte Castille: 'Tout en parlant, comme il l'écrit avec sarcasme dans "La Solitude" "la belle langue de [son] siècle", Baudelaire entreprend une démolition de l'idéologie que ce langage était chargé d'exprimer.'[50] But while this 'antagonism' undoubtedly underpins *Le Spleen de Paris*—and in particular an antagonism towards the public discourse of the press—I would like in the remaining chapters of this book to explore some of the ways in which Baudelaire's resistance to the public discourse of his day is informed not only by a negative spirit of critique and 'opposition' but also by a more positive spirit of celebration and an invitation to otherness. There are many 'fêtes' in *Le Spleen de Paris*: from the noisy New Year street party in 'Un Plaisant' to the firework display of the 'fête intérieure' in 'Le Crépuscule du soir', from the fairground scenes of 'La Femme sauvage et la petite-maîtresse', 'Le Vieux Saltimbanque', and 'Le Galant tireur' to the court performance of the buffoon in 'Une mort héroïque'. Insofar as each prose poem is itself a performance—of story, imagery, rhythm, and vocabulary—the reader is invited both to witness and participate in its celebration of the poetic imagination and to share in the possibility of an alternative truth, the truth of beauty.

---

[48] Robb, 'Les Origines journalistiques', 21, 22. On Baudelaire's use of popular sayings and proverbial utterance, see also J. A. Hiddleston, '"Fusée", Maxim, and Commonplace in Baudelaire', *Modern Language Review*, 80 (1985), 563–70, and Rosemary Lloyd, 'Façons de voir, façons de parler: Cliché, pastiche, parodie et jeu dans *Le Spleen de Paris*', *Studi francesi*, 126 (Sept.–Dec. 1998), 510–20.

[49] Robb, 'Les Origines journalistiques', 24.   [50] Robb, 'Les Origines journalistiques', 24–5.

22
The Question of Intent
Mystification and Perplexity

Et cependant écoutez cette petite histoire, où j'ai été singulièrement mystifié par l'illusion la plus naturelle.

('La Corde')

Polyphony and Conjecture

Qui ne sait pas peupler sa solitude, ne sait pas non plus être seul dans une foule affairée.

('Les Foules')

One principal manifestation of this resistant stance towards public discourse as it is staged in *Le Spleen de Paris* is polyphony, the adoption by the poet of a range of different voices, opinions, attitudes, and personas throughout the prose poems. The journalistic hack of 'À une heure du matin' who wants to recover his lost integrity with the production of some fine verse seems rather different from the lyrical lovers and dreamers of 'L'Invitation au voyage' or 'Un hémisphère dans une chevelure', just as the fastidious moralist of 'La Fausse Monnaie' appears to have little in common with the experimental behaviourist of 'Assommons les pauvres!', who in turn differs from the narrator of 'Le Mauvais Vitrier' by resorting to violence in order to prove a theory rather than in a sudden moment of madness. Similarly, the narrator of 'Une mort héroïque' who is so reluctant to comment categorically on the motivations of his protagonists might in all likelihood disapprove of the happy-go-lucky attitude expressed in 'Enivrez-vous'. This list could be extended. To it could be added examples of polyphony *within* individual poems, where the poet's own voice is also the mouthpiece—variously approving, disapproving, or neutral—for the voices of others. Already in the case of 'La Solitude' we have heard an array of such voices, from that of the 'gazetier philanthrope' to those of La Bruyère and Pascal, not to mention the unbridled loquacity of 'un bavard' and 'nos races jacassières'. A kind of conversation or debate thus takes place within these texts, which is figured more formally in poems such as 'L'Étranger,' 'Les Dons des fées', 'Les Vocations', and 'Portraits de maîtresses'. The overrriding effect is one of tension between dogmatism and relativism, and such that the poet's own voice—and his apparent willingness to acknowledge alternative perspectives—implicitly invites the participation of his reader in seeking, though not necessarily reaching, some conclusion in relation to the matter at hand, be it the benefits and disbenefits of solitude or the characteristics of an ideal mistress.

Marie-Ève Thérenty rightly considers the newspaper to be itself quintessentially heteroglossal and—'n'en déplaise à Mikhaïl Bakhtin'—'une œuvre collective et bien plus authentiquement polyphonique que le roman'. With its ever increasing number of different sections and regular column headings she sees it as both mirroring and endeavouring to organize the fractured multiplicity of the tumultuous modern world on which it reports:

> nouvelles de l'étranger, premier-Paris, chronique, débats de la presse, actes du gouvernement, nouvelles et fait divers, correspondance, débats législatifs, débats judiciaires, variétés, Bourses, ports et marchés, petites annonces, informations publicitaires, spectacles, feuilleton composent le puzzle écrit du monde.[1]

So many human activities, so many different voices and registers, so many different forms of textuality: it could be a description of these poems. But is the prose poet of *Le Spleen de Paris* merely mirroring 'le puzzle écrit du monde' for the sake of it, or has he some other end in view?

In *Logiques du dernier Baudelaire: Lectures du 'Spleen de Paris'* Steve Murphy begins his discussion—under the title 'Logiques du cabotin (En guise d'introduction)'—by focusing on this question. Were Sartre and before him Jules Vallès right in condemning Baudelaire for simply hamming it up, for indulging in mystificatory ventriloquism for the sheer pleasure and mischief of it, or did he, in performing for effect, expressly wish to provoke his readers in particular ways? Did he wish to lead them, as it were, up the hermeneutical garden path? Murphy believes so, and bases his readings in *Logiques du dernier Baudelaire* on this belief:

> Baudelaire aura essayé de programmer au moins partiellement les réactions du lecteur et, plus précisément, de proposer pour certains des 'petits poèmes en prose' des parcours interprétatifs variés où les divergences vont parfois jusqu'à la contradiction.[2]

Murphy grants immediately that Baudelaire's own position as the orchestrator of this polyphony—of these widely divergent narrative personas and registers, of these contradictions and blind alleys—is not in itself neutral. His choice of subject matter bespeaks a clear desire to engage with specific ethical and political issues,

---

[1] Thérenty, *La Littérature au quotidien*, 48, 81.   [2] *Logiques du dernier Baudelaire*, 26.

and poems such as 'Assommons les pauvres!' are plainly designed to shock a mindset that today we might call 'progressive' and was then called 'philanthrope'.[3] At the same time, Murphy argues, the strategy of polyphony is intended to allow the author of *Le Spleen de Paris* to avoid being pigeon-holed as representative of particular political or philosophical positions and indeed to air certain especially subversive or radical ideas without fear of his being assumed to espouse them himself. The first-person voice in these prose poems is thus absolutely not to be taken at face value:

> C'est pourquoi dans *Le Spleen de Paris*, l'emploi de la première personne est souvent un leurre—un piège dans lequel le lecteur doit tomber, avant de s'en extraire en s'apercevant que les locuteurs des poèmes sont soumis à des ironies qui montrent que Baudelaire ne partage ni leurs perceptions, ni leurs valeurs morales.[4]

As Richard Burton and Dolf Oehler had shown earlier, and as we have seen from 'La Solitude', the Baudelaire of the prose poems is keenly alive to the political debates of his own time and, within this context, simultaneously repelled by the intransigent utopianism of the left and moved to compassion and anger by the widespread social injustice for which he holds the right responsible. His sympathy is with the outcasts and downtrodden of modern society, of which, as many critics have pointed out, *Le Spleen de Paris* provides an extensive gallery, and his hatred is reserved above all for the do-gooders who expect to get away with fine words and fail completely to remedy the injustice.[5] And no one more so, as Oehler has suggested, than Arsène Houssaye himself, the editor of *L'Artiste*, who since 1851 had, like Castille, given his allegiance to the new Emperor.[6] For this is the man who could write a prose poem as hypocritically sentimental and aesthetically unremarkable as 'La Chanson du vitrier' (first published in 1850). As many commentators have observed, Baudelaire's reference to this particular 'tentative nouvelle' in his dedicatory letter to Houssaye is finely two-edged:

> Vous-même, mon cher ami, n'avez-vous pas tenté de traduire en une *chanson* le cri strident du *Vitrier*, et d'exprimer dans une prose lyrique toutes les désolantes

---

[3] At the end of 'Assommons les pauvres!', for example, the poet warns the beggar: 'souvenez-vous, si vous êtes réellement philanthrope, qu'il faut appliquer à tous vos confrères, quand ils vous demanderont l'aumône, la théorie que j'ai eu la *douleur* d'essayer sur votre dos'.

[4] *Logiques du dernier Baudelaire*, 28.

[5] See Patrick Labarthe, '*Le Spleen de Paris* ou le livre des pauvres', in Jean-Paul Avice and Jérôme Thélot (eds), *Hommage à Claude Pichois: Nerval, Baudelaire, Colette* [in *L'Année Baudelaire*, 5] (Paris: Klinksieck, 1999), 99–118.

[6] Oehler, *Le Spleen contre l'oubli*, 312–13. Richard Burton also provides a useful account of Arsène Houssaye in his article 'Destruction as Creation: "Le Mauvais Vitrier" and the Poetics and Politics of Violence', *Romanic Review*, 83: 3 (1992), 297–322 (307–11).

suggestions que ce cri envoie jusqu'aux mansardes, à travers les plus hautes brumes de la rue?

Tried but not succeeded... Baudelaire has no sympathy with this attempt at a song in prose nor with the story it tells. In Houssaye's prose poem[7] twelve refrains of 'Oh! vitrier!'—at once the street-cry of the glazier and (implicitly) the poet's own apostrophic lament—are intercalated with eleven quasi-stanzaic paragraphs which tell how on a busy Parisian street, where everyone else is driven by the imperatives of money, sex, or vanity, the poet alone hears the glazier—a tall, thin, pale, long-haired, ginger-bearded hybrid of 'Jésus-Christ et Paganini'—bemoaning his lack of trade that day and his consequent hunger. For he is a martyr to the absence of broken windows. 'J'allai à lui', the poet tells us, before reporting his own words of address to the exhausted, starving man, who steadies himself against the wall like a tottering drunk: 'Mon brave homme, il ne faut pas mourir de faim.' As if he had a choice in the matter... Our charitable poet then invites him for a drink, which causes the man to faint and thus break some of the new glass he is carrying on his back ('la moitié de son capital'). Sufficiently recovered, the glazier recounts how the woman with whom he lives ('Pauvre chère gamelle où tout le régiment a passé!') and their seven children are starving also, and yet proudly he refuses to seek charitable aid. Whereupon he leaves to return home to face this destitution anew, but, Houssaye's poet believes, 'un peu moins triste que le matin,—non point parce qu'il avait rencontré la charité, mais parce que la fraternité avait trinqué avec lui'. And the poet himself? 'Et moi, je m'en revins avec cette musique douleureuse qui me déchire le cœur: "Oh! vitrier!"' This is the kind of language and sentimentality that Oehler has in mind when he describes 'Le Gâteau' as 'une apologie secrète de la révolte de Juin,[8] qui dit tout le mépris dans lequel elle tient la doucereuse rhétorique libérale', and he sees Baudelaire's response to Houssaye's 'La Chanson du vitrier' as informing *Le Spleen de Paris* as a whole:

A cette version parfaitement hypocrite d'une 'communication sans domination' entre un bourgeois émotif et un prolétaire christique, Baudelaire oppose, dans *Le Spleen de Paris*, un modèle de communication et de comportement, lequel ne peut se comprendre autrement que comme commentaire de la philanthropie doucereuse du siècle première version. Ce que Baudelaire entreprend dans 'Le Mauvais Vitrier', mais aussi dans 'Assommons les pauvres!', dans 'Le Gâteau' et

---

[7] For Houssaye's text see i. 1309–11. For a detailed analysis see Murphy, *Logiques du dernier Baudelaire*, 337–49.
[8] An allusion to the public protest from 23 to 26 June 1848 by French workers objecting to the planned closure of the national workshops set up under the Second Republic, following the Revolution in Feb. 1848, and which were intended to provide work and income for the unemployed. The protests were brutally repressed by the National Guard, with several thousand people either killed or injured, and some 4,000 deported to the new French colony of Algeria. This event was seen as marking the defeat of radical/socialist republicanism.

d'autres poèmes en prose, c'est de mettre à nu la morale publique par le moyen d'une autodénonciation.[9]

For Oehler, then, the Baudelaire of the prose poems—of 'Le Spleen de Paris, cette tentative unique de saper le feuilleton du dedans'—is on the side of the radicals and strongly allergic to liberal cant. Hence the poet's desire to resist stereotypes and formulaic ideological positions: 'Baudelaire imagine des actions fantastiques qui paraissent abstruses, pour briser des structures mentales encroûtées, pour sortir de débats politiques stériles.'[10] Murphy, by contrast, cautions against the perception of a radical Baudelaire, reminding us of the poet's scepticism about progress, and suggesting instead that 'Baudelaire voit dans le contexte social une variation historique sur une "nature humaine" en définitive assez fixe.' But since the individual embodies this human nature within a specific historical and social context, then 'la représentation de sa perception exigerait que ce contexte soit convoqué dans toute tentative artistique de cerner son existence.'[11] Murphy considers Le Spleen de Paris, therefore, as being less political than 'anthropological' in nature, while at the same time seeing within the apparent diversity and polyphony of the poems a fundamental unity of purpose: 'Le volume n'a sans doute pas le système allégorique officiel, en partie linéaire, des Fleurs du Mal, mais par des récurrences et par un réseau de recoupements, l'intertextualité interne de ces "petits poëmes en prose" fait système.'[12] In short, as Murphy concludes, this polyphonic 'system' of repetition and interconnection in Le Spleen de Paris bespeaks a vision of society which, 'tout en donnant sa place à ce qui relève de la circonstance et de l'éphémère, tient la souffrance et la misère pour des phénomènes anthropologiques, qui ne disparaîtront jamais et qu'il serait vain d'espérer abolir par des modifications de la société'.[13]

Other critics have been equally alive to the polyphony of Le Spleen de Paris and the agendas that may or may not be hidden within its diversity and multiplicity. Writing a decade before Murphy's Logiques du dernier Baudelaire, Rosemary Lloyd and Sonya Stephens argued that Baudelaire's prose poetry 'owes much of its tensile strength to contradictions between what the narrators say and what the text reveals, between speech and gesture, and between the interpretation of gesture offered within a particular prose poem, and the meanings the reader may infer from imagery, sound patterning, irony, or intertextual references'.[14] They describe Baudelaire's 'narrators' as seeking 'to seduce their readers into a quite false sense

---

[9] Oehler, Le Spleen contre l'oubli, 328, 314. [10] Oehler, Le Spleen contre l'oubli, 333, 325–6.
[11] Murphy, Logiques du dernier Baudelaire, 31.
[12] Murphy, Logiques du dernier Baudelaire, 31.
[13] Murphy, Logiques du dernier Baudelaire, 680–1.
[14] Sonya Stephens and Rosemary Lloyd, 'Promises, Promises: The Language of Gesture in Baudelaire's "Petits Poèmes en prose"', Modern Language Review, 88: 1 (Jan. 1993), 74–83 (74). Steve Murphy welcomes and notes the recentness of this approach in his 'L'Hiéroglyphe et son interprétation: L'Association des idées dans "Le Tir et le cimetière"', Bulletin baudelairien, 30: 2

of secure partnership' and (in relation to 'Un plaisant') of the 'narrative voice' setting 'a trap of the sort frequently encountered in the prose poems, for the intended French reader can join the condemnation only by self-condemnation'.[15] Indeed, they argue, '[t]he narrators of these prose poems ['La Fausse Monnaie', 'Les Yeux des pauvres', 'Le Gâteau', and 'Le Vieux Saltimbanque'] [...] consistently reveal themselves to be dishonourable.'[16]

Similarly, Maria Scott has focused on what she calls Baudelaire's 'ironic pseudo-selves' in *Le Spleen de Paris*. Acknowledging the work of Lloyd and Stephens, and avowedly following Murphy's example in *Logiques du dernier Baudelaire*, she has examined in detail the unreliability of the poet-narrators in *Le Spleen de Paris* and highlighted just how many of the texts themselves thematize the problematic nature of reading and/or interpretation.[17] She shows how the 'shifting perspectives' of the prose poems constantly wrongfoot readers and leave them at a loss for coherence and answers, advancing by way of authorial intention a 'hypothesis of textual ruse' and a 'hypothesis of hoax'.[18] Unlike Murphy, Scott sees no systematic unity in the collection ('a collection whose most signal trait is its defiance of systemization'), and, unlike Sonya Stephens, she sees no 'unified self lurking behind a narratorial mask'.[19] But she nevertheless insists, as Murphy does, 'that the poet's self-representation in *Le Spleen de Paris* is, crucially, not to be trusted'.[20]

So why the hoax? In her 'Conclusion' Scott suggests not a political but a personal motivation on Baudelaire's part: 'a conscious design in the collection' that relates to the public's misunderstanding of his previous work, and above all *Les Fleurs du Mal*:

(1995), 61–84 (66). Patrick Labarthe takes up the theme in *Patrick Labarthe présente 'Petits Poèmes en prose' de Charles Baudelaire* (Paris: Gallimard [Foliothèque], 2000), 155–60.

[15] This echoes the idea put forward by Oehler and discussed above that Baudelaire effects a critique of liberal cant by having narrators deploy it in such a way as to 'denounce' themselves by the very act of giving voice to it. (*Le Spleen contre l'oubli* was first published in German in 1988.)

[16] Stephens and Lloyd, 'Promises, Promises', 76, 75, 79.

[17] See Maria C. Scott, *Baudelaire's 'Le Spleen de Paris': Shifting Perspectives* (Aldershot: Ashgate, 2005), 5, 6.

[18] Scott, *Baudelaire's 'Le Spleen de Paris'*, 14, 203. Cf. also, more recently, Jean-Michel Gouvard, for whom Baudelaire's prose poems are subversive by creating a sense of discomfort and communicational overload on the part of the reader: 'Il n'est pas possible de déterminer quelle est la "bonne" interprétation, car l'intention de Baudelaire n'est pas de délivrer "un" message, quel qu'il soit. [...] la visée première est de dérouter le lecteur, en mettant en place des dispositifs qui instaurent une polyphonie troublante, qui frôle parfois la cacophonie. C'est en déstabilisant le lecteur dans ses routines que *Le Spleen de Paris* se révèle particulièrement subversif, et critique, bien plus que par les allusions plus ou moins explicites à la société du Second Empire et à la Bohème qui émaillent le texte' (*Charles Baudelaire, 'Le Spleen de Paris'*, 101).

[19] Scott, *Baudelaire's 'Le Spleen de Paris'*, 14, 12. She refers to the claim in Sonya Stephens, *Baudelaire's Prose Poems: The Practice and Politics of Irony* (Oxford: Oxford University Press, 1999) that 'there is a unifying identity between the different [narratorial] voices' (62). See Scott, *Baudelaire's 'Le Spleen de Paris'*, 4.

[20] Scott, *Baudelaire's 'Le Spleen de Paris'*, 12.

Reacting against an audience that had failed to understand his practice of extracting the poetic and the heroic from the prosaic world around him, Baudelaire may have decided to exploit this very weakness. In other words, he may have chosen to return the favour of his own 'humiliation par le malentendu'.[21]

Though she acknowledges that 'Le Crépuscule du soir' and 'La Solitude' were published before the trial of Les Fleurs du Mal, she contends nevertheless that all the prose poems bespeak Baudelaire's 'extreme antipathy towards his public' and recalls how the projected prefaces to a subsequent edition of Les Fleurs du Mal repeatedly express 'the violent scorn inspired in him by the alleged vulgarity of his contemporaries'. In particular she points to Baudelaire's frustration that readers (and magistrates) assumed that the poetic persona who speaks in Les Fleurs du Mal was automatically and necessarily him. She points to the 'desire for revenge' expressed on a number of occasions in his correspondence and suggests the possibility that 'Baudelaire's resentment at the public's confusion of his own person with the subject matter of the verse collection gave rise to an ironic response in the form of prose poems that actually invite a similar recognition.' Hence the fact, she notes, that in several of these poems (for example, 'Enivrez-vous', 'Le Mauvais Vitrier', and 'Assommons les pauvres!') 'the author of Le Spleen de Paris seems at times to caricature his own public persona [...] as a hedonistic and profoundly amoral individual'. And hence too, perhaps, the title of the work, which may indicate that it was inspired by the writer's 'horreur de Paris'.[22]

In acknowledging the role of the reader in constructing the meanings of Le Spleen de Paris both Scott and Murphy[23] have (like Lloyd and Stephens before them) made important contributions to our understanding of Baudelaire's prose poems. But the principal implication of their approach remains, as in the analyses of Oehler and Burton, that what matters is for the reader to work out what Baudelaire himself thought. Where Scott argues in essence that we are being taught a lesson for reading badly, Murphy proposes (in the final section of his 'Introduction', 'Comment faire réfléchir le lecteur?') that the polyphony of problematic voices in Le Spleen de Paris is designed to provoke us into seeing, as it were independently and for ourselves, a unity of meaning that would otherwise remain hidden, a single truth about human nature as it is manifest in the circumstances of the historical moment: 'Il s'ensuit que l'exégète est amené au moins à formuler l'hypothèse d'une signification globale du recueil, obtenue par le biais d'une série de déductions tirées de la mise en confrontation des aspects *implicites* de ces

---

[21] For this quotation from Mon cœur mis à nu, see Fusées, ed. Guyaux, 91; i. 685.
[22] Scott, Baudelaire's 'Le Spleen de Paris', 204–7. For the quotation see Corr., i. 457 (20 Feb. 1858).
[23] See Logiques du dernier Baudelaire, 675: 'C'est dire que Le Spleen de Paris donne un rôle particulièrement important au lecteur, rôle tantôt gratifiant (il y trouvera bon nombre de motifs de satisfaction), tantôt ingrat (il est l'objet de provocations et peut se sentir désorienté).'

poèmes.'[24] But I would argue that what matters to Baudelaire is that readers should ignore him and think for themselves: that they should engage independently, as Murphy suggests, with the various political, ethical, philosophical, and aesthetic issues that are raised by the poems and keep thinking about them[25]—*but without necessarily seeking to come to a conclusion or even believing that a conclusion is either possible or desirable*, least of all desired by the author himself. In this respect we might perhaps imagine the poet of *Le Spleen de Paris* rather as Flaubert wants us to imagine his own 'impersonal' narrator:

> C'est un de mes principes, qu'il ne faut pas *s'écrire*. L'artiste doit être dans son œuvre comme Dieu dans la création, invisible et tout-puissant; qu'on le sente partout, mais qu'on ne le voie pas.[26]

For Baudelaire, as for Flaubert, 'la bêtise humaine consiste à vouloir conclure', which is just what 'les races jacassières' with their 'effusions oratoires' are constantly trying to do and indeed believe that they have succeeded in doing in exemplary fashion. Solitude is dangerous! But Baudelaire's poet seeks on the contrary to wean his readers from a reliance on authoritative pronouncement, on the lawgiving of norm and cliché and convention, and to countenance the possibility of alternative legislations: of endeavouring to becoming lawgivers themselves while recognizing the difficulty, and perhaps even the impossibility, of ever reaching a sure and final judgement. As J. A. Hiddleston has written:

> ce qui motive et explique les ambiguïtés et la prétendue mystification de l'œuvre de Baudelaire [i.e. *Le Spleen de Paris*], c'est moins sa modernité ou les conséquences de l'ironie romantique, bien qu'elles jouent un rôle important dans l'esthétique qui les informe, que la difficulté, voire l'impossibilité, de faire des jugements moraux, ou plus précisément d'établir une position sûre à partir de laquelle on pourrait les faire avec certitude et bonne foi.[27]

---

[24] *Logiques du dernier Baudelaire*, 30.
[25] A similar approach is adopted by David Evans towards the status of the 'poetic idea' within the prose poems and Baudelaire's awareness of its 'fundamental instability': 'Poetry requires a redefinition of its most basic elements: poet, poem, rhythm and reader, who henceforth undertakes a necessarily irresolvable search for a poetic value constantly deferred by a set of mystificatory mechanisms' (*Rhythm, Illusion and the Poetic Idea*, 127).
[26] Flaubert, *Correspondance*, ed. Jean Bruneau and Yvan Leclerc, ii. 691 (letter to Mademoiselle Leroyer de Chantepie, 18 Mar. 1857). A similar parallel has been noted by Gisèle Sapiro between Flaubert's 'impersonal' narrator and Baudelaire's presentation of himself as a 'comédien' in the note with which he prefaced the poems of 'Révolte' in the 1857 edition of *Les Fleurs du Mal*. See *La Responsabilité de l'écrivain: Littérature, droit et morale en France (XIXe–XXIe siècle)* (Paris: Éditions du Seuil, 2011), 311.
[27] 'Mobile et motivation chez Baudelaire', *L'Année Baudelaire*, 15 (2012), 61–71 (65). See also 71: 'Ici comme ailleurs ma conviction est que Baudelaire a la clairvoyance, je dirais même la candeur, de montrer qu'il n'y a point de position totalement innocente à partir de laquelle on peut passer jugement'.

Qui parle?

Tant poète que je sois, je ne suis pas aussi dupe que vous voudriez le croire.

('La Femme sauvage et la petite-maîtresse')

As an answer to this question about a unifying voice in *Le Spleen de Paris* Baudelaire's notorious dedicatory letter to Arsène Houssaye may, as Michele Hannoosh has suggested, provide a clue, for it raises the very question of authorial intention. Ostensibly a statement of friendship and writerly solidarity, this text has been seen as constituting a preface, and even as 'a prose-poem about prose-poems'.[28] Certainly it contains so many layers of irony and allusion that it is very difficult to derive a clear and unambiguous meaning from it, rather like the prose poems themselves.[29] Where Baudelaire had striven hard to organize the poems of *Les Fleurs du Mal* into meaningful patterns and to arrange them within an eloquent overall structure, now contingency is seemingly the goal, a random assembly of disparate works to be read in any order the reader so wishes. Except that in this very disorder lies its order:

Mon cher ami, je vous envoie un petit ouvrage dont on ne pourrait pas dire, sans injustice, qu'il n'a ni queue ni tête, puisque tout, au contraire, y est à la fois tête et queue, alternativement et réciproquement. Considérez, je vous prie, quelles admirables commodités cette combinaison nous offre à tous, à vous, à moi au lecteur. Nous pouvons couper où nous voulons, moi ma rêverie, vous le manuscrit, le lecteur sa lecture; car je ne suspends pas la volonté rétive de celui-ci au fil interminable d'une intrigue superflue. Enlevez une vertèbre, et les deux morceaux de cette tortueuse fantaisie se rejoindront sans peine. Hachez-la en nombreux fragments, et vous verrez que chacun peut exister à part. Dans l'espérance que quelques-uns de ces tronçons seront assez vivants pour vous plaire et vous amuser, j'ose vous dédier le serpent tout entier. (i. 275)

---

[28] Ross Chambers, 'Baudelaire's Dedicatory Practice', *SubStance*, 56 (1988), 5–17 (9). See also Stephens, *Baudelaire's Prose Poems*, 15. Cheryl Krueger suggests 'reading it not as the manifesto we would like it to be, but rather as one of the collection's many telling stories'. See her *The Art of Procrastination: Baudelaire's Poetry in Prose* (Newark: University of Delaware Press, 2007), 58.

[29] For Stephens these difficulties of reading reflect a dysfunctional socio-political and linguistic context. She argues that this letter 'figures the exchange economy into which the prose poems are launched. [...] in its duplicitous discursive strategies, it sets up a dysfunctional circuit of communication which prefigures the conflicting discursive and ideological discourses of the poems themselves' (*Baudelaire's Prose Poems*, 29). Of the poems she writes: 'In making available different meanings and in staging oppositional discursive relationships in a genre which is itself dependent on contrasting formal modes, the *Petits Poèmes en prose* constitutes a textual encounter representative of the dysfunctional social and linguistic encounters it stages' (22).

Instead of a collection of verse poems that proceeds from birth to death and evokes the journey of life, here is a group of texts about which we are invited to think that we shall never make head nor tail of them, a work, in short, that has lost the superfluous plot. And yet, we are told, every text is both head *and* tail, a beginning and a conclusion, or a conclusion (like an 'idée reçue', say) that is only the beginning of a conjecture and a further quest for conclusion. And so the satanic verses of Les Fleurs du Mal are followed in Le Spleen de Paris by a serpent in prose, a textual temptation—or generous invitation—to eat of the Tree of Knowledge, a combination of parts endowed with those popularly supposed capacities of the snake to reconnect when severed or to form two new living creatures out of one. Or, more accurately, the supposed capacities of a worm, of 'les vers': the worm of verse has turned and become a prosaic instrument of resistance against those who would lay down the law on our behalf, telling us what is true or not true, dictating to us what we should or should not do. As though there were a God, or providence—or indeed the 'Celui-là seul qui sait pourquoi' so desperately but so fruitlessly appealed to by the poet-narrator of 'Mademoiselle Bistouri'—who might authorize such lawgiving.

In the second paragraph of the dedicatory letter we can, therefore, begin to intimate a new reading of the title *Le Spleen de Paris*. Baudelaire here describes how, on reading Aloysius Bertrand's *Gaspard de la nuit* (1842) for the twentieth time, the idea occurred to him (not immediately therefore!) that he might himself attempt something similar and apply to the description of modern life—'ou plutôt d'*une* vie moderne et plus abstraite' (i. 275)—the same process or procedure ('procédé') as Bertrand had applied in his own description of 'la vie ancienne, si étrangement pittoresque' (i. 275). By 'procédé' Baudelaire appears to mean simply Bertrand's use of a 'poetic' prose style but not necessarily the kind of writing that he now immediately goes on to define, famously, in the third paragraph:

> Quel est celui de nous qui n'a pas, dans ses jours d'ambition, rêvé le miracle d'une prose poétique, musicale, sans rythme et sans rime, assez souple et assez heurtée pour s'adapter aux mouvements lyriques de l'âme, aux ondulations de la rêverie, aux soubresauts de la conscience?

Here attributing to all and sundry what is in fact his own unique (and, in the event, genre-creating) aspiration—namely, to express the duality of 'surnaturalisme et ironie' (or 'les fleurs du Mal') in a new kind of prose—Baudelaire then asserts that such an ambition derives principally not from Bertrand (nor from the allegedly commonplace writerly ambition of others) but from the city itself: 'C'est surtout de la fréquentation des villes énormes, c'est du croisement de leurs innombrables rapports que naît cet idéal obsédant.' So it seems as though the serpentine divisibility and interchangeability of the texts that constitute the multiple unity of *Le Spleen de Paris* may express the innumerable criss-crossing relationships that

THE QUESTION OF INTENT 515

constitute the life of a city. This is the city in general—and therefore the city of Paris in particular—seen as a site of transit and 'correspondance', of countless interconnections—personal, social, vehicular, moral, intellectual, philosophical, aesthetic—that may or may not be random, that may or may not demonstrate a pattern, but do constitute a multiple unity.

Yet just what model *is* the poet following? Here Baudelaire implies that Arsène Houssaye himself has led the way in 'La Chanson du vitrier'. But, as we have seen, Houssaye's poem is a pious, sentimental evocation of urban poverty, and as Baudelaire's own prose poem 'Le Mauvais Vitrier' shows (and as will be discussed below) there are 'alternative' ways of treating that subject.[30] Houssaye may have tried, but he has not necessarily succeeded. No more than Baudelaire himself has succeeded, it seems:

> Sitôt que j'eus commencé le travail, je m'aperçus que non seulement je restais bien loin de mon mystérieux et brillant modèle, mais encore que je faisais quelque chose (si cela peut s'appeler *quelque chose*) de singulièrement différent, accident dont tout autre que moi s'enorgueillerait sans doute, mais qui ne peut qu'humilier profondément un esprit qui regarde comme le plus grand honneur du poète d'accomplir *juste* ce qu'il a projeté de faire.

Who or what is 'mon mystérieux et brillant modèle'? Bertrand's *Gaspard de la nuit*? Or Houssaye? And so Baudelaire is being ironic and only too glad *not* to have emulated 'La Chanson du vitrier'? Or is the model that 'ideal obsédant', allegedly pursued by everyone, of a 'poetic prose' that combines the supple reverie of lyricism with the sudden somersaults and double-takes of a reflexive awareness? But, as almost all commentators on the prose poems remark, Baudelaire's formulation of this ideal of prose poetry seems to fit very well with the prose poems themselves, just as these poems do seem to mirror in their multiple complexities the teeming and confusing life of a city. So what, then, has he produced by accident and what in fact had he intended to produce that was different?

Michele Hannoosh has persuasively suggested that Baudelaire is here mindful of the arguments on which the court case against *Les Fleurs du Mal* had turned. Where six months earlier Flaubert had been acquitted on the grounds of his own (good) moral character and of his alleged (worthy) authorial intentions (to depict vice the better to guard his reader against it), the same prosecuting counsel, Pinard, now reversed his line of argument and contended that the effect of a work on the reader (through the depiction of vice), was in itself, irrespective of its

---

[30] 'Le Mauvais Vitrier' was the last of the nine poems included along with the dedicatory letter in the issue of *La Presse* published on 26 Aug. 1862 and thus played the part of an alternative and reciprocal 'queue' to the 'tête' that was the letter, a 'bad' glazier to answer Houssaye's 'good' one. A further five poems appeared the next day, and six more on 24 September. Houssaye subsequently refused to publish the final six poems that Baudelaire had sent him. See i. 1305–6.

author's character and intentions, and irrespective also of the overall tenor of the work in which the offending passages occurred, to be judged offensive to public decency. Where Flaubert's counsel had successfully mounted their defence on the ground that the offending passages in *Madame Bovary* had been illegitimately taken out of context, Pinard now successfully argued that fragments of text could on their own and in isolation exert a pernicious influence on public morals. As Hannoosh puts it: 'Authorial intention is thus irrelevant before the power of the text, and the meaning of the part is self-sufficient, not subordinated to, or modified by, the larger whole.'[31] As a result of Pinard's arguments, six of the thirteen indicted poems from *Les Fleurs du Mal* were therefore condemned as being necessarily conducive to the stimulation of the senses 'par un réalisme grossier et offensant pour la pudeur' (i. 1182). Thus, as Hannoosh also argues, we see here enacted in the judicial proceedings of a French court in the middle of the nineteenth century the 'death of the author' and a move from the unproblematic intentionality assumed by positivist literary critics (and by the judges who had acquitted Flaubert) to a view of literature as effect, of literature as constituted by the reader's response.[32]

Accordingly, Hannoosh sees the dedicatory letter as 'a lesson in the practice of reading' and as 'alluding, whether consciously or not, to the kind of reading the judges had performed'. She sees a knowing irony, therefore, in all this talk of an accident:

> This may indeed be one of the main effects of the trial of the *Fleurs du mal*. It represented those very features of a 'modern' reading practice which Baudelaire would so brilliantly exploit in the *Petits poèmes en prose*: the reader/flâneur wandering aimlessly through the text, submitting to the momentary shocks of a fragmented reading experience, unconcerned with 'what precedes or follows', the work emerging accidentally, like the chance intersections of urban phenomena which inspire the form of the volume, independently of the author's intentions. The poems treat this with high irony, creating a dizzying range of conflicting interpretations, stylistic registers, parodic clichéd discourses and ambiguous ideological positions, a confusing multiplicity of poetic voices and subjectivities to choose from, making the poems into the kind of commodity, and the reader into the kind of 'consumer', so undermined in the text.[33]

---

[31] See her 'Reading the Trial of the *Fleurs du mal*', *Modern Language Review*, 106 (2011), 374–87 (381).
[32] This shift is discussed at greater length in Sapiro, *La Responsabilité de l'écrivain*, 285–91.
[33] 'Reading the Trial of the *Fleurs du mal*', 387. In drawing this conclusion Hannoosh refers her reader specifically to Stephens's discussion of Baudelaire's engagement with media politics (in *Baudelaire's Prose Poems*, 81–90).

In addition, Hannoosh sees this letter as being of a piece with the 'projets de préface' (i. 181-6) drafted by Baudelaire in response to the court's verdict on *Les Fleurs du Mal*, and she draws attention to the terms in which, in notes prepared for his defence counsel, Baudelaire sought to defend his work, notably on the ground of the morality of the collection taken as a whole and also on the ground of his own sincerity in expressing a horror of evil. She takes this defence at face value and accordingly considers the description of *Le Spleen de Paris* as accidental to constitute 'high irony' on the part of a writer who still embraced a traditional view of literature and how we should read it:

> The literary values brought out in Flaubert's trial were classical ones: the work judged as a whole, the reader interpreting correctly or not the message which the work contained; those present in Baudelaire's trial were, for better or worse, resolutely modern—fragmented, random, non-narrative, haphazard, appropriate to a state of distraction and to the commodification of life in the modern city. The trial may have been a perfect example *avant la lettre* of that modern reading practice which the prose poems simultaneously reflect, ironize, and expose.[34]

In support of her argument she cites Baudelaire's remark in his first draft preface that the debate surrounding the 'morality' of *Les Fleurs du Mal* has proved to him yet again 'que ce siècle avait désappris toutes les notions classiques relatives à la littérature' (i. 181), and she notes: 'The context is those who believe the book will do either harm or good, in either case a confusion of beauty and morality.'[35] But, as I have tried to show throughout this book, Baudelaire finds beauty in a certain kind of moral seriousness, and to speak of confusion here is itself misleading. In this draft preface Baudelaire does indeed state that he himself will never 'confondre l'encre avec la vertu' (i. 181), and in decrying those who have 'unlearnt' all 'classical' notions of literature he has in mind those who advocate an overt didactic function for literature, an attitude he associates with the current vogue for 'Progress' and a crass philistinism and anti-intellectualism. But fortunately there are those who resist such an attitude: 'Mais il est des carapaces heureuses que le poison lui-même n'entamerait pas' (i. 181). And plainly Baudelaire considers himself one of them.[36]

In this first draft he then goes on directly to describe the nature of his resistance by sketching a possible defence of the nature and purpose of poetry, and specifically verse poetry: 'la distinction du Bien d'avec le Beau', 'la Beauté dans le Mal', versification as satisfying our 'immortels besoins de monotonie, de symétrie et de

---

[34] 'Reading the Trial of the *Fleurs du mal*', 387.
[35] 'Reading the Trial of the *Fleurs du mal*', 386-7, and 387 n. 47.
[36] Cf. the second draft: 'La France traverse une phase de vulgarité. Paris, centre et rayonnement de bêtise universelle. Malgré Molière et Béranger, on n'aurait jamais cru que la France irait si grand train dans la voie du *Progrès*.—Questions d'art, *terra incognitae*. Le grand homme est bête' (i. 182).

surprise', 'l'adaptation du style au sujet', 'la vanité et [le] danger de l'inspiration' (i. 182). As we have already seen, what he is advocating here is not formalism, or Art for Art's Sake, but the 'poetic idea': a form of writing in which 'style' is adapted to 'sujet' (in the case of *Les Fleurs du Mal*, the 'poetic idea' that he here calls 'la Beauté dans le Mal') in such a way that the two are indissociable (and always have been in the best 'classical' tradition of the literature of the past) and not in such a way that style is merely the means to express some pre-existing moral, philosophical, or religious position.

For Baudelaire, as later for Marshall McLuhan, the medium is the message. In *Le Spleen de Paris*, I would argue, Baudelaire is not, as Stephens and Hannoosh contend, satirizing a consumer society that has lost all notion of truth and value but rather setting up in opposition—in resistance—to those who, like Flaubert's Homais, believe they have all the answers. This is the Baudelaire who claimed that our most fundamental human right is the right to contradict ourselves, to forsake the supposed virtue of consistency and, by implication, to embrace the new virtue of conjecture. This is the Baudelaire who in *Le Peintre de la vie moderne* values Constantin Guys' depictions of Parisian life in sketch and water colour because they prompt moral considerations, and the Baudelaire who believes that the voicing of these conjectures is the best form of art criticism: 'Les considérations et les rêveries morales qui surgissent des dessins d'un artiste sont, dans beaucoup de cas, la meilleure traduction que le critique en puisse faire; les suggestions font partie d'une idée mère, et, en les montrant successivement, on peut la faire deviner' (ii. 712). The prose poems of *Le Spleen de Paris* may perhaps be seen, therefore, as the verbal equivalents of such drawings and as texts in which the 'idée mère' is the poetic voice itself: the voice of 'l'Étranger', a unique kind of discourse that transgresses the normal rules of moral, political, and/or philosophical commentary while all the time striving, in alliance with its readers, towards some provisional truths of its own. Within the dissonant and fragmented polyphony there is indeed one single unifying voice: a voice of resistance, but at the same time a voice of comedy and fantasy and dream, the alternative voice of the cloud-gazer.

If these prose poems can be called 'lycanthropes', then that is perhaps because they themselves ceaselessly shift their shape, like clouds in the sky. Almost all commentators on *Le Spleen de Paris*, including those discussed in this chapter, see such shape-shifting as worrisome: as disruption and fragmentation, as incoherence and impossibility, as being symptomatic of the alienation and dysfunction that allegedly characterize our experience of modernity. With scholarship and insight they search for substantive meaning where meaning itself seems at once suspect and elusive. But what if we were to see this cloudy shape-shifting as liberating, as a celebratory performance of the power of the poetic imagination to rethink our world? If Oehler is right to see Baudelaire's prose poems as 'cette tentative unique de saper le feuilleton du dedans', that is not only because they subvert the political and cultural assumptions of the discourse that fills the upper reaches of the page, but more especially because they represent a wholly other mindset and invite us to learn its language. And since, for Baudelaire, beauty, like meaning, is not an inherent attribute but the production of an effect, we can begin to see how the radical form of polyphonic writing on display in *Le Spleen de Paris* may have an aesthetic as well as a political or ethical function, and indeed how a certain form of aesthetic effect—namely, the provocation of conjecture in the reader—may itself in turn be regarded as having an ethical as well as an aesthetic integrity. To my knowledge no critic other than Jean-Luc Steinmetz has ever affirmed that these extraordinary poems might be beautiful, but then he himself is also a poet:

> Plusieurs générations se sont mises à l'épreuve de ces textes indéfinissables. Il n'est pas dit que, malgré la richesse des études poétiques en ce siècle comme en l'autre, leur singulière beauté puisse être l'objet d'analyses qui les délivreraient enfin de leur ambiguïté foncière.[37]

Such a prospect seems unlikely and even unwelcome. For the 'singular beauty' of these texts lies in their very resistance to critical analysis, as though we were reading them not through the windows of 'Les Fenêtres', be they open or closed, but through broken panes of glass. As Steinmetz himself has since commented in relation to 'Les Fenêtres': '"Je te défends de plaire" forme l'une des maximes de Baudelaire. L'éventualité de la beauté dans les *Petits poèmes en prose* est repoussée *ad infinitum*.'[38]

Broken Panes: 'Le Mauvais Vitrier'

> Nouvelles *Fleurs du Mal* faites. À tout casser, comme une explosion de gaz chez un vitrier.
> (letter to Poulet-Malassis, 29 April 1859 (*Corr.* i. 568))
> Ce qu'on peut voir au soleil est toujours moins intéressant que ce qui se passe derrière une vitre.
> ('Les Fenêtres')

The question of the poet's role and function as an alternative lawgiver comes firmly to the fore in 'Le Mauvais Vitrier', the last of the nine poems published on 26 August 1862 in *La Presse* and thus framing them by silently alluding back to Houssaye's 'La Chanson du Vitrier', mentioned in the dedicatory letter. Baudelaire's glazier has received extensive critical attention and a range of diverse

---

[37] *Le Spleen de Paris*, ed. Steinmetz, 7.   [38] 'Ontoscopie (sur "Les Fenêtres")', 164.

interpretations. According to the poet-narrator himself this street-seller is ostensibly 'mauvais' because he carries with him no coloured glass, which, the poet maintains, is what inhabitants of 'des quartiers pauvres' require: 'de[s] vitres qui fassent voir la vie en beau'.[39] So the poet has no wish for merely transparent glass (Realism?) but wants instead (on behalf of the poor? for himself?) coloured panes (imaginative 'vers/verres'?) that will allow the observer to see 'la vie', as it were, 'en rose'. Or, conversely, is the poet-narrator a parodic representation of the 'general reader' who wants from poetry (literature, art) not truth but the rose-tinted spectacles of escapist illusion and the sentimental compassion of Houssaye's own prose poem?

Or should we, given the setting in a 'quartier pauvre', look for a more specific, political meaning in this poem? Steve Murphy has shown that 'vitrier' was a slang term for a particular group of trigger-happy, window-breaking soldiers—the *chasseurs de Vincennes*—who had been involved in the suppression of the workers' insurrection in June 1848 and again in carrying out Louis-Napoléon's coup of December 1851 and so would have been for Baudelaire a term connoting reactionary violence. In Murphy's reading, therefore, Baudelaire is obliquely denouncing Arsène Houssaye as a 'mauvais vitrier' because he is a 'vendeur de valeurs fausses, d'une fraternité factice, et surtout d'un réalisme sous-réel'.[40] Building on Murphy's analysis Richard Burton has discussed how at that time 'the *vitrier* in the standard sense of "glazier" was already a figure of some ambiguity with regard to both his professional and political activities' and analyses 'some ways in which that ambiguity may be linked to the ambiguity, or inadequacy, of Houssaye's political posturings during and after 1848 and his related posturings as a writer'.[41] In particular Burton sees in the *vitrier*'s cry 'the discordant swan-song not only of a dying street-trade but of a superseded socio-economic order, a whole urban culture now in the process of being swept away by the onward march of Haussmannization'.[42] Accordingly, and equating the first-person narrator of

---

[39] As Jonathan Culler points out, the poet's complaint is generated by a literalization of the figure 'voir la vie en beau'. See his 'Baudelaire and Poe', *Zeitschrift für französische Sprache und Literatur*, 100 (1990), 61–73 (70). Culler argues that Baudelaire's recurrent use of this technique ('the generation of an allegorical narrative through the literalization of a phrase or a figure') derives from Poe (71) and he gives further examples from 'Le Galant Tireur' (cf. 'tuer le temps') and 'Les Dons des fées' (cf. 'le don de plaire') (72). On Baudelaire's use of what he himself called 'un calembour en action', see also Burton, 'Destruction as Creation', 317; Lloyd, 'Façons de voir, façons de parler', 518; Murphy, *Logiques du dernier Baudelaire*, 366; and Georges Kliebenstein, 'Baudelaire et le principe de déplaisir (À propos d'"Un plaisant")', in Murphy (ed.), *Lectures du 'Spleen de Paris'*, 79–96 (89–91). For discussion of the possible pun on 'pot (Poe) de fleurs' and an associated reference to *Les Fleurs du Mal*, see Culler, 'Baudelaire and Poe', 70, and Burton, 'Destruction as Creation', 317 n. 56. Baudelaire's literalization of the figure (of speech) is central to the deconstructive readings of Barbara Johnson in her *Défigurations du langage poétique*.

[40] Steve Murphy, 'Le Mauvais Vitrier' ou la crise du verre', *Romanic Review*, 82: 3 (1990), 339–49 (348), and his *Logiques du dernier Baudelaire*, 374–80.

[41] Burton, 'Destruction as Creation', 298–9.   [42] Burton, 'Destruction as Creation', 303.

'Le Mauvais Vitrier' with Baudelaire himself, he sees 'the *vitrier* who staggers breathlessly into Baudelaire's room and text as the relic of a by-gone age, a *petit industriel* survivor in an era of high capitalism' and argues that 'Baudelaire's violent hatred of the *vitrier* [...] is [...] wholly in line with his political, ideological and artistic "position" as it evolved in the wake of the December coup.'[43] Consequently he sees the poem as 'a dramatization [...] of a political-ideological and artistic struggle taking place simultaneously within Baudelaire and between him and certain orthodoxies or myths of both the Second Republic and the Second Empire'.[44]

Briefly put, Burton sees Baudelaire as caught between a former self who had between February 1848 and December 1851 'aligned himself unreservedly with the radical republican left' and then subsequently adopted 'a pessimistic reactionary ideology that was as opposed to the optimistic materialism of the Second Empire as it was to the optimistic idealism of the Second Republic'.[45] For Burton, therefore, as for Murphy, Houssaye is the 'real *mauvais vitrier*', and the flowerpot that descends on his inadequate glass is aimed at 'the showy superstructure of Second Empire progressivism'.[46] At the same time, in Burton's view, that destructive flowerpot expresses Baudelaire's rage at the passivity with which the Parisian working class had accepted defeat. For the poet this 'mauvais vitrier' is one who 'has lost all the idealism, all the utopian fervour that characterized his forebears—perhaps him himself—in 1848. He has no '"vitres magiques", no "vitres de paradis", to give hope or vision of "la vie en beau"',[47] and so the narrator (and, for Burton, therefore Baudelaire also) is himself now a 'vitrier' in the slang sense of one who smashes glass in violent opposition to the insurrectionary poor. Finally, the poet-narrator is also the author of Les Fleurs du Mal so that '"Le Mauvais Vitrier" thus represents, and itself strikingly enacts, a comprehensive break with the false values and aesthetic of Republic and Empire alike, conducted in the name of, and through the agency of, a "pot de fleurs": the "true" aesthetic and values of *Les Fleurs du Mal* and of Baudelaire's new inventions [sic], the *petit poème en prose*.'[48]

As this shows and as Burton readily acknowledges, a political reading 'in no way undercuts or supersedes the more common "aesthetic" interpretation of "Le Mauvais Vitrier" as a violent protest against realism and naturalism in art and in favour of the kind of *surnaturalisme* practised by Baudelaire and a handful of others'.[49] But it may also be that this is not the only 'aesthetic' interpretation that is

---

[43] Burton, 'Destruction as Creation', 306.
[44] Burton, 'Destruction as Creation', 312.
[45] Burton, 'Destruction as Creation', 312–13.
[46] Burton, 'Destruction as Creation', 314.
[47] Burton, 'Destruction as Creation', 316.
[48] Burton, 'Destruction as Creation', 319.
[49] Burton, 'Destruction as Creation', 317. For 'a useful restatement of this view' Burton refers his reader to Francis Heck, '"Le Mauvais Vitrier": A Literary Transfiguration', *Nineteenth-Century French Studies*, 14: 3–4 (Fall–Winter, 1986), 260–8.

possible, not least because, as Sonya Stephens and Maria Scott in particular have shown, the multiple ironies of action, statement, and register in the text prevent any simple identification of Baudelaire with his poet-narrator.[50] One particular feature of this poem lies in its similarity to the inaugural prose poems 'Le Crépuscule du soir' and 'La Solitude' where a particular question at issue—there the benefits and disbenefits of, respectively, dusk and solitude, here the unpredictability and inexplicability of certain acts of sudden violence—is presented in terms of the narrator's own behaviour as compared with that of his 'friends'. Moreover, in all three cases the human type at the centre of the debate is the 'rêveur'. 'Le Mauvais Vitrier' begins as follows:

> Il y a des natures purement contemplatives et tout à fait impropres à l'action, qui cependant, sous une impulsion mystérieuse et inconnue, agissent quelquefois avec une rapidité dont elles se seraient crues elles-mêmes incapables.

This psychological phenomenon—here stated as an incontrovertible fact while in itself nevertheless open to doubt—is then illustrated by the behaviour of three anonymous procrastinators ('tel qui', 'tel qui', 'ou [qui]') and then by three friends ('Un de mes amis', 'Un autre', 'Un autre'). In a prose poem that has often been read as comic—André Breton, for example, included it in his *Anthologie de l'humour noir*[51]—these illustrations are indeed quite daft. A man who delays going home for an hour in case his concierge gives him bad news; a man who takes a fortnight (for reasons here unstated) to open a letter; a man who waits six months before doing something he should have done a year ago... Are these really the most convincing examples of contemplative natures unfit for action (as poets themselves, of course, are stereotypically thought to be)? Nonetheless, says the narrator, they all 'se sentent quelquefois brusquement précipités vers l'action par une force irrésistible, comme la flèche d'un arc'.

As to the three 'friends', they are no more convincing as psychological test cases. The first—'le plus inoffensif rêveur qui ait existé'—once set fire to a forest to see if it would burn as quickly as people said it would, and when ten times in a row it didn't, he tried an eleventh time and it did. So, hardly violence on the spur of the moment then... The second also plays with fire since he is given to lighting his cigar in the vicinity of a keg of gunpowder. Like you do. But why? For all sorts of reasons: '"pour voir, pour savoir, pour tenter la destinée" [the man's own words?], pour se contraindre lui-même à faire preuve d'énergie, pour faire le joueur, pour connaître les plaisirs de l'anxiété, pour rien, par caprice, par désœuvrement'.

---

[50] See Stephens, *Baudelaire's Prose Poems*, 64–71, and Scott, *Baudelaire's 'Le Spleen de Paris'*, 189–95.

[51] As noted in Scott, *Baudelaire's 'Le Spleen de Paris'*, 189.

You name it, for the narrator himself has lost the plot. Undeterred, the latter reasserts his thesis: 'C'est une espèce d'énergie qui jaillit de l'ennui et de la rêverie; et ceux en qui elle se manifeste si inopinément sont, en général, comme je l'ai dit, les plus indolents et les plus rêveurs des êtres.' As to the third friend, he is quite capable of suddenly throwing his arms round an old man in the street: on an impulse, but also, it seems, as a matter of course. But why? Who knows! 'Parce que... parce que cette physionomie lui était irrésistiblement sympathique? Peut-être; mais il est plus légitime de supposer que lui-même il ne sait pas pourquoi.' Or maybe just for the hell of it? For badness? Because he has the devil in him? After all, if this excessively timid man regards entering a café or theatre booking office as the equivalent of entering the Underworld to be met by Minos, Aeacus, and Rhadamantys, the three judges of the dead standing watch over the entrance, then presumably the enthusiastic embrace of an elderly stranger quite plainly represents a most infernal act.

As in both 'Le Crépuscule du soir' and 'La Solitude' Baudelaire is here using the prose poem to demonstrate 'la bêtise de vouloir conclure' and in this case to question the authority of those who claim (like the 'gazetier philanthrope') to be experts in the field of human behaviour. As in 'Le Crepuscule du soir' and 'La Solitude' the emphasis is on the difficulty of understanding—let alone making sweeping statements about—a certain facet of human experience. Some fear the coming of night, while others, like the poet, welcome it: some advise that solitude is dangerous, while others, like the poet, advocate its benefits. Here the unpredictable actions of the 'rêveur' constitute the puzzle in question:

> Le moraliste et le médecin, qui prétendent tout savoir, ne peuvent pas expliquer d'où vient si subitement une si folle énergie à ces âmes paresseuses et voluptueuses, et comment, incapables d'accomplir les choses les plus simples et les plus nécessaires, elles trouvent à une certaine minute un courage de luxe pour exécuter les actes les plus absurdes et souvent même les plus dangereux.

This time, though, there appears to be no equivalent of La Bruyère or Pascal to rule on the matter, and the narrator himself seems to be a decidedly suspect guide. His first three examples ('tel qui') concern banal acts of delayed resolve that can hardly be seen as inexplicable displays of manic energy. It is not fecklessness but fear of bad news that deters the first and possibly the second procrastinator, while the unknown task facing the third may, for all we know, warrant his reluctance. As for the three 'friends', the first two act with premeditation and out of a spirit of quasi-scientific experimentation, and the third is an 'enthusiast' who, for all his commendable embrace of the Other, would appear to be more or less off his head. The possibility therefore arises that the narrator is simply creating a spurious category of human behaviour that allows him to grace his own (self-indulgent? petulant? insane?) act of flower-pot violence with the respectability of an acknowledged syndrome. In the hermeneutic vacuum left by both moralist and medic he cites his own behaviour as a new source of authority:

> J'ai été plus d'une fois victime de ces crises et de ces élans, qui nous autorisent à croire que des Démons malicieux se glissent en nous et nous font accomplir, à notre insu, leurs plus absurdes volontés.

Many readers of this poem have noted the similarity between these demons and Poe's 'Imp of the Perverse', though without necessarily acknowledging the difference between Poe's focus on the irrational 'perverseness' of our occasional impulse to self-harm and Baudelaire's insistence on our 'perversity': that is, our deep-seated and seemingly irresistible urge to commit 'wicked' or injurious deeds. Moreover there is a clear parallel between the poet-narrator's comment about demons and Baudelaire's statement to Flaubert that he had always been 'obsédé par l'impossibilité de me rendre compte de certaines actions ou pensées soudaines de l'homme sans l'hypothèse de l'intervention d'une force méchante extérieure à lui' (*Corr.*, ii. 53). But still we may need to guard against directly identifying Baudelaire with a poet-narrator who appears determined to present his dubious act of pot-throwing not only as the symptom of a recognizable pattern of human behaviour but *also* both as a joke and as evidence of a quasi-Faustian pact. Thus the poet-narrator concludes his narrative with an expression of putative wisdom and a bravado that recalls his earlier, absurd reference to the 'courage de luxe' that allows a man to open a letter or face his concierge: 'Ces plaisanteries nerveuses ne sont pas sans péril, et on peut souvent les payer cher. Mais qu'importe l'éternité de la damnation à qui a trouvé dans une seconde l'infini de la jouissance?' This final incongruity between dropping a flower-pot and selling your soul, compounding that inherent in the previous comparison of the flower-pot itself to an 'engin de guerre', serves to cast the seriousness of this prose poem into final and retrospective doubt, such that the reader may now recall the parenthesis introduced by the narrator just as he begins to tell us how he woke up one morning feeling grumpy and bored and 'impelled' to 'faire quelque chose de grand, une action d'éclat'. In retrospect we see the punning humour in that reference to 'une action d'éclat', and indeed the irony of the clause that follows: 'et j'ouvris la fenêtre, hélas!' For all will hinge on the question of window-panes and how they get broken.

The parenthesis in question reads as follows:

> (Observez, je vous prie, que l'esprit de mystification qui, chez quelques personnes, n'est pas le résultat d'un travail ou d'une combinaison, mais d'une inspiration fortuite, participe beaucoup, ne fût-ce que par l'ardeur du désir, de cette humeur, hystérique selon les médecins, satanique selon ceux qui pensent un peu mieux que les médecins, qui nous pousse sans résistance vers une foule d'actions dangereuses ou inconvenantes.)

Translating 'mystification' as hoax, Maria Scott notes here the distinction between impromptu hoaxes and those that are premeditated and argues for a further distinction between the narrator who favours the former and a 'poet (as distinct from the narrator)' who 'enjoys the kind of mystification that requires effort and artifice'. For her it is this poet who here in 'Le Mauvais Vitrier' has written in such a way as 'to trap the very readers whose naively literal, positivistic response to [*Les Fleurs du Mal*] had so galled the poet', and who in other prose poems sets similar traps for those who would automatically identify the first- or third-person voices of these poems with that of Baudelaire himself.[52] But perhaps we can instead read 'mystification' positively and rather more in the sense of a conscious intention to puzzle or bewilder, to open questions up for consideration and debate, to make readers think again:[53] in short, to open windows. And this, as Baudelaire knows, is a dangerous activity: 'et j'ouvris la fenêtre, *hélas!*' (my emphasis).[54] To put it another way, he, too, is playing with fire and risking an explosion.[55]

As in 'Le Crépuscule du soir' the question of causation is central to 'Le Mauvais Vitrier'. There, it will be recalled, the poet notes (in both versions) that 'bien qu'il ne soit pas rare de voir la même cause engendrer deux effets contraires, j'en suis toujours comme intrigué et alarmé'. Here the poet's puzzlement continues. People—'des natures purement contemplatives et tout à fait impropres à l'action', people like his friend, 'le plus inoffensif rêveur qui ait existé', people such as poets—do all sorts of funny things and sometimes quite out of the blue. Why? Mental illness ('hystérie')? Or because they are possessed by demons? Or is there perhaps method in their madness ('le résultat d'un travail ou d'une combinaison')? Through the multiplicity and diversity and incoherence of its proposed explanations, and in particular through the insistent contrast between incontrovertible statement and unanswered questions, 'Le Mauvais Vitrier' demonstrates

---

[52] See Scott, *Baudelaire's 'Le Spleen de Paris'*, 190, 192.
[53] On this approach to 'mystification', see Scott Carpenter, 'Mystification et esthétique moderne', *Romantisme* 156 (2012), 13–24, and in particular his discussion (19–23) of some of Baudelaire's prose poems, including 'Le Mauvais Vitrier'. Carpenter concludes: 'En dernier lieu, si la mystification moderne refuse de révéler sa vérité, c'est parce qu'elle comporte une mise en question fondamentale du "vrai". Elle s'écarte du mystère (au sens religieux) en faisant comprendre que les vérités révélées sont toujours des leurres, et que la mystification, loin d'être un cas exceptionnel, est devenue la norme de l'expérience moderne' (24).
[54] For Ross Chambers in *An Atmospherics of the City* this action represents 'for my argument, the most significant moment in all Baudelaire [...] the poet narrator throws his window wide open to the noise of the city, in a gesture that encapsulates Baudelaire's own (never complete) renunciation of the magical refracting windowpane of idealizing aesthetics in favor of an atmospherics of noise—one that, by this time, will have shed its supernatural reference completely' (32).
[55] See Richard D. E. Burton, 'Bonding and Breaking in Baudelaire's *Petits Poèmes en prose*', *Modern Language Review*, 88: 1 (Jan. 1993), 58–73 for an account of 'the principal moments of breaking, cutting, exploding, or unbinding in the *Petits poèmes en prose*' (61). Burton tentatively attributes the prevalence of these images and narrative actions to (i) 'the scissile, dislocating nature of the modern city' (66–7); (ii) the poet's interest, relating to his 'Catholicism' (68), in the diabolical origins of violence; and (iii) a possible parallel between 'the breakdown of poetic form and [Baudelaire's] mental and physical breakdown' (69).

to its readers just how difficult it is, in fact, to see. For this reason it may be that—and again as in 'La Solitude'—the work of Frédéric Bastiat, liberal economist and friend of Hippolyte Castille, is of relevance to an understanding of this poem. In 1850 Bastiat published a short work of some sixty pages entitled *Ce qu'on voit et ce qu'on ne voit pas, ou L'Économie politique en une leçon*[56] where, in his first paragraph, he introduces as the principal subject of his book the question of cause and effect:

> Dans la sphère économique, un acte, une habitude, une institution, une loi n'engendrent pas seulement un effet, mais une série d'effets. De ces effets, le premier seul est immédiat; il se manifeste simultanément avec sa cause, *on le voit*. Les autres ne se déroulent que successivement, *on ne les voit pas*; heureux si on les *prévoit*.

Bad economists observe only the immediate and visible effect and are unaware of the law of unintended consequences; good economists pay heed both to the visible and to the foreseeable effect(s) insofar as they are able. The difference is 'enormous' because it is 'almost always' the case that when the immediate effect is favourable, the longer-term consequences are not so, and vice versa. Moreover, Bastiat argues, the same holds true 'en hygiène, en morale' (cf. Baudelaire's 'moraliste' and 'médecin'?): 'Souvent, plus le premier fruit d'une habitude est doux, plus les autres sont amers. Témoin: la débauche, la paresse, la prodigalité' (cf. dropping a flower-pot and eternal damnation?). For Bastiat, immediate gratification—embraced 'non seulement par penchant, mais par calcul'—is therefore deleterious in its consequences and accounts for 'l'évolution fatalement douloureuse de l'humanité'. Short-termism is the root of all evil. From the cradle onwards we are slow to learn because at first we see only immediate effects, but with time we gradually learn from experience such that 'nous ne pouvons manquer de finir par savoir que le feu brûle, à force de nous brûler' (like the first two friends in 'Le Mauvais Vitrier'?). Much better, argues Bastiat, to learn to foresee consequences than to have to keep learning from experience—or making the same mistake twice.[57]

By way of illustrating the central argument of this book subtitled 'L'Économie politique en une leçon', Bastiat begins with a chapter entitled 'La Vitre cassée'.[58] Here he examines a stereotypical situation in which Jacques Bonhomme's son has broken a window-pane and people console his father with clichés: 'A quelque

---

[56] (Paris: Guillaumin & Cie). The work was republished on multiple occasions throughout the remainder of the century and into the next. First translated into English in 1859, it quickly went through several editions. It has been described as the work for which Bastiat is 'best remembered'. See under 'Frédéric Bastiat (1801–50) Pioneering French Economist', in Simon Blackburn (ed.), *The Oxford Dictionary of Philosophy* (3rd edn, Oxford: Oxford University Press, 2016).
[57] *Ce qu'on voit*, 1–2.   [58] *Ce qu'on voit*, 4–7.

chose malheur est bon. De tels accidents font aller l'industrie. Il faut que tout le monde vive. Que deviendrait les vitriers, si l'on ne cassait jamais de vitres?' The glazier comes and earns six francs, which is good: *'C'est ce qu'on voit.'* But if anyone concludes from this that breaking window-panes is good because it stimulates the economy, they are ignoring the fact—*'ce qu'on ne voit pas'*—that the six francs Jacques Bonhomme spends on the glass cannot now be spent on something else. (Bastiat thus theorizes what has come to be known as an 'opportunity cost'.) Hence any form of destruction (or other inhibition of the creation and accumulation of capital wealth) represents an overall loss to society, and protectionists are therefore wrong to seek to stimulate the economy by legislating on the basis of this belief that such destruction (or targeted inhibition) is beneficial: such as 'ce bon M. de Saint-Chamans' who has so carefully calculated (and described in *Le Moniteur industriel*) the profits that industry would make if the city of Paris were to be destroyed by fire (or perhaps by Baudelaire's 'friend'?).

Basing himself on this example of a broken window-pane, Bastiat then proceeds in his book to question under a series of headings (public sector workers, infrastructure investment, subvention of the arts, etc.) the alleged benefits of state intervention in a free market economy, arguing, for example, that in seeing the indubitable benefits of spending tax revenue on good causes, we fail to see what else the money so raised could have been spent on by the taxpayer and to the benefit of the economy as a whole. Whatever one's views on Bastiat's liberal economics, it is plain that the whole thrust of his book derives from his demolition of the easy assumptions implicit in what he calls 'ce dicton vulgaire: "Que deviendrait les vitriers, si l'on ne cassait jamais de vitres!"'[59] Several commentators have suggested that 'Le Mauvais Vitrier' may derive from the idiomatic expression 'casser les vitres' (meaning to create a commotion) or 'qui casse les vitres les paie' (on the need to accept responsibility), but the particular 'dicton' foregrounded by Bastiat is thus perhaps an equally—and perhaps more—plausible cause of the effect that is 'Le Mauvais Vitrier'. It is not known whether Baudelaire read Bastiat's 'political economy in one lesson' and so it cannot be known whether it played a part in the writing of 'Le Mauvais Vitrier', but, as we saw earlier, his reference to Robinson Crusoe in both versions of 'La Solitude' suggests that he was at least familiar with his ideas. Less problematically, Bastiat's work indicates that the saying in question was widely known in mid-nineteenth-century France and would therefore most probably have been known to Baudelaire and his readers. But where Bastiat is keen to refute the particular false logic that underlies the 'dicton', Baudelaire is more concerned to confound reliance on popular sayings *tout court*, and in 'Le Mauvais Vitrier' he narrates a comic act of violence (note: no

---

[59] *Ce qu'on voit*, 7.

glaziers were hurt in the performance of this act) that symbolizes this confounding.

Houssaye's 'La Chanson du Vitrier' was first published in the first edition of his *Poésies complètes* in 1850, in the same year therefore as Bastiat's *Ce qu'on voit et ce qu'on ne voit pas*, but was almost certainly written before it (or at the very least without knowledge of it). Nevertheless within the text Houssaye presents what would appear to have been a widespread recognition that a glazier's lot depends on the misfortune of others. His 'vitrier' has found no work that day:

> Depuis le matin, il avait crié plus de mille fois:
>
> Oh! vitrier!
>
> Quoi! pas un enfant tapageur n'avait brisé une vitre de trente-cinq sous! pas un amoureux, en s'envolant la nuit par les toits, n'avait cassé un carreau de six sous! Pas une servante, pas une bourgeoise, pas une fillette, n'avaient répondu, comme un écho plaintif:
>
> Oh! vitrier! (i. 1310)

Hence the glazier's starving exhaustion and subsequent collapse in which he breaks some of his glass worth 'trois francs dix sous, la moitié de son capital! car je ne pus empêcher ses carreaux de casser' (i. 1310). Houssaye's poet does, therefore, try to prevent disaster (even if the offer of alcohol to a hungry and already tottering man might be thought ill advised), and he appears wholly unaware of any irony that when a glazier breaks *his own* glass, that really isn't good for business. Baudelaire, however, appears to acknowledge this irony as he rewrites Houssaye's narrative and substitutes for the charitable host a pot-dropping prankster who carefully aims not at the glazier himself but at 'le rebord postérieur de ses crochets' and thereby causes him, like Houssaye's latter-day Christ, to break his own glass: 'le choc le renversant, il acheva de briser sur son dos toute sa pauvre fortune ambulatoire qui rendit le bruit éclatant d'un palais de cristal crevé par la foudre'. Like Zeus hurling thunderbolts, Baudelaire's poet has smashed this particular Crystal Palace to smithereens—as though administering justice.[60]

As Burton has noted, this image recalls the opening paragraphs of the section entitled 'Des écoles et des ouvriers' in the *Salon de 1846* in which Baudelaire equates realism with republicanism and attributes a lack of originality in contemporary painting (with the honourable exceptions of Delacroix and Ingres) to a wanton eclecticism deriving from 'une liberté anarchique qui glorifie l'individu'

---

[60] Michele Hannoosh has proposed in '"Le Mauvais Vitrier" devant la justice' (*L'Année Baudelaire*, 22 (2018), 125–9) a reading of this particular action as a parodic re-enactment of the court's condemnation of *Les Fleurs du Mal*: 'le poème montre une scène de justice parodique. Celle-ci tourne en ridicule la Justice qui a condamné le poète des *Fleurs du Mal* comme un "mauvais vitrier" pour avoir montré un "réalisme grossier" au lieu de "la vie en beau"' (129).

(ii. 492). The section begins with an account of the critic's enthusiasm during a riot as he observes a policeman hitting a republican 'insurgent' with the butt of his rifle:

Crosse, crosse un peu plus fort, crosse encore, municipal de mon cœur; car en ce crossement suprême, je t'adore, et te juge semblable à Jupiter, le grand justicier. L'homme que tu crosses est un ennemi des roses et des parfums, un fanatique des ustensiles [...] Crosse religieusement les omoplates de l'anarchiste! (ii. 490)

Rather than apprenticing themselves subserviently to the masters and learning new skills in an 'école', the artists of 1846 see themselves as independent workers but are thereby condemned to promiscuous imitation and the mere assembly of pictorial cliché: 'Les singes sont les républicains de l'art' (ii. 492).[61] For Burton, the 'mauvais vitrier' with his transparent panes of glass represents this equation of republicanism and realism, while the poet-narrator's violence epitomizes Baudelaire's conception of the creative process as inherently 'explosive': 'Artistic creation was itself for Baudelaire a process of rupture, wrenching, and release, a sometimes violent unleashing of repressed energies.'[62] In support of his argument he adduces the poet's comparison of his newly completed poems for 'Tableaux parisiens' in 1859 to 'une explosion de gaz chez un vitrier' (*Corr.*, i. 568). But where Burton sees an explosive creativity as the *cause* of the poet's destructive action, one might perhaps also see it as an *effect* of that action: an effect felt not by the glazier (whose reaction to the thunderbolt is not recorded) but by the reader for whom (as the very proliferation of critical commentary on this prose poem itself demonstrates) multiple possibilities of interpretation have been opened up, like a window, by the ludic mystifications of the text. For it is no accident, no 'inspiration fortuite', that the poet-narrator should intervene parenthetically just before he tells us the story of his 'action d'éclat': ostensibly to say that the idea of playing a practical joke (by asking an awkwardly laden glazier to climb the narrow stairs to his room on the sixth floor when he the poet has no intention of buying any glass) came to him just as suddenly and spontaneously as it occurred to his dreamy friend to see how quickly a forest can be set ablaze, but also, and more importantly, implicitly to warn us that we ourselves are precisely about to be mystified also—deliberately and creatively mystified—by this cruel act of his.

Like the kaleidoscope (etymologically, the means of seeing beautiful forms or 'ideas') to which Baudelaire thought of comparing his prose poems in the draft dedicatory letter to Houssaye, this text is itself like an assembly of glass shards that

---

[61] For further discussion of 'Des écoles et des ouvriers' see Burton, 'Destruction and Creation', 317-19, and Gretchen van Slyke, 'Riot and Revolution in the *Salon de 1846*', *French Forum*, 10: 3 (Sept. 1985), 295-306.
[62] Burton, 'Destruction and Creation', 319.

appear to have one pattern before some readerly rotation of the text creates another. But, as with a kaleidoscope, each pattern has a necessity and validity of its own. This is perhaps what Baudelaire had in mind when in some unpublished notes ('Notes précieuses') he observes that there is 'rien de plus beau que le lieu commun',[63] and it may also be why, as Théophile Gautier recalled, he himself liked in conversation to make strange and inscrutable pronouncements as though he were merely stating a commonplace truth:

> D'un air très simple, très naturel et parfaitement détaché, comme s'il eût débité un lieu commun à la Prudhomme sur la beauté ou la rigueur de la température, il avançait quelque axiome sataniquement monstrueux ou soutenait avec un sang-froid de glace quelque théorie d'une extravagance mathématique, car il apportait une méthode rigoureuse dans le développement de ses folies.[64]

Here in 'Le Mauvais Vitrier' we are similarly presented with a ludic performance that appears absurd but nevertheless has a logic of its own. For in the end the poet—as the polyphonic voice of the text who both warns of pranks and commits them—does reject the kind of transparent meaning potentially symbolized by the glazier's uncoloured panes (his own prose poem demonstrates that fact), and he does also prefer to see 'la vie en beau': not 'la vie en rose' as allegedly desired by the poor, but 'en beau': a world that can give rise to the kaleidoscopic possibilities of imaginative conjecture that Baudelaire sees as constitutive of the experience of beauty.

For the writer of these prose poems everyday sayings such as 'Que deviendrait les vitriers, si l'on ne cassait jamais de vitres!' can thus be an object of fascination, and perhaps for one reason in particular: they themselves are authorless, issuing from no single voice of authority, and simply *there*, a law unto themselves. This question of authorial wisdom and intention lies at the heart of *Le Spleen de Paris*, and it recurs repeatedly in 'Le Mauvais Vitrier' through the continual contrasting of sententious affirmation and expressions of perplexity ('Il me serait d'ailleurs impossible de dire pourquoi'), and also in its ambivalence as to whether a number of unwise human actions ('une foule d'actions dangereuses ou inconvenantes') are spontaneous or planned, 'inspired' by irresistible devilish impulse or else 'le résultat d'un travail ou d'une combinaison'. Thus the poem further recalls the dedicatory letter to Houssaye in which Baudelaire claims to have to have tried to follow one model and to have produced something entirely different. For in this

---

[63] *Fusées*, ed. Guyaux, 131, and i. 670. Cf. also Baudelaire's account of a conversation with Delacroix: 'nous causâmes tout d'abord de lieux communs, c'est-à-dire des questions les plus vastes et les plus profondes' (*Salon de 1859*, ii. 624).
[64] Théophile Gautier, 'Préface aux Œuvres complètes', in Guyaux (ed.), *Baudelaire: Un demi-siècle de lectures*, 468.

way he himself drives a wedge between 'Baudelaire' and not only his various poet-narrators but also the prose poems themselves, which apparently and as though by accident, speak with a voice of their own:

> Sitôt que j'eus commencé le travail, je m'aperçus que non seulement je restais bien loin de mon mystérieux et brillant modèle, mais encore que je faisais quelque chose (si cela peut s'appeler 'quelque chose') de singulièrement différent, accident dont tout autre que moi s'enorgueillirait sans doute, mais qui ne peut qu'humilier profondément un esprit qui regarde comme le plus grand honneur du poète d'accomplir *juste* ce qu'il a projeté de faire.

Here is the poet who rejects the Romantic notion of 'inspiration' (whether divine or satanic) and firmly agrees with Poe in seeing 'composition' as a willed and conscious act. And yet he has unwittingly produced something that anyone else would be proud of. But what? Perhaps a form of accidental beauty? Poems where the beauty will derive not from him but from the reader's own response? Poems that at first we can make neither head nor tail of but which gradually reveal a whole series of kaleidoscopic patterns? Poems in which a form of disorder, or dissonance, becomes an alternative form of order and harmony: 'un petit ouvrage dont on ne pourrait pas dire, sans injustice, qu'il n'a ni queue ni tête, puisque tout, au contraire, y est à la fois tête et queue, alternativement et réciproquement'. It would be unjust to think otherwise, since to think *otherwise* is just what these prose poems are intended to make their readers do. For the poet has indeed managed to 'accomplir juste ce qu'il a projeté de faire', not least because the projectile in question is a thing of beauty, a container in which flowers may grow and bloom.

With clear and entertaining intent Baudelaire thus smashes through the paradox and contradiction inherent in a certain conception of the poet as an ineffectual dreamer, like the 'âme oisive et divagante' denigrated by others in 'La Solitude'. For if poets are so ineffectual, why then do people—like Hippoltye Castille or the magistrates who condemned some of the poems in Les Fleurs du Mal—believe them to represent such a danger to social order and the moral welfare of the nation? In this respect Baudelaire foreshadows the Mallarmé of La Musique et les Lettres who wryly assures his university audiences that the Poet cannot be both the etiolated degenerate recently denounced by Max Nordau *and* the sort of bomb-throwing anarchist who has been causing so much havoc in the Assemblée nationale.[65] In the view of both these writers society seeks to marginalize the Poet as being at once useless and dangerous, and in that contradiction lies

---

[65] See *Unacknowledged Legislators*, 597.

evidence of society's fear and a source of comfort for the Poet that the cause of Poetry is not without its effects. As the last of the nine prose poems published in *La Presse* on 26 August 1862 'Le Mauvais Vitrier' constitutes a comic and provocative statement of the capacity of the Poet, whether in prose or in 'vers/ verres', to break the glass of a suspect transparency and to assume the perplexing voice of an Étranger.

23
The Voice of the Stranger
Reality and Imagination

> Eh! qu'aimes-tu donc, extraordinaire étranger?
> ('L'Étranger')
> L'étrangeté est une des parties intégrantes du beau.
> ('Edgar Poe, sa vie et ses œuvres', ii. 302)
> Chaque homme porte en lui sa dose d'opium naturel, incessamment sécrétée et renouvelée[.]
> ('L'Invitation au voyage')

When Baudelaire published his prose poems in *La Presse* in the late summer and autumn of 1862, circumstances had changed since Soulié launched his butterfly of war in 1836. Delphine Gay had died in 1855, and Girardin had sold *La Presse* in 1856, though he later reassumed editorial control in December 1862. During this period the paper's circulation had fallen abruptly from 40,000 in 1855 to under 18,000 for the year 1860–1.[1] Nevertheless the publication of two-fifths of Baudelaire's eventual collection of fifty prose poems in its *feuilleton* in August and September constituted—some eighteen months after the appearance of the second edition of *Les Fleurs du Mal*—a major unveiling, to a significantly large readership, of this notorious and unorthodox poet's 'tentative nouvelle'. As we have seen, the *feuilleton* was already well established as a site of counter-discourse, and so there is nothing remarkable as such about Baudelaire's use of the prose poem as a mode of resistance within the context of the Parisian press. But, as we have also seen, and despite Soulié's call to arms, there was something essentially cosy about the relationship between the two 'floors' of *La Presse*. A *feuilleton* that included a historical novel by Dumas did not pose much of a threat to the bourgeois-liberal ideology of the press baron whose wife presided over its contents. Indeed the visual relationship between upper and lower 'floors' in itself implied an 'upstairs, downstairs' relationship between master and servant, between the governors and the governed, as though the role of the arts in national life was really no more than that of a court jester, like Fancioulle in 'Une mort héroïque', or of a street entertainer on a public holiday, like the subject of 'Le Vieux Saltimbanque'.

---

[1] See Roger Bellet, *Presse et journalisme sous le Second Empire* (Paris: Armand Colin, 1967), 313.

Here, therefore, was a further dualistic assumption for Baudelaire to dismantle. What if the prose poem were to replace the doxa of the governors with doxa of its own and become the alternative lawgiver? What if the prose poem were to go further and break down the very idea that humanity is necessarily divided into the governors and the governed by demonstrating how the process of writing and being read offers the most appropriate path towards a potentially universal self-governance? I have discussed elsewhere how Germaine de Staël, prevented by her sex from being an actual lawgiver, saw literature as the most powerful form of alternative legislation and established the role model of the lyric poet as an 'outlaw' (exemplified by Corinne) such that many future writers, including Baudelaire, started also to write as 'outlaws'. As the major poets and writers of nineteenth-century France, and notably Vigny, began to accept that they were being irretrievably marginalized within the power structures of society, they came to believe that 'the purpose of creative writing was and remains to bear witness to an alternative, non-establishment set of principles and values'.[2] Chateaubriand had been France's Minister for Foreign Affairs, Lamartine had briefly been de facto Prime Minister, and Hugo continued in exile to be the rallying point of republicanism before becoming a Senator and grandfatherly *éminence grise* after 1871: but all were ultimately 'unacknowledged legislators' who withdrew from the public arena into their book-lined studies, into rooms of their own. Vigny, by contrast, knew already in the aftermath of the July Revolution of 1830—the 'lawyers' Revolution'—that the poet was condemned to eternal opposition. As he puts it in *Stello* (1831–2): 'Le poète, apôtre de la vérité toujours jeune, cause un éternel ombrage à l'homme du pouvoir, apôtre d'une vieille fiction.'[3] Hence the docteur Noir's famous prescriptions: 'Séparer la vie poétique de la vie politique', 'Seul et libre accomplir sa mission', and hence too the new importance attached to solitude: 'la solitude seule est la source des inspirations. *La solitude est sainte*'[4]—that is, the dangerous solitude denounced by Hippolyte Castille and defended by Baudelaire.

A Double Room of his Own

Une chambre qui ressemble à une rêverie

('La Chambre double')

As we saw in the previous chapter, one major effect of the polyphony of *Le Spleen de Paris*, both as a collection and within individual prose poems, is that no single

---

[2] *Unacknowledged Legislators*, 159.
[3] *Œuvres complètes*, ii. (ed. Bouvet), 664. Cf. also ii. 655: 'il y aura toujours antipathie entre l'homme du pouvoir et l'homme de l'art'.
[4] *Œuvres complètes*, ii. (ed. Bouvet), 662.

voice predominates, and certainly no one single voice with an identifiable set of opinions. In this respect, and as already suggested, the poet-narrator(s) of *Le Spleen de Paris* resemble(s) the impersonal narrators of Flaubert's novels who provide an impassive viewing point from which to take in a whole vista of multiple and conflicting perspectives belonging to the various characters and other observers who figure within the novels themselves. But, as we also saw, that impassive viewing point is in itself (for both writers) a unifying voice, the voice of the Poet who leaves space for the reader's own conjectures. As Flaubert phrased it in a letter to Louise Colet in August 1853: 'Ce qui me semble, à moi, le plus haut dans l'Art (et le plus difficile), ce n'est ni de faire rire, ni de faire pleurer, ni de vous mettre en rut ou en fureur, mais d'agir à la façon de la nature, c'est-à-dire de *faire rêver*.'[5]

Baudelaire's representative of this impassive viewing point is the 'Étranger' who is introduced at once in the first of the nine poems published in *La Presse* on 26 August 1862 and subsequently the first in the collection as a whole. Indeed we should perhaps regard this text and not the dedicatory letter to Arsène Houssaye as the more appropriate preface for the eventual collection of fifty prose poems.[6] For here is Baudelaire's own radical new version of the 'nouvelles de l'étranger' that customarily figured in the 'upper floor' of the newspaper: not so much news from abroad as an interview with the representative of that 'autre monde' in which poetry is true, the land of clouds:[7]

—Qui aimes-tu le mieux, homme énigmatique, dis? ton père, ta mère, ta sœur ou ton frère?
—Je n'ai ni père, ni mère, ni sœur, ni frère.
—Tes amis?
—Vous vous servez là d'une parole dont le sens m'est resté jusqu'à ce jour inconnu.
—Ta patrie?
—J'ignore sous quelle latitude elle est située.
—La beauté?
—Je l'aimerais volontiers, déesse et immortelle.

---

[5] *Correspondance*, ed. Bruneau, ii. 417.
[6] In *Le Spleen de Paris*, ed. Cervoni and Schellino, the editors relegate this letter to their dossier of editorial documentation and commentary on the grounds that, even though Asselineau and Banville chose to present it before the poems in the first complete (posthumous) edition of *Le Spleen de Paris* in 1869, it pertains only to the circumstances of the 1862 publication of the prose poems in *La Presse* and cannot therefore serve appropriately in its traditional role as a preface to the collection of all fifty poems. (See pp. 30 and 237–40.)
[7] As Steve Murphy suggests (*Logiques du dernier Baudelaire*, 176-7), we can also read the interlocutor's difficulty in determining the Étranger's identity as a reflection of the reader's incipient difficulty in coming to terms with the generic identity of the prose poem itself.

—L'or?
—Je le hais comme vous haïssez Dieu.
—Eh! qu'aimes-tu donc, extraordinaire étranger?
—J'aime les nuages... les nuages qui passent... là-bas... là-bas... les merveilleux nuages!

Where *Les Fleurs du Mal* gave us a catechism in the form of a summary of 'le Mal', here the opening text of *Le Spleen de Paris* gives us a more traditional catechistic sequence of question and answer[8] but with a view to imparting a strictly secular lesson. The opening question perhaps echoes Christ's statement in Luke 14: 26[9] as he addresses the 'great multitudes' that went with him: 'If any man come to me, and hate not his father, and mother, and wife, and children, and brethren, and sisters, yea, and his own life also, he cannot be my disciple.' That is to say, he who would serve God through following and proclaiming the teaching of Christ must be ready to put this vocation before all other claims, filial or conjugal, and be ready even to lay down his life in the service of the Lord. Since the speaker who addresses the first question in 'L'Etranger' is later said by the Étranger to hate God, he is clearly not trying to recruit this 'stranger' to the service of the Church. The Étranger is an 'homme énigmatique' who knows no allegiance, neither to family nor friends, neither to country nor to material wealth. Only to clouds. And so there is one deity he *could* love: 'La beauté [...] déesse et immortelle'.[10]

In this way *Le Spleen de Paris* opens with the disconcerting suggestion that the poet of these prose poems is a new sort of poet: not a poet come to preach the Christian lesson of love, like Lamartine or Hugo or countless other more orthodox Roman Catholic poets for whom the beauty of verse is a reflection of divine Creation and an instrument of moral instruction, but a poet who simple loves clouds: passing clouds, marvellous clouds, the clouds of wondrous and fantastical shapes that draw the eye away from the here and now and towards not heaven but that other sky-world—'là-bas'—in which Poetry is the Word of Beauty. And, like

---

[8] A possible debt to a popular nineteenth-century parlour game has also been suggested. See Robert T. Cargo, 'Baudelaire's "L'Étranger" as Parlor Game', *Nineteenth-Century French Studies*, 8: 1–2 (Fall–Winter, 1979–80), 76–8.

[9] As suggested, for example, by Hiddleston, *Baudelaire and 'Le Spleen de Paris'*, 6, but contested by Murphy, *Logiques*, 172–3. Others have been readier to hear an echo of the first sentence in Rousseau's *Rêveries du promeneur solitaire*: 'Me voici donc seul sur la terre, n'ayant plus de frère, de prochain, d'ami, de société que moi-même.' See, for example, Christian Leroy, 'Les Petits Poèmes en prose "palimpsestes" ou Baudelaire et *Les Rêveries du promeneur solitaire* de Rousseau', in Jean Delabroy and Yves Charnet (eds), *Baudelaire: nouveaux chantiers* (Villeneuve d'Ascq: Presses universitaires du Septentrion, 1995), 61–70 (62), and Henri Scepi, 'Le plus proche et le plus lointain', in Murphy (ed.), *Lectures du 'Spleen de Paris'*, 153–67 (159–61). Scepi sees a further (ironic) parallel with Chateaubriand's René, who describes himself as 'sans parents, sans amis, pour ainsi dire seul sur la terre' (see 161–2).

[10] Cf. Beckett's famous statement in his 'Hommage à Jack B. Yeats': 'L'artiste qui joue son être est de nulle part. Il n'a pas de pays. Et il n'a pas de frères.' See Samuel Beckett, *Disjecta: Miscellaneous Writings and a Dramatic Fragment*, ed. Ruby Cohn (London: John Calder, 1983), 148–9.

Mallarmé's 'littéraire' (discussed earlier at the beginning of Chapter 20), this poet is at once 'gratuitous', seemingly without a 'useful' social role as family man, loyal friend, or defender of the nation, and 'vain' or pointless, since his only purpose in life is to gaze at the sky. He is 'l'Étranger': a loner, in his own literary minority of one, a solitary (like the individualist of 'La Solitude'), and (like the poet of 'Le Crépuscule du soir') the inhabitant of an endlessly fascinating twilight zone between reality and imagination. That the poet should present himself in the stereotypical and here parodic guise of a cloud-gazer[11] constitutes a challenge to the more alert reader of *La Presse* precisely to realize that there is more to cloud-gazing—that is, to conjecture—than meets the conventional eye.[12]

The following poem, 'Le Désespoir de la vieille', may be read as a no less disconcerting acknowledgement of the dangers of reader reception (a theme more explicitly evident in the eighth of these nine opening poems, 'Le Chien et le flacon'). The poet-stranger, or alternative lawgiver, writes from within his solitude to be read by his fellow human beings and engages, perforce, with the human condition: writing, say, about our journey from childhood to old age, that journey on which the poet of *Les Fleurs du Mal* takes his readers. The poet performs for us a shared experience and, if he is a genius ('l'enfance retrouvée à volonté'), with a childlike innocence of perception. But the members of his reading public may not feel quite the same way. And here these readers are, the apple of the poet-journalist's eye: 'ce joli enfant à qui chacun faisait fête, à qui tout le monde voulait plaire', and yet quite possibly just as vulnerable and ill furnished as the poet himself. But this pretty little toothless, hairless child sees no resemblance whatsoever between itself and the balding, shrivelled hag inanely grinning at it in the hope of a delighted response. Where is the beauty of verse? What are these wrinkles of prose? And so the 'bonne vieille' retreats into the 'solitude éternelle' of her 'conscience dans le Mal': time is the victor ('l'âge est passé de plaire'), joy gives way to tears, innocence and the willing bestowal of love are replaced by horror and howling disgust. A familiar human lament at the fading of beauty has been transformed into the poignant expression of a failed meeting of hearts and minds.

---

[11] Jean-Michel Gouvard sees a reference to Lamartine's fondness for clouds, and therefore to a particular type of Romantic poetry that Baudelaire himself despised. See Gouvard, *Charles Baudelaire, 'Le Spleen de Paris'*, 104–5.
[12] On 'L'Étranger' as a lesson in the pitfalls of readerly interpretation, see Maria Scott, 'Baudelaire's "L'Étranger" and the Limits of Mind-Reading', *L'Esprit créateur*, 58: 1 (Spring 2018), 32–47. Scott sees the poem as 'a covert attack on Houssaye' (38), arguing from two intertextual allusions—to Houssaye's use of the maxim 'Dis-moi qui tu aimes, et je te dirai qui tu es' and to a hostile review of Houssaye's recent biography of Voltaire (*Le roi Voltaire*) that mocks a bourgeois, money-minded Houssaye as an inauthentic would-be dreamer-poet—for the possible interpretation of of the stranger 'not as a Baudelairean alter ego but as a representation of Houssaye' (41). More broadly, Scott sees this poem as paradigmatic of those poems in *Le Spleen de Paris* that present 'apparently readable others' only to 'remind us that other people's minds are never fully accessible' (44) and 'that the inferences we make about strangers are always based on an understanding of contexts that is incomplete and prone to change' (45).

The old woman ends up talking to herself, like this prose poem also perhaps, reflecting on an illusory and childish prettiness that understandably but unjustifiably refuses to see its own future in ugliness. For this very ugliness here assumes a quasi-fugal beauty of its own through the careful formal and thematic symmetries of the poem. In four paragraphs whose length is chiastically arranged, the dualities of similarity and difference, infancy and decrepitude, innocence and knowledge, delight and despair, cynosure and isolation, are performed: point and counterpoint come and go, accompanied by rhythmic repetitions ('à qui', à qui'; 'comme elle', 'comme elle') and in simple narrative progressions ('l'enfant épouvanté se débattait [...] et remplissait [...]'; 'la bonne vieille se retira [...] et elle pleurait') that evoke the innocence of a bedtime story.

The solitude of the poet-stranger, comparable with that of a lonely old woman whose beauty is lost and yet who wishes to please, recurs again in 'Le "Confiteor" de l'artiste' where, like the old woman reduced to talking to herself, the first-person poet-artist 'confesses' to himself his own despair and the hopelessness of his task: 'Cesse de tenter mes désirs et mon orgueil! L'étude du beau est un duel où l'artiste crie de frayeur avant d'être vaincu.' Like the preceding poem this one begins in delight and ends in defeat. Here the delight, like that of an old woman seeing a resemblance between herself and an 'infant' (from the Latin 'infans' = unspeaking), derives from the solitary poet's fulfilling sense of oneness both with and within the (unspeaking) phenomenal world: 'Solitude, silence, incomparable chasteté de l'azur!' Now there does seem to be a match between self and other, a 'correspondance': 'une petite voile frissonnante à l'horizon, et qui par sa petitesse et son isolement imite mon irrémédiable existence'. But soon this sense of oneness ('toutes ces choses pensent par moi, ou je pense par elles') becomes unbearable in its intensity, as though the poet-artist needed to recover a sense of his own separateness and difference, his own 'étrangeté': 'Et maintenant la profondeur du ciel me consterne; sa limpidité m'exaspère. L'insensibilité de la mer, l'immuabilité du spectacle, me révoltent...'. His own nervous system signals the rejection of sameness just as the howling infant screamed the house down: 'Mes nerfs trop tendus ne donnent plus que des vibrations criardes et douleureuses.' The poet thrills to be at one with the world—like Rousseau in the second and fifth 'Promenades' of his *Rêveries du promeneur solitaire*—but also needs to be different.

From this intense and ultimately intolerable spectacle of an unfeeling and unchanging uniformity of nature we move at once in 'Un plaisant' to its opposite in the city, and yet to an opposite that also threatens to overwhelm the solitary poet: 'C'était l'explosion du nouvel an: chaos de boue et de neige, traversé de mille carrosses, étincelant de joujoux et de bonbons, grouillant de cupidités et de désespoirs, délire officiel d'une grande ville fait pour troubler le cerveau du solitaire le plus fort.' Like the rue du Bac in Houssaye's 'La Chanson du vitrier', where the poet is alone 'au milieu de tous ces passants qui à pied ou en carrosse allaient au but,—à l'or, à l'amour, à la vanité' (i. 1309), this city is filled with a crowd made up of solitary self-interests; but whereas Houssaye's poet believes that he alone sees Christ and the persecuted poor, Baudelaire's poet sees an ass being wished a 'Happy New Year' by a 'beau monsieur' of the most self-satisfied kind. Whereas Houssaye's poet is filled with lachrymose compassion and proceeds to compound the glazier's poverty by unintentionally destroying half his stock, Baudelaire's poet is angry: 'je fus pris subitement d'une incommensurable rage contre ce magnifique imbécile, qui me parut concentrer en lui tout l'esprit de la France'. Imagine reading that in *La Presse* in 1862! But the angry poet turns the tables with his ironies. The 'beau monsieur' is ostensibly to be pitied for his subjugation to the sartorial requirements of these public celebrations, for he is 'cruellement cravaté et emprisonné dans des habits tout neufs'. But the real victim here is the ass: 'harcelé par un malotru armé d'un fouet', an ass who nevertheless secures its fortuitous, asinine victory by failing to see 'ce beau plaisant' as it continues to 'courir avec zèle où l'appelait son devoir'. But who in fact is the object of the poet's rage, who is this 'magnifique imbécile'? The well-dressed, patronizing fool who represents the self-satisfaction of the Second Empire bourgeoisie, or perhaps the ass as the symbol of a passive and unthinking working class that allows itself to be whipped by a loutish owner class and fails to see the huge divisions in wealth and status that bespeak a profound social injustice? Either way, the poet wonders, is the world a madhouse in which he alone is sane (cf. 'délire officiel d'une grande ville fait pour troubler le cerveau du solitaire le plus fort')? In solitude lies wisdom and strength and the means to survive a world governed by the whip.

Whether in nature or in the city, therefore, the Étranger is vulnerable and responds with consternation, exasperation, and revolt (in the last paragraph of 'Le "Confiteor" de l'artiste') or (here in 'Un plaisant') with rage. If only the ruling class were indeed simply a joke, if only the world were not mad. And so, if read as following on from these poems in a sequence (which nevertheless the professedly random nature of the collection in no way obliges us to do), 'La Chambre double' can be seen to offer the description of a refuge, a symbolic place—like the twilit balcony of 'Le Crépuscule du soir' or the prose poem itself—in which the poetic imagination may 'voluptuously' co-habit with 'l'Idole, la souveraine des rêves'. After public revelry, private rêverie. Here is a place for the 'fête intérieure' celebrated in 'Le Crépuscule du soir', for this is the chamber of the imagination:

Une chambre qui ressemble à une rêverie, une chambre véritablement *spirituelle*, où l'atmosphère stagnante est légèrement teintée de rose et de bleu.
L'âme y prend un bain de paresse, aromatisé par le regret et le désir.—C'est quelque chose de crépusculaire, de bleuâtre et de rosâtre; un rêve de volupté pendant une éclipse.

Here once more, like the sunset that is compared in 'Le Crépuscule du soir' to a 'jupe éclatante' overlaid with a dark veil, the realm of the imagination is figured in terms of half-light and half-colours. At its centre, recumbent like a woman or a cat or indeed Beauty 'herself', is the 'Idole', a word cognate with 'Idée', the poetic idea or 'idée mère' at the centre of the poet's creativity. But the poet's room of his own is a double room, as is this prose poem with its two equal groups of nine paragraphs divided by a middle paragraph-partition that records a moment of abrupt transition: 'Mais un coup terrible, lourd, a retenti à la porte'. The text, like the imaginary space it describes, is a room to be shared first with 'l'Idole' and then with 'le Spectre', the ghost of time and etymologically (from the Latin 'specere' = to look at) also something seen (for those who see things). Two forms of perception, therefore: the one creative, the other a sight of death...two forms of perception called beauty and melancholy.

During his cohabitation with the 'Idole' the poet is granted the experience not only of timelessness ('Le Temps a disparu; c'est l'Éternité qui règne, une éternité de délices')—an experience reprised in 'L'Horloge' by gazing into the eyes of a cat—but also (as with the Paris of 'Tableaux parisiens', discussed in Chapter 18) of what Proust calls 'un peu de temps à l'état pur': that is, not a moment *outside* time but a simultaneous and, as it were, panoptic situation *within* past, present, and future, here described (in terms that recall the paradisiacal moments of 'Parfum exotique' and 'La Chevelure') as 'un bain de paresse, aromatisé par le regret et le désir'. But during his cohabitation with 'le Spectre', when the imagination and the poetic idea are replaced by reality and the seen, the 'magical' chamber is replaced by a hovel and his 'féconde paresse' turns into an 'éternel ennui'. In the first room the inanimate becomes animate and participates in the living world of the poetic imagination. The furniture seems to be dreaming and walking in its sleep, shifting shape in imitation of dreamy human beings and cloud-gazing poets: 'Les meubles ont des formes allongées, prostrées, alanguies. Les meubles ont l'air de rêver'. The fabrics speak in silence, like the poet's own poetry on the page: 'Les étoffes parlent une langue muette, comme les fleurs, comme les ciels, comme les soleils couchants.' There are no pictures on the wall because they would provide too direct a representation of the seen compared with the 'rêve pur' and 'l'impression non analysée' that constitute the medium of the imagination and, as we saw earlier, afford 'la suffisante clarté et la délicieuse obscurité de l'harmonie'. And here the 'Idole' presides, 'la souveraine des rêves', exerting with its own powers of perception and its capacity to reflect the world an irresistible and avowedly predatory power to fascinate and to hold the gaze of the other: 'Voilà bien ces yeux dont la flamme traverse le crépuscule; ces subtiles et terribles *mirettes*, que je reconnais à leur effrayante malice! Elles attirent, elles subjuguent, elles dévorent le regard de l'imprudent qui les contemple.' But here in this chamber at the timeless hour of a fiery dusk, the poet—already aware in 'Le "Confiteor" de l'artiste' that '[l]'étude du beau est un duel où l'artiste crie de frayeur avant d'être vaincu'—stands ready to 'ad-mire' these '*mirettes*'[13] and to give himself up to imaginative conjecture: 'Je les ai souvent étudiées, ces étoiles noires qui commandent la curiosité et l'admiration.' Despite the dangers and the paradoxical blackness of the stars, the poet thanks his own lucky stars for this perfect moment: 'A quel démon bienveillant dois-je d'être ainsi entouré de mystère, de silence, de paix et de parfums?'

But in the second room a different sovereign reigns: 'le Temps règne en souverain maintenant', 'Oui! le Temps règne; il a repris sa brutale dictature.' Where the female 'Idole ("sur ce trône de rêverie et de volupté") 'subjugated' a willing admirer, the male 'Spectre' enslaves and dictates. And now, like the ass in 'Un plaisant', it is the poet's turn to be driven forward, goaded like an ox by the 'double aiguillon' of a clock's two hands: '"Et hue donc! bourrique! Sue donc, esclave! Vis donc, damné!"' Where before he had lived in a dream-room without the 'abomination' and 'blasphemy' of pictorial decoration, now he is condemned to inhabit a pauper's hovel in which Time makes its relentless passage as directly visible as a crassly representational picture on the wall. Dust, wear and tear, an untended hearth; manuscripts unfinished and endlessly revised, almanacs with dates, and clocks that tick. In the first room the poet had known a perfect moment, but in this room the only perfect moment is the last: 'Il n'y a qu'une Seconde dans la vie humaine qui ait mission d'annoncer une bonne nouvelle, la *bonne nouvelle* qui cause à chacun une inexplicable peur.' Time is an obituary, an official newspaper record of death and destruction—like the 'petites annonces' sitting just above the *feuilleton*. Instead of the 'nouvelles de l'étranger' represented by the innovative prose poem, Time brings long-familiar news of forfeit and destitution, of deadlines and dead-ends:

> C'est un huissier qui vient me torturer au nom de la loi; une infâme concubine qui vient crier misère et ajouter les trivialités de sa vie aux douleurs de la mienne; ou bien le saute-ruisseau d'un directeur de journal qui réclame la suite du manuscrit.

As at the end of 'Rêve parisien', the dream is over, and the poet feels '[l]a pointe des soucis maudits' (l. 56) as it enters his soul. The furniture of his imagination is about to be seized under the law of the real world; the voluptuous 'Idole' is now a destitute whore; the 'rêve pur' and 'l'impression non analysée' have to be abandoned in favour of 'l'art défini, l'art positif' of a newspaper article—unless, of course, it is the manuscript of this prose poem that remains to be completed!

For that is the final twist: 'La Chambre double' provides its own evidence that the first room can subsume the second. As we saw in 'Une charogne', the body needs to decompose before its essential shape can be resurrected, and from out of

---

[13] A slang term for 'eyes', comparable in register with 'peepers'.

this 'decay into dream' ('Les formes s'effaçaient et n'étaient plus qu'un rêve') a new and more essential beauty emerges. Here in 'La Chambre double' it seems that paradise has been lost: 'La chambre paradisiaque, l'idole, la souveraine des rêves, la *Sylphide*, comme disait le grand René, toute cette magie a disparu', and this paradise is figured especially as a scent: 'Une senteur infinitésimale du choix le plus exquis, à laquelle se mêle une très légère humidité, nage dans cette atmosphère, où l'esprit sommeillant est bercé par des sensations de serre chaude'; 'ce parfum d'un autre monde, dont j'enivrais avec une sensibilité perfectionnée'. Within the 'autre monde' of the imagination the poet has lived a separate life: 'Ô béatitude! ce que nous nommons généralement la vie, même dans son expansion la plus heureuse, n'a rien de commun avec cette vie suprême dont j'ai maintenant connaissance et que je savoure minute par minute, seconde par seconde!'

Like the experience of plenitude described in terms of scents at the end of 'Correspondances', this experience of paradise is thus an experience of beauty: of something rare, almost not there, barely tangible, of a mind caught between waking and sleeping and subject to physical sensation, like a baby being rocked or a plant being nurtured in a hothouse: the experience of something like an 'ébauche', the beginnings of a picture, or like a conjecture, the beginnings of an idea. But in the second room this paradisiacal scent is replaced by 'une fétide odeur de tabac mêlée à je ne sais quelle nauséabonde moisissure. On respire ici maintenant le ranci de la désolation.' Now there is a stink ('fétide') and a stomach-turning stench of rot: not the perfume of paradise but the acrid reek of decomposition, of 'desolation'—etymologically, an excessive solitude, and, by a false etymology, a sunless darkness where nothing grows. Once there was expansion, now we have a 'monde étroit'; once there was delight, now we have 'dégoût'. Each element of the first room has its spectral counterpart, including the 'Idole': here, 'la fiole de laudanum' with its treacherous promise of access to a 'paradis artificiel' of the kind denounced in *Les Paradis artificiels* as ephemeral and ultimately harmful.

But it is precisely through the artifice of art that the poet can transcend the duality of timeless imagination and timebound reality by means of an imagined space that combines them both, a prose poem entitled 'La Chambre double' in which through the deployment of careful symmetries what seems like a sequence of defeat—delight followed by desolation—can be turned into a mirror-like emblem of beauty and melancholy sharing a room of their own. In this respect 'La Chambre double' constitutes a paradigm for several others poems in *Le Spleen de Paris*: for those that precede it (the move from anticipation to disappointment in 'Le Désespoir de la vieille', from 'délice' to 'malaise' in 'Le "Confiteor" de l'artiste', from the explosion of celebration to the explosion of rage in 'Un plaisant') and, as we shall see, for several of those that follow. The prose poem—itself seemingly divided between the magic of poetry and the banality of prose—can create a harmonious space for the co-habitation of 'Idole' and 'Spectre' (so nearly 'Idéal' and 'Spleen'), of the synchronic and the diachronic, of timeless dream and timebound narrative. As Jacques Rancière has argued in his rejection of Benjamin's Baudelaire, this is 'rêverie' not as a manifestation of alienation and withdrawal but as an alternative way of living and thinking in the world:

> La rêverie n'est pas le repliement sur le monde intérieur de celui qui ne veut plus agir parce que la réalité l'a déçu. Elle n'est pas le contraire de l'action mais un autre mode de la pensée, un autre mode de rationalité des choses. Elle n'est pas le refus de la réalité extérieure mais le mode de pensée qui remet en question la frontière même que le modèle organique imposait entre la réalité 'intérieure' où la pensée décidait et la réalité 'extérieure' où elle produisait ses effets.[14]

Accordingly, and as was the case in 'Tableaux parisiens', these first prose poems show us a poet who is caught between going out and staying in. Both the natural world and the city have sent the Étranger back to this 'chambre double', but now in 'Chacun sa chimère' and 'Le Fou et la Vénus' the poet ventures forth once more: onto a dusty plain and into a sunny parkland that are each in their way also 'double spaces', combining nature and artifice. In 'Chacun sa chimère' the flâneur wanders in a kind of dream landscape from which, as in 'Rêve parisien', '[l]e végétal irrégulier' (l. 8) has been banished: 'Sous un grand ciel gris, dans une grande plaine poudreuse, sans chemins, sans gazon, sans un chardon, sans une ortie, je rencontrai plusieurs hommes qui marchaient courbés.' But here organic irregularity is absent not because the poet imagines a fairy urban architecture of mineral purity but because, in anticipation of *En attendant Godot*, this is the sterile landscape of the Absurd, of spleen and sunless 'desolation': 'la poussière d'un sol aussi désolé que [c]e ciel'. And beneath this featureless sky without sun—and doubtless without God—and across this featureless plain, these men simply walk:

> Je questionnai l'un de ces hommes, et je lui demandai où ils allaient ainsi. Il me répondit qu'il n'en savait rien, ni lui, ni les autres; mais qu'évidemment ils allaient quelque part, puisqu'ils étaient poussés par un invincible besoin de marcher.

Like the ass whipped on by his driver, or the poet goaded by time, these men are ridden by some monstrous and illusory purpose—'une énorme Chimère'—and on they walk 'sous la coupole spleenétique du ciel'. But even though this landscape of melancholy is all 'desolation', they themselves show no sign of despair: for, exhausted and resigned, they are condemned to hope.

As for the poet, the old sequence repeats itself, from mystery to misery: his eagerness to know ('Je questionnai', 'je lui demandai', 'Chose curieuse à noter')

---

[14] Jacques Rancière, 'Le Goût infini de la République', in Rancière, *Le Fil perdu: Essais sur la fiction moderne* (Paris: La Fabrique éditions, 2015), 105. (Previously published as 'The Infinite Taste of the Republic', trans. Elissa Marder and Gina Stamm, *Yale French Studies*, 125-6 (2014), 30–44.)

and his own compulsion to 'comprendre ce mystère' give way, as the men pass out of sight and beyond the horizon of human curiosity, to a total lack of interest: 'mais bientôt l'irrésistible Indifférence s'abattit sur moi, et j'en fus plus lourdement accablé qu'ils ne l'étaient eux-mêmes par leurs écrasantes Chimères'. But as in previous poems this passage from interest to ennui is articulated within a sequence of symmetrically arranged paragraphs (reminiscent of the concentric stanzaic structure of 'La Chevelure') that wrests harmonious order from a narrative of directionless travel. The undifferentiated landscape of the first paragraph is recalled by the poet's indifference in the last; the arrival of the men in the second mirrors their departure in the sixth; the description of the Chimeras riding the men in the much longer third paragraph is reversed in the similarly long fifth paragraph as a description of the men's response under this burden; and the pivotal fourth paragraph contains the moment of meeting and dialogue between poet and men.

Having left the natural world and the city behind (presuming once again that we choose to read these poems in the order in which they were presented in *La Presse* and later in the posthumous complete edition), this poet-artist has now exchanged the dual perspective of his own room for an allegorical landscape of the mind, and one that may quite probably have been inspired by Goya[15] (as Aloysius Bertrand had been inspired by Callot and Rembrandt).[16] Among Goya's *Caprichos*, a series of eighty prints in etching and aquatint, there is one (no. 42: 'Tú que no puedes')—thus preceding no. 43, the more famous print entitled 'El sueño de la razón produce monstruos'—that depicts two men bent double, each under the weight of a large donkey, an image that has been thought to allegorize the subjugation of the Spanish people under an asinine government. Perhaps taking his cue from 'capricho', derived from the Latin 'caper' = goat, Baudelaire turns Goya's donkey into a Chimera, the mythological hybrid animal of antiquity that is usually depicted as a lion with a goat's head protruding from its back. As they submit to their 'invincible besoin de marcher', these men are each saddled with a monstrous, 'capricious' illusion—for example, that there is some point to all their walking.

In 'Le Fou et la Vénus' two by now familiar patterns repeat themselves. First, we move once more from delight to defeat, here figured respectively as '[l]'extase universelle des choses' and the statue's refusal (akin to that of the child in 'Le Désespoir de la vieille') to acknowledge a desperate supplicant. Second, the concentric arrangement of seven paragraphs: the first and last paragraphs feature a gaze ('l'œil brûlant du soleil', 'l'implacable Vénus regarde au loin') and establish

---

[15] A suggestion first made by Jacques Crépet (see i. 1313).
[16] In 'Bohémiens en voyage', a similarly allegorical account of the human journey through life, Baudelaire himself is thought to have had a Callot etching in mind, as also in the final paragraph of 'Les Veuves'. See i. 864–5.

a contrast between the park swooning blissfully in the hot sunshine 'comme la jeunesse sous la domination de l'Amour' and the 'fou' pleading desperately at the feet of a towering statue of Venus; the second and sixth paragraphs extend the parallel with reference to an expressive silence ('L'extase universelle des choses ne s'exprime par aucun bruit', 'Et ses yeux disent'); and the third and fifth paragraphs describe a quasi-religious offering up to the heavens ('rivaliser avec l'azur', 'les fait monter vers l'astre'; 'lève des yeux [...] vers l'immortelle Déesse'). The poem pivots on the middle paragraph in which the poet's own act of perception ('j'ai aperçu') intervenes within this triangular gazing of sun, clown, and statue and notes the central duality of 'idéal' and 'spleen': 'Cependant, dans cette jouissance universelle, j'ai aperçu un être affligé.' Where 'Un plaisant' described the loud greeting by an unconscious joker amidst the cacophony of a New Year party, here a silent jester wordlessly implores Beauty herself amidst 'une orgie silencieuse' that is '[b]ien différente des fêtes humaines'.

This 'fou' is the Étranger's alter ego. When asked about '[l]a beauté', as we saw, the latter replies: 'Je l'aimerais volontiers, déesse et immortelle.' Here the 'fou' tells Venus: 'Cependant je suis fait, moi aussi, pour comprendre et sentir l'immortelle Beauté! Ah! Déesse! ayez pitié de ma tristesse et de mon délire!' But though he is, like the Étranger, a loner without family or friends, the 'fou' contrasts with him in his abjection, which is both individual and social. On the one hand, he views himself as 'le dernier et le plus solitaire des humains, privé d'amour et d'amitié, et bien inférieur en cela au plus parfait des animaux'. He is therefore without love, so that in imploring Venus he is not just worshipping Beauty. And unlike the Étranger he cannot be simply a private cloud-gazer but must perform at the behest of power. The poet describes him as the classic court jester, a *buffo* like Fancioulle in 'Une mort héroïque': 'un de ces fous artificiels, un de ces bouffons volontaires chargés de faire rire les rois quand le Remords ou l'Ennui les obsède, affublé d'un costume éclatant et ridicule, coiffé de cornes et de sonnettes'. With his cuckold's horns he looks like a goat, a human hybrid born of whimsical and capricious fancy, and his job is silently to perform, as though in a 'fête humaine', and to alleviate the spleen of those whose important tasks of governance fill the 'haut-de-page' above him.

This presentation of poetic writing as a process of performance and reception, adumbrated in 'Le Désespoir de la vieille', is now explicitly allegorized in 'Le Chien et le flacon', where once more but this time in comic mode we encounter the rhythm of delighted anticipation (on the part of the tail-wagging dog as well as the gift-bearing dog-owner) and sad disappointment (expressed in a reproachful bark and human insult). The subtle perfume of Beauty so delicately described in 'La Chambre double' and recalling that evoked at the end of 'Correspondances' is here offered as the best that money can buy to a dog-public that would rather sniff excrement. Why treasure the prose poem when you can gnaw on the bone of juicy gossip provided by an 'écho de Paris'? Why? Because, as we discover in 'Le

Mauvais Vitrier', the prose poem can offer a kaleidoscopic vision to delight the reader's eye with seemingly fixed but ceaselessly changing patterns of meaning, like the firework display of the 'fête intérieure' at the end of 'Le Crépuscule du soir'.

Cloud-Gazing

> J'aime les nuages...les nuages qui passent...là-bas...là-bas...les merveilleux nuages!
>
> ('L'Étranger')

As a cloud-gazer and lover of beauty the Étranger recurs in a number of guises throughout *Le Spleen de Paris* where he continues to testify to the power of the creative imagination to provoke nebulous conjecture. In 'Les Vocations' (first published in 1864), the first-person narrative opens in a symbolic place of beauty at dusk:

> Dans un beau jardin où les rayons d'un soleil automnal semblaient s'attarder à plaisir, sous un ciel déjà verdâtre, où des nuages d'or flottaient comme des continents en voyage, quatre beaux enfants, quatre garçons, las de jouer sans doute, causaient entre eux.

Life is on the cusp: as day gives way to night and autumn leads from summer to winter, so childhood play is superseded by adult conversation (and 'enfant' quickly followed by 'garçon'), and the four boys imagine their future. For one, his vocation lies in the theatre, while for another it lies with God; one boy anticipates only the joys of sex, while another is drawn to the life of a travelling musician. And all these speculations are shared beneath 'travelling continents' of golden cloud, huge, mutable lands of possibility. The theatre is a place of beauty as make-believe: 'Ah! c'est bien beau!', the first boy exclaims, and he delights in the physical beauty and fine dress of its protagonists, whom he wishes to emulate. For in this world suffering seems not to matter in the end: 'On a peur, on a envie de pleurer, et cependant l'on est content...'.

For the second boy, a little passing cloud—'ce petit nuage isolé'—is the seat of God Himself as it passes towards a liminal horizon between visibility and invisibility and between certainty and trust, leaving in his eyes 'une inexprimable expression d'extase et de regret', like an ocular 'chambre double'. The third boy, by contrast, is not one for clouds. Impatient with his companions for their faith in the illusory worlds of theatre and religion, a night in bed with a sleeping maid has convinced him of the merits of a world you can see and, more especially, touch. As the rays of sunset lend his unruly ginger hair the comic semblance of 'une auréole sulfureuse de passion', so it is plain to see that this satanic figure is not going to spend his life searching for 'la Divinité dans les nuées, et qu'il la trouverait fréquemment ailleurs'. But the fourth boy, reminiscent of the passing figures in 'Chacun sa chimère' and anticipating the poet of 'Any where out of the world', wants simply to wander lonely as a cloud: 'Il m'a souvent semblé que mon plaisir serait d'aller toujours droit devant moi, sans savoir où, sans que personne s'en inquiète, et de voir toujours des pays nouveaux. Je ne suis jamais bien nulle part, et je crois que toujours je serais bien mieux ailleurs que là où je suis.' Bored at home, with parents who never take him to the theatre and a private tutor who is too mean to do so, ignored by a God who seems oblivious to his boredom and having no maid to sleep with, he too, like the Étranger, is alone in the world and tempted to fall in with three travelling musicians whose way of life seems to fit the pattern of his dreams. The first three boys do not share this 'vocation', but the poet-narrator identifies an alter ego: 'ce petit était déjà un *incompris* [...] j'eus un instant l'idée bizarre que je pouvais avoir un frère à moi-même inconnu'. Perhaps the Étranger, self-professedly without kin, has a brother after all. Darkness falls, for we cannot see beyond this crepuscular moment: only in our mind's eye can we follow their separate fortunes, 'chacun allant, à son insu, selon les circonstances et les hasards, mûrir sa destinée, scandaliser ses proches et graviter vers la gloire ou vers le déshonneur'. But which boy will do which? How is the path of life to be charted in all its contingency? Does 'vocation' equate to destiny or mere random accident?

In 'Les Projets', first published in 1857 with five other 'poèmes nocturnes' ('Le Crépuscule du soir', 'La Solitude', 'L'Horloge', 'La Chevelure', and 'L'Invitation au voyage'), the protagonist is another loner and to be found at the outset 'se promenant dans un grand parc solitaire'. Introduced simply as 'Il' by an equally anonymous third-person narrator, this solitary walker wonders in what setting 'she' (his ideal companion and perhaps beauty itself) might be placed to best effect: as a princess on the marble steps of this palace with its great park, or, as his life partner, in the more private, tropical setting suggested by an engraving in a shop window that he passes in the street. Stimulated by this picture his imagination embarks on a mental journey in which the richness of the language used to evoke this setting conveys the sensual stimulation and delight he dreams of sharing with 'le rêve de ma vie'—not so much the ideal companion, perhaps, as his own life lived as a dream. But soon, passing now along a great avenue, his eye and imagination are caught by 'une auberge proprette' and this more proximate, cosy vision of a paradise that includes a very large bed. Finally—'en rentrant seul chez lui, à cette heure où les conseils de la Sagesse ne sont plus étouffés par les bourdonnements de la vie extérieure'—the narrator realizes that though his feet have done the walking, it is his imagination that has done the travelling: 'Pourquoi contraindre mon corps à changer de place, puisque mon âme voyage si lestement?' Once again, as in 'Le Crépuscule du soir', dusk allows the seemingly urgent demands of reality to fade so that the imagination may come into full 'enjoyment' of its 'fête intérieure'. From parkland to street to avenue, from palace to log cabin to pretty little inn, the mind has gradually learnt to dispense with the stimuli of the physical world in the creation of its own dreamworld and learnt the wisdom also of that old adage that it is better to travel than to arrive: 'Et à quoi bon exécuter des projets, puisque le projet est en lui-même une jouissance suffisante?'

For the sexual fantasist there is no need to leave his own bed, especially if there is someone else in it. In 'Un hémisphère dans une chevelure' (originally entitled 'La Chevelure') the cloud-gazer has only to bury the hemisphere of his own face in the black abundance of his lover's curls there to dream—with eye and ear and nose and mouth and touch of hand—of being half a world away: 'Mon âme voyage,' 'Tes cheveux contiennent tout un rêve.' I could eat you, he reflects in the ardour of his desire, and he does: 'Quand je mordille tes cheveux élastiques et rebelles, il me semble que je mange des souvenirs.' He has entered a dreamworld in which the sensual delights of the present bring with them all the sensual delights of the past, an imaginative land of plenty—like the land of Cockaigne celebrated in 'L'Invitation au voyage'. A creation of medieval myth, and akin to El Dorado, this is a land of 'luxe, calme, et volupté' in which anything goes and everything can be had, a world of sensual adventures—and, for Baudelaire's poet-narrator, a paradise so easily entered, like somewhere he would like to visit 'avec une vieille amie'. And this poem aspires to be his invitation, something presented 'à la femme aimée, à la sœur d'élection', the description of a place 'où tout vous ressemble, mon cher ange'—even a cuisine ('poétique, grasse et excitante') that offers the prospect of further edible delight. And so powerful now is his imagination that this place *is* this woman: 'Ces trésors, ces meubles, ce luxe, cet ordre, ces parfums, ces fleurs miraculeuses, c'est toi.' And this woman, like this place, like this invitation, is beauty: 'Pays singulier, supérieur aux autres, comme l'Art l'est à la Nature, où celle-ci est réformée par le rêve, où elle est corrigée, embellie, refondue.' As in 'Les Projets', the creation of this ideal imaginative space, furnished like an apartment, is in itself sufficient to preclude the need to go there, just as in 'L'Horloge' the very act of writing the poem—'un madrigal vraiment méritoire, et aussi emphatique que vous-même'—already achieves the purpose it may have been designed to serve: 'En vérité, j'ai eu tant de plaisir à broder cette prétentieuse galanterie que je ne vous demanderai rien en échange.'

In this way the cloud-gazer is both a loner and yet also a creator of his own peopled universe, as we discover further in 'Les Foules': 'Multitude, solitude: termes égaux et convertibles pour le poète actif et fécond. Qui ne sait pas peupler sa solitude, ne sait pas non plus être seul dans une foule affairée.' Again as in 'Tableaux parisiens', the poet of *Le Spleen de Paris* is torn symbolically between staying in his room (as La Bruyère and Pascal recommend) or going out to mingle with his fellow human beings (as Poe suggests in *The Man of the Crowd*, which itself begins by quoting La Bruyère's reference to 'ce grand malheur de ne pouvoir être seul'). The second group of *Petits Poèmes en prose* published in the *feuilleton* of *La Presse* (on 27 August 1862) begins with 'À une heure du matin', where the poet returns to his room after a long, hard day out in the world of the city ('Horrible vie! Horrible ville!') and double-locks his door. 'Enfin! seul!', the poem begins, as though it were itself a place of refuge from the printed world above it ('nous posséderons le silence, sinon le repos'). During his long day of exile from the Pascalian sanctuary of his home the poet has endured the terrible reality of human interaction: discovering all the ignorance, self-righteousness (in the editor of a review!), insincerity, tiresome demands, and insulting, patronizing behaviour of which his fellow man and one 'sauteuse' are capable, and then discovering also how in his own relations with others he himself is nothing but a *mythomane*. To be with others is to play-act. Indeed—as though remembering his own rôle in 'Le Mauvais Vitrier'?—he has boasted of 'plusieurs vilaines actions que je n'ai jamais commises' and denied 'quelques autres méfaits que j'ai accomplis avec joie'. '[D]élit de fanfaronnade, crime de respect humain', he calls these fictions, the invention of false selves under the pressure of human intercourse. Perhaps straight-talking and honest truths are impossible out in the crowd? Perhaps only poetry is pure, the poetry that he now hopes to write by way of self-redemption here in this 'bain de ténèbres' that recalls the darkness of 'Le Crépuscule du soir' and its invitation to a 'fête intérieure'. The rhetorical extravagance of the poet's prayer in the last paragraph might perhaps be read, therefore, not so much as an occasion for ridicule but as a mask concealing the true predicament of the Étranger,[17] another '"Confiteor" de l'artiste' on the part of the author of *Les Fleurs du Mal*, who here pulls no punches with his 18,000 readers:

> Mécontent de tous et mécontent de moi, je voudrais bien me racheter et m'enorgueillir un peu dans le silence et la solitude de la nuit. Âmes de ceux que j'ai aimés, âmes de ceux que j'ai chantés, fortifiez-moi, soutenez-moi, éloignez de moi le mensonge et les vapeurs corruptrices du monde, et vous, Seigneur mon Dieu! accordez-moi la grâce de produire quelques beaux vers qui me prouvent à moi-même que je ne suis pas le dernier des hommes, que je ne suis pas inférieur à ceux que je méprise!

---

[17] This putative choice between readings of the prayer has been central to many accounts of the poem. For a recent overview and judicious analysis of this issue and, more broadly, of the poem as a reflection of the growing mid-nineteenth-century interest in the *journal intime*, see Lewis, *Intimacy and Distance*, 81–92. Drawing a comparison with Flaubert's famous statement that 'l'ironie n'enlève rien au pathétique. Elle l'outre au contraire', Lewis writes that 'it could be argued that the pathos of "À une heure du matin" is in fact further heightened by the shadow of irony' (88). For Flaubert's comment see his *Correspondance*, ed. Bruneau, ii. 172.

But the cloud-gazer of *Le Spleen de Paris* is writing in prose, not verse, and as Jean-Luc Steinmetz nicely puts it: 'Ce qui, dans *Les Fleurs du Mal*, était malgré tout sublime par une esthétique valorisante ne connaît plus désormais de belles excuses.'[18] And therein lies the prose poet's greatest challenge: 'Sois toujours poète, même en prose.' How to respect the claims of poetry and beauty while remaining true to the reality of 'le Mal', of what in 'La Chambre double' he describes—allegorically and therefore poetically—as the horrible retinue of Time: 'tout son démoniaque cortège de Souvenirs, de Regrets, de Spasmes, de Peurs, d'Angoisses, de Cauchemars, de Colères et de Névroses' (i. 281)? In the prose of *Le Spleen de Paris*, by embracing the quotidian and the decrepit, the trivial and the absurd, by deploying a polyphony of voices and registers from the purple passage to the expletive and the 'argotique', the poet as Étranger borrows some of the techniques of a prose writer like Poe[19] to push against and test the coherence of the poetic 'dream': resisting the ease of nebulous rêverie and yet lovingly engaging with its shifting shapes in paragraphs of finely chosen rhythm and vocabulary, going out into a world of moral mess and coming home to the double room of the prose poem there to arrange it as question and puzzle, as comic conundrum and beautiful surmise.

Like a performer of masques, his strategy is to stage verbal spectacles of empathy with those who, like him, are outsiders and to present these performances in a variety of artistic modes: as comedy or fairy-story, as painting or music. Where false prophets like Castille tell us what to think, this alternative lawgiver takes us into the lives of other people and through his empathy allows us also to experience the reality of a life 'below stairs' in the urban basement of Paris or in any other place of teeming human habitation, but without the novelistic nuisance of a plot. And as the cloud-gazer gazes at the ever-changing, kaleidoscopic patterns of human experience, so he gazes also at the gaze of others and tries to fathom the depths of suffering or knowledge or mystery—or beauty—to be found in the eye of the beheld.

For this reason the eyes of other people, and especially of women, come to serve in *Le Spleen de Paris* as invitations to the journey of wonderment, as sources of beauty. In 'Le Désir de peindre' the poet-artist catches a vanishing glimpse of beauty and wants to capture it permanently in his paint-words: 'Je brûle de peindre celle qui m'est apparue si rarement et qui a fui si vite, comme une belle chose regrettable derrière le voyageur emporté dans la nuit.' As the poet travels forward in space-time, 'elle' vanishes ('Comme il y a longtemps déjà qu'elle a disparu!') and yet continues to remain by virtue of the poet's insistent use of the

---

[18] *Le Spleen de Paris*, ed. Steinmetz, 37.
[19] 'Cf. Baudelaire's comment in his 'Notes nouvelles sur Edgar Poe': 'l'auteur d'une nouvelle a à sa disposition une multitude de tons, de nuances de langage, le ton raisonneur, le sarcastique, l'humoristique, que répudie la poésie, et qui sont comme des dissonances, des outrages à l'idée de beauté pure' (ii. 330).

present tense: 'Elle est belle, et plus que belle; elle est surprenante.' Unlike in the poem 'À une passante' there is no question here of 'love', and 'elle' appears to denote beauty itself (of which surprise and 'étrangeté' are for Baudelaire always essential ingredients), inspiring in the Étranger not sexual desire but 'le désir de peindre'. And this beauty is of the kind celebrated at the end of 'Le Crépuscule du soir' as a combination of darkness and explosive light: 'En elle le noir abonde: et tout ce qu'elle inspire est nocturne et profond. Ses yeux sont deux antres où scintille vaguement le mystère, et son regard illumine comme l'éclair: c'est une explosion dans les ténèbres.' Instead of ejaculation we have the firework display of the imagination, a 'fête intérieure'; and instead of the destructive sexual desire we find portrayed in Les Fleurs du Mal we have here—through the presence of beauty—the *happy* desire of an artist. 'Malheureux peut être l'homme', the poem begins, 'mais heureux l'artiste que le désir déchire!' And such beauty is paradoxical, cosmic, lunatic!

> Je la comparerais à un soleil noir, si l'on pouvait concevoir un astre noir versant la lumière et le bonheur. Mais elle fait plus volontiers penser à la lune, qui sans doute l'a marquée de sa redoutable influence[.]

A black sun might symbolize the life-creating energy to be felt as the imagination of the night replaces the reality of the day, but the more logical image is of the moon, shining at night and figuring the illumination cast within the imagination in its dark remove from daylight visibility. But this lunar beauty is not that of some cold sterile moon on a frosty night ('la lune blanche des idylles, qui resemble à une froide mariée') but of something dynamic and storm-tossed: 'la lune sinistre et enivrante, suspendue au fond d'une nuit orageuse et bousculée par les nuées qui courent'; not the calm, unsullied beauty of innocent dreams ('la lune paisible et discrète visitant le sommeil des hommes purs'), but the raging and resistant beauty of a captive roughly subjugated by the witches of Thessaly (traditionally known for their power to draw down the moon) and made to dance 'sur l'herbe terrifiée!' In the final two paragraphs of the poem, beauty as 'elle' now becomes more evidently a woman: not a woman to be possessed but, rather, a gaze by which to be possessed: 'Il y a des femmes qui inspirent l'envie de les vaincre et de jouir d'elles; mais celle-ci donne le désir de mourir lentement sous son regard.' Woman, like beauty, is here a desired effect, and this effect is one of fascination and fear, like witnessing the 'miracle d'une superbe fleur éclose dans un terrain volcanique'. As the source of this effect the woman represents beauty as a breath of fresh air, inhaling 'l'inconnu et l'impossible' through 'des narines mobiles' and exhaling it in joyous laughter 'avec une grâce inexprimable'. Here is the 'déesse' whom the Étranger could love, this cloud-gazer slowly dying beneath the gaze of the moon: the artist and his beauty, and both of them—as we learn in 'Les Bienfaits de la lune', which follows 'Le Désir de peindre'—'lunatiques'.

But to be gazed on by the moon, it seems, is not an undivided blessing (and nor is 'une certaine Bénédicta' in the poem that follows 'Les Bienfaits de la lune'). For in *Le Spleen de Paris* there are no undivided blessings: every room is double. Those who have been gazed on by the moon—'qui est le caprice même'—can only love and be loved by those who have been similarly gazed upon, companions under the curse of wistful melancholy and 'le reflet de la redoutable Divinité, de la fatidique marraine, de la nourrice empoisonneuse de tous les *lunatiques*'. The woman at whose feet the poet now lies—he like the sad buffoon of 'Le Fou et la Vénus', she ('maudite chère enfant gâtée') reminiscent of the 'little madam' of 'La Femme sauvage et la petite-maîtresse'—has been forever marked, since the cradle, by the silent visit of the moon. Inhabitant of the clouds at which the Étranger gazes, moonlight knows no impediment, and glass panes are of no consequence: 'Et elle descendit moelleusement son escalier de nuages et passa sans bruit à travers les vitres.' And she leaves her own particular imprint of beauty: 'Tu seras belle à ma manière. Tu aimeras ce que j'aime et ce qui m'aime: l'eau, les nuages, le silence et la nuit.' Here also are the things that delight the poet of *Le Spleen de Paris*: not only the clouds, the silence, and the night that we have already met so often, but also (the moon tells the sleeping infant) 'la mer immense et verte; l'eau informe et multiforme' (cf. 'Déjà!', 'Le Port'); 'le lieu où tu ne seras pas' (cf. 'Any where out of the world'); and 'les parfums qui font délirer' ('La Chambre double' and *passim*). In loving the goddess of beauty in the form of woman the poet as Étranger loves these selfsame emblems of insubstantiality and elusiveness, which the moon now enumerates afresh as though casting her seductive spell: and, like the woman, he too must suffer. As the moon has gently squeezed the throat of the baby so that she will always be on the verge of crying, so too this woman can be loved only by those whom the moon has similarly squeezed—someone like the poet for whom beauty is always associated with 'le Mal'. For is it not true that the most powerful effect of beauty is to move us to tears? At any rate, readers of *Le Spleen de Paris* can become *lunatiques* themselves as they learn to listen to the voice of the Stranger imprinted beneath their gaze... and perhaps with a lump in their throat.

24
The Poet in the World
Empathy and Performance

> être lui-même et autrui.
> ('Les Foules')
>
> Le propre des vrais poètes—pardonnez-moi cette petite bouffée d'orgueil, c'est le seul qui me soit permis—est de savoir sortir d'eux-mêmes, et comprendre une toute autre nature.
> (letter to Mme Aupick, 9 Jan. 1856 (*Corr.*, i. 334))

In the first nine poems of *Le Spleen de Paris*, those first published together in *La Presse* on 26 August 1862 and framed by 'L'Étranger' and 'Le Mauvais Vitrier', the focus is principally on the poet as a solitary artist, preoccupied with his own dualistic experience of beauty and melancholy while also fearful of his reception by the public at large. In 'À une heure du matin', the poem with which the second group of poems began on 27 August, this figure of the conflicted and estranged poet—'[m]écontent de tous, mécontent de moi'—is recalled and foregrounded. But subsequently, against this backdrop of a vexed relationship between poet and world, 'Les Foules' presents an alternative mode of intercourse, that of art itself. Instead of being divided between the 'horrible' world outside and the refuge of poetry within, like the poet of 'À une heure du matin' (and perhaps like the poet of *Les Fleurs du Mal*?), the poet of 'Les Foules' (and of *Le Spleen de Paris*?) now takes his imagination out with him into that world and inhabits it with his empathy. Recalling the Étranger in the poem of that title, the poet of 'Les Foules' is also without family or other ties so that, unencumbered, he can enter the lives of other people as though they were each of them a blank page just waiting to be ghost-written: 'Le poète jouit de cet incomparable privilège, qu'il peut à sa guise être lui-même et autrui. Comme ces âmes errantes qui cherchent un corps, il entre, quand il veut, dans le personnage de chacun. Pour lui seul, tout est vacant'. Castille had warned that solitude is dangerously anti-social, fostering melancholic introspection and suicidal thoughts, but for Baudelaire the death of self through imaginative empathy (for the *lunatique* reader as well as for the artist) is the means to a genuine life of community: 'Le promeneur solitaire et pensif tire une singulière ivresse de cette universelle communion.' The egotist ('fermé comme un coffre') and the couch-potato ('le paresseux, interné comme un mollusque') are missing out on the 'jouissances fiévreuses' that come from giving oneself unconditionally to the world of experience: 'cette ineffable orgie, [...] cette sainte prostitution de l'âme qui se donne tout entière, poésie et charité, à l'imprévu qui se montre, à l'inconnu qui passe'. Together we can all gaze at the shifting shapes of clouds and die slowly, happily, beneath the light of '[l]a Lune qui est le caprice même'.

For the poet of 'Les Foules' this experience of 'communion' through empathy puts him in mind of '[l]es fondateurs de colonies, les pasteurs de peuples, les prêtres missionnaires exilés au bout du monde', that is, of solitary leaders of humankind. They too, he imagines, must know something of these 'mystérieuses ivresses' as they live among 'la vaste famille que leur génie s'est faite', like the poet who has found a universal family through imagination and fellow-feeling. Moreover, and perhaps surprisingly, he sees himself as being, like them, a moral leader who in this particular prose poem is teaching a quasi-Christian lesson of humility: 'Il est bon d'apprendre quelquefois aux heureux de ce monde, ne fût-ce que pour humilier un instant leur sot orgueil, qu'il est des bonheurs supérieurs au leur, plus vastes et plus raffinés.' Here therefore, as later in 'Assommons les pauvres!', the Étranger has 'toutes les élucubrations de tous ces entrepreneurs de bonheur public' very firmly in his sights. But as a moral leader his own preferred method of instruction is not the pastoral or priestly pronouncement of some fixed doctrine, still less the ambition to colonize the minds of his readers, but rather the performance of empathy. Like those ageing Romans who sought to revitalize themselves by bathing in blood and to whom Baudelaire alludes at the end of 'Spleen [iii]' (ll. 15–18), the poet of 'Les Foules' draws renewed strength from 'un bain de multitude', immersing himself in the lives of others by putting himself in their place.[1] Only by leaving his room and undertaking this performance can he himself hope to live life to the full: 'celui-là seul peut faire, aux dépens du genre humain, une ribote de vitalité, à qui une fée a insufflé dans son berceau le goût du travestissement et du masque, la haine du domicile et la passion du voyage'. Unlike the lunar godmother of 'Les Bienfaits de la lune' with her poisonous gift of melancholic repose, this fairy godmother offers the excitement of discovery and the thrill of shape-shifting polyphonic performance.

Public Spaces: Street, Park, Fairground, Boulevard

C'est surtout vers ces lieux que le poète et le philosophe aiment diriger leurs avides conjectures.

('Les Veuves')

---

[1] Cf. Baudelaire's account of De Quincey's experience of London life as a returning young adult in *Les Paradis artificiels*: 'L'ancien écolier veut revoir cette vie des humbles; il veut se plonger au sein de cette foule de déshérités, et, comme le nageur embrasse la mer et entre ainsi en contact plus direct avec la nature, il aspire à prendre, pour ainsi dire, un bain de multitude' (i. 468). Further intertextual parallels are to be found in Poe's *The Man of the Crowd*.

This new performative role for the Étranger is already manifest in 'La Femme sauvage et la petite-maîtresse', the poem which comes between 'À une heure du matin' and 'Les Foules' within the traditional ordering of *Le Spleen de Paris*. The text, framed in quotation marks, consists entirely of an imagined monologue in which a man, weary of his female companion's endless complaints, resolves to teach this 'little madam' a lesson. Where the poet of 'Les Foules' wants to humble the smug, this man wishes to 'cure' a woman whose tiresome whingeing he regards as deriving entirely from 'la satiété du bien-être et l'accablement du repos'. To hear her sighs anyone would think she suffered more than the most destitute of old women, but he wants to teach her 'ce que c'est que le vrai malheur'.[2] Accordingly he takes her to a fairground ('au milieu d'une fête') where together they observe the strangest of freak shows: a man has chained his wife in a cage in the costume of a wild animal, feeding her on live chickens and rabbits and beating her with a stick, and all by kind permission of the magistrates ('cela va sans dire'). The woman herself is 'incontestablement malheureuse', though she has the small consolation of being something of a celebrity. But she knows no better: 'dans le monde où elle a été jetée, elle n'a jamais pu croire que la femme méritât une autre destinée'. Now, however, thanks to this spectacle, the 'little madam' will herself know better, or, rather, know worse. For her companion has no time for such ignorance of how the other half lives: 'À voir les enfers dont le monde est peuplé, que voulez-vous que je pense de votre joli enfer, vous qui ne reposez que sur des étoffes aussi douces que votre peau.'

By taking her to see this husband-and-wife fairground performance, he has shown her the institution of marriage in its rawest and most primordial state ('Telles sont les mœurs conjugales de ces deux descendants d'Ève et d'Adam'), marriage in which women are enslaved and abused by tyrannical and cruel men, and all with the approval of the licensing authorities.[3] By attending this performance and viewing it on both a literal and a metaphorical basis the speaker wants to

---

[2] A possible parallel suggests itself here with the Baudelaire who undertook to depict the cruel realities of depression in *Les Fleurs du Mal* as a form of riposte to the lachrymose sentimentality of 'l'École mélancolico-farceuse' (ii. 52) and out of scorn for 'toutes les fadaises de la mélancolie apprise' (ii. 649). See above Chapter 4, 'Baudelaire's Melancholy'.

[3] This aspect of the text (among many) is taken up by Debarati Sanyal in her brilliant deconstructive reading of the poem in 'Peindre, non la chose, mais l'effet qui l'a produite: défigurations du féminin dans "La Femme sauvage et la petite-maîtresse"', in Murphy (ed.), *Lectures du 'Spleen de Paris'*, 251–60. Writing partly to pay 'homage' (255) to Barbara Johnson's *Défigurations du langage poétique*, Sanyal argues that 'la modernité baudelairienne', far from consisting in an 'ensemble de pratiques esthétiques visant à l'autonomie, à la déréalisation des objets, à la désincarnation des corps, au culte de la forme et à l'autoréflexivité' (259), instead foregrounds in radical ways (anticipating Judith Butler's ideas on performative gendering) how the figurative 'constructs' the material world of things: 'Baudelaire remet en cause l'opposition entre nature et figure, matière et représentation, fond et forme. Loin d'enfermer le texte dans un formalisme stérile, les moments métapoétiques de "La Femme sauvage et la petite-maîtresse" impliquent profondément la poésie dans la constitution des corps et des choses. Dans ce poème, la fameuse réflexivité baudelairienne, c'est-à-dire la mise en abîme de la représentation, pose le corps comme problème dans un cadre non seulement esthétique, mais aussi social, juridique et matériel' (259–60).

demonstrate the speciousness of his companion's mindset, founded as he believes it to be on mere affectation and preciosity: 'Et que peuvent signifier pour moi tous ces petits soupirs qui gonflent votre poitrine parfumée, robuste coquette? Et toutes ces affectations apprises dans les livres, et cette infatigable mélancolie, faite pour inspirer au spectateur un tout autre sentiment que la pitié?' This moaning minnie has learnt the lines of the wrong performance. She needs to get out more and cease her '*précieuses* pleurnicheries', or else the speaker will imitate the violent role of the fairground husband: 'je vous traiterai en *femme sauvage*, ou je vous jetterai par la fenêtre, comme une bouteille vide'. For this speaker turns out to be a poet, as ready to defenestrate his lover as the poet-narrator of 'Le Mauvais Vitrier' had been keen to smash a glazier's glass: 'Tant poète que je sois, je ne suis pas aussi dupe que vous voudriez le croire.'

As in 'Les Foules', therefore, the imparting of a moral lesson demands theatricals ('le goût du travestissement et du masque'): pretentious ways uncritically borrowed from a book are to be countered by public exposure to pretence, just as simpering self-pity is to be cured by the shock treatment of real empathy. Coming after 'Les Foules', the poems 'Les Veuves' and 'Le Vieux Saltimbanque' both demonstrate this empathy in action, as the poet-narrator chances upon fellow-loners, respectively in a public park and on the occasion of a public holiday. Here on display is the loneliness to be felt in a crowd, and particularly of a crowd taken up with festivity. Taking his cue from the eighteenth-century moralist Vauvenargues, who (we are informed) saw public gardens as a place of private grief, the poet of 'Les Veuves' views the municipal park as a kind of living museum of melancholy, of multiple solitudes: 'Ces retraites ombreuses sont les rendez-vous des éclopés de la vie.' Thwarted ambition and failed designs, broken hearts and hollow victories, all have come to hide away, but they cannot escape the 'œil expérimenté' of the poet's empathy: 'C'est surtout vers ces lieux que le poète et le philosophe aiment diriger leurs avides conjectures. Il y a là une pâture certaine.' With this expert eye the poet 'déchiffre' the tell-tale signs of the human world passing before him, and in this case its widows. And which of them is the more to be pitied: the widow (whom he follows) who walks forever alone on each of the 365 days of the year, or the widow (whom he chances on) who walks with a young child with whom she cannot share the knowledge of her grief? This very question may serve to prompt readers into providing their own answers and thus to enter imaginatively into the lives of these women in an attempt to calibrate the degrees of their suffering. And here they are, these two particular women, keeping their distance from the crowd as they seek private solace from the playing of a regimental band (as in 'Les Petites Vieilles') or the music of an open-air orchestral concert. For these women, too, are avatars of the Étranger and foreshadowed in 'Le Désespoir de la vieille': the first is 'évidemment condamnée, par une absolue solitude, à des habitudes de vieux célibataire', while the second is 'seule, toujours seule', despite the company of her child.

One afternoon in autumn, and thus in a temporal context comparable with that of 'Le "Confiteor" de l'artiste', 'Les Vocations', and 'Le Crépuscule du soir', the first of these two widows sits in solitude ('à l'écart', 'loin de la foule'), but a solitude filled with 'la consolation bien gagnée d'une de ces lourdes journées sans ami, sans causerie, sans joie, sans confident'. Like the friendless Étranger who could love beauty, and like the loveless Fou who implores his Venus in another public park, she has come here to sit alone with the beauty of music and to mingle with a different crowd, for overhead stretches one of those skies 'd'où descendent en foule les regrets et les souvenirs'. The second widow illustrates apartness in a different way, as the poet describes a scene of social exclusion from festivity in which the excluded are the true lovers of beauty. With a judicious gaze of conjecture that falls short of automatic self-identification with these social outcasts the poet observes a fundamental duality at work. 'Je ne puis jamais m'empêcher', he tells us, 'de jeter un regard, sinon universellement sympathique, au moins curieux, sur la foule des parias qui se pressent autour de l'enceinte d'un concert publique. L'orchestre jette à travers la nuit des chants de fête, de triomphe ou de volonté.' Within this precinct of the idle rich, not a care in the world: 'Ici rien que de riche, d'heureux; rien qui ne respire et n'inspire l'insouciance et le plaisir de se laisser vivre.' With the repetition of 'ri' (in 'rien', 'riche', and 'rien') followed by its repeated reversal (in 'respire', 'inspire', and 'plaisir', further echoed in 'vivre'), together with the repetition of vowel sounds in 'Ici' and 'heureux', the poet here performs some linguistic music of his own, evoking the steady, rhythmic ease of the haves whom nothing can perturb. Nothing... 'excepté l'aspect de cette tourbe qui s'appuie là-bas sur la barrière extérieure, attrapant gratis, au gré du vent, un lambeau de musique, et regardant l'étincelante fournaise intérieure'.

In a scenario that anticipates the smaller-scale scene described in 'Les Yeux des pauvres'—the poet comments here that '[c]'est toujours chose intéressante que ce reflet de la joie du riche au fond de l'œil du pauvre'—the have-nots ('la tourbe') observe the idle rich at play and witness mere philistine pretence: 'les oisifs, fatigués de n'avoir rien fait, se dandinent, feignant de déguster indolemment la musique'. But, in contrast to this effortless emptiness of the wealthy mind, the poor are all eyes and all ears, desperate to catch 'un lambeau de musique' as though it were a rag with which to clothe themselves in their destitution. And among them is this second widow (comparable with the woman glimpsed in 'A une passante') whom the poet describes as 'une femme grande, majestueuse, et si noble dans tout son air, que je n'ai pas souvenir d'avoir vu sa pareille dans les collections des aristocratiques beautés du passé'. Like the first widow this woman separates herself from the crowd ('la plèbe à laquelle elle s'était mêlée et qu'elle ne voyait pas'), but she is already unique and without equal, a form of beauty incarnate and in solitary communion with the beauty of the music and the luminosity of festivity: 'elle regardait le monde lumineux avec un œil profond, et elle écoutait en hochant doucement la tête'. Like the poet with his expert eye, she can see—and listen—more deeply: he in tune with her grief, she in tune with this alternative dimension of living that is beauty. The world of the idle rich is a world of self-reflection and self-regard ('Les robes traînent en miroitant; les regards se croisent') while the world of poetry and music is a world of communication in which both eye and ear are turned outwards to the other, a community of fellow-feeling within the potential void of our solitude. The 'éclopés de la vie' may shun the 'regard insolent des joyeux et des oisifs', as we are told in the first paragraph under the auspices of Vauvenargues, but this prose poem shows just how—pressing against the barrier that separates the *feuilleton* from the *haut-de-page*—poetry can meet that insolent gaze of entitlement with the authority of its own widowed majesty.

In 'Le Vieux Saltimbanque' the poet's empathy finds expression in the world of the fairground on a public holiday: one of those licensed occasions ('une de ces solennités') when 'le peuple' is granted a day off 'pour compenser les mauvais temps de l'année'. Like a tatter of music, then, or a crumb from the rich man's table, the 'people' are given the opportunity to forget 'la douleur et le travail' of their everyday lives and, briefly, to become once more like children. The children themselves don't have to go to school, while for the grown-ups this exceptional day constitutes 'un armistice conclu avec les puissances malfaisantes de la vie, un répit dans la contention et la lutte universelles'. Here, as in 'Les Veuves', there is an 'atmosphère d'insouciance', but this time it is shared by all, not only the 'people' but even by '[l]homme du monde lui-même et l'homme occupé de travaux spirituels'. Not to mention the poet himself, who participates fully in the festivity: 'Pour moi, je ne manque jamais, en vrai Parisien, de passer la revue de toutes les baraques qui se pavanent à ces époques solennelles.' Through an accumulation of verbs and plural nouns the poet evokes the multiple activities and explosive cacophony of the scene, which he summarizes: 'Tout n'était que lumière, poussière, cris, joie, tumulte [...] Et partout circulait, dominant tous les parfums, une odeur de friture qui était comme l'encens de cette fête.' Here are the people brought together not by Holy Communion but by the smell of fries and a communion of fairground performers: 'les saltimbanques, les faiseurs de tours, les montreurs d'animaux et les boutiquiers ambulants'—a communion of insistent plurality and action in which just one single person stands alone and motionless at the entrance to his own sad version of a candlelit chapel:

> Au bout, à l'extrême bout de la rangée de baraques, comme si, honteux, il s'était exilé lui-même de toutes ces splendeurs, je vis un pauvre saltimbanque, voûté, caduc, décrépit, une ruine d'homme, adossé contre un des poteaux de sa cahute; une cahute plus misérable que celle du sauvage le plus abruti; et dont deux bouts de chandelles, coulants et fumants, éclairaient trop bien encore la détresse.

There follows a contrasting accumulation of verbs in the negative ('Il ne riait pas, le misérable! Il ne pleurait pas, il ne dansait pas', etc.) that culminates in a dead-end: 'Il était muet et immobile.' This man is as far removed from life and festivity as it is possible to be without actually being dead. His is a world of pluperfects and of an imperfect that now betokens not repeated action but a permanent and immutable state: 'Il avait renoncé, il avait abdiqué. Sa destinée était faite.' Above all his art has deserted him, and his rags are real: 'de haillons comiques, où la nécessité, bien plus que l'art, avait introduit le contraste [between wealth and poverty]'.

Here again the poet's 'expert eye' has been caught by an embodiment of the Étranger, with whom he now empathizes not only in this figure of the street entertainer but also in the person of the old poet whom this elderly man appears metaphorically to represent, someone who is also without friends or family or child:

> Je viens de voir l'image du vieil homme de lettres qui a survécu à la génération dont il fut le brillant amuseur; du vieux poète sans amis, sans famille, sans enfant, dégradé par sa misère et par l'ingratitude publique, et dans la baraque de qui le monde oublieux ne veut plus entrer!

But what are the implications for the poet of this prose poem? The sight of the 'vieux saltimbanque' has left him 'obsédé par cette vision' and with a sudden feeling of 'douleur'. Does his painful empathy derive from the man's present destitution or from this picture of his own potential future fate? In the present the poet has been engaging fully in the festivity before him and so perhaps he could be seen to represent a new kind of poetry, like that figured later, for example, in 'Les Bons Chiens' ('J'invoque la muse familière, la citadine, la vivante').[4] But perhaps he, too, as a 'modern' poet, will be overtaken by time and fashion and sink into the oblivion of the unread and the unheard? Or is there another lesson to be learnt from his empathy with this aged entertainer who puts him in mind of an elderly man of letters? For, like the second widow in 'Les Veuves' who gazes on the luminous concert with her 'œil profond', this man is also a seer: 'Mais quel regard profond, inoubliable, il promenait sur la foule et les lumières'. Is this a portrait of the vatic poet of a bygone age who can see beyond the contingencies of the here and now and perceive some eternal verity, whereas the poet-narrator of this text is blinded by his immersion in the life of the present? Or is the old man simply a *Doppelgänger* in the double room of time? For 'Le Vieux Saltimbanque' articulates a now familiar rhythm, first introduced in 'Le Désespoir de la vieille': delight before defeat, childhood before old age, a similarity between the young and the old that the young cannot yet see and that the old can only contemplate in solitary

---

[4] Cf. Stevens, *Baudelaire's Prose Poems*, 53: 'The separation of the narrator from this figure is, then, the differentiation of the modern poet from an outmoded form of lyricism, but one to which the narrator nevertheless feels he owes some debt.'

silence (as the widow, too, must suffer in silence the grief that her child cannot grasp). For a moment the poet himself has again been caught between the two, here the childlike people and the old man, able to share in both perspectives before being swept away by 'un grand reflux de peuple, causé par je ne sais quel trouble' (the paradise of the people's childlike joy has thus now also been replaced by disquiet) and thereby prevented from expressing his empathetic solidarity by the gesture of a monetary offering—a failure now perhaps redeemed by the act of the poem itself.

The dialectic of the gaze, manifest in 'Les Veuves' and also in 'Le Vieux Saltimbanque', is central to 'Les Yeux des pauvres'. Comparable with 'La Femme sauvage et la petite-maîtresse' in being addressed in the first person by the poet to a tiresome female companion ('Ah! vous voulez savoir pourquoi je vous hais aujourd'hui'), it foregrounds how a lack of empathy can be a source of conjugal, social, and generational disharmony. Where, for example, in 'Le "Confiteor" de l'artiste', the poet's sense of unity with the world is evident in a form of selflessness ('car dans la grandeur de la rêverie, le *moi* se perd vite!'), here in 'Les Yeux de pauvres' we encounter a kind of 'dialogue des aveugles'. Seated one evening outside a glittering new café on one of Haussmann's not yet quite completed boulevards, the poet and his companion, having earlier resolved upon mutual empathy and to think and feel as one ('nos deux âmes désormais n'en feraient plus qu'une'), now fail to see eye to eye:

> Je tournais mes regards vers les vôtres, cher amour, pour y lire *ma* pensée; je plongeais dans vos yeux si beaux et si bizarrement doux, dans vos yeux verts, habités par le Caprice et inspirés par la Lune, quand vous me dîtes: 'Ces gens-là me sont insupportables avec leurs yeux ouverts comme des portes cochères!'

Here she is, the 'maudite chère enfant gâtée' of 'Les Bienfaits de la lune'. The bothersome goggling eyes of which she complains number six in total and belong respectively to a father, his small son, and another, younger child whom the father carries on his arm: 'ces six yeux contemplaient fixément le café nouveau avec une admiration égale, mais nuancée diversement par l'âge'. Each pair of eyes has a different perspective on the wonderful décor of this café, which nevertheless for all of them represents beauty ('Que c'est beau!'). The adult sees wealth and perhaps unjust expropriation ('tout l'or du pauvre monde est venu se porter sur ces murs'); the boy sees exclusion ('une maison où peuvent seuls entrer les gens qui ne sont pas comme nous'); and the toddler sees, joyously, but has no view ('une joie stupide et profonde'). And the poet-narrator? '[J]'étais attendri par cette famille d'yeux, mais je me sentais un peu honteux de nos verres et de nos carafes.' But his companion cannot tolerate the gaze of others. Thus each participant in this scenario of seeing has their own emotional and intellectual response, but here there is no communion, no meeting of hearts and minds: 'Tant il est difficile de

THE POET IN THE WORLD 561

s'entendre, mon cher ange, et tant la pensée est incommunicable, même entre gens qui s'aiment!' A comic portrayal of amatory discord thus becomes a figure for the difficult and delicate lines of communication between the seer and the seen and perhaps also between poets and their readers.[5]

'Les Yeux des pauvres' follows 'La Belle Dorothée', where the poet views the world through a very particular lens of poverty. Here adopting a third-person persona the poet observes a form of beauty that belies a terrible underlying reality: a woman walking along the street in the suffocating midday heat, the only living thing at this siesta hour ('une espèce de mort savoureuse'), proud, strong, triumphant, lazily at ease in her body and coquettishly at one with her beauty... but on her way to earn money so that she can buy the freedom of her 11-year-old sister 'qui est déjà mûre, et si belle!' Like an unfolding mystery her ambulant presence in the text is presented as a series of progressively more eloquent clues to the final, awful truth: that she, a freed slave, must work as though a slave (and implicitly as a prostitute) in order to accumulate enough money to buy the freedom of a sister whose pubescence renders her imminently vulnerable to a similar fate. The sun, the sand, the sea, the heat, the darkness of her skin, the blackness of her hair, the bare feet (unlike those of marble goddesses locked up in European museums), the overriding desire to please despite her status as an 'affranchie'... the poet invites us into her story, detail by detail, finally presenting us with questions to which we may already have begun to envisage the answers: 'quel puissant motif fait donc aller ainsi la paresseuse Dorothée, belle et froide comme le bronze?' 'Pourquoi a-t-elle quitté sa petite case [...]?' Gradually the description of her home becomes more and more indicative of a tropical location, while the colonial nature of this setting is revealed by the poet's idle speculation: 'Peut-être a-t-elle un rendez-vous avec quelque jeune officier qui, sur des plages lointaines, a entendu parler par ses camarades de la célèbre Dorothée.' But the final paragraph reveals how distant we are from the world of a ball at the Paris Opera, and also how, beneath the picturesque beauty of this scene in which a woman in a pink silk dress walks languidly down the street in the protective shade of a red umbrella, there lies not only the reality of sex work and slavery but also a

---

[5] For discussion of the problematics and ideological implications of seeing in this prose poem, see Robert St Clair, 'Writing Poetry Against the Grain: Or, What Can Be Seen in "Les Yeux des pauvres"', *French Forum*, 39: 1 (Winter 2014), 49–63. St Clair writes: 'As readers, we are ultimately left wondering what sort of order makes possible the disorder, injustice, and human wreckage we behold in the eyes of the poor' (55); 'Baudelaire also draws attention to the centrality, pitfalls, and aporias of reading as such, and to the potential risks involved in mistaking one's perspective or projections for a faithful map of reality (which may just be one helpful way of thinking about ideology)' (61). See also his 'Misères de la poésie: micro-lecture des économies de la violence dans "Les Yeux des pauvres"', in Murphy (ed.), *Lectures du 'Spleen de Paris'*, 307–20. For a reading of the poem, by contrast, as the representation of a new democratic openness and transparency in society, see Maurice Samuels, 'Baudelaire's Boulevard Spectacle: Seeing Through "Les Yeux des pauvres"', *Yale French Studies*, 125–6 (2014), 167–82.

story of sisterly devotion.[6] This woman who apparently cares so much about her own beauty and seemingly wants only to fish for compliments from French officers transpires to be a model of virtue. Fortunately the slave-owner is 'trop avare pour comprendre une autre beauté que celle des écus'. But we readers too, for all the knowingness of our empathy, need perhaps to remember that there is moral as well as physical beauty.

Resistance Comedy

le goût du travestissement et du masque
('Les Foules')

Je me suis résigné à être moi-même. Pourvu que je sois amusant, vous serez content, n'est-ce pas?
(letter to Arsène Houssaye, Christmas 1861 (*Corr.*, ii. 208))

In *Le Spleen de Paris* the empathy of this alternative poet-lawgiver thus takes the form of imaginatively inhabiting those who warrant compassionate attention and of inviting the reader to see beyond the surface of such lives, to uncover a backstory and to understand a reality that is most probably not their own. At the same time each reader is a potential 'petite maîtresse', all of us needing to be cured of our airs and graces: to be shown the hollowness of piety, say, or the absurdity of a political opinion, or the silliness of fairy-story assumptions. Through the poet's own comic performances readers may be led to look at themselves in a mirror and laugh. But surely, asks the poet of 'Le Miroir', that does not make sense 'puisque vous ne pouvez vous y voir qu'avec déplaisir?' Pompously, the 'homme épouvantable' invokes the 'immortel principles' of the Revolution and the belief that all men are equal before the law: *ergo*, he can look at his ugly face if he wants to. Comically, the poet may be suggesting that his readers should have every right—and opportunity—to see just how 'épouvantable' each of us may be. 'Hypocrite lecteur,—mon semblable,—mon frère'...

In 'Les Tentations ou Eros, Plutus et la Gloire' we learn again about hypocrisy. The poet recounts a hellish dream of his in which '[d]eux superbes Satans et une Diablesse' paid him a visit one night, wreathed in sulphur (like the naughty boy who enjoyed sleeping beside a maid in 'Les Vocations'), and how each tempted him with a special gift (comparable with those distributed in the preceding poem

---

[6] Dorothée Dormeuil, the person whom Baudelaire met on the Île de Bourbon (now the Île de la Réunion) and on whom this prose poem is based, in fact had two sisters who were still slaves. See Alexander Ockenden, 'Baudelaire, Lacaussade and the Historical Identity of "La Belle Dorothée"', *French Studies Bulletin*, 35: 3 [no. 132] (Autumn 2014), 64–8. Ockenden suggests that Baudelaire may have helped Dorothée financially (while paying her as a prostitute), since one of the two sisters, the 10-year-old Marie Dormeuil, was bought out of slavery ten days after Baudelaire's arrival in the island.

'Les Dons des fées'). The first Satan offers the poet the power of love: 'tu connaîtras le plaisir, sans cesse renaissant, de sortir de toi-même pour t'oublier dans autrui', which provides him with a devilish opportunity to be ironic about empathy: 'Grand merci! je n'ai que faire de cette pacotille d'êtres qui, sans doute, ne valent pas mieux que mon pauvre moi.' The second offers the poet the power of wealth, which gives him a devilish opportunity to deny that the poverty of others is of any interest to him: 'Je n'ai besoin, pour ma jouissance, de la misère de personne.' And the third emissary from Hell—'la Diablesse'—offers him fame, or at least the renown symbolized by a gigantic trumpet garlanded with the titles of 'tous les journaux de l'univers'. Though sorely tempted ('"Diable!" fis-je, à moitié subjugué, "voilà qui est précieux!"'), this gives the comic poet his opportunity to turn 'la séduisante virago' down: he has seen this ageing lady of wholly resistible charms ('dont la beauté garde la magie pénétrante des ruines') drinking with 'quelques drôles de [s]a connaissance'. In a manner that foreshadows Laforgue's *Moralités légendaires* Baudelaire here debunks a whole mythology of satanic temptation by means of bathos, incongruity (two Satans? a she-devil just a little 'sur le retour'?), and much elaborate and grotesquely bizarre descriptive detail, and he pokes fun at the basic premise of this mythology: namely, that temptation is there to be withstood. On waking, the poet bitterly regrets 'une si courageuse abnégation' and wishes he'd said 'yes'. Alas, it is too late. *Carpe noctem*!

But what, then, are we to make of the fact that these three gifts are already his? Empathy, writing about the poor, and publication in the press? 'Les Tentations' was itself published together with the empathetic 'La Belle Dorothée' in the *Revue nationale et étrangère* in June 1863, and together they were the first of Baudelaire's prose poems to appear since the twenty published the previous year in *La Presse*. Bluff and double bluff? Is this poet both ironizing his previous work and, as the writer of the dedicatory letter who had then introduced his collection as a serpent, here reaffirming his satanic credentials while continuing (in 'La Belle Dorothée') to turn the subject matter of poverty and abuse into a new kind of beauty? Or does he simply wish to amuse, as he had declared privately to Houssaye in an earlier letter (at Christmas 1861) where he speaks frankly of having begun writing the prose poems as a pastiche of *Gaspard de la nuit* and then desisted: 'mais j'ai bien vite senti que je ne pouvais pas persévérer dans ce pastiche, et que l'œuvre était inimitable. Je me suis résigné à être moi-même. Pourvu que je sois amusant, vous serez content, n'est-ce pas?' (*Corr.*, ii. 208).

Comedy is perhaps the feature of these texts mostly commonly passed over by critics, either because it can be taken as read (and no one likes to have a joke explained) or because the poems seem to call for more intricate and sophisticated readings. Yet comedy, as in Laforgue's *Moralités légendaires*, is a powerful instrument of resistance to cant and ready-made thinking, and in this respect the 'comique absolu' is even more effective than the 'comique significatif'. The inscrutability of the polyphonic poet of *Le Spleen de Paris* derives from his dead-pan expression. Thus, in 'Les Dons des fées' (preceding 'Les Tentations'), the whole rigmarole of fairy godmothers blessing babies at birth is given an entertaining new look. Not only can fairies run out of stock, but then they go and give the greatest gift of all—'le don de plaire'—to the son of 'un pauvre petit commerçant' who irritatingly doesn't understand the value of what he's been given and pesters the overworked fairy for an explanation. Because why *would* he understand, given that he is 'sans doute un de ces raisonneurs si communs, incapables de s'élever jusqu'à la logique de l'Absurde'? The distribution of life's blessings is a random business, and fairies make mistakes. Lighten up!

In 'Laquelle est la vraie?', whose heroine has also been blessed ('une certaine Bénédicta'), the fairy-story is again a source of fun, and here of a Voltairean kind. In 'Ce qui plaît aux dames', a *conte en vers* first published in the *Contes de Guillaume Vadé* (1764), Voltaire had drawn for comic purposes on the tradition of the so-called 'loathly lady', itself part of Arthurian legend. The figure of the 'loathly lady' dates back at least to the late fourteenth-century chivalric romance *Sir Gawain and the Green Knight*, featuring the crone Morgan le Fay, and is also central to Chaucer's *The Wife of Bath's Tale* of the same period. In the traditional story a knight who has been dispatched on a mission to discover 'what women want' proves his worth by marrying an old hag who, when the knight proceeds undeterred to fulfil his conjugal role on their wedding night, promptly turns into the most beautiful young woman a man could possibly desire. That he (like the reader of 'La Belle Dorothée'?) should have been persuaded by moral worth rather than physical beauty is thus rewarded.[7]

In 'Laquelle est la vraie?' Baudelaire turns the story round. The poet has met a beautiful young woman, so beautiful that she soon dies (as all illusion must!). Following her burial he then sees, trampling on her newly dug grave 'avec une violence hystérique et bizarre', 'une petite personne qui ressemblait singulièrement à la défunte'. This little person announces that she is the 'real' Bénédicta and that the poet will just have to love her the way she is: 'C'est moi, une fameuse canaille! Et pour la punition de ta folie et de ton aveuglement, tu m'aimeras telle que je suis!' In a further twist to the traditional tale the poet then stamps his own foot on the softened earth and sinks in up to the knee: 'comme un loup pris au piège, je reste attaché, pour toujours peut-être, à la fosse de l'idéal'. The chivalric hero has turned into a comic lover (cf. the term of affection 'mon loup') with one foot in the grave, condemned in possible perpetuity to enact the sequence that informs so many of these prose poems: an abrupt and sorry transition from delight to disillusion, from

---

[7] For further discussion of 'Ce qui plaît aux dames' and this literary tradition, see Voltaire, *Candide and Other Stories*, trans. and ed. Roger Pearson (rev. edn, Oxford: Oxford University Press [Oxford World's Classics], 2006), xxiv–xxx. Charles Nodier's celebrated 'conte fantastique' *La Fée aux miettes* (1832) also derives from this tradition.

paradise to an ineradicable sense of loss, and from 'idéal' to 'spleen'—where 'spleen' feeds like worms on the decomposing 'idéal'.[8]

The poet as comic entertainer, already on stage in 'Le Chien et le flacon', 'La Femme sauvage et la petite-maîtresse', and 'Les Tentations', has further performances to give. In 'Le Joueur généreux' he meets the Devil himself, at last! And on the streets of Paris (where else?). What's more, the Devil has been wanting to meet him... Together they go gambling in an infernal basement paradise of the kind where men lose the will to go home to their wives and children (not to mention the soup). Surrounded by 'des visages étranges d'hommes et de femmes, marqués d'une beauté fatale', the poet feels empathy—'une sympathie fraternelle'—with a whole new set of eyes: 'je dirais que jamais je ne vis d'yeux brillant plus énergiquement de l'horreur de l'ennui et du désir immortel de se sentir vivre'. He and the Devil are now best mates: 'À votre immortelle santé, vieux Bouc!' And thus, with heroic unconcern, the poet gambles away his soul: 'une chose si impalpable, si souvent inutile et quelquefois si gênante'. For the Devil is a great comedian himself (as we know from *De l'essence du rire*), possessed of 'une suavité de diction et une tranquillité dans la drôlerie que je n'ai trouvées dans aucun des plus célèbres causeurs de l'humanité'. No left-wing journalist he. More like a writer of prose poems. And clever, of course, like an undercover agent. The only time he ever thought his power might be undermined was when a preacher told his flock: 'Mes chères fréres, n'oubliez jamais, quand vous entendrez vanter le progrès des lumières, que la plus belle ruse du diable est de vous persuader qu'il n'existe pas.' Those humanitarian do-gooders are actually doing the Devil's work for him! And so, with the wit of a Voltairean *conte philosophique*, the poet continues to report on what he has learnt from his 'audience' with the Devil: about his work with the academies, for example, and about his cordial if distant relationship with God, despite 'le souvenir d'anciennes rancunes'. And when the Devil (who can sometimes be a 'bon diable') offers him in return for his soul 'la possibilité de soulager et de vaincre, pendant toute votre vie, cette bizarre affection de l'Ennui, qui est la source de toutes vos maladies et de tous vos misérables progrès', well, the poet can only pray to God that it may be so: 'Mon Dieu! Seigneur, mon Dieu! faites que le diable me tienne sa parole!' As if the 'vieux bouc' could ever be trusted...

Thus, with the straightest of faces, the poet (and well-known author of *Les Fleurs du Mal*?) here acts out his sympathy for the devil and plays the role of a 'joueur généreux' himself in letting us in on the secrets of his conversation, even if,

---

[8] For a reading of this poem as an ironic and reflexive allegory of Baudelaire's embrace of poetry in prose, see Régine Foloppe, *Baudelaire et la vérité poétique* (Paris: L'Harmattan, 2019), 262–4. Cf. also Labarthe, *'Petits Poèmes en prose'*, 49: 'Le "double" dissemblable de la défunte, tout armé qu'il est de sa vive ironie, plaide pour une voie négative, celle qui, de l'Idéal enseveli, ferait naître une autre poésie, dont le terreau serait la Mort.' Labarthe sees the poem as an ironic take on the tradition of the 'tombeau poétique'.

quite understandably, there were one or two 'principes fondamentaux dont il ne me convient pas de partager les bénéfices et la propriété avec qui que ce soit'. The devil's secrets are not for 'philanthropic' sharing as though they were taxable items in a socialist economy. Or is the poet in fact a double agent? Comically pretending to approve while in fact, like the preacher, urging us towards 'la conscience dans le Mal'? Less a devil's advocate than a poet who wants to blow Satan's cover? In 'La Fausse Monnaie', which precedes 'Le Joueur généreux, that at least seems to be the message: 'On n'est jamais excusable d'être méchant, mais il y a quelque mérite à savoir qu'on l'est; et le plus irréparable des vices est de faire le mal par bêtise.' Here again we find the poet's empathy with the poor focused on a gaze:

> Je ne connais rien de plus inquiétant que l'éloquence muette de ces yeux suppliants, qui contiennent à la fois, pour l'homme sensible qui sait y lire, tant d'humilité, tant de reproches. Il y trouve quelque chose approchant cette profondeur de sentiment compliqué, dans les yeux larmoyants des chiens qu'on fouette.

In this case the poet believes that his friend was pretending to give this poor man a coin of significant value—all the while knowing it to be counterfeit—in order to give him the pleasure of a delightful surprise. But another gaze reveals his error: 'Je le regardai dans le blanc des yeux, et je fus épouvanté de voir que ses yeux brillaient d'une incontestable candeur.' His friend had not been pretending, but now he is, letting the poet believe that his motive was to cause pleasurable surprise whereas in fact he simply wanted to appear charitable on the cheap. But for the poet it would have been so much more interesting if the donation had been intended as an experiment to see what happened next, rather as the narrator of the preceding poem, 'Une mort héroïque', wonders if the Prince is conducting a psychological experiment on Fancioulle. Might the possession of this counterfeit coin have led the beggar to acquire many genuine ones? Or might it have landed him in prison? And so the poet's conjectures multiply: 'Et ainsi ma fantaisie allait son train, prêtant des ailes à l'esprit de mon ami et tirant toutes les déductions possibles de toutes les hypothèses possibles.' But what he describes as his 'rêverie' is interrupted by the banal truth of his friend's mean-spirited act. Can we infer from this perhaps that for the poet the creative imagination of a knowing prankster (as, previously, was the poet-narrator of 'Le Mauvais Vitrier) or an experimental behaviourist (as, later, will be the poet-narrator of 'Assommons les pauvres!') is altogether of more value and interest? Because it would have constituted a conscious, willed exploration of cause and effect as opposed to this tawdry act of meanness that merely illustrates the natural 'perversity' of human beings? Or is the poet mocking his own tendency to overcomplicate things? Indeed have the fairies given him a tiresome gift? For his 'misérable cerveau' is 'toujours occupé à chercher midi à quatorze heures (de quelle fatigante faculté la nature m'a fait cadeau!)'. And so he is always keen to find a 'sentiment compliqué' in the simplest gaze and even in the eyes of a dog? Certainly his predecessor in 'Une mort héroïque' seemed similarly reluctant to jump to conclusions about what he saw. Empathy may not be as easy as it looks!

Be that as it may, these poems ('Les Tentations', 'Le Joueur généreux', 'La Fausse Monnaie') suggest that the poet of *Le Spleen de Paris* takes pleasure in poking fun at himself. Compare also 'Perte d'auréole', which offers a comic take on the poet's decision to slum it in prose:

> Eh! quoi! vous ici, mon cher? [an anonymous interlocutor rhetorically exclaims.] Vous, dans un mauvais lieu! vous, le buveur de quintessences! vous, le mangeur d'ambroisie! En vérité, il y a de quoi me surprendre.

He has lost his halo in the mud while crossing a busy boulevard and lacked the courage to retrieve it. But what matter? As we all know: 'à quelque chose malheur est bon'. He can now write what he likes: 'Je puis maintenant me promener incognito, faire des actions basses, et me livrer à la crapule, comme les simples mortels.' What's more, he can have a laugh at the thought of some 'mauvais poète' or other wearing the halo with contented pride. This, then, is the poet who in the immediately preceding poems has already been lowering the tone, like the cloud-gazing Étranger of 'La Soupe et les nuages', for example, who faithfully records the words of his beautiful beloved as she punches him in the back and yells: 'Allez-vous bientôt manger votre soupe, sacré bougre de marchand de nuages?' As to the 'actions basses' and 'la crapule', these are to be found in 'Portraits de maîtresses', where four 'vétérans de la joie', now filled with the 'tristesse froide et railleuse' of a cynical middle age, kill time ('qui a la vie si dure') by drinking and smoking and discussing their former, unsatisfactory mistresses: the one who wanted to wear the trousers, the frigid one who ended up having six children and no orgasms, the glutton who could have been exhibited as a fairground freak (the 'monstre polyphage'), and finally Little Miss Perfect whose tedious perfection served only as a permanent reproach—until her lover drowned her in a pond because there was simply no other way. At least the no less murderously inclined husband of 'Le Galant Tireur' (which follows 'Portraits de maîtresses') is able to take out his conjugal hatred at a shooting range by blasting the head off a doll who looks like his wife. But really he, too, has gone there just to '*tuer* le Temps'.

The narrator of these poems has a black sense of humour, of the sort that notices the sign over a bar—'À la vue du cimetière. Estaminet'—and begins to make puns about 'bière'. Beer or no bier, the poet's third-person account of his flâneur ('notre promeneur') permits the vicarous reflection that here is a perfect illustration of a *memento mori*, just like those skeletons the ancient Egyptians used to have with them at a feast in case anyone forgot to seize the moment and enjoy themselves. Surely the owner of the bar must know his Horace ('Carpe diem'), not to mention the teachings of Epicurus and the poets who follow them. Like the poet of 'Enivrez-vous' perhaps: 'Il faut être toujours ivre. Tout est là: c'est l'unique question'; 'Mais de quoi? De vin, de poésie ou de vertu, à votre guise. Mais enivrez-vous.'[9] So the 'promeneur' duly enters to drink 'un verre de bière en face des tombes' (with their own 'vers de bière') before visiting the graveyard itself, which is bursting with organic life beneath a warm, intoxicated sun: tall, luxuriant grass, 'un tapis de fleurs magnifiques engraissées par la destruction', and, filling the air, '[u]n immense bruissement de vie [...] la vie des infiniments petits'. Death, where is thy sting? Even the adjacent shooting-range adds to the sense of festivity as the shots ring out like 'l'explosion des bouchons de champagne' amidst the 'symphonie en sourdine' of the buzzing insects. But there is a 'trouble-fête' (comparable with 'je ne sais quel trouble' that interrupts the jollities in 'Le Vieux Saltimbanque'): a grumpy voice complains loudly from its tomb about all the racket (so much for 'rest in peace') and curses mankind for its scheming impatience ('Maudites soient vos ambitions, maudits soient vos calculs, mortels impatients') in practising the art of killing beside a sanctuary of death. For we really don't need to practise. Dying comes easy. Take it from those who know, those who have long since hit that particular target: 'ceux qui depuis longtemps ont mis dans le But, dans le seul but de la détestable vie!' To the classic instance of a *memento mori* represented by the contiguity of a bar and a cemetery is thus comically added a different lesson: why learn to cause death when it will kill us all in the end? Like war.

This comedy of violence is an insistent feature of *Le Spleen de Paris*, and rarely without a political dimension. Already in 'Le Gâteau' we have been shown how ridiculously easy it is to unleash destruction. Here we have a cloud-gazing 'promeneur' telling us in the first person how he has found himself in a snowy mountainous region (reminiscent of Rousseau's Savoy) and able to look *down* on the clouds beneath him, together with the 'passions vulgaires' of our petty humanity. In short, he is on a high:

> Bref, je me sentais, grâce à l'enthousiasmante beauté dont j'étais environné, en parfaite paix avec moi-même et avec l'univers; je crois même que, dans ma parfaite béatitude et dans mon total oubli de tout le mal terrestre, j'en étais venu à ne plus trouver si ridicules les journaux qui prétendent que l'homme est né bon[.]

But, as usual, 'idéal' is followed by 'spleen': a man has to eat. But what he eats becomes a bone of contention. The fake news of man's goodness peddled by the press is soon under threat from two starving boys who fight tooth and nail over

---

[9] Jean-Michel Gouvard sees a parody of Hugolian verse and of 'Pan' in particular as contributing to the ironic subtext of 'Enivrez-vous'. See *Charles Baudelaire, 'Le Spleen de Paris'*, 101–3.

the slice of bread that our kind 'promeneur' has charitably bestowed on one of them—who believes it to be 'cake'. For, quite clearly, neither is instinctively a socialist: 'aucun n'en voulant sans doute sacrifier la moitié pour son frère'. Consequently the first boy—'[l]e légitime propriétaire du gâteau', doubtless representative of an oppressed and hungry populace duped by the urban myth of a royal lady recommending the consumption of brioche—defends his property by sinking 'ses petites griffes dans les yeux [where else?] de l'usurpateur'. In the end the prize itself is destroyed by the fight, and 'ces petits hommes' are left with nothing. The cookie has crumbled. Our post-Rousseauean walker can but sadly reflect: 'Il y a donc un pays superbe où le pain s'appelle du *gâteau*, friandise si rare qu'elle suffit pour engendrer une guerre parfaitement fratricide!' At any rate it looks as though Hippolyte Castille and his 'philanthropic' friends have got it wrong. For the Devil moves in mysterious ways his destruction to perform, not least in an age of revolutions.

In 'Assommons les pauvres!' (first submitted for publication in 1865 but refused) the poet-narrator is himself the comic perpetrator of violence, and all because he has read the wrong sort of book. Set 'il y a seize ou dix-sept ans' and thus at the (precisely and knowingly approximate) time of the 1848 Revolution, the poem tells how the poet has self-isolated for a fortnight to devour his own choice of sugary confection ('J'avais donc digéré,—avalé, veux-je dire,—toutes les élucubrations de tous ces entrepreneurs de bonheur public'), which has left him 'dans un état d'esprit avoisinant le vertige ou la stupidité'—and sorely needing a drink. Dazed and dumb, he heads for a bar, vaguely resolved to carry out an experiment (of a kind that the narrators of 'Une mort héroïque' and 'La Fausse Monnaie' might have approved of) to see if he can get the poor to stand on their own two feet. In this respect he is therefore representative of a particularly hard-line response to 'la question sociale'. And seemingly the experiment works: 'ô miracle! ô jouissance du philosophe qui vérifie l'excellence de sa théorie!' By beating up a beggar (said to be in his sixties) he has provoked a resistance and made a man of him. Like so many of the cast in *Le Spleen de Paris* this man is the possessor of a gaze: 'un de ces regards inoubliables qui culbuteraient les trônes, si l'esprit remuait la matière, et si l'œil d'un magnétiseur faisait mûrir les raisins'. A potential revolutionary, then, but of implausible efficacy. The poet, for his part, has the devil in him: 'un Démon d'action, un Démon de combat', which, as the references to Lélut and Baillarger suggest,[10] may account for this moment of

---

[10] Louis-Francisque Lélut (1804–77), a doctor specializing in mental illness, was the author of *Du démon de Socrate: Spécimen d'une application de la science psychologique à celle de l'histoire* (1836) and *L'Amulette de Pascal, pour servir à l'histoire des hallucinations* (1846) in which he presented Socrates and Pascal as case studies of mental 'alienation'. Jules Baillarger (1809–90), a neurologist and psychiatrist and author of *Des hallucinations* (1842), was a specialist in the area of what we now call bi-polar disorder.

madness that entitles the poet to a 'brevet de folie' (as might also his behaviour in 'Le Mauvais Vitrier' where he describes himself as 'ivre de ma folie').

The comedy of the violence here, as in 'Le Gâteau', derives from placing a simple fist-fight within such an elaborate intellectual context, in this case of Stoic philosophy, political ideology, and psychiatric medicine, and bespeaks Baudelaire's fundamental scepticism about theorizing human behaviour beyond the simple recognition of our 'perversité naturelle'. Hence the Parthian shot with which he ends the poem: 'Qu'en dis-tu, citoyen Proudhon?' For all that he was a 'bon bougre' in Baudelaire's eyes, the author of *Qu'est-ce que la propriété? ou, Recherches sur le principe du droit et du gouvernement* (1840) was too wedded to the objective of radical social reform and to the faith in Progress on which such radicalism was founded.[11] By way of comic retort Baudelaire therefore has the pugilist of 'Assommons les pauvres!' enact the very violence against the poor of which the Second Republic was guilty in suppressing the workers' revolt of June 1848, itself a protest against the abolition of the workshops that were intended to enable them, precisely, to stand economically on their own two feet.[12] In this way, the poem pokes fun at the earnestness and self-bestowed worthiness of 'ces entrepreneurs de bonheurs publics' and, through its own sense of comedy, urges everyone to have a laugh and take a break. If the exclamation mark in the title were an emoji, it would feature a broad smile.

In this respect 'Assommons les pauvres!' is of a piece with 'Le Joujou du pauvre', which begins: 'Je veux donner l'idée d'un divertissement innocent. Il y a si peu d'amusements qui ne soient pas coupables!' Here, both in the title and in the tone, the ludic is the name of the game. Already in the second paragraph the poem turns us readers into self-contradicting theorists: 'Quand vous sortirez le matin avec l'intention décidée de flâner sur les grandes routes'. Surely 'flânerie' is all about aimlessness? Yet here again we have a poet with an experimental aim, as though he were a theorist of human behaviour like Lélut and Baillarger. Instead of beating up 60-year-old beggars, how about giving random 'penny toys' to destitute children on the street? Just to see the look on their face? 'Vous verrez leurs yeux s'agrandir démesurément.' And it is the ludic potential of the toy that matters, not its intrinsic worth. Witness the poor little rich kid with his gorgeous doll gazing at a poor little poor kid whose only toy is a rat: 'Les parents, par économie sans doute, avaient tiré le joujou de la vie elle-même.' The owner of the doll is himself dressed like a doll and imprisoned behind 'la grille d'un vaste jardin', while the owner of the rat is as dirty as a rat—but free, unlike his pet who lives 'dans une boîte grillée'. Each is an object of art: the one 'habillé de ces vêtements de

---

[11] See *Corr.*, ii. 563, and *'Le Spleen de Paris'*, ed. Steinmetz, 211 n. 1.

[12] For a detailed account of the many complexities, ambiguities, and intertextual allusions of 'Assommons les pauvres!', set against earlier critical readings of the poem, see Murphy, *Logiques du dernier Baudelaire*, 393–432. As Murphy notes: 'On ne peut [...] déduire l'idéologie de Baudelaire de celle de ce locuteur de toute évidence farfelu' (431).

campagne si pleins de coquetterie', the other like an unwashed coach: 'un de ces marmots-parias dont un œil impartial découvrirait la beauté, si, comme l'œil du connaisseur devine une peinture idéale sous un vernis de carrrossier, il le nettoyait de la répugnante patine de la misère'. The 'poète-déchiffreur' with his 'œil expérimenté' now has the knowing eye of an art-specialist, able to restore a masterpiece of humanity from beneath the grime and yellowing varnish of neglect. One message, then, is apparently clear: class is a question of wealth and surface, but beneath the dirty surface of life 'liberté, fraternité, égalité' are just waiting to show themselves in all their pristine glory. For the poem seems to end with knowing emphasis: 'Et les deux enfants se riaient l'un à l'autre fraternellement, avec des dents d'une *égale* blancheur.' And, indeed, which of the boys is actually the poorer? The free urchin or Little Lord Fauntleroy? Or is the title in fact a reference to the poet-narrator himself, a *pauvre type* whose idea of fun is to fill his pockets with toy figures and then toy with destitute children as though he were tossing titbits to stray cats? For doll and rat, read urchin and cat? For the poet of *Le Spleen de Paris* is himself a street performer in the theatre of the world.

25
The Beauty of the Prose Poem

> Le joujou est la première initiation de l'enfant à l'art.
> (*Morale du joujou*, i. 583).
>
> Toutes ces choses pensent [...] mais musicalement et pittoresquement, sans arguties, sans syllogismes, sans déductions.
> ('Le "Confiteor" de l'artiste')

'Le Joujou du pauvre' offers us the prose poem as pure *divertissement*, neither innocent nor culpable but a knowing performance of contrasts and parallels, seeming to present a moral and possibly political message but in fact giving us the opportunity to delight in an array of verbal and thematic patterns: the prose poem as a scrap of fun to be tossed before its readers (the poet's pets) during the street performance of a literary flâneur. As we know from Baudelaire's earlier prose piece *Morale du joujou* (1853), from which this prose poem derives,[1] he regarded the child playing with a toy as a kind of primal scene of the artistic imagination: 'Cette facilité à contenter son imagination témoigne de la spiritualité de l'enfance dans ses conceptions artistiques. Le joujou est la première initiation de l'enfant à l'art' (i. 583). Moreover the 'penny toys' listed there (i. 584) are also those distributed by the poet in 'Le Joujou des pauvres': 'le polichinelle plat, mû par un seul fil; les forgerons qui battent l'enclume; le cavalier et son cheval dont la queue est un sifflet', and in *Morale du joujou* they explicitly illustrate a message to be found also in the prose poem: 'Croyez-vous que ces images simples créent une moindre réalité dans l'esprit de l'enfant que ces merveilles du jour de l'an, qui sont plutôt un hommage de la servilité parasitique à la richesse des parents qu'un cadeau à la poésie enfantine?' (i. 584).

Street Art, or the Beauty of Inclusion

> Quelles bizarreries ne trouve-t-on pas dans une grande ville, quand on sait se promener et regarder? La vie fourmille de monstres innocents.
> ('Mademoiselle Bistouri' (i. 355))
>
> Je chante le chien crotté.
> ('Les Bons Chiens' (i. 361))

---

[1] On the transformation of one into the other, see Franck Bauer, 'Le Poème en prose: Uun joujou du pauvre?', *Poétique*, 109 (1997), 17–37.

The same lesson could be inferred, *mutatis mutandis*, from a comparison of poetry in verse with poetry in prose: the worth of the text derives from the reader's imaginative response and not from the supposed intrinsic value or prestige of the source. This in turn might be the lesson of 'Les Bons Chiens', which is explicitly dedicated to an artist—Joseph Stevens (1816-92)—who was celebrated for his paintings of animals, and notably dogs. As the last of the prose poems in *Le Spleen de Paris* this text constitutes, whether by chance or Baudelairean design, the 'queue' that the collection is said, in the dedicatory letter, not to possess and thus the counterpart of its allegedly absent 'tête', represented by the opening poem 'L'Étranger'. But since, as we are told also, the collection has neither head nor tail only because 'tout, au contraire, est à la fois tête et queue, alternativement et réciproquement', then it is perhaps also true that 'L'Etranger' and 'Les Bons Chiens' stand in a reciprocal relationship of mirroring since both concern the poet as representative of the alternative and the outcast. At the same time, being a 'queue' about dogs, the poem recalls 'Le Chien et le flacon', where the dog (representing the reading public) is said to be 'frétillant de la queue, ce qui est, je crois, chez ces pauvres êtres, le signe correspondant du rire et du sourire'. Certainly the tone of 'Les Bons Chiens' is one of tail-wagging jubilation, so that at first the poet invokes the irreverent spirit of Laurence Sterne (1713-68) as his muse. In explicit preference to the scientific spirit of the celebrated naturalist, the comte de Buffon (1707-88)—and so this is not going to be some learned scientific account of canines—the poet calls on the author of *Tristram Shandy* and *A Sentimental Journey through France and Italy* ('sentimental farceur, farceur incomparable!') to inspire him to 'un chant digne de toi' 'en faveur des bons chiens, des pauvres chiens'. In particular he recalls the famous episode in *Tristram Shandy* when Tristram gives his ass a macaroon to eat—by way of an experiment.[2] Not only does this link the poem to 'Un plaisant' (through the allusion to an ass) but also, for the reader familiar with the detail of Sterne's novel, to those several poems where the idea of experiment or quasi-scientific demonstration is central to the story or anecdote in question ('La Femme sauvage et la petite-maîtresse', 'Le Joujou du pauvre', 'Une mort héroïque', 'La Fausse Monnaie', 'Assommons les pauvres!'). At the same time these experiments also illustrate the comedy of the prank as it is performed throughout *Tristram Shandy* and which in turn has its own counterpart in 'Le Mauvais Vitrier'.

But in this final prose poem of *Le Spleen de Paris* the poet is resolved, culturally speaking, to slum it, and so he rejects even the subversive model of Laurence Sterne:

---

[2] See *Le Spleen de Paris*, ed. Steinmetz (ed), 212 n. 3. For discussion of the intertextual allusions to Sterne, see Margery A. Evans, 'Laurence Sterne and *Le Spleen de Paris*', *French Studies*, 42 (1988), 165-76, and her *Baudelaire and Intertextuality*, 105-9.

> Arrière la Muse académique! Je n'ai que faire de cette vieille bégueule. J'invoque la Muse familière, la citadine, la vivante, pour qu'elle m'aide à chanter les bons chiens, les pauvres chiens, les chiens crottés, ceux-là que chacun écarte, comme pestiférés et pouilleux, excepté le pauvre dont ils sont les associés, et le poète qui les regarde d'un œil fraternel.

Thus, in a spirit of celebratory irreverence that eschews the prudery of the *bien-pensants* and aligns the poet with the poor in a solidarity of the outcast, this particular poet honours all the 'éclopés de la vie' ('Les Veuves') who have figured in the preceding poems: the good, the bad, and the ugly, marginalized by society but placed centre-stage in this diverse poetry of the street. The canine world is also the world of the homeless beggar, the flâneur, the bohemian, and the fairground performer, and all are the true subjects of this mongrel genre, the prose poem:

> Je chante le chien crotté, le chien pauvre, le chien sans domicile, le chien flâneur, le chien saltimbanque, le chien dont l'instinct, comme celui du pauvre, du bohémien et de l'histrion, est merveilleusement aiguillonné par la nécessité, cette si bonne mère, cette vraie patronne des intelligences!

But even as he insists on the lowliness of his subjects, the poet also foregrounds—and more emphatically than in any other poem in *Le Spleen de Paris*—his own status as a singer and popular bard. The reference to the Muse, the repetition of 'je chante', the triumphant language of assertion and self-confidence in ridiculing the pampered pets of the rich ('À la niche, tous ces fatigants parasites!'), the delight in multiplicity and diversity and sheer urban busyness, all point to the presence of the lyric poet as street artist and defender of the down-and-out. The well-known Parisian journalist and theatre director Nestor Roqueplan (1804–70) had once written a *feuilleton* article entitled 'Où vont les chiens?', as though really he had no idea.[3] But this poet knows: 'Où vont les chiens, dites-vous, hommes peu attentifs? Ils vont à leurs affaires.'

Honouring Stevens, who also knows where dogs go, the poet of 'Les Bons Chiens' simulates the wide variety of the artist's subjects with his own lists of canine types and itemizes their manifold pursuits, in all weathers, with a proliferation of verbs ('ils vont, ils viennent, ils trottent, ils passent sous les voitures') and a miscellany of objectives ('excités par les puces, la passion, le besoin ou le devoir'). In fact they are just like human beings: 'Comme nous, ils se sont levés de bon matin, et ils cherchent leur vie ou courent à leurs plaisirs.' Like urban commuters, some will spend the night in the suburbs and then come in for

---

[3] On Baudelaire's debt to this *feuilleton* in the writing of 'Les Bons Chiens', see Graham Chesters, 'Sur "Les Bons Chiens" de Baudelaire', *Revue d'histoire littéraire de la France*, 80: 3 (May–June 1980), 416–21.

lunch at a restaurant in the Palais-Royal (albeit a hand-out from the kitchen door); others will travel more than five leagues to be fed by charitable elderly spinsters; and others, who live still further away, will proceed to the city only on appointed days, minded to have sex: 'Et ils sont tous très exacts, sans carnets, sans notes et sans portefeuilles.' Moreover, as may be seen in the poet's evocation of Stevens's painting (*Intérieur de saltimbanque*) featuring two dogs left alone in 'la chambre du saltimbanque absent', all dogs resemble their owners: 'Mais regardez, je vous prie, ces deux personnages, intelligents, habillés de vêtements à la fois éraillés et somptueux, coiffés comme des troubadours ou des militaires.' And intelligent they are too, carefully (if self-interestedly) guarding the contents of a cauldron simmering on the stove as though they were the witches in *Macbeth*.[4] For they are also actors ('de si zélés comédiens'), and, like all actors, they will soon have to face not only 'l'indifférence du public' but also 'les injustices d'un directeur qui se fait la grosse part et mange à lui seul plus de soupe que quatre comédiens'. But here at home they can have some soup of their own and doubtless gaze at clouds.

Thus dogs become the objects of the poet's empathy and compassion, both as artists and as emblems of the dispossessed, just as they also raise important questions—here in the final poem of *Le Spleen de Paris*—about society's treatment of the artist and about the rewards that artists may or may not expect to receive for their work. In comically suggesting that there should be a welfare state for dogs, the poet may also have himself in mind:

> Que de fois j'ai contemplé, souriant et attendri, tous ces philosophes à quatre pattes, esclaves complaisants, soumis ou dévoués, que le dictionnaire républicain pourrait aussi bien qualifier d'"officieux", si la république, trop occupée du *bonheur* des hommes, avait le temps de ménager l'*honneur* des chiens!

For his own part the poet has often wondered—'qui sait, après tout?'—whether dogs that are especially patient, courageous, and hard-working may receive their reward in heaven ('un paradis spécial pour les bons chiens'). After all, Swedenborg claims that even Muslims and Protestants have heavens of their own ('un pour les Turcs et un pour les Hollandais!'). And the poet himself? His reward comes here on earth (indeed in a Belgian bar called 'The Prince of Wales')[5] and takes the form of a public acknowledgement by Joseph Stevens that 'il était bon et honnête de chanter les pauvres chiens'. The poem thus ends with the story—based on a real event—of how, in recognition of his poetic talents, Stevens gave Baudelaire his own waistcoat: 'un beau gilet, d'une couleur à la fois riche

---

[4] See Jérôme Thélot, 'Une citation de Shakespeare dans "Les Bons Chiens"', *Bulletin baudelairien*, 24: 2 (Dec. 1989), 61–6.
[5] See Richard D. E. Burton, 'Baudelaire's Indian Summer: A Reading of "Les Bons Chiens"', *Nineteenth-Century French Studies*, 22: 3–4 (1994), 466–86 (476–8).

et fanée, qui fait penser aux soleils d'automne, à la beauté des femmes mûres et aux étés de la Saint-Martin'.

In the poem this act of donation may perhaps be read as a cabaret version of the ceremony of coronation that inaugurated a new poet laureate on the Capitoline in Rome, the ceremony later re-enacted in honour of Petrarch and imagined by Staël for her heroine at the beginning of *Corinne*. But instead of a laurel wreath—let alone a halo—a waistcoat is here the ritual symbol of poetic authority (perhaps serving also to recall Gautier's famous waistcoat worn at the so-called 'battle' on the occasion of the first night of *Hernani* in 1830). Thus the poet of 'Les Bons Chiens' begins his poem by rejecting the fancy credentials that might be bestowed by 'la muse académique'; continues by comparing himself not to those great writers Virgil and Theocritus but to the humble shepherds in their eclogues who, as a reward for singing their bucolic songs, could look forward to 'un bon fromage, une flûte du meilleur faiseur, ou une chèvre aux mamelles gonflées'; and ends by comparing himself to Pietro Aretino (1492–1556), the Renaissance poet and writer of comedies, best known for his political satire, sixteen sonnets on lust (the *Sonetti lussuriosi*, written to accompany a series of engravings illustrating sexual positions), and the exciting private life of an outlaw (homosexuality, blackmail, extortion, and numerous acts of physical violence). Aretino is reputed to have suffocated to death, throttled by an excess of laughter.

Another 'farceur incomparable', therefore, or so it would seem—like the poet of *Le Spleen de Paris* who ends his last poem in the collection by repeating his description of the 'beautiful' waistcoat. For the waistcoat is beautiful not so much because of how it looks—'d'une couleur à la fois riche et fanée'—but because of its effect, because of the things this colour brings to mind: autumn sunshine, beautiful women of a certain age, Indian summers... Only this time the order has changed slightly, as have the details, so that the collection ends on a particularly suggestive note:

> Et toutes les fois que le poète endosse le gilet du peintre, il est contraint de penser aux bons chiens, aux chiens philosophes, aux étés de la Saint-Martin et à la beauté des femmes très mûres.

The beautiful women are now '*très* mûres' (my emphasis), no doubt in part for the rhythm of the sentence but also because their 'maturity', indeed their 'ripeness', is the source of their power over the poet's imagination. Compare 'Un cheval de race', where the older woman ('Le Temps et l'Amour l'ont marquée de leurs griffes') is all the more beautiful: 'Elle est vraiment laide [...] squelette même; mais aussi elle est breuvage, magistère, sorcellerie! en somme, elle est exquise.' For in the nearness of the end lies a new beginning: 'Elle aime comme on aime en automne; on dirait que les approches de l'hiver allument dans son cœur un feu nouveau.' The waistcoat in 'Les Bons Chiens' is thus a kind of visual emblem of the 'fête intérieure' celebrated in the prose poem 'Le Crépuscule du soir' and throughout *Le Spleen de Paris*: of the festival celebrated by an imagination set alight by the imminence of darkness and death, and exploding in a firework display of creativity and poetic performance.

As such, this waistcoat, now so proudly worn, constitutes a symbolic costume for the poet, his own more suggestive and poetic equivalent of the traditionally idiotic costume worn by the buffoon in 'Le Fou et la Vénus', 'un costume éclatant et ridicule, coiffé de cornes et de sonnettes'. (Fancioulle's, by contrast, is never described in 'Une mort héroïque'). Less a stand-up comic and more a painter of modern life, this poet shows throughout *Le Spleen de Paris* how it is possible to think in pictures. As foregrounded in particular by 'Les Yeux des pauvres' (and as was true of 'Tableaux parisiens'), eyes are everywhere in these poems, reflecting the world and expressing the response and/or intentions of the viewer: be it the eyes of the clown in 'Le Fou et la Vénus' ('Et ses yeux disent:—"Je suis le dernier et le plus solitaire des hommes"') or 'ces subtiles et terribles *mirettes*' of the Idole in 'La Chambre double', 'que je reconnais à leur effrayante malice!'; the 'œil profond' of the second widow in 'Les Veuves', the 'regard profond, inoubliable' of the 'vieux saltimbanque' or the time-telling eye of a cat in 'L'Horloge'; the ravenous eyes of the children in 'Le Gâteau'; or, in 'Les Vocations', the extraordinary look in the eye of those who have caught a glimpse of their destiny—be it the second boy, who 'observait avec une fixité étonnante je ne sais quel point du ciel', or the third, who 'avait, en faisant son récit, les yeux écarquillés par une sorte de stupéfaction de ce qu'il éprouvait encore', or the fourth, who 'avait dans son œil et dans son front ce je ne sais quoi de précocement fatal qui éloigne généralement la sympathie'. In many of the poems the simple act of seeing is invested in this way with an enormous power of thought.

And thereby we, too, are invited to see. As epitomized by 'Les Fenêtres', many images are exhibited before the visual imagination of the reader: street scenes, like the New Year festivities of 'Un plaisant' or the fair in 'Le Vieux Saltimbanque'; the public parks of 'Le Fou et la Vénus' and 'Les Veuves'; the graveyard of 'Le Tir et le cimetière'; the mountain scenery of 'Le Gâteau' or the exotic setting of 'La Belle Dorothée'; interiors, as in 'La Chambre double' and 'L'Invitation au voyage' (where the room is hung with 'des peintures béates, calmes et profondes, comme les âmes de artistes qui les créèrent'), or the basement gambling den of 'Le Joueur généreux'. As 'Les Projets' demonstrates, the creative imagination can fashion its own landscapes and settings as a way of 'thinking' desire. Or as 'Le Désir de peindre' also shows, the 'désir de peindre' constitutes a way to 'peindre le désir'. Indeed that is what desire is, an imaginary journey to an imagined place of possession, as in 'Any where out of the world (N'importe où hors du monde)' where the destination matters less than the leaving. 'Cette vie est un hôpital où chaque malade est possédé du désir de changer de lit.' Here is the 'mal de vivre' of *Les Fleurs du Mal*, the world of 'Spleen [i]' in which restless desire reduces us to the condition of a mangy cat striving to settle its bony frame on the cold tiles of the floor or of a dead poet whose ghost 'erre dans la gouttière' like the very poor rhymester we can hear that he has become. But this 'mal de vivre' is a problem that can be alleviated by the imagining of alternatives, by accepting the restlessness as part of our condition and turning its destructive dynamic into creative momentum: Lisbon? Rotterdam? Indonesia? Finland? The North Pole?! 'N'importe où! n'importe où! pourvu que ce soit hors de ce monde!' As the poet asserts in 'Les Fenêtres', to see and imagine is to think and feel our situation in the world: 'Qu'importe ce que peut être la réalité placée hors de moi, si elle m'a aidé à vivre, à sentir que je suis et ce que je suis?' Like looking at that tiny sail in 'Le "Confiteor" de l'artiste', shimmering far away on the blue horizon 'et qui par sa petitesse et son isolement imite mon irrémédiable existence, mélodie monotone de la houle'... as though our own lonely little life resembled a sailing boat launched like a toy upon the musical waters of time. For sound, too, is a way of thinking 'le mal de vivre' and the beauty of desire, of beauty as 'la promesse du bonheur'.

Music, or the Beauty of Shape

un mystique fandango

('Le Thyrse')

As a symbol of poetic authority, here conferred by a fellow-artist, the waistcoat of 'Les Bons Chiens' recalls that other intriguing symbol of authority presented in *Le Spleen de Paris*, the thyrsus. In the prose poem entitled 'Le Thyrse', first published in December 1863 and dedicated to the Hungarian-born pianist and composer Franz Liszt (1811–86), the poet begins at once by explaining the title: 'Qu'est-ce qu'un thyrse? Selon le sens moral et poétique, c'est un emblème sacerdotal dans la main des prêtres ou des prêtresses célébrant la divinité dont ils sont les interprètes et les serviteurs.' But immediately he takes pains to demystify this sacred object: 'Mais physiquement ce n'est qu'un bâton, un pur bâton, perche à houblon, tuteur de vigne, sec, dur et droit.' Yet then in turn, through the richness of his own description, he transforms the thyrsus into something much more than just a stick, no longer a sacerdotal staff but the emblem of an erotic dance of geometric shapes. Indeed it is 'une gloire', the sacred symbol of Christian iconography, akin to 'une auréole', featuring a radiant sunburst and denoting the presence of God. But in this case the 'divinité' in question is beauty, 'déesse et immortelle':

> Autour de ce bâton, dans des méandres capricieux, se jouent et folâtrent des tiges et des fleurs, celles-ci sinueuses et fuyardes, celles-là penchées comme des cloches ou des coupes renversées. Et une gloire étonnante jaillit de cette complexité de lignes et de couleurs, tendres ou éclatantes. Ne dirait-on pas que la ligne courbe et

la spirale font leur cour à la ligne droite et dansent autour dans une muette adoration? Ne dirait-on pas que toutes ces corolles délicates, tous ces calices, explosions de senteurs et de couleurs, exécutent un mystique fandango autour du bâton hiératique?

Many readers of the poem[6] have noted the similarity between this description and Baudelaire's account in his dedicatory letter to Houssaye of what he was ostensibly trying to achieve through this new form of the prose poem: 'le miracle d'une prose poétique, musicale, sans rythme et sans rime, assez souple et assez heurtée pour s'adapter aux mouvements lyriques de l'âme, aux ondulations de la rêverie, aux soubresauts de la conscience?' Moreover the opposites foregrounded here in the letter and in 'Le Thyrse' appear to map easily onto further well-known Baudelairean dualities: 'vaporisation' and 'centralisation', 'surnaturalisme' and 'ironie', 'idéal' and 'spleen'... and poetry and prose. But why choose to honour Liszt with this particular emblem? Baudelaire had encountered the thyrsus in De Quincey's *Suspiria de profondis* and worked it into his translation-cum-paraphrase of the same author's *Confessions of an Opium-Eater* in *Les Paradis artifiels* (i. 444, 515), where it serves as an image for the (self-diagnosed) digressive character of De Quincey's thought processes, especially under the influence of drugs: 'cette pensée est le *thyrse* dont il a si plaisamment parlé avec la candeur d'un vagabond qui se connaît bien' (i. 515). As in 'Le Thyrse', but here in metaphorical application to De Quincey's cast of mind, Baudelaire insists on the simplicity of the stick itself in comparison with its decoration: 'Le sujet [of De Quincey's réflexions] n'a pas d'autre valeur que celle d'un bâton sec et nu; mais les rubans, les pampres et les fleurs peuvent être, par leurs entrelacements folâtres, une richesse précieuse pour les yeux. La pensée de De Quincey n'est pas seulement sinueuse; le mot n'est pas assez fort: elle est naturellement spirale' (i. 515). But in applying the figure of the thyrsus to the musical art of Liszt, Baudelaire not only calls attention to its traditional function as an 'emblème sacerdotal' but also mobilizes the distinction between stick and decoration to articulate the profound tensions which he sees as constitutive of Liszt's genius and, by extension, of the creative process itself. The stick is no longer just a stick and no longer the less interesting partner in the dance. It now *is* the thyrsus and an emblem of Liszt's creative will, around which the imagination twirls its gorgeous shapes like variations on a musical theme, or like an orchestra playing in response to a conductor's baton and his interpretation of a score:

Le bâton, c'est votre volonté, droite, ferme et inébranlable; les fleurs, c'est la promenade de votre fantaisie autour de votre volonté; c'est l'élément féminin

---

[6] For a summary see Stephens, *Baudelaire's Prose Poems*, 36–7, and n. 16. For Johnson's deconstructive reading of 'Le Thyrse' as a model of difference, see her *Défigurations du langage poétique*, 62–5.

exécutant autour du mâle ses prestigieuses pirouettes. Ligne droite et ligne arabesque, intention et expression, roideur de la volonté, sinuosité du verbe, unité du but, variété des moyens, amalgame tout-puissant et indivisible du génie[.]

In Graeco-Roman mythology the thyrsus was a sacred wand or staff held by Dionysus/Bacchus himself or by officiants of his cult, whose followers, the so-called Bacchantes (including satyrs and maenads), would dance and carouse in celebration of the god of wine and fertility and to the accompaniment of music. Thus also Liszt:

> Le thyrse est la représentation de votre étonnante dualité, maître puissant et vénéré, cher Bacchant de la Beauté mystérieuse et passionnée. Jamais nymphe exaspérée par l'invincible Bacchus ne secoua son thyrse sur les têtes de ses compagnes affolées avec autant d'énergie et de caprice que vous agitez votre génie sur les cœurs de vos frères.

A virtuoso pianist, Liszt was also a composer and, as this image of a brandished thyrsus recalls, a conductor. Among his most famous works were the *Hungarian Rhapsodies*, composed mostly between 1846 and 1853, in which he sought to incorporate (and in a sense also to conserve) tunes and other elements from the folk—and particularly gypsy—music of his native Hungary. In addition, in 1859, he published (in French) *Des Bohémiens et de leur musique en Hongrie* in which he describes—and indeed seeks verbally to imitate[7]—this gypsy music. In 1861 Wagner introduced Baudelaire to Liszt, who gave him a copy of this book by way of reciprocating the poet's earlier gift of *Les Paradis artificiels*, and Liszt's descriptions of gypsy music, and in particular of the art of improvisation (for which as a pianist he himself was renowned), have been shown to inform some of Baudelaire's own descriptive language both in 'Le Thyrse' and in the narrative account of the itinerant musicians in the latter part of 'Les Vocations' (which immediately precedes 'Le Thyrse' in *Le Spleen de Paris* but was first published two months after it).[8] For Liszt, as for the poet of 'Les Vocations', these musicians represent what the composer himself calls the 'out-law', describing them as follows: 'Les Zigeuner ne connaissent pas plus de dogmes, de lois, de règle, de discipline en musique qu'ailleurs. Tout leur est bon, tout leur est permis, pourvu

---

[7] See Sarga Moussa, 'Les Bohémiens de Liszt', in *Le Mythe des Bohémiens dans la littérature et les arts en Europe* (Paris: L'Harmattan, 2008), 223–42.

[8] See Christian Doumet, 'Céder ou ne pas céder aux "Vocations" (Baudelaire face à la musique)', in Pierre Sorlin, Marie-Claire Ropars-Wuilleumier, Michell Lagny (eds), *L'Art et l'hybride* (Paris: Presses universitaires de Vincennes, 2001), 25–52; and Barbara Bohac, 'Baudelaire et Liszt: Le Génie de la rhapsodie', *Romantisme*, 151 (2011), 87–99.

que cela leur plaise.'⁹ Hence in 'Les Vocations' the attraction which they hold for the fourth boy in 'Les Vocations': 'Il m'a souvent semblé que mon plaisir serait d'aller toujours droit devant moi, sans savoir où, sans que personne s'en inquiète, et de voir des pays nouveaux.'

The errancy and 'lawlessness' of these travelling players is reflected in the improvisatory nature of their music, and in particular of the rhapsody. For Barbara Bohac, therefore, 'Le Thyrse' constitutes a celebration of Liszt as 'le génie de la rhapsodie', of Liszt who had himself for several years led a similarly itinerant life touring Europe as a celebrated pianist. For her the multiple intertextual links to Liszt's book that are present in Baudelaire's prose poem, and especially the imagery of sinuous, spiralling flora, are the poet's way of representing 'la parenté profonde entre la musique du compositeur et celle des Bohémiens, toutes deux gouvernées par le libre jeu de la fantaisie'.¹⁰ She notes nevertheless the discrepancy between Liszt's celebration of the rhapsodic or improvisatory nature of gypsy music and Baudelaire's lifelong rejection of the idea of poetic 'inspiration', and seeks to resolve the discrepancy:

> Si le feuillage sinueux du thyrse peut figurer la composante bohémienne, ou hongroise, de l'œuvre de Liszt, la ligne droite lui donne une allure plus baudelairienne. Le thyrse devient donc le parfait symbole de deux fraternités spirituelles: celle qui unit Liszt aux 'Zigeuner' et celle qui unit Baudelaire à Liszt. Cette dernière passe par un culte de la volonté, l'idéal d'un art à la fois libre, rebelle aux règles, et éminemment lucide, maîtrisé.¹¹

Finally, she proposes a parallel between Liszt's aim to collect and preserve gypsy music (both in his book and in the *Hungarian Rhapsodies*) and Baudelaire's recording of modern life in *Le Spleen de Paris*. Noting that the word 'r(h)apsodique' derives from the figure of the rhapsode, the professional performer of epic poetry in ancient Greece, and recalling Baudelaire's early ambition to 'rechercher quel peut être le côté épique de la vie moderne' (*Salon de 1846*, ii. 493), she sees Baudelaire's prose poems as Parisian rhapsodies:

> Avec sa prose poétique ondoyante et soumise au caprice de la fantaisie, *Le Spleen de Paris* pourrait esquisser par ses 'tronçons' une autre épopée que l'épopée bohémienne, l'épopée de la civilisation moderne, dont Paris serait le berceau et Baudelaire le rhapsode.¹²

---

⁹ *Des Bohémiens et de leur musique en Hongrie* (Paris: Boudilliat, 1859), 221. Quoted by Bohac, 'Baudelaire et Liszt', 91. For 'out-law', see *Des Bohémiens*, 94.
¹⁰ Bohac, 'Baudelaire et Liszt', 95.   ¹¹ Bohac, 'Baudelaire et Liszt', 97.
¹² Bohac, 'Baudelaire et Liszt', 98.

But the figure of the 'rhapsode' is central to 'Le Thyrse' for another reason also. In the final phrases of the eulogy that takes up the last paragraph of the poem, addressed to Liszt himself, the poet celebrates him as 'chantre de la Volupté et de l'Angoisse éternelles, philosophe, poète et artiste'. In part this alludes to the striking co-presence of joy and sadness that Liszt himself saw as especially characteristic of gypsy music and which at the end of 'Les Vocations' the boy, too, particularly notes: 'une musique si surprenante qu'elle donne envie tantôt de danser, tantôt de pleurer, ou de faire les deux à la fois'. And clearly a parallel may be seen here with the ubiquitous co-presence of 'idéal' and 'spleen' in Baudelaire's own work. But by calling Liszt a 'chantre' and a 'poète' the poet of 'Le Thyrse' is indeed here affiliating this musical artist to the ancient tradition of the poet as public singer, as rhapsode, and in so doing he may be recalling the long essay entitled 'De la situation des artistes, et de leur condition dans la sociéte' that the 23-year-old Liszt published in six instalments in the Gazette musicale de Paris between May and October 1835.[13] In essence he complained that musicians were treated as mere entertainers and as society's servants and proposed instead, robustly (and in capital letters), that musicians should henceforth regard themselves as artists entrusted with a sacred mission: 'Dans la certitude des convictions que nous avons acquises, nous crions sans relâche qu'une grande œuvre, qu'une grande MISSION religieuse et sociale est *imposée* aux artistes.' Explicitly he appeals to ancient precedent: 'En contemplant les magnifiques destinées que le génie de l'antiquité assignait à la musique; en évoquant les législateurs et les philosophes illustres qui instruisirent les peuples au son de la lyre, nous nous sommes demandés "quelle pouvait être la cause de cette déchéance, de cette abdication sociale de la musique moderne, et comment ceux qui étaient les premiers avaient consenti à se faire les derniers?"' Then, so that no one shall be left in any doubt as to his meaning and intentions, he proceeds to set out a missionary programme that aligns musicians explicitly with ideals of moral and artistic progress proclaimed by Germaine de Staël some three decades earlier and subsequently espoused by Hugo and other 'mages' and 'prophètes' in the domain of the arts:

> Or, afin qu'on ne nous reproche point d'employer ces mots au hasard, dans un sens vague ou indéterminée,—pour traduire d'ailleurs d'une manière efficace les sympathies générales que le parallélisme ininterrompu du progrès de l'art et du progrès moral et intellectuel des artistes ne fait qu'accroître et rendre chaque jour plus vives;—pour aider enfin de notre mieux la réalisation de cet avenir que tous

---

[13] For a detailed account of this essay see Ralph P. Locke, 'Liszt on the Artist in Society', in Christopher H. Gibbs and Dana Gooley (eds), *Franz Liszt and his World* (Princeton: Princeton University Press, 2006), 292–302. On the context see Joseph-Marc Bailbé, 'De Liszt à Berlioz: Réflexions sur la condition de l'artiste-musicien', *Romantisme*, 57 (1987), 7–16.

pressentent, que tous veulent, nous appelons TOUS LES MUSICIENS, tous ceux qui ont un sentiment large et profond de l'art, à établir entre eux un lien commun, fraternel, religieux, à *instaurer* une *société universelle*, ayant pour but (1) De provoquer, d'encourager et d'activer le mouvement ascendant, l'extension et le développement indéfini de la musique; (2) D'élever et d'ennoblir la condition des artistes, en remédiant aux abus, aux injustices qui les frappent, et en déterminant les mesures nécessaires dans l'intérêt de leur dignité.[14]

'Musicians of the world, unite!' At the end of his long article, by way of summarizing earlier instalments, Liszt itemizes his practical recommendations: the introduction of music into the curriculum of primary schools and its 'propagation' in other types of school, which would entail '*la création* d'une nouvelle musique religieuse'; the reform of church music, and particularly plainchant; music festivals to bring philharmonic societies together as in England and Germany; opera productions, orchestral concerts, and chamber music recitals, all to be organized by the Conservatoire; 'une ÉCOLE PROGRESSIVE [d]e musique', founded by 'des artistes éminents' and separate from the Conservatoire, with branches in the provinces; a new professorial chair in the history and theory of music; the publication of affordable musical scores by every composer, whether ancient or modern, and illustrating the entire history of music from popular song to Beethoven's Ninth Symphony, this series of published scores to be called the 'PANTHÉON MUSICAL'. The very first of these recommendations is for the inauguration of a new musical competition comprising three categories of music (religious, dramatic, symphonic) to be held every five years in the Louvre, lasting a month, with the winning entries to be published at the expense of the state: 'En d'autres termes,—la fondation d'un nouveau MUSÉE', by which Liszt means a 'museum' in its original sense of a place, sometimes a temple, dedicated to the muses, and set aside for the performance and study of the arts.[15]

Of all these recommendations, clearly imprinted with the model and terminology of the poet-musician in ancient Greece but also heavily influenced by Saint-Simonianism and the teachings of Liszt's close friend, the radical Roman Catholic priest the abbé de Lamennais (1782–1854), the most controversial was the call for new forms of religious music.[16] Liszt believed that such innovation could serve to restore religious fervour by conveying the messages of a re-energized, humanitarian Christian faith in the freshly rethought musical languages of symphonic and operatic art. 'Chantre [...] philosophe, poète et artiste': Liszt was not 'just' a pianist, and Baudelaire is clearly aware of this other, 'missionary' role advocated,

---

[14] *Gazette musicale de Paris*, 2e année, no. 41 (11 Oct. 1835), 333.
[15] *Gazette musicale de Paris*, 2e année, no. 41 (11 Oct. 1835), 333.
[16] See Locke, 'Liszt on the Artist in Society', 293.

adopted, and performed by the composer of the *Hungarian Rhapsodies*. So his prose poem bestows the thyrsus on someone who can be compared to priests and priestesses 'célébrant la divinité dont ils sont les interprètes et les serviteurs'. But in Baudelaire's tribute Liszt's 'divinity' is very much music itself rather than the Christian god worshipped by Lamennais or, in their own particular ways, by those other poet-prophets Chateaubriand, Lamartine, and Hugo. The thyrsus is the conductor's baton by means of which he directs the performance of this 'divine' music with the 'volonté, droite, ferme et inébranlable' of a fervent adept.

Rather than representing (as Bohac suggests) a combination of Baudelairean 'maîtrise' with Liszt's rhapsodic improvisation, the thyrsus can be seen instead to figure the perplexing duality that lies at the heart of all poetic and artistic production, the duality of what the poet calls 'intention et expression'. Does the artwork come unbidden to the artist, or is it consciously created? In 'Le Thyrse' the poet asks this question *twice* and in slightly different terms:

> Et quel est, cependant, le mortel imprudent, qui osera décider si les fleurs et les pampres ont été faits pour le bâton, ou si le bâton n'est que le prétexte pour montrer la beauté des pampres et des fleurs?
> Ligne droite et ligne arabesque, intention et expression, roideur de la volonté, sinuosité du verbe, unité du but, variété des moyens, amalgame tout-puissant et indivisible du génie, quel analyste aura le détestable courage de vous diviser et de vous séparer?

Has the beauty of the flowers and the vines been made, or is it found, already there and just waiting to be displayed? Is the process of artistic creation a straight line of willed and conscious intention, actively directed at a particular target, or is it instead the more or less passive provision of support for a directionless yet self-regulating performance of diverse shapes and sundry arabesques? In this 'mystique fandango', just how—as Yeats was later to ask in 'Among School Children'—'can we know the dancer from the dance?' As the use of the word 'verbe' (in the sense of 'language') here suggests, the poet is talking as much about poetry as he is about the 'language' of music (and in ancient Greece poetry and music were one and the same). Moreover the very repetition of the question— albeit with 'imprudence' replaced by 'détestable courage' as the only plausible basis for trying to distinguish between baton and vine—calls attention to the nature of 'Le Thyrse' itself as a work of literary and symbolic art. The dash that separates 'vos frères' from 'Le bâton, c'est votre volonté' is a visual hinge connecting the two parts of a diptych (or implying a pause before a musical reprise?) which itself separates out the literal from the symbolic. In the first part we move from a factual description of the thyrsus, through the rhetorical question that states the impossibility of attributing priority of importance to either the stick or the vine, to a comparison of the thyrsus (addressed directly to the dedicatee himself) with the 'duality' of Liszt (explicitly) and (implicitly) with his conductor's baton.

In the second part we move similarly from a symbolic description of the thyrsus as a figure for the duality of Liszt, through the rhetorical question about the analyst, to a further direct address to Liszt (ending in 'je vous salue en l'immortalité') as a ubiquitous European genius and as both itinerant musical performer and a writer of books. In this final paragraph, the emblem of 'la gloire' said to burst forth from the thyrsus is now equated with Liszt's piano-playing ('où les pianos chantent votre gloire'), while the duality of 'énergie' and 'caprice' with which at the end of the first part he was said to conduct here returns in his double role as performer and writer: 'improvisant', 'confiant au papier vos méditations abstruses'.

'Le Thyrse' is thus itself a nexus of dualities in which the literal and the symbolic, the musician and the poet, the intended and the improvised, the willed and the capricious, the prosaic and the poetic perform their own 'mystique fandango' of ever-shifting geometric shapes (for example, of parallel and opposition or of thematic assertion and repetitive variation). Above all the text demonstrates tight structural design and verbal control, and for this reason we may perhaps infer an implicit note of warning against the dangers of rhapsodic improvisation. In the *Salon de 1859*, as we saw earlier, Baudelaire expresses his reservations about 'fantaisie', or what we might call a freewheeling imagination:

> car la fantaisie est d'autant plus dangereuse qu'elle est plus facile et plus ouverte; dangereuse comme la poésie en prose, comme le roman, elle ressemble à l'amour qu'inspire une prostituée et qui tombe bien dans la puérilité ou dans la bassesse; dangereuse comme toute liberté absolue. (ii. 644)

Fantasy thus represents a form of promiscuity which is the opposite of art, a temporary and capricious infatuation rather than something more constructed and lasting. Above all, it simply mirrors the disorder of the world rather than consciously and wilfully creating patterns in the manner which Baudelaire believes essential:

> Mais la fantaisie est vaste comme l'univers multiplié par tous les êtres pensants qui l'habitent. Elle est la première chose venue interprétée par le premier venu; et, si celui-là n'a pas l'âme qui jette une lumière magique et surnaturelle sur l'obscurité naturelle des choses, elle est une inutilité horrible, elle est la première venue souillée par le premier venu. Ici donc, plus d'analogie, sinon de hasard; mais au contraire trouble et contraste, un champ bariolé par l'absence d'une culture régulière. (ii. 644–5)

In 'Le Thyrse', by contrast, we see how intentional analogy is the lord of the dance, a creative (erotic) duality from which all manner of 'correspondance', or interconnection, derives. For this reason 'Le Thyrse' also constitutes a model for the prose poem as Baudelaire believes it should be: not just as a combination of lyrical 'ondulations de la rêverie' with ironic, deflating, and 'unpoetic' 'soubresauts de la conscience', but a combination of the contingent and the constructed. Where the orderliness of verse poetry has difficulty in accommodating the disorderly in life (and even in 'Tableaux parisiens'), prose poetry can perform and 'empathize' with this disorderliness, but at the same time it must above all (because total licence is dangerous) keep a tight hold on its material through the construction of verbal and structural patterns, the 'beautiful ideas' of the kaleidoscope. Like the verse poem, the prose poem must combine content and form in such a way that they become inextricable one from the other. The thyrsus is thus also the symbol of the 'poetic idea' in which 'intention' and 'expression' are themselves inseparable—and of a world of things that think 'musicalement et pittoresquement'. For all that 'rhapsody' may suggest inspiration and improvisation, its etymology—to sew a song—tells us that a text must always be carefully stitched, or a fabric artfully woven from the music of life.[17]

Life's Harmonies, or the Beauty of Rhythm

les musiques de la vie

('Déjà')

Le rythme est nécessaire au développement de l'idée de beauté, qui est le but le plus grand et le plus noble du poème.

('Notes nouvelles sur Poe', ii. 329)

In January 1866 Baudelaire wrote to Sainte-Beuve from Brussels and described how, despite his increasingly poor health, he was attempting to continue with his work on *Le Spleen de Paris*. Citing the example of Sainte-Beuve's own *Vie, poésies et pensées de Joseph Delorme* (1829), he hopes that one day he will be able to reveal 'un nouveau Joseph Delorme accrochant sa pensée rapsodique [*sic*] à chaque accident de sa flânerie et tirant de chaque objet une morale désagréable'. But, he says, the more 'accidental' the topic, the more difficult the creative challenge: 'que les bagatelles, quand on veut les exprimer d'une manière à la fois pénétrante et légère, sont donc difficiles à faire!' (*Corr.*, ii. 583). Here Baudelaire's use of the term 'rhapsodique' needs to be read in the light of his explicit gloss in *Les Paradis artificiels* (i. 428), where in its application to the experience of smoking hashish the

---

[17] On Mallarmé's subsequent enactment of the analogy between poetry and needlework in *Un coup de Dés*, see my 'Mallarmé and Poetry: Stitching the Random', in Christopher Prendergast (ed.), *A History of Modern French Literature: From the Sixteenth Century to the Twentieth Century* (Princeton and Oxford: Princeton University Press, 2017), 495–513.

word describes both a benefit and a very real danger: 'le mot "rhapsodique", qui définit si bien un train de pensées suggéré et commandé par le monde extérieur et le hasard des circonstances'. Baudelaire has borrowed the word from a character (Augustus Bedloe) in one of Poe's stories (*A Tale of the Ragged Mountains*), who describes the power of opium to 'revêtir tout le monde extérieur d'une intensité d'intérêt' and to produce 'tout un monde d'inspirations, une procession magnifique et bigarrée de pensées désordonnées et rhapsodiques'. For Baudelaire this 'rhapsodic' effect is common to both opium and hashish, but he argues that it is much stronger in the case of hashish: 'Ici, le raisonnement n'est plus qu'une épave à la merci de tous les courants, et le train de pensées est *infiniment plus* accéléré et plus *rhapsodique*'. Opium, he says, is 'un séducteur paisible', where hashish is 'un démon désordonné'.

In terms of Baudelaire's own artistry in *Le Spleen de Paris* it is clear that the benign 'rhapsodic' effect of imaginative engagement with the surrounding world must be kept under control if the malign effects of freewheeling 'fantaisie'—notably, unconnectedness or merely random connections (cf. 'Ici donc, plus d'analogie, sinon de hasard')—are to be avoided. For him, beauty cannot be an accidental effect, though it can be an effect of the accidental where that effect has been artistically contextualized: for example, the fortuitous double meaning of 'bière', which serves to provoke serious conjecture about the relationship between 'ivresse' and death thanks to the context of the prose poem in which it is foregrounded ('Le Tir et le cimetière'). Accordingly, in many of these prose poems we find the poet's imagination engaged in a kind of two-way process whereby the imagination lays itself open to the world of experience (and the contingencies of language) and then actively shapes what the imagination receives, and yet in such a way that it becomes ambiguous—and ultimately both unknowable and irrelevant—whether the world itself or the work of the creative imagination may, as with the two partners in the dance of the thyrsus, claim priority. Thus, for example, in 'Le "Confiteor" de l'artiste' (as we have already partly seen), we find the poet describing a moment of beauty in just these terms. Towards the end of an autumn day he gazes with '[g]rand délice' at the immensity of the sea and the sky. Immersed in silence and solitude and the 'incomparable chasteté de l'azur!', he loses himself in the spectacle which in turn loses itself in him: 'toutes ces choses pensent par moi, ou je pense par elles (car dans la grandeur de la rêverie, le *moi* se perd vite!)'. And the effect is a new language of art quite different from the language of rational analysis: 'elles pensent, dis-je, mais musicalement et pittoresquement, sans arguties, sans syllogismes, sans déductions'.

This ability of the world to 'think' musically, as though independently of the poet, is featured elsewhere, and often in relation to the sea. In 'Le Crépuscule du soir' (as we have also partly seen) the moment of peace that follows the busyness of the day is figured as a union of human response and the visible external world: 'leurs pensées prennent maintenant les couleurs tendres et indécises du crépuscule'. The 'pauvres esprits fatigués du labeur de la journée' are absorbed into the scene before them, which now colours their thoughts. At once, and in parallel with this, the noise of the world's suffering is heard by the poet but similarly transformed, as it were by the art of the world itself: 'un grand hurlement, composé d'une foule de cris discordants, que l'espace transforme en une lugubre harmonie, comme celle de la marée qui monte ou d'une tempête qui s'éveille'. By contrast with 'Le "Confiteor" de l'artiste', where the artist 'confesses' his failure to sustain the intensity of his experience of beauty ('Ah! faut-il éternellement souffrir, ou fuir éternellement le beau?'), here the suffering belongs to the day and is replaced by the 'fête intérieure' of the nocturnal imagination.

In 'Déjà!' the experience is threefold and once again involves both the sea and a music of space. As a ship nears port the passengers are relieved at the prospect of journey's end, but for the poet the sight of land means saying goodbye to 'cette incomparable beauté' that derives from the extraordinarily *human* life of the sea and a concomitant, panoptic experience of time:

> Moi seul j'étais triste, inconcevablement triste. Semblable à un prêtre à qui on arracherait sa divinité, je ne pouvais, sans une navrante amertume, me détacher de cette mer si monstrueusement séduisante, de cette mer si infiniment variée dans son effrayante simplicité, et qui semble contenir en elle et représenter par ses jeux, ses allures, ses colères et ses sourires, les humeurs, les agonies et les extases de toutes les âmes qui ont vécu, qui vivent et qui vivront!

In the previous poem, 'Enivrez-vous', which itself follows 'Le Thyrse' and its account of the priesthood of beauty, the poet has already offered the advice encapsulated in the title as the best response to this transience of spiritual intoxication and the loss of beauty. It suffices, '[p]our n'être pas les esclaves martyrisés du Temps', to look the world in the face (as into the eye of a cat in 'L'Horloge') and ask it what the time is. For the answer will always be: 'Il est l'heure de s'enivrer!' Beauty is always waiting, ready to be found again as soon as lost. Here in 'Déjà', which takes up this theme of transience in its own title, the renewal of 'ivresse' is provided by the land itself, supposed cause of beauty's loss: 'une terre magnifique, éblouissante. Il semblait que les musiques de la vie s'en détachaient en un vague murmure, et que de ses côtes, riches en verdure de toute sorte, s'exhalait, jusqu'à plusieurs lieues, une délicieuse odeur de fleurs et de fruits.' As in 'Le Thyrse' the structure of the poem comprises a double tripartite sequence: for the passengers, from discontent through arrival ('Enfin!') to delight, and for the poet, from contentment through arrival ('*Déjà!*') to delight: two contrasting journeys towards a landfall that proves, in the last paragraph, to offer the same totality of sensual satisfaction for passengers and poet alike. Only by travelling can one arrive:

Cependant c'était la terre, la terre avec ses bruits, ses passions, ses commodités, ses fêtes; c'était une terre riche et magnifique, pleine de promesses, qui nous envoyait un mystérieux parfum de rose et de musc, et d'où les musiques de la vie nous arrivaient en un amoureux murmure.

The Étranger is now at one with 'nous' in an unBenjaminian world of commodity and festivity, united with his fellow-passengers and with humankind at large by a whispered language of love and the smell of roses. Recalling the 'muette adoration' at the centre of the 'mystique fandango' of 'Le Thyrse', here too is further evidence to support the poet's assertion in 'Les Foules' that '[l]e promeneur solitaire et pensif tire une singulière ivresse de cette universelle communion'. Where once Rousseau and Lamartine had communed with God through the divinely created beauty of nature, Baudelaire's poet communes—and communicates—with humanity through the medium of beauty itself: the 'musiques de la vie' to be seen in the infinite variety of the sea and to be heard coming off the land of human passions. This beauty is a beauty of effect, an effect registered by the poet's imagination and then both conveyed and further provoked by his own poetic language, composed in tune with the rhythms and harmonies of life that issue—'musicalement et pittoresquement'—from the world.

The polyphony that is such a feature of the deployment of the poetic 'je' in *Le Spleen de Paris* is itself a reflection of this form of communion—of community and communication—achieved through the agency of beauty. Just as in the performance of the poetic idea we cannot know the dancer from the dance, so we cannot distinguish any given poet-persona from the particular prose poem that gives it voice. The poetic 'je' is thus one of the many forms, one of the 'musiques de la vie', by which the prose poem shapes the contingencies of human experience into the *work* of art, and as such it is comparable with the other 'beautiful ideas' that comprise this kaleidoscope. Already we have noted how symmetry and number play their part in the structure of many of the poems. Witness, for example, the chiastically arranged paragraphs of 'Le Désespoir de la vieille' and the mirrored paragraphing of 'Chacun sa chimère', or the diptychs of 'La Chambre double' (two groups of nine paragraphs around a 'hinge' paragraph) and 'Le Thyrse'. Each doubling is a formal reflection of the 'irremediable' and inevitable passage from delight to disappointment that is synonymous with the passage of time itself and with 'le Mal' of our human condition. Other poems are even more clearly marked by number: three 'projects', four 'vocations', three 'temptations', four 'portraits de maîtresses', two widows, two hungry boys eager for 'cake', two little boys playing with toys (or a pet). Similarly, the titles themselves appear to treat the world of human experience as a numerical computation, be it single persons ('L'Étranger', 'La Belle Dorothée', 'Mademoiselle Bistouri') and single objects ('Le Gâteau', 'L'Horloge', 'La Corde'), or the pairings that (ironically) suggest the fables of La Fontaine ('Le Chien et le flacon', 'Le Fou et la Vénus', 'Le Tir et le cimetière'), or the several pluralities of people ('Les Foules', 'Les Veuves') and objects ('Les Fenêtres').

In the case of those poems that are mostly evidently narrative, such as 'Le Mauvais Vitrier', 'Le Gâteau', 'Une mort héroïque', 'La Corde', and 'Mademoiselle Bistouri', the traditional straight line of a story in the past tense is itself the 'shape' of the poem, but this shape is relativized as simply *one* way of figuring the geometry of our human experience (and in particular the experience of time) when set beside all the other poetic patterns and shapes in Le Spleen de Paris. In these poems human experience may be placed outside time ('L'Étranger') or else confronted with eternity ('L'Horloge'), or it may consist of individual moments: of exquisitely intense perception ('Le "Confiteor" de l'artiste'), of discord ('Les Yeux de pauvres') or transition ('Le Crépuscule du soir') or delight ('Un hémisphère dans une chevelure'); of anticipation ('Les Projets', 'Les Vocations') or retrospect ('Un plaisant'), of experiment ('Le Joujou du pauvre') or death ('Une mort héroïque'). But even when the poem seems particularly concerned to embed a sequence of moments within a narrative logic, another narrative shape may be forming itself in parallel, an allegory perhaps (as in 'Le Mauvais Vitrier', 'Le Gâteau', 'Une mort héroïque'), that requires a form of binocular reading through which we see the poem as another version of the 'double room'. Even in 'La Corde', than which, in the words of Steve Murphy, '[a]ucun poème du *Spleen de Paris* ne paraît plus profondément enraciné dans le réel',[18] a 'double-story' is evident in the implicit but insistent parallels between, on the one hand, the attitudes and behaviour of the protagonists, notably the child's parents, and, on the other hand, of the (evidently unreliable) narrator himself who demonstrates a singular lack of empathy and compassion.[19] In its depiction of illusion and hypocrisy the poem creates a kind of mirror-effect that renders the suicide of this boy every bit as puzzling—and therefore open to conjecture—as the death of Fancioulle or the dropping of a flowerpot. Indeed this example demonstrates particularly well how the deployment of multiple poet-narrators throughout Le Spleen de Paris can serve to 'shape' these poems by creating a quasi-kaleidoscopic array of shifting perspectives. In these ways some of Baudelaire's prose poems come close to exhibiting the complex, crafted shaping of narrative point-of-view to be found in the novels of Flaubert.

Given this idea that the world itself may 'think' musically, it is tempting to see the poetic idea of some of these poems as comprising specifically musicological structures. Clearly the form of the rhapsody itself—being a free composition in one single movement of exuberant or emotional tonality—might be thought to

---

[18] Murphy, *Logiques du dernier Baudelaire*, 551.
[19] See in particular Scott, *Baudelaire's 'Le Spleen de Paris'*, 181–8, where Scott analyses these parallels and summarizes earlier critical readings of the poem that reach a similar conclusion.

suit poems such as 'Enivrez-vous' or 'Un hémisphère dans une chevelure', while the traditional three-part structure of a sonata (exposition, development, recapitulation/resolution) might be seen reflected in a poem such as 'L'Invitation au voyage', which opens by stating the existence of the land of Cockaigne, develops this theme through varied description while also restating it ('Un vrai pays de Cocagne, te dis-je'), and then recapitulates it in a different 'key' by equating it with the poet's imagined lover ('Ne serais-tu pas encadrée dans ton analogie [...]?'). Moreover, this particular structure, loosely applied, might be seen also to inform those poems that begin by stating a 'truth' before either illustrating or refuting it with an anecdote or description and then drawing a conclusion. 'Le "Confiteor" de l'artiste' and 'Le Mauvais Vitrier' offer the clearest examples of this, but so also, to a lesser extent, do 'Les Foules', 'Les Veuves', 'Le Joujou du pauvre', 'La Solitude', 'La Corde', 'Les Fenêtres', 'Le Désir de peindre', and 'Any where out of the world'. And a similar structure underpins those poems that begin with a chance sighting or meeting and then go on to elaborate on the consequences and/or significance of this 'accident': as, for example, in 'Un plaisant', 'Chacun sa chimère', 'La Fausse Monnaie', 'Le Joueur généreux', 'Le Tir et le cimetière', and 'Mademoiselle Bistouri'.

Underlying these tripartite structures is the reassuring, 'harmonious' view of life as quite simply having a beginning, a middle, and an end, a sequence most comfortably provided in the traditional format of the fairy-story (here echoed ironically in 'Les Dons des fées' and 'Les Tentations'). By being taken from 'Once upon a time' to 'lived happily ever after', the reader (or listener) is taken on a safe and familiar journey through time towards a destination of perpetual happiness that is the opposite of death. But in *Le Spleen de Paris* the walks and journeys that are literally or metaphorically undertaken in the poems are never one-way. The beauty celebrated and created in them is the beauty of the to-and-fro, of the ceaseless coming and going of a gypsy *flânerie*: the beauty of errancy and itinerancy, of homelessness and restlessness, of wandering outside the pale—be it of genre, tradition, orthodoxy, assumption, or expectation. This beauty derives from a dynamic and provisional sense of plenitude and interest, of a festivity forever glimpsed, forever lost, and yet forever regained; from a delight in the dissonance and incongruities of life, in the comic and the bizarre and the capricious, in a dissonance at once honoured and yet accommodated within a set of harmonic relations taken also from life: like a double-room under a single roof. And nowhere in *Le Spleen de Paris* are these characteristics of Baudelairean beauty more succinctly celebrated than in 'Le Port', which might itself be read as the description of a prose poem:

Un port est un séjour charmant pour une âme fatiguée des luttes de la vie. L'ampleur du ciel, l'architecture mobile des nuages, les colorations changeantes de la mer, le scintillement des phares, sont un prisme merveilleusement propre à amuser les yeux sans jamais les lasser. Les formes élancées des navires, au gréement compliqué, auxquels la houle imprime des oscillations harmonieuses, servent à entretenir dans l'âme le goût du rythme et de la beauté. Et puis, surtout, il y a une sorte de plaisir mystérieux et aristocratique pour celui qui n'a plus ni curiosité ni ambition, à contempler, couché dans le belvédère ou accoudé sur le môle, tous ces mouvements de ceux qui partent et de ceux qui reviennent, de ceux qui ont encore la force de vouloir, le désir de voyager ou de s'enrichir.

This port is contemplated from the perspective of a certain kind of artist, of one who has taken a step back from the arena of passion ('une âme fatiguée des luttes de la vie', 'celui qui n'a plus ni curiosité ni ambition'), of an Étranger who is tired and yet never tires of seeing. The port itself constitutes an emblematic site and sight of comings and goings, and so of the relentless drive of human agency and human desire. As a hub of energy it is filled with change, variety, and movement. Here, gathered together within one single vista, are the amplitude of the sky (recalling 'l'expansion des choses infinies'), the architecture of the clouds beloved of the Étranger (and of the poet who neglects his soup), and the polychromatic lightshow of 'Le Crépuscule du soir'. Here, too, is the eurhythmic ship of *Fusées* and 'Le Beau Navire': reaching for the sky, powered by the complex thyrsus of its rigging, and conveyed upon the music of the waves.

Similar to a kaleidoscope, all these elements that make up the symbolic locus of the port are together described as a prism, a geometrically precise block of glass through which light is resolved into a spectrum of separate colours, transforming the undifferentiated glare of a blinding ennui into the individual details of a revelatory 'ivresse'.[20] Observed from a 'belvédère' (etymologically, a place from which to see something beautiful), this port is beauty itself: a therapeutic place of rest and benign stasis ('séjour', 'couché', 'accoudé') in which the human being, worn out by life, is emotionally and spiritually revived and sustained by the vitality of rhythm and harmonious movement ('des oscillations harmonieuses', 'le goût du rythme et de la beauté). 'Môle' derives etymologically from the Greek 'molos', meaning 'struggle', coming then to mean a breakwater that protects against the force of the waves and also, within the context of Roman antiquities, a tomb.[21] So this port offers respite and security in the face of life's tumult and the approach of a death foretold by weariness. 'Charmant', 'merveilleusement propre', this port of beauty is a source of magic and miracle, and it produces the most particular effect, 'une sorte de plaisir mystérieux et aristocratique': an effect that is at once 'mysterious', because elusive and (etymologically) like a sacred truth not to be divulged;

---

[20] Cf. Mallarmé's comment on *Un coup de Dés*: 'comme il ne s'agit pas, ainsi que toujours, de traits sonores réguliers ou vers—plutôt, de subdivisions prismatiques de l'Idée' (*Œuvres complètes*, ed. Marchal, i. 391).
[21] See *Dictionnaire historique de la langue française*, ed. Alain Rey, under 'môle'.

and 'aristocratic' because (etymologically) ruled by the best—by the government of the imagination. In this way the port manifests the three principal attributes of the beauty of Baudelaire—desire, melancholy, and conjecture: 'C'est quelque chose d'ardent et de triste, quelque chose d'un peu vague, laissant carrière à la conjecture.' And to and from this port, as we learn at the end of 'L'Invitation au voyage', there are always further journeys for a poet to make, whether in verse or in prose, the journeys of an imagination borne up by the buoyancy of beauty:

> C'est encore toi, ces grands fleuves et ces canaux tranquilles. Ces énormes navires qu'ils charrient, tout chargés de richesses, et d'où montent les chants monotones de la manœuvre, ce sont mes pensées qui dorment ou qui roulent sur ton sein. Tu les conduis doucement vers la mer qui est l'Infini, tout en réfléchissant les profondeurs du ciel dans la limpidité de ta belle âme;—et quand, fatigués par la houle et gorgés des produits de l'Orient, ils rentrent au port natal, ce sont encore mes pensées enrichies qui reviennent de l'Infini vers toi.

Conclusion
Beauty and the Poet as Alternative Lawgiver

> le beau multiforme et versicolore, qui se meut dans les spirales infinies de la vie.
> (*Exposition universelle*, ii. 578)
>
> Tâchez de concevoir un *beau banal*!
> (*Exposition universelle*, ii. 578)

Beauty

> nous avons créé à notre usage un jardin de vraie beauté.
> ('Le Poème du hachisch', i. 441)

I have attempted in this book to display a Baudelaire who engages throughout his work, in both theory and practice, with the purpose of poetry in the world. For him the fundamental role of poetry, and of art in general, is to instigate 'beauty'—to capture, to create, and to provoke in his reader a particular and exceptional viewing-point, like the belvedere in 'Le Port'. The function of poetry, and of art in general, lies in the capacity to provide structures of perception and understanding—'legislations'—with which, from this belvedere, the reader of poetry and the receiver of art may articulate their own relationship with the world from within the especial circumstances of their own lives. Beauty for Baudelaire resides simultaneously in the phenomenal world itself and in the nature of our response both to that world and to works of art that represent it. As such his work constitutes 'that fully realized poetry' later defined by Seamus Heaney as 'a poetry where the co-ordinates of the imagined thing correspond to and allow us to contemplate the complex burden of our own experience'.[1] The beauty of Baudelaire comprises 'correspondances' that lie not between nature and heaven but between us and the world.

---

[1] In 'The Redress of Poetry', his inaugural lecture as Oxford Professor of Poetry, in *The Redress of Poetry* (London and Boston: Faber and Faber, 1995), 1–16 (10).

Central to these 'objective' and 'subjective' modes of beauty is harmony—'cette grande loi d'harmonie générale' (ii. 626): harmony as a pattern of combination that attracts and holds human attention by juxtaposing movement and stasis, complex diversity and a single shape, in unique and surprising ways: *'le beau est toujours bizarre'* (ii. 578). Hence, for example, the beauty of the sea: 'Douze ou quatorze lieues (sur le diamètre), douze ou quatorze lieues de liquide en mouvement suffisent pour donner la plus haute idée de beauté qui soit offerte à l'homme sur son habitacle transitoire.'[2] Herein, too, lies the 'charme infini et mystérieux' to be derived from observing a ship under sail, as it is described in *Fusées*, f. 22 and which has served throughout this book as an eloquent expression of Baudelaire's conception of beauty. First, this spectacle demonstrates 'la régularité et la symétrie qui sont un des besoins primordiaux de l'esprit humain, au même degré que la complication et l'harmonie', and, second, 'la multiplication successive et [...] la génération de toutes les courbes et figures imaginaires opérées dans l'espace par les éléments réels de l'objet'. Beauty is the geometry of human desire: 'L'idée poétique qui se dégage de cette opération du mouvement dans les lignes est l'hypothèse d'un être vaste, immense, compliqué, mais eurythmique, d'un animal plein de génie, souffrant et soupirant tous les soupirs et toutes les ambitions humaines.'[3]

Rather like the ship itself, jibing and tacking, Baudelaire's ideas about the role and function of poetry and art underwent a series of significant shifts and metamorphoses in the course of a writing career that nevertheless spanned little more than a quarter of a century. In his art criticism from the mid-1840s onwards, as we saw in Part I, beauty for him lies very much in the unique personal vision expressed by the individual artist, notably Delacroix. The successful painter or poet has a fresh take on the world—the 'impeccable naïveté' (ii. 578) afforded by the individual's 'tempérament'—which must not be inhibited or homogenized by rules and norms and schools, but which must nevertheless be served by the carefully acquired and already well-established skills and techniques of the artistic medium in question: by the rule of thumb rather than the pronouncements of university professors. For 'il y a dans les productions multiples de l'art quelque chose de toujours nouveau qui échappera éternellement à la règle et aux analyses de l'école!' (ii. 578). The perception of beauty, by artist/poet or spectator/reader, depends significantly on the element of surprise, of novelty and difference. Hence, in *Exposition universelle*, Baudelaire's rejection of a classical aesthetic that, for him, simply results in 'une vaste unité, monotone et impersonnelle, immense comme l'ennui et le néant' (ii. 578). If beauty is to hold our gaze it must disconcert us, and so it requires '[c]ette dose de bizarrerie qui constitue et définit

---

[2] From *Mon cœur mis à nu*, f. 55, in *Fusées*, ed. Guyaux, 106; i. 696. Antoine Compagnon infers potential allusions to the alexandrine and the sonnet in these seemingly random numbers (*Baudelaire devant l'innombrable*, 84).
[3] *Fusées*, ed. Guyaux, 70; i. 663–4.

l'individualité, sans laquelle il n'y a pas de beau' (ii. 579). Being unorthodox, being alternative, is what grants 'le beau' its licensed authority: 'C'est son immatriculation, sa caractéristique' (ii. 578). In *Fusées*, f. 13 he suggests further that oddity is essential to aesthetic beauty because it implies life: 'Ce qui n'est pas légèrement difforme a l'air insensible;—d'où il suit que l'irrégularité, c'est-à-dire l'inattendu, la surprise, l'étonnement sont une partie essentielle et la caractéristique de la beauté.'[4]

The fundamental importance of this individuality of vision as a prerequisite of beauty accounts for Baudelaire's early wariness of sculpture (in the *Salon de 1846*) on the grounds that the sculpted object—by being potentially seen from any number of different perspectives and in any number of different lights—thus escapes the control of the sculptor whose own unique, originary perspective is thereby lost. As a result the artist's work may be seen as beautiful for reasons other than those that were intended: 'il arrive souvent, ce qui est humiliant pour l'artiste, qu'un hasard de lumière, un effet de lampe, découvrent une beauté qui n'est pas celle à laquelle il avait songé' (ii. 487). Yet, as we saw in Chapter 12, the Baudelaire who writes about sculpture in the *Salon de 1859* is there much readier to welcome it as a source of beauty because it sets the imagination of the viewer free: 'le fantôme de pierre s'empare de vous pendant quelques minutes, et vous commande, au nom du passé, de penser aux choses qui ne sont pas de la terre' (ii. 670). And this is the more usual Baudelaire, always quick to state—from his earliest writings onwards and before he first read Poe—that beauty is an effect, so that the role of the spectator or reader is itself an indispensable element in its being. In this way beauty becomes a form of dialogue between artist and receiver, each attentive to the particulars of the phenomenal world ('forme, attitude et mouvement, lumière et couleur, son et harmonie' (ii. 132)) and together tapping into the laws that govern the universe they share—the *nomoi*, as they were called in ancient Greece, or what Baudelaire in his article on Hugo calls 'la morale des choses':

> La musique des vers de Victor Hugo s'adapte aux profondes harmonies de la nature; sculpteur, il découpe dans ses strophes la forme inoubliable des choses; peintre, il les illumine de leur couleur propre. Et, comme si elles venaient directement de la nature, les trois impressions pénètrent simultanément le cerveau du lecteur. De cette triple impression résulte la *morale des choses*. (ii. 132)

For this reason, as we saw in Chapters 2 and 3, beauty is also envisaged as a performance. The artist or poet becomes a kind of double agent, participating in the realities of human experience while separately fashioning a work of art that patterns those realities. Thus in *La Fanfarlo*, for example, the poet Samuel Cramer is described as 'comédien par le tempérament' (i. 554), while in the review of

---

[4] *Fusées*, ed. Guyaux, 60; i. 656.

Madame Bovary Baudelaire refers to Flaubert's 'zèle de comédien' when describing the novelist's desire to think and feel his way into the character of Emma, 'de se dépouiller (autant que possible) de son sexe et de se faire femme' (ii. 81). Like the comic actor in *De l'essence du rire* who, the better to provoke laughter, must pretend to be unaware of how laughable he is, so the poet-artist creates beauty as though in ignorance of the fundamental futility of artistic creativity in a world governed by time and destruction, a world experienced by humankind as an irremediable state of ill-being, or 'le Mal'. As we have seen in Part II, the emphasis in the earlier manifestations of what would become *Les Fleurs du Mal* is very much on this experience of ill-being, or melancholy, itself seen as an essential ingredient in the kind of beauty Baudelaire had identified, for example, in Delacroix's paintings of women. In 'Les Fleurs du Mal' (1855) this melancholy begins to be counterbalanced by a kind of 'anti-melancholy' whereby certain human activities or states of being are more positively explored as possible alternatives to the tragedy of desire depicted in the Lesbos poems or to the sense of indifferentiation portrayed in *Les Limbes* where life is experienced as a living death. Yet in the first edition of *Les Fleurs du Mal* melancholy continues to dominate, with the final poem—'La Mort des artistes'—giving the last word in the collection to the failure of art to 'piquer dans le but, de mystique nature', that is, to achieve some form of transcendence of the human condition through beauty.

But after 1857, and quite possibly goaded into a more militant resistance by having been put on trial for impiety and obscenity, Baudelaire seems to have come—through his new preoccupation with the idea of a *constructive* imagination—to a more robust conception of beauty: of beauty as the manifestation of an imagination that has the power to govern the world by reshaping our ways of seeing it. A melancholic condition of disintegration and loss can now be resisted by a form of beauty that thrives on the decomposed, like maggots on a corpse, and enacts, like alchemy, a process of transmutation—for example, of erotic experience—through an increasingly assertive performance and display of aesthetic creativity. In 'Hymne à la Beauté', newly added to the revised architecture of the 1861 *Les Fleurs du Mal*, beauty is no longer a missed target but a magical power that opens the doors of conjecture onto infinite vistas of the unknown—even, and particularly, as one strolls along the familiar streets of Paris.

Beauty itself now feeds on contingency and clutter, transforming both into a shapeliness that, like the sea or a ship under sail, has the power to hold both poet and reader in thrall. This experience of beauty is like having a new soul 'qui jette une lumière magique et surnaturelle sur l'obscurité naturelle des choses' (ii. 645)— anticipating Picasso's celebrated statement that the purpose of art is to 'wash the dust of daily life off our souls'. Baudelaire's evolving and increasingly radical conception of beauty culminates in the 'fête intérieure' of his prose poems, where he invents a new and unique way of engaging with the world in language: a language framed as 'the voice of the stranger', setting itself against the conventional discourses of philosophy, religion, politics, and ethics, and, like a novel without a plot, combining narrative, description, and dialogue with the humour and irony of a subversive mischievousness to produce an original form of... of itself, something entirely *sui generis*: of poetry that can be in prose, of texts both self-sufficient and yet assembled in a collection, like a kaleidoscope—an instrument with which (etymologically) to 'see beauty' with each turn of the tube.

For all the twists and turns in Baudelaire's lifelong engagement with beauty, nevertheless, there remain three constants in his thinking: beauty is relative, beauty requires a beholder, and beauty is right. 'Chaque siècle, chaque peuple ayant possédé l'expression de sa beauté et de sa morale', he contends in the opening section of the *Salon de 1846* (ii. 419), and he makes the point again in the last: 'on peut affirmer que puisque tous les siècles et tous les peuples ont eu leur beauté, nous avons inévitablement la nôtre' (ii. 493). Hence that key adjustment in his famous definition in *Fusées*, f. 16: 'J'ai trouvé la définition du Beau,—*de mon Beau*. C'est quelque chose d'ardent et de triste, quelque chose d'un peu vague, laissant carrière à la conjecture' (my emphasis). As these statements suggest, beauty is relative *because* it depends on the beholder; and if the beholder is to perceive beauty—that is, to perceive either something in the world or else represented in a work of art as being both harmonious and strange, then the beholder must be familiar enough with the elements being observed both to be surprised by the new way(s) in which they have been brought together and also to understand and to accept the essential consonance that has permitted the harmonious reconciliation of dissonant items. From this logical requirement—that the unknown can only be accessed from the known—stems the combination of 'eternity' and 'transience' that has so often been taken as the very definition of Baudelaire's 'modernity', as the source of his instigation of the notion of the avant-garde,[5] and as evidence of a paradigmatic fall into history that is synonymous with the social alienation of human beings within an age of capitalism in Second Empire France. And yet his definition is perhaps less radical and more straightforward than these claims might suggest, being potentially applicable as much to the Greeks who first set eyes on the Venus de Milo or to the Italians of the Renaissance who were permitted to view the Mona Lisa:

> Toutes les beautés contiennent, comme tous les phénomènes possibles, quelque chose d'éternel et quelque chose de transitoire,—d'absolu et de particulier. La beauté absolue et éternelle n'existe pas, ou plutôt elle n'est qu'une abstraction écrémée à la surface générale des beautés diverses. L'élément particulier de chaque beauté vient des passions, et comme nous avons nos passions particulières, nous avons notre beauté. (ii. 493)

[5] See Paul de Man, 'Lyric and Modernity, in his *Blindness and Insight: Essays in the Rhetoric of Contemporary Criticism* (2nd edn, London: Methuen, 1983), 166–86.

For all observers of these famous beauties, whether now or long ago, what is 'beautiful' involves a combination of the particular and timebound (items of dress, for example, however scanty) and some general and 'eternal' quality such as harmony or symmetry (of body shape, say, or pictorial composition). In his opposition to the uniformity of the classical idealized type Baudelaire is not so much proposing a new kind of beauty as reminding his readers of what beauty has always consisted in, and this so that they may more readily countenance the presence in today's work of art of a freckled beggar-girl, say, or an Afro-Caribbean head of hair, rather than a falling shift or the distant landscape of Montefeltro.

When he returns to this idea in *Le Peintre de la vie moderne* and proposes what he calls 'une théorie rationnelle et historique du beau, en opposition avec la théorie du beau unique et absolu', he makes a similar point, though the skimmed cream has now become a heavenly cake:

> Le beau est fait d'un élément éternel, invariable, dont la quantité est excessivement difficile à déterminer, et d'un élément relatif, circonstanciel, qui sera, si l'on veut, tour à tour ou tout ensemble, l'époque, la mode, la morale, la passion. Sans ce second élément, qui est comme l'enveloppe amusante, titillante, apéritive, du divin gâteau, le premier élément serait indigestible, inappréciable, non adapté et non approprié à la nature humaine. Je défie qu'on découvre un échantillon quelconque de beauté qui ne contienne pas ces deux éléments. (ii. 685)

Here Baudelaire not only echoes his own earlier claims in the *Salon de 1846* that art provides spiritual nourishment ('Vous pouvez vivre trois jours sans pain;— sans poésie, jamais', 'vous avez besoin d'art' (ii. 415)), but also now gives clear priority to the 'eternal' element of beauty as the essential foodstuff of the soul— and *this* because the spectacle of beauty provides a spectacle of what is 'right'. Whereas in 1846 he sought principally to reject a timeless classical art in the name of a 'modern' art that could renew itself by integrating the warp and woof of the contemporary world, here in 1859—and two years after his trial—he wants to emphasize the value of beauty as an alternative form of justice.

This equation of beauty and justice appears in a number of Baudelaire's writings around this time (1857–60), and thus in the period during which the poetic argument of the first edition of *Les Fleurs du Mal* (a resigned acceptance of 'le Mal')) was being transformed into the poetic argument of the second (a militant resistance to 'le Mal' through the 're-creations' of art). Thus in the 'Notes nouvelles sur Edgar Poe' (1857) (as discussed in Chapter 11), Baudelaire sidesteps the alleged binary of the useful and the beautiful by quoting Poe's contention that Horace's 'irritable race of poets' is in fact better placed than anyone else to be judges (like the Baudelaire who in the same year writes overtly in his review of *Madame Bovary* as though he were summing up a legal debate). Indeed, unlike the magistrates who found the author of 'Lesbos' to be guilty of obscenity, poets *never* find the innocent guilty, but they *do* find injustice in all sorts of places where the powers that be (and who want to remain that way) 'fail' to see it: 'Les poètes voient l'injustice, *jamais* là où elle n'existe pas, mais fort souvent là où des yeux non poétiques n'en voient pas du tout' (ii. 330-1). And this, says Poe (and says Baudelaire), is because they can see right: '[c]ette clairvoyance n'est pas autre chose qu'un corollaire de la vive perception du vrai, de la justice, de la proportion, en un mot du Beau' (ii. 331). Thanks to their 'exquisite' sense of beauty—of harmony and 'rightness'—poets and artists also have a sharp eye for what is *not* 'right': 'Un artiste n'est un artiste que grâce à son son sens exquis du Beau,—sens qui lui procure des jouissances enivrantes, mais qui en même temps implique, enferme un sens également exquis de toute difformité et de toute disproportion' (ii. 330). For Baudelaire this equivalence of beauty and 'rightness' constitutes 'une excellente et irréfutable apologie' (ii. 331) for all poets, and (as discussed in Chapters 1 and 11) he reinforces his paraphrase of Poe by making his own further, seemingly 'scandalous' claim: 'et je ne crois pas qu'il soit scandalisant de considérer toute infraction à la morale, au beau moral, comme une espèce de faute contre le rythme et la prosodie universels' (ii. 334).

In his essay on Gautier of 1859 Baudelaire similarly places emphasis on the truthfulness of beauty, and here in relation to the work of the person most closely associated with 'l'art pour l'art' and thus supposedly with the pursuit of beauty to the exclusion of all other concerns. Baudelaire sees Gautier the poet as deploying the imagination to create an alternative and more authentic form of truthfulness: 'L'imagination du lecteur se sent transportée dans le vrai; elle respire le vrai; elle s'enivre d'une second réalité créée par la sorcellerie de la Muse' (ii. 121)—an accolade that recalls (as discussed in Chapter 13) Baudelaire's own view of poetry as offering 'ce qu'il y a de plus réel, [...] ce qui n'est complètement vrai que dans *un autre monde*' (ii. 59). As to Gautier the celebrated art critic, this time the accolade relates closely to the view presented in the 1861 edition of *Les Fleurs du Mal* of beauty as constituting a means of resistance to 'le Mal': 'Nul n'a mieux su que lui exprimer le bonheur que donne à l'imagination la vue d'un bel objet d'art, fût-il le plus désolé et le plus terrible qu'on puisse supposer. C'est un des privilèges prodigieux de l'Art que l'horrible, artistement exprimé, devienne beauté, et que la *douleur* rythmée et cadencée remplisse l'esprit d'une *joie* calme' (ii. 122-3).[6] Here we are granted a rare glimpse of what Baudelaire considers the 'effect' of beauty actually to consist in, as opposed to his repeated statements that beauty depends on the participation and individual contribution of the spectator—such as we find, for example, at the beginning of the section on landscape painting in the *Salon de 1859*: 'Si tel assemblage d'arbres, de montagnes, d'eaux et de maisons, que nous appelons un paysage, est beau, ce n'est pas par lui-même, mais par moi, par ma

---

[6] Cf. a similar comment about 'l'art pur' in *Le Peintre de la vie moderne*: 'l'art pur, c'est-à-dire la beauté particulière du mal, le beau dans l'horrible' (ii. 722).

grâce propre, par l'idée ou le sentiment que j'y attache' (ii. 660). Now from the description of Gautier's art criticism we can infer that for Baudelaire the perception of beauty, itself derived from rhythm and cadence, engenders a state of 'calm joy'—and indeed a state of happiness.

A further and more sustained perspective on how Baudelaire envisages the effect of beauty is provided in Les Paradis artificiels (1860), where he describes at the very outset, in a section entitled 'Le Goût de l'infini', the particular feeling and state of mind (the 'paradise') that drug-users seek to induce artificially but which, if we are lucky, can be experienced—and perhaps has been experienced—by us all, and without resort to opium or hash:

> Il est des jours où l'homme s'éveille avec un génie jeune et vigoureux. Ses paupières à peine déchargées du sommeil qui les scellait, le monde extérieur s'offre à lui avec un relief puissant, une netteté de contours, une richesse de couleurs admirables. Le monde moral ouvre ses vastes perspectives, pleines de clartés nouvelles. L'homme gratifié de cette béatitude, malheureusement rare et passagère, se sent à la fois plus artiste et plus juste, plus noble, pour tout dire en un mot. (i. 401)

Beatitude: in Christian theology, a 'beatific' or blessed state enjoyed by the chosen few, a condition of perfect happiness, of serenity and calm joy. Or, in secular terms, a wow moment, a perfect moment, a buzz, the feeling that all is right with the world, that it is very good indeed to be alive: 'cet état exceptionnnel de l'esprit et des sens, que je puis sans exagération appeler paradisiaque, si je le compare aux lourdes ténèbres de l'existence commune et journalière' (i. 401). In these opening paragraphs Baudelaire offers his own mini-version of the first chapter of the Book of Genesis, the early life of man in the space of a morning. Some days we wake up feeling great, 'avec un génie jeune et vigoureux'. Emerging from sleep at the dawn of time, eyes newly opened, humankind beholds Creation as all things bright and beautiful: 'le monde extérieur s'offre à lui avec un relief puissant, une netteté de contours, une richesse de couleurs admirables'. The world is at once our oyster and an open book: 'Le monde moral ouvre ses vastes perspectives, pleines de clartés nouvelles.' Bliss is it in that dawn to be alive, but to feel like an artist is very heaven: 'L'homme gratifié de cette béatitude, malheureusement rare et passagère, se sent à la fois plus artiste et plus juste, plus noble, pour tout dire en un mot.' Beauty, justice, happiness. 'Pour tout dire en un mot'? The word 'noble' derives from the Latin *noscere*, meaning to know or to begin to know.[7] Baudelaire may or may not have been aware of this etymology, but 'noble' is an appropriate word to describe the effect of Baudelaire's beauty since it evokes the prayer at the end of

---

[7] See *Dictionnaire historique de la langue française*, ed. Rey, under 'noble'.

'Les Litanies de Satan' and the knowingness that is central to the poetic argument of *Les Fleurs du Mal*. Reunited with Satan beneath the Tree of Knowledge (both Lucifer and ourselves as sons and daughters of Adam and Eve being returning exiles from paradise) the poet-artist re-enters a garden of Eden that is beauty, created not by drugs but by art, not by passive submission (or 'inspiration') but through a willed act of creation, a 'beginning to know': 'un Infini que j'aime et n'ai jamais connu' as he calls it in 'Hymne à la Beauté', where the title implies the creation of a new God and a new Creation.

In 'Le Goût de l'infini' Baudelaire goes on to explore with humour the alternative methods by which this beatific state might be brought about (i. 401–2). Maybe by clean living, 'une bonne hygiène' and 'un régime de sage'? Except that it often seems to occur when the body has been abused! Through prayer and spiritual devotion perhaps? Surely they would be especially conducive to 'cette santé morale, si éclatante et si glorieuse' that we experience in such moments. But no, for sometimes the experience seems to occur 'après de coupables orgies de l'imagination, après un abus sophistique de la raison, qui est à son usage honnête et raisonnable ce que les tours de dislocation sont à la saine gymnastique?' There is simply no rhyme or reason to it. Just as going to the gym may land you with a sprain, so, conversely, an unabstemious overdose of imagining and thinking—or listening to Wagner's music, say[8]—can bring you a sudden revelation of paradise. And so it amounts to a secular form of grace: 'comme une véritable grâce, comme un miroir magique où l'homme est invité à se voir en beau, c'est-à-dire tel qu'il devrait et pourrait être; une espèce d'excitation angélique, un rappel à l'ordre sous une forme complimenteuse' (ii. 402). Beauty seen in this light is thus a moral force, a polite reminder that really and truly there is a better way, a kind of justice. By an act of grace we come to know that fair is indeed fair... 'plus artiste et plus juste'. Moreover the word 'beauté' derives from the Latin 'bellus', itself originally a diminutive of 'bonus,—um', meaning good:[9] Art for Art's Sake is also Art for Goodness' Sake.

This experience of 'béatitude' in 'Le Goût de l'infini' is comparable with the blessed state described in the first part of 'La Chambre double', published two years later in *La Presse*: 'Ô béatitude! ce que nous nommons généralement la vie, même dans son expansion la plus heureuse, n'a rien de commun avec cette vie suprême dont j'ai maintenant connaissance et que je savoure minute par minute, seconde par seconde!' Here, too, the perfect moment comes suddenly, surprisingly, and for no apparent reason: 'Sur ce lit est couchée l'Idole, la souveraine des

---

[8] This state of 'béatitude' recurs in Baudelaire's article on Wagner, where he again compares it to the effect of opium: 'Il semble parfois, en écoutant cette musique ardente et despotique, qu'on retrouve peintes sur le fond des ténèbres, déchiré par la rêverie, les vertigineuses conceptions de l'opium' (ii. 785). Indeed he has become addicted to this music: 'Ma volupté avait été si forte et si terrible, que je ne pouvais m'empêcher d'y vouloir retourner sans cesse' (ii. 785).

[9] See *Dictionnaire historique de la langue française*, ed. Rey, under 'Beau, bel'.

rêves. Mais comment est-elle ici? Qui l'a amenée? quel pouvoir magique l'a installée sur ce trône de rêverie et de volupté? Qu'importe? la voilà! je la reconnais.' Her name is Beauty, an 'idole', an 'idée', an 'idée poétique', the counterpart of the treacherous opiate that awaits in the 'other room' of spleen: 'Dans ce monde étroit, mais si plein de dégoût, un seul objet connu me sourit: la fiole de laudanum; une vieille et terrible amie; comme toutes les amies, hélas! féconde en caresses et en traîtrises.' Here in miniature is the argument of *Les Paradis artificiels*: we must beware 'le ravage moral causé par cette dangereuse et délicieuse gymnastique' (i. 428). Drug-induced states of bliss are not to be trusted, whether bestowed by the 'séducteur paisible' that is opium or the 'démon désordonné' of hashish (i. 428).

For drug-usage saps the will and imperils the *constructive* powers of the imagination, whereas a poetry consciously wrought ('la rédemption par le travail' (i. 441))—perhaps a prose poem like 'La Chambre double' that can unite 'idéal' and 'spleen' under one roof—will see us through the night-time of the soul. Or a prose poem like 'Le Gâteau' perhaps, where we learn that the calm joy of a beautiful morning cannot last because we will always need lunch:

> Bref, je me sentais, grâce à l'enthousiasmante beauté dont j'étais environné, en parfaite paix avec moi-même et avec l'univers; je crois même que, dans ma parfaite béatitude et dans mon total oubli de tout le mal terrestre, j'en étais venu à ne plus trouver si ridicules les journaux qui prétendent que l'homme est né bon;—quand la matière incurable renouvelant ses exigences, je songeai à réparer la fatigue et à soulager l'appétit causés par une si longue ascension.

But this latter-day Rousseau wandering by his mountain lake need not fear. Not only does he have his own divine cake to hand (aka 'un gros morceau de pain'), but there is also something he can take to restore his energy after such a long climb towards the high of beauty: 'un certain élixir que les pharmaciens vendaient dans ce temps-là aux touristes pour le mêler dans l'occasion avec de l'eau de neige'. A medicine to help with altitude-sickness? Or, better still, an elixir to induce 'l'ivresse de l'art' with which this poet-narrator can veil the afternoon melancholy brought on by the sorry sight of two boys fighting over his 'cake' and destroying it in the process: 'Ce spectacle m'avait embrumé le paysage, et la joie calme où s'ébaudissait mon âme avant d'avoir vu ces petits hommes avait totalement disparu.' For the narrator of 'Le Mauvais Vitrier', by contrast, the day has started badly: 'Un matin, je m'étais levé maussade, triste, fatigué d'oisiveté'—in stark contrast to the 'blessed' prospect of another day in paradise enjoyed by one who awakes 'avec un génie jeune et vigoureux' and 'se sent à la fois plus artiste et plus juste, plus noble'. But in his case, too, as for the hungry mountaineer, what follows is violence and destruction, lending weight to the contention made in 'Le Poème du hachisch' that 'les vices de l'homme, si pleins d'horreur qu'on les suppose, contiennent la preuve (quand ce ne serait que leur infinie expansion!) de son goût de l'infini' (i. 402). As Mallarmé's faun will soon discover also, afternoons are difficult. But for Baudelaire, already attuned to the rhythms of the 'drame solaire', there remains the further prospect of a delicious 'harmonie du soir' and a 'crépuscule' in which to celebrate the 'fête intérieure' of a redemptive beauty and 'la promesse du bonheur' (ii. 686): 'nous avons créé à notre usage un jardin de vraie beauté'.

Lawgiving

Ma chère mère, vous ignorez tellement ce que c'est qu'une existence de poète[.]
   (letter to Mme Aupick, 20 December 1855 (*Corr.*, i. 327))

C'est un *moi* insatiable du *non-moi*, qui, à chaque instant, le rend et l'exprime en images plus vivantes que la vie elle-même, toujours instable et fugitive.
   (*Le Peintre de la vie moderne*, ii. 692)

Lawgiving may be defined as the attempt to fit the apparently contingent into a pattern, a way to have the world make sense. For the scientist this process consists in establishing the laws of nature, laws that have the power to predict outcomes on the basis of some discovered relationship of cause and effect. For the moralist or political scientist this process is similar in that aspects of human behaviour are examined with a view to determining causal links between actions, but in this case the resultant laws are not only descriptive but also, potentially, prescriptive: in the form of a moral code or ethical system, of a civil code or body of civil law, of a political ideology, or of a religion. For the poet and artist the creation of pattern from contingency is also central: whether it involves words, or paint, or sounds, whether the means of patterning be register, rhythm, and prosody, or drawing and colour, or scale and chord, the objective is to bestow expressive power on the random. In that sense harmony and eurhythmy are forms both of beauty and of lawgiving.

  For Victor Cousin, whose neo-Platonic aesthetic theory loomed over the cultural landscape of nineteenth-century France, the prime cause of art was God.[10] Founding his aesthetic theory on his own Catholic faith, Cousin sought to counter the materialism and relativism of Enlightenment empiricism by (re)-asserting the objective validity of truth, beauty, and goodness as interrelated spiritual manifestations of the divine that are accessible to human reason.[11]

---

[10] See Chapter 1 n. 27.
[11] Such a view was and remains central to the Roman Catholic faith. Article 41 of *The Catechism of the Catholic Church* (1993) states: 'All creatures bear a certain resemblance to God, most especially

Hence, for Cousin, art is essentially moral and religious and has the capacity to confer on its materials 'un caractère mystérieux qui s'adresse à l'imagination et à l'âme': 'Toute œuvre d'art [...] jette l'âme dans une rêverie gracieuse ou sévère qui l'élève vers l'infini.'[12] By beginning *Les Paradis artificiels* with a section entitled 'Le Goût de l'infini' Baudelaire is thus engaging with a central contemporary debate about the religious and metaphysical function of art and about the nature of beauty, and what emerges is a radically new version of Cousin's trinity. God is absent, except as the putative and ironically celebrated source of human creativity (briefly discussed above at the end of Chapter 10): 'nous avons accompli le seul miracle dont Dieu nous ait octroyé la licence!' (i. 441). In God's absence Baudelaire establishes a new hierarchy wherein 'le vrai' and 'le bien' are no longer on a par with beauty as reflections of the divine but now subsidiary to it, being themselves both reflections *of* beauty and reflected *in* beauty. On that bright new morning described at the beginning of 'Le Goût de l'infini' the human being awakes and feels 'à la fois plus artiste et plus juste, plus noble': 'le beau,' 'le vrai', and 'le bien' are here restated and rearranged, not now as a reflection of God but as the haunting possibility of a better life here on earth: 'une espèce de hantise, mais de hantise intermittente, dont nous devrions tirer, si nous étions sages, la certitude d'une existence meilleure et l'espérance d'y atteindre par l'exercice journalier de notre volonté' (i. 402). And in that creative exercise of our human will—'la rédemption par le travail'—lies the power of art as a form of resistance to 'le mal de vivre'.

In the course of writing this book I have come to believe that the originality of Baudelaire's contribution to the history of modern French poetry was essentially threefold. First, he substituted Beauty for God as the foundation of a poet's authority. Second, he rejected a widely shared and deeply rooted Western reliance on the Christian theology of evil and redemption in favour of a secular ethics based on the role of the poetic imagination and the redemptive value of human creativity and human work. And, third, he created in the prose poem a radically new form of writing that demands to be read in a new way: not to be 'understood' in any traditional sense of that word but to be read and reread and pondered and remembered and reread anew by a reader content to turn the kaleidoscope and be content with each new pattern of meaning that presents itself to the eye. Rimbaud's *Illuminations* (themselves metaphorical glassware); Mallarmé's verse

---

man, created in the image and likeness of God. The manifold perfections of creatures—their truth, their goodness, their beauty [—] all reflect the infinite perfection of God.'

[12] Victor Cousin, *Du vrai, du beau et du bien* (Paris: Didier, 1853), 188. On Cousin's part in the emergence of 'l'Art pour l'Art', see Albert Cassagne, *La Théorie de l'art pour l'art en France chez les derniers romantiques et les premiers réalistes* (Paris: Hachette, 1906 [Geneva: Slatkine Reprints, 1979]); repr. (with a preface by Daniel Oster) Seyssel: Champ Vallon, 1997), 68–73, and Sapiro, *La Responsabilité de l'écrivain*, 169–70.

(from 1868 onwards), his later prose poems, his *poëmes critiques*, and above all *Un coup de Dés*; Apollinaire's *Alcools* and *Calligrammes*; Surrealism, and in particular Breton's experiments with 'le hasard objectif': all are forms of alternative lawgiving that will later similarly ask us, as does *Le Spleen de Paris*, to think and see (literally so in the cases of *Un coup de Dés* and *Calligrammes*) according to a new and shifting set of rules and to read without the comfort of an easy conclusion.

For Baudelaire there was no Fall, no Original Sin, in the orthodox Roman Catholic sense of those terms, but rather the moral law of diminishing returns, the irremediably downward, deathly spiral of time-bound human desire; just as also for Baudelaire there was no life after death but rather the possibility of multiple resurrections within life itself, re-creations to be effected through the agency of memory, imagination, and artistic craft. For him the specific art of poetry can give us access through language onto the realm of the spiritual, of beauty: not a world of the soul beyond the grave but a world of the soul in parallel with the here-and-now; not beauty as a self-sufficient, immutable ideal but beauty as an ephemeral subjective effect: an effect of depth, mysteriousness, and stimulus, of an unknowable—an uncertainty—that asks tantalizingly, excitingly, impossibly, to be known. For Baudelaire, poetry offers us an alternative dimension of existence: not the negative resort of escape and despair but rather a positive locus of mental and emotional sustenance—an oasis, an island of *exotic*[13] 'parfums', a rich domain of 'féconde paresse' where the sterile inactivity of ennui, consequent on the death of desire, is replaced by the vitality of conjecture and the racing pulse of endless imaginings. For the author of *Les Fleurs du Mal* and *Le Spleen de Paris*, poetry—whether in verse or in prose—offers the possibility of a wild surmise, opening up for us, in the manner of Delacroix's paintings, 'de profondes avenues à l'imagination la plus voyageuse' (ii. 431).

If Baudelaire's work, as so many have asserted, represents the advent of 'modernity'—and this even or particularly in the form of an 'anti-modernity'[14]—then the appositeness of such a claim derives not only from his rejection of orthodox religious faith and his promotion of art as a secular form of salvation through the effort of human creativity, but also from his new conception of poetry as an instrument rather than a container, of poetry not as gift-wrapped thought but as travel ticket and quasi-narcotic substance, the means to a trip. If we compare

---

[13] From the Greek *exotikos*, where *exo-*, meaning 'outside', connotes the foreign and the strange, the world of the Étranger.

[14] See Antoine Compagnon, *Les Antimodernes: De Joseph de Maistre à Roland Barthes* (Paris: Gallimard, 2005; repr. 2016), and his 'Avant-Propos' to *Baudelaire: L'Irréductible* (Paris: Flammarion, 2014): 'Nul n'illustrait mieux que [Baudelaire] la résistance moderne au monde moderne. L' "anti-modernité" représentait en effet à mes yeux [in *Les Antimodernes*] la modernité authentique, celle qui résistait à la vie moderne, au monde moderne, tout en y étant irrémédiablement engagée' (8). See also the special issue of *L'Année Baudelaire* (18/19 (2015)) edited by Compagnon with Matthieu Vernet, under the title 'Baudelaire antimoderne'.

Baudelaire with Paul Bénichou's three 'mages romantiques' (Lamartine, Hugo, Vigny) we can see that he shares Vigny's pursuit of a secular world-view but with a degree of philosophical and moral scepticism that precludes the possibility of a poem being a 'perle de la pensée'—that is, Vigny's ideal of a lasting, highly wrought perpetuation of hard-won and universally valid human wisdom. If he shares with Lamartine the belief that poetry is a form of active verbal response to the uncertainties of our human condition, he sees it as his aim not to lend prayer-like expression to some pre-existing mystery but rather to *create* mystery; not to simulate, in a poetics of murmur, the silent worship offered up to God by Nature, but to transform that Nature and to bring into existence, through a quasi-sexual act of voluptuous engagement and procreation, a world that will express *his* heart and *his* mind—an act described at the end of 'Paysage' as 'cette volupté | D'évoquer le Printemps avec ma volonté, | De tirer un soleil de mon cœur, et de faire | De mes pensers brûlants une tiède atmosphère'. And if he shares with Hugo the ambition to express 'le *mystère de la vie*' (ii. 131) he does so not as though (in the manner of *Les Contemplations*) the poet were seeking to re-enact the Creation but rather as one who is creating new worlds of his own. Where Hugo, like Moses delivering God's truth, sees in the poetic image an act of worship since the very possibility of simile and metaphor derives from the laws intrinsic in a divinely created and divinely ordered universe, Baudelaire, like Orpheus in tune with nature, begins with chaos—the chaos of a disparate, fragmented, transitory world of sensual experience—and orders that chaos with the patterns of poetry. And where Hugo's universe is governed by the *nomos*, or law, of spiritual redemption, the onward march of Progress towards the light and the ultimate transmutation of all matter into spirit through love, Baudelaire's universe is a world of mud waiting to be transformed into gold by the new laws of the poet-alchemist, the laws of structure and rhythm and prosody, the laws of Number, the laws of the poetic idea.

Baudelaire is, then, a *nomothète*. For Pierre Bourdieu he is so because, with Flaubert, he succeeded in modifying the 'rules' or *doxa* by which literary art was judged. But Baudelaire is a *nomothète* also, and more importantly, in the sense of being an 'alternative lawgiver' *within* his work: a poet who invites his readers to embark upon a fundamental recasting of their habitual moral and intellectual take on the world and thereby to renew perception and revitalize the experience of living. This is poetry not as statement or doctrine or propaganda, not as approval or confession or lament, but poetry as probing investigation, as contradiction and conjecture, as invitation and illicit celebration: poetry as resistance. At the end of his landmark study of Baudelaire published in 1956, Lloyd Austin concludes that 'c'est malgré son "message" que Baudelaire est un grand poète'. For Austin the 'message'—which he dismisses as 'rétrograde' because he sees Baudelaire as a political and religious reactionary in hock to De Maistre and an orthodox Roman Catholic belief in original sin—is somehow separate from his achievement as a 'poet': 'La gloire de Baudelaire est d'avoir [...] renouvelé l'expression poétique.'

What really matters, he says, is his 'recherche de la perfection artistique'.[15] But for Baudelaire 'form' and 'content' were one and the same, and his poetry, whether in verse or in prose, is predicated on the indissoluble relationship between beauty and melancholy that has been my principal focus throughout this book.

Central to his role as an alternative lawgiver is the belief that through poetry he can give expression to the contradictions and dualities that inform human experience, but without resolving or reducing them to some ostensibly coherent philosophy or system of ethics. Poetry is an alternative form of discourse that honours uncertainty. As mentioned in Part I, Baudelaire relates in his article on the Exposition universelle of 1855 how he used to wish he could formulate some hard-and-fast theory of art that would then allow him to 'prêcher à [s]on aise' and pontificate like all those professors at the École des Beaux-Arts. But he has now realized that 'un système est une espèce de damnation qui nous pousse à une abjuration perpétuelle; il en faut toujours inventer un autre, et cette fatigue est un cruel châtiment'. Life exceeds system, however flexible that system may be:

> Et toujours mon système était beau, vaste, spacieux, commode, propre et lisse surtout; du moins il me paraissait tel. Et toujours un produit spontané, inattendu, de la vitalité universelle venait donner un démenti à ma science enfantine et vieillote, fille déplorable de l'utopie. (ii. 577)

Hence his robust view that self-contradiction should be regarded as a virtue. Why indeed should truth be thought to reside exclusively, if indeed at all, in consistency and immutability of mind? Is that not the foolishness of Voltaire's Pangloss: 'Je suis toujours de mon premier sentiment, répondit Pangloss, car enfin je suis philosophe: il ne me convient pas de me dédire.'[16] For Baudelaire by contrast, misquoting Alphonse de Custine, '[a]pprendre c'est se contredire—il y un degré de conséquence qui n'est qu'à la portée du mensonge' (i. 710). Consistency and convention are intrinsically suspect, and to think alternatively is indeed a human right: 'Parmi les droits dont on a parlé dans ces derniers temps' (he noted at some unknown date for the benefit of his fellow-writer Philoxène Boyer (1829–67)), 'il y en a un qu'on a oublié, à la démonstration de laquelle *tout le monde* est intéressé,—le droit de se contredire' (i. 709). Indeed the world itself—'ce vaste système de contradictions' (i. 546), as he calls it his 'Choix de maximes consolantes sur l'amour' (1846)—would appear to require it.

Thus Baudelaire, too, is an 'officiant of uncertainty', but in a very different way from his immediate predecessors in the history of nineteenth-century poetry. For them the uncertainty was essentially ontological. Why are we here? Is there a God?

---

[15] Austin, *L'Univers poétique de Baudelaire*, 338, 339, and 340 respectively.
[16] Voltaire, *Romans et contes*, ed. Frédéric Deloffre and Jacques Van den Heuvel (Paris: Gallimard [Bibliothèque de la Pléiade], 1979), 228.

For Lamartine, this was a cause of particular anguish. Following the death of his mother in November 1829 he asserts with grief: 'Dieu n'est qu'un mot rêvé pour expliquer le monde' ('Le Tombeau d'une mère', l. 14), and in 'Le Désert, ou l'Immatérialité de l'âme' (drafted in 1835 but published only in 1856) he speculates that 'Dieu n'est qu'une idée', leaving him with a one-word answer to the conundrum of life: 'MYSTÈRE'. Lamartine's 'mystère' is Hugo's 'problème', which he attempts to solve by positing (in *Les Contemplations*) his divine narrative of redemption through love. For Vigny the question is otiose, an object of intellectual disdain, and he refers with indifference to 'la Cause pour toujours incertaine'.[17] And Baudelaire? For him, too, the question simply does not arise. The term 'Dieu' is merely implicit shorthand for 'la Cause pour toujours incertaine', as when at the end of 'Le Poème du hachisch' he attributes to divine authority the possibility of a secular redemption through creativity. Otherwise the nearest we get to a divinity is the 'divin gâteau', or the Goddess of Beauty herself: the 'déesse' implored by the buffoon in 'Le Fou et la Vénus' and whom the Étranger would be glad to adore. Beauty, then: a substitute for God and source of a beneficent and creative uncertainty.

I have suggested elsewhere (while discussing poetry as 'a mode of perception and knowledge that constitutes and maps a "strategic gap" between the sensual and the conceptual') that we might abandon the traditional narrative which sees in nineteenth-century French poetry 'a progression away from Romantic confidence, through Baudelairean irony, to *fin-de-siècle* doubt and failure: as it might be, from the Hugolian prophet, via [Baudelaire's] 'La Muse malade', to Mallarmé's nonexistent Book'. Instead we might consider that 'the history of nineteenth-century French poetry turns primarily on a prolonged and repeated attempt to reimagine the divine, and that it demonstrates a movement away from the idea that God exists but, sadly, is inconceivable and ineffable, to the idea that God does not exist and that, thank goodness, thank language, we can figure the divine as we please. In this account, the history of nineteenth-century French poetry is the story not of a Fall but of a secular emancipation.' Of 'Baudelaire and his successors' I wrote that their 'revolution lay in a poetry that frames the ineffable, intimating the unsayable with poems that leave gaps. The truth, if it exists at all, lies in the blank spaces between the words, the brief flash of a very fragmentary illumination. Once, God and the divine were the default, a mysterious truth and perfection that we are prevented from seeing by our mortal limitations, but that we may perhaps glimpse through art. Now it is a lack of mystery that is the default of our drab, monotonous, spleen-bound, sense-bound lives, and the function of art is to open up vistas of conjecture, to *create* a mysterious gap between the facile certainties of sensual

---

[17] See *Unacknowledged Legislators*, 582–4.

and intellectual experience, a nowhere-land for the divine.'[18] Hence, amongst many possible examples, Paul Éluard's famous comments in L'Évidence poétique, the lecture he gave in London at the Internationalist Surrealist Exhibition organized by Roland Penrose in June 1936: 'Le poète est celui qui inspire bien plus que celui qui est inspiré. Les poèmes ont toujours de grandes marges blanches, de grandes marges de silence où la mémoire ardente se consume pour recréer un délire sans passé.'[19]

In this new narrative Baudelaire remains therefore a pivotal figure: no longer as the 'post-Romantic' ironist and pessimist who destroyed but as the servant of a beauty that creates and set its subjects free. Here is beauty as relative, requiring the participation of the beholder, and here is beauty as right: as a force for moral good and as a form of truthfulness. Where at the end of his 'Ode on a Grecian Urn' Keats has the urn itself proclaim its timeless message that 'Beauty is truth, truth beauty', Baudelaire might agree—but only because he sees both as provisional, time-bound, and elusive. For him neither beauty nor truth is something waiting to be discovered but rather each is something that requires to be constructed, a coherence to be wrought within the paradoxically systematic chaos ('ce vaste système de contradictions') of our contingent world. Or as Michel Foucault puts it: 'L'homme moderne, pour Baudelaire, n'est pas celui qui part à la découverte de lui-même, de ses secrets et sa vérité cachée; il est celui qui cherche à s'inventer lui-même.'[20]

For Foucault 'modernity' is not a historical moment but an attitude of mind, and 'Baudelaire' is his name for that attitude. Alluding to the binary of the 'eternal' and the 'transient', Foucault argues that we should see Baudelaire not simply as accepting the transience and historicity of the present ('ce mouvement perpétuel') but as finding more in it than meets the eye: 'cette attitude volontaire, difficile, consiste à ressaisir quelque chose d'éternel qui n'est pas au-delà de l'instant présent, ni derrière lui, mais en lui'.[21] For him this is the distinction that Baudelaire himself makes in Le Peintre de la vie moderne between the mere flâneur and the 'painter of modern life', epitomized by Constantin Guys: 'Ainsi il va, il court, il cherche. Que cherche-t-il? À coup sûr, cet homme, tel que je l'ai dépeint, ce solitaire doué d'une imagination active, toujours voyageant à travers "le grand désert d'hommes", a un but plus élevé que celui d'un pur flâneur, un but plus général, autre que le plaisir fugitif de la circonstance. Il cherche ce quelque chose qu'on nous permettra d'appeler la "modernité"' (ii. 694).

---

[18] See 'Strategic Gaps: Poetry and the Sixth Sense from Chateaubriand to Mallarmé', Dix-Neuf, 19: 2 (2015), 113–29 (114, 126).
[19] Éluard, Œuvres complètes, ed. Marcelle Dumas and Lucien Scheler (2 vols, Paris: Gallimard [Bibliothèque de la Pléiade], 1968), i. 511–21 (515).
[20] 'Qu'est-ce que les Lumières?', Magazine littéraire, 309 (April 1993), 61–73 (68).
[21] 'Qu'est-ce que les Lumières?', 67.

For Baudelaire, therefore 'modernité' is synonymous with what he calls 'beauty' in that both denote a patterned meaningfulness in the life about us; and so the poet as servant of beauty and as the 'painter of modern life' is a living, walking, thinking kaleidoscope, gazing from his belvedere at a crowd that looks very much, once again, like that ship under sail described in *Fusées*, f. 16 and to be found also in 'Le Port', where '[l]es formes élancées des navires, au gréement compliqué, auxquels la houle imprime des oscillations harmonieuses, servent à entretenir dans l'âme le goût du rythme et de la beauté':

> Ainsi l'amoureux de la vie universelle entre dans la foule comme un immense réservoir d'électricité. On peut aussi le comparer, lui, à un miroir aussi immense que la foule; à un kaléidoscope doué de conscience, qui, à chacun de ses mouvements, représente la vie multiple et la grâce mouvante de tous les éléments de la vie. C'est un *moi* insatiable du *non-moi*, qui, à chaque instant, le rend et l'exprime en images plus vivantes que la vie elle-même, toujours instable et fugitive.
>
> (ii. 692)

Here is Baudelaire himself, the alternative poet-lawgiver of modern life, finding movement and gracefulness and multiplicity amidst the fleeting instabilities of human experience and conferring them back, through his linguistic art, upon life itself. And this life that he adds to life is what he also calls beauty: like an electrical charge, conducted and bestowed on the words we speak—so that we may see straight and in a better light.

The Beauty of Redress

> Que serait une société, que serait une littérature qui accepteraient M. Charles Baudelaire pour leur poète?
> (Armand de Pontmartin, 'Les Poètes et la poésie française en 1861')[22]

---

[22] *Revue des Deux Mondes*, 1 Aug. 1861. On the context see Pichois and Ziegler, *Baudelaire*, 422–3. Also Marielle Macé, 'Le *Navire Baudelaire*: Imagination et hospitalité', *Littérature*, 177 (2015), 100–13. In her article, where she quotes Pontmartin (109), Macé recalls how in October 2013 the Italian government proposed to hold a day of national mourning for migrants drowned while crossing the Mediterranean in their attempt to reach Europe. While this proposal was not in the event accepted, Macé sees it as a commendable act of imagination whereby human beings of foreign nationality who had not set foot on Italian soil were nevertheless embraced and mourned as fellow-citizens by representatives of the Italian state. She sees this as a politics of the imagination ('La politique doit être imaginée' (109)) and Baudelaire as its origin: 'Cette mise en première ligne de l'imagination, jusque dans ses enjeux politiques, notre culture moderne la doit sans aucun doute à Baudelaire' (109). In particular she sees here a politics of 'mental hospitality', such as Baudelaire illustrates in 'Le Cygne' by his expression of solidarity and empathy with fellow exiles (such as Andromaque and Hugo), and which is both a prerequisite of progressive social attitudes and synonymous with what Baudelaire calls 'l'admirable faculté poétique' (*Corr.*, i. 327).

This, then, is the beauty of Baudelaire, and it does indeed have a modern look to it. In his published lecture entitled 'Joy or Night: Last Things in the Poetry of W. B. Yeats and Philip Larkin', Seamus Heaney concludes by affirming that here, as in his preceding Oxford lectures, he has 'repeatedly tried to establish [...] that the goal of life on earth, and of poetry as a vital factor in the achievement of that goal, is what Yeats called in "Under Ben Bulben" the "profane perfection of mankind"'. And he elaborates on this claim by referring to a group of writers who could just as pertinently and persuasively, I believe, have included Baudelaire:

> In order to achieve that goal, therefore, and in order that human beings bring about the most radiant conditions for themselves to inhabit, it is essential that the vision of reality which poetry offers should be transformative, more than just a printout of the given circumstances of its time and place. The poet who would be most the poet has to attempt an act of writing that outstrips the conditions even as it observes them. The truly creative writer, by interposing his or her perception and expression, will transfigure the conditions and effect thereby what I have been calling 'the redress of poetry'. The world is different after it has been read by a Shakespeare or an Emily Dickinson or a Samuel Beckett because it has been augmented by their reading of it. Indeed, Beckett is a very clear example of a writer who is Larkin's equal in not flinching from the ultimate bleakness of things, but who then goes on to do something positive with the bleakness. For it is not the apparent pessimism of Beckett's world-view that constitutes his poetic genius: his excellence resides in his working out a routine in the playhouse of his art which is both true to the depressing goings-on in the house of actuality and— more important—a transformation of them. It is because of his transformative way with language, his mixture of word-play and merciless humour, that Beckett the writer has life, and has it more abundantly than the conditions endured by Beckett the citizen might seem to warrant. [-] We go to poetry, we go to literature in general, to be forwarded within ourselves. The best it can do is to give us an experience that is like foreknowledge of certain things which we already seem to be remembering. What is at work in this most original and illuminating poetry is the mind's capacity to conceive a new plane of regard for itself, a new scope for its own activity.[23]

'Transformative', 'outstrips the conditions even as it observes them', 'not flinching from the ultimate bleakness of things, but who then goes on to do something positive with the bleakness', 'the playhouse of his art', 'the writer has life, and has it more abundantly', 'a new plane of regard for itself', 'a new scope for its own activity'... We could be reading about *Les Fleurs du Mal* and *Le Spleen de Paris*.

---

[23] Heaney, *The Redress of Poetry*, 159–60.

More broadly, what I have called 'the beauty of Baudelaire' shares many characteristics with Heaney's conception of poetry as a form of 'redress', itself a legal term. In his first Oxford lecture the newly inaugurated Professor of Poetry begins by reflecting somewhat resignedly that '[p]rofessors of poetry, apologists for it, practitioners of it, from Sir Philip Sidney to Wallace Stevens, all sooner or later are tempted to show how poetry's existence as a form of art relates to our existence as citizens of society—how it is "of present use"'. Acknowledging that '[b]ehind such defences and justifications, at any number of removes, stands Plato, calling into question whatever special prerogatives or useful influences poetry would claim for itself within the *polis*', Heaney then—master of his brief—turns the tables on the author of the *Republic*: 'Yet Plato's world of ideal forms also provides the court of appeal through which poetic imagination seeks to redress whatever is wrong or exacerbating in the prevailing conditions.' Here speaks the poet of *North*, resident of Bellaghy until it became a Provisional IRA stronghold and subsequent bard of the Wicklow Mountains. 'Moreover', Heaney continues, '"useful" or "practical" responses to those same conditions are derived from imagined standards too: poetic fictions, the dream of alternative worlds, enable governments and revolutionaries as well.' But there is a big difference between the poet and the ideologue: 'It's just that governments and revolutionaries would compel society to take on the shape of their imagining, whereas poets are typically more concerned to conjure with their own and their readers' sense of what is possible, or desirable, or, indeed, imaginable'—or, as Baudelaire would argue, with the sense of what is, at least in the moment, more 'real' and 'true': 'ce qu'il y a de plus réel, c'est ce qui n'est complètement vrai que dans *un autre monde*'. And for Heaney as for Baudelaire the word 'noble' is key. Quoting from Wallace Stevens's essay 'The Noble Rider and the Sounds of Words', where Stevens concludes that the nobility of poetry 'is a violence from within that protects us from a violence without', Heaney adds his own gloss: 'It is the imagination pressing back against the pressure of reality.'[24] Baudelaire's resistance hero is one such noble rider.

As Stevens shows, and as Heaney knew, this 'pressure of reality' can include the pressure to protest, to participate in 'the politics of subversion, of redressal, of affirming that which is denied voice'. The revolutionaries of 1848, for example, will want the poet to join them on the barricades and for poetry to be a form of direct action (in the style, say, of Pierre Dupont). Similarly, as Heaney discusses, poets have always been called on in time of strife to supply propaganda and to meet 'the common expectation of solidarity'—whether it be an English poet at the Front required to 'dehumanize' his German adversary during the First World War, or an Irish poet 'in the wake of the 1916 executions' pressured 'to revile the tyranny of the executing powers'... or, by implication, another Irish poet in the

---

[24] Heaney, *The Redress of Poetry*, 1.

midst of the Troubles. But a poet who conceives of poetry as a form of redress will resist not by deferring to the common protest but by refusing to go with the flow. 'Obedience to the force of gravity. The greatest sin', writes Simone Weil in *Gravity and Grace,* from her own Christian perspective, and as here quoted: resistance to the prevailing theology of the Fall might be Baudelaire's retort. Heaney draws on the work of several writers and on several meanings of 'redress' to build a composite picture of this power of poetry to 'protest' by other means: to resist, to counterbalance in order to redress the balance, to set to rights by offering alternatives. His own solidarity is with the poets of the twentieth century, 'from Wilfred Owen to Irina Ratushinskaya', 'who from principle, in solitude, and without any guarantee of success, were drawn by the logic of their work to disobey the forces of gravity. These figures have become the types of an action that gains value in proportion to its immediate practical ineffectiveness.'[25] Sympathetic as many poets may very well be to a wide range of causes, for Heaney those poets who discharge the function of poetry as a mode of redress in the sense of 'proclaiming and correcting injustices' are 'in danger of slighting another imperative, namely, to redress poetry *as* poetry, to set it up as its own category, an eminence established and a pressure exercised by distinctly linguistic means'. Poets, as it were, need to watch their language: 'Poetry cannot afford to lose its fundamentally self-delighting inventiveness, its joy in being a process of language as well as a representation of things in the world.'[26]

The problem is age-old: how can poetry weigh anything in the scales of justice? Socrates' disparagement of Ion as 'a light thing' and Malherbe's celebrated remark that a poet is of no more use to the state than a good skittles-player, Hugo's statement that after the Terror a poet can no longer write madrigals or Adorno's misgivings about what it might mean to write lyric poetry after Auschwitz... the list could be extended; and perhaps with Auden's apparently straightforward concession in his memorial poem for Yeats that poetry 'makes nothing happen'? Except that those words might also mean (though in the context of the poem they appear not to) that poetry can make a happening out of nothing. Be that as it may, Heaney constructs a strong and subtle argument for poetry as a form of 'redress': for 'poetry's possible service to programmes of cultural and political realignment' (he has briefly been alluding to the poetry of feminism, post-colonialism, and Irish nationalism), and of 'poetry as an upright, resistant, and self-bracing entity within the general flux and flex of language'. And then, anxious not to 'give the impression that [poetry's] force must always be exercised in earnest, morally premeditated ways', the new Professor ends with his own act of redress: 'On the contrary, I want to profess the surprise of poetry as well as its reliability':

---

[25] Heaney, *The Redress of Poetry,* 2–4.   [26] Heaney, *The Redress of Poetry,* 5–6, 5.

I want to celebrate its given, unforeseen thereness, the way it enters our field of vision and animates our physical and intelligent being in much the same way as those bird-shapes stencilled on the transparent surfaces of glass walls or windows must suddenly enter the vision and change the direction of the real birds' flight. In a flash the shapes register and transmit their unmistakable presence, so the birds veer off instinctively. An image of the living creatures has induced a totally salubrious swerve in the creatures themselves. And this natural, heady diversion is also something induced by poetry[.][27]

For Baudelaire, too, '*le beau est toujours bizarre*', and it conduces to 'cette santé morale, si éclatante et si glorieuse' (i. 401) that was so strongly manifest on the bright and beautiful morning of 'Le Goût de l'infini'. As it happens, those 'bird-shapes' are known technically as 'manifestations', which lends new vigour to the cliché of a 'haunting beauty'.

Reflecting on this 'salubrious swerve', Heaney is reminded of one further meaning of 'redress', one used in the hunting field: 'To bring back (the hounds or deer) to the proper course', and he finds this sense of the word appropriate also: 'In this "redress" there is no hint of ethical obligation; it is more a matter of finding a course for the breakaway of innate capacity, a course where something unhindered, yet directed, can sweep ahead into its full potential.'[28] Like Baudelaire's 'conjecture' perhaps, launched and guided along the 'profondes avenues' that poetry has opened up for 'l'imagination la plus voyageuse'? A sudden swerve of recognition ('hypocrite lecteur,—mon semblable,—mon frère!') that makes us change course by virtue of the 'heady diversion' he calls 'l'ivresse de l'art'?

Baudelaire is not Larkin, or Beckett, or Heaney. The 1848 Revolution and its aftermath are not the Troubles. But if we are to continue to see Baudelaire as in some way or other the instigator of what we consider to be 'modern' poetry, then we need, I believe, to rethink the nature of his modernity and to 'go forward' beyond the Benjaminian model of 'a lyric poet in the era of high capitalism'. If Baudelaire is to be viewed as the 'writer' or 'painter' of modern life, then it is the *way* he writes and the frame of poetic mind from within which he writes—seeing poetry and 'beauty' as forms of resistance—that make him eligible for that title, and eligible for the very reasons set out by Heaney in his own attempt to account for the public value of poetry. In a slightly earlier essay, 'The Interesting Case of Nero, Chekhov's Cognac and a Knocker', with which he prefaces *The Government of the Tongue*, Heaney notes that whereas Wilfred Owen, confronted by the horrors of the Great War, 'sponsors an art which seems to rebuke beauty', Osip Mandelstam, by contrast, 'and at an equally high price', 'sponsors all over again the Keatsian proposition that beauty is truth, truth beauty':

---

[27] Heaney, *The Redress of Poetry*, 15.   [28] Heaney, *The Redress of Poetry*, 15.

He is a burning reminder of the way in which not only the words 'truth' and 'justice' may be salvaged from the catastrophe of history, but the word 'beauty' also: a reminder that humanity is served by the purely poetic fidelity of the poet to all words in their pristine being.[29]

In our postmodern age, assailed by pandemic and threatened with apocalypse by a warming climate while continuing to be overwhelmed by the 'catastrophic' history of two world wars, the Holocaust, and (since Heaney's lectures) the events and aftermath of 9/11, the words 'truth', justice', and 'beauty' seem light indeed. But if we read Baudelaire's 'beauty' as a synonym for Heaney's 'redress', it becomes easier to see it for what it is: the capacity of poetry, whether in verse or prose, to 'bring us back to the proper course', to 'redeem' and 'buy us back' from lazy thinking and tired perceptions, and doubtless too from a thousand hypocrisies; and to cause us, as though it were a luxury toy ('cet objet de luxe qu'on nomme Poésie' (ii. 344)),[30] to re-imagine the world in a spirit of playful experiment and celebratory seriousness. Like a kaleidoscope, and comparable also with those other instruments of vision mentioned in *Morale du joujou*, ludic aids to the modern seer: the 'stéréoscope' ('qui donne en ronde bosse une image plane') and then the 'phénakisti[s]cope', which Baudelaire cites as an example of the 'joujou scientique' that may be too expensive for some parents to afford but which is certainly able to 'développer dans le cerveau de l'enfant le goût des effets merveilleux et surprenants' (i. 585). The phenakistoscope was a toy Baudelaire had known in his own childhood. Invented in 1832 and introduced into France the following year,[31] with a name derived etymologically from the Greek words for 'to deceive the eye', this plaything consisted of a spinning cardboard disc on which a sequence of fixed images of sequential actions served to create the optical illusion of fluid movement. As such it is considered to be a forerunner of the motion picture: of stasis turned into movement by the process of 'animation'[32]—akin perhaps to that of the painter of modern life who adds life to life. For Baudelaire the work of art is just such an instrument of beauty, a way of presenting a sequence of patterns that are in their own way strange, harmonious, and right. But, as with these toys, such patterns are only provisional, mere playful invitations to see one form of order that will soon be replaced by another. Beauty is the poet's new

---

[29] Seamus Heaney, *The Government of the Tongue: The 1986 T. S. Eliot Lectures and Other Critical Writings* (London: Faber and Faber, 1989), xi–xxiii (xix–xx).

[30] Cf. Flaubert in a letter to René de Maricourt, 4 Jan.[1867]: 'Nous sommes des ouvriers de luxe; or, personne n'est assez riche pour nous payer' (*Correspondance*, ed. Bruneau, iii. 585).

[31] He describes it to his half-brother Alphonse in a letter of 23 Nov. 1833 (*Corr.*, i. 22).

[32] See Marit Grøtta, *Baudelaire's Media Aesthetics: The Gaze of the Flâneur and 19th-Century Media* (New York and London: Bloomsbury, 2015), 8–9, 76–84, and 92–3. Grøtta argues that 'Baudelaire's aesthetics can be conceived, to a large degree, as a media aesthetics, and that montages, moving images, and 3-D images are features that are central to Baudelaire's aesthetics' (1).

authority, but it is also protean, and, as we know from the dedicatory letter to Houssaye, it may also be accidental.

With which we return to the fundamental question raised at the beginning of this book in the Preface (and throughout *Unacknowledged Legislators*). Who is in charge here? Writers with their fond intentions, or beauty which may have a mind of its own? Moses or Orpheus? The bright idea or the graft of craft? Both or all, of course: like Wordsworth's 'first Poetic spirit of our human life' which '[c]reates, creator and receiver both, | Working but in alliance with the works | Which it beholds'. Or indeed like Emma Bovary. For, states Baudelaire, women will thank Flaubert for raising the female sex 'à une si haute puissance, si loin de l'animal pur et si près de l'homme idéal, et de l'avoir fait participer à ce double caractère de calcul et de rêverie qui constitue l'être parfait' (ii. 83–4). Not all women may agree, even though—or not least because—they recognize that by 'l'homme idéal' is meant a stereotype of pure will to set against that other false, female stereotype of pure sentiment. But here the critic is suggesting that, far from being 'le poète hystérique' (ii. 83), Emma Bovary represents 'l'être parfait': an incarnation of that omnipotent governing body we call the creative imagination, itself combining 'calcul' and 'rêverie', and whose rule we may elect to accept by participating in the beauty of Baudelaire.

Bibliography

Primary Sources

Baudelaire

Œuvres complètes, ed. Claude Pichois (2 vols, Paris: Gallimard [Bibliothèque de la Pléiade], 1975–6).
Correspondance, ed. Claude Pichois and Jean Ziegler (2 vols, Paris: Galllimard [Bibliothèque de la Pléiade], 1973).
Correspondance, ed. Claude Pichois and Jérôme Thélot (Paris: Gallimard [Folio classique], 2000).
Lettres à Baudelaire, ed. Claude and Vincenette Pichois (Neuchâtel: Éditions de la Baconnière, 1973).
Charles Baudelaire: Nouvelles lettres (ed. Claude Pichois) (Paris: Fayard, 2000).
Fusées, Mon cœur mis à nu, et autres fragments posthumes, ed. André Guyaux (Paris: Gallimard [Folio classique], 2016).
Edgar Allan Poe, sa vie et ses ouvrages, ed. W. T. Bandy (Toronto and Buffalo, Colo.: University of Toronto Press, 1973).
La Fanfarlo, ed. Claude Pichois (Monaco: Éditions du Rocher, 1957).
La Fanfarlo: Le Spleen de Paris (Petits Poèmes en prose), ed. David Scott and Barbara Wright (Paris: GF Flammarion, 1987).
L'Atelier de Baudelaire: 'Les Fleurs du Mal': Édition diplomatique, ed. Claude Pichois and Jacques Dupont (4 vols, Paris: Champion, 2005).
Les Fleurs du Mal, ed. Antoine Adam (Paris: Garnier frères, 1961).
Les Fleurs du Mal, ed. Graham Chesters (London: Duckworth [Bristol Classical Press], 1995).
Les Fleurs du Mal, ed. Claude Pichois (rev. edn, Paris: Gallimard, 1996).
Le Spleen de Paris: Petits Poèmes en prose, ed. Max Milner (Paris: Imprimerie nationale, 1979).
Le Spleen de Paris. (Petits Poèmes en prose), ed. Jean-Luc Steinmetz (Paris: Le Livre de poche [Classiques], 2003).
Le Spleen de Paris (Petits Poèmes en prose), ed. Robert Kopp (Paris: Gallimard, 2006).
Le Spleen de Paris, ed. Aurélia Cervoni and Andrea Schellino (Paris: Flammarion, 2007).
Petits Poèmes en prose (Le Spleen de Paris), ed. Henri Daniel-Rops (Paris: Les Belles Lettres, 1962).
Petits Poèmes en prose (Le Spleen de Paris), ed. Henri Lemaitre (Paris: Garnier frères, 1962).
Petits Poèmes en prose (Le Spleen de Paris), ed. Marcel A. Ruff (Paris: Garnier-Flammarion, 1967).
Petits Poèmes en prose, ed. Robert Kopp (Paris: Corti, 1969).
Salon de 1846, ed. David Kelley (Oxford: Clarendon Press, 1975).

Baudelaire's reception

Bandy, W. T. (ed.), *Baudelaire Judged by his Contemporaries (1845–1867)* (New York: Columbia University, 1933).

Bandy, W. T. and Claude Pichois (eds), *Baudelaire devant ses contemporains* (Monaco: Éditions du Rocher, 1957).

Carter, A. E., *Baudelaire et la critique française 1868–1917* (Columbia: University of South Carolina Press, 1963).

Guyaux, André (ed.), *Baudelaire: Un demi-siècle de lectures des 'Fleurs du mal' (1855–1905)* (Paris: PUPS [Presses de l'Université Paris-Sorbonne], 2007).

Other Primary Sources

Aristotle, *Problems*, ed. and trans. Robert Mayhew and David C. Mirhady (2 vols, Cambridge, Mass.: Harvard University Press, 2014).

Asselineau, Charles, et al., *Fontainebleau: Paysages, légendes, souvenirs, fantaisies. Hommage à C. F. Denecourt* (Paris: Hachette, 1855).

Balzac, Honoré de, *Écrits sur le roman*, ed. Stéphane Vachon (Paris: Librairie Générale Française [Le Livre de poche], 2000).

Bastiat, Frédéric, *Capital et rente* (Paris: Guillaumin & Cie, 1849).

Bastiat, Frédéric, *Ce qu'on voit et ce qu'on ne voit pas, ou L'Économie politique en une leçon* (Paris: Guillamin & Cie, 1850).

Bastiat, Frédéric, *Harmonies économiques* (Paris: Guillaumin & Cie, 1850).

Bastiat, Frédéric, *La Loi* (Paris: Guillaumin & Cie, 1850).

Beckett, Samuel, *Proust/Samuel Beckett: Three Dialogues/Samuel Beckett & Georges Duthuit* (London: John Calder, 1965).

Beckett, Samuel, *Disjecta: Miscellaneous Writings and a Dramatic Fragment*, ed. Ruby Cohn (London: John Calder, 1983).

Bertrand, Aloysius, *Gaspard de la nuit: Fantaisies à la manière de Rembrandt et de Callot*, ed. Max Milner (Paris: Gallimard, 1980).

Bertrand, Aloysius, *Gaspard de la nuit: Fantaisies à la manière de Rembrandt et de Callot*, ed. Henri Scepi (Paris: Gallimard [Folioplus Classiques], 2011).

Castille, Hippolyte, 'Critique littéraire: Romanciers contemporains. I. M. H. de Balzac', in Stéphane Vachon (ed.), *Balzac* (Paris: Presses de l'Université de Paris-Sorbonne [Collection Mémoire de la critique], 1999), 133–41.

Castille, Hippolyte, 'Réponse aux adhérents du *Travail intellectuel*', *Le Travail intellectuel*, no. 2 (15 Sept. 1847), 1–2.

Castille, Hippolyte, *Histoire de la seconde République française* (4 vols, Paris: Victor Lecou, 1854–6).

Catechism of the Catholic Church (Vatican City: Libreria Editrice Vaticana, 1993).

Chateaubriand, François-René de, *Génie du christianisme*, ed. Pierre Reboul (2 vols, Paris: Garnier-Flammarion, 1966).

Desbordes-Valmore, Marceline, *Bouquets et prières* (Paris: Dumont, 1843).

Éluard, Paul, *Œuvres complètes*, ed. Marcelle Dumas and Lucien Scheler (2 vols, Paris: Gallimard [Bibliothèque de la Pléiade], 1968).

Flaubert, Gustave, *Correspondance*, ed. Jean Bruneau and Yvan Leclerc (5 vols, Paris: Gallimard [Bibliothèque de la Pléiade], 1973–2007).

Gautier, Théophile, *Mademoiselle de Maupin*, in *Romans, contes et nouvelles*, ed. Pierre Laubriet (2 vols, Paris: Gallimard [Bibliothèque de la Pléiade], 2002).

Gautier, Théophile, *Œuvres poétiques complètes*, ed. Michel Brix (Paris: Bartillat, 2004).

Heaney, Seamus, *The Government of the Tongue: The 1986 T. S. Eliot Lectures and Other Critical Writings* (London: Faber and Faber, 1989).
Heaney, Seamus, *The Redress of Poetry* (London: Faber and Faber, 1995).
Hugo, Victor, *Œuvres complètes*, ed. Jacques Seebacher, Guy Rosa, et al. (15 vols, Paris: Robert Laffont, 1985–90).
La Bruyère, Jean de, *Les Caractères, ou Les Mœurs de ce siècle*, ed. Antoine Adam (Paris: Gallimard [Folio], 1975).
Lamartine, Alphonse de, *Cours familier de littérature* (28 vols, Paris: Chez l'auteur, 1856–70).
Liszt, Franz, 'De la situation des artistes, et de leur condition dans la sociéte', *Gazette musicale de Paris*, 2e année, no. 41 (11 Oct. 1835), 332–3.
Mallarmé, Stéphane, *Œuvres complètes*, ed. Bertrand Marchal (2 vols, Paris: Gallimard [Bibliothèque de la Pléiade], 1998–2003).
Mallarmé, Stéphane, *Divagations*, trans. Barbara Johnson (Cambridge, Mass., and London: The Belknap Press of Harvard University Press, 2007).
Mallarmé, Stéphane, *Correspondance 1854–1898*, ed. Bertrand Marchal (Paris: Gallimard, 2019).
Plato, *Early Socratic Dialogues*, ed. Trevor J. Saunders (rev. edn, London: Penguin Books, 2005).
Plato, *Laws*, ed. Trevor J. Saunders (rev. edn, London: Penguin Books, 2004).
Plato, *Republic*, trans. C. D. C. Reeve (Indianapolis and Cambridge, Mass.: Hackett, 2004).
Poe, Edgar Allan, *Collected Works of Edgar Allan Poe*, ed. Thomas Ollive Mabbott (3 vols, Cambridge, Mass., and London: The Belknap Press of Harvard University Press, 1969–78).
Poe, Edgar Allan, *Selected Writings*, ed. David Galloway (Harmondsworth: Penguin Books, 1967).
Poe, Edgar Allan, *Œuvres en prose*, traduction par Ch. Baudelaire, ed. Y.-G. Le Dantec (Paris: Gallimard [Bibliothèque de la Pléiade], 1951).
Proudhon, Pierre-Joseph, *La Guerre et la paix: Recherches sur le principe et la constitution du droit des gens* (2 vols, Paris: E. Dentu, 1861).
Proudhon, Pierre-Joseph, *Théorie de la propriété* (Paris: Librairie internationale, 1866).
Proust, Marcel, *A la recherche du temps perdu*, ed. Jean-Yves Tadié (4 vols, Paris: Gallimard [Bibliothèque de la Pléiade], 1987–9).
Rousseau, Jean-Jacques, *Œuvres complètes*, ed. Bernard Gagnebin and Marcel Raymond (5 vols, Paris: Gallimard [Bibliothèque de la Pléiade], 1959–95).
Ruskin, John, *'Unto this Last' and Other Writings*, ed. Clive Wilmer (rev. edn, London: Penguin Books, 1997).
Shelley, Percy Bysshe, *Shelley's Poetry and Prose*, ed. Donald H. Reiman and Neil Fraistat (2nd edn, New York and London: Norton, 2002).
Staël, Germaine de, *De la littérature considérée dans ses rapports avec les institutions sociales*, ed. Gérard Gengembre and Jean Goldzink (Paris: Flammarion, 1991).
Staël, Germaine de, *Corinne*, ed. Simone Balayé (Paris: Gallimard [Folio classique], 1985).
Staël, Germaine de, *De l'Allemagne*, ed. Simone Balayé (2 vols, Paris: Garnier Flammarion, 1968).
Staël, Germaine de, *Delphine*, ed. Béatrice Didier (2 vols, Paris: Flammarion, 2000).
Verlaine, Paul, 'Charles Baudelaire', in *Œuvres en prose complètes*, ed. Jacques Borel (Paris: Gallimard [Bibliothèque de la Pléiade], 1972), 599–612.
Vigny, Alfred de, *Œuvres complètes* (2 vols), ed. François Germain and André Jarry (vol. i) and Alphonse Bouvet (vol. ii) (Paris: Gallimard [Bibliothèque de la Pléiade], 1986–93).

Vigny, Alfred de, *Journal d'un poète*, in *Œuvres complètes*, ed. Fernand Baldensperger (2 vols, Paris: Gallimard [Bibliothèque de la Pléiade], 1948-50).
Voltaire, *Romans et contes*, ed. Frédéric Deloffre and Jacques Van den Heuvel (Paris: Gallimard [Bibliothèque de la Pléiade], 1979).
Voltaire, *Candide and Other Stories*, trans. and ed. Roger Pearson (rev. edn, Oxford: Oxford University Press [Oxford World's Classics], 2006).
Wagner, Richard, *Quatre poèmes d'opéras traduits en prose française, précédés d'une Lettre sur la musique* (Paris: Librairie nouvelle [A. Bourdilliat et Cie], 1861).
Wordsworth, William, *The Major Works*, ed. Stephen Gill (Oxford: Oxford University Press [Oxford World's Classics], 2000).

SECONDARY SOURCES

Works on Baudelaire

Abbott, Helen, *Between Baudelaire and Mallarmé: Voice, Conversation and Music* (Farnham: Ashgate, 2009).
Abbott, Helen, *Parisian Intersections: Baudelaire's Legacy to Composers* (Oxford and New York: Peter Lang, 2012).
Abbott, Helen, *Baudelaire in Song: 1880-1930* (Oxford: Oxford University Press, 2017).
Acquisto, Joseph, *The Fall Out of Redemption: Writing and Thinking Beyond Salvation in Baudelaire, Cioran, Fondane, Agamben, and Nancy* (New York and London: Bloomsbury, 2015).
Acquisto, Joseph, 'Styles of Life, *Poéthique*, and Irony in Charles Baudelaire', *Nineteenth-Century French Studies*, 48: 1-2 (Fall-Winter, 2019-20), 114-29.
Austin, Lloyd James, *L'Univers poétique de Baudelaire: Symbolisme et symbolique* (Paris: Mercure de France, 1956).
Avice, Jean-Paul, 'La Théologie usée de Baudelaire', *L'Année Baudelaire*, 7 (2003), 81-90.
Badesco, Luc, 'Baudelaire et la Revue Jean Raisin: La Première Publication du "Vin des Chiffonniers"', *Revue des sciences humaines*, 85 (Jan.-March 1957), 57-88.
Bauer, Franck, 'Le Poème en prose: Un joujou du pauvre?', *Poétique*, 109 (1997), 17-37.
Bayle, Corinne, *Nocturne de l'âme moderne: 'Le Spleen de Paris' de Charles Baudelaire* (Mont-Saint-Aignan: Presses universitaires de Rouen et du Havre, 2014).
Benedetto, L[uigi] F[oscolo], 'L'Architecture des *Fleurs du Mal*', *Zeitschrift für französische Sprache und Literatur*, 39 (1912), 18-70.
Bénichou, Paul, 'Le Satan de Baudelaire', in Guyaux and Marchal (eds), *'Les Fleurs du mal': Actes du colloque de la Sorbonne*, 9-23.
Benjamin, Walter, *Charles Baudelaire: A Lyric Poet in the Era of High Capitalism*, trans. Harry Zohn (London and New York: Verso, 1973).
Bercot, Martine, '"Nouvelles *Fleurs du Mal*": idéalisme et désillusion', in Bercot et al., *'Les Fleurs du Mal': L'Intériorité de la forme*, 41-54.
Bercot, Martine, et al., *'Les Fleurs du Mal': L'Intériorité de la forme. Actes du colloque du 7 janvier 1989* (Paris: SEDES, 1989).
Bercot, Martine, and André Guyaux, *Dix études sur Baudelaire* (Paris: Champion, 1993).
Bernard, Suzanne, *Le Poème en prose de Baudelaire jusqu'à nos jours* (Paris: Nizet, 1959).
Bersani, Leo, *Baudelaire and Freud* (Berkeley, Los Angeles, and London: University of California Press, 1977).

Bertrand, Jean-Pierre, 'Une lecture médiatique du *Spleen de Paris*', in Thérenty and Vaillant (eds), *Presse et plumes*, 329-37.
Billy, Dominique, *Les Formes poétiques selon Baudelaire* (Paris: Honoré Champion, 2015).
Blin, Georges, *Baudelaire* (Paris: Gallimard, 1939).
Blin, Georges, *Le Sadisme de Baudelaire* (Paris: Corti, 1948).
Blood, Susan, 'Mimesis and the Grotesque in "L'Albatros"', in Thompson (ed.), *Understanding 'Les Fleurs du Mal'*, 1-15.
Bohac, Barbara, 'Baudelaire et Liszt: Le Génie de la rhapsodie', *Romantisme*, 151 (2011), 87-99.
Bonnefoy, Yves, 'Préface' [to *Les Fleurs du Mal*], in Baudelaire, *Œuvres complètes*, ed. Lloyd James Austin (2 vols, Paris: Club du meilleur livre, 1955), reproduced in Bonnefoy, *L'Improbable, suivi de Un rêve fait à Mantoue* (rev. edn, Paris: Mercure de France, 1980), 29-38, and in *Sous le signe de Baudelaire*, 11-18.
Bonnefoy, Yves, 'Préface', in Starobinski, *La Mélancolie au miroir*, 7-8.
Bonnefoy, Yves, 'Que signifie J.G.F.?', *L'Année Baudelaire*, 9-10 (2005-6), 65-70, reprinted in *Sous le signe de Baudelaire*, 331-9.
Bonnefoy, Yves, *Sous le signe de Baudelaire* (Paris: Gallimard, 2011).
Brix, Michel, 'Claude Pichois et l'interprétation de Baudelaire', *L'Année Baudelaire*, 9/10 (2007), 71-7.
Brombert, Victor, 'City Images and the "Dream of Stone"', *Yale French Studies*, 32 (1964), 99-105.
Brombert, Victor, '"Le Cygne" de Baudelaire: Douleur, souvenir, travail', in *Études baudelairiennes*, 3 (1973), 254-61.
Brombert, Victor, 'The Will to Ecstasy: The Example of Baudelaire's "La Chevelure"', *Yale French Studies*, 50 (1974), 54-63; trans. and republished as '*La Chevelure* ou la volonté de l'extase', in Bercot and Guyaux (eds), *Dix études sur Baudelaire*, 61-9.
Brunel, Pierre, 'Lesbos', in Bercot et al., *'Les Fleurs du Mal': L'Intériorité de la forme*, 85-90.
Burton, Richard D. E., *Baudelaire in 1859: A Study in the Sources of Poetic Creativity* (Cambridge: Cambridge University Press, 1988).
Burton, Richard D. E., 'Baudelaire and Lyon: A Reading of "Paysage"', *Nottingham French Studies*, 28: 1 (March 1989), 26-38.
Burton, Richard D. E., *Baudelaire and the Second Republic: Writing and Revolution* (Oxford: Clarendon Press, 1991).
Burton, Richard D. E., 'Destruction as Creation: "Le Mauvais Vitrier" and the Poetics and Politics of Violence', *Romanic Review*, 83: 3 (1992), 297-322.
Burton, Richard D. E., 'Bonding and Breaking in Baudelaire's *Petits Poèmes en prose*', *Modern Language Review*, 88: 1 (Jan. 1993), 58-73.
Burton, Richard D. E., 'Baudelaire's Indian Summer: A Reading of "Les Bons Chiens"', *Nineteenth-Century French Studies*, 22: 3-4 (1994), 466-86.
Burton, Richard D. E., 'Poet, Painter, Lover: A Reading of "Les Bijoux"', in Thompson (ed.), *Understanding 'Les Fleurs du Mal'*, 214-23.
Butor, Michel, *Histoire extraordinaire: Essai sur un rêve de Baudelaire* (Paris: Gallimard, 1961).
Calasso, Robert, *La Folie Baudelaire*, trans. Alastair McEwen (London: Allen Lane, 2012 [first published in Italian in 2008]).
Cargo, Robert T., 'Baudelaire's "L'Étranger" as Parlor Game', *Nineteenth-Century French Studies*, 8: 1-2 (Fall-Winter, 1979-80), 76-8.
Carpenter, Scott, *Acts of Fiction: Resistance and Resolution from Sade to Baudelaire* (University Park, Pa: Pennsylvania State University Press, 1996).

Carpenter, Scott, 'Entre rue et boulevard: Les chemins de l'allégorie chez Baudelaire', *Romantisme*, 134 (2006), 55-65.
Carpenter, Scott, 'Mystification et esthétique moderne', *Romantisme*, 156 (2012), 13-24.
Cassagne, Albert, *Versification et métrique de Ch[arles] Baudelaire* (Paris: Hachette, 1906; repr. Geneva: Slatkine, 1982).
Cellier, Léon, *Baudelaire et Hugo* (Paris: Corti, 1970).
Chambers, Ross, '"L'Art sublime du comédien" ou le regardant et le regardé: Autour d'un mythe baudelairien', *Saggi et richerche di letteratura francese*, 10 (1971), 189-260.
Chambers, Ross, 'Baudelaire et l'espace poétique: A propos du "Soleil"', in Yves Bonnefoy et al., *Le Lieu et la formule: Hommage à Marc Eigeldinger* (Neuchâtel: Éditions de La Baconnière, 1978), 111-20.
Chambers, Ross, 'Seeing and Saying in Baudelaire's "Les Aveugles"', in Robert L. Mitchell (ed.), *Pre-Text, Text, Context: Essays on Nineteenth-Century French Literature* (Columbus, Oh.: Ohio State University Press, 1980), 147-56.
Chambers, Ross, '"Je" dans les 'Tableaux parisiens' de Baudelaire', *Nineteenth-Century French Studies*, 9: 1-2 (1980-1), 59-68.
Chambers, Ross, 'Trois paysages urbains: Les Poèmes liminaires des *Tableaux parisiens*', *Modern Philology*, 80: 4 (May 1983), 372-89.
Chambers, Ross, 'Baudelaire's Street Poetry', *Nineteenth-Century French Studies*, 13: 4 (Summer, 1985), 244-59.
Chambers, Ross, 'The Storm in the Eye of the Poem: Baudelaire's "A une passante"', in Mary Ann Caws (ed.), *Textual Analysis: Some Readers Reading* (New York: Modern Language Association of America, 1986), 156-66.
Chambers, Ross, 'Are Baudelaire's "Tableaux parisiens" about Paris?', in Anna Whiteside and Michael Issacharoff (eds), *On Referring in Literature* (Bloomington and Indianapolis: Indiana University Press, 1987), 95-110.
Chambers, Ross, 'Baudelaire's Dedicatory Practice', *SubStance*, 56 (1988), 5-17.
Chambers, Ross, 'Perpetual Abjuration: Baudelaire and the Pain of Modernity' [review article of Burton, *Baudelaire in 1859*, and Maclean, *Narrative as Performance*], *French Forum*, 15: 2 (May 1990), 169-88.
Chambers, Ross, 'Recycling the Ragpicker: "Le Vin des chiffonniers"', in Thompson (ed.), *Understanding 'Les Fleurs du Mal'*, 176-91.
Chambers, Ross, 'Baudelaire's Paris' [2005], in Lloyd (ed.), *The Cambridge Companion to Baudelaire*, 101-16.
Chambers, Ross, 'On Inventing Unknownness: The Poetry of Disenchanted Reenchantment (Leopardi, Baudelaire, Rimbaud, Justice)', *French Forum*, 33 (2008), 15-36.
Chambers, Ross, 'Daylight Spectre: Baudelaire's "The Seven Old Men"', *Yale French Studies*, 125: 6 (2014), 45-65; incorporated in *An Atmospherics of the City*.
Chambers, Ross, *An Atmospherics of the City: Baudelaire and the Poetics of Noise* (New York: Fordham University Press, 2015).
Charnet, Yves, '"L'Orage rajeunit les fleurs": Lettre à Claude Pichois', in Guyaux and Marchal (eds), *'Les Fleurs du Mal': Actes du colloque de la Sorbonne des 10 et 11 janvier 2003*, 41-52.
Chatterjee, Ronjaunee, 'Baudelaire and Feminine Singularity', *French Studies*, 70 (2015), 17-32.
Chesters, Graham, 'Sur "Les Bons Chiens" de Baudelaire', *Revue d'histoire littéraire de la France*, 80 (1980), 416-21.

Chesters, Graham, *Baudelaire and the Poetics of Craft* (Cambridge: Cambridge University Press, 1988).
Combe, Dominique, 'L'Esthétique kantienne et la genèse de l'"art pur": Baudelaire et le romantisme', in Isabelle Bour, Éric Dayre, and Patrick Née (eds), *Modernité et romantisme* (Paris: Champion, 2001), 27-49.
Combe, Dominique, 'Le "poème épique condamné": Baudelaire, Hugo et Poe', in Guyaux and Marchal (eds), *'Les Fleurs du Mal': Actes du colloque de la Sorbonne des 10 et 11 janvier 2003*, 53-64.
Compagnon, Antoine, *Baudelaire devant l'innombrable* (Paris: Presses de l'Université de Paris-Sorbonne, 2003).
Compagnon, Antoine, 'Notes sur notes', in *Baudelaire toujours: Hommage à Claude Pichois, L'Année baudelairienne*, 9-10 (2005-6), 105-12.
Compagnon, Antoine, *Baudelaire: L'Irréductible* (Paris: Flammarion, 2014).
Cornulier, Benoît de, 'Métrique des *Fleurs du Mal*', in Bercot et al., *'Les Fleurs du Mal': L'Intériorité de la forme*, 55-76.
Cornulier, Benoît de, 'Pour l'analyse du sonnet dans *Les Fleurs du Mal*', in Murphy (ed.), *Lectures de Baudelaire: 'Les Fleurs du Mal'*, 197-236.
Cornulier, Benoît de, 'La Versification des *Fleurs du Mal*', in *L'Atelier de Baudelaire. 'Les Fleurs du Mal': édition diplomatique*, ed. Pichois and Dupont, iv. 3543-65.
Culler, Jonathan, 'Intertextuality and Interpretation: Baudelaire's "Correspondances"', in Christopher Prendergast (ed.), *Nineteenth-Century French Poetry: Introductions to Close Reading* (Cambridge: Cambridge University Press, 1990), 118-37.
Culler, Jonathan, 'Baudelaire and Poe', *Zeitschrift für französische Sprache und Literatur*, 100 (1990), 61-73.
Culler, Jonathan, *Baudelaire's Satanic Verses: The Cassal Lecture, 6 October 1994* (London: University of London, 1994); published in a revised version as 'Baudelaire's Satanic Verses', *Diacritics*, 28: 3 (Fall 1998), 86-100.
Culler, Jonathan, 'Baudelaire's Destruction', *MLN*, 127: 4 (Sept. 2012), 699-711.
Derrida, Jacques, *Donner le temps. 1: La Fausse Monnaie* (n.p. [Paris]: Galilée, 1991).
Dotoli, Giovanni, *Baudelaire-Hugo: Rencontres, ruptures, fragments, abîmes* (Fasano and Paris: Schena and Presses de l'Université de Paris-Sorbonne, 2003).
Doumet, Christian, 'Céder ou ne pas céder aux "Vocations" (Baudelaire face à la musique)', in Pierre Sorlin, Marie-Claire Ropars-Wuilleumier, and Michell Lagny (eds), *L'Art et l'hybride* (Paris: Presses universitaires de Vincennes, 2001), 25-52.
Dubray, Jean, *Pascal et Baudelaire* (Paris: Classiques Garnier, 2011).
Dufour, Pierre, '*Les Fleurs du Mal*: Dictionnaire de mélancolie', *Littérature*, 72 (1988), 30-54.
Dufour, Pierre, 'Formes et fonctions de l'allégorie dans la modernité des *Fleurs du Mal*', in Bercot et al., *'Les Fleurs du Mal': L'Intériorité de la forme*, 135-47.
Dupont, Jacques, 'Baudelaire et Colette: Du côté de Lesbos', *L'Année Baudelaire*, 5 (1999), 155-67.
Eigeldinger, Marc, 'Baudelaire et la conscience de la mort', in Eigeldinger, *Poésie et métamorphoses* (Neuchâtel: Éditions de la Baconnière, 1973), 137-54.
Etheridge, Kate, '"Grâces sataniques": Laughter, Redemption, and Poetic Self-Awareness in *Les Fleurs du Mal*', in Charlie Louth and Patrick McGuinness (eds), *Gravity and Grace: Essays for Roger Pearson* (Cambridge: Legenda (Modern Humanities Research Association), 2019), 70-84.
Evans, David, *Rhythm, Illusion and the Poetic Idea: Baudelaire, Rimbaud, Mallarmé* (Amsterdam: Rodopi, 2004).

Evans, Margery A., 'Laurence Sterne and *Le Spleen de Paris*', *French Studies*, 42 (1988), 165–76.
Evans, Margery A., *Baudelaire and Intertextuality: Poetry at the Crossroads* (Cambridge: Cambridge University Press, 1993).
Fairlie, Alison, 'Some Remarks on Baudelaire's *Poème du haschisch*', in Will Moore, Rhoda Sutherland, and Enid Starkie (eds), *The French Mind: Studies in Honour of Gustave Rudler* (Oxford: Clarendon Press, 1952), 291–317.
Fairlie, Alison, *Baudelaire: 'Les Fleurs du Mal'* (London: Edward Arnold, 1960).
Ferran, André, *L'Esthétique de Baudelaire* (Paris: Hachette, 1933; republished by Nizet, 1968).
Finch-Race, Daniel, 'Placelessness in Baudelaire's "Les Sept Vieillards" and "Les Petites Vieilles"', *Modern Language Review*, 110 (2015), 1011–26.
Foloppe, Régine, *Baudelaire et la vérité poétique* (Paris: L'Harmattan, 2019).
Fondane, Benjamin, *Baudelaire et l'expérience du gouffre* (Paris: Seghers, 1947).
Genovali, Sandro, *Baudelaire, o della dissonanza* (Florence: La Nuova Italia, 1971).
Gilman, Margaret, '"L'Albatros" again', *Romanic Review*, 41: 2 (April 1950), 96–107.
Gilman, Margaret, *Baudelaire the Critic* [1943] (New York: Octagon Books, 1971).
Godfrey, Sima, 'Baudelaire's Windows', *L'Esprit créateur*, 22: 4 (1982), 83–100.
Goulbourne, Russell, 'The Sound of Silence...*Points de suspension* in Baudelaire's *Les Fleurs du Mal*', *Australian Journal of French Studies*, 36: 2 (May–Aug. 1999), 200–13.
Gouvard, Jean-Michel, *Charles Baudelaire, 'Le Spleen de Paris'* (Paris: Ellipses, 2014).
Gouvard, Jean-Michel, '*Le Spleen de Paris* de Charles Baudelaire: Des "petits genres journalistiques" aux "petits poèmes en prose"', *Mémoires du livre/Studies in Book Culture*, 8: 2 (Spring 2017). https://doi.org/10.7202/1039699ar.
Gouvard, Jean-Michel, 'Sur les notions d'égalité, de fraternité et de citoyenneté dans *Le Spleen de Paris*', in Murphy (ed.), *Lectures du 'Spleen de Paris'*, 297–306.
Grøtta, Marit, *Baudelaire's Media Aesthetics: The Gaze of the Flâneur and 19th-Century Media* (New York and London: Bloomsbury, 2015).
Guégan, Stéphane, 'À propos d'Ernest Christophe: D'une allégorie l'autre', in Guyaux and Marchal (eds), *'Les Fleurs du Mal': Actes du colloque de la Sorbonne des 10 et 11 janvier 2003*, 95–106.
Guerlac, Suzanne, *The Impersonal Sublime: Hugo, Baudelaire, Lautréamont* (Stanford, Calif.: Stanford University Press, 1990).
Guyaux, André, 'Baudelaire et Victor Hugo', in Elio Mosele (ed.), *George Sand et son temps: Hommage à Annarosa Poli* (3 vols, Geneva: Slatkine, 1994), i. 143–56.
Guyaux, André and Bertrand Marchal (eds), *'Les Fleurs du Mal': Actes du colloque de la Sorbonne des 10 et 11 janvier 2003* (Paris: Presses de l'Université Paris-Sorbonne, 2003).
Guyaux, André and Henri Scepi (eds), *Lire 'Le Spleen de Paris'* (Paris: Presses de l'Université Paris-Sorbonne, 2014).
Guyaux, André, 'Des "habitantes de l'île de Lesbos"?', *L'Année Baudelaire*, 22 (2018), 107–14.
Hannoosh, Michele, 'Etching and Modern Art: Baudelaire's *Peintres et aquafortistes*', *French Studies*, 43 (1989), 47–60.
Hannoosh, Michele, *Baudelaire and Caricature: From the Comic to an Art of Modernity* (University Park, Pa: Pennsylvania State University Press, 1992).
Hannoosh, Michele, 'Reading the Trial of the *Fleurs du mal*', *Modern Language Review*, 106 (2011), 374–87.
Hannoosh, Michele, '"Le Mauvais Vitrier" devant la justice', *L'Année Baudelaire*, 22 (2018), 125–9.

Heck, Francis, '"Le Mauvais Vitrier": A Literary Transfiguration', *Nineteenth-Century French Studies*, 14: 3-4 (Fall—Winter, 1986), 260-8.
Hiddleston, J. A., '"Fusée", Maxim, and Commonplace in Baudelaire', *Modern Language Review*, 80 (1985), 563-70.
Hiddleston, J. A., 'Baudelaire et le rire', *Études baudelairiennes*, 12 (1987), 85-98.
Hiddleston, J. A., *Baudelaire and 'Le Spleen de Paris'* (Oxford: Clarendon Press, 1987).
Hiddleston, J. A., *Baudelaire and the Art of Memory* (Oxford: Clarendon Press, 1999).
Hiddleston, J. A., 'Mobile et motivation chez Baudelaire', *L'Année Baudelaire*, 15 (2012), 61-71.
Hovasse, Jean-Marc, 'Les Signes de Hugo au cygne de Baudelaire', in Claude Millet, Florence Naugrette, and Agnès Spiquel (eds), *Choses vues à travers Hugo: Hommage à Guy Rosa* (Valenciennes: Presses universitaires de Valenciennes, 2008), 367-76.
Howells, Bernard, *Baudelaire: Individualism, Dandyism and the Philosophy of History* (Oxford: Legenda, 1996).
Jackson, John E., *La Mort Baudelaire: Essai sur 'Les Fleurs du Mal'* (Neuchâtel: Éditions de la Baconnière, 1982).
Jackson, John E., *Mémoire et subjectivité romantiques: Rousseau, Hölderlin, Chateaubriand, Nerval, Coleridge, Baudelaire, Wagner* (Paris: Corti, 1999), 130-68.
Jackson, John E., *Baudelaire* (Paris: Le Livre de poche, 2001).
Jackson, John E., *Baudelaire sans fin: Essais sur 'Les Fleurs du Mal'* (Paris: Corti, 2005).
Jackson, John E., *Baudelaire et la sacralité de la poésie* (Geneva: Droz, 2018).
Johnson, Barbara, *Défigurations du langage poétique: La Seconde Révolution baudelairienne* (Paris: Flammarion, 1979).
Jossua, Jean-Pierre, 'Quelques interprétations de la religion de Baudelaire', *Recherches de science religieuse*, 94 (2006), 169-91.
Kaplan, Edward K., *Baudelaire's Prose Poems: The Esthetic, the Ethical and the Religious in 'The Parisian Prowler'* (Athens, Ga: University of Georgia Press, 1990); trans. into French as *Baudelaire et Le Spleen de Paris: L'Esthétique, l'éthique et le religieux* (Paris: Classiques Garnier, 2015).
Kelley, David, 'L'Art: L'Harmonie du beau et de l'utile', *Romantisme*, 5 (1972), 18-36.
Killeen, Marie-Chantal, 'Pastoral Womanscapes (Baudelaire, Tournier, Jablonka)', *Modern Language Review*, 113 (2018), 321-37.
Killick, Rachel, '"Sorcellerie évocatoire" and the Sonnet in *Les Fleurs du Mal*', *Dalhousie French Studies*, 2 (1980), 21-39.
Killick, Rachel, 'Espaces du moi, espaces de la ville: Forme et signification dans quatre poèmes de "Tableaux parisiens"', *Essays in French Literature*, 39 (2002), 153-70.
Killick, Rachel, 'Baudelaire's Versification: Conservative or Radical?', in Lloyd (ed.), *The Cambridge Companion to Baudelaire*, 51-68.
Kliebenstein, Georges, 'Baudelaire et le principe de déplaisir (À propos d' "Un plaisant")', in Murphy (ed.), *Lectures du 'Spleen de Paris'*, 79-96.
Kopp, Robert, 'Le Spleen baudelairien: De la mélancolie à la dépression', in Clair and Kopp (eds), *De la Mélancolie*, 171-89.
Krueger, Cheryl, *The Art of Procrastination: Baudelaire's Poetry in Prose* (Newark: University of Delaware Press, 2007).
Krueger, Cheryl (ed.), *Approaches to Teaching Baudelaire's Prose Poems* (New York: Modern Language Association of America, 2017).
Labarthe, Patrick, *Baudelaire et la tradition de l'allégorie* (Geneva: Droz, 1999; rev. edn. 2015).

Labarthe, Patrick, 'Locus amoenus, locus terribilis dans l'œuvre de Baudelaire', *Revue d'histoire littéraire de la France*, 99 (1999), 1021–45.
Labarthe, Patrick, '*Le Spleen de Paris* ou le livre des pauvres', in Jean-Paul Avice and Jérôme Thélot (eds), *Hommage à Claude Pichois: Nerval, Baudelaire, Colette*, in *L'Année Baudelaire*, 5 (1999), 99–118.
Labarthe, Patrick, *Patrick Labarthe présente 'Petits Poèmes en prose' de Baudelaire* (Paris: Gallimard [Foliothèque], 2000).
Labarthe, Patrick, 'De l'usage des archaïsmes dans *Les Fleurs du Mal*', in *Relais: Dix études réunies en hommage à Georges Blin* (Paris: Corti, 2002), 119–47.
Labarthe, Patrick, 'Une poétique ambiguë: les "correspondances"', in Guyaux and Marchal (eds), *'Les Fleurs du Mal'; Actes du colloque de la Sorbonne*, 121–42.
Labarthe, Patrick, 'Le "Tombeau de Jeanne": Lecture d' "Un fantôme"', in Yoshikazu Nakaji (ed.), *Baudelaire et les formes poétiques* (*La Licorne* [Presses universitaires de Rennes], 83 (2008), 79–95.
Labarthe, Patrick, 'Baudelaire, Paris et "le palimpseste de la mémoire"', *L'Année Baudelaire*, 18: 19 (2014–15), 245–61.
Laforgue, Pierre, 'Baudelaire, Hugo et la royauté du poète: Le Romantisme en 1860', *Revue d'histoire littéraire de la France*, 96 (1996), 966–82.
Laforgue, Pierre, *Ut pictura poesis: Baudelaire, la peinture et le romantisme* (Lyon: Presses universitaires de Lyon, 2000).
Laforgue, Pierre, 'Sur la rhétorique du lyrisme en 1850: "Le Flacon" de Baudelaire', *Poétique*, 126 (2001), 245–52.
Laforgue, Pierre, *Œdipe à Lesbos; Baudelaire, la femme, la poésie* (Paris: Eurédit, 2002).
Laforgue, Pierre, '1857/1861: Histoire, allégorie et modernité', in Murphy (ed.), *Lectures de Baudelaire: 'Les Fleurs du Mal'*, 45–56.
Laforgue, Pierre, 'Baudelaire et la royauté du spleen: Le Poète, la mélancolie et la révolution', in Guyaux and Marchal (eds), *'Les Fleurs du Mal': Actes du colloque de la Sorbonne des 10 et 11 janvier 2003*, 143–60.
Laforgue, Pierre, *Politiques de Baudelaire: Huit études* (Paris: Eurédit, 2014).
Laforgue, Pierre, 'Portrait de l'artiste en chien ("Les Bons Chiens", "Le Vieux Saltimbanque", "Le Chien et le flacon")', in Murphy (ed.), *Lectures du 'Spleen de Paris'*, 321–31.
Launay, Claude, *Claude Launay présente 'Les Fleurs du Mal' de Charles Baudelaire* (Paris: Gallimard, 1995).
Lawler, James R., *Poetry and Moral Dialectic: Baudelaire's 'Secret Architecture'* (Madison-Teaneck: Fairleigh Dickinson University Press, 1997).
Leakey, Felix, 'Baudelaire: The Poet as Moralist', in L. J. Austin, Garnet Rees, and Eugène Vinaver (eds), *Studies in Modern French Literature presented to P. Mansell Jones by pupils, colleagues and friends* (Manchester: Manchester University Press, 1961), 196–219.
Leakey, Felix, 'A *Festschrift* of 1855: Baudelaire and the *Hommage À C. F. Denecourt*', in J. C. Ireson, I. D. Macfarlane, and Garnet Rees (eds), *Studies in French Literature Presented to H. W. Lawton* (Manchester: Manchester University Press, and New York: Barnes & Noble Inc., 1968), 175–202.
Leakey, Felix, *Baudelaire and Nature* (Manchester and New York: Manchester University Press and Barnes & Noble, Inc., 1969).
Leakey, Felix, *Collected Essays, 1953–1988*, ed. Eva Jacobs (Cambridge: Cambridge University Press, 1990).
Leroy, Christian, 'Les *Petits Poèmes en prose* "palimpsestes" ou Baudelaire et *Les Rêveries du promeneur solitaire* de Rousseau', in Jean Delabroy and Yves Charnet (eds), *Baudelaire:*

BIBLIOGRAPHY 629

Nouveaux Chantiers (Villeneuve d'Ascq: Presses universitaires du Septentrion, 1995), 61–70.
Lloyd, Rosemary, *Baudelaire et Hoffmann: Affinités et influences* (Cambridge: Cambridge University Press, 1979).
Lloyd, Rosemary, *Baudelaire's Literary Criticism* (Cambridge: Cambridge University Press, 1981).
Lloyd, Rosemary, 'Façons de voir, façons de parler: Cliché, pastiche, parodie et jeu dans *Le Spleen de Paris*', *Studi francesi*, 126 (Sept.–Dec. 1998), 510–20.
Lloyd, Rosemary, 'Baudelaire sonneteer: Flare to the Future', in Ward (ed.), *Baudelaire and the Poetics of Modernity*, 101–23.
Lloyd, Rosemary, *Baudelaire's World* (Ithaca, NY: Cornell University Press, 2002).
Lloyd, Rosemary, *The Cambridge Companion to Baudelaire* (Cambridge: Cambridge University Press, 2005).
Lloyd, Rosemary, *Charles Baudelaire* (London: Reaktion Books, 2008).
Lloyd, Rosemary, 'Engendering Performance in Les Fleurs du Mal', *Dix-Neuf*, 17: 1 (Apr. 2013), 24–36.
Lonke, Joycelynne, *Baudelaire et la musique* (Paris: Nizet, 1975).
Lübecker, Nikolaj, 'Twenty-First Century Baudelaire? Affectivity and Ecology in "Le Crépuscule du soir"', *Modernism/modernity*, 27: 4 (Nov. 2020), 689–706.
Macé, Marielle, 'Baudelaire, une esthétique de l'existence', *L'Année Baudelaire*, 18: 19 (2014–15), 49–67.
Macé, Marielle, 'Le *Navire Baudelaire*: Imagination et hospitalité', *Littérature*, 177 (2015), 100–13.
MacInnes, John W., *The Comical as Textual Practice in 'Les Fleurs du Mal'* (Gainesville, Fla.: University of Florida Press, 1988).
Maclean, Marie, *Narrative as Performance: The Baudelairean Experiment* (London, Routledge, 1988).
McLees, Ainslie Armstrong, *Baudelaire's 'Argot plastique': Poetic Caricature and Modernism* (Athens, Ga, and London: University of Georgia Press, 1989).
Marchal, Bertrand, 'La Nature et le péché', *Études baudelairiennes*, 12 (1987), 7–22.
Marchal, Bertrand, 'Baudelaire, Barbier, Gautier et "Le Mauvais Moine"', *L'Année Baudelaire*, 6 (2002), 127–41.
Marchal, Bertrand, 'De quelques comparaisons baudelairiennes', *L'Année Baudelaire*, 9–10 (2007), 189–201.
Marder, Elissa, *Dead Time: Temporal Disorders in the Wake of Modernity (Baudelaire and Flaubert)* (Stanford, Calif.: Stanford University Press, 2001).
Marder, Elissa, 'From Poetic Justice to Criminal "Jouissance": Poetry by Other Means in Baudelaire', *Yale French Studies*, 125: 6 (2014), 69–84.
Marder, Elissa, 'Baudelaire's Feminine Counter-Signature: "Mademoiselle Bistouri"'s Photographic Poetics', *Nineteenth-Century French Studies*, 46: 1–2 (Fall–Winter, 2017–18), 1–25.
Massin, Jean, *Baudelaire entre Dieu et Satan* (Paris: Julliard, 1945).
Masson, Bernard, 'Sur la "spiritualité" baudelairienne', in Bercot et al., *'Les Fleurs du Mal': L'Intériorité de la forme*, 77–84.
Mathieu, Jean-Claude, *'Les Fleurs du Mal' de Baudelaire* (Paris: Hachette, 1972).
Mathieu, Jean-Claude, 'Une charogne', in Guyaux and Marchal (eds), *'Les Fleurs du Mal': Actes du colloque de la Sorbonne*, 161–80.
Mathias, Paul, *La Beauté dans 'Les Fleurs du Mal'* (Grenoble: Presses universitaires de Grenoble, 1977).

Maulpoix, Jean-Michel, 'Le Spleen baudelairien: Une mélancolie moderne', in Ann-Déborah Lévy-Bertherat, *Poétiques du néant: Leopardi, Baudelaire, Pessoa* (Paris: SEDES, 1998), 23–38.
Melzer, Françoise, *Seeing Double: Baudelaire's Modernity* (Chicago: University of Chicago Press, 2011).
Milner, Max, *Le Diable dans la littérature française de Cazotte à Baudelaire (1772–1861)* (2 vols, Paris: Corti, 1960).
Milner, Max, *Baudelaire, enfer ou ciel, qu'importe!* (Paris: Plon, 1967).
Milner, Max, 'Baudelaire et le surnaturalisme', in *Le Surnaturalisme français: Actes du colloque organisé à l'Université Vanderbilt les 31 mars et le 1er avril 1978* (Neuchâtel: Éditions de la Baconnière, 1979), 31–49.
Miner, Margaret, *Resonant Gaps: Between Baudelaire and Wagner* (Athens, Ga, and London: University of Georgia Press, 1995).
Morisi, Ève, *Capital Letters: Hugo, Baudelaire, Camus and the Death Penalty*. (Evanston, Ill.: Northwestern University Press, 2020).
Mossop, D. J., *Baudelaire's Tragic Hero: A Study of the Architecture of 'Les Fleurs du Mal'* (Oxford: Clarendon Press, 1961).
Murphy, Margueritte S., *Material Figures: Political Economy, Commercial Culture, and the Aesthetic Sensibility of Charles Baudelaire* (Amsterdam and New York: Rodopi, 2012).
Murphy, Steve, 'Le Mauvais Vitrier' ou la crise du verre', *Romanic Review*, 82: 3 (1990), 339–49.
Murphy, Steve, 'L'Hiéroglyphe et son interprétation: L'Association d'idées dans "Le Tir et le cimetière"', *Bulletin baudelairien*, 30: 2 (1995), 61–84.
Murphy, Steve, 'La Scène parisienne: Lecture d'"Une mort héroïque" de Baudelaire', in Keith Cameron and James Kearns (eds), *Le Champ littéraire, 1860–1900* (Amsterdam: Rodopi, 1996), 49–61, republished in a revised version in *Logiques du dernier Baudelaire*, 113–60.
Murphy, Steve (ed.), *Lectures de Baudelaire: 'Les Fleurs du Mal'* (Rennes: Presses universitaires de Rennes, 2002).
Murphy, Steve, *Logiques du dernier Baudelaire: Lectures du 'Spleen de Paris'* (Paris: Honoré Champion, 2003).
Murphy, Steve, 'Effets et motivations: quelques excentricités de la versification baudelairienne', in Patrick Labarthe (ed.), *Baudelaire: Une alchimie de la douleur. Études sur 'Les Fleurs du Mal'* (Paris: Eurédit, 2003), 265–98.
Murphy, Steve, 'A propos de quelques rimes et vents paradoxaux de Baudelaire', *L'Année Baudelaire*, 9–10 (2005–6), 231–51.
Murphy, Steve, 'De la prose poétique au poème en prose: Baudelaire, Bertrand et la confusion des genres', in Henri Scepi (ed.), *Le Genre et ses qualicatifs*, in *La Licorne*, 105 (2013), 81–109.
Murphy, Steve (ed.), *Lectures du 'Spleen de Paris'* (Rennes: Presses universitaires de Rennes, 2014).
Murphy, Steve, '"L'Œuvre sans nom": origines, structures et (dés)inscriptions génériques', in Murphy (ed.), *Lectures du 'Spleen de Paris'*, 105–25.
Natta, Marie-Christine, *Baudelaire* (Paris: Perrin, 2017).
Née, Patrick, 'Du "poète hystérique" chez Baudelaire', *L'Année Baudelaire*, 16 (2012), 111–30.
Née, Patrick, 'Baudelaire et l'hystérie en son temps (1800–1860)', *Revue d'histoire littéraire de la France*, 116 (2016), 841–56.

Newmark, Kevin, 'Who Needs Poetry? Baudelaire, Benjamin, and the Modernity of "Le Cygne"', *Comparative Literature*, 63: 3 (2011), 269-90.
Newmark, Kevin, 'Now you see it, now you don't: Baudelaire's Modernity', *Nineteenth-Century French Studies*, 44: 1-2 (Fall-Winter 2015-16), 1-24.
Nurse, Peter H., 'Les Aveugles de Baudelaire', *L'Information littéraire*, 8 (Nov.-Dec. 1966), 219-22, reprinted as 'Baudelaire, Les Aveugles', in Peter H. Nurse (ed.), *The Art of Criticism: Essays in French Literary Analysis* (Edinburgh: Edinburgh University Press, 1969), 193-203.
Ockenden, Alexander, 'Baudelaire, Lacaussade and the Historical Identity of "La Belle Dorothée"', *French Studies Bulletin*, 35: 3 [no. 132] (Autumn 2014), 64-8.
Oehler, Dolf, *Le Spleen contre l'oubli. Juin 1848: Baudelaire, Flaubert, Heine, Herzen* (Paris: Payot et Rivages, 1996).
Oehler, Dolf, 'Baudelaire's Politics', trans. Rosemary Lloyd, in Lloyd (ed.), *The Cambridge Companion to Baudelaire*, 14-30.
Olmsted, William, *The Censorship Effect: Baudelaire, Flaubert, and the Formation of French Modernism* (New York: Oxford University Press, 2016).
Pachet, Pierre, *Le Premier Venu: Essai sur la politique baudelairienne* (Paris: Denoël, 1976).
Paraschas, Sotirios, 'Baudelaire, the *Flâneur*, and the Author as Prostitute', in Paraschas, *The Realist Author and Sympathetic Imagination* (London: Maney [Legenda], 2013), 104-24, 183-7.
Patty, James S., 'Baudelaire's Knowledge and Use of Dante', *Studies in Philology*, 53 (1956), 599-611.
Pichois, Claude, *Baudelaire: Études et témoignages* (rev. edn, Neuchâtel: Éditions de la Baconnière, 1967).
Pichois, Claude and Jean-Paul Avice (eds), *Dictionnaire Baudelaire* (Tusson: Du Lérot, 2002).
Pichois, Claude and Jean Ziegler, *Charles Baudelaire* [1987; 1996] (rev. edn, Paris: Fayard, 2005).
Planté, Christine, 'Voix du mal', in Guyaux and Marchal (eds), *'Les Fleurs du Mal': Actes du colloque de la Sorbonne des 10 et 11 janvier 2003*, 181-99.
Pommier, Jean, *La Mystique de Baudelaire* (Paris: Belles Lettres, 1932; repr. Geneva: Slatkine, 1967).
Poulet, Georges, 'Baudelaire', in *Les Métamorphoses du cercle* (Paris: Plon, 1961), 397-432.
Poulet, Georges, *La Poésie éclatée: Baudelaire/Rimbaud* (Paris: Presses universitaires de France, 1980).
Prévost, Jean, *Baudelaire: Essai sur la création et l'inspiration poétiques* (Paris: Mercure de France, 1953).
Raser, Timothy, *A Poetics of Art Criticism: The Case of Baudelaire* (Chapel Hill: University of North Carolina, 1989).
Raymond, Marcel, *De Baudelaire au surréalisme* (Paris: Corti, 1940).
Raymond, Marcel, 'Baudelaire et la sculpture', in *Journées Baudelaire: Actes du colloque (Namur-Bruxelles, 10-13 octobre 1967)* (Brussels: Académie royale de langue et de littérature françaises, 1968), 66-74.
Richard, Jean-Pierre, 'Profondeur de Baudelaire', in *Poésie et profondeur* (Paris: Éditions du Seuil, 1955), 91-162.
Richter, Mario, *Baudelaire, 'Les Fleurs du Mal': Lecture intégrale* (2 vols, Geneva: Slatkine, 2001).
Richter, Mario, 'Réflexivité et représentation du poète dans Les Fleurs du Mal', in Murphy (ed.), *Lectures des 'Fleurs du Mal'*, 71-88.

Robb, Graham, 'Baudelaire, Lucan, and "Une mort héroïque"', *Romance Notes*, 30: 1 (Fall 1989), 69–75.
Robb, Graham, 'Les Origines journalistiques de la prose poétique de Baudelaire', *Les Lettres romanes*, 14 (1990), 15–25.
Robb, Graham, *La Poésie de Baudelaire et la poésie française 1838–1852* (n.p.: Aubier, 1993).
Rubin, Vivien L., 'Two Prose Poems by Baudelaire: "Le Vieux Saltimbanque" and "Une mort héroïque"', *Nineteenth-Century French Studies*, 14: 1–2 (1985–6), 51–60.
Rueff, Martin, 'Le Cadre infini—sur la poétique baudelairienne', *Littérature*, 177 (2015), 21–37.
Ruff, Marcel, *L'Esprit du mal et l'esthétique baudelairienne* (Paris: Armand Colin, 1955).
Runyon, Randolph Paul, *Intratextual Baudelaire: The Sequential Fabric of the 'Fleurs du Mal' and 'Spleen de Paris'* (Columbus, Oh.: Ohio State University Press, 2010).
St Clair, Robert, 'Writing Poetry Against the Grain: Or, What Can Be Seen in "Les Yeux des pauvres"', *French Forum*, 39: 1 (Winter 2014), 49–63.
St Clair, Robert, 'Misères de poésie: micro-lecture des économies de la violence dans "Les Yeux des pauvres"', in Murphy (ed.), *Lectures du 'Spleen de Paris'*, 307–20.
Samuels, Maurice, 'Baudelaire's Boulevard Spectacle: Seeing Through "Les yeux des pauvres"', *Yale French Studies*, 125–6 (2014), 167–82.
Sanyal, Debarati, 'Conspiratorial Poetics: Baudelaire's "Une Mort héroïque"', *Nineteenth-Century French Studies* 27: 3–4 (1999), 305–22.
Sanyal, Debarati, *The Violence of Modernity: Baudelaire, Irony, and the Politics of Form* (Baltimore: Johns Hopkins University Press, 2006).
Sanyal, Debarati, 'Peindre, non la chose, mais l'effet qui l'a produite: Défigurations du féminin dans "La Femme sauvage et la petite-maîtresse"', in Murphy (ed.), *Lectures du 'Spleen de Paris'*, 251–60.
Sartre, Jean-Paul, *Baudelaire* (Paris: Gallimard, 1963).
Scepi, Henri, 'Le plus proche et le plus lointain' [on 'L'Étranger'], in Murphy (ed.), *Lectures du 'Spleen de Paris'*, 153–67.
Schellino, Andrea, 'Baudelaire et la prostitution "*fraternitaire*": A propos de "La Solitude"', *Méthode! Revue de littérature* [Université de Pau], 24 (Autumn 2014), 183–94.
Schellino, Andrea, 'Existe-t-il un "cycle de Félicité' dans l'œuvre en vers de Baudelaire?', *Revue d'histoire littéraire de la France*, 117 (2017), 697–706.
Schofer, Peter, '"Une mort héroïque": Baudelaire's Social Theater of Cruelty', in *Theater and Society in French Literature*, ed. Claude Kurt Abraham et al. (Columbia: University of South Carolina [French Literature Series, 15], 1988), 50–7.
Schulz, Gretchen, '"La Géante": Feminine Proportions and Lyric Subjectivity', in Thompson (ed.), *Understanding 'Les Fleurs du Mal'*, 35–48.
Scott, David, 'Baudelaire, le sonnet et la poétique symboliste', *L'Année Baudelaire*, 4 (1998), 45–59.
Scott, Maria, *Baudelaire's 'Le Spleen de Paris': Shifting Perspectives* (Aldershot: Ashgate, 2005).
Scott, Maria, 'Baudelaire's "L'Étranger" and the Limits of Mind-Reading', *L'Esprit créateur*, 58: 1 (Spring 2018), 32–47.
Scott, Maria, '*État présent*: Baudelaire', *French Studies*, 74 (2020), 83–101.
Séginger, Giselle, 'Éthique et poésie', in Guyaux and Marchal (ed.), *'Les Fleurs du Mal': Actes du colloque de la Sorbonne*, 231–45.
Seiller, Philippe, 'Pour un *Baudelaire et Pascal*', in Bercot et al., *'Les Fleurs du Mal': L'Intériorité de la forme*, 5–16.

Stamelman, Richard, 'The Shroud of Allegory: Death, Mourning, and Melancholy in Baudelaire's Work', *Texas Studies in Literature and Language*, 25: 3 (Fall 1983), 390-409.

Starobinski, Jean, 'L'Encre de la mélancolie', *Nouvelle Revue française*, 21 (Mar. 1963), 410-23; reprinted as '"Un éclat sans fin pour mon amour"', in *L'Encre de la mélancolie*, 611-23.

Starobinski, Jean, 'Sur quelques répondants allégoriques du poète', *Revue d'histoire littéraire de la France*, 67 (1967), 402-12.

Starobinski, Jean, 'Les Rimes du vide: Une lecture de Baudelaire', *Nouvelle Revue de psychanalyse*, 11 (1975), 133-43; republished as 'Les Rimes du vide: une lecture d'"Horreur sympathique"', in Guyaux and Marchal (eds), *'Les Fleurs du Mal': Actes du colloque de la Sorbonne*, 269-80, and as 'Les Rimes du vide' in *L'Encre de la mélancolie*, 455-69.

Starobinski, Jean, 'Bandello et Baudelaire (*Le Prince et son bouffon*)', in *Le Mythe d'Étiemble: Hommages, études et recherches: inédits* (Paris: Didier Érudition, 1979), 251-59; reprinted in *L'Encre de la mélancolie*, 499-513 (506-13).

Starobinski, Jean, 'Rêve et immortalité chez Baudelaire', *Corps écrit*, 7 (1983), 45-56; reprinted as 'Baudelaire metteur en scène' in *L'Encre de la mélancolie*, 421-35.

Starobinski, Jean, 'Les Proportions de l'immortalité', *Furor*, 9 (May 1983), 5-19, reprinted in *L'Encre de la mélancolie*, 437-54.

Starobinski, Jean, *La mélancolie au miroir: Trois Lectures de Baudelaire* (Paris: Julliard, 1989).

Starobinski, Jean, 'Le Regard des statues', *Nouvelle revue de psychanalyse*, 50 (1994), 45-64; reprinted in *L'Encre de la mélancolie*, 471-98.

Starobinski, Jean, 'Le Poème d'invitation', in Starobinski, *Le Poème d'invitation, précédé d'un entretien avec Frédéric Wandelère et suivi d'un propos d'Yves Bonnefoy* (Geneva: La Dogana, 2001), 51-88.

Steinmetz, Jean-Luc, 'Une fable des origines', in Steve Murphy (ed.), *Lectures du 'Spleen de Paris'*, 97-104.

Steinmetz, Jean-Luc, 'Ontoscopie (sur "Les Fenêtres")', in André Guyaux and Henri Scepi (eds), *Lire 'Le Spleen de Paris'* (Paris: Presses de l'Université Paris-Sorbonne, 2014), 159-66.

Stephens, Sonya, *Baudelaire's Prose Poems: The Practice and Politics of Irony* (Oxford: Oxford University Press, 1999).

Stephens, Sonya and Rosemary Lloyd, 'Promises, Promises: The Language of Gesture in Baudelaire's "Petits Poèmes en prose"', *Modern Language Review*, 88: 1 (Jan. 1993), 74-83.

Stierle, Karlheinz, 'Baudelaires "Tableaux parisiens" und die Tradition des "tableau de Paris"', *Poetica*, 6 (1974), 285-322, republished in English translation as 'Baudelaire and the Tradition of the *Tableau de Paris*', *New Literary History*, 11: 2 (Winter 1980), 345-61.

Thélot, Jérôme, 'Une citation de Shakespeare dans "Les Bons Chiens"', *Bulletin baudelairien*, 24: 2 (Dec. 1989), 61-6.

Thélot, Jérôme, *Baudelaire: Violence et poésie* (Paris: Gallimard, 1993).

Thélot, Jérôme, 'Pour une poétique de la faim', in Guyaux and Marchal (eds), *'Les Fleurs du Mal': Actes du colloque de la Sorbonne des 10 et 11 janvier 2003*, 281-93.

Thélot, Jérôme, 'La Conversion selon Baudelaire', in Thélot, *L'Immémorial: Études sur la poésie moderne* (n.p.: Les Belles Lettres, 2011), 19-44.

Thélot, Jérôme, 'Prosodie et histoire', *L'Année Baudelaire*, 18/19 (2014-15), 263-79.

Thompson, William J. (ed.), *Understanding 'Les Fleurs du Mal': Critical Readings* (Nashville: Vanderbilt University Press, 1997).

Tilby, Michael J., 'Les Fleurs du Mal in Limbo: The Non-appearance of Les Limbes Revisited', French Studies Bulletin, 36 [no. 135] (Summer 2015), 20–4.

Tortonese, Paulo, 'Baudelaire et la philosophaillerie moderne', in André Guyaux and Sophie Marchal (eds), La Vie romantique: Hommage à Loïc Chotard (Paris: Presses de l'Université Paris-Sorbonne, 2003), 483–522.

Tortonese, Paulo, 'Baudelaire romantique et antiromantique', L'Année Baudelaire, 18/19 (2015), 149–66.

Vaillant, Alain, Baudelaire, poète comique (Rennes: Presses universitaires de Rennes, 2007).

Van Slyke, Gretchen, 'Riot and Revolution in the Salon de 1846', French Forum, 10: 3 (Sept. 1985), 295–306.

Van Slyke, Gretchen, 'Les Épiciers au musée: Baudelaire et l'artiste bourgeois', Romantisme, 55 (1987), 55–66.

Vitry, Alexandre de, 'Baudelaire et ses "frères"', Revue d'histoire littéraire de la France, 119 (2019), 289–304.

Vouga, Daniel, Baudelaire et Joseph de Maistre (Paris: Corti, 1957).

Ward, Patricia A. (ed., with the assistance of James S. Patty), Baudelaire and the Poetics of Modernity (Nashville: Vanderbilt University Press, 2001).

Wetherill, P. M., Charles Baudelaire et la poésie d'Edgar Allan Poe (Paris: Nizet, 1962).

Wing, Nathaniel, 'The Poetics of Irony in Baudelaire's La Fanfarlo', Neophilologus, 49: 2 (Apr. 1975), 165–89.

Wing, Nathaniel, Limits of Narrative: Essays on Baudelaire, Flaubert, Rimbaud and Mallarmé (Cambridge: Cambridge University Press, 1986).

Wing, Nathaniel, 'Poets, Mimes and Counterfeit Coins: On Power and Discourse in Baudelaire's Prose Poetry', Paragraph, 13 (1990), 1–18.

Yee, Jennifer, '"La Beauté": Art and Dialogism in the Poetry of Baudelaire', Neophilologus, 102: 1 (2018), 1–14.

Yee, Jennifer, 'Baudelaire and the Chinese Object', L'Esprit créateur, 58: 1 (Spring 2018), 101–13.

Zanetta, Julien, 'Enfance contre poncif: Théâtre et banalité', Littérature, 177 (2015: 1), 38–47.

Zanetta, Julien, 'Baudelaire, vies héroïques', Revue d'histoire littéraire de la France, 117 (2017), 667–82.

Zanetta, Julien, Baudelaire, la mémoire et les arts (Paris: Classiques Garnier, 2019).

Other

Abrams, M. H., The Mirror and the Lamp: Romantic Theory and the Critical Tradition (London, Oxford, and New York: Oxford University Press, 1971 [first published 1953]).

Bailbé, Joseph-Marc, 'De Liszt à Berlioz: Réflexions sur la condition de l'artiste-musicien', Romantisme, 57 (1987), 7–16.

Banville, Théodore de, Petit traité de poésie française (rev. edn, Paris: Librairie de l'Écho de la Sorbonne, 1875).

Barot, Odysse, Émile de Girardin, sa vie, ses idées, son œuvre, son influence (Paris: Michel Lévy, 1866).

Bellet, Roger, Presse et journalisme sous le Second Empire (Paris: Armand Colin, 1967).

Bénichou, Paul, Le Temps des prophètes: Doctrines de l'âge romantique (Paris: Gallimard, 1977).

Bénichou, Paul, L'École du désenchantement: Sainte-Beuve, Nodier, Musset, Nerval, Gautier (Paris: Gallimard, 1992).

Bénichou, Paul, Selon Mallarmé (Paris: Gallimard, 1995).

Benjamin, Walter, *The Origin of German Tragic Drama*, trans. John Osborne (London: NLB, 1977).
Benjamin, Walter, *The Arcades Project*, trans. Howard Eiland and Kevin McLaughlin (Cambridge, Mass., and London: Belknap Press of Harvard University Press, 1999).
Berrios, G. E., 'Melancholia and Depression during the 19th Century: A Conceptual History', *British Journal of Psychiatry*, 153: 3 (1988), 298-304.
Blackburn, Simon (ed.), *The Oxford Dictionary of Philosophy* (3rd edn, Oxford: Oxford University Press, 2016).
Bonnefoy, Yves, 'La Mélancolie, la folie, le génie—la poésie', in *Mélancolie: génie et folie en Occident: En hommage à Raymond Klibansky (1905-2005)* (Paris: Gallimard, 2005), 14-22.
Boutin, Aimée, 'Rethinking the Flâneur: Flânerie and the Senses', *Dix-Neuf*, 16: 2 (July 2012), 124-32.
Boutin, Aimée, *City of Noise: Sound and Nineteenth-Century Paris* (Urbana, Ill.: University of Illinois Press, 2015).
Bourdieu, Pierre, *Les Règles de l'art: Genèse et structure du champ littéraire* ([1992] rev. edn., Paris: Éditions du Seuil, 1998).
Brierre de Boismont, Alexandre, *Du suicide et de la folie suicide* (Paris: Germer Baillière, 1856).
Brix, Michel, *Le Romantisme français: Esthétique platonicienne et modernité littéraire* (Louvain and Paris: Peeters and Société des études classiques, 1999).
Burt, E. S., *Poetry's Appeal: Nineteenth-Century French Lyric and the Political Space* (Stanford, Calif.: Stanford University Press, 1999).
Cassagne, Albert, *La Théorie de l'art pour l'art en France chez les derniers romantiques et les premiers réalistes* (Paris: Hachette, 1906 (Geneva: Slatkine Reprints, 1979); repr. (with a preface by Daniel Oster) Seyssel: Champ Vallon, 1997).
Catani, Damian, *Evil: A History in Modern French Literature and Thought* (London: Bloomsbury, 2013).
Caws, Mary Ann and Hermine Riffaterre (eds), *The Prose Poem in France: Theory and Practice* (New York: Columbia University Press, 1983).
Caygill, Howard, 'Walter Benjamin's Concept of Allegory', in Rita Copeland (Ed.), *The Cambridge Companion to Allegory* (Cambridge: Cambridge University Press, 2010).
Chambers, Ross, *Mélancolie et opposition: Les Débuts du modernisme en France* (Paris: Corti, 1987).
Chévrier, Alain, *Le Décasyllabe à césure médiane: Histoire du tarantara* (Paris: Garnier, 2011).
Citron, Pierre, *La Poésie de Paris dans la littérature française de Rousseau à Baudelaire* (2 vols, Paris: Les Éditions de minuit, 1961).
Clair, Jean and Robert Kopp (eds), *De la Mélancolie* (Paris: Gallimard, 2007).
Clark, T. J., *The Absolute Bourgeois: Artists and Politics in France 1848-1851* (London: Thames and Hudson, 1973).
Compagnon, Antoine, *Les Antimodernes: De Joseph de Maistre à Roland Barthes* (Paris: Gallimard, 2005).
Compagnon, Antoine, *Les Chiffonniers* (Paris: Gallimard, 2017).
Culler, Jonathan, *Theory of the Lyric* (Cambridge, Mass.: Harvard University Press, 2015).
Davison, Kenneth, 'Historical Aspects of Mood Disorders', *Psychiatry*, 5: 4 (2006), 115-18.
De Man, Paul, 'Lyric and Modernity', and 'The Rhetoric of Temporality', in De Man, *Blindness and Insight: Essays in the Rhetoric of Contemporary Criticism* (2nd edn, London: Methuen, 1983), 166-86, 187-228.

De Man, Paul, 'Anthropomorphism and Trope in the Lyric', in De Man, *The Rhetoric of Romanticism* (New York: Columbia University Press, 1984), 239–62.

Dictionnaire historique de la langue française, ed. Alain Rey (Paris: Dictionnaires Le Robert, 1998).

Disegni, Silvia, 'Les poètes journalistes au temps de Baudelaire', in Silvia Disegni (ed.), *Poésie et journalisme au XIXe siècle en France et en Italie*, in *Recherches et travaux* [Grenoble], 65 (2005), 83–98.

Disegni, Silvia, 'Poème en prose et formes brèves au milieu du XIXe siècle', in Marie-Ève Thérenty and Guillaume Pinson (eds), *Microrécits médiatiques: Les Formes brèves du journal, entre médiations et fiction*, in *Études françaises*, 44: 3 (2008), 68–85.

Edelman, Nicole, *Les Métamorphoses de l'hystérique: Du début du XIXe siècle à la Grande Guerre* (Paris: Éditions La Découverte, 2003).

Esquirol, Étienne, 'Mélancolie', in *Dictionnaire des sciences médicales par une société de médecins et de chirurgiens* (60 vols, Paris: Panckoucke, 1818–22), xxxii [1819].

Foucault, Michel, 'Qu'est-ce que les Lumières?', *Magazine littéraire*, 309 (Apr. 1993), 61–73.

Gefen, Alexandre, *L'Idée de littérature: De l'art pour l'art aux écritures d'intervention* (Paris: Corti, 2021).

Gendre, André, *Évolution du sonnet français* (Paris: Presses universitaires de France, 1996).

Goldstein, Jan, *Console and Classify: The French Psychiatric Profession in the Nineteenth Century* (Cambridge: Cambridge University Press, 1987).

Hamon, Philippe, *L'Ironie littéraire* (Paris: Hachette, 1996).

Jackson, John E., *Mémoire et création poétique* (Paris: Mercure de France, 1992).

Jackson, John E., *La Poésie et son autre: Essai sur la modernité* (Paris: Corti, 1998).

James, Tony, *Dream, Creativity, and Madness in Nineteenth-Century France* (Oxford: Oxford University Press, 1995).

Johnson, Barbara, 'Anthropomorphism in Lyric and Law', *Yale Journal of Law and the Humanities*, 10: 2 (1998), 549–74.

Jouanna, Jacques, 'Aux racines de la mélancolie: La Médecine grecque est-elle mélancolique?', in Clair and Kopp (eds), *De la Mélancolie*, 11–51.

Kalifa, Dominique, Philippe Régnier, Marie-Ève Thérenty, and Alain Vaillant, *La Civilisation du journal: Histoire culturelle et littéraire de la presse française aux XIXe siècle* (Paris: Nouveau Monde éditions, 2011).

Kelley, Donald R. and Bonnie G. Smith, 'What was Property? Legal Dimensions of the Social Question in France (1789–1848)', *Proceedings of the American Philosophical Society*, 128: 3 (Sept. 1984), 200–30.

Klibansky, Raymond, Erwin Panofsky, and Fritz Saxl, *Saturn and Melancholy; Studies in the History of Natural Philosophy, Religion, and Art* (London: Nelson, 1964).

Kristeva, Julia, *Soleil noir: Dépression et mélancolie* (Paris: Gallimard, 1987).

LaCapra, Dominick, *Madame Bovary on Trial* (Ithaca, NY: Cornell University Press, 1982).

Ladenson, Elisabeth, *Dirt for Art's Sake: Books on Trial from 'Madame Bovary' to 'Lolita'* (Ithaca, NY: Cornell University Press, 2007).

Lawler, James, *Edgar Poe et les poètes français* (Paris: Julliard, 1989).

Leclerc, Yvan, *Crimes écrits: La Littérature en procès au XIXe siècle* (Paris: Plon, 1991).

Lemonnier, Léon, *Edgar Poe et les poètes français* (Paris: Éditions de la Nouvelle Critique, 1932).

Lewis, A. J., 'Melancholia: A Historical Review', *Journal of Mental Science*, 80 (1934), 1–42.

Lewis, Philippa, *Intimacy and Distance: Conflicting Cultures in Nineteenth-Century France* (Cambridge: Legenda (MHRA), 2017).

Lewis, Roy, *On Reading French Verse: A Study of Poetic Form* (Oxford: Clarendon Press, 1982).

Lloyd, Rosemary, *The Land of Lost Content: Children and Childhood in Nineteenth-Century French Literature* (Oxford: Oxford University Press, 1992).
Locke, Ralph P., 'Liszt on the Artist in Society', in Christopher H. Gibbs and Dana Gooley (eds), *Franz Liszt and his World* (Princeton: Princeton University Press, 2006), 292–302.
McGuinness, Patrick, *Poetry and Radical Politics in Fin de Siècle France: From Anarchism to Action Française* (Oxford: Oxford University Press, 2015).
Maulpoix, Jean-Michel, *Du lyrisme* (3rd edn, Paris: Corti, 2000).
Maulpoix, Jean-Michel, *Le Poète perplexe* (Paris: Corti, 2002).
Melmoux-Montaubin, Marie-Françoise, *L'Écrivain-journaliste au XIXe siècle: Un mutant des lettres* (Saint-Étienne: Cahiers intempestifs, 2003).
Michel, Arlette, 'La Morale du roman: Balzac répond à Hippolyte Castille', *L'Année balzacienne*, 4 (2003), 225–47.
Morienval, Jean, *Les Créateurs de la grande presse en France: Émile de Girardin, H. de Villemessant, Moïse Millaud* (Paris: Éditions Spes, s.d. [1934]).
Monroe, Jonathan, *A Poverty of Objects: The Prose Poem and the Politics of Genre* (Ithaca, NY and London: Cornell University Press, 1987).
Moussa, Sarga, 'Les Bohémiens de Liszt', in *Le Mythe des Bohémiens dans la littérature et les arts en Europe* (Paris: L'Harmattan, 2008), 223–42.
Murat, Michel, 'Le Dernier Livre de la bibliothèque', in Murat, *La Langue des dieux modernes* (Paris: Classiques Garnier, 2012), 45–59.
Newmark, Kevin, *Beyond Symbolism: Textual History and the Future of Reading* (Ithaca, NY and London: Cornell University Press, 1991).
Paraschas, Sotirios, *Realist Author and Sympathetic Imagination* (London: Maney, 2013).
Pearson, Roger, *Mallarmé and Circumstance: The Translation of Silence* (Oxford: Oxford University Press, 2004).
Pearson, Roger, 'Flaubert's Style and the Idea of Literary Justice', *Dix-Neuf*, 17: 2 (July 2013), 156–82.
Pearson, Roger, 'Strategic Gaps: Poetry and the Sixth Sense from Chateaubriand to Mallarmé', *Dix-Neuf*, 19: 2 (2015), 113–29.
Pearson, Roger, *Unacknowledged Legislators: The Poet as Lawgiver in Post-Revolutionary France: Chateaubriand–Staël–Lamartine–Hugo–Vigny* (Oxford: Oxford University Press, 2016).
Pearson, Roger, 'Mallarmé and Poetry: Stitching the Random', in Christopher Prendergast (ed.), *A History of Modern French Literature: From the Sixteenth Century to the Twentieth Century* (Princeton and Oxford: Princeton University Press, 2017), 495–513.
Prendergast, Christopher, *Paris and the Nineteenth Century* (Oxford: Blackwell, 1982).
Prigent, Hélène, *Mélancolie: les métamorphoses de la dépression* (Paris: Gallimard, 2005).
Prigent, Hélène, 'Mélancolie antique: Une philosophie de l'image?', in Clair and Kopp (eds), *De la mélancolie*, 75–93.
Radden, Jennifer (ed.), *The Nature of Melancholy: From Aristotle to Kristeva* (Oxford: Oxford University Press, 2000).
Radden, Jennifer, 'Is This Dame Melancholy? Equating Today's Depression and Past Melancholia', *Philosophy, Psychiatry, and Psychology*, 10: 1 (Mar. 2003), 37–52.
Rancière, Jacques, 'Le Goût infini de la République', in Rancière, *Le Fil perdu: Essais sur la fiction moderne* (Paris: La Fabrique éditions, 2015), 94–112. (Previously published as 'The Infinite Taste of the Republic', trans. Elissa Marder and Gina Stamm, *Yale French Studies*, 125: 6 (2014), 30–44.)
Rigoli, Juan, *Lire le délire: Aliénisme, rhétorique et littérature en France au XIXe siècle* (Paris: Fayard, 2001).
Rufus of Ephesus, *On Melancholy*, ed. Peter E. Pormann (Tübingen: Mohr Siebeck, 2008).

Rushworth, Jennifer, *Discourses of Mourning in Dante, Petrarch, and Proust* (Oxford: Oxford University Press, 2016).
Sandras, Michel, *Lire le poème en prose* (Paris: Dunod, 1995).
Sapiro, Gisèle, *La Responsabilité de l'écrivain: Littérature, droit et morale en France (XIXe-XXIe siècle)* (Paris: Éditions du Seuil, 2011).
Schulz, Gretchen, *Sapphic Fathers: Discourses of Same-Sex Desire from Nineteenth-Century France* (Toronto: University of Toronto Press, 2015).
Scott, Clive, *French Verse-Art: A Study* (Cambridge: Cambridge University Press, 1980).
Scott, David, *Sonnet Theory and Practice in Nineteenth-Century France: Sonnets on the Sonnet* (Hull: University of Hull, 1977).
Scott, David, *Pictorialist Poetics: Poetry and the Visual Arts in Nineteenth-Century France* (Cambridge: Cambridge University Press, 1988).
Söllner, Fritz, 'The Use (and Abuse) of Robinson Crusoe in Neoclassical Economics', *History of Political Economy*, 48: 1 (2016), 35–64.
Starobinski, Jean, *Histoire du traitement de la mélancolie des origines à 1900* (Basel: Geigy, 1960).
Starobinski, Jean, *Portrait de l'artiste en saltimbanque* (Geneva and Paris: Éditions d'Art Albert Skira and Flammarion, 1970).
Starobinski, Jean, *L'Encre de la mélancolie* (Paris: Éditions du Seuil, 2012).
Stierle, Karlheinz, *Der Mythos von Paris: Zeichen und Bewusstsein der Stadt* (Munich and Vienna: Carl Henser Verlag, 1993); trans. into French by Marianne Rocher-Jacquin as *La Capitale des signes: Paris et son discours* (Paris: Éditions de la Maison des sciences de l'homme, 2001).
Terdiman, Richard, *Discourse/Counter-Discourse: The Theory and Practice of Symbolic Resistance in Nineteenth-Century France* (Ithaca, NY: Cornell University Press, 1985).
Thérenty, Marie-Ève, *La Littérature au quotidien: Poétiques journalistiques au XIXe siècle* (Paris: Éditions du Seuil, 2007).
Thérenty, Marie-Ève, and Alain Vaillant (eds), *Presse et plumes: Journalisme et littérature au XIXe siècle* (Paris: Nouveau Monde Éditions, 2004).
Thérenty, Marie-Ève and Guillaume Pinson (eds), *Microrécits médiatiques: Les Formes brèves du journal, entre médiations et fiction*, in *Études françaises*, 44: 3 (2008).
Todorov, Tzvetan, 'La Poésie sans le vers', in *Les Genres du discours* (Paris: Éditions du Seuil, 1978), 116–31.
Toal, Catherine, *The Entrapments of Form* (New York: Fordham University Press, 2016).
Vachon, Stéphane (ed.), *Balzac* (Paris: Presses de l'Université de Paris-Sorbonne [Collection Mémoire de la critique], 1999).
Vadé, Yves, *Le Poème en prose et ses territoires* (Paris: Belin, 1996).
Vaillant, Alain, 'Métamorphoses littéraires. 2: La Modernité littéraire', in Kalifa et al., *La Civilisation du journal*, 1523–31.
Vaillant, Alain and Marie-Ève Thérenty, *1836: l'an I de l'ère médiatique, étude littéraire et historique du journal 'La Presse' d'Émile de Girardin* (Paris: Nouveau Monde Éditions, 2001).
Vincent-Munnia, Nathalie, *Les Premiers Poèmes en prose: Généalogie d'un genre dans la première moitié du dix-neuvième siècle français* (Paris: Champion, 1996).
Vines, Lois Davis, 'Poe in France', in Lois Davis Vines (ed.), *Poe Abroad: Influence, Reputation, Affinities* (Iowa City: University of Iowa Press, 1999), 9–18.
White, Michael, 'Robinson Crusoe', in *The New Palgrave Dictionary of Economics* (London: Palgrave Macmillan, 2019: article first published in *The New Palgrave Dictionary of Economics*, 2nd edn, 2008).

Index

Page numbers in bold indicate pages of particular relevance to the indexed item.

BAUDELAIRE'S POETRY IN VERSE

Collections

Les Lesbiennes (*see also* Lesbos) 14, **128–48**, 151, 164, 182, 184, 336
Les Limbes 14, 128, 131, **150–8**, 164, 169, 176, 181, 182, 185, 186, 194–5, 243, 364, 427, 457, 597
'Les Fleurs du Mal' [1855] 14, **160–75**, 181, 182, 183, 184, 185, 186, 243, 365, 371, 457, 472, 597
Les Fleurs du Mal [1857, 1861, and 1869] ix, xi, 1, 2, 4 n.10, 6, 8, 10, 13, 14, 15, 16, 18, 39, 42, 43, 45, 46, 50, 51, 55, 58, 58–9, 64, 65, 66, 69, 71, 81, 84, 85, 86, 87, 92, 97, 98, 104, 105 n.48, 107, 109, 110 n.3, 112, 115, 116, 117, 118, 119, 120, 121, 123, 124, 125, 126, 127, 128, 131, 132, 133 n.17, 135, 141, 144, 151, 152 n.36, 153, 154, 155, 156, 158, 160, 161, 162, 165, 167 n.12, 169, 170, 172, 173, 175, 176, 177, 179, 181, **182–239**, 243, 244, 246, 261, 267, 269, 279, 282, 286, 290, 296, 328, **333–453**, 457, 458, 461, 470 n.41, 476, 486, 489, 493, 510, 511, 513, 514, 515, 516, 517, 518, 521, 525, 528 n.60, 531, 533, 536, 537, 549, 550, 551, 553, 555 n.2, 565, 577, 597, 599, 600, 602, 606, 612
'Spleen et idéal' 127 n.4, 144, 156, 164 n.8, 170, 171, 176, 178, 179, 180, 181, **182–227**, 243, 339, **341–405**, 406, 407, 408, 409, 412, 415, 418, 421, 425, 427, 434, 435, 437
'Tableaux parisiens' 16, 127, 152 n.36, 156, 157, 173, 183, 186, 189 n.14, 209, 211, 328, 331, 364 n.1, 379, 382, 403, 404, **406–53**, 493, 529, 540, 543, 548, 577, 586
'Le Vin' 132, 176, 180, 208, 404, 406, 407, 408, 435
'Fleurs du Mal' 121, 131, 135, 141, 144, 148, 149 n.32, 162, 169, 176, 179, 202, 338, 339, 363, 369, 404, 406, 408, 422
'Révolte' 84, n.19, 161, **172–3**, 176, 177, 180, 406, 407, 408, 435, 512 n.26
'La Mort' 132, **154–6**, 176, 179, 180, 185, 186, 210, 221, 406, 407, 427

'Nouvelles *Fleurs du Mal*' 100, **127 n.3**, 458–9 n.10
Les Épaves 102, **127 n.2**, 127 n.3, 133 n.17, 175, 459 n.10

Individual Poems

'Abel et Caïn' **173**, 177, 389
'À celle qui est trop gaie' 127 n.2, 127 n.4, **132–3**, 161 n.3, 209, 353, 369 n.2, 371
'À la Belle aux cheveux d'or' 168 n.15, 170
'Alchimie de la douleur' 104, 210, **215–16**, 223, 365, 380 n.11, 393 n.45, 397
'Allégorie' **148**, 150
'Au lecteur' 27, 46, 66, 97, 118, 125, 126, 128 n.7, 135, 146, 161, **162–4**, 165, 166 n.10, 176, 178, **179**, 180, 185, 197, 217, 230, 362, 382, 397, 411, 422, 476
'À une dame créole' 337, 381, 391 n.37, 393 n.44, 457 n.3
'À une Madone' 296, 343, 353, 374, **378–9**, 380, 383
'À une Malabaraise' 457 n.3, 458 n.10
'À une mendiante rousse' 169 n.16, 171, 379 n.9, 392, 398, 409, 411, **412–13**, 424, 425 n.25, 432, 435, 438, 444, 448, 449, 450, 453
'À une passante' 107, 391 n.37, 393 n.45, 409, 414, 416, 427, 435, 436, 437, 438, 448–9, 449, 450, 551
'Avec ses vêtements ondoyants...' 176 n.27, 358, 364, 374, 382, 393 n.46

'Bénédiction' 75 n.9, 178, 179, 180, 181, **186–8**, 189, 190, 207, 209, 210, 215, 396, 397, 403 n.62, 409, 412
'Bien loin d'ici' 459 n.10
'Bohémiens en voyage' 169 n.16, **171–2**, 173, 177, 200, 220 n.19, 393 n.43, 544 n.16
'Brumes et pluies' 379 n.9, 382, 393, 417–18, 425 n.25, 426, 435, 448

'Causerie' 209, 210, 217 n.14, 374, 377, 379, 380, 391 n.37, 393 n.46
'Chanson d'après-midi' 353, **380**, 381, 392, 398, 399
'Chant d'automne' 353, 374, 377, 380, 397, 398
'Châtiment de l'orgueil' 200, 201, 216, 457 n.3
'Ciel brouillé' 167 n.12, 359, 373, 376–7, 398, **399**, 451
'Confession' 128 n.7, 165, 170, 369 n.2, **371–2**, 392, 396, 397, 398, 416 n.12
'Correspondances' 190, **191–8**, 199, 200, 201, 209, 210, 211, 212, 213, 214, 227, 230, 307, 312, 344, 355, 357, 362, 373, 374, 378, 391 n.37, 393 n.45, 397, 404, 410, 416, 423, 463 n.25, 542, 545

'Danse macabre' 282, 284, 290, 296, 383, 409, 414, 416, 417, 421, 427, 435, 439, 441, 444, 450
'De profundis clamavi' 128 n.5, 128 n.7, **151**, 166, 169, 170, 176, 177, 364, 365, 366, 374, 393 nn.45 and 47
'Don Juan aux enfers' 116, 200, 201, 210, 216, 383 n.12, 457 n.3
'Duellum' 209, 353, **366**, 367, 368, 391 n.37, 393 n.46

'Élévation' 75 n.9, 180, **190**, 191, 193, 196, 198, 207, 210, 375 n.4, 397, 404, 409, 410, 412, 464
'Épigraphe pour un livre condamné' 8–9, 458 n.10
'Épilogue [I]' 120, 121, 122, 132, 173, 221, 418, 420 n.19
'Épilogue [II]' 120, 121, 132, 221, 233 n.13, 418

'Femmes damnées' ['Comme un bétail pensif...'] 121, 128, 135, **141–4**, 147, 338, 422, 440
'Femmes damnées. Delphine et Hippolyte' 127 n.2, 127 n.4, 135, **138–41**, 144
'Franciscae meae laudes' 176 n.27, 343, **380–1**, 397, 398, 399

'Harmonie du soir' 176 n.27, 369 n.2, **372–3**, 375, 377, 380, 389, 390, 397, 398, 458
'Horreur sympathique' 104, 106, 210, **216–17**, 218, 223, 380 n.11, 382, 393 n.44, **394–5**, 397
'Hymne' 458 n.10
'Hymne à la Beauté' 15, 16, 58, 193, 204, **208–9**, 214, 215, 227, 282, **341–3**, 351, 352, 353, 364, 365, 383, 391, 404, 597, 602

'J'aime le souvenir de ces époques nues...' **190**, 193, 198, 396–7, 463 n.25
'Je n'ai pas oublié...' 379 n.9, 417, 425 n.25, 435, 438, 450
'Je t'adore à l'égal de la voûte nocturne...' **356**, 373
'Je te donne ces vers...' 176 n.27, 343, 353, 366, 367, 368, 374, 392 n.41, **393–4**

'La Béatrice' **148**, 150, 151, 177
'La Béatrix' 151 n.35, 176, 364
'La Beauté' 16, 176 n.27, **201**, 202, 204, 205, 208, 353, 382, 390, 393 n.45
'La Chevelure' 183, 209, 289, 337, **345–52**, 355, 356, 357, 359, 362, 363, 368, 376, 377, 380, 382, 398, 404, 413, 436, 487, 540, 544
'La Cloche' 152 n.37
'La Cloche fêlée' 128 n.5, 128 n.7, **152**, 169, 212 n.6, 375, 380, 382, 393 nn.46 and 47
'La Comédie humaine' (*see* 'Le Masque')
'La Destruction' 128 n.7, 141, 145, 147, **160–2**, 163, 169, 170, 186, 187, 196, 202, 219, 340, 369, 370, 393 n.46, 406, 472, 477
'La Fin de la journée' 155, 177, 210, 222
'La Fontaine de sang' **148**, 150, 169 n.16, 393
'La Géante' 105 n.48, **201–2**, 204, 208, 345, 353, 368, 393 n.46
'L'Albatros' 207, 396, 397, 404, 421
'La Lune offensée' 459 n.10
'L'Âme du vin' **131–2**, 233, 435 n.2, 457
'La Mort des amants' 128 n.5, **154**, 392, 393 n.44, 395
'La Mort des artistes' 128 n.5, 132, **154–5**, 177, 181, 233, 279, 279 n.14, 283, 393 n.43, 597
'La Mort des pauvres' **154–5**, 157, 169 n.16, 177, 188, 391 n.37, 393 n.44
'L'Amour du mensonge' 327–8, 409, 417, 435, 441, **443–4**
'L'Amour et le crâne' 128 n.7, **149–50**, 163, 169, 296, 383, 392, 406
'La Muse malade' **198–9**, 393 n.44, 393 n.47, 609
'La Muse vénale' 198, **199**, 205, 393
'La Musique' 180, 310 n.4, 379 n.10, 382, 390, 392, 393 n.46
'La Pipe' 180–1, 197, 379 n.10, 382, 393 n.43
'La Prière d'un païen' 459 n.10
'La Rançon' 169 n.16, **171**, 173, 459 n.10
'La servante au grand cœur...' 105 n.48, 379 n.9, 417, 425 n.25, 426, 435, 438 n.4, 439, 450
'L'Aube spirituelle' 128 n.7, 165–6, 170, 369 n.2, 371, **372**, 393 n.45
'L'Avertisseur' 458 n.10
'La Vie antérieure' 128 n.7, 164, 166, 200, 393

'La Voix' 458 n.10
'La Volupté' (see 'La Destruction')
'Le Balcon' 366, **367–9**, 372, 378, 388
'Le Beau Navire' 374, 377, 390, 392, 397, 398, **399–402**, 592
'Le Chat' ['Viens mon beau chat…'] 365, 367, 368, 374, 392, 393 n.46, 395 n.52
'Le Chat' ['Dans ma cervelle se promène…'] 373, 377, 382, 398, 399
'Le Couvercle' 127 n.3, 459 n.10
'Le Crépuscule du matin' 156, **157–8**, 166, 169 n.16, 379 n.9, 403, 412, 416, 418, 424, 425 n.25, 426, 427 n.27, 435, 438, 442, 451, **452–3**, 463, 464
'Le Crépuscule du soir' **156–7**, 158, 161, 169 n.16, 379 n.9, 403, 412, 418, 424, 425 n.25, 426, 427 n.27, 434, 435, 445, 449, 463, 464
'Le Cygne' 67, 104, 105, 183, 234 n.14, 412, 413, 414, 415, 416, 420–1, 423, 424, 425, 426, **427–9**, 430, 433, 434, 435, 438–9, 441, 443, 449, 450, 451, 611 n.22
'L'Examen de minuit' 458 n.10
'Le Flacon' 132, 176 n.27, 233, 343, 363, 369 n.2, **374–6**, 379, 398, 399
'Le Flambeau vivant' 176 n.27, 369 n.2, 371, 391 n.37, 393 n.46, 398
'Le Gouffre' **100–1**, 459 n.10
'Le Goût du néant' 210, **215**, 380 n.11, 390, 398
'Le Guignon' 128 n.7, 164, 169–70, 200, 393 n.45
'Le Jet d'eau' 389 n.26, 459 n.10
'Le Jeu' 211, 379 n.9, 417, 425 n.25, 426, 435, 436, **441–3**, 450
'Le Léthé' 127 n.2, 127 n.4, **144–5**, 209, 353, 365
'Le Masque' 176 n.28, **204–6**, 208, 209, 282, 296, 353, 383
'Le Mauvais Moine' 128 n.5, **152–3**, 198, 199–200, 214 n.8, 229 n.6, 239, 355, 391 n.37, 393 n.44
'Le Monstre' 459 n.10
'Le Mort joyeux' 128 n.5, **152**, 155, 177, 180, 379 n.10, 382, 383, 393 n.44
'L'Ennemi' 128 n.7, 164, 169, 391 n.37, 393 n.46, 425
'Le Poison' 176 n.27, 343, 373, 376, 380, 390, 392, **398**, **399**
'Le Possédé' 209, 339, 353, **366–7**, 368, 373, 374, 382, 392
'Le Rebelle' 116, 458–9 n.10
'Le Reniement de saint Pierre' 59, 84 n.19, 103, 169 n.16, 171, **172–3**, 177, 217, 220
'Le Rêve d'un curieux' 155, 169, 177, 210, 222, 227, 393 n.44
'Le Revenant' 180, 379 n.10, 381, 383, 393, 398

'Les Aveugles' 116, 173, 393 n.45, 410, 414, 416, 421, 423, 434, 435, **440–1**, 448, 449, 450
'Les Bijoux' 127 n.2, 127 n.4, **202–4**, 206, 208, 209, 353
'Lesbos' 121, 122, 127 n.2, 127 n.4, 130, **135–8**, 140, 141, 142, 143, 148 n.31, 162, 220, 388, 457 n.3, 599
'Les Chats' 128 n.5, **153–4**, 380, 382, 393 n.45, 457 n.3
'Les Deux Bonnes Sœurs' **147–8**, 393 n.44
'Le Serpent qui danse' **358–61**, 363, 364, 373, 374, 376, 379, 380, 392, 399
'Les Hiboux' 128 n.5, **153–4**, 380, 382, 393 n.45
'Les Litanies de Satan' 116, 123, **173–5**, 177, 178, 198, 389, 602
'Les Métamorphoses du vampire' 127 n.2, 127 n.4, **150**, 169 n.16
'Le Soleil' 180, 181, **188–9**, 190, 198, 207, 397 n.57, 409, 411, 412, 415, 416, 423, 425 n.25, 426, 435, 440, 463 n.25
'Les Petites Vieilles' 67, 116, 183, 211, 299, 403 n.62, 407, 409, 412, 413, 414, 416, 417, 421, 422, 423, 424, 425, 426, 427, **429–30**, 431, 432–3, 434, 435, 436, 445, 449, 450, 556
'Les Phares' **124–5**, 198, 397
'Les Plaintes d'un Icare' 459 n.10
'Le Spleen' 151 n.35, 152 n.37, 170, 177, 365
'Le Squelette laboureur' 96 n.20, 105, 152 n.36, 157, 412, 416, 427, 433, 435, **436–7**, 446–7, 449, 450
'Les Sept Vieillards' 183, 211, 299, 331, 412, 414, 415 n.10, 415–16, 416, 417, 418 n.16, 421–2, 423, 425, 426, 427, **430–2**, 434, 435, 436, **439–40**, 441, 444, 445, 449, 449–50, 450
'Les Yeux de Berthe' 459 n.10
'Le Tonneau de la haine' 128 n.5, 128 n.7, **151**, 165, 166, 169, 177, 180, 181, 379 n.10, 393
'Le Vampire' 128 n.7, 169, 170, 177, 365, 374, 398 n.59
'Le Vin de l'assassin' 392 n.40, 407, 435
'Le Vin des amants' 393, 407–8, 408, 435
'Le Vin des chiffonniers' 10, 131 n.16, 169 n.16, 407, 408, 423, 435, 457
'Le Vin du solitaire' 393 n.45, 407, 435
'Le Voyage' 69, 125, 155, 156, 168, 181, 210, 219, **222–7**, 236, 237, 339, 362, 396, 404–5, 411
'L'Héautontimorouménos' 9 n.21, 104, 105 n.48, 176 n.27, 210, **217–18**, 220, 261, 353, 380, 382, 397
'L'Homme et la mer' 200
'L'Horloge' 170, 210, **221**, 222, 376, 380, 383, 397, 408, 414, 425, 426

'L'Idéal' 128 n.5, **152**, 189 n.13, 201, 202, 205, 208, 353, 383 n.12, 391 n.37, 393 n.46
'L'Invitation au voyage' 128 n.7, **166–7**, 170, 181, 196 n.24, 374, 377, 389 n.26, 390, 392, 397, 398, **402–3**
'L'Irrémédiable' 104, 105, **123–4**, **125**, 164, 175, 176 n.27, 210, **218–21**, 366, 380, 382, 397, 407, 423
'L'Irréparable' 128 n.7, 153, 156 n.40, 166, **168–9**, 170, 374, 377, 392, 399
'Lola de Valence' 459 n.10

'Madrigal triste' 458 n.10
'Moesta et errabunda' 128 n.7, **167–8**, 170, 343, 353, 380, 381, 458

'Obsession' 101, **210–15**, 216, 221, 223, 230, 355, 373, 380 n.11, 381, 382, 383, 393 n.46, 432 n.33

'Parfum exotique' 204, 209, 233, 337, 343, **344–5**, 352, 353, 355, 356, 357, 359, 362, 370, 374, 377, 380, 387, 388, 391 n.37, 392, 404, 540
'Paysage' 189 n.14, **408–11**, 414, 416, 417, 421, 425, 426, 432, 433, **434–5**, **437–8**, 440, 442, 445, 446, 450, 478, 490 n.13

'Que diras-tu ce soir…' 369 n.2, **370**, 371, 387, 391 n.37, 393 n.46

'Recueillement' 126, 157, 373, 459 n.10
'Remords posthume' 128 n.7, 166, **168**, 170, 363, 365, 374, 375, 378, 393 n.43
'Rêve parisien' 105, 211, 412, 416, 417, 426, 433, 435, 436, 442, 443, 444, 450, **451–2**, 541
'Réversibilité' 128 n.7, **165**, 169, 170, 369 n.2, 371

'Sed non satiata' **357**, 359, 380, 387, 388, 391 n.37, 392, 404
'Semper eadem' 343, 353, 366, 369, 374, 393 n.46
'Sépulture' 180, 215, 379 n.10, 382, 383, 393 n.46
'Sisina' 343, 353, 380, 391 n.37, 393 n.44
'Sonnet d'automne' 343, 353 n.11, 380, **381–2**, 392 n.41, 393 n.43
'Spleen' [I] ('Pluviôse, irrité…') 128 n.5, **153**, 214–15, **234–6**, 382, 391 n.37, 393 n.44, 398, **577–8**
'Spleen' [II] ('J'ai plus de souvenirs…') 105, 106 n.50, 164 n.6, 214–15, **234–6**, 286, 382, 394, 398
'Spleen' [III] ('Je suis comme le roi…') 81, 99, 214–15, **234–6**, 382, 398, 554

'Spleen' [IV] ('Quand le ciel bas et lourd…)' 214–15, **234–6**, 382, 398
'Sur *Le Tasse en prison* d'Eugène Delacroix' 97, **101–3**, 296, 459 n.10

'Tous imberbes alors…' **129–30**, 147, 196 n.25
'Tout entière' 176 n.27, **369–70**
'Tristesses de la lune' 180, 379 n.10, 381–2, 391 n.37, 393 n.46, 463 n.25
'Tu mettrais l'univers entier dans ta ruelle…' 356

'Une charogne' 171, **230–2**, 340, 364, 365, 392, 396, 415, 447, 541
'Une gravure fantastique' 296, 380, 383, 388
'Une martyre. Dessin d'un maître inconnu' **145–7**, 296, 383, 392, 396, 406, 407, 408
'Une nuit que j'étais près d'une affreuse Juive…' 365, 374, 393
'Un fantôme' 209, 214 n.8, **353–5**, 362, 363, 366, 368, 369, 391, 392, **395–6**, 398, 404
'Un voyage à Cythère' 128 n.7, 143, **148–9**, 150, 151, 152, 159–60, 161, 169, 178, 181, 220, 406, 434

'Vers pour le portrait de M. Honoré Daumier' 296

BAUDELAIRE'S PROSE POEMS

Poèmes nocturnes 184, 458, 487
Le Spleen de Paris [*Petits poèmes en prose*] ix, xi, 12, 16, 60 n.23, 63, 64, 65 n.30, 69, 72, 98, 107, 117, 239, 244, 278, 328, 331, 418, 419, 437, 443, 444, 451 n.21, **455–593**, 606, 612

Individual Prose Poems

'Any where out of the world' 458, 492, 552, **577–8**, 591
'Assommons les pauvres!' 458, 492, 493, 505, 506, 511, 554, 566, **569–70**, 573
'À une heure du matin' 478, 492, 503, 505, **549**, 553, 555

'Chacun sa chimère' 492, 496, **543–4**, 547, 589, 591

'Déjà!' 492, 502, 552, **588–9**

'Enivrez-vous' 492, 505, 511, 568, **588**, 591

'La Belle Dorothée' 492, 502, **561–2**, 563, 564, 577, 589
'La Chambre double' 83, 105, 488, 492, 496, **539–42**, 543, 545, 550, 552, 577, 589, 602, 603

'La Corde' 491, 492, 502, 589, **590**, 591
'La Fausse Monnaie' 490, 492, 502, 505, 510, **566–76**, 569, 573, 591
'La Femme sauvage et la petite-maîtresse' 492, 504, 552, **555–6**, 560, 565, 573
'Laquelle est la vraie?' ['L'Idéal et le réel'] 478 n.62, 492, 552, **564–5**
'La Solitude' 16, 183, 457, 458, 461, **466–81**, 486 n.5, 487, 488, 492, 493, 494, 504, 505, 507, 511, 522, 523, 526, 527, 531, 537, 547, 591
'La Soupe et les nuages' 83, 215, 418 n.16, 458, 475, 492, **567**
'Le Chien et le flacon' 492, 496, 537, **545–6**, 565, 573, 590
'Le "Confiteor" de l'artiste' 71 n.3, 492, 496, **538**, 539, 540, 542, 549, 557, 560, 578, 587, 588, 590, 591
'Le Crépuscule du soir' 16, 183, 457, 458, **461–6**, 478, **481–4**, 486, 487, 492, 504, 511, 522, 523, 525, 537, 539, 540, 546, 547, 548, 549, 551, 557, 576, 587, 590, 592
'Le Désespoir de la vieille' 492, 496, **537–8**, 542, 544, 545, 556, 559, 589
'Le Désir de peindre' 492, **550–1**, 577, 591
'L'Étranger' 492, 496, 505, 518, **535–7**, 546, 547, 549, 551, 553, 556, 557, 559, 573, 589, 590, 592, 609
'Le Fou et la Vénus' 492, 496, 543, **544–5**, 552, 577, 590, 609
'Le Galant Tireur' 458, 492, 504, 520 n.39, **567**
'Le Gâteau' 488, 492, 501, 502, 508, 510, **568–9**, 577, 589, 590, 603
'Le Joueur généreux' 490, 491, 492, **565**, 566, 577, 591
'Le Joujou du pauvre' 488, 492, 502, **570–1**, 572, 573, 590, 591
'Le Mauvais Vitrier' 491, 492, 496, 501, 505, 511, 515, **519–32**, 545–6, 549, 553, 556, 566, 570, 573, 590, 591, 603
'Le Miroir' 492, 502, **562**
'Le Port' 492, 496, 552, **591–3**, 594, 611
'Les Bienfaits de la lune' 492, 551, **552**, 554, 560
'Les Bons Chiens' 458, 490 n.13, 492, 559, **573–7**
'Les Dons des fées' 492, 505, 520 n.39, 563, **564**, 591
'Les Fenêtres' **444–5**, 492, 519, 576, 578, 590, 591
'Les Foules' 62, 458, 488, **548–9**, **553–4**, 555, 556, 589, 590, 591
'Les Projets' 458, 487, 492, **547–8**, 548, 577, 590
'Les Tentations ou Eros, Plutus et la Gloire' 492, **562–3**, 565, 567, 591

'Les Veuves' 458, 488, 492, **556–8**, 559, 560, 574, 577, 590, 591
'Les Vocations' 492, 502, 505, **546–7**, 557, 562, 577, 580–1, 582, 590
'Les Yeux des pauvres' 492, 510, 557, **560–1**, 577, 590
'Le Tir et le cimetière' 492, **567–8**, 577, 587, 590, 591
'Le Thyrse' 487, 492, **578–86**, 588, 589
'Le Vieux Saltimbanque' 75 n.10, 458, 488, 491, 492, 504, 510, 533, 556, **558–60**, 568, 577
'L'Horloge' 458, 487, 492, 496, 540, 547, 548, 577, 588, 589, 590
'L'Invitation au voyage' 167 n.11, 458, 487, 488, 492, 505, 547, 577, 591

'Mademoiselle Bistouri' **418–19**, 420, 458, 492, 589, 590, 591

'Perte d'auréole' 188, 458, 492, 501, 502, **567**
'Portraits de maîtresses' 492, 502, 505, **567**

'Un cheval de race' 492, 496, 576
'Une mort héroïque' 14, **72–84**, 107, 206, 492, 504, 505, 533, 545, 566, 569, 573, 577, 590, 590
'Un hémisphère dans une chevelure' (formerly 'La Chevelure') 352, 458, 487, 492, 505, 547, **548**, 590, 591
'Un plaisant' 492, 496, 500, 502, 504, 510, 520 n.39, **538–9**, 542, 545, 573, 576, 590, 591

OTHER WORKS BY BAUDELAIRE

'Choix de maximes consolantes sur l'amour' 336–7, 608
'Conseils aux jeunes littérateurs' 22–3, 25, 26

De l'essence du rire 14, **56–9**, 64, 67, 73, 75, 112, 217, 218, 275, 363, 414, 565, 597
draft prefaces to *Les Fleurs du Mal* 41–2, 50, 84, 517
'Du vin et du hachisch' 24, 54, 70, 71, 430, 457

'Edgar Allan Poe, sa vie et ses ouvrages' 38, 244, 245, **246–53**, 258 n.15, 259 n.17, 263, 286, 289
'Edgar Poe, sa vie et ses œuvres' 244, 245, 246–7, 247, 248, 249, 252 n.9, 262 n.22, 263
Exposition universelle. 1855. Beaux-Arts 28, 30, 33, 34, 35, 55 n.15, 66, 111, 123 n.33, 332, 391 n.35, 595, 608

Fusées 9 n.20., 45–6, 109, 111 n.4, 112, 119, 202, 217, 296, 301, 305, 320, 323, 324, 338, 339, 340, 401, 401–2, 403, 432, 592, 595, 596, 598, 611

Hygiène 100, 119

La Fanfarlo **99–100, 337–8**, 457–8, 596
'L'Art philosophique' 40
Le Catéchisme de la femme aimée 336
'L'École païenne' 35, 43, 201, 452
Le Peintre de la vie moderne 29, 33, 55, 60, 61, 63, 119 n.28, 171, 227, 233, 244, 266, 282, **315–29**, 338, 339, 372, 413, 419, 432, 447–8, 518, 599, 600 n.6, 610
'Les Drames et les romans honnêtes' 23, 38, 470
Les Paradis artificiels 46 n.33, 55, 160, 161–2, 214 n.8, **237–9**, 296, 433, 489, 542, 554 n.1, 579, 580, 586, **601–3**, 605, 609
'L'Œuvre et la vie d'Eugène Delacroix' 28, 30, **331–2**

Mon cœur mis à nu 45, 58, 122, 229–30, 494, 511 n.21
Morale du joujou 572

'Notes nouvelles sur Edgar Poe' 35 n.21, 37–8, 123 n.33, 244, 245, 247, **253–64**, 265, 289, 291, 550 n.19, 599
'Notes sur *Les Liaisons dangereuses*' 115 n.10

Pauvre Belgique! 21
'Peintres et aquafortistes' 60 n.23
'Puisque réalisme il y a' 34

'Quelques caricaturistes étrangers' 54 n.13, 60, 61 n.26
'Quelques caricaturistes français' 60, 414

'Réflexions sur quelques-uns de mes contemporains. I. Victor Hugo' 38–9, 41–4, 244, 490
'Réflexions sur quelques-uns de mes contemporains. II. Auguste Barbier' 37, 391
'Réflexions sur quelques-uns de mes contemporains. III. Marceline Desbordes-Valmore' 6
'Richard Wagner et *Tannhaüser* à Paris' x, 25, 30, 34, 244, 403 n.63, 489

Salon de 1845 ix, x, 25, 28, 101 n.37, 245, 266, 290
Salon de 1846 x, xi, 18, 25–7, 28, 29 n.15, 30, 31, 37, 40, 44–5, 55, 56, 60, 61, 79, 108, 128, 141 n.24, 171, 176, 245, 266, 271 n.7, 278, 279, 290, 304, 315, 317, 331, 336, 419, 445–6, 447 n.13, 448, 528–9, 581, 596, 598, 599
Salon de 1859 15, 28, 30, 31 n.17, 33–4, 53, 57, 98, 104, 106, 209, 244, 253, **265–85**, 287, 290, 292, 294, 306, 310, 312, 313, 330, 343, 352, 390, 391 n.36, 446, 530 n.63, 585, 596, 600

'Théodore de Banville' 28 n.12
'Théophile Gautier' [1859] 24, 30 n.16, 35 n.21, 35 n.22, 37, 108, 244, 262 n.22, **290–6**, 299, 311, 489, 600–1
'Théophile Gautier' [1861] 244, 292 nn.11 and 12, 294 nn.13 and 14

General Index

Abbott, Helen 389 n.26
Abrams, M. H. 273 n.10
Acquisto, Joseph 209 n.3, 236
Adam, Antoine 133 n.17, 161 n.3, 162 n.4, 204 n.34, 214 n.8, 216 n.11, 218 n.17
Adorno, Theodor W. 614
Aeschylus 212 n.6, 298, 308
Amphion 36, 133
Ancelle, Narcisse 298 n.18, 300 n.23
Antony, St 142, 477
Apollinaire, Guillaume
  Alcools 606
  Calligrammes 606
Arabian Nights 162
Aretino, Pietro 576
Aristotle 94, 102 n.38
Art for Art's Sake 10, 14, 23, 35, 37, 39, 40, 57, 296, 330, 412, 452, 518, 602, 605 n.12
Ashley-Cooper, Anthony, Earl of Shaftesbury 468 n.35
Asselineau, Charles 7 n.16, 126, 184 n.6, 459 n.10, 470 n.40, 485, 493 n.20, 535 n.6
Auden, W. H. 296, 614
Augier, Émile
  Gabrielle 23
Augustine, St 63, 178, 480
Austin, Lloyd James 192, 195 n.23, 607–8
Autard de Bragard, Mme 337

Babou, Hippolyte 128
Bacon, Francis 31 n.17
Badesco, Luc 10 n.23.
Baillarger, Jules 7, 569, 570
Bakhtin, Mikhail 506
Ballanche, Pierre-Simon 134
Balzac, Honoré de 116, 245, 297, 319, 332, 415, 469–70
  Béatrix 99 n.30
  La Comédie humaine 176, 469
  La Fille aux yeux d'or 129, 145
  La Vieille Fille 495
Bandy, W.T. 18 n.38, 246 n.4
Banville, Théodore de 71, 108, 113, 116, 386, 392, 462 n.18, 485, 493 n.20, 500, 535 n.6
  La Lanterne magique 500
  Petit traité de poésie française 386, 392

Barbereau, Auguste 54
Barbey d'Aurevilly, Jules 175 n.25, 185
Barbier, Auguste 37
  Iambes 293
Barot, Odysse 495 n.26
Barthes, Roland 97 n.22
Bastiat, Frédéric 468, 473–6, 480, 481, 526–8
  Capital et rente 480
  Ce qu'on voit et ce qu'on ne voit pas 526–8
  Harmonies économiques 473–4, 480 n.66
  La Loi 475–6
Baudrillart, Henri 468 n.34
Bauer, Franck 572 n.1
Beckett, Samuel 69, 536 n.10, 615
  En atttendant Godot 543
Becquet, Just 282
Beethoven, Ludwig van 108, 583
Bellet, Roger 533 n.1
Benedict, Saint 94 n.14, 477
Bénichou, Paul ix, 115–18, 163 n.6, 478–9 n.64, 607
Benjamin, Walter 11, 62–3, 86, 140, n.23, 141 n.25, 236, 415 n.10, 419, 424, 431 n.31, 433 n.34, 543, 615
Béranger, Pierre-Jean de 2, 108 n.1, 389, 468, 517 n.36
Bernard, Suzanne 459 n.11, 491, 502, 503 n.42
Berrios, G. E. 91 n.1, 93 n.7
Bersani, Leo 75 n.9
Bertrand, Aloysius 485, 544
  Gaspard de la nuit: Fantaisies à la manière de Rembrandt et de Callot 485, 486, 487, 502, 514, 563
Bertrand, Jean-Pierre 500 n.33, 504
Billy, Dominique 389, 391 n.37, 392 nn.39, 40, and 42, 393 n.47, 394 nn.50 and 53, 396, 397, 403 n.61
Blin, Georges 14 n.33
Blood, Susan 207 n.2
Boccaccio, Giovanni 94
Bohac, Barbara 580 n.8, 581, 584
Boileau (Nicolas Boileau-Despréaux) 388
Bonald, Louis de 134, 253
Bonnefoy, Yves 94–5, 98, 217 n.15, 229
Borel, Pétrus 473, 490
Bourdieu, Pierre 26–7, 607

646 GENERAL INDEX

Boyer, Philoxène 252 n.9, 608
Braquemond, Félix 175
Breton, André 522, 606
Brière [or Brierre] de Boismont, Alexandre 7, 234 n.15
  Du suicide et de la folie suicide 153 n.38, 234 n.15
Brix, Michel 18
Brombert, Victor 232 n.9
Brueghel, Pieter (Brueghel the Elder) 54 n.13
Buffon, Georges Louis Leclerc, comte de 292 n.12, 573
Burton, Richard 10, 10 n.23, 11, 244 n.1, 408 n.1, 416 n.13, 493-4, 507, 511, 520-1, 525 n.55, 528-9, 575 n.5
Butler, Judith 555 n.3
Butor, Michel 470 n.40
Byron, George Gordon 108 n.1, 109, 250, 290

Calasso, Roberto 389 n.32, 441 n.8
Callot, Jacques 172, 544
Camoëns, Luis Vaz de x
Camus, Albert 100
Cargo, Robert T. 536 n.8
Carpenter, Scott 2 n.6, 525 n.53
Carter, A. E. 18, n.38
Cassagne, Albert 386, 387, 389, 605 n.12
Castille, Hippolyte 467-78, 500, 504, 507, 526, 531, 534, 550, 553, 569
  Histoire de la seconde République française 470-1
Catani, Damian 118 n.25, 442 n.10
Catechism of the Catholic Church 178-9, 604-5 n.11
Cellier, Léon 297, 299 n.22
Chambers Ross 10 n.23, 12 n.29, 16 n.35, 73 n.4, 74 n.8, 103-4 n.39, 188 nn.10 and 12, 409, 410 n.4, 411 n.5, 417, 419-20, 426 n.26, 440 nn.6 and 7, 449 nn.16 and 17, 450 n.19, 451 n.21, 513 n.28, 525 n.54
Chapelle (Claude-Emmanuel Luillier) 248
Charles d'Orléans 229
Charnet, Yves 231 n.8
Chartier, Alain 93
Chateaubriand, François René de ix, 9, 11, 12-13, 26, 36, 48, 50, 51, 53, 80, 95, 108, 112, 113, 114, 115, 122, 124, 125, 134, 193, 195, 196, 198, 211, 272, 288, 289, 292 n.12, 297, 423, 462, 463 n.22, 472, 498, 504, 534, 584
  Atala 502
  Essai sur les révolutions 114, 472
  Génie du christianisme 26, 36, 48, 50, 193, 472
  René 114, 130, 193, 289, 536 n.9, 542
Chatelain, Clara de 462, 464

Chatterjee, Ronjaunee 432 n.32
Chaucer, Geoffrey
  The Wife of Bath's Tale 564
Chénier, André 167 n.13
Chesters, Graham 212 n.6, 348 n.8, 357 n.14, 388, 449 n.17, 574 n.3
Chévrier, Alain 392 n.39
Chopin, Frédéric 487
Christophe, Ernest 176 n.28, 204, 206, 282, 290, 383, 414, 427, 442
Citron, Pierre 415 n.10, 418 n.16, 424 n.22
Cladel, Léon
  Les Martyrs ridicules 30, 40 n.28
Cleopatra 111
Clésinger, Auguste 282
Colet, Louise 25 n.7, 535
Colletet, Guillaume 248
Combe, Dominique 490 n.13
Compagnon, Antoine 10 n.23, 14 n.33, 17-18, 119 n.27, 129 n.10, 595 n.2, 606 n.14
Condillac, Étienne Bonnot de 133
Constant, Benjamin 120
  Adolphe 130 n.14
Corinna 134
Corneille, Pierre
  Polyeucte 275-6
Cornulier, Benoît de 393 n.48
Corot, Jean Baptiste Camille 28
Courbet, Gustave 318
Cousin, Victor 37, 200, 291, 293, 325, 469, 604-5
Crépet, Jacques 544
Crowe, Catherine 269-71, 275, 290
  The Night Side of Nature, or Ghosts and Ghost Seers 269
Culler, Jonathan 161 n.3, 192-3, 195 n.23, 340 n.6, 520 n.39
Custine, Alphonse de 608

Daily News 496
Daily Telegraph 496
Damian, St Peter 94 n.14
Daniel, John Moncure 246 n.4, 250 n.8, 289 n.7
Daniel-Rops, Henri 491
Dante x, 94, 97 n.22, 99, 105, 120, 176, 200, 208, 364, 441
  Divine Comedy 120, 127 n.1, 142 n.27, 158, 176-81, 185, 193
Daubrun, Marie 168 n.15, 169, 170, 217 n.14, 343, 379 n.8, 414
Daumier, Honoré 319, 418 n.16
Da Vinci, Leonardo 124
Davison, Kenneth 91 n.1, 92 n.4, 96 n.22, 100 n.32
Deburau, Jean-Gaspard 75 n.10

Defoe, Daniel 473
  Robinson Crusoe 472–3, 475, 477, 527
Delacroix, Eugène 6, 7, 10, 25, 27, 28–9, 30, 33, 37, 45, 55, 56, 64, 96, 97, 102, 103, 104, 108, 111, 112, 124, 176, 200, 202, 216 n.11, 234, 266, 271, 273 n.9, 290, 299 n.22, 301, 328, 331–2, 390, 415 n.11, 444, 447, 528, 530 n.63, 595, 597, 606
Delasiauve, Louis 93 n.7
De Maistre, Joseph 12, 63, 122, 165, 261, 324, 420, 607
De Man, Paul 62, 194 n.21, 210 n.4, 598 n.5
Denecourt, Claude-François 462, 464, 465
De Quincey, Thomas 55 n.15, 214 n.8, 554 n.1, 579
Desbordes-Valmore, Marceline 6, 125, 388
  Élegies et romances 183
Deschamps, Antony 176 n.29
Deschamps, Émile 176 n.29
Desdemona 111
Desnoyers, Fernand 462, 463 n.25, 464, 465, 467, 477
Diaz, José-Luis 116 n.14
Diderot, Denis 245
  La Religieuse 129, 147
  Les Bijoux indiscrets 203
Dionysus 143
Disegni, Silvia 501
Dormeuil, Dorothée 562 n.6
Dorval, Marie 129 n.10
Doumet, Christian 580 n.8
Drouet, Juliette 129 n.10
Du Bellay, Joachim 235
  Les Regrets 228
Dubray, Jean 14 n.33
Du Camp, Maxime 225 n.21
  Chants modernes 225 n.21
Dufour, Pierre 105 n.48
Dumas, Alexandre [Dumas père] 533
  Antony 318
  Kean ou Désordre et génie 23
  La Comtesse de Salisbury 495
Dupont, Jacques 110 n.3, 140 n.23
Dupont, Pierre 22, 25, 35, 37, 131, 171 n.18, 388, 420, 613
Dürer, Albrecht 96, 101
Duval, Jeanne 170, 204 n.34, 217, 343
Dylan, Bob 216 n.12, 388

Edelman, Nicole 6 n.14
Eliot, T.S. 60
Éluard, Paul 610
Emerson, Ralph Waldo 37 n.27
Empedocles 92

Esquirol, Étienne 92
Etheridge, Kate 9 n.21
Euripides 428
Eurydice 143, 158
Evans, David 15 n.34, 386 n.8, 390–1 n.34, 490 n.13, 512 n.25
Evans, Margery 573 n.2
Ezekiel 43

Fairlie, Alison 388
Ferran, André 297 n.18
Ficino, Marsilio 94 n.14, 96
Finch-Race, Daniel 449 n.17
Fiorentino, Pior Angeli 176
Flaubert, Gustave 1, 2, 3, 4, 5, 8, 25 n.7, 37, 40, 50, 52, 116, 208 n.2, 450, 470 n.42, 512, 515–17, 518, 524, 535, 549 n.17, 590, 597, 607, 616 n.30, 617
  Bouvard et Pécuchet 208 n.2
  L'Éducation sentimentale 12 n.29, 450
  Madame Bovary 1, 2–5, 7, 8, 40, 50, 277, 332, 516, 597, 599, 617
Foloppe, Régine 565 n.8
Foucault, Michel 610
Fourier, Charles 43, 253
Fraisse, Armand 391, 410
Franceschi, Jules 282
Freud, Sigmund 105–6 n.48, 106
  'Mourning and Melancholia' 94
Friedrich, Caspar David 105
Fulton, Alice 340 n.6

Garibaldi, Giuseppe 496
Gauguin, Paul 344
Gautier, Théophile 6, 7, 10, 16, 23, 25, 28, 30, 35, 50, 51, 108, 116, 169 n.16, 177, 182, 260 n.18, 290–6, 297, 299, 301, 304, 307, 311, 313, 315, 319, 324, 328, 330, 331, 384–5, 386, 412, 446 n.12, 462 n.18, 484, 497, 530, 576, 600
  Albertus 291
  Émaux et camées 50, 384, 385, 412
  España 294
  La Comédie de la Mort 294
  Mademoiselle de Maupin 23, 35 n.22, 50, 129, 291
Gavarni, Paul 201, 319, 414
Gay, Delphine (Mme Émile de Girardin) 497, 533
  Gazette musicale de Paris 582–3
Gefen, Alexandre 388 n.24
Gendre, André 387 n.16
Genovali, Sandro 195 n.23
Gide, André
  Les Caves du Vatican 258

648 GENERAL INDEX

Gilman, Margaret 28 n.14, 207 n.2, 244 n.1
Girardin, Émile de 495, 498, 499, 533
Godard, Jean-Luc
   Sympathy for the Devil 216 n.12
Goethe, Johann Wolfgang von 49, 113, 114, 245, 253, 297
   Faust 111, 370
Goldstein, Jan 91 n.1, 100 n.34
Gouvard, Jean-Michel 480 n.66, 490 n.12, 490 n.14, 491, 502, 510 n.18, 537 n.11, 568 n.9
Goya, Francisco 61 n.26, 124, 544
Gray, Thomas
   'Elegy Written in a Country Churchyard' 164 n.7
Grøtta, Marit 616 n.32
Guégan, Stéphane 204 n.35
Guizot, François 24
Guyaux, André 7 n.16, 14 n.33, 17, 18 n.38, 129 n.10, 297 n.18
Guys, Constantin 6, 16, 27, 29, 63, 227, 233, 290, 307, 314–29, 330, 331, 343, 414, 415 n.11, 447, 518, 610

Hamon, Philippe 412 n.6
Hannibal 223 n.20
Hannoosh, Michele 2 n.3, 60–4, 65, 66 n.31, 73–7, 83 n.18, 491, 513, 515–18, 528 n.60
Harpocrates 279
Haussman, Georges Eugène (Baron Haussman) 415, 450, 560
Heaney, Seamus 22, 372, 594, 612–16
Hébert, Émile 284
Heck, Francis 521 n.49
Heine, Heinrich 28, 55, 108 n.1
Hermes Trismegistus 162
Hetzel, Pierre-Jules 486 n.7
Hiddleston, J. A. 57 n.17, 73 n.4, 77 n.12, 83 n.18, 457, 491, 504 n.48, 512, 536 n.9
Hildegard of Bingen 96 n.22
Hippocrates 92
Hobbes, Thomas 56
Hoffmann, Ernst Theodor Amadeus 245
Homer 176, 428, 433
Hood, Thomas 278 n.13
   'The Bridge of Sighs' 278 n.13
Horace 167 n.13, 176, 262, 567, 599
Houssaye, Arsène 63, 480 n.66, 485, 486, 489, 496, 503 n.44, 507–8, 513, 515, 520, 529, 530, 535, 537 n.12, 617
   'La Chanson du vitrier' 507–9, 515, 519, 520, 528, 538
Hovasse, Jean-Marc 297 n.18
Howells, Bernard 23 n.3

Hugo, Victor ix, 9–10, 11, 13, 16, 25, 28–9, 37, 38–9, 41–4, 48, 49, 50, 51, 53, 55, 65, 77 n.12, 117, 125, 129 n.10, 134, 159, 184, 185, 192, 193 n.20, 196, 215, 264, 269, 272, 274, 276 n.12, 290, 293, 294, 296–306, 307, 311, 313, 315, 328, 330, 331, 387 n.17, 392 n.38, 397, 412, 415, 446, 462 n.18, 488, 490, 534, 536, 582, 584, 596, 607, 609, 611 n.22, 614
'À la Colonne' 293
'À l'Arc de Triomphe' 293, 415 n.10, 446
Châtiments 38
Hernani 25, 387 n.17, 499, 576
La Légende des siècles 184, 300, 302, 306, 490
'La Pente de la rêverie' 300, 302
Les Contemplations 13, 38, 41, 42, 53, 126, 183, 184, 266, 271, 279, 297, 300, 302, 303, 304–5, 306, 392 n.38, 415, 607, 609
Les Feuilles d'automne 183
'Les Mages' 124
'Les Malheureux' 126
Les Misérables 12, 39, 122, 126, 415
Les Orientales 37, 183
Notre-Dame de Paris 300
Odes et poésies diverses [later *Odes et ballades*] 49, 183
'Préface de *Cromwell*' 290, 317

Illustrated London News 227, 315
Ingres, Jean Auguste Dominique 56, 528

Jackson, John E. 97 n.24, 105 n.47, 152 n.36, 229 n.6, 231 n.8, 232 n.11, 233 n.12, 236 n.18
Jagger, Sir Mick 216 n.12
James, Tony 91 n.1
Janin, Jules 108 n.1, 462 n.18
Janmot, Louis 101 n.37
Jesus 36, 66, 70, 78, 84 n.19, 124, 143, 161, 172, 173, 177, 180 n.33, 181, 186, 200, 213, 237, 251, 252, 253, 276, 431, 477, 508, 528, 536, 539
John (of Patmos), St 174
John Paul, St 178
John the Baptist, St 177
Johnson, Barbara 210 n.4, 460 n.15, 491, 520 n.39, 555 n.3, 579 n.6
Johnson, Samuel 100 n.32
Jossua, Jean-Pierre 14 n.33
Jouanna, Jacques 91 n.1
Journal des Débats 497, 498
Jouy, Étienne de 497

Kant, Immanuel 51–2
Kaplan, Edward K. 491

Keaton, Buster 66
Keats, John 610
　'Ode on a Grecian Urn' 610
　'Ode to a Nightingale' 155
　'On First Looking into Chapman's
　　Homer' 289
Kelley, David 11
Kelley, Donald R. 468 n.34
Killick, Rachel 393 n.48, 423 n.20, 449 n.17
Klibansky, Raymond 91 n.1, 93 nn.9 and 10,
　94 nn.11, 13 and 14, 96, 97 n.23, 102 n.38,
　129 n.13
Kliebenstein, Georges 520 n.39
Kopp, Robert 103 n.39, 234 n.15, 491
Kraepelin, Emil 93
Kristeva, Julia 94, 104 n.39
Krueger, Cheryl 491, 513 n.28

Labarthe, Patrick 69 n.1, 73 n.4, 395, 412 n.6,
　428 n.28, 491, 507 n.5, 565 n.8
La Bruyère, Jean de 292 n.12, 476, 479, 505, 523,
　548, 549
　Les Caractères 476
LaCapra, Dominick 2 n.3,
Laclos, Pierre Choderlos de 245
Ladenson, Elisabeth 2 n.3, 3 n.7, 4 n.8, 8 n.19
Laforgue, Jules
　Moralités légendaires 563
Laforgue, Pierre 11, 12, 100 n.34, 137 n.21,
　148 n.31, 188 n.9, 297 n.18
Lamartine, Alphonse de ix, 9, 11, 13, 25, 48, 50,
　51, 52, 53, 65, 117, 125, 134, 185, 192, 196,
　208, 215, 272, 289, 293, 397, 462 n.18,
　463 n.22, 468, 488, 534, 536, 537 n.11,
　584, 589, 607, 609
　Des destinées de la poésie 290
　'Dieu' 273
　Harmonies poétiques et religieuses 53, 183
　'Le Désert, ou l'immatérialité de l'âme' 609
　'Le Tombeau d'une mère' 609
　Méditations poétiques 52, 53, 183
　Nouvelles méditations poétiques 127 n.3
Lamennais, Félicité Robert de 120, 583, 584
Laplace, Pierre-Simon 303
Laprade, Victor de 51, 463 n.22
La Presse 63, 458, 478, 481, 485, 486, 488, 489,
　490, 495–9, 519, 532, 533, 535, 537, 539,
　549, 553, 563, 602
Larkin, Philip 615
L'Artiste 2, 100, 176 n.27, 489, 490, 507
La Semaine 469
Lavater, Johann Kaspar 43, 336
Lawler, James 185 n.7, 246 n.4
Lazarus 180 n.33, 375

Leakey, Felix 388, 462 n.19, 463 n.25, 464 n.26,
　469 n.36
L'Écho des marchands de vins 128
Leclerc, Yvan 2 n.3, 127 n.2
Leconte de Lisle, Charles Marie René 49, 116,
　395 n.51
　Poèmes antiques 49
Le Figaro 485, 490, 502 n.39
Le Gil Blas 500
Leibniz, Gottfried Wilhelm 119
Lélut, Louis 7, 569, 570
Lemaître, Henri 491
Lemer, Julien 458 n.8
Le Messager de l'Assemblée 128, 457
Le Moniteur 496
Le Moniteur industriel 527
Le Parnasse contemporain 100, 127 n.3, 458 n.10
Le Présent 183, 417, 458, 485, 487
Leroy, Christian 536 n.9
Lesbos 112, 121, 122, 130, 132, 133, 134, 136,
　137, 138, 139, 141, 145, 147, 148, 149, 156,
　158, 159, 160, 162, 164, 169, 170, 179, 185,
　186, 201, 209, 220, 224, 243, 260, 336, 340,
　342, 343, 404, 406, 407, 408, 418, 440, 597
Le Siècle 495, 500 n.31
Les Lesbiennes de Paris 129
Le Tintamarre 470
Le Travail intellectuel 468
L'Événement 491
Le Voleur 496 n.27
Lewis, A. J. 91 n.1, 93 n.8
Lewis, Philippa 495 n.24, 549 n.17
Lewis, Roy 348 n.8
Libre-Échange 468
L'Indépendance belge 485
Liszt, Franz 34, 311, 314, 487, 578, 579–85
Lloyd, Rosemary 2 n.5, 5 n.12, 12, 168 n.14, 297
　n.18, 386 n.9, 504 n.48, 509–10, 511,
　520 n.39
Locke, John 51
Locke, Ralph P. 582 n.13
Longfellow, Henry Wadsworth 246
Lonke, Joycelynne 314 n.8
Louis-Napoléon (Napoléon III) 11, 117, 297,
　470, 520
Louis-Philippe I 128
Lübecker, Nikolaj 484 n.67
Lucan 176
Lucifer 112, 118, 174, 200, 219, 220, 367
Lycurgus 133, 135

Macé, Marielle 315–16 n.9, 438 n.5, 611 n.22
McGuinness, Patrick 25 n.8, 469 n.35
MacInnes, John. W. 59, 62

McLees, Ainslie Armstrong 60
McLuhan, Marshall 518
Maenads 143
Magdalen, Mary 111
Malherbe, François de 614
Mallarmé, Stéphane 32, 115, 237, 244, 251,
    459–60 n.12, 460–1, 463 n.23, 484 n.68, 492,
    531, 537, 586 n.17, 604, 605–6, 609
  Divagations 473
  'La Gloire' 463 n.23
  La Musique et les Lettres 21 n.1, 290,
    460–1, 531
  'Le Pitre châtié' 442 n.9
  'Mimique' 76 n.11
  'Tombeau [de Verlaine]' 151
  Un coup de Dés 586 n.17, 592 n.20, 606
Mandelstam, Osip 615–16
Mantegna, Andrea 238
Marchal, Bertrand 14 n.33
Marmontel, Jean-François 133
Marot, Clément 389 n.26
Marx, Karl 468
Mathieu, Jean-Claude 17
Maturin, Charles 109
  Melmoth 218 n.17
Melmoux-Montaubin, Marie-Françoise 500 n.31
Melzer, Françoise 431 n.31
Ménard, Louis [*pseud.* Louis de Senneville]
  Prométhée délivré 40
Mendès, Catulle 458 n.7
Mercier, Louis-Sébastien 415 n.10
Mercure de France (formerly *Mercure
    galant*) 498
Mercure français 498
Meryon, Charles 446
Michel, Arlette 470 n.41
Michelangelo (Buonarotti) 124, 152, 201, 282
Michelet, Jules 117, 468
Mill, John Stuart 468 n.35
Milner, Max 61 n.28, 115 n.10, 118 n.25,
    173 n.21, 270 n.4, 491, 502
Milton, John 94 n.14, 112, 118
  'Il Penseroso' 93
  Paradise Lost 112
Miner, Margaret 314 n.8
Molière (Jean-Baptiste Poquelin) 57, 517 n.36
Molinari, Gustave 468
Mona Lisa 111
Monselet, Charles 463
Montaigne, Michel de
  'Des cannibales' 255
Morel, Jean 407
Moreau [de Tours], Jacques Joseph 7
Morienval, Jean 495 n.25

Moses x, 9, 36, 51, 120, 134, 135, 136, 159, 172,
    217, 483, 617
Mossop, D. J. 110 n.3
Moussa, Sarga 580 n.7
Murat, Michel 459 n.11
Murger, Henri (also Henry) 462 n.18, 503
  Scènes de la vie de Bohème 503
Murphy, Margueritte S. 11 n.27
Murphy, Steve 11, 15 n.35, 73 n.4, 75 n.10, 82
    n.16, 226 n.22, 475 n.56, 486 n.5, 491,
    506–7, 508 n.7, 509, 510, 511–12, 520, 521,
    535 n.7, 536 n.9, 570 n.12, 590
Musset, Alfred de 51, 98, 116, 289, 462 n.18,
    463 n.22
  Contes d'Espagne et d'Italie 183
  Gamiani, ou deux nuits d'excès 129
  La Confession d'un enfant du siècle 130 n.14

Nacquart, Raymond 183
Nadar (*see* Tournachon)
Natta, Marie-Christine 128 n.6, 192 n.15,
    462 nn.16 and 21
Née, Patrick 6–7, 8 n.19, 100 n.34, 101 n.35
Neri, Élisa 380
Nero 80–1
Nerval, Gérard de [Gérard Labrunie] 116,
    462 n.18
  'El Desdichado' 186
Newmark, Kevin 210 n.4
Newton, Sir Isaac 303
Nicodemus 276
Nodier, Charles 116, 564 n.7
nomos, nomoi 36 n.23, 41–5, 47–8, 51, 56, 87,
    296, 301, 303, 305, 329, 596, 607
Nordau, Max 531
Nouvelle Revue de Paris 485
Nurse, Peter H. 440, n.6

Ockenden, Alexander 562 n.6
Odysseus 222
Oehler, Dolf 11, 12, 470 n.42, 507–9, 510 n.15,
    511, 518
Olmsted, William 2 n.3
Orpheus x, 36, 51, 70, 71, 133, 137, 143, 158, 186,
    220, 607, 617
Ovid x, 176, 216, 339, 428
  Metamorphoses 137 n.21
Owen, Wilfred 614, 615
Oxyrynchus Papyri 134

Pachet, Pierre 11
Paganini, Niccolò 70, 337, 508
Panofsky, Erwin 91 n.1, 93 nn.9 and 10, 94 nn.11,
    13, and 14, 96, 97 n.23, 102, n.38, 129 n.13

Pascal, Blaise 56, 101 n.36, 213, 480–1, 484, 505, 523, 548
Pearson, Roger 4 n.9, 7 n.18, 10–11, 12 n.31, 13, 23 n.5, 24 n.6, 32 n.20, 36 n.23, 36 n.24, 36 n.25, 51 n.8, 51 n.9, 52 n.12, 76 n.11, 95 n.18, 116 n.15, 120 n.30, 121 n.31, 134 n.18, 165 n.9, 183 nn.4 and 5, 188 n.11, 193 n.20, 253 n.11, 267 n.1, 276 n.12, 288 n.5, 289 n.6, 298 n.20, 302 n.24, 304 n.25, 442 n.9, 450 n.20, 460 n.12, 463 n.23, 477 n.59, 477 n.61, 479 n.64, 484 n.68, 489 n.9, 491 n.15, 531 n.65, 534 n.2, 564 n.7, 586 n.17, 609 n.17, 610–11
Pelloquet, Théodore 462 n.17
Penguilly-l'Haridon, Octave 391 n.36
Penrose, Roland 610
Petrarch 97 n.22, 576
Phidias 298
Picasso, Pablo 597
Pichois, Claude 6, 23 n.4, 100, 101, 119 n.27, 128 n.9, 129 n.10, 133 n.17, 162 n.4, 170 n.17, 186 n.8, 192 n.15, 204 n.34, 214 n.8, 216 n.11, 221, 246 n.4, 314 n.8, 338 n.3, 369 n.2, 386 n.12, 388 n.22, 389 n.26, 391 n.36, 491, 492
Pinard, Ernest 4, 515–16
Pindar 134
Planche, Gustave 129 n.10
Plato 36 n.23, 47–8, 133, 134, 136, 188, 219, 613
Ion 7 n.18, 54, 265, 614
Laws 36 n.23, 47
Republic 36 n.23, 47–8, 477 n.61, 613
Symposium 470 n.37
Poe, Edgar Allan 6, 10, 16, 30, 31 n.17, 32 n.18, 38, 44–5, 108 n.1, 109, 123, 243–64, 285, 286–90, 291, 309, 312, 313, 329, 391, 489, 520 n.39, 531, 550, 596, 599, 600
A Descent into the Maelstrom 251
'Anastatic Printing' 31, n.17
A Tale of the Ragged Mountains 587
Berenice 251
Eureka 251
Histoires extraordinaires (trans. Baudelaire) 247
Ligeia 31 n.17
Magnetic Revelation 244–5, 251
Marginalia 262
Nouvelles histoires extraordinaires (trans. Baudelaire) 247, 258 n.15, 259 n.17
'The Bells' 289
The Black Cat 251, 258–9
The Gold-Bug 251
The Imp of the Perverse 258–9, 261, 524
The Man of the Crowd 320, 549, 554 n.1

The Murders in the Rue Morgue 251
'The Philosophy of Composition' 289–90
The Poetic Principle 44–5, 250, 262–3, 287–8, 291
'The Raven' 249, 289–90
Pommier, Jean 192
Pontmartin, Armand de 611 n.22
Poulet, Georges 61 n.28
Poulet-Malassis, Auguste 127 n.2, 140 n.23, 175, 309 n.3, 310
Prendergast, Christopher 411 n.5, 411–12 n.6, 415 n.10, 420 n.19, 425 n.23, 434 n.1, 438 n.3
Prévost, Jean 392 n.39, 394
Prigent, Hélène 97 n.22
Proserpina 151–2, 357
Proudhon, Pierre-Joseph 12, 468 n.34, 480, 493–4, 570
Qu'est-ce que la propriété? 468 n.34, 570
Proust, Marcel 97 n.22, 540
À la recherche du temps perdu 425 n.24
Puget, Pierre Paul 124
Pythagoras 92, 279

Quinet, Edgar 117

Rabelais, François 57, 218
Racine, Jean 428, 433
Radden, Jennifer 92 nn.2, 3, and 6, 94, 95–6, 102 n.38
Rancière, Jacques 543
Raphaël 238
Ratushinskaya, Irina 614
Raymond, Marcel 270 n.4, 284
Rembrandt 124, 544
Rétif de la Bretonne, Nicolas 248
Revue de Paris 2, 169 n.16, 172 n.19, 182, 246
Revue des Deux Mondes 128, 151 n.35, 160, 183, 457
Revue européenne 311
Revue fantaisiste 458, 485, 488
Revue française 407
Revue nationale et étrangère 563
Revue nouvelle 101–2
Richard, Jean-Pierre 231 n.8
Richter, Mario 226 n.22
Rigoli, Juan 6 n.14., 91 n.1
Rimbaud, Arthur
Illuminations 605
Robb, Graham 129 n.10, 151 n.33, 195 n.22, 386–89, 390, 502–4
Ronsard, Pierre de 389 n.26, 395, 412, 413, 433
Rops, Félicien 175, 177
Robespierre, Maximilien de 23 n.5

Roqueplan, Nestor 574
Rousseau, Jean-Jacques 12, 122, 133, 255, 325, 467, 473, 474, 488, 538, 568, 589, 603
  Discours sur l'inégalité 255, 473, 474
  Les Rêveries du promeneur solitaire 475, 536 n.9, 538
Rubens, Peter Paul 124, 301
Rubin, Vivien L. 73 n.4
Rueff, Martin 316 n.9
Ruff, Marcel 171 n.18, 491
Rufus of Ephesus 141
Runyon, Randolph 404 n.63
Rushworth, Jennifer 97 n.22
Ruskin, John 468 n.35
  Unto this Last 468 n.35

Sabatier, Apollonie 133 n.17, 165, 170, 185, 343, 369, 372 n.3, 380, 404
Sade, Donatien Alphonse François, marquis de 171 n.18, 261, 338
Saint-Amant, Marc-Antoine Girard de 248
Sainte-Beuve, Charles Augustin 7 n.16, 21, 51, 101 n.36, 116, 129, 297, 298 n.18, 486 n.7, 586
  Vie, poésies et pensées de Joseph Delorme 586
  Volupté 130
Saint-Simonianism 120, 583
Samuels, Maurice 561 n.5
Sand, George 129 n.12, 462, 466
Sandras, Michel 459 n.11
Santerre, Antoine Joseph 479 n.65
Sanyal, Debarati 73 n.4, 82, 555 n.3
Sapiro, Gisèle 2 n.3, 512 n.26, 516 n.32, 605 n.12
Sappho 8, 129 n.10, 133, 134–5, 137–8, 158, 159, 162, 209, 340, 342
Sartre, Jean-Paul 321, 506
Satan 57, 58, 108, 112, 115–18, 120, 121, 122, 137, 158, 159, 161, 164, 171, 173, 174, 175, 185, 209, 221, 227, 243, 342, 426 n.26, 477, 485, 566
Satan Trismegistus 162–3, 170, 179
Saxl, Fritz 91 n.1, 93 nn.9 and 10, 94 nn.11, 13, and 14, 96, 97 n.23, 102 n.38, 129 n.13
Scepi, Henri 536 n.9
Schellino, Andrea 336 n.2, 480, n.66, 491, 535 n.6
Schiller, Friedrich 49, 113, 114
Schofer, Peter 73 n.4, 77 n.12, 82 n.14
Scott, Clive 348 n.8
Scott, David 393 n.48
Scott, Maria 72–3 n.4, 74 n.7, 81 n.13, 82 n.15, 491, 510–11, 522, 525, 537 n.12, 590 n.19
Scott, Sir Walter 253

Semaine théâtrale 470
Senancour, Étienne Pivert de
  Obermann 130 n.14, 289
Senneville, Louis de (*see* Ménard, Louis)
Shaftesbury, Earl of (*see* Ashley-Cooper)
Shakespeare, William 176, 229, 297
  Hamlet 111
  Macbeth 152, 201, 328, 575
Shelley, Percy Bysshe 36
  Defence of Poetry x, 36, 267 n.1
Sidney, Sir Philip 613
Sir Gawain and the Green Knight 564
Smith, Bonnie G. 468 n.34
Socrates 54, 265, 614
Söllner, Fritz 473 n.48
Solon 36, 133, 135
Sophocles 308
Soulié, Frédéric 497, 533
Southern Literary Messenger 246 n.4, 250 n.8
Staël, Germaine de ix, 9, 11, 13, 24, 36, 48–9, 50, 51, 52, 53, 55, 56, 112, 113, 114, 115, 122, 125, 134, 137, 192, 288–9, 298 n.20, 317, 533, 576, 582
  Corinne 13, 48, 114, 134, 288, 289, 534, 576
  Delphine 50 n.5, 134, 288 n.5
  De la littérature 50 n.5, 113, 317
  De l'Allemagne 13, 49, 113, 192
Stamelman, Richard 83 n.18, 103 n.39, 433 n.34
Starobinski, Jean 73, n.4, 74, 75 n.10, 77 n.12, 91 n.1, 94, 98, 103–7, 129 n.13, 145 n.29, 151 n.34, 153 n.38, 167 n.13, 196 n.25, 228, 234 n.14, 394, 491
St Clair, Robert 561 n.5
Steinmetz, Jean-Luc 445 n.11, 457 nn.2 and 5, 458 nn.6 and 9, 459 n.11, 519, 550
Stendhal (Marie-Henri Beyle) 317
  De l'amour 336
  Racine et Shakespeare 317
Stephens, Sonya 60 n.25, 73 n.4, 74 n.7, 75 n.10, 82 n.17, 491, 509–10, 511, 513 n.29, 516 n.33, 518, 522, 559 n.4
Sterne, Laurence 245, 573
  A Sentimental Journey through France and Italy 573
  Tristram Shandy 573
Stevens, Joseph 573
Stevens, Wallace 613
Stierle, Karlheinz 415 n.10
Stuart Mill, John 468 n.35
Sue, Eugène 415
  Le Juif errant 431 n.30
Surrealism 606
Swedenborg, Emanuel 43, 192, 253, 312, 575
Swinburne, Algernon Charles 4 n.10

GENERAL INDEX 653

Taine, Hippolyte 23 n.4
Tasso, Torquato x, 102, 103, 104
   Jerusalemma liberata 103
Teixier, Edmond 425 n.23
Tennyson, Lord Alfred 108 n.1, 290
Terdiman, Richard 460 n.13
Thackeray, William Makepeace 319
Theocritus 409, 490 n.13, 576
Thélot, Jérôme 575 n.4
Thérenty, Marie-Ève 498–502, 503 nn.42 and 47, 504, 506
Thompson, John Reuben 246 n.4
Thoré, Théophile 246
Thucydides 36 n.23
Tilby, Michael J. 128 n.6
Toal, Catherine 260 n.18
Todorov, Tzvetan 459 n.11
Töppfer, Rodolphe 37 n.27
Tortonese, Paulo 37 n.27
Tournachon, Gaspard Félix (*pseud.* Nadar) 11
Toussenel, Alphonse 258 n.14

Vadé, Yves 459 n.11
Vaillant, Alain 14 n.33, 60, 64–6, 403–4 n.63, 499 n.29, 500 n.31, 501 n.36
Valdès Leal, Juan de 295
Valéry, Paul 14
Vallès, Jules 506
Van Slyke, Gretchen 27 n.11, 529 n.61
Vauvenargues, Luc de Clapiers, marquis de 556
Velázquez, Diego 301
Verlaine, Paul x
Vernet, Carle 414
Véron, Théodore 128 n.6
Veronese, Paulo 301
Vigny, Alfred de ix, 9, 11, 13, 23, 24, 48, 49, 50, 52, 53, 113, 123, 125, 181, 182, 183, 297, 397, 488–90, 491 n.15, 534, 607
   De Mademoiselle Sedaine et de la propriété littéraire 23 n.5
   'Éloa' 180 n.33
   'Hélena' 135
   Les Destinées 13, 49, 125, 183, 489
   'Moïse' 186 n.8

'Paris' 120, 425 n.23
Poèmes antiques et modernes 183, 488
Stello 13, 23 n.5, 186 n.8, 247, 534
Vincent-Munnia, Nathalie 459 n.11
Vines, Lois Davis 246 n.4
Virgil 120, 176, 185, 189 n.14, 409, 428, 433, 490 n.13, 576
Virgin Mary 78, 111, 178, 378
Vitry, Alexandre de 480 n.66
Voltaire (François-Marie Arouet) 44, 57, 537 n.12, 565
   Candide 608
   'Ce qui plaît aux dames' 564
Von Trier, Lars 96 n.19

Wagner, Richard x, 6, 10, 16, 25, 34, 290, 307–14, 315, 319, 324, 328, 330, 331, 484, 580, 602
   Lohengrin 34, 309, 311, 312, 313, 314
   Tannhaüser, 309, 310, 311 n.5, 312, 313
Watteau, Jean Antoine 124, 149
Weber, Carl Maria von 487
Weil, Simone 614
   Gravity and Grace 614
Wetherill, P.M. 290 n.8
White, Michael 473 n.48
Wilberforce, William 468 n.35
Wilmer, Clive 468 n.35
Wing, Nathaniel 73 n.4, 99 n.29
Wordsworth, William x, 52 n.11, 55, 446 n.12, 617
   'Lines written a few miles above Tintern Abbey' 52 n.11
   The Excursion 446 n.12
   The Prelude x

Yeats, W. B. 296, 584, 612, 614
Young, Edward
   Night-Thoughts 487
Yee, Jennifer 201 n.31

Ziegler, Jean 128 n.9, 192 n.15
Zimmermann, Johann Georg 467
   Über die Einsamkeit 467
Zurburán, Francisco de 295